PRIVACY AND POWER

Edward Snowden's leaks exposed fundamental differences in the ways Americans and Europeans approach the issues of privacy and intelligence gathering. Featuring contributions from leading commentators, scholars, and practitioners from both sides of the Atlantic, the book documents and explains these differences, summarized in these terms: Europeans should "grow up" and Americans should "obey the law." The book starts with a collection of chapters acknowledging that Snowden's revelations require us to rethink prevailing theories concerning privacy and intelligence gathering, explaining the differences and uncertainty regarding those aspects. An impressive range of experts reflect on the law and policy of the NSA-Affair, documenting its fundamentally transnational dimension, which is the real location of the transatlantic dialogue on privacy and intelligence gathering. The conclusive chapters explain the dramatic transatlantic differences that emerged from the NSA-Affair with a collection of comparative cultural commentary.

RUSSELL A. MILLER is Professor of Law at the Washington and Lee University School of Law where his research and teaching focuses on comparative constitutional law. He is the author and editor of a number of books, including *The Constitutional Jurisprudence of the Federal Republic of Germany* (3rd edn. 2012) and *U.S. National Security, Intelligence and Democracy* (2008). He has lectured and published extensively in the United States and Germany on the issues of privacy and intelligence oversight.

PRIVACY AND POWER

A Transatlantic Dialogue in the Shadow
of the NSA-Affair

Edited by

RUSSELL A. MILLER

Washington and Lee University, Virginia

CAMBRIDGE
UNIVERSITY PRESS

CAMBRIDGE
UNIVERSITY PRESS

University Printing House, Cambridge CB2 8BS, United Kingdom

One Liberty Plaza, 20th Floor, New York, NY 10006, USA

477 Williamstown Road, Port Melbourne, VIC 3207, Australia

314-321, 3rd Floor, Plot 3, Splendor Forum, Jasola District Centre, New Delhi - 110025, India

79 Anson Road, #06-04/06, Singapore 079906

Cambridge University Press is part of the University of Cambridge.

It furthers the University's mission by disseminating knowledge in the pursuit of education, learning and research at the highest international levels of excellence.

www.cambridge.org
Information on this title: www.cambridge.org/9781316609101
10.1017/9781316658888

First published 2017
First paperback edition 2018

A catalogue record for this publication is available from the British Library

Library of Congress Cataloging in Publication data
Names: Miller, Russell A., 1969– editor.
Title: Privacy and power : a transatlantic dialogue in the shadow of the NSA-Affair / edited by Russell A. Miller, Washington and Lee University, Virginia.
Description: Camridge [UK] ; New York : Cambridge University Press, 2016. | Includes bibliographical references and index.
Identifiers: LCCN 2016031806| ISBN 9781107154049 (Hardback) | ISBN 9781316609101 (pbk.)
Subjects: LCSH: Intelligence service–Law and legislation. | Intelligence service–International cooperation. | Electronic surveillance–Law and legislation. | Government information–Access control. | Privacy, Right of. | Data protection–Law and legislation. | United States. National Security Agency/Central Security Service. | Snowden, Edward J., 1983– | Leaks (Disclosure of information)
Classification: LCC K3278 .P75 2016 | DDC 342/.0412–dc23 LC record available at https://lccn.loc.gov/2016031806

ISBN 978-1-107-15404-9 Hardback
ISBN 978-1-316-60910-1 Paperback

CONTENTS

CONTRIBUTORS

ANDREW BORENE is an American attorney and executive. A former Associate Deputy General Counsel at the U.S. Department of Defense and veteran U.S. Marine Corps intelligence officer, he was Counselor to Steptoe & Johnson LLP's national security practice while writing this chapter. He is editor-in-chief of American Bar Association publications on *Human Rights Law*, *International Humanitarian Law*, and *U.S. Intelligence Law*. In corporate roles, Mr. Borene has provided business leadership within publicly held international companies, directed corporate development at a defense technology startup, and served as program manager for U.S. government contracts. He earned a JD at the University of Minnesota Law School, a BA in Economics at Macalester College, and completed executive education in international development at Harvard University. He is a Senior Fellow with the University of Minnesota's Technological Leadership Institute, Chairman of Minneapolis' Cyber Security Summit, Defense Council with the Truman National Security Project, and an Adjunct Professor at American University. Mr. Borene would like to thank Alice Beauheim Borene for her valuable support and suggestions on early versions, along with Tony Busch, a student at the Washington University School of Law, for his research assistance on this chapter. All opinions expressed in Mr. Borene's chapter are personal and do not reflect official positions of organizations with which he has been or is affiliated.

IAN BROWN is Professor of Information Security and Privacy at the University of Oxford's Internet Institute, where his research focuses on surveillance, privacy-enhancing technologies, and Internet regulation. He has acted as an expert witness for the English High Court, U.K. Investigatory Powers Tribunal, and European Court of Human Rights; and given evidence to the U.K., German, and European parliaments. In 2014–15, Professor Brown was a Knowledge Exchange Fellow with the Commonwealth Cybercrime Initiative and U.K. National Crime Agency.

He has consulted for the United Nations, Council of Europe, OECD, U.S. Department of Homeland Security, European Commission, and many private sector organizations. He holds a PhD in computer science from University College London. His chapter (coauthored with Halperin, Hayes, Scott, and Vermeulen) was produced with the support of the Open Society Foundations and the Economic and Social Research Council (grant number ES/L01310X/1).

STEPHEN CHOVANEC is a 2016 graduate of the Washington and Lee University School of Law.

ROGER CROCKETT is Professor of German at Washington and Lee University where, for twenty-three years, he chaired the German and Russian Department. Previously he taught for twelve years at Texas A&M University. He has published on Friedrich Dürrenmatt, most notably a monograph *Understanding Friedrich Dürrenmatt* with South Carolina Press, and he currently has two book-length translations of works by Dürrenmatt in submission. His scholarship includes several articles on Viennese folk comedy of the nineteenth century and he is the coeditor of a three volume edition of the works of Hans Sachs. Professor Crockett earned his PhD from the University of Illinois in 1979.

ELS DE BUSSER holds a PhD from Ghent University, Belgium, and is Lecturer and Researcher, Law Program and Centre of Expertise Cybersecurity at The Hague University of Applied Sciences, the Netherlands. Until early 2016 she was Head of the Department of European Criminal law at the Max Planck Institute for Foreign and International Criminal Law in Freiburg, Germany. Her research is focused on European and international cooperation, information exchange, and data protection in criminal matters, especially in the transatlantic relationship. Her book *Data Protection in E.U. and U.S. Criminal Cooperation* (2009) was awarded the 2014 Siracusa Prize for Young Penalists by the Association Internationale de Droit Pénal (AIDP) and the International Institute of Higher Studies in Criminal Sciences (ISISC).

CHRISTOPH ENGEL is a director of the Max Planck Institute for Research on Collective Goods at Bonn, Germany, and professor of law at the universities of Bonn, Osnabrück, and Rotterdam. He specializes in behavioral and, in particular, experimental law, and economics. Part of his work is foundational. For instance, he investigates the motivating force of (utilitarian) social preferences, as well as (deontological) rule following. Another part of his work is applied. He has tested copyright trade to determine whether the "blockbuster" rule of German law applies. Professor Engel's papers have been published in journals such as the *Journal of Empirical Legal Studies*, the *American Law and Economics Review*, *Duke Law Journal*, the *Journal of Economic Behavior and Organization*, and *Perspectives on Psychological Science*. Professor Engel's chapter first appeared in expanded form in the *Duke Law Journal* (2015). It is reproduced here in edited form by permission.

MARC ENGELHART is head of the Max Planck Research Group on "The Architecture of Public Security Regulation" and head of the section for business and economic criminal law at the Max Planck Institute for Foreign and International Criminal Law in Freiburg, Germany. He studied law at the Universities of Freiburg, Germany (where he also completed his PhD), and Edinburgh, United Kingdom, and has been a researcher at the Max Planck Institute since 2003. His work and publications concentrate on comparative criminal law and in recent years on the preventive aspects of criminal law, police law, and the law of the secret services. From February 2014 to the end of January 2015 he was a visiting scholar at the Institute of Criminology, University of Cambridge, and at the Centre for Criminology, University of Oxford, working on preventive justice in English law.

JOSHUA FAIRFIELD is a Professor of Law at the Washington and Lee University School of Law where his research and teaching focuses on big data privacy, digital property, electronic contracts, and virtual communities. His articles on protecting consumer interests in an age of mass-market consumer contracting regularly appear in top journals, and his policy pieces on consumer protection and technology have appeared in the *New York Times*, *Forbes*, and the *Financial Times*. In 2012–13 he was awarded a Fulbright Grant to study transatlantic privacy law at the Max Planck Institute for Research on Collective Goods in Bonn, Germany. He was elected a member of the American Law Institute in 2013, and is an Advisory Board member of the Future of Privacy Forum. Prior to his career in the law Professor Fairfield was a technology entrepreneur, serving as the director of research and development for the language-learning software company Rosetta Stone. He is currently writing a book for Cambridge University Press entitled *OWNED: Property, Privacy, and the New Digital Serfdom*. Professor Fairfield's chapter first appeared in expanded form in the *Duke Law Journal* (2015). It is reproduced here in edited form by permission.

KLAUS FERDINAND GÄRDITZ studied at the University of Bonn (1995–98) and completed his First and Second State Exams in 1999 and 2001. He was awarded his doctorate in law with a dissertation in criminal procedural law in 2001. Professor Gärditz has been an attorney-at-law and judge at an Administrative Court from 2002 to 2004. His academic posts include service as an assistant professor of public law (*Wissenschaftlicher Assistent*) at the University of Bayreuth (2004–09); completion of a postdoctoral thesis (*Habilitation*) in administrative law (2008); and a Chair of Public Law at the University of Bonn since April 2009. He has also been a deputy judge at the Constitutional Court of North Rhine-Westphalia since July 2014, and judge of appeal at the Higher Administrative Court of North Rhine-Westphalia since March 2015. Professor Gärditz has been a legal expert on constitutional and administrative law subjects for various parliamentary committees on the federal and state levels and for private companies, including network firms. He also has served as counsel representing governments and parliaments in litigation in administrative and constitutional courts. Professor Gärditz thanks Dr. Carl-Friedrich Stuckenberg (LLM) for his sterling comments on the criminal liability questions in his chapter.

MORTON H. HALPERIN is a Senior Advisor to the Open Society Foundations and the Open Society Policy Center. Dr. Halperin worked for many years for the American Civil Liberties Union (ACLU). He was Director of the Center for National Security Studies from 1975 to 1992; from 1984 to 1992 he was also the Director of the Washington Office of the ACLU. Dr. Halperin has testified more than fifty times before congressional committees on civil liberties issues. He served in the Clinton, Nixon, and Johnson administrations; in the Defense and State Departments; on the staff of the National Security Council; and as the Director of the Policy Planning Staff at the Department of State (1998–2001). He is the author of numerous books and articles on national security and civil liberties, including *The Lawless State* (1976) and *Bureaucratic Politics and Foreign Policy* (2006).

SARAH HARTMANN is a research associate at the Institute for Information, Telecommunications and Media Law at the University of Münster, Germany. She studied law in Bremen, Paris, and Münster. After passing her first State Exam in law in 2013 she began working at the Institute for Information, Telecommunications, and Media Law and is currently developing her dissertation on press regulation in convergent media environments. Her research interests are focused on human rights in European and international media and data protection law.

BEN HAYES is a Fellow of the Transnational Institute, an Associate of the Human Security Collective, and a researcher at the Peace Research Institute, Oslo. He also works as an independent consultant. Dr. Hayes' counterterrorism work includes groundbreaking research into the proliferation and impact of terrorist "blacklists" (e.g., on human rights and conflict resolution) and the impact of counter-terrorism laws on charities, development, and "civil society" organizations. He has a PhD from Magee College awarded by the University of Ulster in 2008.

LAURA HEINS is the author of *Nazi Film Melodrama* (2013) and various articles on German film history and media theory. She has been a professor at Tulane University and the University of Virginia.

STEFAN HEUMANN is a member of the Management Board at the Berlin think-tank *Stiftung Neue Verantwortung* and a cofounder of its privacy project, which seeks to engage policy makers, civil society, and businesses in a debate on how privacy needs to and can be protected in the age of big data and mass surveillance. He is also a member of the Freedom Online Coalition Working Group 3, "Privacy and Transparency Online." He holds a PhD in political science from the University of Pennsylvania. For valuable feedback, criticism, and feedback on earlier drafts of this chapter, Dr. Heumann would like to thank his colleagues Thorsten Wetzling, Ben Scott, and the participants of the "Transatlantic Dialogue on Surveillance Methods" symposium hosted by the Max Planck institute in Freiburg in December 2014. He also extends special gratitude to Russell Miller for pushing him to sharpen his arguments and making many helpful suggestions for the improvement of the chapter.

BERND HOLZNAGEL (Dr., LLM, Dipl-Soz) is a professor for Constitutional Law, Administrative Law, European Law, and Administrative Sciences at the University of Münster where he is also the Director of the Institute for Information, Telecommunications, and Media Law. Professor Holznagel studied law and sociology in Berlin. After postgraduate LLM studies at McGill University in Montreal, Canada, he received his PhD at the University of Hamburg (1990). He finished his habilitation *Broadcasting Law in Europe – The Path to a Common Law in the European Broadcasting System* at the University of Hamburg in 1995. It received a special award issued by the European Group of Public Law during its Spetses Reunion in 1996. Professor Holznagel is member of the academic advisory council of the *Bundesnetzagentur* (Federal Network Agency for Electricity, Gas, Telecommunications, Post, and Railway). His research interests include Public Law and Regulatory Law (Media, Telecommunication, Energy, Data Protection/Security, and State Aid Law).

SARAH HOROWITZ has a PhD from the University of California, Berkeley, and is Associate Professor of History at Washington and Lee University. She is the author of *Friendship and Politics in Post-Revolutionary France* (2013) and articles on the relationship between politics, gender, the emotions, and privacy in the nineteenth century. She is currently working on a study of sex scandals in modern France. Professor Horowitz thanks Russell Miller for encouraging her to write this chapter and for his helpful comments on an earlier draft. She is also grateful to Margaret Hu, members of the German Law in Context seminar, and Professor Hu's Cybersecurity Policy and Privacy Law seminar for their thoughtful questions and suggestions.

MARGARET HU is Assistant Professor of Law at Washington and Lee University School of Law. Her research interests include the intersection of immigration policy, national security, cybersurveillance, and civil rights. Previously, she served as senior policy advisor for the White House Initiative on Asian Americans and Pacific Islanders, and also served as special policy counsel in the Office of Special Counsel for Immigration-Related Unfair Employment Practices, Civil Rights Division, U.S. Department of Justice, in Washington, D.C. Professor Hu's articles include "Biometric ID Cybersurveillance," "Small Data Surveillance v. Big Data Cybersurveillance," "Big Data Blacklisting," and "Taxonomy of the Snowden Disclosures." Professor Hu extends deep gratitude to those who offered comments on drafts of this chapter, or who offered perspectives and expertise on this research, including danah boyd, Andy Briggs, Andrew Christensen, Josh Fairfield, Amos Guiora, Erik Luna, Russell Miller, Steve Miskinis, Ralf Poscher, John Radsan, Andrew Selbst, Jeff Powell, and the participants of the "Privacy and Power: Transatlantic Dialogue in the Shadow of the NSA-Affair" Symposium, hosted by the University of Freiburg, KORSE Centre for Security and

Society, in Freiburg, Germany. Professor Hu also thanks the following for research assistance: Rossana Baeza, Emily Bao, Lauren Bugg, Russell Caleb Chaplain, Maureen Edobar, Cadman Kiker, Kirby Kreider, Madeline Morcelle, Markus Murden, Kelsey Peregoy, and Cole Wilson.

EVA JOBS is a Historian at the Bundeswehr Military History Museum and a PhD candidate at the University of Marburg. In her dissertation she addresses the role trust, secrecy, and betrayal play in transatlantic intelligence cooperation. Her historical analysis highlights not only the importance of personal relationships but also demonstrates the effects of rituals, values, and habit. She has held positions as a Visiting Scholar at the University of North Carolina, Chapel Hill, and a Research Fellow at the American Institute for Contemporary German Studies (AICGS). Ms. Jobs holds a master's degree from Philipps University, Marburg. In 2011–12 she was a research assistant for the Independent Research Commission for the History of the German Intelligence Service (BND) in Berlin and Washington, D.C. Ms. Jobs wishes to thank Russell Miller and Sebastian Jobs for their comments and criticisms.

RONALD D. LEE is a partner of Arnold & Porter LLP in Washington, D.C., where his practice focuses on national security, cybersecurity, and privacy law. He served as General Counsel of the U.S. National Security Agency from 1994 to 1998 and as Associate Deputy Attorney General, U.S. Department of Justice, from 1998 to 2000. Mr. Lee graduated from Princeton University with highest honors. He received an MPhil in International Relations from the University of Oxford, where he attended Balliol College as a Rhodes Scholar, and a JD from Yale Law School. He served as a law clerk to Justice John Paul Stevens, United States Supreme Court, and as a law clerk to Judge Abner J. Mikva, United States Court of Appeals for the District of Columbia Circuit. He is an elected member of the American Law Institute and regularly writes and speaks on cybersecurity, privacy, counterterrorism, national security, and government contracts. Mr. Lee acknowledges with gratitude the assistance of Nicholas L. Townsend and Tom McSorley, both of Arnold & Porter LLP, in the preparation of this chapter. Mr. Lee's chapter presents the author's personal views and not those of any organization with which the author is or has been affiliated.

JOHANNES MASING is a Justice of the Federal Constitutional Court of Germany and a Professor of Law at the University of Freiburg in Germany, where he holds the chair for Constitutional Law. At the Court he serves on the First Senate where he is the reporting justice for the right to free speech, freedom of information and the press, the general right of personality, data protection law, and the right of assembly. Justice Masing was a visiting professor at the University of Pennsylvania, repeatedly at the Université Paris 1, Paris 2, and Lyon 3, as well as at the Jagellonian University of Kraków. As a visiting scholar he spent six months at the University of Michigan. In 2007, Justice Masing was granted the Gay Lussac Humboldt award. Before taking up his post in Freiburg, Justice Masing taught in Augsburg, Heidelberg, and Bielefeld. He was a judicial law clerk for Justice Böckenförde at the Federal Constitutional Court.

RUSSELL A. MILLER is a Professor of Law at the Washington and Lee University School of Law where his research and teaching focuses on comparative law theory and methods, German law and legal culture, comparative constitutional law, and public international law. He has authored and edited a number of books in these fields, including *The Constitutional Jurisprudence of the Federal Republic of Germany* (with Donald Kommers; 3rd edn. 2012) and *U.S. National Security, Intelligence and Democracy: From the Church Committee to the War on Terror* (2009). He was a 2013–14 Research Fellow at the Center for Security and Society at the University of Freiburg. Professor Miller is the cofounder and Editor-in-Chief of the *German Law Journal*.

KONSTANTIN VON NOTZ is Deputy Chairman of the Alliance 90/The Greens in the German *Bundestag*, where he has served since 2009. In the *Bundestag* Dr. von Notz has held a number of committee assignments with central importance for issues involving technology, the Internet, and privacy. He has been his party's spokesman of the Committee on Political Strategy for the Internet, and the Committee of Inquiry for NSA Surveillance. During the seventeenth term of the *Bundestag*, Dr. von Notz served as spokesman for the Study Commission on the Internet and Digital Society. He studied law and earned a PhD in law at the University of Heidelberg and practiced law as an attorney in Mölln, Schleswig-Holstein prior to entering the parliament. Dr. von Notz thanks Nils Leopold (LLM), who was the legal advisor in Dr. Notz's office, for his collaboration on this chapter.

DAWN CARLA NUNZIATO is Professor of Law at the George Washington University in Washington, D.C., where she codirects the Global Internet Freedom and Human Rights Project. She is an internationally recognized expert in the area of free speech and the Internet and has taught Internet law courses and been an invited presenter on Internet free speech issues around the world, including at Harvard, Yale, Oxford, the Organization for Security and Cooperation in Europe (OSCE) in Vienna, the European University Institute in Florence, the Munich Intellectual Property Law Center, Tsinghua University in Beijing, the Center for Studies on Freedom of Expression and Access to Information in Buenos Aires, and the Instituto Tecnológico Autónomo de México in Mexico City. She has published widely in national and international journals and is the author of *Virtual Freedom: Net Neutrality and Free Speech in the Internet Age*. Professor Nunziato is grateful to Lauren Pyle and Ken Rodriguez for providing excellent research and library assistance in connection with this chapter. She is also grateful to Professor Todd Peterson and Professor Russell Miller for their helpful comments on earlier drafts, and to Dean Blake Morant for financial support of her research and writing.

ANNE PETERS is Director of the Max Planck Institute for Comparative Public Law and International Law in Heidelberg, Germany. She is also a professor at the universities of Heidelberg, Freie Universität Berlin, and Basel (Switzerland). She has been a member (substitute) of the European Commission for Democracy through Law (Venice Commission) in respect of Germany (2011–15) and served as the President of the European Society of International Law (2010–12). Born in Berlin in 1964, Professor Peters studied at the universities of Würzburg, Lausanne, Freiburg, and Harvard. Her books (authored and coedited) include: *Jenseits der Menschenrechte* (2014) [*Beyond Human Rights* (Cambridge University Press, 2016)]; *Transparency in International Law* (Cambridge University Press, 2013); *Oxford Handbook of the History of International Law* (2012; ASIL certificate of merit); *Conflict of Interest in Global, Public and Corporate Governance* (Cambridge University Press, 2012); *The Constitutionalization of International Law* (2011); *Non-state Actors as Standard Setters* (Cambridge University Press, 2009); *Women, Quotas and Constitutions* (1999). Professor Peters thanks Stephen Chovanec for excellent research assistance, and Russell Miller for his help editing and polishing the chapter.

RALF POSCHER is Director of the Institute for Philosophy of Law at the University of Freiburg, where he is also the Managing Director of the Centre for Security and Society. His areas of research cover national security law, fundamental rights, and legal theory. His writings in English on security law include "The Moral and Legal Risks of Interventions" in the *Journal of Institutional and Theoretical Economics*; "Surveillance and Data Protection in the Conflict between European and American Legal Cultures" (with Russell Miller) in *American Institute for Contemporary German Studies Working Papers*; and "Terrorism and the Constitution – Looking at the German Case" in *Dissent*. He received a doctorate and habilitated at Humboldt University of Berlin.

SUMMER RENAULT-STEELE has degrees in Continental Philosophy and the History of Philosophy from Villanova University. Her research combines the resources of feminist philosophy with German and French critical theory in the aesthetic analysis of figurative language, film, and new media. Her translations, interviews, and reviews have appeared in *Epoché: A Journal for the History of Philosophy*; *PhaenEx: A Journal of Existential and Phenomenological Theory and Culture*; and the *American Philosophical Association Newsletter on Feminism and Philosophy*. Her most recent work, based on her dissertation "Unravel the Girl, Unravel the World: Critical Theory, Gender, and the Crisis of Modernity," is forthcoming with *Philosophia: A Journal of Continental Feminism*.

SUSANA SÁNCHEZ FERRO teaches Constitutional Law at the Universidad Autónoma de Madrid. She holds a PhD in Constitutional Law from the Universidad Autónoma de Madrid and completed her training at Saarland University and University of California, Berkeley. She held a Fulbright Scholarship to take part in the U.S. Institute Winter 2005 Program: "U.S. National Security: American Foreign Policy Formulation in an Era of Globalization," which was organized by the U.S. Department of State at the University of Delaware. She is the author of the book *State Secrets Privilege* (2006) and several articles dealing with the tensions between national security and fundamental rights. Professor Sánchez Ferro took part as an expert in the discussions that led to the elaboration of The Global Principles on National Security and the Right to Information. She has been a visiting scholar at the London School of Economics and Political Science (2009) and at the University of Freiburg (2014).

JENS-PETER SCHNEIDER is a professor of Public Law at the University of Freiburg. Among other topics he has taught German, European, and Comparative Administrative Law at the Universities of Freiburg (since 2010), Osnabrück (2000–10), and Hamburg (1993–2000). Professor Schneider has been a Visiting Research Fellow at Brasenose College,

Oxford, and in 2006 he established the annual International Seminar on European and Comparative Law together with colleagues from the Universities of Birmingham, Oxford, Strasbourg, and Tilburg. He is cofounder and coordinator of the Research Network on E.U. Administrative Law (ReNEUAL). His publications address issues of German and European constitutional, regulatory, and administrative law, as well as comparative law. E.U. data protection law and E.U. information management law are a special focus of his work. Professor Schneider's chapter is based on a presentation at the symposium "Privacy and Power – A Transatlantic Dialogue in the Shadow of the NSA-Affair" held at the University of Freiburg in July 2014, and on a talk held at the Columbia Law School. He is grateful for the comments he received at these events.

BEN SCOTT is Senior Advisor to the *Stiftung Neue Verantwortung* in Berlin and the Open Technology Institute at New America in Washington, D.C. Previously, he was Policy Adviser for Innovation at the U.S. Department of State, and for six years he led the Washington office for Free Press, a nonprofit organization dealing with media and communications policy. Before joining Free Press, Dr. Scott worked as a legislative aide handling telecommunications policy for then-Rep. Bernie Sanders (I-VT) in the U.S. House of Representatives. He holds a PhD in communications from the University of Illinois.

MATHIAS VERMEULEN is a research fellow at the Free University of Brussels. He previously worked for the U.N. Special Rapporteur on The Protection of Human Rights while Countering Terrorism, the Belgian Intelligence Oversight Committee, and the European University Institute in Florence.

SILJA VÖENEKY is Co-Director of the Institute for Public Law as well as Professor of Public International Law, and the Ethics of Law at the University of Freiburg. She was a member of the German Ethics Council, where she was head of the working group "Biosecurity." During the 2015–16 academic year she was a Visiting Fellow at Harvard Law School (Human Rights Program). Her areas of focus include humanitarian law, environmental law, human rights law, the relation of ethics and law, bioethics and biolaw, and especially questions on how to govern existential risks. With respect to the latter, she is the head of the research group Regulation and Governance of Existential Risks (LGER). Professor Voeneky was also a member of the Board of Directors for the Freiburg platform of the Network for Civil Security Law in Europe (KORSE); She is a member of the Standing Committee Science and Ethics of the Leopoldina (National Academy of Sciences). Professor Voeneky is grateful to Ms. M. Roseman (Human Rights Program Harvard Law School), Commander I. Park (Royal Navy, Fellow Harvard Law School), and Dr. C. Draghici (Fellow Harvard Law School) for their helpful remarks. She is also thankful for the valuable support of Mr. F. Beck, Mr. J. Juergensen, and Mr. D. Wisehart (University of Freiburg).

ALEC WALEN is Professor at Rutgers University, with a joint appointment in Law, Philosophy, and Criminal Justice. He has published numerous articles and chapters on topics in criminal law, constitutional law, and national security law, as well as moral philosophy, including: "Human Dignity and Proportionality: Deontic Pluralism in Balancing" (with Mattias Kumm) in *Proportionality and the Rule of Law: Rights, Justification, Reasoning* (2014); "Transcending the Means Principle" in *Law and Philosophy* (2014); and "A Unified Theory of Detention, with Application to Preventive Detention for Suspected Terrorists" in the *Maryland Law Review* (2011). Professor Walen thanks the following people for their help in discussing this chapter in its developmental stages: David Cole, Jennifer Daskal, Jonathan Hafetz, Erin Islo, Russell Miller, Cymie Payne, Ralf Poscher, and the participants at the Privacy and Power Symposium at the University of Freiburg in July 2014. A longer version of this chapter can be found in 16 *German Law Journal* 1131 (2015).

BENJAMIN WITTES is a Senior Fellow in Governance Studies at the Brookings Institution and Editor-in-Chief of *Lawfare*.

LUCIA ZEDNER, FBA, is Professor of Criminal Justice and Law Fellow, Corpus Christi Senior Research Fellow, All Souls College, University of Oxford, and Conjoint Professor, Faculty of Law, University of New South Wales, Sydney. She was elected as a Fellow of The British Academy in 2012. She has held visiting fellowships at universities in Germany, Israel, America, and Australia. Her publications include *Women, Crime, and Custody in Victorian England* (1991); *Child Victims* (1992, with J. Morgan); *The Criminological Foundations of Penal Policy* (2003, coedited with A. Ashworth); *Criminal Justice* (2004); *Security* (2009); *Principles and Values in Criminal Law and Criminal Justice* (2012, coedited with Julian Roberts); *Prevention and the Limits of the Criminal Law* (2013, coedited with A. Ashworth and P. Tomlin); and *Preventive Justice* (2014, with A. Ashworth). Her present research interests include criminal law and criminal justice, surveillance, security, border control, and counterterrorism. Professor Zedner is grateful to the participants, and especially to Russell Miller, at the symposium "Transatlantic Dialogue on Surveillance Methods" held at the Max Planck Institute for Foreign and International Criminal Law in Freiburg in December 2014. She is also grateful to Professor Ian Brown of the Oxford Internet Institute for helpful feedback and comments. Finally, Professor Zedner thanks Cian Ó Concubhair for his valuable research assistance on this chapter.

ACKNOWLEDGMENTS

The essential transatlantic dialogue on the issues of personal information privacy and intelligence gathering that this book urges is already underway. Most of the chapters in this volume began as contributions to several transatlantic collaborations and programs dating back to the days immediately after the first media reports covering Edward Snowden's leaks. A number of remarkable institutions have helped to foster that exchange and supported the publication of this book.

None did more than the Center for Security and Society at the University of Freiburg, which hosted one platform in the Network for Civil Security Law in Europe (KORSE). The KORSE network, with funding from the German Federal Ministry of Education and Research, aimed to promote interdisciplinary and international research on legal issues related to European security. Several of the contributors to this book had close ties to KORSE, including its Directors (Ralf Poscher, Jens-Peter Schneider, and Silja Vöneky). Other contributors (Russell Miller, Susana Sánchez-Ferro, and Alec Walen) enjoyed generous KORSE research fellowships at the University of Freiburg. Most importantly, KORSE hosted a two-day, transatlantic symposium in the summer of 2014 at which early versions of many of the book's chapters were presented and discussed by a range of American and European commentators and practitioners.

The *German Law Journal*, in cooperation with the School of Law and the German and Russian Department at Washington and Lee University, extended and expanded the conversation in the framework of the "German Law in Context Seminar" that took place at Washington and Lee University in the fall of 2014. The seminar featured lectures from several of the book's contributors (Roger Crockett, Laura Heins, Bernd Holznagel, Sarah Horowitz, and Summer Renault-Steele).

The discussion resumed at a two-day symposium in December 2014 that was hosted by the Max Planck Institute for Foreign and International Criminal Law in Freiburg, Germany. Carolin Hillemanns (a Senior Research Fellow at the Max Planck Institute) and Margaret Hu (Washington and Lee University School of Law) provided visionary leadership for that program. Because many of these chapters were contributions to these particular discussions they are shaped by and respond to those distinct conversations and contexts. This gives them twofold value: they document the tenor of the discourse in the immediate aftermath of Snowden's revelations; and they lay a foundation for developments in the years since 2013.

The project also served as the basis for immensely productive conversations between me and young Germans, who are particularly passionate about these issues. The book's chapters formed part of the curriculum for the sessions of Working Group 6 at the 2015 *Studienstiftung* Summer Academy in Neubeuern, Germany. Similarly, the book's chapters served as the curriculum for a series of lectures I was invited to give at the University of Greifswald in December 2015. In those settings my faculty colleagues – Andreas Paulus and Uwe Kischel – offered invaluable insight and proved to be lively discussion partners on these questions.

My work on this volume was supported by the American Institute for Contemporary German Studies (AICGS) and the Max Planck Institute for Comparative Public Law and Public International Law (Heidelberg, Germany). I was in residence at the AICGS as a DAAD Research Fellow in May and June 2015. The AICGS, located in Washington, D.C., has a vast and impressive network of experts and contacts. I enjoyed remarkable conditions there for productive work on this project. My understanding of these matters especially benefitted from conversations with AICGS President Jackson Janes and Senior Research Associate Parke Nicholson. The Heidelberg MPI supported my research stay in 2015–16, when I finished the writing and editing for this book. The conversations I had with the Institute's immensely competent research staff proved to be a great asset. The MPI's directors, Armin von Bogdandy and Anne Peters, were generous with their resources and their time. This experience confirmed my conviction that the Heidelberg MPI is my true scholarly *Heimat*.

The editors and staff at Cambridge University Press (including Finola O'Sullivan, Rebecca Roberts, and Lorenza Toffolon) made a significant contribution to the dialogue as well. They showed great enthusiasm for the project, offered valuable wisdom and insight on the book's substance, and demonstrated remarkable patience and professionalism during the book's production. Washington and Lee University law students Stephen

Chovanec and Hengyi Jiang provided tireless and always-professional research and editorial assistance throughout my work on the book.

I mention these institutions and events not only because I want to acknowledge the role they played in helping realize my vision for this book. I also want to demonstrate that there is genuine – even determined – interest in a transatlantic dialogue on these and many other important issues. These programs and institutions show that the infrastructure is in place to pursue this important conversation.

This book's title deliberately draws on the title of Daniel Solove's seminal article, "Privacy and Power: Computer Databases and Metaphors for Information Privacy," 53 *Stanford Law Review* 1393 (2001). Rosa Ehrenreich also used the phrase in the title to her essay reacting to Jeffrey Rosen's excellent book *The Unwanted Gaze* (2001). That essay published as "Privacy and Power," 89 *Georgetown Law Journal* 2047 (2000–01). The book's contributors and I are indebted to these (and many other) pioneers in this field. I hope they appreciate the old axiom that "imitation is the sincerest form of flattery."

Finally, I want to thank my family for accompanying me in and supporting this work.

Introduction

Privacy and Power: A Transatlantic Dialogue in the Shadow of the NSA-Affair

BY RUSSELL A. MILLER

A Introduction

Edward Snowden's disclosures in the early summer of 2013 have had a roiling, still-unfolding effect. The consequences of the former National Security Agency (NSA) contractor's revelations are intensely disputed. One version of the story is that Snowden's courageous and visionary acts helped galvanize a new and more focused global debate about privacy in our digital, big-data epoch.[1] This debate, in turn, has spurred a number of policy and legal reforms that seek, on one hand, to reinforce communications privacy and data protection while, on the other hand, imposing greater constraints and oversight on states' intelligence services.[2] As Snowden hoped, the West's fundamental commitment to privacy has been revived and reinforced for a new era.[3] But there is another version of the story according to which Snowden's traitorous conduct

---

[1] *See, e.g.,* Interview by Amy Goodman of James Risen, Pulitzer Prize winning investigative journalist with the N.Y. TIMES (Oct. 14, 2014), www.democracynow.org/2014/10/14/james_risen_on_nsa_whistleblower_edward (claiming that Snowden "sparked a new national debate on surveillance).

[2] *See* Andrea Peterson, *A Year after Snowden Revelations, Government Surveillance Reform Still a Work in Progress,* WASH. POST (June 5, 2014), www.washingtonpost.com/news/the-switch/wp/2014/06/05/a-year-after-snowden-revelations-government-surveillance-reform-still-a-work-in-progress/ (arguing that the "move toward greater openness is arguably an incredible shift of policy in a very short period of time."). *But see* Sarah Childress, *How the NSA Spying Programs Have Changed since Snowden,* PBS (Feb. 9, 2015), www.pbs.org/wgbh/frontline/article/how-the-nsa-spying-programs-have-changed-since-snowden/ (alleging that the actual changes implemented "just feel like gestures.").

[3] *See, e.g.,* David Miranda & Joseph Huff-Hannon, *Edward Snowden Inspires Global Treaty for Online Privacy,* ROLLING STONE (Sept. 24, 2015), www.rollingstone.com/politics/news/edward-snowden-inspires-global-treaty-for-online-privacy-20150924.

imperiled essential intelligence initiatives to the advantage of the West's determined and deadly enemies, with frightening consequences.[4] Compounding this view is the suggestion that Snowden's leaks confirm that intelligence services, for the most part, have kept within the legal boundaries ordained by their democratically legitimate masters.[5] There is no evidence, it is argued, that the far-reaching power to watch us has been used to undermine liberties such as the right to democratic participation, the right to free speech, the right to freely assemble, the freedom of religion, or the right to property.[6]

One of the most confounding – and significant – features of the NSA-Affair is that these disputed narratives have a strong transatlantic correlation. This claim can be exaggerated on the basis of overly broad generalizations. Still, thanks to Edward Snowden, it is clearer now than ever before that a vast chasm exists between American and European perspectives on privacy and intelligence gathering.[7] In fact, the different reactions to Edward Snowden's leaks on the opposite sides of the Atlantic reveal that there is hardly another issue about which

---

[4] See Scott Shane, *After Paris Attacks, C.I.A. Director Rekindles Debate Over Surveillance*, N.Y. TIMES (Nov. 16, 2015), www.nytimes.com/2015/11/17/us/after-paris-attacks-cia-director-rekindles-debate-over-surveillance.html?_r=0; James Gordon Meek *et al.*, *Intel Heads: Edward Snowden Did "Profound Damage" to U.S. Security*, ABC NEWS (Jan. 29, 2014), http://abcnews.go.com/Blotter/intel-heads-edward-snowden-profound-damage-us-security/story?id=22285388; John Bolton, *Edward Snowden's Leaks Are a Grave Threat to U.S. National Security*, THE GUARDIAN (June 18, 2013, 7:30 AM), www.theguardian.com/commentisfree/2013/jun/18/edward-snowden-leaks-grave-threat ("Whatever his grandiose claims, the NSA leaker has betrayed his country by gifting China moral equivalence for its cyber warfare."); Tom Risen, *Pentagon Report Says Snowden's NSA Leaks Risk Lives*, U.S.NEWS & WORLD REP. (Jan. 9, 2014, 3:38 PM), www.usnews.com/news/articles/2014/01/09/pentagon-report-says-snowdens-nsa-leaks-risk-lives.

[5] See Chris Strohm, *NSA Use of Facial Recognition Stays within Legal Boundary*, BLOOMBERG BUSINESS (June 3, 2014, 2:29 PM), www.bloomberg.com/news/articles/2014-06-03/nsa-use-of-facial-recognition-stays-within-legal-boundary; Doug Stanglin, *Federal Judge: NSA Phone Surveillance Legal*, USA TODAY (Dec. 27, 2013, 2:20 PM), www.usatoday.com/story/news/nation/2013/12/27/new-york-nsa-phone-surveillance/4219055/.

[6] PRIVACY AND CIVIL LIBERTIES OVERSIGHT BOARD, REPORT ON THE SURVEILLANCE PROGRAM OPERATED PURSUANT TO SECTION 702 OF THE FOREIGN INTELLIGENCE SURVEILLANCE ACT (2014) (the Board found "no evidence" of improper use).

[7] See Francesca Bignami, *European versus American Liberty: A Comparative Privacy Analysis of Antiterrorism Data Mining*, 48 B.C. L. REV. 609 (2007). One of the reasons this cultural divide exists may stem in part from each continent's experience with World War II. In Germany, internal security services were very visible and feared. They sought to persecute part of the German populace. In America, the main threat was painted as being overseas, and so internal security services like the FBI were seen as heroes attempting to root out enemy spies.

transatlantic attitudes diverge so sharply. Americans and Europeans have very different views about privacy and the power of intelligence services.[8] Americans do not understand Europeans' outrage over the collection of seemingly meaningless and mostly innocent information that, when deployed creatively, has pragmatic value for promoting security and commercial innovation. Europeans, and especially Germans, do not understand Americans' seeming indifference toward the profound personal privacy implicated by access to highly revealing telecommunications and Internet data. The so-called "NSA-Affair" – as it is referred to in Germany – once again profoundly and painfully demonstrates that there are "significant privacy conflicts between the United States and the European Countries – conflicts that reflect unmistakable differences in sensibilities about what ought to be kept private."[9]

Especially as we are examining these issues in the tumultuous wake left behind by Snowden's revelations, there are at least two reasons why this divergence matters.

First, transatlantic disagreement over the political and legal meaning of privacy calls into question the widespread conviction that privacy is a shared and fundamental Western value.[10] The concept of the "West" retains its power, in the supposed-West and the supposed-East.[11] But the tensions surrounding the NSA-Affair have revealed that the concept can become the source of misunderstanding when dramatically different values emerge and come into conflict *between* Western societies. In part, the transatlantic discord over privacy and intelligence gathering is surprising because it exposes fissures in what was thought to be a foundation of shared social and political ideals among Western democracies.[12] At a

---

[8] James Q. Whitman, *The Two Western Cultures of Privacy: Dignity versus Liberty*, 113 YALE L.J. 1151 (2004).

[9] *Id.* at 1155.

[10] Gus Hosen & Maria-Martina Yalamova, *International Co-Operation and Intercultural Relations: Reconciling the Security and Privacy Agendas*, in 2 CROSS-CULTURAL INTERACTION: CONCEPTS, METHODOLOGIES, TOOLS, AND APPLICATIONS 818, at 822 (Info. Resources Mgmt. Ass'n, 2014).

[11] *See, e.g.,* Carey Goldberg, *Differences Between East and West Discovered in People's Brain Activity*, THE TECH (Mar. 4, 2008), http://tech.mit.edu/V128/N9/culture.html; Alix Spiegel, *Struggle For Smarts? How Eastern And Western Cultures Tackle Learning*, NPR (Nov. 12, 2012, 3:29 AM), www.npr.org/sections/health-shots/2012/11/12/164793058/struggle-for-smarts-how-eastern-and-western-cultures-tackle-learning.

[12] *See, e.g.,* CHARLES WALDSTEIN, THE EXPANSION OF WESTERN IDEALS AND THE WORLD'S PEACE (1899); NIALL FERGUSON, CIVILIZATION: THE WEST AND THE REST (2011).

time when the West is confronted with serious external challenges,[13] it is imperative that we pursue an honest, nuanced, and critical reflection on the values that supposedly bind us together.

The chapters in this book – either embodying or directly engaging with the different transatlantic reactions to the NSA-Affair – pose a challenge to the fundamental assertion that privacy is a Western (not to mention universal) human right. The critical insight that emerges in this respect is that a concept such as privacy, especially when expressed as a national norm, necessarily reflects a society's culture and identity.[14] The comparative lawyer Pierre Legrand argued that "the objectives pursued by legal actors in a given society can only be determined and understood if account be taken of the culture of which they are also the reflection."[15] With that lesson in mind, the following chapters repeatedly demonstrate that our different notions of privacy as a legal concept are rooted in different histories, different social and cultural forces, different political traditions and institutions, different legal cultures, and different economic conditions and orientations.[16] On these terms, there is no privacy. There are only *privacies*.

Second, there are tremendously important practical consequences for the diverging transatlantic views on privacy that have been exposed by the NSA-Affair. The intense misunderstanding on these issues threatens to undermine essential cooperation on security and commerce.

America and Europe cooperate in important ways on security and intelligence.[17] Both sides of this partnership view it as necessary to

---

[13] Bridget Kendall, *How Does Russia View the West?*, BBC (Aug 10, 2015), www.bbc.com/news/world-europe-33821589 ("If you ask Western policy makers about the main security threats facing Europe, they come up with two: Jihadists from the so-called Islamic State and President Vladimir Putin's Russia."); Gareth Jennings, *West "Must Unite" to Face-Off Simultaneous Threats from Islamic State and Russia*, IHS JANE's 360 (Nov. 16, 2015), www.janes.com/article/56033/west-must-unite-to-face-off-simultaneous-threats-from-islamic-state-and-russia.

[14] *See* Irwan Altman, *Privacy Regulation: Culturally Universal or Culturally Specific?*, 33 J. Soc. Issues 66 (1977); Stephan Richter & Jan Philipp Albrecht, *NSA Spying on Europe Reflects the Transatlantic Culture Gap*, The Guardian (Oct. 30, 2013, 7:19 AM), www.theguardian.com/commentisfree/2013/oct/30/nsa-spying-europe-transatlantic-culture-gap.

[15] Pierre Legrand, *Comparative Legal Studies and Commitment to Theory*, 58 Mod. L. Rev. 262, 263 (1995).

[16] Altman, *supra* note 14 ("[T]he behavioral mechanisms by which accessibility is controlled are probably unique to the particular physical, psychological, and social circumstances of a culture.").

[17] Richard J. Aldrich, *Transatlantic Intelligence and Security Cooperation*, 80 Int'l Affairs 733 (2004) (describing the "awkward challenges" that face "western intelligence cooperation").

their respective interests.[18] If that is true, then restoring the trust that was shattered by the NSA-Affair must be a priority, especially as long as we face common – and deadly – threats.[19] This book, with its plain and accessible presentation of our differences, can help us reframe and refashion a common posture that delivers as much cooperation, and as much security, as possible, despite our significant differences.

America and Europe are also indispensable commercial partners, especially in fields that implicate telecommunications data. Our digital ships – full of commercially relevant and valuable data – used to sail in and out of one another's "safe harbors."[20] As a result of the NSA-Affair, this is no longer to be taken for granted. The value of the trade interests thought to be harmed by the NSA-Affair has been calculated to be in the billions.[21] It touches the travel, telecommunications, information technology, and banking industries.[22] Seemingly in reaction to the NSA-Affair, the Court of Justice of the European Union (CJEU) has repeatedly pressed for a distinctly European approach to data protection with

---

[18] John M. Nomikos, *Transatlantic Intelligence Cooperation, the Global War on Terrorism, and International Order, in* INTERNATIONAL ORDER IN A GLOBALIZING WORLD 161, at 161 (Yannis A. Stivachtis ed., 2007) ("The process [of intelligence cooperation] must be a joint transatlantic partnership which emphasizes shared beliefs, values, and interests; addresses more constructively the differences and greivances; and builds a future upon the recognition that all face a common enemy, one that can be effectively contained and eliminated only through a recognition of mutual interests and the use of multilateral alliances, strategies, and action.").

[19] *See* GEORG MASCOLO & BEN SCOTT, OPEN TECHNOLOGY INSTITUTE, LESSONS FROM THE SUMMER OF SNOWDEN: THE HARD ROAD BACK TO TRUST (2013), http://wcfia.harvard .edu/files/wcfia/files/mascolo_summerofsnowden_0.pdf?m=1383852775.

[20] *See* Mark Scott, *Data Transfer Pact Between U.S. and Europe Is Ruled Invalid*, N.Y. TIMES (Oct. 6, 2015), www.nytimes.com/2015/10/07/technology/european-union-us-data-collection.html; Julia Fioretti & Foo Yun Chee, New European, U.S. Data Transfer Pact Agreed, REUTERS (Feb. 2, 2016, 1:15 PM), www.reuters.com/article/us-eu-dataprotection-usa-accord-idUSKCN0VB1RN.

[21] DANIELLE KEHL *ET AL.*, OPEN TECHNOLOGY INSTITUTE, SURVEILLANCE COSTS: THE NSA's IMPACT ON THE ECONOMY, INTERNET FREEDOM & CYBERSECURITY (2014), www.scribd.com/doc/235335954/OTI-Surveilance-Costs-Final; Sam Gustin, *NSA Spying Will Cost U.S. Tech Titans Billions, and That's Just the Start*, MOTHERBOARD (July 28, 2014, 11:00 PM), http://motherboard.vice.com/read/nsa-spying-will-cost-us-tech-titans-billions-and-thats-just-the-start.

[22] *See, e.g.*, KEHL *ET AL.*, *supra* note 21, at 11 ("The NSA disclosures have similarly been blamed for Brazil's December 2013 decision to award a $4.5 billion contract to Saab over Boeing, an American company that had previously been the frontrunner in a deal to replace Brazil's fleet of fighter jets.").

serious consequences for transatlantic trade.[23] These questions created a significant sticking point in the negotiations over a Transatlantic Trade and Investment Partnership.[24] To preserve, let alone "maximize," the value of the stable and mutually beneficial transatlantic economy, it is necessary to have the authentic and constructive conversation about privacy and intelligence gathering that this book promotes.

Or maybe we are making too much of the tension surrounding the NSA-Affair? It is possible, instead, to see our deep and persistent transatlantic interdependence on security and commercial matters as evidence that these events have not cut out the root of transatlanticism. According to this interpretation, Americans and Europeans have to be close enough to one another to make such a falling out possible in the first place. Seen in this light, the NSA-Affair might be little more than yet another spat in an otherwise constant and secure relationship. Before I survey the book's contents and offer some introductory reflections on the lessons they teach, I want to respond to the challenge this suggestion poses to the book's underlying thesis. The NSA-Affair is more than just a common tiff between old and steady friends. We would be wise to take it more seriously than that. It is clear to me that Americans and Europeans differ fundamentally on the issues most closely linked to the NSA-Affair.

B   Different Reactions to the NSA-Affair

The terms Americans and Europeans – especially Germans – use to describe the NSA-Affair suggest profound differences regarding privacy and intelligence gathering. This is confirmed by polling results and anecdotes that reflect different reactions to Snowden and the different values Americans and Europeans assign to privacy. Finally, the differences are also clear in the way scholars in the United States and Germany think and write about privacy.

I   What's in a Name? – And Other Anecdotes

Throughout this book the phrase "NSA-Affair" is used to describe the political and legal turmoil – both domestic and international – loosed by

---

[23] Christopher Kuner, *The European Union and the Search for an International Data Protection Framework*, 2 GRONINGEN J. INT'L L. 55 (2014).

[24] Mary Bottari, *NSA Spying Scandal Roils U.S.–E.U. Trade Negotiations*, HUFFINGTON POST (Nov. 10, 2013, 5:25 PM), www.huffingtonpost.com/mary-bottari/us-eu-trade-negoti ations_b_4251035.html.

Edward Snowden's disclosure of some of the NSA's extensive data collection and intelligence gathering activities.[25] But that phrase suggests critical unease (if not hostility tinted with intimations of illegality) towards the operations exposed by Snowden.[26] The NSA's programs qualify as an "affair" if they are scandalous – that is, unethical or illegal. In this sense, the use of the phrase "NSA-Affair" is a concession to the anger the revelations have stirred in many Europeans.[27] That concession, however, seems to conflict with the book's central claim, which is that, as a result of different cultural and legal traditions concerning privacy and intelligence gathering, Americans and Europeans have reacted differently to the news that the NSA is collecting immense amounts of their telecommunications data. The book starts from the premise that Americans and Europeans do not equally share the view that these programs are scandalous. That is the case – despite the book's adoption of the phrase "NSA-Affair." The developments swirling around Snowden's revelations are not seen in singularly appalling terms by Americans. It is largely the German media that has referred to the story as the "NSA-Affäre," with all of the accompanying negative connotations of that label.[28] References to the "NSA-Affair" in the American media mostly involve reports describing the German reaction to the

---

[25] *See* Tom McCarthy, *Edward Snowden Identifies Himself as Source of NSA Leaks – as It Happened*, THE GUARDIAN (June 9, 2013, 5:16 PM), www.theguardian.com/world/2013/jun/09/nsa-secret-surveillance-lawmakers-live. *See, generally, The NSA Files*, THE GUARDIAN, www.theguardian.com/us-news/the-nsa-files (last visited Feb. 13, 2016); *NSA Spying Scandal*, SPIEGEL ONLINE, www.spiegel.de/international/topic/nsa_spying_scandal/ (last visited Feb. 13, 2016).

[26] Charly Wilder, *"Out of Hand": Europe Furious Over U.S. Spying Allegations*, SPIEGEL ONLINE (Oct. 24, 2013, 1:17 PM), www.spiegel.de/international/world/angry-european-and-german-reactions-to-merkel-us-phone-spying-scandal-a-929725.html.

[27] *Id. See also* Alison Smale, *Anger Growing Among Allies on U.S. Spying*, N.Y. TIMES (Oct. 23, 2013), www.nytimes.com/2013/10/24/world/europe/united-states-disputes-reports-of-wiretapping-in-Europe.html; Alissa J. Rubin, *French Condemn Surveillance by N.S.A.*, N.Y. TIMES (Oct. 21, 2013), www.nytimes.com/2013/10/22/world/europe/new-report-of-nsa-spying-angers-france.html; Jay Newton-Small, *U.S. Allies Still Angry at Snowden's Revelations of U.S. Spying*, TIME (Oct. 4, 2013), http://nation.time.com/2013/10/04/u-s-allies-still-angry-at-snowdens-revelations-of-u-s-spying/.

[28] *See, e.g.*, Kai Biermann, *Eine Telefonnummer reicht, um Menschen zu töten*, ZEIT ONLINE (Oct. 15, 2015, 6:09 PM), www.zeit.de/politik/2015-10/nsa-affaere-untersuchungsausschuss-metadaten-brandon-bryant-aussage; *NSA-Affäre: Weißes Haus soll Bundesregierung Freigabe der Selektorenliste überlassen haben*, SPIEGEL ONLINE (Aug. 12, 2015, 4:20 PM), www.spiegel.de/politik/deutschland/nsa-affaere-weisses-haus-soll-selektoren-freigabe-nicht-untersagt-haben-a-1047820.html; *NSA-AFFÄRE*, SÜDDEUTSCHE ZEITUNG, www.sueddeutsche.de/thema/NSA-Aff%C3%A4re (last visited Feb. 13, 2016).

story.[29] Even more telling is the fact that Snowden's revelations have not widely earned the label "NSA-gate" or "Snowden-gate" from the American media. That would be in keeping with the tiresome American practice of borrowing the suffix "-gate" from the Nixon-era "Watergate scandal" to create a catchy name for nearly every contemporary controversy.[30] This is true for even the most banal crises in pop culture and politics, but it has not been the way Americans think about Snowden.[31] Americans may be more conflicted than Europeans, who seem to regard the story exclusively as a scandal. Only parts of the story – for only some Americans – qualify as an "affair" (or a "-gate"). As a convenience, the developments of the last several years are referred to in this book as the NSA-Affair. But that is not meant to obscure the fact – fundamental to this book's project – that the labels Americans and Europeans have used to refer to the story reflect the countries' significant differences on the issue.

Besides the very different ways in which they refer to the NSA-Affair, other anecdotes point to the radically different responses to Snowden's revelations in America and Europe. Germans, in particular, have sought to recognize Snowden as an advocate for freedom. German universities have attempted to bestow honorary degrees or other awards of distinction on Snowden. The Academic Senate of the Free University of Berlin granted Snowden an "honorary membership" in appreciation for his "exceptional commitment to transparency, justice and freedom."[32] The philosophy department at the University of

---

[29] See Mirko Hohmann, *The German NSA Affair and the Need for Reform in Berlin*, LAWFARE (Sept. 17, 2015, 7:12 AM), www.lawfareblog.com/german-nsa-affair-and-need-reform-berlin; Democrats Ramshield, *After the NSA Affair, the German Government is Steering towards a Serious Confrontation with the U.S.*, DAILY KOS (Feb. 20, 2014, 8:03 AM), www.dailykos.com/story/2014/2/20/1278992/-After-the-NSA-affair-the-German-government-is-steering-towards-a-serious-confrontation-with-the-US.

[30] Alex Campbell, *Turning a Scandal into a '-gate'*, BBC (May 11, 2013), www.bbc.com/news/magazine-22464422.

[31] There are a plethora of sources on either side of the debate, some praising Snowden and others attempting to bury him. *See supra* note 1, note 4. However, the only usage of the phrase "Snowdengate" in mainstream print media comes from the Telegraph review of the Laura Poitras film CITIZENFOUR. *See* Tim Robey, *Citizenfour Review: "Everybody Needs to See It,"* TELEGRAPH (Oct. 16, 2014), www.telegraph.co.uk/culture/film/filmreviews/11166711/Citizenfour-review-Edward-Snowden.html.

[32] *AStA FU Informs Edward Snowden about His Honorary Membership and Demands Asylum for Edward Snowden*, ASTA FU (June 23, 2014), www.astafu.de/content/asta-fu-informs-edward-snowden-about-his-honorary-membership-and-demands-asylum-edward-snowd.

Rostock sought,[33] but was ultimately denied,[34] the chance to award Snowden an honorary doctorate. Just blocks from the marvelously restored baroque Frauenkirche, a private landowner has named a plaza in Dresden's Neustadt district "Edward Snowden Paltz."[35] There have been efforts in Berlin and Cologne to name streets after Snowden.[36] There have been few such gestures of veneration in the United States,[37] where Snowden instead faces a federal criminal indictment that could result in a lengthy prison sentence.[38] Perhaps worse than the government's strong condemnation, it seems that the American public does not care about Snowden at all. One commentator wondered if Snowden's revelations have grown stale or have "proven to be inaccessible or not titillating enough for the American public."[39] Americans'

---

[33] *Germany: Snowden Approved for Honorary Doctorate*, N.Y. TIMES (May 14, 2014), www.nytimes.com/2014/05/15/world/europe/germany-snowden-approved-for-honorary-doctorate.html.

[34] Rick Noack, *The Global Cult of Edward Snowden Keeps Growing*, WASH. POST (June 23, 2015), www.washingtonpost.com/news/worldviews/wp/2015/06/23/the-global-cult-of-edward-snowden-keeps-growing/ ("When a German university wanted to award Snowden an honorary doctorate, the German federal government stepped in and prohibited the public institution from pursuing its plan.").

[35] *Id.*

[36] Adam Taylor, *The Not-so-Subtle Diplomatic Tactic of Renaming Streets to Troll other Countries*, WASH. POST (June 25, 2015), www.washingtonpost.com/news/worldviews/wp/2014/06/25/the-not-so-subtle-diplomatic-tactic-of-renaming-streets-to-troll-other-coun tries/ (discussing the renaming of a street in Berlin); German Artist Pushes for "Snowden Street" near U.S. Embassy, ALJAZEERA AMERICA (Oct. 31, 2013, 3:38 PM), http://amer ica.aljazeera.com/watch/shows/the-stream/the-stream-officialblog/2013/10/31/ german-artist-pushesforsnowdenstreetnearusembassy.html; *Berlin Activists Want to Rename Major Streets Around the World "Snowden Street"*, MOTHERBOARD (Oct. 30, 2013, 10:30 AM), http://motherboard.vice.com/blog/berlin-activists-want-to-rename-major-streets-around-the-world-snowden-street.

[37] *Artists Who Displayed Edward Snowden Statue in New York Park Escape Charges*, THE GUARDIAN (May 6, 2015, 8:01 PM), www.theguardian.com/us-news/2015/may/07/artists-edward-snowden-statue-new-york-park-charges.

[38] Peter Finn & Sari Horwitz, *U.S. Charges Snowden with Espionage*, WASH. POST (June 21, 2013), www.washingtonpost.com/world/national-security/us-charges-snowden-with-espi onage/2013/06/21/507497d8-dab1-11e2-a016-92547bf094cc_story.html; *U.S. vs. Edward J. Snowden Criminal Complaint*, WASH. POST, http://apps.washingtonpost.com/g/docu ments/world/us-vs-edward-j-snowden-criminal-complaint/496/ (last visited Feb. 13, 2016). For the possible federal penalties, *see* 18 U.S.C.A. § 641 (2016); 18 U.S.C.A. § 793 (2016); 18 U.S.C.A. § 798 (2016).

[39] Adam Chandler, *What It Takes to Make People Care about NSA Surveillance*, ATLANTIC (Apr. 6, 2015), www.theatlantic.com/national/archive/2015/04/naked-selfies-and-the-nsa/389778/. The tepid response to Oliver Stone's film *Snowden*, which released in the fall of 2016, might be additional evidence of the American public's unfamiliarity with or

disinterest in Snowden and his revelations led another commentator to wonder if "Americans have largely accepted the reality of the surveillance state in their lives."[40]

II   Surveying the NSA-Affair

It is hard to imagine a stronger contrast in responses to the NSA-Affair. But American and European differences with respect to personal information privacy and intelligence gathering – and the resulting different reactions to Snowden's revelations – are not just reflected in labels and anecdotes. Social science research and survey data confirm these differences. First, these sources suggest that there are fundamental differences between America and Germany on the issue of personal information privacy. Second, they suggest that there are differences between America and Germany more specifically with respect to the NSA-Affair.

1   Data Privacy as an Abstract Question

At the most fundamental level some social science research claims to have confirmed that there are distinct national cultures.[41] That research, which builds upon the characteristics of national culture described by Gerard Hofstede,[42] assigns the United States and Germany to different (albeit adjacent) clusters of national culture, identified respectively as the "Anglo" and the "Germanic Europe" cultural groups.[43] Building from these claims, many authors in the area of information science claim to have "identified a relationship between national culture and attitude to information privacy."[44] Concerns about personal information privacy are

---

disinterest in Snowden and the NSA-Affair. The first of five reasons for the film's poor-showing at the box office offered by an article in *The Wrap* was that "people don't know/care about Snowden." *See* Beatrice Verhoeven, *5 Reasons Why "Snowden" Couldn't Hack It at the Box Office*, THE WRAP (Sept. 18, 2016), www.thewrap.com/snowden-box-office-not-hack-joseph-gordon-levitt/.

[40] Marc Ambinder, *Does the Public Still Care about the NSA?*, THE WEEK (Jan. 29, 2014), http://theweek.com/articles/452113/does-public-still-care-about-nsa.

[41] GEERT HOFSTEDE, CULTURAL CONSEQUENCES: INTERNATIONAL DIFFERENCES IN WORK RELATED VALUES (1980); GEERT HOFSTEDE, CULTURES AND ORGANIZATIONS: SOFTWARE OF THE MIND (1991).

[42] *Id.*

[43] CENTER FOR CREATIVE LEADERSHIP, LEADER EFFECTIVENESS AND CULTURE: THE GLOBE STUDY (2014), www.ccl.org/leadership/pdf/assessments/GlobeStudy.pdf.

[44] Sophie Cockcroft, *Culture, Law and Information Privacy*, in Proceedings of European and Mediterranean Conference on Information Systems 2007 (EMCIS2007) June 24–26,

stronger, the research suggests, in societies characterized by higher levels of power equality, higher levels of communitarianism, and higher levels of uncertainty avoidance.[45] In one study Germans were found to be twice as likely as Americans to be concerned about personal information privacy.[46] Social and information scientists seem willing to attribute this result to a German national culture that is – at least relative to America – more egalitarian, more communitarian, and more averse to uncertainty.[47]

The "Privacy Index" produced by the German Internet and technology consultancy company EMC substantiates the claim that Americans and Germans have different expectations with respect to personal information privacy.[48] The report found, for example, that Germans are much less willing than Americans – by almost 20 percentage points – to trade some privacy for greater convenience.[49] In fact, Germany was the most

[45] Steven Bellman et al., International Differences in Information Privacy Concerns: A Global Survey of Consumers, 20 INFO. SOC. 313, 315 (2004).

[46] Id. at 321 ("[T]he IBM privacy survey, which used national probability samples from the United States and Germany (IND = 67), found that Americans were twice as likely to be classified as "low" in privacy concern compared to Germans."); See also IBM Multi-National Privacy Survey Consumer Report 14, IBM (Oct. 1999), ftp://www6.software.ibm.com/software/security/privacy_survey_oct991.pdf.

[47] Nale Lehmann-Willenbrock et al., Observing Culture: Differences in U.S.-American and German Team Meeting Behaviors, 17 GROUP PROCESSES INTERGROUP RELATIONS 252, 254 (2014) (noting that Germany is a country that ranks high on the Uncertainty Avoidance Index, while the U.S. ranks low; and also that "Germans are considerably less individualistic than U.S.-Americans."). See also Germany, HOFSTEDE CENTRE, http://geert-hofstede.com/germany.html (last visited Feb. 13, 2016) (rating Germany's Power Distance, or the likelihood of acceptance of uneven power distribution, at 35; rating Germany's Individualism at 67; and rating Germany's Uncertainty Avoidance at 65); United States, HOFSTEDE CENTRE, http://geert-hofstede.com/united-states.html (last visited Feb. 13, 2016) (rating the U.S.'s Power Distance, at 47; rating the U.S.'s Individualism at 91; and rating the U.S.'s Uncertainty Avoidance at 46); by comparing these metrics we see that the U.S. is more accepting of unequal power distribution, less risk-averse, and far more individualistic.

[48] See EMC², THE EMC PRIVACY INDEX GLOBAL & IN-DEPTH COUNTRY RESULTS (2014), www.emc.com/collateral/brochure/privacy-index-global-in-depth-results.pdf (hereinafter EMC² IN-DEPTH RESULTS). See also Steve Rosenbush, EMC's New Index Shows Public Is Deeply Conflicted Over Privacy, WALL ST. J. (June 12, 2014, 5:16 PM), http://blogs.wsj.com/cio/2014/06/12/emcs-new-index-shows-public-is-deeply-conflicted-over-privacy/. See generally EMC Privacy Index, EMC², www.emc.com/campaign/privacy-index/index.htm (ranking nations based on the "willingness to trade privacy for greater convenience and benefits online.").

[49] EMC² IN-DEPTH RESULTS, supra note 48 (polling indicated that while 56% of Americans would be unwilling to "trade some privacy for greater convenience and ease," 71% of German respondents were unwilling.).

conservative of the study's fifteen countries in this regard,[50] a posture colorfully symbolized by Germans' suspicion towards a number of data-based consumer innovations, including Google's "Street View."[51] It also forms a part of Germans' embrace of the CJEU's recent data protection jurisprudence, including the demand that Google respect a European "right to be forgotten."[52] Underscoring their general aversion to trading privacy for convenience – even in the commercial or consumer context – EMC's "Privacy Index" reported that Germans were more likely than Americans to believe that the law should prohibit businesses from buying and selling data without an individual's consent.[53]

Significantly, one of the forms of "convenience" the EMC study took into account was "protection from terrorist and/or criminal activity."[54] The "Privacy Index" did not publish the separate national results with respect to this "value." But in the global sample, protection against terrorism scored as the second highest "convenience value" and was the value for which the most subjects were willing to sacrifice privacy.[55] This is in line with the stance of a large majority of Americans. A *Washington Post*–Pew Research Center survey from 2013 showed that 62 percent of Americans felt that it was "important for the government to investigate terrorist threats, even if those investigations intrude on personal privacy."[56]

---

[50] *Id.*

[51] Claire Cain Miller & Kevin J. O'Brien, *Germany's Complicated Relationship with Google Street View*, N.Y. TIMES (Apr. 23, 2013), http://bits.blogs.nytimes.com/2013/04/23/germanys-complicated-relationship-with-google-street-view/. *See also Data Collected by Google Cars*, GOOGLE (Apr. 27, 2010), http://googlepolicyeurope.blogspot.com/2010/04/data-collected-by-google-cars.html.

[52] *See* Google Spain SL and Google Inc. v Agencia Española de Protección de Datos (AEPD) and Mario Costeja González, 2014 E.C.J. C-131/12, ¶ 14 (May 13). *See also* Alan Travis & Charles Arthur, *EU Court Backs "Right to be Forgotten": Google Must Amend Results on Request*, THE GUARDIAN (May 13, 2014, 9:06 AM), www.theguardian.com/technology/2014/may/13/right-to-be-forgotten-eu-court-google-search-results; Samuel Gibbs, *Google to Extend "Right to be Forgotten" to all Its Domains Accessed in EU*, THE GUARDIAN (Feb. 11, 2016, 7:40 AM), www.theguardian.com/technology/2016/feb/11/google-extend-right-to-be-forgotten-googlecom.

[53] EMC[2] IN-DEPTH RESULTS, *supra* note 48 (while 92% of Germans thought that businesses should be legally barred from selling consumer information without consent, only 88% of Americans felt the same way.).

[54] *Press Release, Global Internet Privacy Study Reveals Consumers' Conflicting Views*, EMC² (2014), www.emc.com/about/news/press/2014/20140612-01.htm.

[55] *Id.*

[56] John Cohen, *Most Americans Back NSA Tracking Phone Records, Prioritize Probes Over Privacy*, WASH. POST (June 10, 2013), www.washingtonpost.com/politics/most-ameri

A Microsoft poll suggested, however, that this is a "value" for which Germans are less willing to sacrifice their privacy.[57]

A study conducted by the Boston Consulting Group (BCG) further reinforces the claim that Americans and Germans have different expectations with respect to personal information privacy.[58] The published report shows that, across a broad range of categories, Germans are far more likely than Americans to consider data to be "moderately" or "extremely" private, including: social network information (14% higher); information about media usage and preferences (10% higher); dialed-phone-number history (9% higher); exact location data (6% higher); and surfing history (5% higher).[59] One exception to this clear trend that is relevant to the NSA-Affair is BCG's finding that Germans are less likely than Americans to believe that email information is moderately or extremely private (15% lower).[60] The BCG study also reveals that Germans are more concerned than Americans about the privacy of personal information in precisely the industrial sectors implicated by the NSA-Affair, including: the social media sector (19% higher); the mobile phone sector (16% higher); and the search engine sector (12% higher).[61] Germans, however, are far less concerned than Americans about sharing private data with the government (17% lower).[62]

2   Different Reactions to Snowden and the NSA-Affair

This very limited survey of a small sample of polling data does not prove the existence of a fundamental difference between Americans and Europeans on the question of personal information privacy. But it provides ballast for this book's foundational assumption: that Americans and Europeans have responded in very different ways to the NSA-Affair. Whatever questions remain open about differences regarding privacy on a broader cultural level, there can be little doubt about our dramatically different responses to Snowden and the NSA intelligence gathering operations he disclosed. Europeans are inclined to see Snowden as a hero who cast light on highly intrusive and unnecessary surveillance

---

cans-support-nsa-tracking-phone-records-prioritize-investigations-over-privacy/2013/06/10/51e721d6-d204-11e2-9f1a-1a7cdee20287_story.html.

[57] *Developing Countries Are More Willing to Trade Privacy for Security*, HELP NET SECURITY (Jan. 24, 2014), www.net-security.org/secworld.php?id=16257.

[58] John Rose *et al.*, *Data Privacy by the Numbers*, BCG.PERSPECTIVES (Feb. 19, 2014), www.bcgperspectives.com/content/Slideshow/information_technology_strategy_digital_economy_data_privacy_by_the_numbers/#ad-image-0.

[59] *Id.* at slide 4.   [60] *Id.* at slide 4.   [61] *Id.* at slides 6–7.   [62] *Id.* at slides 6–7.

programs.[63] Americans are inclined to see Snowden as a well-intentioned criminal who jeopardized valuable antiterrorism programs.[64] A large majority of Germans (61%) approved of Snowden's actions, even if they were illegal.[65] Sixty percent see him as a "hero" and not as a "criminal."[66] A growing percentage of Germans, having eventually reached a near majority, are in favor of offering Snowden asylum.[67] In about the same time period PEW Research registered a slight increase in the percentage of Americans who believe the government should pursue a criminal case against Snowden (up from 54% in the summer of 2013 to 56% in the winter of 2014).[68] On the basis of a survey conducted in the days immediately following the media's initial extensive coverage of Snowden's disclosures, PEW Research reported that a narrow majority of Americans found the NSA's intelligence gathering operations to be acceptable (56%).[69] This was a slight increase over the result PEW Research obtained in January 2006 (48%).[70] In June 2013 – at the height

---

[63] Steven Nelson, *Edward Snowden Unpopular at Home, A Hero Abroad, Poll Finds*, U.S. NEWS (Apr. 21, 2015), www.usnews.com/news/articles/2015/04/21/edward-snowden-unpopular-at-home-a-hero-abroad-poll-finds ("In Germany and Italy, 84 percent of adults familiar with Snowden view him positively."); Harriet Torrey, Edward Snowden Emerges as a Cult Hero in Germany, WALL ST. J. (Sept. 24, 2014, 7:17 AM), www.wsj.com/articles/edward-snowden-emerges-as-a-cult-hero-in-germany-1411557452.

[64] James Stephens & Edward Snowden: Not a Hero, STANFORD DAILY (Oct. 19, 2015), www.stanforddaily.com/2015/10/19/edward-snowden-not-a-hero/;   Teklehaymanot Yilma, *NSA PRISM Program: Edward Snowden a Hero? Hardly*, MIC (June 13, 2013), http://mic.com/articles/48343/nsa-prism-program-edward-snowden-a-hero-hardly#.dFe EzjjON.

[65] *Spying Fallout: German Trust in United States Plummets*, SPIEGEL ONLINE (Nov. 8, 2013), www.spiegel.de/international/germany/nsa-spying-fallout-majority-of-germans-mistrust-united-states-a-932492.html.

[66] *Id.*

[67] *Id. See also* Sonya Hepinstall, *Germans See Snowden As Hero But Don't Favor Asylum: Poll*, REUTERS *(Nov. 7, 2013)*, www.reuters.com/article/us-usa-security-snowden-ger many-idUSBRE9A60W920131107 ("46 percent were in favor of offering Snowden political asylum in Germany, with 48 percent against.").

[68] *See Public Split over Impact of NSA Leak, but Most Want Snowden Prosecuted*, PEW RESEARCH CENTER (June 17, 2013), www.people-press.org/2013/06/17/public-split-over-impact-of-nsa-leak-but-most-want-snowden-prosecuted; Seth Motel, *NSA Coverage Wins Pulitzer, but Americans Remain Divided on Snowden Leaks*, PEW RESEARCH CENTER (Apr. 15, 2014), www.pewresearch.org/fact-tank/2014/04/15/nsa-coverage-wins-pulitzer-but-americans-remain-divided-on-snowden-leaks/.

[69] Cohen, *supra* note 56.

[70] *Americans Taking Abramoff, Alito and Domestic Spying in Stride*, PEW RESEARCH CENTER (Jan. 11, 2006), www.people-press.org/2006/01/11/americans-taking-abramoff-alito-and-domestic-spying-in-stride/ (48% of Americans thought "government

of the sensational coverage of Snowden's leaks – a majority of Americans believed that the NSA's programs helped prevent terrorist attacks (53%).[71] At the same time, a majority of Germans were found to be critical of the NSA programs.[72]

III   Different Perspectives on Privacy in Scholarship

The significant American and European differences regarding data protection are also evident in the work of privacy scholars.

German privacy scholars, for example, are inclined to see technology almost exclusively as an ominous threat. They devote large parts of their work to documenting the new and ever-deeper ways technology is intruding upon our privacy. Peter Schaar, the former Federal Commissioner for Data Protection and Information Freedom (*Bundesbeauftragter für Datenschutz und Informationsfreiheit*) has written a representative manifesto entitled *Das Ende der Privatsphäre* (*The End of Privacy*).[73] His alarm taps into an awareness of the fact that IBM punch-card technology was used in the Nazis' 1938 census, which helped the *Reich* develop the demographic profiles it needed to implement the Holocaust.[74] Computing technology, Schaar warns, can lead to an all-encompassing surveillance state of the kind Orwell imagined.[75] The book's first fifty pages constitute a careful accounting of the many ways in which Orwell's vision is now being realized. Schaar concludes, for example, that the Internet "has a shadowy side."[76] He warns against the state's collection of data about our normal activities and the grave risks for data protection that result from our deepening "*Vernetzung*."[77] The most threatening possibility, Schaar notes, comes from the role technology is coming to play in the health care sector, including digital and networked records keeping and data driven or biometric research and treatment.[78] Christine Hohmann-Dennhardt, in an essay published during her service as a

---

monitoring telephone and email communications of Americans suspected of having terrorist ties without first obtaining permission from the courts" was "generally right.").

[71] *See Public Split Over Impact of NSA Leak, but Most Want Snowden Prosecuted*, Pew Research Center (June 17, 2013), www.people-press.org/2013/06/17/public-split-over-impact-of-nsa-leak-but-most-want-snowden-prosecuted.

[72] *See Spying Fallout: German Trust in United States Plummets*, Spiegel Online (Nov. 8, 2013, 12:07 PM), www.spiegel.de/international/germany/nsa-spying-fallout-majority-of-germans-mistrust-united-states-a-932492.html.

[73] Peter Schaar, Das Ende der Privatsphäre (2009).   [74] *Id.* at 38.   [75] *Id.* at 40.

[76] *Id.* at 42.   [77] *Id.* at 49, 54.   [78] *Id.* at 75–78.

Justice at the Federal Constitutional Court, also lamented the way in which technology seems to have rendered privacy an "antiquated description of an idyllic condition that belongs to the past."[79] The year before he joined the Federal Constitutional Court as the reporting justice for matters concerned with, *inter alia*, personal liberty and data protection, Wolfgang Hoffmann-Reim wrote about the "new risks" resulting from "new technologies," a development he compared to an arms race.[80] Spiro Simitis, one of Germany's best-known experts in the field of data protection,[81] takes a similar approach, expressing particular concern about the ways in which technology is helping businesses track – perhaps even manipulate – consumers' shopping activities.[82] If they do so at all, these German scholars only reluctantly acknowledge the ways that the same technologies have improved our lives.

The general skepticism toward technology in German privacy scholarship is accompanied by a contrasting pastoral, quasi-spiritual conceptualization of privacy. Wolfgang Schmale and Marie-Theres Tinnefeld represent the most extreme version of this posture. In their book *Privatheit im digitalen Zeitalter* (*Privacy in the Digital-Age*) they draw on the *Bible's* "Garden of Eden" as a metaphor for privacy because it points to the deeply rooted cultural significance we place on the need for a protected retreat in which we can think and compose ourselves in full acceptance of nature and our bodies.[83] The tangible garden, Schmale and Tinnefeld believe, should help us to understand the abstract notion of data protection in more concrete terms.[84] Sadly, they miss the chance to point out that it is in no small part the technology of a company called "Apple" that has chased us from privacy's paradise.[85] Schmale and Tinnefeld see the European Union, with its culture and tradition of rights, as the "paradise" in

---

[79] Christine Hohmann-Dennhardt, *Freiräume – Zum Schutz der Privatheit*, 59 NEUE JURISTISCHE WOCHENSCHRIFT 545 (2006).

[80] Wolfgang Hoffmann-Reim, *Informationelle Selbtsbestimmung in der Informationsgesellschaft - Auf dem Wege zu einem neuen Konzept des Datenschutzes*, 123 ARCHIV DES ÖFFENTLICHEN RECHTS 513, 517–18 (1998).

[81] *See, e.g.*, BUNDESDATENSCHUTZGESETZ – KOMMENTAR (Spiros Simitis ed., 8th ed. 2014).

[82] Spiros Simitis, *Datenschutz—eine notwendige Utopie*, in SUMMA—DIETER SIMON ZUM 70. GEBURTSTAG 511 (Rainer Maria Kiesow *et al.* eds., 2005).

[83] WOLFGANG SCHMALE & MARIE-THERES TINNEFELD, PRIVATHEIT IM DIGITALEN ZEITALTER 11 (2014).

[84] *Id.* at 18.

[85] They do connect the fruit of the Tree of Knowledge – and the expulsion from the garden– with the end of privacy, which is linked with the onset of shame. *Id.* at 20.

which privacy can be restored.[86] Hohmann-Dennhardt, taking a more secular turn, compared privacy to Roseau's garden, in which one lives in simple harmony with nature.[87] Simitis also understands data protection as part of an effort to fashion a utopian paradise.[88] Schaar sees something of the sacred in privacy. He approvingly quotes Philippe Quéua, the former Director of the UNESCO's Division on Information and Society, who called privacy the "foundation of human dignity and the sacred nature of the human person."[89] It is this quasi-spiritual approach to privacy that helps make sense of Schmale's and Tinnefeld's appeal for data and information aestheticism.[90]

Working with these grand themes, perhaps it is not surprising that German scholars have taken a broad and abstract approach to privacy and data protection.[91] This is also in keeping with German legal culture's impulse to work in abstract and general terms.[92] Hohmann-Dennhardt's approach is representative of this feature of German privacy law scholarship. Describing a broad, general theory of privacy, she maps the concentric spheres of privacy that are derived from (themselves nearly indeterminate) constitutional protections of dignity and personal liberty.[93] These spheres, in turn, create and condition the right to data protection.[94] This includes, without nuanced consideration for the almost infinite possibilities each contains, an intimate sphere, a private sphere, and the public sphere.[95] One consequence of this broad conceptual approach is that German privacy scholars must struggle to account for the different meaning the broadly construed notion of privacy should be given in the public law and private law contexts.[96]

---

[86] *Id.* at 144.   [87] Hohmann-Dennhardt, *supra* note 79, at 546.

[88] Simitis, *supra* note 82, at 527.   [89] SCHAAR, *supra* note 73.

[90] They attribute this to the Federal Constitutional Court's *Census Act Case* (1983). *See* SCHMALE & TINNEFELD, *supra* note 83, at 86.

[91] *See* HANS PETER BULL, INFORMATIONELLE SELBSTBESTIMMUNG – VISION ODER ILLUSION? 28 (2d ed. 2011) ("From the beginning the German Data Protection law was comprehensive and, therefore, too abstract.") (Russell Miller translation).

[92] *See* Russell Miller & Ralf Poscher, *Kampf der Kulturen: Der präventive deutsche Datenschutz liegt quer zur pragmatischen Rechtskultur in Amerika – Eine Harmonisierung muss scheitern,* FRANKFURTER ALLGEMEINE ZEITUNG (Nov. 28, 2013).

[93] *See* GRUNDGESETZ [GG] [BASIC LAW] arts. 1(1) and 2(1), *translation at* www.gesetze-im-internet.de/englisch_gg/; Census Act Case, 65 BVerfG 1 (1983). *See also* Hohmann-Dennhardt, *supra* note 79, at 546.

[94] *See* Hohmann-Dennhardt, *supra* note 79, at 546; Chapter 2 in this volume.

[95] *See* Hohmann-Dennhardt, *supra* note 79, at 546.

[96] *See, e.g.,* SCHMALE & TINNEFELD, *supra* note 83, at 123.

Finally, German privacy scholarship commonly gives a central role to international and supranational law. All of the writers in this brief survey appeal to and strongly assert the authority of international and European law in this area. Schaar, for example, concludes that the global character of data flows makes data protection a "new responsibility for the United Nations" in the same way that environmental protection has emerged as a global concern of the United Nations.[97] I have already referred to the hope Schmale and Tinnefeld place in the European Union as the source for a more vigorous data protection regime.[98] Simitis reminds us that the right to informational self-determination is a constitutional protection under national *and* supranational law.[99]

Daniel Solove, America's leading privacy scholar, sees things differently.[100] First, Solove takes a more balanced approach to technology. He acknowledges that technology raises concerns about privacy.[101] But Solove leaves space for an alternative view of these developments by acknowledging that "not everyone is concerned."[102] He is less willing than the German privacy scholars to see technology in exclusively menacing terms. On one hand, he characterizes many of the problems facing privacy as traditional or historical concerns, including risks to communications privacy (going back to the eras of letters, telegraphs, and telephones),[103] risks resulting from information collection and surveillance (going back to ancient Jewish law and the original "peeping Tom" in the middle ages),[104] and risks resulting from information processing and aggregation (going back to the accelerating use of computers in the 1960s).[105] These are old problems that are not exclusively linked to advances in technology. Nor is technology, for Solove, exclusively a threat. He is able to acknowledge the benefits of modern technology, even in areas (such as consumer data aggregation) that Schaar vilifies. "Identification is connecting information to individuals," Solove explains.[106] While accepting that "identification" creates special problems, Solove recognizes that it also provides many benefits.[107] Solove obviously cares a great deal about privacy. But he does not succumb to German scholars' neo-Luddism.

---

[97] SCHAAR, *supra* note 73, at 235.
[98] *See* SCHMALE & TINNEFELD, *supra* note 83, at 137–144.
[99] Simitis, *supra* note 82, at 519.
[100] *See* DANIEL J. SOLOVE, UNDERSTANDING PRIVACY (2008).   [101] *Id.* at 4.
[102] *Id.* at 5.   [103] *Id.* at 61–62.   [104] *Id.* at 107–08.   [105] *Id.* at 118.
[106] *Id.* at 122.   [107] *Id.* at 122–23.

Solove's most significant contribution to the theory of privacy is precisely his rejection of the broad and abstract approach adopted by German privacy scholars. Solove proposes a pragmatic, context-specific understanding of privacy. His is a "pluralistic" and not a "unitary" theory.[108] Most conceptions of privacy suffer, Solove explains, because they are too broad. This is true of Brandeis' and Warren's famous conclusion that privacy is the "right to be let alone."[109] It is true of the notion that privacy involves a right to limit others access to the self, which Solove sees as "too broad and vague."[110] It is also true of the idea that privacy involves the right to control one's personal information. This approach is too broad, Solove explains, "because there is a significant amount of information identifiable to us that we do not deem as private."[111] According to Solove, each of these general theories of privacy (and others I have not mentioned here) suffers from being "too vague" or "too broad."[112] To solve this problem – which is a central part of the German approach to privacy – Solove proposes treating "privacy" as an "umbrella term that refers to a wide and disparate group of related things."[113] Those "things," Solove urges, must be assessed pragmatically in their specific contexts. He quotes Serge Gutwirth, who observed that "Privacy . . . is defined by its context and only obtains its true meaning within social relationships."[114] With this admonition in mind, Solove proposes differentiated concepts of privacy for distinct circumstances, including private relations in the family, privacy relating to one's body and sex, privacy associated with the home, and privacy connected with communications.[115]

One consequence of Solove's highly differentiated and pragmatic approach is that he does not have to struggle to have an encompassing theory account for different public law and private law frameworks, as the German scholars must. Instead, his approach to privacy allows him to conceptualize discrete privacy protections for concrete circumstances. In this way, the resulting protection operates only at the level of public or private conduct (or below that level) and is adapted to the needs of the respective legal and factual context.

Finally, Solove constructs his theory of privacy with only the slightest reference to international and supranational norms. Perhaps in keeping with the contextualism of his theory, Solove is largely concerned with an American theory of privacy, for Americans, and derived from American law.

---

[108] *Id.* at 9.   [109] *Id.* at 16, 18.   [110] *Id.* at 20.   [111] *Id.* at 25.   [112] *Id.* at 29.
[113] *Id.* at 45.   [114] *Id.* at 47.   [115] *Id.* at 50.

IV   Conclusion

It seems there are different cultural expectations of personal information privacy in America and Europe. These differences have produced significantly different reactions to the revelations of the NSA's data collection and intelligence gathering activities. The question remains: How are these cultural differences reflected in the two countries' legal regimes for privacy – and how do those legal regimes help foster these cultural differences? That is the territory covered by this book.

C   The Book: A Transatlantic Dialogue in the Shadow of the NSA-Affair

This book documents and discusses the different American and European perspectives on personal information privacy and intelligence gathering from an interdisciplinary perspective. There is quite a lot of positive law here. But, as a comparative law endeavor that seeks not only to report on these profound differences but also hopes to explain them, several contributions reach beyond the relevant treaty or statutory provisions, and beyond the latest court decisions from Luxembourg, Karlsruhe, or Washington. Instead, there are insightful efforts to give the questions a theoretical and sociocultural foundation. In this way, the book also models the approach – and depth of understanding – that will be necessary for any productive dialogue on these issues across the Atlantic in the coming years.

The book proceeds in five parts, each of which is introduced here with a brief reflection on the lessons the respective chapters offer and how they interact with one another.

I   Part One: Privacy and Data Protection for the Digital Age

Part One lays a conceptual foundation for the book with a collection of chapters that acknowledge that Snowden's revelations require us to rethink prevailing theories concerning privacy and intelligence gathering.[116] Sarah Horowitz critically examines the easy use many have made of the Panopticon as a metaphor for governments' intelligence gathering practices in the era of ubiquitous computing and big data. For all the insight it provides us today, Horowitz argues that especially

---

[116] *Id.* at 12.

Foucault's theory of the Panopticon and state power does not adequately account for the voluntary and private dimensions of the NSA-Affair.

Russell Miller, delving deep into the context of the American and German constitutional privacy regimes, establishes that the two countries have radically different approaches to these issues. This insight counsels greater respect for and acceptance of these differences, especially as the basis for the transatlantic dialogue. More controversially, his survey poses a significant challenge to attempts to frame privacy in abstract or universal terms.

Joshua Fairfield and Christoph Engle instead see a profound similarity in American and European notions of privacy: privacy has a significant collective or communitarian aspect that is independent of the traditional understanding of privacy as a personal and subjective right. Neglect of this collective dimension in most theoretical approaches to privacy, they argue, has helped to confound efforts to enhance privacy protection. Viewing privacy as a collective good (or its diminishment as a collective bad), Fairfield and Engle suggest a number of practical policy measures that would help us to avoid losing (more) privacy in a tragedy of the commons scenario.

Ralf Poscher, contradicting the trend in German and European law, wonders if data protection is a "right" at all. He sees in the jurisprudence of the German and European courts the settled practice of deriving data protection from other protected interests (dignity or liberty) and its application as a prophylactic enhancement of other discrete constitutional protections (freedom of speech, freedom of assembly, freedom of religion). Poscher's provocative thesis contributes to the transatlantic dialogue that this volume hopes to facilitate by casting light on the fact that the *ex ante* character of Europe's "no-right data protection" regime fits awkwardly (at best) with the fact-centric and *ex post* character of American legal culture.

II Part Two: Framing the Transatlantic Debate

The conceptual differences and uncertainty regarding personal information privacy and intelligence gathering that emerge in Part One are emphatically on display in the two contributions to Part Two of the book. Chapters from Anne Peters and Benjamin Wittes colorfully embody and frame the transatlantic debate on the NSA-Affair.

Peters, with an admirable command of the international and domestic legal doctrine, argues that the NSA programs exposed by Snowden are illegal. She proceeds in three steps. First, she systematically maps the scope of protections against espionage, surveillance, and data collection (relying in particular on the UN Charter and the ICCPR). Second, she argues that NSA's programs constituted a serious infringement of the relevant legal protections. Finally, she concludes that the programs were disproportionate. On the basis of this analysis, Peters demands the United States should "obey the law." This is the appeal for "privacy" in the book's title.

Wittes responds with a characteristically strong dose of realpolitik in which he advances three arguments. First, he insists that the activities of the American Intelligence Community are subject to consequential legal limits and effective political oversight in ways that the Intelligence Communities in other countries – including Germany – are not. Second, he notes that a widening divergence between German and American foreign policy justifies America's interest in Germany and Germans as targets of espionage and intelligence gathering. Third, Wittes makes the pragmatic observation that intelligence services, by their very nature, defy international legal controls. Leaning heavily on the last point, Wittes concludes that it is an unavoidable reality of international relations that countries spy on one another – on their friends as well as their enemies – and that these activities necessarily take place in the shadows. Recalling that Israeli espionage against the United States had not meaningfully disrupted the Israeli-American relationship, *Wittes* urges the Germans to "grow up." This is the concession to "power" in the book's title.

These chapters are more than just the uncritical reassertion of a tired cliché about Europeans' insistence on positive law in pursuit of a cosmopolitan vision that contrasts with Americans' resort to the pragmatics of power in defense of national interests. That old difference, almost perfectly exemplified by Peters and Wittes, is at the core of Europeans' and Americans' very different political and legal postures on these issues. That old difference forms the unique framework within which the transatlantic dialogue on privacy and intelligence gathering – including most of this book's remaining chapters – operates. Peters and Wittes, when read together as representative of the strained transatlantic dialogue over the NSA-Affair, present us with two fundamental questions. On one hand, how can Americans and Germans negotiate the different priorities we place on the national and the universal? On the other hand, how can Americans and Germans negotiate the different priority we place on political and legal legitimacy?

III   Part Three: Transatlantic Perspectives on the NSA-Affair

In Part Three of the book, an impressive range of experts from the United States and Europe – reflecting on the law and policy of the NSA-Affair – provide concrete answers to the questions posed by Peters and Wittes. Two central lessons emerge from this dialogue of experts. The first is the banal – but too-easily forgotten – insight that American and European views on these issues cannot be reduced to a single or unitary position. There are American defenders *and* American critics of the NSA, as the chapters from Ron Lee and Alec Walen demonstrate. Some Germans are more concerned than others about the privacy risks presented by intelligence gathering, as the chapters from Konstantin von Notz and Klaus Gärditz demonstrate. The second is that the NSA-Affair does not raise a narrow legal question. Instead, it involves issues of the broadest significance (the old privacy versus security challenge) while implicating a number of more discrete legal subjects, including constitutional law (privacy, free speech, separation of powers, due process), administrative law, and private law. The transnational nature of the issues is an additional complication. The complexity of the NSA-Affair means that this collection of voices from the United States and Europe is not – and could not be – meticulously representative. Still, it is a highly effective sample, the breadth of which permits some cautious generalizations. First, there is more evidence of a fundamental transatlantic disagreement on the issues of privacy and intelligence gathering.[117] But the left–right ideological dimension of the NSA-Affair – generally applicable on both sides of the Atlantic – is also on display. Second, Americans and Germans can seem to agree on the hypocrisy involved in the German outrage over the NSA's operations, especially considering the weak oversight applied to the German intelligence services' operations.[118] Third, the question of the extraterritorial application of constitutional protections is not as settled as it might seem in either U.S. or German law.[119] Fourth, even proponents of data protection measures (such as the newly minted European "right to be forgotten") are concerned about the way those measures might conflict with or erode other cherished liberty interests (such as the freedom of speech).[120]

---

[117] *See* Chapters 7, 9, 12, and 15 in this volume.
[118] *See* Chapters 9, 13, and 14 in this volume.
[119] *See* Chapters 10 and 15 in this volume.   [120] *See* Chapters 11 and 16 in this volume.

1   American Voices

The American contributions are led by Ron Lee's chapter. He was the NSA's General Counsel for a number of years. From that position of experience, Lee understands the NSA-Affair as stark evidence that we are in a new era with respect to privacy and intelligence gathering. He then documents the significant reforms the United States has implemented in response to that reality. These include increased transparency, increased judicial oversight, and new executive branch rules and review mechanisms. *Lee's* conviction that America's intelligence operations conform to the rule of law are confirmed by the legal challenges the NSA's programs have faced (and largely survived) in U.S. courts and by the enactment of the USA FREEDOM Act in the summer of 2015.

Margaret Hu, who also did service in the executive branch in Washington, DC, is less sanguine. In her chapter Hu presents the troubling – but very real – prospect that American "kill decisions" are being made on the basis of the kind of metadata the NSA has been collecting. This extreme scenario is an invitation, Hu argues, to critically examine the "scientific validity and logic" behind big-data decision making. Hu asks us to consider how the law might be framed to account for the risks inherent in correlative analyses, and by doing so she calls into question the very foundation of the NSA's dramatic prioritization of big-data intelligence gathering and analysis.

Andrew Borene joins Wittes and Lee in defending the legitimacy and efficacy of the legal regime for controlling and overseeing America's Intelligence Community. It is an unblushing piece of advocacy, especially valuable for the insight it gives privacy advocates on both sides of the Atlantic into the perspective of those who would give "power" the greater priority in this book's dichotomous title. Borene points to the accountability problems associated with the prominent role played by EU figures and institutions in the continent's post-Snowden rebuke of American policy and practice. The European Union, Borene argues, pursues its privacy agenda without itself having to bear the burden of a proper security mandate, which remains a matter for the domestic law and policy of the Member States.

Alec Walen is not impressed with the executive and legislative branch oversight outlined by Wittes, Lee, and Borene. He insists that the NSA's collection of the content of communications should satisfy the constitutional privacy protection provided by the Fourth Amendment to the U.S. Constitution. That privacy guarantee, Walen argues, is also owed to people who have no ties to the United States. Walen builds his provocative argument for the extraterritorial application of the Fourth Amendment by reference to the broad values that inform the commitment to privacy and with an impressively close reading of the existing Supreme Court precedent.

The American contributions conclude with Dawn Nunziato's chapter on the First Amendment implications of the "right to be forgotten" announced by the CJEU in the *Google Spain Case*. Having surveyed the free speech limits the American jurisprudence has come to tolerate, Nunziato is less worried about the substantive First Amendment protections implicated by the "right to be forgotten." Instead, she is concerned that the administration of the right will undermine or evade "First Amendment due process" requirements, including notice and the opportunity to be heard. She argues that the CJEU's deletion regime (which is to be implemented by private Internet search engine operators such as Google) neglects those procedural guarantees. Nunziato highlights the confounding way privacy law can conflict with other liberty interests and she poignantly reveals the complex way that public authority interacts with – and in this case, is dependent on – nonstate actors when it comes to privacy law and policy.

2   European Voices

The European contributions open with the authoritative views of Konstantin von Notz. On the one hand, von Notz expresses profound respect for privacy rights. On the other hand, he expresses profound skepticism toward the American and German intelligence services, which he sees as singular threats to our enjoyment of privacy. As the Green Party's spokesman for the *Bundestag's* NSA Committee of Inquiry, these positions might seem entirely predictable. But they are a necessary contribution to this volume for precisely that reason. As much as Lee and Borene clearly speak from the perspective of American intelligence "hawks," von Notz fully embodies the views of European data protection "religionists." He writes about un-checked intelligence agencies and the chilling effects that can result from their collection of all our communications data. Without von Notz's passionate and informed voice, this book would function more like a monologue than the transatlantic dialogue it hopes to both document and facilitate. Still, von Notz is less clear about the path he sees to increased control of democratic states' intelligence services. He confirms the impressive contribution made by the *Bundestag's* Committee of Inquiry (especially when it has been allowed to pursue the interests of the opposition parties), but Germany's parliamentary system of government leaves him doubtful about the long-term prospects for legislative branch oversight. What is left? Von Notz suggests a thick statutory regime for control and oversight enforced by the judiciary.

In two dramatic steps Stefan Heumann confirms von Notz's doubts. First, he establishes that the German *Bundesnachrichtendienst* (Foreign Intelligence Service – BND) is an extremely active and effective intelligence agency. This contrasts with the widely held view that the BND is a modest or bumbling institution. Second, he argues that the BND is not rigorously controlled under German law. In his survey of the history of the German Intelligence Community, Heumann points out that the BND operated for decades without statutory authority. The statutory regime, when it finally came, provided only loose standards that invited the intelligence services' permissive – and secret – interpretation. Heumann characterizes the German oversight mechanisms as victims of design flaws meant to keep them weak and ineffectual.

Marc Engelhart's chapter deepens Heumann's critique by way of a troubling case study. Engelhart argues that the decade-long program of xenophobic crime and murder carried out in Germany by the National Socialist Underground (NSU) involved disturbing intelligence abuses and failures unlike anything yet attributable to the NSA's extensive intelligence gathering operations.[121] Worse, in Engelhart's view, one of the consequences of the tragic NSU story seems to have been the expansion of the intelligence services' powers, especially through the erosion of the doctrine that strictly separated the German state's intelligence gathering and law enforcement functions.

Walen, in his contribution, challenged the accepted notion that American constitutional law does not follow the flag overseas. Klaus Gärditz presents the opposite paradox by arguing, against an emerging consensus, that there are fundamental limits on the application of the German constitution to foreign intelligence operations, including data collection and communications surveillance. Gärditz's chapter is an example of the doctrinal integrity and precision that characterizes the best German legal scholarship. In this respect, it might have been another example of the positivism embodied by Peters chapter. Except that Gärditz's contribution is also extraordinarily pragmatic. He concludes that the limited application of the constitutional and statutory privacy regime is justified

---

[121] *But see* Chapter 8 in this volume.

because the law – including the basic rights – should have a less signifi-cant role in Germany's increasingly robust foreign policy. Gärditz's chapter, reinforcing realism with command of the doctrine, might pro-vide a model for American scholarship on these subjects.

Johannes Masing, a Justice at the German Federal Constitutional Court, offers only a cautious endorsement of the CJEU's *Google Spain Case*. He celebrates the CJEU's strong assertion of the privacy protections secured by the European Union's Charter of Fundamental Rights. But unlike Nunziato, in her survey of American law, Masing sees risks for substantive free speech guarantees in the delisting regime established by the Court. The "right to be forgotten," Masing argues, does not adequately account for the complexity and nuance of the German juris-prudence on free speech. Ultimately, Masing worries that the CJEU's approach emphasizes privacy at the expense of free speech interests, thereby threatening the German jurisprudence that "has promoted open and critical public discourse."

IV   Part Four: Transnational Legal Responses to Privacy and Intelligence Gathering

The NSA-Affair has prompted some domestic legal reform, especially in the United States and Germany.[122] But several factors have focused privacy advocates' attention on international and supranational frame-works as additional – if not the *primary* – venues for imposing legal restraints on intelligence services and for securing new, more robust protection for personal information privacy in our networked, digital era. The first factor is the widespread belief that the American domestic political culture lacks the will (in more conspiratorial views, it is thought that American politics lacks the power) to truly curb the country's intelli-gence services. This would suggest that the basis for restraining the NSA must be lodged outside the United States, perhaps in international law.

---

[122] *See, e.g.*, Directive on Signals Intelligence Activity (PPD-28), 2014 Daily Comp. Pres. Doc. (Jan. 17, 2014), www.fbi.gov/about-us/nsb/fbis-policies-and-procedures-presiden tial-policy-directive-28-1; Uniting and Strengthening America by Fulfilling Rights and Ensuring Effective Discipline Over Monitoring Act of 2015 (or the USA FREEDOM Act of 2015), 5 U.S.C. § 552 (2012); *Entwurf für neues BND-Gesetz: Eine Art No-Spy-Klausel für Europa?*, Tagesschau.de (Jan. 18, 2016), *available at* www.tagesschau.de/inland/ bnd-reform-103.html; *Einigung auf Geheimdienstreform: Koalition nimmt BND an die Leine*, Tagesschau.de (Nov. 13, 2015), *available at* www.tagesschau.de/inland/bnd-reform-101.html.

The second factor is the evident transnational or transboundary character of the phenomena involved in the NSA-Affair. This includes the global ambitions and capacities of the American and European intelligence services. It also includes the transnational flow of telecommunications and Internet data, which sloshes indiscriminately across old national boundaries, channeled through a worldwide market by undersea cables and orbiting satellites. In this reality, the jurisdictional limits of domestic law mean that it cannot be the solution. Worse, domestic law might merely foster false confidence while establishing a cynical framework for symbiotic privacy abuses pursuant to which countries do for each other what they cannot themselves do at home. Only a single, harmonized, and international framework could put an end to this game. The third factor is the emergence of the European Union as the central regulator of data protection – and an increasingly important guarantor of personal privacy – for the vast and lucrative European market. In the European context, these issues can now be addressed only from a supranational perspective, through the European Union's supranational institutions, and by way of the European Union's multilevel normative framework.

Part Four of the book documents the NSA-Affair's fundamentally transnational dimension. This is the real location of the transatlantic dialogue on privacy and intelligence gathering. On the one hand, Europeans – Peters, for example – will assert international law standards in their critiques of the United States. On the other hand, the U.S. government and American firms must respond and adapt to EU standards for data protection. Both of these regimes are discussed here.

1   International Law

Ian Brown and his coauthors accept that international law must be part of the solution to the difficult problems exposed by the NSA-Affair. The alternative, they remind us, is an equally disturbing fragmentation of the Internet into closed national alcoves with incompatible technological infrastructure. That, truly, would be the death of all that the Internet promised to become. Their provocative thesis, however, is that the credible and effective American regime for controlling and overseeing surveillance and data collection would have to be the model on which the international regime is based. Especially with the post-Snowden reforms in mind, Brown and his coauthors bluntly conclude that the American regime now provides greater clarity and more meaningful judicial oversight for the operations of the Intelligence Community than any

European system of intelligence law. It is a provocative thesis that seems to substantiate the positions taken by Wittes, Borene, and Lee. Brown and his coauthors support the thesis with a thorough comparative survey of the existing regimes for controlling surveillance and intelligence gathering. Without missing the irony, they conclude that the United States now comes closer to fulfilling the standards for personal information privacy secured by the European Convention on Human Rights than do the states parties to the Convention.

Silja Voeneky might disagree with this conclusion. But she, too, is convinced that an answer to the NSA-Affair must be found in international law. Voeneky productively maps the problems and possibilities for international law in this area. Voeneky identifies some of the problems, including difficult questions about the extraterritorial application of international obligations; the seeming conflict between privacy rights and states' undeniable duties to promote security and protect life; and the absence of a customary law prohibition on espionage. But Voeneky sees potential in merging security and human rights law. Intelligence gathering, she suggests, might find a concrete – but better defined – basis in collective security agreements. Yet, states' human rights commitments would limit intelligence gathering to the most strictly proportional operations. Despite her innovative effort, Voeneky can only conclude that, at best, international law provides an ambiguous and fragmented response to the NSA-Affair. Where law stumbles in this way, Voeneky urges greater respect for privacy as a reaffirmation of our highest values. But whose values? On what terms?

Susana Sanchez-Ferro needs international law to address only a discrete issue: transnational intelligence sharing. Privacy is clearly at stake in the way states' collect and share intelligence with one another. But Sanchez-Ferro does not have to tackle big values conflicts such as "privacy and power." Instead, she urges a concrete set of rules for a seemingly narrow range of actions. Sampling policies from a few commendable domestic systems (especially Holland), Sanchez-Ferro argues that an international intelligence sharing regime should, among other elements, (1) provide foreseeability, (2) involve a form of preliminary assessment of potential partners' human rights records, and (3) limit the shared intelligence to only that content which is necessary.

2   European Law

Jens-Peter Schneider's chapter surveys the NSA-Affair's ripples in EU law. It opens the collection of chapters on European Law for two reasons.

First, Schneider's map provides a useful structure for the other treatments of European law in this section, including examinations of the following issues: the ill-fated Data Retention Directive; the rights to privacy and data protection found in the Charter for Fundamental Rights; and the adequacy standard applied to transfers of data outside the European Union under the Data Protection Directive. Second, Schneider's survey is largely concerned with the CJEU's recent jurisprudence. The themes I mention above might be more commonly identified by the names of CJEU decisions: *Digital Rights Ireland* (April 2014); *Google Spain* (May 2014); and *Schrems* (October 2015). Schneider seems to welcome the prominent role the Court has played in Europe's reaction to the NSA-Affair. And he credits the European Parliament's activism. Still, he acknowledges that the CJEU has in part been forced to take the lead in these matters by the passivity and reluctance of the Commission and Council. This story exposes a disquieting element of the European privacy agenda, which has largely been shaped by the least popularly accountable institution in a supranational framework for governance that itself suffers from nagging and significant democratic deficiencies.[123]

The counter-majoritarian pathology plaguing the European privacy agenda is lost on Lucia Zedner who – in her fine chapter on the short, unhappy life of the EU data retention regime (both in Europe broadly and in the United Kingdom in particular) – warmly endorses the "*judicial* opinion that retention of metadata interferes unwarrantedly with rights to privacy and protection of personal data" while expressing dismay at the fact that the Directive's data retention program "prompted relatively little *public* debate or controversy" and stirred almost no "*public* outcry."[124]

Bernd Holznagel and Sarah Hartmann provide a thorough analysis of the CJEU's *Google Spain Case*. They share Nunziato's procedural concerns about the implementation of the "right to be forgotten." They offer a concrete set of proposals for improving the delisting procedure, including rights of participation and arbitral review. But unlike Zedner, Holznagel and Hartmann are aware of the hegemonic potential of the CJEU's privacy agenda. They share, for example, Masing's concerns about the

---

[123] *See, e.g.*, Russell A. Miller, Schrems v. Commissioner: *A Biblical Parable of Judicial Power*, VERFBLOG (Oct. 7, 2015), *available at* http://verfassungsblog.de/schrems-v-com missioner-a-biblical-parable-of-judicial-power/.
[124] *See* Chapter 21 in this volume. (emphasis added).

way the *Google Spain Case* crudely prioritizes privacy over the highly nuanced approach to free speech protection developed over the last decades by the German Federal Constitutional Court. They worry that the German Constitutional Court's *So Lange* jurisprudence permits the CJEU to substantially reframe Germany's traditional free-speech regime. And Holznagel and Hartmann unambiguously reject claims that the "right to be forgotten" should be applied across non-European search engine platforms all around the world. "Given the profound differences between privacy regimes around the world," they explain, "it would be presumptuous for one regime to assume sovereignty of interpretation over the content accessible to users through search engines worldwide."

Els de Busser's chapter is largely concerned with the terms under which intelligence information may be exchanged for use in law enforcement proceedings. But this is a close relative of the commercial data transfers out of the European Union that the Data Protection Directive prohibits unless the receiving country provides Europeans with an adequate level of data protection. The Commission, in the Safe Harbor Agreement with the United States, concluded that the United States satisfied this requirement. De Busser reports on the *Schrems Case*, in which the CJEU – in the darkening shadow of the NSA-Affair – rejected that conclusion. In explaining that result and the general conflict between U.S. and European data protection law, de Busser provides us with a compact introduction to the central elements of European data protection. On the one hand, this includes an expansive definition of the terms "personal data" and "privacy." On the other hand, the protections consist in: (1) the strict application of the separation of the state's law enforcement and intelligence functions, (2) the requirement that data are collected and used only according to clear and narrowly framed legislation, (3) the requirement that data are used or transferred only for the purposes that justified their original collection, (4) the requirement that data are collected and used only as strictly necessary to advance a legitimate state interest, and (5) that requirement that the proportionality principle apply to the collection and use of data. The problem with the "adequacy" requirement, de Busser concludes, is that almost no one lives up to this standard. There are significant deviations among the EU's Member States (which need not be fatal because the adequacy requirement does not apply to intra-European transfers). The differences between the United States and the European Union are even more substantial, suggesting that the

"Privacy Shield Agreement" that was hastily crafted to replace the "Safe Harbor Agreement" after the *Schrem's Case*, is doomed to fail as an another experiment in reconciling two irreconcilable cultures of privacy.

V   Part Five: Transatlantic Reflections on the Cultural Meaning of Privacy and Intelligence Gathering

There it is again: The United States and Europe – Germany in particular – differ significantly in their understanding of and approaches to privacy and intelligence gathering. This is clearly confirmed, as a matter of substance and style, in the law and policy examined in this book's first four parts. Yet documenting these profound differences begs for an attempt at a deeper explanation for the dissimilarity. Part Five of this book represents that attempt. It is not a comprehensive collection of commentary from scholars of history, political economy, anthropology, or the social sciences. Instead, it is a small collection of comparative cultural commentary focusing on literature and film. It aims to give the participants in the transatlantic dialogue, which sometimes might seem mutually incomprehensible, the insight and understanding that can result from critical engagement with culture. These chapters do not pretend to tell us, in the causal sense, why things are the way they are. They aim, instead, to foster openness toward the other's difference – and critical reflection on one's inherited position – by considering some cultural treatments of privacy and intelligence gathering. This is the interpretive understanding we can develop through an encounter with narrative, which helps to shape meaning and understanding.

The first three chapters examine the way privacy and surveillance have been treated in German cinema and literature. Together they provide the important insight that, while the experiences of the Nazi era and with the East German Stasi loom large in the German understanding of the NSA-Affair, there are also themes that transcend those specific experiences and reach deeper into the collective German psyche. These include a pastoral romanticism that sits uncomfortably with modernity and technological progress. They also include persistent reservations about industrialization and the resulting American commercial empire.

Laura Heins' excellent chapter opens this section of the book with an examination of contemporary German cinema's exaggerated fascination with the East German Stasi. In films such as *Das Leben der Anderen* (*The*

Lives of Others), Heins discovers sympathetic portrayals of Stasi agents that contrast sharply with the unease Germans have expressed over the NSA-Affair. Heins wonders if an important distinction is that East German monitoring and control consisted in personalized – sometimes deeply intimate – human intelligence gathering as opposed to the highly impersonal, abstracted signals intelligence pursued by the NSA. Heins suggests that this is part of a broader yearning for solidity in the face of increasing social "liquidity" and the alienation brought on by the very technologies the NSA exploits. Heins profoundly recognizes that each of us produces and consumes ever-increasing volumes of data, "but not a lot of personal attention" of the kind the Stasi lavished on the subjects of their surveillance.

Roger Crockett uses an examination of Hans Fallada's life – and sorrowful book *Every Man Dies Alone* – to graphically depict the brutal nature of the Nazi surveillance state. Fallada's experiences – and the experiences of his doomed characters – reveal just how pervasive and oppressive this regime of monitoring and control was. It might be easy to dismiss the increasingly remote Nazi era as a basis for contemporary Germans' deep reservations about intelligence gathering. After all, the NSA-Affair seems to be an altogether different phenomenon with its own actors and involving wholly new surveillance methods. But Crockett's essay suggests that anxiety for state monitoring and control crept into and then corroded the trust that members of families should be able to expect from one another. Surely this experience has been passed on to the postwar generations, not just by literature such as Fallada's book, but also as part of Germany's social DNA.

Summer Renault-Steele suggests, however, that the German preoccupation with surveillance predates Hitler's SS and Gestapo. She offers Fritz Lang's Weimar era films about the character "Dr. Mabuse" – and the reception the films were given by film critics – as evidence of a long-standing disquiet for mass culture and modern technology. Renault-Steele notes that Lang and others were troubled by the way that modern technology and mass culture rendered the individual as little more than an object: as the target of Dr. Mabuse's omnipresent and all-seeing surveillance, in the case of the former; as the consumer in the modern industrialized market, in the case of the latter. Renault-Steele notes that there are already hints of resentment for American cultural and economic imperialism in the films and film criticism of the Weimar era. That long thread might weave prominently into the fabric of contemporary Germans' response to the NSA-Affair.

Part Five's final two chapters take up American cultural treatments of privacy and intelligence gathering.

Eva Jobs' survey of the espionage genre in literature and film produces the remarkable insight that it has largely been an Anglo-American interest. One looks in vain, Jobs concludes, for positive depictions of spies in German culture. In passing, she wonders if this has something to do with a German tradition that regards spying as dishonorable. Closely examining two of the best-loved American films in the genre (*Three Days of the Condor* and *Enemy of the State*) Jobs sees a conflicting presentation of the intelligence services. As institutions, they are portrayed as sinister and unchecked. But the individuals working for the intelligence services can achieve heroic status. Jobs argues that this tension is a productive complexity, allowing Americans – and the American Intelligence Community – to contest and grapple with, through popular culture, the threats posed by intelligence gathering while at the same time crediting the valuable contribution the Intelligence Community makes to promoting America's security. This constitutes another forum for the political debate over "privacy and power." Or, as Jobs puts it, it is "catharsis through fiction."

Russell Miller and Stephen Chovanec see Laura Poitras' award-winning film *CITIZENFOUR* (which documents the first days of the Snowden leaks) as a contribution to the political debate surrounding the NSA-Affair. But, for Miller and Chovanec, the film's two significant shortcomings do its political agenda more harm than good. First, it is an act of documentary surveillance that is meant to serve as a critique of surveillance. Second, the film has to rely on unsubstantiated fear as its critique of surveillance, in much the same way as the Intelligence Community relies on unsubstantiated fear to justify surveillance.

E Conclusion

This book is meant to be an honest reckoning with the different transatlantic perspectives on the issues involved in the NSA-Affair. That has involved documenting and demonstrating what might roughly be characterized as Europe's cosmopolitan legalism ("obey the law"), on the one hand, and America's pragmatic realpolitik ("grow up"), on the other hand. More importantly, these chapters give informed Americans and Europeans an opportunity to consider the underlying sociocultural dynamics that should allow us to better comprehend these significant differences. I hope the book will help us better understand each other – on both the legal and cultural planes. That is bound to be a better place to begin if we have any hope of a constructive dialogue in the face of the current crisis.

In fact, these chapters illuminate the contours of what might be a way forward through the NSA-Affair. Europeans will insist on anchoring the legitimacy of State authority, including intelligence activities, in the law. But they might be invited to soften their legal dogmatism to give some weight to a jurisprudence that credits law's expressive and aspirational functions. It can take law a long time to establish an enforceable reality. Until the day that international law truly serves as a limit on America's foreign intelligence activities, the legal regime to which Peters and Voeneky so passionately refer will continue to serve as a beacon and as a common vocabulary for American and European policy-makers and diplomats. For the time being, this would lend international law some value in the strained transatlantic relationship, even if it does not seem likely that it will exert Austinian force on the United States. Americans, for their part, might be persuaded to expand the *ex post facto* causes of action available to individuals for harms suffered as a result of intelligence gathering or data protection abuses. This would sit well with America's common law regulatory culture while offering Europeans some role for law in the intelligence context. Are we already seeing this in the form of the ombudsperson anticipated by the new "Privacy Shield" and in legislative proposals that would grant Europeans some form of judicial redress for data protection violations? There are obvious limits to this possibility, including the justiciability and confidentiality issues that dog the existing regime of lawsuits. But these barriers could be overcome with some modest reform. The United States also might adopt laws offering greater protection for whistle blowers and the media that publicizes their disclosures. This aligns with the realpolitik that Wittes attributed to American policy in the area of intelligence gathering. If the Intelligence Community is not good enough to keep its work secret, then the logic of realpolitik might suggest that the Intelligence Community should have to live with and learn from its failures.

America, however, will continue to chiefly insist on the integrity of political processes and institutions as the basis for the legitimacy of its intelligence activities. American policy more or less reflects the will of the American public, expressed through the electoral process. Americans seem to be convinced that the ballot box – and other political processes – are adequate to control state power, even in the context of national security and intelligence gathering. This is a deeply rooted faith, reinforced in this context by the work of the historic Church Committee and by the ongoing, effective Congressional oversight it helped establish. Several of the book's American contributors – and some of the Europeans – pointed to President Obama's Signals Intelligence Policy Directive and the USA FREEDOM Act as examples of the rationality of this view. This confidence is reinforced by the seeming hypocrisy of the European stance, considering that several of the book's contributors (American and European alike) noted the weak nature of Germany's intelligence oversight regime. This deserves the careful self-reflection that the *Bundestag's* Committee of Inquiry is giving it.

The larger conceptual gap remains Europe's commitment to a cosmopolitan politics that conflicts with the priority America places on its national interests. In the context of the European Union, the Europeans have made a half-century's experience with the processes of opening and relaxing state sovereignty. That has largely been a process of mutual self-interest pursued in gradual steps that create their own momentum towards deeper integration. That process, as several of the book's European contributors noted, has gained particular resonance in the areas of privacy and data protection. The same gradualism should be deployed in relations with the United States on the issues of privacy and intelligence gathering.

These are surely just some of the lessons this book offers in the hopes of strengthening our essential transatlantic dialogue. But perhaps the most important lesson the book teaches is that Americans and Europeans should come to acknowledge – and respect – that we have fundamental differences on the issues of privacy and intelligence gathering.

PART ONE

Privacy and Data Protection for the Digital Age

1

Foucault's Panopticon

A Model for NSA Surveillance?

BY SARAH HOROWITZ

A Introduction

Michel Foucault had a profound impact on how scholars think about questions of power, knowledge and privacy. His 1975 *Surveiller et punir: Naissance de la prison* (*Discipline and Punish: The Birth of the Prison*) is arguably his most famous work.[1] Along with George Orwell's *1984*,[2] Foucault's book – and its meditation on the nature and power of the "Panopticon" – has become one of the touchstones for how we talk about surveillance today. This has been especially true in the wake of Edward Snowden's revelations and the alarm raised over the intrusive power of the National Security Agency (NSA). Indeed, Snowden himself used the term "Panopticon" to describe NSA surveillance, as has the award-winning documentary filmmaker Laura Poitras, while columnists on both the left and the right have adopted Foucault's term to decry the actions of the U.S. government.[3]

---

[1] Michel Foucault, Surveiller et Punir: Naissance de la prison (1975); for the English translation, *see* Michel Foucault, Discipline and Punish: The Birth of the Prison (Alan Sheridan trans., 1995). Unless otherwise noted, all citations are to the English translation.

[2] George Orwell, Nineteen Eighty-Four (Everyman's Library, 1992) (1949).

[3] For Snowden's use of this term, *see* Barton Gellman, *Code Name "Verax": Snowden, In Exchanges with Post Reporter, Made Clear He Knew Risks*, Wash. Post (June 9, 2013), www.washingtonpost.com/world/national-security/code-name-verax-snowden-in-exchanges-with-post-reporter-made-clear-he-knew-risks/2013/06/09/c9a25b54-d14c-11e2-9f1a-1a7cdee20287_story.html. For Poitras, *see* Michael Silverberg, *The Next Chapter in the Snowden Leaks May Unfold in a New York Museum*, Quartz (May 30, 2014), http://qz.com/214831/the-next-chapter-in-the-snowden-leaks-may-unfold-in-a-new-york-museum/. Other invocations of the Panopticon can be found in James B. Rule, *The Price of the Panopticon*, N.Y. Times (June 11, 2013), www.nytimes.com/2013/06/12/opinion/the-price-of-the-panopticon.html?_r=1&; Reid Smith, *The Surveillance State in Your Head*, Am. Conservative (July 19, 2013), www.theamericanconservative.com/articles/the-

Because Foucault's theoretical model of surveillance has surfaced in the contemporary debate, this chapter lays out his arguments and situates them in the context of his larger body of work. In particular, it focuses on his idea of the Panopticon as a central model and metaphor for the relationship between power and knowledge in modern societies. Foucault's work has enormous value for helping us to understand certain elements of the NSA-Affair because he shows how forms of surveillance that are known but hidden can transform human behavior and because of his efforts to reconcile liberal democracies with surveillance states. Yet, his theory of the Panopticon obscures as much as it clarifies in the NSA-Affair. The Foucauldian Panopticon is more effective in reshaping its citizens than the NSA is. In contrast to what Foucault posited, Snowden's revelations led to increased political activity around the issues of data collection and surveillance, not passivity. Additionally, because Foucault sees the state as having primacy over other entities that wield power, his theories cannot adequately address the intrusive role that Internet and telecommunications companies play, nor the complex interactions between these private entities and the state. Despite its wide currency, Foucault's model of the Panopticon does not fully account for how power and surveillance work in the modern era.

B   Foucault: Privacy and Power in the Panopticon

Foucault's published works include texts on sexuality, psychiatry and mental institutions, and the criminal justice system.[4] Many of his writings revolve around two central questions. The first is the issue of knowledge: how knowledge is produced, for what purposes, and how it is used.[5] For Foucault, this was no abstract question. Knowledge is not

surveillance-state-in-your-head/. The use of the Panopticon as a trope in writings on the NSA-Affair is discussed more fully in Section C I of this chapter.

[4] On sexuality, *see* MICHEL FOUCAULT, HISTOIRE DE LA SEXUALITÉ: LA VOLONTÉ DE SAVOIR (1976) [hereinafter Savoir]; MICHEL FOUCAULT, HISTOIRE DE LA SEXUALITÉ: L'USAGE DES PLAISIRS (1984); MICHEL FOUCAULT, HISTOIRE DE LA SEXUALITÉ: LE SOUCI DE SOI (1984). On psychiatry and mental institutions, *see* MICHEL FOUCAULT, HISTOIRE DE LA FOLIE À L'ÂGE CLASSIQUE: FOLIE ET DÉRAISON (1961). On criminal justice, *see* FOUCAULT, *supra* note 1.

[5] For instance, *Discipline and Punish* discusses how the "sciences of man" like "psychology, psychiatry, pedagogy, criminology, and so many other strange sciences" arose out of the state's efforts to control populations. FOUCAULT, *supra* note 1, at 226. MICHEL FOUCAULT, LES MOTS ET LES CHOSES: UNE ARCHÉOLOGIE DES SCIENCES HUMAINES (1966) discusses

produced for the sake of knowledge itself but is instead deeply bound up in the practices of power.[6] For example, Foucault argued that states expand their power by collecting and systematizing knowledge about their citizens and using that knowledge to classify and control individuals.[7] For Foucault, knowledge was power in a very real and practical sense. Another of Foucault's major concerns is how institutions (especially those that are state run) interact with the "self."[8] Foucault's works on prisons, mental asylums, hospitals, and schools explored how they came to have power over individuals and attempted to shape them in the state's desired image. These institutions collect knowledge about the populations they serve (including through the creation of disciplines such as criminology and sociology to study criminals and psychiatry to study the mentally ill), classify individuals according to whether they are deemed "normal" or "abnormal" (e.g., criminals or the insane), isolate those judged "abnormal" in prisons or clinics, and attempt to impose preferred or ordained values on these captive populations.[9] In other words, knowledge production is intimately linked to the power of institutions – and often to the power of the state itself. These institutions' practices of observation can be quite sinister as they use their authority to socially segregate, silence dissent, and impose norms on individuals.

---

the question of the categorization of knowledge. On the relationship between sexology, knowledge and state power, see SAVOIR, *supra* note 4. On the question of knowledge as central to Foucault's thought, *see, e.g.*, LISA DOWNING, THE CAMBRIDGE INTRODUCTION TO MICHEL FOUCAULT (2008), vii, where she begins her work by stating, "A reading of the works of Michel Foucault (1926–1984) does not so much equip us with new pieces of knowledge, or even teach us new and different ways of knowing. Rather, it invites us to share in a radical calling into question of the ways in which knowledge itself operates. Foucault argues that all forms of knowledge are historically relative and contingent, and cannot be disassociated from the workings of power."

[6] Thus, Foucault states the following in DISCIPLINE AND PUNISH: "We should admit rather that power produces knowledge (and not simply by encouraging it because it serves power or by applying it because it is useful); that power and knowledge directly imply one another; that there is no power relation without the correlative constitution of a field of knowledge, nor any knowledge that does not presuppose and constitute at the same time power relations." FOUCAULT, *supra* note 1, at 27.

[7] *See, e.g.*, FOUCAULT *supra* note 1, at 192.

[8] This question is particular apparent in the works cited in note 4, where he discusses these questions with respect to the disciplines of psychiatry, sexology and criminology. *See also* CLARE O'FARRELL, MICHEL FOUCAULT 110 (2005). *See also Id.* at 192.

[9] FOUCAULT, *supra* note 1, at 199.

Discipline and Punish: The Birth of the Prison focuses on these issues through the lens of the criminal justice system.[10] Foucault discusses the transition from early modern penal styles, in which criminals were punished publicly and by torture,[11] to a more modern penal regime in which punishments were moved behind closed doors and relied far less on the infliction of pain.[12] The transition Foucault documents was in part achieved through legal reforms across Europe that restricted the use of torture.[13] It would be possible to read this shift as evidence of humane progress. According to this version, at the advent of the modern era governments became less interested in displaying their power through humiliation and torment and came to act more humanely, largely as a result of self-imposed limits on their power.[14] Foucault was more critical. He argued that this shift actually involved an increase in the power of states. In his words, "The expiation that once rained down upon the body must be replaced by a punishment that acts in depth on the heart, the thoughts, the will, the inclinations."[15] The goal of punishment was no longer to touch the body, but to reshape the soul through efforts at reforming criminals and rehabilitating the condemned. Corrections no longer lasted for a few gruesome hours, but for a lifetime, as deviant individuals were remade into docile citizens who would support the state without critique or challenge. In Foucault's critical assessment states became more powerful in the modern era by extending their control to the inner lives of citizens while seeming to renounce the power to inflict pain.[16]

---

[10] A short useful introduction to DISCIPLINE AND PUNISH Is DOWNING, *supra* note 5, at 75–85. A longer account can be found in Alan D. Schrift, *Discipline and Punish, in* A COMPANION TO FOUCAULT 137–53 (Christopher Falzon, Timothy O'Leary & Jana Sawicki eds., 2013). For a discussion of Foucault's work within the field of surveillance studies, see DAVID LYON, THE ELECTRONIC EYE: THE RISE OF SURVEILLANCE SOCIETY 62–79 (1994).

[11] FOUCAULT, *supra* note 1, at 32–69.   [12] *Id.* at 16–24.   [13] *Id.* at 3–10.

[14] In the Anglophone world, this narrative is often called "Whig history" and refers to a teleological account of history that relies on a notion of progressive liberation. *See* HERBERT BUTTERFIELD, THE WHIG INTERPRETATION OF HISTORY (1931). *See also* Adrian Wilson & T.G. Ashplant, *Whig History and Present-Centered History*, 31 HIST. J. 1 (1988).

[15] FOUCAULT, *supra* note 1, at 16.

[16] This move to disrupt a commonly held narrative of human liberation and progress over time is a common one in Foucault's work. *See also* SAVOIR, *supra* note 4. It should be said that historians do not necessarily accept Foucault's conclusions or chronology. For a more optimistic view of the decline of public torture, see LYNN HUNT, INVENTING HUMAN RIGHTS: A HISTORY (2008). Susan Dwyer Amussen highlights how early modern forms of punishment used violence as a means to reach the soul. *See* Susan Dwyer

The emblem of this newly expanded state authority is the Panopticon, an architectural ideal proposed by the British philosopher Jeremy Bentham in the late eighteenth century as a model for a new type of prison.[17] At the center of the Panopticon is a guard tower. A ring of cells surrounds this tower and "all that is needed, then, is to place a supervisor in a central tower and to shut up in each cell a madman, a patient, a condemned man, a worker or a schoolboy."[18] The guard can see all of the inmates all of the time, but inmates can see neither who is in the tower nor one another. Isolated as they are, the inmates are unable to interact with one another in order to resist authority collectively or, if working, waste any time that could be spent laboring.

The lines of sight in the Panopticon are central to the functioning of this system. The fact that guards can always see the inmates induces "in the inmate a state of conscious and permanent visibility that assures the automatic functioning of power."[19] In other words, the individuals who are confined to the Panopticon will always do as they are supposed to because at any one moment they could be under observation.[20] But because inmates cannot see into the tower, it does not matter if anyone is inside the guard tower. If there is someone, the identity of that person is irrelevant (a small child or a visitor serves equally well as an armed

---

Amussen, *Punishment, Discipline, and Power: The Social Meanings of Violence in Early Modern England*, 34 J. BRIT. STUD. 1 (1995). Petrus Cornelis Spierenburg critiques Foucault's narrative for describing an abrupt shift away from torture and public forms of punishment when in fact this transition happened over the course of centuries. *See* Petrus Cornelis Spierenburg, *Punishment, Power, and History: Foucault and Elias*, 28 SOC. SCI. HIST. 607 (2004).

[17] Bentham's writings on the Panopticon can be found in JEREMY BENTHAM AND MIRAN BOŽOVIČ, THE PANOPTICON WRITINGS (1995). For a discussion of Bentham's work and the relationhip between Foucault's ideas and Bentham's, see ANNE BRUNON-ERNST, BEYOND FOUCAULT: NEW PERSPECTIVES ON BENTHAM'S PANOPTICON (2012). On the history of Bentham's prison project, see JANET SEMPLE, BENTHAM'S PRISON: A STUDY OF THE PANOPTICON PENITENTIARY (1993).

[18] FOUCAULT, *supra* note 1, at 200.   [19] *Id.* at 201.

[20] Foucault and the Panopticon have thus been central to arguments about what is often termed the "chilling effect" of contemporary surveillance practices in that they make citizens more passive and disengaged out of fear that the state is watching them. *See, e.g.*, GLENN GREENWALD, NO PLACE TO HIDE: EDWARD SNOWDEN, THE NSA AND THE US SURVEILLANCE STATE 170–209 (2014); Neil M. Richards, *The Dangers of Surveillance*, 126 HARV. L. REV. 1948–52 (2013); DAVID LYON, SURVEILLANCE AFTER SEPTEMBER 11, 52–55, 152 (2003); DANIEL SOLOVE, UNDERSTANDING PRIVACY, 109, 178, 193 (2008); BRUCE SCHNEIER, DATA AND GOLIATH: THE HIDDEN BATTLES TO COLLECT YOUR DATA AND CONTROL YOUR WORLD 95–99 (2015). On the chilling effect of surveillance, see also Section C I ("The Panoptican as a Valuable Insight into the NSA-Affair") of this chapter.

guard) as is their motivation for observing, whether because of "the curiosity of the indiscreet, the malice of a child, the thirst for knowledge of a philosopher who wishes to visit this museum of human nature, or the perversity of those who take pleasure in spying and punishing."[21]

Bentham's model Panoptic prison was never built, although it did influence the design of prisons and institutions, including factories and hospitals, in the nineteenth and twentieth centuries.[22] Foucault was less interested in the practicalities and realities of Bentham's project than in the way the Panopticon could illuminate how power functions in modern societies. In the Panopticon power is both anonymous and omnipresent: anonymous in the sense that those in the Panopticon do not know who is observing them (or if anyone actually is doing so), omnipresent in the sense that this power depends on us knowing all the time that someone could be observing us. Foucault understood that the Panopticon is intended to reshape its inmates and to alter not only their behavior but also their minds. Through the mechanics of surveillance those in the Panopticon are disciplined and become self-disciplining as they internalize the norms that the institution wants to instill, whether those norms consist in blunt obedience to the state or the value of hard work. Foucault quotes Bentham's enumeration of the benefits of the Panopticon: "*Morals reformed – health preserved – industry invigorated – instruction diffused – public burdens lightened.*"[23] Crucially, these alterations in the habits and attitudes of inmates can occur without the application of a great deal of force. Observation and isolation displace the infliction of physical pain as the central mechanisms of social discipline.[24]

Foucault viewed Panoptic power as being distributed throughout society while at the same time maintaining a central role for the state among all the entities that wield power. For both Foucault and Bentham, prisons were only one possible use for Panoptic structures and other institutions could also benefit from a regime of discipline through

---

[21] FOUCAULT, *supra* note 1, at 202.
[22] On the history of Bentham's prison project, see SEMPLE, *supra* note 17. On the influence of Bentham's prison design in the United States in the nineteenth century, *see* ANNA VEMER ANDRZEJEWSKI, BUILDING POWER: ARCHITECTURE AND SURVEILLANCE IN VICTORIAN AMERICA 13–41 (2008). Andrzejewski's work discusses the issue of surveillance more generally in American architecture.
[23] Quoted in FOUCAULT, *supra* note 1, at 207 (emphasis in original).
[24] It should be said, of course, that ultimately what backs up the power of isolation and observation is the ability to inflict violence, should inmates misbehave. On this issue in Bentham's thought, *see* SEMPLE, *supra* note 17, 126–27.

observation. Foucault listed hospitals, mental asylums, schools, and factories as being capable of operating through the principle of control through surveillance.[25] Some of these institutions are state run, others (such as schools) could be in either private or public hands, but the inclusion of factories in Foucault's list underscores that the Panopticon was not exclusively a mechanism for the state's control over individuals.[26] Employers could also use Panoptic principles – either through direct visual observation or instruments like time cards – to extend control over their workers. In these instances the aim was to increase efficiency and output rather than reduce crime or other antisocial behavior. Foucault thus saw Panoptic power as a tool for state and non-state actors, particularly as he understood that those who wielded it wanted the same thing: the creation of what he terms "docile bodies."[27] The docility that one set of institutions instilled in its inmates would help the other institutions. Schools would teach children how to behave so that they could be good workers and obedient citizens; prisons would reform antisocial individuals with the hopes of turning them into model factory employees; factories would boost the state's economy and prevent worker unrest to further stabilize the authority of the government. Foucault's model imagines a world where the state and the capitalist bourgeoisie work together and often have interests that are aligned with one another.[28] In other works, Foucault elaborated on the idea that power was not just the property of the state. In a 1982 essay titled "The Subject and Power," he states, "It is certain that in contemporary societies the

---

[25] FOUCAULT, *supra* note 1, at 200–01.

[26] On the Panopticon as a form of control over labor, both agricultural and industrial, see Alessandro Stanziani, *The Traveling Panopticon: Labor Institutions and Labor Practices in Russia and Britain in the Eighteenth and Nineteenth Centuries*, 51 COMP. STUD. SOC. & HIST. 715 (2009). SEMPLE, *supra* note 17, also discusses that Bentham saw the Panopticon as a model for educational institutions as well as for workhouses.

[27] Most notably, "docile bodies" is the title of a chapter in DISCIPLINE AND PUNISH in a section called "Discipline." This is a direct translation from the French of "les corps dociles." *See* FOUCAULT, *supra* note 1, at 137–71 (Fr.).

[28] The notion of a bourgeoisie in league with the state has, of course, a long history, most notably in Marxist thought. See for example KARL MARX & FRIEDRICH ENGELS, THE MANIFESTO OF THE COMMUNIST PARTY, Part II (1848). On Foucault's relationship with Marxist thought, see DOWNING, *supra* note 5, at 5, where she states "Foucault's position in *Discipline and Punish* ultimately differs from a Marxist analysis of class oppression, owing to the specific nature of the Foucaldian concept of *homo docilis* or disciplined body, which is found everywhere in society, not just in the toiling classes but in the classroom, the army and the prison, since the workings of what Foucault would call disciplinary power saturate the whole of society."

state is not simply one of the forms or specific situations for the exercise of power – even if it is the most important – but that in a certain way all other forms of power relations must refer to it. But this is not because they are derived from it; it is rather because power relations have come more and more under state control."[29] Thus, although Foucault saw that many different actors wield power in society, he also maintained that the state has primacy among them and becomes increasingly dominant over time.

In Foucault's description, Panoptic power is both generalized and targeted. At the end of *Discipline and Punish*, Foucault writes that the book was meant to "serve as a historical background to various studies of the power of normalization and the formation of knowledge in modern society."[30] In other words, the institutions that Foucault discusses are representative of how power operates in the contemporary era through the processes of knowledge collection and a particular type of highly visible anonymity. Foucault was saying that even those of us who are not in prisons, mental institutions, hospitals, factories, or schools are still subject to forms of anonymous observation that are intended to tame us. Yet individuals in modern societies do not shoulder the burden of Panoptic power equally. To this end, Foucault spoke of the importance of the power to classify. He writes,

> disciplinary power from the beginning of the nineteenth century in the psychiatric asylum, the penitentiary, the reformatory, the approved school and, to some extent, the hospital … function[ed] according to a double mode; that of binary division and branding (mad/sane; dangerous/harmless; normal/abnormal); and that of coercive assignment, of differential distribution (who he is; where he must be; how he is to be characterized; how he is to be recognized; how a constant surveillance is to be exercised over him in an individual way, etc.).[31]

Those placed on the "wrong" side of the divide – the mad, the dangerous, the abnormal – are subject to more control and surveillance than those deemed sane, harmless and normal.

Foucault's exploration of the politics of discipline, institutions, and surveillance has three discernible roots: his political activism, his sexual orientation, and Europe's twentieth-century history. At the end of the first chapter of *Discipline and Punish*, he states that a wave of prison

---

[29] Michel Foucault, *The Subject and Power*, 8 Criti. Inq. 777, 793 (1982).
[30] Foucault, *supra* note 1, at 308.   [31] *Id.* at 199.

revolts was one of the inspirations for this work. During the 1970s, the decade in which this work was published, Foucault was heavily involved in campaigns for prison reform in France.[32] He was one of the founders of the *Groupe d'information sur les prisons* (GIP), an organization that sought to raise awareness of prison conditions and turn the gaze of the citizens to an investigation of the coercive powers of the state.[33] GIP's aims were to reverse the processes that Foucault saw at work in *Discipline and Punish*, such as the shift toward punishments that were hidden from view and the construction of a state that sought to watch and control its citizens without itself being seen.[34] Left unstated in this work was the issue of Foucault's queer sexuality.[35] For much of Foucault's life homosexuality was considered a mental disorder.[36] Given these circumstances it is easy to understand how the power of the state and medical professionals to classify individuals as either sane or insane was particularly troubling for Foucault.[37] Moreover, despite the fact that his sexual and romantic relationships were with men, Foucault often resisted the label of "homosexual" precisely because he saw that the imposition of this identity was a tool of power. In *The History of Sexuality* he described how the notion of homosexuality as a fixed and defining trait of individuals emerged in the nineteenth century as states and institutions sought to classify (and control) individuals whose sexual acts were nonreproductive.[38]

Foucault was also writing precisely at a moment when French citizens and intellectuals were increasingly preoccupied with questions about

---

[32] DAVID MACEY, THE LIVES OF MICHEL FOUCAULT: A BIOGRAPHY 157–82 (1993); DIDIER ERIBON, MICHEL FOUCAULT 224–37 (Betsy Wing trans., 1991).

[33] Perry Zurn, *Publicity and Politics: Foucault, the Prisons Information Group, and the Press*, 17 RADICAL PHILOS REV. 43 (2014) and Michael Welch, *Counterveillance: How Foucault and the Groupe d'information sur les Prisons Reversed the Optics*, 15 THEOR. CRIMINOL. 301 (2011).

[34] Zurn, *supra* note 33; Welch, *supra* note 33.

[35] On Foucault's sexuality, *see* MACEY, *supra* note 32, at 14–15; ERIBON, *supra* note 32, at 26–30.

[36] On the medical stigmatization of homosexuality, *see* Vernon A. Rosario, THE EROTIC IMAGINATION: FRENCH HISTORIES OF PERVERSITY (1997). On the general history of homosexuality in post-war France, *see* Julian Jackson, LIVING IN ARCADIA: HOMOSEXUALITY, POLITICS, AND MORALITY IN FRANCE FROM THE LIBERATION TO AIDS (2009). On the social stigmas and laws used to prosecute homosexuals in Foucault's time, *see* MACEY, *supra* note 32, at 30.

[37] On the autobiographical strain in Foucault's work with particular respect to issues of psychiatry and sexuality, *see* ERIBON, *supra* note 32, at 27–29.

[38] SAVOIR, *supra* note 4; Jon Simons, *Power, Resistance, and Freedom*, in A COMPANION TO FOUCAULT, *supra* note 10, at 301, 317.

France's wartime collaboration with Nazi Germany.[39] The story of the invidious use of population statistics during World War II would largely confirm Foucault's claims about the reasons why states seek information about their citizens.[40] Of course, the Holocaust demonstrated the ultimate danger of the power of states to identify and classify.[41] The fact that Nazi racial laws redefined Jewishness from being about religion to being about ancestry revealed how identity classification was a top-down process imposed on individuals.[42] Nazi conquest frequently resulted in censuses designed to locate Jews so that they could be targeted for deportation to concentration camps.[43] In turn, death rates were sometimes correlated with the quality of a country's statistical measurements. In the Netherlands about 75% of the Jewish population died in the Holocaust, in part because of the thoroughness of prewar population registration systems, which the Nazis were able to use in their quest to target Jews for extermination.[44] The French case is instructive. France, similar to other countries conquered by or collaborating with Nazi Germany, had to move from a traditional census system that measured population percentages to a new model that was designed to follow individuals and track them through their lifetimes.[45] These efforts were the origins of the French INSEE code – a national identification number similar to the American Social Security number.[46] The digits themselves were initially intended to record an individual's professional skills as well as heritage and the first digit classified individuals as Jewish or not.[47] The

---

[39] HENRY ROUSSO, THE VICHY SYNDROME: HISTORY AND MEMORY IN FRANCE SINCE 1944 (1991).

[40] On the use of French population statistics to assist with the German Holocaust, see EDWIN BLACK, IBM AND THE HOLOCAUST: THE STRATEGIC ALLIANCE BETWEEN NAZI GERMANY AND AMERICA'S MOST POWERFUL CORPORATION 292–332 (2001).

[41] On the issue of Foucault, classification and the Nazi state, see Alan Milchman & Alan Rosenberg, Michel Foucault, Auschwitz, and the Destruction of the Body, in POSTMODERNISM AND THE HOLOCAUST, 205 (Alan Milchman & Alan Rosenberg eds., 1998).

[42] JOSEPH W. BENDERSKY, A CONCISE HISTORY OF NAZI GERMANY 142 (2007).

[43] William Seltzer, Population Statistics, the Holocaust and the Nuremberg Trials, 24 POPUL. & DEV. REV. 511, 514–527 (1998).

[44] Id. Additionally, the Nazi extermination efforts were aided by the careful work of Jacobus Lambertus Lentz, the Inspector of Population Registries during World War II. Lentz, whose motto was "to record is to serve," does not seem to have been motivated by anti-Semitism or adherence to Nazi beliefs, but rather by a desire to record so much information about individuals that, in his words, "a paper human" could stand in for "the natural human." Quoted in BLACK, supra note 40, at 304.

[45] Seltzer, supra note 43, at 525–26.   [46] BLACK, supra note 40, at 321.

[47] Id. at 319, 321–22.

original goal of the INSEE code was to allow the state to find Jews as well as workers who might be able to further the state's productive capacity.[48] Both the origins of the INSEE code and the wartime population censuses occurred in 1941, when Foucault was an adolescent. While he never explicitly engaged with these episodes in French (and his personal) history, it is easy to suppose that Foucault's lived experiences with the classificatory impulses of the state informed his sense of the degree to which information gathering was hardly a neutral process, and his understanding of the human costs of classification, identification, and monitoring.[49]

C The NSA as the Panopticon?

I The Panopticon as a Valuable Insight into the NSA-Affair

In the immediate aftermath of Edward Snowden's revelations, journalists and commentators seized upon Foucault's model of the Panopticon in their discussions the NSA's surveillance practices. Their writings show the variety of ways Foucault's work has been applied to contemporary questions about power, the state, and knowledge. Some authors used the Panopticon as a synonym for widespread state surveillance.[50] Likewise,

---

[48] *Id.* at 321. However, in many ways, the French story is quite complicated. The man in charge of population statistics in France (René Carmille) was actually working for the resistance; not only did he not register who was Jewish and who was not, his aim was also to locate individuals who had military or occupational skills that the resistance could use. Partly as a result of his efforts, the death rate of French Jews was far lower than in other occupied countries. BLACK, *supra* note 40, at 329–32.

[49] For instance, Foucault once spoke of the men and women of his generation in the following terms: "The menace of war was our background, our framework of existence. Then the war arrived. Much more than the activities of family life, it was these events concerning the world which are the substance of our memory. I say "our" because I am nearly sure that most boys and girls in France at this moment had the same experience. Our private life was really threatened. Maybe that is the reason why I am fascinated by history and the relationship between personal experience and those events of which we are a part. I think that is the nucleus of my theoretical desires." Quoted in ERIBON, *supra* note 32, at 10.

[50] *See, e.g.,* Julian Sanchez, *Snowden Showed Us Just How Big the Panopticon Really Was. Now It's Up to Us*, THE GUARDIAN (June 5, 2014, 4:02 PM), www.theguardian.com/commentisfree/2014/jun/05/edward-snowden-one-year-surveillance-debate-begins-future-privacy; Sean Gallagher, *Building a Panopticon: The Evolution of the NSA's XKeyscore*, ARS TECHNICA (Aug. 9, 2013, 7:45 AM), http://arstechnica.com/information-technology/2013/08/building-a-panopticon-the-evolution-of-the-nsas-xkeyscore/; Emile Simpson, *The Panopticon Paradox*, FP (Dec. 24, 2013), www.foreignpolicy.com/articles/2013/12/24/the_panopticon_paradox_nsa_war_on_terror.

references to the Panopticon served as a shorthand for how states increase their power through violating our privacy.[51] In many of these instances, Foucault's ideas were invoked only in passing and not fully discussed. Other commentators have used Foucault's claim that surveillance creates a passive citizenry as a way to explain the perils of NSA surveillance.[52] For example, in *No Place to Hide: Edward Snowden, The NSA, and the U.S. Surveillance State*, Glenn Greenwald cites Foucault's work as helping us understand why "every oppressive state views mass surveillance as one of its most critical instruments of control."[53] Greenwald concludes that the United States is to be regarded as one of these oppressive states. What emerges from these references is the sense that, for a certain segment of the general public, invoking Foucault provides a way to conjure the dangers of mass data collection. But scholars in surveillance studies have suggested that the theory of the Panopticon is not particularly applicable to contemporary surveillance practices because the scope and effects of NSA surveillance and data collection are not very similar to the Panoptic observation that interested Foucault.[54] In the following parts of this chapter I discuss how Foucault's description of the Panopticon can help us understand many elements of the NSA-Affair, including the drive to classification among both governments and private firms and the nature of a state that is powerful while also offering us protections against its power. Some studies also show that surveillance can make us compliant and obedient in ways similar to those identified by Foucault. But in many respects Foucault's Panopticon is an uncomfortable fit with the NSA-Affair. Surveillance can produce

---

[51] *See, e.g.,* John Lanchester, *The Snowden Files: Why the British Public Should Be Worried about GCHQ,* The Guardian (Oct. 3, 2013, 2:01 PM), www.theguardian.com/world/2013/oct/03/edward-snowden-files-john-lanchester and Rule, *supra* note 3.

[52] *See, e.g.,* Smith, *supra* note 3; Ray Pensador, *The Surveillance State as Foucault's Panopticon,* Daily Kos (Sept. 11, 2013, 3:01 AM), www.dailykos.com/story/2013/09/11/1238013/-The-Surveillance-State-As-Foucault-s-Panopticon; John L. Sullivan, *Uncovering the Data Panopticon: The Urgent Need for Critical Scholarship in an Era of Corporate and Government Surveillance,* 1 Pol. Econ. Comm. 89 (2013).

[53] Greenwald, *supra* note 20, at 176.

[54] Siva Vaidhyanathan, *The Rise of the Cryptopticon,* 17 Hedgehog Rev. (Spring 2015), www.iasc-culture.org/THR/THR_article_2015_Spring_Vaidhyanathan.php; Miguelángel Verde Garrido, *Contesting a Biopolitics of Information and Communications: The Importance of Truth and Surveillance after Snowden,* 13 Surveill. & Soc'y. 153 (2015). Vaidhyanathan suggests that contemporary surveillance practices do not particularly affect our behavior and are more hidden than what Foucault suggests. The latter claim is an argument that Verde shares, as he also discusses how individuals' surveillance practices can be used to resist state power.

resistance as well as docility. Foucault's theories are a better guide to state surveillance than commercial data collection, a fact that is hardly surprising given his emphasis on state power. We need to look elsewhere to understand the nature and dangers of the data collection carried out by technology companies. Foucault's ideas are problematic in an instance where much of the NSA's data comes from non-state commercial entities with which we willingly interact. Fundamentally, both the practices of the NSA and the responses to the revelations about this surveillance are far more complex than any simple application of Foucault's model of power in the Panopticon.

One of the major advantages of using Foucault's Panopticon as a model for contemporary surveillance practices is that he manages to reconcile liberal democracy with a strong surveillance state. Central to much of Foucault's work is the idea that the developments we take to be liberating in fact have the effect of expanding state control. In *Discipline and Punish*, he described how the new and less violent forms of punishment of the early nineteenth century seem to be a sign of freedom from the coercive power of the state but are not (or are not entirely). Contemporary governments can provide legal protections, limit their power, and even offer avenues for public political participation. Yet they may still control us through mechanisms that are less visible, lighter, and perhaps more effective than the more brutal means of control of early modern states. In this respect, Foucault offers a better model for NSA surveillance than George Orwell does. The state of Oceania, in which *1984* is set, spies on its citizens extensively.[55] But unlike the Foucauldian state, the government of Oceania is hyper-visible and brutally totalitarian. Orwell imagines a centralized dictatorship that constantly broadcasts itself on Telescreens and tortures its citizens to "correct" thought crimes.[56] Orwell's novel presents a slippery slope argument: this is what we might become if we give up our freedoms and give in to state surveillance.[57]

---

[55] At the beginning of the novel, Orwell describes how each household has a device called a "telescreen" that "received and transmitted simultaneously. Any sound that Winston [the protagonist of the novel] made, above the level of a very low whisper, would be picked up by it; moreover, so long as he remained within the field of vision which the metal plaque commanded, he could be seen as well as heard." ORWELL, *supra* note 2, at 4.

[56] For a description of telescreens, *see id.* For an overview of the state apparatus, *see id.* at 6. For a description of the torture that the state inflicts on Winston for his thought crimes, *see id.* at 295–300.

[57] For this interpretation of Orwell's novel as presenting a possible future for Western societies, *see* Julian Symons, *Introduction*, NINETEEN EIGHTY-FOUR, *supra* note 2.

Foucault, in contrast, aimed to reveal the hidden mechanisms of the states in which we actually live: their norms have embedded themselves in our minds even as we think we are free and have control over the government. Orwell rails against totalitarian states. Foucault shows us how liberal states present their own form of domination.

Some of the principles of present-day surveillance practices also fit with Foucault's model of how power and knowledge work together. For instance, his description of the drive to classify resonates with what the surveillance scholar David Lyon calls the "phenetic fix," a practice central to modern surveillance cultures. This is the effort "to capture personal data triggered by human bodies and to use these abstractions to place people in new social classes of income, attributes, habits, preferences, or offences, in order to influence, manage, or control them."[58] Foucault's work is also an important reminder that the burdens of surveillance do not fall on everyone equally. For individuals placed into certain categories (in the current context the classifications "Arab," "Muslim," or "non-United States person" have particular gravity), state control is often more visible and more coercive than for those who fall outside these groupings.

Foucault's description of power as distributed throughout society helps us to understand how surveillance practices have become central to the workings of both private industry and governments and to elements of the relationship between the two. Even before Edward Snowden's revelations it was widely known that both states and technology companies engage in the practice of phenetic fixing, whether for the purpose of market segmentation or to decide who is to be considered a threat.[59] The NSA-Affair also revealed how much the government depends on private firms for its information gathering and the complicity between the state and private companies.[60] Moreover, Foucault's claims about the

---

[58] David Lyon, *Editorial Surveillance Studies: Understanding Visibility, Mobility and the Phenetic Fix*, 1 SURVEILL. & SOC'Y. 1, 3 (2002).

[59] On these issues, *see, e.g.*, LYON, *supra* note 10, at 91–114, 136–47.

[60] On this as central to Snowden's revelations, *see, e.g.*, Ewen MacAskill and Gabriel Dance, *NSA Files: Decoded. What the Revelations Mean for You*, THE GUARDIAN (Nov. 1, 2013), www.theguardian.com/world/interactive/2013/nov/01/snowden-nsa-files-surveillance-revelations-decoded. However, the question of private actors' obligation to provide information to the intelligence community was not a new one, as librarians resisted provisions of the Patriot Act that they turn over patron information to the government. *See* April Glaser, *Long Before Snowden, Librarians Were Anti-Surveillance Heroes*, SLATE (June 3, 2015, 3:17 PM), www.slate.com/blogs/future_tense/2015/06/03/usa_freedom_act_before_snowden_librarians_were_the_anti_surveillance_heroes.html. However, the reforms enacted by the USA Freedom Act in the summer of 2015 are likely to deepen

normalization of Panoptic surveillance in modern societies can help us understand the degree to which commercial entities have lowered our expectations of privacy in ways that benefit both them and the state. Numerous studies have noted distinct generational gaps in attitudes towards privacy, as those who have grown up on social media are more willing to share information online and have fewer concerns about commercial data collection.[61] This lower expectation of privacy may explain why those under thirty have a more favorable view of the NSA than older generations: they are already used to giving away their information.[62] This suggests that technology and telecommunications companies further the power of the state in at least two ways. First, they provide governments with valuable data. Second, they facilitate a downward realignment of our expectation of privacy.[63] There is, however, a notable difference between what Foucault described and the NSA's practices. The information that Internet companies collect relates here not to the production side (the efficiency of workers) but to consumption (the viewing, searching, and communication practices of users). As will be discussed later in this chapter, this distinction is perhaps more significant than it might initially appear because it has led to a divergence between the interests of technology firms and the government.

Foucault's theories are also useful for civil libertarians who want to make arguments about the importance of curtailing surveillance efforts. His focus is resolutely on the effects of monitoring practices on the behavior and minds of ordinary citizens. For many, this is the ultimate danger of surveillance: that it will fundamentally change who we are and how we act and make it less likely that we will dissent or resist the power

---

these relationships between internet companies and the government, as they temporarily oblige private actors to retain data for state access. *See* Mike DeBonis, *Congress Turns Away from post-9/11 Law, Retooling U.S. Surveillance Powers*, WASH. POST (June 2, 2015), www.washingtonpost.com/politics/senate-moves-ahead-with-retooling-of-us-surveillance-powers/2015/06/02/28f5e1ce-092d-11e5-a7ad-b430fc1d3f5c_story.html.

[61] *See* Zeljka Zorn, *Privacy Expectations and the Generation Gap*, HELP NET SECURITY (Sept. 14, 2010), www.net-security.org/article.php?id=1487; Caroline Lancelot Miltgen & Dominique Peyrat-Guillard, *Cultural and Generational Influences on Privacy Concerns: A Qualitative Study in Seven European Countries*, 23 EUR. J. INFO. SYS. 103, 115–117 (2014); Center for the Digital Future, USC Annenberg School for Communication and Journalism, *Is Online Privacy Over?* (Apr. 22, 2013), www.digitalcenter.org/online-priv acy-and-millennials-0413/.

[62] *Most View the CDC Favorably; VA's Image Slips*, PEW RESEARCH CENTER (Jan. 22, 2015), www.people-press.org/2015/01/22/most-view-the-cdc-favorably-vas-image-slips/.

[63] Verde Garrido, *supra* note 54, at 155–56.

of the state.[64] In calling on Foucault, those who want to decry the government's practices get around the public's lack of sympathy for terrorists by shifting our attention away from questions about security and toward issues of privacy in ways that are concrete and immediately relevant to our lives.[65] Additionally, the theory of the Panopticon makes the details of the surveillance programs less relevant than the fact of widespread surveillance. It does not matter whether the NSA had records of the content of phone calls or just of the metadata; nor is it terribly important whether the NSA had "direct access" to the servers of technology firms, one of the bones of contention between these companies and Edward Snowden.[66] Foucault's writings shift us away from thinking about what the NSA is actually doing and toward an analysis of what effects state surveillance – imagined in the abstract – is having on us.

A number of studies confirm Foucault's claims about the chilling effect of surveillance. After the Snowden revelations the PEN American Center reported that many writers are now less inclined to pursue sensitive topics that might lead them to being placed under closer government scrutiny.[67] Likewise, a study of Internet use revealed that in the wake of the NSA-Affair, individuals in both the United States and abroad were less likely to undertake Google searches that might attract the government's attention.[68] Studies done prior to 2013 found some of the same effects as well. In an exploration of how activist organizations responded

---

[64] *See, e.g.*, GREENWALD, *supra* note 20, at 3; Amory Starr, Luis A. Fernandez, Randall Amster, Lesley Wood & Manuel J. Caro, *The Impacts of State Surveillance on Political Assembly and Association: A Socio-Legal Analysis*, 31 QUAL. SOC. 251 (2008). Though this last work was written before Snowden's revelations, it is an in-depth treatment of the effects of surveillance on protest movements.

[65] Examples of this type of argumentation are GREENWALD, *supra* note 20, at 182–209; RULE *supra* note 3; SCHNEIER, *supra* note 20, at 91–107. All three works discuss how surveillance programs have been used as a tool against domestic dissent and bring up the FBI's wiretapping of civil rights leaders in particular.

[66] Kashmir Hill, *Facebook Denies Giving NSA Direct Access to Its Servers; Microsoft Says It Only Turns Over Info for "Specific Accounts,"* FORBES (June 6, 2013, 7:31 PM), www.forbes.com/sites/kashmirhill/2013/06/06/facebook-denies-giving-nsa-direct-access-to-its-servers; Michael B. Kelley, *Part Two of Snowden's Guardian Interview Could Rekindle the PRISM "Direct Access" Debate*, BUS. INSIDER (July 8, 2013, 1:39 PM), www.businessinsider.com/snowden-says-nsa-has-direct-access-to-tech-companies-2013-7.

[67] *Chilling Effects: NSA Surveillance Drives U.S. Writers to Self-Censor*, PEN AM. (Nov. 12, 2013), www.pen.org/sites/default/files/2014-08-01_Full%20Report_Chilling%20Effects%20w%20Color%20cover-UPDATED.pdf.

[68] Alex Marthews & Catherine Tucker, *Government Surveillance and Internet Search Behavior*, SSRN (Aug. 28, 2013), http://papers.ssrn.com/sol3/papers.cfm?abstract_id=2412564.

to increased government surveillance after the 1999 Seattle WTO protests, five scholars of social movements detailed the toxic effect that
surveillance has on political organizations.[69] Individuals dropped out of
activism for fear of being subject to government attention. If they stayed
in the organizations, they declined prominent roles to avoid attracting
surveillance; for the same reason, organizations refused to work with
other groups that they thought the government might be monitoring. As
a result, activist groups became increasingly isolated from each other.
Organizations also shifted their activities away from those that directly
challenged state power (such as civil disobedience) to those that were
seen as safer (such as educational efforts).[70] Psychologists have found
that individuals who think they might be subject to surveillance show a
stronger attachment to conventional moral norms than those who do
not.[71] All of this could be taken as signs of the docility the Panopticon is
designed to produce. We are changing our behavior to suit the state. But
we might also be changing our very beliefs.

II   The Limits on Using the Panopticon to Understand the NSA-Affair

Following Foucault's reflection on the Panopticon too closely may blind
us to crucial elements of the public's reactions to Snowden's revelations
as well as to the complexity of the interactions between the government,
private industry, and individuals. A first problem is the issue of resistance. Foucault has been criticized for paying less attention to human
agency than to the forces that attempt to control us.[72] In particular,
although Foucault allows for the possibility of resistance in his work,
the model of the Panopticon does not credit the degree to which surveillance can spur political engagement with and opposition to state power.[73]
Secondly, the primacy of the state – as opposed to market forces – in
Foucault's thought means that he is less able to help us understand the
relationship between surveillance, private companies, and personal
behavior in the modern world. Government surveillance, on one hand,
and data collection among Internet companies, on the other hand, are

---

[69] Starr *et al.*, *supra* note 64.   [70] *Id.* at 258–68.
[71] Pierrick Bourrat, Nicolas Baumard & Ryan McKay, *Surveillance Cues Enhance Moral
Condemnation*, 9 EVOL. PSYCHOL. 191 (2011).
[72] For a discussion of this issue, *see* Raymond Caldwell, *Agency and Change: Re-Evaluating
Foucault's Legacy*, 14 ORGANIZATION 769 (2007).
[73] Schrift, *supra* note 10, at 150–51.

informed by different logics and produce different dangers. Foucault is far better at uncovering the workings of state power than those of private enterprises.

Among social scientists who study the psychological effects of surveillance there is no clear consensus on how the knowledge that we are being watched shapes political activity.[74] While docility is one outcome, so are hostility and anger. Both of these can lead to political mobilization. One common effect of government surveillance is distrust, as individuals may become suspicious of the state and even of each other, particularly if the government relies on human intelligence as well electronic surveillance.[75] At the most basic level, rising degrees of distrust suggest a lack of acceptance of the surveillance state; government intrusion may not wear us down so much as make us increasingly hostile to the state's encroachment. Distrust can also have positive political effects. After all, suspicious journalists will uncover the failings of the state more rapidly than trusting ones. Wariness provokes watchdog groups to call for governmental transparency and accountability. And insiders will increasingly blow the whistle on what they see as the troublesome conduct of illegitimate actors. The political theorist and historian Pierre Rosanvallon has argued that suspicion gives rise to types of political engagement that supplement electoral forms of participation.[76] Distrust may turn a watched citizenry into the watchers, in ways that recall Foucault's own prison activism. Anger is another possible response to state surveillance. The political scientists Samuel Best and Brian Krueger suggest that individuals react to surveillance with either anxiety or anger.[77] Individuals, they explain, become anxious when they feel they have no control over the government's

---

[74] In addition to the other works cited in this paragraph on how surveillance does not lead to conformity, *see also* Brian S. Krueger, *Government Surveillance and Political Participation on the Internet*, 23 Soc. Sci. Comput. Rev. 439 (2005), which contains references to both sides of the debate.

[75] Starr *et al.*, *supra* note 64; Sarah Horowitz, *Policing and Problem of Privacy in Restoration-Era France, 1815–30*, 27 French Hist. 45 (2013).

[76] Pierre Rosanvallon, Counter-Democracy: Politics in an Age of Distrust (2008). In this, Rosanvallon is in part arguing against the work of Robert Putnam, who has described trust as necessary to the functioning of democracies. Robert Putnam, Making Democracy Work: Civic Traditions in Modern Italy (1993); Robert Putnam, Bowling Alone: The Collapse and Revival of American Community (2000).

[77] Samuel J. Best & Brian S. Krueger, *Government Monitoring and Political Participation in the United States: The Distinct Roles of Anger and Anxiety*, 39 Am. Pol. Res. 85 (2011).

intrusions.[78] In turn, this anxiety leads to a disengagement from politics as they seek to avoid drawing the state's attention.[79] But Best and Krueger note that individuals also may become angry if they feel that the government's actions are wrong and that they are capable of effecting change.[80] This anger can spur political activity, including citizens' attempts to reform the political system that places them under surveillance.[81] The first reaction (anxiety) more or less corresponds to Foucault's model. The second reaction (anger) is a more dynamic vision of the effects of surveillance. Best and Krueger suggest that anger is also the more common response to the rise of the American security state; contemporary surveillance practices, then, do not so much lead to passivity as engagement.[82] Indeed, the NSA-Affair itself provides some evidence in support of Best and Krueger's argument. Snowden's revelations sparked a massive and sustained debate over privacy, security, and surveillance.[83] In the wake of the Affair, civil liberties groups filed lawsuits against the NSA, and the outcry against government overreach fueled the emergence of a libertarian contingent among Republicans in Congress whose members have been willing to break ranks with the party leadership on issues of surveillance and security.[84] This political realignment was integral to the 2015 passage of the USA FREEDOM Act, which restricted the NSA's surveillance powers.[85] Historically, too, surveillance states have sparked activism and protest. This was true in the mid eighteenth century, when the perceived over-policing of Paris provoked days of rioting, and in the early nineteenth century, when the outcry against the French state's practices of spying on its citizens weakened the successive post-revolutionary regimes.[86] During World War II, Nazi efforts to register Jewish businesses and individuals in the

---

[78] *Id.* at 89–90.   [79] *Id.* at 91–92, 97.   [80] *Id.* at 80.   [81] *Id.* at 103.   [82] *Id.* at 97.

[83] Scott Shane, *Snowden Sees Some Victories, From a Distance*, N.Y. TIMES (May 19, 2015), www.nytimes.com/2015/05/20/world/europe/snowden-sees-some-victories-from-a-distance.html; Maria Helen Murphy, *The Pendulum Effect: Comparisons between the Snowden Revelations and the Church Committee. What Are the Potential Implications for Europe*, 23 INFO. & COMM. TECH. L. 192 (2014).

[84] Wes Bruer, *Civil Liberties Groups File Lawsuit against NSA*, CNN (Mar. 10, 2015, 6:36 PM), www.cnn.com/2015/03/10/politics/nsa-spying-lawsuit-aclu/; Sabrina Siddiqui, *Congress Passes NSA Surveillance Reform in Vindication for Snowden*, THE GUARDIAN (June 3, 2015, 2:28 AM), www.theguardian.com/us-news/2015/jun/02/congress-surveillance-reform-edward-snowden.

[85] Shane, *supra* note 83.

[86] ARLETTE FARGE, THE VANISHING CHILDREN OF PARIS: RUMOR AND POLITICS BEFORE THE FRENCH REVOLUTION (1991); Horowitz, *supra* note 75.

Netherlands led to protests.[87] These forms of opposition may not be perfectly efficacious. For instance, the Dutch outcry against discriminatory registration efforts did little to change the fact that about three-quarters of Dutch Jews died in the Holocaust. Still, they show that surveillance can produce resistance as well as docility, in contrast to Foucault's model of the Panopticon.

Resistance has also manifested itself in less politicized forms, as individuals have switched to Internet services that offer more privacy protections. Many in the US are choosing to move their shopping and financial transactions offline out of concerns about NSA surveillance.[88] Additionally, firms that promise to protect consumers' privacy have seen a surge of interest in the wake of the NSA-Affair.[89] Those not living in the United States have even more options to maintain their privacy, and many international customers have opted to use non-US firms for their technology needs. Indeed, one estimate stated that American companies could lose one-quarter of their revenue due to the disclosures about NSA surveillance.[90] To reassure customers, US-based firms have also instituted privacy measures, such as smartphones that offer automatic encryption.[91] Because consumers have come to see privacy as desirable, it has become a commodity: a selling point for upstart firms looking to break into the market and a necessity for established firms seeking to keep their market share.

Relying on Foucault's theories also obscures questions about nongovernmental surveillance and the relationship between private industry, the state, and the individual. Foucault can help us understand where, how, and why Internet companies and governments work together to gather information on individuals. But he does not allow us particular insight into the differences between these two types of surveillance.

---

[87] BLACK, *supra* note 40, at 306.

[88] Steve Rosenbush, *Post-Snowden, Some Internet Usage Is Contracting, Study Finds*, WALL ST. J. (Apr. 3, 2014, 5:44 PM), http://blogs.wsj.com/cio/2014/04/03/post-snowden-some-internet-usage-is-contracting-study-finds/.

[89] *Episode 568: Snoops, Hackers and Tin Foil Hats*, NPR: PLANET MONEY (Sept. 12, 2014, 10:50 AM), www.npr.org/blogs/money/2014/09/12/347179145/episode-568-snoops-hackers-and-tin-foil-hats (podcast).

[90] Claire Cain Miller, *Revelations of N.S.A. Spying Cost U.S. Tech Companies*, N.Y. TIMES (Mar. 21, 2014), www.nytimes.com/2014/03/22/business/fallout-from-snowden-hurting-bottom-line-of-tech-companies.html?_r=0.

[91] Trevor Timm, *Your iPhone Is Now Encrypted. The FBI Says It'll Help Kidnappers. Who Do You Believe?*, THE GUARDIAN (Sept. 30, 2014, 7:15 AM), www.theguardian.com/commentisfree/2014/sep/30/iphone-6-encrypted-phone-data-default.

As discussed earlier in this chapter, Foucault saw Panoptic power as a tool for both private industry and governments while at the same time maintaining that the power of non-state actors is ultimately tied to – and feeds – the power of the state. Foucault's emphasis on state power is not surprising given that postwar France was known for its *étatisme* and government interference in the market.[92] Recent decades have seen a shift away from this *dirigiste* model in France. There is a more general trend involving nation-states' loss of power to the private sector, including large corporations, financial institutions, criminal networks, and terrorist organizations.[93] Foucault is not a particularly good guide to the operations of power in our globalized and privatized world. His theories offer more insight into state-based surveillance than into data collection undertaken by technology and telecommunications companies.

Foucault's model of Panoptic power presupposes that in some ways governments and private industry have interests that are aligned with each other; both, for instance, want to create a class of docile workers/ citizens.[94] But in some cases Snowden's revelations both exposed and exacerbated fissures between the American government and US-based companies. In the wake of the NSA-Affair polls found that many people came to have considerable distrust for technology and telecommunications companies – hardly something good for their bottom lines.[95] It is not surprising that major firms – including Google, Facebook, Apple, and Microsoft – have publically argued for stricter limits on the government's authority to demand the data these private firms have collected.[96]

---

[92] On this issue, *see* JONAH LEVY, TOCQUEVILLE'S REVENGE: STATE, SOCIETY, AND ECONOMY IN CONTEMPORARY FRANCE (1999).

[93] On the shift away from dirigisme in France, *see id.* On the more general decline in the power of nation-states, *see, e.g.,* SUSAN STRANGE, THE RETREAT OF THE STATE: THE DIFFUSION OF POWER IN THE WORLD ECONOMY (1996).

[94] It should be said that Foucault allows for the possibility that the entities that wield power do not work in lockstep with one another. In the words of Clare O'Farrell, "All these relations of power at different levels work together and against each other in constantly shifting combinations." O'FARRELL, *supra* note 8, at 100. However, what he presents in DISCIPLINE AND PUNISH is a world where the state and private firms work together (if unconsciously) for the same ends.

[95] Jaikumar Vijayan, *Snowden Leaks Erode Trust in Internet Companies, Government,* COMPUTERWORLD (Apr. 4, 2014, 8:23 AM), www.computerworld.com/article/2489544/ data-privacy/snowden-leaks-erode-trust-in-internet-companies–government.html.

[96] *Reform Government Surveillance,* www.reformgovernmentsurveillance.com/ (last visited Nov. 23, 2015).

Foucault's theories are not particularly good at allowing us to understand the divergence of interests between governments and private firms.

Additionally, the theory of the Panopticon does not necessarily match the business model around which commercial forms of data collection are built. Companies monitoring their customers have different aims than teaching users to be docile and passive. They want to figure out how to attract users and sell them the goods and services their advertisers offer. The niche marketing that firms like Facebook and Google engage in relies on them knowing what makes us different than others. In the words of Siva Vaidhyanathan, "These companies are devoted to tracking our eccentricities because they understand that the things with which we set ourselves apart from others are the things about which we are most passionate."[97] That is precisely what we are most willing to spend our money on. Thus, Internet firms do not want us to become like everyone else and to conform to externally imposed norms. Instead, they want to sort us into various categories of oddballs. Moreover, the pay-off for this targeted marketing is the offer of convenience and services that individuals highly value, such as free email, cloud-based storage, or an easy way to connect to our social networks.[98] In those circumstances it is no longer accurate to treat private data collection as a zero-sum manipulation of the individual. Instead, it is a bargained-for exchange in which the individual stands to gain something, too.

The dangers that individuals run in giving their personal information to governments and technology firms are also different in notable respects. Here again Foucault is more helpful for allowing us to think about state surveillance than commercial data collection. States have the power of coercion and they arrest us based on the data that they have about us. This is the world Foucault describes: coercion may be lighter in modern states than their predecessors, but it is never absent. When privacy advocates talk about the dangers of technology and telecommunications firms' data collection they talk about a different set of risks to our privacy, some of which Foucault highlighted and others which he did not anticipate. These companies have the power to shape what information we see and when, to market to us based on our location, political

---

[97] Vaidhyanathan *supra* note 55.

[98] On the history of this pay-off, see John Naughton, *We Wanted the Web for Free – but the Price Is Deep Surveillance*, THE GUARDIAN (Aug. 24, 2014, 3:30 AM), www.theguardian.com/technology/2014/aug/24/deep-surveillance-is-price-of-a-free-web-advertising.

preferences, or even mood, for instance. Many in surveillance studies are thus concerned about the manipulation that these firms can engage in, whether that comes in the form of targeting us for certain types of advertisements when we are particularly vulnerable or swaying our vote during election time.[99] Likewise, the information that private companies collect is used in ways that are often discriminatory, such as to offer the same goods or services at different prices to different individuals, or to judge creditworthiness based on data about one's social network.[100] Foucault certainly had something to say about this last problem and the use of information to classify individuals and treat people in these categories differently, but he was not particularly interested in questions about information flows. Ultimately, too, targeted marketing relies on tactics of seduction and the cultivation of consumer desire as opposed to the disciplinary-based model that Foucault proposes.[101] In these instances Foucault is able to understand how governments and private industry are similar to each other. But he does not illuminate the more distinctive features of the interaction between the market, the individual, and surveillance.

Lastly, there is the question of volition. We have to give the state certain information about ourselves and our activities – and there are penalties if that information is inaccurate. Yet the same is not the case with technology and telecommunications firms. No entity forces us to perform Google searches when we could go to the library to find the same information, or use cloud storage instead of USB flash drives for our personal documents. (Of course, many of us are highly integrated into the services of technology companies and quitting them would present enormous practical hurdles.) In many cases, too, there are no penalties for giving these firms inaccurate information about ourselves.[102] Indeed, privacy advocates recommend giving false information

---

[99] SCHNEIER, *supra* note 20, at 113–16; Robert Epstein, *How Google Could Rig the 2016 Election*, POLITICO (Aug. 19, 2015), www.politico.com/magazine/story/2015/08/how-google-could-rig-the-2016-election-121548_full.html.

[100] SCHNEIER, *supra* note 20, at 109–13 and LYON, *supra* note 10, at 145.

[101] LYON, *supra* note 10, at 74–75.

[102] There are, of course, exceptions. One is Facebook's "real name" policy, which has been the subject of a great deal of criticism recently. *See* Lil Miss Hot Mess (@lilmisshotmess), *Facebook's "Real Name" Policy Hurts Real People and Creates a New Digital Divide*, THE GUARDIAN (June 3, 2015), www.theguardian.com/commentisfree/2015/jun/03/facebook-real-name-policy-hurts-people-creates-new-digital-divide. Another issue is defamation and bullying on social media. *See* Roy Greenslade, *23% Increase in Defamation Actions as Social Media Claims Rise*, THE GUARDIAN (Oct. 20, 2014, 7:06 AM),

to companies as a way to shield ourselves from their intrusive gazes and to misdirect their sorting algorithms.[103] Once again, Foucault's model of the Panopticon is more helpful in thinking about state surveillance – which is not voluntary – than it is for thinking about our interactions with private data collection efforts. At least in theory, the latter involves a greater degree of personal choice. If we want to think of the Internet as a vast Panopticon designed to systematically collect information about us, then we must also consider the many ways that we, the inmates, have admitted ourselves into the asylum.

D   Conclusion

Foucault's model of the Panopticon is an insightful starting place for discussions about power, surveillance, and privacy. It forces us to think about how forms of surveillance that are known but invisible are particularly intrusive. It should also lead us to consider the central role that classification plays in the modern surveillance state and commercial data collection processes. Foucault is also helpful in orienting our attention towards the psychological effects of surveillance and his work allows us to think about how a state that seems to have limited its power may be adopting even more disturbing methods that allow it to wield extraordinary control over its citizens. Foucault's theory of Panoptic surveillance, however, should not be our end point for an analysis of the surveillance state and the NSA-Affair in particular. Foucault's theory is far more helpful for understanding government surveillance than that undertaken by technology firms. And if his model has an appealing simplicity to it, in describing a world in which a centralized state works in tandem with the capitalist bourgeoisie to impose its norms on a passive citizenry, that is not the world in which the NSA-Affair has unfolded. That is a world in which NSA surveillance takes place within the context of a far more complex relationship between the security state, market forces, and citizens.

www.theguardian.com/media/greenslade/2014/oct/20/medialaw-social-media;   Michael Martinez, *Charges in Rebecca Sedwick's Suicide Suggest "Tipping Point" in Bullying Cases*, CNN (Oct. 28, 2013, 9:17 AM), www.cnn.com/2013/10/25/us/rebecca-sedwick-bullying-suicide-case/.
[103]   SCHNEIER, *supra* note 20, at 217–18.

2

A Rose by any Other Name?

The Comparative Law of the NSA-Affair

RUSSELL A. MILLER

A   Introduction

The NSA-Affair once again demonstrates that there are "significant privacy conflicts between the United States and the countries of Western Europe – conflicts that reflect unmistakable differences in sensibilities about what ought to be kept private."[1] These differences are shaped by and reflected in discordant regulatory regimes for the protection of privacy in the face of the state's surveillance and intelligence gathering activities. These distinct legal regimes are a familiar topic of study for comparative lawyers and social scientists.[2] Interest in the subject as an academic matter, as well as the general public's dismay over the stark differences, are partly fueled by the assumption that Americans and Europeans share a foundation of common (Western and democratic) values and have similar normative orders that place great importance

---

[1] James Q. Whitman, *The Two Western Cultures of Privacy: Dignity Versus Liberty*, 113 YALE L.J. 1151, 1155 (2004). See Introduction in this volume.

[2] *See, e.g.*, H.C. Gutteridge, *The Comparative Law of the Right to Privacy*, 47 L.Q. REV. 203 (1931); F.P. Walton, *The Comparative Law of the Right to Privacy*, 47 L.Q. REV. 219 (1931); Edward Lewis, *Responsibility for Privacy in the Middle Ages*, 19 J. Comp. Legis. & INT'L L. 77 (1937); T.L. Yang, *Privacy: A Comparative Study of English and American Law*, 15 INT'L & COMP. L. Q. 175 (1966); Brian Walsh, *The Judicial Power and the Protection of the Right of Privacy*, 1 DUBLIN UNIV. L.J. 3 (1976–1977); Stephen R. Barnett, *The Right to One's Own Image: Publicity and Privacy Rights in the United States and Spain*, 47 AM. J. COMP. L. 555 (1999); Francesca Bignami, *European versus American Liberty: A Comparative Privacy Analysis of Antiterrorism Data Mining*, 48 B. C.L. REV. 609 (2007); Bignami, Francesca, *Cooperative Legalism and the Non-Americanization of European Regulatory Styles: The Case of Data Privacy*, 59 AM. J. COMP. L. 411 (2011); Konrad Lachmayer, *The Challenge to Privacy from Ever Increasing State Surveillance: A Comparative Perspective*, 37 UNSWLJ 748 (2014); Ronald J. Krotoszynski, Jr., *Reconciling Privacy and Speech in the Era of Big Data: A Comparative Legal Analysis*, 56 WM. & MARY L. REV. 1279 (2014–2015).

on the protection of personal privacy.[3] But this assumption is not correct. As the NSA-Affair demonstrates, when it is taken too far or asserted too bluntly, assumptions about American and European convergence on the issue of privacy can be the source of considerable misunderstanding.

Our different notions of privacy are the consequence of different histories, different social and cultural forces, different political traditions and institutions, and different legal cultures. James Whitman masterfully captured much of this thick explanation in his 2004 article "The Two Western Cultures of Privacy: Dignity Versus Liberty."[4] Whitman's examination of French and German legal history led him to conclude that a continental tradition of interpersonal respect, dignity, and honor forms the basis of contemporary European privacy law. "To the continental way of seeing things," Whitman explained, "what matters is the right to control your public image."[5] American privacy law, Whitman remarked, must accommodate and account for other values, including the strong American commitment to the free press and the free market. The privacy law that grew up around those values, Whitman explained, gives greater priority to privacy as an expression of the control one enjoys over her property. "To the American mind," Whitman concluded, "what matters is sovereignty within one's own home."[6]

Whitman's article provides valuable insight into the different transatlantic cultures – and laws – of privacy that have been exposed by the NSA-Affair. But for a number of reasons specific to the NSA-Affair, there are some important limits to his article's explanatory force for the current debate.

First, Whitman was largely concerned with the *private law* of privacy, including tort and property law. He was mostly interested in defamation law and in the protection of consumer and credit information by private firms. The NSA-Affair, however, involves privacy protection against the actions of public authorities, in the form of intelligence services (albeit sometimes working in tandem with private commercial actors). The current transatlantic privacy debate more extensively involves comparative constitutional law.

Second, the NSA-Affair involves a distinct kind of privacy that is uniquely linked to new technologies that have evolved and developed

---

[3] *See, e.g.,* HAROLD J. BERMAN, LAW AND REVOLUTION (I): THE FORMATION OF THE WESTERN LEGAL TRADITION (1983); HAROLD J. BERMAN, LAW AND REVOLUTION (II): THE IMPACT OF THE PROTESTANT REFORMATIONS ON THE WESTERN LEGAL TRADITION (2006).

[4] Whitman, *supra* note 1.   [5] *Id.* at 1161.   [6] *Id.*

in the decade since Whitman's article appeared. Whitman was interested in broader privacy concerns that somewhat loosely intermingled several of Roger Clarke's typologies of privacy.[7] The NSA programs, however, more narrowly involve what others have described as the meaningful intersection of "privacy of communication" and "privacy of data and image."[8] These discrete types of privacy have particular and enhanced meaning as a result of our pervasive use of new and deeply revealing technologies. I distinguish between the wider concept of privacy that interested Whitman and the narrower concept of privacy involved in the NSA-Affair by referring to the former as "personal privacy" in a broad sense and the latter as "personal information privacy" in a narrower sense.

Third, American and especially German reactions to the NSA's data collection programs either do not align with the interests that informed Whitman's conclusions, or they defy some of Whitman's most fundamental assumptions. For example, German alarm over the NSA's collection of telecommunications data does not seem to be motivated by the dignitarian interest in "guaranteeing that people see you the way you want to be seen."[9] Germans are outraged that the American government collected the information, and might use it to maintain comprehensive individual profiles for each of us, regardless of whether the NSA uses the information to harm an individual's image or to humiliate her in public. This is an interest in privacy for privacy's sake, regardless of the use that is made of the collected information. It is not concerned with the public exposure of intimate details to others – often by the media – that animated many of the European privacy cases Whitman discussed. As another example, Americans' general disinterest in the revelations of the NSA's widespread collection of domestic telephone metadata defies Whitman's conclusion that American privacy law, at its core, revolves around "suspicions of the police and other officials."[10] Why, despite general distrust for their government, do Americans seem nonplussed by Snowden's disclosures about the invasive activities of their government? With respect to the NSA-Affair, many of the usual assumptions

---

[7] Roger Clarke, "Introduction to Dataveillance and Information Privacy, and Definitions of Terms," *Xamax Consultancy*, Aug. 1997, www.rogerclarke.com/DV/Intro.html. *See* Rachel Flynn *et al.*, *Seven Types of Privacy, in* EUROPEAN DATA PROTECTION: COMING OF AGE 3, 6–7 (Serge Gutwirth *et al.* eds., 2013).

[8] Flynn *et al.*, *Seven Types of Privacy, supra* note 7.   [9] Whitman, *supra* note 1, at 1161.

[10] *Id.* at 1164.

about privacy and the power of the state – in both Germany and the United States – must be reconsidered.

These departures from Whitman's foundational comparative law work on privacy justify this chapter, which seeks to document and explain the different American and German notions of privacy that are at stake in the distinctly constitutional setting of the NSA-Affair. First, I will account for the separate sociolegal contexts in which American and German constitutional law operate. As it turns out, these dissimilar frameworks are thick with meaningful differences in history, political culture, and legal culture. Second, moving to a concrete, functional legal comparison with respect to the issue of privacy, I will highlight the institutional and doctrinal differences in the two countries' constitutional law. These regimes are distinguished by different constitutional texts, different political infrastructures, different courts, different privacy jurisprudences, and different constitutional teleologies.

These insights into the many differences between America and Germany regarding privacy should contribute to understanding on both sides of the Atlantic, despite the prevailing disillusionment and disdain. Greater understanding, rooted in an appreciation of these differences, is necessary so that the essential transatlantic dialogue can continue, even in the shadow of the NSA-Affair.

B The Different Sociolegal Contexts of Privacy

The different reactions to the NSA-Affair in America and Germany, including the different constitutional responses to the issues of privacy and intelligence gathering, are a product of the countries' very different sociolegal contexts. Quite a lot might be captured by this broad lens. But three sociolegal elements have particular relevance. The two countries have different histories regarding privacy and intelligence gathering. The two countries have different political cultures that lead policy makers in the two systems to strike different balances with respect to the protection of privacy and the threat posed by terrorism. Finally, the legal conception of privacy (including the constitutional law) in the two countries is a product of their different legal cultures.

I Different Histories

A common explanation for Americans' and Germans' different responses to the NSA-Affair is that their reactions reflect the disparate experiences they have made with respect to terrorism and their countries' use of personal surveillance. On both points America and Germany have very different histories.

On one hand, while the American government has long had an excessive interest in collecting information about its citizens,[11] Americans have not had to confront brutal and invidious totalitarian dictatorships such as those that used personal information to terrorize all Germans between 1933 and 1945, and East Germans between 1949 and 1990.[12] On the other hand, the contemporary American acceptance of government intelligence gathering reflects the still-recent trauma of the September 11, 2001, terrorist attacks in the United States.[13] Germany has its own history with terrorism.[14] And Germany is a potential target of the current brand of Islamist terrorism.[15] Yet the terror of the German Autumn is now several generations old and the country, unlike its European neighbors in Spain, England, and France,[16] has so far avoided

---

[11] *See, e.g.*, Seymour Hersh, "Huge C.I.A. Operation Reported in U.S. Against Antiwar Forces, Other Dissidents in Nixon Years," N.Y. Times, Dec. 22, 1974, at 1; Ray Downs, "A Brief History of the U.S. Government Spying on Its Citizens," VICE (June 14, 2013), www.vice.com/read/a-brief-history-of-the-united-states-governments-warrentless-spying.

[12] *See* ERIC A. JOHNSON & KARL-HEINZ REUBAND, WHAT WE KNEW: TERROR, MASS MURDER, AND EVERYDAY LIFE IN NAZI GERMANY (2005); ANNA FUNDER, STASILAND: STROIES FROM BEHIND THE BERLIN WALL (2002).

[13] *See, e.g.*, Jared Keller, *Why Don't Americans Seem to Care about Government Surveillance?*, PAC. STANDARD (June 12, 2013), www.psmag.com/politics-and-law/why-dont-americans-care-about-government-surveillance-60011; Mark Landler & Dalia Sussman, "Poll Finds Strong Acceptance for Public Surveillance," N.Y. Times (Apr. 30, 2013), www.nytimes.com/2013/05/01/us/poll-finds-strong-acceptance-for-public-surveillance.html?pagewanted=all&_r=0.

[14] *See, e.g.*, Bernhard Blumenau, *The United Nations and West Germany's Efforts against International Terrorism in the 1970s, in* AN INTERNATIONAL HISTORY OF TERRORISM: WESTERN AND NON-WESTERN EXPERIENCES 65 (Jussi M. Hanhimäki & Bernhard Blumenau eds., 2013).

[15] *See Germany Still on Alert after Tip about Possible Islamic State Terror Attack*, VICE (Jan. 1, 2016), https://news.vice.com/article/germany-still-on-alert-after-tip-about-possible-islamic-state-terror-attack; Police in German City Warn of Islamist Terrorism Threat, DW (Feb. 28, 2015), www.dw.com/en/police-in-german-city-warn-of-islamist-terrorism-threat/a-18286410.

[16] *See Paris Attacks: What Happened on the Night*, BBC (Dec. 9, 2015), www.bbc.com/news/world-europe-34818994; "The Worst Islamist Attack in European History," *The Guardian* (Oct. 31, 2007), www.theguardian.com/world/2007/oct/31/spain; *The Worst Islamist Attack in European History*, THE GUARDIAN (Oct. 31, 2007, 10:27 AM), www.theguardian.com/world/2007/oct/31/spain; Melissa Gray, *3 Stabbed at London Tube Station in Terror Attack, Police Say*, CNN (Dec. 7, 2015, 9:24 AM), www.cnn.com/2015/12/05/europe/london-tube-stabbings/.

bloody Islamist terror attacks.[17] The experience Germans made (and have been socialized to remember in subsequent generations) with Nazi and East German authoritarian surveillance and control helps to explain why German law places such a high priority on personal information privacy as a fundamental liberty protection.[18] Germans have every reason to prioritize privacy and no recent terrorist trauma that would suggest the need to sacrifice privacy in the name of security.

America's spies, domestic and foreign, have not been angels.[19] But comparisons with the Gestapo and Stasi are fallacious.[20] The FBI has played a role in curtailing personal freedoms.[21] The CIA has killed and sown the seeds of bloody discord around the world.[22] But it cannot be said that the American intelligence community was a central cog in one of history's largest and most gruesome genocides, or that it implemented one of history's most thorough, invasive, and sinister regimes of surveillance and social control.[23] It is an unfortunate fate, but that is a distinctly

---

[17] *See* Melanie Amann, *et al.*, *Keeping Its Composure: Germany Seeks Calm after French Attack*, Spiegel Online (Jan. 12, 2015), www.spiegel.de/international/germany/germany-plans-no-new-terror-laws-in-wake-of-charlie-hebdo-attack-a-1012188.html ("'Our composure is that of a country that has not faced a fundamental test of this kind yet. But when push comes to shove, we have stuck together until now. I am confident that this would also be true in the case of a terrorist attack,' says [German] Interior Minister [Thomas] de Maizière."); Tristiana Moore, *Is Germany Europe's Next Terrorism Target?*, TIME (Nov. 19, 2010), http://content.time.com/time/world/article/0,8599,2032203,00 .html.

[18] *See* Kenneth A. Bamberger & Deirdre K. Mulligan, Privacy on the Ground: Driving Corporate Behavior in the United States and Europe 198–99 (2015); Eric Gujer, *Germany: The Long and Winding Road*, *in* Safety, Liberty, and Islamist Terrorism: American and European Approaches to Domestic Counterterrorism 62, at 63 (Gary J. Schmitt, ed. 2010).

[19] *See, generally*, Arthur S. Hulnick, Fixing the Spy Machine: Preparing American Intelligence for the Twenty-first Century (1999); Jamie Smith, Grey Work: Confessions of an American Paramilitary Spy (2015).

[20] *See* Nina Khrushcheva, *NSA as "Big Brother"? Not Even Close*, Reuters (June 28, 2013), http://blogs.reuters.com/great-debate/2013/06/28/nsa-as-big-brother-not-even-close/.

[21] *See, e.g.*, Tim Weiner, Enemies: A History of the FBI (2012) (In one instance, FBI Director was accused of leading an "assault on the most sacred principles of our Constitutional liberties.")

[22] *See* Smith, *supra* note 19; Nick Cullather, Secret History, Second Edition: The CIA's Classified Account of Its Operations in Guatemala 1952–1954 (2d ed., 2006); William Blum, Killing Hope: U.S. Military and CIA Interventions since World War II (2004).

[23] *See* Jacques Delarue, The Gestapo: A History of Horror (Pen & Sword Books 2008); Jens Gieseke, The History of the Stasi: East Germany's Secret Police, 1945–1990 (David Burnett trans., Berghahn Books 2014).

German history.[24] The intrusions on privacy with which the American public has been confronted – including the programs revealed by Snowden – are a pale reflection of the domestic terror German governments have (relatively recently) inflicted on their citizens with the help of secret, state-sanctioned surveillance and intelligence gathering.[25]

But it is not only the different quality (or quantity) of intelligence abuses that distinguishes the American and German histories. The consequences of the abuses, once exposed, also differ in significant ways. Americans have come to understand that intelligence abuses inevitably come to light and can be met with democratic responses inside the state's institutions and structures. This is the enduring lesson of the Church Committee.[26] It has also been true in the post-9/11 era. The scandal involving the Terrorist Surveillance Program prompted President Bush to discontinue the NSA initiative and to place future surveillance programs under the authority of the Foreign Intelligence Surveillance Act and the Foreign Intelligence Surveillance Court.[27] Snowden's revelations have generated significant reform, including President Obama's Policy Directive 28 and the USA FREEDOM Act.[28] By contrast, the only outcome of the extreme intelligence abuses Germans endured in the twentieth century (under the Nazis and in East Germany) was the complete dissolution of the respective states. External forces were needed in both cases – with respect to the German Reich and the German Democratic Republic – to overcome the political cultures that had fostered and facilitated massive surveillance regimes. Unlike the Americans, the Germans have not experienced the corrective possibility of an existing democratic system confronting their worst intelligence abuses.[29]

---

[24] *See, e.g.,* Bryn Caless & Steve Tong, Leading Policing in Europe: An Empirical Study of Strategic Police Leadership 46 (2015) ("Few other regimes ... were as ruthless, single minded and unaccountable as the Gestapo/KGB/Stasi.")

[25] *See* Delarue, *supra* note 23; Gieseke, *supra* note 23.

[26] *U.S. National Security, Intelligence and Democracy: From the Church Committee to the War on Terror* (Russell A. Miller ed., 2008).

[27] *See* Letter from Alberto R. Gonzalez, Attorney General of the United States, to Senator Patrick Leahy and Senator Arlen Specter, Jan. 17, 2007, http://graphics8.nytimes.com/packages/pdf/politics/20060117gonzales_Letter.pdf.

[28] Press Release, The White House, Office of the Press Sec'y, Presidential Policy Directive/PPD-28, at 5 (Jan. 17, 2014); Uniting and Strengthening America by Fulfilling Rights and Ending Eavesdropping, Dragnet-collection and Online Monitoring Act [USA FREEDOM Act], Pub. L. No. 114–23, 129 Stat. 268 (2015).

[29] The *Bundestag's* NSA Committee of Inquiry may change this tradition. *See* Chapter 12 in this volume.

II Different Political Cultures

The NSA's surveillance programs are justified as essential (and successful) tools for discovering and preventing (and later, prosecuting) terrorist
attacks. This is the business of fear. Terror spreads it and governments
struggle to allay it.[30] Whether one or the other forces has gained a
definitive advantage, it may be enough to conclude that Islamist terrorism has proven to be an enduring and resilient and destructive phenomenon. Western societies are surely right to be more fearful because of the
successes of al Qaeda and ISIS.

A country's response to this fear (legal or otherwise) is affected by
many factors. It is the most straightforward republican calculation, but
one factor is the degree to which the political class is required to be
attuned and accountable to popular sentiments, such as fear of terrorism.
The American and German political systems calibrate this dynamic
differently. According to typologies originally mapped by comparative
political scientists such as Arend Lijphart, American politics are seen as
more majoritarian while German politics are seen as more consensual.[31]
Democracies classified as majoritarian are characterized by high levels of
subsystem autonomy and intense competition for majoritarian support
among elites.[32] Consensual democracies are characterized by limited
subsystem autonomy and deliberate efforts on the part of elites to take
actions that counteract the potentially destabilizing impulses of shifting
majorities. Confirming Germany's classification as a consensual democracy, Ralf Dahrendorf famously described German politics as "government by elite cartel."[33] Elsewhere Lijphart has used the concepts "mass
political culture" and "elite political culture" to describe these distinct
democratic approaches.[34]

A number of features in the two systems confirm these labels. America
is a heterogeneous society with strong subsystem autonomy. Politics in
the United States harnesses these forces through multilevel and nearly
constant competition in the formation of governing majorities and for

---

[30] See, e.g., PETER R. NEUMANN & M.L.R. SMITH, THE STRATEGY OF TERRORISM: HOW IT
WORKS, AND WHY IT FAILS (2008); ALAN M. DERSHOWITZ, WHY TERRORISM WORKS:
UNDERSTANDING THE THREAT, RESPONDING TO THE CHALLENGE (2008).

[31] See, e.g., AREND LIJPHART, PATTERNS OF DEMOCRACY (1999). See also J. TYLER DICK-
OVICK & JONATHAN EASTWOOD, COMPARATIVE POLITICS 452 (2013).

[32] Arend Lijphart, Consociational Democracy, 21 WORLD POLIT. 207 (1969).

[33] RALF DAHRENDORF, SOCIETY AND DEMOCRACY IN GERMANY 276 (1967).

[34] See, e.g., Arend Lijphart, Comparative Politics and the Comparative Method, 65 AM. POL.
SCI. REV. 682 (1971).

the framing of policy. The majoritarian and accountability elements of the systems are institutionally secured through biennial, direct elections for Congress and the (seeming) direct election of the president.[35] The autonomy of subsystems can be seen in the relative lack of party discipline and the mélange of civil society advocates, activists, and lobbyists.[36] Germany is a homogenous society with weaker subsystem autonomy. Elites in Germany have seized on these factors to fashion and maintain a governing consensus. In its most benign form, this has served as a curative to the highly fractious and unstable politics of the Weimar era.[37] Germany's consensus politics are facilitated by a number of structures, including the so-called *Parteinstaat* (which almost exclusively privileges the traditional political parties in the democratic process); proportional, party-based election of half the parliamentarians; and the proportional-parliamentary election of the chancellor.[38] Grand coalitions featuring the largest center-right parties (CDU-CSU) and the largest center-left party (SPD) are a prominent example of Germany's consensus politics.[39] Two of the last three governments have been formed through grand coalitions of this type.[40]

The distinct political cultures and the institutions that reinforce them produce different conditions with respect to the control and oversight of intelligence services – and by extension, the two societies' understanding of privacy. The strict separation of powers in America's Madisonian system, for example, permits Congress to play a significant role in overseeing the executive's intelligence gathering operations. This can be reinforced by frequent partisan splits between the presidency and the

---

[35] U.S. CONST. art. II, § 2–3. *See, e.g.*, ROBERT ALAN DAHL, HOW DEMOCRATIC IS THE AMERICAN CONSTITUTION? 73 (2003).

[36] *See, e.g.*, Brian Beutler, "The American Right, Not the 'Tea Party,' Is the GOP's Big Liability," NEW REPUBLIC (May 21, 2014), https://newrepublic.com/article/117845/gop-primary-victories-aside-republicans-still-have-gop-base-problem ("[T]he real issue isn't whether the 'Tea Party,' now vanquished, has been a liability for the Republican Party, but whether the Republican electorate is fractious and reactionary, and has thus kept the Senate out of reach for Republicans two cycles in a row. The answer is yes.").

[37] *See, e.g.*, Hans Peter Schwarz, *Woran scheitern deutscher Bundeskanzler?*, *in* 60 JAHRE BONNER GRUNDGESETZ – EINE GLÜCKTE VERFASSUNG? 29 (Christian Hillgruber & Christian Waldhoff eds., 2010.

[38] *See, e.g.*, DONALD P. KOMMERS & RUSSELL A. MILLER, THE CONSTITUTIONAL JURISPRUDENCE OF THE FEDERAL REPUBLIC OF GERMANY 269 (3rd ed., 2012).

[39] Lijphart, *supra* note 32, at 213.

[40] *See "Grand Coalition" Returns to Germany*, DW (Dec. 16, 2013), www.dw.com/en/grand-coalition-returns-to-germany/a-17299248 (explaining the most recent coalition agreement and mentioning that the last grand coalition ran from 2005 to 2009.).

Congressional majority. Again, this was the lesson of the Church Committee.[41] Especially in the wake of the September 11, 2001, terrorist attacks, an interbranch and bipartisan security consensus formed in America that undermined the possibility that checks and balances would be an adequate brake on the government's intelligence gathering activities.[42] Still, Congress found extremely rare common ground to enact the USA FREEDOM Act in 2015, a move that one commentator described as a signal "that the days when Congress gave maximal deference to the executive branch might finally be over."[43] The success of this reform was also a product of America's strong subsystem autonomy, which helps to explain the emergence and political success of the "Tea Party" movement.[44] The Tea Party movement has, in part, been animated by libertarian concerns about government overreach, including on issues of intelligence gathering and security.[45] The Senate Intelligence Committee's historic "Study of the Central Intelligence Agency's Detention and Interrogation Program" may be a more inspiring example of the possibility in the American system for interbranch oversight.[46] The *Bundestag's* intermingled relationship with the chancellor and her cabinet – typical of the parliamentary model – leaves the German parliament with a smaller role in controlling the executive's intelligence function. The success of the *Bundestag's* Investigative Committee on the NSA-Affair, for example, will largely depend on the engagement of the parliamentary opposition, which holds only four of the Committee's

---

[41] U.S. NATIONAL SECURITY, *supra* note 26.

[42] *See, e.g.,* FREDERICK A. O. SCHWARTZ & AZIZ Z. HUQ, UNCHECKED AND UNBALANCED: PRESIDENTIAL POWER IN A TIME OF TERROR (2008).

[43] Scott Lemieux, *How Congress Learned to Stop Bowing to President Obama on National Security*, THE WEEK (June 8, 2015), http://theweek.com/articles/558953/how-congress-learned-stop-bowing-president-obama-national-security.

[44] *See* Beutler, *supra* note 36 (Beutler notes that the emergence of the Tea Party ideology and candidates in 2010 was politically successful enough to cost mainstream Republican candidates several elections. He also points out that while "[i]t's true that 'Tea Party' candidates, defined narrowly, have only lost two or three seats over the last four years, and won a bunch of seats in 2010 ... establishment candidates lost everywhere in 2012.").

[45] *See* Scott Clement, *Tea Party Privacy Concerns Skyrocket, Poll Finds*, WASH. POST (July 26, 2013), www.washingtonpost.com/news/the-fix/wp/2013/07/26/tea-party-privacy-concerns-skyrocket-poll-finds/.

[46] Senate Select Committee on Intelligence – Committee's Study of the Central Intelligence Agency's Detention and Interrogation Program (December 13, 2012), *available at* https://web.archive.org/web/20141209165504/;http://www.intelligence.senate.gov/study 2014/sscistudy1.pdf.

sixteen seats.[47] With these structural differences in mind, it is not surprising that the American judiciary has shown more restraint than the German judiciary in its review of privacy and intelligence gathering cases.

III   Different Legal Cultures

The different legal traditions prevailing in America and Germany also provide a sociolegal explanation for the different reactions to the NSA-Affair in the two countries.

The civil law tradition prevalent in Germany typically seeks to identify and conceptualize social phenomena as abstractions and independent of any discrete, actually occurring circumstances.[48] This leads to a preemptive regulatory culture in which everything is already legally framed in advance of any particular iteration of the anticipated events actually taking place.[49] Through comprehensive and systematic statutory regimes and the deployment of deductive logic, the German lawyer lives in a world in which everything is always already regulated, including access to and use of individuals' personal information.[50] The common law tradition prevalent in America typically works from the concrete facts of a particular case to identify the applicable rule.[51] The American lawyer lives in a world that is less oriented toward systematic, *ex ante* prevention.[52] The common law does not try to regulate potential problems. Rather, problems are addressed by the law when they actually arise.[53]

From the perspective of the German legal understanding, surveillance, data collection, and data storage are themselves a violation of the abstract rule protecting informational self-determination. From the American perspective, the *potential* misuse of personal information data is less the concern. It is much more important that an actual abuse can be demonstrated. With this in mind, for Americans the issue is whether – although the NSA can be said to have pursued

---

[47] *See* Chapter 12 in this volume.

[48] *See, e.g.,* H. PATRICK GLENN, LEGAL TRADITIONS OF THE WORLD 132 (5th ed. 2014).

[49] *See* Russell Miller & Ralf Poscher, *Kampf der Kulturen: Der präventive deutsche Datenschutz liegt quer zur pragmatischen Rechtskultur in Amerika – Eine Harmonisierung muss scheitern,* FRANKFURTER ALLGEMEINE ZEITUNG (Nov. 28, 2013). *See also* Chapter 4 in this volume.

[50] *Id.*   [51] *See, e.g.,* GLENN, *supra* note 48, at 236.

[52] *See* Miller & Poscher, *supra* note 49.   [53] *Id.*

disproportionate and ill-conceived programs – the personal information resulted in manipulation and misuse.

C The Different Constitutional Law of Privacy

The NSA-Affair is a constitutional law problem: Have public authorities, through their intelligence gathering activities, intruded upon the
individual privacy interests secured by the constitution's basic rights?
A thoughtful examination of the two countries' constitutional systems
reveals dramatic differences with respect to privacy. These regimes are
distinguished by different constitutional texts, different courts, different jurisprudences, and different constitutional teleologies. It all adds
up to some very different constitutional law with respect to the
question of personal information privacy. These differences provide
profound insight into the two countries' different reactions to the
NSA-Affair.

I Different Constitutional Texts

If constitutional text is the beginning of constitutional analysis,[54] then
American and German constitutional law start from very different
places with respect to the issue of personal information privacy. It is
an old trick, for example, to note that the U.S. Constitution never uses
the term "privacy" while the German constitution does.[55] Article 10 of
the Basic Law provides that "the *privacy* of correspondence, posts and
telecommunications shall be inviolable."[56] More than its mere invocation of the term "privacy," Article 10 is significant because it establishes a concrete constitutional protection for the exact activities
involved in the NSA-Affair. With its modern outlook, Article 10 also
seems to better anticipate the contemporary forms of electronic communication – such as email and smart phone usage – that are central

---

[54] *See* Peter M. Shane, *Analyzing Constitutions, in* THE OXFORD HANDBOOK OF POLITICAL
INSTITUTIONS 191, at 192 (R. A. W. Rhodes, *et al.* eds. 2006) ("[W]hat legal materials
say – that is, the history and wording of constitutions . . . significantly determines how
they are interpreted.").

[55] *See* Edward J. Eberle, *Human Dignity, Privacy, and Personality in German and American
Constitutional Law*, 1997 UTAH L. REV. 963, 975–79 (1997).

[56] GRUNDGESETZ [GG] [Basic Law] art. 10, *translation at* www.gesetze-im-internet.de/
englisch_gg/ (emphasis added).

to reimagining privacy for our digital age.[57] Naturally, America's eighteenth century text is more awkwardly suited to that agenda.[58]

Of course, constitutional law is not bound to the narrowest construction of the charter's text. Slightly broader readings of both constitutions reveal a number of liberty protections that serve the same interests as those we imagine to be involved in privacy.[59] Without using the term "privacy," the Fourth Amendment to the U.S. Constitution protects Americans from unreasonable searches and seizures "in their persons, houses, papers, and effects."[60] This has been extended to include some of the forms of communication covered by Article 10 of the German Basic Law.[61] Both constitutions also protect against government intrusions into the home.[62]

The Basic Law, however, prominently includes text that identifies and protects liberty interests and values that can be more easily read to be constituent elements of privacy. Articles 2 and 1 of the Basic Law, for example, are clear and very expressive commitments to personal freedom and human dignity.[63] The human condition to which these protections aspire – including the relationship to government – obviously involves an inviolable intimate sphere.[64] America's Due Process Clause has been put to similar use, but without the same clarity and expressive force.[65] Similarly, the Eight Amendment to the U.S. Constitution, which prohibits "cruel and unusual punishments," asserts a dignified (privacy

---

[57] *See* Thomas Fetzer & Christopher S. Yoo, *New Technologies and Constitutional Law, in* ROUTLEDGE HANDBOOK OF CONSTITUTIONAL LAW 485, at 492 (Mark Tushnet *et al.* eds., 2013).

[58] *Id.* at 490–91; *see also* MARK TUSHNET, THE CONSTITUTION OF THE UNITED STATES OF AMERICA: A CONTEXTUAL ANALYSIS 1 (2D ED., 2015) ("[I]t seems clear that the problems of privacy posed by GPS and similar modern technologies are different in kind from the problems of intrusive searches with which the framers were familiar. In nations with more recent constitutions, constitutional provisions address modern problems of privacy directly. The United States must do so in some other way.").

[59] *See, e.g.,* Jacqueline E. Ross, *Germany's Federal Constitutional Court and the Regulation of GPS Surveillance,* 6 GERMAN L.J. 1805 (2005). *See also* Katja de Vries, *Privacy, Due Process, and the Computational Turn, in* PRIVACY, DUE PROCESS AND THE COMPUTATIONAL TURN: THE PHILOSOPHY OF LAW MEETS THE PHILOSOPHY OF TECHNOLOGY 9, at 17–19 (Mireille Hildebrandt & Katja de Vries eds., 2013).

[60] U.S. CONST. amend. IV.   [61] *See* Fetzer & Yoo, *supra* note 57, at 490–91.

[62] U.S. CONST. amends. III, IV. BASIC LAW art. 13.   [63] Basic Law arts. 1, 2.

[64] KOMMERS & MILLER, *supra* note 38, at 405.

[65] OTIS H. STEPHENS *ET AL.*, AMERICAN CONSTITUTIONAL LAW, VOLUME 2 at 406 (6th ed. 2015).

respecting) image of the human condition, but does so chiefly in the limited circumstances of the state's penal function.

II Different High Courts

The American and German high courts have played different roles in striking the balance between privacy and security. The American Supreme Court has shown considerable restraint, invoking a range of justiciability rules and doctrines to demur when presented with these cases. The German Federal Constitutional Court has been more assertive. This is, in part, a consequence of the distinct nature of the courts themselves.

The German Federal Constitutional Court has a wide-open jurisdictional mandate that almost ensures that it will be asked to resolve cases raising personal information privacy issues. Importantly, the Constitutional Court does not enjoy the Supreme Court's discretionary authority to pick the cases it hears.[66] Once the cases come, the Constitutional Court cannot avoid ruling on them.[67] A number of devices guarantee that the cases will reach the Constitutional Court. First, the Constitutional Court has developed a *Schutzplficht* (Duty to Protect) jurisprudence.[68] Traditionally, constitutional basic rights were understood to defend individuals from the state's abuses.[69] These are often described as "negative rights."[70] This is still the predominant understanding of the liberty protections in the U.S. Constitution.[71] Some of the basic rights in the German constitution, however, explicitly call on the state to take affirmative steps to promote the liberty interest identified by the Basic Law. The clearest example of this can be found in the protections for marriage, family, and children secured by Article 6. Paragraph 1, for example, insists that "marriage and the family shall enjoy the special

---

[66] KOMMERS & MILLER, *supra* note 38, at 12 ("The FCCA [Federal Constitutional Court Act] requires the Court to accept for decision any complaint if it is constitutionally significant or if the failure to accept it would work a grave hardship on the complainant.").

[67] Peter E. Quint, *Leading a Constitutional Court: Perspectives from the Federal Republic of Germany*, 154 U. PA. L. REV. 1853, 1862 (2006).

[68] *Id.* ("[E]very person filing a Constitutional Complaint is, in principle, entitled to a decision on the merits.").

[69] ROBERT ALEXY & JULIAN RIVERS, A THEORY OF CONSTITUTIONAL RIGHTS 288 (2013).

[70] *Id.*

[71] JAMES A. CURRY *ET AL.*, CONSTITUTIONAL GOVERNMENT: THE AMERICAN EXPERIENCE 15 (5th ed. 2003).

protection of the state."[72] Paragraph 4 provides that "every mother shall be entitled to the protection and care of the community."[73] But even where the text of the basic right seems limited to providing a negative liberty protection, the Constitutional Court found that the constitution imposes a duty on the German state to take affirmative measures to protect citizens from intrusions upon the freedoms secured by the basic rights. In its seminal *Lüth Case*, the Constitutional Court explained that this *Schutzpflicht* results from the fact that the Basic Law insists on the establishment of an "objective order of values" for German society.[74] Under this doctrine it is not enough that the state may have refrained from intruding on someone's privacy. The state has the duty to do what it can to ensure that Germans are enjoying a full measure of privacy, as a component of Germany's objective order of values. In this way, inaction (or inadequate action) on the part of the state might lead to a constitutional violation of the protected right via the state's *Schutzpflicht*.[75] This radically expands the Constitutional Court's role in the polity.[76]

Added to this sweeping substantive mandate is the large and accommodating number of jurisdictional paths leading to the Constitutional Court. The most relevant of these is the Constitutional Court's duty to rule on "constitutional complaints, which may be filed by any person alleging that one of his basic rights ... has been infringed."[77] This is a permissive and informal process that does not involve burdensome court fees, that does not require highly stylized pleadings, and that does not require the complainant to be represented by counsel.[78] The Constitutional Court receives and resolves thousands of these complaints each year. The constitutional complaint jurisdiction has served as the basis for a number of the Constitutional Court's most prominent recent personal information privacy cases.[79]

---

[72] BASIC LAW art. 6(1).   [73] BASIC LAW art. 6(4).

[74] KOMMERS & MILLER, *supra* note 38, at 442, 444.   [75] *Id.* at 444–45.   [76] *Id.* at 445.

[77] BASIC LAW art. 93(4a).

[78] Ralf Rogowski & Thomas Gawron, *Constitutional Litigation as Dispute Processing: Comparing the U.S. Supreme Court and the German Federal Constitutional Court, in* CONSTITUTIONAL COURTS IN COMPARISON: THE U.S. SUPREME COURT AND THE GERMAN FEDERAL CONSTITUTIONAL COURT 1, at 8 (Ralf Rogowski & Thomas Gawron eds., 2002) ("The Federal Constitutional Court understands itself as a 'citizens' court.' In filing a constitutional complaint, it is not necessary for a citizen to hire a legal representative.").

[79] *See, e.g.*, Data Mining Case, 115 BVerfG 320 (2006); Online Computer Surveillance Case, 120 BVerfGE 274 (2008); Data Stockpiling Case, 125 BVerfGE 260 (2010); Anti-Terror Data Act Case, 133 BVerfGE 277 (2013).

In cases involving intelligence gathering activities the Constitutional
Court has also established a permissive standing doctrine. This contrasts
with the approach taken by the U.S. Supreme Court, which has strictly
enforced the standing requirement in intelligence cases, expressing what
one lower court recently described as the presumption that "Congress is
tasked in the first instance with achieving the right balance" between
liberty and security.[80] Justice Alito, in his opinion for the Supreme Court
in *Clapper v. Amnesty International*, explained that "we have often found
a lack of standing in cases in which the Judiciary has been requested to
review actions of the political branches in the fields of intelligence
gathering and foreign affairs."[81] In *Clapper* the Supreme Court found
that rights advocates lacked standing to challenge the portions of the
Foreign Intelligence Surveillance Act under which many of the NSA's
surveillance and data collection programs operate because the advocates'
belief that their legitimate activities would nevertheless lead to surveillance was not enough to establish a "certainly impending" and "fairly
traceable" constitutional injury.[82] The Supreme Court insisted that "an
objectively reasonable likelihood" that the plaintiffs' communications
would be intercepted at some point in the future was too attenuated
and speculative to meet the standing doctrine's "injury in fact" standard.[83] The Supreme Court was unconcerned that more definitive evidence of an injury would be nearly impossible to develop with respect to
the NSA's highly secretive operations, noting in particular the importance of maintaining the separation of powers – and judicial restraint
generally – in the context of the government's intelligence gathering
activities.[84] The German Constitutional Court has taken the opposite
approach. The Constitutional Court Act generally requires that parties
bringing a complaint show that they have been "directly and currently
affected" by the alleged constitutional violation.[85] But the Constitutional
Court has recognized that the intelligence services' strategic surveillance
represents an exception to this rule. The secrecy of surveillance measures,
the Constitutional Court explained, means the surveillance might never

---

[80] 785 F.3d 787, 793 (2d Cir. 2015).   [81] 568 U.S. ___, 133 S.Ct. 1138, 1147 (2013).
[82] *Id.*   [83] *Id.*
[84] *Id. See* Jewel v. NSA, Order Denying Plaintiffs' Motion for Partial Summary Judgment
and Granting Defendants' Motion for Partial Summary Judgment, U.S. DC – Northern
Dist. Calif., No. C 08-04373 JSW (Feb. 10, 2015); Wikimedia Foundation *et al.* v. NSA,
Memorandum Opinion, U.S. D.C. – District of Maryland, No. l:15-cv-662 (Oct. 23,
2015); Obama v. Klayman, 800 F.3d 559 (D.C. Cir. 2015).
[85] § 90 Abs. 1 BVerfGG.

be discovered by potential complainants and that, consequently, the state might be able to evade constitutional limits on the exercise of its power.[86] In these circumstances, the Constitutional Court ruled, it would be enough to establish standing if the complainant can show "with some probability" that his or her constitutional rights have been harmed.[87] Under this approach, rights advocates similar to those who were denied the right to sue in *Clapper* and in other American cases have succeeded in establishing standing before the Constitutional Court in recent privacy and intelligence gathering cases.[88]

III   Different Privacy Jurisprudence

The American and German courts have developed dissimilar jurisprudences on the issues of personal information privacy. German law resorts to a general concept of privacy derived from Articles 2 and 1 of the Basic Law. American law recognizes discrete privacy interests to which it extends distinct legal protections. The privacy interests implicated by the NSA-Affair are chiefly a concern of the Fourth Amendment to the U.S. Constitution. Both courts are increasingly aware of the challenge modern telecommunications technology poses to their respective traditions. The German jurisprudence seems better adapted to the new circumstances, which some theorists say now requires a "mosaic" understanding of privacy, as demonstrated by the two systems' confrontation with Global Positioning System (GPS) surveillance.

1   German Jurisprudence

A number of recent cases decided by the Constitutional Court have recognized a right to personal information privacy in surveillance or data collection scenarios on the basis of the Court's pioneering jurisprudence that conceived a right to "informational self-determination."[89] The right was first articulated in the 1983 *Census Act Case*.[90] The Constitutional Court demanded that the parliament amend the federal census statute to ensure that there would be no abuses in the collection, storage, use, and transfer of the personal data gathered during the census. The

---

[86]   G10 Act Case, 67 BVerfGE 157, 169–70 (1984).   [87]   *Id.*

[88]   *See, e.g.,* Online Data Surveillance Case, 120 BVerfGE 274 (2008); Counter-Terrorism Database Case, 133 BVerfGE 277 (2013).

[89]   Census Act Case, 65 BVerfGE 1, preamb. ¶ 2 (1983).

[90]   Census Act Case, 65 BVerfGE 1 (1983).

Constitutional Court demonstrated remarkable foresight – with respect to technology, data collection, and the potential for the chilling effects of surveillance – when articulating the basis for the new right. The Constitutional Court explained:

> The individual's decisional authority needs special protection in view of the present and prospective conditions of automatic data processing. It is particularly endangered because . . . the technical means of storing highly personal information about particular persons today are practically unlimited, and information can be retrieved in a matter of seconds with the aid of automatic data processing, irrespective of distance. Furthermore, such information can be joined to other data collections – particularly when constructing integrated information systems – to produce a partial or virtually complete personality profile, with the person concerned having insufficient means of controlling either its veracity or its use. The possibilities of acquiring information and exerting influence have increased to a degree hitherto unknown and may affect the individual's behavior because of the psychological pressure which public awareness may place upon the individual.[91]

The Constitutional Court derived the right to informational self-determination from the general personality and dignity protections secured by Articles 2 and 1 of the Basic Law.[92] That constitutional doctrine has provided a foundation for a general concept of privacy that finds relevance in a number of settings, including the contexts considered by Whitman in his 2004 article.[93] The easy application of this general privacy interest in circumstances as various as transsexual rights and information privacy is a consequence, as I explained above, of the German legal culture's preference for abstract concepts.[94]

The right to informational self-determination has taken on increasing relevance as Germany pursued its own counterterror measures in the wake of the September 11, 2001, attacks in the United States. Despite upholding challenged international telephone wiretaps, in 2003 the Constitutional Court reaffirmed the principle that the state may not intrude on communications and that the official use or storage of any information with respect to individuals not suspected of criminal activity is absolutely prohibited.[95] As in other cases, the Constitutional Court also reiterated the view that the right to one's personal information protects not only the content of communications but also the circumstances

---

[91] *Id.*   [92] *Id.*   [93] Whitman, *supra* note 1.   [94] *See* GLENN, *supra* note 48.
[95] Telecommunications Case, 107 BVerfGE 299 (2003).

surrounding them, including when, how often, and with whom the communications took place.[96]

In 2006 the Constitutional Court decided the *Data Mining Case*,[97] the first of several decisions involving the constitutionality of advanced monitoring technologies. In the *Data Mining Case* the Constitutional Court invalidated a state counterterrorism statute that permitted the local police to filter out information from various electronic sources, both public and private, in order to identify persons (mainly Islamic students) whose activities and associations might target them as potential terrorists.[98] The Constitutional Court virtually characterized the procedure as a fishing expedition and therefore an infringement of the right to informational self-determination in violation of the personality and dignity clauses of Articles 2 and 1 of the Basic Law.[99] The Constitutional Court acknowledged that the right is not absolute and may be regulated in the public interest, particularly when the danger of terrorism is real.[100] But any balance between liberty and security, the Constitutional Court ruled, must be proportional.[101]

The *Online Computer Surveillance Case*, decided in 2008, was a landmark ruling in defense of the "right to the confidentiality and integrity of information technological systems."[102] The Constitutional Court derived this right from the general personality protection secured by Articles 2 and 1 of the Basic Law. The case involved challenges to a state law that empowered intelligence officials to conduct surveillance and collect data by covertly infiltrating computer systems through the Internet.[103] The decision extended the Basic Law's privacy protection to personal computers. The Constitutional Court explained that "today's personal computers can be used for a wide variety of purposes, some for the comprehensive collection and storage of highly personal information ... corresponding to the enormous rise in the importance of personal computers for the development of the human personality."[104] The right to informational self-determination, said the Constitutional Court, protects individuals against the disclosure of personal data unless surveillance and data collection is necessary to avoid a "concrete danger" to human life or the security of the state.[105] The Constitutional Court noted, "the fundamental right to the integrity and confidentiality of

---

[96] *Id.*   [97] Data Mining Case, 115 BVerfGE 320 (2006).   [98] *Id.*   [99] *Id.*
[100] *Id.*   [101] *Id.*   [102] Online Computer Surveillance Case, 120 BVerfGE 274 (2008).
[103] *Id.*   [104] *Id.*   [105] *Id.*

information technology systems is to be applied ... if the empowerment
to encroach covers systems that, alone or in their technical networking,
contain personal data of the person concerned to such a degree that
access to the systems facilitates insight into significant parts of the life of
a person or indeed provides a revealing picture of his or her personality."[106] The Constitutional Court concluded that general exploratory
online searches based on mere suspicion of some remote danger, however serious, is constitutionally impermissible.[107]

In the *Data Stockpiling Case*, decided in 2010, the Constitutional Court
ruled that a European Union Directive requiring the mass storage of
mobile and fixed-line telephone calls and e-mail traffic violated the
personality clause of the Basic Law.[108] The Constitutional Court ordered
these records to be deleted immediately and insisted on legislative measures designed to place strict controls on the use of such information.[109]
The laws challenged in the *Data Stockpiling Case* were amendments to
the Telecommunications Act and the Code of Criminal Procedure (*Strafprozessordnung*) enacted in 2007 to satisfy the European Union Directive.[110] The data subject to the challenged Directive's stockpiling regime
included information derived from landline, wireless, fax, SMS, and e-
mail communications that would be necessary to reconstruct by whom,
when, how long, with whom, and from where a telecommunications act
had been conducted.[111] Additionally, changes to the Telecommunications Act and Code of Criminal Procedure expanded both the justifications for the state's acquisition of the stockpiled data from the private
service providers and the uses to which the state might put the information.[112] In a maneuver that allowed it to show respect to the European
Union, the Constitutional Court held that the stockpiling of telecommunications data by private service providers was not a *per se* constitutional
violation. Instead, the Constitutional Court focused its disapproval on
the German Parliament's implementing laws, concluding that they did
not adequately protect the deeply intimate sphere of human personality
protected by the general privacy right.[113] The Constitutional Court
explained that the addresses, phone numbers, dates, times, and locations
revealed in the data, if examined over any length of time, could be used to
sketch a deeply personal and revealing portrait of a subject's political
associations, personal preferences, inclinations, and weaknesses.[114]

---

[106] *Id.*   [107] *Id.*   [108] Data Stockpiling Case, 125 BVerfGE 260 (2010).
[109] *See* Chapter 21 in this volume.   [110] Data Stockpiling Case, *supra* note 108.
[111] *Id.*   [112] *Id.*   [113] *Id.*   [114] *Id.*

The Constitutional Court continued to closely supervise Germany's counterterrorism measures to ensure respect for personal information privacy in its 2013 decision in the *Counter-Terrorism Database Case*.[115] On the basis of a statute enacted in 2006 a new centralized counter-terrorism database was to be established to facilitate the exchange of data between law enforcement and intelligence agencies.[116] Once again concerned with the general privacy protection secured by Articles 2 and 1 of the Basic Law, the Constitutional Court ruled that a number of the law's provisions violated the right to informational self-determination, even if the basic structure of the database was constitutionally sound.[117] The Constitutional Court was reassured by the fact that the qualified agencies would only be able to access the database in urgent and exceptional circumstances.[118] But the Constitutional Court found that the law provided too much executive discretion, cast too wide a net for potential subjects, permitted a too extensive use of the available data, did not require adequate documentation, and lacked adequate oversight and reporting safeguards.[119]

2 American Jurisprudence

American courts, if they are willing to engage with the issues raised by the NSA-Affair, have largely been concerned with the discrete privacy protection provided by the Fourth Amendment to the U.S. Constitution. The broader notion of privacy, anchored in the due process clauses of the Fifth and Fourteenth Amendments, has not played a role. The latter protection was the basis for the decisions in which the Supreme Court articulated a general right to privacy in deeply intimate matters, such as family and reproduction issues.[120] This – and the free speech limits on privacy rights – was the constitutional doctrine and history that chiefly interested Whitman.[121] The courts' avoidance of the more general privacy interests derived from due process reminds us of the fragmented, context-specific nature of America's common law jurisprudence.

The Fourth Amendment was implemented in response to the British practice of issuing general search warrants that lacked probable cause.[122]

---

[115] Counter-Terrorism Database Case, 133 BVerfGE 277 (2013).   [116] *Id.*   [117] *Id.*
[118] *Id.*   [119] *Id.*
[120] *See, e.g.,* Griswold v. Connecticut, 381 U.S. 479 (1965); Roe v. Wade, 410 U.S. 113 (1973).
[121] Whitman, *supra* note 1.
[122] R. Carter Pittman, *The Supremacy of the Judiciary: A Study of Preconstitutional History,* 40 ABAJ 389 at 391 (quoting Justice Horace Gray Jr.).

And, to the degree that it secures protection of the individual against the overwhelming power of the state, the Fourth Amendment also is a reflection of the founding precepts of American democracy.[123] In its seminal decision in *Katz v. U.S.*, the Supreme Court rejected the traditional jurisprudence, which had aligned the Fourth Amendment's privacy protection with notions of property and trespass.[124] The Court in *Katz* emphatically declared that "the Fourth Amendment protects people, not places."[125] The substance of this protection consists in the requirement that government searches may be performed only when authorized by a detailed and specific warrant that has been issued by a neutral and detached magistrate on the basis of sworn evidence demonstrating probable cause.[126] The Court has, however, identified a number of exceptions to the Fourth Amendment's warrant requirement, permitting searches that are otherwise "reasonable."[127] Some contend that these exceptions have swallowed the rule, leaving the Fourth Amendment a hollow form that no longer provides meaningful privacy protection.[128]

A threshold question is what constitutes a "search" for Fourth Amendment purposes. Far more than the substantive elements of Fourth Amendment protection, this preliminary issue has complicated the application of the Fourth Amendment to intelligence gathering cases. After *Katz* the occurrence of a "search" no longer depended on evidence that the state had made a physical intrusion into a private space. Instead, the Court found an intrusion into Katz's *personal sphere of privacy*. In *Katz* a wiretap had been placed on the outside of a glass pay-phone box permitting law enforcement officers to listen to Katz's phone conversation.[129] Although no physical intrusion into the pay-phone box had taken place, the Court reasoned that Katz had a subjective expectation that "the words he utters into the mouthpiece will not be broadcast to the world" and that society would accept Katz's expectation as reasonable.[130] This is now the standard for determining whether a "search" has taken place, without

---

[123] *See* Bruce A. Newman, Against That "Powerful Engine of Despotism:" The Fourth Amendment and General Warrants at the Founding and Today (2007).

[124] 389 U.S. 347 (1967).   [125] *Id.* at 351.

[126] Thomas McInnis, The Evolution of the Fourth Amendment 51–56 (2009).

[127] *Id* at 75.

[128] *See, e.g.*, Brando Simeo Starkey, *A Failure of the Fourth Amendment & Equal Protection's Promise: How the Equal Protection Clause Can Change Discriminatory Stop and Frisk Policies*, 18 Mich. J. Race & L. 131 (2012).

[129] Katz, 389 U.S. at 348.   [130] *Id.* at 352.

which the substantive protections of the Fourth Amendment will not apply: (1) a person "has exhibited an actual (subjective) expectation of privacy" and (2) society is prepared to recognize that this expectation is (objectively) reasonable.[131]

The Supreme Court applied this standard in *Smith v. Maryland* and found that a Fourth Amendment search had not occurred.[132] This is relevant because the circumstances of the *Smith* case might be seen as closely analogous to those involved in the NSA-Affair. In *Smith*, law enforcement officers collected evidence of the suspect's telephone contacts by installing a "pen register" on his telephone line at the telephone company's offices.[133] An electronic device, the pen register records only the numbers called from a particular telephone line. The content of phone calls is not documented. The Court concluded that neither of the elements necessary for a Fourth Amendment *search* existed in the case. First, Smith did not have a subjective expectation in the privacy of the telephone numbers he dialed. The Court reasoned:

> We doubt that people in general entertain any actual expectation of privacy in the numbers they dial. All telephone users realize that they must "convey" phone numbers to the telephone company, since it is through telephone company switching equipment that their calls are completed. All subscribers realize, moreover, that the phone company has facilities for making permanent records of the numbers they dial, for they see a list of their long-distance (toll) calls on their monthly bills. In fact, pen registers and similar devices are routinely used by telephone companies "for the purposes of checking billing operations, detecting fraud, and preventing violations of law."[134]

Second, the Court found that a subjective expectation of privacy with respect to the phone numbers one dials – as unlikely as that expectation would be – cannot be regarded as objectively reasonable.[135] Society appreciates, the Court explained, that electronic equipment is used extensively to track and catalogue the telephone numbers called from any particular phone. At the very least, the Court concluded, this is common (and commonly known) because it is necessary for the telephone company to keep billing records.[136] The Court ruled that, in dialing the telephone numbers, Smith held that information out to third parties (at least the telephone company). Exposing information in such

---

[131] *Id.* at 361.   [132] 442 U.S. 735 (1979).   [133] *Id.* at 737.
[134] *Id.* at 742 (quoting United States v. New York Tel. Co., 434 U.S. 159, 174–75 (1977)).
[135] *Id.* at 743.   [136] *Id.* at 742.

an indiscriminate way, which stripped it of any subjective or objective expectation of privacy, meant that the government's collection of the telephone numbers involved only the acquisition of nonprivate information.[137] On the basis of the third-party doctrine the Supreme Court ruled that search had occurred and that the Fourth Amendment had no applicability to the case whatsoever.

Judge William Pauley of the Southern District of the New York Federal District Court drew on the obvious parallels between the facts in the *Smith* case and the NSA's bulk telephony metadata collection programs when he dismissed a Fourth Amendment challenge to the NSA's surveillance measures in December 2013.[138] Citing *Smith*, Judge Pauley ruled that phone users had no reasonable expectation of privacy that would give them Fourth Amendment rights, especially with respect to information they voluntarily provide to third parties, such as telephone companies.[139] On appeal from Judge Pauley's order, the U.S. Court of Appeals for the Second Circuit found that the NSA's bulk telephony metadata collection program exceeded the surveillance authority established by the relevant statutory provisions.[140] But the Appeals Court refused to rule on the constitutional issues in the case even as it expressed grave misgivings about the continuing adequacy of the *Smith* case and the third-party doctrine for ensuring privacy under present technological conditions.[141]

In a separate case, Judge Richard Leon of the District of Columbia Federal District Court acted on similar misgivings and refused to be bound by *Smith*. Judge Leon found that the likelihood that the NSA's bulk telephony metadata collection program violated the Fourth Amendment was adequate to justify a preliminary injunction against the programs and to allow the constitutional challenge to go forward on the merits.[142] Troubled by the "Orwellian" character of the NSA program,[143] Judge Leon sought to distinguish – in quantity and quality – the information collected by the NSA from the information collected by the government in the *Smith* case. Judge Leon found that, for at least four reasons, the claimant had a reasonable expectation of privacy in the

---

[137] *Id.* at 743–46.
[138] American Civil Liberties Union v. James Clapper, 959 F.Supp.2d 724, No. 13-3994 (S.D. New York, Dec. 28, 2013).
[139] *Id.* At 750–52.
[140] American Civil Liberties Union v. James Clapper, 785 F.3d 787 (2d. Cir. 2015).
[141] *Id.* at 792.   [142] Klayman v. Obama, 957 F.Supp.2d 1 (D. D.C. 2013).
[143] *Id.* at 33.

telephone data collected by the NSA. First, even if the short-term use of the pen register in *Smith* was reasonably foreseeable, there is no reasonable expectation that the government will engage in a long-term data collection effort of the kind involved in the NSA program (lasting half a decade or more).[144] Second, the anticipated third-party exposure of telephone numbers in the *Smith* case is a mere sliver of the vast amount of personally revealing information the NSA can now collect on the basis of telecommunications activities as a result of a quantum technological leap in the years since *Smith* was decided.[145] Third, the use to which phones were put in the *Smith* era is not at all comparable with today's deeply personal use of telephones and other technologies.[146] Fourth, while there might have been an expectation in the *Smith* era that the government could hope for the assistance of the private telephone company in obtaining a person's telephone data, there is no reasonable expectation of the deeply synergistic cooperation that takes place between the NSA and telecommunications firms.[147] Nevertheless, the U.S. Court of Appeals for the District of Columbia Circuit, in the appeal to Judge Leon's order, found that the plaintiffs had not satisfactorily established standing to bring the lawsuit and ordered the case back to Judge Leon for additional consideration of the standing question.[148]

In at least two other lawsuits filed in response to the NSA-Affair, the first-instance courts found that the *Smith* precedent and the third-party doctrine precluded a Fourth Amendment Challenge to the NSA's data-collection programs.[149]

3 Mosaic Privacy and the GPS Cases

The German jurisprudence, dating back to the *Census Act Case*, has been conscious of the distinct privacy harm that could result from the accumulation of personal information data. In its recent cases the Constitutional Court has sought to strengthen constitutional privacy protection in response to the sweeping personal portrait our ever-more extensive use of technology makes it possible for the state to develop from mere telecommunications metadata. This approach is in line with what is referred to as the "mosaic" theory of privacy,

---

[144] *Id.* at 32. [145] *Id.* at 32–33. [146] *Id.* at 33–36. [147] *Id.* at 32–33.
[148] Obama v. Klayman, 800 F.3d 559 (D.C. Cir. 2015).
[149] *See* Smith v. Obama, 24 F.Supp.3d 1005 (D. Idaho 2014); U.S. v. Muhtorov, No. 1:12-cr-00033-JLK (D. Colo.).

which seeks to account for intrusive conduct as a "collective whole" rather than as isolated incidents.[150]

The American jurisprudence is just beginning to struggle with the dramatic challenge contemporary telecommunications technology poses for privacy. If the courts will hear the cases at all (by overcoming justiciability issues and the third-party doctrine), then so far they have hewn to the traditional "sequential" approach to enforcing the Fourth Amendment.[151] The clearest move in the direction of the mosaic approach occurred in the *U.S. v. Jones* case decided by the Supreme Court in 2012.[152] Jones challenged the government's use of a GPS device as a violation of the Fourth Amendment. The device had been placed on Jones's car without the authority of a judicial warrant and it allowed the police to track all of Jones's movements by car for twenty-eight days.[153] The resulting 2,000 pages of data were used to support Jones's arrest and as evidence leading to his conviction for drug offenses.[154] The Supreme Court ruled that the use of the GPS device constituted an illegal "search" under the Fourth Amendment.[155] Justice Scalia wrote the opinion for the Court, but justified the result on the property intrusion that took place when law enforcement agents placed the GPS device on Jones's car. "It is important to be clear about what occurred in this case," Justice Scalia wrote. "The Government physically occupied private property for the purpose of obtaining information."[156] Justice Scalia's opinion embraced the sequential approach to the Fourth Amendment. It was the single intrusion onto Jones's property that established the constitutional violation and not the accumulation of data the GPS device allowed the law enforcement agents to collect. It also revived the pre-Katz property/ trespass approach to privacy. Justice Scalia approvingly noted that "our Fourth Amendment jurisprudence was tied to common-law trespass."[157] This is one of the important insights in Whitman's 2004 article.[158] It is also a significant step away from the mosaic theory of privacy. But five of the Supreme Court's justices wrote or joined concurring opinions that embraced the mosaic theory in various degrees. Justice Alito and three other justices, for example, would have found that the government's use of the GPS device violated Jones's reasonable expectation of privacy because the duration of the surveillance was exceptional for such an

---

[150] Orin S. Kerr, *The Mosaic Theory of the Fourth Amendment*, 111 MICH. L. REV. 311, 320 (2012).
[151] *Id.* at 316–17.   [152] 132 S.Ct. 945 (2012).   [153] *Id.* at 947.   [154] *Id.* at 947–49.
[155] *Id.* at 949.   [156] *Id.* at 949.   [157] *Id.* at 949.   [158] Whitman, *supra* note 1, at 1207.

ordinary criminal enterprise.[159] This indicates these justices' conscious-ness of the significance of the government's ability to accumulate data over time. Justice Sotomayor explicitly invoked the mosaic theory in a separate opinion. Justice Sotomayor worried about technology's ability to generate "a precise, comprehensive record of a person's public movements that reflects a wealth of detail about her familial, political, professional, religious, and sexual associations."[160] The inexpensive opportunity to assemble "a substantial quantum of intimate information" and to store that information indefinitely, Justice Sotomayor urged, should be taken into account when considering the reasonableness of a person's expectation of privacy.[161] Justice Sotomayor was straining for an approach to the Fourth Amendment that would prevent the government from intruding upon the private interests revealed by the "sum" of discrete data.[162] Justice Sotomayor also expressed her lack of confidence in the Smith precedent and the third-party doctrine, calling that approach "ill-suited to the digital age, in which people reveal a great deal of information about themselves to third parties in the course of carrying out mundane tasks."[163]

The German Constitutional Court decided a GPS surveillance case in 2005, finding that no constitutional violation occurred when law enforce-ment agents installed a GPS device on the complainant's car, giving the authorities constant and complete information about the complainant's movement by car for almost three months.[164] The Constitutional Court nevertheless laid down a number of conditions for the use of GPS surveillance. First, consistent with the mosaic approach to personal information privacy, the Constitutional Court insisted that any around-the-clock use of these methods must not lead to the development of a detailed profile of the suspect's personality.[165] If it does, then the infor-mation must be discarded.[166] Second, the Constitutional Court explained

---

[159] Jones, 132 S.Ct. at 964 (Alito, J., concurring in judgment) ("Under this approach, relatively short-term monitoring of a person's movements on public streets accords with expectations of privacy that our society has recognized as reasonable ... But the use of longer term GPS monitoring in investigations of most offenses impinges on expect-ations of privacy. For such offenses, society's expectation has been that law enforcement agents and others would not – and indeed, in the main, simply could not – secretly monitor and catalogue every single movement of an individual's car for a very long period. In this case, for four weeks, law enforcement agents tracked every movement that respondent made in the vehicle he was driving.").

[160] *Id.* at 955 (Sotomayor, J., concurring).   [161] *Id.* at 956 (Sotomayor, J., concurring).
[162] *Id.* at 956 (Sotomayor, J., concurring).   [163] *Id.* at 957 (Sotomayor, J., concurring).
[164] Global Positioning System Case, 112 BVerfGE 304 (2005).   [165] *Id.*   [166] *Id.*

that such measures are permissible only with regard to crimes of major importance, such as murder, aggravated robbery, extortion, and money laundering.[167] Finally, the Constitutional Court instructed legislators to keep abreast of advances in surveillance technology and, if necessary, to pass laws that would prevent security agencies from using them to interfere with the right of informational self-determination.[168] These standards, despite the outcome in the case, reinforce the mosaic orientation of Germany's privacy jurisprudence by taking account of the risk that surveillance data might do more harm when accumulated and by signaling the Constitutional Court's sensitivity to the way that technological developments can affect privacy.

The two courts' GPS cases were incongruent, and they seemingly contradicted the two countries' expected positions on personal information privacy and surveillance. On the one hand, Jones's constitutional privacy interests were vindicated by the U.S. Supreme Court. On the other hand, the Constitutional Court found no constitutional violation in the government's use of a GPS device over a three month period. But the GPS cases should not be read as a dramatic shift away from the distinct American and German jurisprudences I have outlined. The *Jones* case, at least in part, was decided on the basis of Justice Scalia's insistence on a sequential approach to assessing Fourth Amendment claims and his revival of the archaic trespassory approach to privacy. The Constitutional Court's *Global Positioning System Case* involved the clear confirmation of concerns that orient the German jurisprudence toward the mosaic approach to privacy.

IV   Different Constitutional Teleologies

For Germans, the more important constitutional question arising from the NSA-Affair might be whether they can insist that the U.S. Constitution's privacy guarantees – whatever they may be with respect to the American government's intelligence activities – apply as limits on the NSA's collection of telecommunications data from Germans in Germany. This, essentially, is the question of the extraterritorial effect of the U.S. Constitution. German frustration on this point depends on two assumptions. First, Germans seem to believe that the Basic Law applies (perhaps without limit) to the extraterritorial activities of the German state.

---

[167] *Id.*   [168] *Id.*

Second, Germans have the impression that the Supreme Court has concluded that the U.S. Constitution has no extraterritorial effect. The constitutional reality is more complex than this. Still, the issue of extraterritoriality exposes the two constitutional systems' fundamentally different teleologies.

The Basic Law does not have unlimited extraterritorial effect.[169] And particularly with respect to Germany's foreign intelligence gathering activities, the German Government has historically insisted that Article 10 of the Basic Law does not apply.[170] Yet, as a general matter, the Basic Law has greater extraterritorial effect than the U.S. Constitution.[171] In the wake of the NSA-Affair there has been increasing pressure to clearly and definitively apply the Basic Law's liberty protections to Germany's foreign intelligence operations.[172] Advocates for extraterritoriality point to Article 1(3) of the Basic Law, which makes the constitution's basic rights binding "as directly applicable law" on the legislature, the executive, and the judiciary.[173] This simple and unambiguous commitment, it is argued, is not territorially limited.[174]

---

[169] BASIC LAW pmbl. ("This Basic Law thus applies to the entire German people." The Basic Law contemplates some extraterritorial application, but very clearly states in the beginning to which class of people it applies.). *See, generally*, Galia Rivlin, *Constitutions Beyond Borders: The Overlooked Practical Aspects of the Extraterritorial Question*, 30 B.U. INT'L L.J. 135 (2012).

[170] *See* KOMMERS & MILLER, *supra* note 38, at 415 (Discussing the Federal Constitutional Court's decision in the Telecommunications Surveillance Act Case of 1999.).

[171] While the Federal Constitutional Court has limited German intelligence collection in several cases, the United States has made it clear that it will decline to provide Fourth Amendment protections to noncitizens abroad. *See, e.g.*, Philip Oltermann, *U.S. Will Not Enter Bilateral No-Spy Deal with Germany, Reports Media*, THE GUARDIAN (Jan. 14, 2014, 8:05 AM), www.theguardian.com/world/2014/jan/14/us-not-entering-no-spy-agreement-germany-media.

[172] *See* Michael Nienaber & Matthias Sobolewski, *Germany Vows Tougher Control of Spy Agency After New Revelations*, REUTERS (Oct. 15, 2015, 9:20 AM), www.reuters.com/article/us-germany-spying-idUSKCN0S91O920151015; Malik Baumgärtner et al., *America's Willing Helper: Intelligence Scandal Puts Merkel in Tight Place*, SPIEGEL ONLINE (May 4, 2015, 5:42 PM), www.spiegel.de/international/germany/bnd-intelligence-scandal-puts-merkel-in-tight-place-a-1031944.html; Kay-Alexander Scholz, *The BND Affair: "No Better Partner than the USA"*, DW (Apr. 24, 2015), www.dw.com/en/the-bnd-affair-no-better-partner-than-the-usa/a-18407523.

[173] BASIC LAW art. 1(3).

[174] *See* Jan-Hendrik Dietrich, *Of Toothless Windbags, Blind Guardians and Blunt Swords: The Ongoing Controversy about the Reform of Intelligence Services Oversight in Germany*, 2015 INTELL. & NAT'L SECUR., DOI: 10.1080/02684527.2015.1017246 (2015), at 17–18, http://dx.doi.org/10.1080/02684527.2015.1017246.

It is likely – although it is not absolutely settled – that the U.S. Constitution offers little in the way of protection against the NSA's data-collection activities in Germany.[175] The text of the United States Constitution provides no language, such as Article 1(3) of the Basic Law, that can be said to clearly and definitively resolve the question of its application to foreigners or beyond America's territorial jurisdiction. The Supreme Court's jurisprudence on the question also has not resulted in a single, bright-line rule. It would be incorrect to say, for example, that the U.S. Constitution never applies to U.S. government actions undertaken outside America's territorial jurisdiction and having an effect on non-Americans.[176] But this may be of little comfort in the context of the NSA-Affair because the Court has definitively held, with regard to the more discrete question of the extraterritorial application of the Fourth Amendment for the benefit of foreigners, that the United States Constitution does not apply.[177] In its decision in *United States v. Verdugo-Urquidez* a majority of the Court found that the Fourth Amendment protections are limited to the *people* who constitute the "national community" (primarily citizens) or those with a connection to the United States that approximates membership in the national community.[178] Based on this limiting principle, the Supreme Court concluded that searches and seizures taking place outside America's jurisdiction are not limited by the Fourth Amendment.[179] In support of this position the Supreme Court cited a number of cases that "emphatically" rejected the extraterritorial application of more universally oriented liberty protections (such as the Fifth Amendment's right to be free from self-incrimination).[180] One of these cases expressed, in almost bemused terms, the extreme novelty of the possibility: "Such extraterritorial application of organic law would have been so significant an innovation in the practice of governments that, if intended or apprehended, it could scarcely have failed to excite contemporary comment. Not one word can be cited. No decision of this Court supports such a view."[181]

---

[175] *See* Alec Whalen, *Fourth Amendment Rights for Nonresident Aliens*, 16 GERMAN L.J. 1131 (2014) (While he is arguing that it is possible to extend Fourth Amendment protections to nonresident aliens, Whelan points out that "[t]he dominant view in the American legal community … is that there is nothing constitutionally wrong, or even suspect, about such targeting of nonresident aliens.").

[176] *See, e.g.*, Boumedine v. Bush, 553 U.S. 723 (2008).

[177] *But see* Chapter 10 in this volume.   [178] 494 U.S. 259 (1990).   [179] *Id.* at 261.

[180] *Id.* at 260.

[181] U.S. v. Verdugo-Urquidez, 494 U.S. 259, 269 (1990) (*quoting* Johnson v. Eisentrager, 339 U.S. 763, 784 (1950)).

The countries' different approaches to the question of extraterritoriality can be explained, in part, by reference to the two constitutions' distinct purposes, or teleologies. One prominent objective of the Basic Law was to integrate Germany into a cosmopolitan normative order.[182] This is exemplified by the Preamble, which declares that the German people adopted the Basic Law with "the determination to promote world peace as an equal partner in a united Europe."[183] This commitment naturally justifies the extraterritorial application of the Basic Law.[184] In sharp contrast to this, the most prominent objectives of the U.S. Constitution were to fashion and frame a new American polity, in part by demarcating and defining a distinct, domestic order of rights that dramatically departed from the then-prevailing universal normative order. This is exemplified by the Preamble, which declares that the American people were concentrated on forming "a more perfect Union" with decidedly national purposes, including "domestic tranquility," the "common defence," and to secure "the Blessings of Liberty to ourselves and our Posterity."[185] Where the German Basic Law is outward looking, the U.S. Constitution looks inward.[186]

D   Conclusion

The different responses to the NSA-Affair in America and Germany are embodied in – and fostered by – the two countries' different constitutional privacy regimes.

The American approach shows greater confidence in the political process for striking the balance between privacy and security. When

---

[182] KOMMERS & MILLER, *supra* note 38, at 302.

[183] BASIC LAW, pmbl. *See* JUSTIN O. FROSINI, CONSTITUTIONAL PREAMBLES: AT A CROSSROADS BETWEEN POLITICS AND LAW (2012).

[184] *See* FROSINI, *supra* note 183, at 80–82.   [185] U.S. CONST. pmbl.

[186] *See, e.g.*, PETER E. QUINT, THE IMPERFECT UNION: CONSTITUTIONAL STRUCTURES OF GERMAN UNIFICATION 298 (1997) (Pointing out that the very fact that article 24(1) contemplates the ability to give "sovereign rights to international organizations" reflects "outward-looking aspects of the Basic Law"); Angioletta Sperti, *United States of America: First Cautious Attempts of Judicial Use of Foreign Precedents in the Supreme Court's Jurisprudence*, in THE USE OF FOREIGN PRECEDENTS BY CONSTITUTIONAL JUDGES 393 (Tania Groppi & Marie-Claire Ponthoreau eds., 2013) (Pointing out that American constitutional law has been traditionally inward looking.); *but see* Noah Feldman, *When Judges Make Foreign Policy*, N.Y. TIMES (Sept. 25, 2008), www.nytimes.com/2008/09/28/magazine/28law-t.html?_r=0 (illustrating the inward looking view of the United States constitution as being a conservative stance, and claiming that there is a more liberal, outward looking interpretation).

the courts become involved they enforce a specialized constitutional privacy right that has been calibrated to respond to the state's surveillance and intelligence gathering activities. This jurisprudence, so far, has not embraced the mosaic approach to privacy, which seems to better account for the comprehensive and intimate uses to which we put technology today. The German approach emphasizes the judicial enforcement of a broad and general concept of privacy. In its sensitivity to technology's ubiquity and the deeply revealing portraits that can be developed through the accumulation of a vast amount of discrete data, the German jurisprudence has been a pioneer of the mosaic approach to privacy.

The American constitutional regime is largely inward looking while the German constitutional regime looks outward.

Most profoundly, operating in their unique sociolegal contexts, the two constitutional privacy regimes offer very different visions of personhood. On the one hand, the German Constitutional Court has imagined and enforced a substantive and objective vision of personhood that includes a protected private and intimate sphere. The state is obliged to help realize this vision. On the other hand, the American courts have reinforced individuals' freedom of action, including the autonomy to dispose of one's privacy. This is an autonomous and subjective vision of personhood.

The challenge posed by the NSA-Affair is not to fashion and enforce a harmonized approach to privacy, but to come to accept that "a rose by any other name would smell as sweet."[187] In coming to appreciate and respect our different transatlantic notions of privacy, we have the best chance at acting productively to restore the invaluable transatlantic relationship.

---

[187] WILLIAM SHAKESPEARE, ROMEO AND JULIET, act 2, sc. 2.

3

Privacy as a Public Good

BY JOSHUA FAIRFIELD AND CHRISTOPH ENGEL

"We must all hang together, or assuredly we will all hang separately."

– Benjamin Franklin

A Introduction

Privacy is commonly studied as a private good: my personal data is mine to protect and control, and yours is yours. This conception of privacy misses an important component of the policy problem. An individual who is careless with data exposes not only extensive information about herself, but about others as well.[1] As a result, the protection of privacy requires group coordination.[2] The negative externalities imposed on nonconsenting outsiders by such carelessness can be productively studied in terms of welfare economics. If all relevant individuals maximize private benefit, and expect all other relevant individuals to do the same, neoclassical economic theory predicts that society will achieve a suboptimal level of privacy. This prediction holds even if all individuals cherish privacy with the same intensity. As the neoclassical economics literature would have it, the struggle for privacy is destined to become a tragedy.

But the experimental public goods literature offers some hope. Just as in real life, people in experiments cooperate in groups at rates well above those predicted by neoclassical theory. Groups can be aided in their struggle to produce public goods by institutions, such as communication, framing, or sanction. With these institutions, communities can manage public goods without heavy-handed government intervention. Legal scholarship has not fully engaged this problem in these terms. In this

---

[1] See Mark MacCarthy, *New Directions in Privacy: Disclosure, Unfairness and Externalities*, 6 I/S: J.L. & Pol'y for Info' Soc'y 1, 5 (2011).
[2] See Julie E. Cohen, *What Privacy Is For*, 126 Harv. L. Rev. 1904, 1927 (2013).

chapter, we explain why privacy has aspects of a public good, and we draw lessons from both the theoretical and the empirical literature on public goods to inform the policy discourse on privacy.

Our proposed shift may help explain the still-simmering transatlantic tensions surrounding the commercial use of data on the one hand, and the debate over government use of that information as revealed in the NSA-Affair on the other hand. It offers a new understanding of privacy, the social and legal concept at the center of the transatlantic debate. It also addresses the commercial–government data conduit (exemplified by the Prism program) that gave rise to the current debate,[3] explaining why individual-focused privacy protections in both Europe and the United States have fallen short.

A public good is a social benefit that risks not being produced because everyone can share in it equally, whether they contribute to it or not.[4] In the technical language of economics, a public good is a nonrival and nonexcludable resource.[5] Such goods pose a social dilemma – although society is better off if the good is produced, it is against each individual's best interest to expend resources contributing to the production of the good.[6] Public goods run the gamut, from clean air to national defense.[7] Consumption by one person does not affect consumption by another, and no one can be excluded from consuming.[8] A public bad is the mathematical mirror image of a public good.[9] Here, the costs of a public good are not borne by any one person, but rather all suffer. Public bads, like polluted water, filthy air, or public security risks caused by lax data practices (consider the counterintelligence threat posed by a combination of the recent United States Office of Personnel Management hack with a search for .mil addresses from data released by hackers from the adultery site Ashley Madison, for a

---

[3] See Barton Gellman & Laura Poitras, *U.S., British Intelligence Mining Data from Nine U.S. Internet Companies in Broad Secret Program*, WASH. POST (June 7, 2013), www.washingtonpost.com/investigations/us-intelligence-mining-data-from-nine-us-inter net-companies-in- broadsecret-program/2013/06/06/3a0c0da8-cebf-11e2-8845-d970ccb0 4497_story.html.

[4] See infra. See also RICHARD CORNES & TODD SANDLER, THE THEORY OF EXTERNALITIES, PUBLIC GOODS, AND CLUB GOODS 9 (2d ed. 1996).

[5] See CORNES & SANDLER, *supra* note 4, at 9.   [6] See id.   [7] See id.

[8] RICHARD POSNER, ECONOMIC ANALYSIS OF LAW (2011); *see also* CORNES & SANDLER, *supra* note 4, at 8–9.

[9] See Bruce Yandle, *Mixed Goods and Bads*, 19 PUB. CHOICE 95 (1974); Kenneth R. Richards, *Framing Environmental Policy Instrument Choice*, 10 DUKE ENVTL. L. & POL'Y F. 221, 268 (2000).

vivid example)[10] are mathematically identical to public goods, with only the framing of the question differing: Are we creating something from which we all benefit (clean air) or avoiding the creation of something that harms everyone (smog)?[11]

By applying tools from behavioral and experimental economics to the still-intractable legal problem of privacy, we hope to shift the debate surrounding privacy protection. If the theories espoused here are correct, and we believe the science strongly shows that they are, there will and must be a sea change in how law addresses privacy. The social, legal, and self-regulatory tools that we use and promote now are focused on empowering individuals. They must equally be focused on empowering groups.

Why should a bystander's privacy be at risk if another discloses information about herself? One source of risk is immediate and palpable. Information about one person is also information about others.[12] If a machine-learning algorithm knows where someone is at a given time, it can predict where a spouse or friend is as well. Such network analysis is central to intelligence surveillance, where sussing out the network of who knows whom is often the most important work. Another source of risk is remote and concealed, but potentially even more dangerous. Big data companies collect large amounts of information about everyone.[13] They then mine this data for patterns.[14] For instance, imagine paying higher insurance premiums because a sibling has cancer, or because a parent posts something about his heart disease, or a relative self-identifies as suffering from a particular mental illness.[15] Alternatively, imagine not receiving a job offer because an algorithm has identified that the distance an employee lives from work strongly correlates with higher turnover.[16]

---

[10] See David Jackson and Kevin Johnson, *China Suspected in Massive U.S. Government Data Breach*, USA Today (June 5, 2015, 12:42 PM), www.usatoday.com/story/news/nation/2015/06/04/obama-office-of-personnel-management-data-breach/28495775/; Steve Ragan, *Ashley Madison Hackers Publish Compromised Records*, CSO (Aug. 18, 2015, 4:53 PM) www.csoonline.com/article/2973036/vulnerabilities/ashley-madison-hackers-publish-compromised-records.html.

[11] See James Andreoni, *Warm-Glow Versus Cold-Prickle: The Effects of Positive and Negative Framing on Cooperation in Experiments*, 110 Q.J. Econ. 1 (1995).

[12] See Neil M. Richards, *The Dangers of Surveillance*, 126 Harv. L. Rev. 1934, 1939 (2013).

[13] See MacCarthy, *supra* note 1, at 7.

[14] See Neil M. Richards, *The Dangers of Surveillance*, 126 Harv. L. Rev. 1934, 1939 (2013) (quoting danah boyd & Kate Crawford, *Six Provocations for Big Data* 6 (Sept. 21, 2011)).

[15] See MacCarthy, *supra* note 1, at 26.   [16] See id.

Individual control of data is a fundamentally flawed concept because individuals cannot know what the data they reveal means when aggregated with billions of other data points.[17] For example, people who buy felt pads for their furniture are more likely to pay back loans because they are conscientious with their belongings. Or, people who log into their credit card accounts at 1 AM may be showing signs of financial anxiety. And people who use credit cards at drinking establishments are more likely to default on loans than people who use credit cards at the dentist.[18] Big data firms learn these things by gathering colossal datasets from millions of people, and mining the resulting pools of information.[19] No matter how healthy or credit trustworthy or committed to your work you may be, you may not receive affordable health insurance, a home loan, or job offer because of the correlations that can be ascertained from the data of others.

If one believes in the effectiveness of incentivizing, informing, and empowering individual citizens to protect their own privacy, this is very bad news. As long as the immediate benefit from disclosing your data exceeds the ensuing long-term risk for your own privacy, you will give away your data. This prediction holds even if all individuals cherish privacy with the same intensity. As the theoretical literature would have it, the struggle for privacy will fail.[20]

But there is hope. Both in the field and under the tightly controlled conditions of a lab, groups have effectively produced public goods.[21] The tragedy can be overcome. Good will alone is not enough. Instead, group rules or structural conditions must trigger and channel contributors' sense of altruism and equity.[22] This works even better if an institution

---

[17] *See, e.g.,* Bruce Schneier, Data and Goliath: The Hidden Battles to Collect Your Data and Control your World 18–19 (2015); Anna Bernasek & D.T. Mongan, All You Can Pay: How Companies Use Our Data To Empty Our Wallets (2015).

[18] *See* Charles Duhigg, *What Does Your Credit Card Company Know About You?,* N.Y. Times (May 12, 2009), www.nytimes.com/2009/05/17/magazine/17credit-t.html?page wanted =all&_r=0.

[19] *See* Bernasek & Mongan, *supra* note 17, at 143–55 (describing the "new gold rush" of big-data datamining).

[20] *See* Garrett Hardin, *The Tragedy of the Commons,* 162 Science 1243 (1968); for an application to privacy and information, *see* Dennis D. Hirsch, *Protecting the Inner Environment: What Privacy Regulation Can Learn from Environmental Law,* 41 Ga. L. Rev. 1, 10 (2006).

[21] *See, e.g.,* John O. Ledyard, *Public Goods, A Survey of Experimental Research, in* The Handbook of Experimental Economics 111 (John H. Kagel & Alvin E. Roth, eds., Princeton 1995).

[22] *See* Andreoni, *supra* note 11, at 11.

actively foments cooperation.[23] Luckily, privacy is by no means the only public good. Clean air, safety, roads, and the common defense all share the same incentive structure.[24] Privacy policy thus need not reinvent the wheel; it can already benefit from the solutions that have been developed and tested in these areas.

The behavioral economics literature – which asks how people actually behave in these situations – draws a clearer picture than the excessively rigorous pure-theory public goods of neoclassical economics.[25] In neoclassical economics, a dilemma results from a difference between individual and social benefit.[26] The individual is best off if she ignores the negative or positive effects that her action entails for others.[27] The neoclassical literature therefore supposes that individually informed and empowered actors will act against group social welfare.[28] But the experimental literature shows repeatedly that the neoclassical picture is too pessimistic. A rich literature[29] has tested and rejected the theoretical prediction that groups will completely fail to produce public goods.[30]

---

[23] *See, e.g.*, James Andreoni & Larry Samuelson, *Building rational cooperation*, 127 J. ECON. THEORY 117, 122 (2006).

[24] *See, e.g.*, RICHARD CORNES & TODD SANDLER, THE THEORY OF EXTERNALITIES, PUBLIC GOODS, AND CLUB GOODS 517 (2d ed. 1996); Paul M. Schwartz, *Property, Privacy, and Personal Data*, 117 HARV. L. REV. 2055, 2084–85 (2004).

[25] *See* Christine Jolls *et al.*, *A Behavioral Approach to Law and Economics*, 50 STAN. L. REV. 1471 (1998).

[26] *See* Richard Warner & Robert H. Sloan, *Behavioral Advertising: From One-Sided Chicken to Informational Norms*, 15 VAND. J. ENT. & TECH. L. 49, 55 (2012).

[27] *See id.*

[28] *See* CORNES & SANDLER, *supra* note 4; Hardin, *supra* note 20; TODD SANDLER, COLLECTIVE ACTION: THEORY AND APPLICATION (1992); TODD SANDLER, ECONOMIC CONCEPTS FOR THE SOCIAL SCIENCES (2001); TODD SANDLER, GLOBAL COLLECTIVE ACTION (2004); Margaret M. Blair & Lynn A. Stout, *Trust, Trustworthiness, and the Behavioral Foundations of Corporate Law*, 149 U. PA. L. REV. 1735, 1751 (2001); Jennifer L. Radner, *Phone, Fax, and Frustration: Electronic Commercial Speech and Nuisance Law*, 42 EMORY L.J. 359, 404–05 (1993) (citing EJAN MACKAAY, ECONOMICS OF INFORMATION AND LAW 4, 117 (1982)).

[29] Surveys are provided by Ledyard, *supra* note 21; Jennifer Zelmer, *Linear Public Goods. A Meta-Analysis*, 6 EXP. ECON. 299–310 (2003); Ananish Chaudhuri, *Sustaining Cooperation in Laboratory Public Goods Experiments: A Selective Survey of the Literature*, 14 EXP. ECON. 47–83 (2011).

[30] *See* Reinhard Selten, *The Chain Store Paradox* 9 THEORY & DECIS. 127–59 (1978); Robert W. Rosenthal, *Games of Perfect Information, Predatory Pricing and the Chain Store Paradox*, 25 J. ECON. THEORY 92–100 (1981); David M. Kreps *et al.*, *Rational Cooperation in the Finitely Repeated Prisoners' Dilemma*, 27 J. ECON. THEORY 245–52 (1982); Robert J. Aumann & Lloyd S. Shapley, *Long Term Competition: A Game Theoretic Analysis*, in COLLECTED PAPERS 395 (R.J. Aumann ed., 2000).

This chapter mines the behavioral economics literature to find new approaches to privacy protection that permit groups to sustain cooperation and protect privacy even without direct government intervention. We suggest a focus on empowering groups. We suggest leveraging inequity aversion, reciprocity, and normativity to lessen exploitation among group members.[31] We suggest positive framing to promote altruism.[32] We suggest that communication and (private) sanctions are key components of group coordination.[33] With these tools, there is a chance to sustain privacy without relying on governmental intervention.[34]

In the current broader context of the Snowden disclosures, we suggest that these tools are particularly useful because, while governments can certainly help by encouraging use of the behavioral tools we mention here, it is not necessary for the government to directly implement or oversee them for the tools to be effective. This is good news. Government is a primary beneficiary of consumers' inability to collectively protect privacy. Governments on both sides of the Atlantic have not acted strongly to limit their own access to the information citizens provide about one another. Following public outcry in Europe and the USA FREEDOM Act reforms in the United States, the conduit from consumer to corporation to government will become even more important, and less likely to be directly restricted by any government. Government, as an institution, is therefore unlikely to serve the role of the single institution coordinating citizens' response to a collective action problem. This political reality points toward solutions that groups themselves can use to resolve social dilemmas and coordinate in the face of the collective action problem posed by privacy.

B   The Gap in Law and Policy

The problem of privacy online is often not what one says about oneself, but what others say.[35] Big data exacerbates this problem beyond gossip

---

[31] See David A. Dana, *Adequacy of Representation After Stephenson: A Rawlsian/behavioral Economics Approach to Class Action Settlements*, 55 EMORY L.J. 279, 303 (2006).

[32] See Stephanos Bibas, *Plea Bargaining Outside the Shadow of Trial*, 117 HARV. L. REV. 2463, 2512 (2004).

[33] See Richard H. McAdams, *Beyond the Prisoners' Dilemma: Coordination, Game Theory, and Law*, 82 S. CAL. L. REV. 209, 218 (2009).

[34] See *id.*; Blair & Stout, *supra* note 28, at 1771.

[35] See Daniel J. Solove, *Introduction: Privacy Self-Management and the Consent Dilemma*, 126 HARV. L. REV. 1880, 1892 (2013).

and thoughtless comments. Big data allows users to reveal critical information about other people without understanding that they are doing so.[36] Even by revealing what their interests and disinterests are, users train machine-learning algorithms to predict the behavior of other people, forming the basis for targeted behavioral advertising (or targeted behavioral intelligence surveillance for that matter),[37] and creating the potential for abuse by other interested actors.

I Toxic Data Accumulation

Central to our thesis is the idea that large pools of data can exert a corrosive effect on social welfare.[38] There are two salient features of accumulated data that make it potentially toxic. The first is that data accumulates across time. Humans do not remember contributing the information, and do not take precautions against misuse. The second is accumulation across sources. Again, humans do not adequately account for the fact that what they tell one counterparty will be communicated many times to many others. In both senses, the accumulated data is experienced as toxic: it can harm people in ways they did not foresee. Because of these effects, Bruce Schneier has referenced information as a form of data pollution.[39] For example, assume that because of a youthful indiscretion, you carried a drug conviction, for which you paid a penalty, or suppose that you had engaged in political protests that create a risk of employer backlash. Decades ago that would have been the end of it, because the information was not concatenated with other datasets or stored in an easily searchable fashion. Now, a conviction or involvement in a politically unpopular cause can result in exclusion from the economy because the information is permanently recorded and spreads into easily searchable databases. Stale data damages the ability of citizens to reinvent

---

[36] See MacCarthy, *supra* note 1, at 24; Richards, *supra* note 14, at 1939 (quoting danah boyd & Kate Crawford, *Six Provocations for Big Data* 6 (Sept. 21, 2011)); Solove, *Introduction*, *supra* note 35, at 1881; Terence J. Lau, *Towards Zero Net Presence*, 25 Notre Dame J.L. Ethics & Pub. Pol'y 237, 244 (2011).

[37] See, e.g., Riva Richmond, As *"Like" Buttons Spread, So Do Facebook's Tentacles*, N.Y. Times (Sept. 27, 2011, 03:51 PM), http://bits.blogs.nytimes.com/2011/09/27/as-like-buttons-spread-so-do-facebooks-tentacles/?_php=true&_type=blogs&_r=0.

[38] See id.

[39] See Bruce Schneier, *The Tech Lab: Bruce Schneier*, BBC (Feb. 26, 2009, 11:54 AM), http://news.bbc.co.uk/2/hi/technology/7897892.stm.

themselves, increases the risk of identity theft, increases price discrimination, and through filter bubbling (the practice of limiting search results based on the searching party's profile)[40] decreases the ability of citizens to make informed choices drawn from a range of data sources, among a number of other potential effects.[41]

We take Schneier's intuition one step further. Given that data can be toxic, we ask why groups of people remain willing to continue pouring data into those pools. One stock response, which we find unconvincing, is that people do not care about privacy.[42] The answer we advance here is that there are divergent incentives between groups and individuals. This answer is particularly elegant: public goods theory explains why everyone might deeply cherish privacy, yet still contribute to privacy-damaging stores of data, just as everyone likes clean air, but individuals still pollute.

We find these divergent incentives in practice. Social media provides rich troves for data researchers.[43] Users disclose data about shops they visit, the trips they take, the routes they drive, the food they eat, and increasingly the people they encounter.[44] Users tag photographs of one another on Facebook.[45] Users reference one another in geolocated social media posts. They comment on one another's walls.[46] They take photographs of one another with Snapchat, and post commented pictures to Instagram.[47] Consumers do this in the mistaken belief that data is

---

[40] *See* ELI PARISER, THE FILTER BUBBLE: HOW THE NEW PERSONALIZED WEB IS CHANGING WHAT WE READ AND HOW WE THINK (2011).

[41] These are the risks that animate the emerging European "right to be forgotten." *See* Case C-131/12, Google Spain SL v. Agencia Espanola de Protección de Datos (AEPD), INFOCURIA – CASE-LAW CT. JUST. (May 13, 2014), http://curia.europa.eu/juris/docu ment/document.jsf;jsessionid=9ea7d0f130d58fa348967d244833bad1c86381ec1189.e34Ka xiLc3eQc40LaxqMbN4Oc3aKe0?text=&docid=152065&pageIndex=0&doclang=EN& mode=lst&dir=&occ=first&part=1&cid=385379 [hereinafter Google Spain CJEU]. *See also* Chapters 11, 16, 20, and 22 in this volume.

[42] *See* Bruce Schneier, *Google and Facebook's Privacy Illusion*, FORBES (Apr. 6, 2010, 6:00 AM), www.forbes.com/2010/04/05/google-facebook-twitter-technology-security-10-privacy.html.

[43] *See* Michael Birnhack, *Reverse Engineering Informational Privacy Law*, 15 YALE J.L. & TECH. 24, 85 (2013).

[44] *See id.* at 86.

[45] *See* James Grimmelmann, *Saving Facebook*, 94 IOWA L. REV. 1137, 1145–46 (2009).

[46] *See* Jason Mazzone, *Facebook's Afterlife*, 90 N.C. L. REV. 1643, 1653 (2012).

[47] *See* Nick Bilton, *Disruptions: Indiscreet Photos, Glimpsed Then Gone*, N.Y. TIMES (May 6, 2012, 5:24 PM), http://bits.blogs.nytimes.com/2012/05/06/disruptions-indiscreet-photos-glimpsed-then-gone/; *see also* Josh Constine, *Instagram Now Lets Anyone Tag You [Or Brands] In Photos, Adds Them to "Photos of You" Profile Section*, TECHCRUNCH (May 2, 2013), http://techcrunch.com/2013/05/02/instagram-photo-tagging/.

ephemeral, or because of too-often-broken promises that consumer data can be kept safe from other consumers or malicious third parties.[48]

Ubiquitous smartphones permit users to contribute data about themselves and others on a constant basis.[49] There are fewer places to hide from social media–enabled computing, since other people carry it with them.[50] Engaging with social media is therefore not an individual choice. It is an inevitable outcome of being in almost any social situation. Location information is a particularly powerful example of how one person's data can affect others. Cellphones track individuals' location precisely, and by proxy, the locations of others.[51] Knowledge of where one person is, augmented by knowledge of that person's social network, can help to identify and locate those who are regularly in proximity to that person.[52] Aggregated data contributions train machine-learning algorithms, such that the data offered by one person trains an algorithm that impacts someone else.[53] Consider Facebook, which has recently applied for a patent for inferring the creditworthiness of an individual based on the financial responsibility of the people in that individual's social network.[54] Machines need ground truth to learn. Each subject's contributions of data serve to train the algorithm to develop rules that will then be applied to others.[55] In no sense, then, does our privacy rest solely in our individual hands.

---

[48] *See* Catherine Shu, *Confirmed: Snapchat Hack Not a Hoax, 4.6M Usernames And Numbers Published*, TECHCRUNCH (Dec. 13, 2013), http://techcrunch.com/2013/12/31/hackers-claim-to-publish-list-of-4–6m-snapchat-usernames-and-numbers/; *see also* Press Release, Federal Trade Commission, Snapchat Settles FTC Charges That Promises of Disappearing Messages Were False, (May 18, 2014), www.ftc.gov/news-events/press-releases/2014/05/snapchat-settles-ftc-charges-promises-disappearing-messages-were.

[49] *See* Thomas H. Chia, *Fighting the Smartphone Patent War with Rand-Encumbered Patents*, 27 BERKELEY TECH. L.J. 209, 231 (2012).

[50] *See* Peter Swire, *Social Networks, Privacy, and Freedom of Association: Data Protection vs. Data Empowerment*, 90 N.C. L. REV. 1371, 1381–82 (2012).

[51] *See* Lau, *supra* note 36, at 245; *see also* U.S. Gov't Accountability Office, GAO-12-903, *Mobile Device Location Data: Additional Federal Actions Could Help Protect Consumer Privacy* 11–13 (2012).

[52] *See* James Risen & Laura Poitras, *NSA Gathers Data on Social Connections of U.S. Citizens*, N.Y. TIMES (Sept. 28, 2013), www.nytimes.com/2013/09/29/us/nsa-examines-social-networks-of-us-citizens.html?pagewanted=all&_r=0.

[53] *See* MacCarthy, *supra* note 1, at 21.

[54] *See* Susie Cagle, *Facebook Wants to Redline Your Friends List*, PAC. STANDARD (Aug. 24, 2015), www.psmag.com/nature-and-technology/mo-friends-mo-problems-might-have-to-defriend-joey-with-the-jet-ski-bankruptcy.

[55] *See* DEPARTMENT OF HOMELAND SECURITY S&T/INNOVATION FAST PROJECT, PRIVACY IMPACT ASSESSMENT FOR THE FAST PROJECT 1, www.dhs.gov/xlibrary/assets/privacy/privacy_pia_st_fast.pdf (2008).

II Privacy's Individualism Bias

Privacy theorists differ famously and widely on the proper conception of privacy,[56] but these many theories tend to share an underlying theoretical assumption. Most dominant theories of privacy view privacy through the lens of individualism.[57] Some approaches may touch on the social dimension of privacy,[58] but they do not strongly engage the social dilemma of privacy.[59]

The traditional right to privacy contemplates an individual's control of information that originates from or bears on that individual and is therefore hers exclusively to reveal or protect. It does not focus on the spillover effects of information that is not about me, or you, but us. The traditional approach does not focus on group coordination as an increasingly significant part of the problem, or on known solutions to the social dilemma.

Modern privacy approaches have developed and intensified the emphasis on individual notice, choice, and control over information flows.[60] For

---

[56] See Daniel J. Solove, *Conceptualizing Privacy*, 90 CAL. L. REV. 1087, 1099–1123 (2002).

[57] See Robert C. Post, *The Social Foundations of Privacy: Community and Self in the Common Law Tort*, 77 CAL. L. REV. 957, 958 (1989) ("[P]rivacy rests upon an individualist concept of society.").

[58] See Paul M. Schwartz, *Privacy and Democracy in Cyberspace*, 52 VAND. L. REV. 1609, 1663 (1999); *see also* Robert C. Post, *The Social Foundations of Privacy: Community and Self in the Common Law Tort*, 77 CAL. L. REV. 957, 963 (1989); Amitai Etzioni, *A Communitarian Perspective on Privacy*, 32 CONN. L. REV. 897, 899 (2000); *see also* AMITAI ETZIONI, THE LIMITS OF PRIVACY 15 (Basic Books 1999).

[59] We are not the first to note this emphasis on individualism. *See* PRISCILLA REGAN, LEGISLATING PRIVACY: TECHNOLOGY, SOCIAL VALUES, AND PUBLIC POLICY 228, 231 (N.C. PRESS 1996) ("The question, then, is whether privacy can be considered a public good . . . . Recognition that privacy has some features of a public or collective good would make clearer the institutional or organizational interests in personal information and the weaknesses of a market solution in providing privacy protection."). Regan further writes, "in policy debates in the United States, the emphasis has been on achieving the goal of protecting the privacy of individuals rather than curtailing the surveillance activities of organizations. . . . It was thought that by protecting individual privacy, the surveillance activities of organizations and the government would be checked." *Id.* at 3. Thus, "[a]lthough privacy is viewed as a boundary separating the individual from society, the dominant assumption has been that only the individual has an interest in that boundary . . . ." *Id.* at 23. The result has been an emphasis on an atomistic individual and the legal protection of his or her rights." The results have not been positive for privacy theory. "[I]ndividualistic conception of privacy does not provide a fruitful basis for the formulation of policy to protect privacy. *See id.* at xiv.

[60] See REGAN, *supra* note 59, at 24–41 (tracing the post-*Right to Privacy* history of overemphasis on individualism through legal and philosophical thought).

example, privacy-as-control has emerged as a dominant theory of informational privacy,[61] in part because it promises individuals (rightly or wrongly) the ability to both disclose and control dissemination of information online.[62] Privacy-as-control's operationalizing regime of notice and choice demonstrates the dominance of individualism in modern privacy law.[63] Notice and choice depends entirely and explicitly on individuals. Such regimes attempt to ensure that individuals know what is being done with their information, and have some choice as to how or whether that data is used. Notice is provided to the individual about information pertaining to the individual, and the choice is the individual's to make.

This is not to say that notice and choice is not useful, merely that individual-focused education and empowerment appear to yield diminishing returns. Consumers quite rationally do not read the carefully drafted privacy policies.[64] Even if they did, privacy controls are often left unused because of time costs of vigilance or complexity.[65] Yet, even if individualized notice-and-choice did function as desired (and it does not), then there would still be a problem. The notice-and-choice approach to privacy assumes incorrectly that the individual is the predominant unit in the privacy conversation, and thus that each individual can and should manage information solely about herself.[66] This is an oversight.[67] By consenting to information gathering a user becomes a

---

[61] See James Q. Whitman, *The Two Western Cultures of Privacy: Dignity Versus Liberty*, 113 YALE L.J. 1151, 1167 (2004); Charles Fried, *Privacy*, 77 YALE L.J. 475 (1968); Jeffrey Rosen, THE UNWANTED GAZE: THE DESTRUCTION OF PRIVACY IN AMERICA 5 (2000); Thomas Nagel, CONCEALMENT AND EXPOSURE 4 (2002)); ALAN F. WESTIN, PRIVACY AND FREEDOM (1967); *see also* Paul Schwartz, *Internet Privacy and the State*, 32 CONN. L. REV. 815, 820 (1999).

[62] See MacCarthy, *supra* note 1, at 10.   [63] See REGAN, *supra* note 59, at 27.

[64] See Solove, *Introduction*, *supra* note 35, at 1884; Daniel J. Solove & Woodrow Hartzog, *The FTC and the New Common Law of Privacy*, 114 COLUM. L. REV. 583, 667 (2014); Yannis Bakos *et al.*, *Does Anyone Read the Fine Print? Testing a Law and Economics Approach to Standard Form Contracts*, 43 J. LEGAL STUD. 1 (2014); Florencia Marotta-Wurgler, *Does Contract Disclosure Matter?*, 168 J. INST. & THEO. ECON. 94 (2012); Florencia Marotta-Wurgler, *Does Increased Disclosure Help? Evaluating the Recommendations of the ALI's "Principles of the Law of Software Contracts"*, 78(1) U. CHI. L. REV. 165 (2011).

[65] See Emil Protalinski, *Survey: Facebook, Google privacy policies are incomprehensible*, ZDNet (May 4, 2012, 5:58 AM), www.zdnet.com/blog/facebook/survey-facebook-google-privacy-policies-are-incomprehensible/12420.

[66] See, e.g., Kenneth A. Bamberger & Deirdre K. Mulligan, *Privacy on the Books and on the Ground*, 63 STAN. L. REV. 247, 247 (2011).

[67] See MacCarthy, *supra* note 1, at 20.

conduit for gathering information about her entire social network, whether or not others in that network have consented.[68]

The individualism bias also crosses major cultural and legal divides in privacy law. For example, approaches to privacy appear at first blush to play out differently on each side of the Atlantic.[69] One narrative is that the United States focuses on liberty,[70] while the European Union focuses on human dignity.[71] Yet both philosophies look at privacy as a matter best resolved by informing and empowering individuals. In both Europe and the United States, the presumed goal is for fully informed individuals to consent to the use of their individual data. The problem remains: the data does not impact that individual alone.

The Atlantic divide in privacy theory, therefore, cloaks an underlying and deeper similarity.[72] In both legal orders, individuals consent to the use of data that impacts nonconsenting third parties.[73] Both the liberty and dignity approaches focus on empowering and informing individuals, rather than improving group coordination.[74] U.S. and European law differ on whether individuals must opt in or opt out of data collection and processing.[75] But both traditions locate the problem and its solution with the individual deciding in isolation – the individual must opt in or opt out.[76] In both the United States and Europe, the law provides tools to help individuals understand and control information that directly concerns them. Both traditions lack tools that help groups of individuals

---

[68] *See* Daniel J. Solove, *Conceptualizing Privacy*, 90 CAL. L. REV. 1087, 1104 (2002); Michal Kosinski *et al.*, *Private Traits and Attributes Are Predictable from Digital Records of Human Behavior*, 110 PNAS 5802, *passim* (2013); Jennifer Goldbeck, *Smart People Prefer Curly Fries*, SLATE (Oct. 7, 2014, 7:48 AM), www.slate.com/articles/technology/future_tense/2014/10/youarewhatyoulike_find_out_what_algorithms_can_tell_about_you_based_on_your.html.

[69] *See id.* at 1106.   [70] *See* Whitman, *supra* note 61, at 1155.

[71] *Id.* at 1161. *See also* Chapter 2 in this volume.

[72] *See* Whitman, *supra* note 61, at 1163.

[73] *See* Omer Tene & Jules Polonetsky, *Big Data for All: Privacy and User Control in the Age of Analytics*, 11 NW. J. TECH. & INTELL. PROP. 239, 285 (2013).

[74] *See* Whitman, *supra* note 61, at 1167–68.

[75] *Compare* Directive 95/46/EC of the European Parliament and of the Council of 24 October 1995 on the Protection of Individuals with Regard to the Processing of Personal Data and on the Free Movement of Such Data, 1995 O.J. (L 281) 31 (requiring opt-in consent within a purpose-based collection framework) with U.S. – E.U. Safe Harbor Overview, EXPORT.GOV, http://export.gov/safeharbor/eu/eg_main_018476.asp (requiring consumers to opt out if they do not want their data used, but otherwise exempting Safe Harbor participants from E.U. opt-in restrictions).

[76] *See* Tene & Polonetsky, *supra* note 73, at 260–62.

manage coordination problems. And both traditions have little to no protection for spillover effects of information – information about person A that nevertheless imposes negative effects on person B, and everyone else.[77]

Given the interdisciplinary and transnational nature of this collection of essays, we will risk a guess as to how these differing conceptions might impact adoption of the recommendations we make here. U.S. law in particular has emphasized individualism, as we argue above, and because of that focus we believe that recognition of the basic collective nature of privacy will face an uphill battle for adoption in U.S. courts and legislatures, as will any solution that smacks of communitarianism. What will be more palatable from a U.S. perspective is that we do not rely on government as a central institution to moderate the collective action problem. Indeed, given that government is a primary beneficiary of the current mass surveillance regimes, we do not think government can act as an uninterested institution that will moderate the collective action problem of privacy. Our anecdotal observation is that by leveraging social media tools to gather information on citizens, government has exacerbated the problem. By casting the tools we suggest as self-help, although of the group rather than the individual variety, it may be possible to avoid triggering a knee-jerk reaction against group-empowering tools.

European legal traditions may perhaps be more open to communitarian solutions. Here the barriers to adoption may be different. The tools we describe are grounded in the discipline of behavioral law and economics. There may be some resistance to the ideas described here on the grounds that it would be more convincing to express them in deontological rather than economic terms. Nor do we discount such explanations. Our hope is that these arguments would add an economic helping hand to deontological intuitions about the role of individuals in relation to society. The fact that these tools have been tested in the laboratory and are likely to work adds additional support to the argument.

III   Toward Privacy as a Public Good

The legal literature is not entirely empty of the suggestion that privacy can be profitably studied as a true public good.[78] For example, Paul

---

[77] See Lau, *supra* note 36, at 266.

[78] See, e.g., Paul M. Schwartz, *Property, Privacy, and Personal Data*, 117 HARV. L. REV. 2055, 2084–85 (2004) [hereinafter *Property, Privacy, and Personal Data*]; Paul M. Schwartz,

Schwartz notes that "information privacy functions as a type of public good, like clean air or national defense"[79] and that "[p]rivacy, from a constitutive perspective, is also a 'public good.' Information privacy is a kind of commons that requires some degree of social control to construct and then preserve."[80] Priscilla Regan discusses the "collective value" of privacy, which she "derive[s] from the economists' concept of collective or public goods." Regan suggests that "[r]ecognition that privacy has some features of a public or collective good would make clearer the institutional or organizational interests in personal information and the weaknesses of a market solution in providing privacy protection."[81] We take this suggestion as an invitation for a full analysis of privacy in light of the public goods literature of the past several decades.[82]

We note a nascent literature that draws on existing environmental regulatory approaches to propose solutions to the problem of toxic data.[83] The eco-privacy literature shares a base set of concerns with our public goods analysis. For example, Dennis Hirsch analogizes spam to pollution,[84] suggesting that privacy (in this sense, freedom from spam) is subject to a tragedy of the commons.[85] Michael Froomkin uses a similar characterization: "Many mass-data collection activities, particularly those that take place in or through public spaces can be usefully analogized to pollution of the private sphere."[86] Eben Moglen notes that "[surveillance] is not the first, the last, or the most serious of the various forms of environmental crisis brought on in the last two centuries by industrial

---

Privacy and Democracy in Cyberspace, 52 VAND. L. REV. 1609 (1999); Paul M. Schwartz, *Internet Privacy and the State*, 32 CONN. L. REV. 815 (2000); Paul M. Schwartz, *Regulating Governmental Data Mining in the United States and Germany: Constitutional Courts, the State, and New Technology*, 53 WM. & MARY L. REV. 351 (2011); Edward J. Janger & Paul M. Schwartz, *The Gramm-Leach-Bliley Act, Information Privacy, and the Limits of Default Rules*, 86 MINN. L. REV. 1219, 1253–54 (2002).

[79] See Schwartz, *Property, Privacy, and Personal Data, supra* note 78, at 2084–85.

[80] Edward J. Janger & Paul M. Schwartz, *The Gramm-Leach-Bliley Act, Information Privacy, and the Limits of Default Rules*, 86 MINN. L. REV. 1219, 1253–54 (2002).

[81] See REGAN, *supra* note 59, at 231; *see also* MacCarthy, *supra* note 1, at 23.

[82] See Schwartz, *Property, Privacy, and Personal Data, supra* note 78, at 2076, 2085.

[83] See Hirsch, *supra* note 20, at 10 (2006); Dennis D. Hirsch, *The Glass House Effect: Big Data, The New Oil, and the Power of Analogy*, 66 MAINE L. REV. 374 (2014) [hereinafter *Glass House*]; A. Michael Froomkin, *Regulating Mass Surveillance as Privacy Pollution: Learning from Environmental Impact Statements*, 2015 ILL. L. REV. 713 (2015); Eben Moglen, *Snowden and the Future: Part III; The Union, May It Be Preserved*, Columbia L. SCH. (Nov. 13, 2013).

[84] See Hirsch, *supra* note 20 at 15–18.   [85] *See id.* at 24–28.

[86] See Froomkin, *supra* note 83, at 30.

overreaching."[87] There are therefore some similarities between our approach and the framing language of the environmental privacy literature.[88] That literature has the particular advantage of drawing on a rich and successful regulatory tradition, which has ironed some of the kinks out of helping industrial communities find and implement low-cost, high-value changes. As such, it provides a strong set of analogies for how to craft and maintain political coalitions to resolve particularly harmful collective action problems.

Yet there are some important differences. Where the environmental privacy literature draws on environmental law and the history of environmental regulation for inspiration, we draw on public goods models and experiments, and hence focus on the behavioral dimension of the question. Environmental law is chiefly shaped by the experience of government in seeking to reign in large-scale polluters.[89] As a result, the environmental privacy literature suggests government action or legislation to resolve the collective action problem of privacy.[90] In the privacy context, however, government is both a primary polluter and a major beneficiary (through the intelligence services and law enforcement) of group failure to coordinate. Although judges and consumer protection agencies can certainly play a role in developing pro-privacy solutions, avoiding the need for direct government administration of our suggested tools is particularly useful under present circumstances. Therefore, where the example of environmental law suggests regulation to resolve collective action problems, we suggest group tools to sustain cooperation with minimal government intervention. Instead of following a Pigouvian approach of seeking government intervention to tax or sanction bad institutional behavior,[91] we follow in the tradition of Coase and Ostrom,[92] and mine the economics literature for tools groups themselves can use to sustain production of public goods, or in this case to maintain privacy.

---

[87] See Moglen, *supra* note 83.

[88] See Hirsch, *Glass House Effect, supra* note 83; *see also* Hirsch, *supra* note 20, at 28.

[89] See Hirsch, *supra* note 20, at 4.

[90] See *id.* at 43; *see also* Froomkin, *supra* note 83, at 33.

[91] See CORNES & SANDLER, *supra* note 4, at 16.

[92] COMM. ON THE HUMAN DIMENSIONS OF SOC. CHANGE ET AL., THE DRAMA OF THE COMMONS (Elinor Ostrom *et al.*, eds., National Academy Press 2002); Ronald Coase, *The Problem of Social Cost*, 3 J. LAW & ECON. 1 (1960).

C   Privacy as a Public Good

This section draws on the past several decades' advances in public goods theory and experiments. The section then highlights certain specific group institutions that appear repeatedly in this literature as being particularly worthy of consideration for building tools to help groups resist the social dilemma of privacy.

One way to perceive the problem clearly is to consider lack of privacy as a public bad, to which we all contribute when we produce digital information about ourselves that has negative spillover effects. Recall that public goods and public bads are mathematically identical; only the framing of the problem changes. The production function for clean air can be expressed as the minimization of the production function for creating pollution. Flipping the framing in this way is a very powerful tool for understanding how privacy is a public good. It is much easier to perceive the problem using the public bads model.

In the online world individuals regularly face the following decision: they are invited to join some Internet platform, knowing (more or less vaguely) that they will indirectly pay by making personal information available. Take the typical social network. The individual damage a user foresees when leading an active online life seems reasonable. A user might reason that the likelihood of negative consequences (such as those suffered by those whose secrets were disclosed in the Ashley Madison hack) is low. The user may feel that her life is simply not that interesting, discounting the possibility of being used as a surveillance conduit for someone who is more interesting, or being placed on a no-fly list based on the statements of friends-of-friends. The user may not perceive individual risk worth abstaining from the immediate and personal benefits conveyed by use of the network. The user knows she will reveal some information about her friends and family. Maybe the user knows one of them to be particularly vulnerable, but does not account for the risk of her own contributions to data about that person – certainly few people understand that a message of sympathy in the event of illness might affect healthcare premiums.

This is precisely the kind of reasoning the public bad model aims to capture. The user's anticipated individual damage is too small to outweigh anticipated benefit. Things would look differently if users were to factor in the negative repercussions of being generous with their private information on the privacy risk faced by others and vice versa. Yet, as long as each user only considers the potential damage to herself, no individual would be concerned that (anticipated) damage outweighs (actual and anticipated) benefit. If an individual does not reflect on the possibility that surveilling authorities might be interested in others in her network,[93] she will not properly measure the damage of her disclosures. If, however, each user were to sum up the potential for damage resulting from her own and everybody else's disclosure, she would see that the social balance is negative, implying that those fully cognizant of social cost would not want to join a social network where the business model is based on disclosing private information.

The public bad of lack of privacy increases over time as more data is stored and machine learning algorithms improve. Individuals are less and less able to control and monitor the damage that their revelations may cause to themselves, let alone to others. Small contributions to the data pool provide bigger results. Individuals who face the social dilemma of privacy face three strong pressures to defect even if they are inclined to cooperate: they realize that their individual efforts will only cost them; that others will likewise defect over time; and that the development of technology tends toward ever greater intrusions on privacy. Under those circumstances it makes sense to give up privacy-seeking behavior and seize what private benefit they can. No wonder, then, that even the most privacy-minded consumers may eventually defect.

D   Applying Public Goods Theory to Privacy Problems

Understanding why groups cooperate or fall apart is essential to devising institutions or tools groups can use to protect their own privacy. This section explores the experimental and classical literature to understand group dynamics and suggest potential paths for group coordination in the face of the social dilemma of privacy.

---

[93] Consider Sondra Arquiett, who was arrested for cocaine possession and agreed to permit DEA agents to inspect her phone in 2010. Without her consent, DEA agents used intimate photographs from her phone to create a Facebook account and interact with fugitives in an attempt to leverage her social network. *See Woman Sues Federal Agent Over Fake Facebook Profile Used in Drug Case*, THE GUARDIAN (Oct. 7, 2014, 3:16 PM), www.theguardian.com/world/2014/oct/07/fake-facebook-dea-agent-lawsuit-sondra-arquiett.

I   Repeated Interaction

Probably the most important feature of sharing private information online is the repeated character of the interaction among those whose privacy is potentially at stake. If two anonymous individuals meet once, it may be that standard economic theory gets it right, and they will treat each other poorly because they will never meet again.

Yet the Internet is not purely organized out of an undifferentiated mass of strangers, but rather nested smaller groups with higher frequencies of repeat play.[94] Within such nested groups, people may reasonably consider the impact defections may have on others' future incentive to cooperate. If I post an embarrassing picture of my friend on Facebook, she might do the same to me tomorrow. In such situations, it is more plausible to model the interaction as a repeated game. Typically it will be appropriate to think of a game that does not have a precisely defined, *ex ante* known end. If one seeks to induce cooperation in groups, this is good news. In a repeated game with an unknown end there is a credible shadow of the future. If it becomes known that I have misbehaved, that is, recklessly shared dangerous information, others may sanction me, or simply start doing the same.[95] The value of future cooperation may sustain present cooperation.

In determining whether to cooperate or defect, players may also consider the chance of other players defecting. This could either be defection in response to the defection of the deciding player, or it might be outright defection given the incentives the group faces. A player will cooperate if a game has a certain length, and she does not expect other players to exploit her. Cooperation can be sustained even if the deciding player believes that there is a chance other players will defect, as long as the game is long enough that the benefits of future cooperation are worth the risk. Thus, cooperation is sustainable in groups when the endpoint of cooperation is not previously established, and other people do not expect necessarily to be exploited.

There is also cause for optimism because the experimental literature does not support the theoretical prediction of complete defection, even when there is a known game end. In experiment after experiment, group

---

[94] *See id.*

[95] Game theorists refer to this result as the "folk theorem." *See* Aumann & Shapley, *supra* note 31. For an application to a public good see David Kreps *et al.*, *Rational Cooperation in the Finitely Repeated Prisoners' Dilemma*, 27 J. ECON. THEORY 245–52 (1982).

members are willing to cooperate at first.[96] This suggests that people come to social dilemmas with life experiences or cultural commitments that make them predisposed to cooperate at higher rates than neoclassical economics would predict.[97] This is likely because people know from experience that they cannot predict when another person may in the future impact their life. Cooperation as a default is a response to the general unpredictability of social life. But repeat play can also corrode cooperation through the repeated experience of being punished by the social dilemma. Effective application of these insights requires accounting for each of these effects. Fostering repeat play among more tightly knit online groups may foster cooperative behavior and reduce intentional malicious disclosures. But repeated fruitless attempts to protect privacy are likely to induce an effect akin to learned helplessness.

Applying this insight to privacy, we note that features that remind users of the value of cooperation given the shadow of the future are built into social networks, but they are not ones commonly expected to produce privacy gains. First, certain social network features remind users that they are repeat players. Friends of friends appear on personal walls. Routine "do you know x? He is a friend of y." reminders are sent out by the social networks in order to encourage users to expand their personal networks.[98] Social networks routinely scrape email lists, for example, to permit users to recreate their network of contacts within the network. There is no reason that these low-level reminders of the connection group members have with one another should be limited to the moment a user joins the network. One might imagine a "make new friends, and keep the old" open-source app that serves to remind users of contacts with whom they have not spoken in some time, thus raising the perception of repeat play at the edges of an individual's network. Even more valuable, given the insights regarding inequity aversion and reciprocity, would be aggressive promotion of the privacy-seeking actions others are taking. Even spreading "likes" of privacy enhancing technologies would help.

---

[96] *See* Ledyard, *supra* note 21, at 146–47.

[97] For a study of cultural constraints that produce ordered systems without government intervention, *see* ROBERT C. ELLICKSON, ORDER WITHOUT LAW: HOW NEIGHBORS SETTLE DISPUTES 123–27 (1991).

[98] *See* Nick Bilton, *Facebook's Killer Feature: The Mutual Friends List*, N.Y. TIMES (Dec. 2, 2009, 6:06 PM), http://bits.blogs.nytimes.com/2009/12/02/facebooks-killer-feature-the-mutual-friends-list/.

It should similarly be possible to ameliorate the corrosive effects of repeat play. One step would be to give full force to consumer expectations of privacy through simplified terms of service and opt-in permission each time the information is reshared or sold forward. Even simpler tools might assist. For example, users are already partially empowered to de-link their social network content from posts or un-flag from photographs that purport to represent them. This means that, although they cannot control viral outbreaks of content about them, they may have some ability to manage the degree to which their data is used by others without consent. Individual actions taken to minimize the damage of others' disclosures should provide users with strong, immediate feedback and verifiable results. This would help to avoid the corrosion engendered by repeated experiences of failure.

II   Group Characteristics

This subpart turns from an examination of repeated interaction to an analysis of the impact of group composition. Groups respond to incentives, but in ways that reflect the shared costs of creating or damaging resources that benefit group members.[99] Thus, the observable characteristics of the group matter.[100]

1   Size

Social diffusion is popularly understood to reduce incentives to take individual, positive, costly action. The well-known murder of Kitty Genovese is often used as an example to demonstrate the impact of diffuse responsibility on an individual's incentive to help.[101] Based on this intuition, early experimental efforts focused on the effect of increasing group size on cooperation.[102] Because social networks are colossal, and because we intuit that group size affects the ability to coordinate to achieve group outcomes, group size is a natural place to start mining the literature for insights about social networks and privacy.[103]

---

[99] See generally Ledyard, supra note 21, at 113.   [100] See id.
[101] See Tal Z. Zarsky, Thinking Outside the Box: Considering Transparency, Anonymity, and Pseudonymity As Overall Solutions to the Problems of Information Privacy in the Internet Society, 58 U. MIAMI L. REV. 991, 1008 (2004).
[102] See R. Mark Isaac and James M. Walker, Group Size Effects in Public Goods Provision: The Voluntary Contributions Mechanism, 103:1 Q. J. ECON. 179 (1988).
[103] Id.

The experimental findings both confirmed and challenged received wisdom. Although experimental evidence supported the claim that increases in group size lead to decreases in the ability of the body to allocate resources efficiently – in this case, by securing enough contributions to a public good – it did not support the hypothesis that increasing numbers alone decreased group coordination.[104] Instead, Isaac and Walker, who have tested this question in the lab, found that the less players received from cooperating (their marginal per capita return, or MPCR), the less the players cooperated to produce the public good.[105] From this literature we can draw several insights. First, the MPCR, or, in the case of a public bad, the marginal per capita loss, within social media may not be high enough to sustain cooperation to avoid accumulating public bads. Isaac and Walker flagged high-number, low MPCR systems as those most likely to be plagued by efficiency problems. This describes social media networks and mobile social media fairly directly. In these systems, the losses are so small and nonspecific that users may over-contribute to the system without realizing it. Tiny amounts of damaging data, logged from thousands of different sources, may not incentivize users to avoid loss. In the same way, smaller amounts of per capita return, when spread across a larger number of players, are less likely to induce efficient contribution to a public good.

Despite this, it appears that, with a sufficient MPCR,[106] even large groups can produce public goods.[107] Later experiments by Isaac, Walker, and Williams confirmed that larger groups can be more efficient than small ones at producing public goods.[108] These results provide a ray of hope for large social networks, or large groups of friends nested within such networks. From these results we draw two suggestions: increase the marginal per capita reward for privacy-seeking behavior, and keep nested groups tight. Keeping nested groups tight and intimately connected might foster positive cooperation and increase the value of MPCR as a tool for promoting more cooperation. One user's contributions of data impact those close to her much more strongly. Small, tightly nested

---

[104] *Id.*   [105] *Id.* at 179–82.

[106] Although the impact of MPCR declines in larger groups, the effect remains positive and significant.

[107] *See* Ananish Chaudhuri, *Sustaining Cooperation in Laboratory Public Goods Experiments: A Selective Survey of the Literature*, 14 Exp. Econ. 47–83 (2011).

[108] *See* R. Mark Isaac and James M. Walker, *Group Size and the Voluntary Provision of Public Goods: Experimental Evidence Utilizing Large Groups*, 54 J. Pub. Econ. 1, 30 (1994).

groups are the best place to leverage MPCR, since the users not only have an effect on each other, but care about the effects they have.[109] A good example of useful tools would be controls, already enabled in certain networks, which permit users to differentiate between narrow groups of family and friends, and broader groups of acquaintances. The weight of MPCR would be multiplied by the personal investment of the user in nearby group members. Tools to protect the privacy of friends will help nested groups produce privacy.[110] The MPCR of privacy in the narrower circle is higher, the connections tighter, and the probability of future cooperation likewise higher.

2   Player Heterogeneity and Conditional Cooperation

The literature that followed then began to look more closely at group composition in order to find out why some groups can provide public goods and others fail.[111] As one commenter notes, "the most notable [recent] finding in the area is that many participants behave as 'conditional cooperators,' whose contribution to the public good is positively correlated with their beliefs about the contributions to be made by their group members."[112] Conditional cooperators are not altruists. They do not aim at improving other individuals' utility irrespective of who those others are or what these others do. But if conditional cooperators are sufficiently optimistic that others will resist the temptation to exploit them, then they are willing to resist that temptation as well. In the context of online information sharing conditional cooperation implies that an individual is willing to resist the immediate urge to post some piece of information (and thereby to expose others to informational risk) as long as she is sufficiently optimistic that many others will also be cautious. Thus, *who* one plays with is as important as the rules of the game or the number of players.[113]

The motives that drive conditional cooperation are not yet finally settled. Two explanations have found considerable experimental support: distributional equity ("inequity aversion")[114] and reciprocity.[115] Inequity

---

[109] *Id.*   [110] *Id.*   [111] *See* Chaudhuri, *supra* note 107, at 48.   [112] *See id.* at 49.

[113] *See id.*

[114] *See* Chaudhuri, *supra* note 107, at 50, *citing* Ernst Fehr & Klaus Schmidt, *A Theory of Fairness, Competition and Cooperation*, 114 Q. J. ECON. 817–68 (1999) and Gary Bolten & Axel Ockenfels, *ERC: A Theory of Equity, Reciprocity and Competition*, 90 AM. ECON. REV. 166–93 (2000).

[115] *See* Chaudhuri, *supra* note 107, at 50, *citing* Matthew Rabin, *Incorporating Fairness into Game Theory and Economics*, 80(5) AM. ECON. REV. 1281 (1993) and Martin

aversion exclusively looks at outcomes. A person is inequity averse if she cares not only about absolute profit, but also about relative profit. Inequity averse individuals do not want to get less than others, and also possibly feel uncomfortable when they get more than others. In the context of online information sharing, inequity aversion could support conditional cooperation if the typical user of the platform in question perceives most other users to act as she will. If that is the case, by misbehaving herself she exposes others to inequity (in the form of risk or damage) while she reaps the immediate gains from disclosing information. If she is sufficiently averse to doing that, this may suffice to support an environment where little potentially critical information is leaking out. Yet the more this individual is skeptical about the behavior of others on that same platform, the more she faces the risk of being herself the one who suffers from their irresponsible behavior. That would lead to disadvantageous inequity. In line with the experimental evidence, models of inequity aversion tend to assume that the disutility from being exploited is more pronounced than the disutility from being an exploiter.[116] Yet, if the individual is sufficiently optimistic about the behavior of relevant others, then the risk of being exploited herself becomes negligible.

The difficulty with inequity aversion is that it may cause groups to coordinate on bad outcomes. If being treated equally is more important to individuals than being treated well (in the absolute sense), groups may choose to coordinate on the easier and worse every-person-for-themselves defection outcome in a social dilemma, rather than on the harder and better coordinated outcome that maximizes social welfare. Applying this insight to the privacy context, one is more likely to cooperate in an environment in which each person is perceived to benefit from privacy equally. If privacy protections are perceived to have an unequal impact, individuals are more likely to defect, especially if they fear being disadvantaged. Inequity aversion may explain the strength of the "nothing to hide" fallacy that plagues privacy discussions. The claim does not at first make sense: as Daniel Solove has repeatedly argued, even those with

---

Dufwenberg & Georg Kirchsteiger, *A Theory of Sequential Reciprocity*, 47 GAMES & ECON. BEHAV. 268 (2004).

[116] *See* Ernst Fehr & Klaus M. Schmidt, *A Theory of Fairness, Competition, and Cooperation*, 114 Q. J. ECON. 817 (1999). For the empirics, *see* Mariana Blance *et al.*, *A Within-Subject Analysis of Other-Regarding Preferences*, 72 GAMES & ECON. BEHAV. 321 (2011).

nothing to hide suffer nonzero costs of surveillance.[117] Why then resist privacy rules that benefit both oneself and others?

One possible answer suggested by the experimental evidence above is that individuals may assume that bad actors benefit from privacy more than other people. Because the bulk of the population consider themselves not to be bad actors, they consider themselves comparatively disadvantaged by such an outcome. It is difficult to find any other reason to resist rules that offer a small benefit to me and a large benefit to someone else. Law enforcement and intelligence community advocates leverage inequity aversion to focus public opinion on low-privacy outcomes by pairing the "nothing to hide" fallacy with an equally inaccurate suggestion that the only people being surveilled are bad actors, outsiders, or (in the U.S. context) non-U.S. persons. Increases in privacy would supposedly benefit ostensible bad actors more than decent citizens.

Leveraging inequity aversion to create privacy will have two components. First, education initiatives could focus on the benefit of privacy to each person and smoothing out perceptions of unequal outcomes in privacy protection. Second, initiatives could help coordinate users on the better equality option of group coordination, rather than the worse equality option of individual defection. Inequity-averse groups want everyone to be equal – equally well off, or equally harmed. By anchoring expectation on the equal benefits of privacy to all, rather than the dystopian equality of no privacy at all, such initiatives may focus the effect of inequity aversion on generating socially positive outcomes.

Reciprocity, the other explanation for conditional cooperation, focuses on perceived intentions rather than outcomes. If reciprocity is the driving force, then conditional cooperation obtains as long as the individual observes or believes that a sufficient fraction of the relevant others is acting in good faith.[118] We may refuse to participate in the production of public goods because we do not trust others to participate. Conversely, we may be willing to cooperate on the condition that we receive sufficiently strong evidence of others' intent. Thus, "studies have found that players are much more likely to cooperate in a social dilemma when they

---

[117] See Daniel J. Solove, *Why Privacy Matters Even if You Have Nothing to Hide*, CHRON. HIGHER EDUC. (May 15, 2011), https://chronicle.com/article/Why-Privacy-Matters-Even-if/127461/.

[118] Margaret M. Blair & Lynn A. Stout, *Trust, Trustworthiness, and the Behavioral Foundations of Corporate Law*, 149 U. PA. L. REV. 1735, 1772 (2001).

expect their fellow players to cooperate."[119] Evidence of outcomes may or may not be informative about others' intentions. If the other person's actions directly and predictably caused harm to the conditional cooperator, the cooperator might reasonably infer bad intent. More importantly, if the other person could have acted to cause clear harm, and did not, trust may build, fostering cooperation on group goals. If one were able to prove that a negative outcome was caused by random chance, and not by the bad intent of other group members, then a conditional cooperator motivated by reciprocity would continue to be willing to cooperate despite a bad outcome.

Applied to online privacy, reciprocity theory yields significantly different policy suggestions than does inequity aversion. Here, we must increase trust rather than smooth perceptions of outcomes. For example, reciprocity could work to sustain cooperation with respect to correlated information, as with the prototypical picture in which others feature together with me. In such a case, the outcome provides good information about the intent of the poster. For eBay, Instagram, Facebook, LinkedIn, Twitter, and other channels that permit actions from which intention can be inferred, reciprocity can be expected to play a significant role. But information about intentions is much more difficult to get if the main risk is other people providing grist for better pattern recognition by machine-learning algorithms. What is needed is an expression of the positive intentions of others. Advertisements where one actor deletes an embarrassing photo of someone else, or advertising campaigns highlighting steps one can take to protect the privacy of others will help to generate a sense of positive intent on the part of other group members. Testimonials, repeat experience, or reputation-rating systems for friends within narrow social circles can help build a sense of who is trustworthy and who is not. This trust-building within social circles cuts against the current approach, which is to promote through schools and advertising that no one can be trusted online. That approach triggers negative views of others' intentions, causing conditional cooperation to fail as each person seeks to protect herself alone. Indeed, the negative view of others' intentions would cause reciprocity-based conditional cooperation to fail even without any experienced negative consequences of others' bad actions.

---

[119] *See id.*

III   Tools to Resist Social Dilemmas

The tools that foster coordination in groups are different from those needed by individuals to protect their private interests. Indeed, the two types are in conflict. The economics literature, both experimental and classical, indicate four tools that increase group coordination: the marginal value of investing in the public good, the ability of members to communicate with one another, the possibility of sending a targeted reaction (often a sanction) to those whose behavior an individual condemns, and changing the light in which individuals view privacy's dilemma.

As we have suggested above, we believe these tools are best implemented and used by groups to coordinate group protection of privacy. The role of government is trickier. Intelligence and law enforcement wings of government benefit from citizens' inability to stop providing information about one another. But government is not monolithic. Independent judges, consumer protection agencies, and data protection authorities can help groups develop and use tools to protect their own privacy from companies. And this will curtail intelligence surveillance, given the company-to-intelligence data conduit. Thus, when we discuss regulatory enforcement of consumer preferences, we do not suggest that the FTC or European DPAs should directly intervene or administer these tools, but that they should enforce consumer preferences and foster development and use of tools that help groups manage privacy's social dilemma.

1   Marginal Per Capita Return

As long as the return from individual private investment exceeds the individual marginal payoff from the public good, classical theory would predict that individuals would continue to defect without regard to the cooperation or defection of all other players. If classical theory were correct, marginal increases in the payout players receive from contributing to a public good would not positively impact cooperation until the individual payout for public good investment exceeded the individual reward for being selfish. In the experimental literature, however, group cooperation is improved significantly by increases in the marginal payoff for contributing.[120] In the lab, cooperation increases as the ratio of

---

[120] *See* Ledyard, *supra* note 21, at 141 (citing R. Mark Isaac *et al.*, *Public Goods Provision in an Experimental Environment*, 26 J. PUB. ECON. 51 (1985), and R. Mark Isaac *et al.*,

payout for investing in a public good rises relative to the level of payout on investments in purely private gain. The effect is confirmed and powerful.[121]

The important policy question for privacy is whether modest incremental increases in the value of privacy-seeking behavior are useful, or whether we must resolve the problem by raising the individual payoff of investment in privacy until it exceeds the value of selfish behavior, thus dissolving the social dilemma. The experimental results lead us to believe that increasing the payoff from privacy-seeking behavior, or decreasing the payoff from ignoring the side effects on others' privacy for that matter, will encourage public coordination on better privacy outcomes even if careless behavior remains individually profitable. We do not have to raise the payout from privacy seeking to a level higher than the individual payout from using privacy-intrusive services. Modest marginal increase in the payoff of privacy-seeking behavior ought to increase the overall amount of privacy society produces.

A practicable way to increase the payout for privacy-seeking behavior is to provide consumers with a method for communicating their expectations and an enforcement mechanism to ensure those expectations are met. For example, one might consider the current dearth of enforcement surrounding consumer-set do-not-track flags. The flag is a feature in every mainstream browser. Consumers must incur time costs to understand and set the do-not-track flag in their browser. Even if they do so, however, companies continue to take the "no" of a consumer as a "yes." Regulatory agencies have not enforced the consumer's preferences. As a result, the investment of time by the consumer in understanding and configuring even this most basic privacy technology yields no return. It would be neither legally nor technically complicated to require companies to respect the flag. Doing so would raise the payoff for the consumer's investment in privacy, causing those within the population

---

Divergent Evidence on Free Riding: An Experimental Examination of Possible Explanations, 43 PUB. CHOICE 113 (1984).).

[121] *See* Ledyard, *supra* note 21, at 150, surveying the literature on increased MPCR, including R. Mark Isaac et al., *Public Goods Provision in an Experimental Environment*, 26 J. PUB. ECON. 51 (1985); Oliver Kim & Mark Walker, *The Free Rider Problem: Experimental Evidence*, 43 PUB. CHOICE 3 (1984); R. Mark Isaac & James M. Walker, *Group Size Effects in Public Goods Provision: The Voluntary Contributions Mechanism*, 103 Q. J. ECON. 179 (1988); J. Brown-Kruse & D. Hummels, *Gender Effects in Laboratory Public Goods Contribution: Do Individuals Put Their Money Where Their Mouth Is?*, 22 J. ECON. BEHAV. & ORG. 255 (1993).

who are willing to cooperate at this higher payoff to do so. In short, the MPCR literature suggests that small, incremental, and above all politically feasible measures to increase the payout from consumers' privacy-seeking behavior are well worth the candle even if they fall short of making investment in privacy pay out more than self-interested behavior.

2   Communication

Because social dilemmas are a coordination problem, communication is a powerful tool to foster group cooperation.[122] Groups that can communicate can coordinate, and those that cannot are severely hampered.[123] As an intuitive matter, therefore, the presence of robust means of communication between group members ought to be a good way for them to coordinate on the creation of public goods such as privacy. But classical theory predicts that communication will have no impact on a social dilemma. In a dilemma, each player should defect regardless of the actions of other players – and regardless of how much the players have been able to communicate with one another about their interests and plans. This prediction holds no matter what other players might say about their intentions.[124]

Experiments have again shown some interesting divergence from classical theory. In experiments, permitting participants to identify and communicate with one another increases the provision of public goods.[125] Lifting the veil of anonymity is a rather powerful technology for increasing cooperation in dilemma situations.[126] Cooperation further increases if individuals have a chance to talk to each other,[127] and if they

---

[122] *See* Ledyard, *supra* note 21, at 141 (citing R. Dawes *et al.*, *Behavior, Communication and Assumptions About Other People's Behavior in a Commons Dilemma Situation*, 35 J. PERS. & SOC. PSYCHOL. 1 (1977)).

[123] *See* Rick Wilson & Jane Sell, *"Liar, Liar ..." Cheap Talk and Reputation in Repeated Public Goods Settings*, 41 J. CONFLICT RESOL. 695 (1997).

[124] *See* Ledyard, *supra* note 21, at 156.

[125] *See* Ledyard, *supra* note 21, at 156 (citing R. Dawes *et al.*, *Behavior, Communication, and Assumptions about Other People's Behavior in a Commons Dilemma Situation*, 35 J. PERS. & SOC. PSYCHOL. 1 (1977); R. Mark Isaac *et al.*, *Public Goods Provision in an Experimental Environment*, 26 J. PUBLIC ECON. 51 (1985); R. Mark Isaac & James M. Walker, *Communication and Free Riding Behavior: The Voluntary Contribution Mechanism*, 26 ECON. INQ. 585 (1988); R. Mark Isaac & James M. Walker, *Costly Communication: An Experiment in a Nested Public Goods Problem*, LAB. RES. POL. ECON. 269–86 (T. Palfrey, ed., 1991).).

[126] Bruno Frey & Iris Bohnet, *Identification in Democratic Society*, 26 J. SOCIO-ECON. 25 (1997).

[127] Gary Charness & Martin Dufwenberg, *Promises and Partnership*, 74 ECONOMETRICA 1579 (2006).

are given the ability to check and verify whether their fellow participants have followed through on their announced intentions.[128] Cheap, non-binding talk does not appear to increase cooperation. Rather, the effect appears to rely on communication occurring in a setting in which group members can assess the commitment of other players to contributing to the public good. Two broad causes of the effect have been posited from this research: the ability to communicate may promote mutual promises to cooperate, or it may build group identity and cohesion.[129]

These results provide both some insight and challenges for the provision of privacy online. It is difficult to imagine a digital privacy scenario in which participants do not have some capacity to communicate. On one hand, as communication enables group coordination on welfare-maximizing outcomes, this is positive. On the other hand, the specific public good sought here is privacy, which can be damaged by malicious or thoughtless communication of information. There can be significant tension in identifying people and communicating information about them in the name of privacy. The key appears to be to provide reliable feedback about the privacy practices of actors when compared to their past promises, not necessarily disclosing further information about the actor's real-world identity. For example, it is not at all common practice for participants in laboratory experiments, even those testing communication, to share real names or other identifying information, yet their ability to communicate during the experiment helps sustain cooperation. Pseudonymity is not merely failed anonymity – it presents the real and useful option for people to build stable reputations and relationships and communicate with one another while limiting the impact of revealing real-world information. For example, the power of pseudonymity to build community while protecting the vulnerable was underscored by the Hamburg Data Protection Authority when it required Facebook to reverse its vaunted real-name policy and permit pseudonyms.[130] The action protected vulnerable populations (e.g., drag queens) who needed

---

[128] *See* J. Sell & R.K. Wilson, *The Effects of Signaling on the Provisioning of Public Goods*, Discussion Paper, Workshop in Political Theory and Policy Analysis, Indiana University (1990); *see also* Ledyard, *supra* note 21, at 156–57.

[129] *See* Sell & Wilson, *supra* note 128, at 698.

[130] *See Klarnamenpflicht: Hamburger Datenschützer fordert Pseudonyme auf Facebook*, SPIEGEL ONLINE (July 28, 2015, 8:42 PM), www.spiegel.de/netzwelt/netzpolitik/face book-hamburger-datenschuetzer-fordert-recht-auf-pseudonyme-a-1045739.html; *Facebook in Germany Privacy Battle over Users' Fake Names*, BBC (July 29, 2015), www.bbc .com/news/technology-33702674.

the ability to construct a professional identity while protecting other portions of their lives.[131]

3 Sanction

Some individuals do not care about others, or they even enjoy seeing them in trouble. Happily, in those populations that have been rigorously tested, they are not in the majority.[132] But for those in the population who remain indifferent to the costs of their behavior to others, identification and communication open up the possibility of shaming.[133] Shaming is a social sanction, which is frequently used as a reaction to informational damage. Spread rumors about a sister-in-law and you can expect to be ostracized at family gatherings. Air dirty laundry on Facebook and expect to be de-friended.

Such commonsense intuitions are borne out in the public goods experimental literature. Studies repeatedly show that the availability of social sanctions is a very effective technology for securing the provision of a public good.[134] But sanctions often cost the sanctioning party.[135] Worse, if one person polices the environment, she bears the risk that others might pursue a vendetta against her.[136] Even if one considers the risk of gang-up or the costs of imposing sanctions to be small, most people find it unpleasant to assume the role of the cop. In the technical language of welfare economics: vigilance and sanctioning are contributions to a second order public good.[137] Yet the experimental evidence suggests that, from a policy perspective, one has to be much less

---

[131] *Facebook in Germany Privacy Battle over Users' Fake Names, supra* note 130.

[132] *See* Joseph Henrich & Robert Boyd, *"Economic Man" in Cross-Cultural Perspecvive*, 28 BEHAV. & BRAIN SCI. 795 (2005).

[133] William S. Neilson, *A Theory of Kindness, Reluctance, and Shame for Social Preferences*, 66 GAMES & ECON. BEHAV. 394 (2009).

[134] Ernst Fehr & Simon Gachter, *Cooperation and Punishment in Public Goods Experiments*, 90 AM. ECON. REV. 980 (2000); Ernst Fehr & Simon Gachter, *Altruistic Punishment in Humans*, 415 NATURE 137 (2002).

[135] *See* Martin Sefton *et al.*, *The Effects of Rewards and Sanctions in Provision of Public Goods*, 45 ECON. INQ. 671 (2007).

[136] *See* Nikos S. Nikiforakis, *Punishment and Counter-Punishment in Public Good Games: Can We Really Govern Ourselves?*, 92 J. PUB. ECON. 91 (2008); Nikos S. Nikiforakis & Dirk Engelmann, Feuds in the Laboratory? A Social Dilemma Experiment (U. of Melbourne Dep't of Econ., Research Paper 1058, 2008), http://fbe.unimelb.edu.au/__ data/assets/pdf_file/0006/802734/1058.pdf.

[137] Douglas D. Heckathorn, *Collective Action and the Second-Order Free-Rider Problem*, 1 RATION. & SOC'Y 78 (1989); Toshio Yamagishi, *The Provision of a Sanctioning System as a Public Good*, 51 J. PERS. & SOC. PSYCHOL. 110 (1986).

concerned about this second-order public good, compared with the original first-order public good. Society can rely on people being upset about others misbehaving, and trying to get them under control.

In principle, this is good news for the protection of privacy. Informal sanction and social ostracism for bad actors is the norm across many online platforms. Features of most platforms support some form of sanction, and the sanction also has the additional effect of limiting access to private information by the offender. If I act irresponsibly on a social network, for example, I will be de-friended and my access to information reserved for the in-group will be revoked. If I act irresponsibly on a discussion site by revealing the personal details of other posters, I will be banned. Yet sanction depends on repeat play and identification, discussed above. In order for a group to impose a sanction, they must know who has defected against group interest, and they must have a mechanism that can deter future defection. Future defection only matters if the member to be sanctioned is a member of a future potentially cooperative group that knows, and can in turn also sanction, the offender. Mediating the balance between sanction and privacy can be challenging, but there are already good solutions in place. Distributed database technology based on trustless public ledgers, such as that used by World Table or other distributed-ledger comment-curating systems, permit users to create persistent pseudonymous identities across multiple platforms: a worldwide online pseudonymous reputation. Once they do, the reputation of the pseudonym can serve as a sanctionable resource. Those with established reputations will be trusted. Those without will not, because they – like eBay sellers with no reputation ranking – will be perceived as attempting to avoid sanction.

4   Framing

Mathematically, public goods and public bads are identical.[138] We have found the public bad story convincing, since in a public bad game the cooperative decision is not to contribute to the public bad, just as with social media one strong cooperative decision is not to contribute data that bears on or concerns others. Yet it may be that psychologically speaking, conceiving of privacy as a public good could have a salutary effect on attempts to help groups control third-party generated

---

[138] *See* Andreoni, *supra* note 11.

information online.[139] In a highly cited experiment, James Andreoni demonstrated that framing impacts contributions to a public good, or, conversely, abstention from contributing to a public bad.[140] The pessimistic view of a public bad, or a "cold prickle" as Andreoni described it, seemed to encourage defection.[141] The optimistic view of a public good seemed to engender contribution to the public good, described by Andreoni as a "warm glow."[142] In short, even though the decision to contribute private information that impacts others may be most accurately described as a public bad, it may perhaps be usefully described to groups seeking to avoid the negative effects of this bad as a public good. In discussing the problem with the public, it may well be better to encourage social network participants to protect the privacy of other members of their social network than to avoid contributing to the pools of data that can have toxic effects on those members. The one construction may create a warm glow, while the other yields only a cold prickle.

The economic literature refers to such interventions as "valence framing": the structure of the interaction, or the payoffs, is represented in some alternative form. An even more subtle intervention is called "label framing."[143] Some cue evokes some context that, one has reason to believe, will change how individuals act. For instance, it has been shown that experimental participants are much more likely to cooperate in a dilemma game if this game is called a "community game," rather than a "Wall Street game."[144] Likewise, participants cooperate more if the situation is described as a "joint project" or "jointly protecting against danger," rather than "competition."[145]

Given this, it matters more than ever how society talks about privacy. If those seeking to jointly protect themselves against commercial and government exploiters of data do face a public goods problem, as this article has sought to demonstrate, it may help to name it as such. Too few seem to see their information-sharing behavior in that light. The experimental evidence suggests that it might be helpful just to let them know.

---

[139] *See* Woodrow Hartzog & Frederic Stutzman, *Obscurity by Design*, 88 Wash. L. Rev. 385, 417 (2013).

[140] *See id.*   [141] *See* Andreoni, *supra* note 11, at 13.   [142] *See id.*

[143] *See* Martin Dufwenberg et al., *The Framing of Games and the Psychology of Play*, 73 Games & Econ. Behav. 459 (2011).

[144] *See* Ross Lee & Andrew Ward, Naive Realism in Everyday Life. Implications for Social Conflict and Misunderstanding. Values and Knowledge (1996).

[145] Christoph Engel & David Rand, *What Does "Clean" Really Mean? The Implicit Framing of Decontextualized Experiments*, 122 Econ. Lett. 386 (2014).

Merely encouraging people to contribute to the public good of privacy may drive up investment in privacy-protecting behavior.

Conversely, if society continues to debate privacy in purely individualistic terms, as it has largely done until this point, then the experimental evidence indicates that the individual focus will lead to the underprovision of privacy. An "every person for herself" mentality will predominate, reducing cooperative behavior. Worse, as individuals fail in the face of the social dilemma, they will be individually blamed. Under the individual privacy narrative, people who do not benefit from privacy must not be trying hard enough. This chapter has taken an initial step toward countering this narrative, by naming the dilemma of privacy for what it is, and by encouraging a positive framing for a longstanding conundrum of social interaction: privacy is a public good.

E   Conclusion

The current focus on privacy individualism has left a large gap in theory. The focus on empowering individuals has induced policymakers to overlook important tools for protecting privacy. The relevant privacy unit is the group, rather than the individual. Social dilemmas pit individuals against each other, and individual incentives cut against group welfare. In many ways, the more educated and empowered individuals are, the worse the social dilemma becomes for the group.

The public goods model has a broad range of tools suggested by the theoretical and experimental economic literatures that have gone underexplored thus far in the privacy debate. Policymakers should consider the size, composition, and cohesion of online groups when they attempt to create an environment conducive to privacy protection. Tools should not be centered on individual rights of review and deletion, which have proven largely ineffective. Rather, tools should focus on group communication, sanction, and fostering a sense of repeat play and community. Even the way that we speak about the nature of the problem can have an impact on whether people cooperate to produce the public good of privacy.

The problem of privacy among and within the transatlantic privacy cultures is, we believe, not one of differing governance, at least in this instance. Rather, transatlantic privacy cultures share a commitment to the individual as the source and sovereign of private information. When individualism fails, each transatlantic privacy paradigm fails. We believe one reason that treating privacy as a private good fails is that privacy is a social dilemma: we do not adequately account for what we reveal about one another. This social dilemma causes consumers to fail to protect the personal information of those in their networks. That failure is exploited by companies. Those companies pass that information along to governments.

To address consumer protection issues such as the one we raise here is to set fire to the surveillance state's feet of clay. Governments simply do not have the ability to raise the kind of taxes needed to rival the commercial apparatus of surveillance. They can barely build the facilities needed to tap the commercial Panopticon.[146] If we are to turn off the tap of government surveillance, then we will have to do so at the source: commercial information. There are many reforms needed. But one of the most basic is that we must recognize the group nature of the problem.

---

[146] *See* Chapter 1 in this volume.

4

The Right to Data Protection

A No-Right Thesis

BY RALF POSCHER

A   Introduction

For advocates of data protection worldwide, the revelations in the context of the NSA-Affair must seem like nightmares of total surveillance come true. But with regard to the legal remedies to protect personal data against state collections, the situation on both sides of the Atlantic could hardly be more different. Whereas American advocates of data protection have to struggle for every specific data protection regulation, like the USA FREEDOM Act,[1] in Europe the general right to data protection is recognized as a fundamental right. For American advocates of stronger data protection rights, Europe (and especially Germany) must seem like the Promised Land.

In 1983, drawing on the Basic Law's protection of personal liberty and human dignity,[2] the German Federal Constitutional Court announced a right to informational self-determination – as the right to data protection is named and framed under the German constitution.[3] This right has had an astonishing career: numerous laws have been tailored to meet its demands. It provides the basis for contemporary general data protection codes.[4] It also has been woven into the fabric of many administrative regulations – such as the different German police codes – in which now almost the majority of rules are concerned with data protection issues.[5]

---

[1] USA FREEDOM Act of 2015, H.R. 2048, 114th Cong. (2015).

[2] GRUNDGESETZ [GG][BASIC LAW], art. 2., *translation* at http://www.gesetze-im-internet .de/englisch_gg/index.html.

[3] BVerfG 1 BvR 209/83, Dec. 15, 1983, ¶¶ 41–43, http://dejure.org/dienste/vernetzung/ rechtsprechung?Text=1%20BvR%20209/83.

[4] *See, e.g.,* Bundesdatenschutzgesetz (BDSG) (Federal Data Protection Code), Jan. 14, 2003, BGBl. I, at 66 (Ger.).

[5] *See, e.g.,* Polizeigesetz (PolG) (Police Code of the State of Baden-Württemberg), Jan. 13, 1992, §§ 19–25, 37–48a, GESETZESBLATT [GBL.] [LAW GAZETTE] 1992, 1 (Ger.); Gesetz

Dozens of Federal Constitutional Court decisions have invoked the right,[6] especially in the area of national security legislation.[7] The Constitutional Court has used the right to curb or even invalidate laws designing new data collection and storage initiatives.[8]

Across Europe the protection of personal data is accepted as an offspring of the right to privacy provided by the European Convention on Human Rights.[9] The European Court for Human Rights has issued a number of decisions controlling and curbing national data collection efforts.[10] In its sphere, the Court of Justice of the European Union acknowledged a right to the protection of personal data even before the Charter of Fundamental Rights of the European Union came into force.[11] The Charter, which entered into force following the ratification of the Treaty of Lisbon in 2009, made the right to data protection an explicitly guaranteed right of European primary law. Article 8 § 1 of the Charter of

über die Aufgaben und Befugnisse der Bayerischen Staatlichen Polizei [Polizeiaufgaben-gesetz – PAG] [Police Mission Code of the state of Bavaria], Sept. 14, 1990, arts. 30–49, GESETZ- UND VERORDNUNGSBLATT [GVBL.] [LAW GAZETTE] 1990, 397 (Ger.); Polizei-gesetz des Landes Nordrhein-Westfalen [PolG NRW] [Police Code of the state of North Rhine-Westphalia], July 25, 2003, §§ 11–33, GESETZ UND VERORDNUNGSBLATT [GV. NRW.] [LAW GAZETTE] 2003, 441 (Ger.).

[6] See, e.g., BVerfG, 1 BvR 239/90, June 11, 1991, http://dejure.org/dienste/vernetzung/rechtsprechung?Text=BverfG%2084,%20192; BVerfG, 1 BvR 1564/92, Mar. 7, 1995, http://www.servat.unibe.ch/dfr/bv092191.html; BVerfG, 1 BvR 2111/94, July 8, 1997, http://www.servat.unibe.ch/dfr/bv096171.html; BVerfG 118, 168; BVerfG 120, 351; BVerfG, 1 BvR 2074/05, Mar. 11, 2008, http://www.servat.unibe.ch/dfr/bv120378.html.

[7] See, e.g., BVerfG, 1 BvR 518/02, Apr. 4, 2006, http://www.servat.unibe.ch/dfr/bv115320.html; BVerfG, 1 BvR 370, 595/07, Feb. 27, 2008; BVerfG, 1 BvR 1215/07, Apr. 24, 2013, http://www.servat.unibe.ch/dfr/bv133277.html.

[8] See, e.g., BVerfG, 1 BvR 518/02, Apr. 4, 2006, http://www.servat.unibe.ch/dfr/bv115320.html; BVerfG, 1 BvR 2074/05, Mar. 11, 2008, http://www.servat.unibe.ch/dfr/bv120378.html; BVerfG, 1 BvR 1215/07, Apr. 24, 2013, http://www.servat.unibe.ch/dfr/bv133277.html; MARION ALBERS, INFORMATIONELLE SELBSTBESTIMMUNG (2005); Gabriele Britz, Informationelle Selbstbestimmung zwischen rechtswissenschaftlicher Grundsatzkritik und Beharren des Bundesverfassungsgerichts, in OFFENE RECHTSWISSENSCHAFT 561 (Wolfgang Hoffmann-Riem ed., 2010); Wolfgang Hoffmann-Riem, Informationelle Selbstbestimmung als Grundrecht kommunikativer Entfaltung, in "DER NEUE DATENSCHUTZ". DATENSCHUTZ IN DER INFORMATIONSGESELLSCHAFT VON MORGEN 11 (Helmut Bäumler ed., 1998).

[9] Art. 8 of European Convention for the Protection of Human Rights and Fundamental Freedoms, as amended by Protocols Nos. 11 and 14 (1950) [hereinafter ECHR].

[10] See, e.g., Leander v. Sweden, App. No. 9248/81, Eur. Ct. H.R. (Ser. A) at 116–6 (1987); Rotaru v. Romania, App. No. 28341/95 Eur. Ct. H.R.(2000); Weber & Saravia v. Germany, App, No. 54934/00, Eur. Ct. H.R. (2006).

[11] Case C-275/06, Promusicae v. Telefónica de España, 2008 E.C.R. I-271, § 63; Case 553/07, College van Burgemeester en Wethouders van Rotterdam v. Rijkeboer, 2009 E.C.R. I-3889, § 46, §§ 48–49.

Fundamental Rights of the European Union reads: "Everyone has the right to the protection of personal data concerning him or her." Recently, the Court of Justice of the European Union issued rulings on the Data Retention Directive,[12] the so-called "right to be forgotten,"[13] and the safe harbor treaty between the European Union and the United States.[14] These decisions, relying on Article 8, made strenuous and strict demands for data privacy.

From a perspective outside Europe it must seem that data protection is well established as a specific fundamental right in Germany and Europe.

B The Issue of Substance

A closer look, however, reveals that Europe is still not at ease with the right to data protection. Above all, it is not clear what the right to data protection is actually about. What, as a substantive matter, does the right actually protect? Fundamental rights usually protect a general or specific liberty or equality interest.[15] But what, specifically, should that be in the case of the right to data protection? This is a question that has haunted the right to data protection since its origins and has been at the center of a more recent wave of criticism leveled against the right, especially in Germany.[16] The critics challenge the conception of the right to data

---

[12] Joined Cases C-293/12 & C-594/12, Digital Rights Ireland v. Minister for Commc'n, Marine and Nat. Res. and others and Kärntner Landesregierung and others v. Seitlinger and others. *See* Chapter 21 in this volume.

[13] Case C-131/12, *Google Spain and Google v. AEPD and Costeja González*. See Chapters 22, 16, 11, and 20 in this volume.

[14] Case C-362/14, Schrems v. Data Protection Commissioner, 2015.

[15] Think of, for example, the right to marriage. *See* Loving v. Virginia, 388 U.S. 1, 12 (1967); Obergefell v. Hodges, 135 S. Ct. 1732 (2015). *See also* Dworkin, *Taking Rights Seriously*, 5ᵀᴴ Impr. 184–206, 266–78 (1987).

[16] Marion Albers, *Zur Neukonzeption des grundrechtlichen "Daten"schutzes*, in Herausforderungen an das Recht der Informationsgesellschaft 113 (Andreas Haratsch *et al.* eds., 1996); Albers, *Informationen als neue Dimension im Recht*, 33 Rechtstheorie (RTh) 61 (2002); Albers, *supra* note 8; Albers, *Umgang mit Personenbezogenen Informationen und Daten*, in 2 Grundlagen des Verwaltungsrechts, No. 107 (Wolfgang Hoffmann-Riem, Eberhard Schmidt-Aßmann & Andreas Vosskuhle eds., 2d ed., 2012); Britz, *supra* note 8; Hans Peter Bull, *Zweifelsfragen um die informationelle Selbstbestimmung – Datenschutz als Datenaskese*, 59 Neue Juristische Wochenschrift (NJW) 1617 (2006); Bull, *Informationsrecht ohne Informationskultur?*, 24 Recht der Datenverarbeitung (RDV) 47 (2008); Bull, Informationelle Selbstbestimmung – Vision oder Illusion? (2d ed., 2011); McKay Cunningham, *Next Generation Privacy: The Internet of Things, Data Exhaust, and Reforming Regulation by Risk of Harm*, 2 (2) Groningen Journal of International Law (GroJIL) 115 (2014); Wolfgang Hoffmann-Riem,

protection, especially in the light of the ever faster-developing electronic hyper-connectedness in a world of ubiquitous computers, sensors, virtual worlds and the Internet of things. These developments were neither anticipated nor do they seem to be properly reflected in contemporary data protection conceptions.

In the early stages of its data protection jurisprudence, the German Federal Constitutional Court seemed to have linked the idea with a kind of property rights conception of personal data.[17] The Court explained that the individual has a "right to determine himself, when and in which boundaries personal data is disseminated."[18] This was something like an owner's right to determine herself when she allows someone to use her property. The property approach to data protection has been much ridiculed as naïve in our contemporary technologically interconnected and socially networked reality, in which a vast spectrum of personal data is disseminated and exchanged at all levels almost all of the time.[19] Data simply does not possess the kind of exclusivity that would justify drawing a parallel with property ownership.[20] The Constitutional Court seems to have recognized this. It has not explicitly revoked the formula, but it has

---

Informationelle Selbstbestimmung in der Informationsgesellschaft. Auf dem Wege zu einem Neuen Konzept des Datenschutzes, 123 ARCHIV DES ÖFFENTLICHEN RECHTS (AöR) 513 (1998); Hoffmann-Riem, *supra* note 8; Michael Kloepfer, *Geben moderne Technologien und die europäische Integration Anlaß, Notwendigkeit und Grenzen des Schutzes personenbezogener Informationen neu zu bestimmen?*, *in* 1 VERHANDLUNGEN DES ZWEIUND-SECHZIGSTEN DEUTSCHEN JURISTENTAGS, No. 66, 81–82 (1998); Karl-Heinz Ladeur, *Datenschutz – Vom Abwehrrecht zur Planerischen Optimierung von Wissensnetzwerken*, 24 DATENSCHUTZ UND DATENSICHERHEIT (DuD) 12 (2000); Ladeur, *Das Recht auf informationelle Selbstbestimmung: Eine Juristische Fehlkonstruktion?*, 62 DIE ÖFFENTLICHE VERWALTUNG (DÖV) 45 (2009); Rainer Pitschas, *Informationelle Selbstbestimmung Zwischen Digitaler Ökonomie und Internet*, 22 DuD 139, 146 (1998); Hans-Heinrich Trute, *Der Schutz Personenbezogener Information in der Informationsgesellschaft*, 53 JURISTENZEITUNG (JZ) 822, 824–29 (1998); Trute, *Verfassungsrechtliche Grundlagen*, *in* HANDBUCH DATENSCHUTZRECHT 156, ¶ 11, ¶¶ 21–24 (Alexander Roßnagel ed., 2003).

[17] There is a certain parallel between this conceptualization of the right to privacy and its scope under the U.S. Supreme Court's early Fourth Amendment jurisprudence. The Supreme Court, until Katz v. U.S. (1967), applied the Fourth Amendment only to searches and seizure of a citizen's personal property and effects. *See, e.g.*, Olmstead v. United States, 277 U.S. 438 (1928). Privacy in this era was tied in substance to a property right.

[18] BVerfG, 1 BvR 209/83, Dec. 15, 1983, http://www.servat.unibe.ch/dfr/bv065001.html ("Befugnis des Einzelnen, grundsätzlich selbst zu entscheiden, wann und innerhalb welcher Grenzen persönliche Lebenssachverhalte offenbart werden.").

[19] Albers, *supra* note 16, at 81; Ladeur, *supra* note 16, at 46–47.

[20] *See* Chapter 3 in this volume.

made decreasing use of it and makes no reference to it all in more recent decisions on the subject.[21] Thus, reviving the critique of the Constitutional Court's early property conceptualization of data protection is beside the point. But even if everybody can agree that the right to data protection is not akin to a property interest in one's personal data, the question nevertheless remains what specifically the right to data protection is. What kind of right is it and what is the specific liberty interest it protects?

The answer to this question is especially important in the context of this book's engagement with transatlantic differences relating to privacy and intelligence gathering. If Europeans do not really know what they are talking about when they invoke the right to informational self-determination, then it will remain difficult to communicate about these issues with their partners who come from different legal traditions and, thus, have different conceptions of data protection and privacy.[22]

My answer to this question is that the right to data protection is not a specific right at all. Rather, it is a systematic modal enhancement of potentially every other fundamental right. On these terms, the right to data protection is not a fundamental right with equal standing alongside the others in the canon. Instead, it is a modification of other already existing fundamental rights. The "data protection modification" would be an enhancement in that fundamental rights usually only protect against actual infringements of or at least concrete risks of the violation of liberty or equality interest, whereas the right to data protection enhances those rights by providing a preemptive protection against abstract dangers that accompany the collection, storage, and processing of personal data.[23] Despite appearances, Article 8 of the Charter of Fundamental Rights of the European Union is not an independent fundamental right, but a systematic enhancement of potentially every other fundamental right guaranteed in the Charter. Data protection would thus also be an issue distinct from traditional conceptions of privacy, like the privacy of the home or of mail and telecommunication. Data protection also concerns privacy, but not every privacy issue is also

---

[21] *See, e.g.,* BVerfG, 1 BvR 233833/03, 360, Mar. 10, 2008, https://dejure.org/dienste/vernet zung/rechtsprechung?Text=BverfG%20120,%20351; BVerfG, 1 BvR 2074/05, 397–98, Mar. 11, 2008, http://www.servat.unibe.ch/dfr/bv120378.html.

[22] *See* Chapters 2 and 6 in this volume.

[23] *See* Orla Lynskey, *Deconstructing Data Protection*, 63 INT. COMP. L.Q. 569 (2014) (Highlighting, the "protective" character of the right to data protection.).

an issue of data protection. The body scanner that shows the image of the person naked is a traditional issue of privacy, which protects against infringements on zones of shame and guarantees a right to be let alone, but not an issue of data protection. An issue of data protection, however, would be the storage of the scanner's raw data, which bears the abstract danger of access to images of the naked body and thus the abstract danger of a traditional infringement of privacy. Data protection enhances potentially every fundamental right, including the right to privacy.

First, I will present some phenomenological evidence that justifies this "no-right" characterization of data protection. Second, I will explain what the specific enhancement is about and what makes it so specific. I will conclude with some remarks about how my thesis might contribute to the understanding of the transatlantic legal cultural divide concerning data protection and how such a conception might help to mitigate the turbulence that arose in the shadow of the NSA-Affair.

C The Evidence

A number of factors provide evidence for the thesis that data protection is not an independent fundamental right. To begin, one can point to the principle's origin in the jurisprudence of the German Federal Constitutional Court. The Court has always associated data protection with the general fundamental right to personal freedom and it is largely presented as a spinoff of that right.[24] The Court, however, has also associated data protection with other constitutional rights, such as the freedom of assembly.[25] Significantly, the Federal Constitutional Court regards the collection of personal data in the context of assemblies as an infringement of the right to assembly in Article 8 of the Basic Law and not as an infringement of the general right to personal freedom.[26] Further evidence is provided by the fact that the Court liberally extends the right to data protection to corporate bodies,[27] even though it is very reluctant to extend the right to personal freedom (with a partial basis in the guarantee

---

[24] BVerfG, 1 BvL 19/63, 6–8, July 16, 1969, http://www.servat.unibe.ch/dfr/bv027001.html; BVerfG, 1 BvR 209/83, 41–5, Dec. 15, 1983, http://www.servat.unibe.ch/dfr/bv065001.html.

[25] BVerfG, 1 BvR 209/83, 43, Dec. 15, 1983, http://www.servat.unibe.ch/dfr/bv065001.html.

[26] BVerfG 68, 315, 349; BVerfG, 1 BvR 2492/08, 368–70, Feb. 17, 2009, http://www.servat .unibe.ch/dfr/bv122342.html.

[27] BVerfG, 60 NJW 2464, 2471 (2007); BVerfG, 67 NJW 1581 (2014).

of human dignity) to legal persons.[28] The right to data protection does not seem so closely connected to the right of personal freedom that it cannot be extended beyond its scope.

The conjoined presentation of data protection and another, underlying right has also been the case in the European jurisprudence.[29,30,31] Data protection is guaranteed in a special article of the Charter of Fundamental Rights. Still, the Court of Justice of the European Union almost never cites Article 8 of the Charter as an independent right.[32] The Court usually invokes Article 8 only in conjunction with the right to privacy secured by Article 7.[33]

Data protection does not seem to stand on its own feet in the jurisprudence of the Court of Justice of the European Union. Instead, the interest in data protection needs another right to support it. Even more in line with the no-right thesis are hints in recent decisions of the Court of Justice of the European Union that data protection might be associated with other rights, such as the freedom of expression.[34] Thus, even when data protection is codified as an explicit, independent fundamental right (as it is in the Charter), it is nevertheless regarded as an accessory to other, more traditional fundamental rights.

Daniel Solove's nearly exhaustive list of harms that might be caused by the collection, storage, and processing of personal data provides further evidence for the no-right thesis. In his wonderful article, "Nothing to Hide," Solove cites more than a dozen affronts that might be caused by data collection.[35] They include the loss of life and liberty,

---

[28] BVerfG, 58 NJW 883 (2005); BVerfG, 67 NJW 1581 (2014). On the general inapplicability of the guarantee of human dignity to legal persons, *see* BVerfG, 1 BvR 2172/96, 242, Feb. 26, 1997, http://www.servat.unibe.ch/dfr/bv095220.html.

[29] Leander v. Sweden, Eur. Ct. H.R. ¶ 48.

[30] Rotaru v. Romania, Eur. Ct. H.R., ¶¶ 42–46; Weber & Saravia v. Germany, Eur. Ct. H.R. ¶¶ 143–44; Uzun v. Germany, Eur. Ct. H.R., ¶¶ 44–48.

[31] Weber & Saravia v. Germany, Eur. Ct. H.R. ¶¶ 145–46.

[32] Case C-543/09, Deutsche Telekom v. Germany, 2011 E.C.R. I-3441, ¶¶ 49–53, 66; Case C-70/10, Scarlet v. SABAM, 2011 E.C.R. I-11959, ¶ 50.

[33] Joined Cases C-92/09 & C-93/09, Schecke and Eifert v. Hesse, 2010 E.C.R. I-11063, ¶¶ 47, 52; Joined Cases C-293/12 & C-594/12, *Digital* Rights Ireland v. Minister for Commc'n, Marine and Nat. Res. and others and Kärntner Landesregierung and others v. Seitlinger and others, 2014 E.C.R. I-238, ¶¶ 53, 60, 65.

[34] Joined Cases C-293/12 & C-594/12, Digital Rights Ireland v. Minister for Commc'n, Marine and Nat. Res. and others and Kärntner Landesregierung and others v. Seitlinger and others, ¶ 28.

[35] Daniel J. Solove, *"I've Got Nothing to Hide" and Other Misunderstandings of Privacy*, 44 SAN DIEGO L. REV. 745 (2007).

infringements on property interests and on the freedom of expression, violations of privacy, and denials of due process guarantees. Solove's list suggests that the essence of data protection cannot be pinned down to just a single liberty or equality interest. Instead, it potentially involves many protected interests.

An approach that regards data protection as a mere modulation of other fundamental rights could also explain why it is usually associated with a *general* liberty or privacy right. *General* liberty and privacy rights serve a kind of subsidiary function in the context of data collection. Often, a measure does not have an impact on any more specific liberty or equality interest or such an impact cannot be foreseen at the time the measure is taken. Thus, the potential harm that might be caused by the data collection often will be foreseeable only for a general liberty and equality interest. Thus, it is no accident that data protection is often connected to rights that protect such general liberty and equality interests, such as the right to personal freedom in the German constitution, the right to privacy in the Charter of Fundamental Rights of the European Union, or the right to respect for the privacy of the home and family life in the European Convention on Human Rights. But the relation between data protection and these more general rights is subsidiary and not exclusive.

D   The Characteristics the Data Protection Enhancement of Fundamental Rights

If the idea that data protection is not a fundamental right on its own but a systematic enhancement of other fundamental rights has gained some plausibility, then the crucial question is what kind of enhancement it provides. Fundamental rights usually protect against actual infringements. For example, the State encroaches upon your right of personal freedom if you are incarcerated; or your right to freely assemble is infringed when your meeting is prohibited or dispersed by the police; or your freedom of expression is violated when you are prevented from expressing your political views. In some cases your fundamental rights might be involved when there is a concrete danger that such infringements are about to happen.[36] What is unique about data protection,

---

[36] *See* BVerfG, 2 BvR 1060/78, June 19, 1979, www.servat.unibe.ch/dfr/bv051324.html, where the Court saw it as an infringement of the right to physical integrity to proceed with a criminal trial if the defendant runs the risk to suffer a heart attack during the trial.

however, is its preemptive character that protects not only against concrete but also abstract dangers that are involved with the collection and storage of personal data. Data protection preemptively protects against violations of liberty or equality interests that are potentially connected to the *use* of collected and stored personal data.[37]

The collection of data as such does no harm. This has often been expressed with the idea that data has to become information in certain contexts before it can prove its relevance.[38] It is only the use of data in certain contexts that might cause a violation of liberty or equality interests. The collection of personal data about political or religious convictions of citizens by the state is generally prohibited, for example, because of the potential that it could be misused by the state to discriminate against certain political or religious groups. Data protection demands a justification for the collection of personal data even if such misuse is only an abstract danger.[39] It does not require concrete evidence that misuse of the data has taken place, or even that such a misuse is about to occur.

If data protection is essentially about abstract dangers, then it is clear how we must look at data protection issues. They have to be evaluated against the background of the question: To what extent does a certain form of data collection pose an abstract danger for the exercise of what kind of fundamental right? To look at data collection issues in this way raises a few important implications.

See also BVerfG, 1 BvR 542/62, July 25, 1963, www.servat.unibe.ch/dfr/bv017108.html (life-threatening brain surgery with the aim to determine criminal accountability); BVerfG , 1 BvR 614/79, 220, Oct. 3, 1979, http://dejure.org/dienste/vernetzung/rechtspre chung?Text=BverfG%2052,%20214 (eviction of a suicidal tenant) and RALF POSCHER, GRUNDRECHTE ALS ABWEHRRECHTE 388–90 (2003).

[37] See, e.g., the collection of comprehensive data in the course of a nation-wide census is not in itself an imminent threat, but is dangerous because of the potential (mis-)use of the masses of the gathered mass data. See BVerfG, 1 BvR 209, Dec. 15, 1983, http://www.servat .unibe.ch/dfr/bv065001.html. The collection of data for an anti-terrorism or anti-Nazism database is problematic because of *potential* negative impacts for those mentioned in it. See BVerfG, 1 BvR 1215/07, Apr. 24, 2013, http://www.servat.unibe.ch/dfr/bv133277.html.

[38] Albers, *Neukonzeption, supra* note 16, at 121–23, 131–33; Albers, *supra* note 16, at 75; Albers, *supra* note 8, at 87–148; Albers, *Umgang, supra* note 16, at 7–28; Britz, *supra* note 8, at 566–68.

[39] See, e.g., the examples mentioned in note 37. This preemptive protection against state action is not to be confused with the duties to protect against *unlawful* infringements of liberty interests by *third parties*. See Poscher, *supra* note 36, at 380-7 (on the duty to protect under the German basic law). As far as such duties to protect are accepted, data protection would also address preemptive dimensions of these duties.

First, it implies a more systematic perspective on data collection measures. On the one hand, it gives us some perspective on the ever-more absurd idea that each and every act of data processing constitutes an infringement of a fundamental right. Otherwise, it would have to be accepted that modern data-processing chips perform millions, if not billions, of fundamental right infringements in just fractions of seconds. But, if data protection is understood as protection against abstract dangers, then we do not have to look at the individual acts of data processing. Instead, we can concentrate on the whole data-processing system and its context to evaluate the abstract danger it poses. Factors that can lower the abstract threat connected with the processing of personal data are the transparency and reliability of the data-processing systems, the level of independent oversight, the accountability of the operating officials, and other design features that aim at securing individual privacy. Whether or not – and to which degree – such measures are implemented thus has a direct impact on the legal evaluation of data-collection measures. On the other hand, it is important to determine the quantity and quality of the abstract danger connected with a data-collection measure. In the first instance, data collection measures can be designed in a way that any specific abstract danger can be eliminated. Body scanners, for example, can be designed and programmed so that the raw data gets deleted as soon as an avatar displaying a positive or negative signal is generated. With the deletion of the data, no abstract danger connected to the raw data collection remains. The scanning itself, and any follow-up measures like body searches, do not concern data protection. Instead, they concern traditional aspects of traditional rights such as the right to privacy or equality if, for example, physical disabilities are detected and become the basis for discriminatory treatment. But these rights-infringing actions no longer have anything to do with data protection.

Second, an abstract danger of data collection can only be relevant if it surpasses the general risk level of data dissemination. This might explain, for example, why the German Federal Constitutional Court does not see an infringement of data protection if the government seeks access to information about a citizen that is otherwise publicly available in the Internet.[40] Data is accessed, collected, and even stored. It does not, however, pose a danger that exceeds the general risk level that is

---

[40] BVerfG, 1 BvR 370/07, Feb. 27, 2008, www.servat.unibe.ch/dfr/bv120274.html.

connected with publically available data on the Internet. If, however, the state systematically gathers the publicly available data and employs inferential big-data technologies to predict habits, attitudes, or even behavior of its citizens, then the general risk level would be exceeded.

Third, the intensity of the data collection measure must be evaluated only if the abstract danger surpasses such a threshold. Here again, it is not so much the individual datum or the individual data collection measure that is of concern. Instead, the concern is focused on the system into which the personal data is entered and the systematic protections that the system provides.

E   The Comparative Uptake

The preemptive and accessory character of the right to informational self-determination might help to contribute to a better understanding of the transatlantic differences about data protection standards. First, the general preemptive character of the right to data protection runs counter to the American legal culture and political tradition. Anglo-American pragmatism informs a legal culture that is less oriented toward systematic preemption. Instead, in keeping with the common law tradition, American law develops in response to distinct, actual cases.[41] The common law does not try to regulate potential problems. Rather, problems are addressed by the law when they actually arise. A systematic preemptive right to data protection, which provides protection against mere potential harm, does not fit easily with this legal tradition. Accordingly, American data protection law is also more pragmatic and less conceptually broad. It is oriented toward responding to specific misuses of personal information, but does not provide a general legal protection against mere potential threats.[42]

This is reflected, for example, in the curious fact that the idea of "chilling effects" was first developed in American free speech cases[43] and picked up

---

[41] See H. PATRICK GLENN, LEGAL TRADITIONS OF THE WORLD 241 passim (5th ed. 2014).

[42] For the U.S approach, see Patricia L. Bellia, Federalization in Information Privacy Law, 118 YALE L.J. 868 (2008); Leslie Francis, Privacy and Health Information: The United States and the European Union, 103 KY. L.J. 419, 428–31 (2014–2015). With regard to the fragmented character of U.S. data protection law, it has even been claimed that "privacy is on its deathbed in America." See Stephanie Segovia, Privacy: An Issue of Priority, 11 HASTINGS BUS. L.J. 193, 200 (2015).

[43] For the origins of the U.S. Supreme Court's argumentative use of "chilling effects," see Wieman v. Updegraff, 344 U.S. 183, 195 (1952) (Frankfurter, J., concurring); Walker v.

much later in German constitutional law to establish the right to data protection,[44] which gives chilling effects a broader systematic importance.[45] And there are obvious differences in the collective political experiences of many European countries and the United States that support the more cautious European approach. Most prominent is the experience of a – or as in the German case two – totalitarian regimes, which subdued their population not least by means of personal data collection. This explains the sensitivity with regard to personal data in many European countries.

A second point has been raised by James Whitman, who highlights the fact that personal dignity and reputation play a much more important role in many continental legal systems.[46] Similarly, Susanne Baer has characterized the difference between the U.S. and the German constitutional systems as one between a system based on equality, on the one hand, and dignity, on the other hand.[47] Both studies show a stronger focus on the protection of personal dignity and reputation in at least some European legal systems. Since the general liberty and privacy rights that form the subsidiary base of the right to data protection are interpreted very much in the light of the dignity component, it is not surprising that the structural modification as well as the material liberty interest on which data protection depends are less well developed in the American legal culture. The root foundations of the no-right thesis helps shed light on the structural and material reasons for the transatlantic differences on the issue of data protection.

F   An Outlook

Whatever other cultural, legal, and political differences are in play, further discussions should take these differences into account. For a transatlantic dialogue and cooperation on data exchange, the sketched

---

City of Birmingham, 388 U.S. 307, 345 (1967) (Brennan, J., dissenting). In Lamont v. Postmaster General, 381 U.S. 301, 307 (1965), the Court relies on the same idea when it invokes the notion of "deterring effects."

[44] BVerfG, 1 BvR 209, 43, Dec. 15, 1983, www.servat.unibe.ch/dfr/bv065001.html;3.

[45] See, e.g., BVerfG, 1 BvF 1/84, 183, Nov. 4, 1986, www.servat.unibe.ch/dfr/bv073118.html; BVerfG, 1 BvR 2378/98, 354, www.servat.unibe.ch/dfr/bv109279.html, and the denial of standing in Laird v. Tatum, 408 U.S. 1, 13 (1972).

[46] James Q. Whitman, *The Two Western Cultures of Privacy: Dignity Versus Liberty*, 113 YALE L.J. 1151 (2004).

[47] SUSANNE BAER, WÜRDE ODER GLEICHHEIT? ZUR ANGEMESSENEN GRUNDRECHTLICHEN KONZEPTION VON RECHT GEGEN DISKRIMINIERUNG AM BEISPIEL SEXUELLER BELÄSTIGUNG AM ARBEITSPLATZ IN DER BUNDESREPUBLIK DEUTSCHLAND UND DEN USA 159–220 (1995). *See* Chapter 2 in this volume.

no-right conception of data protection might prove more flexible than the alternatives. First, it would advise against overly broad approaches to the topic. Europe will not convince the United States to adopt a general preemptive right to data protection and the United States cannot force Europe to give up on the idea. Realizing that the right to data protection is about abstract dangers for diverse liberty or equality interests would recommend a piecemeal approach,[48] which first identifies the specific liberty and equality interests that are in play in a certain area of data exchange in order to specify what interests are really at stake. The exchange of passenger data, for example, might raise specific worries with regard to no-fly lists, which might be mitigated by more transparency, oversight, and the institutionalization of reliable corrective procedures as part of the data-exchange treaties.[49]

The more systemic, no-right approach to data protection implies developing systemic risk reduction strategies tailored to the material interests involved in a specific area, selecting from a wide array of instruments: implementation of privacy enhancing technologies,[50] independent monitoring mechanisms, minimization of data collection and data storage tailored to the specific aims, and serious material thresholds for the use of data. The assessment of the abstract dangers involved could also take into account the fact that, at least in some areas, the potential for harm has to be evaluated differently if the data is collected by a foreign government with at least less legal and factual power over the individuals involved. Besides risk-reduction strategies addressing the design of data collection systems, the transparency of the systems could reduce the objective dangers involved as well as contribute to distinctions between subjective fears and objective dangers of importance to the fundamental rights analysis. Additionally, transparency produces the surplus benefit of building mutual trust. Following an approach along these lines should make it possible to find a compromise, at least in some of the areas concerned that reduces the abstract dangers of data collection and storage to a level acceptable to both sides. Such a piecemeal approach would not deliver an all-encompassing solution that cuts through the knot, but it could provide real progress in transatlantic relations in the shadow of the NSA-Affair.

---

[48] Cunningham, *supra* note 11, at 141–44.
[49] Agreement Between the United States of America and the European Union on the Use and Transfer of Passenger Name Records to the United States Department of Homeland Security, Dec. 14, 2011, 2012 O.J. (L 215) 5.
[50] See Chapter 3 in this volume.

PART TWO

Framing the Transatlantic Debate

PART TWO

5

Privacy, *Rechtsstaatlichkeit*, and the Legal Limits on Extraterritorial Surveillance

BY ANNE PETERS

A Introduction

In early 2015, both the UN General Assembly and the UN Human Rights Council issued resolutions on "The Right to Privacy in the Digital Age," in which each body "affirms that the same rights that people have offline must also be protected online, including the right to privacy."[1] Both resolutions welcome the 2014 report by the High Commissioner for Human Rights on the same topic.[2] The General Asssembly explicitly "calls upon all States: (a) To respect and protect the right to privacy, including in the context of digital communication and (b) To take measures to put an end to violations of those rights and to create the conditions to prevent such violations, including by ensuring that relevant national legislation complies with their obligations under international human rights law."[3]

Already in 2013, the UN General Assembly had approved a relevant resolution.[4] In both General Assembly Resolutions the Assembly

---

[1] G.A. Res. 69/166, ¶ 3, The Right to Privacy in the Digital Age (Dec. 18, 2014). Identical wording in Human Rights Council, U.N. Doc. A/HRC/28/L.27 ¶ 3, The Right to Privacy in the Digital Age (Mar. 24, 2015).

[2] Human Rights Council, U.N. Doc. A/HRC/27/37, ¶ 20, The Right to Privacy in the Digital Age: Report of the Office of the High Commissioner for Human Rights (June 30, 2014).

[3] G.A. Res. 69/166, *supra* note 1, at ¶ 4.

[4] G.A. Res. 68/167 (Dec. 18, 2013). The resolution was sponsored by Brazil and Germany. The resolution reaffirms the human right to privacy. It calls upon states to take measures to put an end to violations of these rights, G. A. Res. 68/167, ¶ 4(b); calls upon states to review their procedures, practices and legislation concerning the extra-territorial surveillance of private communications, G.A. Res. 68/167, ¶ 4(b); and it also calls upon states to establish independent oversight mechanisms capable to ensure transparency and accountability of state surveillance of communications, G.A. Res. 68/167, ¶ 4(d). Although the draft resolution did not mention the United States or the National Security Agency (NSA), it was evidently a reaction to the NSA's surveillance activities in countries around the world. Those activities had been exposed by former NSA contractor Edward Snowden only a few months earlier.

expressed its deep concern for "the negative impact that surveillance and/
or interception of communications ... may have on the exercise and
enjoyment of human rights."[5] The two Resolutions' express reference to
"extraterritorial surveillance and/or interception of communications, as
well as the collection of personal data, in particular when carried out on a
mass scale"[6] confirmed that the General Assembly had in mind America's recently exposed surveillance and data collection programs – the
NSA-Affair.

This chapter aims to substantiate the General Assembly's, the UN
Human Rights Council's, and the UN High Commissioner's unease
over the international human rights implications of the programs
exposed by Edward Snowden. I will argue that as currently practiced –
in most cases and in the current circumstances – America's extraterritorial programs are unlawful under international law. I have in mind
surveillance, intercepting communications, and collecting personal
data. Following the lead of the UN documents I focus on international
human rights law. But I will also briefly examine possible violations of
other international law regimes, including the law of diplomatic
relations.

B   International Human Rights: Privacy and the Confidentiality of Correspondence

Surveillance via the Internet (the interception and collection of electronic data – including so-called metadata and communications content) may violate the human rights to privacy and to the confidentiality
of correspondence, as those protections are guaranteed by international
law.[7] Ordinary citizens enjoy these rights. But so do government officials. Public persons – including government officials – must tolerate a
greater degree of intrusion on these rights due to their exposure in
public life. But this is a distinction of degree and not a categorical
exclusion.[8]

---

[5] *Id.* at preamble at 2; G.A. Res. 69/166, *supra* note 1, preamble at 2.

[6] G.A. Res. 68/167, preamble (Dec. 18, 2013); G.A. Res. 69/166, preamble (Dec. 18, 2014).

[7] *See* MICHELE NINO, TERRORISMO INTERNAZIONALE, PRIVACY E PROTEZIONE DEI DATI
PERSONALI (2012).

[8] *See* Von Hannover v. Germany, App. No. 59320/00, 1, 28, 2004-VI Eur. Ct. H.R. 41, 71.
See also infra note 80.

These rights are expressed in Article 12 of the Universal Declaration of Human Rights.[9] The rights to privacy and confidential correspondence are also codified in Article 17 of the International Covenant on Civil and Political Rights (ICCPR).[10] It may well be that the guarantee already has the status of customary international law.

I   Scope: Ratione Materiae

The right to privacy is not merely the "right to be let alone."[11] Its essence concerns an individual's autonomous development in the community and the ability to communicate with others in order to fulfill her personal development.[12] Privacy, for these reasons, is intertwined with the right to freedom of expression: the two are mutually dependent upon one another, and both facilitate the ability of individuals to participate in free and democratic societies. The right to privacy also protects an individual's autonomy to choose what information she wants to share and with whom. "Correspondence," in its broadest meaning, involves communication with others.

In the digital age, the two rights specified in Article 17 ICCPR may have taken on new meaning and relevance. What is new with regard to privacy and correspondence as they involve the Internet? What do these two rights mean in that medium? The Human Rights Covenant does not

---

[9] G.A. Res. 217 A(lll), art. 12, U.N. Doc. A/810, Universal Declaration of Human Rights (Dec. 10, 1948) ("No one shall be subjected to arbitrary interference with his privacy, family, home or correspondence, nor to attacks upon his honour and reputation. Everyone has the right to the protection of the law against such interference or attacks.").

[10] International Covenant on Civil and Political Rights art. 17, Dec. 19, 1966, S. Exec. Doc. No. E, 95-2 (1978), 999 U.N.T.S. 171 ("1. No one shall be subjected to arbitrary or unlawful interference with his privacy, family, home or correspondence, nor to unlawful attacks on his honour and reputation. 2. Everyone has the right to the protection of the law against such interference or attacks.") [hereinafter ICCPR].

[11] For the classic conception of privacy under U.S. Constitutional law, see Samuel D. Warren and Louis D. Brandeis, The Right to Privacy, 4 Harv. L. Rev. 193, 193 (1890) ("Later, there came a recognition of man's spiritual nature, of his feelings and his intellect. Gradually the scope of [the right to life] broadened; and now the right to life has come to mean the right to enjoy life, – the right to be let alone; the right to liberty secures the exercise of extensive civil privileges; and the term "property" has grown to comprise every form of possession – intangible, as well as tangible.").

[12] Martin Scheinin (Special Rapporteur on the Promotion and Protection of Human Rights and Fundamental Freedoms while Countering Terrorism), Rep. of the Spec. Rapporteur on the Promotion and Protection of Human Rights and Fundamental Freedoms while Countering Terrorism, U.N. Doc. A/HRC/13/37, ¶ 11, Dec. 28, 2009).

mention the telephone, let alone the Internet. The text dates from 1966, when telephones were less ubiquitous and the Internet did not exist. But the provision has been applied to these technologies. For example, the UN Human Rights Committee's General Comment 16 of 1988 already referred to "electronic surveillance" and suggested a ban: "Surveillance, whether electronic or otherwise, interceptions of telephonic, telegraphic and other forms of communication, wire-tapping and recording of conversations should be prohibited."[13] But is this recommendation still valid today? Every child today – especially the so-called digital native – knows that the Internet is not a private realm. Surely our privacy expectations have changed. Are email or Facebook posts just modern, high-tech postcards – with their contents revealed to the world? We know that these communications are not confidential. In fact, the advantages and efficiency they offer in part depend on their lack of confidentiality.

But the postcard analogy is a poor fit with respect to today's mass electronic surveillance. First, it does not fit with regard to the content of data, which includes areas of life that almost never appear in postcards, including health data and financial transactions. Second, it does not fit with regard to the quantity of data a person produces today, which would have to consist in thousands – if not millions – of postcards being sent by each of us all day long. Third, it does not fit with regard to the use to which communications data can now be put, including algorithmic processing that can eerily predict the next book we want to read. It would be impossible to construct the same kind of comprehensive personal profile of someone based on the postcards they sent. And in any case, privacy (as other human rights) has a settled, essential content. It does not vary with the oscillation of our reasonable expectations. The right to privacy is guaranteed even in long periods of ruthless dictatorship – when people do not expect confidentiality for their correspondence and have long ago forgotten the delights of personal privacy.

Both privacy and the confidentiality of correspondence are protected by the Human Rights Covenant, even in the Internet.[14] This means that the 2013 General Assembly Resolution does not articulate new law, not

---

[13] Human Rights Committee, U.N. Doc. HRI/GEN/1/Rev.9 (Vol. I), ¶ 8, CCPR General Comment No. 16: Article 17 (The Right to Respect of Privacy, Family, Home and Correspondence, and Protection of Honour and Reputation) (Apr. 8, 1988).

[14] MANFRED NOWAK, U.N. COVENANT ON CIVIL AND POLITICAL RIGHTS: CCPR COMMENTARY 401 (N. P. Engel ed., 2d ed., 2005); SARAH JOSEPH ET AL., THE INTERNATIONAL COVENANT ON CIVIL AND POLITICAL RIGHTS: CASES, MATERIALS, AND COMMENTARY 491 (2d ed., 2004) (quoting General Comment 16).

even a new interpretation of the law. It only clarifies the existing human rights protection of privacy in the Internet.

II   What Constitutes an Interference?

The following activities may constitute an interference with the right to privacy: intercepting, collecting (especially bulk-collection, that is collection of big data without any suspicion against the person whose data are collected), storing, and the further distribution of communications data. Another type of interference would occur when data are not sufficiently secured by the authorities so that data are lost or obtained by unauthorized persons.[15] The U.N. High Commissioner's report on Privacy in the Digital Age even held that "[t]he very existence of a mass surveillance programme ... creates an interference with privacy."[16]

It is interesting to consider whether a distinction might be made between content data and data *about* the communication (often called "metadata") when thinking about how the right to communications privacy might be infringed. Would that difference require us to calibrate different forms of infringement? After all, metadata mostly include so-called traffic data, including information about who communicates when and with whom.[17] Usually, the content of a communication is not revealed by metadata. For this reason it has been debated whether collection of metadata (e.g., data on a persons' location generated with Global Positioning Satellite [GPS] technology) constitutes an interference with the right to privacy.[18] In line with the recent judgment of the Court of Justice of the European Union on the Data Retention Directive,[19] and with the mentioned UN High Commissioner

---

[15] See NOWAK, *supra* note 14, at 388.

[16] Human Rights Council, U.N. Doc. A/HRC/27/37, ¶ 20, The Right to Privacy in the Digital Age: Report of the Office of the High Commissioner for Human Rights (June 30, 2014).

[17] See David Goldman, *Obama and NSA: So What Is Metadata Anyway?*, CNN (Jan. 17, 2014, 3:57 PM) http://money.cnn.com/2014/01/17/technology/security/obama-metadata-nsa/.

[18] U.S. v. Jones, 132 S.Ct. 945 (2012) (Holding that using a GPS tracking device constitutes a search within the meaning of the 4th Amendment). *But see* Bundesverfassungsgericht [BVerfG] [German Federal Constitutional Court] Apr. 12, 2005, 112 BVerfGE 304 (the Global Positioning System case, holding that limited use of GPS within the penal code was not a violation of the Basic Law's guarantee of privacy.).

[19] Joined Cases C293/12 & C594/12, Digital Rights Ireland and Seitlinger and Others, [2014] WLR (D) 164, ¶¶ 26, 29. See Federico Fabbrini, *Human Rights in the Digital Age: The European Court of Justice Ruling in the Data Retention Case and Its Lessons*

Report,[20] I submit that it does. In any case, the distinction between content data and metadata is rapidly fading. It is fading because those engaged in monitoring communications can now construct an almost comprehensive personal profile on the basis of metadata, including the places a person goes, the meals she takes on an airplane, the phone numbers she dials, the products she purchases, the websites she visits – and on and on – into a nearly infinite range of behaviors and experiences that constitute a person's life-world. All of this, when strategically surveyed, can say as much or more about a person than the content of her communications. To conclude, the collection of metadata can also constitute an interference with the human right secured by Article 17 ICCPR.[21]

III   Extraterritoriality

Even if the scope of the protection provided by Article 17 has been implicated, a preliminary objection to the application of the ICCPR to the NSA's programs remains. Is the United States at all bound by the International Covenant for Civil and Political Rights when the NSA intercepts and collects data abroad?[22] The traditional debate over the "territorial" extent of a state's international human rights obligations takes on new meaning in cyberspace, which is not a terrestrial place at all.[23] There are two concrete aspects to this issue. First, as a technological matter, the interference with the privacy of communication on the

---

for Privacy and Surveillance in the U.S., 28 Harv. Hum. Rts. J. 65–95 (2015). See also Chapter 21 in this volume.

[20] Human Rights Council, The Right to Privacy in the Digital Age, supra note 16, ¶¶ 19–20.

[21] Martin, Scheinin, LIBE Committee Inquiry on Electronic Mass Surveillance of E.U. Citizens, Statement by Professor Martin Scheinin in the Hearing of Oct. 14, 2013 Before the European Parliament, Speaking Notes, at 2–6, www.europarl.europa.eu/meetdocs/2009_2014/documents/libe/dv/scheinin_/scheinin_en.pdf.

[22] The U.S. ratified the Covenant in 1992 but deposited a number of reservations, understandings and declarations. This included the Senate's statement that the provisions of the Covenant are not self-executing. This means that they cannot be invoked before U.S. Courts. But it does not mean that the state, as an international legal person, is not bound by the Covenant. See Jack Goldsmith, The Unexceptional U.S. Human Rights RUDs, 3 U. St. Thomas L.J. 311 (2005).

[23] The extant case-law on the extraterritorial application of human rights covenants, e.g. the ECHR in Iraq, can therefore only offer limited guidance. See, e.g., Hassan v. U.K., App. No. 29750/09, HUDOC (Sept. 16, 2014), http://hudoc.echr.coe.int/eng#{"fulltext": ["hassan v. uk"],"documentcollectionid2":["GRANDCHAMBER","CHAMBER"],"itemid": ["001-146501"]} (for the extra-territorial applicability of the ECHR).

Internet almost always takes place somewhere other than where the communication originates.[24] Second, modern communication infrastructure (not to mention modern communication itself) consists in multinational or transnational networks that defy international law's traditional state-centric paradigm. An email travels a route through the quickest and best fibers, often through many states, sometimes returning to its jurisdiction of origin like a boomerang having traveled far afield only to return home. In the same way, the communications data that ought to be protected by Article 17 is stored on servers located in a number of different states. For example, Google stores the data generated by its users around the world at thirteen server clusters located in the United States, Chile, Taiwan, Singapore, Finland, Belgium, Ireland, and the Netherlands.[25] Often, the same data is located on servers in different states as a form of backup.[26] Users do not know where their data are stored and where their data travel. For these reasons the traditional principles of extraterritorial jurisdiction do not seem wholly appropriate for this sector and these intelligence activities.[27]

Nevertheless, the traditional principles – which will need some modification – constitute a valuable starting place. Article 2(1) of the ICCPR is the pertinent provision: "Each State Party to the present Covenant undertakes to respect and to ensure to all individuals within its territory and subject to its jurisdiction the rights recognized in the present Covenant, without distinction of any kind, such as race, colour, sex, language,

---

[24] Barton Gellman, Julie Tate & Ashkan Soltani, *In NSA-Intercepted Data, Those Not Targeted Far Outnumber the Foreigners Who Are*, WASH. POST (July 5, 2014), www.washingtonpost.com/world/national-security/in-nsa-intercepted-data-those-not-targeted-far-outnumber-the-foreigners-who-are/2014/07/05/8139adf8-045a-11e4-8572-4b1b969b6322_story.html ("Upstream intercepts data on the move as it crosses the U.S. junctions of global voice and data networks.") This allows NSA to intercept foreign traffic as it moves through servers based on American territory.

[25] *Data Center Locations*, GOOGLE, www.google.com/about/datacenters/inside/locations/.

[26] ASHISH GUPTA ET AL., MESA: GEO-REPLICATED, NEAR REAL-TIME, SCALABLE DATA WAREHOUSING, http://static.googleusercontent.com/media/research.google.com/en//pubs/archive/42851.pdf (Describes Google's database management software, which "is a data warehouse that is truly cloud enabled (running on dynamically provisioned generic machines with no dependency on local disks), is geo-replicated across multiple datacenters, and provides strong consistent and ordered versioning of data.").

[27] In at least two instances of extra-territorial surveillance/data collection, the ECtHR held the surveilling viz. collecting state bound by art. 8 ECHR. *See* Weber v. Germany, App. No. 54934/00, 2006-XI Eur. Ct. H.R. 309; Liberty v. U.K., App. No. 58243/00, HUDOC (July 1, 2008), http://hudoc.echr.coe.int/eng#{"fulltext":["liberty v. uk"],"documentcollectionid2":["GRANDCHAMBER","CHAMBER"],"itemid":["001-87207"]}.

religion, political or other opinion, national or social origin, property, birth or other status."[28] The key word for determining the Covenant's scope *ratione loci* is "jurisdiction."[29]

The prevailing view is that the two conditions in this provision, namely "territory" and "jurisdiction," are an alternative. The "and" is disjunctive, not conjunctive.[30] A state is bound either within its territory or *vis-à-vis* persons under its "jurisdiction," even if the affected persons are not situated within the state's territory.[31] This is the settled jurisprudence of the ICCPR's monitoring body, the United Nations Human Rights Committee.[32] It was developed in individual communications in Uruguayan cases. The leading case, *Lopez Burgos* (decided in 1981), involved the kidnapping of an Uruguayan trade union activists by Uruguyan secret service agents in Buenos Aires, Argentina.[33] The Human Rights Committee held that the Covenant binds the state without regard to "the place where the violation occurred."[34] Jurisdiction of the violating state is established, the Committee explained, when there is a "relationship between the individual and the state."[35] In that case the Covenant was applicable to the agents' activity outside Uruguay. In other words, "jurisdiction" is not about territory. Instead, it refers to the factual causal

---

[28] The parallel but not identical provision in the ECHR is Article 1 – Obligation to Respect Human Rights: "The High Contracting Parties shall secure to everyone within their jurisdiction the rights and freedoms defined in Section I of this Convention."

[29] The concept of "jurisdiction" has various functions and meanings with regard to different questions arising in international law. Besides determining the geographical scope of the covenant, "jurisdiction" is also relevant for the *attribution* of human rights interferences and for the jurisdiction of the monitoring body. "Jurisdiction" as a factor determining the gegraphical scope of application does not establish or confirm a state's competence to prescribe, adjudicate, and enforce. Quite to the contrary, the concept of jurisdiction here seeks to limit these competences. The obligation to respect human rights can be compared to a "rule-of-law mortgage" attached to the state's exercise of its authority.

[30] *See* Human Rights Committee, Lopez Burgos v. Uruguay, No. 52/1979, U.N. Doc. A/36/40, ¶ 12.3 (July 29, 1981).

[31] Human Rights Committee, U.N. Doc. CCPR/C/21/Rev.1/Add.13, ¶ 10, General Comment 31, Nature of the General Legal Obligation on States Parties to the Covenant (2004).

[32] *See* Sophie Vidal Martins v. Uruguay, No. R.13/57, U.N. Doc. Supp. No. 40 (A/37/40) at 157 (1982) (Concerning the denial of passport in an Uruguayan embassy in Mexico, the Human Rights Committee held that the ICCPR was applicable to Uruguay even if the affected person was in Mexico. The Committee then found a violation of the freedom of movement.). *See also* Human Rights Committee, Gueye v. France, No. 196/1985, U.N. Doc. CCPR/C/35/D/196/1985 (1989). (Pension denial of Senegalese former French soldiers in Senegal triggered the application of Article 2 of the ICCPR to France.).

[33] Human Rights Committee, Lopez Burgos v. Uruguay, *supra* note 30.   [34] *Id.* at ¶ 12.2.

[35] *Id.* at ¶ 12.2–12.3.

link between a state and a human rights violation.[36] The Human Rights Committee drew upon Article 5(1) of the Covenant, which states that "nothing in the present Covenant may be interpreted as implying ... any right to engage in any activity ... aimed at the destruction of any of the rights ... to a greater extent than is provided for in the present Covenant."[37] In line with this reasoning the Human Rights Committee has insisted that the Covenant does not permit a state party to take actions on the territory of another state that would constitute a violation of the Convention if those actions took place within that state's territory.[38]

The International Court of Justice followed this reasoning in its advisory opinion on the Israeli Wall from 2004.[39] The Court found that Israel was bound by the ICCPR in territories merely occupied by Israel.[40] The Court referred to the ICCPR's "object and purpose,"[41] to the "constant practice of the Human Rights Committee,"[42] and to the historical argument that the Covenant's drafters "did not intend to allow States to escape" their human rights obligations.[43] All of this made it seem "natural" that the Covenant also applies outside a state's territory.[44] But the ICJ's conclusion that a state is bound by the Covenant "in the exercise of its jurisdiction outside its own territory"[45] begs the question: *when* exactly does the state exercise jurisdiction outside its territory?

There have been phases when the U.S. rejected the extraterritorial application of the ICCPR, and thus denied that it was bound by the Covenant's limitations when acting outside its territory.[46] This position is immaterial if the alleged rights violation is the result of actions performed within the territory of the United States – as is the case when the surveillance of communications is ordered by an American agency operating in the United States. The U.S. Supreme Court embraced this reasoning when it confirmed the applicability of the U.S. Constitution's

---

[36] NOWAK, *supra* note 14, at 114 ("States parties are ... responsible for violations of the Covenant that their agents commit upon the territory of another State.").

[37] ICCPR, *supra* note 10, art. 5(1).

[38] Human Rights Committee, Celiberti v. Uruguay, No. 56 /1979, U.N. Doc. A/36/40, ¶ 10.3 (July 29, 1981). *Id.*: "In line with this, it would be *unconscionable to so interpret* the responsibility under article 2 of the Covenant as to permit a State party to perpetrate violations of the Covenant on the territory of another State, which violations it could not perpetrate on its own territory." (emphasis added).

[39] Legal Consequences of the Construction of a Wall in the Occupied Palestinian Territory, Advisory Opinion, 2004 I.C.J. 136 ¶¶ 102–11 (July 9).

[40] *Id.* at 111.   [41] *Id.* at 109.   [42] *Id.*   [43] *Id.*   [44] *Id.*   [45] *Id.* at ¶ 111.

[46] Aldo S. Zilli, *Approaching the Extraterritoriality Debate: The Human Rights Committee, the U.S. and the ICCPR*, 9 SANTA CLARA J. INT'L. L. 399, 410 (2011).

habeas corpus protections to governmental acts ordered in the territory of the United States but having their effect on detainees in the Guantanamo Bay prison camp in Cuba.[47]

Moreover, the U.S. position on extraterritoriality may not be as clear as it is often depicted. The ICCPR was drafted over the course of nearly a decade (1947–1954). During the elaboration of the Covenant the President of the drafting committee, Eleanor Roosevelt, insisted on the mention of "territory" in Article 2(1) in order to avoid that the United States would be saddled with affirmative duties to enforce rights in foreign territories under U.S. occupation.[48] This was an especially acute concern on the part of the Americans with respect to the German people under Allied authority and occupation after World War II.[49] A broader survey of the *travaux préparatoires* shows that the drafters did not intend to rule out the Covenant's extraterritorial applicability.[50] And when the United States ratified the ICCPR in 1992, the Senate did not issue a reservation or declaration seeking to limit the Covenant's authority over the United States to acts taken in American territory. Had the Senate intended any territorial limitation it would most likely have expressed it, as the fourteen different reservations, understandings, and declarations attached to the Senate's advice and consent show.[51] Additionally, in America's First Periodic Country Report under the Covenant from 1994, the issue of territoriality was not mentioned.[52] The United States asserted the extraterritorial limit on the Covenant's applicability for the first time in 1995 during the discussion of 1994 Country Report before the UN Human Rights Committee.[53] America's sudden concern for the issue was motivated by the country's intervention in Haiti, which was ongoing at the time of the proceedings before the UN Human Rights Committee. Still, in its Fourth Periodic Country Report (2012), the U.S. stated that it "is mindful

---

[47] Rasul *et al.* v. Bush, 542 U.S. 466 (2004). *See* Chapter 10 in this volume.

[48] Peter Margulies, *The NSA in Global Perspective: Surveillance, Human Rights, and International Counterterrorism*, 82 FORDHAM L. REV. 2137, 2144–46 (2014).

[49] *Id.* at 2144.

[50] *See* Marko Milanovic, *Human Rights Treaties and Foreign Surveillance: Privacy in the Digital Age*, 56 HARV. INT'L L.J. 81, 102–08 (2015); Sarah H. Cleveland, *Embedded International Law and the Constitution Abroad*, 110 COLUM. L. REV. 225, 251–53 (2010). *But see* NOWAK, *supra* note 14, at 43.

[51] U.S. Reservations, Declarations, and Understandings, International Covenant on Civil and Political Rights, 138 Cong. Rec. S4781-01 (daily ed., Apr. 2, 1992).

[52] Initial Report of States Parties due in 1993: United States of America, U.N. Doc. CCPR/C/81/Add.4 (Aug. 24, 1994).

[53] Milanovic, *supra* note 50, at 105.

[of] General Comment No. 31," and that it was "aware of the jurisprudence of the ICJ."[54] The latter reference was an invocation of the ICJ's 2004 advisory opinion on the Israeli Wall, which, as noted earlier, embraced the extraterritorial effect of the Covenant.[55] Further clouding the matter, no clear position on the issue emerged in America's response (published in July 2013) to UN Human Rights Committee's reaction to America's Fourth Periodic Report and comments. This left the UN Human Rights Committee to express in April 2014, in its final observations on the United States' Fourth Periodic Report, its "regrets that the State party continues to maintain the position that the Covenant does not apply with respect to individuals under its jurisdiction, but outside its territory ... The Committee is concerned about the surveillance of communications in the interest of protecting national security, conducted by the National Security Agency (NSA) *both within and outside the United States*, through the bulk phone metadata surveillance programme."[56]

As a minimum, and pursuant to the UN Human Rights Committee's established jurisprudence, the jurisprudence of the International Court of Justice, and State practice, states are obliged to respect ICCPR rights of persons under the acting state's *"authority"/"power" or effective control*. The concepts of "authority" or "power," which have been forwarded in the cyber-context as an alternative to the more traditional criterion of "effective control."[57] But these new criteria have not yet been clearly

---

[54] Fourth Periodic Report of the United States of America to the United Nations Committee on Human Rights Concerning the International Covenant on Civil and Political Rights, U.N. Doc. CCPR/C/USA/4, ¶ 505 (Dec. 30, 2011); Human Rights Committee, General Comment 31, *supra* note 31, referring to the Wall opinion (*supra* note 39). *But see* Summary Record of the 1405th meeting: United States of America, U.N. ESCOR Hum. Rts. Comm., 53d Sess., 1504th mtg. at 7, 20, U.N. Doc. CCPR/C/SR 1405 (1995).

[55] Wall Opinion, *supra* note 39.

[56] Human Rights Committee, U.N. Doc. No. CCPR/C/USA/CO/4 (Apr. 23, 2014), ¶¶ 4, 22, Concluding observations on the fourth periodic report of the United States of America (emphasis added).

[57] Human Rights Council, The Right to Privacy in the Digital Age, *supra* note 16, ¶ 33: "The notions of 'power' and 'effective control' are indicators of whether a State is exercising 'jurisdiction' or governmental powers, the abuse of which human rights protections are intended to constrain"; ¶ 34: "It follows that digital surveillance therefore may engage a State's human rights obligations if that surveillance involves the State's exercise of power or effective control in relation to digital communications infrastructure, wherever found, for example, through direct tapping or penetration of that infrastructure (...)." See in this sense already the U.S. Department of State, Office of the Legal Advisor, *Memorandum Opinion on the Geographic Scope of the International Covenant on Civil and Political Rights* (Oct. 19, 2010) (Koh ICCPR Opinion) which was not endorsed by the U.S. government.

defined. I submit that virtual control through direct surveillance may amount to the exercise of such "authority" or "power." On these grounds, the United States is bound to respect ICCPR privacy rights of persons who are under direct American surveillance independent of their location outside U.S. territory.[58] In the face of this rule, the U.S. position seems to be uncertain and in flux. Moreover, the narrow interpretation the U.S. Americans have given the issue was disputed from the moment it was articulated in 1995.[59] If the United States categorically refuses to be bound by the Covenant in extraterritorial constellations, then that posture seems to conflict with international law obligations to which the United States has subscribed and is bound.

IV   Violation

Persons who are surveilled – whose electronic communications data are intercepted, stored, or collected – are protected by an international human right to privacy and the confidentiality of their correspondence. But these rights are not absolute. They may be lawfully restricted. A violation of the Covenant occurs only if the interference amounts to an unjustified limitation, which Article 17 CCPR refers to as an "unlawful or arbitrary interference" with privacy and correspondence.[60] In its practice regarding other limitable rights in the Covenant, the UN Human Rights Committee has considered at least six factors when determining whether a violation has occurred. For example, in its General Comment No. 27 (concerning the limitable right to freedom of movement in Article 12),[61] the UN Human Rights Committee insisted that a restriction of the right to Freedom of Movement: (1) be based on a law; (2) not

---

[58] *See, e.g.,* Andreas Fischer-Lescano, *Der Kampf um die Internetverfassung,* 69 JURISTEN-ZEITUNG 965, 969 (2014) (extraterritorial appplicability because of the "disciplining effect" of surveillance.); Milanovic, *supra* note 50, at 118–20 (applicability based on a distinction between positive obligations to protect (with no extraterritorial application) and negative obligations to respect (which Milanovic finds to apply also extraterritorially).

[59] Theodor Meron, *Extraterritoriality of Human Rights Treaties,* 89 AM. J. INT'L L. 78 (1995).

[60] ICCPR, *supra* note 10, art. 17(1); NOWAK *supra* note 14, at 382 ("it was stressed above all that "arbitrary"clearly went beyond "unlawful"and contained an element of "capriciousness"); JOSEPH ET AL. *supra* note 14, at 481 ("The term 'unlawful' means that no interference can take place except in cases envisaged by the law.").

[61] Human Rights Committee, U.N. Doc. CCPR/C/21/Rev.1/Add.9, General Comment 27, Freedom of movement (art. 12) (1999).

compromise the essential core of the right; (3) not be undertaken pursuant to state authority that enjoys sweeping discretion; (4) be strictly
necessary to achieve the state's legitimate objectives; (5) conform with
other rights secured by the Covenant; and (6) be proportional.[62] These
factors are today equally applicable to all rights granted by the Covenant.
Specifically with regard to the United States' extraterritorial surveillance
program, the Commitee recommended that "the State party should ...
take all necessary measures to ensure that its surveillance activities, *both
within and outside the United States*, conform to its obligations under the
Covenant, including Article 17; in particular, measures should be taken
to ensure that any interference with the right to privacy complies with the
principles of *legality, proportionality and necessity, regardless of the
nationality or location of the individuals whose communications are
under direct surveillance.*"[63] Also, the High Commissioner on Human
Rights stated in its 2014 Report on Privacy in the Digital Age that "the
overarching principles of legality, necessity and proportionality" must
guide limitations of the right to privacy under Article 17 CCPR.[64] In
practice this test aligns itself with the term employed in the European
Convention, namely, that restrictions on rights "must be necessary in a
democratic society." That formula has also been applied by the Human
Rights Committee for limitation of ICCPR-rights.[65] It seems that falling
short on any one of these requirements is enough to qualify the state's
interference with communications privacy as "unlawful and arbitrary,"
and therefore as a violation of the Article 17.

---

[62] The U.N. Human Rights Committee also referred to some procedural requirements in the
case of restrictions on the freedom of movement, including the minimization of administrative obstacles to enjoyment of the right and expeditious proceedings providing the
state's reasoning for any denial of the right. *Id.* at 11–18 (Paragraph 18 also notes some of
the "bureaucratic barriers" states have implemented to restrict freedom of movement and
points out that "the Committee has criticized provisions requiring individuals to apply
for permission to change their residence or to seek the approval of the local authorities of
the place of destination, as well as delays in processing such written applications. States'
practice presents an even richer array of obstacles making it more difficult to leave the
country, in particular for their own nationals." The Committee goes on to enumerate
some of the state practices that might be objectionable, and stresses that any restrictions
be in conformity with Article 12(3)).

[63] Human Rights Committee, ¶ 22, Concluding Observations on the Fourth Periodic Report
of the United States of America, *supra* note 56 (emphasis added).

[64] Human Rights Council, ¶ 23, The Right to Privacy in the Digital Age, *supra* note 16.

[65] Human Rights Committee, General Comment 27, *supra* note 61, Freedom of movement
(art. 12).

The American regime for communications surveillance and data-collection trips – fatally – over several of these conditions.

First, it is arguable that the entire electronic mass surveillance architecture under which the NSA operates lacks a clear legal basis. The Foreign Intelligence Surveillance Act (FISA)[66] and its many amendments (especially including Section 215 of the USA Patriot Act,[67] which served as the basis for the NSA's PRISM initiative and the collection of communications data and content in Europe and elsewhere around the world) are vague and overbroad. The legal basis for an infringement of the right to communications privacy – even if drawn from an international treaty between the surveilling and surveilled states – must be forseeable (not just a secret treaty) and sufficiently precise: "[R]elevant legislation must specify in detail the precise circumstances in which such interferences [with communications privacy] may be permitted."[68] But Section 215 is almost cynically nebulous. It requries only that the appropriate Executive Branch official apply for an order permitting the collection of so-called business records from the secretive Foreign Intelligence Surveillance Court.[69] The application only needs to demonstrate that the surveillance will not involve a U.S. person "solely upon the basis of activities protected by the first amendment to the Constitution of the United States."[70] Further specifications are drawn from Presidential Executive Order 12333.[71] But it is equally vague. For example, it tautologically limits the American intelligence community to the pursuit of "information constituting foreign intelligence."[72]

---

[66] Foreign Intelligence Surveillance Act of 1978 [FISA], Pub. L. No. 95–511, 92 Stat. 1783 (codified as amended in scattered sections of 50 U.S.C.); Uniting and Strengthening America by Providing Appropriate Tools Required to Intercept and Obstruct Terrorism Act [USA PATRIOT Act] of 2001, Pub. L. No. 107–56, 115 Stat. 272 (codified as amended in scattered sections of 8 U.S.C., 12 U.S.C., 15 U.S.C., 18 U.S.C., 20 U.S.C., 31 U.S.C., 42 U.S.C., 47 U.S.C., 49 U.S.C., 50 U.S.C., 51 U.S.C.); Protect America Act of 2007, Pub. L. No. 110–55, 121 Stat. 552 (codified as amended in scattered sections of 50 U.S.C.); FISA Amendments Act of 2008, Pub. L. No. 110–261, 122 Stat. 2436 (codified as amended in scattered sections of 50 U.S.C.).

[67] USA PATRIOT Act of 2001 § 215, 50 U.S.C. § 1861 (2012).

[68] Human Rights Committee, *supra* note 13, at ¶ 8, General Comment 16 (1988) [hereinafter General Comment 16].

[69] 50 U.S.C. § 1861(b)(1)(A) (codified as amended by FISA § 501 (b)(1)(A), USA PATRIOT Act § 215).

[70] 50 U.S.C. § 1861(a)(1) (codified as amended by FISA Sec. 501(a)(1), USA PATRIOT Act § 215).

[71] Exec. Order No. 12,333, 3 C.F.R. 200 (1981), reprinted as amended in 50 U.S.C. § 3001 (2012).

[72] *Id.* at (2.3)(b).

Second, it is arguable that, in some instances, the essential core of privacy has been harmed by the NSA's surveillance programs. This would be true even if we *only* take account of the collection of metadata. As discussed earlier, this can happen when the state's collection of metadata allows it to develop a deeply intimate, comprehensive personality profile. For example, the websites someone visits and the phone numbers this person calls and the news and entertainment media she consumes can reveal accurate and profoundly private information about sexual identity and sexual preferences. Of course, the controversial PRISM program involved the more invasive collection of communications content.

Third, it is arguable that America's global surveillance regime does not conform with other human rights provisions. For example, mass electronic surveillance of this kind implicates the right to nondiscrimination,[73] and it casts an impermissible "chill" on the freedoms of expression and association.[74]

Finally, it is arguable that the NSA's surveillance programs are substantially disproportionate. On one hand, the depth of the intrusion is, in many cases, serious. On the other hand, the information secured is often of questionable value to the stated goal of interdicting and combatting terrorism.[75] Addressing the former concern, several factors lead to the conclusion that the NSA's programs constitute a particularly intense intrusion on the right. First, it must be conceded that mass surveillance is far more troubling than targeted surveillance. Targeted surveillance is conducted based on the reasonable suspicion that the target is involved in illegal activity, and that this surveillance is necessary to gather evidence. Mass surveillance, however, collects data on a large group. This collection is still intended to collect evidence of illegal activity. But the number of subjects of mass surveillance that are committing illegal acts is vanishingly small in comparison to those that are not. Furthermore, the vast majority of the subjects of mass surveillance are under no suspicion whatsoever. Second, the fact that the surveillance often involves communications that take place in private settings such as one's home or the use of one's personal computer – as opposed to taking place in the public sphere

---

[73] ICCPR, *supra* note 10, at art. 26; Human Rights Committee, U.N. Doc. HRI/GEN/1/Rev.9, General Comment 18 (1989).
[74] ICCPR, *supra* note 10, at arts. 19, 22.
[75] Ian Brown & Douwe Korff, *Terrorism and the Proportionality of Internet Surveillance*, 6 EUR. J. CRIMINOL. 119 (2009).

(such as traffic enforcement cameras or airport security screening) –
suggests that these programs constitute a severe intrusion on the right.[76]
Third, as noted in other places in this chapter, these surveillance regimes
involved information that is profoundly private and intensely intimate. It
is different – in kind – from more publicly exposed information such as
participation in open assemblies or published commentary. On the side
of the scale registering the NSA programs as particularly intense intrusions on the right to communications privacy, it is also necessary to note
that the NSA programs are not strictly regulated. The NSA can liberally
collect data,[77] store them forever,[78] and faces few limits on sharing
data with state institutions outside the intelligence community, including
law enforcement authorities.[79] Finally, the status of the person on whom
data are collected might counsel for the conclusion that the intrusion
on the right to communications privacy is especially intense. Ordinary
citizens, as a rule, may reasonably expect more privacy than public

---

[76] *See* Katz v. U.S., 389 U.S. 347 (1967) (In this case a Fourth Amendment violation was
found when a wiretap was placed on a telephone booth, because the defendant had a
"reasonable expectation of privacy.").

[77] 50 U.S.C. § 1861 (2012); Exec. Order No. 12, *supra* note 71, at 333(1.7)(c)(1); Joseph D.
Mornin, *Note: NSA Metadata Collection and the Fourth Amendment*, 29 BERKELEY
TECH. L.J. 985 (2014). *See* Administration White Paper: Bulk Collection of Telephony
Metadata Under Section 215 of the USA PATRIOT Act 2 (Aug. 9, 2013), http://big
.assets.huffingtonpost.com/Section215.pdf.

[78] Mornin, *supra* note 77, at 987 (citing Administration White Paper: Bulk Collection of
Telephony Metadata Under Section 215 of the USA PATRIOT Act 2 as saying "there is
no reasonable expectation of privacy in [metadata], which is routinely collected by
telecommunications service providers for billing and fraud detection purposes.").

[79] Eric J. Holder, TOPSECRET//COMINT//NOFORN//20310108, MINIMIZATION PROCED-
URES USED BY THE NATIONAL SECURITY AGENCY IN CONNECTION WITH ACQUISITIONS
OF FOREIGN INTELLIGENCE PURSUANT TO Section 702 OF THE FOREIGN INTELLIGENCE
SURVEILLANCE ACT OF 1978, AS AMENDED (Oct. 31, 2011), www.aclu.org/files/assets/
minimization_procedures_used_by_nsa_in_connection_with_fisa_sect_702.pdf), at 8 (§
5(2), saying that domestic communications do not need to be destroyed if "the communication does not contain foreign intelligence information but is reasonably believed to
contain evidence of a crime that has been, is being, or is about to be committed. Such
communication may be disseminated (including United States person identities) to
appropriate Federal law enforcement authorities, in accordance with 50 U.S.C. §§ 1806
(b) and 1825(c), Executive Order No. 12333, and, where applicable, the crimes reporting
procedures set out in the August 1995 "Memorandum of Understanding: Reporting of
Information Concerning Federal Crimes," or any successor document. Such communications may be retained by NSA for a reasonable period of time, not to exceed six months
unless extended in writing by the Attorney General, to permit law enforcement agencies
to determine whether access to original recordings of such communications is required
for law enforcement purposes.").

figures.[80] On the other side of the balance, one factor underscoring the necessity and proportionality of extraterritorial surveillance is the fact that the acting state has less alternative means at its disposal than in the domestic context to achieve its security-related objectives.

Beyond this nuanced assessment of the intensity of the intrusion resulting from programs such as PRISM, it might also be argued that "bulk data collection" (so called "big data collection without suspicion" or *"anlasslose Speicherung"*) is an inherently disproportionate burden on the enjoyment of the right.[81] I cannot go so far. In fact, the huge flood of data collected by programs such as PRISM literally cannot be read and analyzed. It must be admitted that some of the sting of the intensity of this burden on the right is mitigated by the realization that, by necessity, some (unknowable) portion of all the data collected by NSA will never be read or analyzed by the authority.[82] A significant portion of the data will go untouched in any penetrating sense and will only be accessed for anonymized and abstract keyword searches.[83] Consistent with this mitigating characterization, the German Federal Constitutional Court has

---

[80] EUR. PARL. RES. 1165, ¶¶ 6–7 (1998); Von Hannover v. Germany (No. 2), App. No. 40660/08, 2012-I Eur. Ct. H.R. 399, 440 ("[A] distinction has to be made between private individuals and persons acting in a public context, as political figures or public figures. Accordingly, whilst a private individual unknown to the public might claim particular protection of his or her right to private life, the same is not true of public figures."); Baumgartner v. United States, 322 U.S. 665, 673–74 (1944) N.Y. Times v. Sullivan, 376 U.S. 254, 270 (1964); Hustler v. Falwell, 485 U.S. 46 (1988).

[81] *See* Brown & Korff, *supra* note 75. *But see* Article 29 Data Protection Working Party, Opinion of the European Data Protection Supervisor on the Proposal for a Directive of the European Parliament and of the Council on the Retention of Data Processed in Connection with the Provision of Public Electronic Communication Services and Amending Directive 2002/58/EC, 1868/05/EN WP 113, at 4 (Oct. 21, 2005), http:// ec.europa.eu/justice/policies/privacy/docs/wpdocs/2005/wp113_en.pdf ("Traffic data retention interferes with the fundamental right to confidential communications guaranteed to the individuals by Article 8 of the European Convention on Human Rights. In a democratic society, any interference with this fundamental right can be justified if it is necessary in the interests of national security."); Francesca Bignami, *Privacy and Law Enforcement in the European Union: The Data Retention Directive*, 8 CHI. J. INT'L L. 233, 246–49 (2007).

[82] *See* Julia Angwin, *NSA Struggles to Make Sense of Flood of Surveillance Data*, WALL ST. J. (Dec. 25, 2013, 10:30 PM), www.wsj.com/articles/SB10001424052702304202204579252022823658850. *But see* Derrick Harris, *Here's How the NSA Analyzes All That Call Data*, GIGAOM (June 6, 2013, 3:13 PM), https://gigaom.com/2013/06/06/heres-how-the-nsa-analyzes-all-that-call-data/.

[83] Harris, *supra* note 82 ("[T]he good news is that the vast majority of people are still anonymous even in this sea of data: There's just too much data to care until someone pops up in the bad guys' networks or gets on the agency's radar.")

found that big data is not *inherently* disproportionate unless the data are collected without any discernible aim, such as the effort to interdict and combat terrorism and other serious crimes.[84]

On the other side of the proportionality analysis – concerning the value of the information obtained through an intrusion upon the right to communications privacy – a shocking insight is that many of the surveillance methods implicated by the NSA programs (such as cable splitting fibers, phantom viewers combined with a local splitter, or FinSpy[85]) are not very effective at exposing the plans of terrorists.[86]

For all of these reasons a host of the NSA's activities will probably turn out to be disproportionate when closely examined on the facts.[87] The means and the ends are – generally speaking – out of balance: a deep and significant intrusion on the right to communications privacy generates little benefit.

V   The Privacy of Foreigners

An issue often discussed in U.S. circles is whether international human rights law imposes stricter limits on a state when taking actions that affect its citizens while providing less rigorous protection for other states' citizens.[88] According to this understanding German citizens would be owed less international law protection against surveillance undertaken by American intelligence agencies than U.S. citizens could demand against the actions of their government. There is no reason to credit this claim. The ICCPR protects persons against discrimination.[89] And every State Party to the Covenant undertakes "to respect and to ensure to all individuals ... the rights recognized in the Covenant, without distinction of any kind such as race ... or other status."[90] Citizenship or nationality is a protected "status" under the terms of Article 2 of the ICCPR.[91] Distinctions based on nationality are inherently

---

[84] Bundesverfassungsgericht [BVerfG] [Federal Constitutional Court] Mar. 2, 2010, 125 BVerfGE 260 (2010) (Data Retention Case).

[85] Martin Scheinin, *E.U.-Funded Study: Electronic Mass Surveillance Fails – Drastically*, JUSTSECURITY (Oct. 14, 2014, 8:01 AM), http://justsecurity.org/16336/eu-funded-study-electronic-mass-surveillance-fails-drastically/ (detailing a study that exhibits the failings of these systems).

[86] Scheinin, *supra* note 85.   [87] *See* Fischer-Lescano, *supra* note 58, at 970.

[88] For a discussion, *see* Milanovic, *supra* note 50, at 87–101.

[89] ICCPR, *supra* note 10, art. 26.   [90] *Id.* art. 2.

[91] Human Rights Committee, General Comment 18, *supra* note 73, at ¶ 7.

suspect.[92] This means that the burden is on the state invoking the distinction to show that "the criteria for such differentiation are reasonable and objective and [that] the aim is to achieve a purpose which is legitimate."[93] For example, a state may legitimately distinguish between citizens and noncitizens in the context of voting rights,[94] or with regard to border crossings.[95] But it is difficult to see how citizenship serves as a legitimate distinction with regard to surveillance and the communications privacy secured by Article 17.[96] The United States owes Germans and Americans equal protection of privacy under international law.

C   Other International Law Limitations[97]

The interception of communications – authorized and carried out by government officials, agents, and authorities – seems to constitute espionage.[98] Throughout history states have surely used spies to attempt to gather information about other states.[99] Despite (or maybe because of) this widespread practice, there are no specific international law norms that prohibit or regulate espionage. In this sense, espionage – as such – is not prohibited under treaty-based international law.[100] And because

---

[92] Human Rights Committee, General Comment 15, ¶ 2, U.N. Doc. HRI/GEN/1/Rev. 9 (1986).

[93] Human Rights Committee, General Comment 18, *supra* note 73, at ¶ 13.

[94] ICCPR, *supra* note 10, at art. 25; Human Rights Committee, U.N. Doc. CCPR/C/21/ Rev.1/Add.7, ¶ 3, General Comment 25 (57) (1996).

[95] Human Rights Committee, General Comment 15, *supra* note 92, at ¶¶ 5–6.

[96] Human Rights Council, The Right to Privacy in the Digital Age, supra note 16, at ¶¶ 35–36. *Cf.* for the ECHR-violation through directing anti-terror measures (especially detention) specifically against non-citizens A. v. U.K., App. No. 3455/05, 2009-II Eur. Ct. H.R. 137, 143 (the Court found "that the derogating measures were disproportionate in that they discriminated unjustifiably between nationals and non-nationals.").

[97] This section draws on Anne Peters, *Surveillance Without Borders? The Unlawfulness of the NSA-Panopticon, Part I*, EJIL TALK! (Nov. 1, 2013), *available at* www.ejiltalk.org/ surveillance-without-borders-the-unlawfulness-of-the-nsa-panopticon-part-i/.

[98] *See* Lt. Col. Geoffrey B. Demarest, *Espionage in International Law*, 24 DENV. J. INT'L L. & POL'Y 321, 325 (1996).

[99] *See* HUGO GROTIUS, THE LAW OF WAR AND PEACE, Book III, ch. IV xviii 655 (F. Kelsey translation, Oxford, 1925) ("[S]pies, whose sending is beyond doubt permitted by the law of nations – such as the spies whom Moses sent out, or Joshua himself — if caught are usually treated most severely.").

[100] For example, art. 46 of AP I to the Geneva Conventions, entitled "Spies", assumes that spying in armed conflict happens; Demarest, *supra* note 98, at 321 ("[I]ntelligence activities are now accepted as a common, even inherent, attribute of the modern state.").

everybody does it, it must be equally true that customary international law does not prohibit it, Benjamin Wittes' argument seems to go.[101]

This posture aligns with the traditional understanding of international law, which advances the following framework: that which is not prohibited is allowed.[102] But maybe this sovereigntist presumption is no longer warranted in our age of interdependence.[103] In any case, the following may form the basis for additional international law violations as a consequence of the NSA-Affair.

I   State Sovereignty, Nonintervention, and the Prohibition on Extraterritorial Governmental Acts

Espionage might constitute an *intervention* that is prohibited by international law.[104] But the principle of nonintervention is generally deemed to be breached only if there is an element of "coercion."[105] This would be lacking in the circumstances surrounding the NSA-Affair. After all, the NSA's surveillance did not seek to pressure – or "coerce" – the states in which the programs operated to make specific policy choices or take specific actions.

Spying might, however, violate the principle of *sovereign equality of states*.[106] "Westphalian sovereignty," to borrow the term used by Stephen Krasner to describe one component of state sovereignty,[107] essentially means state control over the *domaine réservé*. Nonpublic communications among government figures (including Chancellor Angela Merkel's telephone calls with other public officials) certainly belong to this *domaine réservé*.[108] States have no right to gather another state's confidential political information. Even under a presumptive, general

---

[101]   *See* Chapter 6 in this volume.

[102]   The Case of the S.S. Lotus (Fr. v. Turk.), 1927 P.C.I.J. (ser. A) No. 10 (Sept. 7); Hugh Handeyside, *The Lotus Principle in ICJ Jurisprudence: Was the Ship Ever Afloat?*, 29 MICH. J. INT'L L. 71, 72 (2007).

[103]   *See* Ashley Deeks, *An International Legal Framework for Surveillance*, 55 VA. J. INT'L L. 291 (2015).

[104]   U.N. Charter art. 2, ¶ 4; G.A. Res. 2625 (XXV), U.N. GAOR, 25th Sess., Supp. No. 18, U.N. Doc A/8018, at 123 (Oct. 24, 1970).

[105]   ICJ, Military and Paramilitary Activities in and against Nicaragua (Nicaragua v. U.S.A.), Merits, Judgment, ICJ Reports (1986), 14, ¶ 205.

[106]   U.N. Charter art. 2, ¶ 1.

[107]   Stephen D. Krasner, *Abiding Sovereignty*, 22 INT'L POL. SCI. REV. 229, 231 (2001).

[108]   *See* JACK GOLDSMITH & TIM WU, WHO CONTROLS THE INTERNET? ILLUSIONS OF A BORDERLESS WORLD 184 (2006).

expectation of transparency, states are not obliged to make all their internal decision-making processes public.[109] After all, this would inhibit politics and policy making. For this reason, surveilling and gaining access to other countries' confidential intragovernmental communications might be seen as an interference with state sovereignty in its most traditional sense.

U.S. governmental acts performed within the territory of other states might also violate the international legal *principles on the allocation of state jurisdiction* (which are, one could say, one facet of the principle of state sovereignty). States can assert the authority to act outside their territory only if there is a sufficient jurisdictional link between the state and the situation supposedly requiring its extraterritorial action. This link might be the perilous effects for the United States (including its armed forces and citizens located abroad) of suspected criminal acts.[110] But the potential harm the United States faces from the abstract threat of global terrorism seems too remote to constitute "effects" in the sense of the international rules on the exercise of extraterritorial state jurisdiction. America's expansive and indiscriminate surveillance programs seem to be *prima facie* breaches of those principles.

The United States' surveillance regime also may have violated the *general principle of good faith* it was obliged to uphold as part of the international law governing treaty practice.[111] After all, the NATO Agreement is a treaty of alliance pursuant to which the parties have pledged to furnish one another "mutual aid."[112] Within such a regime the principle of good faith, which generally governs treaty relationships, is particularly important.[113] In these circumstances the principle of good faith might crystallise into a more specific obligation of *loyalty* or *comity* towards the treaty partners. Spying on one's allies is distasteful – despite

---

[109] *See, e.g.,* U.S. v. Nixon, 418 U.S. 683 at 708 (1974) ("The expectation of a President to the confidentiality of his conversations and correspondence . . . has all the values to which we accord deference for the privacy of all citizens and, added to those values, is the necessity for protection of the public interest in candid, objective, and even blunt or harsh opinions in Presidential decisionmaking.").

[110] RESTATMENT (THIRD) OF FOREIGN RELATIONS LAW OF THE UNITED STATES (1987) § 402 lit. d).

[111] Vienna Convention on the Law of Treaties art. 26, May 23, 1969, 1155 U.N.T.S. 331 (noting, of course, that the United States is not a party to the Vienna Convention).

[112] North Atlantic Treaty art. 3, Apr. 4, 1949, 63 Stat. 2241, 34 U.N.T.S. 243.

[113] Vienna Convention on the Law of Treaties, *supra* note 111, at art. 26.

Benjamin Wittes' attempt to make it a less bitter pill to swallow.[114] It might also be illegal.

It is irrelevant when and to what extent the U.S. President was informed about concrete surveillance measures. It will be no defense in international law that the nation's head of government was ignorant of the offending programs (as President Obama seemed to suggest).[115] All measures taken by U.S. state organs (and the NSA undoubtedly counts) are attributable to the state as an international legal subject and are capable of triggering the state's responsibility for substantive violations of international law.[116]

The United States might nonetheless benefit from Germany's consent, which would be a valid defense against claims that the U.S. interfered with Germany's state sovereignty or disregarded the prohibition on extraterritorial actions within the territory of another state.[117] But, in order to preclude wrongfulness, consent must be given prior to the actions that would constitute a breach of international law.[118] Further-more, the challenged action must be covered by the consent given (i.e., be "within the limits" of the consent, as the ILC Articles on State Responsi-bility put it[119]).

Has Germany consented to America's conduct in this case? As brought to light by a German historian, Germany concluded a number of inter-national (and partly secret) treaties with the United States in the 1950s and 1960s.[120] These agreements might embody Germany's prior consent to secret surveillance conducted by the United States in Germany. One of them is the Agreement to Supplement the Agreement between the Parties to the North Atlantic Treaty regarding the Status of their Forces with respect to Foreign Forces stationed in the Federal Republic of Germany

---

[114] *See* Chapter 6 in this volume.

[115] Martha T. Moore, *NSA Denies Obama Knew of Spying on German Leader*, USA TODAY (Oct. 27, 2013, 11:27 PM), www.usatoday.com/story/news/nation/2013/10/27/rogers-house-intelligence-chief-nsa-europe/3282161/.

[116] *Draft Articles on Responsibility of States for Internationally Wrongful Acts* art. 4, *in* Rep. Of the Int'l Law Comm'n, 53d Sess., Apr. 23–June 1, July 2–Aug. 10, 2001, U.N. Doc. A/CN.4/L.602/Rev.1; GAOR, 53d Sess., Supp. No. 10, U.N. Doc. A/56/10 (2001).

[117] *Id.* art. 20.

[118] *Id.* at 73 (Commentary on Article 20 of the Draft Articles on Responsibility of States, para. 3).

[119] *Id.* at 73–74, art. 20.

[120] JOSEF FOSCHEPOTH, ÜBERWACHTES DEUTSCHLAND: POST- UND TELEFONÜBERWACHUNG IN DER ALTEN BUNDESREPUBLIK (2d ed. 2013).

(August 3, 1959).[121] A second relevant treaty might be the *Administrative Agreement between the Government of the Federal Republic of Germany and the Government of the United Kingdom of Great Britain and Northern Ireland with respect to Law on Article 10 of the Basic Law* (October 28, 1968).[122] A third relevant agreement is a *note verbale* entitled *Surrender of the Allied Reserved Rights for Surveillance of Post and Telecommunications, the Verbal Note of the U.S. Embassy Confirmed by the Foreign Ministry* (May 27, 1968).[123] The latter note confirms a "principle of international law" pursuant to which "any military commander is entitled to take, in the event of an immediate threat to his armed forces, the *appropriate* protective measures that are *necessary* to remove the danger."[124] This is not a broad consent to American surveillance in Germany. Instead, it confirms the basic notions that undergird the human rights protections I described earlier. For example, it only allows for proportionate and necessary surveillance measures. In any case, the *note verbale* cannot be read as German consent to disproportionate and unnecessary measures. As a final point, it is not acceptable to read these agreements as a blank check for America's excessive surveillance measures in Germany. This is not the kind of informed and qualified consent that would serve as a justification for an internationally wrongful act.

II   The Law of Diplomacy

The United States also may have breached the law of diplomacy by conducting surveillance activities at and through its embassies abroad, including in Berlin.[125] Article 3(1)(d) of the Vienna Convention on Diplomatic Relations states: "The functions of a diplomatic mission consist *inter alia* in . . . ascertaining by all *lawful means* conditions and developments in the receiving State, and reporting thereon to the

---

[121] Agreement to supplement the agreement of June 19, 1951 between the parties to the North Atlantic Treaty regarding the status of their forces with respect to foreign forces stationed in the Federal Republic of Germany, Aug. 3, 1959, 14 U.S.T. 531, 481 U.N.T.S. 262.

[122] *See* FOSCHEPOTH, *supra* note 120.   [123] *Id.*

[124] This is my translation of the German text reprinted in FOSCHEPOTH, Doc. No. 18b, ¶ 6, pp. 297–98.

[125] *See also* Ingrid Wuerth, *Indonesia and China Question Use of Embassies for Spying*, LAWFARE (Nov. 1, 2013, 12:00 PM), www.lawfareblog.com/2013/11/indonesia-and-china-question-use-of-embassies-for-spying/.

Government of the sending State."[126] The lawful means referred to by this provision include – first and foremost – the domestic law of the receiving state. Of course, most states have criminalized spying (whether it aims to acquire state secrets by accessing governmental communications or collect private information through surveillance of private communications). For example, the German Criminal Code (*Strafgesetzbuch*) forbids "spying on state secrets" (*Auskundschaften von Staatsgeheimnissen*).[127] It also criminalizes "breaches of confidential communication" and "spying and intercepting data."[128] The NSA programs exposed by Edward Snowden would count as unlawful under these domestic criminal provisions and, therefore, as violations of the proper function of a diplomatic mission as provided by international law.

D   European Human Rights Obligations

The international law I have outlined binds the United States and should have precluded many of the NSA's surveillance programs. But the NSA-Affair also has European human rights law implications. Germany (and other European states) probably violated the right to privacy guaranteed by the European Convention on Human Rights (ECHR)[129] by concluding bilateral agreements with the United States, by tolerating U.S. activities, and by engaging in surveillance programs

---

[126] Vienna Convention on Diplomatic Relations art. 3(1)(d), Apr. 18, 1961, 23 U.S.T. 3227, 500 U.N.T.S. 95 (emphasis added). *See* Case Concerning United States Diplomatic and Consular Staff in Tehran (U.S. v. Iran), 1980 I.C.J. 3, 39 (May 24) ("[T]he 1961 Convention ... take[s] account of the difficulty that may be experienced in [...] determining exactly when exercise of the diplomatic function, expressly recognized in Article 3 (1) (d) of the 1961 Convention, of 'ascertaining by all lawful means conditions and developments in the receiving State' may be considered as involving such acts as 'espionage' or 'interference in internal affairs.'").

[127] STRAFGESETZBUCH [StGB] [PENAL CODE], May 15, 1871, BUNDESGESETZBLATT, Teil I [BGBI. I] 3322, as amended, § 96 (Ger.).

[128] *Id.* at §§ 201, 202a, 202b (Ger.).

[129] European Convention on Human Rights art. 8, Nov. 4, 1950, E.T.S. 5 ("Article 8 – Right to Respect for Private and Family Life. 1. Everyone has the right to respect for his private and family life, his home and his correspondence. 2. There shall be no interference by a public authority with the exercise of this right except such as is in accordance with the law and is necessary in a democratic society in the interests of national security, public safety or the economic wellbeing of the country, for the prevention of disorder or crime, for the protection of health or morals, or for the protection of the rights and freedoms of others.").

themselves.[130] Under the *Matthews* principle, ECHR member states are not allowed to avoid their obligations under the Convention by asserting other, conflicting international law committments. This rule emerged recently, long after European states concluded Cold War joint intelligence agreements.[131] Still, the *Matthews* principle applies to the current constellation of events and circumstances. The European Court of Human Rights (ECtHR) case law has fleshed out the legal require-ments posed by Article 8 of the ECHR for national surveillance meas-ures, interception, storage, and the exchange of data.[132] This means that

---

[130] *See* Big Brother Watch v. UK, App. No. 58170/13, HUDOC (lodged Sept. 4, 2013), http://hudoc.echr.coe.int/eng?i=001-140713#{"itemid":["001-140713"]} (various privacy-activists and NGOs filed complaint claiming that the U.K.'s surveillance regime notably with regard to monitoring the U.S. American surveillance programs fall short of the standard of art. 8 ECHR). The lawfulness of the E.U. member states' own programs will not be further analysed in this chapter. See for an assessment D. Bigo/S. Carrera/N Hernandez/J Jeandsboz/J Parkin/F Raggazzi/A Scherrer, National Programmes for mass surveillance of personal data in E.U. Member States and their compatibility with E.U. law: Study (Directorate General for Internal Policies: Policy Department Citizens' Rights and Constitutional Affairs, Sept. 2013). The study concludes that it "could be argued that large-scale surveillance practices in E.U. member states constitute a systematic and persistent breach of the Union's values as foreseen in Article 7 TEU"(at p. 42).

[131] *See* James I. Walsh, *Intelligence Sharing in the European Union: Institutions Are Not Enough*, 44 J. Common Mkt. Stud. 625, 631 (2006) ("The Berne Group, or Club of Berne, was formed in the 1970s as a forum for the security services of six E.U. Member States.").

[132] Malone v. U.K., App. No. 8691/79, HUDOC, ¶ 79 (Aug. 2, 1984) http://hudoc.echr.coe.int/eng#{"fulltext":["8691/79"],"documentcollectionid2":["GRANDCHAMBER","CH-AMBER"],"itemid":["001-57533"]} (legal framework on interception of telephone calls was not clear and precise enough, and therefore violation of art. 8); Rotaru v. Romania, App. No. 28341/95 2000-V Eur. Ct. H.R. 109 (Romanian legal framework on secret surveillance did not satisfy the standards of clarity and protection against abuse as required by art. 8); Weber v. Germany, App. No. 54934/00, 2006-XI Eur. Ct. H.R. 309 (exchange of data); Cemalettin Canlı v. Turkey, App. No. 22427/04, HUDOC (Nov. 18, 2008), http://hudoc.echr.coe.int/eng#{"fulltext": ["canli v. turkey"]," documentcollectionid2":["GRANDCHAM-BER","CHAMBER"],"itemid":["001-89623"]} (inter-agency data exchange); Liberty v. U.K., App. No. 58243/00, ¶ 56 et seq., HUDOC (July 1, 2008), http://hudoc.echr.coe.int/eng#{"fulltext":["liberty   v.   uk"],"documentcollectionid2":["GRANDCHAMBER","CHAM-BER"],"itemid":["001-87207"]} (deficient legal framework on surveillance); S. and Marper v. U.K., App. No. 30562/04, 2008-V Eur. Ct. H.R. 167 (storage of personal data incl. DNA profile); Dalea v. France, App. No. 964/07, HUDOC (Feb. 2, 2010), http://hudoc.echr.coe.int/eng#{"appno":["964/07"],"itemid":["001-97520"]} (correction of data in the Schengen data-base) (Fr.); Kennedy v. U.K., App. No. 26839/05, ¶ 118 et seq., HUDOC (May 18, 2010), http://hudoc.echr.coe.int/eng#{"fulltext":["kennedy v uk"],"documentcollectionid2":["GRAN DCHAMBER","CHAMBER"],"itemid":["001-98473"]} (surveillance of (internal) communi-cation with a scrutiny of the British legislation; interceptions occurred in the course of a crimininal investigation for murder; no violation of art. 8); Uzun v. Germany, App. No. 35623/05, 2010-VI Eur. Ct. H.R. 1 (GPS-surveillance of a terror suspect).

member states of the ECHR are not only bound to respect these standards in their own surveillance activities, but they must also refrain from collaborating with a third state and assisting that state's violations of privacy through surveillance measures. Such collaboration may take the form of providing data and granting a third party state access to communication systems. Quite to the contrary, member states of the ECHR are obliged to protect persons under their jurisdiction from threats to human rights emanating from third actors, including foreign states.[133] In fact, this duty of protection may require the member states to take effective diplomatic and legal measures against the United States in response to the the NSA's surveillance and data-collection programs.[134] Positive obligations arising from the ECHR, such as this one, are normally requirements that states act ("obligations of conduct"), not requirements that states guarantee results. States do not need to undertake all expedient steps no matter what burden or costs they might involve.[135] When assessing whether a burden resulting from a positive obligation under the ECHR is tolerable, it is reasonable to take into account the member states' desire to avoid a costly political or diplomatic dispute with a foreign state. But the overall balance between the pursuit of the positive obligation and minimizing the resulting burden must result in an adequately sufficient level of human rights protection.[136] One among the minimally burdensome steps a member state might be expected to take to satisfy this positive obligation is the earnest consideration of the termination of the conflicting bilateral accords that were concluded in the 1960s.[137] It would go too far, however, to say that the positive obligation under the

---

[133] *See* Osman v. United Kingdom, [1998] Eur. H.R. Rep. 101, ¶ 115; El-Masri v. Macedonia, App. No. 39630/09, HUDOC (Dec. 13, 2012), http://hudoc.echr.coe.int/sites/eng/pages/search.aspx?i=001-115621#{"itemid":["001-115621"]}; Von Hannover v. Germany, App. No. 59320/00, 1, 28, 2004-VI Eur. Ct. H.R. 41.

[134] Soering v. United Kingdom, (1989) 11 E.H.R.R. 439 (Holding that should the United Kingdom decide to extradite Soering to the U.S., they would be violating art. 3).

[135] Plattform "Ärzte für das Leben" v. Austria, App. No. 10126/82, ¶¶ 33–34, HUDOC (June 21, 1988), http://hudoc.echr.coe.int/eng#{"fulltext":["10126/82"],"documentcollectionid2":["GRANDCHAMBER","CHAMBER"],"itemid":["001-57558"]}.

[136] ANNE PETERS & TILMANN ALTWICKER, EUROPÄISCHE MENSCHENRECHTSKONVENTION: MIT RECHTSVERGLEICHENDEN BEZÜGEN ZUM DEUTSCHEN GRUNDGESETZ 32 (2d ed. 2012).

[137] *Germany ends spy pact with U.S. and U.K. after Snowden*, BBC (Aug. 2, 2013), www.bbc.com/news/world-europe-23553837.

ECHR requires Member States to institute a complaint against the United States before an international court or tribunal.[138]

E Domestic Constitutional Law

In most – if not all – of the states where the NSA was revealed to be pursuing its surveillance programs, the citizens enjoy a domestic constitutional right to communications privacy that is independent of the international human rights law protection I have outlined. But the fundamental rights embodied in Europe's domestic constitutions only limit the power of the respective state. They do not limit the United States. Still, the European states' responsibility under their own constitutional law may be implicated if they condone, tolerate, or – despite their knowledge of the American activities – refrain from protesting and seeking to end the NSA's surveillance measures on their territory. This justifies a consideration of the relevant domestic constitutional law.

In Germany, for example, the secrecy of communications is secured by Article 10 of the German Basic Law (*Grundgesetz*).[139] This is not an absolute protection. Similar to other fundamental rights provided by the Basic Law, Article 10 explicitly provides that it may be restricted by law.[140] The principal relevant legislation in Germany is the so-called G10-Act (Gesetz zur Beschränkung des Brief-, Post und Fernmeldegeheimnisses).[141] The G10-Act permits intrusions on communications privacy in the interest of Germany's national security and to repel "dangers to the troops of the non-German contracting parties of the NATO treaty."[142] That Act allows for different types of state intrusions

---

[138] *See* Soering v. U.K., *supra* note 134 (The Court in Soering in no way forbade the U.K. from extraditing Soering, realizing that would implicate the relationship between a member state and a non-member state. Instead, it merely declared a damages judgment *should* the U.K. extradite Soering.).

[139] GRUNDGESETZ [GG] [BASIC LAW] art. 10.

[140] *Id.*, art. 10(2) ("Restrictions may be ordered only pursuant to a law. If the restriction serves to protect the free democratic basic order or the existence or security of the Federation or of a Land, the law may provide that the person affected shall not be informed of the restriction and that recourse to the courts shall be replaced by a review of the case by agencies and auxiliary agencies appointed by the legislature.").

[141] Gesetz zur Beschränkung des Brief-, Post- und Fernmeldegeheimnisses in der Fassung des Gesetzes zur Änderung des Strafgesetzbuches, der Strafprozeßordnung und anderer Gesetze (Verbrechensbekämpfungsgesetz) [Crime Control Act], Oct. 28, 1994, BGBl. I, at 3186; geändert durch das Begleitgesetz zum Telekommunikationsgesetz (BegleitG) [Act Accompanying the Telecommunications Act], Dec. 17, 1997, BGBl. I, at 3108. [Hereinafter G10-Act].

[142] *Id.* at § 1 (my translation).

on the fundamental right, including "targeted surveillance" (in pursuit of specific individuals for whom there is tangible criminal suspicion)[143] and "strategic surveillance" (involving generalized, nonspecific surveillance of the kind usually associated with a state's foreign intelligence services).[144] The G10-Act imposes specific and concrete conditions on these surveillance measures. First, only specific German agencies can perform the permissible surveillance, notably the German Federal Intelligence Service (*Bundesnachrichtendienst*) but also including the German Military Counter-Intelligence Service (*Militärischer Abschirmdienst*) and the Federal and State domestic intelligence agencies known as the Offices for the Protection of the Constitution (*Verfassungsschutzbehörden*).[145] Second, surveillance must be undertaken in pursuit of one of a limited number of justifications. Targeted surveillance requires "actual grounds for the suspicion" that the subject has committed or is planning to commit a listed criminal offense.[146] Strategic surveillance is limited to the collection of information that is necessary for discrete national security objectives.[147] Third, all surveillance measures are subject to specific approval and oversight procedures.[148] Fourth, there are strict limits on the retention, use, and distribution of data collected.[149] Finally, the affected persons must be informed (after the fact) that they were the object of surveillance measures and they are guaranteed access to nonjudicial and – eventually – judicial remedies.[150] When the German Federal Constitutional Court has reviewed constitutional privacy complaints as a result of communications surveillance measures similar to those permitted by the G10-Act, it has strictly applied the proportionality principle.[151] Needless to say, these preconditions and limits have not been met in the course of the NSA's extensive surveillance of German communications.[152] The German Parliament has opened an investigation into the NSA-Affair and its impact on Germany, in part to clarify what German authorities knew about the NSA's surveillance activities,

---

[143] *Id.* at §§ 3–4.   [144] *Id.* at §§ 5–8.   [145] *Id.* at § 1.   [146] *Id.* at § 3.

[147] *Id.,* at § 5.   [148] *Id.* at §§ 9–11, 14–15.   [149] *Id.* at §§ 4, 6–7.

[150] *Id.* at § 12; 125 BVerfGE 260, *supra* note 84.

[151] *See, e.g.,* Bundesverfassungsgericht [BVerfG] [Federal Constitutional Court] Apr. 12, 2005, 112 BVerfGE 304 (the GPS case); Bundesverfassungsgericht [BVerfG] [Federal Constitutional Court] Feb. 27, 2008, 120 BVerfGE 274 (the Online Computer Surveillance case); *see also* 125 BVerfGE 260, *supra* note 84.

[152] Sven Becker *et al.*, *New NSA Revelations: Inside Snowden's Germany File*, SPIEGEL ONLINE (June 18, 2014, 4:20 PM), www.spiegel.de/international/germany/new-snowden-revelations-on-nsa-spying-in-germany-a-975441.html.

when they knew about them, and whether they facilitated or participated in the programs.[153] That information may point to constitutional violations on the part of German authorities, either for direct intrusions upon Germans' constitutionally protected communications privacy or for having tolerated American communications surveillance.

F   Commercial Actors and Privacy Rights

A full understanding of the NSA-Affair also must account for the fact that American-based commercial actors (such as Google and Microsoft) – and not just state intelligence agencies – contributed to the intrusions on Germans' communications privacy. This part of the story has three distinct bases. First, commercial interests have developed (and continue to develop at a breathtaking pace) the technology we now use to communicate and that the NSA manipulates in its pursuit of communications data. Second, when allowing state intelligence agencies to access their communications data or infrastructure, businesses are usually complying with laws that require them to do so.[154] In fact, most states require private Internet and telecommunications service providers to conti?niously collect and preserve communications metadata and content.[155] But it is also the case that commercial actors voluntarily take measures that facilitate surveillance, in part because they hope to profit from the collection and use of data their users produce. Third, standard setting in this sphere is often private, or consists in a hybrid of public-private norms. For example, the European Telecommunication Standards Institute (ETSI) drafts standards that are meant to regulate the interception of foreign cloud-based services by European governments.[156]

---

[153] Einsetzung eines Untersuchungsausschusses, DEUTSCHER BUNDESTAG: DRUCKSACHE 18/843 (March 18, 2014). *See* for the ongoing work www.bundestag.de/bundestag/ausschuesse18/ua/1untersuchungsausschuss. *See* von Notz chapter in this volume.

[154] 47 U.S.C. §§ 1001–10 (2012); 50 U.S.C. §§ 1885–85b (2012); G10-Act, *supra* note 141, at § 2.

[155] Directive 2006/24/EC of the European Parliament and of the Council of 15 March 2006 on the Retention of Data Generated or Processed in Connection with the Provision of Publicly Available Electronic Communications Services or of Public Communications Networks and Amending Directive 2002/58/EC, 2006 O.J. (L105) 54. *See also* Chapter 21 in this volume.

[156] European Telecommunication Standards Institute, Cloud Standards Coordination Final Report (Nov. 2013), www.etsi.org/images/files/Events/2013/2013_CSC_Delivery_WS/CSC-Final_report-013-CSC_Final_report_v1_0_PDF_format-.PDF.

Each of these factors suggest that, normatively speaking, private commercial interests bear some form of responsibility for the harm done to privacy. But, in the traditional international law framework, these actors are not directly bound to respect the human right to privacy as it is guaranteed by the ICCPR. Private businesses are not parties to the international human rights covenants, which oblige and are addressed only to the state parties.

If it were accepted that private commercial entities had the capacity to possess rights and duties flowing from international law (international legal personality), then they would be obliged to observe customary international law and general principles of international law. But international business entities have not yet been saddled with concrete and firm international law duties to respect specific human rights such as the right to privacy. So far, private actors have been found to be bound to respect the *corpus* of *jus cogens* norms – on the understanding that these are "absolute" norms in terms of substance and with regard to their potential addressees ("debtors").[157] Importantly, the ECJ held that Google Spain, "the operator of the search engine as the person determining the purposes and means of that activity must ensure, within the framework of its responsibilities, powers and capabilities, that the activity meets the requirements of Directive 95/46/EC in order that the guarantees laid down by the directive may have full effect and that effective and complete protection of data subjects, in particular of their right to privacy, may actually be achieved."[158] Thus, the Court held a private operator directly bound to an E.U. Directive although such Directives are formally addressed to the E.U. Member States only. Still, the question of "direct" human rights obligations of private actors, flowing from the E.U. Fundamental Rights Charter, the ECHR, or international human rights covenants has so far not been answered positively by the case-law.

---

[157] *See* Human Rights Council, Rep. of the Independent International Commission of Inquiry on the Syrian Arab Republic, UN Doc. A/HRC/19/69, ¶ 106 (Feb. 22, 2012) ("at a minimum, human rights obligations constituting peremptory international law (*ius cogens*) bind States, individuals and non-State collective entities, including armed groups. Acts violating *ius cogens* – for instance, torture or enforced disappearances – can never be justified.").

[158] Case C-131/12, Google Spain SL v. Agencia Española de Protección de Datos (AEPD), ¶ 38, InfoCuria – Case-Law Ct. Jus. (May 13, 2014), http://curia.europa.eu/juris/document/document.jsf;jsessionid=9ea7d0f130d58fa348967d244833bad1c86381ec1189.e34KaxiLc3e Qc40LaxqMbN4Oc3aKe0?text=&docid=152065&pageIndex=0&doclang=EN&mode=lst& dir=&occ=first&part=1&cid=385379.

Additionally, in some constellations, commercial actors' data-gathering activities will trigger the international responsibility of particular states. If Google and Microsoft have committed themselves to providing data on Internet communication to U.S. authorities, then their collection, storage, and transmission of data could – under quite narrow conditions – be attributable to the United States. This would only be the case if their private actions – which contribute to a violation of the communications privacy secured by Article 17 of the ICCPR – have been taken "under the direction and control" of the American government.[159]

State parties are also obliged to protect individuals from private actors. This is stated specifically in Article 17(2) of the ICCPR: "everyone has the right to the protection of the law against such interference or attacks."[160] This includes a duty to enact "extraterritorial" legislation.[161] By this I mean the sending state's domestic laws that regulate business entities – even when they act abroad – if they possess the sending-state's nationality, and maybe on the basis of further links. On this analysis the United States is obliged to enact adequate (domestic) legislation to prevent Google's contribution to or participation in human rights abuses.[162]

Finally, under the Ruggie Principles (UN Guiding Principles on Human Rights and Transnational Corporations and Other Business Enterprises)[163] transnational corporations incur a kind of "soft" international "responsibility" for the protection of privacy and

---

[159] *Draft Articles on Responsibility of States for Internationally Wrongful Acts, supra* note 116, at art. 8 ("The conduct of a person or group of persons shall be considered an act of a State under international law if the person or group of persons is in fact acting on the instructions of, or under the direction or control of, that State in carrying out the conduct." Commentary provided in the cited source points out in ¶ 2 that "[m]ost commonly, cases of this kind will arise where State organs supplement their own action by recruiting or instigating private persons or groups who act as 'auxiliaries' while remaining outside the official structure of the State.") (at p. 47).

[160] ICCPR, *supra* note 10, at art. 17(2).

[161] *See* General Comment 16, *supra* note 13, at ¶ 1 ("The obligations imposed by this article require the State to adopt legislative and other measures to give effect to the prohibition against such interferences and attacks as well as to the protection of this right."); NOWAK, *supra* note 14, at 379 ("Article 17 [has] a certain emphasis on the *positive obligation of States to protect privacy* against interference and attacks from others." Emphasis Nowak's.).

[162] *See* General Comment 16, *supra* note 13, at ¶¶ 8–10.

[163] Special Rep. of the Secretary-General, *Guiding Principles on Business and Human Rights: Implementing the United Nations "Protect, Respect and Remedy" Framework*, Annex § II (A) ¶ 12, Annex § II(B) ¶ 18, U.N. Doc. A/HRC/17/31 (Mar. 21, 2011) ("Ruggie report"). On Business responsibility, including human rights due diligence requirements see ¶¶ 11–24.

correspondence.[164] Under these principles commercial enterprises must identify the adverse impacts their business practices may have on the right to privacy and freedom of correspondence.[165] In response to these adverse impacts the commercial enterprises must seek to avoid the harm where possible and to mitigate the intrusion on privacy where it is unavoidable.[166] And finally, business must establish or contribute to processes that enable remediation for violations.[167]

G   Conclusion

Practically speaking, what are the possible consequences of this extensive indictment mapping the illegality (both international and domestic) of the NSA's surveillance and data collection programs?

Individual communications against the United States under the ICCPR are inadmissibile because the United States did not submit to that procedure.[168] An interstate complaint remains a possibility, although that mechanism has never been used. It has largely been avoided out of fear that it would cause a political and diplomatic nuisance. At the very least, the UN Human Rights Committee can remark America's noncompliance in its periodic reports. In fact, the Committee has already done so.[169]

Violations of the law of diplomatic relations might have more bite because they open the way to the International Court of Justice (ICJ). As far back as 1972 the United States ratified the Optional Protocol of the Vienna Convention on Diplomatic Relations Concerning the Compulsory Settlement of Disputes (April 18, 1961).[170] Significantly, the United

---

[164] The normative quality of the Ruggie Principles is moderate: According to their own terms, the" Guiding Principles' normative contribution lies not in the creation of new international law obligations". *Id.* at ¶ 14.

[165] *Id.* at ¶¶ 12, 18.   [166] *Id.* at ¶ 19.   [167] *Id.* at ¶ 22.

[168] The U.S.A. did not ratify OP 1 to the ICCPR.

[169] Human Rights Committee, Concluding observations on the fourth periodic report of the U.S.A., *supra* note 56 ("Applicability of the Covenant at national level: . . . 4. The Committee regrets that the State party continues to maintain the position that the Covenant does not apply with respect to individuals under its jurisdiction, but outside its territory, despite the interpretation to the contrary of article 2, paragraph 1, supported by the Committee's established jurisprudence, the jurisprudence of the International Court of Justice and State practice . . .)."

[170] Vienna Convention on Diplomatic Relations Concerning the Compulsory Settlement of Disputes, Apr. 18, 1961, 23 U.S.T. 3227, 500 U.N.T.S. 95 (entered into force for the U.S. Dec. 13, 1972); Optional Protocol of the Vienna Convention on Diplomatic Relations

States has not withdrawn from this Optional Protocol as it did with respect to the Optional Protocol on Consular Relations.[171] Article 1 of the Optional Protocol foresees that "[d]isputes arising out of the interpretation or application of the Convention shall lie within the compulsory jurisdiction of the International Court of Justice and may accordingly be brought before the Court by an application made by any party to the dispute being a Party to the present Protocol."[172] Given that both Germany and the United States are parties to the Optional Protocol, Germany could institute proceedings before the ICJ alleging a breach of the Diplomatic Relations Convention. There is precedent for exactly that kind of dramatic maneuver. Under the now-rescinded authority of the Optional Protocol to the Consular Relations Convention, Germany brought and won a complaint against the United States before the ICJ.[173]

The goal of international (or domestic) adjudication – and institutional monitoring and comments of the kind conducted by the UN Human Rights Committee – would be to underscore two fundamental principles. In precise terms, it would confirm that communications privacy as secured by law is an essential human right. In more general terms, it would remind us that all states – even a state with America's vast power – are subject to the rule of law. In both cases the message is the same: the United States should obey the law.

My confidence that the United States will also come to acknowledge the benefits of doing so (just as some think America did after its controversial invasion of Iraq in 2003) leads me deeper into the embrace of the law. One important way forward out of the shadow of the NSA-Affair will be *law making*. Considering its global importance, this will necessarily involve a dialogue with the United States.[174] First, the UN Human Rights Committee should issue a General Comment on the right

Concerning the Compulsory Settlement of Disputes, Apr. 18, 1961, 23 U.S.T. 3374, 500 U.N.T.S. 223 (entered into force for the U.S. Dec. 13, 1972).

[171] Vienna Convention on Consular Relations, Apr. 24, 1963, 21 U.S.T. 77, 596 U.N.T.S. 261 (entered into force for the U.S. Dec. 24, 1969); Optional Protocol to the Vienna Convention on Consular Relations concerning the Compulsory Settlement of Disputes, Apr. 24, 1963, 596 U.N.T.S. 487 (entered into force for the U.S. Dec. 24, 1969, withdrawn from by the U.S. Mar. 7, 2005) [hereinafter Consular Relations Optional Protocol].

[172] Consular Relations Optional Protocol, *supra* note 171, at art. 1.

[173] LaGrand Case (Ger. v. U.S.), 2001 I.C.J. 466 (June 27).

[174] See for a European call for such a dialogue Krystyna Kowalik-Banczyk, *Les Aspects Transfrontaliers des Infractions a la Vie Privée par la Surveillance de Masse de la Part de Agents Étatiques*, 119 REVUE GÉNÉRALE DE DROIT INTERNATIONAL PUBLIC 383 (2015).

to privacy in the digital age. Unfortunately, the Committee does not seem to consider this a priority to which it should devote its scarce resources. Second, the work of the UN Human Rights Council, building on its 2014 resolution, "The right to privacy in the digital age," should be welcomed.[175] It is laudable that the Human Rights Council established a mandate for a special rapporteur on privacy.[176] Third, the Council of Europe – the Assembly or the Council of Ministers – could ask the Venice Commission to issue an opinion. Most importantly, stakeholder forums should be created. It is imperative that the business sector be involved in any standard settting activity.

A hard law option would be an optional or amending protocol to the ICCPR in order to highlight communications privacy, especially in the Internet. Insiders are hesitant in this regard, in part because it will be difficult to arrive at an agreed text. More importantly, they worry that by acknowledging the need for an Additional Protocol, they would be inviting an *e contrario* argument that digital privacy is not yet covered by the Covenant. In any case, it is uncertain (as always) how many states would ratify such a protocol.

Much work lies ahead for concerned international law scholars. The UN Human Rights Committee published its General Comment on Privacy and Secrecy of Correspondence in 1988.[177] Mark Zuckerberg, the cofounder of Facebook, was only four years old at the time. The world has changed immeasurably since then, and the field of communications has been pushed along by technological advances almost unimaginable just a decade ago. There is no sign of this warp-speed evolution slowing. International law concepts must be reconceived and reimagined for the digital age and the challenges posed by cyberspace. As legal scholars, we must think of ways to adapt and translate traditional principles for our times. We must, for example, transliterate our understanding of "territorial sovereignty" to account for "digital sovereignty." We must adapt our notion of "state security" so that it functions for "cyber security" as well. These interpretations are needed to make international law adequate to the real challenges it faces. It is an open question – a question that will be answered in the first instance by scholarly debate – whether we can translate "post card" as "email," or

---

[175] Human Rights Committee, U.N. Doc. A/HRC/28/L.27 (Mar. 24, 2015).

[176] *Id.* at ¶ 4. The Human Rights Council then appointed Mr. Joseph Cannataci (Malta) as Special Rapporteur at its 29th regular session (2015), for a period of three years.

[177] General Comment 16, *supra* note 13.

"effective control" (a term needed for determining jurisdiction) as "virtual control." Our new ideas should not cling too tightly to the past. But neither should our answers for the future give up on the core constitutional achievement of the past: the protection of liberty and human rights.

We should keep in mind that the Internet plays an extremely valuable positive role in upholding human rights (by making violations public, and exposing them to worldwide rebuke). The Internet can play an indispensable role in guaranteeing human security (precisely by helping to identify, prevent, track, and combat terrorist and criminal activities). The Internet can also foster democracy (by furnishing education, information, transparency, participation, and e-voting). Inversely, as the European Court of Human Rights reminded us in *Weber and Saravia v. Germany* (a case involving telephone surveillance), "a system of secret surveillance for the protection of national security may undermine or even destroy democracy under the cloak of defending it."[178] Democracy, the rule of law, and privacy rights must therefore be vigilantly protected in the era of Internet-based surveillance.

---

[178] *See* Weber, *supra* note 27, at ¶ 106.

6

Privacy, Hypocrisy, and a Defense of Surveillance

BY BENJAMIN WITTES

A   Introduction: Different Notions of Privacy

Defending the NSA in a conversation with Germans these days is a bit like ascending the pulpit at a Southern Baptist Church on Sunday morning to speak on behalf of the Devil.[1] Despite this, I hope the following reflections are taken as a good-faith contribution to this project's important efforts to promote honest and productive dialogue between the United States and Germany on issues of "privacy and power" in the shadow of the NSA-Affair.

I want to start with a broad point that Russell Miller has touched on in his chapter introducing this project. Part of the difficulty the transatlantic dialogue faces is that we have one word – *privacy* – that means extraordinarily different things depending on who is invoking it and what culture he or she comes from.[2] I can offer some additional – random but important – examples of this. The legal system with which the United States is most closely related is Britain's. Yet, if you look at American and British wiretapping law in the criminal context (not in the national security context), some very striking differences emerge. In the United States it is relatively hard to get a wiretap warrant.[3] You need a warrant from a judge confirming the existence of probable cause.[4] But, once you

---

[1] I am indebted to Stewart Baker for this vivid analogy.   [2] *See* Chapter 2 in this volume.
[3] *See, e.g.*, James Q. Whitman, *The Two Western Cultures of Privacy: Dignity versus Liberty*, 113 Yale L.J. 1151, 1159 (2004) (comparing the rates at which wiretapping occurs between America and various European nations); Ryan Gallagher, *What Country Monitors Communications the Most: U.S., U.K., Canada, or Australia?*, Slate (July 18, 2012, 11:45 AM), www.slate.com/blogs/future_tense/2012/07/18/wiretapping_and_subscriber_information_requests_by_law_enforcement_in_u_s_australia_canada_u_k_.html (demonstrating that the per capita rate of wiretapping is substantially higher in the U.K. than in the U.S.). *But see* United States Courts, Table 7 Authorized Intercepts Granted Pursuant to 18 U.S.C. § 2519 as Reported in Wiretap Reports, Wiretap Report 2012, www.uscourts.gov/uscourts/Statistics/WiretapReports/2012/Table7.pdf (showing that 99.9% of all wiretap requests since 2002 have been granted.).
[4] U.S. Const. amend. IV (protecting against unreasonable search and seizure, and requiring probable cause for the issuance of a warrant); 18 U.S.C. § 3123(a)(1) (2012) (requiring a

get that wiretapping order, the evidence obtained – and any new evidence or "fruit" it produces – can be used in criminal proceedings.[5] In Britain, as a general matter, the exact opposite is true.[6] It is quite easy to get a wiretap order. The minister can order it and there is no obligation to secure prior judicial approval.[7] On the other hand, the evidence obtained may guide the investigation but is almost invariably not admissible in the criminal proceedings.[8] Both of these systems are deemed to be necessary to protect privacy and they are precisely the inverse of one another. Something similar surfaces when one looks to Germany. There are some things the famously privacy-conscious German state can get away with that would provoke riots in the streets if implemented in the United States. I have in mind, for example, the duty in Germany to register your residence with local authorities every time you move. Imagine what would happen if you told a bunch of Texans that the police were entitled to know where they live! The discrepancies go on and on. In the United States, we have a certain capricious interest in the privacy of gun ownership. After the Newtown school shooting,[9] for example, the suburban New York newspaper *The Journal News* published information about

court order to place wiretap devices); 18 U.S.C. § 2516 (2012) (enumerating the possible offenses which may warrant wiretapping).

[5] 18 U.S.C. § 2515 (2012) (prohibiting the admission as evidence of only improperly gathered information).

[6] *See supra* note 3; *supra* note 4.

[7] Regulation of Investigatory Powers Act, 2000, c. 1, § 3 (U.K.). *See* Oxford Pro Bono Publico, *Legal Opinion on Intercept Communication* 9 (Jan. 2006) www2.law.ox.ac.uk/opbp/OPBP%20Intercept%20Evidence%20Report.pdf; *See also* Eric Weiner, *Wiretapping, European-Style*, SLATE (Feb. 14, 2006, 6:39 AM), www.slate.com/articles/news_and_polit ics/how_they_do_it/2006/02/wiretapping_europeanstyle.single.html.

[8] Regulation of Investigatory Powers Act, 2000, c. 1, § 17(1) (U.K.). Oxford, *supra* note 7, at 10. *See also Using Intercept Evidence in Court "Not Yet Viable,"* BBC (Dec. 10, 2009, 3:18 PM), http://news.bbc.co.uk/2/hi/uk_news/8405109.stm. *But see* Deborah Summers *et al.*, *Brown Approves Use of Wiretap Evidence*, THE GUARDIAN (Feb. 6, 2008, 10:49 AM), www.theguar dian.com/politics/2008/feb/06/uk.ukcrime (demonstrating that the British government is considering ways to implement the use of wiretapped communications as evidence).

[9] *See* James Barron, *Nation Reels after Gunman Massacres 20 Children at School in Connecti-cut*, N.Y. TIMES (Dec. 14, 2012), www.nytimes.com/2012/12/15/nyregion/shooting-reported-at-connecticut-elementary-school.html?pagewanted=all&_r=0; Tom McCarthy, *Shooting in Newtown, Connecticut School Leaves 28 Dead*, THE GUARDIAN (Dec. 14, 2012, 1:37 PM), www.theguardian.com/world/us-news-blog/2012/dec/14/newtown-connecticut-school-shooting-live; *Sandy Hook Elementary School Shooting: Newtown, Connecticut Administrators, Students among Victims, Reports Say*, HUFFINGTON POST (Dec. 12, 2012, 10:28 AM), www.huffingtonpost.com/2012/12/14/sandy-hook-elementary-school-shoot ing_n_2300831.html.

gun owners in Westchester and Rockland counties. The report was entitled "The Gun Owner Next Door: What You Don't Know About the Weapons in Your Neighborhood,"[10] and it included addresses and interactive maps. The report relied on public records that documented people who had or who were registered to own firearms.[11] The gun-owning community went crazy about this invasion of their privacy.[12] This was widely regarded as a significant privacy violation in America. But I suspect that, if you published information in Germany about gun owners, it would not be thought of in the language of privacy. In Switzerland, to cite another example, there is a much cherished tradition of "banking privacy," which is a concept unknown outside of the Cayman Islands and a few other countries.[13]

My point is that it is very easy to talk in abstract, formalistic terms about privacy. But when it comes to Americans and Germans, we are not actually talking about the same thing. You cannot ask questions about the meaning of privacy – not in any productive sense – until you know more about the different values that are served by different societies' different legal notions of privacy. One factor in this pluralistic exercise is the different kinds of responsibility governments assume for the societies they govern. This difference may help justify an infringement of privacy in one country that would not be permitted in another.

---

[10] Dwight R. Worley, *The Gun Owner Next Door: What You Don't Know about the Weapons in Your Neighborhood*, Journal News Lohud (Dec. 23, 2012), www.lohud.com/apps/pbcs.dll/article?AID=2012312230056&gcheck=1.

[11] *Id.*

[12] *See* Christine Haughney, *After Pinpointing Gun Owners, Paper Is a Target*, N.Y. Times (Jan. 6, 2013), www.nytimes.com/2013/01/07/nyregion/after-pinpointing-gun-owners-journal-news-is-a-target.html?pagewanted=all&_r=0; David Carr, *Guns, Maps and Data That Disturb*, N.Y. Times (Jan. 14, 2013), www.nytimes.com/2013/01/14/business/media/guns-maps-and-disturbing-data.html; Nick Carbone, *Outrage After New York Paper Posts Map of Gun Owners' Names and Addresses*, TIME (Dec. 26, 2012), http://newsfeed.time.com/2012/12/26/outrage-after-new-york-paper-posts-map-of-gun-owners-names-and-addresses/; Henry Blodget, *Gun Owners Freak Out After Newspaper Publishes Their Names and Addresses*, Business Insider (Dec. 26, 2012, 10:58 AM), www.businessinsider.com/gun-owners-freak-out-after-newspaper-publishes-their-names-and-addresses-2012-12?IR=T.

[13] *See* Gracielle R. Cabungeal, *Paradise Lost – Searching for New (Off) Shores: The State of Bank Secrecy, Fiduciary Mistrust, and International Estate Planning After the Financial Crisis*, 25 Quinnipiac Prob. L.J. 67, 83 (2011) (discussing the vanishingly few countries with banking privacy laws); M. V., *Swiss Bank Secrecy: A Whistleblower's Woes*, Economist (July 19, 2014, 11:05 AM), www.economist.com/blogs/schumpeter/2014/07/swiss-bank-secrecy.

The point that people mean very different things when they talk about privacy in the intelligence context has been driven home to me in significant ways over the last few years.

Professor Anne Peter's contribution to this project captures one approach to privacy.[14] It is an effective summary of an international law framing for the subject. And I think it very fairly represents the way a lot of people think about the NSA and its work.

But another approach comes into view as a consequence of the considerable time I have spent, on a personal and professional level, with people who work at the NSA. I have talked with them about how they – and their institution – navigate the increased public concern with privacy and the heightened scrutiny being given to their work. After all, almost by definition, this is not an agency that deals much with the public.[15] The NSA is not like the FBI. The FBI holds press conferences when it undertakes investigations and it has agents that testify in every criminal proceeding in which it is involved in developing evidence. This is not the way of the NSA. Despite its massive payroll and budget – and even bigger mandate – the NSA used to have a press office consisting of only two people. Those public relations officers have described their job in the pre-Snowden era as consisting of picking-up the phone when it rang and getting the caller off the phone as quickly as possible without having said anything themselves. And that is how *they* described their job. The NSA is an agency that has very little experience with, and very little expertise in, engaging the public. There is good reason, after all, that the NSA used to be called – and only half-jokingly – the "No Such Agency."[16] This all leads to a marked dissonance between the way the NSA's activities are understood by the public (particularly in the era since the Snowden revelations) and the way NSA understands itself. I can assure you that

---

[14] *See* Chapter 5 in this volume.

[15] *See, e.g.,* Steven Aftergood, *Secrecy and Accountability in U.S. Intelligence,* FED'N AM. SCIENTISTS (Oct. 9, 1996), www.fas.org/sgp/cipsecr.html (quoting National Security Council Intelligence Directive No. 12 as saying "any publicity, factual or fictional, concerning intelligence is potentially detrimental to the effectiveness of an intelligence activity and to the national security").

[16] *See* James Bamford, *The Agency that Could Be Big Brother,* N.Y. TIMES (Dec. 25, 2005), www .nytimes.com/2005/12/25/weekinreview/25bamford.html?pagewanted=all; Anne Gearna, *"No Such Agency" Spies on the Communications of the World,* WASH. POST (June 6, 2013), www .washingtonpost.com/world/national-security/no-such-agency-spies-on-the-communications-of-the-world/2013/06/06/5bcd46a6-ceb9-11e2-8845-d970ccb04497_story.html; KATHLEEN HILL & GERALD HILL, THE ENCYCLOPEDIA OF FEDERAL AGENCIES AND COMMISSIONS 63 (2004).

the NSA thinks about individuals' privacy – as it pursues the mandate it has been given by a democratically elected government – in ways that are very different from the approach that others such as Professor Peters take.

B   Privacy and the NSA: A Political and Procedural Approach

Let me try to characterize how the NSA perceives itself and its approach to privacy. To do this I am going to don the persona of an "NSA insider." Please do not assume that this reflects any specific conversations, or that I am quoting someone, because that is really not the case. Instead, these are distilled perspectives based on my familiarity with the institution and the people who work for it. In pursuing this effort I am going to pause from time-to-time to make comparisons with Germany. It might even seem that I am picking on Germany a bit. But the comparison is invited by the specific framing of this project – as a dialogue between Germans and Americans on "privacy and power" in the shadow of the NSA-Affair. I want to be clear that these comparative points could have been made with reference to the laws and institutions of nearly any other democratic country. The conversation and the view of the NSA would be largely the same.

First, the NSA considers itself a very highly regulated and supervised institution. And, in fact, it is supervised and regulated in ways that no comparable international service of any intelligence-collecting country, including Germany, is supervised. When it collects intelligence against a domestic target, the NSA is required to get a judicial warrant. And the NSA has to get a judicial warrant when it collects intelligence against a U.S. person anywhere. This bears repeating. The NSA must obtain a prior judicial warrant. Actually, when working in the domestic sphere, the work is generally done by the FBI with the NSA's help, not by the NSA itself. In these circumstances, surveillance is only undertaken pursuant to a Foreign Intelligence Surveillance Act (FISA) "probable cause warrant" that must be issued by the Foreign Intelligence Surveillance Act Court (FISA Court) in advance of the intelligence gathering initiatives. It is true that when the NSA acts abroad against non-U.S. persons – even when using domestic servers to collect data – it does not obtain specific prior approval for each individual act of surveillance. But those collection policies are not totally unsupervised. The FISA Court plays a supervisory role here, too.[17] Those initiatives are closely reviewed by the FISA

---

[17] 50 U.S.C. § 1881 (2012).

Court.[18] The NSA secures approval from the FISA Court every year for its policies[19] – including its minimization procedures, which are meant to ensure that its activities abroad have the smallest possible impact on Americans.[20] Those policies are also closely reviewed by the Senate and the House Intelligence Committees.[21] The NSA operates under layers of judicial and legislative-branch review that are very close and very probing.

There is no analog for this kind of intelligence supervision in many other countries.[22] There is no comparable presurveillance judicial review of policies and procedures for sister intelligence services in other countries. The BND (*Bundesnachrichtendienst* – German Federal Intelligence Service), for example, does not operate with similar restraints.[23] In Germany, when the BND conducts what I understand is its strategic surveillance, there is no prior judicial approval. Instead, the BND works on the basis of ministerial orders and approval granted by the quasi-parliamentary G10 Commission.[24]

Second, it is broadly misunderstood just how detailed the statutory regime framing and limiting American intelligence activities is. In the limited context of the collection of telecommunications metadata, the general impression that we did not know what the NSA was authorized to do is generally correct. In this sense, Snowden's disclosures were "revelations" in the truest sense. But that impression is totally misplaced with respect to nearly every other facet of the NSA's activities. Any reasonably literate student of U.S. law who followed the debates in 2007 and 2008 that led to the enactment of the Protect

---

[18] 50 U.S.C. § 1881 (2012). *See* EDWARD C. LIU *ET AL.*, CONG. RESEARCH SERV., R43459, OVERVIEW OF CONSTITUTIONAL CHALLENGES TO NSA COLLECTION ACTIVITIES AND RECENT DEVELOPMENTS (2014).

[19] 50 U.S.C. § 1881a(l)(3) (2012).   [20] 50 U.S.C. § 1881a(l)(1) (2012).

[21] 50 U.S.C. § 1881 (2012).

[22] *See* VODAFONE LAW ENFORCEMENT DISCLOSURE REPORT (June 2014), www.vodafone.com/content/dam/sustainability/2014/pdf/operating-responsibly/vodafone_law_enforcement_disclosure_report.pdf.

[23] *See* Gesetz über den Bundesnachrichtendienst [BNDG] [Federal Intelligence Service Act], Dec. 20, 1990, BGBl. I at 2954, §§ 2, 12; Gesetz zur Beschränkung des Brief-, Post- und Fernmeldegeheimnisses [G10 Act], Aug. 13, 1968, BGBl. I at 949, §§ 5, 10–13, 15. *See also* Chapter 13 in this volume.

[24] *See* Christopher Wolf, Dir., Global Privacy and Info. Mgmt Practice at Hogan Lovells U.S. LLP, Address Before the Privacy and Civil Liberties Oversight Board: A Transnational Perspective on Section 702 of the Foreign Intelligence Surveillance Act 11–12 (Mar. 19, 2014), www.pclob.gov/Library/20140319-Testimony-Wolf.pdf. *See also* Russell A. Miller, *Intelligence Oversight – Made in Germany, in* GLOBAL INTELLIGENCE OVERSIGHT: GOVERNING SECURITY IN THE TWENTY-FIRST CENTURY (Zachary Goldman ed., *forthcoming* 2016).

America Act[25] and the FISA Amendments Act[26] knew exactly what the NSA was being authorized to do. There were extensive and highly contested debates over it at the time the laws were passed. I was party to them. I wrote a number of pieces saying what the laws authorized.[27] I wrote to support these legislative developments. The American Civil Liberties Union (ACLU) publically advocated against these reforms.[28] There was no dispute – except at the extreme and most detailed margins of the new regime – about what the NSA would be authorized to do under Section 702. This public, legislative debate was concerned with both domestic and foreign intelligence powers. The policies that people are now pretending to find so alarming were debated in public; passed by Congress (not once, but twice); reauthorized by Congress four years later; and have been subject to extensive oversight by both of the congressional intelligence committees and by the FISA Court. Again, there is no analog in most other countries to the degree of legislative elaboration over time that has taken place with respect to foreign intelligence in the United States.

Third, the NSA's compliance program merits our attention. It is an almost neurotic, highly detailed system that ensures compliance with very specific rules.[29] Errors are counted, corrected, and disclosed.[30]

---

[25] Protect America Act of 2007, Pub. L. No. 110–55, 121 Stat 552 (current version at 50 U.S.C. § 1803, 1805a–1805c (2012)).

[26] FISA Amendments Act of 2008, Pub. L. No. 110–261, 122 Stat 2436 (codified as amended in scattered sections of 18 U.S.C. and 50 U.S.C.).

[27] Benjamin Wittes, *Congress, the Attorney General and the Foreign Intelligence Surveillance Act*, NEW REPUBLIC (Aug. 6, 2007), www.brookings.edu/research/opinions/2007/08/06natio nalsecurity; Benjamin Wittes, *The Law On Wiretapping*, NEW REPUBLIC (Aug. 18, 2007), www.brookings.edu/research/opinions/2007/08/18governance-wittes; Benjamin Wittes, *The Democrats and Bush Don't Really Disagree Much on FISA*, NEW REPUBLIC (Oct. 15, 2007), www.brookings.edu/research/opinions/2007/10/15nationalsecurity.

[28] *See, e.g., ACLU Analysis of the Protect America Act*, ACLU (Aug. 29, 2007), www.aclu.org/ national-security/aclu-analysis-protect-america-act.

[29] Exec. Order No. 12333(1.6)(b)–(c), 46 FR 59941, *reprinted as amended in* 50 U.S.C. § 3001 (2012) (declaring that any possible violations of federal law by employees of the agency be reported to the Attorney General, and also requiring that any intelligence gathering activities that might be "unlawful or contrary to executive order or presidential directive" be reported to the President's Intelligence Oversight Board and to the Director of National Intelligence.). *See* Memorandum from George Ellard, Inspector Gen., Patrick J. Reynolds, Acting Gen. Counsel, & Gen. Keith B. Alexander, Dir. of NSA to the Chairman, Intelligence Oversight Board, DOCID 4165279 (Apr. 5, 2012), www.nsa.gov/public_info/_files/IOB/ FY2012_1Q_IOB_Report.pdf (an example of a compliance report).

[30] Jane Chong, *The NSA Documents, Part VII: The Compliance Report*, LAWFARE (Aug. 24, 2013, 6:10 PM), www.lawfareblog.com/2013/08/the-nsa-documents-part-vii-the-compli ance-report/.

I have a story that helps illustrate the heavily regulated and scrutinized nature of the NSA's work. I was testifying before the Senate Intelligence Committee on reform of FISA. Timothy Edgar had also been called to testify and he was appearing before the committee at the same time as me. Tim is a very thoughtful civil libertarian who ended up going into the Intelligence Community as a privacy watchdog and came out with some very interesting thoughts on the relationship between the Intelligence Community and civil liberties advocates in civil society.[31] Before we started our testimony, Tim told me he was annoyed because he had found four typos in his written statement to the committee. Tim said to me, "that's one more than I usually allow myself." We were standing next to John DeLong when he said this and he heard Tim's remark. DeLong was then the head of compliance at the NSA. Without missing a beat, he quipped, "If that were [the NSA], we would have to report each of those errors to the FISA Court and the Intelligence Committees."

He is not exaggerating: Every error is counted; every error is reported.

The stereotype is to think of Germans as bureaucratic and as obsessed with compliance with picayune rules. But this is American bureaucracy pursuing an almost weirdly meticulous documentation of the activities of the Intelligence Community. These procedural safeguards – involving political-branch reporting, oversight, and transparency – are a big part of Americans' conception of privacy and the rule of law in this space. Again, it has no analog in any other country.

Despite the fundamental differences I have highlighted, the shock and awe over the Snowden revelations also should have been mitigated by the fact that the legal regimes for intelligence gathering in the United States and many other countries have some profound similarities. This means that the activities pursued by the NSA are not as singular as America's many foreign critics would like to portray them. The similarities between these legal regimes – in their fundamental demands – are greater than most people understand. I am referring, for example, to the fundamental demands on telecommunications companies, and the fundamental burdens that they potentially present to citizens.

---

[31] TIMOTHY H. EDGAR, SENATE SELECT COMM. ON INTELLIGENCE, 113TH CONG., A SHIELD AND A SWORD: REFORMING THE FOREIGN INTELLIGENCE SURVEILLANCE ACT (Sept. 26, 2013), www.intelligence.senate.gov/130926/edgar.pdf.

In the same way as the United States does, for example, Germany also requires that telecommunications be built in such a way as to facilitate interceptions when those interceptions are lawfully required.[32]

This point, in turn, invites consideration of yet another set of differences. But here the differences reveal Germany to be the country that is less protective of telecommunications privacy. I do not pretend to be an expert on German surveillance law.[33] But as I understand it, there are requirements in German law that involve intrusions on telecommunications privacy that are not countenanced by U.S. law. One example of this "role reversal" is that when you sign up for Internet service in Germany, the subscriber information is presented to a centralized database that can then be queried.[34] The United States has nothing like that. Another example of Germany's less-than-absolute protection of telecommunications privacy is that German law, like the FISA Amendments Act, tolerates very broad collection of data with one end in Germany.[35] German law allows this, by the way, without regard of the legality of the interception in the country at the other end.[36]

---

[32] 47 U.S.C. § 1002 (2012). Telekommunikationsgesetz [TKG] [Telecommunications Act] § 88(1) (1996).

[33] *See, e.g.,* Miller, *supra* note 24; Russell A. Miller, *Balancing Security and Liberty in Germany,* 4 J. Nat'l Security L. & Pol'y 369 (2010); Christian DeSimone, *Pitting Karlsruhe Against Luxembourg? German Data Protection and the Contested Implementation of the E.U. Data Retention Directive,* 11 German L.J. 291 (2010); Paul M. Schwartz, *Regulating Governmental Data Mining in the United States and Germany: Constitutional Courts, the State, and New Technology,* 53 Wm. & Mary L. Rev. 351 (2011).

[34] Telekommunikationsgesetz [TKG] [Telecommunications Act] §§ 111–113 (1996).

[35] Gesetz über den Bundesnachrichtendienst [BNDG] [Federal Intelligence Service Act], Dec. 20, 1990, BGBl. I at 2954, § 2(1.4); Gesetz über den Bundesnachrichtendienst [BNDG] [Federal Intelligence Service Act], Dec. 20, 1990, BGBl. I at 2954, §§ 2, 12; Gesetz zur Beschränkung des Brief-, Post- und Fernmeldegeheimnisses [G10 Act], Aug. 13, 1968, BGBl. I at 949, § 3.

[36] Gesetz über den Bundesnachrichtendienst [BNDG] [Federal Intelligence Service Act], Dec. 20, 1990, BGBl. I at 2954, § 1(2) (authorizing the BND "zur Gewinnung von Erkenntnissen über das Ausland, die von außen- und sicherheitspolitischer Bedeutung für die Bundesrepublik Deutschland sind, die erforderlichen Informationen und wertet sie aus [to gain knowledge about foreign countries that are of foreign and security policy importance for the Federal Republic of Germany, the necessary information and evaluates them.]" with no provision made respecting the domestic laws of the foreign target). *See* Lothar Determann & Karl T. Guttenberg, *On War and Peace in Cyberspace – Security, Privacy, Jurisdiction-,* 41 Hastings Const. L.Q. 875 (2014) (illustrating that international law has no prohibition on spying, and just as the United States broke German domestic law by intercepting signal traffic, so too would any interception of United States signals by a foreign intelligence agency be a breach of American domestic law, and the United States would have no recourse).

This is just a glimpse into the frame-of-mind of those who work at the NSA. They feel themselves to be dramatically more constrained – by law – than their counterparts in other countries. But they are now accused of being an out-of-control entity that is indiscriminately sucking up information all over the world. The reality and the criticism are so incompatible that I am left wondering what has truly motivated the intense European condemnation. Given the disparity, it is hard to believe that the European alarm is really about great differences in the rule of law.

C   If Not the Rule of Law, Then What's Behind Europe's Alarm over the NSA?

One explanation for the European hysteria is simple hypocrisy.[37] After all, we have recently learned that Germany is also not above spying on its friends, including the United States. And when it does so, it is not constrained by the same legal restrictions that limit the NSA.[38]

But perhaps there is something else going on that might explain the disparity between the legal reality in the United States – especially as

---

[37] See, e.g., Nikolaus Blome et al., Targeting Turkey: How Germany Spies on Its Friends, SPIEGEL ONLINE (Aug. 18, 2014, 2:14 PM), www.spiegel.de/international/germany/german-considers-turkey-to-be-official-target-for-spying-a-986656.html.

[38] See, e.g., David Francis, Spies Like Us: Germany Spies on Allies, Too, FP (Aug. 18, 2014, 9:36 PM), http://foreignpolicy.com/2014/08/18/spies-like-us-germany-spies-on-allies-too/; Tony Todd, Paris Also Snoops on U.S., Says French Former Spy Boss, FRANCE 24 (Oct. 26, 2013), www.france24.com/en/20131024-nsa-france-spying-squarcini-dcri-hollande-ayrault-merkel-usa-obama/ (quoting the former head of France's counter-espionage and counter-terrorism agency as saying "The French intelligence services know full well that all countries, whether or not they are allies in the fight against terrorism, spy on each other all the time . . .. The Americans spy on French commercial and industrial interests, and we do the same to them because it's in the national interest to protect our companies. . . .. There was nothing of any real surprise in this report. No one is fooled."); Denver Nicks, Report: U.K. Spy Agency Stored Millions of Webcam Images, TIME (Feb. 27, 2014), www.time.com/10117/nsa-leaks-edward-snowden-gchq-yahoo-webcam-spying/ (demonstrating that the United Kingdom's signal interception service has copied millions of photos while spying on webcam chats both in their own country and in the U.S., in addition to other countries); Greg Miller, Backlash in Berlin over NSA Spying Recedes as Threat from Islamic State Rises, WASH. POST (Dec. 29, 2014) www.washingtonpost.com/world/national-security/backlash-in-berlin-over-nsa-recedes-as-islamic-state-rises/2014/12/29/c738af28-8aad-11e4-a085-34e9b9f09a58_story.html (claiming that despite public outrage, German intelligence agencies have continued to cooperate with U.S. agencies, with German officials describing the situation as a broken marriage where divorce is not an option).

experienced by those who work at the NSA – and the way media all over
Europe, particularly but not exclusively in Germany, portrays the American Intelligence Community?[39] Giving Europeans the benefit of the
doubt here, I want to propose five other possible explanations for the
disparity. I think all of them bear some resemblance to the reality – or
part of the reality. And, by the way, I think that hypocrisy is also part of
the reality

The first huge difference between the United States and other intelligence services – at least in the immediate aftermath of the Snowden
revelations – is that our intelligence services got caught. Snowden
exposed the activities of the American Intelligence Community. Getting
caught is one of the cardinal sins in the intelligence business. There is an
old joke that rattles around the CIA. It is a bit of a morbid joke. It goes
like this: "If it were legal under local law, you wouldn't need us to do it."
And there is something to that. You do not have a clandestine intelligence service to do things that people are going to be thrilled about if
they are exposed. You have a clandestine service to do things that are *not*
legal under other countries' local law. You need clandestine services to do
things that are not pleasant or popular, but that you want to get away
with nonetheless. The NSA does a lot of things that are not legal under
local law,[40] as Europeans now know. The NSA does a lot of things that
are not pleasant. The NSA does a lot of things that are not nice and
polite. But it is doing things that America wants to be able to do. One of
the big things is that we did not "get away with it."

As time wears on and we learn more about European intelligence
practices, this difference erodes. Many of us have long known that
European intelligence services are also involved in unsavory operations
around the world.[41] We expected that they would not be able to keep up
the appearances of propriety forever, especially in light of the vast
quantity and global scope of the information Snowden stole. Our suspicions have now been confirmed. The German parliamentary investigation into the NSA-Affair and materials provided to Wikileaks have
turned up evidence showing that the BND was deeply involved in quite
a lot of the NSA's intelligence gathering in Europe, including operations

---

[39] *See* Chapters 24, 27, and 28 in this volume.
[40] Exec. Order No. 12333(1.7)(c)(1), 46 FR 59941, *reprinted as amended in* 50 U.S.C. § 3001
(2012) (authorizing the NSA to "[c]ollect (including through clandestine means), analyze,
produce, and disseminate foreign intelligence").
[41] *See* Chapter 9 in this volume.

targeting close German partners such as France.[42] And, as noted above, they have also not been above spying on the United States. Now that the Europeans have been caught in the act, too, they will have to adjust their righteous posture towards the United States.

A second difference – and I think that maybe this is the most important point – is simply the scale of the NSA's capabilities.[43] We are debating in the language of law something that is not really about the law. It is about the fact that this is an awesomely powerful agency that has developed impressive capabilities. I would call the NSA's capacity "unique" or "singular" except that the Russians and Chinese are also very good at signals intelligence (even if they are primarily focused on stealing intellectual property rather than more typical clandestine espionage activities).[44] The NSA has extraordinary capabilities.[45] The big difference between what it is empowered to do and what other intelligence services are empowered to do is not actually a function of law. It is a function of technical ability and scale.[46] The NSA is more legally constrained than any other intelligence agency in the world. But it also acquires more information than any other intelligence agency in the world (despite those limits) because of the breadth, size, and scope of its capabilities.

The NSA's immense capabilities point to a third difference. The NSA's power reflects the scale of U.S. intelligence ambitions. German intelligence is fundamentally about protecting Germany from internal and

---

[42] See German BND spy agency "helped U.S. target France," BBC (Apr. 30, 2015), www.bbc.com/news/world-europe-32529277; Ian Traynor, Coverup Claims over Revelation that Germany Spied on E.U. partners for U.S., THE GUARDIAN (Apr. 30, 2015, 9:53 AM), www.theguardian.com/world/2015/apr/30/germany-spied-on-european-partners-on-behalf-of-us-for-years

[43] See The Black Budget, WASH. POST (Aug. 29, 2013), www.washingtonpost.com/wp-srv/special/national/black-budget/; Andrew MacAskill & Sanjeev Miglani, Insight: Indian Intelligence Agency on the Cheap Hampers War on Militants, REUTERS (Nov. 7, 2014, 9:10 AM), http://in.reuters.com/article/2014/11/07/india-security-intelligence-idINKB N0IR04820141107; Bernd Debusmann, U.S. Intelligence Spending – Value for Money?, REUTERS (July 16, 2010), http://blogs.reuters.com/great-debate/2010/07/16/us-intelli gence-spending-value-for-money/ (serving to illustrate the vast differences in spending when comparing U.S. intelligences to other nations' intelligence services).

[44] See OFFICE OF THE NATIONAL COUNTERINTELLIGENCE EXECUTIVE, FOREIGN SPIES STEALING U.S. ECONOMIC SECRETS IN CYBERSPACE 4–6, B-1 (Oct. 2011), www.ncix.gov/publications/reports/fecie_all/Foreign_Economic_Collection_2011.pdf.

[45] See Barton Gellman & Greg Miller, "Black Budget" Summary Details U.S. Spy Network's Successes, Failures and Objectives, WASH. POST (Aug. 29, 2013), www.washingtonpost.com/world/national-security/black-budget-summary-details-us-spy-networks-successes-fail ures-and-objectives/2013/08/29/7e57bb78-10ab-11e3-8cdd-bcdc09410972_story.html.

[46] Id.

external threats.[47] Germany does not send troops all over the world. You can argue with the breadth of U.S. foreign policy; a lot of people do. But the scale of American intelligence ambitions is a reflection of the fact that there is no part of the world in which the United States is not engaged on a systematic, long-term basis. This includes military, civilian, and trade interests. The scale of American intelligence ambitions follows the scale of American foreign policy ambitions.

This brings me to a fourth difference. America's massive intelligence operations reflect the scale of America's national security responsibilities, including responsibilities to other countries.[48] I think Germans would do well to reflect on this point. The United States has taken responsibility for providing security for a lot of countries other than itself, including Germany. Other countries have willingly ceded that responsibility to the United States, not the least because it has provided them a budgetary windfall. The United States takes this responsibility very seriously and sometimes that obliges the United States to engage in activities that its many security beneficiaries do not find appealing. This is a two-edged sword. The chief beneficiaries of U.S. intelligence gathering – after the United States itself – are America's European allies. If the United States scaled back its counterterrorism efforts, the first place major terrorist problems would emerge is Europe, not the United States. This has produced a dependent and asymmetrical relationship in which Germany and other countries do not have to do certain things because America does it for them. But this comes with a scale of intelligence ambitions – responsibilities, really – that Europeans are able to avoid. In some respects, Europeans have helped to put the NSA in its current position. It cannot choose to neglect its vast intelligence gathering mandate without inflicting a very real cost on America's allies. It is simply a question of whether certain things that we all want done are going to get done.

---

[47] Gesetz über den Bundesnachrichtendienst [BNDG] [Federal Intelligence Service Act], Dec. 20, 1990, BGBl. I at 2954, § 1(2); Gesetz über die Zusammenarbeit des Bundes und der Länder in Angelegenheiten des Verfassungsschutzes und über das Bundesamt für Verfassungsschutz [BVerfSchG] [Constitutional Protection Act] Dec. 20, 1990, BGBl. I at 2954, § 3.

[48] JAMES M. McCORMICK, THE DOMESTIC SOURCES OF AMERICAN FOREIGN POLICY: INSIGHTS AND EVIDENCE 2–18 (2012) (illustrating the impact globalization has on the United States and the growing security concerns that have resulted from the process of globalization).

A final reason for the current tension between the U.S. and Germany is the truism that America got caught spying *on Germany*. This is particularly meaningful, in part, because of the radical asymmetry between the two countries in security and intelligence matters. That asymmetry has given these events a rude – even obnoxious and in-your-face – feel. This is especially true of the revelations concerning America's efforts to treat Chancellor Merkel and other German government figures as surveillance targets. But it is also shaped by the more general sentiment that America should not have been gathering intelligence on its allies. Apparently there is something offensive about that to many Germans – though perhaps less offensive when the BND engages in similar activities.

If what I am talking about here is hurt feelings, disappointment, and betrayal, then the message I have may well sound impolite or blunt. But it must be said all the same: Get over it. Countries spy on each other. Even close friends and allies. And as we now know, this truism includes German spying efforts.

Those tough words merit the following, powerful illustration. At the height of the U.S.–Israel relationship, when it was at its closest and Israel was taking three billion dollars a year in aid from the United States,[49] Israel ran Jonathan Pollard as an agent against the United States.[50] He got caught (he stole nuclear submarine codes – at the peak of the Reagan-era Cold War), he was charged with espionage, he pleaded guilty, and he was sentenced to life in prison in 1987.[51] That is where Pollard sat for nearly thirty years, until he

---

[49] JEREMY M. SHARP, CONG. RESEARCH SERV., RL33222, U.S. FOREIGN AID TO ISRAEL 28 (2012) (claiming that U.S. aid to Israel from 1971 to 2012 averaged $2.6 billion a year, and that in 1985, the year Pollard was caught, Congress "pass[ed] a special economic assistance package of $1.5 billion" for Israel); JIM ZANOTTI, CONG. RESEARCH SERV., RL33476, ISRAEL: BACKGROUND AND U.S. RELATIONS 29–30 (2014) (demonstrating the Memoranda of Understanding signed between the United States and Israel in the years immediately after Pollard's arrest); CLYDE R. MARK, CONG. RESEARCH SERV., IB82008, ISRAELI-UNITED STATES RELATIONS CRS-2(2005) (characterizing the Reagan era as the most pro-Israel administration in spite of the diplomatic difficulties that occurred in the 1980s).

[50] Adam Taylor, *Jonathan Pollard: Why Israel Wants Him Free, Why the U.S. Doesn't, and What Might Happen Next*, WASH. POST (Mar. 31, 2014), www.washingtonpost.com/blogs/world views/wp/2014/03/31/jonathan-pollard-why-israel-wants-him-free-why-the-u-s-doesnt-and-what-might-happen-next/.

[51] RONALD J. OLIVE, CAPTURING JOHNATHAN POLLARD (2006).

was granted parole at the end of 2015.[52] For all of that, Pollard is a national hero in Israel.[53]

What was the effect of this incident on U.S.–Israel relations? There was almost no effect. Allies spy on each other. As I have noted, even the Germans have been known to spy on the U.S.[54] There are good reasons for Americans and Germans to spy on each other. German–American relations are close, but the countries' interests are not identical. Germany pursues a very different foreign policy in a lot of ways. Germany, for example, has a totally different relationship to Russia than America does. Chancellor Merkel has frequent phone conversations with Russia's President Putin. It is right that America should want to know what they are saying. And it just so happens that the NSA can help the American government find that out.

It can work the other way around, too. There are several counter-terrorism initiatives in the United States that the European Union, spurred largely by Germany, has sought to frustrate.[55] The Passenger Name Record (PNR) database in the computer system for flight reservations is one example.[56] American attempts to access the Society for Worldwide Interbank Financial Telecommunication database, which

---

[52] Devlin Barrett, *Israeli Spy Pollard Will Be Released in November, Lawyers Say*, WALL ST. J. (July 28, 2015), www.wsj.com/articles/israeli-spy-pollard-will-be-released-in-novem ber-lawyers-say-1438104728.

[53] Karl Vick, *Israelis See Pollard as Hero and Hostage*, TIME (Apr. 1, 2014), www.time.com/ 45048/pollard-hero-hostage-in-israel/. Every Israeli Prime Minister seeks Pollard's release. RICHARD A. BEST, JR. AND CLYDE MARK, JONATHAN POLLARD: BACKGROUND AND CONSIDERATIONS FOR PRESIDENTIAL CLEMENCY, CRS REP. RS20001 (Jan. 31, 2001) (stating that after acknowledging that Pollard was a spy for Israel, both Prime Ministers Netanyahu and Barak requested his release). *See also* Taylor, *supra* note 64.

[54] *See German Federal Intelligence Service Taps Hillary Clinton's Phone Call*, NDR.DE (Aug. 15, 2014, 6:00 PM), www.ndr.de/nachrichten/German-Federal-Intelligence-Ser vice-taps-Hillary-Clintons-phone-call-,spying100.html. *See also* Blome *supra* note 49.

[55] Paul de Hert and Bart de Schutter, *International Transfers of Data in the Field of JHA: The Lessons of Europol, PNR, and Swift, in* JUSTICE, LIBERTY, SECURITY: NEW CHALLENGES FOR E.U. EXTERNAL RELATIONS 299 (Bernd Martenczuk and Ser-vaas van Thiel eds., 2008) www.vub.ac.be/LSTS/pub/Dehert/242.pdf (illustrating the difficulties the U.S. and E.U. have had in reaching an agreement regarding the access of PNR and SWIFT information.).

[56] Agreement Between the United States of America and the European Union on the Use and Transfer of Passenger Name Records to the United States Department of Homeland Security, U.S.-E.U., Dec.14, 2011, TIAS 12-701; Magda Fahsi, *A Divided Europe Wants to Protect Its Personal Data Wanted by the U.S.*, L'OBS AVEC RUE 89 (Mar. 4, 2008), http://rue89.nouvelobs.com/2008/03/04/a-divided-europe-wants-to-protect-its-personal-data-wanted-by-the-us.

tracks international money transfers (used by more than 10,500 banks internationally), is another example.[57] As a number of contributions to this book document and discuss, the Court of Justice of the European Union, in a number of recent cases, has taken an extremely critical stance towards American data protection practices and policies.[58] These sources of information are really important to some major entities in the U.S. government, but the United States is fighting with Europeans about them all the time.[59]

Do not take me the wrong way when I raise this point. I am not complaining about European behavior here. Germany has a different conception of its strategic objectives than America does. And Germany has a different conception of the value of privacy. It remains mysterious to me why Europeans think information about passengers on commercial airlines is so private, but that is probably a discussion for another day and related to my earlier point about the cultural contingency of privacy in general. It is enough for me to say here that there is clearly some cultural and strategic difference involved, and Europeans are entitled to pursue their interests in those respects to the fullest of their capabilities. Europeans are entitled to have a fetish about PNR data.

But, if there are a lot of different questions about which we do not see eye-to-eye – and I mean disagreement in an ongoing, systematic way about the most prominent geopolitical issues – then we cannot be surprised when we discover that the relationship is not close enough to preclude intelligence gathering activities between the United States and Germany.

---

[57] The Agreement between the United States of America and the European Union on the processing and transfer of Financial Messaging Data from the European Union to the United States for the purposes of the Terrorist Finance Tracking Program, U.S.-E.U., June 28, 2010, TIAS 10-801; Hans-Jürgen Schlamp, *"The Americans Want to Blackmail Us": European Parliament Balks at U.S. Data Deals*, SPIEGEL ONLINE (Oct. 7, 2010, 5:29 PM), www.spiegel.de/international/europe/the-americans-want-to-blackmail-us-european-par liament-balks-at-us-data-deals-a-721811-2.html.

[58] *See* Chapters 16, 23, 20, and 21 in this volume.

[59] *See, e.g., Privacy vs. Security: E.U. Eyes Massive Collection of Air Passenger Data*, SPIEGEL ONLINE (Dec. 10, 2012, 4:05 PM), www.spiegel.de/international/europe/european-parlia ment-to-debate-own-database-for-flight-passengers-a-871953.html. *See also* Richard Connor, *E.U. to Share Air Passenger Data with U.S., Despite German Concerns*, DW (Dec. 14, 2011), www.dw.de/eu-to-share-air-passenger-data-with-us-despite-german-con cerns/a-15599854. *But see* Dario Sarmadi, *Berlin Calls for E.U.-Wide Retention of PNR Flight Data*, EurActiv.com (Oct. 30, 2014, 8:18 AM), www.euractiv.com/sections/infoso ciety/berlin-calls-eu-wide-retention-pnr-flight-data-309604.

I have the same reaction to American complaints about China's industrial espionage in the technology sector. This is what I say to those Americans who complain about Chinese behavior: "Grow up." The Chinese have a different conception of their national security than America does. In fact, their conception of national security includes stealing America's intellectual property.[60] The proper response to this is not a lot of whining. The proper response is to raise the price to the Chinese for conducting those programs so that they come to believe that it is in their strategic interest to stop. That is what I tell Americans.

D Conclusion

That is what I have to say to Germans now in the shadow of the NSA-Affair: "Grow up." America is going to spy on Germany until all of our interests are sufficiently aligned in all of the important areas and the two countries have a common understanding of what merits protection and what does not merit protection. Until that far-off day (and I doubt we should really be hoping for it to come to pass) America is going to spy on Germany. And Germany will resist American security and intelligence programs to the extent of its capabilities and to the extent it disagrees with U.S. policy.

I would like to mention one final thing that I think helps to explain the dichotomy between the United States and Germany over these issues. And that is the point that I started with. It is a profoundly different conception of privacy. In the U.S. model, privacy protection against the intelligence community has its origins in 1978 when a layer of judicial review was placed between intelligence targets and the FBI (concerning domestic intelligence gathering) and the NSA (concerning intelligence gathering with an overseas nexus).[61] The United States imposed a series of very elaborate procedures and established a number of executive-branch oversight mechanisms. Americans imposed significant congressional oversight as well. And where revelations about the practices of the intelligence community show that there have been departures from

---

[60] See Richard A. Clarke, Op-Ed – How China Steals Our Secrets, N.Y. TIMES (Apr. 3, 2012), www.nytimes.com/2012/04/03/opinion/how-china-steals-our-secrets.html?_r=0; see also Paulo Shakarian et al., The Dragon and the Computer: Why Intellectual Property Theft is Compatible with Chinese Cyber-Warfare Doctrine, http://arxiv.org/ftp/arxiv/papers/1309/1309.6450.pdf.

[61] The Foreign Intelligence Surveillance Act of 1978, Pub.L. No. 95–511, codified at 50 U.S.C. § 1804.

the rules in place – or if the world situation changes as radically as it did after the September 11, 2001 terrorist attacks – then America has a very open, very public debate about reforms to this legal framework. This happened again as Americans reacted to the Snowden revelations. After a lengthy public and political debate – in part spurred by judgments of the courts – Congress enacted the USA FREEDOM Act with support from both parties in both houses.[62] It is not a perfect law and, not surprisingly, almost no one is perfectly happy with it. But it does establish some new and significant limits on the NSA's intelligence gathering operations. That is the way that America has sought to protect privacy: through public debate, judicial and congressional oversight, and the political process. It is a totally different approach to the German rights-based, formalistic, and judicially enforced understanding of privacy protection.[63] Most certainly it is not a set of formalistic propositions about what the word privacy, as used in an international human rights treaty, means.[64]

I think the biggest part of this problem between Germany and America – here in the shadow of the NSA-Affair – is that we are talking past one another when it comes to what privacy really is. Americans and Germans do not mean the same things when they talk about privacy or how the interests involved in the concept should be protected. Americans and Germans are not fully acknowledging the relative responsibilities of their respective countries in the world. And Americans and Germans are not being honest about the fact that – although we are close – we do not see eye-to-eye on a lot of important issues. In the meantime, the United States will continue gathering foreign signals intelligence.

---

[62] USA FREEDOM Act, Public Law 114–23 (June 2, 2015).
[63] *See* Chapter 2 in this volume.
[64] International Covenant on Civil and Political Rights, Dec. 16, 1966, 999 U.N.T.S. 171.

PART THREE

Transatlantic Perspectives on the NSA-Affair

I American Voices

7

Sensing Disturbances in the Force

Unofficial Reflections on Developments and Challenges in the U.S.–Germany Security Relationship

BY RONALD D. LEE

A   Introduction

"*Alles hat ein Ende; nur Wurst hat zwei.*"[1] This German aphorism provides a suitable starting point for a few personal and unofficial reflections on the state of security and intelligence relations and policy between the Government of the United States of America and the Government of Germany as of mid-2015. These relations remain in a state of flux, indeed perturbation, in the wake of highly publicized and unauthorized disclosures of classified information (leaks) by Edward Snowden that *The Guardian*, the *Washington Post*, the *New York Times*, and the German news magazine *Der Spiegel* have published. These disclosures, and the resulting surprise and anger of the German government and people, as well as of their counterparts across the European Union, have damaged U.S. - German political, security, and diplomatic relations. To highly pessimistic observers, this damage signaled *das Ende* – the end of an exceptionally close and productive period of U.S. - German political, military, and security cooperation and alignment that has been one of the defining features of post-World War II global politics. To less pessimistic observers – or to those willing to take a longer view less focused on recent headlines – this crisis marks not an epochal end but, perhaps, two less cataclysmic ends.

First, the unauthorized disclosures marked the end of an era in which the United States and Germany could avoid discussing the question of whether one nation conducted intelligence activities against the other, or against intelligence targets in the other country. The constellations of political, social, and institutional forces in the two countries after the

---

[1] Everything has an end to it; only sausage has two ends.

unauthorized disclosures simply ruled out continuing any explicit or tacit understanding – if one ever existed – not to raise these issues at the highest levels of government.

Second, the unauthorized disclosures heralded the end of a long period in which political and constitutional debate about the conduct of, authority for, and limits on national intelligence activities by the United States took place on a purely domestic basis. These issues had been an exclusive matter of the framework of the United States Constitution, the civil liberties rights and protections that it embodies, and the laws, history, and culture of the United States. The domestic orientation of the debate remains of crucial and central importance in the United States and it was the pivot-point for congressional consideration and public discussion of intelligence reform legislation enacted in 2015.[2] The foreign implications of the unauthorized disclosures, however, have widened the field of vision of American policy discussions surrounding these issues.

The significance of this pivot away from an exclusively domestic focus should be fully emphasized: A brief recap of the long history of this purely domestic oversight of U.S. surveillance activities is appropriate here. For most of the history of the United States the executive branch, headed by the President, exercised sole and exclusive decision making authority over the conduct of intelligence operations.[3] It was not until 1967, almost two centuries after the founding of the Republic, that the United States Supreme Court ruled that electronic surveillance by the U.S. Government implicated constitutional protections.[4] And it was not until the mid-1970s that Congress began to play a significant role in oversight of the intelligence community. Congress became involved in the wake of revelations regarding President Richard Nixon's use of wiretapping

---

[2] *See* Uniting and Strengthening America by Fulfilling Rights and Ensuring Effective Discipline Over Monitoring (USA FREEDOM) Act, Pub. L. No. 114–23, 129 Stat. 268 (codified as amended in 50 U.S.C.A. § 1801 et seq. (West 2015)); *see also* Foreign Intelligence Surveillance Court ("FISC") Opinion 15–77 (June 19, 2015), www.fisc.uscourts.gov/sites/default/files/BR%2015-77%2015-78%20Memorandum%20Opinion.pdf.

[3] *See, e.g.,* BRIAN KILMEADE & DON YAEGER, GEORGE WASHINGTON'S SECRET SIX: THE SPY RING THAT SAVED THE AMERICAN REVOLUTION (2014); CHRISTOPHER ANDREW, FOR THE PRESIDENT'S EYES ONLY: SECRET INTELLIGENCE AND THE AMERICAN PRESIDENCY FROM WASHINGTON TO BUSH (1995).

[4] *See* Katz v. United States, 389 U.S. 347 (1967) (holding that wiretap of a phone call made from a phone booth – with a device attached to the outside of the booth – implicated the Fourth Amendment to the United States Constitution's prohibition against unreasonable searches and seizures because persons have a reasonable expectation of privacy in phone conversations conducted in private).

against his administration's domestic political opponents (such as Vietnam War protesters) and covert Central Intelligence Agency ("CIA") operations involving assassination attempts against foreign leaders. As a result, a U.S. Senate committee chaired by Senator Frank Church conducted public hearings and an extensive investigation of the CIA, the NSA, and the FBI. The Church Committee – as the Senate Select Committee to Study Governmental Operations with Respect to Intelligence Activities came to be known – produced fourteen reports on U.S. intelligence operations and a number of reform recommendations.[5] One of the reforms was the enactment of the Foreign Intelligence Surveillance Act of 1978 ("FISA"),[6] a statute that places the executive branch's conduct of domestic electronic surveillance activities for foreign intelligence purposes on a statutory footing and provides oversight by both the Congress and the judiciary.[7]

FISA protects the rights of both "United States persons" and persons other than United States persons, but requires higher showings of intelligence and national security need before the executive branch may conduct electronic surveillance against United States persons.[8] Many of the most heated electronic surveillance and intelligence issues in the United States since the enactment of FISA have related to the appropriate balance to be struck between the privacy rights of U.S. persons and the national security needs of the U.S. Government. Notably, the FISA Amendments Act of 2008 now regulates the U.S. government's collection

---

[5] *See* S. Res. 21, 94th Cong. (1975); S. Rep. No. 94–755 (1976); S. Rep. No. 94–465 (1975). *See also* Loch K. Johnson, A Season of Inquiry: The Senate Intelligence Investigation (1985); Frank John Smist, Congress Oversees the United States Intelligence Community, 1947–1994 (1994); U.S. National Security, Intelligence and Democracy: From the Church Committee to the War on Terror (Russell A. Miller ed., 2008). In the House of Representatives, a similar committee chaired by Otis Pike (known as the "Pike Committee") also investigated the intelligence community. *See* H.R. Res. 138, 94th Cong. (1975).

[6] Foreign Intelligence Surveillance Act of 1978, Pub. L. 95–511, 92 Stat. 1783 (1978).

[7] This is an oversimplification of the statutory reach of the Foreign Intelligence Surveillance Act as originally enacted in 1978. But it captures the primary point for the present purpose: That the conduct of intelligence activities by the United States not regulated by FISA (and other statutes enacted after 1978) remains the sole province of the Executive Branch. *See, e.g.,* Exec. Order No. 12,333, 46 Fed. Reg. 59941 (Dec. 4, 1981).

[8] For example, a non-U.S. person is an agent of a foreign power and can become an intelligence target if, among other statutory criteria, he or she "engages in international terrorism," whereas a U.S. person must "knowingly engage[]" in international terrorism "for or on behalf of a foreign power" in order to qualify as an "agent of a foreign power" for the purposes of intelligence gathering. 50 U.S.C.A. § 1801(b)(West).

of foreign intelligence involving the participation of United States-based Electronic Communications Service Providers, such as Internet e-mail providers. This is the case where the targets are U.S. persons and non-U.S. persons.[9] But it is fair to say that most of the U.S. controversy and legislative and public debates about the pros and cons of FISA reform related to the provisions targeting U.S. persons.[10]

For these reasons it should come as no surprise that much of the intellectual fabric and the anchor-points of U.S. discussions about the appropriate conduct of intelligence activities focuses on U.S. constitutional and domestic law norms. The new facets of the debate that have opened up – about the proper balancing between U.S. national security imperatives and the rights of the citizens of the E.U. and indeed citizens of all nations – further animates and complicates an already robust debate about protecting the rights of U.S. persons while developing and deploying the nation's intelligence capabilities to protect the nation and its allies that has been ongoing for at least forty years in the United States.

With this backdrop in place, this chapter proceeds in four parts. First, I summarize U.S. – German tensions over U.S. intelligence activities. And it is a dynamic and evolving story. For both these reasons, I traverse it lightly here. Second, I summarize the principal aspects of the U.S. government's reactions and responses to the unauthorized disclosures of U.S. surveillance activities. These reactions are important foundational facts for any assessment of the efforts and initiatives that have sought to address the perturbations in U.S. – German security cooperation, to ameliorate the harms to the bilateral relationship caused by the unauthorized disclosures, and to suggest a few potential paths forward into the future. Third, I offer selected observations and reflections on factors in the external environment that complicate and condition global technology companies' efforts to do business and to comply with both U.S. and E.U. (and E.U. nation-state) legal requirements. These points serve as context and a foundation for the chapter's fourth part in which I suggest a few discussion topics on which serious, informed observers of the two countries' constitutions, laws, governments, public policies, and cultures might make significant contributions.

---

[9] *See* 50 U.S.C.A. §§ 1881a; 1881b (West 2015).
[10] *See, e.g.*, 154 Cong. Rec. S6108-11 (daily ed. June 25, 2008) (remarks of U.S. Senator Russ Feingold Opposing H.R. 6304, FISA Amendments Act of 2008).

B   U.S.–German Tensions over Intelligence Activities

On June 5, 2013, *The Guardian* published the first article, in any news source, reporting on classified documents obtained by Edward Snowden.[11] German Interior Minister Hans-Peter Friedrich travelled to Washington shortly after the disclosures and met with several high-level Obama administration officials, stating "[t]he most important thing was that all parties with whom we have held talks here in the United States understand that the people of Germany and Europe are extremely aware and sensitive when it comes to protection of privacy and protection of liberty[.]"[12] A few days later, Chancellor Angela Merkel released an eight-point program for strengthening "privacy protection at the international level."[13] The Chancellor's proposals included the signing of E.U. and United Nations ("UN") agreements on privacy and surveillance, as well as holding "expert-level talks" with the United States and asking a "very concrete list of questions."[14]

Work towards any productive resolution of Germany's concerns with U.S. surveillance activities was dealt a major setback in October 2013, when the press reported that Chancellor Merkel's cell phone may have been monitored by U.S. intelligence agencies.[15] German Foreign Minister Guido Westerwelle informed the United States Ambassador to Germany that the German government was "absolutely astounded" by the allegations, and Chancellor Merkel herself characterized the substance of these claims as a breach of trust.[16] The German Parliament initiated a Parliamentary inquiry into the allegations including a review of whether

[11] Glenn Greenwald, *NSA Collecting Phone Records of Millions of Verizon Customers Daily*, THE GUARDIAN (June 5, 2013, 6:05 AM), www.theguardian.com/world/2013/jun/06/nsa-phone-records-verizon-court-order.

[12] Press Release, The Federal Chancellor, Investigations Continue (July 16, 2013), www.bundeskanzlerin.de/ContentArchiv/EN/Archiv17/Artikel/2013/07/2013-06-28-internetdaten_en.html.

[13] Press Release, The Federal Chancellor, Germany Is a Country of Freedom (July 19, 2013), www.bundeskanzlerin.de/ContentArchiv/EN/Archiv17/Artikel/2013/07/2013-07-19-bkin-nsa-sommerpk.html.

[14] *Id.*

[15] Press Release, The Press and Information Office of the Federal Government, Chancellor's Mobile Phone Might Have Been Monitored by American Intelligence Agencies (Oct. 24, 2013), www.bundeskanzlerin.de/ContentArchiv/EN/Archiv17/Pressemitteilungen/BPA/2013/10/2013-10-24-merkel-obama-telefonat.html.

[16] Press Release, The Federal Chancellor, Breach of Trust (Oct. 25, 2013), www.bundeskanzlerin.de/ContentArchiv/EN/Archiv17/Artikel/2013/10/2013-10-24-bkin-datenausspaehung.html.

and to what extent German government officials were aware of and complicit in the NSA's activities in Germany and Europe,[17] and the E.U. commenced numerous reviews and bilateral discussions with the United States.[18] The German government cancelled a contract with the United States' second largest telecommunications company, which had been providing network infrastructure for Berlin-Bonn tele-communications between ministries.[19] Germany's Interior Ministry stated that "the relationships between foreign intelligence agencies and companies revealed in the course of the NSA-Affair show that especially high demands must be made of the federal government com-munications infrastructure that is critical for security."[20] Germany's most senior prosecutor launched an investigation into determining whether individuals involved in the surveillance of Chancellor Merkel's phone can be identified and charged with criminal espionage.[21] U.S. – German rela-tions were further complicated when it was reported that Germany had intercepted phone calls made by former Secretary of State Hillary Clinton and current (until January, 2017) Secretary John Kerry. The German government sought to excuse these interceptions by characterizing them as accidental.[22] Perhaps in an effort to prevent future diplomatic rows (or at least diffuse the continued public perception that tensions remained

---

[17] See Establishment of a Committee of Inquiry, DEUTSCHER BUNDESTAG: DRUCKSACHEN [BT] 18/843 (Mar. 18, 2014), www.bundestag.de/blob/284528/a89d6006f28900c4f46e56 f5e0807ddf/einsetzungsantrag_englisch-docx-data.pdf (Eng. trans.). See also Snowden-Enthüllungen: Bundestag einigt sich auf NSA-Ausschuss, SPIEGEL ONLINE (Mar. 14, 2014, 12:21 PM), www.spiegel.de/politik/deutschland/nsa-affaere-bundestag-einigt-sich-auf-untersuchungsausschuss-a-958630.html; Marcel Fürstenau, German Parliament to Inquire Into NSA, DW (Mar. 20, 2014), www.dw.de/german-parliament-to-inquire-into-nsa/a-17510640. See Chapter 12 in this volume.

[18] See, e.g., Claus Hecking & Stefan Schultz, Spying "Out of Control": E.U. Official Questions Trade Negotiations, SPIEGEL ONLINE (June 30, 2013, 2:46 PM), www.spiegel.de/inter national/europe/eu-officials-furious-at-nsa-spying-in-brussels-and-germany-a-908614 .html; Daniel Basteiro, Divided EU Responds To NSA Spying Scandal, THE WORLD POST (Oct. 25, 2013, 5:05 PM), www.huffingtonpost.com/2013/10/25/eu-nsa-spying_n_ 4164559.html.

[19] See Anton Troianovski & Danny Yadron, German Government Ends Verizon Contract, WALL ST. J. (June 26, 2014, 2:54 PM), www.wsj.com/articles/german-government-ends-verizon-contract-1403802226.

[20] Id.

[21] Matthew Schofield, Germany Opens Criminal Probe Into U.S. Tapping of Merkel's Phone, McCLATCHYDC (June 4, 2014), www.mcclatchydc.com/2014/06/04/229350/germany-opens-criminal-probe-into.html?sp=/99/117.

[22] Germany Accused of Spying on Kerry and Clinton, BBC (Aug. 16, 2014), www.bbc.com/ news/world-europe-28819625.

high between Germany and the U.S. over the spying allegations), "current and former U.S. officials" were quoted in the media saying that the CIA had issued a "stand down order" to cease espionage against Western European allies, including Germany.[23] But, as the *Bundestag's* investigation continued and information continued to trickle into the media, German-American relations continued to simmer over these issues. The Americans flatly rejected German gestures towards a bi-lateral no-spy agreement.[24] The German government ordered the expulsion of the CIA's Berlin Station Chief when it was discovered, in mid-summer 2014, that America had a paid informant working inside the German Federal Intelligence Service (BND).[25] The Germans' alarm over the NSA-Affair, however, turned into awkward self-reflection in the spring of 2015 as documents published by WikiLeaks and media reports disclosed German government awareness of U.S. intelligence activities in Germany[26] and that the BND had given assistance to the U.S. government.[27]

C Summary of U.S. Government Reactions to Unauthorized Disclosures

I Initial Reaction

Across the Atlantic, the United States government's initial reaction to the Snowden disclosures in June 2013 was one of focused outrage towards the extensive leak of highly classified information. Almost immediately, the Director of National Intelligence, James Clapper, issued a statement condemning the disclosures as threatening "potentially long-lasting and irreversible harm to [the United States'] ability to identify and respond

---

[23] *Espionage Against Allies Put on Hold While Risks and Rewards Are Examined*, U.S. NEWS & WORLD REP. (Sept. 19, 2013, 9:42 PM), www.usnews.com/news/politics/articles/2014/09/19/ap-exclusive-cia-halts-spying-in-europe.

[24] Philip Oltermann, *U.S. Will Not Enter Bilateral No-spy Deal with Germany, Reports Media*, THE GUARDIAN (Jan. 14, 2014, 8:05 AM), www.theguardian.com/world/2014/jan/14/us-not-entering-no-spy-agreement-germany-media.

[25] *CIA Station Chief Ordered out of Germany Has Left, U.S. Confirms*, THE GUARDIAN (July 17, 2014, 2:15 PM), www.theguardian.com/world/2014/jul/17/cia-station-chief-germany-us-leaves.

[26] *BND-Affäre: Kanzleramt soll schon 2008 vor NSA-Spionage gewarnt worden sein*, SPIEGEL ONLINE (Apr. 26, 2015, 1:45 PM), www.spiegel.de/politik/deutschland/bnd-affaere-kanzleramt-soll-schon-frueh-vor-nsa-umtrieben-gewarnt-worden-sein-a-1030722.html.

[27] Thomas Sparrow, *The NSA's Eyes in Europe*, POLITICO (May 12, 2015, 5:35 AM), www.politico.eu/article/nsa-merkel-bnd-spying-scandal/.

to the many threats facing our nation."[28] Simultaneously, Clapper ordered the release of additional records relating to the disclosed surveillance program, citing the need to contextualize the program and describe its limits.[29] General Keith Alexander, Director of the NSA until March 2014, was less diplomatic in his response to the disclosures, which he characterized as "sensational." General Alexander suggested that "their timing ha[d] been carefully orchestrated to inflame and embarrass."[30]

Snowden's disclosures have steadily continued to surface in the press,[31] and the responses from the U.S. government have reflected, in various combinations and with varying degrees of relative emphasis, six themes articulated by General Alexander in a speech during the month following the initial disclosures.[32] First, the U.S. government has resolutely defended the intelligence programs at the center of the disclosures as necessary for national security.[33] Second, it has emphasized internal safeguards that are in place to protect against abuse of its national capabilities and the use of data that have been collected.[34] Third, the U.S. government has asserted that the benefits of the intelligence programs are not theoretical, and that such surveillance has directly led to the disruption of terror plots.[35] Fourth, the U.S. government has pointed to the participation of all three branches of government in oversight

---

[28] Press Release, Office of the Director of National Intelligence ("ODNI"), DNI Statement on the Recent Unauthorized Disclosures of Classified Information (June 6, 2013), www.dni.gov/index.php/newsroom/press-releases/191-press-releases-2013/868-dni-statement-on-recent-unauthorized-disclosures-of-classified-information.

[29] Id.

[30] Keith B. Alexander, Director, Nat'l Security Agency ("NSA"), Statement to the NSA/CSS Workforce (June 25, 2013), www.nsa.gov/public_info/speeches_testimonies/25jun13_dir.shtml.

[31] See Timeline of Edward Snowden's revelations, AL JAZEERA AMERICA., http://america.aljazeera.com/articles/multimedia/timeline-edward-snowden-revelations.html (last visited Nov. 23, 2015).

[32] See Keith B. Alexander, Director, NSA, General Keith Alexander Speaks at AFCEA's Conference (June 28, 2013), www.nsa.gov/public_info/_files/speeches_testimonies/Transcript_of_GEN_Alexanders_AFCEA_Keynote_Speech_27_June_2013.pdf.

[33] See, e.g., Press Release, ODNI, DNI Clapper: Defunding FISA Business Records Program Risks Dismantling Important Intelligence Tool (July 24, 2013), www.dni.gov/index.php/newsroom/press-releases/191-press-releases-2013/899-dni-clapper-defunding-fisa-business-records-program-risks-dismantling-important-intelligence-tool.

[34] See, e.g., Press Release, NSA, Press Statement on 30 July 2013, www.nsa.gov/public_info/press_room/2013/30_July_2013.shtml.

[35] See, e.g., Keith B. Alexander, Director, NSA, Keynote Address by General Keith Alexander, Director, National Security Agency, Black Hat USA 2013, (July 31, 2013), www.nsa.gov/public_info/_files/speeches_testimonies/Transcript_of_GEN_Alexanders_Black_Hat_Speech_31_July_2013.pdf.

of the U.S. government's programs, including briefing the U.S. Senate Select Committee on Intelligence ("SSCI"), the House Permanent Select Committee on Intelligence ("HPSCI"), and engagement with the FISA Court.[36] Fifth, the government has noted that the United States is not alone among nations in its surveillance activities.[37] Finally, U.S. government officials have continued to reiterate the assertion that the unauthorized disclosures, because they purportedly have provided adversaries with an understanding of the U.S. government's capabilities, "have caused significant and irreversible damage to our nation's security."[38]

At the direction of President Obama, the government has also continued to declassify documents related to the U.S.' electronic surveillance programs,[39] and to directly address news reports in situations in which the government believes reports have "mischaracterize[d]" aspects of such programs.[40] While condemning Snowden's actions, President Obama and other officials have also acknowledged that the public discussion engendered by the Snowden disclosures has been valuable.[41] And, as described below, this discussion appears to have played a role in significant changes to several of the U.S. government's surveillance programs and policies,[42] including the significant revisions to the U.S. government's bulk collection of telephony metadata and to permitted

---

[36] See, e.g., Letter from George Ellard, Inspector Gen., NSA, to Charles E. Grassley, Sen., U.S. Senate (Sept. 11, 2013), www.nsa.gov/public_info/press_room/2013/grassley_letter.pdf.

[37] See, e.g., Press Release, ODNI, DNI Statement on Inaccurate and Misleading Information in Recent Le Monde Article (Oct. 23, 2013), www.dni.gov/index.php/newsroom/press-releases/191-press-releases-2013/951-dni-statement-on-inaccurate-and-misleading-information-in-recent-le-monde-article-security.

[38] See, e.g., Claudette Roulo, Leaks Damage National Security, NSA Director Says, U.S. DEP'T DEFENSE (June 28, 2013), http://archive.defense.gov/news/newsarticle.aspx?id=120387.

[39] See, e.g., Press Release, ODNI, DNI Clapper Declassified Intelligence Community Documents Regarding Collection Under Section 501 of FISA (Sept. 10, 2013), www.dni.gov/index.php/newsroom/press-releases/191-press-releases-2013/927-draft-document.

[40] See Press Release, ODNI, Joint Statement: NSA and Office of the Director of National Intelligence (Aug. 22, 2013), www.dni.gov/index.php/newsroom/press-releases/191-press-releases-2013/917-joint-statement-nsa-and-office-of-the-director-of-national-intelligence.

[41] See, e.g., Barack Obama, President, U.S., Remarks by the President on Review of Signals Intelligence (Jan. 17, 2014), www.whitehouse.gov/the-press-office/2014/01/17/remarks-president-review-signals-intelligence; Interview by Chris Anderson with Richard Ledgett, Jr., Deputy Director, NSA, in Wash. D.C. (Mar. 20, 2014), www.nsa.gov/public_info/_files/speeches_testimonies/TED_Transcript_With_R._Ledgett_March_20_2014.pdf.

[42] See, e.g., Press Release, The White House Office of the Press Sec'y, Presidential Policy Directive – Signals Intelligence Activities, Presidential Policy Directive/PPD 28 (Jan. 17, 2014), www.whitehouse.gov/the-press-office/2014/01/17/presidential-policy-directive-signals-intelligence-activities.

public reports by recipients of national security legal process achieved by the USA FREEDOM Act that was enacted in June 2015.[43]

II   "Transparency" Reforms

The first significant change, after the leaks, to the way electronic surveillance for national security purposes operates in the United States was brought about first by several internet service providers through the Foreign Intelligence Surveillance Court (the "FISC"), the judicial body granted jurisdiction over certain components of the national security legal infrastructure. Shortly after the initial Snowden disclosures, several leading U.S. Internet companies sought permission from the government to publish additional data about the scope of surveillance requests the companies had received, through new or existing "transparency reports" on the companies' websites.[44] They sought this permission because several national security surveillance statutes permit the government to prohibit the recipient of national security orders from disclosing information about or the existence of these orders.[45] These non-disclosure authorities appear to be used frequently. For example, 97 percent of all National Security Letters include a non-disclosure order.[46] The impetus for their interest in publishing this data was the erroneous reporting in June and July 2013, apparently based on a misunderstanding or mischaracterization of documents leaked by Snowden, that the United States government had unfettered "direct access" to the servers of these and many other service providers.[47]

---

[43] Uniting and Strengthening America by Fulfilling Rights and Ensuring Effective Discipline Over Monitoring (USA FREEDOM) Act, Pub. L. No. 114–23, 129 Stat. 268 (2015).

[44] Dieter Bohn, *Facebook, Microsoft Rolling FISA National Security Request Numbers into Transparency Reports*, VERGE (June 14, 2013, 9:29 PM), www.theverge.com/2013/6/14/4432060/facebook-to-include-national-security-requests-in-transparency-report.

[45] See 18 U.S.C.A. § 2709(c); 50 U.S.C.A. § 1805(c)(2)(B); 50 U.S.C.A. § 1861(d); 50 U.S. § 1881a(h)(4) (2012)(West).

[46] See THE PRESIDENT'S REVIEW GROUP ON INTELLIGENCE AND COMMUNICATIONS TECHNOLOGIES, LIBERTY AND SECURITY IN A CHANGING WORLD, REPORT AND RECOMMENDATIONS 92 (Dec. 12, 2013), www.whitehouse.gov/sites/default/files/docs/2013-12-12_rg_final_report.pdf [hereinafter REVIEW GROUP].

[47] See, e.g., Amended Motion for Declaratory Judgment of Google Inc.'s First Amendment Right to Publish Aggregate Information About FISA Orders at 2–3, Docket No. Misc. 13-03 (FISC Sept. 9, 2013), www.fisc.uscourts.gov/sites/default/files/Misc%2013-03%20Motion-1.pdf.

While the U.S. government initially granted permission to individual companies to disclose a limited amount of additional data, these companies – and their customers and the public generally – expressed dissatisfaction with the scope of the "transparency reporting" the government had permitted. For various business, legal, and philosophical reasons, seven major internet service providers filed motions in the FISC, beginning in August 2013, seeking a court order declaring that the government could not legally prohibit the reporting of "aggregate" surveillance request data that was not tied to an individual request or revelatory of specific targets or investigations.[48]

At first, the government opposed the motions by filing a brief that asserted sweeping authority under existing law to prohibit the disclosure of any data about surveillance requests. The government justified its position by citing the danger of revealing too much about the government's surveillance capabilities.[49] The government's opposition was based on the assertion that permitting the release of even aggregate data on a company level (such as, Company A released between 100 and 200 national security letters in the six-month period between X date and Y date), when aggregated, would expose how and where the government conducts surveillance. This, the government explained, would open opportunities for potential surveillance targets to switch to systems or platforms the government does not, or does not often, target.[50]

In late January 2014, however, Deputy Attorney General James Cole, of the United States Department of Justice, released a letter (the "Cole Letter") and a memorandum setting forth what was functionally a settlement between the parties involved in the FISC transparency litigation.[51] The Cole Letter provided guidance for the companies, and "similarly situated" service providers, on the scope of aggregate data that could be reported.[52] The Cole Letter contemplates two "options" for companies

---

[48] *See generally* Docket Nos. Misc. 13-03, 13-04, 13-05, 13-06, 13-07 (FISC 2013).

[49] *See* Response of the United States to Motions for Declaratory Judgment by Google Inc., Microsoft Corporation, Yahoo! Inc., Facebook Inc., & LinkedIn Corporation at 8-11, Docket Nos. Misc. 13-03, 13-04, 13-05, 13-06, 13-07, (FISC Sept. 30 2013), www.fisc.uscourts.gov/sites/default/files/Misc%2013-03%20Motion-21.pdf.

[50] *Id.*

[51] Letter from James M. Cole, Deputy Att'y Gen., U.S. Dep't of Justice, to Colin Stretch, Vice President & Gen. Couns., Facebook Inc., *et al.* (Jan. 27, 2014), www.justice.gov/iso/opa/resources/366201412716018407143.pdf.

[52] The letter also provided for a six month delay in reporting certain data, and a two year delay for data related to the surveillance of a "new capability," which is a service not previously surveilled under a given authority. It seems that this latter provision was

seeking to publish a transparency report. First, a company may report, in six month increments, the number of requests, and separately the number of affected user accounts, for each individual legal provision granting the government a particular national security surveillance authority in "bands" of "0–1000."[53] Alternatively, a company could choose to report only the total number of national security requests (pursuant to all the various surveillance authorities) within a six month period in "bands" of "0–250."[54] Congress largely adopted this framework in the USA FREEDOM Act, enacted on June 2, 2015, adding a two extra reporting "bands" of 100 and 500 for slightly different sets of data while at the same time imposing these reporting limitations not only on parties to the original transparency litigation but on all recipients of government national security requests for information.[55]

While some companies have continued to question whether these limitations are constitutional,[56] public discussion of "transparency reporting" has quieted. Nevertheless, almost every major Internet service provider and telecommunications company's website in the United States now includes a "transparency report," driven in large part by the public discussion over the scope of the government's intelligence activities.[57]

III   Stored Communications Act Litigation

Internet service providers went to court to push back on the U.S. government's surveillance authority in other ways. A leading Internet service provider, for example, sued in federal district court in New York

---

included to mitigate some of the danger the government alleged would result from reporting aggregate data. Without the delay, according to the government, adversaries could be put on notice too quickly when a previously unsurveilled service – like a new messaging application – was targeted.

[53] Letter from James M. Cole, *supra* note 51.   [54] *Id.*

[55] Uniting and Strengthening America by Fulfilling Rights and Ensuring Effective Discipline Over Monitoring (USA FREEDOM) Act, Pub. L. No. 114–23, 129 Stat. 268 § 603 (codified as amended 50 U.S.C.A. § 1873 (West 2015)).

[56] *See, e.g.*, Twitter, Inc. v. Lynch, No. 14-cv-04480-YGR, 2015 WL 5970295 (N.D. Cal. Oct. 14, 2015).

[57] *See, e.g.*, FACEBOOK, GOVERNMENT REQUESTS REPORT, https://govtrequests.facebook.com/ (last visited Nov. 24, 2015); VERIZON, VERIZON'S TRANSPARENCY REPORT FOR THE FIRST HALF OF 2015, http://transparency.verizon.com/ (last visited Nov. 24, 2015); GOOGLE, ACCESS TO INFORMATION, www.google.com/transparencyreport/ (last visited Nov. 24, 2015).

to quash a warrant acquired by the government pursuant to the Stored Communications Act ("SCA") after the company determined that the non-content data being sought in the warrant was stored on a company-owned server located in Dublin.[58] Some view the thirty-year-old SCA, which was originally enacted to provide additional privacy protections for electronic communications and to provide the government processes for acquiring such communications, as archaic in its contemplation of the role, function, and scope of electronic communications. These observers have criticized the statute for providing different levels of protection to a digital communication based less on its sensitivity than on how the circumstances of the proposed disclosure of that content fit within statutory terms that were enacted decades before the particular form of digital content or its particular mode of transmittal existed or was even contemplated.[59] Nevertheless, the courts have given the law broad applicability to the modern Internet and digital landscape, including e-mail providers, text messages, and social media.[60]

In the recent legal action, the company asserted that traditional territorial limits on search warrants, which usually may be issued to conduct searches only within the territorial jurisdiction of the issuing court, applied equally to warrants acquired pursuant to the SCA.[61] The SCA grants the government authority to acquire electronic communications data, but the law also references, among other processes for obtaining such information, the traditional warrant process.[62] The company advanced two arguments. On one hand, the company claimed that the government did not have the authority under the SCA to obtain its data located outside of the territorial jurisdiction of U.S. federal courts. On the

---

[58] *See* Stored Communications Act, Pub. L. 99–508, 100 Stat. 1848 (1986); In re Warrant to Search a Certain E-Mail Account Controlled and Maintained by Microsoft Corporation, 15 F. Supp. 3d 466 (S.D.N.Y. 2014), rev'd, 829 F.3d 197 (2d Cir. 2016). A petition for rehearing is pending at the time of publication.

[59] *See, e.g.,* Center for Democracy and Technology, Statement of James X. Dempsey, Vice President for Public Policy, before the Senate Committee on the Judiciary (Sept. 22, 2010), https://cdt.org/files/pdfs/20100922_jxd_testimony_ecpa.pdf (criticizing the SCA because "technology has advanced dramatically since [the law was passed], and the statute has been outpaced").

[60] *See, e.g.,* Konop v. Hawaiian Airlines Inc., 302 F.3d 868, 876 (9th Cir. 2002); Crispin v. Christian Audigier Inc., 717 F.Supp.2d 965, 982 (C.D. Cal. 2010); *In re* Application of the U.S. for an Order Pursuant to 18 U.S.C. § 2703(d), 830 F. Supp. 2d 114 (E.D. Va. 2011).

[61] Center for Democracy and Technology, Statement of James X. Dempsey, *supra* note 59, at 3.

[62] *Id.*

other hand, the company claimed that the SCA did not expand the traditional territorial limits on search warrants. The court rejected these arguments. First, the court held that the SCA authorized a search warrant, served on a U.S. company, for data it controlled on servers overseas. Second, the court held that this broad jurisdiction was one of the reasons the law was passed. In other words, the court reasoned that, given the nature of electronic data, the SCA was enacted to permit the issuing of search warrants for electronic communications stored outside the territorial boundaries of a given court's jurisdiction. After this manuscript went to press, the United States Court of Appeals for the Second Circuit reversed the District Court, holding that the SCA does not authorize a U.S. court to issue a SCA warrant against a U.S.-based service provider for the contents of a customer's electronic communications stored outside the U.S.[63]

IV   Review and Revisions to the Bulk Phone Metadata Collection Program

The most significant revisions to the U.S. legal framework for intelligence activities spurred, at least in part, by the Snowden disclosures involve White House and Congressional efforts to reform the "bulk phone metadata collection" program that was the subject of one of the initial Snowden disclosures. The government has since acknowledged that the program, undertaken pursuant to the "business records" provision of the Foreign Intelligence Surveillance Act, entailed the ongoing collection of all "telephony metadata" from telecommunications providers, with the purpose of analyzing such data to discern connections between known investigative targets and new targets of interest.[64] Over the past several years, Congress, Obama administration officials, and the President himself have stated views on both the merits and drawbacks of the program, and on potential changes to it.

In August 2013, the President organized a "Review Group on Intelligence and Communications Technologies" charged with making recommendations "designed to protect [U.S.] national security and advance [U.S.] foreign policy while also respecting our long standing commitment

---

[63] *Id.* at 10–11.

[64] *See In re* Application of the FBI for an Order Requiring the Production of Tangible Things From [Redacted], Docket No. BR 13–80 (FISC Apr. 25, 2013), www.dni.gov/files/documents/PrimaryOrder_Collection_215.pdf.

to privacy and civil liberties, recognizing our need to maintain the public trust (including the trust of our friends and allies abroad), and reducing the risk of unauthorized disclosures."[65] The Review Group issued its report on 12 December 2013. Among other recommendations for reform to the existing surveillance legal infrastructure, the report recommended ending the metadata collection program in its current form and shifting to a system where such data is held by private parties and accessed by the government only pursuant to an individualized court order.[66]

On January 23, 2014, the Privacy and Civil Liberties Oversight Board (the "PCLOB"), an independent government agency charged with assessing the civil liberties implications of intelligence activities, issued a more direct criticism of the metadata program, asserting not only that it needs to be reformed but that, in its existing form, it was not supportable by either the U.S. Constitution or the statutory provision on which the metadata program was based.[67] The PCLOB also challenged assertions by intelligence officials that the program had played a role in thwarting attacks against the United States, stating bluntly: "The Board is not aware of any instances in which the use of [the] telephone records directly contributed to the disruption of a terrorist plot."[68] The PCLOB assessed and criticized in detail each instance the government had cited as a "success story" for the program.[69] The PCLOB called for the ending of the bulk records program without recommending any specific replacement or alternative.[70]

In January 2014, a week before the PCLOB released its report on the bulk metadata program, President Obama also announced a series of reforms to foreign signals intelligence activities in light of the recommendations of the President's Review Group.[71] The President announced that, effective immediately, the use of data collected through the bulk metadata program would be curtailed, and directed that the Attorney General should begin the process of developing options for a new approach to the collection and storage of the data.

---

[65] REVIEW GROUP, *supra* note 46, at 1.   [66] *Id.* at 24–25.

[67] PRIVACY AND CIVIL LIBERTIES OVERSIGHT BOARD, REPORT ON THE TELEPHONE RECORDS PROGRAM CONDUCTED UNDER SECTION 215 OF THE USA PATRIOT ACT AND ON THE OPERATIONS OF THE FOREIGN INTELLIGENCE SURVEILLANCE COURT (Jan. 23, 2014), www.pclob.gov/SiteAssets/Pages/default/PCLOB-Report-on-the-Telephone-Records-Program.pdf.

[68] *Id.* at 148.   [69] *Id.* at 149–55.   [70] *Id.* at 168–69.

[71] *See, e.g.*, Obama, *supra* note 41; Press Release, The White House Office of the Press Sec'y, *supra* note 42.

In March 2014, the President outlined a proposal to replace the bulk metadata collection program with a new program that would permit the government to obtain such records only pursuant to individual orders from the FISC and that would require service providers to maintain such records only for as long as they currently do. The President suggested that the appropriate way forward would be through the passage of new legislation embodying these reforms.

While this debate amongst policymakers was unfolding publicly, the courts were reaching disparate conclusions about the bulk collection of telephone metadata by the U.S. government. In late December 2013, two federal lower court judges issued contradictory opinions on the constitutionality and legality of the program.[72] One held that the program was authorized by law and authorized under existing doctrine regarding the scope of the U.S. Constitution's protections against "unreasonable searches";[73] the other held the opposite: that the program constitutes an unreasonable search and is therefore unconstitutional.[74] In a somewhat unexpected turn of events, the first appeals court to consider this issue, the Second Circuit Court of Appeals, reversed the lower court opinion upholding the legality of the program in May 2015, finding that the program was not authorized by statute.[75] The Second Circuit did not, however, reach the issue of whether the program was constitutional, narrowing the scope and import of its ruling.

More importantly, the Second Circuit deferred implementation of its ruling in light of the USA FREEDOM Act, pending at the time (and subsequently enacted on June 2, 2015), that directly addresses the bulk program, revising the statutory provision on which the program was originally based and making some changes to the way it is administered. The Act makes a number of changes to the government's intelligence gathering authorities. Specifically, as to the bulk metadata program, the law purports to ban the "bulk" collection of telephone call records. Instead, the law authorizes the government to seek from service providers "the production on an ongoing basis of call detail records created before, on, or after the date of the application relating to an authorized investigation[.]"[76] In practice, the law creates a scheme

---

[72] *See* ACLU v. Clapper, 959 F. Supp. 2d 724 (S.D.N.Y. 2013); Klayman v. Obama, 957 F. Supp. 2d 1 (D.D.C. 2013). *See also* Chapter 2 in this volume.
[73] *See* 959 F. Supp. 2d at 749–52.   [74] *See* 957 F. Supp. 2d at 37–42.
[75] ACLU v. Clapper, 785 F.3d 787 (2d Cir. 2015).
[76] USA FREEDOM Act § 101, 50 U.S.C. § 1861 (West 2015).

where service providers will retain call records (as required already by another federal regulation) and the government may upon the issuance of a court order collect such data with respect to particular search terms, rather than itself collect all such call records.

For now, it seems that the USA FREEDOM Act has settled the debate (subject to expected continued litigation) over what changes need to be made to balance the government's asserted need to collect telephony metadata in national security investigations and concerns over the collection and storage of vast amounts of such data.

V   Privacy Rights of Non-U.S. Persons

The Obama Administration also indicated that it would push for reforms to existing laws, and the creation of new laws, aimed at acknowledging and protecting the privacy interests of non-U.S. persons. First, President Obama issued Presidential Policy Directive PPD-28 in January 2014, which ordered changes to U.S. signals intelligence practices, and, notably, acknowledged the civil liberties interests of non-U.S. persons, stating: "[A]ll persons have legitimate privacy interests in the handling of their personal information. U.S. signals intelligence activities must, therefore, include appropriate safeguards for the personal information of all individuals, regardless of the nationality of the individual to whom the information pertains or where that individual resides."[77]

These sentiments concerning the privacy interests of U.S. persons and non-U.S. persons alike echoed the December 2013 report from President Obama's Review Group. The report contains numerous recommendations that touch on the privacy interests of all persons—regardless of nationality. For example, the group recommended that the U.S. government undertake surveillance of non-U.S. persons "directed *exclusively* at the national security of the United States or our allies[,]" and not for other "illegitimate ends, such as theft of trade secrets or obtaining commercial gain for domestic industries[.]"[78] The group also specifically recommended applying the Privacy Act of 1974, which governs the U.S. government's treatment of sensitive personal data in its possession, "the same way to both U.S. persons and non-U.S. persons, ... absen[t] ... a specific and compelling showing[.]"[79] On the specific issue of the surveillance of foreign leaders and foreign governments, the

---

[77] Press Release, The White House Office of the Press Sec'y, *supra* note 42.
[78] REVIEW GROUP, *supra* note 46 at 29–30.   [79] *Id.* at 30.

Review Group recommended considering, among other factors, whether "the other nation [is] one with whom we share values and interests ... and whose leaders we should accord a high degree of respect and deference[.]"[80] Finally, the group recommended that the government explore formal arrangements between the United States and "a small number of closely allied governments,.... regarding intelligence collection guidelines and practices with respect to each others' citizens[.]"[81] While the current policy debate has focused primarily on the reform of the bulk metadata collection program, these additional issues remain open and unresolved.

In his January 2014 speech, President Obama also defended the U.S. intelligence agencies as "consistently follow[ing] protocols designed to protect the privacy of ordinary people" and "not abusing authorities" while doing an extraordinarily difficult job. He went on to clarify that "[o]ur intelligence agencies will continue to gather information about the intentions of governments, as opposed to ordinary citizens, around the world in the same way that the intelligence services of every other nation does" and he stated that "[w]e will not apologize simply because our services may be more effective."[82]

In light of these sentiments, the U.S. Attorney General, who was Eric Holder at that time, announced at a June 2014 meeting of U.S. and E.U. home affairs and justice ministers in Greece that the Administration would seek to pass legislation granting E.U. citizens "the same right to seek judicial redress for intentional or willful disclosures of protected information and for refusal to grant access or to rectify any errors in that information."[83] While the Administration subsequently announced minor changes to the way non-U.S. information collected by the U.S. government may be stored and used, non-U.S. persons continued for the time being to have no right of action to go to court to protect their information.[84] Legislation providing such a right of action was then introduced in Congress, and enacted into law, but the the law limits the right of a non-U.S. person to sue U.S. agencies under the Privacy Act for alleged privacy violations to citizens of designated foreign countries

---

[80] *Id.* at 32.   [81] *Id.* at 33.   [82] Obama, *supra* note 41.

[83] Ben Gilbert, *United States Planning Legislation to Offer Europeans the Same Privacy Rights as U.S. Citizens*, ENGADGET (June 27, 2014, 9:43 AM), www.engadget.com/2014/06/27/united-states-europe-privacy.

[84] David E. Sanger, *President Tweaks the Rules on Data Collection*, N.Y. TIMES (Feb. 3, 2015), www.nytimes.com/2015/02/03/world/president-tweaks-the-rules-on-data-collection.html.

and under the same restrictions that apply to U.S. citizens suing under the Privacy Act.[85] Nevertheless, the executive branch has not previously advocated legislation directly addressing the privacy rights of non-U.S. persons.

Neither American policy-makers nor the American courts seem inclined to extend significant privacy protections to non-U.S. persons.[86] Still, the increasing attention given to the concern suggests a perceptible shift away from the entrenched exceptionalism and exclusive focus on the rights of U.S. persons that has long-characterized these debates in the United States. This may be one of the most significant consequences of the NSA-Affair.

D   Observations, Outlook, and Challenges

In framing a multi-dimensional discussion of U.S. – German relations – and potential solutions for easing transatlantic differences on intelligence operations and policy – it is not sufficient to consider developments within and between the governments of the United States and of Germany. The global geopolitical and security environment provides an essential backdrop to the NSA-Affair. The fifteen year time span preceding the NSA-Affair encompasses the era in which terrorism became one of the chief security concerns for established democracies. This period includes the following events, which, when taken together, add-up to a new defense and security constellation: the interdiction of the Millennium bomb plot at Los Angeles International Airport on New Year's Eve 1999, the terrorist attacks of September 11, 2001 (New York, Virginia, and Pennsylvania), the terrorist attack of March 11, 2004 (Madrid), the terrorist attack of July 7, 2005 (London), and the terrorist attack of November 26–29, 2008 (Mumbai). This period also coincides with the economy's increasing dependence on technology, which expands the scope for nearly-cataclysmic vulnerability. The global economy now extensively relies on networked computer systems and Internet companies, and many hundreds of millions of users around the world embrace the "cloud" for storage and processing of personal and sometimes highly personal information. This fifteen-year period witnessed more rapid evolutions and challenges for technology companies, individual users, and intelligence agencies than perhaps any preceding fifteen or even twenty-five year

---

[85] *See*, The Judicial Redress Act of 2015, Pub. L. No. 114-26.
[86] *But see* Chapter 10 in this volume.

period. Nor is the pace likely to slow in the foreseeable future. Indeed, the rate of technological and economic change continues to accelerate.

Moreover, the Internet companies upon which governments, international organizations, enterprises, and individual users around the world rely for their daily operations, connectivity, data-storage, and continuity of operations are subject to additional constraints and their responses to those constraints in turn affect the challenges and options that governments have. I do not intend to provide comprehensive coverage of these developments here. Instead, I want to single out just two constraints: (1) the demand of these companies' users for greater confidentiality of their communications and other personal data after the revelations that began in 2013 and (2) E.U. data protection laws and enforcement mechanisms. My goal is to illustrate by example the dynamic and rapidly changing nature of the economic, business, and technological environments. Governments on both sides of the Atlantic must function in these complex and dynamic environments and, within the rule of law and the applicable frameworks of civil liberties and human rights, pursue their protective missions in the interest of their citizens.

I   Technology Companies' Technological Responses

In the wake of the Snowden revelations, users around the world called for more disclosures relating to both government surveillance requirements and Internet companies' responses to these requirements. Technology companies stepped up their efforts to provide greater privacy in a number of ways. First, they pursued informal dialogue with the executive branch. Second, they pursued litigation in federal court to obtain government authorization to disclose more detailed and fine-grained information about the number and types of surveillance orders they had received. But individuals and companies also made clear their demand for greater protection of the confidentiality of their communications.[87] Internet companies have responded in additional ways, reflecting the many and sometimes conflicting concerns and pressures from consumers, end users in the United States and in many other countries, governments, investors, media organizations, the public, and nongovernmental organizations. They have endorsed legislative proposals to provide additional constraints on the executive branch's intelligence

---

[87] *See, e.g.,* Amended Motion for Declaratory Judgment, *supra* note 47.

activities and to increase judicial and legislative oversight. In some cases, Internet companies have made public statements equating intelligence agencies' activities with criminal activities. For example, one tech executive stated in a blog post that he was "confused" and "frustrated" by the repeated reports of the behavior of the U.S. government, expressing surprise that his company's engineers must work against both "criminals" and "our own government."[88] Similarly, a coalition of leading companies have expressed the "strong" belief that change is needed to ensure that government surveillance programs operate under a legal framework that is rule-bound, narrowly tailored, transparent, and subject to oversight.[89]

Internet companies have also pursued technological efforts seeking to place their users' communications and information beyond the reach of intelligence agencies, or to attempt to reassure their users that the companies have made every reasonable effort to do so. Ira Rubinstein and Jorys van Hoboken summarized these measures in an article.[90] These initiatives include encrypting communications between end users' computers (client computers) and servers, and encrypting bulk data transfers of customer communications and information between data centers within a company's networks where such transfers had not always been encrypted. In addition to bulk encryption implemented by the cloud services providers, the surveillance revelations have also given new impetus to explorations of a variety of other encryption-based technologies that in effect place less plaintext user information within the reach of Internet companies. These include (a) advanced techniques implemented on servers that provide services to users without the service provider having access to the plain, unencrypted text of the users' queries or activities; (b) encryption at the client level of e-mail communications or of chat sessions; and (c) techniques based on "crowd-sourcing" such as Tor, which rely on a distributed architecture of machines operated by independent actors to make surveillance more difficult by obscuring the origin of communications, and peer-to-peer file synchronization tools such as Bittorent Sync that distribute a user's files among other

---

[88] Mark Zuckerberg, CEO of Facebook, FACEBOOK (Mar. 13, 2014), www.facebook.com/zuck/posts/10101301165605491.

[89] *See Reform Government Surveillance*, www.reformgovernmentsurveillance.com/ (last visited Nov. 24, 2015).

[90] *See* Joris V.J. van Hoboken & Ira S. Rubinstein, *Privacy and Security in the Cloud: Some Realism About Technical Solutions to Transnational Surveillance in the Post-Snowden Era*, 66 ME. L. REV. 487 (2014).

peer-connected devices without using a centralized server on whose operator a government can serve a surveillance order.[91] While these technologies are varied and operate in different ways, they uniformly remind observers of one of the defining characteristics of law and policy debates in the Internet industry: No issue, no challenge, and no resolution remains static for long because of the speed with which new technologies are developed, deployed, and sometimes adopted.

II Article 29 Data Protection Working Party, 819/14/EN, WP215, Opinion 04/2014 on Surveillance of Electronic Communications for Intelligence and National Security Purposes

European readers will not need a summary of European views and actions on the application of European human rights laws to alleged United States intelligence activities. Indeed, it would be folly for an observer from the United States to try to offer one.[92] The episode that follows illustrates European legal concerns in order to underscore the enormous cross-pressures operating on Internet companies based in the United States that collect, transmit, and process data of users located in almost every country of the world.

On April 10, 2014, the Working Party on the Protection of Individuals with Regard to the Processing of Personal Data issued Opinion 04/2014 on surveillance of electronic communications for intelligence and national security purposes (the "Opinion").[93] The Opinion makes several points of particular relevance for a transatlantic discussion of these issues:

First, the Opinion distinguishes between the surveillance programs run by intelligence services of E.U. Member States and the intelligence services of third countries that collect data of E.U. citizens. The Opinion concludes that under the data protection principles based on the European Convention on Human Rights and Council of Europe Convention 108 on the protection of personal data, the intelligence services of E.U. Member States must meet the requirements of necessity and proportionality and "[u]nder no circumstances surveillance programs

---

[91] Id. at 516–18.

[92] For European contributors, See, e.g., Chapters 5, 20, and 21 in this volume.

[93] Article 29 Data Protection Working Party, Opinion 04/2014 on Surveillance of Electronic Communications for Intelligence and National Security Purposes, 819/14/EN WP 215 (Apr. 10, 2014), www.cnpd.public.lu/fr/publications/groupe-art29/wp215_en.pdf [hereinafter Opinion].

based on the indiscriminate, blanket collection of personal data" can meet those requirements.[94] The Opinion does not define what it means by the "indiscriminate, blanket collection of personal data."

Second, the Opinion concludes that while the national security exemption written into the European treaties and the European data protection directive exempts data collection and processing by the intelligence services of E.U. Member States, the data privacy laws apply fully to the intelligence activities of other countries.[95] A follow-on "working document" issued in December 2014, by the Article 29 working party recognizes, however, that "a Member State may claim that a threat to the national security of a (partner or ally) third country also forms a part of this Member State's own national security, thus making E.U. law inapplicable."[96]

The Opinion further provides that all requirements in the European data protection directive governing international transfers of personal data to countries outside of the E.U. must be respected including an adequate level of data protection in the receiving state, transfers in line with the original purpose for which the data were collected, and the existence of a legal basis for fair and lawful processing.[97] Where such transfers are sought by intelligence or law enforcement authorities outside the E.U., the Article 29 Working Document expressly states that access to data stored in an E.U. Member State or under E.U. jurisdiction requires the formal request of mutual legal assistance through existing official channels.[98] The working party does not directly address situations where such data is not stored in the E.U. or otherwise under E.U. jurisdiction.

The Opinion then comes to the primary point for any transatlantic discussion of these issues: "Companies need to be aware that they may be acting in breach of European law if intelligence services of third countries gain access to the data of European citizens stored on their servers or comply with an order to hand over personal data on a large scale."[99] Here, too, the Opinion does not define "data on a large scale" or guide companies on how they would identify demands or orders for such data.

---

[94] Opinion at 6.   [95] *Id.*

[96] Article 29 Data Protection Working Party, Working Document on Surveillance of Electronic Communications for Intelligence and National Security Purposes, 14/EN WP 228, at 26 (Dec. 5, 2014), www.europarl.europa.eu/meetdocs/2014_2019/documents/libe/dv/13_wp29_wd228_/13_wp29_wd228_en.pdf [hereinafter Working Document].

[97] Opinion at 7.   [98] Working Document at 45.   [99] Opinion at 7.

The Opinion does not rule out enforcement action against companies that the Opinion considers to have provided personal data of E.U. nationals on a large scale to third countries.

The Opinion then returns to the subject of meaningful oversight mechanisms of the intelligence services, through Parliamentary scrutiny and oversight by a data protection authority or another suitable independent body.[100] Because third-country intelligence services are a component of sovereign governments that are not E.U. members and, by definition, therefore their demands on multi-national technology companies are not subject to E.U. data protection laws, the Opinion seems to leave highly uncertain the question of what these companies should do when faced with both compulsory legal process from third-country intelligence services for data relating to E.U. nationals and the threat of E.U. enforcement. This predicament is actual, not theoretical.

The Opinion provides two high-level indications for companies with operations in E.U. Member States:

(1) It states that data controllers "established in the E.U. or making use of equipment in a Member State must respect their obligations under E.U. law," and suggests that data protection authorities "may suspend ... data flows foreseen in the transfer instruments where there is a substantial likelihood that the data protection principles are being violated and that continuing transfers would create an imminent risk of grave harm to the data subject."[101] This conclusion may be more theoretical than practical, as the data protection authorities may not even learn of such allegedly violative data flows.

(2) The Opinion also states that third country intelligence services "must not have direct access to private sector data processed in the E.U."[102] The Opinion does not define what it means by "direct access" or how the data protection enforcement authorities in the E.U. would learn of or act in respect of "direct access" arrangements.

These two brief excursions into the external environments beyond the bilateral security and policy relationships underscore the cross-cutting pressures under which companies providing Internet-based services operate and the challenges of finding a lasting resolution of transatlantic differences.

---

[100] Opinion at 8.   [101] Opinion at 14.   [102] Opinion at 15.

E   Topics for Transatlantic Discussion

I close this chapter by suggesting three areas for productive and detailed discussions across the Atlantic on these issues.

First, it must be determined if there is a sincere and widespread interest in Germany (and the E.U. generally) in quickly and dramatically lowering transatlantic tensions on intelligence operations and policy matters, and reaching a resolution or at least an accommodation. The alternative may be a collective sense that resolution is not possible, at least not in the short- to medium-term, for various political, institutional, legal, and nation-specific reasons.

Second, if some trust-building and tension-lowering means are possible, the appropriate fora and processes for this détente must be identified. Any initiative in this respect will also require us to decide what information should be publicly available as a baseline for this dialogue.

Third, it must be determined how the U.S. and German scholarly, non-governmental, and legal practice communities can best contribute to these fora and processes. Are there particular legal, institutional, or constitutional issues on either side of the Atlantic that require illumination and exegesis as inputs to this dialogue?[103] One such issue is further study of the laws, institutions, and practices relating to systematic (bulk or unmediated) governmental access to data in many nations of the world.[104] This volume is a productive first-step on these three points.

F   Conclusion

It is far too early to predict how the U.S. – German bilateral discussions on these issues will proceed, how they will conclude, or whether the outcome will be a stable and appropriate balancing of national security, business and electronic commerce, and individual rights considerations. We know only that the discussions are hugely consequential and that the public debate, as rich as it is and will be, will not be able to take into

---

[103] *See, e.g.,* Chapter 2 in this volume.

[104] *See* Ira Rubinstein, Gregory Nojeim, & Ronald D. Lee, *Systematic Government Access to Personal Data: A Comparative Analysis*, 4 Int'l Data Privacy L. 2 (2014), http://papers.ssrn.com/sol3/papers.cfm?abstract_id=2444414; H. Cate, Jares X. Dempsey, and Ira S. Rubstein, *Systemtac Government Access to Private–Sector Data*, Int'l Data Privacy 2 (2012), *available at* http://idpl.oxfordjournals.org/content/2/4/195.full.pdf+html.

account much of the private and in many cases classified[105] information known to the various governments that are involved. We can also conclude that the conduct of intelligence operations – and the constitutional oversight of those intelligence operations – in an age of widespread and global reliance on the Internet will require exquisitely difficult and sometimes nearly real-time legal, political, and operational judgments.

[105] "Classified information" refers to information, generally relating to the national security or foreign policy of a government, that the government in question safeguards through a variety of measures, including criminal penalties for the unauthorized dissemination of the information.

8

Metadeath

How Does Metadata Surveillance
Inform Lethal Consequences?

BY MARGARET HU

A Introduction

The disclosures by former National Security Agency (NSA) contractor Edward Snowden[1] appear to reveal the extent to which the Intelligence Community relies upon bulk metadata surveillance technologies.[2]

---

[1] Only two individuals reportedly hold the full complement of Snowden's archived documents: journalist and attorney Glenn Greenwald and journalist and documentary filmmaker Laura Poitras. George Packer, *The Holder of Secrets: Laura Poitras's Closeup View of Edward Snowden*, NEW YORKER (Oct. 20, 2014). The Snowden disclosures were first revealed by Greenwald on June 5, 2013. For an extensive historical account of the Snowden disclosures, see GLENN GREENWALD, NO PLACE TO HIDE: EDWARD SNOWDEN, THE NSA, AND THE U.S. SURVEILLANCE STATE (2014) at 12. Multiple scholars have addressed the legality and constitutionality of the Snowden disclosures and modern surveillance architecture. *See, e.g.*, Laura K. Donohue, *Section 702 and the Collection of International Telephone and Internet Content*, 38 HARV. J.L. & PUB. POL'Y 117 (2015); Laura K. Donohue, *Bulk Metadata Collection: Statutory and Constitutional Considerations*, 37 HARV. J.L. & PUB. POL'Y 757 (2014); Orin S. Kerr, *A Rule of Lenity for National Security Surveillance Law*, 100 VA. L. REV. 1513 (2014); Peter Margulies, *Dynamic Surveillance: Evolving Procedures in Metadata and Content Collection After Snowden*, 66 HASTINGS L.J. 1 (2014); Stephen I. Vladeck, *Big Data Before and After Snowden*, 7 J. NAT'L SEC. L. & POL'Y 333 (2014); Christopher Slobogin, *Panvasive Surveillance, Political Process Theory, and the Nondelegation Doctrine*, 102 GEO. L.J. 1721 (2014); Nathan A. Sales, *Domesticating Programmatic Surveillance: Some Thoughts on the NSA Controversy*, 10 I/S: J.L. & POL'Y INFO. SOC'Y 523 (2014); Patrick Toomey & Brett Max Kaufman, *The Notice Paradox: Secret Surveillance, Criminal Defendants, & the Right to Notice*, 54 SANTA CLARA L. REV. 843 (2014); RACHEL LEVINSON-WALDMAN, BRENNAN CTR. FOR JUSTICE, WHAT THE GOVERNMENT DOES WITH AMERICANS' DATA 9 (2013); Paul Ohm, *Electronic Surveillance Law and the Intra-Agency Separation of Powers*, 47 U.S.F. L. REV. 269 (2012).

[2] *See, e.g.*, Jeremy Scahill & Glenn Greenwald, *The NSA's Secret Role in the U.S. Assassination Program*, INTERCEPT (Feb. 10, 2014); Greg Miller, Julie Tate & Barton Gellman, *Documents Reveal NSA's Extensive Involvement in Targeted Killing Program*, WASH. POST (Oct. 16, 2013). Barton Gellman & Ashkan Soltani, *NSA Tracking Cellphone Locations*

As General Michael Hayden, former Director of the Central Intelligence Agency (CIA) and the NSA, confirmed after the Snowden disclosures, "We kill people based on metadata."[3] This implies that metadata surveillance is now used to help inform drone strikes and targeted killing practices.[4] But the Snowden disclosures pose this question as well: Are we killing people based on big data[5] and not

---

Worldwide, Snowden Documents Show, WASH. POST (Dec. 4, 2013). Scholars and experts have documented how the NSA, CIA, and other intelligence organizations capitalize on technological innovation in the evolution and expansion of intelligence gathering tools and methods. *See, e.g.,* JAMES BAMFORD, THE SHADOW FACTORY: THE ULTRA-SECRET NSA FROM 9/11 TO THE EAVESDROPPING ON AMERICA (2008); JAMES BAMFORD, THE PUZZLE PALACE: INSIDE THE NATIONAL SECURITY AGENCY AMERICA'S MOST SECRET INTELLIGENCE ORGANIZATION (1982); William C. Banks, *Programmatic Surveillance and FISA: Of Needles in Haystacks,* 88 TEX. L. REV. 1633 (2010); Peter P. Swire, *Privacy and Information Sharing in the War on Terrorism,* 51 VILL. L. REV. 951 (2006).

[3] David Cole, *"We Kill People Based on Metadata,"* N.Y. REV. BOOKS (May 10, 2014); Lee Ferran, *Ex-NSA Chief: "We Kill People Based on Metadata,"* ABC NEWS (May 12, 2014). From the Snowden disclosures, it appears that metadata surveillance is potentially justified under several legal authorities: Section 215 of the USA PATRIOT Act, Section 702 of the Foreign Intelligence Surveillance Act (FISA) Amendments Act of 2008, and Executive Order 12333. Section 215 of the USA PATRIOT Act authorized the collection of "tangible things" that were "relevant to an authorized investigation . . . [to] protect against international terrorism or clandestine intelligence activities." USA PATRIOT Act, § 215, U.S.C. § 1861(a)(1) (2012), § 1861(b)(2)(A) (2012). Section 215 of the USA PATRIOT Act expired on June 1, 2015, and was replaced by the USA FREEDOM Act. P.L. 114-23 (2015). Section 702 of the FISA Amendments Act authorizes the Attorney General and the Director of National Intelligence to target non-U.S. persons reasonably believed to be outside the United States for surveillance. P.L. 110-261, § 101, 50 U.S.C. §§ 1881-1881g , 50 U.S.C. § 1881a(b). Executive Order 12333 delegates to the Attorney General the power to authorize intelligence gathering pursuant to collection, dissemination and retention protocols set forth by the Order. 46 Fed. Reg. 59,941 (Dec. 4, 1981), as amended by E.O. 13284, 68 Fed. Reg. 4,075 (Jan. 23, 2003); E.O.13355, 69 Fed. Reg. 53,593 (Aug. 27, 2004); and E.O. 13470, 73 Fed. Reg. 45,325 (July 30, 2008).

[4] *See, e.g.,* Scahill & Greenwald, *supra* note 2 ("[An anonymous member of JSOC's [Joint Special Operations Command] High Value Targeting task force explained that] the NSA 'geolocates' the SIM card or handset of a suspected terrorist's mobile phone, enabling the CIA and U.S. military to conduct night raids and drone strikes to kill or capture the individual in possession of the device."). The JSOC "is a subunified command of the U.S. Special Operations Command (USSOCOM)" within the U.S. government. ANDREW FEICKART, U.S. SPECIAL OPERATIONS FORCES: BACKGROUND AND ISSUES FOR CONGRESS, CONG. RES. SERV. 7 (Apr. 28, 2015). USSOCOM maintains the "responsibility for synchronizing planning for global operations to combat terrorist networks." *Id.* at Summary.

[5] "Big data" is difficult to define, as it is a newly evolving field and the technologies that it encompasses are evolving rapidly as well. Multiple authors have addressed the characteristics of "big data" and the challenges posed by big-data technologies. *See, e.g.,* VIKTOR MAYER-SCHÖNBERGER & KENNETH CUKIER, BIG DATA: A REVOLUTION THAT WILL

intelligence?[6] In a small-data[7] world, human analysts were capable of converting data into intelligence.[8] The Snowden disclosures and other reports have revealed that in a big-data world, it appears that we now

TRANSFORM HOW WE LIVE, WORK, AND THINK (2013); JULES J. BERMAN, PRINCIPLES OF BIG DATA: PREPARING, SHARING, AND ANALYZING COMPLEX INFORMATION (2013); PRIVACY, BIG DATA, AND THE PUBLIC GOOD: FRAMEWORKS FOR ENGAGEMENT (Julia Lane, Victoria Stodden, Stefan Bender & Helen Nissenbaum eds., 2014); ROB KITCHIN, THE DATA REVOLUTION: BIG DATA, OPEN DATA, DATA INFRASTRUCTURES & THEIR CONSEQUENCES (2014).

[6] "Data is not intelligence" is a quote from an NSA document released by the Snowden disclosures. *See* Peter Maass, *Inside NSA, Officials Privately Criticize "Collect It All" Surveillance*, INTERCEPT (May 28, 2015). According to some experts, the Snowden disclosures "suggest that analysts at the NSA have drowned in data since 9/11, making it more difficult for them to find the real threats." *Id.* "The titles of the documents capture their overall message: 'Data Is Not Intelligence,' 'The Fallacies Behind the Scenes,' 'Cognitive Overflow?' 'Summit Fever' and 'In Praise of Not Knowing.' Other titles include 'Dealing With a 'Tsunami' of Intercept' and 'Overcome by Overload?'" *Id.*

[7] "'Small data,' like 'big data,' has no set definition." Andrew Guthrie Ferguson, *Big Data and Predictive Reasonable Suspicion*, 163 U. PA. L. REV. 327, 329 n.6 (2015). "Small data" has been described in the following way: "Generally, small data is thought of as solving discrete questions with limited and structured data, and the data are generally controlled by one institution." *Id.* (citing JULES J. BERMAN, PRINCIPLES OF BIG DATA: PREPARING, SHARING, AND ANALYZING COMPLEX INFORMATION 1–2 (2013)). In many important recent works, scholars and experts have observed the transformational nature of emerging technologies of the Information Society – such as the Internet, digital culture, technological innovations in surveillance capacities – and the legal and privacy implications of such transformative technological developments. *See, e.g.*, JOHN GILLIOM & TORIN MONAHAN, SUPERVISION (2013); SIMON CHESTERMAN, ONE NATION UNDER SURVEILLANCE (2011); CONSTITUTION 3.0: FREEDOM AND TECHNOLOGICAL CHANGE (Jeffrey Rosen & Benjamin Wittes eds., 2011); SUSAN LANDAU, SURVEILLANCE OR SECURITY: THE RISKS POSED BY NEW WIRETAPPING TECHNOLOGIES (2010); JONATHAN ZITTRAIN, THE FUTURE OF THE INTERNET – AND HOW TO STOP IT (2008); DAVID LYON, SURVEILLANCE STUDIES: AN OVERVIEW (2007); LAWRENCE LESSIG, CODE VERSION 2.0 (2006); JACK GOLDSMITH & TIM WU, WHO CONTROLS THE INTERNET? (2006) MARK POSTER, INFORMATION PLEASE: CULTURE AND POLITICS IN THE AGE OF DIGITAL MACHINES (2006); A. Michael Froomkin, *The Death of Privacy?*, 52 STAN. L. REV. 1461 (2000).

[8] Historically, it appears that in a small-data world, intelligence gathering methods have relied upon human intelligence, including human sensory perception analysis, and other communication gathering and analytic methods that have depended upon human judgment and human decisionmaking; traditional evidence based upon analog data and paper-based files; traditional intelligence collection methods, such as traditional signals intelligence and other traditional communications interception; and other data analytic tools that have centered upon traditional research approaches, such as hypothesis-driven methods. *See, e.g.*, ROBERT M. CLARK, INTELLIGENCE COLLECTION (2014); ROBERT WALLACE & H. KEITH MELTON, WITH HENRY R. SCHLESINGER AND FOREWARD BY GEORGE TENET, SPYCRAFT: THE SECRET HISTORY OF THE CIA'S SPYTECHS FROM COMMUNISM TO AL-QAEDA (2008). "'[I]ntelligence comes from the brains of [human] analysts.'" Maass, *supra* note 6 (quoting Dr. Thomas Fingar, Deputy Director of National Intelligence for

resort to algorithms and supercomputing tools, and other forms of artificial intelligence, because we do not have the human capacity to analyze all of the data collected.[9] Some within the NSA have concluded that "data is not intelligence[.]"[10] In fact, some experts have explained that big-data projects an algorithmic hologram rather than reflecting reality.[11]

Whether the hologram of big-data cyber surveillance is more accurate and reliable than the reality of human intelligence and traditional signals intelligence appears to be openly debated within the NSA.[12] According to one Snowden document, "the author of a 'SIGINT [Signals Intelligence] Philosopher' column wrote that if the NSA was a corporation, it could have the following mission statement: 'building informed decision makers – so that targets do not suffer our nation's wrath unless they really deserve it – by exercising deity-like monitoring of the target.'"[13] The "deity-like monitoring" of individuals was impossible prior to the advent of metadata surveillance and other technological advances that have facilitated ubiquitous cyber surveillance in the Information Age and Big-Data Revolution.[14] Similarly, traditional surveillance methods did not necessarily entail "building" decision makers though supercomputing

Analysis, in an NSA document titled "Data Is Not Intelligence," www.documentcloud.org/documents/2088973-data-is-not-intelligence.html).

[9] Maass, *supra* note 6.

[10] The NSA document that refers to the concept that "data is not intelligence" was released as a part of the Snowden disclosures. *Id.* Specifically, the quote is attributed to Dr. Thomas Fingar, Deputy Director of National Intelligence for Analysis, from an opening statement at a symposium sponsored by the Intelligence and National Alliance, "a non-profit, non-partisan public policy forum focusing on intelligence and national security issues." *Id.* According to the Snowden disclosures, the NSA document was issued by the SID [Signals Intelligence Directorate] on September 18, 2007, and is available at www.documentcloud.org/documents/2088973-data-is-not-intelligence.html. *Id.*

[11] *See, e.g.,* Telephone Interview by Seth Fletcher with Jaron Lanier (Oct. 15, 2013), www.scientificamerican.com/article/lanier-interview-how-to-think-about-privacy/ ("And that's why we have scientists and theories . . . to talk about the structure of reality, not just trend lines. So anything relying on big data and trend lines will hit a wall at some point because [those statistical] models don't actually fit the structure of reality."); *see also* Margaret Hu, *Small Data Surveillance v. Big Data Cybersurveillance,* 42 PEPP. L. REV. 773, 836–40 (2015).

[12] *See, e.g.,* Maass, *supra* note 6.   [13] *Id.*

[14] *See, e.g.,* MAYER-SCHÖNBERGER & CUKIER, *supra* note 5, at 157. *See also* David Lyon, *Surveillance, Snowden, and Big Data: Capacities, Consequences, Critique,* BIG DATA & SOC., July–Dec. 2014, at 1, 2; Mark Andrejevic, *Surveillance in the Big Data Era,* in EMERGING PERVASIVE INFORMATION AND COMMUNICATION TECHNOLOGIES (PICT): ETHICAL CHALLENGES, OPPORTUNITIES, AND SAFEGUARDS 56 (Kenneth D. Pimple ed., 2014).

advances. Historically, surveillance tools served human decision making processes.[15] The big-data world has inverted multiple collection and decision making processes.[16] From the Snowden disclosures, it appears that humans now serve big-data cyber surveillance processes.[17]

Leaving aside for the moment the legal and constitutional challenges of this new era of big-data cyber surveillance, the technological challenges that accompany big-data tracking and "deity-like monitoring" are many. Primary among these are "collect-it-all"[18] cyber surveillance tools that are excessively blunt and over inclusive.[19] The question of whether we can appropriately use metadata and other digital data rather than traditional intelligence to inform lethal consequences can be framed this way: Whether big-data cyber surveillance facilitates a more "precise" version of a supercomputing-generated big-data "virtual reality" than the human

---

[15] *See, e.g.,* CLARK, *supra* note 8; WALLACE, *supra* note 8; *see also,* Hu, *supra* note 11.

[16] *See, e.g.,* Bruce Schneier, *Surveillance by Algorithm,* SCHNEIER ON SECURITY (Mar. 5, 2014); *see also* Ira "Gus" Hunt, Presentation at Gigaom Structure Data Conference: The CIA's "Grand Challenges" with Big Data (Mar. 20, 2013) [hereinafter Hunt CIA Presentation] (video and transcript available at https://gigaom.com/2013/03/20/even-the-cia-is-struggling-to-deal-with-the-volume-of-real-time-social-data) ("When I started as analyst years ago inside the CIA . . . . It was the world of the few to the many in terms of information flows . . . . The Social Mobile Cloud world has completely inverted that model and has gone to this complex many-to-many model.").

[17] *See, e.g.,* Maass, *supra* note 6 ("The documents noted the difficulty of sifting through the ever-growing haystack of data. For instance, a 2011 document titled 'ELINT Analysts – Overcome by Overload? Help is Here with IM&S' outlined a half dozen computer tools that 'are designed to invert the paradigm where an analyst spends more time searching for data than analyzing it.'").

[18] GREENWALD, *supra* note 1, at 97 (citing NSA slide from Snowden disclosures titled, "New Collection Posture," quoting NSA data collection procedure as "Collect-it-All"), http://glenngreenwald.net/pdf/NoPlaceToHide-Documents-Compressed.pdf; *see also* David Cole, *"No Place to Hide" by Glenn Greenwald, on the NSA's Sweeping Efforts to "Know it All,"* WASH. POST (May 12, 2014).

[19] *See, e.g.,* Comments by James Chipman, *Reforming NSA Surveillance: Where Do We Go From Here?* Panel Discussion, *Cybersecurity + Law Enforcement: The Cutting Edge Symposium,* Hosted by Roger Williams University Law School and the *Roger Williams University Law Review,* http://law.rwu.edu/event/cybersecurity-law-enforcement-cutting-edge-symposium. *See also* PRIVACY AND CIVIL LIBERTIES OVERSIGHT BD. (DAVID MEDINE, CHAIRMAN; RACHEL BRAND; ELISEBETH COLLINS COOK; JAMES DEMPSEY & PATRICIA WALD), REPORT ON THE TELEPHONE RECORDS PROGRAM CONDUCTED UNDER SECTION 215 OF THE USA PATRIOT ACT AND ON THE OPERATIONS OF THE FOREIGN INTELLIGENCE SURVEILLANCE COURT 39 (Jan. 23, 2014) (citing Opinion and Order, No. PR/TT [*redacted*] (FISA Ct.) ("PR/TT Op.") at 23); Klayman v. Obama, 2015 U.S. Dist. LEXIS 151826, at 39 (D.D.C. Nov. 9, 2015) (describing the Section 215 program as a "breathtakingly broad metadata collection Program").

fallibility of small-data "reality."[20] Thus, at the dawn of the Big-Data Revolution, whether the projection of a big-data hologram can be fairly championed for its "precision"[21] deserves close scrutiny. Understanding exactly why "data is not intelligence" in a big-data world helps to discern the limits of algorithmic-driven decision making; and why further interrogation may be necessary before big data can be ascribed high intelligence value and significant evidentiary weight.

Moreover, bulk metadata surveillance and other cyber surveillance developments in contemporary surveillance architecture[22] invite a critical legal focus on the stark distinctions between small-data surveillance[23] and big-data cyber surveillance[24] methods. As the NSA and other intelligence organizations have increasingly exploited newly available mass-data surveillance, or dataveillance,[25] and other cyber surveillance tools,[26]

---

[20] See Hu, *supra* note 11, at 839 n.289 (quoting interview with Jaron Lanier where Lanier posits that big data creates a "seductive illusion" of reality, however, does not "actually reflect the structure of reality.").

[21] See, e.g., Comments by Glenn Greenwald, *Contact Presents: An Evening with Glenn Greenwald*, Washington and Lee University, Oct. 20, 2015 (notes on file with author); see also James Risen & Laura Poitras, *N.S.A. Collecting Millions of Faces from Web Images*, N.Y. Times, June 1, 2014, at A1.

[22] Several important works have been published in recent years, shedding light on mass surveillance technologies, and the policy and programmatic framework of cyber surveillance and covert intelligence gathering. *See, e.g.*, JULIA ANGWIN, DRAGNET NATION: A QUEST FOR PRIVACY, SECURITY, AND FREEDOM IN A WORLD OF RELENTLESS SURVEILLANCE 17–18 (2014); SHANE HARRIS, @WAR: THE RISE OF THE MILITARY-INTERNET COMPLEX (2014); DANA PRIEST & WILLIAM M. ARKIN, TOP SECRET AMERICA: THE RISE OF THE NEW AMERICAN SECURITY STATE 128–55 (2011); SHANE HARRIS, THE WATCHERS (2010); ROBERT O'HARROW, NO PLACE TO HIDE 8, 10 (2005); JEFFREY ROSEN, THE NAKED CROWD: RECLAIMING SECURITY AND FREEDOM IN AN ANXIOUS AGE (2004).

[23] *See generally*, Hu *supra* note 11.

[24] See, e.g., LESSIG, *supra* note 7, at 209 (describing cyber surveillance or "digital surveillance" as "the process by which some form of human activity is analyzed by a computer according to some specified rule.... [T]he critical feature in each [case of surveillance] is that a computer is sorting data for some follow-up review by some human.").

[25] Roger Clarke is attributed with introducing the term "dataveillance." See Roger A. Clarke, *Information Technology and Dataveillance*, 31 COMM. ACM 498 (1988). Clarke describes dataveillance as the systematic monitoring or investigation of people's actions, activities, or communications through the application of information technology. *Id.*; see also LYON, *supra* note 7, at 16; MARTIN KUHN, FEDERAL DATAVEILLANCE: IMPLICATIONS FOR CONSTITUTIONAL PRIVACY PROTECTIONS (2007).

[26] The Snowden disclosures have included multiple high-profile revelations on newly emerging data surveillance, or dataveillance tools, and cyber surveillance methods, and information specific to their implementation. *See, e.g.*, Glenn Greenwald, *NSA Collecting Phone Records of Millions of Verizon Customers Daily*, THE GUARDIAN (June 6, 2013); Barton Gellman & Laura Poitras, *U.S., British Intelligence Mining Data from Nine U.S.*

new and unresolved legal and constitutional questions have presented themselves.[27] The legal framework in place to analyze the legality and constitutionality of big-data cyber surveillance methods such as bulk metadata surveillance – and the intelligence activities it supports – remains unclear.[28] Clarity will not be achieved without better understanding what metadata is and the purposes for which it has traditionally been used.

Metadata is data about data.[29] For example, while bulk metadata surveillance programs indiscriminately collect the time of a call or an email address of millions of recipients and senders,[30] the content of the call or the content of the email is not included.[31] Prior to the big-data revolution, metadata was not considered meaningful under traditional surveillance methods.[32] Due to technological restrictions, for instance, the content of the call was significant and distinguishing the content of a call from the metadata associated with it was not significant. This is

---

Internet Companies in Broad Secret Program, Wash. Post (June 7, 2013); T.C. Sottek & Josh Kopstein, *Everything You Need to Know About PRISM,* Verge, (July 13, 2013); Scott Shane, *No Morsel Too Minuscule For All-Consuming N.S.A., From Spying on Leader of U.N. to Tracking Drug Deals, an Ethos of 'Why Not?',* N.Y. Times (Nov. 3, 2013) A1, A10; Ellen Nakashima & Barton Gellman, *Court Gave NSA Broad Leeway in Surveillance, Documents Show,* Wash. Post (June 30, 2014).

[27] Several scholars have noted how transformative technological shifts have also transformed methods of governance and surveillance as a tool of governance. *See, e.g.,* Jack M. Balkin, *Old-School/New-School Speech* Regulation, 127 Harv. L. Rev. 2296, 2297 (2014); Jack M. Balkin, *The Constitution in the National Surveillance State,* 93 Minn. L. Rev. 1 (2008) [hereinafter Balkin, *National Surveillance State*]; Jack M. Balkin & Sanford Levinson, *The Processes of Constitutional Change: From Partisan Entrenchment to the National Surveillance State,* 75 Fordham L. Rev. 489 (2006); Lior Jacob Strahilevitz, *Signaling Exhaustion and Perfect Exclusion,* 10 J. Telecomm. & High Tech. L. 321 (2012); David Lyon, *Biometrics, Identification and Surveillance,* 22 Bioethics 499 (2008); Erin Murphy, *Paradigms of Restraint,* 57 Duke L.J. 1321 (2008).

[28] *See, e.g.,* ACLU v. Clapper, 785 F.3d 787, 794 (2d Cir. 2015). *See also infra* notes 38, 84.

[29] Bruce Schneier, *Metadata = Surveillance,* Schneier on Security (Mar. 13, 2014).

[30] *See, e.g.,* Office of the Privacy Commissioner of Canada, Metadata and Privacy: A Technical and Legal Overview at 1 (2014) ("Simply put, metadata is data that provides information about other data. It is information that is generated as you use technology . . . .").

[31] *See, e.g.,* Bruce Schneier, *NSA Surveillance Program Reaches "Into the Past" to Retrieve, Replay Phone Calls,* Wash. Post (Mar. 18, 2014).

[32] *See, e.g.,* Schneier, *Surveillance by Algorithm, supra* note 16 ("[M]ost alarming of all, drone targeting is partly based on algorithmic surveillance") (citing Bruce Schneier, *Everything We Know About How the NSA Tracks People's Physical Location,* Schneier on Security (Feb. 11, 2014). *See also* Scahill & Greenwald, *supra* note 2 ("According to a former drone operator for the military's Joint Special Operations Command (JSOC) who also worked with the NSA, the agency often identifies targets based on controversial metadata analysis and cell-phone tracking technologies.").

because metadata in a small-data world could not be quantified in exponentially increasing volumes and could not inform meaningful inferences.[33] The supercomputing technologies to collect, store, and analyze bulk metadata in the millions, billions, and trillions of units did not exist.[34] The algorithms – and the massive volumes of metadata and other data fed into big data's algorithms – did not exist.[35] Metadata, thus, was not considered valuable information in of itself. Yet, metadata – data about data, such as information on the time and location of a telephone call, but, not information on the substance of the conversation of the telephone call – is now a critical part of the data backbone that supports big-data cyber surveillance architecture.[36]

Big-data cyber surveillance architecture is better understood now than ever before in light of the Snowden disclosures.[37] Despite the Snowden disclosures, however, the exact manner in which big-data cyber surveillance programs specifically are used to link information gleaned from the cyber surveillance to specific national security decision making protocols are still largely unknown.[38] Applying what we know about the scientific

---

[33] MAYER-SCHÖNBERGER & CUKIER, *supra* note 5, at 26.

[34] *See, e.g.*, NATIONAL RESEARCH COUNCIL'S COMMITTEE ON THE FUTURE OF SUPERCOMPUTING, GETTING UP TO SPEED: THE FUTURE OF SUPERCOMPUTING 31 (Susan L. Graham, Marc Snir & Cynthia A. Patterson eds., 2005).

[35] *See, e.g.*, KITCHIN, *supra* note 5, at 100.

[36] Experts increasingly describe big-data surveillance in architectural terms. *See, e.g.*, BRUCE SCHNEIER, DATA AND GOLIATH: THE HIDDEN BATTLES TO COLLECT YOUR DATA AND CONTROL YOUR WORLD 48 (2015) ("This has evolved into a shockingly extensive, robust, and profitable surveillance architecture."). *See also* GREENWALD, *supra* note 1; JENNIFER STISA GRANICK, AMERICAN SPIES: MODERN SURVEILLANCE, WHAT IT IS, & WHY YOU SHOULD CARE (forthcoming 2016); Margaret Hu, *Taxonomy of the Snowden Disclosures*, WASH. & LEE L. REV. (forthcoming 2015).

[37] *See, e.g.*, Edward Wasserman, *Protecting News in the Era of Disruptive Sources*, *in* AFTER SNOWDEN: PRIVACY, SECRECY, AND SECURITY IN THE INFORMATION AGE 116 (Ronald Goldfarb ed., 2015) (hereinafter AFTER SNOWDEN); Jon L. Mills, *The Future of Privacy in the Surveillance Age*, *in* AFTER SNOWDEN.

[38] Although the Snowden disclosures have revealed that there is an apparent connection between NSA cyber surveillance and CIA drone strikes, the exact nature of that link has not been disclosed. *See, e.g.*, Greg Miller, Julie Tate & Barton Gellman, *Documents Reveal NSA's Extensive Involvement in Targeted Killing Program*, WASH. POST (Oct. 16, 2013); Greg Miller, *Plan for Hunting Terrorists Signals U.S. Intends to Keep Adding Names to Kill Lists*, WASH. POST (Oct. 23, 2012). Increasingly, the U.S. government has conducted drone strikes where the identity of the target is unknown, but, whose data signature is suspect. The United States in recent years has attempted to "[s]ecur[e] permission to use these 'signature strikes' [that] would allow the agency to hit targets based solely on intelligence indicating patterns of suspicious behavior . . . ." Greg Miller, *Broader Drone Tactics Sought*, WASH. POST, Apr. 19, 2012, at A1. *See also supra* note 3.

principles of big data to how big-data tools are integrated into national security decision making is a speculative exercise. To deepen the conversation on the legality and constitutionality of newly emerging cyber surveillance methods, a close understanding of the data science that underscores big-data tools is increasingly necessary.[39] Covert intelligence methods that are increasingly data science-dependent cannot be properly interrogated under the rule of law without scientific validity determinations.[40] Therefore, despite the speculative nature of this exercise, the logic and scientific validity of metadata surveillance should be questioned in all instances, but especially in circumstances where "we kill people based on metadata."[41] That might, in turn, inform a court's assessment of whether such processes are rationally related to the governmental purpose or, at a minimum, assist a court with balancing privacy rights and other constitutional protections against the claimed paramount of national security interests advanced by the measures.

This chapter asks whether and how the Snowden disclosures imply that big-data tools, such as metadata surveillance, may now be used to inform targeted killing and drone strikes. As multiple national security experts have observed, drone strikes have become a cornerstone of modern counterterrorism policy.[42] Much scholarship has been dedicated to the important question of whether and how modern targeted killing decision making protocols and programs are lawful.[43] Yet, those

---

[39] *See, e.g.*, ACLU v. Clapper, 785 F.3d 787, 794 (2d Cir. 2015) (relying on Yves-Alexandre de Montjoye, Laura Radaelli, Vivek Kumar Singh & Alex "Sandy" Pentland, *Unique in the Shopping Mall: On the Reidentifiability of Credit Card Metadata*, 347.6221 Science J. 536–39 (2015)). "'[I]nformation that could traditionally only be obtained by examining the contents of communications' and that is therefore 'often a proxy for content.'" *Id.* (citing Joint App'x 50 (Declaration of Professor Edward W. Felten [Professor of Computer Science and Public Affairs at Princeton University])).

[40] *See, e.g.*, GRANICK, *supra* note 36; Hu, *Big Data Cybersurveillance*, *supra* note 11; Peter Margulies, *Rage Against the Machine?: Automated Surveillance and Human Rights* 33 (forthcoming 2016), http://ssrn.com/abstract=2657619.

[41] Cole, *supra* note 3; *see also* JEREMY SCAHILL, DIRTY WARS (2013); DAVID E. SANGER, CONFRONT AND CONCEAL: OBAMA'S SECRET WARS AND SURPRISING USE OF AMERICAN POWER 241–70 (2012); DANIEL KLAIDMAN, KILL OR CAPTURE: THE WAR ON TERROR AND THE SOUL OF THE OBAMA PRESIDENCY 41 (2012).

[42] *See, e.g.*, Thomas Gibbons-Neff, *U.S. Drone Policies a "Slippery Slope" for Continuous Wars, Report Finds*, WASH. POST (June 26, 2014) ("Targeted drone strikes have become a centerpiece of the Obama administration's counterterrorism policy . . . .").

[43] Multiple scholars are carefully examining the legal implications of targeted killing policies and drone strikes. *See, e.g.*, Martin S. Flaherty, *The Constitution Follows the Drone: Targeted Killings, Legal Constraints, and Judicial Safeguards*, 38 HARV. J.L. & PUB. POL'Y 21 (2015); Oren Gross, *The New Way of War: Is There a Duty to Use Drones?*, 67 FLA.

analytical efforts operate in the absence of an informed public debate about the data science underpinning cyber surveillance tools, and why the logic and science of big-data cyber surveillance should be made more transparent. Even where the surveillance is covert, transparency can take the form of a more public interrogation of the principles of logic and scientific validity of the big-data tools engaged by the Intelligence Community. Thus, understanding the logic and limits of bulk metadata surveillance is necessary, especially where it might be the basis for the death of a target.[44]

L. Rev. 1 (2015); Gregory S. McNeal, *Targeted Killing and Accountability*, 102 Geo. L.J. 681 (2014); Douglas Cox & Ramzi Kassem, *Off the Record: The National Security Council, Drone Killings, and Historical Accountability*, 31 Yale J. Reg. 363 (2014); David W. Opderbeck, *Drone Courts*, 44 Rutgers L.J. 413 (2014); Matthew Craig, *Targeted Killing, Procedure, and False Legitimation*, 35 Cardozo L. Rev. 2349 (2014); Jenny-Brooke Condon, *Illegal Secrets*, 91 Wash. U.L. Rev. 1099 (2014); Jennifer Daskal, *The Geography of the Battleflield: A Framework for Detention and Targeting Outside the 'Hot' Conflict Zone*, 171 U. Pa. L. Rev. 1165 (2013); Amos Guiora, *Legitimate Target: A Criteria-Based Approach to Targeted Killing* (2013), Deborah Pearlstein, *Enhancing Due Process in Targeted Killing*, American Constitution Society Issue Brief (Oct. 2013); Kevin Jon Heller, *'One Hell of a Killing Machine': Signature Strikes and International Law*, 11 J. Int'l Crim. Just. 89 (2013); Kenneth Anderson, *The Secret "Kill List" and the President*, 3 J.L.: Periodical Laboratory of Leg. Scholarship 93 (2013); Richard Murphy & Afsheen John Radsan, *Notice and an Opportunity to Be Heard Before the President Kills You*, 48 Wake Forest L. Rev. 829 (2013); Alberto R. Gonzales, *Drones: The Power to Kill*, 82 Geo. Wash. L. Rev. 1 (2013); Leila Nadya Sadat, *America's Drone Wars*, 45 Case W. Res. J. Int'l L. 215 (2012); Carla Crandall, *Ready . . . Fire . . . Aim! A Case for Applying American Due Process Principles Before Engaging in Drone Strikes*, 24 Fla. J. Int'l L. 55 (2012); Pardiss Kebriaei, *The Distance Between Principle and Practice in the Obama Administration's Targeted Killing Program: A Response to Jeh Johnson*, 31 Yale L. Pol'y Rev. 151 (2012); Mark V. Vlasic, *Assassination & Targeted Killing-A Historical and Post-Bin Laden Legal Analysis*, 43 Geo. J. Int'l L. 259 (2012); Robert Chesney, *Who May Be Killed? Anwar al-Awlaki as a Case Study in the International Legal Regulation of Lethal Force*, in Y.B. of Int'l Humanitarian L. (M.N. Schmitt *et al.* eds., 2011); Lesley Wexler, *Litigating the Long War on Terror: The Role of al-Aulaqi v. Obama*, 9 Loy. U. Chi. Int'l L. Rev. 159 (2011); Philip Alston, *The CIA and Targeted Killings beyond Borders*, 2 Harv. Nat'l Sec. J. 283 (2011); Kenneth Anderson, *Targeted Killing in U.S. Counterterrorism Strategy and Law*, in Legislating the War on Terror: An Agenda for Reform (Ben Wittes ed., 2009); Richard Murphy and Afsheen John Radsan, *Due Process and Targeted Killing of Terrorists*, 31 Cardozo L. Rev. 405 (2009); Daphne Barak-Erez & Matthew C. Waxman, *Secret Evidence and the Due Process of Terrorist Detentions*, 48 Colum. J. Trans. L. 3 (2009).

[44] In one NSA document released through the Snowden disclosures, an author summarized the statements of Dr. Thomas Fingar, Deputy Director of National Intelligence for Analysis, explaining that he had "called for 'transparency' in intelligence analysis; that is, that all analysis has to be reproducible." *See Maass, supra* note 6 (discussing "Data Is Not Intelligence," www.documentcloud.org/documents/2088973-data-is-not-intelligence

This chapter proceeds in four parts. After this Introduction, Part B discusses how metadata surveillance may inform targeted killing decisions. Part C elaborates how bulk metadata surveillance may be driven by the big-data logic of algorithmic intelligence.[45] Important scholarship has explored the "death of privacy" in the digital age.[46] Part D concludes that "metadeath" is not only a way to descriptively capture the potential lethal consequences of metadata surveillance in a big-data world, but is also a term to describe a new way of conceptualizing how "bulk metadata collection" is contributing to the "metadeath of privacy" in an age of ubiquitous cyber surveillance.

B   The Snowden Disclosures and Recent Targeted Killing Disclosures

The first surveillance program revealed by the Snowden disclosures on June 5, 2013, is commonly referred to as the NSA's "bulk telephony metadata collection program."[47] The "bulk telephony metadata" surveillance method exposed new legal complexities and oversight challenges in the modern landscape of big-data cyber surveillance. Post-Snowden litigation[48] and

---

.html). The author's summary appears to suggest that Dr. Fingar advocated for a more robust application of the scientific method. The summary, for example, included the statement: "Following established common standards will help ensure transparency." *Id.* The U.S. Court of Appeals for the Second Circuit, when reviewing the legality of the bulk telephony metadata program that had been revealed by the Snowden disclosures, discussed the need for methods to assess the justification for the metadata surveillance and the reasonableness of the data collection. *See* ACLU v. Clapper, 785 F.3d 787, 824 (2d Cir. 2015) (asserting the need to gauge "reasonableness of the government's assertions of the necessity of the data collection").

[45] *See, e.g.,* Leo Pape & Arthur Kok, *Real-World Limits to Algorithmic Intelligence, in* Artificial General Intelligence 394–400 (Jurgen Schmidhuber, Kristinn R. Thorisson & Moshe Looks eds., 2011).

[46] Daniel J. Solove, The Digital Person: Technology and Privacy in the Information Age 3; A. Michael Froomkin, *The Death of Privacy?,* 52 Stan. L. Rev. 1461, 1475 (2000); David Brin, The Transparent Society 8–9 (1998).

[47] *See, e.g.,* Adam Liptak & Michael S. Schmidt, *Judge Upholds N.S.A.'s Bulk Collection of Data on Calls,* N.Y. Times (Dec. 27, 2013); *see also* Obama v. Klayman, No. 14–5001, slip op. at 2 (D.C. Cir. Aug. 18, 2015). Section 215 of the USA PATRIOT Act expired on June 1, 2015, and was replaced by the USA FREEDOM Act. P.L. 114–23 (2015).

[48] The bulk telephony metadata collection program, as had been legally justified under Section 215 of the USA PATRIOT Act, faced multiple legal challenges under several legal theories, with lawsuits filed in federal court immediately following the Snowden disclosures. *See* Klayman v. Obama, 957 F. Supp. 2d 1, 9 (D.D.C. 2013) (finding that court lacked jurisdiction to review Administrative Procedure Act [APA] claim but could hear Fourth

legislative reform efforts[49] illustrate that proper oversight of bulk metadata collection is a fraught exercise and has not yet resolved the question of exactly how "we kill people based on metadata." Therefore, whether and how the "bulk telephony metadata collection program" or other metadata surveillance programs operate to inform drone strikes is largely unknown. The difficulty and frustration surrounding proper oversight is caused in no small measure by the new and revolutionary nature of big-data – a revolution at its infancy.[50]

It is difficult to conceive how metadata, for instance, is being converted into algorithmic intelligence and artificial intelligence. It is even more difficult to conceive how, from the Snowden disclosures, it appears that big-data decision making may be displacing other traditional forms of national security decision making, such as the policy choices that had been dependent upon human intelligence and traditional signals intelligence. To help understand this displacement, it is instructive to refer to a

---

Amendment constitutional challenges to NSA's conduct; and granting motion for injunction, however, staying the order pending appeal); Obama v. Klayman, 800 F.3d. 559, 561 (D.C. Cir. 2015) (reversing district court and remanding for further proceedings); Klayman v. Obama, 2015 U.S. Dist. LEXIS 151826, at 21–59 (D.D.C. Nov. 9, 2015) (concluding plaintiff's claim that Section 215 program is unconstitutional under the Fourth Amendment has a likelihood of success on the merits and ordering injunction, blocking the final 20 days of the Section 215 program, prior to the implementation of the USA FREEDOM Act's reforms to metadata collection); Obama v. Klayman, 1:13-cv-00851-RJL (D.C. Cir. Nov. 16, 2015) (granting emergency motion for a stay pending appeal); Klayman v. Obama, 2015 U.S. App. LEXIS 20216 (D.C. Cir. Nov. 20, 2015) (denial of emergency petition for rehearing en banc); ACLU v. Clapper, 959 F. Supp. 2d 724 (S.D.N.Y. 2013) (dismissing complaint in part on grounds that subscribers do not have legitimate expectation of privacy in telephony metadata held by third parties under Fourth Amendment precedent); ACLU v. Clapper, 785 F.3d. 787, 792 (2d. Cir. 2015) (vacating dismissal of complaint, finding that bulk collection of telephone metadata exceeded scope of statutory authority, remanding for argument on constitutional issues, and affirming district court's denial of preliminary injunction); ACLU v. Clapper, 2015 U.S. App. LEXIS 12244 (2d. Cir. June 9, 2015) (ordering stay of proceedings pending parties' supplemental briefing in light of passage of USA FREEDOM Act); ACLU v. Clapper, 2015 U.S. App. LEXIS 18862 (2d. Cir. Oct. 29, 2015) (denying motion for preliminary injunction, declining to reach constitutional issues for prudential reasons, and remanding for further proceedings in district court); Hu, *supra* note 11, at 808.

[49] Congress passed the USA FREEDOM Act in the wake of the Snowden disclosures, *supra* note 47 (imposing new statutory limits to how and when NSA can collect metadata records, and requiring that NSA identify specifically the information sought); Andrea Peterson, *A Year After Snowden Revelations, Government Surveillance Reform Still a Work in Progress*, WASH. POST (June 5, 2014).

[50] *See, e.g.*, KITCHIN, *supra* note 5, at 2; Lisa Gitelman & Virginia Jackson, *Introduction, in* 'RAW DATA' IS AN OXYMORON 1–14 (Lisa Gitelman ed., 2013); MAYER-SCHÖNBERGER & CUKIER, *supra* note 5, at 7.

single sentence from a 2010 NSA document released through the Snowden disclosures that explains: "'It's not just the traditional communications we're after: It's taking a full-arsenal approach that digitally exploits the clues a target leaves behind in their regular activities on the [Inter]net to compile biographic and biometric information' that can help 'implement precision targeting.'"[51] The term "targeting" in this document does not appear to be defined. But the term "targeting" in the defense and intelligence context has been defined as "[t]he process of selecting and prioritizing targets and matching the appropriate response to them, considering commander's objectives, operational requirements, capabilities, and limitations."[52] In a small-data world "traditional communications" and traditional national security evidence – such as human intelligence and traditional signals intelligence – were used to support killing decisions and other tactical decisions taken by the military and the Intelligence Community.[53] What is not clear from the Snowden disclosures is whether algorithmic intelligence may now be used to inform killing decisions. In other words, if "we kill people based on metadata," then it is important to recognize the new role of big-data tools in national security policy making.

The Bureau of Investigative Journalism estimates that "there have been at least 514 US drone strikes in Pakistan, Somalia and Yemen since the first in November 2002."[54] To date, various media reports indicate that between 3,000 to 4,700 individuals total have been killed by drone attacks.[55] One U.S. Senator, Lindsey Graham (R-SC), has estimated the death toll of the drone strike program at 4,700,[56] a figure that "matches

---

[51] Risen & Poitras, *supra* note 21. *See* U.S. DEPT. OF DEFENSE, OFFICE OF COUNTERINTELLI-
GENCE, DEFENSE CI & HUMINT CENTER, DEFENSE INTELLIGENCE AGENCY, GLOSSARY
(UNCLASSIFIED), TERMS & DEFINITIONS OF INTEREST FOR DoD COUNTERINTELLIGENCE
PROFESSIONALS, at GL-167 (2011), http://fas.org/irp/eprint/ci-glossary.pdf; *see also Id.*
(defining the counterintelligence community's use of the word "target" as "1) An entity
or object considered for possible engagement or other action; 2) in intelligence usage, a
country, area, installation, agency, or person against which intelligence operations are
directed; 3) an area designated and numbered for future firing; and 4) in gunfire support
usage, an impact burst that hits the target.").

[52] *Id.*   [53] *See supra* note 8 and accompanying text.

[54] Chris Woods & Jack Serle, *Hostage Deaths Mean 38 Westerners Killed By US Drone
Strikes, Bureau Investigation Reveals*, BUREAU OF INVESTIGATIVE JOURNALISM
(Apr. 23, 2015).

[55] *See, e.g.*, Scott Neuman, *Sen. Graham Says 4,700 Killed in U.S. Drone Strikes*, NPR: THE
TWO-WAY (Feb. 21, 2013); Micah Zenko, *America's 500th Drone Strike*, COUNCIL ON
FOREIGN RELATIONS (Nov. 21, 2014).

[56] Dylan Matthews, *Everything You Need to Know about the Drone Debate, in One FAQ*,
WASH. POST ONLINE (Mar. 8, 2013).

the high end of a tally by the London-based Bureau of Investigative Journalism.... [stating] the number killed in drone strikes in Pakistan, Yemen and Somalia is between 3,072 and 4,756."[57]

From some reports, only a fraction of those killed have been classified as "high-level targets."[58] In one study by the New America Foundation, for instance, only 2.3 percent of those killed in Pakistan by drone attacks (approximately seventy individuals) can be classified as high value.[59] Some experts have concluded that hundreds of those killed by drone strikes, including upwards of 881 civilians and 176 children, can be classified as "collateral damage."[60] Micah Zenko, Senior Fellow at the Council on Foreign Relations and an expert on drone strikes, has explained that, "[As of April 23, 2015,] 'an average of separate counts of American drone strikes by three organizations, the New America Foundation, the Bureau of Investigative Journalism and The Long War Journal, finds that 522 strikes have killed 3,852 people, 476 of them civilians. But those counts, based on news accounts and some on-the-ground interviews, are considered very rough estimates.'"[61]

Thus far, media reports indicate that ten U.S. citizens have been killed by drone strikes outside of the United States[62] According to public sources, of the several U.S. citizens killed, it appears that only one target was intentional (Anwar al-Awlaki).[63] In 2011 it was previously disclosed

---

[57] Agence France-Presse, *U.S. Senator Says Drones Death Toll Is 4700*, Telegraph (Feb. 21, 2013) ("A spokesman told AFP [Agence France-Presse] that the senator 'quoted the figure that has been publicly reported and disseminated on cable news.'").

[58] *See, e.g.*, Int'l Human Rights & Conflict Resolution Clinic at Stanford Law Sch. & Global Justice Clinic at N.Y. Univ. Sch. of Law, Living Under Drones (2012) ("The number of 'high-level' targets killed as a percentage of total casualties is extremely low – estimated at just 2%.") (citing Peter Bergen & Megan Braun, Drone is Obama's Weapon of Choice, CNN (Sept. 6, 2012)).

[59] *Id. See also, Drone Wars: Pakistan, Key Findings*, New America Found. Rep. ("Only 58 known militant leaders have been killed in drone strikes in Pakistan, representing just 2% of the total deaths."); Dan Gettinger, *The Disposition Matrix*, Center for the Study of the Drone, Bard College, Apr. 25, 2015) ("[O]f the 2,500–3,500 estimated deaths from drones in Pakistan, 70 individuals – around 2.3% – were ranking members of al-Qaeda. The remainder were mid-to-low level commanders and fighters or civilians.").

[60] *Id.* ("[F]rom June 2004 through mid-September 2012, available data indicate that drone strikes killed 2,562–3,325 people in Pakistan, of whom 474–881 were civilians, including 176 children.").

[61] Scott Shane, *Drone Strikes Reveal Uncomfortable Truth: U.S. Is Often Unsure About Who Will Die*, N.Y. Times (Apr. 23, 2015).

[62] Woods & Serle, *supra* note 54; *see also* Jere Van Dyk, *Who Were the 4 U.S. Citizens Killed in Drone Strikes?*, CBSNEWS (May 22, 2013).

[63] *Id.*

that four U.S. citizens had been killed through drone strikes. The United States has acknowledged that Anwar al-Awlaki was specifically targeted as a threat and was killed in Yemen through a drone strike on September 30, 2011.[64] Samir Khan, also a U.S. citizen, was killed in the same drone attack.[65] It was reported that Khan, who was an associate of Anwar al-Awlaki and an al-Qaeda operative, was driving in the same vehicle as Anwar al-Awlaki.[66]

Two weeks later, on October 14, 2011, the sixteen-year-old son of Anwar al-Awlaki, Abdulrahman al-Awlaki, was killed in a drone strike in Yemen.[67] Abdulrahman al-Awlaki was born in the United States in the state of Colorado and did not have any known ties to terrorism; however, "[f]ormer White House press secretary Robert Gibbs, stated that his death was justified, and that he 'should have had a more responsible father.'"[68] On November 16, 2011, Jude Kenan Mohammad, a twenty-three-year-old U.S. citizen born in the state of Florida, was killed by a drone strike in Pakistan.[69] The United States acknowledged his death was a result of a CIA drone "signature strike" on May 22, 2013.[70] Former U.S. Attorney General Eric Holder has stated that three out of the four Americans who were killed by drones had not been specifically targeted (Samir Khan, Abdulrahman al-Awlaki, and Jude Kenan Mohammad). But A.G. Holder failed to explain how these deaths could be justified.[71] It appears the government's position is that the three nontargeted U.S. citizens killed by drone strikes were not included on the Kill List and must be characterized as "collateral damage."[72]

---

[64] *Id.*

[65] Peter Bergen, *Opinion: Target an American with Drones?*, CNN (Feb. 11, 2014).

[66] *See* Mark Mazzetti et al., *How a U.S. Citizen Came to Be in America's Cross Hairs*, N.Y. TIMES (Mar. 9, 2013).

[67] *Id.*

[68] Conor Friedersdorf, *How Team Obama Justifies the Killing of a 16-Year-Old American*, THE ATLANTIC (Oct. 24, 2012).

[69] Scott Shane & Eric Schmitt, *One Drone Victim's Trail from Raleigh to Pakistan*, N.Y. TIMES (May 22, 2013).

[70] Van Dyk, *supra* note 62.

[71] *See* Letter from Eric Holder, U.S. Att'y Gen., to Patrick J. Leahy, U.S. Senator (May 22, 2013).

[72] "In practice, the United States has targeted with lethal force only one of its own citizens: Anwar al-Awlaki. Three others, including Awlaki's teenage son and propagandist Samir Khan, have been killed in drone strikes, but none of them appears to have been the target of the strike; all were considered collateral damage." Daniel Byman & Benjamin Wittes, *How Obama Decides Your Fate if He Thinks You're a Terrorist*, THE ATLANTIC (Jan. 3, 2013).

In addition to the four U.S. citizens discussed above, the Bureau of Investigative Journalism reported that an additional six U.S. citizens have been killed by drone strikes.[73] The Bureau of Investigative Journalism explained that it gathered its data "over the past four years through an extensive analysis of thousands of media reports and NGO filings, as well as from court papers and leaked government documents."[74] In January 2015, the following three Americans were killed in drone strikes in Pakistan: Warren Weinstein, Ahmed Farouq, and Adam Gadahn.[75] The Bureau of Investigative Journalism also reported that the identities of two Americans who were killed in drone strikes in Pakistan on November 7, 2008, remain unknown. Another American, Kemal Darwish, was killed in a drone strike in Yemen on November 3, 2002.[76]

On April 23, 2015, the White House issued an apology for the accidental killing of two hostages during a drone strike in Pakistan in January 2015.[77] The apology drew widespread media attention to the U.S. policy of "signature strikes," drone strikes against individuals where the identities of the targets are unknown.[78] The methods for intelligence gathering that lead to a Kill List nomination are covert and, thus, the criteria or data signature necessary to justify a signature strike is unknown.[79]

The claim, "we kill people based on metadata," however, raises the question of whether big-data techniques are used to isolate suspicious data rather than suspicious people.[80] For example, "[a]ccording to a former drone operator for the military's Joint Special Operations Command (JSOC) who also worked with the NSA, the agency often identifies targets based on controversial metadata analysis and cell-phone tracking technologies."[81] The drone operator elaborates, "'People get hung up that there's a targeted list of people [on the Kill List],' he says. 'It's really like we're targeting a cell phone. We're not going after people – we're going after their phones, in the hopes that the person on the other end of that missile is the bad guy.'"[82] Given this statement, careful attention should be given to the scientific validity and logic of the assignment of

---

[73] Chris Woods & Serle, *supra* note 54.   [74] *Id.*   [75] *Id.*   [76] *Id.*   [77] *Id.*

[78] *See, e.g.*, Lev Grossman, *Drone Home: They Fight for America Abroad, But What Happens When Drones Return Home?*, Time, Feb.11, 2013, at 26, 30 ("According to reports in the New York Times and elsewhere, the Obama Administration conducts so-called signature strikes, which are aimed not at specific high-level targets but at any person or people whose behavior conforms to certain suspicious patterns."). *See also supra* note 118.

[79] *Id.*   [80] *See, e.g.*, Hu, *Big Data Cybersurveillance*, *supra* note 11.

[81] Scahill & Greenwald, *supra* note 2.   [82] *Id.*

evidentiary weight to "suspicious" metadata or other digital data deemed "suspicious." This careful attention is especially warranted where experts have noted that risks may attach to decision making based on algorithmic intelligence that may assess correlative results that are not necessarily causative.[83]

C The Logic and Limits of Algorithmic Intelligence

It is still unknown the extent to which algorithmic methods and other big-data tools are used in targeted killing, signature strikes, and drone strikes.[84] The discussion below focuses on how the logic and underlying reasoning of big-data technology – which facilitates a combination of abductive, inductive, and deductive reasoning[85] – may now support metadata-based inferences of suspicion or inferences of guilt.[86] Without this type of careful interrogation, policy makers may be at risk of assuming that increased collection of personally identifiable data, aggregation of multiple databases, and use of more sophisticated data-mining tools and complex algorithms will lead to a more accurate result in precision targeting.[87] But too little criticism has been leveled at the

---

[83] *See, e.g.,* MAYER-SCHÖNBERGER & CUKIER, *supra* note 5, at 7 ("Most strikingly, society will need to shed some of its obsession for causality in exchange for simple correlations: not knowing *why* but only *what*"); *Id.* at 169 ("Correlations do not imply causation"); PRESIDENT'S COUNCIL OF ADVISORS ON SCIENCE AND TECHNOLOGY ("PCAST"), BIG DATA AND PRIVACY: A TECHNOLOGICAL PERSPECTIVE x (May 2014) ("[D]ata fusion can result in the identification of individual people, the creation of profiles of an individual, and the tracking of an individual's activities. More broadly, data analytics discovers patterns and correlations in large corpuses of data, using increasingly powerful statistical algorithms.").

[84] *See, e.g.,* Schneier, *Surveillance by Algorithm, supra* note 16 ("[M]ost alarming of all, drone targeting is partly based on algorithmic surveillance") (citing Bruce Schneier, *Everything We Know About How the NSA Tracks People's Physical Location,* SCHNEIER ON SECURITY (Feb. 11, 2014)). *See also* Scahill & Greenwald, *supra* note 2 ("According to a former drone operator for the military's Joint Special Operations Command (JSOC) who also worked with the NSA, the agency often identifies targets based on controversial metadata analysis and cell-phone tracking technologies.").

[85] Rob Kitchin, *Big Data, New Epistemologies and Paradigm Shifts,* BIG DATA & SOCIETY, Apr.–June 2014, at 1, 5 ("In contrast to new forms of empiricism, data-driven science seeks to hold to the tenets of the scientific method, but is more open to using a hybrid combination of abductive, inductive and deductive approaches to advance the understanding of a phenomenon.").

[86] *See, e.g.,* Margaret Hu, *Big Data Blacklisting,* 67 FLA. L. REV. 1735 (2015).

[87] *See, e.g.,* MAYER-SCHÖNBERGER & CUKIER, *supra* note 5, at 12, 161; *see also* Danielle Keats Citron & David Gray, *Addressing the Harm of Total Surveillance: A Reply to Professor Neil*

efficacy of the tools that purportedly justify this assumption and, thus, the methodology of these programs may remain incompletely examined, especially given the covert nature of big-data cyber surveillance.

Algorithmic intelligence is considered a form of artificial intelligence.[88] From the Snowden disclosures, it appears that decision makers and policy makers place great and increasing reliance on this new form of intelligence. Because artificial intelligence relies on "building decision makers" or programming designed to create consistent results, it is argued that algorithmic intelligence is not prone to human error or human biases.[89] Likewise, to proponents of big-data cyber surveillance methods, algorithmic intelligence may appear to be a more technologically efficient method of processing data in the same manner in which humans would analyze information,[90] even though big-data is dissimilar in the manner in which information is factually grounded and scientifically controlled in a small-data sense.[91]

The sheer volume of data sets and databases allow for the development of complex algorithms that are calibrated to detect anomalous results or capture predictive analytics (e.g., pattern analysis and anticipated behavioral patterns based upon historical or contextual data sets and statistically similarly situated comparators).[92] As one expert explained: "[Big data] differs from the traditional, experimental

---

Richards, 126 HARV. L. REV. F. 262 (2013); Matt Sledge, *CIA's Gus Hunt on Big Data: We "Try to Collect Everything and Hang on to It Forever,"* HUFFINGTON POST (Mar. 20, 2013).

[88] *See, e.g.,* MAYER-SCHÖNBERGER & CUKIER, *supra* note 5, at 11–12; E. TYUGU, ALGORITHMS AND ARCHITECTURES OF ARTIFICIAL INTELLIGENCE 1–2 (2007).

[89] *See, e.g.,* Danielle Keats Citron & Frank Pasquale, *The Scored Society: Due Process for Automated Predictions,* 89 WASH. L. REV. 1, 3–4 (2014) ("Automated systems are claimed to rate all individuals in the same way . . . . [However, b]ecause human beings program predictive algorithms, their biases and values are embedded into the software's instructions, known as the source code and predictive algorithms. Scoring systems mine datasets containing inaccurate and biased information provided by people") (footnote omitted).

[90] *See, e.g.,* MAYER-SCHÖNBERGER & CUKIER, *supra* note 5, at 169 ("[T]he promise of big data is that we do what we've been doing all along – profiling – but make it better, less discriminatory, and more individualized."). *See also* EVGENY MOROZOV, TO SAVE EVERYTHING, CLICK HERE: THE FOLLY OF TECHNOLOGICAL SOLUTIONISM (2013).

[91] Some experts have explained that big data is more of a philosophy than a science. *See, e.g.,* KITCHIN, *supra* 5, at 2 (explaining big data requires a more "philosophical perspective"); STEVEN FINLAY, PREDICTIVE ANALYTICS, DATA MINING AND BIG DATA: MYTHS, MISCONCEPTIONS AND METHODS 14 (2014) ("Rather than getting hung up on a precise definition of Big Data, an alternative perspective is to view Big Data as a philosophy about how to deal with data . . .").

[92] MAYER-SCHÖNBERGER & CUKIER, *supra* note 5, at 1–12.

deductive design in that it seeks to generate hypotheses and insights 'born from the data' rather than 'born from the theory'."[93] Big-data products are not purely the result of deductive reasoning and consequently defy traditional syllogistic logic. In contrast to small-data deductive reasoning, algorithmic intelligence offers a form of probable reasoning based upon correlative evidence rather than any showing of causation.[94]

Because little is known about the exact algorithmic intelligence methods that may utilize metadata to inform targeted killing, understanding the big-data logic of a nonclassified big-data program used by the U.S. Department of Homeland Security (DHS) can be instructive in explaining the limitations of the logic of algorithmic-driven decision making. For example, a big-data approach might start with the following premise: "All Social Security Numbers are stored in the Social Security Administration's Numident database.[95] John Doe produced a Social Security Number that was screened over the Internet[96] and does not match[97] the Social Security Administration's Numident

---

[93] Kitchin, *supra* note 85, at 5–6 (citing Steve Kelling S., Hochachka W., Fink D., *Data-Intensive Science: A New Paradigm for Biodiversity Studies*, 59 BioScience 613 (2009)); *see also* Omer Tene & Jules Polonetsky, *Big Data for All: Privacy and User Control in the Age of Analytics*, 11 Nw.J. Tech. & Intell. Prop. 239 (2013).

[94] *See, e.g., supra* note 83.

[95] One DHS big-data program identified by the White House in a recent report discussing potential big-data challenges is the E-Verify program. *See, e.g.,* Exec. Office of the President, Big Data: Seizing Opportunities, Preserving Values 52–53 (2014). The E-Verify program, jointly operated by the DHS and the Social Security Administration (SSA), screens potential hires through online software provided by DHS and accessed through the Internet, and attempts to "verify" the identity or citizenship status of a worker based upon complex statistical algorithms and multiple databases. *Id. See also* Fred H. Cate, *Government Data Mining: The Need for a Legal Framework*, 43 Harv. C.R.C.L. L. Rev. 436, 469 (2008) (describing the SSA's Numident database).

[96] *See, e.g., Electronic Employment Verification Systems: Needed Safeguards to Protect Privacy and Prevent Misuse: Hearing Before the Subcomm. on Immigration, Citizenship, Refugees, Border Sec., & Int'l Law of the H. Comm. On the Judiciary,* 110th Cong. (2008) ("In almost every case, a mismatch will occur either because the employee is actually not authorized to work . . . ; because the employee has not yet updated his or her records with SSA . . . ; or because the employer made an error inputting information into the system.").

[97] Social Security Number no-matches can occur through E-Verify, but can also occur through SSNVS, HAVA, etc. *See, e.g., Senate Bill Implementing Help America Vote Act (HAVA) Would Disenfranchise Thousands of New Yorkers,* Brennan Ctr. for Justice at N.Y. Univ. Sch. of Law (Mar. 21, 2005) (describing how Social Security Number mismatches under HAVA database screening can disenfranchise voters).

database.[98] Therefore, John Doe is neither a U.S. citizen nor a lawful resident of the United States,[99] and/or is likely perpetrating identity fraud."[100] Even assuming the first sentence offers a true statement, that all Social Security Numbers are stored in the Numident database, the second sentence takes correlative evidence as established fact,[101] especially given statistical probabilities. Because algorithmic intelligence takes correlative evidence as true, big-data technologies permit invalid conclusions to determine questions of citizenship. DHS contends that the results of the big-data program confirm identity and citizenship status approximately 94 percent of the time.[102] Relying on the logic outlined above, DHS then concludes that there is a 94 percent chance that John Doe is not who he says he is and, based on this "no match" result, an employer may begin a process that may result in the denial of employment for the person flagged as suspicious through the database screening.[103]

There are multiple inferential leaps within each proposition of the above syllogism that is predicated upon an automated and database-derived epistemology.[104] At best, a data mismatch allows for only one conclusion based on established fact in a small-data sense: that there is a data mismatch. The mismatch can occur, for example, as a result of simple human error (e.g., data processor who incorrectly inputted the

---

[98] See, e.g., WESTAT, FINDINGS OF THE E-VERIFY PROGRAM EVALUATION (2009), www.uscis .gov/USCIS/E-Verify/E-Verify/Final%20E-Verify%20Report%2012-16-09_2.pdf (report submitted to DHS).

[99] See E-Verify Memorandum of Understanding at www.uscis.gov/USCIS/E-Verify/Cus tomer%20Support/Employer%20MOU%20(September%202009).pdf (explaining time procedures for final nonconfirmation under E-Verify based on inference that the individual is not lawfully present in the U.S.).

[100] See, e.g., U.S. GOV'T ACCOUNTABILITY OFFICE, GAO-11–146, EMPLOYMENT VERIFICA-TION: FEDERAL AGENCIES HAVE TAKEN STEPS TO IMPROVE E-VERIFY, BUT SIGNIFICANT CHALLENGES REMAIN 3 (2010) [hereinafter GAO, 2010 E-Verify Report].

[101] See, e.g., MAYER-SCHÖNBERGER & CUKIER, supra note 5, at 7 ("[Big data correlations and probabilities] overturns centuries of established practices and challenges our most basic understanding of how to make decisions and comprehend reality.").

[102] How E-Verify Works and How It Benefits American Employees and Workers: Hearing before the Subcomm. on Immigration & Border Sec. of the H. Comm. on the Judiciary, 113th Cong. 14–17 (1st Sess. 2013) (written testimony of Soraya Correa, Associate Director, U.S. Citizenship and Immigration Services) ("[Ninety-four] percent of Final Nonconfirmations [FNCs] were issued correctly to employees not authorized for work.").

[103] Id.

[104] See, e.g., MAYER-SCHÖNBERGER & CUKIER, supra note 5; Tene & Polonetsky, supra note 93, at 270.

Social Security Number into the database in the first instance; John Doe accidentally transposed a number in his Social Security Number at the time he produced a Social Security Number for identity verification purposes; Internet database screening technology could be flawed and algorithms could be inadequately constructed; individuals conducting the database screening could have incorrectly entered the Social Security Number or other personally identifiable data into the Internet screening system).[105] Thus, a data mismatch does not even allow one to conclude that the data produced does not match the data located within any given database.[106]

Yet, in a big-data world, traditional deductive reasoning may be in a process of displacement in some decision making protocols. The mass aggregation of data and big-data analysis of data – for example, the synthesis of multiple databases that may allow for algorithmic results to glean conclusions from complex supercomputing-enabled analyses – may serve as a proxy for established fact.[107] The results of sophisticated algorithms facilitate confidence in big data-driven conclusions. In other words, "there is a real risk that the benefits of big data will lure people into applying the techniques where they don't perfectly fit, or into feeling overly confident in the results of the analyses. As big-data predictions improve, using them will only become more appealing, fueling an obsession over data."[108] The result of big-data tools in this way appears to take the form of statistically verifiable truth.[109] The massive amounts of data collected, aggregated, and analyzed appear to make truth quantifiable.[110]

---

[105] *See, e.g.,* U.S. DEP'T HOMELAND SEC., U.S. CITIZENSHIP & IMM. SERVS., *Westat Evaluation of the E-Verify Program: USCIS Synopsis of Key Findings and Program Implications* (Jan. 28, 2010) (citing *supra* note 98).

[106] Cate, *supra* note 95, at 469 (observing that the error rate of SSA's Numident database was found to be 4.1% – in other words, 17.8 million records "contained discrepancies in the name, date of birth or citizenship status of the numberholder or concerned deceased individuals" (internal quotation marks omitted).

[107] *See, e.g.,* Tene & Polonetsky, *supra* note 93, at 251; MAYER-SCHÖNBERGER & CUKIER, *supra* note 5, at 179.

[108] MAYER-SCHÖNBERGER & CUKIER, *supra* note 5, at 170.

[109] Tene & Polonetsky, *supra* note 93, at 241 ("The Obama Administration has recently announced a new, multi-agency big-data research and development initiative aimed at advance the core scientific and technological means of managing, analyzing, visualizing and extracting information from large, diverse, distributed, and heterogeneous data sets.").

[110] *See, e.g.,* MAYER-SCHÖNBERGER & CUKIER, *supra* note 5, at 79–97 ("Today we have the tools (statistics and algorithms) and the necessary equipment (digital processors and storage) to perform similar [knowledge-enhancing or "unlock[ing] insights"] tasks much

This follows advances in what scholars have characterized as rationalized surveillance that appears to be scientifically supportable: an empirically-based method for deriving conclusions.[111]

The limits of algorithmic intelligence in the nonclassified big-data context can be informative in the classified context. The Snowden disclosures have especially illuminated how big-data tools have revolutionized the Intelligence Community's activities. Some of these disclosures have discussed the manner in which targeted killing decision making may rely upon data gathered through dataveillance-cyber surveillance systems.[112] For example, "a collection of records in the Snowden trove ... make clear that the drone campaign – often depicted as the CIA's exclusive domain – relies heavily on the NSA's ability to vacuum up enormous quantities of e-mail, phone calls and other fragments of signals intelligence, or SIGINT."[113] In one program, the NSA "collects [cell phone] locations in bulk because its most powerful analytic tools – known collectively as CO-TRAVELER – allow it to look for unknown associates of known intelligence targets by tracking people whose movements intersect."[114] The Snowden disclosures revealed that this type of metadata analytics is used to inform the targeted killing program.[115]

At most, in a small-data sense, a data match in the CO-TRAVELER analytics program can show that two cell phones are in close geographic proximity to one another for extended periods of time. The data match

faster, at scale, and in many different contexts... [D]atafication represents an essential enrichment in human comprehension. With the help of big data, we will no longer regard our world as a strong of happenings that we explain as natural or social phenomena, but as a universe comprised essentially of information.").

[111] See, e.g., MAYER-SCHÖNBERGER & CUKIER, supra note 5, at 97 ("Today, we are a numerate society because we presume that the world is understandable with numbers and math [e.g., empirical-based vision of world] ... Tomorrow, subsequent generations may have a 'big-data consciousness' – the presumption that there is a quantitative component to all that we do, and that data is indispensable for society to learn from [e.g., datafication-based vision of world with statistics, algorithms, correlations, and probabilities]. The notion of transforming the myriad dimensions of reality into data probably seems novel to most people at present. But in the future, we will surely treat it as a given.").

[112] See, e.g., Barton Gellman & Ashkan Soltani, NSA Tracking Cellphone Locations Worldwide, Snowden Documents Show, WASH. POST (Dec. 4, 2013).

[113] See, e.g., Miller, Tate & Gellman, supra note 2.   [114] Gellman & Soltani, supra note 2.

[115] See, e.g., Miller, Tate & Gellman, supra note 2 ("[A] collection of records in the Snowden trove [] make clear that the drone campaign – often depicted as the CIA's exclusive domain – relies heavily on the NSA's ability to vacuum up enormous quantities of e-mail, phone calls and other fragments of signals intelligence, or SIGINT.").

does not permit the conclusion that a "co-traveler" is a terrorist or a close associate of a terrorist. If the government tracks the cell phone of person A – a terrorist target (e.g., Anwar al-Awlaki) – and discovers person A's cell phone is in close geographic proximity with the cell phone of person B (e.g., for the sake of argument, 16-year-old son of Anwar al-Awlaki, Abdulrahman al-Awlaki) – a data match through the CO-TRAVELER analytics program will only yield information that the cell phones of person A and B are in close geographic proximity. Big data may be limited in its ability to reveal information on whether person B is also a terrorist target based on correlative and statistical methods.[116] The fact that two cell phones are in close geographic proximity does not allow for an inference that two individuals are co-travelers under small-data reasoning. Further, a co-traveler is not a co-terrorist using traditional deductive reasoning and small-data logic. In short, big-data tools using correlational analysis, alone or under risks of misapplication and over-emphasized value, may be unable to establish that an individual co-traveler is a terrorist simply because correlational analysis is not intended to establish cause. From an examination of the sea of hundreds of Snowden disclosures revealed thus far, of which the CO-TRAVELER program is just one, therefore, it appears the inductive-deductive-abductive reasoning of big data is assuming greater prominence in intelligence gathering. This allows for the increasing risk that data is mistaken for intelligence. Additionally, this helps to explain why the traditional deductive reasoning of small-data and human logic by human analysts may be increasingly marginalized in contemporary big-data intelligence decision making.[117]

D   Conclusion

In a big-data world, metadata is simply one form of digital data. And metadata surveillance is simply one type of big-data cyber surveillance. Therefore, the assertion, "We kill people based on metadata," could be potentially rephrased as, "We kill people based on big-data."

---

[116] *See, e.g.,* Scahill & Greenwald, *supra* note 2 (explaining accuracy limits of what metadata-driven intelligence can yield in identifying appropriate targets for drone strikes).

[117] *See, e.g.,* Maass, *supra* note 6; *supra* notes 8, 44; ACLU v. Clapper, 785 F.3d 787, 824 (2d Cir. 2015) (noting the need for "developing knowledge about the far-reaching technological advances that render today's surveillance methods drastically different from what has existed in the past and in understanding the consequences of a world in which individuals can barely function without involuntarily creating metadata that can reveal a great deal of information about them.").

The Snowden disclosures appear to illustrate how emerging and experimental metadata surveillance methods and other big-data cyber surveillance methods can inform a range of actions, some carrying lethal consequences.[118] Yet, from the Snowden disclosures, it also appears that the *apparatus* of contemporary surveillance, in contrast to the *protocols* of traditional surveillance, is best understood as a technologically-derived architecture[119] that spins on an axis of big-data philosophy. Big-data cyber surveillance is uniquely big data–driven in its science and theory.[120] Big data, therefore, can be understood as defining both the apparatus and protocols of contemporary intelligence gathering and contemporary forms of intelligence analysis.

In contrast to traditional surveillance, which depended upon vertical data collection that facilitated drilling down on a particular target, the "collect-it-all" philosophy of big-data cyber surveillance depends upon horizontal data collection that facilitates big-data algorithmic analysis of all data of all potential targets, unknown and known.[121] Put simply, as explained by Gus Hunt, Chief Technology Officer for the CIA, the science and policy rationales of big data "drives us into this mode of: We fundamentally try to collect everything and hang on to it 'forever,' forever being in quotes of course."[122] The tools of big data are unable to

---

[118] Miller, Tate & Gellman, *supra* note 2 ("[D]ocuments provided to The Washington Post by former NSA contractor Edward Snowden . . . reveal the agency's extensive involvement in the targeted killing program that served as a centerpiece of President Obama's counterterrorism strategy."). "[T]he vast majority of drone attacks conducted by the United States have been signature strikes[.]" Kevin Jon Heller, *'One Hell of a Killing Machine': Signature Strikes and International Law*, 11 J. INT'L CRIM. JUST. 89, 89 (2013); *see also* Scott Shane, *Rights Groups, in Letter to Obama, Question Legality and Secrecy of Drone Killings*, N.Y. TIMES (Apr. 13, 2013); Scott Shane, *Election Spurred a Move To Codify U.S. Drone Policy*, N.Y. TIMES, Nov. 25, 2012, at A1.

[119] *Supra* note 36.

[120] Experts are increasingly emphasizing the need to understand the theory of big data. *See, e.g.*, danah boyd & Kate Crawford, *Critical Questions for Big Data: Provocations for a Cultural, Technological, and Scholarly Phenomenon*, 15 INFO. COMM. & SOC'Y 662, 662–79 (2012); Kitchin, *supra* note 85; KITCHIN, *supra* note 50.

[121] *See, e.g.*, Hu, *Big Data Cybersurveillance, supra* note 11, at 804–05 (citing Lyon, *supra* note 14; Slobogin, *supra* note 1; Hunt CIA Presentation, *supra* note 16). *See also* Hunt CIA Presentation, *supra* note 16. Within Hunt's PowerPoint slides, he includes one titled, "Tectonic Technology Shifts." *Id.* The slide juxtaposes "Traditional Processing" and "Mass Analytics/Big Data." *Id.* Under "Mass Analytics/Big Data," Hunt identifies "Horizontal Scaling" of data. *Id.*

[122] Hunt CIA Presentation, *supra* note 16 ("[T]he value of any piece of information is only known when you can connect it with something else which arrives at a future point in time. . . . [S]ince you can't connect dots you don't have, it drives us into this mode of: We fundamentally try to collect everything and hang on to it 'forever.'").

discern what data may or may not be useful in a big-data world, so all data is potentially relevant into the indefinite future.[123] This is why, "according to [one intelligence] official: 'Everybody's a target; everybody with [digital] communication is a target.'"[124] In a big-data world, it appears that because the digital stream of flows of information have been inverted from the geography in which flows of information were generated in a small-data world,[125] the Intelligence Community's "collect-it-all" mission has been redesigned (e.g., the NSA's bulk telephony metadata collection program) to keep pace.

So long as the Intelligence Community perceives bulk metadata as necessary to support a big-data cyber surveillance architecture that has been built for over a decade – an architecture that, based upon modest estimates, reflects an investment of billions[126] – the task of bringing bulk metadata collection under closer oversight is an extraordinarily difficult one.[127] From the Snowden disclosures, in one document, one NSA

---

[123] *Id. See also* LEVINSON-WALDMAN, *supra* note 1, at 8 ("As the nation recently learned – initially from Edward Snowden – the term 'relevance' has been interpreted since 2006 to allow bulk collection of Americans' phone records because some small number of them may at some point in the future be germane to an FBI investigation.") (citing e.g., Glenn Greenwald, *NSA Collecting Phone Records of Millions of Verizon Customers Daily*, THE GUARDIAN (June 5, 2013); Jennifer Valentino-Devries & Siobhan Gorman, *Secret Court's Redefinition of "Relevant" Empowered Vast NSA Data-Gathering*, WALL ST. J. (July 8, 2013)). "Six years after 9/11, a panel of experts convened by the government expressed concern about 'an increasing trend in the post-9/11 era for federal agencies to collect as much information as possible in the event that such information might be needed at a future date.' That accumulation and storage of data poses significant practical problems: it can obscure useful information entirely, complicate analysis, and make data management more difficult." *Id.* at 15 (citing e.g., U.S. GOV'T ACCOUNTABILITY OFFICE, GAO-08–536, ALTERNATIVES EXIST FOR ENHANCING PROTECTION OF PERSONALLY IDENTIFIABLE INFORMATION 35 (2008), www.gao.gov/assets/280/275558.pdf).

[124] James Bamford, *The NSA Is Building the Country's Biggest Spy Center (Watch What You Say)*, WIRED (Mar. 15, 2012); *see also* James Bamford, *Big Brother Is Listening*, THE ATLANTIC (Apr. 2006) (providing an early analysis of NSA collection techniques pre-Snowden disclosures).

[125] Hunt CIA Presentation, *supra* note 16 ("When I started as an analyst years ago inside the CIA . . . . It was the world of the few to the many in terms of information flows . . . . The Social Mobile Cloud world has completely inverted that model and has gone to this complex many-to-many model."). *See also supra* note 17.

[126] DANA PRIEST & WILLIAM M. ARKIN, TOP SECRET AMERICA: THE RISE OF THE NEW AMERICAN SECURITY STATE 24 (2011) ([The National Archives, Information Security Oversight Office] has studied how much the federal government spends just to keep secrets secret. The price tag: $10 billion a year."). "The budget [for intelligence] had been estimated to be $75 billion a year, which did not include all the military's spending on counterterrorism and intelligence." *Id.* at 103.

[127] Maass, *supra* note 6 ("The agency appears to be spending significant sums of money to solve the needles-in-a haystack problem." An NSA document titled, 'Dealing With a

analyst poses this question: "'How many times have you been watching a terrible movie, only to convince yourself to stick it out to the end and find out what happens, since you've already invested too much time or money to simply walk away?'"[128] The analyst then elaborates: "'This 'gone too far to stop now' mentality is our built-in mechanism to help us allocate and ration resources. However, it can work to our detriment in prioritizing and deciding which projects or efforts are worth further expenditure of resources, regardless of how much has already been 'sunk.' As has been said before, insanity is doing the same thing over and over and expecting different results.'"[129]

Interrogating the underlying logic and reasoning of metadata surveillance may assist in evaluating the value of big-data cyber surveillance methods. Currently, there is no conclusive evidence that bulk metadata collection is efficacious.[130] Consequently, an assessment of the efficacy of these rapidly emerging metadata collection methods is integral to any future statutory reform, and future oversight and compliance reform efforts, as well as an evolution of the constitutional inquiry under the Fourth Amendment.

'Tsunami' of Intercept,' explains the challenges that accompany how the speed and volume of data collection will grow exponentially 'almost beyond imagination.' The document referred to a mysterious NSA entity – the 'Coping With Information Overload Office.' This appears to be related to an item in the Intelligence Community's 2013 Budget Justification to Congress, known as the 'black budget' – $48.6 million for projects related to 'Coping with Information Overload.'").

[128] *Id.*   [129] *Id.*

[130] "Based on the information provided to the [Privacy and Civil Liberties Oversight] Board, including classified briefings and documentation, we have not identified a single instance involving a threat to the United States in which the [bulk metadata collection] program made a concrete difference in the outcome of a counterterrorism investigation. Moreover, we are aware of no instance in which the program directly contributed to the discovery of a previously unknown terrorist plot or the disruption of a terrorist attack. And we believe that in only one instance over the past seven years has the program arguably contributed to the identification of an unknown terrorism suspect. Even in that case, the suspect was not involved in planning a terrorist attack and there is reason to believe that the FBI may have discovered him without the contribution of the NSA's program." PRIVACY AND CIVIL LIBERTIES OVERSIGHT BOARD (DAVID MEDINE, CHAIR-MAN; RACHEL BRAND; ELISEBETH COLLINS COOK; JAMES DEMPSEY & PATRICIA WALD), REPORT ON THE TELEPHONE RECORDS PROGRAM CONDUCTED UNDER SECTION 215 OF THE USA PATRIOT ACT AND ON THE OPERATIONS OF THE FOREIGN INTELLIGENCE SURVEILLANCE COURT 111 (Jan. 23, 2014). "And in those few cases where some information not already known to the government was generated through the use of Section 215 records, we have seen little indication that the same result could not have been obtained through traditional, targeted collection of telephone records." *Id.* at 146.

The data science of big-data cyber surveillance such as bulk metadata collection may not be "scientific" in a small-data sense. This is particularly possible if traditional statistical and analytic methods are being misapplied or disregarded, which, at present, is difficult to interrogate. For this reason, the data science and attendant theories of the big-data cyber surveillance methods that inform targeted killing should be made more transparent. Further, even where the surveillance is covert, transparency can take the form of a more public interrogation of the principles of logic and scientific validity of the big-data tools, big-data methods, and big-data analysis procedures engaged by the Intelligence Community. Thus, understanding the logic and limits of bulk metadata surveillance is necessary, especially where it might be the basis for the death of a target.[131]

In conclusion, as of yet, it is unknown whether recently introduced data science technologies, of which bulk metadata surveillance systems are a part,[132] may be appropriately deployed for targeting killing decision making.[133] Yet, bulk metadata surveillance may remain largely unchecked due to an underappreciation of the surveillance implications and the data privacy impact of big-data cyber surveillance methods. Efficacy assessments and more stringent scientific evaluation could assist in the development of the legal

---

[131] *See, e.g.,* Maass, *supra* note 6; *supra* notes 8, 44.

[132] "As data sets become more complex, so do the attached metadata. Metadata are ancillary data that describe properties of the data such as the time the data were created, the device on which they were created, or the destination of a message. Included in the data or metadata may be identifying information of many kinds. It cannot today generally be asserted that metadata raise fewer privacy concerns than data." REPORT TO THE PRESIDENT, BIG DATA AND PRIVACY: A TECHNOLOGICAL PERSPECTIVE, EXECUTIVE OFFICE OF THE PRESIDENT, PRESIDENT'S COUNCIL OF ADVISORS ON SCIENCE AND TECHNOLOGY xi (May 2014). *See also* Donohue, *Bulk Metadata Collection, supra* note 1, at 776 ("The NSA was not the only federal entity making use of new technologies to collect significant amounts of information on U.S. citizens.").

[133] *See, e.g.,* McNeal, *supra* note 43; Pearlstein, *supra* note 43; Heller, *supra* note 43; Anderson, *supra* note 43; Murphy & Radsan, *supra* note 43; Byman & Wittes, *supra* note 72. "[A] former JSOC drone operator recounts, tracking people by metadata and then killing them by SIM card is inherently flawed. The NSA 'will develop a pattern,' he says, 'where they understand that this is what this person's voice sounds like, this is who his friends are, this is who his commander is, this is who his subordinates are. And they put them into a matrix. But it's not always correct. There's a lot of human error in that.'" Scahill & Greenwald, *supra* note 2.

oversight necessary to bring bulk metadata surveillance under proper legal and constitutional review. Metadata surveillance occurs at the meta level. Big data now allows privacy harms to also occur at the meta level. This essay concludes that without redefining privacy harms to encompass the "metadeath of privacy," metadata surveillance, rapidly unfolding in an age of ubiquitous cyber surveillance, may not be viewed as unlawful or unconstitutional.

9

"We're in This Together"

Reframing E.U. Responses to Criminal Unauthorized Disclosures of U.S. Intelligence Activities

BY ANDREW BORENE

A Introduction

Edward Snowden's epic theft[1] and unauthorized disclosure[2] of U.S. government secrets began their run in the global media in June 2013.[3] The flow of revelations – and the media's hunger for them – has not slowed much in the years since.[4] Much of America's extensive intelligence apparatus has effectively been laid bare before the world's eyes. The disclosures revealed an unprecedented amount of embarrassing information about how the U.S. Intelligence Community does business, including alleged intercepts of German Chancellor Angela Merkel's

---

[1] Complaint at 1, United States v. Snowden, No. 1:13 CR 265 (CMH), http://apps.washingtonpost.com/g/documents/world/us-vs-edward-j-snowden-criminal-complaint/496/ (alleging violation of 18 U.S.C. 641 prohibiting theft of government property). Nick Simeone, *Clapper: Snowden Caused "Massive, Historic" Security Damage*, AMERICAN FORCES PRESS SERVICE (Jan. 29, 2014), http://archive.defense.gov/news/newsarticle.aspx?id=121564 (last visited, Nov. 17, 2015).

[2] Complaint at 1, United States v. Snowden, No. 1:13 CR 265 (CMH), http://apps.washingtonpost.com/g/documents/world/us-vs-edward-j-snowden-criminal-complaint/496/ (alleging violations of 18 U.S.C. 793(d) and 18 U.S.C. 798(a)(3) prohibiting unauthorized communication of national defense information and willful communication of classified communications intelligence information to unauthorized persons, respectively) (last visited, Nov. 17, 2015).

[3] Glenn Greenwald, *NSA Collecting Phone Records of Millions of Verizon Customers Daily*, THE GUARDIAN (June 5, 2013), www.theguardian.com/world/2013/jun/06/nsa-phone-records-verizon-court-order (last visited, Nov. 17, 2015).

[4] *See, e.g.*, Margaret B. Kwoka, *Leaking and Legitimacy*, 48 U.C. Davis L. Rev. 1387, 1399 n.60 (2015) (providing examples of continuing media coverage); Ian Black, *NSA Document: Israeli Special Forces Assassinated Top Syrian Military Official*, THE GUARDIAN (July 15, 2015), www.theguardian.com/world/2015/jul/15/nsa-reveals-israeli-commandos-killed-mahmoud-suleiman-syria (last visited, Nov. 17, 2015).

telephone calls,[5] massive bulk collection of metadata,[6] and special programs that monitor terrorist communications on computers, on phones, and even within the virtual worlds of video games.[7] Halting, and at times half-hearted, defenses of such activities from U.S. officials compounded the problem,[8] particularly when ambivalent or unconvincing defenses were added to fashionable European views of the United States as a proponent of security at the expense of civil liberties.[9]

[5] *Embassy Espionage: The NSA's Secret Spy Hub in Berlin*, DER SPIEGEL (Oct. 27, 2013), www.spiegel.de/international/germany/cover-story-how-nsa-spied-on-merkel-cell-phone-from-berlin-embassy-a-930205.html (last visited, Nov. 17, 2015). *But see German Prosecutors Drop Angela Merkel Mobile Phone Spying Investigation*, THE TELEGRAPH (June 12, 2015), www.telegraph.co.uk/news/worldnews/europe/germany/angela-merkel/11669892/German-prosecutors-drop-Angela-Merkel-mobile-phone-spying-investigation.html (last visited, Nov. 17, 2015).

[6] Glenn Greenwald & Ewan MacAskill, *NSA Prism Program Taps in to User Data of Apple, Google, and Others*, THE GUARDIAN (June 7, 2013), www.theguardian.com/world/2013/jun/06/us-tech-giants-nsa-data (last visited, Nov. 17, 2015). The PRISM Program is governed by Section 702 of the Foreign Intelligence Surveillance Act. H.R. 6304, 110th Cong. (2008) (enacted); DIRECTOR OF NAT'L INTELLIGENCE, FACTS ON THE COLLECTION OF INTELLIGENCE PURSUANT TO SECTION 702 OF THE FOREIGN INTELLIGENCE SURVEILLANCE ACT (2013), www.dni.gov/files/documents/Facts%20on%20the%20Collection%20of%20Intelligence%20Pursuant%20to%20Section%20702.pdf (last visited, Nov. 17, 2015).

[7] James Ball, *Xbox Live Among Game Services Targeted by U.S. and U.K. Spy Services*, THE GUARDIAN (Dec. 9, 2013), www.theguardian.com/world/2013/dec/09/nsa-spies-online-games-world-warcraft-second-life (last visited, Nov. 17, 2015).

[8] For example, "Democratic Senator Dianne Feinstein, head of the Senate Intelligence Committee, said . . . that Congress would consider legislation to limit government contractors' access to certain classified information." Meanwhile, President Obama chose his words very carefully in an obvious attempt to avoid all the legal nuance that is necessary to adequately explain the American domestic counterterrorism surveillance regime: "What I can say unequivocally is that if you are a U.S. person, the NSA cannot listen to your telephone calls, and the NSA cannot target your emails . . . and have not." Tabassum Zakaria & John Whitesides, *NSA Head, Lawmakers Defend Surveillance Programs*, ONEIDA DAILY DISPATCH (June 18, 2013), www.oneidadispatch.com/general-news/20130618/nsa-head-lawmakers-defend-surveillance-programs (last visited, Nov. 17, 2015).

[9] *See* Claus Hecking & Stefan Schultz, *Spying "Out of Control": E.U. Official Questions Trade Negotiations*, DER SPIEGEL (June 30, 2013), www.spiegel.de/international/europe/eu-officials-furious-at-nsa-spying-in-brussels-and-germany-a-908614.html (last visited, Nov. 17, 2015); Russell Berman, *The Return of Anti-Americanism*, REAL CLEAR POLITICS (Sept. 18, 2013), www.realclearpolitics.com/articles/2013/09/18/the_return_of_anti-americanism_119974.html (last visited, Nov. 17, 2015). *But see Global Opposition to U.S. Surveillance and Drones, But Limited Harm to America's Image*, PEW RESEARCH CENTER, 24 (July 14, 2014), www.pewglobal.org/files/2014/07/2014-07-14-Balance-of-Power.pdf ("The image of the United States has been tarnished by Snowden's revelations about National Security Agency monitoring of communications around the world, especially in Europe and Latin America.") (last visited, Nov. 17, 2015).

In many political circles in the European Union the persistent response has been outrage, mixed with a self-righteous opportunism. Some E.U. leaders feigned shock that the United States would use its intelligence apparatus to collect information about foreign leaders,[10] despite the obvious fact that this has been one of the purposes of state security services for thousands of years.[11] In Europe, Snowden's revelations have also been a significant impetus to advance the "data protection" agenda.[12]

In this climate, I have several aims. First, I will offer an unblushing defense of the U.S. Intelligence Community by highlighting the democratic oversight mechanisms under which the Intelligence Community operates. The government intelligence apparatus in the United States is better regulated, more transparently authorized, and more closely aligned with the interests of the European Union and its members than at any other time in history. This has been confirmed and reinforced by the reforms implemented by the President and Congress in the wake of the Snowden Affair. All of this establishes that the Americans have acted with respect for and in compliance with the rule of law. Second, I will argue that political attacks from Brussels are unwarranted. After all, the supranational, quasi-federal European Union does not itself possess or

---

[10] *Europe's Feigned Spying "Shock,"* THE POST AND COURIER (July 9, 2013), www.postandcourier.com/article/20130709/PC1002/130709494 (last visited, Nov. 17, 2015); *I Spy, You Spy,* THE ECONOMIST (June 27, 2015), www.economist.com/news/europe/21656108-wikileaks-releases-evidence-american-spying-french-say-they-are-shocked-espionage-revealed (last visited, Nov. 17, 2015).

[11] MICHAEL WARNER, THE RISE AND FALL OF INTELLIGENCE 13 (2014) (describing how ancient Chinese and Indian traditions of Sun Tzu and Kautilya counseled the use of spies for, among other reasons, their ability to manipulate and even assassinate foreign leaders).

[12] Simon Shuster, *E.U. Pushes for Stricter Data Protection After Snowden's NSA Revelations,* TIME (Oct. 21, 2013), world.time.com/2013/10/21/e-u-pushes-for-stricter-data-protection-after-snowden-nsa-revelations/; European Parliament Press Release, Prism: European MEPs Hit Out at U.S. Surveillance of People's Personal Data (Nov. 6, 2013, 11:56 AM), www.europarl.europa.eu/news/en/news-room/content/20130611STO11522/html/Prism-MEPs-hit-out-at-US-surveillance-of-people's-personal-data. The "data protection" movement dates back decades in Europe, but received a boost after the Snowden disclosures. Convention for the Protection of Individuals with Regard to Automatic Processing of Personal Data, Jan. 28, 1981, Eur. T.S. No. 108; POLICY DEPTS., EUR. PARLIAMENT, THE E.U. DATA PROTECTION REFORM SEMINAR FOR JOURNALISTS, 1 (2013), www.europarl.europa.eu/document/activities/cont/201305/20130508ATT65908/20130508ATT65908EN.pdf (discussing a directive passed in 1995) (last visited, Nov. 17, 2015).

exercise a national security mandate. And, in any case, European Union criticism conflicts with European states' interests and intelligence practices.

Mature, even-tempered reactions from E.U. politicians that take the facts of American adherence to the rule of law and the realities of statecraft into account are clearly the best path forward toward the re-normalization of transatlantic security cooperation in the face of real threats to shared European and American liberal democratic values.

B   American Intelligence: Highly Regulated

E.U. outrage in the wake of Edward Snowden's leaks, disingenuous or not, has garnered a considerable amount of attention on the world stage. The outrage is fundamentally misguided because the U.S. Intelligence Community is more regulated and has more sophisticated, transparent, and multifaceted oversight of its activities than other similar security services around the world. Because transparency is exceedingly important in a democracy, the U.S. Constitutional system of "checks and balances" extends to its intelligence activities.[13] Although it is important to acknowledge that, like many other facets of the U.S. Government,[14] corrections of intelligence violations take time,[15] unresolved constitutional issues linger,[16]

---

[13] *See, e.g., Warrantless Surveillance and the Foreign Intelligence Surveillance Act: The Role of Checks and Balances in Protecting Americans' Privacy Rights*, 110th Cong. (2007), www.gpo.gov/fdsys/pkg/CHRG-110hhrg37599/html/CHRG-110hhrg37599.htm (exemplifying Congress' interest in examining the sufficiency of existing checks and balances in preventing civil liberties violations and rectifying any imbalances) (last visited, Nov. 17, 2015). See *also* Manget, *infra* note 23, for an ongoing example of the judicial and legislative branches' responses to executive branch violations of § 215 of the PATRIOT Act.

[14] "A common weakness of [many] checks and balances is that they operate after the fact, often long after." James L. Sundquist, *Needed: A Workable Check on the Presidency*, 10 BROOKINGS BULL. 7, 7–8 (1973).

[15] The Foreign Intelligence Surveillance Act of 1978, which created the Foreign Intelligence Surveillance Court, was largely a congressional reaction to decades of executive branch activities carried out via intelligence operations. Amitai Etzioni, *A Liberal Communitarian Conception of Privacy*, 29 J. MARSHALL J. COMPUT. & INFO. L. 419, 441–42 (2012).

[16] For example, Americans have long debated a so-called "national security exception" to the sweeping protection from warrantless search provided by the Fourth Amendment. U.S. CONST. amend. IV ("The right of the people to be secure in their persons, houses, papers, and effects, against unreasonable searches and seizures, shall not be violated, and no Warrants shall issue, but upon probable cause, supported by Oath or affirmation, and particularly describing the place to be searched, and the persons or things to be seized."). The "national security exception" allowing warrantless searches was a point of contention between the Department of Justice and the Federal Bureau of Investigation as early as the

and the true nature of the judiciary's oversight is rightfully scrutinized.[17]

The American intelligence enterprise is governed with careful attention to the rule of law, and regulated by a large body of publicly available law that delineates every aspect of its activities, including intelligence collection, analysis, dissemination, and use.[18] That body of law is supplemented by executive orders,[19] presidential policy directives,[20] and agency

early 1950s. L. Rush Atkinson, *The Fourth Amendment's National Security Exception: Its History and Limits*, 66 VAND. L. REV. 1343, 1366 (2013). The "national security exception" debate has remained a contentious issue, especially as it has morphed into a bigger debate about the use of general warrants to justify the search and seizure of millions of Americans' (and foreigners') communications without a showing of information about a specific threat connected to a particular individual. *Compare Warrantless Surveillance and the Foreign Intelligence Surveillance Act, supra* note 15, at 23–24 (testimony of Professor Robert F. Turner supporting exclusive executive control over national security investigations), *with* Randy E. Barnett, *The NSA's Surveillance Is Unconstitutional*, WALL ST. J. (July 11, 2013, 6:44 PM), www.wsj.com/articles/ SB10001424127887323823004578593591276402574 (last visited, Nov. 17, 2015).

[17] "From 1979 through 2012, the court overseeing the Foreign Intelligence Surveillance Act has rejected only 11 of the more than 33,900 surveillance applications by the government, according to annual Justice Department reports to Congress." Evan Perez, *Secret Court's Oversight Gets Scrutiny*, WALL ST. J. (June 10, 2013, 7:11 PM), www.wsj.com/articles/ SB10001424127887324904004578535670310514616. However, then-Presiding Judge of the Foreign Intelligence Surveillance Court, Reggie Walton, insisted that "[t]he perception that the court is a rubber stamp is absolutely false. There is a rigorous review process of applications submitted by the executive branch, spearheaded initially by five judicial branch lawyers who are national security experts, and then by the judges, to ensure that the court's authorizations comport with what the applicable statutes authorize." John Shiffman & Kristina Cooke, *The Judges Who Preside over America's Secret Court*, REUTERS (June 21, 2013, 6:59 AM), www.reuters.com/article/2013/06/21/usa-security-fisa-judges-idUSL2N0EV1TG20130621 (last visited, Nov. 17, 2015).

[18] *See* THE U.S. INTELLIGENCE CMTY. LAW SOURCEBOOK (Andrew Borene, Adam Pearlman & Harvey Rishikof eds., 2014); OFFICE OF THE DIR. OF NAT'L INTELLIGENCE, INTELLIGENCE CMTY. LEGAL REFERENCE BOOK (2012), www.dni.gov/files/documents/IC_Legal_ Ref_2012.pdf (last visited Nov. 17, 2015).; U.S. SENATE SELECT COMM. ON INTELLIGENCE, LEGAL RESOURCES , www.intelligence.senate.gov/laws. (last visited Nov. 17, 2015) (listing laws, executive orders, and major statutes governing U.S. intelligence) (last visited Nov. 17, 2015).

[19] *See, e.g.*, Exec. Order No. 12,333, 3 C.F.R. 200 (1981), www.archives.gov/federal-register/ codification/executive-order/12333.html (laying down basic framework for nation's intelligence activities); Exec. Order No. 13,526, 3 C.F.R. 298 (2009-2010), www.gpo.gov/fdsys/ pkg/CFR-2010-title3-vol1/pdf/CFR-2010-title3-vol1.pdf (describing a uniform system for classification, safeguarding, and declassification of national security information) (last visited Nov. 17, 2015).

[20] *See, e.g.*, Directive on Signals Intelligence Activity (PPD-28), 2014 DAILY COMP. PRES. DOC. (Jan. 17, 2014), www.gpo.gov/fdsys/pkg/DCPD-201400031/pdf/DCPD-201400031.pdf; THE WHITE HOUSE, PROTECTING WHISTLEBLOWERS WITH ACCESS TO

regulations. Ultimately, all of the activities regulated by these authorities must be compliant with the U.S. Constitution as the supreme law of the land, adding another layer of legal protections.[21] This legal regime is complemented by oversight from multiple angles, to ensure compliance with the law and to enable an "appropriate" degree of public and intergovernmental transparency within the Intelligence Community.

I heavily emphasize the word "appropriate" with regard to the level of transparency of American intelligence activities because, just like services in Europe and other countries, the American intelligence services must be able to rely on some degree of balanced secrecy to protect their sources and methods.[22] Common sense dictates the fundamental principle that every state intelligence service must have means to safeguard its information from public disclosure in order to plan operations and to provide decisional advantage for its own customers. A state can never provide complete public transparency in secret intelligence programs or, by definition, that state will have no secret intelligence programs.

The U.S. Intelligence Community is subject to comprehensive oversight encompassing all three branches of government. There has been an

---

CLASSIFIED INFORMATION (PPD-19) (Oct. 10, 2012), www.whitehouse.gov/sites/default/files/image/ppd-19.pdf (last visited Nov. 17, 2015).

[21] The judiciary is occasionally asked to review the constitutionality of surveillance and intelligence programs. United States v. U.S. District Court, 407 U.S. 297, 323 (1972) (confirming Fourth Amendment probable cause requirement remains even in the context of a domestic security threat). In accordance with the doctrine of constitutional avoidance almost always choose another route to a decision when one is available so as to leave the Constitution undisturbed. See ACLU v. Clapper, 785 F.3d 787, 808, 824, 826 (2d Cir. 2015) (finding § 215 of the PATRIOT Act did not authorize the bulk collection of metadata and therefore a constitutional review of its compliance with the Fourth Amendment was unnecessary), rev'g 959 F.Supp.2d 724 (S.D.N.Y. 2013), briefs ordered No. 14–42 (2d Cir. June 9, 2015) (order requiring briefs regarding the effect of the USA FREEDOM Act on the case; the Act, signed into law on June 3rd, amended § 215 of the PATRIOT Act).

[22] Many agree that some level of secrecy is necessary for effective intelligence. David Frum, We Need More Secrecy, ATLANTIC (May 2014), www.theatlantic.com/magazine/archive/2014/05/we-need-more-secrecy/359820/ (citing THE FEDERALIST No. 70, at 333 (Alexander Hamilton) (advocating for the executive's use of secrecy) (last visited Nov. 17, 2015).; Rahul Sagar, SECRETS AND LEAKS: THE DILEMMA OF STATE SECRECY 16 (2013) ("there is broad agreement that state secrecy is justified so long as it is used to protect national security and not to conceal wrongdoing"). In practice, the U.S. Government may prevent disclosure of sensitive information in American courts by invoking the "state-secrets privilege," which applies when "there is a reasonable danger" that a disclosure "will expose military matters which, in the interest of national security, should not be divulged." United States. v. Reynolds, 345 U.S. 1, 10 (1953).

increasing degree of legal, administrative, and criminal justice oversight by the judicial branch over the past decades.[23] Policy oversight is administered by Congress. The executive branch provides operational oversight. Another layer of public oversight is afforded through the Freedom of Information Act (FOIA), which includes mechanisms for both declassification and review of excepted classified material that federal courts have characterized as protected secrets.[24] While the mechanisms overseeing the U.S. Intelligence Community are far too plentiful to describe in this chapter, a sampling of the most important elements provides an ample sense of the framework's robustness and integrity.

Congress drafts, revises, debates, and passes all legislation governing the Intelligence Community.[25] Members of Congress and their staffs receive briefings from officials in the Intelligence Community informing them about the nature of intelligence operations and the state of foreign affairs. Congress holds budgetary power over the Intelligence Community, as it does for the rest of the federal government. Furthermore, many appointments of senior intelligence officials must be approved by the Senate, giving that Congressional body considerable influence over the leadership and direction of the Intelligence Community.

Most important for the direct intelligence oversight processes in Congress, however, are specialized committees in both legislative houses: the Senate Select Committee on Intelligence (SSCI)[26] and the House Permanent Select Committee on Intelligence (HPSCI).[27] In the words of Office of the Director of National Intelligence (ODNI) General Counsel Robert Litt, "in effect, we as a society have determined that the Intelligence Committees will act as the people's primary authorized agents and representatives, and the Intelligence Community is transparent with

[23] Frederic F. Manget, *Intelligence and the Rise of Judicial Intervention: Another System of Oversight*, 39 Stud. Intelligence 43 (1996), www.cia.gov/library/center-for-the-study-of-intelligence/kent-csi/vol39no5/pdf/v39i5a06p.pdf (last visited Nov. 17, 2015).

[24] *See* Freedom of Information Act, 5 U.S.C. § 552 (2012); *What Is FOIA?*, Foia.gov, www.foia.gov/about.html (last visited Nov. 17, 2015).

[25] *See, e.g.*, 161 Cong. Rec. S2048 (daily ed. May 21–22 & 31, 2015 & June 1–2, 2015) (U.S. Senate debates and adopts USA FREEDOM Act).

[26] U.S. Senate Select Comm. on Intelligence, www.intelligence.senate.gov/ (last visited Nov. 17, 2015). S. Res. 400, 94th Cong. (1976), www.congress.gov/bill/94th-congress/senate-resolution/400 (creating the SSCI) (last visited Nov. 17, 2015).

[27] U.S. House of Representatives Permanent Select Comm. on Intelligence, http://intelligence.house.gov. (last visited Aug. 4, 2015). H. Res. 658, 95th Cong. (1977), www.congress.gov/bill/95th-congress/house-resolution/658 (last visited Nov. 17, 2015).

them on the people's behalf."[28] In that role as "the people's primary authorized agents," the members and staff of the committees possess security clearances[29] and receive regular, classified briefings updating them on the Intelligence Community's activities.[30]

The two Congressional intelligence committees sprung from revelations in the 1970s, when a host of serious violations committed by the Intelligence Community came to light. These included the Watergate scandal, covert attempts to assassinate foreign leaders and subvert foreign governments, and unauthorized intelligence gathering against American citizens. All of this was documented in the Senate's Final Report of the Select Committee to Study Governmental Operations with Respect to Intelligence Activities.[31] These abuses led to the committees' bicameral predecessors (the "Church Committee" in the Senate and the "Pike Committee" in the House), which investigated the allegations of abuse and subsequently built the foundation for a comprehensive legislative oversight framework including permanent intelligence committees in both houses. ODNI General Counsel Robert Litt explained that

> [s]ince the 1970s, when the Church and Pike Committees exposed genuine abuses by intelligence agencies, our political system has chosen to reconcile the competing needs of secrecy and transparency primarily through the select committees on intelligence of the House and Senate. By law, we are required to keep these committees fully and currently informed of intelligence activities, and we do. We provide them dozens of written notifications each month, and dozens more briefings, covering the full range of activities from covert actions, to satellite construction, to the most recent information about the state of affairs in Ukraine or Syria, and including our intelligence collection programs. And make no mistake – the Intelligence Committees knew about the collection programs that have been exposed. Much of this oversight necessarily takes place in a

[28] Robert Litt, *Address at American University Washington College of Law Freedom of Information Day Celebration*, IC ON THE RECORD (Mar. 17 2014), http://icontherecord .tumblr.com/post/79998577649/as-prepared-for-delivery-remarks-of-odni-general (last visited Nov. 17, 2015).

[29] CONG. RESEARCH SERV., PROTECTION OF CLASSIFIED INFORMATION BY CONGRESS: PRACTICES AND PROPOSALS 1–2 (2006), http://fpc.state.gov/documents/organization/ 66482.pdf (last visited Nov. 17, 2015).

[30] *See* CONG. RESEARCH SERV., CONG. OVERSIGHT OF INTELLIGENCE: CURRENT STRUCTURE AND ALTERNATIVES 1–5 (2010), http://fpc.state.gov/documents/organization/141614.pdf (briefly explaining the structure, function, and authorities of the intelligence committees) (last visited Nov. 17, 2015).

[31] S. REP. NO. 94–755 (1976).

classified format, but the Intelligence Community takes its obligations to these committees very seriously.[32]

In this way, the committees serve as the bedrock of legislative oversight, wielding considerable power over the Intelligence Community and its activities. But these powerful committees do not act alone. The other two branches also participate.

The executive branch supervises Intelligence Community activities from vantage points both inside and outside of the intelligence agencies and entities. Within each agency of the Intelligence Community are offices dedicated in whole or in part to oversight, including Offices of the Inspector General, Offices of General Counsel, and Civil Liberties and Privacy Offices. These offices review policies, conduct audits to ensure that systems are being accessed appropriately, and collaborate on oversight reporting mandated by law.[33]

Much of the work done by the triad of internal oversight offices is rarely if ever exposed to the public; however, the Snowden disclosures gave observers at least one concrete example of internal oversight in action in the so-called LOVEINT violations.[34] The LOVEINT[35] episode was a somewhat sensationalized case in which just one dozen identified NSA employees in the past eleven years misused their collection

---

[32] Litt, *supra* note 28.

[33] *See, e.g.*, U.S. Dept. of Justice, Office of the Inspector Gen., A Review of the FBI's Handling of Intelligence Info. Related to the September 11 Attacks (2004, released 2006), https://oig.justice.gov/special/s0606/final.pdf (last visited Nov. 17, 2015); Offices of the Inspectors Gen. at the Dept. of Def., Dept. of Justice, Cent. Intelligence Agency, Nat'l Security Agency, and Office of the Dir. of Nat'l Intelligence, (U) Report on the President's Surveillance Program (2009, released 2015), www.justice.gov/oig/reports/2015/2009JointIGReportonthePSP.pdf (last visited, Nov. 17, 2015); U.S. Dept. of Homeland Security Privacy Office, Report Assessing the Impact of the Automatic Selectee and No Fly Lists on Privacy and Civil Liberties as Required under Section 4012(b) of the Intelligence Reform and Terrorism Prevention Act of 2004, 108–458 (2006), www.dhs.gov/xlibrary/assets/privacy/privacy_rpt_nofly.pdf (last visited Nov. 17, 2015).

[34] Andrea Peterson, *LOVEINT: When NSA Officers Use Their Spying Power on Love Interests*, Wash. Post (Aug. 24, 2013), www.washingtonpost.com/blogs/the-switch/wp/2013/08/24/loveint-when-nsa-officers-use-their-spying-power-on-love-interests/ (last visited Nov. 17, 2015).

[35] The phrase "LOVEINT" was a reporter's play on the collectively understood short names for conventional intelligence collection disciplines and products (i.e., HUMINT for human intelligence, SIGINT for signals intelligence, COMINT for communications intelligence, GEOINT for Geospatial Intelligence, IMINT for imagery intelligence, and OSINT for Open-Source Intelligence, among others).

capabilities to try to gather information about their romantic interests and, in some cases, their spouses' romantic interests.[36] The breaches in these cases were identified through self-reporting or internal control and audit mechanisms, and the employees in question were terminated, providing a persuasive example of how internal oversight mechanisms are intended to – and do – function.[37]

Outside of the Intelligence Community, the executive branch has a separate set of institutions focused on intelligence oversight. The White House oversees and supervises the Intelligence Community in part through the President's Intelligence Advisory Board (PIAB), which "oversees the Intelligence Community's compliance with the Constitution and all applicable laws, Executive Orders, and Presidential Directives," and provides "the President with an independent source of advice on the effectiveness with which the Intelligence Community is meeting the nation's intelligence needs, and the vigor and insight with which the community plans for the future."[38] The PIAB also supervises the work of the Intelligence Oversight Board (IOB), which "[r]eview[s] the internal guidelines of each agency within the Intelligence Community concerning the lawfulness of intelligence activities," and [i]nform[s] the President of intelligence activities that any member of the Board believes are in violation of the Constitution or laws of the United States, Executive orders, or Presidential directives," among other duties.[39] Both the PIAB and the IOB are staffed by professionals with security clearances that give them access to the Intelligence Community's most

---

[36] Peterson, *supra* note 34.

[37] Mem. from Nat'l Security Agency Inspector Gen. Dr. George Ellard, to Senator Charles Grassley, Ranking Member, Comm. on the Judiciary, U.S. Senate, 1 (Sept. 11, 2013), https://archive.org/stream/799792-nsa-surveillance-09-11-13-response-from-ig-to#page/n0/mode/2up (last visited Nov. 17, 2015).

[38] President's Intelligence Advisory Bd. and Intelligence Oversight Bd., Introduction, www.whitehouse.gov/administration/eop/piab (last visited Aug. 4, 2015). President Dwight D. Eisenhower created the "President's Board of Consultants on Foreign Intelligence Activities," which would eventually become the PIAB. *History*, President's Intelligence Advisory Board And Intelligence Oversight Board, www.whitehouse.gov/administration/eop/piab/history (last visited Nov. 17, 2015).

[39] Exec. Order No. 12,334, 3 C.F.R. 216 (1981), www.archives.gov/federal-register/codification/executive-order/12334.html. President Gerald Ford created the IOB in 1976. President's Intelligence Advisory Bd. And Intelligence Oversight Bd., Introduction, www.whitehouse.gov/administration/eop/piab/history (last visited Nov. 17, 2015).

sensitive documents and afford them special insight into the activities of intelligence agencies.

In addition to these bodies, the Privacy and Civil Liberties Oversight Board (PCLOB) has a specific mandate to ensure that privacy and civil liberties are not unduly compromised by the U.S. Government's counterterrorism efforts. Established in 2004, the PCLOB is independent and bipartisan, and is charged with two principle missions: (1) "review[ing] and analyz[ing] actions the executive branch takes to protect the [n]ation from terrorism, ensuring the need for such actions is balanced with the need to protect privacy and civil liberties," and (2) "ensur[ing] that liberty concerns are appropriately considered in the development and implementation of laws, regulations, and policies related to efforts to protect the [n]ation against terrorism."[40] Since the damaging intelligence revelations of 2013, the PCLOB has emerged as an increasingly powerful and often critical oversight agency.[41]

Various other executive branch agencies and departments also play an oversight role, including the National Security Council, which acts "as the highest executive branch entity that provides review of, guidance for and direction to the conduct of all national foreign intelligence, counter-intelligence, and special activities, and attendant policies and programs,"[42] and the Department of Justice, which prosecutes Intelligence Community employees for abusing their access and for illegally divulging classified information.[43]

---

[40] PRIVACY AND CIVIL LIBERTIES OVERSIGHT BD., WHAT IS THE PRIVACY AND CIVIL LIBERTIES OVERSIGHT BOARD?, www.pclob.gov/ (last visited Nov. 17, 2015). The PCLOB was established by statute. 42 U.S.C. § 2000ee (2012). Several other authorities affect the PCLOB's work. See PRIVACY AND CIVIL LIBERTIES OVERSIGHT BD., ABOUT THE BOARD, www.pclob.gov/about-us.html (last visited Nov. 17, 2015).

[41] See, e.g., PRIVACY AND CIVIL LIBERTIES OVERSIGHT BD., REP. ON THE TELEPHONE REC. PROGRAM CONDUCTED UNDER SECTION 215 OF THE USA PATRIOT ACT AND ON THE OPERATIONS OF THE FOREIGN INTELLIGENCE SURVEILLANCE COURT (2014), www.pclob.gov/library/215-Report_on_the_Telephone_Records_Program.pdf (criticizing the NSA's bulk phone call collection program and offering recommendations for reform); PRIVACY AND CIVIL LIBERTIES OVERSIGHT BD., RECOMMENDATIONS ASSESSMENT REP. (2015), www.pclob.gov/library/Recommendations_Assessment-Report.pdf (reporting on progress of reforms related to recommendations made in the 2014 report cited in this footnote) (last visited Nov. 17, 2015).

[42] Exec. Order No. 12,333, 3 C.F.R. 200 (1981), www.archives.gov/federal-register/codifica tion/executive-order/12333.html (last visited Nov. 17, 2015).

[43] Mem. from Ellard, to Grassley, supra note 37.

C   The Problems with European Condemnations
of the U.S. Intelligence Community

There are a number of problems with European condemnations –
whether from national leaders, European parliamentarians, or others –
of the American Intelligence Community. I have already noted that these
criticisms largely neglect the longstanding and ever-increasing legal control and multibranch oversight under which the U.S. Intelligence Community operates. But implementing proper oversight is a challenge in
Europe as well. Before detailing these European-specific issues, however,
I want to document the criticism to which I am referring. Chiefly, I have
in mind the unrelenting criticism of some E.U. institutions and actors
focusing on the U.S. Intelligence Community's data collection, retention,
and use.[44] Specifically, there are E.U. demands that the United States
increase privacy protections for European citizens. Ideally, for these
critics, this would involve American adherence to E.U. standards
regarding data retention and privacy. The fear is that, if "E.U. citizens
do not have the same level of protections as the U.S. citizens, because of
the practices of the U.S. intelligence services and the lack of effective
protections, [then] they will become the first victims of these systems."[45]

   To an extent, U.S. officials have shown respect for European sensitiv-
ities on these issues.[46] After all, some parts of Europe have direct and

---

[44] For example, in October 2013, "an E.U. parliamentary delegation began a visit Washington to discuss the scale of U.S. spying on its allies. Claude Moraes, the British Labour MP
who is leading the delegation, said the Snowden documents suggested that 'the type of
surveillance that is taking place by intelligence services is completely disproportionate in
the important fight against terrorism and for security'. The allegations resulting from
Snowden's leaks need to be investigated, he said." Paul Hamilos, *Spain Warns of U.S.
Breakdown in Trust after New NSA Revelations*, THE GUARDIAN (Oct. 28, 2013, 2:22 PM),
www.theguardian.com/world/2013/oct/28/spain-warns-us-ambassador-breakdown-trust-
nsa (last visited Nov. 17, 2015).

[45] POL'Y DEP'T C: CITIZENS' RIGHTS AND CONSTITUTIONAL AFFAIRS, EUR. PARLIAMENT,
THE US SURVEILLANCE PROGRAMMES AND THEIR IMPACT ON E.U. CITIZENS' FUNDA-
MENTAL RIGHTS, 7 (2013), www.europarl.europa.eu/meetdocs/2009_2014/documents/
libe/dv/briefingnote_/briefingnote_en.pdf (last visited Nov. 17, 2015). *See, e.g.,* Case C-
362/14, Schrems v. Data Protection Commissioner, INFOCURIA – CASE-LAW CT. JUST.
(Oct.   6,   2015),   http://curia.europa.eu/juris/document/document.jsf?text=&docid=
169195&pageIndex=0&doclang=EN&mode=lst&dir=&occ=first&part=1&cid=391877;
Chapters 16, 20, and 21.

[46] For example, in October 2013, "Jay Carney, the White House press secretary, said . . . that a
White House review of intelligence gathering would be complete by year's end, and that it
would address how to balance national security and privacy. But he stressed: 'The work
that's being done here saves lives and protects the United States and protects our allies . . . .'"

tragic experiences with state surveillance. But Brussels is simply not an appropriate venue for discussions about transatlantic intelligence operations and the legal limitations that should apply to those initiatives. The E.U.-driven attempts to limit American intelligence activities actually contradict both the practices and the interests of individual E.U. Member States.

I   The European Union Is the Wrong Forum for Security and Intelligence Debates

The greatest irony is that the European Union has no authority over intelligence gathering. *European* state intelligence agencies themselves do not adhere to E.U. standards. Even after the Treaty of Lisbon expanded the scope of the E.U.'s powers in 2009, the E.U.'s competences do not extend to intelligence activities and other national security matters.[47] This is important because it puts the European Union in the privileged but distasteful position of serving as a forum for sharp criticisms of America's exercise of a traditional state power that the European Union itself cannot exercise. There can be no doubt that this institution would show considerably greater circumspection in these matters if it also had to bear the responsibility for Europeans' security. It is true that the E.U.'s federal intelligence uniform is clean, but only because it has never been called off the bench to play in the game.

The real guarantors of European security – the Member States themselves – have shown exactly the appropriate levels of discretion in the NSA-Affair. The German government's alarm – as an official matter – has been targeted and measured. There has been no sweeping condemnation of America. The official French reaction, even in the face of revelations that the United States was pursuing intelligence gathering operations against a generation of French presidents and other high-ranking government figures, has been noticeably muted. This can be explained by the fact that these governments – bearing their own heavy security responsibility – maintain their own extensive and intrusive

Andrea Mitchell & Erin McClam, *US Coping with Furious Allies as NSA Spying Revelations Grow*, NBC NEWS, (Oct. 28, 2013, 10:11 PM), www.nbcnews.com/news/other/us-coping-furious-allies-nsa-spying-revelations-grow-f8C11478337 (last visited Nov. 17, 2015).

[47] Treaty of Lisbon Amending the Treaty on European Union and the Treaty Establishing the European Communities, Dec. 13, 2007, 2007 O.J. (C 306), http://eur-lex.europa.eu/legal-content/EN/ALL/?uri=OJ:C:2007:306:TOC (last visited Nov. 17, 2015).

intelligence gathering operations at home and around the world. To be clear, I do not point to these activities as any kind of critique. I share Ben Wittes' view that states always have and always will spy on one another.[48] I mention the Member States' intelligence regimes now only to underscore the almost laughable posture from which European Union leaders and institutions have leveled their criticisms of the American Intelligence Community. It is as if the old proverb has been perverted to read: "with no power comes the great responsibility to point-fingers."

In fact, the European Union has made a mess of the one related electronic surveillance policy area over which it does exercise some authority. The 2006 E.U. Data Retention Directive,[49] which would have obliged Member States to enact domestic legal regimes requiring technology and telecommunications service providers to log and store users' data in a uniform fashion across the European Union, has been ruled illegal by the Court of Justice of the European Union.[50] This judgment was preceded and has been followed by a number of national high court decisions finding that the domestic regimes implementing the 2006 Directive were illegal.[51] All of this has confirmed that questions of

---

[48] *See* Chapter 6 in this volume.

[49] Directive 2006/24/EC, of the European Parliament and of the Council of March 15, 2006, on the retention of data generated or processed in connection with the provision of publicly available electronic communications services or of public communications networks and amending Directive 2002/58/EC, 2006 O.J. (L 105) 54–63, http://eur-lex.europa.eu/LexUr iServ/LexUriServ.do?uri=OJ:L:2006:105:0054:0063:EN:PDF. (last visited Nov. 17, 2015).

[50] Joined Cases C-293/12 & C-594/12, Digital Rights Ir. v. Minister for Comm. (Apr. 8, 2014), http://curia.europa.eu/juris/document/document_print.jsf?doclang=EN&docid= 150642 (last visited Nov. 17, 2015).

[51] The German Federal Constitutional Court ruled the Directive illegal in 2010. *Vorratsdatenspeicherung* [Data Retention], BVerfGE, 1 BvR 256/08, Mar. 2, 2010, www .bundesverfassungsgericht.de/entscheidungen/rs20100302_1bvr025608.htmll. The Romanian Constitutional Court ruled the Directive illegal in 2009. Rom. Const. Ct., Decision no. 1258, 789, Rom. Official Monitor 23, Oct. 8, 2009. The Bulgarian Supreme Administrative Court ruled the Directive illegal in 2008. Bulg. Sup. Admin. Ct., Decision no. 13627, Dec. 11, 2008. *See also*, Katja de Vries, Rocco Bellanova, Paul De Hert, & Serge Gutwirth, *The German Constitutional Court Judgment on Data Retention: Proportionality Overrides Unlimited Surveillance (Doesn't It?)*, *in* COMPUTERS, PRIVACY AND DATA PROTECTION: AN ELEMENT OF CHOICE 3 (Serge Gutwirth, Yves Poullet, Paul De Hert & Ronald Leenes eds., 2011), http://works.bepress.com/cgi/viewcontent.cgi?article= 1052&context=serge_gutwirth. (last visited Nov. 17, 2015). In July 2015, a U.K. Court struck down a data retention section of a 2014 law enacted in response to the European Court of Justice's nullification of the 2006 Data Retention Directive (although it suspended the effect of its judgment for nine months to give the U.K. Government a chance to enact new legislation). Eric Metcalfe, *The Role of Judges under U.K. Surveillance Laws*

security – and intelligence operations as a component of security – are and remain the province of the Member States. As Lucia Zedner documents in her contribution to this volume, especially following the demise of the 2006 Data Retention Directive – the Member States are making their own decisions about whether and how to surveil their citizens, how long to retain classified data, and about other issues that have been the focus of criticisms of the U.S.[52]

II E.U. Member States Do Not Provide Greater Oversight and Control – Worse, They Are also Guilty of Invasive Surveillance

The surveillance laws enacted by some European Member States are more permissive than their U.S. counterparts.[53]

Let me offer some examples. In January 2014, nearly eight months after E.U. representatives expressed their outrage about the metadata collection programs revealed in the Snowden disclosures, France enacted a law authorizing its security services to access telephony and Internet metadata in real time, without approval by a court, "for reasons linked to terrorism, national security, and defense of France's economic and scientific potential."[54] The French authority to collect personal data and communications in defense of economic and scientific interests goes far beyond the NSA's collection mandate and illustrates one of the core disconnects between state interests in Paris and bureaucrats in Brussels. France, in the meantime, has succumbed to terrorism fears in the wake of recent acts of terrorism, including the attacks on the office of *Charlie Hebdo* and a Jewish supermarket (January 2015) and the spree of shootings and suicide-bomb detonations that coincided with a friendly soccer match in Paris between the French and German national teams (November 2015). The reaction has been the enactment of draconian surveillance

---

May Be About to Change, JUST SECURITY (July 31, 2015, 9:00 AM), www.justsecurity.org/ 25134/role-judges-uk-surveillance-laws-change/ (last visited Nov. 17, 2015).

[52] *See* Chapter 21 in this volume.

[53] *See, e.g.*, Stefan Heumann & Ben Scott, *Law and Pol'y in Internet Surveillance Programs: United States, Great Britain and Germany*, IMPULSE 25/13 (Sept. 2013), www.stiftung-nv.de/sites/default/files/impulse.pdf (last visited Nov. 17, 2015).

[54] Winston Maxwell, *France Enacts Law to Facilitate Real-Time Collection of Metadata*, HOGAN LOVELLS CHRONICLE OF DATA PROTECTION (Jan. 7, 2014), www.hldataprotection .com/2014/01/articles/consumer-privacy/france-enacts-law-to-facilitate-real-time-collec tion-of-metadata/. (last visited Nov. 17, 2015).

and security laws – including the declaration of a state of emergency – that allow, among other measures, for phone and email intercepts without judicial authorization.[55] Despite warnings about these measures' errosion of privacy from both American academics[56] and European MEPs,[57] France's constitutional court has ratified most of these security provisions.[58] France is not the only European country with laws authorizing broad intelligence collection that conflict with European politicians' demands for U.S. reforms.

In 2009, Sweden passed the "FRA law"[59] giving the Swedish National Defense Radio Establishment (FRA) the authority to intercept communications if those communications fit one of eight categories, which include terrorism, weapons of mass destruction, and threats to Swedish forces.[60] It "stirred considerable controversy as the law goes beyond the scope of surveillance established by the European Commission."[61] This Swedish authority is nearly indistinguishable from current U.S. mandate for

---

[55] Angelique Chrisafis, *France Passes New Surveillance Law in Wake of Charlie Hebdo Attack*, THE GUARDIAN (May 5, 2015), www.theguardian.com/world/2015/may/05/france-passes-new-surveillance-law-in-wake-of-charlie-hebdo-attack (last visited Nov. 17, 2015).

[56] Comparing the French legislation to American surveillance laws, Sales wrote, "[t]he legislation under review by the Conseil Constitutionnel appears to lack comparable safeguards for privacy, freedom of speech, and the attorney-client privilege. . . . [T]he new law establishes warrantless monitoring as the default form of surveillance (rather than, as in the United States, an exception to the normal requirement of prior judicial approval)." Letter from Nathan A. Sales, Professor, Syracuse University College of Law, to the Paris Bar Ass'n. [*l'Ordre des avocats de Paris*] 4 (July 15, 2015), http://insct.syr.edu/wp-content/uploads/2015/07/Sales_France_surveillance_legislation_analysis_0715.pdf.

[57] *Meeting of the Comm. on Civil Liberties, Justice and Home Affairs*, EUR. PARL. (July 2, 2015), www.europarl.europa.eu/ep-live/en/committees/video?event=20150702-1500-CO MMITTEE-LIBE.

[58] Conseil constitutionnel [CC] [Constitutional Court] decision No. 2015-713DC, July 23, 2015 (Fr.), www.conseil-constitutionnel.fr/conseil-constitutionnel/francais/les-decisions/acces-par-date/decisions-depuis-1959/2015/2015-713-dc/decision-n-2015-713-dc-du-23-juillet-2015.144138.html (last visited Nov. 17, 2015).

[59] LAG OM SIGNALSPANING I FÖRSVARSUNDERRÄTTELSEVERKSAMHET (Svensk författningssamling [SFS] 2008:717) (Swed.), www.riksdagen.se/sv/Dokument-Lagar/Lagar/Svensk forfattningssamling/Lag-2008717-om-signalspanin_sfs-2008-717/ (last visited Nov. 17, 2015).

[60] *Id.*

[61] Merlin Münch, *Do As the Swedes Do? Internet Policy and Regulation in Sweden – a Snapshot*, 2(2) INTERNET POL'Y REV. (May 2013), http://policyreview.info/articles/analy sis/do-swedes-do-internet-policy-and-regulation-sweden-snapshot. (last visited, Nov. 17, 2015). *See also*, Ernesto Van der Sar, *Swedes Massively Protest Wiretap Law*, TORRENT-FREAK (July 7, 2008), https://torrentfreak.com/swedes-massively-protest-wiretap-law-080707/ (last visited, Nov. 17, 2015).

collection and some allege that it is the result of significant collaboration with the U.S. Government.[62]

There is another reason why European governments have been less aggressive than E.U. politicians in their criticism of the United States Since the initial disclosures about the NSA's activities, Member State intelligence services have admitted to or been implicated in exactly the same types of activities that many in Europe have found so objectionable in the conduct of the U.S. Intelligence Community. This includes Spain,[63] France,[64] and others.[65] Germany, perhaps the most disgruntled of the European Member States, has emerged as a particularly embarrassing case. It is now clear that German intelligence agencies closely cooperated with the Americans.[66] Some of these instances even involved German intelligence agencies spying on other Europeans on behalf of the Americans,[67] or, more embarrassingly still, German intelligence agencies spying on U.S. officials, including Secretaries of State Hillary Clinton and John Kerry.[68] But it has not just been the Germans who have been caught in this embarrassing situation. The 2013 disclosures, for example, revealed that Sweden cooperated closely with both the NSA and the U.K.'s GCHQ on computer exploitation programs, indicating that the NSA's activities are not substantively different from those of Member State intelligence agencies.[69] Given that all of the countries mentioned are governed in accordance with the rule of law, this cooperation suggests

---

[62] *Sweden "Worked with the U.S." on Surveillance Law*, SVERIGES RADIO (Oct. 13, 2013), http://sverigesradio.se/sida/artikel.aspx?programid=2054&artikel=5673262 (last visited Nov. 17, 2015).

[63] Paul Hamilos, *Spain Colluded in NSA Spying on Its Citizens, Spanish Newspaper Reports*, THE GUARDIAN (Oct. 30, 2013), www.theguardian.com/world/2013/oct/30/spain-col luded-nsa-spying-citizens-spanish-el-mundo-us ("Spanish agents not only knew about the work of the NSA but also facilitated it . . . .") (last visited Nov. 17, 2015).

[64] *See supra* notes 53–56 and accompanying text.

[65] *Europeans Shared Spy Data with U.S.*, WALL ST. J. (Oct. 29, 2014, 7:31 PM), http://online.wsj.com/news/articles/SB10001424052702304200804579165653105860502 (last visited Nov. 17, 2015).

[66] Hubert Gude, *Mass Data: Transfers from Germany Aid US Surveillance*, DER SPIEGEL (Aug. 5 2013, 12:32 PM), www.spiegel.de/international/world/german-intelligence-sends-massive-amounts-of-data-to-the-nsa-a-914821.html (last visited Nov. 17, 2015).

[67] *German BND Spy Agency 'Helped US Target France,'* BBC (Apr. 30, 2015), www.bbc.com/news/world-europe-32529277 (last visited Nov. 17, 2015).

[68] *Germany Accused of Spying on Kerry and Clinton*, BBC, (Aug. 16, 2014), www.bbc.com/news/world-europe-28819625 (last visited Nov. 17, 2015).

[69] *Sweden's Intelligence Agency Has Access to NSA's XKEYSCORE Program*, INFOSECURITY MAG. (Dec. 12, 2013), www.infosecurity-magazine.com/view/36114/swedens-intelli gence-agency-has-access-to-nsas-xkeyscore-system/ (last visited Nov. 17, 2015).

that collection activities similar to those the U.S. Intelligence Community carries out are widespread among E.U. Member States. If E.U. politicians in Brussels do sincerely hope to serve as the world's cops for international intelligence activities, then their own Member States would be a great constituency with whom to start the policing.

III   E.U. Political Attacks on the U.S. Intelligence Community Gainsay European Security Interests

Condemnations of U.S. intelligence activities are not aligned with European practice. Likewise, they are not aligned with European interests. Shock and outrage in the wake of a long stream of dramatic leaks about secret U.S. intelligence programs was leveraged to demand changes in the U.S.–E.U. relationship, yet security remains a fundamental interest of each European state, and intelligence is an integral part of security.[70]

In the immediate aftermath of the disclosures, the E.U. took self-damaging steps contradicting Member States' interests, even imperiling functional transatlantic cooperation mechanisms countering terrorism and promoting trade.[71] It did all of this in the name of "data protection." In October 2013, for example, the European Parliament passed a non-binding resolution calling for the suspension of the Terrorist Finance Tracking Program, a joint venture between the United States and European countries to track terrorism financing.[72] Further, in March 2014, the European Parliament voted to suspend the Safe Harbor agreement, which creates a streamlined process for U.S. companies to do business in

---

[70] See Richard J. Aldrich, *Transatlantic Intelligence and Security Cooperation*, 80 *Int'l Aff.* 731 (2004).

[71] Resolution of October 23, 2013 on the Suspension of the TFTP Agreement as a Result of US National Security Agency Surveillance, Eur. Parl., www.europarl.europa.eu/sides/getDoc.do?pubRef=-%2f%2fEP%2f%2fTEXT%2bTA%2bP7-TA-2013-0449%2b0%2bDOC%2bXML%2bV0%2f%2fEN&language=EN. *See also*, Monika Ermert, *Brief: European Parliament: No More Bank Data Transfers to US for Anti-Terror Investigations*, Intell. Prop. Watch, (Oct. 23, 2013), www.ip-watch.org/2013/10/23/european-parliament-no-more-bank-data-transfers-to-us-for-anti-terror-investigations/ (last visited Nov. 17, 2015).

[72] European Parliament Press Release, US NSA: Stop Mass Surveillance Now or Face Consequences, MEPs Say (Mar. 12, 2014), www.europarl.europa.eu/news/en/news-room/content/20140307IPR38203/html/US-NSA-stop-mass-surveillance-now-or-face-consequences-MEPs-say (last visited Nov. 17, 2015). *See European Parliament: Suspend Safe Harbor, Data Transfers to United States*, Electronic Privacy Info. Ctr. (Mar. 12, 2014), https://epic.org/2014/03/european-parliament-suspend-sa.html (last visited Nov. 17, 2015).

Europe and meet European data protection standards.[73] As others in this collection note, the Court of Justice of the European Union followed the European Parliament's lead on this matter when it invalidated the Safe Harbor agreement in the *Schrems Case*.[74] The E.U.'s willingness to hold these and other important programs hostage demonstrates a distressing willingness to inflict damage on the U.S.–E.U. relationship and the important work that partnership accomplishes.

Since the end of the World War II the United States has shouldered a disproportionate part of the European defense burden. Indeed, according to the North Atlantic Treaty Organization's (NATO) 2014 report on defense spending, the United States contributes nearly three times more than all the European members combined.[75] Given this incredible disparity, it would seem that, if the European Union wants more of a voice in how the United States conducts security activities, then it should contribute more money, staff, and material to NATO. Contributions need not be confined to conventional defense forces, which would be a significant challenge for smaller European countries. Europeans can contribute in other ways, such as in intelligence sharing. For its part, the American Intelligence Community works very closely with its European Member State counterparts and shares detailed information on direct threats as well as shared strategic interests. If Europe will not carry its fair share of the fiscal and staff burdens for transatlantic security, then at least it should not bite the American hand that has long done this work for Europe.

The value of transatlantic counterterrorism cooperation can hardly be doubted. According to the European Union itself, "[Terrorist Finance Tracking Program] leads shared by U.S. authorities with European governments have helped prevent a number of high-profile attempted terrorist attacks, including a 2006 plan to bring down transatlantic flights

---

[73] Issuance of Safe Harbor Principles and Transmission to European Commission, 65 Fed. Reg. 45, 666 (July 24, 2000). *See* U.S. Dept. of Commerce, Int'l Trade Assoc., Welcome to the U.S. – E.U. Safe Harbor (June 3, 2015), http://export.gov/safehar bor/eu/eg_main_018365.asp (last visited Nov. 17, 2015).

[74] *See* Maximillian Schrems v. Data Protection Commissioner, Case C-362/14 (Oct. 6, 2015), *available at* http://curia.europa.eu/juris/document/document.jsf?text=&docid= 172254&pageIndex=0&doclang=EN&mode=req&dir=&occ=first&part=1&cid=474883. *See also* Chapters 20 and 21 in this volume.

[75] North Atlantic Trade Org., Pub. Diplomacy Div., Financial and Economic Data Relating to NATO Defence, PR/CP(2014)028, at 4, www.nato.int/nato_static/assets/ pdf/pdf_topics/20140224_140224-PR2014-028-Defence-exp.pdf. (last visited, Nov. 17, 2015).

using liquid explosives and an attempted attack on U.S. interests in Germany."[76] To be sure, intelligence cooperation is at its base bilateral, so this cooperation is *de facto* with Member States, not the European Union itself.

D   Re-Normalizing the E.U.–U.S. Relationship

In the years since the Snowden disclosures, the decades-old close relationship between the United States and the European Union has suffered. Still, there are signs that this relationship may be healing. First, the United States has not been deaf to European concerns about privacy and has instituted some major changes to its intelligence processes that respect these European concerns.[77] Second, events unfolding near Europe – primarily in Ukraine, but also including the civil war in Syria and its resulting out-flow of refugees – have reminded the United States and European Union that the distance between them is not so great, and that the value of cooperation remains high.

Citing the damage to U.S. relationships with other countries, in January 2014, President Barack Obama gave a major policy speech outlining his views on intelligence and civil liberties, and describing the changes he planned to institute, including increasing transparency into surveillance activities, extending some privacy protections to non-U.S. Persons, circumscribing U.S. surveillance of allied leaders, and limiting the use of bulk metadata.[78] Contemporaneously, he released Presidential Policy Directive 28 (PPD-28) on signals intelligence detailing specific changes to U.S. signals intelligence collection practices.[79]

PPD-28 itself broke new ground in several ways. First, it decreed that "[p]rivacy and civil liberties shall be integral considerations in the planning of U.S. signals intelligence activities."[80] Additionally, it held that "[t]he United States [will] not collect signals intelligence for the purpose of

---

[76] *Ten Years after 9/11: Transatlantic Progress in the Fight against Terrorism*, EU INSIGHT (Sept. 2011), www.euintheus.org/what-we-do/policy-areas/freedom-security-and-justice/counterterrorism/euinsight-911-9-11/ (last visited, Nov. 17, 2015).

[77] Directive on Signals Intelligence Activity (PPD-28), 2014 DAILY COMP. PRES. DOC. (Jan. 17, 2014), www.fbi.gov/about-us/nsb/fbis-policies-and-procedures-presidential-policy-directive-28-1 (last visited, Nov. 17, 2015).

[78] Remarks on United States Signals Intelligence and Electronic Surveillance Programs, 2014 DAILY COMP. PRES. DOC. (Jan. 17, 2014), www.whitehouse.gov/the-press-office/2014/01/17/remarks-president-review-signals-intelligence (last visited, Nov. 17, 2015).

[79] PPD-28, *supra* note 77.   [80] *Id.* at 2.

suppressing or burdening criticism or dissent, or for disadvantaging persons based on their ethnicity, race, gender, sexual orientation, or religion."[81] These specific limitations brought intelligence collection explicitly in line with constitutional and international law, both of which ensure protection of minority groups and strive to prevent discrimination based on protected characteristics.[82]

PPD-28 also placed limits on how the U.S. Intelligence Community may use signals intelligence collected in bulk, mandating that it may only be used for six purposes:

> (1) espionage and other threats and activities directed by foreign powers or their intelligence services against the United States and its interests; (2) threats to the United States and its interests from terrorism; (3) threats to the United States and its interests from the development, possession, proliferation, or use of weapons of mass destruction; (4) cybersecurity threats; (5) threats to U.S. or allied Armed Forces or other U.S or allied personnel; and (6) transnational criminal threats, including illicit finance and sanctions evasion related to the other purposes named in this section.[83]

This change reflects an awareness of the fact that bulk collection of signals intelligence very often results in the incidental collection of personal information or data of people who pose no threat. Limiting use of bulk data to these six purposes does not necessarily preclude all incidental collection, but it does limit access, and therefore intrusions into the lives and data of innocent people.

Finally and most importantly, PPD-28 laid out the President's plan for safeguarding personal information collected through signals intelligence.

---

[81] *Id.*

[82] *See, e.g.,* U.S. CONST. amend. IV ("The right of the people to be secure in their persons, houses, papers, and effects, against unreasonable searches and seizures, shall not be violated, and no Warrants shall issue, but upon probable cause, supported by Oath or affirmation, and particularly describing the place to be searched, and the persons or things to be seized."); U.S. CONST. amend. XIV, § 1 ("No State shall . . . deny to any person within its jurisdiction equal protection of the laws."). *See, e.g.,* G.A. Res. 217, Universal Declaration of Human Rights art. 2 & 12 (Dec. 10, 1948) (articles covering discrimination and privacy, respectively); G.A. Res. 2200A (XXI), International Convention on Civil and Political Rights, art. 17, ¶ 1 & art. 26 (Dec. 16, 1966); International Convention on the Elimination of All Forms of Racial Discrimination, Dec. 21, 1965, 660, U.N.T.S. 195; European Convention on Human Rights arts. 8 & 14, Nov. 4, 1950, 213 U.N.T.S. 221 (articles covering privacy and discrimination, respectively); Convention for the Protection of Individuals with Regard to Automatic Processing of Personal Data, Jan. 28, 1981, Eur. T.S. No. 108. *But see* Chapter 5 in this volume.

[83] PPD-28, *supra* note 77, at 3.

Crucially, this section of the Directive covers, "as much as feasible consistent with national security,"[84] personal information of all people, not just U.S. persons.[85] "U.S. persons," a category that includes foreigners residing in the United States, have long enjoyed particular protections under U.S. law, including the U.S. Constitution,[86] the Privacy Act of 1974,[87] the Foreign Intelligence Surveillance Act,[88] and Executive Order 12333.[89] Therefore, PPD-28 represents a marked change, and not one

---

[84] *Id.* at 5.

[85] For electronic surveillance purposes, "'United States person' means a citizen of the United States, an alien lawfully admitted for permanent residence ... , an unincorporated association a substantial number of members of which are citizens of the United States or aliens lawfully admitted for permanent residence, or a corporation which is incorporated in the United States, but does not include a corporation or an association which is a foreign power ... ." 50 U.S.C. § 1801(i) (2012).

[86] Like nearly every provision of the U.S. Constitution, the Fourth Amendment does not single out citizens for protections from warrantless searches, and instead refers to "the people," which includes foreigners in the U.S. This remained so when, in United States v. Verdugo-Urquidez, 494 U.S. 259, 271 (1990), Chief Justice Rehnquist writing for a plurality "suggested that a Mexican citizen who had been involuntarily brought into this country for criminal prosecution was not part of 'the people' eligible to invoke the Fourth Amendment. However, he was unable to garner a majority for that view, and Justice Kennedy, whose vote was necessary to the majority in that case, expressly rejected Rehnquist's suggestion that the Fourth Amendment did not extend to all persons present in the United States." David Cole, *Are Foreign Nationals Entitled to the Same Constitutional Rights as Citizens?*, 25 T. Jefferson L. Rev. 367, 371 n.16 (2003).

[87] The Privacy Act of 1974 applies to "individuals," meaning "citizen[s] of the United States or ... alien[s] lawfully admitted for permanent residence." 5 U.S.C. § 552a(a)(2) (2012). This is a more narrow definition than the electronic surveillance definition for U.S. persons, but both include a mix of citizens and aliens within the U.S. so this is the Privacy Act equivalent to U.S. persons. *But see*, Robert Gellman, *Foreigners' Privacy Rights in the U.S.: Little More than a Gesture*, PRIVACY LAWS & BUS. INT'L REPORT 7 (Aug. 2014), www.bobgellman.com/rg-docs/rg-PL&B-PA-Gesture-14.pdf (arguing that federal agencies use so many available exceptions that the Privacy Act of 1974 is of little value to U.S. persons) (last visited Nov. 17, 2015). Some U.S. voices, including the Chief Legal Officer of Google, are calling for an extension of the Privacy Act's protections and privileges to E.U. Citizens. David Drummond, *It's Time to Extend the U.S. Privacy Act to E.U. Citizens*, GOOGLE EUR. BLOG (Nov. 12, 2014), http://googlepolicyeurope.blogspot.co .uk/2014/11/its-time-to-extend-us-privacy-act-to-eu.html (last visited Nov. 17, 2015).

[88] For example, the President may authorize foreign electronic surveillance without a court order for up to one year if the Attorney General certifies that, among other things, "there is no substantial likelihood that the surveillance will acquire the contents of any communication to which a United States person is a party ... ." 50 U.S.C. § 1802(a)(1)(B) (2012).

[89] EO 12333 places numerous restrictions on the collection of intelligence when U.S. persons are involved. For example, Part 2.4 highly restricts the collection of intelligence inside the U.S. or against U.S. persons abroad. Exec. Order No. 12,333, 3 C.F.R. 200 (1981), www.archives.gov/federal-register/codification/executive-order/12333.html. (last visited Nov. 17, 2015).

that has a counterpart in other countries, as European countries' laws governing intelligence and surveillance presently do not include efforts to protect the privacy of noncitizens or nonresidents.[90]

PPD-28 is remarkable because it is an unprecedented explanation of the principles and limits of U.S. intelligence activities. This type of publicly available explanation is not something that European governments have matched, making some European politicians' ferocious criticism of the U.S. intelligence apparatus look overblown in comparison to its muted denunciations of far more secretive surveillance regimes among Member States. In sum, PPD-28 represents a good faith effort to address some of the concerns expressed by Washington's European partners, particularly as they relate to the privacy rights of non-U.S. persons and the perception that the United States overreached in its bulk collection effort, and the Directive is a gesture of conciliation and amelioration, designed to repair and strengthen the transatlantic relationship so that the United States and Europe can better face new challenges and seize growth opportunities together.

Common security interests requiring defense and intelligence cooperation will benefit from a restoration of trust. Allied responses to events in Ukraine, for example, reveal a normalization of transatlantic relationships and security partnerships. Russian Federation President Vladimir Putin's aggressive foreign policy has served as an immediate catalyst for renewed cooperation as U.S. and European leaders recognize that the differences between them are insignificant in comparison to an increasingly belligerent Russia.[91]

To illustrate this point, when German Chancellor Angela Merkel visited the United States in the spring of 2014, she left without the "no-spy" agreement[92] for which domestic political interests in Germany had agitated.[93] But she did not leave empty-handed. The international

---

[90] *See* Russell A. Miller, *Intelligence Oversight – Made in Germany, in* GLOBAL INTELLIGENCE OVERSIGHT: GOVERNING SECURITY IN THE TWENTY-FIRST CENTURY (Zachary Goldman ed., *forthcoming* 2016). *See also* Chapter 15 in this volume. *But see* Chapter 10 in this volume.

[91] Julian Borger, Paul Lewis, & Rowena Mason, *E.U. and U.S. Impose Sweeping Economic Sanctions on Russia*, THE GUARDIAN (July 29, 2014), www.theguardian.com/world/2014/jul/29/economic-sanctions-russia-eu-governments (last visited Nov. 17, 2015).

[92] Ken Dilanian & Kathleen Hennessey, *U.S., Germany Fail to Reach Surveillance Agreement*, L.A. TIMES (May 2, 2014), www.latimes.com/world/europe/la-fg-us-germany-spy-20140503-story.html (last visited Nov. 17, 2015).

[93] Emily Sherwin, *German Media Blast U.S. "No" to No-Spy Agreement*, DEUTSCHE WELLE (Jan. 14, 2014), www.dw.com/en/german-media-blast-us-no-to-no-spy-agreement/a-17361080 (last visited Nov. 17, 2015).

relationship between Germany and the United States, including a commitment to work together on Ukraine and Russia, was strengthened.[94] Despite the tensions about the details of intelligence agreements, observers of the meetings between the Chancellor and President Obama noted that the chemistry between the leaders was still "good."[95] Later, at the G7 summit in June 2015 – at a time when salacious new revelations about U.S. intelligence activities in Europe were breaking – Merkel warmly greeted President Obama, affirming before a crowd that although "we have differences of opinion from time to time, the United States of America is our friend and essential partner with whom we cooperate closely because it's in our mutual interest."[96] Both Washington and Berlin have emerged together at the forefront of the united Western response[97] to the crisis in Ukraine, in the face of aggressive, dangerous and unscrupulous Russian Federation behavior[98] on the edges of Europe.

Despite some very uncomfortable revelations about intelligence collection – for both the United States and many European states – the cooperation on Ukraine is just the first united response to many more 21st century security challenges that will demand close cooperation between the United States and Europe. Conflict across the Atlantic only serves the interests of antidemocratic factions around the world. Neither the United States nor the European Union can effectively make significant headway on shaping the global security environment without the help of the other. Although there will undoubtedly be more embarrassing details for each party from more leaked documents, hopefully leaders in both Europe and the United States will see them for what they are – a distraction created by a criminal act and accentuated by opportunistic

---

[94] Paul Lewis, *Obama and Merkel Warn Russia of Economic Sanctions over Ukraine*, THE GUARDIAN (May 2, 2014), www.theguardian.com/world/2014/may/02/obama-merkel-warn-russia-economic-sanctions-ukraine (last visited Nov. 17, 2015).

[95] Markl Landler, *Merkel Signals that Tension Persists Over U.S. Spying*, N.Y. TIMES, (May 2, 2014), www.nytimes.com/2014/05/03/world/europe/merkel-says-gaps-with-us-over-sur veillance-remain.html (last visited Nov. 17, 2015).

[96] Kate Connolly, *Merkel Welcomes Obama with Beer and Sausage Breakfast before G& Summit*, THE GUARDIAN (June 7, 2015, 7:52 AM), www.theguardian.com/world/2015/jun/07/merkel-obama-beer-sausage-breakfast-g7-summit (last visited Nov. 17, 2015).

[97] Chris Good, *Obama Accuses Putin, Russia of Dishonesty on Ukraine*, ABC NEWS (May 2, 2014), http://abcnews.go.com/Politics/obama-urges-russia-call-off-armed-separatists/story?id=23562277 (last visited Nov. 17, 2015).

[98]. *Obama, Merkel: Russia Must Pull Back*, DAILY BEAST (May 2, 2014), www.thedailybeast.com/cheats/2014/05/02/obama-merkel-russia-must-pull-back.html (last visited Nov. 17, 2015).

media outlets and politicians. The two unions are natural allies – the United States and the European Union will find no other major global partners as capable in security matters, as committed in expanding trade cooperation, and as dedicated to protecting democratic ideals. Unnecessary division between the European Union and the United States will continue to be the least intelligent response to embarrassing revelations about the conduct of Western intelligence services.

10

Fourth Amendment Rights for Nonresident Aliens

BY ALEC WALEN

A Introduction

The U.S. National Security Agency (NSA) has nearly unlimited authority to spy upon citizens of foreign countries while they are outside the United States.[1] Section 702 of the Federal Intelligence Surveillance Act (FISA)[2] allows the NSA to collect the "metadata" of nonresident aliens (NRAs) – the collection of which from U.S. citizens is now of dubious constitutionality[3] – as well as the content of the electronic communications of NRAs. The only precondition for collecting this information – other than that the targets must be NRAs and that the collection must be "conducted in a manner consistent with the Fourth Amendment to the Constitution of the United States"[4] – is that the aim is to "acquire foreign intelligence information."[5] This requirement is so broad that it serves as no meaningful restriction at all.[6]

---

[1] The Federal Intelligence Surveillance Act provides that "the Attorney General and the Director of National Intelligence may authorize jointly ... the targeting of persons reasonably believed to be located outside the United States to acquire foreign intelligence information." 50 U.S.C. § 1881a(a) (2012).

[2] This section was adopted as part of the FISA Amendments Act of 2008, Pub. L. No. 110–261, 122 Stat. 2436 (2008).

[3] See Klayman v. Obama, 957 F. Supp. 2d 1 (D.D.C. Dec. 16, 2013); but see A.C.L.U. v. Clapper, 959 F. Supp. 2d 724 (S.D.N.Y. 2013), vacated, 785 F.3d 787 (2d Cir. 2015) (declining to address the constitutionality of collecting metadata under Section 215 of the PATRIOT Act).

[4] 50 U.S.C. § 1881a(b)(5) (2012).

[5] Such information is defined to include "information with respect to a foreign power or foreign territory that relates to ... the conduct of the foreign affairs of the United States." 50 U.S.C. § 1801 (e)(2) (2012).

[6] Compare Id., with 50 U.S.C. § 1802 (2006) (permitting only the narrower surveillance of foreign powers or their agents, and requiring the government to submit an application for every target of surveillance). See also David Cole, We Kill People Based on Metadata, N.Y. Rev. Books (May 10, 2014), www.nybooks.com/blogs/nyrblog/2014/may/10/we-kill-people-based-metadata/ (noting that FISA's definition of "foreign intelligence" includes "any information that might inform our foreign affairs, which is no restriction at all.").

It goes almost without saying that such targeting of U.S. citizens and resident aliens, without any hint of individualized suspicion either of criminal wrongdoing or of being a threat to national security, would be constitutionally prohibited. The Fourth Amendment protects U.S. citizens and resident aliens "against unreasonable searches and seizures,"[7] and such targeted searching for information without individualized suspicion has long been regarded as unconstitutional.[8] But the dominant view in the American legal community is that there is nothing constitutionally wrong, or even suspect, about targeting of NRAs without an identifiable reason for doing so.[9] The assumption is that the U.S. Constitution – specifically the Fourth Amendment – simply does not provide protection to non-resident aliens.

I contend here that the dominant view of the law is wrong both descriptively and normatively. It is wrong with regard to the proper interpretation of the relevant constitutional case law, because that case law is more open-ended and unclear than the dominant view represents it as being. And it is wrong with regard to the underlying legal and moral principles that should guide the interpretation and development of constitutional law. Those principles call for recognizing that NRAs enjoy the Fourth Amendment's prohibition on unreasonable searches and seizures.

In a companion paper I argue that the case law on constitutional rights for NRAs, as a general matter, was never clearly against extending such rights,[10] and that, in the wake of Boumediene v. Bush,[11] the jurisprudence has moved in favor of extending constitutional protections to NRAs. I also argue that there are strong normative reasons in favor of extending to NRAs the constitutional right not to be unjustly harmed.[12]

---

[7] U.S. Const., Amend. IV. In support of the Fourth Amendment applying to resident aliens, see Yick Wo v. Hopkins, 118 U.S. 356, 369 (1886) (holding that the provisions of the Fourteenth Amendment (and by implication similar provisions in the Bill of Rights) "are universal in their application to *all persons* within the territorial jurisdiction.") (emphasis added).

[8] See Katz v. United States, 389 U.S. 347 (1967).

[9] See, e.g., Privacy and Civil Liberties Oversight Bd., Report on the Surveillance Program Operated Pursuant to Section 702 of the Foreign Intelligence Surveillance Act 86 (July 2, 2014), www.pclob.gov/library/702-Report.pdf (writing that those targeted under Section 702 "lack Fourth Amendment rights because they are foreigners located outside of the United States.").

[10] Alec Walen, *Constitutional Rights for Nonresident Aliens: A Doctrinal and Normative Argument*, Drexel L. Rev. (forthcoming).

[11] Boumediene v. Bush, 553 U.S. 723 (2008).

[12] The "suggestion" that privacy concerns and Fourth Amendment rights are among the "fundamental" rights against unjust harm that must apply outside core U.S. territory goes

In this chapter, I extend those general insights and arguments to the specific case of NRAs' Fourth Amendment privacy rights, especially as those interests apply against the NSA's spying. I proceed in four parts. In Part B, I provide a quick overview of the Fourth Amendment and the concerns raised by NSA spying on NRAs, focusing on the example of its signals intelligence activities in Germany. In Part C, I argue that the case law does not resolve whether NRAs enjoy the Fourth Amendment protection against unreasonable searches and seizures. In Part D, I argue that on the relevant constitutional test for determining whether NRAs benefit from particular constitutional protections – whether extending such protections would be impracticable or anomalous – NRAs should be held to enjoy the Fourth Amendment protection against unreasonable searches and seizures. And in Part E, I argue that there is sufficient reason overall to hold that the reasonableness requirement should be applied to limit NSA spying more than it is limited by FISA § 702.

B   Background on the Fourth Amendment and NSA Spying in Germany

I   Background on the Fourth Amendment

The Fourth Amendment was adopted in reaction to British use of general writs, along with other abusive laws that the colonists came to feel violated their basic right to privacy.[13] It was originally enforced in a limited way, prohibiting only trespass against a person or his or her physical property, but that view was rejected in favor of a broader protection of privacy in *Katz v. United States* in 1967.[14] In *Katz*, the Court held that "the Fourth Amendment protects people, not places."[15] Or, as Justice Harlan framed the issue in his concurring opinion in *Katz*, "a person has a constitutionally protected reasonable expectation of privacy."[16] This excludes protection of information that is in the public

---

back to Downes v. Bidwell, 182 U.S. 244, 282–83 (1901) (listing among the "natural rights enforced by the Constitution," "immunities from unreasonable searches and seizures [and] such other immunities as are indispensable to a free government").

[13] *See* WILLIAM J. CUDDIHY, THE FOURTH AMENDMENT: ORIGINS AND ORIGINAL MEANING 766 (2009) ("Privacy was the bedrock concern of the amendment, not general warrants.").

[14] Katz, 389 U.S. at 347.   [15] *Id.* at 351.

[16] *Id.* at 360. This framing has since become generally accepted.

domain, but protects information that a person could reasonably expect not to be in the public domain.

One can identify two basic conceptions of privacy, and four related reasons to value its protection. Framed in terms of interests, the different conceptions concern primarily (1) concealment: the interest in preventing others from knowing about one's activities and characteristics, and (2) discretion: the interest in controlling when and how others know about one's activities and characteristics.[17] These two interests give rise to four concrete types of value that are served by the protection of privacy.[18] First, there is an objective value in keeping parts of one's life under one's own control, sharing details or intimacies with at most a few select persons. Second, many people subjectively value controlling at least some sorts of information about their lives, sharing details or intimacies with at most a few select persons.[19] Third, the protection of privacy, both in the concealment and the discretion senses, can help prevent a variety of harms that may flow from unwanted information collection and dissemination, including: "(1) breach of confidentiality, (2) disclosure, (3) exposure, (4) increased accessibility, (5) blackmail, (6) appropriation, and (7) distortion."[20] Fourth, a special kind of vulnerability may arise from invasion of privacy in both senses: The government can fish through private information searching for information to use to prosecute (or blackmail) its critics and opponents.[21]

This list of reasons for valuing privacy applies to NRAs as well as to U.S. citizens. The first two concerns do not depend on who is being spied upon or where. The third and fourth diminish somewhat as the distance between the privacy invader and the person whose privacy is invaded grows. A stranger is less likely to engage in blackmail than someone who commences the invasion of privacy looking for information with which to blackmail; and governments are less likely to worry about critics who

---

[17] Daniel J. Solove lists six "general headings, which capture the recurrent ideas in the discourse." Daniel J. Solove, *Conceptualizing Privacy*, 90 CAL. L. REV. 1087, 1092 (2002). I think his list can be usefully boiled down to the two interests listed in the text.

[18] This is just one way of distinguishing the underlying concerns; I make no claim that it is the best way to identify them.

[19] Both this and the first harm can also be understood in terms of dignitary harms. *See* Daniel J. Solove, *A Taxonomy of Privacy*, 154 U. PA. L. REV. 477, 487 (2006).

[20] *Id.* at 525.

[21] *See* Laurent Sacharoff, *The Relational Nature of Privacy*, 16 LEWIS & CLARK L. REV. 1249 (2102) (discussing many examples of government violating privacy rights in order to harass or intimidate its critics and opponents).

are not in the civic body than those who are. Nonetheless, these concerns do not drop away altogether. For example, if the United States discovers that an NRA who it views as dangerous has also engaged in minor criminal activities, it may disclose those facts to the government where that person lives to try to have him arrested and prosecuted, and thereby taken out of action. Likewise, if it sweeps up information from a community and searches for people who are vulnerable to having their information disclosed – imagine someone who is having an extra-marital affair, or who is engaged in homosexual activity in a generally homophobic community – the United States could then blackmail that person into serving as an agent for the United States.[22]

Some wonder if these sorts of privacy concerns are as relevant today, when people disclose so much of themselves on the Internet. But one should not exaggerate the extent to which privacy has lost its significance. Even if more people are now happy to disclose things that would have been thought embarrassing to disclose twenty years ago, that does not mean that they are willing to disclose *everything*. Many people still share intimate information with only a select few people. Reading their email, capturing every keystroke they make on their computers or phones, intercepting photos they post electronically but not on public sites, or registering their location on the basis of smart-phone usage could expose them to all of the harms just mentioned.[23]

II NSA Spying in Germany

The bombshell with regard to NSA spying in Germany was the discovery that the NSA had tapped German Chancellor Merkel's phone.[24] But,

---

[22] These sort of worries explain one of the restrictions President Obama put on the collection of signals intelligence in a Presidential Policy Directive, PPD-28: "The United States shall not collect signals intelligence for the purpose of suppressing or burdening criticism or dissent, or for disadvantaging persons based on their ethnicity, race, gender, sexual orientation, or religion." OFFICE OF THE PRESS SEC'Y, PRESIDENTIAL POLICY DIRECTIVE/PPD-28 1, 3 (2014), http://fas.org/irp/offdocs/ppd/ppd-28.pdf.

[23] *See, e.g.,* Teri Dobbins Baxter, *Low Expectations: How Changing Expectations of Privacy Can Erode Fourth Amendment Protection and a Proposed Solution,* 84 TEMP. L. REV. 599, 612 (2012) (noting how younger people, "digital natives," are less likely to be concerned about their privacy, but nevertheless "are cognizant of privacy issues and are willing to protest when they believe their privacy rights have been violated").

[24] *See* Mark Landler, *Merkel Signals That Tension Persists Over U.S. Spying,* N.Y. TIMES (May 2, 2014), www.nytimes.com/2014/05/03/world/europe/merkel-says-gaps-with-us-over-surveillance-remain.html?_r=0 (describing the repercussions of the report in

while the suggestion of such spying was embarrassing to the United States, and arguably reflected poor judgment given the risk to U.S. – German relations, I will not argue that such spying was unconstitutional. Clearly Chancellor Merkel is "an agent of a foreign power,"[25] and I accept, at least for the sake of the current argument, that the United States' interest in protecting itself against threats provides sufficient constitutional justification for targeting the agents of foreign powers for spying. The driving concern in this chapter is FISA § 702, which allows the collection of the content of any and all communications of NRAs, whether or not they are an agent of a foreign power, if the aim is to "acquire foreign intelligence information."[26]

It could be argued that, despite the laxity of FISA § 702, the United States currently is not doing anything problematic, much less unconstitutional, when it comes to collecting signals intelligence in Germany. One way to make that case is to appeal to Presidential Policy Directive, PPD-28, issued by President Obama in January 2014.[27] It directs the NSA to take the privacy interests of NRAs into account essentially as it would the privacy interests of U.S. citizens. It says, for example, that "U.S. signals intelligence activities must … include appropriate safeguards for the personal information of all individuals, regardless of the nationality of the individual to whom the information pertains or where that individual resides."[28]

One can also argue, as Benjamin Wittes does, that this Directive reflects a stable underlying practice. Wittes argues that Obama was able to use "values-based statements as justifications for policies that already exist, at least *de facto*, for purely functional reasons."[29] According to

---

October 2013 "that the National Security Agency had eavesdropped on Ms. Merkel's phone calls"). *But see* Melissa Eddy, *Germany Drops Inquiry into Claims U.S. Tapped Angela Merkel's Phone*, N.Y. Times (June 12, 2015), www.nytimes.com/2015/06/13/world/europe/germany-drops-inquiry-us-tapped-angela-merkel-phone.html (reporting that an investigation by a German federal prosecutor "had not been able to prove that … the chancellor's phone had been tapped").

[25] *See* 50 U.S.C. § 1881b(c)(1)(B)(ii) (2012) (the section of FISA permitting the collection of foreign intelligence information upon a finding of probable cause that the target is "a foreign power, an agent of a foreign power, or an officer or employee of a foreign power.").

[26] *See supra* note 5.   [27] *See supra* note 22.

[28] *Id.* at 5. Of course, this language leaves it open that what is appropriate varies by the nature of the national context in which the individual lives. *See* Chapter 9 in this volume.

[29] Benjamin Wittes, *The President's Speech and PPD-28: A Guide for the Perplexed*, Lawfare (Jan. 20, 2014, 11:02 AM), www.lawfareblog.com/presidents-speech-and-ppd-28-guide-perplexed.

Wittes, the reason that Obama can use such justifications is that "[g]ood intelligence analysis ... is all about discrimination between what's important and what's not. Privacy is a values name we give to a very similar form of discrimination – only framed from the point of view of the individual."[30] In other words, a "reasonable" respect for privacy – what the Fourth Amendment might afford NRAs – reflects a balance between the need for the information and the interests of the person whose privacy might be infringed to get the information, and, according to Wittes, the costs of sorting through and keeping information, especially when collected in bulk, result in a functionally similar balance being struck.

The claim has also been made that U.S. practice and German practice with regard to signals intelligence are fundamentally similar. "German officials assembled [a] vast database without any 'particularized suspicion of wrongdoing.' They then used search terms to query the data. The U.S. section 702 program uses methods that are substantially similar to the German approach."[31] The import of this claim is that since the European Court of Human Rights upheld the German program,[32] U.S. law under § 702 must also pass muster under international law. And if it passes muster under international law, it is hard to see why the U.S. courts should be more restrictive.

None of these arguments is convincing. First, PPD-28 is a directive, not a statute. It does nothing to change the underlying legal space, as established by § 702, in which the United States can engage in essentially unlimited spying on NRAs. Moreover, the President could revoke it at any time. Second, even granting Wittes his point that good intelligence dovetails with respect for privacy values, it is not clear that the United States would always engage in good intelligence practices. Ideology and politics can drive politicians to adopt bad policy if it suits their political agenda.[33] Third, an important difference between German and American signals intelligence in Germany concerns the role of the courts. The German Constitutional Court ruled that German collection of bulk data

---

[30] Id.

[31] Peter Margulies, The NSA in Global Perspective: Surveillance, Human Rights, and International Counterterrorism, 82 FORDHAM L. REV. 2137, 2159 (2014).

[32] See Weber v. Germany, 2006-XI Eur. Ct. H.R. 309.

[33] See U.S. NATIONAL SECURITY, INTELLIGENCE AND DEMOCRACY: FROM THE CHURCH COMMITTEE TO THE WAR ON TERROR (Russell Miller ed., 2009) (discussing the Church Committee's findings regarding the FBI's malicious accessing of Martin Luther King's communications in order to attack his character for political reasons).

is constitutional, but that "certain provisions concerning transfer of the personal data by the [*Bundesnachrichtendienst*] to other agencies" was unconstitutional.[34] That is exactly the sort of limitation on the German use of bulk signals data that would be unlimited under section 702 (but not under PPD-28).[35] It is the lack of that sort of limitation – failure to put any limits on what can be done with data collected in bulk from NRAs – that could ground a claim that § 702 is facially unconstitutional under the Fourth Amendment. Scanning with a computer to look for key words is one thing. Reading the transmissions, and transferring the content to other agencies, to be used as members of various federal agencies see fit, is another.

C A Careful Reading of the Case Law

Having explained why NRAs have an ongoing concern with the possibilities for NSA spying under § 702, we come now to the question whether the Court has already held that NRAs do not enjoy the benefit of the Fourth Amendment. The standard view, that the Supreme Court has held that the Fourth Amendment does not apply to NRAs, is grounded in a superficial reading of a case called *United States v. Verdugo-Urquidez*.[36] In that case Justice Rehnquist, writing at least nominally for a majority of five justices, held that "the Fourth Amendment [does not] appl[y] to the search and seizure by United States agents of property that is owned by [an NRA] and located in a foreign country."[37] If one counts votes, however, it is clear that Rehnquist got only four votes for the proposition that the Fourth Amendment as a whole does not apply to the search and seizure by United States agents of property that is owned by an NRA and located in a foreign country. Five Justices clearly rejected that position, including Justice Kennedy, who, while signing the majority opinion, wrote a concurring opinion in which he expressed a number of points of disagreement. Unfortunately, it is unclear exactly what Justice

---

[34] Paul M Schwartz, *German and U.S. Telecommunications Privacy Law: Legal Regulation of Domestic Law Enforcement Surveillance*, 54 HASTINGS L.J. 751, 782 (2003). *See* Chapter 2 in this volume.

[35] While the German Constitutional Court may have put some limits on the collection of German bulk data by German authorities, it showed a similarly mistaken lack of concern for NRAs. *See* Chapter 15 in this volume. *See also* Russell A. Miller, *Intelligence Oversight – Made in Germany*, in GLOBAL INTELLIGENCE OVERSIGHT: GOVERNING SECURITY IN THE TWENTY-FIRST CENTURY (Zachary Goldman ed., *forthcoming*).

[36] United States v. Verdugo-Urquidez, 494 U.S. 259 (1990).   [37] *Id.* at 261.

Kennedy rejected in Justice Rehnquist's opinion. As a result, we need to go through various arguments in Rehnquist's *Verdugo-Urquidez* opinion carefully to see if they justify the conclusion that Rehnquist's sweeping rejection of Fourth Amendment rights for NRAs actually attracted the support of a majority on the Court.

I   The Fourth Amendment and "the People"

Justice Rehnquist offered a textual argument against extending Fourth Amendment rights to NRAs, based on the fact that the Fourth Amendment speaks in terms of the right of "the people."[38] Some amendments are framed in terms of "persons,"[39] some in terms of "citizens,"[40] some in terms of "the accused,"[41] and some in terms of "the people."[42] Rehnquist's reading of the overall text of the Constitution "suggest[ed]" to him that "the people" "refers to a class of persons who are part of a national community or who have otherwise developed sufficient connection with this country to be considered part of that community."[43] This "suggestion" was not originally endorsed by five members of the Court in *Verdugo-Urquidez*. Justice Kennedy explicitly rejected it, writing: "I cannot place any weight on the reference to 'the people' in the Fourth Amendment as a source of restricting its protections."[44] But, in the more recent *District of Columbia v. Heller* case, in which the Court recognized an individual right to bear arms under the Second Amendment, five Justices, including Justice Kennedy, embraced Justice Rehnquist's interpretation of "the people" in *Verdugo-Urquidez*.[45] Thus, it might seem that the Court has now endorsed this reading of the Fourth Amendment, cementing the exclusion of NRAs.

There are, however, three reasons why this reading should not be taken as settled law. First, *Heller* cited Rehnquist's reading of "the people"

---

[38] U.S. CONST. amend. IV ("The right of the people to be secure in their persons, houses, papers, and effects, against unreasonable searches and seizures, shall not be violated . . .").

[39] U.S. CONST. amends. V; U.S. CONST. amend. XIV, § 1 (due process clause and equal protection clause).

[40] U.S. CONST. amend. XIV § 1 (privileges and immunities clause).

[41] U.S. CONST. amend. VI.

[42] U.S. CONST. amend. I (assembly clause); amend. II (right to bear arms); amend. IV (right against unreasonable search and seizure); amend. IX (unnamed rights retained by the people); amend. X (rights reserved by the people), and amend. XVII (election of senators).

[43] Verdugo-Urquidez, 494 U.S. at 265.   [44] *Id.* at 276.

[45] District of Columbia v. Heller, 554 U.S. 570, 580 (2008).

only in *dicta*. The quotation of Rehnquist's discussion was used to establish the point that "the Second Amendment right was exercised individually and belongs to all Americans."[46] This use is logically independent of Rehnquist's use in *Verdugo-Urquidez*, which was to exclude NRAs, or indeed resident aliens without "sufficient connection with this country," from benefitting from Fourth Amendment rights.

Second, Rehnquist's reading of "the people" as "a class of persons who are part of a national community or who have otherwise developed sufficient connection with this country to be considered part of that community" clearly cannot fit all uses of the phrase, even within the Bill of Rights. The Tenth Amendment speaks of the powers that are "reserved ... to the people."[47] In this context, it is clear that "the people" refers to the citizenry.[48] And in the context of the Second Amendment, reading "the people" as broadly as Rehnquist does has proven to be difficult for lower courts that have upheld 18 U.S.C. § 922(g)(5). That statute makes it a crime "for any person ... who, being an alien, is illegally or unlawfully in the United States ... to ship or transport in interstate or foreign commerce, or possess in or affecting commerce, any firearm or ammunition." There are aliens who have been in the United States illegally, but who have been living in the U.S. for a long time and who have "developed sufficient connection with this country to be considered part of that community." They would clearly have Fourth Amendment rights, but the courts have found that they do not enjoy Second Amendment rights.[49]

Third, Rehnquist's reading is substantively misguided and should simply be rejected. If one is going to pay close attention to the text, one should have evidence that the word choice was deliberate and significant, as opposed to something adopted simply as a rhetorical flourish. But the historical evidence suggests that the choice of "the people" versus "persons" in the Bill of Rights was not particularly

---

[46] *Id.* at 581.

[47] U.S. CONST. amend. X ("The powers not delegated to the United States by the Constitution, nor prohibited by it to the States, are reserved to the States respectively, or to the people.").

[48] *See* Gerald L. Neuman, *Whose Constitution*, 100 YALE L.J. 909, 972 n.380 (1991) (describing the gap between Justice Rehnquist's reading of "the people" and its use in both the Tenth Amendment and the Preamble to the Constitution).

[49] *See, e.g.*, United States v. Huitron-Guizar, 678 F.3d 1164 (10th Cir. 2012). The petitioner was brought to the United States from Mexico at age three, and was prosecuted for violation of 18 U.S.C. § 922(g)(5) at age 24.

deliberate or significant.[50] Instead, the Bills of Rights adopted by states seemed to use different words essentially for stylistic reasons.[51] Indeed, when one appreciates the compelling stylistic problem of the alternative use of "persons" – "The right of persons to be secure in their persons. . ." – the avoidance of that redundancy becomes by far the most reasonable explanation for the word choice.

II Historical Purpose of the Fourth Amendment

Rehnquist claimed that "[w]hat we know of the history of the drafting of the Fourth Amendment also suggests that its purpose was to restrict searches and seizures which might be conducted by the United States in domestic matters."[52] Rehnquist's argument for this point, while mentioning concerns specific to the Fourth Amendment, is of a piece with concerns that would apply to every part of the Bill of Rights. Yet the best reading of *Boumediene* rejects the conclusion that no part of the Bill of Rights could apply to NRAs.[53] Moreover, there is good reason not to give a lot of weight to the fact that the original concern in adopting the Fourth Amendment (along with the other Amendments) was with restraining the federal government's domestic actions. When these Amendments were adopted there was little reason to be concerned that the federal government might wield its power indiscriminately against other nations.[54] Nowadays, the United States is a global power and its respect for or disregard of the rights of NRAs is a much more pressing concern – practically, morally, politically, and legally.[55]

It is also worth noting that the sorts of limitations on the Fourth Amendment's extraterritorial application that Rehnquist mentions would have applied not only to NRAs but also to citizens.[56]

---

[50] *See* J. Andrew Kent, *A Textual and Historical Case against a Global Constitution*, 95 Geo. L.J. 463, 515 (2007).

[51] *See id.* at 515–16.   [52] Verdugo-Urquidez, 494 U.S. at 266.

[53] *See* Walen, *supra* note 10, Part B.III.

[54] Indeed, early cases show that the U.S. was particularly concerned to respect international law and thereby demonstrate that it was an upstanding member of the international community. See Henfield's Case, 11 F. Cas. 1099, ¶ 5 (C.C.D. Pa. 1793) ("Providence has been pleased to place the United States among the nations of the earth, and therefore, all those duties, as well as rights, which spring from the relation of nation to nation, have devolved upon us.").

[55] *See also* Walen *supra* note 10, Part C.I (discussing the limited relevance of the original understanding of the reach of the Constitution).

[56] *See* Neuman, *supra* note 48, at 973 ("If these data suggest anything, however, it is that *no one* has Fourth Amendment rights outside the nation's borders. . ..").

Originally, that is, the Fourth Amendment applied only *domestically*. But things have changed. Now, according to a pair of circuit court opinions, it applies to U.S. citizens in foreign countries, only not in the same way as it applies domestically: U.S. citizens in foreign countries are protected against unreasonable search and seizure, but are not protected by the Warrant Clause.[57] Rehnquist offered no reason to reject the thought that the extension of Fourth Amendment rights to U.S. citizens abroad should be matched by a similar extension to NRAs.

III   Remaining Arguments

Rehnquist argued that the rejection of the applicability of the Fifth Amendment to NRAs in *Johnson v. Eisentrager*[58] implies that the Fourth Amendment must not apply to NRAs, because the former concerns "the relatively universal term of 'person,'" while the latter "applies only to 'the people.'"[59] I have already argued for the weakness of this textual argument in its own terms. Another problem with the argument is that it presupposes a reading of *Eisentrager* – that it emphatically "reject[ed the] extraterritorial application of the Fifth Amendment"[60] – that was emphatically rejected by the majority in *Boumediene*.[61]

This leaves Rehnquist with one other significant argument against extending Fourth Amendment protections to NRAs: that doing so would be impracticable. Because that is the sort of argument with which a court must ultimately decide the issue,[62] I leave it to the next Part. It is enough, at this point, to conclude that none of Justice Rehnquist's other arguments should be taken to preclude the extension of Fourth Amendment rights to NRAs.

---

[57] *See In re* Terrorist Bombings of U.S. Embassies in E. Afr., 552 F.3d 157 (2d Cir. 2008); *see also* United States v. Stokes, 726 F.3d 880 (7th Cir. 2013).

[58] Johnson v. Eisentrager, 339 U.S. 763 (1950) (holding that German nationals, convicted by a U.S. military tribunal of war crimes and imprisoned in an U.S. Army base in Germany, had no Fifth Amendment due process rights, and no right to habeas corpus).

[59] Verdugo-Urquidez, 494 U.S. at 269.   [60] *Id.*

[61] *See also* Walen, *supra* note 10, Part B.I.

[62] The claim that this is the ultimate standard is not merely a "realist" claim about constitutional law in general; it is a claim about the standard the specific relevant law explicitly uses. *See infra* Part D.

D   The Reasonableness of Applying
the Fourth Amendment to NRAs

The default legal framework, after *Boumediene*, for extending consti-tutional rights, other than *habeas corpus*, to NRAs seems to be to ask whether it would be impracticable or anomalous to do so.[63] I consider here the concerns raised by both Justices Rehnquist and Kennedy with regard to the extension of Fourth Amendment protections to NRAs. I conclude that neither has articulated strong reasons why such an extension should be either impracticable or anomalous.

Rehnquist claimed that extending Fourth Amendment rights to NRAs would be impracticable because it would "disrupt the ability of the political branches to respond to foreign situations involving our national interest."[64] And he claimed that the "global view of [the Fourth Amend-ment's] applicability would plunge [Members of the Executive and Legis-lative Branches] into a sea of uncertainty as to what might be reasonable in the way of searches and seizures conducted abroad."[65]

These are important concerns, but they do not call in any straightfor-ward way for completely rejecting the application of the Fourth Amend-ment to NRAs. They call, rather, for careful and principled consideration of the limits of the Fourth Amendment's global applicability. For example, the Court might want to establish a categorical rule that spying on foreign powers and their agents – including agents of terrorist organ-izations[66] – is constitutionally permitted, at least as long as adequate procedures are in place for minimizing the collection of information from others.[67] The Court might also want to permit the bulk collection of communications from abroad, and the electronic scanning of them for key words, while insisting that there must be probable cause – based, at the very minimum, on analysis of key words and metadata – to believe that they are the messages of agents of a foreign power before individual messages are actually read by humans or passed on to other agencies. These and other such rules would protect NRAs much as citizens are

---

[63] Boumediene v. Bush, 553 U.S. at 759 (2008). *See also* Walen, *supra* note 10, Part B.III (discussing how Justice Kennedy relies on this standard, drawing it from Justice Harlan's concurrence in Reid v. Covert, 354 U.S. 1, 74–75 (1957)).

[64] Verdugo-Urquidez, 494 U.S. at 273–74.   [65] *Id.* at 274.

[66] *See* 50 U.S.C. § 1801(a)(4) (2012) (defining a foreign power to include "a group engaged in international terrorism or activities in preparation therefor").

[67] Thus activity under FISA, 50 U.S.C. § 1802, permitting the targeting of foreign powers or their agents, would be upheld.

currently protected, and it would neither "disrupt the ability of the political branches to respond to foreign situations involving our national interest," nor "plunge [Members of the Executive and Legislative Branches] into a sea of uncertainty."[68]

One of Justice Kennedy's objections to applying the Warrant Clause to searches and seizures overseas can also be raised as an objection to the effect that applying the Fourth Amendment's Reasonableness Clause to NRAs is anomalous. His concern was with "the differing and perhaps unascertainable conceptions of reasonableness and privacy that prevail abroad."[69] The underlying worry concerns the fact that to benefit from the Fourth Amendment right to privacy, one must have a "reasonable expectation of privacy."[70] If judges in the United States cannot be expected to know whether people in, for example, Germany, or China, or Saudi Arabia have a "reasonable expectation of privacy" with regard to the content of their electronic communications, or anything else, then how can they hold that NRAs in those countries enjoy the Fourth Amendment's ban on unreasonable searches and seizures?

This is a deep objection, to which I will respond at some length. But to start it is worth saying that in some sense the answer with regard to the collection of electronic data in Germany and the rest of Western Europe is easy. The importance of privacy in the context of electronic communications is, if anything, stronger in places like Germany than in the United States.[71] Thus there is no reason for U.S. courts to worry that Europeans might not have a reasonable expectation of privacy in the content of their electronic communications. What if they have an even stronger expectation of privacy? That too should not be a problem. Having reached the threshold for constitutional protection, the question then is whether the U.S. has sufficient reason to intrude on their

---

[68] This sort of balancing of interests is essential to any idea of "reasonable" searches and seizures. And this sort of balancing is not at all alien to U.S. Constitutional law. *See, e.g.,* Matthews v. Eldridge, 424 U.S. 319 (1976) (laying out a three-pronged balancing test for the process required by the due process clause before terminating government benefits).

[69] Verdugo-Urquidez, 494 U.S. at 278.   [70] Katz, 389 U.S. at 360 (Harlan, J., concurring).

[71] *See* Ralf Poscher & Russell Miller, *Surveillance and Data Protection in the Conflict Between European and American Legal Cultures,* AMERICAN INST. FOR CONTEMP. GERMAN STUD. (Dec. 9, 2013), www.aicgs.org/issue/surveillance-and-data-protection-in-the-conflict-between-european-and-american-legal-cultures/ (discussing the right of informational self-determination and its anticipatory character) *See also* Introduction in this volume; Chapter 2 in this volume.

privacy in particular ways. That balance, as discussed below,[72] can be struck as it would be in the United States.

The problem is that even if Germans and other Europeans have a sense of privacy more or less like that of U.S. citizens, one might worry that other people do not. As Justice Harlan wrote, explaining the idea of a "reasonable expectation of privacy": "there is a twofold requirement, first that a person have exhibited an actual (subjective) expectation of privacy and, second, that the expectation be one that society is prepared to recognize as 'reasonable.'"[73] Both prongs may seem to present problems for extending the Fourth Amendment to countries outside of Western Europe, particularly those with totalitarian governments, where most people expect to be monitored.

With regard to the first prong – the thought that people in such countries do not have a subjective expectation of privacy – it is important to read Harlan's point correctly. Harlan could not have meant to suggest that when people are beaten down they also lose their rights. The fact that a local government violates the privacy rights of its residents does not give the United States the right to disregard their privacy interests as well. Of course, if the information truly is "public" already – if anyone who wants to get it can get it, say by doing a Google search – then there is no further harm in the United States (or anyone else) collecting it.[74] But if the information is not fully "public," if instead it is in the hands of a local, oppressive government but even *more* damage to a person's privacy interests could be done by the United States also gathering and using that information, then it makes sense to ask whether persons in that situation think that they still have some residual privacy interest. Even in totalitarian regimes, people may still wish to minimize the extent to which their personal information is exposed.

With regard to Harlan's second prong – referring to the expectations of privacy that a society would consider reasonable – it is important to step back and get some perspective on how invoking a reasonable expectation of privacy works in Fourth Amendment jurisprudence. One might think that the job of a court would be to take seriously any professed interest in privacy, determine if it is reasonable, all things considered, and then weigh it against the competing state interest in collecting that information in the particular way the state seeks to collect

---

[72] *See infra* Part E.   [73] Katz, 389 U.S. at 361.

[74] This is not to deny that people have a right to be forgotten. *See* Chapters 22, 16, and 11 in this volume.

it. But that is not how the Fourth Amendment works in practice. Instead, Fourth Amendment jurisprudence seeks to establish a set of categories or rules to guide lower courts. If a plaintiff's complaint falls on the wrong side of the categorical line, he or she is entitled to no Fourth Amendment protection at all. If, however, the complaint falls on the protected side of the line, then a balance must be struck. Thus we find that what can be detected by the noses of well trained dogs is fair game – a plaintiff has no constitutionally protected privacy interest in avoiding the olfactory abilities of government trained dogs sniffing around his or her belongings and discovering illegal substances therein.[75] By contrast, people have a constitutionally protected interest in not having high tech sensory equipment, such as devices that can detect the heat of grow-lights through walls, trained on their homes.[76] People have no constitutional privacy interest protecting their property from being photographed from the air if such photography merely documents what could be seen with the naked eye.[77] But they do have a constitutionally protected interest in their luggage on a bus not being squeezed and assessed for contraband by the police.[78] These and other distinctions aim to strike a balance: to allow the government to use widely available or familiar technology to gather information, but to draw lines so that there are still safe zones where individuals can at least demand that the government show that its interest in getting information is important enough, on a case-by-case basis, to justify the intrusion into his or her privacy. Even if it is hard to discern a principled basis for drawing these lines,[79] knowing how the balance works in particular types of cases, and being able to reason by analogy to get a sense for how this balance is likely to work in other cases, is valuable for people who want to know when and in what ways they can expect the government's intrusions into their private affairs to be regulated.[80] It is also valuable for government agents who want to know when

---

[75] Illinois v. Caballes, 543 U.S. 405 (2005).   [76] Kyllo v. United States, 533 U.S. 27 (2001).

[77] California v. Ciraolo, 476 U.S. 207 (1986); Florida v. Riley, 488 U.S. 445 (1989).

[78] Bond v. United States, 529 U.S. 334 (2000).

[79] Orin Kerr, *Four Models of Fourth Amendment Protection*, 60 STAN. L. REV. 503 (2007) (arguing that it is not that the Court has no principles, but that it has conflicting models that is uses differently, to fit different contexts).

[80] The idea that these lines are there not just to reflect societal expectations of privacy but to help set them explains why the Court has never addressed whether certain subcultures, with different expectations of privacy, do not deserve different standards for constitutionally protected privacy interests. Different standards would undermine the law's function in *setting* reasonable expectations.

and how they can act without having to worry about privacy interests, and for lower courts which have to handle a wide range of more or less novel cases.[81]

This analysis of how Fourth Amendment case law works and what functions it serves provides an important insight into why applying the Fourth Amendment in other countries might be anomalous. In other countries such lines, if they are drawn, can and will be drawn in different ways, just as in this country it could have been drawn in different ways. And it may seem anomalous for U.S. courts to draw such lines under the U.S. Constitution, thereby restricting U.S. government agents operating abroad, if they do not match the lines that would be drawn by the local courts where those agents operate. Why, for example, should the United States deny its agents, operating in country X, the freedom to squeeze packages on a bus if agents of country X do that just as regularly as U.S. airport security personnel inspect all baggage going through airports? But if such lines cannot be drawn on a global scale, then one is thrown back into an image of highly particularistic balancing of privacy and government interests, a methodology quite unrelated to actual Fourth Amendment jurisprudence.

I grant that this is a powerful concern, but as I have just given voice to it, it is exaggerated. There are three reasons to think that extending Fourth Amendment rights to NRAs would not, despite the preceding argument, be anomalous. First, the underlying task of determining when privacy interests are serious enough to put the burden on the government to show that it has sufficient reason to intrude on them makes as much sense outside the United States as inside it, as much sense for NRAs as for U.S. citizens. The task of creating standards that inform the citizenry of the conditions under which they have a sort of safe harbor for privacy cannot be carried out for NRAs. Their social norms will not be informed by U.S. courts. But that is not the only function of determining the balance. The other function is simply to provide U.S. courts with a reasonable sense of when they should hold the government to the task of justifying its intrusions on privacy. *That* task makes as much sense for cases involving NRAs as it does for cases involving residents of the United States.

Second, there is no reason why U.S. courts cannot start with the defaults established by the Supreme Court, and then leave it to the parties

---

[81] This is the sort of utility emphasized by Kerr, *supra* note 79.

to argue that local conditions call for an exception. That is, there is no reason why the U.S. government should not have the burden of showing that acts such as squeezing baggage on busses or reading emails do not intrude upon constitutionally protected privacy interests in some particular country, if indeed it thinks that is the case. And, from the other side, there is no reason why a person who feels violated, for example, by aerial photography of his property cannot argue that such snooping is so unheard of in his or her country that he or she has a constitutional interest in not being subject to it. It is important to remember that even if NRAs have a constitutional interest in not having their emails read, there may be sufficient reason for the government to do it. That's a separate stage of inquiry. The present point is only that courts could handle having to consider whether a different standard for the first stage of the inquiry should apply in a particular country. They can do so by looking to settled case law for a starting framework, and then placing the burden on the parties to argue for divergences from the standard templates.

Third, additional trouble for the U.S. government and courts is unlikely to arise from accommodating different conceptions of privacy. It is unlikely that nonresident aliens could often argue that they benefit from privacy protections that do not apply in the United States, at least not with regard to actions that the United States is likely to want to take. And the U.S. government would, presumably, rarely need to argue that privacy protections in another country are so low that it should be free there to engage in certain practices that would trigger Fourth Amendment concerns at home. Much of what it needs to gather information abroad are the techniques it can also use with regard to U.S. citizens abroad or aliens domestically,[82] contexts in which the Fourth Amendment undoubtedly applies. And if, on occasion, the U.S. government needs to use more aggressive information-gathering techniques, the more defensible and direct route by which the United States could try to justify its actions – if using techniques that would raise Fourth Amendment concerns in the United States[83] – would be to

---

[82] *See* Wittes's points about good intelligence analysis, *supra* notes 29–30 and accompanying text.

[83] Insofar as the NSA gets information that has been turned over to third parties, then no privacy rights are implicated. This is known as the third-party doctrine. *See* Katz, 389 U.S. at 351 ("What a person knowingly exposes to the public, even in his own home or office, is not a subject of Fourth Amendment protection."). Information such as the numbers one has dialed on one's phone counts as public in this way. *See* Smith v. Maryland, 442 U.S. 735 (1979). The content of one's email and voice communication does not count as

argue that in the context where they are being deployed, their use is reasonable, all things considered.

In sum, there is no reason why courts should find that entertaining complaints by NRAs, that their privacy rights have been unconstitutionally violated, should be impracticable or anomalous.

E   The Balance of Considerations

If it is granted that NRAs normally have a reasonable expectation of privacy with regard to the content of their private electronic communications, then the question is whether such an expectation can ground a right under the Fourth Amendment that could restrict the activities of the NSA. To answer that question, one must balance certain interests. As the Supreme Court pointed out in *Maryland v. King*, a court must "weigh the promotion of legitimate governmental interests against the degree to which the search intrudes upon an individual's privacy."[84]

There is no denying that the government has a legitimate and powerful interest in collecting information that may be relevant to preventing terrorist attacks. The questions with regard to FISA § 702 are, first, can it pursue that interest effectively while also respecting the privacy rights of NRAs? Second, is the interest in privacy great enough to outweigh the cost to the government of having to come up with sufficient individualized suspicion before intruding on the privacy of NRAs?

The only way these questions can be answered in favor of upholding the FISA section 702's permission for searching the content of private communications from NRAs, even without individualized suspicion, is if it can be argued (1) that the balance is not the same as it would be in the domestic context (where resident aliens enjoy the same protections as citizens), and (2) that the balance abroad should be different when spying

---

public in this way; the companies that carry it are not receivers of the information; they are mere conduits. See Katz, 389 U.S. at 352 (voice); United States v. Warshak, 631 F.3d 266, 288 (6th Cir. 2010) (email). This chapter assumes that the techniques the NSA is using cannot, in general, be justified under the third-party doctrine. Moreover, even if some techniques can, in that way, be justified, it is unclear that the third-party doctrine can be extended to the kind of general collection and processing of information that the government is now, in the internet age, capable of doing. See United States v. Jones, 132 S. Ct. 945, 957, 964 (2012) (five justices, in two separate concurring opinions, opining that the Fourth Amendment may limit the extent to which the government can track an individual's public information without a warrant).

[84] Maryland v. King, 133 S. Ct. 1958, 1970 (2013) (internal quotation marks omitted).

on U.S. citizens and NRAs. The first prong may be easy enough to establish: the U.S. government has a much richer set of police resources to determine who is suspicious inside the country than out; outside, barring extraordinarily good cooperation with foreign governments, it presumably needs the help of bulk signals intelligence. But the second prong is more difficult. It can be established only in two ways: either the need to spy on NRAs must be, as a general rule, greater than the need to spy on U.S. citizens, or NRAs must possess a weaker version of Fourth Amendment rights than U.S. citizens.

There is little reason to think that the need for information from NRAs is generally greater than from nonresident U.S. citizens. U.S. citizens abroad can engage in terrorism just as well as NRAs. And the NSA may be able to get individualized suspicion on NRAs and non-resident citizens with equal ease. Thus this first basis for striking a different balance between nonresident citizens and NRAs seems to come up short.

The second of these possibilities likewise should not ground an argument for different treatment of NRAs and citizens. The point has already been made that privacy is an important interest; harming it, when the person has a reasonable expectation of privacy, has to be justified. I also argued, in the longer version of this chapter that published elsewhere, that NRAs should enjoy those fundamental rights protections that protect them against unjust harms.[85] These include protections against unjustified harms, even if inflicted for the sake of improving the welfare of U.S. citizens. The balance of interests implicit in the distinction between justified and unjustified harms is exactly what is tracked by the distinction between reasonable and unreasonable searches and seizures. In other words, the Fourth Amendment protection that NRAs enjoy has to be the protection against *unreasonable* searches and seizures, the same protection that U.S. citizens enjoy.

F   Conclusion

I have argued here that NRAs enjoy Fourth Amendment rights not to have their private electronic communications intercepted by the NSA without the same sort of individualized suspicion that protects U.S. citizens. The argument relied on having established elsewhere that nothing in Supreme Court case law clearly implies that NRAs lack

---

[85] *See* Walen, *supra* note 10.

constitutional rights, and that the recent *Boumediene* opinion implies that NRAs have at least some fundamental constitutional rights: those that it would not be impracticable or anomalous for them to have. The argument also relies on having established, in the longer version of this chapter published elsewhere, that there are good normative reasons to hold that NRAs benefit from constitutional rights not to be unjustly harmed.

In this chapter, I build on that foundation. I have argued that NRAs benefit from the Fourth Amendment in a way that would prohibit the NSA from spying on their personal electronic communications without individualized suspicion. The argument appealed to three reasons. First, there is no case law blocking the recognition of Fourth Amendment rights for NRAs generally. Second, there are no good reasons why it is unreasonable – impracticable or anomalous – to extend Forth Amendment rights to NRAs. Finally, there is no reason why NRAs should enjoy Fourth Amendment protections less than non-resident citizens.[86]

This is a radical thesis, as it seems that even those who support a global right to privacy have thought it a claim too far. But at no point was the legal reasoning supporting it controversial. The fact that it is radical is a reflection only of the extent to which those who have opposed the idea that NRAs have constitutional rights have captured the legal imagination. Presumably this is furthered by fear that "we" are vulnerable to "them." But legal and moral legitimacy also requires recognizing how much "they" are vulnerable to "us." We cannot do whatever "we" want to "them." Basic principles of legality and legitimacy require the United States to recognize their rights, the rights of NRAs, which they might assert against "us."

This is also an important thesis because, unless the courts stand up for the Fourth Amendment rights of NRAs, they will remain vulnerable to excessive NSA spying. It may be true that the NSA is not currently violating their right to privacy – no more than it violates the privacy rights of U.S. citizens. But this fact, if it is a fact, depends on a Presidential Directive that this or the next President could revoke. The norms of good signals intelligence may imply that NRAs should

---

[86] One could object that no NRAs would have standing to bring the relevant suit. *See* Clapper v. Amnesty Int'l, 133 S. Ct. 1138 (2013) (holding that U.S. citizens did not have the standing to challenge the constitutionality of FISA § 702). I address this problem in a longer version of this chapter. *See* Alec Walen, *Fourth Amendment Rights for Nonresident Aliens*, 16 GERMAN L.J. 1131 (2015).

normally be safe from abusive NSA misuse of personal data. But there is no guarantee, outside of the Presidential Directive, that the NSA will continue to follow good signals intelligence protocol. The larger legislative framework in which the NSA operates provides no relevant constraints. As such, that framework should be deemed constitutionally invalid on its face.

11

Forget About It?

Harmonizing European and American Protections for Privacy, Free Speech, and Due Process

BY DAWN CARLA NUNZIATO

A Introduction

In May 2014, the Court of Justice of the European Union (CJEU) issued its decision in the case of *Google Spain SL v. Agencia Española de Protección de Datos* (*Google Spain*). This is the now-famous "right to be forgotten" decision, in which the Court ruled that a search engine operator like Google must, upon request from a data subject, remove links that result from searches for an individual's name when those results are "inadequate, irrelevant or no longer relevant, or excessive in relation to the purposes ... carried out by the operator of the search engine."[1] Since the decision was handed down, Google has received requests from European data subjects to remove over one million links to web sites containing information about them and has granted about 40 percent of these requests, including in cases where the web sites at issue contained personal information about their medical, sexual, reproductive, or past criminal activity.[2] Google has implemented the decision by removing links only within its European domains (such as Google.es or Google.de). But data subjects have recently argued that these privacy protections also should apply to a search engine's domains worldwide – to all of Google.com for example. European authorities have agreed that these privacy protections should be implemented globally.[3] Further, the

---

[1] Case C-131/12, Google Spain SL v. Agencia Española de Protección de Datos, 2014 E.C.R. 317, ¶ 94, http://eur-lex.europa.eu/legal-content/EN/TXT/?uri=CELEX:62012CJ0131 [hereinafter *Google Spain*].

[2] *See infra* notes 45–53 and accompanying text.

[3] *See, e.g.,* Samuel Gibbs, *French Data Regulator Rejects Google's Right-to-Be-Forgotten Appeal,* THE GUARDIAN (Sept. 21, 2015), www.theguardian.com/technology/2015/sep/21/french-google-right-to-be-forgotten-appeal (explaining that French data protection

Article 29 Data Protection Working Party – composed of all the data protection authorities in the European Union – has determined that these privacy protections should be implemented globally and not just on E.U. domains.[4] Can the European right to be forgotten be implemented in a manner that accords with U.S. constitutional rights?

Many U.S. commentators responded to the *Google Spain* decision by claiming that it was patently inconsistent with the First Amendment's free speech guarantee[5] and could not withstand constitutional scrutiny in the United States.[6] These commentators contend that if the United States passed a law granting individuals the right to demand that search engines remove links to web sites containing embarrassing, harmful, or offensive personal information about them, such a law would violate the First Amendment.[7]

This view is only partly correct. It fails to recognize the long history within the United States of protecting individuals' privacy rights – protections that have been rendered compatible with First Amendment freedoms.[8] Indeed, for the past century, individuals in the United States have vindicated their privacy rights by bringing actions under the tort of public disclosure of private facts and similar invasion of privacy torts,

---

authority Commission Nationale de l'Informatique et des Libertés (CNIL) ordered Google to remove links to websites containing information on French data subjects from all Google domains, not just from country-specific domains like Google.fr, and CNIL's president has rejected Google's appeal of this order).

[4] Article 29 Data Prot. Working Party, *Guidelines on the Implementation of the Court of Justice of the European Union Judgment on "Google Spain and Inc. v. Agencia Española de Protección de Datos (AEPD) and Mario Costeja González"* C-131/12, WP 225, at 9 (Nov. 26, 2014), http://ec.europa.eu/justice/data-protection/article-29/documentation/opinion-recommendation/files/2014/wp225_en.pdf [hereinafter Article 29 Data Prot. Working Party Guidelines].

[5] *See* U.S. Const. amend. I ("Congress shall make no law ... abridging the freedom of speech ...").

[6] *See, e.g.,* Andrew Hughes, *Does the U.S. Have an Answer to the European Right to Be Forgotten?*, 7 LANDSLIDE 18, 19 (2014) ("[B]oth supporters and detractors of the ECJ ruling agree that such a law is likely impossible in the United States."); Eric Goldman, *Primer on European Union's Right To Be Forgotten*, TECH. & MKTG. L. BLOG (Aug. 21, 2014), http://blog.ericgoldman.org/archives/2014/08/primer-on-european-unions-right-to-be-forgotten-excerpt-from-my-internet-law-casebook-bonus-linkwrap.htm ("The ECJ ruling shocked many Americans because American law would not permit a similar result.")

[7] *See, e.g.,* Jeffrey Toobin, *The Solace of Oblivion*, NEW YORKER (Sept. 29, 2014), www.newyorker.com/magazine/2014/09/29/solace-oblivion ("The American regard for freedom of speech, reflected in the First Amendment, guarantees that the Costeja judgment would never pass muster under U.S. law.").

[8] *See infra* notes 54–64 and accompanying text.

and such claims have often prevailed over First Amendment challenges where the information at issue is not of legitimate interest to the public.[9] Similarly, defamation and related laws allow individuals in the United States to vindicate their reputational and dignitary interests, and such claims have prevailed over First Amendment challenges where the information at issue is not of legitimate interest to the public and where the plaintiffs are not public figures.[10] Contrary to the assertions of the free speech advocates, the First Amendment does not grant the public an absolute right of access to information about other private individuals on matters that are not of public importance. The free speech guarantee does not provide absolute protection for the free flow of information where the content at issue embodies harmful, offensive, or embarrassing information about matters not of public importance. Providing individuals with the right to have links to such information about them removed from search engine results is therefore not necessarily inconsistent with substantive First Amendment freedoms.

The privacy protections recognized in the *Google Spain* decision are not necessarily incompatible with the *substantive* protections provided by U.S. free speech law and the balance U.S. courts have struck over time between privacy and free speech. Yet, as implemented, these privacy protections fail to comport with the *procedural* protections required under the U.S. Constitution. The U.S. Constitution requires that "sensitive tools"[11] be used to distinguish between protected speech and unprotected speech. In particular, the party whose speech is being censored must be provided with notice and an opportunity to be heard by an impartial decision-maker before such censorship occurs. Under the *Google Spain* decision, search engine operators like Google are required to remove links to information about a data subject without affording the publisher or content provider notice or an opportunity to be heard before such a removal decision is implemented. The European "right to be forgotten," as it is currently implemented, is inconsistent with the procedural safeguards for speech required under the United States Constitution.

B   The CJEU's "Right to be Forgotten"

The *Google Spain Case* originated in 2010, when Spanish attorney Mario Costeja González became aware that a Google search of his name

---

[9] *See infra* notes 65–95 and accompanying text.   [10] *Id.*
[11] Bantam Books v. Sullivan, 372 U.S. 58, 66 (1963).

returned links to a Spanish newspaper's 1998 archives containing a notice about the foreclosure of his home.[12] Costeja González claimed that this search result was in violation of his rights under the E.U. Data Protection Directive, which requires that personal data only be processed by data controllers insofar as the data is adequate, relevant, and not excessive in relation to the purpose for which the data is collected and processed.[13] Costeja González initiated proceedings against the newspaper *La Vanguardia* (in which the foreclosure notice originally appeared) and against Google Spain and Google Inc. before the Agencia Española de Protección de Datos (Spanish Data Protection Agency). Costeja González advanced two arguments. First, he argued that the archived notice itself should be removed by the newspaper or altered so that his personal data no longer appeared in connection with the notice.[14] Second, in the alternative, he argued that Google Spain and Google Inc. should be required to remove links to the notice when a search was performed on his name.[15]

The Spanish Data Protection Agency rejected Costeja González's complaint against *La Vanguardia*, observing that the publication of the notice was legally justified and indeed legally required by order of the Ministry of Labour and Social Affairs, which mandated the publication of the auction notice so as to secure as many bidders as possible on Costeja González's foreclosed home.[16] Accordingly, the actual content regarding Costeja González's home foreclosure was not removed from the newspaper's web site (and indeed remains there to this day[17]). But the Agency upheld the complaint against Google Spain and Google Inc., and required these search engines to stop linking to the *La Vanguardia* notice when Costeja González's name was searched.[18] Google Spain and Google Inc. brought actions challenging the Agency's decision before the Audiencia Nacional (National High Court) of Spain, and that court stayed those proceedings and referred the relevant questions to the CJEU.[19]

On the questions referred regarding the application of the E.U. Data Protection Directive, the CJEU reached three conclusions. First, the Court concluded that the search engine operators' activities fell within the scope of "processing personal data."[20] Second, it held that a search

---

[12] See *Google Spain*, *supra* note 1, ¶ 7.   [13] See *id.* ¶ 14.   [14] See *id.* ¶ 15.   [15] See *id.*
[16] See *id.* ¶ 16.
[17] See *Subhasta D'immobles* [Auction of Properties], La Vanguardia (Jan. 19, 1998), http://hemeroteca.lavanguardia.com/preview/1998/01/19/pagina-23/33842001/pdf.html.
[18] See *Google Spain*, *supra* note 1, ¶ 17.   [19] See *id.* ¶ 18.   [20] *Id.* ¶ 41.

engine operator is a "data controller."[21] And third, it concluded that the Directive applies to search engines based outside of Europe whose business operates and profits within Europe.[22] On the basis of these rulings the Court held that Google Inc. and Google Spain were bound by the Directive to process personal data of European data subjects only insofar as the processing was "adequate, relevant, and not excessive in relation to the purpose for which it is collected and/or further processed."[23] Therefore, the Court held, a data subject may require a search engine to remove information that does not comply with these requirements.[24] The Court concluded:

> [I]f it is found, following a request by the data subject ... that the inclusion in the list of results displayed following a search made on the basis of his name of the links to web pages published lawfully by third parties and containing true information relating to him personally is, at this point in time, incompatible with ... the directive because that information appears, having regard to all the circumstances of the case, to be *inadequate, irrelevant or no longer relevant, or excessive in relation to the purposes of the processing at issue* carried out by the operator of the search engine, *the information and links concerned in the list of results must be erased.*[25]

The Court qualified its ruling by observing that, in certain cases, the public's interest in accessing information about an individual who has a role in public life may outweigh the data subject's interest in having the link removed.[26] It noted: "[i]f it appeared, for particular reasons, such as the role played by the data subject in public life, that the interference with the [data subject's] fundamental rights is justified by the preponderant interest of the general public in having ... access to the information in question," then the links should not be removed.[27] Accordingly, the Court established a balancing test under which the search engine operator is required to weigh the data subject's interests in removal against the interests of the general public in accessing information of genuine import to the public.[28] In applying its balancing test, the Court concluded that the interests of the general public in accessing the information about Costeja González in this case did not outweigh his interests in securing removal of this information. The Court explained: "[S]ince in the case in point there do not appear to be particular reasons substantiating a preponderant interest of the public in having, in the context of such a

---

[21] *Id.*   [22] *See id.* ¶ 60.   [23] *Id.*   [24] *See id.* ¶ 88.   [25] *Id.* ¶ 94 (emphasis added).
[26] *See id.* ¶ 97.   [27] *Id.*   [28] *See id.* ¶ 98.

search, access to that information ... , the data subject may ... require those links to be removed from the list of results."[29]

On the issue of how exactly a search engine operator is to implement delisting requests from data subjects, the Court ruled that European data subjects have the right to approach the search engine operator directly with their delisting claims under the Directive and that the search engines must then make a determination whether to grant or deny the delisting request.[30] For this reason, the Court's decision does not merely provide a right of action for data subjects to raise in courts of law; rather, it provides a right of action for data subjects to bring directly to the search engines themselves. The search engines are required to implement a system for evaluating and complying with such requests. As the Court explained, "the data subject may address such a request directly to the operator of the search engine (the controller), which must then duly examine its merits [and determine whether to grant or deny the request]."[31] The Court's decision requires search engines like Google to act as the decision-maker to determine whether to grant or deny a data subject's delisting request in the first instance.[32]

C   Google's Interpretation and Implementation of the Decision

The *Google Spain* decision left a number of issues unresolved, even while search engine operators such as Google were expected to immediately implement a system to allow data subjects to submit delisting requests directly to the operators. In an attempt to secure further guidance on the substantive question of how to balance privacy interests against free speech interests, Google constituted a group of experts – the Advisory Council to Google on the Right to be Forgotten – and charged them with identifying a list of factors that Google should take into account in responding to data subjects' delisting requests.[33] The Council proposed a list of criteria that Google should consider in implementing the CJEU's decision. These criteria include: (1) the data subject's role in public life

---

[29] *Id.*   [30] *See id.* ¶ 77.

[31] Court of Justice of the European Union Press Release No. 70/14, Judgment in Case C-131/12, Google Spain SL, Google Inc. v. Agencia Española de Protección de Datos, Luxembourg (May 13, 2014), http://curia.europa.eu/jcms/upload/docs/application/pdf/2014-05/cp140070en.pdf.

[32] *See* Chapter 16 in this volume.

[33] *See* Final Report, Advisory Council to Google on the Right to be Forgotten, GOOGLE (Feb. 6, 2015), www.google.com/advisorycouncil [hereinafter Google Advisory Report].

(with private figures meriting greater privacy protection than public figures);[34] (2) the nature of the information (with information in the public interest – such as information relevant to political disclosure or relating to criminal activity – meriting greater free speech protections);[35] (3) the source of the content and the motivation to publish it (with information provided by recognized bloggers or professional journalistic entities meriting greater free speech protections);[36] and (4) the severity of a crime and the time that has elapsed since the crime occurred, in cases involving criminal activity (with the recentness and severity of crimes militating against delisting).[37]

Google also sought guidance on the procedures it should follow when administering the delisting regime, including whether to provide the affected content provider with notice and an opportunity to be heard in the context of Google's decision whether to delist the web site.[38] The CJEU's decision was silent on these matters, other than to insist that the search engine operator must duly examine the merits of the issue when the data subject brings a delisting request directly to the search engine operator.[39] The European advisory body on data protection and privacy – the Article 29 Data Protection Working Party – has determined that search engine operators should not inform content providers about an adverse decision even *after* it has been reached and has found that that there is "no legal basis" for giving notice in most circumstances.[40] The Google Advisory Council acknowledged that it had received conflicting advice on the question of notice. Still, the Google Advisory Council concluded that, as a matter of good practice, "the search engine should notify the publishers [of adverse delisting decisions that it had reached]

---

[34] *See id.* at 7.   [35] *See id.* at 9.   [36] *See id.* at 13.

[37] *See id.* at 14; *see also* Jodie Ginsburg, Advisory Council Meeting Brussels (Nov. 4, 2014) ("The current ability of searchers to find information about individuals who have had their conviction spent is incompatible with laws about rehabilitation, such as those in the UK.").

[38] *See* Google Advisory Report, *supra* note 33, at 17.

[39] *See supra* notes 16–32 and accompanying text.

[40] Article 29 Data Prot. Working Party Guidelines, *supra* note 4, at 10 ("Search engines should not as a general practice inform the webmasters of the pages affected by de-listing of the fact that some webpages cannot be acceded from the search engine in response to specific queries ... No provision in E.U. data protection law obliges search engines to communicate to original webmasters that results relating to their content have been de-listed. Such a communication is in many cases a processing of personal data and, as such, requires a proper legal ground in order to be legitimate.").

to the extent allowed by law."[41] Google is apparently adhering to this practice, and indicates in its transparency report that "[i]t is Google's policy to notify a webmaster when pages from their site are removed from our search results based on a legal request."[42] Notably, the CJEU's decision does not require search engine operators to provide notice of their delisting decisions. The Court also did not require that the content provider be given an opportunity to be heard before a delisting decision is made. The Article 29 Data Protection Working Party has indicated that notice, even if provided after the fact, would not be authorized by law in most circumstances.[43] This lack of emphasis on notice to affected content providers is in sharp contrast to the emphasis that the European privacy regime generally places on notice in the context of actions affecting privacy rights.[44]

Since the *Google Spain* decision was handed down in May 2014, Google has received requests to remove links to over one million URLs, and has complied with approximately 40 percent of such requests, removing links to nearly 500,000 URLs.[45] In its transparency report, Google has provided only general information about the types of removal requests it grants and the types that it denies. Specific information about removal requests granted by Google is difficult to acquire, but can be

---

[41] Google Advisory Report, *supra* note 33, at 17.

[42] EUROPEAN PRIVACY REQUESTS FOR SEARCH REMOVALS: FREQUENTLY ASKED QUESTIONS, GOOGLE www.google.com/transparencyreport/removals/europeprivacy/faq (last visited Nov. 28, 2015).

[43] *See* Article 29 Data Prot. Working Party Guidelines, *supra* note 4, at 10.

[44] *See, e.g.,* Directive 95/46/EC of the European Parliament and the Council on the Protection of Individuals with Regard to the Processing of Personal Data and on the Free Movement of Such Data, 1995 O.J. (L 281) 31, art. 2, § h, http://eur-lex.europa.eu/legal-content/EN/TXT/PDF/?uri=CELEX:31995L0046&from=en ("For the purposes of this Directive . . . 'the data subject's consent' shall mean any freely given specific and informed indication of his wishes by which the data subject signifies his agreement to personal data relating to him being processed."); Christine Nicholas, *A Select Survey of International Data Privacy Laws* 9, www.moffatt.com/wp-content/uploads/2014/05/InternationalData PrivacyLaws.pdf, ("E.U. data controllers must tell data subjects what information will be and has been collected, why it was collected, who collected it and who can access it.") (last visited Nov. 28, 2015); Antonella Galetta & Paul de Hert, *A European Perspective on Data Protection and Access Rights* 7, available at http://irissproject.eu/wp-content/uploads/2014/06/European-level-legal-analysis-Final1.pdf (". . . a proper protection of the data subjects' rights is not only linked to the exercise of access rights, but also to the obligation of data controllers to notify data subject[s] about the processing of their personal data.") (last visited Nov. 28, 2015).

[45] *See* EUROPEAN PRIVACY REQUESTS FOR SEARCH REMOVALS, GOOGLE, www.google.com/transparencyreport/removals/europeprivacy/?hl=en (last visited Nov. 28, 2015).

obtained from some sources. BBC News, for example, has created an archive of BBC web sites that have been delisted by Google upon request from data subjects.[46] A review of Google's transparency report and the BBC News archives of delisted websites provides a representative sample of the types of delisting requests Google has granted.

Google has granted data subjects' requests to remove links to websites containing various types of personal information about them, including information about their criminal, medical, sexual, and reproductive histories. In the area of crime reporting, for example, Google has removed links to web pages about an individual who had been convicted of a serious crime but whose conviction was quashed on appeal.[47] It has removed links to articles discussing a crime with the victim's name listed, upon request from the victim of the crime.[48] Google has removed links to news stories identifying a lesbian couple who conceived their children from sperm from an anonymous sperm donor.[49] It removed links to a news story identifying a young woman with facial palsy, which included her first name and an accompanying picture of her and disclosed the fact that she attempted suicide.[50] It removed links to an article identifying a woman who suffered from diabetes during her pregnancy and who did not receive proper prenatal care for this disease.[51] It removed links to news stories about the experience of living with HIV that named and highlighted the experience of two individuals living with the virus.[52] It removed links to several articles quoting and describing the personal experiences and reproductive histories of individuals who had been diagnosed with testicular cancer.[53]

Google appears to be working diligently to implement the delisting process mandated by the CJEU's decision. In many cases, as I explore below, Google's determination that the data subject's privacy rights prevail over the content provider's free speech interests might well

---

[46] See Neil McIntosh, *List of BBC Web Pages Which Have Been Removed from Google's Search Results*, BBC, www.bbc.co.uk/blogs/internet/entries/1d765aa8-600b-4f32-b110-d02fbf7fd379 (last visited Nov. 28, 2015) [hereinafter BBC Delistings]

[47] See European Privacy Requests for Search Removals, *supra* note 45.   [48] *See id.*

[49] See BBC Delistings, *supra* note 46 (delisting http://news.bbc.co.uk/2/hi/uk_news/8229401.stm).

[50] See id. (delisting www.bbc.co.uk/newsbeat/article/20357076/facial-palsy-left-me-isolated-and-bullied).

[51] See id. (delisting http://news.bbc.co.uk/2/hi/health/6390421.stm).

[52] See id. (delisting www.bbc.com/news/health-15982608).

[53] See id. (delisting www.bbc.co.uk/wales/bllcks/me_and_mine).

comport with the outcome that would be reached under substantive U.S. law. The First Amendment does not grant the public an absolute right to access information about other private individuals on matters that are not of public importance, and privacy law in the United States grants private individuals rights and remedies against the publication of embarrassing, harmful content that invades their privacy. But, as I explain below, the *process* through which Google has implemented the CJEU's decision fails to provide the procedural safeguards necessary for the protection of speech under the U.S. Constitution – and indeed under fundamental notions of due process shared by both the U.S. and the European legal systems.

D   Substantive Law: Balancing Privacy and Free Speech Rights Within the United States

The United States' regime for protecting individual privacy – and for protecting freedom of expression – includes meaningful tools to protect individual privacy. Courts have frequently held that individuals' privacy rights under state or federal law trump publishers' free speech rights.[54] Indeed, individuals' privacy rights have prevailed over free speech rights in circumstances similar to those in which Google is now granting delisting requests under its obligations under the *Google Spain* decision. First, federal laws such as the Fair Credit Reporting Act restrict the ability of consumer reporting agencies to report on bankruptcies and criminal proceedings that are beyond a certain number of years old.[55] Second, expungement laws in almost every state allow individuals to have certain criminal records expunged – such that all records of the arrest or court case involving the crime are destroyed, sealed, or otherwise removed from the public record.[56] Third, the common law of defamation grants private individuals meaningful rights and remedies against the publication of false information about them that damages their reputation.[57]

---

[54] *See infra* notes 54–92 and accompanying text.

[55] *See* 15 U.S.C. § 1681 (2012). *See generally* Daniel J. Solove, *Access and Aggregation: Privacy, Public Records, and the Constitution*, 86 MINN. L. REV. 6 (2002) (arguing that attempts to limit the use and accessibility of public records do not violate the First Amendment rights to access government information and to freedom of speech and press).

[56] George L. Blum, *Annotation, Judicial Expunction of Criminal Record of Convicted Adult Under Statute*, 69 A.L.R. 6th 1 (2011).

[57] *See* Dun & Bradstreet v. Greenmoss Builders, 472 U.S. 749 (1985).

Fourth, and most significantly, common law privacy protections provide individuals with the power to effectively combat the publication of information about them that is embarrassing, harmful, or otherwise invasive of their privacy.[58] Such privacy protections have been rendered compatible with the strong free speech and free press rights provided by the First Amendment.[59]

The First Amendment does not erect a barrier to liability for publishing embarrassing, offensive, or other harmful private information about another, where that information is not a matter of legitimate public concern. The Supreme Court has made clear that, in balancing an individual's privacy and reputational interests against free speech interests, the First Amendment's strongest protections extend to information on matters of legitimate public concern, as distinguished from information of purely private concern.[60] While the Court has held that the state may not "constitutionally punish publication of [truthful] information ... about a matter of public significance,"[61] it has also emphasized that the First Amendment's strongest protections are reserved for information on matters of public significance or concern – not on matters of private significance or concern: "Speech on matters of purely private concern is of less First Amendment concern [than speech on matters of public concern]."[62] In cases involving liability for or regulation of speech on matters of private concern the Court has ruled that "[t]here is no threat to the free and robust debate of public issues [and] there is no potential interference with a meaningful dialogue of ideas concerning self-government."[63] Accordingly, the Court has concluded that "[w]hile speech [on matters of private concern] is not totally unprotected by the First Amendment ... its protections are less stringent."[64]

Today, under the privacy laws of most of the American states, the publication of offensive content about an individual on a matter of private concern constitutes an actionable invasion of privacy under the tort claim referred to as "the public disclosure of private fact." As set forth in the Restatement (Second) of Torts, this claim consists in:

---

[58] *See infra* notes 64–92 and accompanying text.
[59] *See infra* notes 60–95 and accompanying text.
[60] *See, e.g.,* Dun & Bradstreet v. Greenmoss Builders, 472 U.S. 749 (1985); Daniel J. Solove, *The Virtues of Knowing Less: Justifying Protections Against Disclosure,* 53 DUKE L. J. 967 (2003) (speech of private concern is less valuable than speech of public concern).
[61] Smith v. Daily Mail Pub. Co., 443 U.S. 97, 103 (1979).
[62] Dun & Bradstreet, 472 U.S. at 759.   [63] *Id.* at 760.   [64] *Id.*

> One who gives publicity to a matter concerning the private life of another is subject to liability to the other for invasion of privacy, if the matter is of a kind that:
>
> (a) would be highly offensive to a reasonable person and
> (b) is not of legitimate concern to the public.[65]

Importantly, truth does not serve as an affirmative defense to a claim brought under this tort claim.[66] Further, the First Amendment does not provide a defense to this tort where the content at issue is on a matter of private concern and is not of legitimate concern to the public or legitimately "newsworthy."[67]

This tort claim encompasses various types of invasions of privacy, including the making available of offensive personal information about an individual's criminal, medical, or sexual history, or other aspects of one's private life, if such information is not of legitimate concern to the public and if publication would be offensive to a reasonable person.[68] There are many court decisions involving individuals who have successfully recovered damages for[69] (or secured an injunction to prevent[70]) the publication of truthful, non-newsworthy, offensive information about them.[71] An examination of representative recent cases demonstrates that the result reached by Google in balancing privacy against free speech interests in implementing its delisting regime is not inconsistent with the balance that might be struck by courts in the United States in similar cases, notwithstanding the protections of the First Amendment. U.S. courts have repeatedly held that the publication of embarrassing medical,

---

[65] RESTATEMENT (SECOND) OF TORTS § 652D (AM. LAW INST. 1977).

[66] See 62A AM. JUR. 2D Privacy § 175 (2011) ("Truth, while a defense to an action of libel, is not a defense to an action for an invasion of the right of privacy.") (footnotes omitted).

[67] See, e.g., Amy Gajda, Judging Journalism: The Turn Toward Privacy and Judicial Regulation of the Press, 97 CALIF. L. REV. 1039 (2009).

[68] Restatement (Second) of Torts § 652D cmt. b (Am. Law Inst. 1977) ("Sexual relations . . . are normally entirely private matters, as are family quarrels, many unpleasant or disgraceful or humiliating illnesses . . . most details of a man's life in his home, and some of his past history that he would rather forget. When these intimate details of his life are spread before the public gaze in a manner highly offensive to the ordinary reasonable man, there is an actionable invasion of his privacy, unless the matter is one of legitimate public interest.").

[69] See infra notes 74–94 and accompanying text.

[70] See, e.g., Commonwealth v. Wisemen, 249 N.E.2d 610 (Mass. 1969) (Court restrains the distribution of documentary film Titicut Follies, which showed inmates of state hospital for the criminally insane nude and in otherwise embarrassing detail, on the grounds that the documentary needlessly invaded the privacy of the mentally ill subjects).

[71] See infra notes 74–94 and accompanying text.

sexual, reproductive, financial, or other private personal information may constitute the basis of a "public disclosure of private fact" tort claim and that such publication is not protected by the First Amendment.[72] Plaintiffs may secure injunctive relief or damages for violation of their privacy rights in such circumstances.[73]

The case of *Doe v. Mills* is illustrative.[74] In that case, several women who were about to undergo abortions brought suit against individuals who were protesting outside an abortion clinic and who displayed plaintiffs' names on large signs, indicating that the women were about to undergo this procedure while imploring them not to "kill their babies." Ruling in the plaintiffs' favor on their "public disclosure of private fact" tort claim, the court held that matters involving an individual's reproductive decisions and medical treatment were private, and that, despite the fact that the subject of abortion in general was a matter of public concern, the identity of these women was a matter of private concern and defendants had no right to publish such information about them.[75]

Similarly, courts have held that publication of matters involving an individual's romantic or sexual relationships may form the basis of a "public disclosure of private fact" tort claim. In *Benz v. Washington Newspaper Publishing Co.*, the plaintiff – a CNN assignment editor – brought suit against a Washington newspaper for publishing a story in its gossip column about the plaintiff's romantic and sexual relations.[76] The court rejected the newspaper's newsworthiness/First Amendment defense and ruled in the plaintiff's favor on her "public disclosure of private fact" tort claim, holding that the plaintiff's personal romantic life was not a matter of public concern. Again, in *Winstead v. Sweeney*, the plaintiff brought a "public disclosure of private fact" tort action against a newspaper for its publication of a feature article on "unique love relationships" in which the plaintiff's ex-husband was quoted revealing personal facts about her sexual and reproductive history, including that she had had several abortions and had joined him in "swapping" partners with another couple.[77] Reversing the trial court's holding that the First Amendment protected the newspaper's

---

[72] *Id.*
[73] *See* Wisemen, 249 N.E.2d at 610 (granting injunctive relief); *See also infra* notes 74–92 and accompanying text (discussing cases granting damages).
[74] Doe v. Mills, 212 Mich. App. 73, 77 (1995).   [75] *See id.* at 84.
[76] *See* Benz v. Washington Newspaper Publ'g Co., 34 Media L. Rep. 2368 (D.D.C. 2006).
[77] Winstead v. Sweeney, 205 Mich. App. 664, 677 (1994).

publication of the story, the appellate court held that the article at issue was not necessarily newsworthy.[78]

Courts have also held that the publication of information about an individual's medical treatment can form the basis of a "public disclosure of private fact" tort claim. A recent case from Georgia involving the publication of hair transplant photographs is illustrative. In *Zieve v. Hairston*, Celento Hairston sued Ronald Zieve and the National Hair Transplant Specialists for airing television commercials depicting before and after pictures of Hairston's hair replacement treatments.[79] Although Hairston had consented to the pictures being broadcast in a limited geographic area, he did not consent to their broadcast near his Georgia home where he had taken steps to keep his hair replacement treatments a secret.[80] Ruling in Hairston's favor, the court held that all three elements of the "public disclosure of private fact" tort claim had been met: "(1) the disclosure of private facts was a public one; (2) the facts disclosed were private, secluded, or secret facts; and (3) the matter made public was offensive and objectionable to a reasonable person of ordinary sensibilities under the circumstances."[81]

In a similar case involving the broadcast of truthful but embarrassing information, a Florida court in *Doe v. Universal Television Grp.* ruled in favor of a woman who had undergone a botched facelift.[82] In that case Doe had agreed to be interviewed on camera in the context of a program about overseas facelift surgeries that had gone wrong, on the condition that her identity – including her image and her voice – be rendered unidentifiable.[83] When the broadcast instead revealed her face and voice in a manner that made it possible to identify her, *Doe* brought a "public disclosure of private fact" tort action against the broadcaster. The court ruled in her favor, rejecting the broadcaster's newsworthiness/First Amendment defense.[84]

In another case involving the broadcast of an individual's likeness, in *Multimedia WMAZ v. Kubach*, an AIDS patient prevailed against a television station that aired seven seconds of his face in the context of a story about AIDS, in violation of the station's express promise to depict his face in a manner that was unrecognizable.[85] The case *Huskey v. NBC* also fits with this jurisprudence.[86] In that case the court ruled that a

---

[78] *Id.* at 674.   [79] *See* Zieve v. Hairston, 266 Ga. App. 753 (2004).   [80] *Id.* at 757.
[81] *Id.* at 756.   [82] *See* Doe v. Universal Television Grp. 717 So. 2d 63 (1988).
[83] *Id.* at 64.   [84] *Id.* at 65.
[85] *See* Multimedia WMAZ v. Kubach, 212 Ga. App. 707 (1994).
[86] *See* Huskey v. NBC, 632 F. Supp. 1282 (N.D.Ill. 1986).

prisoner in a federal penitentiary could proceed with his "public disclosure of private fact" lawsuit against NBC for filming him working out in the prison's exercise room wearing only shorts and with several distinctive tattoos exposed.[87] The court rejected NBC's newsworthiness/First Amendment defense and ruled that Huskey, although a prisoner, did not forgo his privacy rights in his image.[88]

Individuals have also successfully brought "public disclosure of private fact" cases in U.S. courts based on the publication of information about their reproductive and sexual practices and choices. For example, in *Y.G. v. Jewish Hosp. of St. Louis*, the plaintiffs brought suit against a hospital and a television station for broadcasting images of them attending a hospital function commemorating the success of an *in vitro* fertilization program in which they had participated.[89] Although the plaintiffs openly attended the function, they had been assured by the hospital that only persons involved in the IVF program would attend and that no publicity would result.[90] Rejecting the station's newsworthiness/First Amendment defense, the court ruled in favor of the plaintiffs on their public disclosure of private fact claim.[91]

U.S. courts have also held that the publication of personal financial information can form the basis of a "public disclosure of private fact" claim. In *Johnson v. Sawyer*, for example, Johnson successfully sued the Internal Revenue Service (IRS) and the United States government for the disclosure of information from Johnson's tax returns.[92] Johnson had pleaded guilty to crimes involving financial impropriety and had disclosed the financial information at issue to the IRS.[93] Still, the court held that he had not waived his privacy interest in such information and that his financial information was not of legitimate concern to the public.[94]

In sum, privacy law in the United States generally provides individuals with meaningful rights and remedies in circumstances where their personal information has been disclosed or published by another in a manner that is offensive, notwithstanding the protections accorded by the First Amendment. Individuals have successfully invoked the "public disclosure of private fact" tort in many instances to vindicate their privacy interests in their medical, sexual, reproductive, financial and

---

[87] *See id.* at 1292.   [88] *See id.*
[89] *See* Y.G. v. Jewish Hosp. of St. Louis, 795 S.W.2d 488 (Mo. Ct. App. 1990).
[90] *See id.* at 492.   [91] *See id.* at 503.
[92] *See* Johnson v. Sawyer, 129 F.3d 1307 (5th Cir. 1997).   [93] *See id.* at 1309.
[94] *See id.* at 1324.

other personal information, and the First Amendment provides no defense for those who publish[95] or disclose information that would be highly offensive to the reasonable person and is not of legitimate concern to the public. The balance struck by Google in responding to hundreds of thousands of delisting requests after the *Google Spain* decision is not necessarily dissimilar to or inconsistent with the balance that has been struck by U.S. courts in weighing privacy and free speech rights.

E   Procedural Law: According Due Process to Parties Whose Free Speech Rights Are Affected

The balance Google has struck between privacy and free speech rights when responding to delisting requests under the *Google Spain* decision may not be inconsistent with substantive First Amendment freedoms. But the procedures Google has followed when implementing the CJEU's *Google Spain* decision are inconsistent with the due process provisions of the U.S. Constitution[96] – and with fundamental, shared notions of due process generally.[97] A fundamental component of due process is that individuals be accorded *notice* and an *opportunity to be heard* by an impartial decision-maker *before* a decision affecting their rights is rendered.[98] Even assuming that Google is such an impartial

---

[95] Notably, U.S. *statutory* law provides search engines and other Internet intermediaries with immunity for hosting content that invades the privacy of others. *See* Communications Decency Act, 47 U.S.C. § 230(c) (2012); Carafano v. Metrosplash, 339 F.3d 1119 (9th Cir. 2003) (interpreting Section 230(c) to require dismissal of plaintiff's invasion of privacy claim against dating website). But this statutory immunity accorded under Section 230(c) is not mandated by the First Amendment, and may be amended. *See, e.g.*, Petition to Amend Communications Decency Act Section 230, CHANGE, https://www.change.org/p/the-u-s-senate-amend-communications-decency-act-section-230 (last visited Nov. 28, 2015).

[96] *See* U.S. CONST. amend. V ("[N]or shall any person . . . be deprived of life, liberty, or property, without due process of law . . ."); U.S. CONST. amend. XIV, § 1 ("[N]or shall any State deprive any person of life, liberty, or property, without due process of law . . ."); *See also infra* notes 105–28 and accompanying text (setting forth procedures required under the Due Process Clauses before fundamental rights – including free speech rights – may be abridged).

[97] *See infra* notes 109–13 and accompanying text (discussing due process rights under the Universal Declaration of Human Rights and the European Convention on Human Rights).

[98] *See, e.g.*, Cleveland Board of Education v. Loudermill, 470 U.S. 532, 542 (1985) ("In most circumstances procedural due process principles require the state to provide an individual with notice and a hearing before an impartial decision-maker prior to the deprivation of a life, liberty, or property interest."); Marshall v. Jerrico, Inc., 446 U.S. 238, 242 (1980)

decision-maker,[99] the procedure by which it is administering delisting decisions is deficient because – under the guidance provided by European data protection authorities – Google provides neither notice nor an opportunity to be heard to the affected content providers before their free speech rights are determined. The Article 29 Data Protection Working Party concluded that the provision of notice to affected content providers regarding a delisting decision is problematic and has no basis in law.[100] While Google is apparently attempting to provide notice to affected content providers *after* it has reached an adverse decision,[101] such after-the-fact notice is insufficient to satisfy the requirements of due process.

This lack of prior notice to individuals whose free speech rights are implicated is problematic and indeed is in sharp contrast to the emphasis European privacy law places on according notice to individuals before their *privacy* rights are implicated. Under European law, those responsible for controlling data are required to provide meaningful notice to a

("[w]hen someone's ... liberty ... interest is going to be taken by the government, procedural due process principles normally will require that the person receive notice and a hearing prior to the deprivation of the constitutionally protected interest"); Mullane v. Central Hanover Trust Co., 339 U.S. 306, 314 (1950) ("An elementary and fundamental requirement of due process in any proceeding which is to be accorded finality is notice reasonably calculated, under all the circumstances, to apprise interested parties of the pendency of the action and afford them an opportunity to present their objections.").

[99] Impartial decision-makers are those that do not have bias or predisposition against either affected party or side. *See, e.g.,* Marshall v. Jerrico, Inc., 446 U.S. 238, 242 (1980) ("The Due Process Clause entitles a person to an impartial and disinterested tribunal in both civil and criminal cases ... ensuring that no person will be deprived of his interests in the absence of a proceeding in which he may present his case with assurance that the arbiter is not predisposed to find against him."); RONALD D. ROTUNDA & JOHN E. NOWAK 3 TREATISE ON CONSTITUTIONAL LAW: SUBSTANCE AND PROCEDURE § 17.8(g) ("Decision makers are constitutionally unacceptable where they have a personal monetary interest in the outcome of the adjudication or where they are professional competitors of the individual").

[100] *See* Article 29 Data Prot. Working Party Guidelines, *supra* note 4, at 3. The Article 29 Working Party has concluded that *no notice or opportunity to be heard* can or should be provided to the content providers. In its guidelines, the Working Party concluded that "[s]earch engines should not as a general practice inform the webmasters of the pages affected by de-listing of the fact that some web pages cannot be accessed from the search engine in response to a specific name-based query. There is no legal basis for such routine communication under E.U. data protection law." *Id.*

[101] *See* EUROPEAN PRIVACY REQUESTS FOR SEARCH REMOVALS: FREQUENTLY ASKED QUESTIONS, GOOGLE www.google.com/transparencyreport/removals/europeprivacy/faq (last visited Nov. 28, 2015).

data subject before processing a data subject's personal data – including what data will be collected, why it was collected, who collected it, and who can access it.[102] Indeed, the preeminent value on which the E.U. Data Protection Directive was founded is the principle of notice to affected data subjects.[103] It is therefore particularly problematic that decision-makers like Google, in the context of implementing the CJEU's *Google Spain* decision, are not required to provide notice to affected individuals before their free speech rights are implicated.

Providing notice *after the fact* to individuals or entities whose rights are adversely affected without according them an opportunity to be heard before a decision affecting their rights is rendered – while better than no notice at all – is inconsistent with the fundamental requirements of the rule of law and principles of due process. A fundamental component of living under the rule of law is that an individual should be accorded due process in connection with the determination of his or her rights. Due process of law requires that an individual be granted the opportunity to be heard and to state her case to an impartial decision-maker before she is deprived of her fundamental rights – including her right to freedom of expression.[104] The United States Constitution's Due Process provisions require that individuals be provided with fundamental protections before the state can abridge their right to freedom of expression. Fundamental principles of due process require that any such deprivation of individuals' right to freedom of expression occur only as a result of a fair,

---

[102] *See, e.g.,* Directive 95/46/EC of the European Parliament and the Council on the Protection of Individuals with Regard to the Processing of Personal Data and on the Free Movement of Such Data, 1995 O.J. (L 281) 31, art. 2, § h, http://eur-lex.europa.eu/legal-content/EN/TXT/PDF/?uri=CELEX:31995L0046&from=en ("For the purposes of this Directive ... 'the data subject's consent' shall mean any freely given specific and informed indication of his wishes by which the data subject signifies his agreement to personal data relating to him being processed."); Christine Nicholas, *A Select Survey of International Data Privacy Laws* 9, www.moffatt.com/wp-content/uploads/2014/05/InternationalDataPrivacyLaws.pdf, ("E.U. data controllers must tell data subjects what information will be and has been collected, why it was collected, who collected it and who can access it."); Antonella Galetta & Paul de Hert, *A European Perspective on Data Protection and Access Rights* 7, http://irissproject.eu/wp-content/uploads/2014/06/European-level-legal-analysis-Final1.pdf (" ... a proper protection of the data subjects' rights is not only linked to the exercise of access rights, but also to the obligation of data controllers to notify data subject[s] about the processing of their personal data.").

[103] *See* Margaret Rouse, *E.U. Data Protection Directive (Directive 95/46/EC)*, SEARCHSECURITY. CO.UK http://searchsecurity.techtarget.co.uk/definition/EU-Data-Protection-Directive (last visited Nov. 28, 2015).

[104] *See infra* notes 114–28 and accompanying text.

independent, and impartial decision-making process in which affected
parties are provided with meaningful notice and an opportunity to be
heard before a decision is rendered.

The right to due process of law in general is of ancient origin and has
its roots in early English and American law. The right can be traced to
Magna Carta, which provides that "No freeman shall be ... disseised ...
of his liberties ... except ... by the law of the land."[105] One of the earliest
express provisions for such procedural protections of individual rights is
provided in the Fifth Amendment to the U.S. Constitution, which provides that "no person shall ... be deprived of ... liberty ... without due
process of law."[106] Similar language was included in the Fourteenth
Amendment to the U.S. Constitution, providing that "No State shall ...
deprive any person of ... liberty ... without due process of law."[107] Since
the 1800s, procedural due process has been linked to the concept of the
rule of law, in both the U.S. Constitution and subsequently in international and European instruments as well.[108]

In the mid-twentieth century, the drafters of the Universal Declaration
of Human Rights recognized the importance of protecting due process
rights, providing in Article 10 that "Everyone is entitled in full equality to
a fair and public hearing by an independent and impartial tribunal, in the
determination of his rights and obligations ..."[109] The European Convention on Human Rights was the first international human rights
instrument to set forth detailed protections for due process and fair trial
rights. With respect to the determination of civil rights and obligations,
Article 6 of the European Convention provides for the general right to
procedural fairness, including a hearing before a fair, independent, and
impartial tribunal that provides a reasoned judgment. Specifically, Article
6(1) states that "In the determination of his civil rights and
obligations ... everyone is entitled to a fair and public hearing within a
reasonable time by an independent and impartial tribunal established by
law."[110] Article 14 of the International Covenant similarly provides, "[i]n
the determination of ... his rights and obligations ... everyone shall be
entitled to a fair and public hearing by a competent, independent and

---

[105] RICHARD CLAYTON QC & HUGH TOMLINSON QC, THE LAW OF HUMAN RIGHTS 708
    (2009) (quoting clause 39 of Magna Carta of 1215) [hereinafter Clayton & Tomlinson].
[106] U.S. CONST. amend. V.   [107] U.S. CONST. amend. XIV, § 1.
[108] See Clayton & Tomlinson, *supra* note 105, at 709.
[109] G.A. Res. 217 art. 10, Universal Declaration of Human Rights (Dec. 10, 1948).
[110] European Convention for the Protection of Human Rights and Fundamental Freedoms,
    art. 6(1), Nov. 4, 1950, 213 U.N.T.S. 222.

impartial tribunal established by law."[111] In each of these foundational documents and instruments, procedural due process rights and the right to independent, impartial, and fair judicial determinations of one's civil and human rights are recognized as necessary for the meaningful protection of substantive rights, including the right to freedom of expression. Article 6 of the European Convention guarantees procedural fairness "whenever there is a 'determination' of a 'civil right or obligation.'"[112] The European Court of Human Rights has emphasized the centrality of the rights of procedural due process articulated in Article 6(1) and has affirmed that an expansive view of these rights is fundamental to protecting civil and human rights:

> In a democratic society within the meaning of the Convention the right to a fair administration of justice holds such a prominent place that a restrictive interpretation of Article 6(1) would not correspond to the aim and purpose of that provision.[113]

U.S. courts have repeatedly emphasized the importance of due process protections and have held that such protections apply specifically in the context of the deprivation of one's right to freedom of expression. As constitutional commentators Rotunda and Nowak explain,

> In their procedural aspects, the due process clauses require that the government not restrict a specific individual's freedom to exercise a fundamental constitutional right without a process to determine the basis for the restriction ... [In particular,] whenever the government seeks to restrain speech, there must be a prompt procedure to determine whether the speech may be limited in conformity with First Amendment principles.[114]

Before the state deprives an individual of a substantial liberty interest such as the right to freedom of expression, the individual must be accorded: adequate notice of the basis for government action; an opportunity to be heard by the decision-maker; and a determination by an

---

[111] International Covenant on Civil and Political Rights, art. 14, Dec. 16, 1966, 999 U.N.T.S. 171.

[112] European Convention for the Protection of Human Rights and Fundamental Freedoms, art. 6, Nov. 4, 1950, 213 U.N.T.S. 222.

[113] *See* Delcourt v. Belgium (1970), 1 Eur. Ct. H.R. 355, ¶ 25, *cited in* Clayton & Tomlinson, *supra* note 105, at 824.

[114] 3 RONALD D. ROTUNDA & JOHN E. NOWAK, TREATISE ON CONSTITUTIONAL LAW § 17.4 (c), at 85 (5th ed. 2012).

impartial decision-maker.[115] Importantly, when the state seeks to authorize a restriction on an individual's freedom of expression, prior notice to
that individual must be provided: "An elementary and fundamental requirement of due process in any proceeding . . . is notice reasonably calculated,
under all the circumstances, to appraise interested parties of the . . . action
and afford them an opportunity to present their objections."[116] In summary,
a basic requirement of due process of law is that individuals be accorded
notice and an opportunity to be heard by an impartial decision-maker
before a decision adversely affecting their rights is rendered.

In addition, First Amendment jurisprudence embodies its own
requirements of due process. The First Amendment's protection for
freedom of expression not only embodies a substantive dimension of
which categories of speech to protect; it also embodies procedural
dimensions, which require that "sensitive tools" be implemented by
decision-makers to determine whether the speech at issue is protected
or unprotected.[117] As free speech theorist Henry Monaghan explains,
"procedural guarantees play an equally large role in protecting freedom
of speech; indeed, they assume an importance fully as great as the validity
of the substantive rule of law to be applied."[118] U.S. courts have constructed a powerful "body of procedural law which defines the manner in
which they and other bodies must evaluate and resolve [free speech]
claims – [establishing] a First Amendment due process."[119] In implementing the First Amendment's protections for free speech, courts have
developed "a comprehensive system of procedural safeguards designed to
obviate the dangers of a censorship system."[120]

Under the Supreme Court's First Amendment jurisprudence, any
government-mandated restriction of speech must be accompanied by
review by an impartial decision-maker and such review must afford the
affected parties notice and an opportunity to be heard before the
decision-maker renders its decision.[121] The Court's decision in *Bantam
Books v. Sullivan* is illustrative.[122] This case involved a system for

---

[115] *See id.*   [116] Mullane v. Central Hanover Bank & Trust Co., 339 U.S. 306, 314 (1950).
[117] Bantam Books v. Sullivan, 372 U.S. 58, 66 (1963).
[118] Henry Monaghan, *First Amendment "Due Process,"* 83 Harv. L. Rev. 518 (1970)
(internal quotations omitted).
[119] *Id.*   [120] *Id.* (internal quotations omitted).
[121] *See* United States v. Thirty-Seven Photographs, 402 U.S. 363, 372–74; Kingsley Books,
Inc. v. Brown, 354 U.S. 436 (1957); Interstate Circuit, Inc. v. City of Dallas, 390 U.S. 676
(1968); Bantam Books, Inc. v. Sullivan, 372 U.S. 58 (1963).
[122] *See* Sullivan, 372 U.S. 58.

determining which books were legal and which were illegal – in the absence of a procedure that accorded the affected speakers notice and an opportunity to be heard by an impartial decision-maker. In that case, the Rhode Island Commission to Encourage Morality in Youth was charged with investigating and recommending prosecution of booksellers for the distribution of obscene or indecent printed works.[123] The Commission reviewed books and magazines in circulation, and notified distributors in cases in which a book or magazine had been distributed that the Commission found objectionable and for which removal from distribution was ordered.[124] In reviewing the constitutionality of this scheme, the Supreme Court first explained that "the separation of legitimate from illegitimate speech calls for . . . . sensitive tools" and insisted that any such restriction on expression must "scrupulously embody the most rigorous procedural safeguards."[125] The Court condemned the fact that, under the scheme at issue, "the publisher or distributor is not even entitled to *notice and hearing* before his publications are listed by the Commission as objectionable [and ordered for removal]," as well as the fact that there was "no provision whatever for *judicial superintendence* before notices issue or even for *judicial review* of the Commission's determinations of objectionableness."[126] The Court concluded that, in the absence of these essential procedural safeguards, the "procedures of the Commission are radically deficient" and unconstitutional.[127] Courts have similarly held that restrictions on Internet speech that fail to accord these procedural safeguards are constitutionally deficient. In *CDT v. Pappert*, for example, the court held unconstitutional a statute that required the blocking of web sites that allegedly hosted child pornography, where the affected content provider was not provided with notice and an opportunity to be heard by an impartial decision-maker before the blocking became effective.[128]

The Supreme Court has consistently emphasized the importance of providing affected individuals with notice and an opportunity to be heard by an impartial decision-maker before an individual's right to free speech is abridged. Absent such procedural safeguards, state-authorized restrictions on expression are unconstitutional. Under the First Amendment, notice, opportunity to be heard, and a fair determination of one's free speech rights by an impartial decision-maker are essential procedural safeguards.

---

[123] *See id.* at 59.   [124] *See id.* at 61.   [125] *Id.* at 66.   [126] *Id.* at 71 (emphasis added).
[127] *Id.*   [128] *See* CDT v. Pappert, 337 F. Supp. 2d 606 (E.D. Pa. 2004).

In summary, both the Due Process Clause of the United States Constitution and the First Amendment itself require that *before* an individual's speech is restricted through a state-authorized process – including the regime being implemented by Google under the mandates of the CJEU's *Google Spain* decision – affected parties must be accorded notice and have an opportunity to be heard in an impartial decision-making proceeding. European data privacy law similarly recognizes the importance of providing notice to parties whose civil rights are implicated. Indeed, the requirement of prior notice is an essential element of fundamental conceptions of due process shared by both the U.S. and European legal systems. Even if – and this is a big if – Google is considered to be an impartial decision-maker, the current process for evaluating and implementing data subjects' removal requests is radically deficient because it fails to provide affected content providers with notice and an opportunity to the heard before an adverse decision is rendered – foundational requirements of due process under both the U.S. and European systems.

F   Conclusion

Most U.S. commentators on the CJEU's right to be forgotten decision have contended that such a right is incompatible with the First Amendment because they mistakenly believe that free speech rights always outweigh privacy rights in the United States. These commentators misunderstand the balance that U.S. courts have struck between privacy rights and free speech rights. They fail to recognize that courts in the U.S. have protected individuals' privacy rights under the "public disclosure of private fact" tort and that such protections for privacy have been held to be compatible with the First Amendment's protections for free speech. In this chapter, I have highlighted a different incompatibility between the CJEU decision and U.S. constitutional rights – one that emphasizes the procedural protections required under the U.S. Constitution for individuals' fundamental rights – and indeed under fundamental requirements of due process shared by both the U.S. and European legal systems. The privacy protections recognized in the CJEU's decision are not necessarily incompatible with the *substantive* protections provided by U.S. free speech law and the balance U.S. courts have struck between privacy and free speech. But the CJEU's mandate regarding search engine operators' implementation of these protections fails to comport with the fundamental requirements of due process – that the party whose speech is affected be provided with notice and an opportunity to be heard by an impartial decision-maker before a decision adversely affecting such rights is rendered. As the *Google Spain* decision's privacy protections are currently being implemented, search engine operators like Google are required to remove links to information about a data subject without affording the affected speaker notice or an opportunity to be heard before such a removal decision is implemented. The right to be forgotten, as implemented, is therefore inconsistent with fundamental, shared notions of due process.

II   European Voices

12

The Challenge of Limiting Intelligence Agencies' Mass Surveillance Regimes

Why Western Democracies Cannot Give Up on Communication Privacy

BY KONSTANTIN VON NOTZ

A   We Live in Surveillance States

A mass surveillance regime is in place. It works on a global scale and Western intelligence agencies are some of the most significant participants.[1] By "mass surveillance" I mean the indiscriminate collection, storage, and analysis of vast amounts of personal data in telecommunication and IT systems for a wide variety of purposes.[2] Recent developments and documents both from the German Parliament's Committee of Inquiry and from WikiLeaks confirm that especially the NSA and the GCHQ have been using their surveillance programs to spy on German government and administration officials as well as key German businesses. There is also plenty of evidence that cooperation projects between Anglo-American and German intelligence agencies have been misused to carry out massive espionage

---

[1] There is no dispute about the authenticity of the Snowden files. The ongoing publication of the files can be followed here: www.theguardian.com/us-news/the-nsa-files and on the web archive for instance of the ACLU: www.aclu.org/nsa-documents-search. *See* GLENN GREENWALD, NO PLACE TO HIDE: EDWARD SNOWDEN, THE NSA, AND THE U.S. SURVEILLANCE STATE (2014).

[2] The Investigatory committee of the German Bundestag for instance came up with proof that one of the BND-NSA cooperation under the name of "eikonal" was being used by the United States to spy on companies like EADS and Eurocopter, although the operation officially was labeled an antiterror-measure, a (German) liveblog of the partially public hearing sessions to the committee can be found here: https://netzpolitik.org/2015/live-blog-aus-dem-geheimdienst-untersuchungsausschuss-dr-urmann-leiter-der-technischen-aufklaerung-des-bnd/. *See Mass Surveillance*, PRIVACY INT'L, www.privacyinternational .org/node/52; Ben Beaumont, *Easy Guide to Mass Surveillance*, AMNSTY INT'L (Mar. 18, 2015, 12:01 AM), www.amnesty.org/en/latest/campaigns/2015/03/easy-guide-to-mass-surveillance/.

against German and European institutions and companies. Of course, China and Russia also have vast digital surveillance programs in place. It is disturbing to see the similarities between the way these authoritarian regimes and Western democratic countries carry out electronic surveillance.

Metadata, which contain information on a person's location, her communication partners, and her communication habits, have become a key element of this development.[3] The problems arising from this are not inherent to the data.[4] Instead, they result from the information they contain and the potential knowledge that state institutions gain from these data about their citizens. The constant and almost-live knowledge of complete circles of contacts, including individuals' whereabouts and the intensity of contacts at different locations worldwide, forms the basis of a wide-range of measures that endanger freedom and civil rights. There can be no freedom if supposedly free citizens are constantly being watched. The chilling effect of mass surveillance on people – and on civil society more broadly – have long been acknowledged by the German Federal Constitutional Court.[5] The most problematic example of the consequences of these activities is that the information can contribute to extreme decision-making processes: "We kill people based on metadata," remains the undisputed conclusion of former NSA Director Michael Hayden.[6] America's ongoing drone war,[7] dependent as it is on intelligence gleaned from the mass surveillance regime, kills innocent people, flouts international law and human rights norms, and, thereby, serves as another dramatic example of the seriousness of the issue.[8]

---

[3] See Glenn Greenwald, *NSA Collecting Phone Records of Millions of Verizon Customers Daily*, THE GUARDIAN (June 6, 2013, 6:05 PM), www.theguardian.com/world/2013/jun/06/nsa-phone-records-verizon-court-order. These data, when being stored, after E.U. data-protection standards need strong legal safeguards in order to be kept: www.loc.gov/law/help/eu-data-retention-directive/eu.php.

[4] See Chapter 4 in this volume.

[5] Bundesverfassungsgericht [BverfG] [Federal Constitutional Court] Dec. 15, 1983, 65 BVerfGE 1. See GREENWALD, *supra* note 1 at 170–209.

[6] Lee Ferran, *Ex-NSA Chief: 'We Kill People Based on Metadata,'* ABC NEWS (May 12, 2014), http://abcnews.go.com/blogs/headlines/2014/05/ex-nsa-chief-we-kill-people-based-on-metadata/. See Chapter 8 in this volume.

[7] See Steve Coll, *The Unblinking Stare*, NEW YORKER (Nov. 24, 2014), www.newyorker.com/magazine/2014/11/24/unblinking-stare.

[8] INTERNATIONAL HUMAN RIGHTS AND CONFLICT RESOLUTION CLINIC AT STANFORD LAW SCHOOL AND GLOBAL JUSTICE CLINIC AT NYU SCHOOL OF LAW, LIVING UNDER DRONES: DEATH, INJURY, AND TRAUMA TO CIVILIANS FROM U.S. DRONE PRACTICES IN PAKISTAN (2012), www.law.stanford.edu/sites/default/files/organization/149662/doc/slspublic/Stanford-NYU-LIVING-UNDER-DRONES.pdf.

Programs of mass surveillance, such as Boundless Informant, Tempora, Prism, or Upstream, cannot be justified by abstract references to a "war on terror."[9] These programs are not focused on just one, perhaps justifiable aim such as counterterror initiatives. They can also be used to pursue espionage against foreign – even partner – countries. In their scope they affect wide swathes of people from all nations around the world.[10] And once a program is started there are always multiple other causes and urgent needs that can be used to justify further prolongation and extension of already existing programs. The legitimate and important fight against terrorist crimes simply does not justify the formation of a secretive surveillance apparatus that aims for the permanent and indiscriminate surveillance of the communications of governments, administrations, the business world, and a nearly unfathomable number of people regardless of suspicions or concrete threats. The consequences of such a broad surveillance regime on democracy and the enjoyment of protected liberties are unacceptable. And particularly espionage, which seems to be an integral part of NSA/GCHQ surveillance, is regarded as a serious crime in every country around the world. Considering Germany's history, which included two dictatorships that trampled on human rights in unprecedented ways, Germans have a particular responsibility to stand up and speak out against all surveillance regimes threatening basic freedoms.[11]

Now, some years after the media started publishing the Snowden files, Germans know that their foreign intelligence service (the *Bundesnachrichtendienst* or BND) and their domestic spy agency (the *Bundesverfassungsschutz* or BfV) are full participants – actors and not just spectators – in this global mass surveillance regime.[12] Thanks to Edward

---

[9] *See* AMERICA'S WAR ON TERROR (Tom Lansford, Robert P. Watson, & Jack Covarrubias eds. 2009).

[10] *See NSA Spying Scandal*, SPIEGEL ONLINE, www.spiegel.de/international/topic/nsa_spying_scandal/.

[11] *See* Cyrus Farivar, *Long-Standing German Tradition of Data Protection Simply Carrying on, Says Expert*, DW (July 16, 2010), www.dw.com/en/long-standing-german-tradition-of-data-protection-simply-carrying-on-says-expert/a-5809285 ("Historically seen, the Nazis and the Third Reich had lists of people that they thought of as being Jewish. And therefore the Germans were very sensitive or very careful about lists that were made by the federal state."); David Wroe, *German Privacy Gets Tangled in Google's Web*, LOCAL DE (Aug.13, 2010, 3:41 PM), www.thelocal.de/20100813/29141 ("Plenty of commentators have noted that Germany is naturally more sensitive regarding private data because of its Nazi and communist East German history.").

[12] *See* Sven Becker *et al.*, *Indispensable Exchange: Germany Cooperates Closely with NSA*, SPIEGEL ONLINE (July 8, 2013, 5:47 PM), www.spiegel.de/international/world/

Snowden's disclosures and the success of the German Parliament's Committee of Inquiry we now have public knowledge about the BND's cooperation with the NSA and CIA with respect to signals intelligence.[13] So far, there is no evidence that any of the relevant intelligence oversight bodies were informed about those operations. Projects with names such as "eikonal" and "glotaic" are probably only the loose ends of a thick web of initiatives.[14] Still, they are exceptional for the fact that they were carried out on German soil with the aim of sharing the collected data with the NSA and CIA.[15] At least two other operations, involving the BND's collection of data from German providers, have been identified.[16] One of these projects was planned with a Five-Eyes country.[17] It appears that Germany traded its cooperation in collecting data on European and international targets for access to technology and know-how.[18]

The German public learned most of this thanks to the Snowden revelations.[19] Before this bright light was directed on these activities, we could only speculate about the scope of intelligence agencies' surveillance ambitions. Even if some of these activities were carried out under democratically legitimate statutory regimes, the relevant laws on which intelligence agencies base their authority for carrying out mass surveillance are extremely complex and rather indistinct. They leave considerable room for the agencies' flexible and generous interpretations. They should not be understood as legitimation for global mass surveillance. For example, America's post-9/11 intelligence reforms were so hastily enacted that, after the Snowden revelations, many critics could not easily

---

spiegel-reveals-cooperation-between-nsa-and-german-bnd-a-909954.html; transcripts of the inquiry sessions can be found under https://wikileaks.org/bnd-nsa/press/.

[13] Becker et al., supra note 12.

[14] The German government has repeatedly claimed that with regard to the investigative committees narrow focus on Five-Eyes surveillance, other *existing* programs and *ongoing* electronic cooperation could not be revealed.

[15] Transcripts of the public inquiry sessions can be found under https://wikileaks.org/bnd-nsa/press/.

[16] Transcripts of the inquiry sessions can be found under https://wikileaks.org/bnd-nsa/press/.

[17] Up till now details of this GCHQ/ BND operation have remained top secret. See Maik Baumgärtner et al., America's Willing Helper: Intelligence Scandal Puts Merkel in Tight Place, SPIEGEL ONLINE (May 4, 2015, 5:42 PM), www.spiegel.de/international/germany/bnd-intelligence-scandal-puts-merkel-in-tight-place-a-1031944.html.

[18] Numerous witnesses insisted that this was the BND rationale behind the deals, see transcripts of the inquiry sessions, which can be found under https://wikileaks.org/bnd-nsa/press.

[19] See GREENWALD, supra note 1.

discern how the laws were being interpreted by the respective intelligence services. In any case, covertly developed, highly questionable legal interpretations of the law helped extend programs that were not originally meant to serve as a basis for mass surveillance. Secret courts, such as the American Foreign Intelligence Surveillance Court, kept the business of surveillance from the eyes of the public for too long.[20] Often, suspicions about surveillance excesses and abuses were regarded as lunatic or unhinged conspiracy theories.[21] This was true of the public realms in both the United States and Europe. The public outcry that arose in the immediate aftermath of Snowden's earliest disclosures documented the public's shock over these surveillance operations,[22] which were a true novelty to most of us. In about ten years a giant technical apparatus had been built, covertly and without the knowledge of the public against which the system would be directed.[23] Seemingly, it was the conclusion of the intelligence agencies after the Internet had arisen that this was to

---

[20] *See* Elizabeth Goitein & Faiza Patel, *What Went Wrong with the FISA Court*, Brennan Center for Justice (Mar. 18, 2015), www.brennancenter.org/publication/what-went-wrong-fisa-court.

[21] *See* Jesse Walker, *Conspiracies: Five Things They Don't Want You to Know*, Boston Globe (Oct. 20, 2013), www.bostonglobe.com/ideas/2013/10/19/conspiracies-five-things-they-don-want-you-know/RDNUlkp1GW095aSJ2THRGK/story.html ("The phrase "conspiracy theory" is often used as a synonym for "fear of fictional conspiracies." But of course actual conspiracies do exist. Spies, Mafias, and terrorists are real. The FBI really does have a history of infiltrating and disrupting dissident groups. The CIA really did study the effects of LSD by dosing unsuspecting Americans with the drug. In the infamous Tuskegee Experiment, which lasted 40 years, the Public Health Service deliberately refrained from telling hundreds of black patients that they had syphilis, so as to study whether the disease affects blacks and whites in different ways. More recently, we've seen a series of creepy revelations about mass surveillance by the National Security Agency."); Raphael Satter, *Britain Unveils Electronic Mass Surveillance Plan*, Huffpost Tech (June 14, 2012, 2:26 PM), www.huffingtonpost.com/2012/06/14/britain-unveils-electroni_0_n_1597529.html ("British authorities on Thursday unveiled an ambitious plan to log details about every Web visit, email, phone call or text message in the U.K. - and in a sharply-worded editorial the nation's top law enforcement official accused those worried about the surveillance program of being either criminals or conspiracy theorists.").

[22] *See February 11TH, 2014 Was the Day We Fought Back against Mass Surveillance*, https://thedaywefightback.org/the-results/; *STOP WATCHING US*, https://rally.stopwatching.us/; *Congress: This Is a Blackout*, www.blackoutcongress.org/; Adam Gabbat, *Protesters Rally for 'The Day We Fight Back' Against Mass Surveillance*, The Guardian (Feb. 11, 2014, 1:12 PM), www.theguardian.com/world/2014/feb/11/day-fight-back-protest-nsa-mass-surveillance.

[23] James Bamord, Shadow Factory (2008); Shane Harris, The Watchers (2010); Greenwald, *supra* note 1.

be their future home and the perfect platform for action – potentially aiming against everyone.[24] The horrifying events of 9/11 gave these developments an urgent and dramatic push.[25]

But most of the facts about this development still remain hidden in the vaults of secret oversight bodies, government administrations, and the agencies themselves. For now we can only extrapolate from the Snowden material what might be going on. For the German *Bundestag* (Federal Parliament) this situation was troubling enough to justify, by a unanimous vote of all party factions, the establishment of an investigative committee. This is the strongest sword in the German parliamentary oversight system.[26] This development was a consequence of the fact that Germany seemed to have been a particular target in the NSA-Affair. The Snowden materials showed that a significant portion of NSA data came

---

[24] *See* BAMFORD, *supra* note 23 at 47 ("[The 1990s are] the same decade when packetized communications – the e-communications we have all become familiar with – surpassed trfaditional communications. That is the same decade when mobile cell phones increased from 16 million to 741 million – an increase of nearly fifty times. That is the same decade when Internet users went from 4 million to 361 million – an increase of over ninety times."), 184–211; JAMES BAMFORD, BODY OF SECRETS (2001) at 458–59 ("Forty years ago there were five thousand stand-alone computers, no fax machines, and not one cellular phone ... In 1999 there were over 420 million computers, most of them networked. There were roughly 14 million fax machines and 468 million cell phones and those numbers continue to grow.").

[25] Jason Leopold, *Revealed: NSA Pushed 9/11 as Key 'Sound Bite' to Justify Surveillance*, AL JAZEERA AM. (Oct. 30, 2013, 12:09 PM), http://america.aljazeera.com/articles/2013/10/30/revealed-nsa-pushed911askeysoundbitetojustifysurveillance.html ("Under the subheading "Sound Bites That Resonate," the document suggests the statement "I much prefer to be here today explaining these programs, than explaining another 9/11 event that we were not able to prevent."").

[26] *See* German BUNDESTAG, MOTION TABLED BY THE CDU/CSU, SPD, THE LEFT PARTY AND ALLIANCE 90/THE GREENS PARLIAMENTARY GROUPS: ESTABLISHMENT OF A COMMITTEE OF INQUIRY, PRINTED PAPER 18/843 (2014) (Ger.), www.bundestag.de/blob/284528/a89d6006f28900c4f46e56f5e0807ddf/einsetzungsantrag_englisch-docx-data.pdf. *See also Bodies Established to Scrutinise the Work of the Government*, DEUTSCHER BUNDESTAG, www.bundestag.de/htdocs_e/bundestag/function/scrutiny/bodies/245706 ("Committees of inquiry are charged with examining and investigating political and bureaucratic misconduct in the government, the Bundestag and the administration. The work of the committees of inquiry involves the gathering of evidence. A committee of inquiry may interview and swear in witnesses and expert witnesses, order that documents be presented to it and request executive assistance from courts and administrative authorities. At the end of the inquiry, a report is published and a debate held in the Bundestag. As the subjects of these inquiries usually fall within the sphere of competence of the executive, committees of inquiry are, above all, an instrument for the selective scrutiny of the work of the government.").

from Germany.[27] Later, there were indications that Chancellor Merkel's cellphone had been targeted, most likely by U.S. Embassy personal in Berlin.[28] This was only the tip of the iceberg. Secret German documents published by WikiLeaks refer to selector lists in which over seventy other government officials from different German ministries are named as targets of surveillance.[29] At least their phone communications were – or still are – being tapped by the NSA or the GCHQ. The Committee of Inquiry started its work in March 2014, and will likely continue its work to the end of the current legislative period in 2017. The Committee has a large mandate. On one hand, it will study the Snowden files with the help of experts and witnesses.[30] On the other hand, it has been charged with investigating the practices of the German intelligence agencies and Germany's involvement in America's drone war.[31] The Committee is also expected to propose practical and effective solutions for the problems it uncovers.[32] The Committee started its daunting assignment with an examination of the *Bundesnachrichtendienst*, which has around 6,000 employees and which was identified in the Snowden files as an important partner for the NSA despite the fact that Germany does not enjoy the "premium partner" status of the Five-Eyes countries.

Chancellor Merkel's administration, which currently governs in a comfortable Grand Coalition with the Social Democrats, has shown very little interest in the NSA-Affair. In fact, the governing parties managed to crudely suppress the issue in order to keep it from derailing Merkel's reelection campaign in the fall of 2013. The base-line response from the Merkel administration remains the same and is being repeated over and over again: there is no German mass surveillance and we Germans are completely surprised by the revelations.[33] Under the leadership of the

---

[27] Sven Becker *et al.*, *New NSA Revelations: Inside Snowden's Germany File*, SPIEGEL ONLINE (June 18, 2014, 4:20 PM), www.spiegel.de/international/germany/new-snowden-revelations-on-nsa-spying-in-germany-a-975441.html.

[28] Rüdiger Ditz, *NSA Spying Scandal: SPIEGEL Stands Behind Merkel Cell Phone Spying Report*, SPIEGEL ONLINE (Dec. 13, 2014, 11:05 AM), www.spiegel.de/international/germany/nsa-german-federal-prosecutor-seeks-to-discredit-spiegel-reporting-a-1008262.html

[29] *NSA Helped CIA Outmanoeuvre Europe on Torture*, WIKILEAKS (July 20, 2015), https://wikileaks.org/nsa-germany/selectors.html#2.

[30] GERMAN BUNDESTAG, PRINTED PAPER 18/843, *supra* note 26.

[31] *Id* at ¶ B I.1, B I.4, B I.7, B I.8, B I.9, B I.14, B III.1, B III.2.   [32] *Id* at ¶ B III.

[33] Josie Le Blonde, *Angela Merkel Launches Re-election Bid Amid Cacophony of Spying Scandal*, THE GUARDIAN (Aug. 16, 2013, 11:27 AM), www.theguardian.com/world/2013/aug/16/angela-merkel-re-election-german-nsa-spy.

Merkel administration, the *Bundestag* has not yet considered a single initiative aiming at reducing or more strictly regulating German intelligence agencies' mass surveillance activities.[34] Meanwhile, new extensive budgets and new blanket competences have been approved.[35]

The Federal Prosecutor is appointed by the Federal Government and his or her conduct is overseen by the German Minister of Justice. It is particularly disappointing – and it is further evidence of the Merkel administration's disinterest on this issue – that the Federal Prosecutor never opened a full and formal investigation into the criminal implications of the many exposed espionage activities directed against Germany. In any case, the independence of the Federal Prosecutor was called into question when he was fired by the Minister of Justice for improperly opening treason charges against two German journalists.[36]

B   Why Didn't Anyone Notice?

Many Germans see a strong need for an effective intelligence oversight system, not the least for historical reasons. Our experience with the Nazi-Regime and with the Stasi-supported GDR has left many Germans deeply skeptical about the self-correcting powers of democracy and the possibility of efficiently overseeing intelligence agencies. Still, it is dispiriting to discover that the current system has failed so thoroughly and for such a long time. At least five different institutions are supposed to watch the watchers when it comes to signals intelligence. The highly secretive Parliamentary Control Committee (*Parlamentarische Kontrollgremium*

---

[34] *But see Entwurf für neues BND-Gesetz: Eine Art No-Spy-Klausel für Europa?*, TAGESSCHAU.DE (Jan. 18, 2016), *available at* www.tagesschau.de/inland/bnd-reform-103 .html; *Einigung auf Geheimdienstreform: Koalition nimmt BND an die Leine*, TAGESSCHAU.DE (Nov. 13, 2015), *available at* www.tagesschau.de/inland/bnd-reform-101.html.

[35] *See* Alexander Drechsel, *Germany's New Security Policies Come with a Price Tag*, DW (Nov. 14, 2014), www.dw.com/en/germanys-new-security-policies-come-with-a-price-tag/a-18066323 ("Official BND budgetary allowance rose by 28 percent between 2008 and 2014. Next year, government funding will increase to 615 million euros – which looks like a drop in the bucket compared to the billions in the defense budget, but intelligence services don't necessarily disclose their entire capital.").

[36] *Germany Drops Treason Inquiry into Netzpolitik Journalists*, THE GUARDIAN (Aug. 10, 2015, 5:38 PM), www.theguardian.com/world/2015/aug/10/germany-drops-treason-inquiry-netzpolitik-journalists ("The justice minister, Heiko Maas, questioned the decision to open a treason inquiry, and last week he fired the chief federal prosecutor, Harald Range, after the two clashed over public allegations by Range of political interference, which the minister denied.").

or PKGr) is the most important oversight institution because the intelligence agencies are obliged to report there on anything considered relevant to the knowledge of the Parliament.[37] But this committee, as with all German parliamentary committees, consists of MEPs in proportion to the party factions' success in the most recent federal election.[38] The majority party (or parties) that forms the government also holds the majority of the seats in the PKGr. Usually this leads to a rather low interest in robust parliamentary control measures that would be implemented against the governing party's (or parties') government. The PKGr cannot be counted on to do much, in any case, because it is a guardian without a sword. The majority may order inspections at intelligence sites, for example. But the PKGr has nearly no staff, not to mention the necessary technological competence. It does not have the authority to issue orders against the intelligence agencies and it is prohibited from sharing the insights it gains from its oversight activities.[39]

Besides the direct control of the intelligence agencies exercised by the PKGr, German law imposes considerable limits on the collection and use of telecommunications data through a strict regime of telecommunications privacy. The secrecy of telecommunication is enshrined in Article 10 of the German Basic Law.[40] But this is not an absolute protection. Years ago the constitution was amended to permit infringements of this right for the purpose of intelligence gathering.[41] The amended Article 10 required that intrusions on telecommunications privacy be carried out under statutory authorization and following the approval of "auxiliary agencies appointed by the legislature." These auxiliary agencies were meant to take the place of traditional courts, which had always had the

---

[37] Kontrollgremiumgesetz [PKGrG] [Act on Parliamentary Supervision of Federal Intelligence Activities], July 29, 2009, BGBl. I at 2346 (Hereinafter Intelligence Oversight Act.). *See Parlamentarisches Kontrollgremium (PKGr)*, Deutscher Bundestag, www.bundestag.de/bundestag/gremien18/pkgr; *Kontrollgremien*, Deutscher Bundestag, www.bundestag.de/service/glossar/K/-/283814.

[38] *See Function and Responsibilities*, Deutscher Bundestag, www.bundestag.de/htdocs_e/bundestag/committees/function/245820 ("Seats are distributed according to the relative strengths of the parties in Parliament: each parliamentary group has a right to a certain number of places on each of the committees proportional to its share of seats in the Bundestag. The leaderships of the parliamentary groups decide which Members are to sit on which committees, seeking to meet Members' requests as far as possible.").

[39] Intelligence Oversight Act §§ 7–14.

[40] Grundgesetz [GG] [Basic Law], art. 10, *translation at* www.gesetze-im-internet.de/englisch_gg/.

[41] Siebzehntes Gesetz zur Ergänzung des Grundgesetzes [17th Act Amending the Basic Law], June 24, 1968, BGBl. I at 709 (Ger.).

responsibility for authorizing surveillance measures.[42] The resulting law, referred to as the G-10 Act,[43] established an auxiliary agency known as the G-10 Commission.[44] The G-10 Commission is somewhat more effective than the PKGr. Its four active commissioners, nominated by the parties of the German *Bundestag*, work like a quasi-judicial institution. German intelligence agencies must apply to and receive approval from the Commission before undertaking intelligence activities that infringe upon telecommunications privacy.[45] In theory, the Commission's decisions can be challenged in court, provided that the intelligence measures have been concluded and the persons affected learn that their data were being processed.[46] Of course, the latter rarely occurs. There are other shortcomings in the G-10 Commission's effectiveness. The commissioners are not chosen for their competence in information technology; usually they are experienced politicians or lawyers at the end of their careers who serve as volunteers on the Commission.[47] Without a staff to support them, the commissioners are completely overwhelmed by the huge responsibility the law imposes on them. And, in the same way as the PKGr, the law requires the Commission to work in absolute secrecy.[48] There is now clear evidence from the hearings of the Committee of Inquiry that the G-10-Commission was bypassed – when the intelligence agencies presented it with fake requests and doctored annual

---

[42] BASIC LAW, art. 10.

[43] Gesetz zur Beschränkung des Brief-, Post- und Fernmeldegeheimnisses [G 10] [Act Restricting the Privacy of Correspondence, Posts and Telecommunications], June 26, 2001, BGBl. I at 1254, revised 2298, last amended by last amended by Gesetz [G], July 31, 2009, BGBl. I at 2499 (Ger.) (Hereinafter G 10 Act).

[44] G 10 Act § 1 ¶ 2, § 15.   [45] G 10 Act §§ 3 ¶ 2, 9, 10, 15 ¶ 5.

[46] *See* G 10 Act §§ 12, 13.

[47] G 10 Act § 15 ¶ 1 ("The G10 Commission shall comprise a chairperson qualified to hold judicial office, three associate chairpersons and four deputy members who may take part in the meetings with the right to speak and to ask questions. In the event of a tie, the chairperson shall have the deciding vote. The members of the G10 Commission shall remain independent in discharging their duties and shall not be subject to instructions. They shall hold an honorary public office and shall be appointed by the Parliamentary Control Panel after a hearing by the Federal Government for the duration of one legislative term of the German Bundestag, subject to the proviso that their term of office shall not end until the members of the Commission are newly appointed, but no later than three months after the end of the legislative term."); *see* IAIN CAMERON, NATIONAL SECURITY AND THE EUROPEAN CONVENTION ON HUMAN RIGHTS (2000) ("The G10 Commission appointees are not members of parliament, but they are politically affiliated ... They usually consist of lawyers or retired civil servants.").

[48] G 10 Act § 15 ¶ 2.

reports – with the intention of hiding possibly illegal operations behind a formal G-10 application process.[49]

The Federal Data Protection Commissioner (*Bundesbeauftragte für den Datenschutz und die Informationsfreiheit* or BfDI) is charged with overseeing the processing of personal data by federal authorities, including Germany's federal intelligence agencies.[50] The Data Protection Commissioner should be able to walk in and out of the BND's headquarters at any time and ask for any information in order to understand Germany's signal intelligence operations and to check their compliance with the law. Instead, up until today, any major move by the Data Protection Commissioner to control intelligence operations has been countered with the legal argument that the requested data falls under the exclusive scope of the G-10 Act and, therefore, is solely the competence of the G-10 Commission.[51] Playing off two oversight bodies against each other in this manner is an old and well-known game. But it has never attracted the serious attention of policy-makers. It seems that it has been a major gap in the oversight system that may have papered-over illegal practices within the BND for quite a long time.[52]

The last of the oversight institutions is the Federal Authority for IT Security (*Bundesamt für Sicherheit in der Informationstechnik* or BSI).[53] This rapidly growing entity, itself a former arm of the intelligence

---

[49] See *Bundestag Demands Access to Surveillance Lists Involved in NSA Scandal*, Sputnik Int'l (July 30, 2015, 9:16 PM), http://sputniknews.com/europe/20150730/1025228787 .html ("We insist on giving us the opportunity to examine the lists, Hahn said, adding that the G10 Commission was deceived and given false information.").

[50] Gesetz zum Schutz vor Mißbrauch personenbezogener Daten bei der Datenverarbeitung [Bundesdatenschutzgesetz] [BDSG] [Federal Data Protection Act], Dec. 20, 1990, BGBl.I at 2954, as amended by the Act of Sept. 14, 1994, BGBl. I at 2325 (Ger.), §§ 22–26.

[51] See *Transcript: Bundestag Committee of Inquiry into the National Security Agency [Untersuchungsausschuss ("NSA")], Session 31*, 1. Untersuchungsausschuss (2015) (statement of Peter Schaar), https://wikileaks.org/bnd-nsa/sitzungen/31_01/WikiLeaks_Tran script_Session_31_01_from_German_NSA_Inquiry.pdf.

[52] See Baumgärtner, *supra* note 17 ("The four members of the so-called G-10 Commission, for example, meet once a month with high-level intelligence officials in a surveillance-proof room in Berlin's official parliament building, the Reichstag. They are given piles of requests to initiate surveillance operations that they then have to rule on within the space of just a few hours ... Nine members of parliament are on the Parliamentary Control Panel. But they are almost entirely dependent on the good will of the intelligence agencies, which are required to notify the panel of "notable occurrences." But it is up to the agencies themselves to decide what classifies as a "notable occurrence.").

[53] Gesetz über das Bundesamt für Sicherheit in der Informationstechnik [BSIG] [Act to Strengthen the Security of Federal Information Technology], Aug. 14, 2009, BGBl. I at 2821 (Ger.).

agencies, is charged with looking after all IT products that are being used in signal intelligence operations and that might affect people protected by the German constitution. But the certificates of compliance the BSI issues have so far been granted only for superficial intelligence operations.[54] The complex software security checks needed to assess more significant signals intelligence programs are almost impossible to implement – or they require disproportionate resources. Therefore, the intelligence services' hardware and software is not being thoroughly analyzed and cannot be certified as secure. This means that these devices might be covertly deployed to carry out functions that contravene German legal norms and interests. The German Parliament has failed completely in making this important institution an effective means for the protection of Germans' rights.

The Committee of Inquiry has faced extreme pressure from Chancellor Merkel's administration. This has reached such a degree that it is fair to say that the government is stonewalling the Committee. The Committee's rights and powers are guaranteed in an autonomous law,[55] but the possibilities to block or complicate its work are immense. For example, government files on signals intelligence developments and cooperation with the NSA dating back to 2001 were delivered to the Committee in an incomplete condition or with massive security redactions. Key witnesses, especially including Edward Snowden, have been blocked from appearing as witnesses because the Merkel administration fears retaliation from the U.S. government and wants to avoiding adding even more strain to an already troubled transatlantic relationship. Unfortunately, the opposition parties failed with a lawsuit that sought to compel the Merkel administration to facilitate Snowden's appearance as a witness.[56] The complaint was thrown out by the Federal Constitutional Court, which concluded

---

[54] *See* Federal Office for Information Security, *German IT Security Certificates* (Mar. 2015), www.bsi.bund.de/SharedDocs/Downloads/DE/BSI/Zertifizierung/7148_e_pdf.pdf?__blob =publicationFile.

[55] Untersuchungsausschussgesetz [PUAG] [Investigative Committee Act], June 19, 2001, BGBl. I at 1142, last amended by Gesetz [G] May 5, 2004, BGBl. I at 718.

[56] Beschluss vom 04. Dezember 2014 2 BvE 3/14, Antrag im Organstreitverfahren zur Zeugenvernehmung von Edward Snowden in Berlin ist unzulässig Pressemitteilung Nr. 114/2014 vom 12. Dezember 2014, www.bundesverfassungsgericht.de/SharedDocs/ Pressemitteilungen/DE/2014/bvg14-114.html; *Court Disallows Bid to Invite Snowden to Testify in Berlin*, DW (Dec. 12, 2014), www.dw.com/en/court-disallows-bid-to-invite-snowden-to-testify-in-berlin/a-18125067; Ulrkie Dauer, *German Court Dismisses Motion for Edward Snowden Hearing*, WALL ST. J. (Dec. 12, 2014, 9:11 AM), www.wsj.com/ articles/german-court-dismisses-motion-for-snowden-hearing-1418393517.

that, due to the ongoing investigation, there was not an urgent need for the administration to decide.[57] This ill-fated decision misjudges the political reality of majority power in investigative committees. The opposition parties have been forced, due to a procedural suggestion offered by the Constitutional Court, to address their case anew to the Federal Court of Justice.

C   Law in the Hands of Agents?

As a foreign intelligence service, most of the BND's collected data are from crisis regions around the globe, especially from Africa, Afghanistan, the Near East, or the Balkans.[58] Supposedly different forms of mass collection are involved. Rather well-known are German attacks on satellite data flows serving the mentioned regions.[59] But these foreign data-collection initiatives are in conflict with the German constitution. Article 10, and its protection for telecommunications privacy, was conceived as a human right and its scope is rather broad. Once it is applicable, clear and concrete laws are necessary to authorize all relevant administrative actions. A clear majority of scholars are also convinced that Article 10 applies to any kind of telecommunications data that is being processed on German territory by German authorities, no matter where the telecommunications acts or the data collection took place.[60] This, of course,

---

[57] Bundesverfassungsgericht [BverfG] [Federal Constitutional Court] Dec. 4, 2014, BVerfG, 2 BvE 3/14, Rn. (1–42), www.bundesverfassungsgericht.de/SharedDocs/Entscheidungen/DE/2014/12/es20141204_2bve000314.html.

[58] Anton Troianovski, *Germany Halts Some Intelligence Sharing with U.S.*, WALL ST. J. (May 7, 2015, 6:27 PM), www.wsj.com/articles/germany-restricts-some-data-sharing-with-u-s-1431021158 ("The BND, which helped operate the station for years and officially took over in 2004, has used the Bad Aibling site to intercept satellite communications in crisis regions such as the Middle East and Afghanistan, German officials said.").

[59] These data are being processed in Bad Aibling, Bavaria, a former NSA outpost. Millions of metadata are being shared with the NSA each day. They still have personnel stationed on the site.

[60] Paul M. Schwartz, *Systematic Government Access to Private-Sector Data in Germany*, 2 INT'L DATA PRIVACY L. 289, 291 (2012) ("In its G-10 opinion, the Constitutional Court found that the protections of the Basic Law's Article 10 were not limited exclusively to communications that took place entirely within the national borders of Germany. As long as enough of a nexus existed between the surveillance and German territory, the protections of Basic Law, Article 10 were applicable."); Marcel Fürstenau, *NSA Affair: German Committee Calls Intelligence Witnesses*, DW (Oct. 10, 2014), www.dw.com/en/nsa-affair-german-committee-calls-intelligence-witnesses/a-17985607 ("The members of the NSA investigative committee pricked up their ears, when the fully qualified attorney spoke of her understanding of the law as regards the controversial BND surveillance station in Bad

would have far reaching legal consequences for the BND. The agency's legal staff shaped their own rather awkward views of Article 10 and its extra-territorial application. They argue, for instance, that satellite surveillance does not fall within the scope of Article 10 because the place of collection – outer space – is supposedly lawless.[61] This particularly selective legal approach, referred to without any sense of irony as "space theory," had never been trotted out until the Committee of Inquiry took testimony from the BND's privacy compliance officer who had been fighting this approach internally without success.[62]

Another example of the BND's creative interpretation of the law is the agency's definition of "personal data." The accepted broad European data protection definition relies on the mere possibility of data being connectable to a person. But the BND has argued that Afghan telecommunications data are not within the scope of the data protection laws because they cannot be concretely linked to names so long as Afghan telephone directories are not easily accessible. Thus, a huge number of BND data being stored is probably currently not being processed in conformity with European data protection laws. One of the consequences of this is that these data are probably being shared with Five-Eyes countries without any legal restraints, making Germany a partner in the global exchange and circumvention of national protections for the privacy of telecommunications.[63] This combination of opaque intelligence services

---

Aibling. She is firmly convinced that all data that the BND collects there with satellites is legal. Whether the phone that was monitored was in Germany or in Afghanistan, and who was on the other end of the line, should not play a role in the handling of the acquired data, according to the data protection officer."). *See* Chapter 15 in this volume.

[61] Franziska Roscher & Kevin O'Brien, *Under the Shadow of Doubt*, HANDELSBLATT (Aug. 6, 2015), https://global.handelsblatt.com/edition/235/ressort/politics/article/under-the-shadow-of-doubt ("One example is the famous "space theory" that has been put forward there. The Bundesnachrichtendienst (the BND, the German equivalent of the Central Intelligence Agency) is not allowed to surveil within Germany. But from Bad Aibling, which is located in (southern) Germany, it surveils satellite communications in space. And they're of the legal opinion that that's perfectly legal, because space isn't Germany.").

[62] Andre Meister, *Live-Blog aus dem Geheimdienst-Untersuchungsausschuss: "Funktionsträger fallen nicht unter G-10-Schutz"*, NETZPOLITIK.ORG (Nov. 6, 2014, 12:06 PM), https://netzpolitik.org/2014/live-blog-aus-dem-geheimdienst-untersuchungsausschuss-herr-b-und-frau-l-vom-bundesnachrichtendienst/.

[63] The massive amount of exchanged data hints to this as much as witnesses statements on former and recently dropped coperation projects, for quantity aspects *see* Kai Biermann, *BND Liefert NSA 1,3 Milliarden Metadaten – Jeden Monat*, ZEIT ONLINE (May 12, 2015, 8:26 AM), www.zeit.de/politik/deutschland/2015-05/bnd-nsa-milliarden-metadaten.

and secret interpretations of the law has proven to be a real threat to civil rights. All of this calls for a major reform agenda, not just of the oversight system, but also of the legal competences of the German intelligence agencies with regard to signals intelligence.[64]

In principle, German constitutional law calls for all personal data processing to be authorized and regulated by concrete and specific laws that must address the typical privacy risks involved. Disproportionate data collection or data analysis can lead to complete unlawfulness, as has been seen with German and E.U. legislation regarding retention of telecommunications data.[65] In another important decision the Federal Constitutional Court ruled that dragnet surveillance for security purposes can only be carried out when the legitimizing laws have established "current substantial dangers" as an essential condition.[66] Unfortunately, it seems that the whole of the Constitutional Court's jurisprudence from the last fifteen years on these issues has been ignored by both the legislature and the executive, at least with respect to intelligence agencies. And the Federal Constitutional Court might announce a general exception to its judicial review for intelligence agencies in order to free itself from these complex and politically fraught constitutional complaints.[67]

D   The Transatlantic Relationship

The bilateral U.S.–German relationship has suffered from the NSA-Affair. Ironically, it was the attack on Merkel's cellphone and the discovery of a U.S. spy inside the BND – and not the Snowden revelations – that did the most damage to Germans' trust in the United States Rather unimpressed by Germans' alarm, both the Obama and the Merkel administrations were determined to leave this crisis behind. President Obama's Intelligence Directive from 2014 was a necessary but insufficient reaction to the Snowden revelations. It was insufficient because it did not address European interests. The limitations it announced for

---

[64] *See supra* note 34.

[65] Court of Justice of the European Union Press Release No. 54/14 (Apr. 8, 2014), http://curia.europa.eu/jcms/upload/docs/application/pdf/2014-04/cp140054en.pdf.

[66] Bundesverfassungsgericht [BverfG] [Federal Constitutional Court] Apr. 4, 2006, BVerfG, 1 BvR 518/02 Rn. (1–184), www.bundesverfassungsgericht.de/SharedDocs/Entscheidun gen/DE/2006/04/rs20060404_1bvr051802.html.

[67] *See* Bundesverfassungsgericht [BverfG] [Federal Constitutional Court] July 14, 1999, BverfG, 1 BvR 2226/94, 1 BvR 2420/95, 1 BvR 2437/95, www.bundesverfassungsgericht .de/SharedDocs/Entscheidungen/DE/1999/07/rs19990714_1bvr222694.html.

American intelligence gathering were largely aimed at protecting Americans and did little for non-U.S. citizens. This initiative will not build trust between Europe and the United States because it leaves European citizens and companies in the same vulnerable situation as before. The global situation has left little time and space for a deeper mutual understanding of what has actually happened. Especially the Obama administration seems to believe that the Europeans can be pacified with minimal reforms, such as limiting the storage time of bulk-data collection for up to five years if they contain data of E.U. citizens.[68]

This strategy will not succeed in maintaining a lasting and reliable transatlantic relationship. Europeans, and especially the Germans, must expose and confront their own intelligence scandals. Still, they should not duck this basic problem, which has been around for quite a while and which has been covered up for far too long. There is no use in denying that Europe and the United States are deeply divided on issues of privacy as a cultural matter. The differences have become more evident with the ever-growing dominance of the Internet economy. On one hand, Silicon Valley companies have worked aggressively to develop a global digital market in which closely tracking and profiling their customers is a key part of the commercial model. On the other hand, U.S. intelligence agencies will not settle for less than global information dominance. Both goals have long been identified as, at least in their tendency, colliding with both basic human rights and internationally accepted concepts of privacy. For both the European Union and Germany the national data-protection "aquis" forms a complex arrangement of statutory provisions, constitutional standards, and public expectations that cannot be ignored or simply downsized at the negotiation table. The differences are fundamental. European privacy rights, for example, are deeply rooted in the European legal tradition and are being applied universally. The U.S. approach to privacy remains, as a legal concept, very spotty and narrowly defined. Privacy in the American context is less a comprehensive legal concept than it is an ethical concept that has to compete in American

---

[68] Ellen Nakashima and Greg Miller, *Obama Calls For Significant Changes in Collection of Phone Records of U.S. Citizens*, WASH. POST (Jan. 17, 2014), www.washingtonpost.com/politics/in-speech-obama-to-call-for-restructuring-of-nsas-surveillance-program/2014/01/17/e9d5a8ba-7f6e-11e3-95c6-0a7aa80874bc_story.html ("[Obama] also said he will order that certain privacy safeguards given Americans whose data are collected be extended to foreigners, including limits on the use of the information and how long it can be kept.").

society with other societal interests, such as the very strong foundations of freedom of expression.

The further digitalization of the German and American economies and security institutions raises the pressure for finding real solutions for these real differences. A practical example for the urgency we face is the so-called Safe Harbor Agreement, which has been reformed to ensure – in the most minimal fashion – that data transfers of E.U.-based American companies into the United States meet European data protection standards.[69] The Snowden revelations opened the public's eyes to the fact that compliance and adequate data protection standards could not be expected from the previous agreement, which for years was not enforced at all by the American Federal Trade Commission (FTC).[70] The efficacy of the newly minted Privacy Shield will be tested in practice and the courts.[71]

Unfortunately not much has happened on both sides of the Atlantic to assert the rule of law in the unruly world of intelligence gathering since the Snowden files were first published. The American Congress enacted the USA FREEDOM Act in June 2015.[72] But it does not offer much to non-U.S. citizens.[73] And the numerous suggestions for reform by the

---

[69] See *Safe Harbor Privacy Principles: Issued by the U.S. Department of Commerce on July 21, 2000*, EXPORT.GOV, www.export.gov/safeharbor/eu/eg_main_018475.asp; *U.S.–E.U. Safe Harbor Overview*, EXPORT.GOV, www.export.gov/safeharbor/eu/eg_main_018476.asp; Mark Scott, *Data Transfer Pact Between U.S. and Europe Is Ruled Invalid*, N.Y. TIMES (Oct. 6, 2015), www.nytimes.com/2015/10/07/technology/european-union-us-data-collec tion.html?_r=0.

[70] Brian J. McGinnis, *European Court of Justice Invalidates U.S.–E.U. Safe Harbor Agreement*, NAT'L L. REV. (Oct. 9, 2015), www.natlawreview.com/article/european-court-just ice-invalidates-us-eu-safe-harbor-agreement ("After being in effect for nearly 15 years, Safe Harbor compliance by U.S. companies was rarely questioned or enforced by the FTC or the Department of Commerce. Many viewed the Safe Harbor as merely a "promise" of compliance by the United States which turned into a free-for-all in regards to data transfers. The lack of attention and oversight by U.S. authorities, along with revelations regarding U.S. government surveillance, eventually led to the recent case in which the European Court invalidated the Safe Harbor.").

[71] See *E.U. Commission and United States agree on new framework for transatlantic data flows: E.U.–U.S. Privacy Shield*, EUROPEAN COMMISSION PRESS RELEASE (Feb. 2, 2016), available at http://europa.eu/rapid/press-release_IP-16-216_en.htm; Schrems v. Data Protection Commissioner (Case C-362/14), Oct. 6, 2015, availble at http://curia.europa .eu/juris/liste.jsf?num=C-362/14.

[72] Uniting and Strengthening America by Fulfilling Rights and Ensuring Effective Discipline Over Monitoring Act of 2015 [USA FREEDOM Act], Pub. L. No. 114–23, 129 Stat. 268 (2015).

[73] Q & A on the USA FREEDOM Act of 2015, CTR. FOR DEMOCRACY & TECH. (Apr. 28, 2015), https://cdt.org/blog/q-a-on-the-usa-freedom-act-of-2015/ ("To the extent a non-U.S. person, whether inside or outside of the U.S., makes calls to a person

Privacy and Civil Liberties Oversight Board have not been taken up in a significant way.[74] Similarly, the German government has disgracefully failed to react to the most obvious breaches of national and international law both by its own agencies and by the agencies of the Five-Eyes countries. It has never even tried to find an independent position when confronted with the severe encroachments of its closest allies. The relations of our Western democracies on an administrative level seem to be too-entangled to process and handle the mutual betrayal and attacks on civil society by the intelligence community.

Our current IT development offers significant chances and possibilities for the restoration of privacy, but it possesses a totalitarian dynamic that has to be legally tamed and, at the least, democratically controlled. In this situation, it is my conviction that especially our parliaments carry a unique responsibility in pursuing possible a dialogue that should start as basically and broadly as possible in order to avoid blocking out stakeholders and interests. Lawmakers on both sides of the Atlantic should get a feel for this civil society topic and should discuss it in a transparent, public fashion. Major developments like Big Data, Cloud Computing, or Industry 4.0 will affect the lives of everyone in a much broader way than IT has done before. Democratic discourse on the goals of these developments and the right balance with competing or often simply contradictory values and norms such as privacy is the precondition for a lasting solution. A U.S.–German parliamentary initiative could be a leading example for the international community. That would be a profound first step toward ending mass surveillance in order to protect our freedom.

---

in the U.S., the person outside the U.S. will benefit from the end of bulk collection under Section 215. In addition, the bill's FISA Court opinion declassification requirement is not limited to domestic laws, so it should give some insight into how U.S. surveillance authorities apply to non-U.S. persons. The bill's company reporting provisions [Sec. 604] will also shed light on the volume and type of surveillance requests – both domestic and international – the government is making on US internet and telecom companies. Other than that, there is little that is helpful to non-U.S. persons. They are still subject to targeted surveillance under FISA Section 702, and to targeted and bulk surveillance under Executive Order 12333."); *see, e.g.*, Russell A. Miller, *The Tattered German-American Relationship Needs the USA FREEDOM Act*, AICGS ADVISOR (18 May 2015), www.aicgs.org/publication/the-tattered-german-american-relationship-needs-the-usa-freedom-act/.

[74] Mark Gleeson *et al.*, *E.U.–U.S. Data Transfer/Safe Harbor Talks, German IT Security and More: Data Privacy Alert for 27 July 2015*, NAT'L L. REV. (July 18, 2015), www.natlawreview.com/article/eu-us-data-transfersafe-harbor-talks-german-it-security-and-more-data-privacy-alert-.

13

German Exceptionalism?

The Debate About the German Foreign Intelligence Service (BND)

BY STEFAN HEUMANN

A   Introduction

Since John Winthrop's famous reference to the "city upon a hill," American exceptionalism has been the focus of many political and academic debates in the United States and around the world.[1] While American exceptionalism takes many forms, all American exceptionalisms are predicated on the thesis that the United States is so special that it stands apart from all other countries.[2] But every country can be exceptional from its own vantage point. Ideas of a people's unique culture, history, and institutions are the hallmark of any national identity.[3] And many attempts to construct national characteristics in terms of exceptionalism have been met with counter-narratives that seek to debunk the "myth of exceptionalism." These critiques call into question how unique certain historical developments, cultural expressions, and political institutions really are. Upon closer examination we often find that what appears to be exceptional is not really so unique. Two vantage points – the transnational and the comparative – pose particularly strong challenges for any constructs of national uniqueness. Transnational perspectives show how ideas and institutions transcend and flow across

---

[1] *See, e.g.*, James W. Caesar, *The Origins and Character of American Exceptionalism*, 1 AM. POL. THOUGHT 3 (2012); BRIDGING THE ATLANTIC: THE QUESTION OF AMERICAN EXCEPTIONALISM IN PERSPECTIVE (Elisabeth Gläser & Hermann Wellenreuther eds., 2002); GODFREY HODGSON, THE MYTH OF AMERICAN EXCEPTIONALISM (2009); AMERICAN EXCEPTIONALISM AND HUMAN RIGHTS (Michael Ignatieff ed., 2005).
[2] PETER ONUF, AMERICAN EXCEPTIONALISM AND NATIONAL IDENTITY, APSA 2011 ANNUAL MEETING PAPER, http://papers.ssrn.com/sol3/papers.cfm?abstract_id=1902711.
[3] ROGERS. M. SMITH, STORIES OF PEOPLEHOOD: THE POLITICS AND MORALS OF POLITICAL MEMBERSHIP (2003).

national borders.[4] Historical experiences with colonialism, industrializa-tion, or immigration are not uniquely national phenomena. Instead they were part of broader forces that closely linked the states in the west to events and developments around the world. Comparative perspectives have a similar effect. Comparisons point out that while culture and institutions may differ across countries, they are shaped by a set of overarching factors. The combination of factors and their effects may differ across countries. But it is also possible to observe similarities. Comparisons are important to point out both differences and similarities among cases. Comparisons help us better understand the characteristics of individual cases but their nuanced differentiations generally weaken the extreme claims of uniqueness or exceptionalism.

The obsession with exceptionalism is not unique to the United States, even if that is the most prominent contemporary case.[5] This is a familiar debate for Germans as well.[6] Thinking about its role in starting two World Wars – especially with regard to the Nazi-Regime and the Holo-caust – German scholars and intellectuals have been wondering for a long time if there could be anything more "exceptional" than German history.[7] This German exceptionalism is extremely relevant to the NSA-Affair. For unique, historic reasons Germans harbor a strong distrust for government surveillance. Two recent dictatorships abused state power – including extensive surveillance and social control – in order to oppress people. On one hand, the West German Constitution of 1949 was drafted as a direct response to the horrific abuses of state power under the rule of Hitler and National Socialism. On the other hand, the East German government's surveillance of its own citizens helped the Communist regime stay in power. The surveillance of the Eastern German state security services is well documented in the millions of files that have been made accessible to the victims of surveillance by the German

---

[4] Ian Tyrrell, Transnational Nation: United States History in Global Perspec-tive since 1789 (2007).

[5] Reflections on American Exceptionalism (David K. Adams & Cornelius A. van Minnen eds., 1994).

[6] Peter Bergmann, *American Exceptionalism and German "Sonderweg" in Tandem*, 23 Int'l Hist. Rev. 505 (2001).

[7] Most recently, this argument has been made by the German historian Heinrich August Winkler. Winkler sees Germany's unique history as a source for its moral exceptionalism that shapes its policies on refugees. *See* Heinrich August Winkler, *Deutschlands Moralische Selbstüberschätzung*, Frankfurter Allgemeine (Sept. 30, 2015, 10:35 AM), www.faz.net/aktuell/politik/fluechtlingskrise/gastbeitrag-deutschlands-moralische-selb stueberschaetzung-13826534.html.

government after reunification. In addition to these historical experiences, Germans are known to be particularly concerned about their privacy. Some of the world's first data protection laws were enacted in Germany, laying the foundation for comparatively strong data protection institutions in Germany and across Europe.[8]

But has this exceptional history had the effect of endowing Germany with an exceptional legal framework for the control of its intelligence service? Few countries have reacted so strongly to the NSA-Affair. The critique of mass-surveillance programs revealed by Edward Snowden has been unequivocal and strident in German public opinion. Government officials, journalists, and activists are generally in agreement that the surveillance programs of NSA and GCHQ go too far. The political class is particularly concerned that, as far as the NSA is concerned, Germans do not have a right to privacy.[9]

The criticism of the NSA and its Five-Eyes allies rests on the implicit assumption that Germany is not conducting its own invasive intelligence operations, because that is prohibited by law and, in any case, would exceed the capabilities of the German intelligence services. This is what I call "German exceptionalism" regarding Germans' popular understanding of their intelligence regime. But German exceptionalism on this point can only be upheld if comparative and transnational perspectives are ignored. And German exceptionalism faces pressure from other sources. The German Parliament's Committee of Inquiry, which was initially established to examine questions regarding the NSA's mass surveillance of German citizens has brought previously secret information about practices and legal doctrines of the German foreign intelligence agency BND into the public spotlight.[10] Reports by investigative journalists have been another important source for those who seek to understand how the German Federal Foreign Intelligence Service (*Bundesnachrichtendienst – BND*) has managed the transition to digital surveillance technologies. These revelations suggest that Germany's Intelligence Community has been extremely active and no less disingenuous with respect to invasive telecommunications surveillance.[11]

---

[8] HANDBUCH DATENSCHUTZRECHT (Lukas Bauer & Sebastian Reimer eds., 2009).

[9] *De Maizière Kritisiert NSA Lauschaktivitäten*, STERN (June 18, 2015, 9:39 PM), www .stern.de/news2/de-maizi%C3%A8re-kritisiert-nsa-lauschaktivitaeten-6306510.html. *See* Introduction in this volume.

[10] *See* von Chapter 13 in this volume.

[11] Stefan Heumann, *Impulse: Bundesnachrichtendienst unter Beobachtung: Erste Erkenntnisse aus Einanhalb Jahren Überwachungsdebatte*, STIFTUNG NEUE VERANTWORTUNG

This chapter proceeds in four parts. First, I will briefly discuss the political reaction in Germany to the NSA-Affair and link it to the concept of German privacy exceptionalism. Second, I will put the NSA-Affair in the global context of the work and mandate of foreign intelligence agencies, which has evolved considerably during the past two decades. These comparative and transnational perspectives have been lacking in the German debate. But, as I pointed out above, exceptionalisms retain their relevance only if these broader perspectives are ignored. Third, I will very briefly point out some important legal, constitutional, and policy questions regarding the NSA. This analysis will serve as a benchmark for my final step in which I will demonstrate that Germany's statutory, constitutional, and policy framework regarding the BND is not at all exceptional. I will conclude with a few observations on the transatlantic reform debate that I see emerging from the NSA-Affair.

B German Exceptionalism: The German Reaction to the NSA-Affair

The revelations by Edward Snowden generated great interest and debate in Germany. This, in turn, put a lot of pressure on the German government.[12] The first stories about NSA surveillance broke when the political campaigns for the September 2013 national elections began to pick up steam. Initially, the opposition was pretty much alone with its demands for major consequences. During the summer of 2013 the German government was still defending the U.S. government and saw very little reason to discuss the NSA-Affair.[13] The initial calculation by the Merkel government was that this was an issue that would fade away over time. The strategy of playing down the importance of the issue was also driven by strategic calculations regarding the campaign. After Merkel won reelection her party continued to defend transatlantic cooperation and to dismiss the significance of the Snowden revelations.

(Feb. 4, 2015), www.stiftung-nv.de/sites/default/files/impulse_bundesnachrichtendienst_s.heumann_feb_15_1.pdf.

[12] For a more thorough discussion of the post-Snowden surveillance debate, *see* Heumann, *supra* note 11.

[13] In August 2013 – two months after the first media reports – the minister in charge of running the Chancellery declared the Snowden affair to be over after reassuring conversations with U.S. and British government officials. *See Pofalla Erklärt NSA-Affäre für Beendet*, ZEIT ONLINE (Aug. 12, 2013, 6:18 PM), www.zeit.de/politik/deutschland/2013-08/nsa-bnd-pofalla–bundestag-spaehaffaere-snowden-abkommen.

But, when news about the Americans' apparent surveillance of Chancellor Merkel's phone surfaced, the conservatives then joined the left in their denunciations of what they perceived to be a U.S. surveillance apparatus that was out of control.[14] The possibility that U.S. surveillance had targeted Merkel was significant in two regards. First, it created a major problem in the transatlantic partnership. As Merkel put it, "Friends just don't spy on each other."[15] Second, it also created urgency for the German government to come up with some sort of response. Doing nothing risked making the Merkel government look weak and toothless. Even conservatives, usually not known for their criticisms of the U.S. government, had become outraged by the NSA-Affair. The Merkel phone-tapping episode forced the German government to take on an issue that it hoped to ignore. Adding to the pressure has been the steady flow of revelations over the subsequent years providing an ever-fuller picture of the NSA's extensive surveillance operations in Germany or against German targets.[16] All of this forced the government to act.

This background is important for our understanding of what I call German exceptionalism. During the past two decades the BND largely operated outside of the public spotlight. For obvious reasons this was a situation with which the Intelligence Community felt very comfortable. Similar to other agencies shrouded in secrecy, the BND has had its share of scandals.[17] But the parliament and the courts rarely interfered with the work of the BND.[18] For the most part Germany's spies – long headquartered in the remote Bavarian town of Pullach, before a recent move to Berolin – went about their business with little public or parliamentary scrutiny.

---

[14] *Politiker Fordern Klarheit Über Mögliche Überwachung Merkels,* ZEIT ONLINE (Oct. 24, 2015), www.zeit.de/politik/2013-10/deutsche-politiker-verlangen-aufklaerung-ueber-abhoeren-von-merkels-handy.

[15] *Merkel zur Handy-Affäre: "Ausspähen Unter Freunden – Das Geht Gar Nicht,"* SPIEGEL ONLINE (Oct. 24, 2013, 4:49 PM), www.spiegel.de/politik/deutschland/handy-spaehaf faere-um-merkel-regierung-ueberprueft-alle-nsa-erklaerungen-a-929843.html.

[16] Laura Poitras *et al., Cover Story: How the NSA Targets Germany and Europe,* SPIEGEL ONLINE (July 1, 2013, 11:11 AM), www.spiegel.de/international/world/secret-documents-nsa-targeted-germany-and-eu-buildings-a-908609.html; *Snowdens Deutschland Akte: Die Dokumente im PDF Format,* SPIEGEL ONLINE (June 18, 2014, 4:17 PM), www.spiegel.de/netzwelt/web/snowdens-deutschland-akte-alle-dokumente-als-pdf-a-975885.html.

[17] PETER F. MÜLLER & MICHAEL MUELLER, GEGEN FREUND UND FEIND: DER BND, GEHEIME POLITIK UND SCHMUTZIGE GESCHÄFTE (2002).

[18] DEUTSCHER BUNDESTAG: DRUCKSACHE [BT] 16/30400, June 18, 2009 (Ger.), http://dipbt.bundestag.de/dip21/btd/16/134/1613400.pdf.

When the scope and scale of surveillance programs developed by NSA and GCHQ became clear, German government officials reverted to German exceptionalism. They assured the public that the BND had neither the expertise nor the resources to engage in such sweeping surveillance activities. And they reassuringly pointed to the narrow legal constraints and the tight oversight under which the BND operates.[19] The suggestion was that the NSA-Affair provided no reason to take a closer look at Germany's Intelligence Community. But, as the work of the Parliament's Committee of Inquiry unfolded,[20] and as additional media reports and leaks piled-up,[21] it became clear that the BND's hands were also dirty. German exceptionalism in the intelligence field, it turns out, was predicated on the basis that one not ask too many questions.

On paper everything looks fine. There is an intelligence oversight committee in the German parliament (the Parliamentary Control Committee).[22] The G-10 Act and the BND Act govern the BND's operational practices.[23] Under this regime surveillance programs have to be authorized by the G-10 Commission, a group of credible and independent persons appointed by the parliament. In addition, the Chancellery must regularly inform the Parliamentary Control Committee about the work of the BND. Both the Parliamentary Control Committee and the G-10 Commission have broad powers to investigate the intelligence services. But this exceptionalism – the notion that everything is done in conformity with German *Rechtsstaatlichkeit* (rule of law) – has grown harder and harder to maintain. There are numerous, well-documented examples of close cooperation between the BND and the NSA, most notably reports that German intelligence agencies have been given access to the

---

[19] *Kauder: Die Kontrolle der Dienste ist Da*, CDU CSU (June 8, 2013), www.cducsu.de/presse/texte-und-interviews/kauder-die-kontrolle-der-dienste-ist-da; *Meinungsbildung Muss das Parlament Betreiben*, DEUTSCHLANDFUNK (Jan. 20, 2006), www.deutschlandfunk.de/meinungsbildung-muss-das-parlament-betreiben.694.de.html?dram:article_id=62849.

[20] *See 1. Untersuchungsausschuss* ("NSA"), DEUTSHER BUNDESTAG, www.bundestag.de/bundestag/ausschuesse18/ua/1untersuchungsausschuss (last visited Nov. 16, 2015).

[21] Heumann, *supra* note 11.

[22] Gesetz über die parlamentarische Kontrolle nachrichtendienstlicher Tätigkeit des Bundes [Kontrollgremiumgesetz] [PKGrG] [Parliamentary Control Committee Act], July 29, 2009, BGBl. I at 2346 (Ger.).

[23] Gesetz zur Beschränkung des Brief-, Post- und Fernmeldegeheimnisses [Artikel 10-Gesetz] [G-10] [G-10 Act], June 26, 2001, BGBl. I at 1254, 2298, last amended by Gesetz [G], June 12, 2015, BGBl. I at 926, art. 2, § 1 (Ger.); Gesetz über den Bundesnachrichtendienst [BND-Gesetz] [BNDG] [BND Act], Dec. 20, 1990, BGBl. I at 2954, 2979, last amended by Gesetz [G], June 20, 2013, BGBl. I at 1602, art. 7 (Ger.).

controversial XKeyscore Program[24] or aided the Americans by conducting surveillance of discrete communications channels and selectors that implicated other European public officials and European military-industrial interests.[25] But how could such cooperation be possible given that the NSA was an "out of control" entity while the German BND was a bastion of the German *Rechtsstaat*?[26]

The name of the Parliament's Committee of Inquiry, the establishment of which resulted from the growing political pressure to respond to the NSA-Affair, still reflects Germans' hope of maintaining exceptionalism on these issues. It is formally referred to as the "NSA Inquiry Committee" and its main task is to investigate mass surveillance of Germans by the NSA.[27] The opposition parties were able to extend the committee's mandate to include questions regarding the practices of the BND.[28] Perhaps not surprisingly, the Committee of Inquiry has not been able to unearth a lot of new information regarding the NSA. Instead, its most significant contribution has been to shatter the notion of German intelligence exceptionalism.

At this point it is important to briefly elaborate the concept of mass surveillance and the scope of this chapter. The term mass surveillance has become a hotly contested issue in Germany. The main reason is that the Committee of Inquiry is supposed to find out whether mass surveillance is taking place or not. From the perspective of the NSA, the GCHQ, and the BND – and the government officials and parliamentarians who defend these agencies' practices in public – there has been no "mass surveillance." The first question raised to deflect these concerns is to ask where surveillance begins. Does the automatic collection of data already

---

[24] *Schnüffelsoftware XKeyscore: Deutsche Geheimdienste Setzen US-Spähprogramm ein,* SPIEGEL ONLINE (July 20, 2013, 6:00 PM), www.spiegel.de/politik/deutschland/bnd-und-bfv-setzen-nsa-spaehprogramm-xkeyscore-ein-a-912196.html.

[25] Kai Biermann *et al., BND Half NSA beim Überwachen Europäischer Politiker,* ZEIT ONLINE (Apr. 23, 2015, 2:37 PM), www.zeit.de/digital/datenschutz/2015-04/ueberwa chung-bnd-half-nsa-wirtschaftsspionage-europa.

[26] *Spying Together: Germany's Deep Cooperation with the NSA,* SPIEGEL ONLINE (June 18, 2014, 4:20 PM), www.spiegel.de/international/germany/the-german-bnd-and-american-nsa-cooperate-more-closely-than-thought-a-975445.html. *See* Russell A. Miller, *Intelligence Oversight – Made in Germany, in* GLOBAL INTELLIGENCE OVERSIGHT: GOVERNING SECURITY IN THE TWENTY-FIRST CENTURY (Zachary Goldman ed., *forthcoming* 2016)

[27] DEUTSCHER BUNDESTAG: DRUCKSACHE [BT] 18/843, Mar. 18, 2014, www.bundestag.de/blob/284528/a89d6006f28900c4f46e56f5e0807ddf/einsetzungsantrag_englisch-docx-data.pdf.

[28] *Id.*

constitute surveillance, even if most of the data is deleted without any person ever analyzing it? Or does surveillance only occur, if the automatic processing leads to storage? Or can we only speak of mass surveillance when the collected and stored data is selected for further analysis and processing by intelligence officers?

The second question posed as a way of minimizing worry about mass surveillance focuses on what constitutes mass surveillance if the intelligence agencies (for technical and tactical reasons) usually do not want to copy and store all available communication but only a "relevant" share of it. But what does relevant mean? And how large must this share be so that it can be considered mass surveillance?

Even if only cynically posed by the Intelligence Community and its defenders, these are interesting and difficult questions. But they are far beyond the scope of this paper. I introduce only one distinction that I regard as central to the debate over surveillance, namely, whether surveillance is targeted or strategic. In regard to foreign intelligence gathering, the German G-10 Act operates with this distinction. Paragraph 3 of the G-10 Act, for example, deals with surveillance of individual targets.[29] Paragraph 5 deals with so-called strategic surveillance.[30] Strategic surveillance does not involve the targeted collection of specific individuals' communications information. Instead, it involves the filtering, screening and analysis of broad swathes of communications activities in order to identify targets about which there was no previous discrete suspicion. This is the much-referenced search for the "needle in the haystack." And this approach requires that you look at the entire haystack. Whether it is called "bulk collection" or "mass surveillance," it involves data and communications that are screened and processed on a large scale. Significantly, mass-surveillance operations cannot be limited in advance by reference to whether and how much of the screened and processed data and communications are actually relevant to legitimate foreign affairs or national security purposes.

C   The NSA-Affair in a Global Context

Edward Snowden's revelations have given us penetrating insight into the scale and scope of surveillance programs conducted by the NSA and the other Five-Eyes agencies. The best sources concern the United States and

---

[29] G-10 Act § 3.   [30] G-10 Act § 5.

its closest allies, but this does not mean that other foreign intelligence services are refraining from these activities. Snowden's revelations have triggered a global debate.[31] This is a very important, urgently-needed debate about privacy and security in an era of ubiquitous digital technologies and big-data. Naturally, it focuses on the United States and its Five-Eyes partners. After all, Snowden's revelations about the United States' surveillance practices have provided the essential empirical basis for thinking about these important questions.

Yet, the availability of good sources should not lead us to draw the wrong conclusions. Mass surveillance by intelligence agencies is a global phenomenon.[32] The drivers behind the development of these programs in the United States and Great Britain are also present in most states in the developed world. Whether Russia or China, Germany, France, Iran, or Turkey – countries around the globe are trying to realize the intelligence benefits of new technological possibilities. The central difference, for the purpose of the debate over mass surveillance and privacy, is whether a country is a democracy or not. An open debate about the powers and limits of intelligence agencies is possible in democracies such as the United States, Sweden, or Germany. In a democracy such a debate is necessary because public debate, and the consent it helps foster, constitute the basis for the legitimate exercise of state power. This is what distinguishes liberal democracies from Russia or China, which are no less active with respect to mass surveillance but where such a debate cannot take place. Mass surveillance is a global phenomenon. But what I call "legitimate surveillance" – surveillance regulated by law and effectively overseen by parliament and courts – is a distinct subspecies.

The mandate of foreign intelligence agencies during the Cold War was quite clear.[33] Foreign intelligence was needed to learn more about the intentions and capabilities of the adversary. Foreign governments and

---

[31] Allison Kilkenny, *Protesters Worldwide Rally to Support Whistleblower Edward Snowden*, NATION (June 12, 2013) www.thenation.com/article/protesters-worldwide-rally-support-whistleblower-edward-snowden/.

[32] See, for example, the numerous reports on the export of surveillance technology by Privacy International. *Reports*, PRIVACY INT'L, www.privacyinternational.org/reports (last visited Nov. 16, 2015).

[33] For a more detailed discussion of how the practices of the BND should be seen as part of global political and technological transformations, *see* Stefan Heumann & Thorsten Wetzling, *Policy Brief: Strategische Auslandsüberwachung: Technische Möglichkeiten, Rechtlicher Rahmen und Parlamentarische Kontrolle*, STIFTUNG NEUE VERANTWORTUNG (May 2014), www.stiftung-nv.de/sites/default/files/052014_snv_policy_brief_strategische_auslandsuberwachung.pdf.

their militaries were the main targets of intelligence collection.[34] The end of the Cold War was a period of crisis for intelligence agencies. They had lost their core mission. But this crisis did not last long. Organized crime, international terrorism, and failed states became the new *raison d'etre* for foreign intelligence services around the globe. The mandates of the agencies were broadened to include these new fields of activity. Germany was part of a global trend when it added new threats to the list of purposes for which the BND could engage in strategic surveillance (surveillance of entire communications streams not individual targets).[35] The reach of intelligence gathering was also extended beyond classical state actors and institutions. Terrorists and international criminal organizations presented new threats and they greatly increased the number of potential intelligence targets.

At the same time a technological revolution took place. New developments in telecommunications technology opened a wide range of new opportunities for signals intelligence. Four factors are particularly important to understand how new communication technology and their spread around the globe revolutionized the work of intelligence agencies. The first factor seems like a truism, but it is important to fully understand its implications. Signals intelligence largely depends on the availability of signals. Wiretapping a house or tracking suspects in person are labor- and cost-intensive methods and there is no guarantee that they will produce useful intelligence. Crucial information may be simply exchanged outside the home during a conversation on the street or in a café. Smartphones and the everyday use of the Internet have totally changed the picture. Use of the Internet and Smartphones involves the content of those activities as well as information about the users' location, communications channels and partners, and activities. All of this provides signals intelligence with a wealth of new data for exploitation.[36]

---

[34] JOSEF FOSCHEPOTH, ÜBERWACHTES DEUTSCHLAND: POST- UND TELEFONÜBERWACHUNG IN DER ALTEN BUNDESREPUBLIK (2013); Erich Schmidt-Eenboom, *The Bundesnachrichtendienst, the Bundeswehr and SIGINT during the Cold War and Beyond, in* SECRETS OF SIGNALS INTELLIGENCE DURING THE COLD WAR AND BEYOND 129 (Matthew M. Aid & Cees Wiebes eds., 2001).

[35] Bundesverfassungsgericht [BVerfG] [Federal Constitutional Court], July 14, 1999, ENTSCHEIDUNGEN DES BUNDESVERFASSUNGSGERICHTS [BVerfGE] 1 BvR 2226/94, www.bundesverfassungsgericht.de/SharedDocs/Entscheidungen/EN/1999/07/rs1999071 4_1bvr222694en.html (Ger.).

[36] M. Cayford, C. van Gulijk & P.H.A.J.M. van Gelder, *All Swept Up: An Initial Classification of NSA Surveillance Technology, in* SAFETY AND RELIABILITY: METHODOLOGY AND APPLICATIONS 643 (Tomasz Nowakowski *et al.* eds., 2015).

Before the 1990s signal collection was largely limited to phone conversations and faxes that were transmitted via satellite or landlines. In order to capture these signals it is necessary to have physical or geographical access. For landlines this is obvious. But even for satellite communications there were practical constraints in terms of what and where signals intelligence could be collected. Today the Internet is the central communication platform. This means that most information can be accessed from anywhere in the world and flows over global networks. Geographical constraints in regard to accessing communication have become much less relevant.

The first two factors introduced above concern the availability of and access to data. The third and fourth factors address the ability of digital technologies to deal with the huge amounts of data the new paradigm has opened up to intelligence services. Big-data technologies are capitalizing on the steady expansion of computing powers during the past years as predicted by Moore's Law.[37] Huge amounts of data can now be stored and analyzed. In the past a much more targeted approach was necessary simply because the amount of data would have otherwise overwhelmed analysts. This problem has been solved with powerful computers and software that can process huge amounts of data almost instantly.[38]

Finally, storage for the large amounts of data that is being collected is crucial. While not all data needs to be stored permanently, large storage capacities are still necessary for the temporary storage that allows for more sophisticated analysis of collected data. The cost of storage has decreased significantly during the past years. But it is still an important constraint. There is probably no country in the world that can match the storage capacities the United States has provided to the NSA – especially when the new data center in Utah comes online.[39] But other countries are catching up and storage capacity is no longer the scarce resource it was just a few years ago.

The emergence of new threats has been a global phenomenon. The pressure intelligence agencies feel to identify terrorists and their plans before attacks occur is also a global phenomenon. The impact of the

---

[37] R. R. Schaller, *Moore's Law: Past, Present and Future*, 36 IEEE SPECTRUM MAG. 52 (1997).

[38] RANDAL E. BRYANT *ET AL.*, COMPUTING CMTY. CONSORTIUM, BIG-DATA COMPUTING: CREATING REVOLUTIONARY BREAKTHROUGHS IN COMMERCE, SCIENCE AND SOCIETY (Version 8, 2008), http://cra.org/ccc/wp-content/uploads/sites/2/2015/05/Big_Data.pdf. *See* Chapter 8 in this volume.

[39] James Bamford, *The NSA Is Building the Country's Biggest Spy Center (Watch What You Say)*, WIRED (Mar. 15, 2012, 7:24 PM), www.wired.com/2012/03/ff_nsadatacenter/.

terrorist attacks of September 11, 2001, has placed the U.S. Intelligence Community under particularly significant pressure.[40] But we should not forget Paris, London, and Madrid. The French, British and Spanish Intelligence Communities have their own grisly experience with modern terrorism and an accompanying need to be responsive to those threats.[41] Russia and China have also had to deal with terrorist attacks and both countries feel vulnerable to internal unrest.[42]

There have been numerous reasons and justifications for governments around the globe to widen the mandate and powers of their intelligence services. And, while the United States has been enjoying a strong strategic advantage because of its central role in the development and governance of the Internet and the strength of U.S. Internet service providers and technology companies, the importance of the information technology revolution has not gone unnoticed by other countries. It is well known, for example, that China and Russia understand that dominance in cyberspace will be one of the most important geostrategic resources in the twenty-first century.[43]

The pressure on intelligence agencies to take advantage of new technological opportunities to expand surveillance capabilities is a global phenomenon. For countries such as Russia and China the expansion of surveillance powers is unproblematic because they care little about the implications for human rights and the rule of law. For liberal democracies, however, this trend raises questions. Are the legal frameworks and especially the limitations and safeguards to prevent abuse of powers still effective? Does oversight still work? Do decision-makers adequately understand the implications of these technologies for human rights and privacy so that they can find the right balance between privacy and power? Those

---

[40] *See* National Archives and Records Administration, *National Commission on Terrorist Attacks Upon the United States*, www.9-11commission.gov/.

[41] Angelique Chrisafis, *France Passes New Surveillance Law in the Wake of Charlie Hebdo Attack*, THE GUARDIAN (May 5, 2015), www.theguardian.com/world/2015/may/05/france-passes-new-surveillance-law-in-wake-of-charlie-hebdo-attack.

[42] Charles E. Ziegler, *Russia and China in Central Asia*, *in* THE FUTURE OF CHINA-RUSSIA RELATIONS 233 (James Belacqua ed., 2010).

[43] Keir Giles, *Russia's Public Stance on Cyberspace Issues*, 2012 4TH INTERNATIONAL CONFERENCE ON CYBER CONFLICT (C. Czosseck, R. Ottis & K. Ziolkowski eds., 2012), https://ccdcoe.org/publications/2012proceedings/2_1_Giles_RussiasPublicStanceOnCyberInformationWarfare.pdf; Timothy L. Thomas, *Nation-State Cyber Strategies: Examples from China and Russia*, *in* CYBERPOWER AND NATIONAL SECURITY 465 (Franklin D. Kramer, Stuart H. Starr & Larry K. Wentz eds., 2009), http://ctnsp.dodlive.mil/files/2014/03/Cyberpower-I-Chap-20.pdf.

are hard questions. But in liberal democracies we have to face them. And not just the United States. Germany also needs to tackle these issues.

The Snowden documents have taught us a lot about the intelligence agencies' new capabilities. The documents also raise many questions regarding legal frameworks, interpretations of the law by intelligence agencies, and oversight. These problems are not unique to the United States. They are problems that every liberal democracy – at least those operating mass surveillance intelligence programs – must confront. Failing to do so creates the risk of illegitimate intelligence services that are able to evade the basic rule of law frameworks that aim to hold them accountable through effective oversight.

D   Status of Foreigners, Secrecy of the Law, and Oversight

The Snowden documents provide an unprecedented view of the scope and scale of surveillance programs developed by the United States and its partners.[44] They have also raised many questions regarding, on one hand, the constitutional and statutory frameworks meant to constrain the intelligence services, and on the other hand, the effectiveness of political or judicial oversight of the intelligence services. The questions can be grouped under three broad categories that I will briefly consider here. As the comparison between Germany and the United States will show, in regard to legal frameworks and oversight, Germany and the United States are not very far apart. This undermines German officials' claims that Germany is somehow exceptional when it comes to its own national intelligence agency. Quite to the contrary, German law and oversight also allows the German BND to take advantage of the new opportunities of digital technologies and global communication flows for its signals intelligence activities.

I   Broad Authorization and the Problematic Distinction between Foreign and Domestic Intelligence

The Foreign Intelligence Surveillance Act grants a very broad authorization for the collection of "foreign intelligence information."[45]

---

[44] U.N. H.R.C. Rep, The Right to Privacy in the Digital Age, U.N. Doc. A/HRC/27/37 ¶ 29 (June 30, 2014) (a discussion of Secrecy of Law), www.ohchr.org/EN/HRBodies/HRC/RegularSessions/Session27/Documents/A.HRC.27.37_en.pdf.

[45] Foreign Intelligence Surveillance Act (FISA) of 1978, Pub. L. 95-511, 92 Stat. 1783 (codified as amended in 50 U.S.C. ch. 36 (2012)). *See* Chapter 5 in this volume; Chapter 12 in this volume.

FSIA's main purpose was to limit and restrict the collection of intelligence inside the United States. For this reason the FISA framework contains safeguards regarding surveillance of so-called "U.S. persons."[46] The FISA act does not apply to NSA activities abroad involving non-U.S. persons. The President uses his executive authority to authorize surveillance targeting non-U.S. persons without a court order.[47]

The Snowden documents show that the distinction between U.S. persons and non-U.S. persons is very difficult to operationalize.[48] FISA amendments passed in 2001 and 2008 broadened the definition of the kinds of information that can be collected. Prior to 2008, FISA only permitted targeting "foreign powers" or "agents of foreign powers" with surveillance programs. Since 2008, the NSA and other intelligence agencies have been authorized to collect "foreign intelligence information" including "information with respect to a foreign power or foreign territory that relates to . . . the conduct of foreign affairs of the United States." This definition goes far beyond counter-terrorism or national security as the main purposes of intelligence gathering. By broadly authorizing the acquisition of communications where at least one party is outside the United States, the revised standard permits the kind of mass surveillance of foreign communications that was exposed by the Snowden documents.[49]

II   Secrecy About Interpretation and Application of the Laws

One of the co-authors of the USA PATRIOT Act, Congressman Jim Sensenbrenner, has become one of the fiercest critics of the domestic surveillance powers exercised by the NSA.[50] Sensenbrenner claims that

---

[46] The NSA regards U.S. citizens, aliens with permanent residency, U.S. corporations, and associations of U.S. citizens or residents as U.S. persons. *See SIGINT Frequently Asked Questions*, NAT'L SECURITY AGENCY CENTRAL SECURITY SERV., www.nsa.gov/sigint/faqs .shtml#sigint4 (last accessed Nov. 16, 2015).

[47] Scott F. Mann, *Fact Sheet: Executive Order 12333*, CSIS (Feb. 24, 2014), http://csis.org/ publication/fact-sheet-executive-order-12333-0.

[48] Elizabeth Goitein, *The NSA's Backdoor Search Loophole*, BOSTON REV. (Nov. 14, 2013), https://bostonreview.net/blog/elizabeth-goitein-nsa-backdoor-search-loophole-freedom-act.

[49] Stefan Heumann & Ben Scott, *Impulse: Law and Policy in Internet Surveillance Programs*, STIFTUNG NEUE VERANTWORTUNG (Sept. 2013), www.stiftung-nv.de/publikation/law-and-policy-internet-surveillance-programs-united-states-great-britain-and-germany.

[50] Dan Roberts, *Patriot Act Author Prepares Bill to Put NSA Bulk Collection "Out of Business,"* THE GUARDIAN (Oct. 10, 2013, 3:37 PM), www.theguardian.com/world/ 2013/oct/10/nsa-surveillance-patriot-act-author-bill.

the Intelligence Community misused its powers under the USA PATRIOT Act when it collected telephone metadata records on all Americans, an abuse compounded by the fact that the Obama administration did not properly inform Congress about these programs.[51] The secrecy of laws is a main problem here. If courts and the executive do not disclose their interpretation and application of the governing legal regimes, then the rule of law cannot be realized because the legislature cannot ensure that the legal constraints on surveillance it has enacted are being respected. Snowden's documents confirm that the Intelligence Community tends to adopt legal interpretations that maximize its authority to conduct surveillance under the relevant statutes.

III The Dilemma of Oversight: Secrecy Undermines Accountability

Oversight of the secretive Intelligence Community is a major challenge. The Presidential Review Group – convened by President Obama in the wake of the NSA-Affair – identified a list of areas where internal review and oversight should be strengthened.[52] But the Snowden revelations are also a stark reminder of the core dilemmas that plague Congressional oversight. Nobody on the Congressional oversight committees should have been surprised by the revelations because it is their job to know what the Intelligence Community does. If they argue that they did not know, then they are implicitly admitting that oversight does not work. But even if they did know, they could not talk about potential concerns since everything is highly classified. In addition, being part of this ring of secrecy strengthens institutional capture.[53] The overseers come to see themselves as part of the Intelligence Community. Despite her commendable and provocative role in exposing the torture conducted by the CIA, Senator Diane Feinstein is a good example of this. As head of the Senate Select Committee on

---

[51] Jim Sensenbrenner, *How Obama Abused the Patriot Act*, L.A. Times (Aug. 19, 2013), www.latimes.com/opinion/op-ed/la-oe-sensenbrenner-data-patriot-act-obama-2013081 9-story.html.

[52] President's Rev. Grp. on Intelligence & Commc'ns Techs., Liberty and Security in a Changing World (Dec. 12, 2013), www.nsa.gov/civil_liberties/_files/liberty_secur ity_prgfinalreport.pdf.

[53] Michael E. Levine & Jennifer L. Forrence, *Regulatory Capture, Public Interest and the Public Agenda: Towards a Synthesis*, 6 J.L. Econ. & Org. 167 (1990).

Intelligence, Senator Feinstein took on the role as one of the leading public advocates in defense of the NSA.[54]

E   The NSA Committee of Inquiry:
Lots of Questions about the BND

One of the ironies of the Snowden revelations is that Germans now know more about the capabilities and programs of the NSA than they do about their foreign intelligence service. It would be naïve – and as I argue here, it is part of the myth of German exceptionalism – to assume that the BND is as weak and ineffective as it is often characterized in public.[55] Instead, the BND has long been known for its strength in signals intelligence. There is strong technical know-how in Germany and during the Cold War – due to its strategic position close to the Iron Curtain – Germany was an important site for conducting surveillance of satellite communications.[56]

After the Cold War the BND took note of and adapted to the diminishing relevance of satellite communications and the growing importance of IP-based communications.[57] After all, the world's largest Internet exchange point is located in Frankfurt.[58] Many strategically important networks in the Middle East, Eastern Europe, and Russia connect through Frankfurt. The NSA certainly recognized the changing situation, pulling out of satellite surveillance in Germany entirely and requesting the assistance of the BND for access to communications and data flowing

---

[54] Seema Mehta, *Sen. Dianne Feinstein Defends NSA and Need for Intelligence Gathering*, L.A. Times (Feb. 19, 2014), http://articles.latimes.com/2014/feb/19/news/la-pn-feinstein-nsa-foreign-policy-20140219.

[55] The German media and public like to refer to members of the BND as "Schlapphüte" – a German word for floppy hat. The term emphasizes human intelligence collection. In popular imagination secret service officers would use floppy hats to better cover their faces from being recognized. But of course wearing such an unusual hat would make them stand out in any crowd. The term is generally used in the media when failures or incompetence of the service are being discussed. *See, e.g.*, BND-Zentrale
    Schlapphut-Saustall, Berliner Kurier (July 17, 2011), www.berliner-kurier.de/kiez-stadt/bnd-zentrale-schlapphut-saustall,7169128,8681432.html for an example of this usage.

[56] Foschepoth, *supra* note 34.

[57] Stefan Krempl, *NSA-Ausschuss: BND Fühlt Sich von der Politik im Stich Gelassen*, Heise Online (Mar. 19, 2015, 6:08 PM), www.heise.de/newsticker/meldung/NSA-Ausschuss-BND-fuehlt-sich-von-der-Politik-im-Stich-gelassen-2581376.html.

[58] Kai Biermann, *Wo das Deutsche Internet Wohnt*, Zeit Online (Nov. 29, 2012, 6:40 AM), www.zeit.de/digital/internet/2012-11/de-cix-frankfurt.

through the exchange point in Frankfurt. This cooperation went ahead under the code word Eikonal.[59] This operation was characterized by the typically symbiotic relationship that forms the basis for cooperation among intelligence agencies. The NSA wanted data and the BND was interested in further developing its technical capabilities. Through this close cooperation the BND gained insight into the NSA's strategy, operations, and technical capabilities, even if the NSA was as protective of its capabilities as the BND was protective of its data. Given the close relationship to the NSA, it is very hard to believe that the BND would be the only intelligence service worldwide which missed the digital revolution.[60]

In Germany bulk collection is known as "strategic surveillance." The law explicitly authorizes it. Paragraph 5 of the G-10 Act describes the circumstances under which the BND can engage in strategic surveillance. The BND uses these powers. The annual reports of the Parliamentary Control Committee contain figures regarding the number of emails that get filtered out of the Internet traffic by BND selectors. For example, 27 million emails in the area of nonproliferation were filtered in 2010.[61] And this only involves cables between Germany and other countries. So-called foreign-to-foreign traffic does not fall under the G-10 Act – a fact that has drawn criticism from prominent constitutional law experts.[62] Given the specific filters that are used, this number needs to be multiplied by a large factor for the number of emails that needed to be screened in the first place. The German lawyer Niko Härting brought a case at the Federal Administrative Court against strategic surveillance referencing the 2010 statistics. Nobody disputed that strategic surveillance was taking place on a massive scale. But Härting's case was dismissed on the grounds that he lacked standing because he could not prove that he had been personally affected.[63]

---

[59] Von Georg Mascolo, Hans Leyendecker & John Goetz, *Codewort Eikonal – der Albtraum der Bundesregierung*, SÜDDEUTSCHE ZEITUNG (Oct. 4, 2014, 9:12 AM), www.sueddeutsche.de/politik/geheimdienste-codewort-eikonal-der-albtraum-der-bundesregierung-1.2157432.

[60] *Id.*

[61] DEUTSCHER BUNDESTAG: DRUCKSACHE [BT] 17/8639, Feb. 10, 2012, http://dipbt.bundestag.de/dip21/btd/17/086/1708639.pdf.

[62] *Staatsrechtler Sehen BND im Rechtsfreien Raum*, ZEIT ONLINE (May 22, 2014, 6:43 PM), www.zeit.de/politik/deutschland/2014-05/nsa-untersuchungsausschuss-bundesnachrichtendienst. *But see* Chapter 15 in this volume.

[63] *Bundesverfassungsgericht Soll E-Mail-Überwachung des BND Prüfen*, HÄRTUNG (June 10, 2014), www.haerting.de/neuigkeit/bundesverfassungsgericht-soll-e-mail-ueberwachung-des-bnd-pruefen.

Until there is a German Snowden there is no way of knowing the BND's exact capabilities. The most interesting parts of the hearings of the NSA Committee of Inquiry are closed to the public. For understandable reasons the German government does not want to publicly disclose its intelligence methods and capabilities. Thus, only educated inferences from the facts that are in the public record are possible. Budgets and resources make it obvious that NSA and the United Kingdom's GCHQ have far superior capabilities and cast a much wider net in their data-collection programs.[64] But most of the superior capabilities are related to exploiting security weaknesses, breaking encryption, and special cyber operations.[65] Surveillance on an Internet exchange point is technically challenging, but it is not expensive rocket science. Much of the technology is commercially available. Importantly, German law permits it and the BND has strong institutional interests in engaging in exactly those kinds of surveillance operations. If the BND was neither interested in doing it nor capable of doing it, then the NSA Committee of Inquiry would not have so many questions to ask. The findings of the NSA Committee of Inquiry and media reports now make it possible to examine the BND according to the three categories that have been identified as problematic regarding NSA surveillance.

I   Broad Authorization and the Problematic Distinction between Foreign and Domestic

The German BND operates based on a law passed by the German parliament in 1990. Paragraph 1, Section 2 of the BND Act authorizes the agency to gather foreign intelligence relevant to German foreign policy and national security interests. The law authorizes the BND to request data from telecommunications providers for the purposes stated in §1, Section 2.

---

[64] According to the *Washington Post* U.S. national agencies combined have a budget of more than 52 billion USD. *See The Black Budget*, WASH. POST, www.washingtonpost .com/wp-srv/special/national/black-budget/ (last accessed Nov. 16, 2015). MI5, MI6 and GCHQ have a combined budget of about 2.5 billion British Pounds. *See* Frank Gardner, *Budget 2015: What Is the New Joint Security Fund?*, BBC (July 9, 2015), www.bbc.com/ news/uk-33469450. The BND only has a budget of about half a billion Euros. *See* Günther Lachmann, Dirk Banse & Uwe Müller, *Ist der BND Überhaupt zur Gegenspionage Fähig?*, DIE WELT (July 10, 2014), www.welt.de/politik/deutschland/article129980685/Ist-der-BND-ueberhaupt-zur-Gegenspionage-faehig.html.

[65] *Inside TAO: Documents Reveal Top NSA Hacking Unit*, SPIEGEL ONLINE (Dec. 29, 2013, 9:18 AM), www.spiegel.de/international/world/the-nsa-uses-powerful-toolbox-in-effort-to-spy-on-global-networks-a-940969.html.

The law requires a strict separation of the intelligence service from police and law enforcement functions. Paragraph 2, Section 4 mandates the BND to use the method of intelligence gathering with the least disruptive impact on the targeted persons. There also has to be a balance between negative consequences of the surveillance and the intended benefit. As the law's provisions indicate, it was written so broadly that it offers very little concrete guidance regarding the legal limits of surveillance activities.

The BND has a broad mandate to collect foreign intelligence information that serves German foreign policy and national security interests. Still, any activities that interfere with Article 10 of the Constitution (protection of the privacy of correspondence, posts, and telecommunications) are subject to the G-10 Act and to the approval of the G-10 Commission. The G-10 Act more narrowly defines the purposes for the authorization of surveillance programs. Among other justifications for international telecommunications surveillance, the law lists the following as the legitimate purposes for surveillance: the threat of an imminent military attack against Germany, the threat of international terrorist attacks related to Germany, or the international proliferation of arms. But the mandate is broadly defined and also extends to drug trafficking, international money laundering, and human trafficking.

The government treats foreign communications abroad as not covered by Article 10 of the Constitution and, thus not subject to the G-10 Act and the required oversight of the G-10 Commission.[66] From this legal perspective German and U.S. practices are quite similar.[67] Germany imposes no limits and safeguards on the surveillance of entirely foreign communications. This policy means that the G-10 Act's limitations on the purposes for which surveillance can be conducted also do not apply. In regard to the surveillance of foreigners – at least from a legal and constitutional perspective – the BND has as much discretion to act as it sees fit.[68]

---

[66] Thorsten Denkler, *Juristen Werfen BND Verfassungsbruch vor*, SÜDDEUTSCHE ZEITUNG (Feb. 5, 2015, 2:55 PM), www.sueddeutsche.de/politik/nsa-untersuchungsausschuss-juris ten-werfen-bnd-verfassungsbruch-vor-1.1972477; *but see* Comments by the German Fed. Gov't on the Report by Nils Muižnieks, the Comm'r for Human Rights of the Council of Eur., Following his Official visit to Ger. on 24 Apr. and from 4 to 8 May 2015, https://wcd .coe.int/com.instranet.InstraServlet?command=com.instranet.CmdBlobGet&Instranet Image=2808748&SecMode=1&DocId=2308986&Usage=2.

[67] Heumann & Scott, *supra* note 49. *See* Chapter 15 in this volume; Chapter 10 in this volume.

[68] Berthold Huber, *Die strategische Rasterfahndung des Bundesnachrichtendienstes – Eingriffs-befugnisse und Regelungsdefizite*, 66 NEUE JURISTISCHE WOCHENSCHRIFT 2572 (2013).

II   Secrecy About Interpretation and Application of the Laws

The structure of German law governing the BND is not straightforward. The intelligence service's work is governed by a combination of the BND Act, the G-10 Act, and German data protection law. To make things even more complicated, the BND Act frequently references the Law for the Office of the Protection of the Constitution. Government officials and employees of the service point out that the BND strictly observes German law.[69] But what does this actually mean? As pointed out above, the German government claims that the constitutional protections of Article 10 do not apply to the surveillance of foreign communications – even if the data is processed and stored in Germany. Most constitutional law experts, including a former president of the German Federal Constitutional Court, dispute this argument.[70] The effect of the German government's legal opinion is that the core work of the BND – the surveillance of foreigners – is only subject to internal supervision and parameters, including the broad control exercised by the Chancellery. And, as of today, the German government has not provided its full legal opinion on its interpretation of the relevant law to the NSA Committee of Inquiry or the G-10 Commission, even though both bodies have requested it.

The secrecy regarding the interpretation and application of the law makes it very difficult to claim that the BND is strictly fulfilling standards with respect to the rule of law. It is especially hard to believe that the BND has embraced the most conservative interpretation of its controlling statutory framework in light of the hearings of the Committee of Inquiry. The data protection officer of the BND testified before the Committee about a legal dispute with the President of the BND.[71] In that dispute the data protection officer argued that the relevant data protection provisions

---

[69] *Potfalla: Deutsche Geheimdienste befolgen alle Gesetze*, Die Welt (July 25, 2013), www.welt.de/newsticker/news1/article118368374/Pofalla-Deutsche-Geheimdienste-befol gen-alle-Gesetze.html.

[70] Zeit Online, *supra* note 62. In a recent discussion the State Minister of the German chancellery could not name a single constitutional law expert who agrees with the government's position that the BND is not bound by Article 10 of the German constitution. *See* Peter Altmaier, *Der Schwarze in der Grünen Hölle*, Süddeutsche Zeitung (Sept. 23, 2015, 7:47 AM), www.sueddeutsche.de/politik/nsa-debatte-bei-der-heinrich-boell-stiftung-der-schwarze-in-der-gruenen-hoelle-1.2660579. *See* Chapter 15 in this volume.

[71] Lisa Caspari, *Der BND Pfeift auf seine Datenschutzbeauftragte*, Zeit Online (Oct. 9, 2014, 8:25 PM), www.zeit.de/politik/deutschland/2014-10/bnd-nsa-bad-aibling.

in the BND law apply to its operations in Germany. The President of the BND rejected this position, referring instead to the so-called "space theory." Since the data in question was acquired through satellite surveillance, the argument went, the data came from outer space and not German territory. Thus, the BND President concluded, no laws govern how these data are stored, processed, or analyzed.

The BND has also argued that, in certain circumstances, even German citizens do not enjoy G-10 Act protection.[72] If, for example, a German works for a foreign entity such as a government or a business that is considered a legitimate target, then the G-10 Act no longer applies. Under this interpretation of the law, this person's communications can be monitored without requesting approval from the G-10 Commission. This interpretation only applies to communications and data that the individual generates in an official capacity. Article 10 would still protect strictly private communications.

The BND also claims that metadata are not personal data, arguing that metadata cannot be directly connected to a person. Here again the legal interpretation of the BND differs from experts' views about metadata.[73] As the German Federal Constitutional Court has recognized, metadata is often more revealing than the content of communications.[74] But the metadata distinction is very convenient for the service. Data that are not considered personal is subject to much less strict rules regarding collection, processing, and storage. From a legal perspective it is also much easier to share metadata with other services.

German laws also prescribe that new databases have to be checked by its internal data protection officer before they can be operated.[75] During her testimony before the Committee of Inquiry, the BND's data protection

---

[72] Thorsten Denklere, *So Biegt sich der BND das Recht Zurecht*, SÜDDEUTSCHE ZEITUNG (Nov. 27, 2014, 6:24 PM), www.sueddeutsche.de/politik/nsa-ausschuss-so-biegt-sich-der-bnd-das-recht-zurecht-1.2242129.

[73] Andre Meister, *Lieber Bundesnachrichtendienst: Wir Erklären Warum Metadaten sehr wohl Personenbezogene Daten sind*, NETZPOLITIK.ORG (Nov. 14, 2014, 4:30 PM), https://netzpolitik.org/2014/lieber-bundesnachrichtendienst-wir-erklaeren-warum-metadaten-sehr-wohl-personenbezogene-daten-sind/.

[74] Bundesverfassungsgerecht [BVerfG] [Federal Constitutional Court] Mar. 2, 2010, 125 BVerfG 260, 1 BvR 256/08, Rn. (1-345), 189 (2010).

[75] Gesetz über die Zusammenarbeit des Bundes und der Länder in Angelegenheiten des Verfassungsschutzes und über das Bundesamt für Verfassungsschutz [Bundesverfassungsschutzgesetz] [BVerfSchG] [Federal Act on the Protection of the Constitution], § 14, 2, 3, Dec. 20, 1990, BGBl. I at 2954, 2970, last amended by Gesetz [G], June 20, 2013, BGBl. I at 1602, art. 6.

officer admitted that two databases have been fully operational for two years without the required data protection audits.[76] The Committee of Inquiry also discovered that the BND reserves the right to put up to five "communication hops" of a target under surveillance.[77] Communication hops describe the degree of separation between a target and the persons in the target's wider network who can be put under surveillance. One hop would be all direct contacts of the target. The second hop would be the friends of the direct contacts, and so on. The expansion of surveillance to entire networks surrounding a specific target – including anyone within five hops of the target's communications – is highly problematic from a civil liberties perspective.[78] The NSA rules allow for three degrees of separation.[79] The BND's "five hops" rule would be hard to operationalize simply because of the sheer size of the contacts that could be monitored. And it is very questionable whether this makes any sense. But the fact that it is allowed illustrates the lack of effective legal constraints on the BND.

The point here is not whether these interpretations are right or wrong. What is problematic is that these theories show that the BND will pursue a permissive reading of the relevant controlling laws and it need not worry about having its highly controversial interpretations tested in court or scrutinized by independent legal experts. The statutory framework for controlling the BND is exclusively the domain of the intelligence agency's self-interested legal counsel and the politically motivated Chancellery. The BND might very well follow the law. But given what we know so far about the way the BND interprets the law, it does not seem likely that it is imposing meaningful safeguards or limitations on itself through strict interpretations of the framework defining and limiting its authority.[80]

---

[76] Kai Biermann, *Was Macht der BND mit seinen Daten?*, ZEIT ONLINE (Oct. 16, 2014, 4:13 PM), www.zeit.de/digital/datenschutz/2014-10/bnd-internetueberwachung-datenbanken-veras-inbe/seite-2.

[77] Kai Biermann, *Die Neugier des BND Kennt Keine Grenzen*, ZEIT ONLINE (Oct. 10, 2014, 4:18 PM), www.zeit.de/digital/datenschutz/2014-10/bundesnachrichtendienst-5-ebenen-ueberwachung.

[78] Alex Abdo, *Are "Two Hops" Too Many*, ACLU (Mar. 27, 2014, 12:07 PM), www.aclu.org/blog/are-two-hops-too-many.

[79] *Three Degrees of Separation: Breaking Down the NSA's "Hops" Surveillance Method*, THE GUARDIAN (Oct. 28, 2013, 11:58 AM), www.theguardian.com/world/interactive/2013/oct/28/nsa-files-decoded-hops.

[80] Kai Biermann, *Die Anarchos vom BND*, ZEIT ONLINE (Nov. 14, 2014, 4:56 PM), www.zeit.de/politik/deutschland/2014-11/bnd-bundesnachrichtendienst-gesetz-grundrecht.

III　The Dilemma of Oversight: Secrecy Undermines Accountability

The most important check on the BND's activities is the G-10 Commission. The G-10 Commission – like the FISA Court – reviews surveillance orders issued by the relevant ministry and it has the authority to reject the requested surveillance measures, if they do not meet statutory formalities and standards. But if you look at the overall picture of what the BND does, the G-10 Commission only plays a marginal role. The BND is supposed to gather foreign intelligence – it is not charged with monitoring Germans. So, in the light of the German government's interpretation of Article 10 of the Constitution, the G-10 Commission is only involved, if the BND targets German citizens abroad or communication lines between Germany and other countries. Even though the G-10 Commission has a court-like function, it does not review the legal doctrines of the BND and the government.[81] Thus, if the BND determines that certain communications are not subject to the G-10 process, then the G-10 Commission plays no role in evaluating those surveillance measures. Judicial review by the courts is also very limited. Only individuals who were targeted under a G-10 order are supposed to be notified – and only after the file is closed.[82] This gives them at least the opportunity to challenge surveillance orders ex-post. Subjects of strategic surveillance or bulk collection, as well as foreigners, are never notified. Thus, they have no access to the courts to challenge the legality of surveillance programs.

The courts are shut out of the process of supervising the activities of the intelligence services and the role of the G-10 Commission is actually very limited, given that the main focus of the BND is communications of foreigners abroad. This only leaves parliamentary oversight. The Parliamentary Control Committee meets for four hours every month, so long as there are no exceptional circumstances that require an extraordinary briefing.[83] A four-hour meeting every month attended by nine

---

[81] Thorsten Wetzling, *Policy Brief: Das Herzstück der deutschen Geheimdienstreform: Vorschläge für eine starke G10 Kommission*, STIFTUNG NEUE VERANTWORTUNG (Sept. 2015), www.stiftung-nv.de/publikation/Vorschl%C3%A4ge-f%C3%BCr-eine-starke-G10-Kommission.

[82] G-10 Act, § 12.

[83] According to the committee bylaws, the parliamentary oversight committee is only required to meet once every three months. Additional meetings can be requested by the committee or government. DEUTSCHER BUNDESTAG, GESCHÄFTSORDNUNG DES PARLAMENTARISCHEN KONTROLLGREMIUMS, § 3, Feb. 4, 2015 (Ger.), www.bundestag.de/blob/366638/21f40aeb8bfb9ddf36e01511150a2add/go_pkgr-data.pdf.

parliamentarians is the core of German oversight over the foreign and domestic intelligence agencies, which, combined, employ more than 10,000 people.[84] On paper the Committee has the authority to independently examine the BND. But it simply does not have the resources. The secretariat at the Parliament that supports the members of the Committee contains only lawyers. Basic technical understanding of the surveillance methods is utterly lacking. The same is true for the parliamentarians and the G-10 Commission. How can necessity and proportionality of the programs be assessed if there is no understanding of the underlying technology? In this regard the overseers are entirely dependent on the BND, which explains these programs to the oversight bodies.

These are just a few examples. The list of problems with the control of Germany's intelligence services is much longer. For example, there is a lack of whistleblower protections. The strict secrecy requirements that prohibit members of the Parliamentary Control Committee from talking to their colleagues in parliament about potential abuses or problems also undermine effective control of the services. The German system of parliamentary control might be better than that in other countries. But this is more of a reflection of how low the bar is elsewhere than an indication of exemplary practice. If the system is scrutinized, then it quickly becomes obvious that it does not pose any serious counterweight to the quest of the intelligence services for the exploitation of digital technology for surveillance.

F   Conclusion: State of Affairs in the Transatlantic Reform Debate

Striking the right balance between liberty and security is a global problem. Countries such as Russia and China can ignore it. But liberal democracies cannot. The Snowden revelations led President Obama to convene the President's Review Group. The group published a long report with many good recommendations.[85] The U.S. government also has begun to declassify some of the rulings of the secretive FISA Court. The most significant executive action has been the issuance of the

---

[84] Thorsten Denkler, *Bundestagsverwaltung sucht Fünf Trüffelschweine*, SÜDDEUTSCHE ZEITUNG (Mar. 14, 2014, 8:36 AM), www.sueddeutsche.de/politik/kontrolle-der-nachrichten dienste-bundestagsverwaltung-sucht-fuenf-trueffelschweine-1.1911701.

[85] PRESIDENT'S REV. GRP. ON INTELLIGENCE & COMMC'NS TECHS., *supra* note 52.

Presidential Policy Directive 28.[86] The Directive contains good principles such as extending better privacy protections to foreigners. But, as Benjamin Wittes has remarked: "The speech [in which the President announced and outlined the PPD] is a big win for the intelligence community."[87] He went on to note that "The PPD is an exceedingly-clever document, one that conveys and writes into policy a great deal of values without constraining a great deal of practice. A few cases challenging the constitutionality of NSA surveillance practices have been introduced to courts.[88] Whether they will bring about any significant policy changes remains to be seen.

In Germany a domestic reform agenda has emerged out of the NSA Committee of Inquiry. Many parliamentarians and government officials, including the German Minister of Justice, have publicly declared that the legal framework and oversight for the BND are in need of a major overhaul.[89] The Federal Government now seems prepared to pursue reform.[90] It remains to be seen, however, whether Germany will enact laws that set a new international standard and serve as a model for modernizing privacy and security policy in other democratic societies.

The main thesis here is that Germany is not exceptional regarding the conduct and legal framework of its foreign intelligence service. But Germany could become exceptional (at least for a while), if it becomes the first country to enact meaningful and comprehensive reforms in the shadow of the NSA-Affair. This would also put Germany in a position to become a more credible voice for the protection of privacy in the international domain. The threat of inaction, which seems the most

---

[86] Press Release, The White House, Office of the Press Sec'y, Presidential Policy Directive – Signals Intelligence Activities Presidential Policy Directive/PPD-28 (Jan. 17, 2014), www.whitehouse.gov/the-press-office/2014/01/17/presidential-policy-directive-signals-intelligence-activities.

[87] Benjamin Wittes, *The President's Speech and PPD-28: A Guide for the Perplexed*, LAW-FARE (Jan. 20, 2014, 11:02 AM), www.lawfareblog.com/presidents-speech-and-ppd-28-guide-perplexed.

[88] Kara Brandeisky, *NSA Surveillance Lawsuit Tracker*, PROPUBLICA (last updated May 13, 2015), https://projects.propublica.org/graphics/surveillance-suits.

[89] *Geheimdienstaffäre: Heiko Maas Fordert Bessere Kontrolle des BND*, SPIEGEL ONLINE (May 17, 2015, 9:15 AM), www.spiegel.de/politik/deutschland/bnd-affaere-heiko-maas-fordert-mehr-demokratische-kontrolle-a-1034099.html

[90] *See Entwurf für neues BND-Gesetz: Eine Art No-Spy-Klausel für Europa?*, TAGESSCHAU.DE (Jan. 18, 2016), *available at* www.tagesschau.de/inland/bnd-reform-103.html; *Einigung auf Geheimdienstreform: Koalition nimmt BND an die Leine*, TAGESSCHAU.DE (Nov. 13, 2015), *available at* www.tagesschau.de/inland/bnd-reform-101.html.

likely scenario, will just lead to more cynicism. Nobody today can afford to stop using digital technologies. Thus, people will become cynical and lose their faith in democracy, at least if we cannot put in place laws and policies that restore trust in the protection of privacy. This will take a lot of time and effort. But whatever happens next, one thing is clear: the battle over surveillance, privacy, and big data has only just begun.

14

The National Socialist Underground (NSU) Case

Structural Reform of Intelligence Agencies' Involvement in Criminal Investigations?

BY MARC ENGELHART

A Introduction

The NSA-Affair has shed much light on the work of foreign as well as German intelligence agencies and their existing competencies.[1] The debate has concentrated on the far-reaching practices and methods used by American and British agencies giving the impression that the "bad guys" are beyond the Channel/the Atlantic and the "good guys" are the German authorities. Yet, pointing a finger at the foreign services in the NSA-Affair distracted public discussion from a scandal in which German intelligence agencies played a major role: The case of the National Socialist Underground (*Nationalsozialistischer Unter-grund* – NSU), in which a rightwing extremist group committed murders and bombings in Germany, undisturbed, for more than a decade.

This case was unprecedented in regard to the failure of the public authorities to discover the group. It was also unprecedented with respect to the effort that was made afterwards to discover the reasons for this failure. Hence, the case illustrates the changing nature of the intelligence agencies within the German security architecture,[2] especially for the

---

[1] In the following the terms secret services and (intelligence) agencies will be used interchangeably. *See* Chapter 12 in this volume.

[2] *See* MATTHIAS BÄCKER ET AL., BERICHT DER REGIERUNGSKOMMISSION ZUR ÜBERPRÜFUNG DER SICHERHEITSGESETZGEBUNG IN DEUTSCHLAND (2013), www.bmi.bund.de/SharedDocs/Downloads/DE/Broschueren/2013/regierungskommission-sicherheitsgesetzebung.pdf?__blob=publicationFile; Dieter Kugelmann, *Entwicklungslinien eines grundrechtsgeprägten Sicherheitsverwaltungsrechts*, 46 DIE VERWALTUNG 25 (2014).

growing involvement of the services in major criminal investigations.[3]
This chapter begins with an introduction to the NSU case. Then,
I provide a survey of the legal framework within which the intelligence
agencies operate. I continue with an analysis of the services' structure,
tasks, and powers, with particular attention given to their cooperation
with police authorities. Throughout the text, reference will be made to
the NSU case, the problems it brought to light, and the reforms undertaken afterwards.

B   The NSU Case

The NSU is a rightwing extremist group that was likely founded in the late
1990s. The group and its activities were unknown to the public and to the
public authorities until November 4, 2011. That was the date when two of
the group's three main figures committed suicide after being discovered by
the authorities. The investigations revealed that the NSU had been involved
in several serious crimes since the end of the 1990s, especially since the year
2000.[4] Members of the NSU are accused of having killed nine immigrants[5]
and a police officer in different cities all over Germany (what the media has
called the Bosphorus serial murders or "Döner murders"), of having
committed two bombings in Cologne, and a series of more than a dozen
bank robberies. It is assumed that the group's members were motivated by
indiscriminate xenophobia as well as antistate sentiment.[6]

   Investigations undertaken after the discovery of the group showed an
unprecedented failure of state and federal police offices, prosecution
offices, and of state and federal intelligence agencies to investigate the

---

[3] *See* Marc Engelhart, *The Secret Service's Influence on Criminal Proceedings, in* A WAR ON
   TERROR? 505 (Marianne Wade & Almir Maljević eds., 2010); NIKOLAOS GAZEAS, ÜBER-
   MITTLUNG NACHRICHTENDIENSTLICHER ERKENNTNISSE AN STRAFVERFOLGUNGSBEHÖR-
   DEN 286 (2015); Roland Hefendehl, *Die Entfesselung des Strafverfahrens über Methoden
   der Nachrichtendienste*, 158 GOLTDAMMER'S ARCHIV FÜR STRAFRECHT 209 (2011); MAR-
   EIKE REHBEIN, DIE VERWERTBARKEIT VON NACHRICHTENDIENSTLICHEN ERKENNTNISSEN
   AUS DEM IN- UND AUSLAND IM DEUTSCHEN STRAFPROZESS 112 (2011).
[4] *See* Michail Logvinov, *Rechtsterrorismus in Deutschland*, FORUM KRIMINALPRÄVENTION
   (Jan. 2014), at 45; NSU-TERROR. ERMITTLUNGEN AM RECHTEN ABGRUND. EREIGNIS,
   KONTEXTE, DISKURSE 19–56 (Imke Schmincke & Jasmin Siri eds., 2013); Otmar Soukup
   & Wolfgang Barten, *Die Taten des "Nationalsozialistischen Untergrunds (NSU),"* 67
   KRIMINALISTIK 22 (2013). *See also* Armin Pfahl-Traughber, *Die Lehren aus der Nichter-
   kennung der NSU-Serienmorde*, 67 KRIMINALISTIK 17 (2013); *infra* note 8.
[5] Eight persons of Turkish and one of Greek origin.
[6] NSU-TERROR, *supra* note 4, at 19–25; NSU-Report, *infra* note 8, at 75–83.

crimes of the NSU in the years between 2000 and 2011. There had been compelling evidence on which the authorities might have acted. And police and intelligence agencies had been in contact with the main figures of the NSU. Still, the authorities failed to stop the crimes and capture and prosecute the suspects: law enforcement and intelligence services had not been able to connect the different killings or analyze the underlying motivations until 2011. Since then nine parliamentary inquiries, one on the federal and eight on the state level,[7] were formed in order to analyze the scope of and reasons for the German security system's failure to adequately deal with the case.[8] Another committee has been set up (in November 2015) on the federal level in order to address further aspects not already covered by the previous investigations, especially the question: What measures should the authorities have taken?[9] The surviving main figure of the NSU, Beate Zschäpe, and four suspected supporters of the group are currently facing trial in Munich at the Higher Regional Court (*Oberlandesgericht*) for murder and membership in a terrorist organization.[10]

C Framework of the Intelligence Agencies in Germany

Germany does not have one omnipotent intelligence agency but has established several, each of which is charged with a discrete mandate.[11] On the federal level there are three agencies: the Federal Office for the

---

[7] Parliamentary committees of inquiry have been formed in the states of Baden-Württemberg (since 2014), Bavaria (2012–2013), Hessen (since 2014), Northrhine-Westfalia (since 2014), Saxony (2012–2014; second committee since end of 2014) and Thuringia (2012–2014; second committee since end of 2014). For further information on the committees see, generally, NSU-WATCH, www.nsu-watch.info/en/ (last visited (Dec. 8, 2015).

[8] *See* Beschlussempfehlung und Bericht [Decision and Recommendation Report], DEUTSCHER BUNDESTAG: DURCKSACHEN [BT] 17/14600, http://dipbt.bundestag.de/dip21/btd/17/146/1714600.pdf (the 1357 page long report of the federal parliamentary inquiry committee of August 22, 2013) [hereinafter NSU-Report]. *See also* BUNDESMINISTERIUM DES INNERN, ABSCHLUSSBERICHT DER BUND-LÄNDER-KOMMISSION RECHTSTERRORISUMS (2013), www.bmi.bund.de/SharedDocs/Downloads/DE/Broschueren/2013/abschlussbericht-kommission-rechtsterrorismus-lang.pdf?__blob=publicationFile.

[9] *See* Antrag der Fraktionen CDU/CSU, SPD, DIE LINKE. und BÜNDNIS 90/DIE GRÜNEN [Application of the CDU/CSU, SPD, The Left, and The Green Parties] DEUTSCHER BUNDESTAG: DURCKSACHEN [BT] 18/6330, http://dip21.bundestag.de/dip21/btd/18/063/1806330.pdf.

[10] *See* NSU-WATCH, *supra* note 7.

[11] THOMAS WÜRTENBERGER & DIRK HECKMANN, POLIZEIRECHT IN BADEN-WÜRTTEMBERG 40–63 (6th ed., 2005); Christoph Gusy, *Architektur und Rolle der Nachrichtendienste in Deutschland*, 61 AUS POLITIK UND ZEITGESCHEHEN (Issue 18/19) 9 (2014).

Protection of the Constitution (*Bundesamt für Verfassungsschutz* – BfV), the Federal Intelligence Agency (*Bundesnachrichtendienst* – BND), and the Military Counter-Intelligence Service (*Militärischer Abschirmdienst* – MAD). In addition to these federal agencies, each of the sixteen states (*Bundesländer*) has established a State Office for the Protection of the Constitution (*Landesamt für Verfassungsschutz* – LfV). The State Offices vary in size and structure. Yet, in substance and regarding tasks and powers, they resemble the Federal Office. For this reason I will treat the Federal Office and the State Offices together in this chapter.

All the federal agencies and several of the State Offices for the Protection of the Constitution were involved in the NSU case.[12] The involvement of so many agencies (not to mention the police and prosecution services) demonstrates the seriousness of the authorities' failure to uncover the NSU at an earlier stage. A main problem was the poor cooperation among the different agencies. For example, only part of the information of the State Offices for the Protection of the Constitution was shared with the Federal Office, so that no central evaluation and analysis was possible.[13] The agencies did not coordinate their approach to the investigations. And in some cases, agencies showed very little iniative in actively following the cases.[14]

In German law the principle of separation between intelligence agencies and the police (*Trennungsgebot*) is an imperative.[15] This separation is the outcome of negative experiences during the Third Reich. During that period the combination of secret services and police in one office (the Reich Security Main Office – *Reichssicherheitshauptamt*) played an important role in the Third Reich's brutally effective ability to terrorize and control the population.[16] After the war the allied occupying powers insisted upon the separation of secret services and the police within a federal structure.[17] The police primarily received

---

[12] *See* NSU-Report, *supra* note 8, at 371 (LfV Thuringia), 437 (LfV Saxony), 464 (LfV Baden-Württemberg), 446 (BfV), 451 (MAD), 456 (BND).

[13] *Id.* at 852.

[14] The social democratic party (SPD) were especially critical. NSU-Report, *supra* note 8, at 884.

[15] *See, e.g.,* BND-Gesetz [BNDG] [Law on the Federal Intelligence Service], Dec. 20, 1990, BGBl. I at 2954, 2979 § 1 ¶ 1 (stating that no police agency may be affiliated with the BND.).

[16] *See, e.g.,* Friedrich Wilhelm, Die Polizei im NS-Staat 118 (2d ed., 1999).

[17] *See* Alexander Dorn, Das Trennungsgebot in verfassungshistorischer Perspektive 121 (2004).

coercive powers whereas the intelligence agencies primarily received investigative (noncoercive) powers.

D   Structure, Tasks, and Powers

I   Federal Office for the Protection of the Constitution

1   Structure and Tasks

The Federal Office for the Protection of the Constitution is a federal agency (*Bundesoberbehörde*) under the control of the Federal Ministry of the Interior. The BfV is tasked with the collection and analysis of "information, intelligence and other documents" concerning efforts directed against the free democratic basic order (freiheitlich demokratische Grundordnung) or against the existence and security of the Federation or one of its States.[18]

By means of the Act on the Fight Against International Terrorism from 2002,[19] these "classic" tasks have been amended in order to strengthen BfV's role in the fight against terrorism.[20] The new mandate permits the BfV to conduct surveillance of international terrorist activities within Germany even when there is not yet a current danger as defined by police law. The absence of a "current danger" means that the police would not be allowed to take measures to interdict such activities. But it is precisely at this preliminary – intelligence gathering – stage where the BfV operates. The Parliament has extended the application of the terrorism amendment twice and plans to do so another time.[21] Initially it was authorized for a period of five years. This once-temporary measure has become an integral part of the work of the BfV.

Although the BfV – and many of the State Offices for the Protection of the Constitution – were granted the powers to fight terrorism in 2002,

---

[18]   Bundesverfassungsschutzgesetz [BVerfSchG] [Federal Act for the Protection of the Constitution], Dec. 20, 1990, BGBl. I at 2954, 2970, § 3.

[19]   Terrorismusbekämpfungsgesetz [TerrBekG] [Counterterrorism Act], Jan. 9, 2002, BGBl. I at 361, last amended by Gesetz [G] of Jan. 5, 2007 BGBl. I at 2.

[20]   Hans-Ullrich Paeffgen, *"Vernachrichtendienstlichung" von Strafprozess- (und Polizei-) recht im Jahr 2001*, 21 STRAFVERTEIDIGER 336 (2002); Hans-Ullrich Paeffgen, *Vernachrichtendienstlichung des Strafprozesses*, 150 GOLTDAMMER'S ARCHIV FÜR STRAFRECHT 647 (2003).

[21]   The first extension was from 2007 to 2012, the last one from 2012 to 2016. The third extension is from 2016 to 2021. *See* Gesetzentwurf der Bundesregierung [Bill of the Federal Government] DEUTSCHER BUNDESTAG: DURCKSACHEN [BT] 18/5924, http://dip21.bundestag.de/dip21/btd/18/059/1805924.pdf.

their work in the first years was not very successful. These agencies were responsible for gathering intelligence on the activities of the NSU insofar as these activities could be qualified as rightwing extremist and politically motivated criminality. For many years – and until the discovery of the NSU – German authorities underestimated and trivialized rightwing terrorism.[22] From the end of the 1990s there was conclusive evidence that the NSU's ringleaders were rightwing extremists and had access to materials for building bombs. Inexplicably, the intelligence services concluded that no current danger of terrorist attacks existed. Also, because no rightwing extremist group claimed responsibility for bombings in Cologne, the intelligence services did not count them toward their scrutiny of Germany's rightwing extremist scene. Yet, this position contradicted practical national and international experience with similar such attacks. Whereas the authorities demonstrated a troubling lack of initiative in this regard, they overstretched their competences in other cases. For example, in the late-1990s the Thuringia State Office for the Protection of the Constitution had been actively looking to interdict the NSU's ringleaders despite the fact that it lacked the authority to search for and arrest criminals.[23] According to the strict separation between intelligence gathering and criminal investigations, these investigations should have been carried out by the police.

In addition to the lack of due attention to the mounting evidence of the NSU's activities, the structures for fighting rightwing extremism in the BfV in general were weakened when the independent department concerned with rightwing extremism was merged with other departments (such as the unit concerned with leftwing extremism) into one department with a mandate for "German extremism."[24] Similar, critical restructurings took place on the state level.[25] These changes left the BfV systematically "blind in the right eye" and it did not serve as the intended early warning system within the German security structure. It seems now that the intelligence personnel simply could not imagine that the rightwing scene would be capable of committing terrorist acts.[26] The main discussion – and disagreement – within the Parliamentary Committee of

---

[22] See NSU-REPORT, *supra* note 8, at 446–451, 853–855. See also Pfahl-Traughber, *supra* note 4, at 17 ff.

[23] See NSU-REPORT, *supra* note 8, at 883.   [24] *Id.* at 855–56.

[25] See, e.g., Christoph Gusy, *Reform der Sicherheitsbehörden*, 44 ZEITSCHRIFT FÜR RECHTSPOLITIK 230, 231 (2012) (on the LfV Thuringia.).

[26] See NSU-REPORT, *supra* note 8, at 855–56.

Inquiry that was convened to investigate the Intelligence Community's failures in relation to the NSU was how it was possible that so many authorities did not recognize the very real threat from rightwing extremists. Die Linke, Germany's leftist political party, saw the failure as evidence of institutional and structural bias, and perhaps even racism.[27] Indeed, the circumstances suggest that the intelligence agencies and the police authorities allowed their work on the cases to be influenced by commonplace prejudices that led them to concentrate on fruitless theories. It cannot be disputed that a general culture in the intelligence and police communities contributed to the failure.

The NSU case led to some reforms within the BfV. A department for rightwing extremism and terrorism was reestablished with the responsibility for concentrating more on the dangerousness of rightwing groups and persons. The process for handling files also was reorganized and allows for more systematic and comprehensive access to information gathered. With these – rather modest and technical changes – the BfV now seems a bit better prepared than before to monitor rightwing extremism in Germany. Still, hardly any measures have been taken that would erode settled prejudices among intelligence agents in order to improve the quality of the collection and evaluation of information. Wether intelligence personnel are now more capable of analyzing and evaluating the evidence, especially in cases of new threats, remains to be seen.

2   General Powers

The BfV has far-reaching powers to collect information. The agency can gather, process, and use information that is of relevance to fulfilling its tasks.[28] This information can include personal data about individual persons. The agency can use several technical surveillance measures to collect information. For instance, it can track active mobile phones or wiretap private homes.[29] Besides these specific legal grounds for surveillance, the statute only names some of the measures the BfV can use. Instead it allows, in general, the use of "methods, objects and instruments

---

[27] *See* NSU-Report, *supra* note 8, at 988–1002 (for the evaluation by The Left Party.).

[28] *See* Bundesverfassungsschutzgesetz [BVerfSchG] [Federal Act for the Protection of the Constitution], Dec. 20, 1990, BGBl. I at 2954, 2970, § 8 ¶ 1. *See also* Joachim Lampe, *Die Schwierigkeiten mit der Rechtfertigung nachrichtendienstlicher Tätigkeit*, 34 Neue Zeitschrift für Strafrecht 361 (2015).

[29] *See* Bundesverfassungsschutzgesetz [BVerfSchG] [Federal Act for the Protection of the Constitution], Dec. 20, 1990, BGBl. I at 2954, 2970, § 9 ¶¶ 3, 4.

for the secret collection of information" (so-called *nachrichtendienstliche Mittel* – secret service measures). It gives the nonexclusive examples of (confidential) informants, observation, taking of pictures, sound recordings, forged papers, and license plates.[30]

3 Informants

One of the most prominent measures is the use of (confidential) informants (so-called *Vertrauensperson* or V-Person).[31] They are not formally officers of the BfV (such as undercover agents) but instead they work for the agencies on a long-term basis in order to observe persons and groups or to investigate crimes. Informants are often members of the observed groups or otherwise have close contact with the relevant persons. The use of informants by the domestic intelligence services became widely known in 2003 when the government (along with the Federal Parliament and the Federal Council of State Governments) filed a request with the Federal Constitutional Court to have the rightwing *Nationaldemokratische Partei Deutschlands* (National Democratic Party of Germany – NPD) declared unconstitutional and dissolved.[32] The Court closed the case when it was discovered that up to 15 percent of the NPD's leadership, on the national and state levels, were paid informants. The Court found that the evidence brought forward in support of the party-ban proceeding, likely was influenced by the agencies and their informants.[33] A new request to ban the NPD was filed in 2013 and the proceedings are ongoing. The Constitutional Court has again signaled its skepticism toward the use of informants as part of the evidence in the case.[34]

---

[30] *See* Bundesverfassungsschutzgesetz [BVerfSchG] [Federal Act for the Protection of the Constitution], Dec. 20, 1990, BGBl. I at 2954, 2970, § 8 ¶ 2.

[31] *See* Wolfgang Roth, *§§ 1–33, Gesetz zur Regelung des öffentlichen Vereinsrechts (Vereinsgesetz), §§ 1–8 Gesetz über die Zusammenarbeit des Bundes und der Länder in Angelegenheiten des Verfassungsschutzes und über das Bundesamt für Verfassungsschutz (Bundesverfassungsschutzgesetz – BVerfSchG)*, *in* SICHERHEITSRECHT DES BUNDES 983 (Wolf-Rüdiger Schenke, Kurt Graulich & Josef Ruthig eds., 2014); Bundesverfassungsschutzgesetz [BVerfSchG] [Federal Act for the Protection of the Constitution], Dec. 20, 1990, BGBl. I at 2954, 2970, § 8 ¶¶ 26–32.

[32] *See* Klaus Lüderssen, *Staatliche Deliktsbeteiligung durch V-Leute - die Politik gibt jetzt die richtige Antwort*, 21 STRAFVERTEIDIGER 169 (2002).

[33] Bundesverfassungsgericht [BVerfG] [Federal Constitutional Court], Mar. 18, 2003, 107 BVerfGE 339.

[34] *See* Bundesverfassungsgericht [BVerfG] [Federal Constitutional Court], Mar. 19, 2015, BVerfG, 2 BvB 1/13.

In the NSU case informants also played a troubling role.[35] Several informants with close contacts to members of the NSU were working for the BfV and the State Offices for the Protection of the Constitution. They clearly possessed important information on the ringleaders' criminal activities. The selection of informants was just one problem. Some were high-ranking neo-Nazis and serious criminal offenders. The intelligence they provided was dubious. The informants were given only very loose guidance by the intelligence agencies and the high payments they received made it attractive for the informants to constantly provide some (and probably false) information. Disturbingly, it is possible that some of the informants used their payments to help finance the extremist activities they were meant to be monitoring. All of this suggests that the agencies had a significant influence on the extremist organizations, actually helping them to grow in Eastern Germany.[36] Additionally, information provided by the informants was often not shared among the various offices, sometimes in order to keep secret the fact that informants were being used and to protect their identity. In many cases the promise to keep informants' identity secret was a precondition for their work for the intelligence services.[37]

The NPD and the NSU cases showed how commonplace the use of informants is. They also brought to light the uncritical complacency with which the agencies made use of this human intelligence gathering technique. It is quite remarkable that clear and strict standards for technological surveillance exist while the use of informants is not regulated by law. There are no minimum standards for the selection and credibility of informants. The NSU case spurred some reform in this regard. In 2015 the state of Thuringia announced it would no longer make use of informants except in single cases of terrorism.[38] The other states and the Federal Government want to keep the system, but improve it. Therefore, federal and state agencies have developed a new common standard for

---

[35] See NSU-REPORT, *supra* note 8, at 257–312, 856–57 and the special investigation report on informants BT-Drs. 18/6545 of November 4, 2015.

[36] See NSU-REPORT, *supra* note 8, at 888 (critical remarks by the social democratic party (SPD).).

[37] Michael Soiné, *Erkenntnisverwertung von Informanten und V-Personen der Nachrichtendienste in Strafverfahren*, 26 NEUE ZEITSCHRIFT FÜR STRAFRECHT 247 (2007); Christoph Keller & Norbert Wolf, *Verdeckte personale Ermittlungen aus kriminalistischer und rechtlicher Sicht*, 67 Kriminalistik 349, 350 f. (2013).

[38] See Press Release, Thuringian Ministry of Local and Home Affairs, Medieninformation 40/2015 (Mar. 18, 2015), www.thueringen.de/th3/tmik/aktuell/presse/83504/index.aspx.

the selection, management, and deployment of informants. The BfV hosts a central file (VP-Datei) that contains information on the informants working on the federal and state levels since the beginning of November 2015. These measures can help make the use of informants a bit more transparent and effective. But it still does not put their use on a solid legal basis. In order to approach this problem, as will be discussed below, Parliament has moved to set up a new legal framework.

4   Expanded Powers for Investigating Terrorist Activities

Since 2002 the BfV has been authorized to require financial and telecommunications companies to provide information about individuals when there are indications of a serious threat in the areas of its competence, including terrorism.[39] If there are indications of the commission of a serious crime (including high treason, founding a terrorist organization, or murder), then the BfV can also monitor telecommunication and postal correspondence.[40] Since 2007 the BfV also has had the authority to issue a search warrant for persons (in the Schengen information system) without asking the police to do so – as had previously been the case.[41]

Especially the authority to demand information from companies and to issue search warrants demonstrates that the BfV has been assigned powers that traditionally have been regarded as police powers. These powers are special in that they aim at the investigation of individual cases and are not restricted to the examination of a general threatening situation, often categorized as "strategic intelligence."[42] The possibility to issue a search warrant is the first measure that grants the BfV direct access to police data bases.

II   Federal Intelligence Agency

The Federal Intelligence Agency is *the* German foreign secret service with the task of collecting and analyzing foreign information that is relevant

---

[39] *See* Bundesverfassungsschutzgesetz [BVerfSchG] [Federal Act for the Protection of the Constitution], Dec. 20, 1990, BGBl. I at 2954, 2970, § 8a ¶ 2.

[40] *See* Gesetz zur Beschränkung des Brief-, Post- und Fernmeldegeheimnisses [G 10] [Act Restricting the Privacy of Correspondence, Posts and Telecommunications], June 26, 2001, BGBl. I at 1254, revised 2298, § 3, last amended by Gesetz [G], July 31, 2009, BGBl. I at 2499 (Ger.).

[41] *See* Bundesverfassungsschutzgesetz [BVerfSchG] [Federal Act for the Protection of the Constitution], Dec. 20, 1990, BGBl. I at 2954, 2970, § 17 ¶ 3.

[42] Frederick Roggan & Nils Bergemann, *Die "neue Sicherheitsarchitektur" der Bundesrepublik Deutschland*, 61 NEUE JURISTISCHE WOCHENSCHRIFT 876 (2007).

for German foreign and security policy.[43] This includes information about transnational terrorism and organized crime. The collection of information can also be carried out within Germany as long as information about developments outside Germany is collected. The BND has powers similar to the BfV's.[44] Like the BfV it was granted new powers to combat terrorism in 2002 and 2007.

The BND was only partly involved in the NSU case insofar as the relation to foreign terrorist groups (such as Combat 18 or Blood & Honour in Great Britain and Scandinavia) and a possible escape of members of the NSU (to the United States) was concerned.[45] Yet, as no foreigner was part of the group, the BND was not really interested in the case. It took no serious actions and was not actively following the investigation.[46] This resulted, for example, in not investigating important information provided by the foreign services.[47]

The BND could have provided important input to the NSU case as it possesses the special authority to pursue strategic foreign surveillance of telecommunications (*strategische Fernmeldüberwachung*).[48] This can involve the monitoring of all international communication to and from Germany. The aim of this competence is primarily to detect terrorist threats as early as possible. Yet, the power is not limited to the discovery of terrorist scenarios but applies to other serious crimes.[49] Besides terrorist activities, the provision makes strategic intelligence gathering available to combat the narcotics and drugs trade, currency counterfeiting, and internationally organized money laundering. The most remarkable aspect concerning strategic foreign surveillance is that it allows an investigation without any further precondition: there does not have to be a threat within the terms of police law or a suspicion within the rules of

---

[43] See BND-Gesetz [BNDG] [Law on the Federal Intelligence Service], Dec. 20, 1990, BGBl. I at 2954, 2979 § 1 ¶ 2.

[44] See id. at § 2, ¶ 1.   [45] See NSU-REPORT, *supra* note 8, at 149–89.   [46] Id. at 456–60.

[47] Id. at 282, 456–60.

[48] MICHAEL KÖHLER, UNBEGRENZTE ERMITTLUNG UND JUSTIZFREIE BUNDESGEHEIMPOLIZEI: DER NEUE STRAFPROZESS 386–89 (1994); Frederik Roggan, *Neue Befugnisse im Geheimdienstrecht*, in HANDBUCH ZUM RECHT DER INNEREN SICHERHEIT, BERLINER WISSENSCHAFTSVERLAG 412, 417 (Frederik Roggan & Martin Kutscha eds., 2d ed. 2006); Bertold Huber, *Die strategische Rasterfahndung des Bundesnachrichtendienstes*, 67 NEUE JURISTISCHE WOCHENSCHRIFT 2572 (2013).

[49] See Gesetz zur Beschränkung des Brief-, Post- und Fernmeldegeheimnisses [G 10] [Act Restricting the Privacy of Correspondence, Posts and Telecommunications], June 26, 2001, BGBl. I at 1254, revised 2298, § 5, last amended by Gesetz [G], July 31, 2009, BGBl. I at 2499 (Ger.) (for a list of crimes.).

criminal procedure. In short, it allows a criminal investigation without the suspicion of the commission of a criminal offense. Because the BND is quite substantially involved in the investigation of crimes, it can be seen as a "secret criminal police agency."[50]

III Military Counter-Intelligence Service

The Military Counter-Intelligence Service is a central unit of the Federal Armed Forces and is responsible to the Federal Ministry of Defense.[51] Like the BfV, the MAD has the task of collecting and analyzing information on activities directed against the constitution, but only if acitivities are of military relevance.[52] Similar to the BfV and the BND, the task and powers of the MAD were amended in 2002 and 2007 to combat international terrorism. The MAD participates equally in the Counter-Terrorism Brief (since 2007) as well as in the Rightwing-Extremism Brief (since 2012). The MAD is the smallest federal intelligence agency, but it is not less powerful from a legal point of view.

The MAD was involved in the NSU case because of its task of monitoring the extremist and terrorist activities of military personnel. Several members (including two of the ringleaders) and supporters of the NSU were monitored by the MAD during their military service.[53] Some supporters were questioned by the MAD and provided helpful evidence on the NSU's ringleaders.[54] This questioning often took place shortly before the interviewed person left the armed forces and the information collected could not, and often was not, used for further investigations or disciplinary proceedings.[55] Apparently, questioning was undertaken just prior to the end of the subjects' military service because it was intended as a way to recruit informants for other intelligence agencies.[56]

---

[50] See KÖHLER, *supra* note 48, at 386; Roggan, *supra* note 48, at 431.

[51] See Gesetz über den militärischen Abschirmdienst [MADG] [Millitary Counterintelligence Service Act], Dec. 20, 1990, BGBl. I at 2954, 2977, § 1, last amended by Gesetz [G], Nov. 17, 2015 BGBl. I at 1938.

[52] See Gesetz über den militärischen Abschirmdienst [MADG] [Millitary Counterintelligence Service Act], Dec. 20, 1990, BGBl. I at 2954, 2977, § 1 ¶ 1, last amended by Gesetz [G], Nov. 17, 2015 BGBl. I at 1938.

[53] See NSU-REPORT, *supra* note 8, at 219–55.   [54] *Id.* at 451–56.   [55] *Id.* at 846–47.

[56] See NSU-REPORT, *supra* note 8, at 876 for the evaluation by the social democratic party (SPD).

IV   Conclusion

Many of the tasks and powers of the modern intelligence services are devoted to preventing and investigating serious crimes. These serious crimes are quite broadly defined, especially when connected to terrorism. After all, a specific crime of terrorism does not exist in German criminal law. As used in this context the term covers an assortment of criminal offenses connected to terrorist activities. The powers the agencies have acquired during the last decade are substantially similar to traditional police powers. These investigative powers are of a coercive nature because they offer possibilities far beyond the mere collection of publicly available information. Because of the commitment to keeping intelligence and police services separate, the intelligence services have not been regarded as general police agencies.[57] Yet, in substance, equipped with the new powers, the intelligence services have developed into special police authorities.[58] Their involvement in the NSU case illustrates how significant the role of the intelligence services can be in traditional policing.

E   Cooperation of the Intelligence Services and the Police

Traditionally the work of German intelligence services (collecting information on threats to the security of the state or to the public order) was seen as distinct from the tasks of the police (preventing crimes) and the prosecution (prosecuting crimes). This reflected the settled understanding of the principle of separation. Therefore, the secret services and the police/prosecution did not cooperate closely. With the expansion of the tasks and powers of the intelligence services, however, cooperation has become much more important and is an essential element of Germany's security regime.

The NSU case showed that the mechanisms for cooperation in force between the mid-1990s and the discovery of the NSU in 2011 were not working. There was almost no close and structured coordination of the work of the intelligence services and the police.[59] Information was exchanged only on an *ad hoc* basis and followed no clear and

---

[57] *See* DIETER KUGELMANN, POLIZEI- UND ORDNUNGSRECHT 52 (2d ed., 2012).
[58] *See* WOLF-RÜDIGER SCHENKE, POLIZEI- UND ORDNUNGSRECHT ¶ 444 (Müller ed., 8th ed. 2013); WÜRTENBERGER & HECKMAN, *supra* note 11, at ¶ 93.
[59] *See* NSU-REPORT, *supra* note 8, at 829-58.

long-term operational policy. Also, information gathered by the intelligence services was only partly shared with police authorities, was transmitted too late, or requests for information went unanswered or received only partial answers.[60] In some cases, instead of working together constructively, the intelligence services gave the impression that they saw themselves as being in competition with the law enforcement authorities to be the first to produce results.[61] In several instances, an intelligence service actively hindered police investigations by not sharing the necessary information,[62] by not allowing informants to be interviewed,[63] or by not allowing the police to follow evidence hinting at a rightwing extremist background in a murder case.[64] The intelligence services were reluctant to allow the police to interview the personnel who had been involved in investigations or they did not authorize those agents to testify. Even when information was shared with the police, it was not duly used in the investigations by the police, probably because the importance and relevance for the police case was not judged properly. Last but not least, different technical systems impeded the exchange of information.

I   Exchange of Information

The most important form of cooperation between the intelligence agencies and the police is the exchange of information. According to the Federal Constitutional Court the principle of separation, although disputed by a number of scholars,[65] does not exclude the possibility of such an exchange as this would make the work in the field of public security quite inefficient.[66] The principle is only meant to ensure that there is neither an all-embracing informational network among both institutions nor an unlimited right to access the databases of the other institution.

The "traditional path" of cooperation between the intelligence services and the police is governed by the legal doctrine known as "administrative assistance," which allows an exchange of information between public authorities on a case-by-case basis. But the transmission of information is limited to an exchange of nonpersonal information in individual cases

---

[60] *Id.* at 832, 833–53.   [61] *Id.* at 851, 883.   [62] *Id.* at 851, 883.   [63] *Id.* at 836.

[64] *Id.* at 840–41.   [65] *See* GAZEAS, *supra* note 3, at 57–66.

[66] Bundesverfassungsgericht [BVerfG] [Federal Constitutional Court], Apr. 24, 2013, 133 BVerfGE 277. *See also* Helmut Albert, *Gedanken zum Verhältnis von Polizei und Verfassungsschutz, in* BUNDESAMT FÜR VERFASSUNGSSCHUTZ. 50 JAHRE IM DIENST DER INNEREN SICHERHEIT 85 (2000); Kay Nehm, *Das nachrichtendienstliche Trennungsgebot und die neue Sicherheitsarchitektur*, 58 NEUE JURISTISCHE WOCHENSCHRIFT 3289 (2004).

upon the request of another authority. Any further exchange (e.g., the constant transmission of personal information) would require specific parliamentary authorization.

The statutes governing the intelligence services today contain detailed regulations on the exchange of information.[67] The police are allowed to transmit information to the secret services when the information is of relevance for the tasks of the secret services and vice versa.[68] As the institutions are not obliged to transmit information, they can evaluate whether the transmission of information is within their interests or not. An exception is made, for example, when the police receive information about terrorist activities. In these cases the police are obliged to inform the intelligence services.[69] There is no publicly available information on the use of this provision (only the Parliamentary Control Committee receives the information). But one can estimate that a great amount of politically motivated criminality (in 2014 there were 32,700 cases) is reported to the secret services by the police.[70] There is reason to suspect that the exception has become the rule and that the principle of separation has almost no limiting effect in the cases of extremism or terrorism.

Special rules exist for the BND's transmission of information gathered under its authority to conduct strategic surveillance of telecommunications. The transmission of information is generally prohibited but may be allowed in cases where a concrete threat or a concrete suspicion exists.[71] This means that the police can only receive information at the stage at which they would be allowed by law to take action. Information that is not substantial enough to constitute a concrete threat (in terms of police

---

[67] *See* Bundesverfassungsschutzgesetz [BVerfSchG] [Federal Act for the Protection of the Constitution], Dec. 20, 1990, BGBl. I at 2954, 2970, §§ 18–20; BND-Gesetz [BNDG] [Law on the Federal Intelligence Service], Dec. 20, 1990, BGBl. I at 2954, 2979 § 8–9; Gesetz über den militärischen Abschirmdienst [MADG] [Millitary Counterintelligence Service Act], Dec. 20, 1990, BGBl. I at 2954, 2977, § 10–11, last amended by Gesetz [G], Nov. 17, 2015 BGBl. I at 1938. *But see, e.g.,* Hefendehl, *supra* note 3, at 209.

[68] Bernadette Droste, HANDBUCH DES VERFASSUNGSSCHUTZRECHTS 518 (2007); Soiné, *supra* note 37, at 247.

[69] *See* Bundesverfassungsschutzgesetz [BVerfSchG] [Federal Act for the Protection of the Constitution], Dec. 20, 1990, BGBl. I at 2954, 2970, § 18 ¶ 1.

[70] The 2014 report of the BfV is based on the numbers on politically motivated criminality. *See* BUNDESMINISTERIUM DES INNERN, VERFASSUNGSSCHUTZBERICHT 2014 23–29 (2014).

[71] Gesetz zur Beschränkung des Brief-, Post- und Fernmeldegeheimnisses [G 10] [Act Restricting the Privacy of Correspondence, Posts and Telecommunications], June 26, 2001, BGBl. I at 1254, revised 2298, § 7, last amended by Gesetz [G], Dec. 3, 2015, BGBl. I at 2161 (Ger.) (for a list of crimes.).

law) or a suspicion (in terms of the rules of criminal procedure) may never leave the BND. The BND alone decides whether the information is concrete enough to be transmitted. As the BND is not bound by the principle of mandatory prosecution, it can refrain from submitting information when agency's interests justify it (e.g., in order to keep the names of informants secret).

II Counter-Terrorism Database and Rightwing-Extremism Database

In 2006 the landscape for information sharing was completely overhauled in order to promote Germany's counter-terrorism posture. The Parliament established the so-called Counter-Terrorism-Database (*Antiterrordateigesetz* – ATDG).[72] This database is hosted by the *Bundeskriminalamt* (BKA)[73] for joint, automatic access by the police and intelligence services (there is no need to contact the other institutions). Federal and state police are participating in the project as well as the federal intelligence services and the State Offices for the Protection of the Constitution.[74] In 2012 a similar database, the Rightwing-Extremism Database (*Rechtsextremismus-Datei-Gesetz* – RED-G), was established to help combat violent rightwing extremist activities.[75]

The Counter-Terrorism Database contains information on natural persons, legal persons, and on objects that are connected to terrorist activities. The information covers future as well as past activities. The database collects information that will be useful for the prevention, as well as investigation, of terrorist activities. The use of the stored data is not restricted to the objectives for which the Counter-Terrorism Database was created. The information can be used for other purposes, for example, in criminal proceedings of serious crimes.[76]

---

[72] *See* Antiterrordateigesetz [ATDG] [Counterterrorism Database Act], Dec. 22, 2006, BGBl. I at 3409, last amended by Gesetz [G], Dec. 18, 2014, BGBl. I at 2314. See also KATHRIN LUISE LANG, DAS ANTITERRORDATEIGESETZ, 171–251 (2011); Felix Ruhmann-seder, *Informationelle Zusammenarbeit von Polizeibehörden und Nachrichtendiensten auf Grund des "Gemeinsame-Dateien-Gesetzes,"* 12 STRAFVERTEIDIGER-FORUM 184 (2007); Mark Alexander Zöller, *Der Rechtsrahmen der Nachrichtendienste bei der "Bekämpfung" des internationalen Terrorismus*, 56 Juristenzeitung 763 (2007).

[73] Federal Criminal Police Office.

[74] *See* Antiterrordateigesetz [ATDG] [Counterterrorism Database Act], Dec. 22, 2006, BGBl. I at 3409, § 1, last amended by Gesetz [G], Dec. 18, 2014, BGBl. I at 2314.

[75] *See* Rechtsextremismus-Datei-Gesetz [RED-G] [Right-Wing Extrenist Database Act], Aug. 20, 2012, BGBl. I at 1798, last amended by Gesetz [G], Dec. 18, 2014, BGBl. I at 2318.

[76] *See* Antiterrordateigesetz [ATDG] [Counterterrorism Database Act], Dec. 22, 2006, BGBl. I at 3409, § 6, last amended by Gesetz [G], Dec. 18, 2014, BGBl. I at 2314.

In 2013 the Federal Constitutional Court declared parts of the Counter-Terrorism Database unconstitutional because the system did not adequately protect personal information.[77] The Court considered the separation of police and intelligence services in regard to the exchange of information to be necessary, but it also concluded that the main structure of the Counter-Terrorism Database (and the cooperation it facilitates) was constitutional.[78] The Parliament reformed the relevant law in December 2014,[79] taking into account most of the Constitutional Court's objections.[80] But the Parliament also used the reform to expand the possibilities for the involved agencies.[81] Stored data can now also be used for specific projects when defined as a single case of international terrorism.[82] Such data can then be used in order to identify clusters involving persons and objects. Additionally, the revised legislation made the Counter-Terrorism Database a permanent institution.

Information is not only collected on suspects, but also on persons having contact with a suspect (contact person). After the reform in 2014, information about contact persons is to be stored only if the authority expects this person to contribute to the investigation of terrorist activities. Single and accidental everyday contacts are not sufficient. Yet, the criteria are still rather vague and subjective (depending on the discretion of the authority). Up to now, the criteria have not been very efficient in limiting the storage of data on innocent persons: In 2007, about 34 percent of all persons listed in the database were contact persons; in 2011, at 19 percent, the number was lower.[83] This is still a quite substantial

---

[77] Bundesverfassungsgericht [BVerfG] [Federal Constitutional Court], Apr. 24, 2013, 133 BVerfGE 277. *See also* Clemens Arzt, *Antiterrordatei verfassungsgemäß – Trennungsgebot tot?*, 31 NEUE ZEITSCHRIFT FÜR VERWALTUNGSRECHT 1328 (2013); Uwe Volkmann, *Verbund oder Trennung – Zu einem neuen Verhältnis von Polizei- und Nachrichtendiensten*, 35 JURISTISCHE AUSBILDUNG 820 (2014).

[78] *See* Volkmann, *supra* note 77, at 826–29.

[79] Gesetz zur Änderung des Antiterrordateigesetzes und anderer Gesetze [Act Amending the Counterterrorism Database Act and other Laws], Dec. 20, 2014, BGBl. I at 2318.

[80] *See* Thomas Petri, *Das Gesetz zur Änderung des Antiterrordateigesetzes – rechtsstaatliche Korrektur gelungen?*, 3 ZEITSCHRIFT FÜR DATENSCHUTZ 597 (2014).

[81] *See* Norbert Demuth, *Kritik an der Reform der Anti-Terror-Datei*, 105 DEUTSCHE RICHTERZEITUNG 398 (2014).

[82] *See* Antiterrordateigesetz [ATDG] [Counterterrorism Database Act], Dec. 22, 2006, BGBl. I at 3409, § 6a, last amended by Gesetz [G], Dec. 18, 2014, BGBl. I at 2314.

[83] *See* Bericht zur Evaluierung des Antiterrordateigesetzes [Report on the evaluation of the Counterterrorism Database] DEUTSCHER BUNDESTAG: DRUCKSACHEN [BT] 17/12665, 32, http://dip21.bundestag.de/dip21/btd/17/126/1712665.pdf (the evaluation of the ATDG of March 7, 2013 by the federal government).

number of individuals who are not personally involved in terrorist activities, indicating a rather *laissez-faire* approach on the part of the involved authorities. The legislative reform in 2014 helped in this regard, so long as the standard (limiting inclusion in the database to only contact persons who can contribute to investigations) is taken seriously and is based on facts rather than speculation regarding what a person might contribute.

The Counter-Terrorism Database and the Rightwing-Extremism Database are remarkable in several ways. Above all, the principle of separation between police and intelligence services was not seen as a barrier to joint databases and to very intensive informational cooperation.[84] The police can now easily access a much larger amount of data from the intelligence agencies than before and vice versa. The joint databases bridge different technical systems. This can help avoid a disastrous breakdown as occurred in the NSU case. But the price for this potentially greater efficiency is that the constitutional right of informational self-determination is substantially minimized. The pure amount of information that can be stored, the potential to store (biased?) commentaries, and, ultimately, the very broad competence to use information (not only in terrorist proceedings but also in other nonspecified cases of serious crimes) is extraordinary.[85] These broad competences are likely to be challenged in the Constitutional Court.[86]

III   Additional Databases

The same legislation that established the Counter-Terrorism Database in 2006 provided for the possibility to establish other joint databases for the police and the intelligence services to share.[87] These initiatives have to be temporary and limited to certain crimes or certain threats to public

---

[84] *See* Martin Kutscha, *Die Erkenntnisse des Polyphem*, 50 VORGÄNGE (Issue 1) 86 (2012) (speaking of the "secret burial of the principle").

[85] *But see* Arzt, *supra* note 77, at 1328 (partly critiquing the former version of the ATDG); Ruhmannseder, *supra* note 72, at 184; Zöller, *supra* note 72, at 763.

[86] *See* Dominic Hörauf, *Das neue Antiterrordateigesetz*, 33 NEUE ZEITSCHRIFT FÜR VERWALTUNGSRECHT 181 (2015).

[87] *See* BND-Gesetz [BNDG] [Law on the Federal Intelligence Service], Dec. 20, 1990, BGBl. I at 2954, 2979 § 9a; Bundesverfassungsschutzgesetz [BVerfSchG] [Federal Act of the Protection of the Constituiton], Dec. 20, 1990, BGBl. I at 2954, 2970, § 22a; Bundeskriminalamtgesetz [BKAG] [Act of the Federal Bureau of Criminal Investigations], July 7, 1997, BGBl. I at 1650 § 9a, last amended by Verordnung [V] of Aug. 31, 2015.

security – generally those that are covered by the tasks of the intelligence services. The databases can be established by the police or the intelligence services without any further parliamentary action. Only the federal ministries concerned have to approve the establishment of the database. The relevant legal framework contains very general guidelines giving the authorities that establish the new joint databases vast discretion. This type of database could, however, be used for investigations such as the NSU case and would certainly enhance investigations in general.

IV   Organizational Cooperation

The police and intelligence services cooperate in more ways than simply through information sharing. This is not a new development. Traditionally, the police could ask intelligence agents to join the investigation of certain serious crimes against the state. Apart from this case-related cooperation, police and intelligence services have coordinated their work in fields in which their tasks overlap, including in special workshops. In recent years, the coordination has been institutionalized through the establishment of regular group meetings coordinating, for instance, work in the fields of terrorism or political extremism.[88]

In order to institutionalize the coordination between police and intelligence services on a long-term basis, a number of specific centers have been created since 2004. In the fight against terrorism the Joint Antiterror Center (*Gemeinsames Terrorismusabwehrzentrum* – GTAZ)[89] was established in Berlin in 2004.[90] More than 200 members of the federal and state police, the federal intelligence services, and the State Offices for the Protection of the Constitution work there together. Unlike the situation of the Counter-Terrorism Database, the federal attorney general (*Generalbundesanwalt*) also participates in the work of the GTAZ. In order not to merge police and secret services too explicitly the center is divided into two different sections: a police division and an intelligence services division.[91] Both divisions, however, meet in regular panels where

---

[88] Albert, *supra* note 66, at 85; Droste, *supra* note 68, at 577.

[89] Joint anti-terrorism center.

[90] See Niclas-Frederic Weisser, *Das Gemeinsame Terrorismusabwehrzentrum (GTAZ) – Rechtsprobleme, Rechtsform und Rechtsgrundlage*, 29 NEUE ZEITSCHRIFT FÜR VERWALTUNGSRECHT 142 (2011).

[91] The police division is called the "Polizeiliche Informations- und Analysestelle (PIAS)" and, accordingly, the secret service division is called "Nachrichtendienstliche Informations- und Analysestelle (NIAS)".

cases are discussed, potentially threatening situations are evaluated, and information is exchanged. As long as the police and the intelligence services are divided into two sections, there is a certain guarantee that no police officer has direct access to secret services data bases and vice versa. A formal division exists, but in practical terms the two functions are integrated into a unified approach.

Similar structures facilitating cooperation among the police and the intelligence services exist in other areas. In 2006 the Shared Analysis and Strategy Center – Illegal Immigration (*Gemeinsames Analyse- und Strategiezentrum illegale Migration* – GASIM) was created to help coordinate the fight to stem illegal immigration. In 2007 the Shared Internet Center (*Gemeinsames Internet-Zentrum* – GIZ)[92] was tasked with a general analysis of the Internet – in regard to terrorist activities – through the monitoring of extremist websites and by collecting and analyzing publicly available information. In 2011 the National Cyber-Defense Center (*Nationale Cyber-Abwehrzentrum* – Cyber-AZ) was created to address cyber attacks. In the same year the Shared Defense Center – Rightwing Extremism (*Gemeinsames Abwehrzentrum gegen Rechtsextremismus* – GAR) was established in reaction to the discoveries of the NSU's activities.[93] The GAR's mandate was amended in 2012 in order to address extremism and terrorism in general and the center was renamed the Shared Extremism and Terrorism Defense Center (*Gemeinsames Extremismus- und Terrorismusabwehrzentrum* – GETZ).[94]

V Conclusion

The development in regard to informational and organizational cooperation shows that, by now, a very close and intensive connection between police and intelligence services exists. The principle of separation is formally observed. The two communities only work side-by-side (and have not been merged into single or joint offices) and exchange information (they do not have automatic and complete access to each other's databanks).[95] But apart from this formal separation, not many barriers

---

[92] Joint Internet Center.

[93] Christian Rathgeber, *Terrorismusbekämpfung durch Organisationsrecht*, 128 DEUTSCHES VERWALTUNGSBLATT 1009 (2013).

[94] See Martin Kutscha, *Die Antimonie des Verfassungsschutzes*, 31 NEUE ZEITSCHRIFT FÜR VERWALTUNGSRECHT 324 (2013).

[95] See Michael Lysander Fremuth, *Wächst zusammen, was zusammengehört?*, 139 ARCHIV DES ÖFFENTLICHEN RECHTS 32, 52–72 (2014).

remain, especially in regard to the exchange of information when members of both institutions sit together in specialized centers on a permanent basis.[96] In substance, the principle of separation has been reduced to little more than a formality and it no longer guarantees the effective limit of the powers of police and intelligence services.

F   Conclusion: Problems Solved?

I   First Steps

The development since 2000 shows that the intelligence services have been trusted with new tasks and powers, especially in the field of fighting serious crimes. The events of 9/11 and legislation responding to the NSU case led to changes for the agencies. Most prominently, the separation of law enforcment and intelligence agencies is no longer as clear or as meaningful as it had been in the decades after WWII.[97] The rulings of the Federal Constituional Court have upheld the new legislative measures, finding only marginal elements of the regime to be unconstitutional. This new security architecture has survived its constitutional wellness check-up.

The principle of separation is now chiefly observed as an organizational separation between police and secret services. Beyond that, the principle only sets some outer limits. One limit is that the intelligence services cannot exercise investigative powers in order to resolve minor crimes. But they can do this in regard to serious crimes.[98] The power to collect information in secret and without the existence of a concrete threat or suspicion is now primarily limited only by the mandate that the intelligence services act only to prevent or investigate the most serious crimes. The new limitation on the competence of the intelligence services seems to be that they should not function as a general criminal police force.

The last ten years have been dominated by efforts to institutionalize and ease the exchange of information between the police and the intelligence services. Joint centers, shared infrastructure, and common

---

[96] *But see* Fremuth, *supra* note 95, at 69–72; Roggan & Bergemann, *supra* note 42, at 876; Ulrich Sieber, *Grenzen des Strafrechts*, 119 ZEITSCHRIFT FÜR DIE GESAMTE STRAFRECHTS-WISSENSCHAFT 1, 33–34 (2007); Zöller, *supra* note 72, at 763.

[97] Nehm, *supra* note 66, at 3292.

[98] Bundesverfassungsgericht [BVerfG] [Federal Constitutional Court] July 14, 1999, 100 BVerfGE 313.

databases are examples of a joint approach that has been adopted at the state and the federal levels. These new instruments might help Germany to avoid a second NSU case by facilitating access to important information.

A consequence of the intelligence services' new activities is the increasing relevance of their work for criminal cases. The substantive powers of the intelligence services double the possibilities for the initiation of criminal proceedings. On the one hand, there is the conventional criminal proceeding initiated by the police or the prosecution when a concrete suspicion exists. On the other hand, intelligence operations can lead to prosecution when there is as little evidence as the mere indication of a serious crime. In the case of strategic surveillance by the BND, no indication of a crime is necessary at all. The main difference between the two is not only the level of suspicion, which can trigger proceedings, but the almost complete secrecy of the investigative proceedings. This is quite astonishing in a system where the publicity of the criminal proceeding has been regarded as one of the main achievements of the rule of law.

It is also a novelty insofar as the possibilities to control or supervise the intelligence services and their investigations are very limited. Weak oversight by the Parliament is all that exists. The NSU case triggered some reforms in this regard.[99] Yet, a very small number of parliamentarians are charged with overseeing the work of all the intelligence services.[100] Therefore a new control structure is needed that enables a day-to-day and case-by-case control of the services.[101] Especially the use of informants should be given scrutiny and at least controlled in a way similar to the use of secret electronic surveillance measures.[102] More effective oversight might only result from an increased budget and a closer study of the critical aspects of German praxis exposed by the NSU case.

---

[99] Jan-Hendrik Dietrich, *Reform der parlamentarischen Kontrolle der Nachrichtendienste als rechtsstaatliches Gebot und sicherheitspolitische Notwendigkeit*, 46 Zeitschrift für Rechtspolitik 205 (2014); Gusy, *supra* note 25, at 233.

[100] 20 parliamentarians shall control about 11,500 employees.

[101] See Martin H. W. Möllers, *Das neue Bundesgenehmigungsamt, in* NSU-Terrorismus 225–39 (Martin H. W. Möllers & Robert Chr. van Ooyen eds., 2015) (proposing to set up a new permanant control authority.).

[102] *See Taskforce soll Geheimdienste überwachen*, Handelsblatt (July 1, 2014), www .handelsblatt.com/politik/deutschland/mehr-kontrolle-fuer-den-bundestag-taskforce-soll-geheimdienste-ueberwachen/10136656.html (statement of the Head of the parliamentary control committee).

These developments in the field of the intelligence services and their influence on criminal proceedings show a new political approach, not only toward the agencies, but also toward criminal law and police law. These areas are no longer regarded as separate sectors of legislation standing alone but as part of the more comprehensive area of homeland security (*Innere Sicherheit*).[103] Homeland security is understood to include all the tasks of the state in regard to preventing harm to individuals and the state, as well as to fighting crimes.[104] Within the context of homeland security, the traditional borders of criminal law, police law, and the law of the security services have begun to vanish, and the different fields of law have begun to merge.[105]

II Reforms and Open Questions

So far the answer to the threat of terrorism has been to expand the powers of the intelligence services. And the answer to the NSU case has been two-fold: to improve cooperation between the intelligence services and the police; and to strengthen the parliamentary oversight marginally. This is not enough. Although the Parliament has done a lot, the structural problems have hardly been addressed. The NSU case clearly illustrated how problematic the involvement of so many state authorities in one case can be. This raises difficult questions. It may be that the main problems are the mere existence of the secret services – such a large number of them with similar and overlapping tasks and powers – and that these agencies generally lack significant oversight. The issue may not be one of poor cooperation. The large number of authorities in Germany is mainly due to the federal structure. Still, are all the intelligence services and the (specialized) police offices really necessary? In regard to the intelligence services, a strong Federal Office for the Protection of the Constitution with local branches might be far more effective and easier to supervise than the existing system of federal and state offices. The latter are often rather small agencies operating with

---

[103] See Volkmar Götz, *Innere Sicherheit, in* HANDBUCH DES STAATSRECHTS DER BUNDES-REPUBLIK DEUTSCHLAND, BAND IV AUFGABEN DES STAATES 671–99 (Josef Isensee & Paul Kirchof eds., 3rd ed. 2006).

[104] Martin Kutscha, *Innere Sicherheit und Verfassung, in* HANDBUCH ZUM RECHT DER INNEREN SICHERHEIT, BERLINER WISSENSCHAFTSVERLAG, *supra* note 48, at 24.

[105] Sieber, *supra* note 96, at 27–43.

small budgets. Also, the tasks of the MAD could be taken over by a specialized department within the BfV.[106]

In July 2015, the Parliament enacted a structural reform based on the results of investigations into the NSU case.[107] This legislation passed the Federal Council of the State Governments (*Bundesrat*) at the end of September 2015, and became law at the end of 2015. The BfV now has a stronger central office function with the possibility of providing central information systems and other technical and professional support to the state offices. This will improve the central access and storage of collected information and can make the actual work more effective, although the law is not a major reform. If one looks at the development of the Federal Criminal Police Office (*Bundeskriminalamt* – BKA), the central office function was the starting point for the creation of a strong and invaluable federal institution. This is a first step in the right direction for the intelligence services, but it still lacks a solution for a sufficient oversight and leaves the number of offices untouched.

The new law also allows the BfV to continue to use informants, but it restricts their use in several ways: no former criminals of major crimes may be employed, no major payments are allowed, and the informant is not allowed to play a major role within the organization that is under surveillance. In this regard, the legislation will be a major step forward as it will not only be the first statutory regulation of the subject but it also sets clear standards for the use of informants. Unfortunately the legislation does not provide for a clear and substantial control mechanism.

The new regulation, for all its merits, does not address the problematic number of authorities. It also does not adress the problem that similar tasks and powers are assigned to different authorities (redundant competences).[108] Multiplying competences and responsibilities diminishes legal certainty as it is never clear which authority actually has to act

---

[106] *See* BÄCKER ET AL., *supra* note 2, at 268–69.

[107] *See* Gesetz zur Verbesserung der Zusammenarbeit im Bereich des Verfassungsschutzes [Act to Improve Cooperation in Constitutional Protections], DEUTSCHER BUNDESTAG: DRUCKSACHEN [BT] 18/4654, http://dip21.bundestag.de/dip21/btd/18/046/1804654.pdf; Beschlussempfehlung und Bericht des Innenausschusses (4. Ausschuss) [Report and Recommendation of the Committee of Internal Affairs (4th Committee)], DEUTSCHER BUNDESTAG: DRUCKSACHEN [BT] 18/5415, http://dip21.bundestag.de/dip21/btd/18/054/1805415.pdf.

[108] BÄCKER ET AL., *supra* note 2, at 261–70; Gusy, *supra* note 25, at 231. For the data aspect, *see* Michael Ronellenfitsch, *Datenschutzrechtliche Schranken bei der Terrorismusbekämpfung*, 31 DATENSCHUTZ UND DATENSICHERHEIT 561 (2007).

and citizens do not know which actions they can expect from whom. But the rule of law requires that authority and responsibility for each case be clear.[109] In this sense it is problematic that police and intelligence services are partly responsible for the same tasks, have overlapping powers, and in consequence, produce and maintain multiple databases.[110] The easiest and best solution to all of this would be to restrict the involvement of the intelligence agencies in resolving serious crimes, such as those in the area of violent terrorism.[111] This would task the secret services with fighting only the most serious threats to the security of the state and not task them with gathering intelligence on other kinds of transborder organized criminality. This would also reduce fears of an expansive, omni-present secret agency.

The German Parliament has not proven ready to change the present structure. Still, a solution must be found for balancing the far-reaching powers of the intelligence services. In another context something similar has been achieved through the strict adherence to standards developed in the rules of criminal procedure, backed-up by constitutional safeguards. The present involvement of the intelligence services in criminal cases shows that sufficient safeguards do not exist to uphold the high standard that has been achieved in criminal proceedings. Those high standards are a product of our commitment to the rule of law as it developed in the Enlightenment. This involves, for example, the prosecution's responsibility to monitor the police, a safeguard that is diminished when the police work closely with the intelligence services. This particular safeguard is precluded altogether where the agencies "conduct" investigations on their own. This also raises questions about the extent to which public proceedings – and the rights of the defense to challenge evidence that is based on the work of the intelligence services (e.g., based on informants) – can be guaranteed. Expanding the powers of the agencies must be accompanied by an equally vigorous effort to effectively guarantee the rights of all persons affected by investigative measures (suspects, witnesses, third parties, and the general public in regard to measures possible without a suspicion). These problems have not been adequately addressed by the Parliament.

---

[109] Bundesverfassungsgericht [BVerfG] [Federal Constitutional Court], Oct. 9, 1984, 67 BVerfGE 299; Bundesverfassungsgericht [BVerfG] [Federal Constitutional Court], Feb 19, 2002, 104 BVerfGE 249; Veith Mehde, *Terrorismusbekämpfung durch Organisationsrecht*, 54 JURISTENZEITUNG 815 (2005).

[110] BÄCKER ET AL., *supra* note 2, at 261–70.   [111] *See* BÄCKER ET AL., *supra* note 2, at 270.

Last but not least, one of the main issues to be solved is the right approach to take when dealing with complex threats such as terrorism. Expanding criminal law by criminalizing abstract threats (e.g., visits to terrorist camps), and thereby converting the criminal law regime into a kind of "preventive" criminal law (*Präventionsstrafrecht*), will contribute to overlaps with police law and the authority of the intelligence services. The task remains to develop an adequate law for potentially risky behavior, a preventively orientated "security law," within the existing security architecture.[112]

---

[112] See Christoph Gusy, *Vom "Neuen Sicherheitsbegriff" zur "Neuen Sicherheitsarchitektur,"* in INNERE SICHERHEIT IM EUROPÄISCHEN VERGLEICH 71 (Thomas Würtenberger *et al.* eds., 2012); Kugelmann, *supra* note 2, at 52–55; Voßkuhle, Andreas, *Das Verhältnis con Freiheit und Sicherheit – Hat der 11. September 2001 das deutsche Verfassungsrecht verändert?*, in VERFASSUNGSSTAATLICHKEIT IM WANDEL 1101, 1119–20 (Dirk Heckmann *et al.* eds., 2013).

15

Legal Restraints on the Extraterritorial Activities of Germany's Intelligence Services

BY KLAUS GÄRDITZ

A Introduction

In January 2014, the President of the Federal Office for the Protection of the Constitution (*Bundesamt für Verfassungsschutz*) – the German domestic intelligence service – was asked whether German counter-espionage had insight into activities of the National Security Agency (NSA) on German soil. He answered, after boldly interpreting the legal assignment of the NSA: "Our understanding is still that the Americans comply with German law in Germany."[1] This short and incredible answer raises a number of legal questions. After all, most counties engage in intelligence activities abroad while fully aware that these activities are prohibited by the laws of the state in which the operations take place. Working as an agent for an intelligence service of a foreign power is a criminal offense under German and American law.[2] Because Germany is a central hub for security-related activities between Europe, Russia, and the Middle East, it is realistic to assume that foreign intelligence services are active in Germany. With this in mind, the claim that foreign agents are in compliance with German laws is naive or dishonest or mere political posturing. It may as well be the latter. As the old saying goes, all politics is local. Above all, President Maaßen's answer calls into question the legal restraints German law imposes on Germany's foreign intelligence activities.

The murky legal twilight zone in which the German Federal Intelligence Service (*Bundesnachrichtendienst* or BND) fulfills its mandate had never been given special attention by lawyers. This rapidly changed

---

[1] Von Hans-Jürgen Jakobs & Thomas Sigmund in Düsseldorf, *Handelsblatt vom 29.01.2014:* "*Unser Geschäft lebt auch vom Verrat,*" BUNDESAMT FÜR VERFASSUNGSSCHUTZ (Dec. 28, 2014), www.verfassungsschutz.de/de/oeffentlichkeitsarbeit/interviews/int-20140129-hand elsblatt (last visited Nov. 23, 2015).

[2] STRAFGESETZBUCH[StGB][CRIMINAL CODE], § 99; 18 U.S.C. §§ 792–99.

when, at the height of the NSA-Affair, the Federal Parliament (*Bundestag*) established a Committee of Inquiry to examine the activities of the United States' intelligence services, in particular the NSA, on German soil.[3] As part of the Committee's efforts it also received expert testimony and advice on questions of international law and the national law relevant to the conduct of German foreign intelligence operations. The latter seemed rather peripheral to the Committee's charge. But it placed the BND in a serious predicament. Three distinguished legal experts – public law professors, two of whom were former justices of the German Federal Constitutional Court (*Bundesverfassungsgericht*) – offered critical remarks on the scant legal framework governing Germany's foreign intelligence operations. They were particularly troubled by the German government's understanding that domestic constitutional limits do not apply to Germany's extraterritorial intelligence activities and the experts took the unusual move of suggesting that the current foreign surveillance practice is unconstitutional.[4]

B Intelligence Architecture, Foreign Affairs, and the Gentle Power of Juridification

The German Foreign Intelligence Service originates from sources under Allied military occupation. In 1946, in the aftermath of World War II and with the Cold War in Europe already looming, the Western Allies sponsored the recreation of a West German intelligence service out of the rubble of a former *Wehrmacht* intelligence detachment.[5] This nascent agency's chief mandate was to spy on the rising Soviet power in Europe.[6]

---

[3] Antrag der Fraktionen, CDU/CSU, *SPD, DIE LINKE. und BÜNDNIS 90/DIE GRÜNEN*: *Einsetzung eines Untersuchungsausschusses*, Bundestag Drucksache (Dec. 24, 2014), www.bundestag.de/blob/284528/a89d6006f28900c4f46e56f5e0807ddf/einsetzungsantrag_englisch-docx-data.pdf (last visited Nov. 23, 2015). *See* Chapter 12 in this volume.

[4] Mathias Bäcker, Erhebung, Bevorratung und Übermittlung von Telekommunikationsdaten durch die Nachrichtendienste des Bundes – Stellungnahme zur Anhörung des NSA-Untersuchungsausschusses (2014); Wolfgang Hoffmann-Riem, Stellungnahme zur Anhörung des NSA-Untersuchungsausschusses (2014); Hans-Jürgen Papier, Gutachtliche Stellungnahme: Beweisbeschluss SV-2 des ersten Untersuchungsausschusses des Deutschen Bundestages der 18. Wahlperiode (2014). *See* Chapter 13 in this volume; Chapter 10 in this volume.

[5] *See* James H. Critchfield, Auftrag Pullach: Die Organisation Gehlen 1948–1956 (2005).

[6] *See id.*; Josef Foschepoth, Überwachtes Deutschland: Post- und Telefonüberwachung in der alten Bundesrepublik 64–94 (2013); Wolfgang Krieger, Geschichte der Geheimdienste 264–74 (2d ed., 2010).

The organization was formally constituted as a service unit of the U. S. Army and later it was a modest unit within the newly founded CIA.[7] In these manifestations it was not formally chartered or approved by occupational statutory law. Following West Germany's rearmament the organization was placed under the control of the German Federal Government by cabinet order in July 1955, and renamed the *Bundesnachrichtendienst*. The BND was integrated into the federal administrative infrastructure.[8] This, too, was achieved without any statutory basis. It was understood at the time that a foreign intelligence service was a cornerstone in the architecture of foreign and security policy making and therefore a traditional and exclusive concern of the executive branch that lay beyond the competence of statutory authority.

After World War II the parliaments of the West German Federation and states, under the aegis of renewed commitments to individual rights and reestablishment of the rule of law,[9] entered into a long process of more strictly regulating administrative affairs.[10] The effect of this was to restrain executive discretion. Areas of statutorily unregulated executive power were incrementally eliminated and brought under the authority of basic rights and democratic legislation.[11] Foreign policy emerged relatively unscathed from this process, including intelligence gathering abroad. Thus, during the Cold War, the BND remained an obscure power outside the common legal framework of the federal administration. Even the constitutional authority for the establishment of the BND remained unidentified, despite the fact that the Federation is free to establish federal authorities only insofar as the German Constitution (the *Grundgesetz* or Basic Law) provides or permits.[12] In the meantime,

---

[7] See CRITCHFIELD, *supra* note 5. See also KRIEGER, *supra* note 6; TIM WEINER, LEGACY OF ASHES: THE HISTORY OF THE CIA 66–68 (2007).

[8] *Cabinet order of 11 July 1955, based on a letter of the Chancellor of 23 March 1955*, BUNDESNACHRICHTENDIENST (July 11, 1955), www.bnd.bund.de (last visited Nov. 23, 2015); REINHARD KLEE, NEUE INSTRUMENTE DER ZUSAMMENARBEIT VON POLIZEI UND NACHRICHTENDIENSTEN 71–72 (2010); ARMIN SCHOREIT, DIE INNERE SICHERHEIT IN DER BUNDESREPUBLIK DEUTSCHLAND 65–66 (1979); STEFANIE WASKE, MEHR LIAISON ALS KONTROLLE: DIE KONTROLLE DES BND DURCH PARLAMENT UND REGIERUNG 1955–1978 32–33 (2009).

[9] See RAINER WAHL, HERAUSFORDERUNG UND ANTWORTEN: DAS ÖFFENTLICHE RECHT DER LETZTEN FÜNF JAHRZEHNTE 18–31, 35–38 (2006).

[10] *Id.* at 16.

[11] See BVERFG, 2 BvR 41/71, Mar. 14, 1972, http://dejure.org/dienste/vernetzung/rechtspre chung?Text=2%20BvR%2041/71.

[12] GRUNDGESETZ [GG][BASIC LAW], art. 83, *translation at* www.gesetze-im-internet.de/ english_gg/index.html.

this shortcoming has been corrected.[13] But prior to this development the BND's activities were neither legally authorized nor limited by statute. An important exception to this shadowy tradition was the enactment of the G-10 Act in 1968.[14] The G-10 Act, which implemented the highly controversial "emergency" amendments to the Basic Law, authorized the BND to intercept telecommunications for reasons of state security.

The opaque legal vacuum in which the BND prospered was filled-in shortly after the fall of the Iron Curtain and German reunification. In December 1990, the *Bundestag* adopted a law concerned with the collection, storage and distribution of data, including data protection.[15] As part of this law the BND was at last given a statutory charter, which is known as the BND Act.[16] The statute formally established the BND as a federal agency, defined its mandate, and empowered the agency with specific competences. This statutory development was not a reaction to the geo-political upheaval at the end of the 1980s and the resulting fundamental shift of the mission of foreign intelligence after the collapse of the Soviet empire. Plans for the "legalization" of the BND dated back to the early 1980s when no one had the slightest idea of the coming decline of the East Block. Instead, the Parliament was under pressure to enact a statutory regime that would comply with the Federal Constitutional Court's *Census Act Case* from 1983. In the *Census Act Case* the Court adopted a basic right to informational self-determination and demanded that the gathering, handling, and protection of personal data must be regulated by area-specific statutory provisions.[17] The result was a broad-based data protection law, including statutory provisions related to the intelligence services.

C The Rule of Law and Executive Actions Abroad

There has always been a discussion about whether intelligence operations abroad are suitable for statutory regulation at all. Some voices stressed

---

[13] The Federal Constitutional Court identified Article 87(3)1 of the Basic Law, which permits that autonomous federal higher authorities under public law may be established by a federal law for matters on which the Federation has legislative power. See BVerfG, 1 BvR 2226/94, July 14, 1999, www.servat.unibe.ch/dfr/bv100313.html

[14] Gesetz zur Beschränkung des Brief-, Post- und Fernmeldegeheimnisses [Law on the Restriction of the Privacy of Correspondence, Posts and Telecommunications], Aug. 13, 1968, BGBl I at 949 (Ger.).

[15] *Id.* at 2954.

[16] Gesetz über den Bundesnachrichtendienst [BND-Gesetz] [Law on the Federal Intelligence Service], Dec. 20, 1990, BGBl I at 2954, 2979 (Ger.).

[17] BVerfG, 1 BvR 209, Dec. 15, 1983, www.servat.unibe.ch/dfr/bv065001.html.

the difficulty of standardizing intelligence operations, which by their nature require the shadow of secrecy and utmost flexibility.[18] Some argued that the BND had no executive competences on German territory and, thus, needed no statutory foundation.[19] Finally, those close to the Intelligence Community advanced the more fundamental objection that the rule of law – albeit strictly binding within domestic relations – did not restrain intelligence operations abroad.[20] From a constitutional perspective this was and is indefensible. Article 20(3) of the Basic Law stipulates that the executive shall be bound by law and justice.[21] The rule of law applies without exception and independent of the location where an administrative agent acts. There is neither an extraterritorial nor a security exception;[22] and the rule of law remains unimpaired, even in the case of a national emergency.[23] The BND must comply with applicable German laws, even when acting abroad.[24] Nonetheless, constitutional legality can only bind the executive branch to the extent that there are applicable legal norms. Constitutional limits are futile when there is no applicable law seeking to give them force. Whether the administration, including the BND, *requires* a statutory authorization when acting abroad is a completely different question, which will be addressed later in this chapter.

In the context at hand, it is worth mentioning that Article 20(3) of the Basic Law demands only compliance with German law (including directly applicable international law and supranational European law).[25] If

---

[18] Ernst Friesenhahn, *Die Kontrolle der Dienste, in* VERFASSUNGSSCHUTZ UND RECHTSSTAAT 87, 89 (Bundesministerium des Innern ed., 1981). *But see* THOMAS RIEGER, DER BUNDESNACHRICHTENDIENST IM DEMOKRATISCHEN RECHTSSTAAT 130–31 (1986).

[19] Hans Hugo Klein, *Verfassungstreue und Schutz der Verfassung,* 37 VERÖFFENTLICHUNGEN DER VEREINIGUNG DER DEUTSCHEN STAATSRECHTSLEHRER 53, 92 (1979); Klaus Stern, I STAATSRECHT DER BUNDESREPUBLIK DEUTSCHLAND 186 (1977).

[20] Helmut Roewer, NACHRICHTENDIENSTRECHT DER BUNDESREPUBLIK DEUTSCHLAND, 1 PKKG 21 (1987).

[21] GRUNDGESETZ [GG][BASIC LAW], art. 20(3).

[22] *See generally* HORST DREIER, *Commentary on Article 1(3) Grundgesetz, in* I GRUNDGESETZ KOMMENTAR § 44 (Horst Dreier ed., 3rd ed. 2013); Wolfgang Kahl, *Commentary on Article 1(3) Grundgesetz, in* BONNER KOMMENTAR ZUM GRUNDGESETZ § 222 (Wolfgang Kahl, Christian Waldhoff, Christian Walter eds. 2015).

[23] Udo Di Fabio, *Sicherheit in Freiheit,* 61 NEUE JURISTISCHE WOCHENSCHRIFT 421 (2008).

[24] NIKOLAOS GAZEAS, ÜBERMITTLUNG NACHRICHTENDIENSTLICHER ERKENNTNISSE AN STRAFVERFOLGUNGSBEHÖRDEN 152 (2014); Christoph Gusy, *Der Bundesnachrichtendienst,* 17 Die Verwaltung 273 (1984).

[25] *See* Klaus F. Gärditz, *Rechtsstaat (Art. 20 Abs. 3 Grundgesetz), in* BERLINER KOMMENTAR ZUM GRUNDGESETZ 51, 123–26 (Karl Heinrich Friauf Wolfram Höfling eds., 2015), with further references.

German administrative officers wield sovereign powers in a foreign state – with or without that state's consent – they are not constitutionally obliged to comply with the *lex loci*. The BND's intelligence operations abroad might qualify as a violation of the law in the state in which the operation took place. But this would not necessarily constitute a violation of the rule of law under the German constitution. For that to be the case German statutory provisions would have to require compliance with the applicable foreign law. Simply put, legality is relative. And Article 20(3) of the Basic Law merely demands compliance with the German legal order irrespective of the competence of a foreign legal order to qualify the same conduct as illegal under its own, independent conditions of legality.

Finally, the extraterritoriality of intelligence operations is not a legal obstacle to bind German agents to German law. The territorial scope of the application of legal norms is not an issue of legal theory. Instead, it is a discretionary matter for the positive law.[26] Within the loose framework of the international law on jurisdiction any state may adopt legal prescriptions that are extraterritorially applicable. As Germany can exert control of personnel via internationally accepted personal sovereignty, the federal parliament, relying on its legislative competence in foreign affairs,[27] could define the scope of intelligence actions abroad, set relevant preconditions, and establish limits.

D   Requirement of a Statutory Authorization of Intelligence Collection Abroad?

Such a statutory regime *could* regulate intelligence collection abroad. The crucial question is whether the BND (or another intelligence service while acting abroad within its assignment) *requires* a parliamentary statute that authorizes foreign intelligence operations. As Germany is a parliamentary democracy, under the Basic Law executive authority ultimately springs from parliamentary statutes, which equally empower and limit administrative action. Therefore, the requirement of statutory authorization is the constitutional instrument that links parliamentary

---

[26] HANS KELSEN, DAS PROBLEM DER SOUVERÄNITÄT UND DIE THEORIE DES VÖLKERRECHTS 72 (2d ed. 1928).

[27] GRUNDGESETZ [GG][BASIC LAW], art. 73(1). *See* BVerfG, 1 BvR 2226/94, July 14, 1999, www.servat.unibe.ch/dfr/bv100313.html. Federal Governement, Deutscher Bundesag Drucksache 618/88, ¶ 183; Deutscher Bundesag Drucksache 11/4306, ¶ 70; Matthias Bäcker, *Das G 10 und die Kompetenzordnung,* 64 DIE ÖFFENTLICHE VERWALTUNG 840, 842 (2011).

democracy with the rule of law.[28] It is a well-established doctrine that any *significant* decision of the executive branch has to be authorized by a parliamentary statute, which is sufficiently precise (so-called *Wesentlich-keitsdoktrin*).[29] For the purposes of this principle, executive measures are particularly significant if they affect basic rights guaranteed by the constitution.[30] Long-established constitutional doctrine holds that any administrative action interfering with a basic right requires a sufficient statutory authorization.[31] Nonetheless, the form and the degree of statutory regulation depend on context-related practicability and the normative-functional limits of parliamentary legislation.[32] The crucial question is whether basic rights can be affected by foreign intelligence operations.

I Extraterritorial Applicability of Basic Rights

The extraterritorial applicability and regulatory effect of constitutional rights is one of the most difficult fields of constitutional doctrine. The question has not benefited from a coherent set of court decisions and a predictable constitutional structure has not yet emerged. Most countries seem to be reluctant to grant rights universally to everybody (in particular the United States traditionally has a strong concept of territoriality). A reason for this posture is that state responsibility still follows effective control and an unsophisticated universalization of one country's domestic constitutional rights might easily overburden its legal institutions. The German Federal Constitutional Court, in the *Second Register Case*, emphasized that legislation regulating extraterritorial issues must be

---

[28] Oliver Lepsius, *Braucht das Verfassungsrecht eine Theorie des Staates?*, 31 EUROPÄISCHE GRUNDRECHTE-ZEITSCHRIFT 370, 378 (2004).

[29] BVERFG, 1 BvR 230/70, July 22, 1970, http://dejure.org/dienste/vernetzung/rechtspre chung?Text=1%20BvR%20230/70; BVERFG, 1 BvR 1213/85, Mar. 2, 1993, www.servat .unibe.ch/dfr/bv088103.html; BVERFG, 1 BvR 1640/97, July 14, 1998, www.servat.unibe .ch/dfr/bv098218.html; BVERFG, 2 BvR 669/04, May 24, 2006, www.servat.unibe.ch/dfr/ bv116024.html.

[30] BVERFG, 2 BvR 883/73, Oct. 28, 1975, http://dejure.org/dienste/vernetzung/rechtspre chung?Text=2%20BvR%20883/73; BVERFG, 1 BvR 402/87, Nov. 27, 1990, www.servat .unibe.ch/dfr/bv083130.html; BVERFG, 1 BvR 48/94, Aug. 4, 1997, www.servat.unibe.ch/ dfr/bv095267.html; BVERFG, 1 BvR 1640/97, July 14, 1998, www.servat.unibe.ch/dfr/ bv098218.html; BVERFG, 2 BvF 3/90, June 7, 1999, www.servat.unibe.ch/dfr/bv101001 .html; BVERFG, 2 BvR 1436/02, Sept. 24, 2003, www.servat.unibe.ch/dfr/bv108282.html.

[31] BVERFG, 2 BvR 883/73, 40, 237, 249, Oct. 28, 1975; BVERFG, 1 BvL 1/75, 1 BvR 147/75, 47, 46. 79, Dec. 21, 1977; BVERFG, 2 BvL 8/77, 49, 89, 126–27, Aug. 8, 1978.

[32] BVERFG, 1 BvR 1640/97, July 12, 1998, www.servat.unibe.ch/dfr/bv098218.html; Lepsius, *supra note 28*, at 279.

sufficiently flexible to allow the executive to adapt to the practical constraints of a foreign scenario.[33] The Court noted that legal relations abroad typically are more fluid and can be accommodated by legislation. Nonetheless, as a result of globalization, traditional borders have become permeable. States have expanded their jurisdiction. Spheres of regulation now overlap. State organs operate more frequently and more intensely outside the domestic territory. The question "Does the Constitution Follow the Flag?" has acquired a new urgency.[34]

Article 1(3) of the Basic Law provides that the basic rights of the Constitution "shall bind the legislature, the executive and the judiciary as directly applicable law." If the state's sovereign functions are exercised, then the state's organs are bound by the basic rights.[35] This seems to apply regardless of whether the location where public agents operate is *intraterritorial* or *extra*-territorial.[36] Against this background one cannot deny that intelligence services (in particular the BND) acting abroad must comply – at least in principle – with the restrictions imposed by the basic rights under the German constitution.[37] Yet, the German Federal Constitutional Court did not affirmatively establish this rule in its decision concerning the strategic surveillance of international

---

[33] BVerfG, 1 BvF 1/90, Jan. 10, 1995, www.servat.unibe.ch/dfr/bv092026.html.

[34] KAL RAUSTIALA, DOES THE CONSTITUTION FOLLOW THE FLAG? THE EVOLUTION OF TERRITORIALITY IN AMERICAN LAW (2009).

[35] BVerfG, 1 BvR 65/54, Mar. 21, 1957, www.servat.unibe.ch/dfr/bv006290.html; BVerfG, 1 BvR 636/68, May 4, 1971, www.servat.unibe.ch/dfr/bv031058.html; BVerfG, 2 BvR 1258/79, Mar. 25, 1981, www.servat.unibe.ch/dfr/bv057009.html; BVerfG, 1 BvR 2226/94, July 14, 1999, www.servat.unibe.ch/dfr/bv100313.html; Matthias Herdegen, *Kommentierung zu art. 1 Abs. 3 Grundgesetz, in* GRUNDGESETZ 71 (Theodor Maunz & Günter Dürig eds., 2014); Rainer Hofmann, GRUNDRECHTE UND GRENZÜBERSCHREITENDE SACHVERHALTE 13 (1994); Ralf Poscher, *Das Verfassungsrecht vor den Herausforderungen der Globalisierung,* 67 VERÖFFENTLICHUNGEN DER VEREINIGUNG DER DEUTSCHEN STAATSRECHTSLEHRER 160, 191–94 (2008).

[36] Horst Dreier, *supra note 22,* No. 44; Herdegen, *supra note 35,* at 71; Wolfgang Kahl, *Kommentierung zu Art. 1 Abs. 3 Grundgesetz, in* BONNER KOMMENTAR ZUM GRUNDGESETZ 222 (Wolfgang Kahl, Christian Waldhoff & Christian Walter eds., 2014); Martin Nettesheim, *Verfassungsbindung der auswärtigen Gewalt, in* XI HANDBUCH DES STAATSRECHTS § 241 No. 57 (Josef Isensee & Paul Kirchhof eds., 3rd ed., 2014).

[37] Gusy, *supra note 24,* at 283; D. Kreuter & K. Möbius, *Verfassungsrechtliche Vorgaben für nachrichtendienstliches Handeln im Ausland: Extraterritoriale Geltung der Grundrechte?,* 53 BUNDESWEHRVERWALTUNG 146, 147, 149–51 (2009); For dissenting opinions, *see* Heike Krieger, *Die Reichweite der Grundrechtsbindung bei nachrichtendienstlichem Handeln, in* PARLAMENTARISCHE KONTROLLE DER NACHRICHTENDIENSTE IM DEMOKRATISCHEN RECHTSSTAAT 31, 36 (Norbert Röttgen & Heinrich Amadeus Wolff eds., 2009).

telecommunication by the BND. In that case the Court held that binding the executive to basic rights does not define the territorial scope of the application of any specific basic right.[38]

In the absence of a general or abstract resolution of the question the applicability of each specific basic right has to be defined *ratione loci*, *ratione materiae*, and *ratione personae*. This might lead to quite different results. For example, some basic rights (the general freedom right,[39] the freedom of assembly,[40] the freedom of association,[41] or the right to an effective remedy before a court[42]) can only be guaranteed within the German jurisdiction because they require a specific (domestic) institutional-legal infrastructure. Another example is the right to asylum,[43] which can be invoked only by those asylum seekers who reach German soil.[44] In contrast, a number of other rights might be applicable abroad because they are "impact-related" and bind the German state organs whenever and wherever they act. I have in mind, especially, the right to life, physical integrity, and liberty.[45] For example, extraditing a culprit who faces the death penalty, torture, or humiliating treatment in the state that requested extradition can infringe the aforementioned basic right under the German constitution.[46] Many legal uncertainties remain.

II Infringement of Basic Rights by Covert Intelligence Gathering Abroad?

I want to concentrate on two questions that seem to be particularly relevant to the intelligence gathering context. First, can intelligence collection abroad, that is, outside effective control and under the cover of secrecy, be qualified as an infringement of a basic right? Second, who is entitled to invoke a basic right abroad?

---

[38] BVerfG, 1 BvR 2226/94, July 14, 1999, www.servat.unibe.ch/dfr/bv100313.html.
[39] Grundgesetz [GG][Basic Law], art, 2(1).
[40] Grundgesetz [GG][Basic Law], art. 8(1).
[41] Grundgesetz [GG][Basic Law], art. 9(1).
[42] Grundgesetz [GG][Basic Law], art. 19(4).
[43] Grundgesetz [GG][Basic Law], art. 16a(1).
[44] BVerwG, June 26, 1984, 9 C 196/83, BVerwGE 69, 323.
[45] Grundgesetz [GG][Basic Law], art, 2(2).
[46] BVerfG, 2 BvR 2259/04, July 6, 2005, www.servat.unibe.ch/dfr/bv113154.html; BVerfG, 2 BvR 685/03, June 24, 2003, http://dejure.org/dienste/vernetzung/rechtsprechung?Text= BVerfG%20108,%20129. The constitutional jurisprudence is, in fact, a follow-up of the model decision in *Soering* of the European Court of Human Rights. *See* Soering v. United Kingdom 161 Eur. Ct. H.R. (1989).

1   The Territorial Dimension: Sovereign Functions and Effective Control

Article 1(3) of the Basic Law does not address the "state" as a unitary subject of legal attribution. Instead, it refers to specific sovereignty functions by disaggregating statehood and mirroring the classic separation of powers model: the legislature, the executive, and the judiciary.[47] The applicability of basic rights is function-based. The attribution of an action to the Federal Republic of Germany is a necessary but not sufficient condition of basic rights protection. Basic rights protect against the exercise of sovereign authority because these rights are needed when state organs can use their asymmetric power and privileges of legal enforcement, which put citizens at a severe disadvantage. It is generally accepted that basic rights are, at least in principle, applicable even if state organs (domestically) use the forms of private law to achieve administrative aims,[48] the rationale behind this extension of basic rights protection is, again, the connection with government functions. Private law is a practicable and flexible instrument of the administration to fulfill public functions as long as the need to unilaterally enforce a decision is not present. Consequently, basic rights are not applicable where the exercise of sovereign functions – a privilege of the executive under public law – is not even abstractly feasible. This is, in particular, the case with private law transactions of a state or its companies abroad.[49] For the qualification of extraterritorial actions as an interference with basic rights it is not enough that that the source of the extraterritorial effects originates from the domestic exercise of executive functions prescribed by public law.[50]

Germany has no *effective control* over a foreign scene of action unless the location is under military occupation or mandated administration.[51] "Effective control" is also the crucial test that the European Court of

---

[47] Oliver Lepsius, *Funktion und Wandel von Staatsverständnissen, in* Verabschiedung und Wiederentdeckung des Staates im Spannungsfeld der Disziplinen 37, 38 (Andreas Voßkuhle, Christian Bumke & Florian Meinel eds., 2013).

[48] BVerfG, 1 BvR 699/06, Feb. 22, 2001, www.servat.unibe.ch/dfr/bv128226.html; Dreier, *supra note 22*, Nos. 66–69; Dirk Ehlers, *Verwaltung in Privatrechtsform* 100 (1984); Herdegen, *supra note 35*, No. 95; Wolfram Höfling, *Kommentierung zu Art. 1 Grundgesetz, in* Grundgesetz Nos. 106–10 (Michael Sachs ed., 7th ed., 2014).

[49] Nettesheim, *supra note 36*, § 241, No. 66.

[50] Christoph Gusy, *Kommentierung zu § 1 BNDG, in* Sicherheitsrecht des Bundes 47 (Wolf-Rüdiger Schenke, Kurt Graulich & Josef Ruthig eds., 2014).

[51] *See* Legal Consequences of the Construction of a Wall in the Occupied Palestinian Territory, Advisory Opinion, 2004 I.C.J. Rep. 136, 179–89 (July 9).

Human Rights applies to decide whether actions of member states fall "within their jurisdiction" according to Article 1 of the European Convention for the Protection of Human Rights and Fundamental Freedoms.[52] The case law of the European Court of Human Rights is generally used as a guideline for the interpretation of basic rights under the German constitution, in particular, to avoid conflicts arising from diverging civil rights standards.[53] The "effective control" criterion generally is a reasonable approach to balancing responsibility for the protection of basic rights.[54] This is true despite the fact that the European Court of Human Rights stressed the peculiarities of regional treaty interpretation in its leading *Bankovic* decision.[55] With this limitation in mind, in later decisions on the question the European Court of Human Rights did not refer to specific arguments of treaty interpretation but relied instead on a basic rationale of legal attribution: "The exercise of jurisdiction is a necessary condition [...] to be able to be held responsible for acts or omissions imputable to it which give rise to an allegation of the infringement of rights and freedoms."[56] But the Court further explained that a state's jurisdiction – and the sphere of its responsibility – "is primarily territorial." The Court concluded: "the question whether exceptional circumstances exist which require and justify a finding by the Court that the State was exercising jurisdiction extraterritorially must be determined with reference to the particular facts."[57]

Clandestine intelligence gathering abroad cannot be qualified as an "exceptional circumstance" that would establish *de facto* effective control.[58] The *exercise of sovereign functions* is an accepted criterion to

---

[52] Bankovic and Others v. Belgium and Others, App. No. 52207/99, Eur. Ct. H.R. §§ 74–82 (2001); Al-Skeini v. United Kingdom, App. No. 55721/07, 53 Eur. H.R. Rep. 589, §§ 131, 138 (2011); Chagos Islanders v. United Kingdom, App. No. 35622/04, § 70 (2012). For conclusions similar to the author's regarding intelligence actions abroad, *see* Stefan Talmon, *Der Begriff der "Hoheitsgewalt" in Zeiten der Überwachung des Internet- und Telekommunikationsverkehrs durch ausländische Nachrichtendienste*, 69 Juristenzeitung 783, 784–85 (2014).

[53] BVerfG, 2 BvR 1481/04, Oct. 14, 2004, www.servat.unibe.ch/dfr/bv111307.html.

[54] *See* Samantha Besson, *The Extraterritoriality of the European Convention on Human Rights: Why Human Rights Depend on Jurisdiction and What Jurisdiction Amounts to*, 25 Leiden J. Int'l. L. 857–84 (2012).

[55] Bankovic and Others v. Belgium and Others, *supra note 52*, § 80.

[56] Al-Skeini and Others v. United Kingdom, *supra note 52*, § 130.   [57] *Id.* § 132.

[58] *But see* Anne Peters, *Surveillance without Borders: The Unlawfulness of the NSA Panopticon, Part II*, EJIL: Talk!, www.ejiltalk.org/surveillance-without-borders-the-unlawful ness-of-the-nsa-panopticon-part-ii/ (last visited Nov. 23, 2015). This view has never been adopted by the European Court of Human Rights. *See also* Chapter 5 in this volume.

identify state authority, which must conform with basic rights even abroad.[59] For example, acts enacted by consular officers within their official capacity would indisputably be bound by basic rights. In contrast, intelligence service agents, acting abroad under the cover of secrecy and unable to wield any sovereign competences, have at best the merely factual power of a gang of criminals. In particular, intelligence agents cannot enforce a decision to obtain certain information. There is no shadow of imperative hierarchy, which is the essence of wielding sovereign functions. The organizational integration in the German executive in the sense of Article 1(3) of the Basic Law is neither visible nor utilizable. Openly invoking the official assignment of the BND in a foreign country to enforce a covert operation – a rather comical idea – would merely expose the agents to criminal prosecution for espionage. In fact, the official assignment – the very basis of every act in official capacity – must be kept secret by the agents while operating abroad without consent of the state where the operation takes place. Agents may use physical force, coercion, duress, or corruption to obtain intelligence, but this would be an illegal act under the *lex loci delicti*. There is neither functional immunity nor any privilege for spies under international law because they do not openly act in an official capacity.[60] If a clandestine operation to gather intelligence, an espionage plot, or a conspiracy is revealed, then the competent authorities of the state in which the operation is located can immediately arrest and prosecute the actors if they choose to do so.[61] And a victim of an intelligence operation usually could act in legitimate self-defense and fend off an intrusion into his or her privacy. In effect, in a foreign country, intelligence agents have to gather information like private persons, in particular, at full personal risk without effective governmental backing.

Intelligence operations abroad – at least in principle – do not entail sovereign functions within the meaning of Article 1(3) of the Basic Law. An exception may be made, in accordance with the European Court of Human Rights,[62] if German agents use coercion to take a person into

---

[59] Al-Skeini and Others v. United Kingdom, *supra note 52*, § 134.

[60] ANDREAS VON ARNAULD, VÖLKERRECHT 325 (2d ed. 2015).

[61] There is no obligatory tolerance for foreign intelligence operations on domestic territory. *See* Christoph Gusy, *Spionage im Völkerrecht*, 26 NEUE ZEITSCHRIFT FÜR WEHRRECHT 187, 190–94 (1984).

[62] Al-Skeini and Others v. United Kingdom, *supra note 52*, § 136; Chagos Islanders v. United Kingdom, *supra note 52*, § 70.

custody and, thus, *de facto* create a small island of effective control.[63] It would be rather surprising if the BND used such methods for the statutory purpose of intelligence gathering. Furthermore, a purposeful deployment of agents abroad to evade the legal requirements of domestic procedures (like electronically intercepting German telecommunication from abroad) would be measured against German basic rights,[64] especially to close loopholes that could be used for circumventing constitutional restraints. As a result, either asking telecommunication providers to hand over data or tapping the telecommunication (or Internet) exchanges to siphon-off data would be measured against basic rights requirements if the intelligence service is misused to obtain information, which technically could be collected in Germany. Acting extraterritorially would be abusive if the German officials could simply evade the high requirements for telecommunication surveillance under national law or – if appropriate – a formal procedure of legal aid to compel a foreign telecommunications provider to produce evidence. Finally, if BND operatives just buy data abroad (as the BND did in an operation that sought to disclose massive tax evasion via Swiss bank accounts[65]), then the intelligence agency would be bound by the basic rights because data-gathering in that context is a functional part of national proceedings.[66]

2   The Personal Dimension: Foreign State Organs and Basic Rights

Another aspect of foreign intelligence gathering is the *personal scope of protection* of basic rights. Basic rights protect the individual against state power; additionally, they may, under qualified preconditions, oblige the state to offer effective protection against private infringement.[67]

---

[63] *See* Helmut Philipp Aust, 1. Untersuchungsausschuss der 18. Wahlperiode des Deutschen Bundestages: Stellungnahme zur Sachverständigenanhörung am 5. Juni 2014 12 (2014).

[64] Nettesheim, *supra note 36*, § 241, No. 67.

[65] *See* BVerfG, 2 BvR 2101/09, 64, Nov. 9, 2010, Neue Juristische Wochenschrift 2417 (2011); Constitution Court of Rhineland-Palatinate, 24.2.2014 – VGH B 26/13, 8 Zeitschrift für Landes- und Kommunalrecht Hessen, Rheinland-Pfalz und Saarland (LKRZ) 143 (2014).

[66] *See* Section F, *infra*.

[67] For the so-called "duty to protect" (*Schutzpflicht*), *see* BVerfG, 1 BvF 1/74, Feb. 25, 1975, www.servat.unibe.ch/dfr/bv039001.html; BVerfG, 2 BvL 8/77, Dec. 8, 1978, www.servat .unibe.ch/dfr/bv049089.html; BVerfG, 1 BvR 385/77, Dec. 20, 1979, www.servat.unibe .ch/dfr/bv053030.html; BVerfG, 1 BvR 612/72, Jan. 14, 1981, www.servat.unibe.ch/dfr/ bv056054.html.

According to well-established jurisprudence from the Federal Constitutional Court the basic rights comprise objective constitutional values,[68] which have to be transformed into an effective legal order and, thus, require sufficient protective regulation where the effective exercise of individual rights is typically endangered by private actions.[69] But it is always the (individual or associated) citizen who enjoys protection. In contrast, the state, even when it is obliged to act to promote rights protections, is not entitled to claim basic rights. And nothing is changed even if the "harmed" entity is a foreign state.[70] A foreign sovereign is not a private citizen, especially when the foreign state – as in the situations relevant here – is wielding sovereign functions (within its territory). If states are excluded from basic rights' protection, then so are states' official agents when acting within their official capacity. If operations to collect intelligence involve state agents exercising their public functions, then they do not interfere with constitutional basic rights and, thus, require no specific statutory authorization. The same applies for *quasi-state powers* that effectively and durably control a territory and exercise state-like authority (like the Taliban in Afghanistan, autonomous tribes in Pakistan, or the Islamic State in Iraq and Syria).[71]

3   Intelligence Operations Abroad Compared to Military Missions

One might ask whether this sharp contrast between foreign and domestic intelligence affairs (the latter are meticulously regulated) is systematically plausible.[72] To corroborate my position I want to advert to the field of law that is most comparable to secret intelligence operations abroad: the law of armed conflict. Both fields of law comprise extraordinary actions taken to enforce national security on foreign soil and are

---

[68] *See, e.g.*, BVERFG, 1 BvR 400/51, Jan. 15, 1958, www.servat.unibe.ch/dfr/bv007198.html; BVERFG, 1 BvR 619/63, Feb. 26, 1969, www.servat.unibe.ch/dfr/bv026265.html; BVERFG, 1 BvR 424/71, May 29, 1973, www.servat.unibe.ch/dfr/bv035079.html; BVERFG, 1 BvR 911, 927, 928/00, Oct. 26, 2004, www.servat.unibe.ch/dfr/bv111333.html.

[69] *Id.*

[70] Argument *e contrario*, GRUNDGESETZ [GG][BASIC LAW], art. 19(3), *see* BVERFG, 2 BvR 575/05, Feb. 8, 2006, 59 NEUE JURISTISCHE WOCHENSCHRIFT 2907, 2908 (2006).

[71] Consequently, in asylum cases "state persecution" within the meaning of art. 16a(1) of the Basic Law exists when the measures of persecution originate from such quasi-state organizations. *See* BVERFG, 2 BvR, 260, Aug. 10, 2000, 19 NEUE ZEITSCHRIFT FÜR VERWALTUNGSRECHT 1165 (2000); BVerwG, Feb. 20, 2001, 9 C 20/00, 114, 16, 21–24.

[72] In fact, plausibility is refuted by Bäcker. *See* BÄCKER *supra note 4*, at 21.

primarily governed by interstate relations. The law of armed conflict became a touchstone of extraterritorial basic rights doctrine after Germany threw its postwar traditions overboard and started to participate in out-of-area military missions during the 1990s. Military and intelligence operations abroad are in close relationship for several reasons. They are part of the larger subject of foreign affairs. They affect interstate relations governed by international law. They are far outside the state-citizen-relations, for which civil rights are specially tailored. And they require a high degree of flexibility. Despite the fact that military actions entail serious consequences (including the lethal use of force), the rules of military engagement have never been regulated by statutory provisions because the constitution does not require statutory empowerment to use military force in armed conflict. The only exceptions to this are the regime of war crimes,[73] and the deployment of the armed forces in domestic operations, which is regulated in statutory provisions in compliance with strict constitutional limits.[74] But the authorization of military operations abroad flows from the government's deployment order, which is sanctioned by prior parliamentary consent.[75] In action, the rules of engagement are defined by military commands within the international law of armed conflict, which does not *authorize* the use of force but merely establishes general *restraints* on its use. What remains is a highly political international conflict governed by a loose legal framework. This fairly describes intelligence operations, which, in fact, are often interwoven with military security issues. The BND's mandate is to gather intelligence to assist the government's foreign and national security policy with regard to foreign threats. Intelligence obtained remains an issue of foreign policy and security as long as it is not introduced into national administrative or judicial proceedings, which would immediately trigger all legal constraints the constitution and national statutory law places upon the exercise of sovereign functions.

---

[73] Völkerstrafgesetzbuch [International Criminal Law Code] §§ 8–12, June 26, 2002, BGBl I at 2254 (Ger.). This was enacted in the wake of the adoption of the Rome Statute.

[74] Gesetz über die Anwendung unmittelbaren Zwanges und die Ausübung besonderer Befugnisse durch Soldaten der Bundeswehr und Verbündeter Streitkräfte Sowie Zivile Wachpersonen of 12 August 1965 [Law on the Use of Coercive Force and the Exercise of Special Powers by Bundeswehr Soldiers and Allied Forces as well as Civilian Security Guards of 12 August 1965], BGBl I at 796, last amendment by statute, Dec. 21, 2007 BGBl I at 3198 (Ger.).

[75] *See* BVerfG, 2 BvE 3/92, July 12, 1994, www.servat.unibe.ch/dfr/bv090286.html.

4   Human Dignity Restraints on State Actions

On the basis of this analysis, it seems that most of the BND's foreign intelligence gathering actions fall outside the directly binding authority of the constitution's basic rights and, thus, do not trigger the requirement for statutory authorization.[76] Therefore, the BND can invoke the blanket clause in Section 1(2)1 of the BND Act as sufficient authority for these activities. This does not mean that the BND faces no legal restraints. There are the usual limits faced by the executive branch that are independent of an infringement of basic rights.[77] For example, the BND still has the fundamental duty to respect and protect human dignity, which Article 1(1) of the Basic Law makes inviolable. A violation of human dignity can result from the consequences that sovereign actions have, independent of the location where those effects are felt, or the time, or whether they result from the direct interference of state organs. The duty to protect human dignity must be complied with under any circumstances and it forbids a number of actions, including: torture, targeted killings of unarmed civilians, or using interrogation methods that endanger a person's psychic or physical integrity. For example, spying on the intimate details of a foreign official's sexual life with ongoing electronic surveillance in order to create material for effective blackmailing would run afoul of the limits imposed by Article 1(1) of the Basic Law.[78]

III   The Challenge of Transboundary Surveillance

Rapid technological change is a challenge for lawmaking as well as for developing legal doctrine, in particular in the field of technology-sensitive

---

[76] See also Gusy, supra note 50, at 52.

[77] It is worth mentioning that there is an established doctrine that constitutional basic rights do not only guarantee liberal rights to freedom of certain restraints but also require positive actions to establish an objective order under which freedom can practically evolve. See, e. g., BVerfG, 1 BvR 619/63, Feb. 26, 1969, www.servat.unibe.ch/dfr/bv025256.html; BVerfG, 1 BvR 424/71, May 29, 1973, www.servat.unibe.ch/dfr/bv035079.html; BVerfG, 1 BvR 347/98, Dec. 6, 2005, www.servat.unibe.ch/dfr/bv115025.html.

[78] The Court refers to a "core area of private life" (including, in particular, intimate aspects of sexuality), which emerges from human dignity and, thus, is inviolable. It has to be respected and sufficiently protected against secret surveillance measures. See BVerfG, 1 BvR 2378/98, Mar. 3, 2004, www.servat.unibe.ch/dfr/bv109279.html; BVerfG, 1 BvR 668/04, July 27, 2005, http://dejure.org/dienste/vernetzung/rechtsprechung?Text=1%20BvR%20668/04; BVerfG, 1 BvR 370/07, Feb. 27, 2008, www.servat.unibe.ch/dfr/bv120274.html; BVerfG, 2 BvR 236/08, Oct. 12, 2011, www.servat.unibe.ch/dfr/bv129208.html; BVerfG, 2 BvR 2500/09, Dec. 7, 2011, www.servat.unibe.ch/dfr/bv130001.html.

surveillance.[79] Secret surveillance measures abroad pose special and previously unsolved problems because they are technically controlled by agents on German territory but have a specific transboundary impact. "Virtual" searches are replacing physical searches,[80] including operations in which officials act from the German territory to gain remote access to extraterritorial data via Internet surveillance or by tapping satellite communications. In this context the old doctrines of territoriality and international affairs blur. A search action may originate from an agent based in the domestic territory, but the effects could be registered anywhere around the globe. This would be the case for the interception of satellite-based telecommunications or online-searches of computer systems.

Pursuant to Article 10(1) of the Basic Law, the privacy of correspondence, posts, and telecommunication shall be inviolable.[81] Still, Art. 10(2)1 of the Basic Law permits surveillance of telecommunications activities if those measures are ordered pursuant to a statute.[82] The territorial scope of the applicability of Article 10 is highly controversial. The German Federal Constitutional Court reasoned that the protection of Article 10 of the Basic Law is triggered when a sufficient link to domestic affairs exists. On this standard, the Court concluded (with regard to the strategic interception of international telecommunication by the BND) that the technological means enabling the intelligence services to impose automatic surveillance on communication via satellite from the German territory constituted a sufficient link. "The gathering and recording of telecommunication with the aid of receiver units of the *Bundesnachrichtendienst* on German soil," the Court explained, "establishes a technical-informational relation with the participants in communication and [...], thus, a relevant territorial contact."[83] Here the Court establishes an evaluative overall analysis of the territorial connection with Germany. Nonetheless, the German Federal Constitutional Court did not positively frame the scope of protection. First, the Court did not conclusively decide whether territorial contact was a necessary or merely a sufficient

---

[79] BENJAMIN WITTES, LAW AND THE LONG WAR: THE FUTURE OF JUSTICE IN THE AGE OF TERROR 222–23 (2008).

[80] Obviously, the worldwide intercommunication cannot substitute all physical interventions on foreign soil for spying purposes, as the NSA's taps of the internet interchanges (especially in Frankfurt) colorfully illustrates.

[81] GRUNDGESETZ [GG][BASIC LAW], art. 10(1).

[82] GRUNDGESETZ [GG][BASIC LAW], art. 20(2)1.

[83] BVERFG, 1 BvR 2226/94, July 14, 1999, www.servat.unibe.ch/dfr/bv100313.html.

condition of protection.[84] In other words, the Court did not resolve whether Article 10 imposes restraints on state organs even without such a territorial link. Second, the Court merely clarified that a sufficient link exists if at least one participant in communication is either located in the German territory or is a German national. But the protection secured by Article 10 is not limited to German nationals,[85] and it remains unclear whether aliens on foreign territory are protected when both telephone connections are outside the German territory.[86]

The transboundary interception of telecommunication activities originating from German territory is not comparable with secret operations abroad, which I have analyzed in the preliminary considerations. The striking difference is that an agent intercepting communication activities outside the German territory may do so through the operation of surveillance devices located within Germany's territorial jurisdiction. These actions have a public purpose (even if they usually are protected by state secret privileges) and they fulfill an official assignment. This means that the intelligence services can use sovereign power to enforce the required compliance, for example, of private agents (such as telecommunication companies providing network access). Additionally, the Federal Republic of Germany is fully responsible for any conduct of its organs on German territory, which is under the unlimited control of German state organs. By using technology for transboundary interception, the BND does not only avoid risky operations on the ground abroad, but the agency retreats into the German territory. This entails the transformation of the operations from a covert status – lacking any sovereign reinforcement – to the regular fulfillment of a statutory assignment by the administrative

---

[84] Georg Hermes, *Kommentierung zu Artikel 10 Grundgesetz, in* Dreier, *supra note 22*, at margin number 43.

[85] Matthias Bäcker, *Strategische Telekommunikationsüberwachung auf dem Prüfstand*, 17 KOMMUNIKATION & RECHT 556, 559 (2014); Wolfgang Durner, *Kommentierung zu Artikel 10 Grundgesetz, in* Maunz & Dürig, *supra note 35*, No. 186; Berthold Huber, *Die strategische Rasterfahndung des Bundesnachrichtendienstes – Eingriffsbefugnisse und Regelungsdefizite*, 66 NEUE JURISTISCHE WOCHENSCHRIFT 2572, 2574 (2013); Ralf Müller-Terpitz, *Die "strategische Kontrolle" des internationalen Telekommunikationsverkehrs durch den Bundesnachrichtendienst*, 22 JURA 296, 302 (2000); Martin Pagenkopf, *Kommentierung zu Artikel 10 Grundgesetz, in* Sachs, *supra note 48*, No. 11; Mareike Rehbein, DIE VERWERTBARKEIT VON NACHRICHTENDIENSTLICHEN ERKENNTNISSEN AUS DEM IN- UND AUSLAND IM DEUTSCHEN STRAFPROZESS 308 (2011).

[86] Affirmatively Bäcker, *supra note 4*, at 22; Peter Badura, *Der räumliche Geltungsbereich der Grundrechte, in* II HANDBUCH DER GRUNDRECHTE § 47 No. 17 (Detef Merten & Hans-Jürgen Papier eds., 2006); Hermes, *supra note 84*, art. 10 No. 43; Krieger, *supra note 37*, at 38; Müller-Terpitz, *supra note 85*, at 302; Rehbein, *supra note 85*, at 304–08.

branch. Even if transboundary interception is a technological prolongation of the practical scope of surveillance, the locality of action is legally relevant. On these abstract terms, transboundary interception falls within the protection of Article 10 of the Basic Law.

Still, the qualitative threshold that has to be reached by actions in order to trigger the protection of Article 10 of the Basic Law remains an unsolved issue. In contrast to the United States,[87] the German Federal Constitutional Court regards the surveillance of telecommunication metadata as an interception governed by the protections secured by Article 10 of the Basic Law.[88] Nonetheless, it has been convincingly asserted that the constitutionally protected privacy of telecommunication is only affected if the participants are individualized.[89] Thus, a merely "strategic" mass surveillance that scans bulk-metadata to reveal patterns and potential threats without identifying any individuals would not trigger the individual protection of the basic right. The German Federal Constitutional Court has acknowledged the so-called "chilling effects" of secret mass surveillance and thereby partially abandoned the individual character of the basic rights protection.[90] But it is doubtful that this would apply to exclusively foreign communication.

The same standards should apply to *online-searches abroad*. The German Federal Constitutional Court has developed a special basic right to the privacy and integrity of information-based systems that limits secret online-searches.[91] But the territorial scope of this right, which is derived from a general right to privacy, has not yet been tested.[92] Consequently, a search conducted from the German territory should be measured against the privacy right, as online-searches obviously have to be directed against specific individuals. As a result, online-searches abroad require a specific statutory authorization, which the current

---

[87] Compare Smith v. Maryland, 442 U.S. 735, 742. (1979); In re Application of the United States for Historical Cell Site Data, 724 F.3d 600, 608. (5th Cir. 2013); United States v. Forrester, 512 F.3d 500, 509. (9th Cir. 2008); United States v. Graham, 846 F.Supp.2d 384, 388. (D.Md. 2012). *But see* Chapter 10 in this volume.

[88] BVerfG, 1 BvR 1494/78, 67, 157, 172, June 20, 1984; BVerfG, 1 BvR 2226/94, July 14, 1999, www.servat.unibe.ch/dfr/bv100313.html; BVerfG, 1 BvR 256, 263, 586/08, 125, 260, 309, Mar. 2, 2010; BVerfG, 1 BvR 1299/05, 130, 151, 179, Jan. 24, 2012; BVerfGK, 2 BvR 308/04, 5, 74, 82, Feb. 4, 2005.

[89] Durner, *supra note 85*, Nos. 122, 185.

[90] BVerfG, 1 BvR 2226/94, July 14, 1999, www.bundesverfassungsgericht.de/SharedDocs/Entscheidungen/DE/1999/07/rs19990714_1bvr222694.html.

[91] BVerfG, 1 BvR 370/07, Feb. 28, 2008, www.servat.unibe.ch/dfr/bv120274.html.

[92] Grundgesetz [GG][Basic Law], arts. 1 (1), 2(1).

intelligence law does not provide. According to the very high standards the Federal Constitutional Court has created to hedge the risks of an online infiltration of computer systems, a statutory authorization must contain specific safeguards, which the Court also explicitly applied to intelligence authorities. In particular, a specific suspicion must rationally indicate a danger for life, liberty, health, or national security.[93] Still, the preference for a prior warrant issued by a judge, which the Court derived from the principle of proportionality,[94] should not apply to intelligence operations. On the one hand, the protection of national security by extraterritorial intelligence gathering, on the one hand, requires a high degree of secrecy and flexibility. On the other hand, online-searches have only a limited impact on individual freedom rights, at least when compared to police operations or criminal proceedings. Thus, extraterritorial intelligence gathering can be proportionate without the prior involvement of the judicial branch as long as measures ensure that the data obtained dose not seep into regular administrative or national proceedings.

IV   Conclusion

Basic rights have considerably less significance in foreign intelligence affairs than it is often suggested and the experts testifying before the NSA Committee of Inquiry asserted.[95] The constitution applies to every exercise of sovereign authority – everywhere and with no territorial limits – in a strictly formal sense. But the basic rights offer only limited protection against intelligence gathering operations taking place abroad. I must emphasize, however, that the analysis I presented here is not based on a settled body of court decisions and, therefore, it is not yet the accepted doctrine.[96] There remains a great deal of uncertainty regarding the basic rights limits applicable to intelligence activities. This places intelligence operations under a (legal) sword of Damocles. This undesirable situation could be resolved if statutory law provided the BND with sufficient authorization. The benefits of this arrangement would be available even if operations, contrary to the arguments advanced here, were qualified as an interference with basic rights. In the following

---

[93] BVerfG, 1 BvR 370/07, 120, 274, 328–30, Feb. 27, 2008, www.bundesverfassungsgericht.de/ SharedDocs/Entscheidungen/DE/2008/02/rs20080227_1bvr037007.html.

[94] *Id.* at 331.   [95] Bäcker, *supra note 4*, at 22; Papier, *supra note 4*.

[96] As the contrary voices cited above indicate, my arguments will probably be challenged in the academic discourse.

section I will show that the existing statutory regime fails to provide this minimum degree of legal certainty. Perhaps the rather shady uncertainty of the legal framework accommodates the Intelligence Community. Still, the current regulatory deficiencies could be remedied without compromising the Intelligence Community's legitimate interests in secrecy and flexibility. The standard of basic rights' protection applicable outside the German territory would be significantly lower than the standard applicable in domestic affairs. Thus, legislation enacted with sound judgment would not significantly hamper intelligence operations abroad. Instead, it might help to clear those operations from the odium of semi-legality. Even if basic rights are affected, then the German Federal Constitutional Court has stressed that legislation may take into consideration the specific circumstances of foreign affairs and the lack of effective control.[97] This leaves the Parliament enough room for maneuver to adapt the procedural and material standards to the very special requirements of foreign intelligence operations.

E   Actions Abroad in the Statutory Law Relating to the Intelligence Services

German intelligence law embraces a complicated, scattered, and imperfect set of rules. Whereas the competences of the intelligence services acting domestically are narrowly defined and strictly regulated,[98] the statutory framework for foreign operations is still weak.

I   G-10 Act

In Section 5, the Act on Intrusions upon the Privacy of the Post and Telecommunications (G-10 Act) specifically authorizes the BND to intercept "international telecommunication."[99] On request of the BND, the competent federal minister – with the consent of the Parliamentary Control Committee – can authorize a bulk interception and surveillance of bundled communication by using search terms.[100] Surveillance can be

---

[97] BVerfG, 1 BvF 1/90, 41–42, Jan. 10, 1995, http://dejure.org/dienste/vernetzung/rechtspre chung?Text=1%20BvF%201/90.

[98] In particular, see Federal Act on the Protection of the Constitution.

[99] Gesetz zur Beschränkung des Brief-, Post- und Fernmeldegeheimnisses [Law on the Restriction of the Privacy of Correspondence, Posts and Telecommunications], § 5, June 26, 2001, BGBl I at 1254, 2298 (Ger.). The term "G-10" refers to the basic right which is restrained.

[100] Id.

ordered to gather information with the aim of detecting and countering specific high profile security threats, which are enumerated in the statute. This form of bulk surveillance has a deeper impact on privacy than the often-criticized NSA metadata-program because the BND gains access without reasonable suspicion and without a judicial warrant, even to the content of communication. A search term, uttered by a participant in the communications act, triggers the interception. An earlier version of the statutory provision was sanctioned by the German Federal Constitutional Court in 1999 even though legislative reform had extended the scope of surveillance to all forms of bundled communication (and not just satellite communication).[101] Nevertheless, the term "international" has been interpreted to include only cross-border telecommunication connecting an intraterritorial participant with a connection abroad.[102] Thus, purely extraterritorial communication – such as intercepting phone calls between Russia and Ukraine – is not regulated by the G-10 Act at all.

It is generally assumed (and has never been officially denied) that the BND spies on telecommunication abroad. The Federal Government has insisted on the lawfulness of its international surveillance operations and has always asserted that those operations are authorized by the blanket clause of Section 1(2)1 BND Act,[103] a provision that I will discuss below. This proposition has been challenged recently because a statute interfering with basic rights must expressly and specifically name the affected rights in which interference is authorized.[104] But the BND Act does not cite Article 10 of the Basic Law and cannot be interpreted as authorizing an interception of telecommunications.[105] This argument is only valid as long as the relevant surveillance can be qualified as an infringement of basic rights. Of course, this qualification does not apply to strategic mass surveillance and interceptions operated from abroad or directed against targets that are not protected by basic rights.

---

[101] BVerfG, 1 BvR 2226/94, July 14, 1999, www.servat.unibe.ch/dfr/bv100313.html. Thus, data protection activists tried to challenge the constitutionality of the amended G-10.

[102] Gesetzentwurf der Bundesregierung Entwurf eines Gesetzes zur Neuregelung von Beschränkungen des Brief-, Post- und Fernmeldegeheimnisses, Bundestag Drucksache 14/5655, p. 18; Antwort der Bundesregierung auf die Kleine Anfrage der Abgeordneten Andrej Hunko, Jan Korte, Jan van Aken, weiterer Abgeordneter und der Fraktion Die Linke, Bundestag Drucksache 17/9640; p. 6;); Huber (note 97), p. 2572.

[103] See Federal Government, Deutscher Bundesag Drucksache 17/9640, ¶¶ 6, 10.

[104] See GRUNDGESETZ [GG][BASIC LAW], art. 19(1)2. See also BVerfG, 1 BvR 668/04, July 27, 2005, http://dejure.org/dienste/vernetzung/rechtsprechung?Text=1%20BvR%20668/04; BVerfG, 1 BvR 370/07, Feb. 27, 2008, www.servat.unibe.ch/dfr/bv120274.html.

[105] Bäcker, supra note 85, at 560.

II   BND Act

Pursuant to Section 1(2)1 of the BND Act, the BND "collects and analyses intelligence to gather information on foreign countries, which are of relevance regarding foreign affairs and security policy of the Federal Republic of Germany." This provision merely defines the abstract competence of the BND (*Aufgabe*).[106] It does not authorize the service members to exercise actions (*Ermächtigung*) that would entail an encroachment upon basic rights. Thus, Section 1(2)2 of the BND Act explicitly states: "If, within the purview of this act, information, including personal data, is collected, the collection, handling, and use of the data is subject to Section 2-6 and 8-11" of the BND Act. These special provisions undisputedly empower the BND to collect, handle, and analyse personal data. Still, it is not clear whether this entails intelligence collection abroad. The ambiguously worded restriction "within the purview of this act" (*im Geltungsbereich dieses Gesetzes*) is generally understood as limiting the scope of the authorization to the territorial jurisdiction of Germany. This narrow (territorial) interpretation of the law is not explicitly supported by the legislative rationale. Nevertheless, the Federal Government later argued – when defending the authority to intercept international telecommunications before the Federal Constitutional Court in 1999 – that the BND Act was never meant to confine actions taking place outside the German territory.[107] The government reasoned that a statutory authorization is not necessary here. This interpretation has since been accepted because it obviously reflects the official legal opinion of the ministerial bureaucracy that drafted the statute. This interpretation is also indirectly corroborated by the law's drafting history.

---

[106] BVerfG, 1 BvR 2226/94, July 14, 1999, www.servat.unibe.ch/dfr/bv100313.html; Nils Bergemann, *Nachrichtendienste und Polizei, in* HANDBUCH DES POLIZEIRECHTS § 26 (Erhard Denninger/Frederik Rachor eds., 5th ed. 2012); Kreuter & Möbius, *supra note 37*, at 150; Konrad Porzner, *Der Bundesnachrichtendienst im Gefüge der öffentlichen Verwaltung*, 28 DIE VERWALTUNG 235, 242 (1993); NICLAS-FREDERIC WEISSER, DIE ENTWICKLUNG DES BUNDESNACHRICHTENDIENSTES 145 (2014); MARK ALEXANDER ZÖLLER, INFORMATIONSSYSTEME UND VORFELDMASSNAHMEN VON POLIZEI, STAATSANWALTSCHAFT UND NACHRICHTENDIENSTEN 306 (2002).

[107] *See* BVerfG, 1 BvR 2226/94, July 14, 1999, www.servat.unibe.ch/dfr/bv100313.html. A parallel argument was advanced by Germany in the European Court of Human Rights. *See* Weber & Saravia v. Germany, App. No. 54934//00, Eur. Ct. H. R. § 66 (2006). The applicants whose communication was intercepted by the BND both resided in Uruguay and had been infringed as regards telecommunications from their telephone connections in that country, thus, being an extraterritorial act outside the purview of the Convention. The question was not decided as the application was judged to be inadmissible.

The former parliamentary opposition caustically challenged the draft of the cited provision with the argument that it would release the BND from any legal restraints when acting abroad. The opposition regarded this as "intolerable."[108] In the face of this criticism the parliamentary majority neither denied the accusation nor felt the need to iron out a wrinkle and change or clarify the draft.[109] The parliamentary majority's inaction, in the face of this criticism, can be read as an indication that this critique was correct and was (tacitly) accepted.[110] Against this background the authorizing clauses of the BND Act do not apply insofar as the BND is acting abroad. Still, the general assignment in Section 1(2)1 of the BND Act was never meant to restrain the maneuverability of the BND while collecting intelligence in foreign countries. Instead, it was the general assumption when the law was enacted that the intelligence service could fulfill its mission due to its general assignment without any specific authorization, which is exactly what the BND had done throughout the decades before the statutory provisions entered into force. On these terms the BND is authorized by its general assignment to operate abroad and collect intelligence by the means necessary and appropriate in the relevant situation. If the actions concerned do not interfere with basic rights, as I have argued above, then this blanket authorization may be criticized politically but it is in conformity with constitutional requirements.

But this is not a blank check. The BND is limited to collecting information in order to aid the government's foreign and security policy making. Admittedly, the BND Act does not limit the *methods* the federal agents may apply to obtain this information. Yet, the authorization does not cover operations to enforce political decisions abroad (such as targeted killings, coup attempts, violent assaults, sabotage, freeing hostages, or regime change), even if those decisions were based on intelligence gathered by the BND.[111] It would be pure speculation if and to what extent the BND actually fulfills or participates in such covert operations (scandals in the agency's history suggest that the intelligence

---

[108] *See* Deutscher Bundestag Drucksache 11/7235, ¶ 110 (presenting the objections of the Green Parliamentary Faction).

[109] Compare the unspecific answer of the majority in Deutscher Bundestag Drucksache 11/7235, ¶ 110.

[110] For the critical remarks of Parliamentarian Emmerlich (SPD, and at that time in opposition), *see* PLENARY PROTOCOL 11/214, p. 16788.

[111] Gazeas, *supra note 24*, at 151.

service in fact does), but it has been (and still is) the official position that operations comprising the use of force are outside its formal capacity.[112]

Finally, BND personnel acting abroad are not obliged to satisfy the *lex loci actus*. To the contrary, the official assignment of the BND is to collect intelligence, which usually involves criminal offenses; at least espionage aimed at a foreign power or gaining access to confidential or classified official secrets will be criminally outlawed anywhere around the world.[113] Intelligence can be gathered legally by analyzing open sources (by surveying newspapers or monitoring public events), but such soft information could be easily obtained by diplomatic and consular missions, thus making the deployment of intelligence agents unnecessary. The usual foreign operations, justified by the general authorization of Section 1(2)1 of the BND Act, will be missions under the cover of secrecy and carrying the risk of criminal prosecution. Each nation that maintains a foreign intelligence service implicitly accepts that its agents commit criminal offenses abroad. As the BND Act entrusts the BND with the task of collecting intelligence abroad, it is the official duty of the agents to break the law of the state in which they operate and, thus, effectively and secretly to commit acts punishable under foreign law in order to obtain the intelligence the German government hopes to exploit. Operating within this statutory assignment, intelligence officials are protected from criminal liability when acting outside the German territory because the performance of statutory duties provides a justification for extraterritorial actions. This is true even if the actions would be punishable under Section 7(2)1 of the Criminal Code,[114] including wiretapping[115] or intercepting data.[116] Nonetheless, due to the vagueness of the blanket provision in Section 1(2)1 of the BND Act, this framework seems burdened with legal risks. Finally, the legal uncertainty became unbearable and the Bundestag enacted a statutory reform in late October 2016. The reform tightly regulated the foreign surveillance and extra-territorial cooperation of the BND (Sections 6–30, BND Act).

---

[112] Wolfgang Krieger, *The German Bundesnachrichtendienst (BND): Evolution and Current Policy Issues, in* THE OXFORD HANDBOOK OF NATIONAL SECURITY INTELLIGENCE 790, 791 (Loch K. Johnson ed., 2010).

[113] *See* STRAFGESETZBUCH [PENAL CODE], §§ 93–99, Nov. 13, 1998, BGBl I at S. 3322, last amendment, Aug 31, 2015, BGBl I at S. 1474 (Ger.).

[114] STRAFGESETZBUCH [PENAL CODE], § 7(2)1.

[115] STRAFGESETZBUCH [PENAL CODE], § 201.

[116] STRAFGESETZBUCH [PENAL CODE], §§ 202 (a)–(b).

III   Binding Customary International Law

Pursuant to Article 25 of the Basic Law the general rules of international law shall be an integral part of federal law. The Constitution gives them precedence over legislation and provides that they directly create rights and duties for the inhabitants of the German federal territory. Federal territory does not mean a territorial restriction but just "within German jurisdiction."[117] The term "general rules" in the sense of this provision simply means the corpus of universal customary international law.[118] Excluded is treaty based international law, which is, if self-executing, binding as federal statutory law, and more recent statutes prevail over those previously in place (*lex posterior derogat legi priori*).[119] This arrangement means that customary international law is positioned in Germany's legal hierarchy below the Constitution but above federal statutory law.[120] Provided the content of a rule is self-executing, administrative authorities and courts must enforce it,[121] and give it priority over conflicting national law.[122] This rule is not limited to any particular territorial framework. It is also binding on German organs acting abroad, including the BND. *Restraints* imposed on executive actions abroad cannot come into conflict with customary international law,[123] but an *authorization* to gather intelligence abroad without the consent of the operational state could, as foreign territorial sovereignty might be violated.

Nevertheless, espionage as such is not outlawed by international law.[124] State practice proves that states accept espionage as an established reality in

---

[117] Herdegen, *supra note 35*, at 47.

[118] BVerfG, 2 BvG 1/55, Mar. 26, 1957, www.servat.unibe.ch/dfr/bv006309.html; BVerfG, 2 BvR 1506/03, Nov. 5, 2003, http://dejure.org/dienste/vernetzung/rechtsprechung?Ger icht=BVerfG&Datum=05.11.2003&Aktenzeichen=2%20BvR%201506/03.

[119] *See* BVerfG, 1 BvR 548/68, Dec. 17, 1975, www.servat.unibe.ch/dfr/bv041088.html.

[120] BVerfG, 2 BvG 1/55, Mar. 26, 1957, www.servat.unibe.ch/dfr/bv006309.html; BVerfG, 2 BvL 52/71, May 29, 1974, www.servat.unibe.ch/dfr/bv037271.html.

[121] BVerfG, 2 BvR 475/78, Mar. 22, 1983, www.servat.unibe.ch/dfr/bv063343.html; BVerfG, 2 BvM 2/86, Mar. 31, 1987, www.servat.unibe.ch/dfr/bv075001.html; BVerfG, 2 BvR 955/00, Oct. 26, 2004, www.servat.unibe.ch/dfr/bv112001.html.

[122] BVerfG, 2 BvG 1/55, Mar. 26, 1957, www.servat.unibe.ch/dfr/bv006309.html; BVerfG, 2 BvR 544/63, May 14, 1968, www.servat.unibe.ch/dfr/bv023288.html.

[123] Christian Walter & Anke von Ungern-Sternberg, *Piratenbekämpfung vor Somalia*, 65 Die Öffentliche Verwaltung 861, 867 (2012).

[124] Claus Dieter Classen, Fernerkundung und Völkerrecht 162 (1987); Karl Doehring, Völkerrecht No. 1159 (2d ed., 2004); Christoph Gröpl, Die Nachrichtendienste im Regelwerk der deutschen Sicherheitsverwaltung 75–76 (1993); Gusy, *supra note 24*, at 192; John Kish, International Law and Espionage (1995); John F. Murphy, *Cyber War and International Law*, 89 Int'l. L. Stud. 309, 320. (2013); John Radson, *The Unresolved Equation of Espionage and International Law*, 28 Mich. J. Int'l. L. 595 (2007); Michael Soiné, *Die Aufklärung der Organisierten Kriminalität*

foreign affairs and do not treat it as a breach of international law. Instead, most states simply reserve the right to punish it individually as a criminal offense according to national law. This applies to the typical methods of intelligence gathering, including facilitated defections of foreign intelligence agents, bribery,[125] intercepting communications, wiretapping, and surveillance. These are not yet illegal actions under customary international law. Yet, customary law unequivocally protects territorial sovereignty. Under this established principle a state may not wield sovereign functions on foreign territory without the consent of the affected state.[126] This rule likely is not implicated by traditional intelligence operations. First, as I have outlined above, intelligence operations do not entail the exercise of sovereign functions. Second, territorial integrity is violated only if a state, without prior consent, uses *coercive* power (whether in openly exercising sovereign functions or not) in foreign territory. Thus, covert operations involving the use of armed force, kidnapping, or acts of physical sabotage would be forbidden by customary international law.[127] Consequently, such actions are prohibited by Article 25 of the Basic Law. But there are a range of intelligence gathering activities a state may pursue abroad that do not involve the requisite level of coercion. This is particularly true of the so-called "passive" collection of vast quantities of telecommunication metadata that formed the heart of the NSA-Affair. Germany's statutory regime merely has to be interpreted and applied in conformity with international law's prohibition on coercive intervention. Thus, while prohibiting the BND from using such internationally outlawed methods to gather intelligence, there are a number of methods and measures that are fully legal under customary international law.

F   Transfer of Intelligence Collected Abroad into Domestic Proceedings

The restraints the constitution imposes on intelligence missions abroad are relatively weak, compared with the high standards applied in

---

durch den Bundesnachrichtendienst, 59 Die Öffentliche Verwaltung 204, 210 (2006). *But see* Chapter 5 in this volume.

[125] Contrasting and advancing a more strictly constructed prohibition Gérard Cohen-Jonathan & Robert Kovar, *L'espionnage en temps de paix*, 6 Annuaire Français de Droit International 239, 250–51 (1960).

[126] BVerfG, 2 BvR 475/78, Mar. 22, 1983, www.servat.unibe.ch/dfr/bv063343.html; von Arnauld *supra note 60*, No. 335; Karl Neumeyer, IV Internationales Verwaltungsrecht 502–03 (1936); Alfred Verdross & Bruno Simma, Universelles Völkerrecht § 456 (3rd ed., 1984).

[127] Compare Verdross & Simma, *supra note 126*, § 456; von Arnauld, *supra note 60*, Nos. 335, 363–64, 366.

domestic security law. Still, they do not undermine the minimum standards required for the protection of basic rights. To corroborate this it is necessary to recall the unique field of application of intelligence law and its limits. Collecting intelligence abroad is strictly confined to securing information required for foreign and security policy, defined by the Federal Government as head of the executive branch. The intelligence gathered is for high politics, which is a very abstract, broad-scale-orientated, and impersonal level of decision-making. As the German Federal Constitutional Court put it in its *Anti-Terror Data Case*:

> In return and as compensation for the breadth of those competences [i. e. of the intelligence services[128]] to collect data the assignment of intelligence is limited. Disregarding differences between the various intelligence services in detail, competences are basically restrained to observation of and reporting on fundamental threats, which could destabilize the body politic, with the aim to enable a political assessment of the security situation.[129]

Thus, intelligence meant to inform the government's foreign or security policy decisions cannot be used as evidence in domestic administrative or court proceedings

As soon as an operation seemingly producing "political" intelligence is actually part of a domestic (administrative or judicial) process and the person the intelligence gathering action is directed against participates in that proceeding, the intelligence agents have to comply with unfettered constitutional rights. If intelligence legally gathered abroad within the BND's general authority is subsequently to be used in internal proceedings, then the information transfer is treated as an independent interference in basic rights, which has to be tested against undiminished constitutional standards. Whether intelligence is admissible and utilizable as evidence depends on the circumstances under which information was obtained, namely a comprehensible documentation of the circumstances under which evidence was obtained, the potential of a contamination with illegal investigation methods, and the degree of the infringement of basic rights by the evidence transfer. Despite these strict limits, should intelligence be admissible as evidence, then the reliability of the source has to be tested very carefully. Clandestine operations abroad considerably heighten the risk that evidence obtained has been

---

[128] Comment by the author.
[129] BVERFG , 1 BvR 1215/07, Apr. 24, 2013, www.servat.unibe.ch/dfr/bv133277.html

tampered with because effective judicial control of operations is often impractical. German procedural law, in principle, lacks strict statutory rules on the use of evidence; the standard of proof is the considered opinion of the court due to its free appraisal of evidence. For this reason evaluating intelligence is, in the end, a matter of case-by-case consideration and interest-balancing. A more formal procedural framework for gathering and using evidence considerably decreases the chances that intelligence gathered abroad can be used as evidence. Where evidence standards are low, however, such as in the circumstances when time constraints justify emergency police measures to counter an immediate threat, then intelligence might be an appropriate source of evidence because it would be inappropriate to ignore warnings presented by an intelligence service just because the source cannot reliably be tested. In asylum cases in which evidence on alleged political circumstances abroad can be hard to obtain, intelligence disclosed by the BND might be used to remedy a lack of evidence. In administrative procedures not under time pressure (like in extradition or deportation cases) a more careful examination is unavoidable.[130] The highest standards apply to the highly formalized procedure used in criminal cases.[131] Intelligence gathered abroad usually will be relatively worthless, unless it can be corroborated by offering additional evidence. Additionally, to avoid circumvention of the tight restraints on criminal investigations by the prosecuting authorities, intelligence should be tested against the regular requirements of criminal procedure. Thus, a transfer from the Intelligence Community to law enforcement officials for use in a criminal proceeding would be admissible only if a hypothetical measure to obtain the same criminal evidence in regular proceedings would be permitted by law.[132] The same restraints should apply if intelligence is obtained from foreign intelligence services.[133]

---

[130] *See* Chahal v. U.K., App. No. 22414/93, Eur. Ct. H. R. § 131 (1996); ANDREW ASHWORTH & LUCIA ZEDNER, PREVENTIVE JUSTICE 241 (2014).

[131] Detailed discussion by Michael Pawlik, *Zur strafprozessualen Verwertbarkeit rechtswidrig erlangter ausländischer Bankdaten*, 65 JURISTENZEITUNG 693, 695 (2010); Rehbein, *supra note 85.*

[132] *See* STRAFPROZESSORDNUNG [StPO][CODE OF CRIMINAL PROCEDURE], § 161(2) (Ger.). *See also* Gazeas, *supra note 24*, at 534.

[133] Marco Gehrke, *PRISM, TEMPORA und das Deutsche Strafverfahren – Verwertbarkeit der Erkenntnisse Ausländischer Nachrichtendienste*, 33 COMPUTER UND RECHT 749, 754 (2013).

G German Foreign Intelligence Law: A Brief Evaluation

The development of German intelligence law is deeply embedded in the broader ideological context that has shaped the constitution regarding foreign affairs. Germany has a strong constitutional tradition of inter- and supranational institutionalism and cooperation.[134] This tends to expand human rights and tightly hedge state power, in particular, through integration into international institutions. After all, the Basic Law was adopted as the constitution of the global-political project to reintegrate Germany as a member of the community of civilized nations from which it had withdrawn through its barbarism (in which aggressive nationalism and militarism played a significant role).[135] For this reason, postwar Germany lacks a specific constitutional tradition respecting warfare abroad, including the shadowy war concerned with intelligence and counter-intelligence. As German foreign policy began to assume a more active role on the world stage after reunification the constitution (and its introspective tradition of strong internal restraints on state authority) had difficulties keeping pace with a rapidly changing foreign affairs landscape. There are many, vivid examples of the incomplete nature of this evolution, including the ongoing disputes connected with out-of-area operations of the armed forces,[136] the questions about how to integrate military rules of engagement in the system of criminal liability when soldiers use force abroad,[137] and the uncertainty surrounding how German naval forces might detain pirates at the Horn of Africa.[138]

---

[134] *See* GRUNDGESETZ [GG][BASIC LAW], arts. 1(2), 23, 24, 59.

[135] *See, e.g.*, Horst Dreier, *supra note 22*, §§ 23–24; RAINER WAHL, HERAUSFORDERUNGEN UND ANTWORTEN: DAS ÖFFENTLICHE RECHT DER LETZTEN FÜNF JAHRZEHNTE 16–23 (2006); RUDOLF WEBER-FAS, DER VERFASSUNGSSTAAT DES GRUNDGESETZES: ENTSTE-HUNG, PRINZIPIEN, GESTALT 31 (2002).

[136] *See, e.g.*, DANIEL BECK, AUSLANDSEINSÄTZE DEUTSCHER STREITKRÄFTE 271 (2008); Daniel Thym, *Zwischen "Krieg" und "Frieden": Rechtsmaßstäbe für operatives Handeln der Bundeswehr im Ausland*, 63 DIE ÖFFENTLICHE VERWALTUNG (DÖV) 621 (2010); ANGELA WAGNER, DIE GRUNDRECHTSBINDUNG DER BUNDESWEHR BEI AUSLANDSEIN-SÄTZEN (2006); MOUNA A. YOUSIF, DIE EXTRATERRITORIALE GELTUNG DER GRUN-DRECHTE BEI DER AUSÜBUNG DEUTSCHER STAATSGEWALT IM AUSLAND (2007).

[137] Helmut Frister, Marcus Korte & Claus Kreß, *Die strafrechtliche Rechtfertigung militär-ischer Gewalt in Auslandseinsätzen auf der Grundlage eines Mandats der Vereinten Nationen*, 65 JURISTENZEITUNG 10 (2010).

[138] *See, e.g.*, Andreas Fischer-Lescano & Lena Kreck, *Piraterie und Menschenrechte* 47 ARCHIV FÜR VÖLKERRECHT 481, 499 (2009); Walter & Sternberg-Ungern, *supra note 123*, at 861.

The legal framework governing the foreign operations of the intelligence services is another chapter in this unfolding story. And we are just at the beginning of the story. Only a few cases have been litigated and standards are highly controversial. Legal doctrine is embryonic. The scarce and scattered cases that actually depended on basic rights protection abroad do not provide a coherent jurisprudence. The German Federal Constitutional Court is still meandering through these issues, following a "muddling through" approach that has not provided stable and predictable parameters for the parliament. All of this means that the self-righteous political rhetoric of German politicians – from the executive as well as from the legislative branch – directed against America's intelligence activities abroad sharply contrasts with the legal reality in Germany. This casts a shadow over Germans' ostentatious appeal to legality as the paramount guideline in intelligence affairs. The mechanics of parliamentary supervision in this inherently opaque realm – even if bolstered by constitutional and statutory provisions – look more like erratic fumbling about in the fog.[139] In practice, the parliament can only try to impose a tighter grip on these secretive agencies after something has gone terribly wrong; the parliament lacks a continuously exercised, effective, and routine control. As strong authorization needs strict accountability,[140] and German intelligence law does not entail a preventive judicial control, this blunt desideratum remains a gaping wound in the institutional body of the German intelligence architecture. Hence, a central part of the major intelligence reform the German Bundestag enacted in October 2016, is an amendment to the Parliamentary Control Committee Act. The Amendment strengthens and professionalizes parliamentary control over the intelligence agencies. The complete lack of statutory provisions on intelligence operations abroad is another distasteful element. This led the Bundestag, when it amended the BND Act, to introduce detailed provisions on the BND's activities abroad. Whereas the BND is allowed to continue surveillance of foreign telecommunications and cooperate with foreign intelligence authorities, these foreign activities were placed under procedural restraints and safeguards. At least until the reforms implemented by the Bundestag, there was little

---

[139] *See* GRUNDGESETZ [GG][BASIC LAW], art. 45d; Parlamentarisches Kontrollgremiumsgesetz [Act Concerning the Parliamentary Control Committee]; Section 14–15 G-10-Act; Bundeshaushaltsordnung [Federal Budget Act], § 10a(2).

[140] Stephen J. Schulhofer, RETHINKING THE PATRIOT ACT 34, 116 (2005).

justification for the political self-aggrandizement and the pharisaic hypocrisy displayed by Germany in the transatlantic debate.[141]

H   The Law of Intelligence Services as a Globalization-Proof Stronghold?

What can be done about all of this? First, we should be political realists and admit that we need effective institutions of foreign intelligence gathering. The need for reliable information will grow as international threats disaggregate (thus, becoming harder to counter), the central role of clearly aligned states dissolves, and the theater of operations continuously expands. Intelligence services back up policymakers with more or less reliable information that enables them to make responsible decisions, both strategic and tactical. But this requires a holistic perspective.[142] Therefore, modern intelligence covers not only classic security threats but also economic, social, and environmental developments, that is, nonmilitary threats to international stability that have to be dealt with adequately, such as refugee streams, forced migration, climate change, human rights violations, scarcity of raw materials, or economic crises. The current refugee crisis in Europe, which apparently took Germany by surprise,[143] demonstrates the need for a broad scope of reliable intelligence to cope with humanitarian challenges as well as with the security risks that will challenge us for the foreseeable future. A broad belt of instability and civil war surrounds Europe: the Levant, Syria, Iraq, Libya, and Northern Africa (from Algeria to Egypt). Unlike the United States,

---

[141] *See* Jochen Wiemken, *The Raw Proposals of the Social Democratic Party of 16 June 2015*, SPD (June 16, 2015), www.spd.de/aktuelles/129380/20150616_bnd_reform.html (last visited Nov. 22, 2015) (demanding a tighter control of the BND by parliament and a specific statutory regulation of the BND's extraterritorial surveillance activities). *See also Entwurf für neues BND-Gesetz: Eine Art No-Spy-Klausel für Europa?*, TAGESSCHAU.DE (Jan. 18, 2016), *available at* www.tagesschau.de/inland/bnd-reform-103.html; *Einigung auf Geheimdienstreform: Koalition nimmt BND an die Leine*, TAGESSCHAU.DE (Nov. 13, 2015), *available at* www.tagesschau.de/inland/bnd-reform-101.html.

[142] William J. Lahneman, *The Need for a New Intelligence Paradigm*, 23 INT'L J. OF INTELLIGENCE AND COUNTER INTELLIGENCE 201–25 (2010); Franz-Josef Schulz & Raoul Gruninger, *Wirkungsorientierte Operationen: Neue Anforderungen an die sicherheitspolitische Wissensgrundlage*, *in* VERSTEHEN, DASS DIE WELT SICH VERÄNDERT – NEUE RISIKEN, NEUE ANFORDERUNGEN UND DIE TRANSFORMATION DER NACHRICHTENDIENSTE 34 (Heiko Borchert ed., 2005).

[143] The official estimations of the number of refugees to be prepared for in 2015 started with 200,000 in early spring and has soared up to 800,000 (possibly over one Million) in late August 2015.

for Europe the heinous organization "Islamic State" is already a domestic threat. Refugees need timely and effective protection but can also pose a security risk, as they may carry conflicts from their home country right into Germany. Intelligence gathering will be necessary in order to develop the information required to form a foreign policy, counter threats, and thwart humanitarian disaster in our African and Middle East neighborhood.

Considering this, it is more necessary than ever before to distinguish between domestic and foreign intelligence. Concepts of territoriality – intra-territoriality and extraterritoriality – cannot be sufficiently comprehended without observing international developments that mold the spheres of state influence.[144] Despite the evident processes of globalization and legal inter-nationalization, most legal orders distinguish between foreign and domestic issues. For a democracy, which depends on epistemic and political openness and should not try to control or spy on the shaping of public opinion, this difference is even more crucial.[145] The authorization and the degree of discretion an intelligence service wields necessarily will be wider when acting abroad.[146] Covert intelligence operations abroad are not police missions. The deployment of agents to unveil protected official secrets and to spy on foreign nations are more comparable to warfare, but without the bloodshed. Against this background, it is not surprising that western democracies all have organizationally separated foreign and domestic intelligence appar-atuses and established special agencies for collecting intelligence abroad. The Central Intelligence Agency (United States), the Secret Intelligence Service (United Kingdom), and the Direction Générale de la Sécurité Extérieure (France) join Germany's BND as prominent examples.

Forcing foreign intelligence operations into a tight and paralyzing straightjacket of legal constraints would simply put Germany at a severe disadvantage. Broad administrative discretion in gathering intelligence abroad does not necessarily pose a substantial risk for individual free-doms. Unquestionably, an expertocratic security and law enforcement community, which assumes an independent existence and evades public control, can seriously hamper the mechanics of a free democratic

---

[144] RAUSTIALA, *supra note 34*, at 237; *See also* Martin S. Flaherty, *Global Power in an Age of Rights: Historical Commentary*, 1946–2000, , *in* INTERNATIONAL LAW IN THE U.S. SUPREME COURT 416, 441–42 (David L. Sloss, Michael D. Ramsey & William S. Dodge eds., 2011).

[145] *See* RICHARD A. POSNER, PREVENTING SURPRISE ATTACKS: INTELLIGENCE REFORM IN THE WAKE OF 9/11 164–65 (2005).

[146] *But see* BÄCKER, *supra note 4*, at 21.

society.[147] But this risk will not specifically emanate from an agency collecting intelligence *abroad*. Civil rights are rather in danger when domestic police operations and criminal prosecutions are blended with intelligence collection.[148] This is the "blurring of the historical distinction between the role of policing and the role of the intelligence and security communities."[149] The highly formalized and protective requirements of public evidence and confirmed suspicion can be subverted by secret intelligence gathered from sources far outside public control. But the consequence thereof should not be a foreign intelligence service legally stripped to the bone. Instead, the goal should be a strict separation of foreign and domestic intelligence, in particular, by procedural and substantive firewalls that prevent an unregulated flow of information and evidence, even if this will remain difficult to manage and monitor.[150] If sufficient safeguards are established, then it would pose no serious problems to vest the foreign intelligence service with sufficient authority to fulfill its dangerous and difficult assignment. The "security constitution" – a former stronghold of national sovereignty – is increasingly subject to the internationalization of law.[151] But the world remains a territorial order. And global legalism engenders its own ambivalences,[152] especially when law is not backed by real power to enforce it.[153] In this reality a foreign intelligence service has a pivotal role in a nation's foreign affairs architecture. Legislative process should not surrender to regulatory idealism. Instead, the parliament should forge a framework under which legally confined intelligence services can nevertheless fulfill their pragmatic purposes. A combination of standard competences for actions abroad with a subsidiary blanket clause to retain flexibility would do the trick.

---

[147] MICHAEL J. GLENNON, NATIONAL SECURITY AND DOUBLE GOVERNMENT 39–65, 113–18 (2015).

[148] *See* Markus Thiel, DIE "ENTGRENZUNG" DER GEFAHRENABWEHR 45 (2011); Mark A. Zöller, *Der Rechtsrahmen der Nachrichtendienste bei der "Bekämpfung" des internationalen Terrorismus*, 62 JURISTENZEITUNG 763, 767–68 (2007).

[149] Clive Harfield, *The Governance of Covert Investigation*, 34 MELB. U. L. REV. 34, 773, 774 (2010).

[150] SIMON CHESTERMAN, ONE NATION UNDER SURVEILLANCE 236–37 (2011).

[151] Ralf Poscher, *Sicherheitsverfassungsrecht im Wandel, in* DER EIGENWERT DES VERFASSUNGSRECHTS 245, 246 (Thomas Vesting & Stefan Korioth eds., 2011).

[152] ERIC A. POSNER & ADRIAN VERMEULE, THE EXECUTIVE UNBOUND: AFTER THE MADISONIAN REPUBLIC 154–75 (2010).

[153] KLAUS FERDINAND GÄRDITZ, WELTRECHTSPFLEGE 436–44 (2006).

16

Assessing the CJEU's "Google Decision"

A Tentative First Approach

BY JOHANNES MASING

A Introduction

The legal situation that has been created by the Court of Justice of the European Union (CJEU) with its *Google Spain SL* decision raises serious concerns. The decision rightly subjects search engines to the European data protection rules. In the final analysis, however, it risks to reinforce rather than to limit the power of search engine operators, particularly that of Google. The decision thereby generates an imbalance in the equilibrium between personality rights and communication freedoms that threatens to undermine the liberal outline of the right to free speech.

The following considerations represent a tentative first assessment. They are not meant to constitute an evaluation of the decision in dogmatic terms – neither with respect to constitutional law nor European law. In particular they are not concerned with the question whether and, if applicable, to what extent the CJEU interpreted the requirements of the Directive 95/46/EC and the Charter of Fundamental Rights incorrectly. Instead, this chapter aims to provide a preliminary, critical analysis of the actual inconsistencies, conflicts, and shifts in legal policy that result from the Court's decision under current legal standards. I especially seek to assess the consequences of the decision regarding the relation between

This chapter is an English-language translation of a comment that was written in May 2014, in the immediate aftermath of the announcement of the *Google Spain* decision. In that context it was intended for internal academic debates. But bowing to wishes for publication it originally appeared three months later in German as Johannes Masing, *Vorläufige Einschätzung der "Google-Entscheidung" des EuGH*, VERFASSUNGSBLOG (Aug. 14, 2014), *available at* www.verfassungsblog.de/ribverfg-masing-vorlaeufige-einschaetzung-der-goo gle-entscheidung-des-eugh/#.VYLZMFLRZ2A. This version has been revised marginally and some footnotes have been added to make it more accessible to an English speaking reader. It has not been updated.

freedom and personality protection in future Internet communication. In its decision the CJEU was guided by a significant disregard for communication freedoms. Accordingly, in Germany the decision imposes an additional legal layer on the German Federal Constitutional Court's liberal jurisprudence regarding communication freedoms. As regards the question of search engine results the decision supersedes these judgments with a doctrine that disproportionately prioritizes personality protection and obscures obvious alternative approaches that offer more balanced solutions.

Actually, one cause for this is not due to the CJEU's decision. Instead, it lies in the general and undifferentiated framework established by the Data Protection Directive. The proposed General Data Protection Regulation would not remedy this defect. But the design of the forthcoming regulation would be the place to address this deficiency.

B   The Decision and Its Effects

I   *The* Google Spain Case

A Spanish citizen felt that his right of personality had been violated because, even in 2010, the search engine Google listed two pages of the daily newspaper *La Vanguardia* from the year 1998 among the results it presented when the citizen's name was searched.[1] These pages included announcements for the auction of his property due to debts owed to the social security administration at the time.[2] In response to the citizen's complaint the Spanish data protection authority decided in favor of the newspaper, concluding that the challenged information had been lawfully published.[3] But Google Spain and Google Inc. were ordered to remove the respective data from the search results the company produced and to prevent access to the challenged newspaper reports in the future.[4] In legal proceedings challenging this outcome the Spanish courts referred the matter to the CJEU, which confirmed the order on the merits.[5]

---

[1] Case C-131/12, Google Spain SL v. Agencia Española de Protección de Datos (AEPD), ¶ 14, INFOCURIA – CASE-LAW CT. JUST. (May 13, 2014), http://curia.europa.eu/juris/document/document.jsf;jsessionid=9ea7d0f130d58fa348967d244833bad1c86381ec1189.e34KaxiLc3eQc40LaxqMbN4Oc3aKe0?text=&docid=152065&pageIndex=0&doclang=EN&mode=lst&dir=&occ=first&part=1&cid=385379 [hereinafter Google Spain, CJEU].
[2] *Id.*   [3] *Id.* at ¶ 16.   [4] *Id.* at ¶ 17.
[5] S.A.N., Feb. 27, 2012 (Case 725/2010, *Google Spain SL, Google Inc. contra Agencia de Protección de Datos (AEPD), Abogado del Estado,* Número de Identificación Único

II Correct Starting Point

First, I must emphasize that the CJEU's decision is obviously inspired by the intention to embrace its duty to seriously protect fundamental rights, also *vis-à-vis* economic interests, and to provide European fundamental rights with substantive effectiveness.[6] In this respect the decision deserves recognition and should be welcomed without reservation.

The decision is convincing insofar as it conclusively establishes that search engine operators such as Google are subject to European law and the laws of its Member States, no matter where the relevant servers are located.[7]

The CJEU's basic approach, which does not marginalize the significance of the search engines but perceives them as a distinct kind of data processing, is also convincing.[8] Even the mere identification and presentation of web content, without more, can have an impact on personality rights. These actions encroach on fundamental rights[9] and require a distinct justification with regard to the right to informational self-determination and the fundamental rights to respect for private life and to protection of personal data, respectively. Indeed, the significance of search engines as to the protection of personal freedoms may not be understated.

Yet, the conclusions the Court draws from this starting point are counterproductive and lopsided.

(Unique case-law identifier) 28079 23 3 2010 0004781) (Spain), www.poderjudicial.es/cgpj/es/Poder-Judicial/Audiencia-Nacional/Jurisprudencia/Actualidad-Jurisprudencial/Auto-AN-Contencioso-Administrativo–En-recurso-interpuesto-por-Google-Inc–y-Google-Spain-frente-a-resolucion-de-la-Agencia-Espanola-de-Proteccion-de-Datos–la-Sala-acuerda-plantear-cuestion-prejudicial-de-interpretacion-al-Tribunal-de-Justicia-de-la-Union-Europea-sobre-ciertas-normas-de-la-Directiva-95-46-CE-sobre-proteccion-de-datos-personales–entre-otras–sobre-el-alcance-del-derecho-de-cancelacion-y-oposicion-en-relacion-con-el–derecho-al-olvido–en-el-marco-de-la-Directiva- (in Spanish, PDF).

[6] The Court makes this clear throughout the judgment. *See, e.g.*, Google Spain CJEU, *supra* note 1, at ¶ 97 ("[...] it should be held [...] that those rights override, as a rule [...] the economic interest of the operator of the search engine"); Google Spain CJEU, *supra* note 1 at ¶ 34 (employing a broad interpretation of the term "controller"); Google Spain CJEU, *supra* note 1 at ¶ 38 (directive interpretation); Google Spain CJEU, *supra* note 1 at ¶ 39 (responsibility of search engine operator for indexing regardless of indication on host site).

[7] Google Spain CJEU, *supra* note 1, at ¶¶ 48–58.   [8] *Id.* at ¶¶ 35–38, 41.

[9] In the German and European jurisprudence fundamental rights apply in a specific way also between private parties. *See* Donald P. Kommers & Russel A. Miller, The Constitutional Jurisprudence of the Federal Republic of Germany 60, 442 (3d ed. 2012) (referring to the horizontality of rights).

III   The Issues Involved

At the heart of the case is the question, under what conditions may search engines list links to web pages that feature personal data (i.e., information on natural or legal persons). In other words, at what point may private persons demand that a search engine operator refrains from listing the challenged information, thereby rendering the data virtually untraceable. The CJEU detached this issue strictly from the question on the lawfulness of the challenged content (see below), that is, whether information may be put online. Nevertheless, as regards the practical outcome, both issues are closely intertwined. The limitations the CJEU established regarding the listing of personal information through search engine results serve and shall serve to prevent the dissemination of certain information due to its legally offending effects for the person concerned.

In this way the decision materially touches on problems that are usually addressed within the framework of the right to free expression: who is allowed to distribute what kind of information about whom under what conditions? This refers to the tension between, on the one hand, freedom of expression, guarded by the fundamental communication rights, and on the other hand, the protection of the general right of personality.[10]

The legal rules in this area are – at least in Germany – complex. They have occupied courts in the different branches of the judiciary for many years. The constitutional standards that have been developed over the years in this field are correspondingly diverse and graduated.[11] These are just some examples: Whether a statement may be prohibited as an insult or whether it constitutes a protected exercise of freedom of expression is

---

[10] *See, e.g.,* Grundgesetz [GG] [Basic Law], arts. 1, 2 & 5(1)[1], *translation at* www.gesetze-im-internet.de/englisch_gg/; The Charter of Fundamental Rights of the European Union, arts. 7 & 8, 2000/C 364/01; The European Convention on Human Rights, art. 8, Nov. 4, 1950, E.T.S. 5, www.echr.coe.int/Documents/Convention_ENG.pdf. *See also* Christoph Enders, *Schutz der Persönlichkeit und der Privatsphäre, in* IV Handbuch der Grundrechte – Grundrechte in Deutschland: Einzelgrundrechte ¶ 86 (Detlef Merten & Hans-Jürgen Papier eds., 2011).

[11] *See, e.g.,* Dieter Grimm, *Die Meinungsfreiheit in der Rechtsprechung des Bundesverfassungsgerichts,* 48 Neue Juristische Wochenschrift 1697, 1701 et seq. (1995); Matthias Jestaedt, *Meinungsfreiheit, in* V Handbuch der Grundrechte – Grundrechte in Deutschland: Einzelgrundrechte II, ¶ 102, margin no. 81 et seq., 90 et seq. (Detlef Merten & Hans-Jürgen Papier eds., 2013); Franz Schemmer, *Article 5, in* Beck'scher Onlinekommentar zum Grundgesetz margin no. 100 et seq. (Volker Epping & Christian Hillgruber eds., 2015).

subject to variously graduated legal presumptions, requirements of interpretation, and balancing restrictions. Equally sophisticated rules apply to
assessing whether a person may impart facts – and which facts – about
another person. Another complex issue has been how a claim of fact is to
be evaluated, in respect to the question of its veracity, as well as how the
burden of proof regarding this issue is to be allocated. It has often been
necessary to distinguish between the press and individuals in this jurisprudence. Again other specific rules cover the question what information
(and in which situations) is to be excluded from media coverage due to
privacy considerations. Particular requirements also apply to coverage on
pending criminal cases, thus on someone who has been accused but not
yet convicted of criminal conduct.[12] Again, different requirements
govern the dissemination of information about convicted offenders,[13]
and these rules vary with respect to how long ago the conviction took
place and whether media coverage might impede the criminal's social
rehabilitation.[14] In some of these cases the question regarding which
information may be published depends also on administrative decisions,
e.g., when consumers are being informed about particular deficiencies or
risks, or when the names of certain individuals are published as part of
professional sanctions.[15] Both in commercial and in environmental law
the legislature deliberately characterized – through transparency requirements – certain corporate information as public and intended for the

---

[12] See STEPHANOS STAVROS, THE GUARANTEES FOR ACCUSED PERSONS UNDER ARTICLE SIX
OF THE EUROPEAN CONVENTION ON HUMAN RIGHTS (1993). See also Standard Verlags
GmbH v. Austria (No. 3), App. No. 34702/07, HUDOC (Jan. 10, 2012), http://hudoc
.echr.coe.int/eng?i=001-108433#{"itemid":["001-108433"]} (on the question of the disclosure of names during a criminal investigation). In Germany, this issue is known as
"identifizierende Berichterstattung" (identifying media coverage). See Bundesverfassungsgericht [BverfG] [Federal Constitutional Court] Nov. 27, 2008, BVerfG, 1 BvQ 46/08, 62
NEUE JURISTISCHE WOCHENSCHRIFT 350 (2009) (the Holzklotz case); Bundesverfassungsgericht [BverfG] [Federal Constitutional Court] June 13, 2006, BVerfG, 1 BvR
565/06, 59 NEUE JURISTISCHE WOCHENSCHRIFT 2835 (2006) (the Autobahnraser case).

[13] See Bundesverfassungsgericht [BverfG] [Federal Constitutional Court] June 5, 1973,
35 BVerfGE 202 (The Lebach Case, a seminal German Constitutional Court decision,
involved the question whether someone may be clearly identified in a TV documentary
years after he had been convicted of having killed several soldiers during a raid on an
army munitions depot and shortly before his release from prison.).

[14] See 35 BVerfGE 202, at 235.

[15] See Bundesverfassungsgericht [BverfG] [Federal Constitutional Court] Mar. 3, 2014,
BVerfG, 1 BvR 1128/13, 67 NEUE JURISTISCHE WOCHENSCHRIFT [NJW] 2019 (2014)
(publication of the name of a doctor in a professional bulletin after he had been fined for
violations of professional rules).

general public.[16] Yet, to some extent, the legislature also stipulates periods during which certain information may be retained, and may be used by the authorities, provided that it is deleted after that time period lapses (e.g., regulations on the deletion of records concerning criminal convictions from the German Federal Central Criminal Register, and limited disclosure requirements in commercial and insolvency law). Time limits such as these may also affect the use and dissemination of information by individuals.

Most of these regulations have been developed without regard to the particular form of dissemination that is achieved through the Internet. This is the case even though ever-more jurisprudence exists that is tailored to the distinct characteristics of the Internet (e.g., on Internet gateways). It is true that the sustainability of the regime is – in light of the new impact that results from dissemination via the Internet – up for reevaluation and might possibly require adjustments.[17] But it is not possible to determine uniformly and in the abstract whether a modification in criteria is necessary. Instead, this can only be resolved on a case-by-case basis. This process is now fully underway.[18]

One problem that needs to be solved in this context is the permanent availability of information once it has been posted on the Internet. This phenomenon is discussed under the heading of a so-called "right to be forgotten." There are cases pending at the German Federal Constitutional Court that raise the issue.[19]

So far, the tension between those who make a controversial statement and those affected by it has, in principle, been dealt with and determined directly between the opposing parties, both of whom are endowed with their respective rights. For example, a case pending before the German Federal Constitutional Court involves a suit filed against a magazine that published the challenged statement in its online archive. The case raises

---

[16] *See* Christoph Grabenwarter, *Article 5*, *in* GRUNDGESETZ margin no. 187–89 (Theodor Maunz, Günter Dürig, & Roman Herzog eds., 72nd supplement 2014).

[17] *See, e.g.,* Wolfgang Hoffmann-Riem, *Regelungsstrukturen für öffentliche Kommunikation im Internet*, 137 ARCHIV DES ÖFFENTLICHEN RECHTS 509 (2012).

[18] *See The Proposal for a Regulation of the European Parliament and the Council on the Protection of Individuals with Regard to the Processing of Personal Data and on the Free Movement of Such Data (General Data Protection Regulation)*, COM (2012) 11 final (Jan. 25, 2012), http://ec.europa.eu/justice/data-protection/document/review2012/com_2012_11_en.pdf; Hoffmann-Riem, *supra* note 17, at 530.

[19] Bundesverfassungsgericht [BverfG] [Federal Constitutional Court], 1 BvR 16/13 (not yet delivered).

the question whether the magazine may be required to post data in its archive in such a manner that search engines cannot find it. This, however, is not the issue that the CJEU resolved. In *Google Spain* the question was whether the affected party may approach a search engine operator in order to render the challenged statement "invisible" by delisting the relevant link from the search results produced. This is not a proceeding against the person who uttered the statement and it raises the follow-up question, whether and to what extent this conflict can be elevated to a meta-level.

IV   The CJEU's Assumptions

The CJEU's decision relied on four assumptions for the resolution of the substantive conflict in the case.

First, the search engine operator bears full responsibility for the potential violation of the right of personality implicated by the content of web pages listed as a result of a search.[20] The search engine operator is therefore required to check whether the content of the listed web pages may be disseminated with regard to data protection aspects or whether doing so would infringe upon the rights of the persons concerned.[21]

Second, for this determination the question of the lawfulness of the information itself is not relevant.[22] Even if a web site lawfully contains and renders accessible certain information, it does not follow that this information may be listed by the search engine. Listing web pages in response to users' searches is a function governed by different criteria than the question of the content's original expression or publication.[23]

Third, comprehensive balancing is required to determine whether a web site may be listed as the result of a search.[24] All the circumstances of the concrete situation and of the affected person have to be taken into account.[25] This balancing effort is to be conducted independently of any conclusion regarding the lawfulness of the information in question. In particular it should be considered whether the data should be available longer than necessary to fulfill the objectives for which it is collected and processed.[26]

Fourth, in the balancing process a substantial presumption applies in favor of the protection of privacy as safeguarded by Articles 7 and 8

---

[20] Google Spain, CJEU, *supra* note 1, at 38.   [21] *Id.* at ¶ 39.   [22] *Id.* at ¶ 88.
[23] *Id.* at ¶¶ 28–30, 85–88.   [24] *Id.* at ¶¶ 74, 76, 81.   [25] *Id.* at ¶¶ 93–98.
[26] *Id.* at ¶¶ 92–93.

CFREU when name-specific searches and results are involved:[27] In the CJEU's view, "data subject's rights protected by those articles also override, as a general rule, that interest of internet users"[28] but "in specific cases" – for example with regard to public figures – the balancing might reach a different outcome.[29]

V   The Formal Aspect of the Decision: Search Engine Operators' Full Responsibility for the Content of Listed Sites

First and foremost, the Court's decision faces substantial concerns due to its formal approach.

The search engine operator is given full responsibility for the content of the web sites it lists in response to a search query. It seems that this responsibility requires no further preconditions, that is, it does not take effect on a subsidiary but on a primary level. Moreover it applies comprehensively with regard to a particular confirmation.[30] An affected person may take any kind of violation of the right of personality as an opportunity to demand the removal of the listed link from the search engine's results. Consequently, the search engine operator slips into the role of a general instance for complaints regarding personality right violations on the Internet.

In the event of a dispute the search engine operator will have to decide between (at least) two parties whose backgrounds are not fully known. In practical terms the search engine operator has essentially three options to deal with applications for delisting. First, the operator may establish a complaints unit that will remove the challenged link. For obvious reasons such a removal will be mandated without any review (or after a merely rudimental plausibility control) – in order to achieve an efficient, inexpensive, and effective resolution of the case. But such a course of action would be extremely dubious in terms of unrestricted Internet communication. The delisted web sites would no longer be identified by search requests and they would essentially be cut off from their audience without giving the web site provider an opportunity to give an opinion on the issue or to even know about it. It is true that they would still enjoy the freedom to publish statements on the Internet, but these statements would be *de facto* excluded from the general Internet communication without any involvement on the part of the web site provider.

[27] *Id.* at ¶¶ 69, 88.   [28] *Id.* at ¶ 81.   [29] *Id.*   [30] *Id.* at ¶¶ 41, 81–88.

Second, it is conceivable that search engine operators will simply ignore complaints and refer them instead to the data protection authorities. The CJEU explicitly requires the authorities to mandate that search engine operators delist challenged search results when necessary. This approach would allow search engine operators to track evolving policy and wait for the order from data protection authorities before complying by delisting the challenged web sites. This solution is also afflicted with considerable problems. It would ensure that the decision on the adjustment of the interests in free expression and in personality protection would not lie with a private corporation. But data protection authorities would be confronted with an unmanageable number of proceedings. They would become a general authority for communication regulation in private law disputes. This is dubious already in principle. Disputes that had typically been resolved in a decentralized manner in civil proceedings would largely be transferred to the jurisdiction of an authority of presumably considerable proportions and therewith into administrative law. To the extent that these procedures would remain free of charge up to the issuance of the first order, litigation costs would fall on public funds. (Should the state seek to impose cost-covering fees on search engine operators, an approach that recommends itself, one can assume that the search engine operators would abandon this strategy in favor of the previously-mentioned approach.).

Third, considering the requirements established by the CJEU, search engine operators would in fact be required to carry out the necessary balancing. For this they would need to obtain the relevant information. Should search engine operators actually tackle this task they would need to make considerable efforts in order to establish an adequate organization, a transparent procedure (especially safeguarding the right to be heard of the party who published the problematic statement), and regulations on preliminary legal protection. In this way, search engine operators would become private arbitration boards invested with far-reaching decision-making powers on Internet communication. This would have consequences for the publication of and access to the content of information as well.

The search engine operators' generally comprehensive responsibility for the content of web sites does not lead to a restriction of their power. Instead it threatens to further intensify it by endowing them with decision-making authority also as to the content of web sites they list in response to search requests. Admittedly, this responsibility only concerns the question which pages may be listed in the results, and not the question of what may be published on these web sites in the first place. But, if one takes the significance of the results seriously (and it is right to do so), then the general distinction between the permissibility of a search engine's list of links and the permissibility of the content on the listed web sites loses its significance. After all, a web site that is not found by a search engine is essentially excluded from interactive communication relations. In Germany there have been suggestions that legal regulations should empower democratically accountable public authorities to block certain web pages (concerning, e.g., child pornography). This initiative has been heavily criticized by the public.[31] But the attribution of that responsibility to search engine operators is, in my view, far more ominous for the freedom of Internet communication.

VI   The Material Aspect of the Decision: The Categorical Priority of the General Right of Personality

In material terms – according to the CJEU – the decision on the permissibility of a listed link shall be reached without regard to the lawfulness of the listed web site. The legality of the information contained on the web site does not determine the legality of the link. Rather, the Court's requirements for an acceptable listing of web pages are evidently higher and more protective of personality rights than the requirements for the publication of the information in the first instance. The CJEU referred in this context to publications by the press, which usually enjoy privileged publication standards (at least compared to other enterprises). This position is based on the freedom of the press enjoyed by journalists.[32] The Court explained that these standards would not apply for search engine operators. Not all

---

[31] For an account of the debate see *Family Minister vs. Freedom of Speech: Anti-Child Pornography Law Flounders*, SPIEGEL ONLINE (May 29, 2009, 6:18 PM), www.spiegel.de/international/germany/family-minister-vs-freedom-of-speech-anti-child-pornography-law-flounders-a-627447.html.

[32] The so-called "media privilege," *see* Bundesdatenschutzgesetz [BDSG] [Federal Data Protection Act], Jan. 14, 2003, BGBl. I at 66, § 41, last amended Feb. 25, 2015, BGBl. I at 162; Eur. Parl. & Council Directive 95/46/EC, art. 9, O.J. (L 281); Google Spain CJEU, at ¶ 85. *See* DIE PRIVILEGIERUNG DER MEDIEN IM DEUTSCHEN DATENSCHUTZRECHT (Philipp-Christian Thomale ed., 2006).

information that may be published by print media, the Court concluded, may be identified and listed by search engines.[33]

1. The question as to which information may be communicated within the framework of social debates is thus also materially covered with a distinct layer. It limits communication independently from general rules – as far as it is conveyed by search engines – in order to protect the right of personality. Established legal regulations – ranging from transparency obligations to various time limits within which certain information is made accessible – are being overridden by rules for retrieval and listing by search engines. As a consequence, even apart from that layer, the sophisticated requirements lose their authority. The accomplishments of the jurisprudence that enabled an open (even with regard to traditional notions of honor, moral concepts, and claims to social entitlements) and potentially critical public discourse are being suspended as a matter of principle. It puts aside a jurisprudence that had been achieved through an arduous, historic process. This is particularly clear in press law. It is not apparent that the CJEU restricted the delisting measures to outdated news and therewith to the issue of oblivion and the right "to be forgotten".

2. The question of listing Internet content and the consequences of doing so for information involving personal data is instead governed by the requirement of a comprehensive balancing – that at least so far has been devised in general terms only. This does not merely supersede the liberty securing standards of free speech law but, according to the CJEU, also shall be shaped by a categorical primacy of the protection of the general right of personality. When balancing the interests of Internet users with the affected persons' fundamental rights as provided by Articles 7 and 8 CFREU, the Court found that the "data subject's rights protected by those articles also override, as a general rule, that interest of internet users."[34] Thus privacy takes priority over public communication. The balancing might reach a different outcome only "in specific cases," due to the kind of information concerned and the interest of the general public in being able to access it. This would be the case, for example, with regard to public figures.

---

[33] Google Spain CJEU, at ¶¶ 29–30 (referring to the circumstance in which that information has already been published).
[34] *Id.* at ¶ 81.

Under these balancing standards, which rigorously unbundle the question of a right to communicate a link to particular information from the question of the right to communicate that information, the speaker's interest in the distribution of his or her statements is obscured. These interests come into view only indirectly as the relatively weak, general interests of Internet users. In this perspective there is no immediate room for the interests and rights of those who wish to disseminate information on their web page in an unrestricted manner. As little as they are involved in the decision-making process on the removal of links – at least there are no indications for this in the judgment – their interest in the dissemination of information is also not considered. A consequence of this strict uncoupling is that it becomes difficult to justify the extent to which they might assert rights after all. It is not self-evident that a web site host has a claim to be listed or merely to equal treatment by search engines. This is problematic when embedded in the CJEU's approach. If the legality of listing a link depends in substance on the material assessment of the interest in publication *vis-à-vis* the claim to privacy of the affected person, then both parties need to face each other at least with similar rights. In fact, the settled case law of the German Federal Constitutional Court applies a presumption in favor of the legality of speech that deals with issues of general public concern.[35] By repealing this equality of arms through the inadequately strict uncoupling of the right to list a link and the right to express information online, the CJEU gives personality protection disproportionate priority over freedom of expression.

3. The disproportionate priority of personality protection in the face of communication freedoms is also reflected by the CJEU's strong emphasis on purpose-limitations that pertain to data protection law. The CJEU turned the rule, according to which data may not be displayed that is not essential for the execution of the purposes for which it was collected or processed, into the decisive balancing aspect.[36] Here, too, the ambivalence of personality protection and free communication between private persons is not adequately accommodated. Originally, the strict requirements of the purpose-limitations in data protection law were established by the jurisprudence of the German Federal Constitutional Court for data processing by public authorities only. The state –

---

[35] Bundesverfassungsgericht [BVerfG] [Federal Constitutional Court] Jan. 15, 1958, 7 BVerfGE 198, 208 (Lüth Case).

[36] Google Spain CJEU, at ¶¶ 81–88 (with a detailed examination of Directive 95/46/EC).

itself not a holder of freedoms – may process personal data only for the purposes explicitly permitted by law. This principle, in the meantime adopted as a substantial part of data protection in Europe, should not be applied to relationships between private individuals without some modification. In fact, some elements of this concept may be harnessed indirectly and in a modified way for certain relations between private individuals, for example, in regard to the extent of an acquiescence. But an objectified review as to at what point in time which data for which purpose still necessarily requires publication misses the character of an information exchange between private individuals, an exchange that is also with regard to its purpose shaped by individual liberty. Here, the different issues of data protection in the private area and in the area of public authorities are confused.

VII   Questions with Regard to the Scope of the Decision and Subsequent Problems

Due to its factual background the case is shaped by the issue of name-related search requests and possible personality violations that result from the content of the listed web pages. It is doubtful whether the CJEU intended to issue further statements beyond the specific factual constellation of the case, and one should refrain from over-interpreting this decision. According to the logic of its argument, however, the decision implicates consequences that reach far beyond the circumstances of the case.

By assigning the search engine operator a primary and direct responsibility (as "controller") for personality violations that result from listed web sites the rationale of the decision is not confined to name-related search queries. If, on these terms, the search engine provider carries a general responsibility as data controller for the information contained in listed web sites, then he must not list personality-violating web sites at all. This will be the only way to be consistent. Accordingly, even a link to research that refers to auctions in 1998 would be impermissible as long as the real names of the affected property owners are recognizable. Similarly, linking critical statements about – let us say a doctor – would not only be disallowed in the course of name searches but would be prohibited in any case if the concerned person asks for this protection. If such information is contained in a review site, then the search engine operator may not list a link to this site at all.

Moreover, based on the principles announced by the CJEU, the search engine operator's responsibility is actually not restricted to an *ex post* review prompted by a complaint filed by the affected person. Instead, a diligent balancing is part of the search engine provider's general obligations. As noted earlier, the CJEU's decision does not take an explicit position on this point and one should not portray this as an intended consequence. But these consequences follow readily from the Court's reasoning and will be difficult to avoid in future cases.

Particularly striking are the consequences of the decision for search engine results involving data that receives (under Art. 8 section 1 of the Directive 95/46/EC) special protection under European Union law.[37] This includes, notably, all personal data "revealing racial or ethnic origin, political opinions, religious or philosophical beliefs, [or] trade-union membership."[38] If the CJEU burdens search engine operators primarily and in an undifferentiated manner with the data controller's general data protection obligations, then the display of search results regarding such data should be impermissible in virtually all cases, unless the affected person obviously published them herself. This applies as well to listing links that pertain to criminal offenses or criminal convictions. But this is untenable in an open democratic society. The CJEU may not have intended this result. It is not clear how the Court will resolve this issue, given the principles it set out in *Google Spain* regarding the then-clear wording of the Directive, and the explicit refusal to extend the media privilege to search engines. The Advocate General explicitly pointed out this problem.[39]

These subsequent difficulties reveal that this problem is not only inherent in the CJEU's interpretation of the Directive. Instead, it rests as well on the undifferentiated situation of European Union law itself. If the law creates (by way of a comprehensive Directive) only one form of data responsibility, then this responsibility establishes without distinction identical obligations for public as well as private actors of all kinds, thereby reducing communication freedoms to the assertion of "justified interests" and a media privilege. A sophisticated

---

[37] *See* Eur. Parl. & Council Directive 95/46/EC, art. 8(1), O.J. (L 281) 31–50.   [38] *Id.*

[39] Google Spain CJEU, at ¶ 85. For the AG's opinion, *see* Case C-131/12, Google Spain SL v. Agencia Española de Protección de Datos (AEPD), Opinion of Advocate General Jääski- nen, ¶ 124, INFOCURIA – CASE-LAW CT. JUS. (June 25, 2013), http://curia.europa.eu/juris/ document/document.jsf?text=&docid=138782&pageIndex=0&doclang=EN&mode=req& dir=&occ=first&part=1&cid=518199.

response to the multilayered challenges of the Internet society is hardly possible. A substantial protection of fundamental rights must demand adequate and graded provisions already on the regulatory level, where also political choices have their place that are not all directly predetermined by fundamental rights.

The planned reform of data protection law on the European level would be the right place to take up this challenge.[40] In the proposal, however, the present approach is perpetuated. Yet, with a too simple regulatory structure, a differentiated protection of fundamental rights cannot be accomplished.

VIII   Considerations on the Solution of the Substantial Questions

The CJEU's decision is shaped by the attempt to grasp the significance of Internet search engines in terms of data protection law and to address the issue of permanent and ubiquitous data accessibility and the limited efficacy of proceedings brought against web site hosts. In this respect the CJEU focused on search engine operators. It is doubtful whether this one-sided focus on search engines, irrespective of their interlinked cooperation with web site hosts, is the right approach. Instead of this lopsided fixation on isolated single actors in the web, viable solutions might be achieved with attention to the interdependency of the various Internet actors and the interdependent effects of web activities as a whole. The disconnected focus on search engines should be as unsuitable as a one-sided concentration on web site hosts and web service operators.

1. Of course, search engines add significantly to the danger that the Internet poses for the protection of general personality rights. They contribute to the traceability of various pieces of personal information and they have a decisive – but not exclusive – role in the ubiquity and permanent availability of data by all and sundry. They

---

[40] On the draft of a General Data Protection regulation, *see Communication from the Commission to the European Parliament, the Council, the European Economic and Social Committee and the Committee of the Regions: Safeguarding Privacy in a Connected World – A European Data Protection Framework for the 21st Century*, COM (2012) 9 final (Jan. 25, 2012); *Proposal for a Regulation of the European Parliament and of the Council on the Protection of Individuals with Regard to the Processing of Personal Data and on the Free Movement of Such Data (General Data Protection Regulation)*, COM (2012) 11 final (Jan. 25, 2012).

thereby create distinct threads for which they should be held responsible in terms of data protection law.[41]

This applies in any case to constellations in which the threat to the right of personality results from the selection mechanism itself or the generation of additional information by the search engine (e.g., the autocomplete feature). In this respect the German Federal Court of Justice rightly imposed responsibilities on search engine operators under data protection law.[42]

In my view there are further good reasons – in this respect I have to agree with the CJEU – to deny search engine operators the right in specific cases to list links due to the content of the respective web site. But, with regard to the interconnection of the various actors in the web and the effects that come with this situation, the direct obligation of search engine operators should be treated in a sophisticated way.[43]

2. Where the generation of additional information is not itself an issue, a lot argues in favor of interlocking the legality of the listing of a web site closely with the legality of the web site's content. The principle according to which information legally published on the web may also be legally listed as a search engine result has sound reasons on its side. This approach acknowledges that the dissemination of information normally involves (at least) two parties with opposing legal positions between which a balance must be struck. If the scale tips toward freedom of expression, then it seems likely in a free society that this also includes the lawfulness of the free dissemination of the information. With regard to the fundamental relevance of search engines in retrieving information on the Internet, a lot speaks in favor of such a conjunction in most cases.

---

[41] *See, e.g.,* SIVA VAIDHYANATHAN, THE GOOGLIZATION OF EVERYTHING: (AND WHY WE SHOULD WORRY) (2011). *See also* Indra Spiecker genannt Döhmann, *A New Framework for Information Markets: Google Spain*, 52 COMMON MKT. L. REV. 1033 (2015).

[42] Again other questions – also in relation to fundamental rights – result from the marketplace power that in particular the search engine Google possesses. But these issues are located in a different field and are insignificant in the present context.

[43] As this memorandum is not concerned with the final reconstruction of persuasive solutions it will also leave open how these issues are resolved under fundamental rights doctrine. Accordingly, it also does not deepen the question whether the distribution of such obligations constitutes – in terms of fundamental rights doctrine – rather an obligation of the search engine operators by the legislator in the exercise of its protective duties for the benefit of the affected persons or whether it must be regarded as the search engine operators' direct responsibility in data protection law.

This should have consequences for the procedural allocation of such disputes. In normal cases it seems reasonable to leave these disputes (over personality violations by dissemination of personal data) where the conflict occurs: between the parties concerned. The relevant information is at hand and the respective rights and interests may be advocated in an authentic manner, decentralized between the affected person and the person making the statement.

3. Of course the CJEU bases its decision on the fact that the Internet comprises unresolved complexities that make it nearly impossible to secure the protection of persons affected by disseminated information.

The first problem is inherent in the aspect that the Internet does not forget.[44] Originally, certain information may have been legitimately disseminated and, even for the person affected, in an acceptable manner. But, as that information remains retrievable and accessible even after longer periods of time, it can acquire a detrimental significance. Indeed, here the legal system is only in the early stages of adequate solutions. It is doubtful, however, that this is only a problem for search engines. The question for what period of time the dissemination of information may be maintained applies rather and primarily to the liable web site host and, in this respect, should be part of a balancing of interests of the different parties. In Germany, certain regulations and jurisprudence already exist for this concern. They address the relationship between persons that express themselves and those affected. Moreover, such rules may be found in or derived from existing case law. But, to a great extent, they are still missing and the "right to be forgotten" needs to obtain further outlines. A specific problem in this connection are digital archives (notably) of newspapers. In fact, these difficulties are decisively related to indexing by search engines, which are able to retrieve very old reports on individuals and keep them available in the present, to the continuing detriment of the affected persons. Here as well it is arguable that a resolution to the conflict should be pursued – at least on the primary level – between the affected person and the web site host who operates the archive. The archive host is able to configure data in a manner that renders it untraceable for search engines. This approach will locate the dispute on the lawfulness of the enduring availability of certain information between

---

[44] See Google Spain CJEU, at ¶¶ 89–99 (for the Court's reasoning with respect to the "right to be forgotten").

those whose rights are involved and would enable at the same time sophisticated solutions (e.g., the full article may remain accessible, only its discovery through a name-related search might be foreclosed). The necessary technological options are available. If deficiencies should surface, then search engine operators could be required to provide the lacking technological capabilities. A solution on this level would not only feature the above-mentioned advantages of a more appropriate localization of the conflict, it would unfold its effects *vis-à-vis all* search engine operators.

The CJEU sees an additional problem in the fact that, in some cases, it may be virtually impossible to bring actions against the host of personality-violating web sites.[45] The CJEU refers in this respect to the possibility that harmful statements that are being removed from one web site might have been mirrored on other web pages – making proceedings against the respective web site host ineffective in the end. The Court likewise referred to the possibility that harmful statements might be published on web sites that are operated in third countries, where no effective means of redress are available.[46] Indeed, in such cases, it might be necessary to take a supplementary responsibility of search engine operators into account.[47] One could deliberate in this respect whether subsidiary obligations to delist a link might constitute a suitable protective mechanism. For example, the delisting of a link might be available if a successful action against a web site host is frustrated by further publications and not achievable in a bearable way. Here, many different provisions are conceivable that require further elaboration.

In these cases there are good reasons for assigning obligations to search engine operators regarding web sites and the content they impart. Even beyond this, there may be other constellations in which such an obligation for search engine operators may be appropriate. This should also be the practice, for example, in the field of intellectual property violations.[48]

---

[45] *Id.* at ¶ 84 (with regard to the possibility that the host is situated outside the scope of Union law).

[46] *Id.* at ¶¶ 83–84.   [47] *Id.*

[48] Experience shows how such complaints are being dealt with: Thus Google reported in an exemplary manner of 24 million URLs whose deletion was requested; in 97 % of the cases Google conformed to the application – generally without consulting the site operators. Whether this is justified in copyright law that is concerned with on their outset illegal activities, needs no discussion here. For the deletion of links to opinion sites such a practice would pose a genuine problem.

But here, according to the basic idea, it would be a subsidiary obligation. In contrast, it is scarcely plausible that occasional difficulties in legal protection on the web should establish a general, primary, and direct responsibility of search engine operators for the content of web sites they list.

4. A direct and primary involvement of search engine operators in protecting the right to personality might – as a matter of fact – be appropriate where an application for the removal of the respective link can be resolved on the basis of the most minimal individual requirements and therefore it would involve as little knowledge as possible on the lines of conflict that are concretely in question. In this sense one may take the CJEU's decision as an opportunity to reflect on a general restriction of the opening-up function of the Internet. In fact, the decision may be a step toward this.

Based on the fact that the decision focuses on the results of name-specific Internet searches and acts on the assumption that precisely the combination of personal data from different areas of life to a personality profile constitutes a core problem, one might consider creating a right of private persons to opt-out from search engine traceability. We may discuss whether it is a good idea in terms of personality protection to grant an individual the more-or-less unrestricted opportunity to refrain from making her person an object of direct Internet inquiries. Public figures would be excluded from such an opt-out. If this option would not allow for the removal of individual links but only for a complete omission of one's name, then this approach would substantially avoid the objections raised above against a primary responsibility of search engine operators. The right to omission on the Internet would resemble a removal of a name in the telephone book. Information could still be obtained via individual fora. But it would no longer be available in such a comprehensive, world-wide form that can be shaped into a personality profile. This all-or-nothing principle would not only relieve search engine operators of difficult, for them in factual terms barely feasible, decisions. Moreover, a one-sided personality protection in the face of freedom of expression could be evaded at least to some extent: Individuals would no longer be able to simply pick-out statements and to filter-out only undesirable coverage – in order to avoid a controversy with the uttering person. An application would no longer pose a lopsided enforcement of self-perception at the expense of the external perception. Instead, it would constitute a categorical retreat from the general public to a private sphere or into self-defined fora.

Such a concept would result in a far-reaching constraint of the Internet's informational function. The opening-up function of the Internet would be substantially limited and would include only those persons who wish to be found, or at least those who do not object to their exposure in the Internet. One might debate such a concept in terms of legal policy. The individual would be offered a differentiated decision regarding fora in which she divulges data and to which segments of the public – without the opportunity to unilaterally immunize herself against critique in these fora as well. Admittedly, even in this constellation, the issue persists that the person making a statement (e.g., a blogger) is deliberately cut off from presenting information, commentaries, and critique in a way that renders them retrievable by everyone. One might consider this an acceptable solution for mere private citizens. Of course, the constrictive concession of such a primary right to address an application for a removal to search engine operators does not solve all problems. The incentives for search engine operators to prematurely assume citizens' privacy based on a simple application persist, as do numerous difficulties with necessary distinctions. Should an opt-out option apply also to accredited professionals (physicians, attorneys) or nonprominent officials (teachers), businessmen, and others? What design does a delisting require if several persons bear the same name? Does it apply to legal entities as well?

Whether one wishes to deprive the Internet of its opening-up function in this extent is a far-reaching question that deserves a prudent resolution. It would be appropriate to resolve this issue explicitly as a matter of policy and not primarily as a matter of judicial decisions – even if a framework requirement of fundamental rights exists, the preservation of which is a central responsibility of the courts. The upcoming reform of data protection law on the European level provides an opportunity for such a political determination.

Certainly, the establishment of such a categorical but limited right to the elimination of name-related searches does not conform to the CJEU's approach. The Court demanded a case-by-case balancing and a decision on the particular link listed by a search engine. That process must account for all relevant circumstances. The practical consequences of this remain to be seen. But it is not a remote apprehension that the Court's approach does not only alternatively establish an opt-out option for name-related searches, but also an opt-out option in relation to disliked coverage at the expense of the persons making the statements in question and the freedom of communication in general.

C Open Questions

This chapter does not suggest how the German Federal Constitutional Court will deal with these issues in the future. Indeed, this matter is scarcely resolvable in an abstract manner. Everything depends on which cases are submitted in what constellations.

Notably the issue whether, to what extent, and in what form the German Federal Constitutional Court is able to guarantee fundamental rights protection in this area has been avoided. There is no question that the CJEU assumed – as always – precedence for its ruling and implements the Union's fundamental rights here. Whether national fundamental rights remain applicable alongside that regime would require closer review. Considering the CJEU's basic assumption that the Directive strives for a full harmonization of law on this issue,[49] there are good reasons to deny this from the perspective of the CJEU and to assume an exclusive fundamental rights protection through Union law. Yet, one might ponder – based as well on the jurisprudence of the CJEU – whether a concurrent fundamental rights protection should apply. After all, the Directive and the CJEU's decision leave ample scope for implementation and balancing.[50] It is unclear whether the elaboration of this scope is understood as an application of exhaustive and mandatory Union law, which leads to an exclusive fundamental rights protection by the Charter of Fundamental Rights. Similarly, it is unclear whether the CJEU's decision establishes a regime for the national level that is merely guided by Union law and appertains to an area in which Union fundamental rights and national rights overlap. It is unnecessary to consider how the German Federal Constitutional Court should approach these issues and what procedural or material conclusions would need to be drawn. This is also true for the question whether the German Federal Constitutional Court – if one assumes exclusive fundamental rights protection by the European Union's Charter of Fundamental Rights – is indeed effectively discharged of its duty to provide for the protection of fundamental rights.

Likewise, this chapter does not seek to resolve the way in which the issues raised by the CJEU's decision might be mitigated in a factual manner. The decision concerns by its nature only a specific constellation that might be applied narrowly and may also be defused in its explosive potential – irrespective of its abstract premises. Despite its presumption

---

[49] Google Spain CJEU, at ¶¶ 53–54, 58.   [50] *Id.* at ¶ 58.

in favor of personality protection in relation to the Internet users' communication interests, the decision leaves margins for balancing that allow for the listing of links with personal data to a larger extent than merely in the case of public figures. The decision therefore opens up more room for freedom of communication than might be presumed. One may also ask if it is necessary to take seriously the Court's insistence on disconnecting delisting criteria and the criteria for determining the legality of the content, in cases other than the one at hand. Moreover, a restrictive reading might not completely rule out a legal arrangement that subjects the complaint to the search engine provider to a subsidiary requirement. Similar to any court ruling, the CJEU's decision contains ambiguities that may be used to catch at least the extreme effects of its approach. Only the right to have links to an outdated newspaper announcement on an auction in a legal situation that did not offer any specific solutions for the issue has been concretely resolved. Still, as is illustrated by Google's reactions, the consequences of the decision are considerable.[51] The decision creates, both in practical as well as in legal terms, structures that render an appropriate balance between the protection of personality and free communication in a democratic society extremely difficult to achieve.

---

[51] Google has created a web site on which the deletion of personal data can be requested, specifically referring to the judgment. *See Legal Help*, GOOGLE, https://support.google .com/legal/contact/lr_eudpa?product=websearch (last visited Nov. 24, 2015).

PART FOUR

Transnational Legal Responses to Privacy and
Intelligence Gathering

I   International Law

17

Toward Multilateral Standards for Foreign Surveillance Reform

BY IAN BROWN, MORTON H. HALPERIN,
BEN HAYES, BEN SCOTT, AND MATHIAS VERMEULEN

A   Introduction

Edward Snowden's revelations about the mass surveillance capabilities of the United States' National Security Agency (NSA) and its partners have created a unique opportunity for democratic states to work toward the adoption of multilateral, human rights-compliant standards for government surveillance conducted against the nationals of other countries. There is certainly much to debate about citizens' privacy concerns *vis-à-vis* their national security services. But the core foreign policy problem is that there are no clear national standards protecting the privacy of one nation's citizens from the intelligence gathering operations of another nation. Moreover, to the extent that such standards can be derived from international law, there are few or no mechanisms of oversight or accountability that could give meaningful effect to such guarantees.[1] These problems are compounded by the global nature of the Internet's infrastructure, where the distinction between foreign and domestic Internet communications is often difficult to discern.

The NSA conducts intelligence gathering operations that intercept and store enormous quantities of data from global communications networks. These bulk collection programs are conducted either by collecting data directly from the cables and servers that carry them,[2] or by

---

[1] *See* Chapter 21 in this volume.

[2] 50 U.S.C. § 1881(a) (2010) for targeting of communications of foreign persons located outside the U.S.A., for foreign intelligence purposes; authorized by Exec. Order No. 12,333, 3 C.F.R 200 (1981 Comp.), *reprinted in* 50 U.S.C. § 401 (Supp. V 1981) outside the U.S.A. *See also* Spencer Ackerman, *NSA Reformers Dismayed after Privacy Board Vindicates Surveillance Dragnet*, THE GUARDIAN (July 2, 2014, 02:47 PM), www.theguardian.com/world/2014/jul/02/nsa-surveillance-government-privacy-board-report.

compelling commercial service providers to supply such information.[3] These data "haystacks" are later searched for operational intelligence "needles." There is now an intense debate over how to restrict and control both the interception and the analysis of all of these communications.[4] This chapter focuses on the rules that govern the communications of private individuals who live outside the country that has collected their data, and who, because of their status as foreigners, do not enjoy the same privacy protections as the collecting state's citizens.

While the United States may be unique in terms of its sheer capacity to collect data, many states with established national security structures engage in broadly similar practices, intercepting communications in real time and compelling service providers to retain and disclose data.[5] The general failure to recognize the privacy rights of nonnationals is by no means limited to the United States or its partners in the so-called "Five-Eyes" alliance (United Kingdom, Canada, Australia, and New Zealand). On the contrary, few if any countries – democratic or otherwise – offer the kinds of protections for foreign nationals subject to their intelligence-gathering operations that have been demanded of the U.S. government in the aftermath of the NSA-Affair.

The Member States of the United Nations have taken tentative steps in the direction of new international standards regarding the right to privacy in the context of extraterritorial and transnational surveillance programs, including the appointment of a new Special Rapporteur on privacy.[6] But it is inconceivable that the surveillance reforms being debated in the shadow of the NSA-Affair can be achieved through a UN Convention, an additional protocol to the International Covenant on Civil and Political Rights (ICCPR), or ushered in through the adoption of a "digital bill of rights."[7]

---

[3] Id.

[4] See, e.g., David Murakami Wood and Steve Wright, Surveillance and Security Intelligence after Snowden (Part 1), 13 SURVEILLANCE & SOC'Y No. 2 (2015); EUROPEAN UNION AGENCY FOR FUNDAMENTAL RIGHTS, SURVEILLANCE BY INTELLIGENCE SERVICES: FUNDAMENTAL RIGHTS SAFEGUARDS AND REMEDIES IN THE E.U. (2015) [hereinafter E.U. SAFEGUARDS AND REMEDIES].

[5] See, e.g., E.U. member state practice described in EU SAFEGUARDS AND REMEDIES, supra note 4.

[6] The Right to Privacy in the Digital Age, U.N. Doc. A/C.3/69/L.26/Rev.1 (Nov. 19, 2014), www.un.org/ga/search/view_doc.asp?symbol=A/C.3/69/L.26/Rev.1.

[7] Adam Alexander, Digital Surveillance 'Worse Than Orwell,' Says New UN Privacy Chief, THE GUARDIAN (Aug. 24, 2015, 02:50 PM), www.theguardian.com/world/2015/aug/24/we-need-geneva-convention-for-the-internet-says-new-un-privacy-chief ("The first UN

In the absence of coordinated and systematic reform at the international level, it is more likely that public outrage over the NSA-Affair might instead encourage moves toward "technological sovereignty."[8] This would involve the push for a set of proposals to create protected, national information infrastructures, following the model currently used in China and other less-open states.[9] This could damage the norms and technical standards that support an open, global Internet, which is a major foreign policy objective of most democratic states and which is widely embraced as a global public good.[10]

This chapter attempts to map a path toward new international standards for foreign intelligence collection. The aims of this new regime are to achieve increased transparency, control, and oversight of national surveillance practices. We first compare the major reform initiatives to date as they relate to foreign surveillance and its oversight. This exercise suggests that the legal framework for foreign intelligence collection in the United States – as enhanced by the Presidential Policy Directive of January 2014 and the USA FREEDOM Act enacted in the summer of 2015 – contains clearer rules and greater limits than the equivalent regime of almost all E.U. Member States. The new American framework falls short of many expectations. Still, with respect to foreign nationals, it provides the authority to collect, use, and share data. It also establishes considerable oversight of these activities. In the absence of clear and specific rules in other countries, ironically the United States now serves as a baseline for foreign surveillance standards. This is the case despite the

---

privacy chief has said the world needs a Geneva convention style law for the internet to safeguard data and combat the threat of massive clandestine digital surveillance."). *See* Geneva Academy of International Humanitarian Law and Human Rights, *The Right to Privacy in the Digital Age: Meeting Report*, GENEVA ACADEMY (Feb. 2014), www.geneva-academy.ch/docs/ResearchActivities/Report_TheRightoPrivacy.pdf.

[8] TIM MAURER, ROBERT MORGUS & ISABEL SKIERKA MIRKO HOHMANN, TECHNOLOGICAL SOVEREIGNTY: MISSING THE POINT? 54 (2015), *available at* www.newamerica.org/down loads/Technological_Sovereignty_Report.pdf ("Technological sovereignty has been used as an umbrella term to suggest a spectrum of different technical and non-technical proposals, ranging from the construction of new undersea cables to stronger data protection rules. Many of them are not new but have developed greater political traction over the past year.").

[9] *Id.*

[10] *Id. See also* Hamadoun I. Touré, *Statement from the ITU Secretary-General Dr Hamadoun I. Touré*, ITU (Mar. 17, 2014), www.itu.int/en/osg/Pages/statement-march2014.aspx ("I would like to reiterate what I have said many times: the Internet is a global public good and therefore all nations and peoples should have an equal say in its running and development").

fact that the European Convention on Human Rights, which requires the protection of the rights of all those within States parties' jurisdiction, sets a higher general standard than that which results from the U.S. government's interpretation of its international human rights law obligations – especially the American insistence that its human rights obligations only apply within its territory.[11]

Our goal is to identify options that would set a high ceiling rather than a low floor for human rights protection and accountability. In this vein, we attempt to identify key issues relevant to all signals intelligence reform efforts. We also hope to provide an analytical framework to guide the development of new standards with sensitivity for realistic options for reform.

B Proposals for Surveillance Reform

For all the shock and outrage generated by the NSA-Affair, many of the current questions around extraterritorial surveillance capabilities, national sovereignty, human rights protection and the need for international agreements limiting the interception of communications had already been raised by the European Parliament's 2001 report on "the existence of a global system for the interception of private and commercial communications (ECHELON interception system)."[12] More proposals for surveillance reform have been tabled since the Snowden disclosures, the four most prominent of which we draw on to help frame the discussion that follows.

First are the thirteen "necessary and proportionate" principles, elaborated prior to the Snowden revelations. These principles seek to codify and apply international human rights law obligations to all forms of communications surveillance.[13] Second are the five principles for

---

[11] UN Human Rights Committee, Concluding Observations on the Fourth Report of the United States of America para. 4, CCPR/C/USA/CO/4 (Apr. 23, 2014) ("The Committee regrets that the State party continues to maintain the position that the Covenant does not apply with respect to individuals under its jurisdiction, but outside its territory.").

[12] *Report on the Existence of a Global System for the Interception of Private and Commercial Communications (ECHELON interception system) (2001/2098(INI))*, European Parliament Temporary Committee on the ECHELON Interception System (July 11, 2001), http://cryptome.org/echelon-ep-fin.htm#13.

[13] *International Principles on the Application of Human Rights to Communications Surveillance* (May 2014), https://en.necessaryandproportionate.org/TEXT [hereinafter Necessary and Proportionate Principles].

surveillance reform endorsed by eight of the United States's best known technology companies in December 2013. These market actors urged governments around the world to enact the recommended measures and to put them into practice.[14] Third are the forty-six recommendations of President Obama's Review Group on Intelligence and Communications Technologies – some of which were influential in the more limited Presidential Policy Directive and USA FREEDOM Act, both of which were implemented in the wake of the NSA-Affair.[15] Fourth is the report of the European Parliament Civil Liberties (LIBE) Committee special enquiry into the NSA-Affair.[16] Table 1 provides a summary of the different sets of principles, with an emphasis on how they relate to state surveillance of nationals of other countries.

The four sets of principles/proposals include some broadly similar provisions, such as: restrictions on the large-scale "bulk collection" revealed in Edward Snowden's documents; enhanced disclosure of the legal authorities underpinning orders that compel companies to provide data about their customers; increased transparency around the number and nature of such orders; and better oversight of the agencies conducting communications surveillance. Yet, the proposals differ markedly in their approach, scope, and substance, particularly with regard to forms of judicial control, the rights of subjects of foreign surveillance, and obligations *vis-à-vis* data use and minimization. In particular, the "necessary and proportionate" principles developed by civil society groups make no distinction between surveillance by police or intelligence agencies, or between investigative and preventative measures.[17] Instead, they are

---

[14] *Global Government Surveillance Reform: The Principles* (Dec. 9, 2013), www .reformgovernmentsurveillance.com [hereinafter Company Principles].

[15] *Liberty and Security in a Changing World: Report and Recommendations of The President's Review Group on Intelligence and Communications Technologies*, THE WHITE HOUSE (Dec. 12, 2013), www.whitehouse.gov/sites/default/files/docs/2013-12-12_rg_final_report .pdf [hereinafter Obama Review Group]; Directive on Signals Intelligence Activity (PPD-28), 2014 DAILY COMP. PRES. DOC. (Jan. 17, 2014), www.fbi.gov/about-us/nsb/fbis-pol icies-and-procedures-presidential-policy-directive-28-1 [hereinafter PPD-28]; Uniting and Strengthening America by Fulfilling Rights and Ensuring Effective Discipline Over Monitoring Act of 2015 or the USA FREEDOM Act of 2015, 5 U.S.C. § 552 (2012).

[16] *Report on the US NSA Surveillance Programme, Surveillance Bodies in Various Member States and Their Impact on E.U. Citizens' Fundamental Rights and on Transatlantic Cooperation in Justice and Home Affairs*, Eur. Parl. Committee on Civil Liberties, Justice and Home Affairs (Feb. 21, 2014), www.europarl.europa.eu/sides/getDoc.do?pubRef=-// EP//TEXT+REPORT+A7-2014-0139+0+DOC+XML+V0//EN [hereinafter European Parliament Report].

[17] Necessary and Proportionate Principles, *supra* note 13, Scope of Application.

Table 1 *Summary of Reform Proposals*

Issue	Necessary and Proportionate	Company Principles	Obama Review Group	European Parliament
Mandatory retention of metadata	*a priori* data retention or collection should never be required of service providers[a]	limitations on governments' ability to compel service providers to disclose user data that balances need for data in limited circumstances with users' privacy interests[b]	U.S. government should introduce a system in which metadata is held by private providers or by a private third party; access to such data should be permitted only with an order from FISC[c]	Report refers to opinion of Advocate-General Cruz Villalòn on Directive 2006/24/EC concluding that data retention as a whole is incompatible with Article 52(1) of the Charter of Fundamental Rights of the European Union[d]
Bulk collection	prohibited; see minimization, below	prohibited[e]	end to collection and storage of *all* mass, undigested, nonpublic personal information; any program involving collection or storage of such data must be narrowly tailored to serve an important government interest[f]; agencies should	calls on the U.S. authorities and the E.U. Member States, where this is not yet the case, to prohibit blanket mass surveillance activities[h]; points to world's leading technology companies' call for sweeping changes to

					national surveillance laws, including an international ban on bulk collection of data[i]
Data mining	not addressed	not addressed	Civil Liberties Impact Assessments to ensure that any big data and data-mining programs are statistically reliable, cost-effective and protective of privacy[j]	examine feasibility of creating software allowing targeted information acquisition[g]	not addressed
Judicial control	an independent, impartial, and competent authority capable of establishing that other available less invasive investigative techniques have been considered[k]	reviewing courts should be independent and include an adversarial process[l]	duly enacted laws or properly authorized executive orders[m]; create position of Public Interest Advocate to represent privacy and civil liberties interests before FISC[n]		respect the principles of legality, necessity, proportionality, due process and transparency, in line with the standards of the European Convention on Human Rights as regards data protection, privacy, and the presumption

Table 1 (*cont.*)

Issue	Necessary and Proportionate	Company Principles	Obama Review Group	European Parliament
				of innocence[o]; strict limits on duration and scope of any surveillance ordered unless its continuation is duly justified by the authorizing/oversight authority[p]
Disclosure of legal authorities	see notification, below	disclosure of important rulings in a timely manner so that the courts are accountable to the public[q]	detailed information about legal authorities requiring third parties to hand over personal data to be made available on a regular basis (with strong presumption of transparency for unclassified programs)[r]; nondisclosure orders may only be issued subject to judicial	convinced that secret laws and courts violate the rule of law[u]

468

Rights of subjects of foreign surveillance	access to a fair and public hearing within reasonable time by an independent, competent, and impartial tribunal established by law, except in cases of emergency when there is imminent risk of danger to human life[v]	not addressed	calls on the U.S. to revise legislation without delay so as to recognize the privacy and other rights of E.U. citizens, to provide for judicial redress for E.U. citizens, to put rights of E.U. citizens on an equal footing with rights of U.S. citizens, and to sign the Optional Protocol allowing for complaints by individuals under the ICCPR[y]	USG should apply 1974 Privacy Act to both U.S. persons and non-U.S. persons[w] and explore understandings or arrangements regarding intelligence collection guidelines and practices with respect to each others' citizens with a small number of closely allied governments[x]	finding of reasonable grounds[s] and last for no longer than 180 days without judicial re-approval[t]
Notification of data subjects	individuals should be notified of decisions authorizing communications	not addressed	respect the principle of user notification[i]		not envisaged

Table 1 (*cont.*)

Issue	Necessary and Proportionate	Company Principles	Obama Review Group	European Parliament
	surveillance with enough time and information to enable them to appeal unless notification would seriously jeopardize the purpose for which the surveillance is authorized[z]			
Data minimization	data accessed must be confined to what is reasonably relevant and any excess information collected must be promptly destroyed or returned to the impacted individual[ii]	not addressed	extend provisions on data minimization for U.S. citizens in S.215 of Patriot Act to National Security Letters; PPD-28 effectively extends provisions to all subjects of signals intelligence[iii]	not addressed except as general principle for governance of the Internet[iv]
Onward transmission/	surveillance data can only be accessed by the specified authority and	not addressed	no dissemination of information about non-U.S. persons	not addressed

purpose limitation	used for purpose for which authorization was given[v]	unless the information is relevant to protecting the national security of the United States or its allies[vi]	
Transparency	governments to publish periodic reports and other information relevant to communications surveillance[vii]	companies to publish the number and nature of government demands for user information; governments should also promptly disclose this data publicly[viii]	recipients of orders may publicly disclose on a periodic basis general information about the number of such orders, the number complied with, general categories of information and number of users affected unless government makes compelling demonstration that disclosures endanger national security[ix]; government should publicly disclose on a regular basis general data about such orders[x]	only refers to transparency in general terms; calls for E.U. proposal on standardized general terms and conditions for online and telecommunications services[xi]

Table 1 (*cont.*)

Issue	Necessary and Proportionate	Company Principles	Obama Review Group	European Parliament
Oversight	independent mechanisms that ensure transparency and accountability and have the authority to access all potentially relevant information about state actions, including, where appropriate, access to secret or classified information, to evaluate whether the state has been transparently and accurately publishing information about the use and scope of communications surveillance	strong checks and balances[xiii]	Director of National Intelligence should establish a mechanism to monitor the collection and dissemination activities of the Intelligence Community to ensure they are consistent with the determinations of senior policymakers. To this end, the Director of National Intelligence should prepare an annual report on this issue to the National Security Advisor, to be shared with the Congressional	should be based on both democratic legitimacy (strong legal framework, ex ante authorization and ex post verifcation) and adequate technical capability and expertise – the majority of current E.U. and U.S. oversight bodies dramatically lack both, in particular the technical capabilities[xv]; should include power to conduct on-site visits, a robust set of powers of interrogation, adequate resources

techniques and powers[xii]

intelligence committees[xiv]

and technical expertise, strict independence *vis-à-vis* their respective governments, and a reporting obligation to their respective parliaments[xvi]

[a] Necessary and Proportionate Principles, *supra* note 13, Integrity of communications systems.

[b] Company principles, *supra* note 14, para. 1.

[c] Obama Review Group, *supra* note 15, Recommendation 5.

[d] European Parliament Report, *supra* note 16, Preamble.

[e] Company principles, *supra* note 14, para. 1.

[f] Obama Review Group, *supra* note 15, Recommendation 4.

[g] Obama Review Group, *supra* note 15, Recommendation 20.

[h] European Parliament Report, *supra* note 16, para. 21.

[i] European Parliament Report, *supra* note 16, para. 17.

[j] Obama Review Group, *supra* note 15, Recommendations 35 & 36.

[k] Necessary and Proportionate Principles, supra note 13, Proportionality & Competent Judicial Authority.

[l] Company principles, *supra* note 14, para. 2.

[m] Obama Review Group, *supra* note 15, Recommendation 13.

n Obama Review Group, *supra* note 15, Recommendation 35.

o European Parliament Report, *supra* note 16, para. 22.

p European Parliament Report, *supra* note 16, para. 77.

q Company principles, *supra* note 14, para. 2.

r Obama Review Group, *supra* note 15, Recommendation 7.

s That disclosure would significantly threaten the national security, interfere with an ongoing investigation, endanger the life or physical safety of any person, impair diplomatic relations, or put at risk some other similarly weighty government or foreign intelligence interest.

t Obama Review Group, *supra* note 15, Recommendation 8.

u European Parliament Report, *supra* note 16, para. 14.

v Necessary and Proportionate Principles, *supra* note 13, Due process.

w Obama Review Group, *supra* note 15, Recommendation 14.

x Obama Review Group, *supra* note 15, Recommendation 21.

y European Parliament Report, *supra* note 16, para. 30.

z Necessary and Proportionate Principles, *supra* note 13, "User notification" Principle (Such authorization must granted by the authority authorizing the surveillance and the individual affected should be notified as soon as the risk is lifted or within a reasonably practicable time period, whichever is sooner, and in any event by the time the communications surveillance has been completed.).

i European Parliament Report, *supra* note 16, para. 22.

ii Necessary and Proportionate Principles, *supra* note 13, Proportionality & Competent Judicial Authority.

iii Obama Review Group, *supra* note 15, Recommendation 3; *see also* PPD-28, *supra* note 15, § 4(a)(i) o.c.

iv European Parliament Report, *supra* note 16, para. 106.

v   Necessary and Proportionate Principles, *supra* note 13, Proportionality & Competent Judicial Authority.

vi Obama Review Group, *supra* note 15, Recommendation 13(4).

vii Necessary and Proportionate Principles, *supra* note 13, Public Oversight.

viii Company Principles, *supra* note 14, para. 2.

ix Obama Review Group, *supra* note 15, Recommendation 9.

x   Obama Review Group, *supra* note 15, Recommendation 10.

xi European Parliament Report, *supra* note 16, para. 62.

xii Necessary and Proportionate Principles, *supra* note 13, Public oversight.

xiii Company principles, *supra* note 14, para. 2.

xiv Obama Review Group, *supra* note 15, Recommendation 18.

xv European Parliament Report, *supra* note 16, para. 74.

xvi European Parliament Report, *supra* note 16, para. 79.

designed to apply "regardless of the purpose for the surveillance – law enforcement, national security, or any other regulatory purpose."[18] They also make no distinction between the rights of nationals and nonnationals subject to surveillance by a particular government.[19] Finally, they urge that the data subject be notified that surveillance has taken place and that he or she be given full access to a judicial process in order to pursue a challenge to the warrant or order that authorized the surveillance measures.[20]

At the other end of the spectrum, the "company principles" make no mention of individual rights and assume instead that, given adequate opportunity, communications service providers and data controllers will always advocate in their customers' best interests and challenge those surveillance requests they deem to be overbroad or illegitimate.[21] Between these approaches lie the proposals presented by President Obama's review panel. Among its comprehensive forty-six recommendations, the panel urged extending protections in the 1974 Privacy Act to non-U.S. persons, which the Presidential Policy Directive (PPD) of January 2014 went some way toward meeting,[22] and recommended the introduction of a "Public Interest Advocate" into the proceedings of the Foreign Intelligence Surveillance Court,[23] an idea taken up in the USA FREEDOM Act's *amicus curiae* provisions.[24]

It should be repeated, however, that these and other standards proposed by the Review Group (and even the much weaker version adopted by the President in the PPD) mean that U.S. law has by far the most specific and transparent statement of principles, procedures, and oversight for foreign intelligence collection.[25] Any international attempt to raise these standards to a higher level will have to recognize the United States as the new benchmark, and point toward tighter controls in other states.

---

[18] Necessary and Proportionate Principles, *supra* note 13, Preamble.
[19] Necessary and Proportionate Principles, *supra* note 13, Changing Technology and Definitions.
[20] Necessary and Proportionate Principles, *supra* note 13, User Notification and Right to Effective Remedy.
[21] Company Principles, *supra* note 14.
[22] Obama Review Group, *supra* note 15, Recommendation 14; PPD-28, *supra* note 15, Preamble ("Our signals intelligence activities must take into account that all persons should be treated with dignity and respect, regardless of their nationality or wherever they might reside, and that all persons have legitimate privacy interests in the handling of their personal information.").
[23] Obama Review Group, *supra* note 15, Recommendation 28.
[24] 50 U.S.C. § 1803(i) (2010).   [25] *See* Chapter 6 in this volume.

C   A Roadmap for Multilateral Standards

The global political and economic pressure generated by the NSA-Affair provides an opportunity to modernize standards across the democratic world so that the legal regime ensures respect for privacy especially by accounting for the way that information technology is transforming social and material life, and with those changes, the capacity for states to conduct surveillance.

This opportunity will be missed if attempts are not made to establish a process that genuinely involves multiple stakeholders and, thereby, seeks to bridge the gaps between the views of different interest groups and the silos in which they continue to operate. More research, new ideas, and much discussion are required from across the wide-range of interested communities. But it is already clear that the *lacuna* in human rights protection caused by foreign intelligence gathering and exchange can only be addressed through a transnational process anchored in common goals and shared objectives. We suggest focusing specifically on three overarching questions with a focus on how they relate to SIGINT collection and the privacy rights (or lack thereof) of foreign nationals/ noncitizens:

I.   What laws and procedures authorizing surveillance should be upgraded or put in place?
II.   What rules should govern the operational practice?
III.   What methods of oversight and accountability should apply to these laws and practices?

These questions reflect the existing structure of surveillance policy and practice in most countries and can be answered by considering what intelligence agencies should be allowed to do, how they should be allowed to do it, and how their actions should be scrutinized and held in compliance with fundamental rights and democratic responsibilities.

I   Laws and Procedures for Authorizing Surveillance

Three fundamental issues must be addressed in order to establish a clear procedure for seeking authorization of communications surveillance for SIGINT purposes: the justification, the scope, and the scale of the surveillance.

The first issue is the specific national security purposes for which surveillance may be justified. The U.S.'s Presidential Policy Directive

(PPD) offers a point of departure insofar as it moves beyond mere "relevance" to national security or foreign policy (the standard that has long provided a catch-all justification for American SIGINT operations).[26] But even the PPD leaves a large gap to the international human rights law requirements argued for by the UN High Commissioner for Human Rights and Special Rapporteur on human rights and counter-terrorism,[27] whose interpretation is that any interference in the right to privacy on national security or foreign policy grounds must be legitimate, proportionate, narrowly proscribed, and necessary in a democratic society.[28]

The second issue is the standard of privacy protection that applies extraterritorially to the communications of persons subject to foreign intelligence collection. Most states pay little attention to the privacy rights of nonnationals affected by SIGINT collection.[29] In a departure from this tradition, the UN Special Rapporteur on human rights and counter-terrorism concluded "States are legally bound to afford the same protection to nationals and nonnationals, and to those within and outside their jurisdiction."[30]

Current law and practice relies overwhelmingly on distinctions that technology has rendered more difficult, if not impossible, to draw. For example, most legal regimes seek to enforce distinctions between internal and external communications, citizens and noncitizens, content and traffic.[31] The effect of these distinctions is that they permit the use of a lower standard of protection for communications data relating to extra-territorial communications acts, foreign nationals, and "mere" metadata. It is clear that international law places an obligation on states to

---

[26] Exec. Order No. 12,333, § 3.5(e) 3 C.F.R 200 (1981 Comp.), *reprinted in* 50 U.S.C. § 401 (Supp. V 1981) ("*Foreign intelligence* means information relating to the capabilities, intentions, or activities of foreign governments or elements thereof, foreign organizations, foreign persons, or international terrorists.").

[27] The Right to Privacy in the Digital Age – Report of the Office of the United Nations High Commissioner for Human Rights, U.N. Doc. A/HRC/27/37 (June 30, 2014); Report of the UN Special Rapporteur on the Promotion and Protection of Human Rights and Fundamental Freedoms While Countering Terrorism, U.N. Doc. A/69/397 (Sept. 23, 2014).

[28] *Id.*   [29] *See* Chapter 15 in this volume.

[30] Report of the UN Special Rapporteur on the Promotion and Protection of Human Rights and Fundamental Freedoms While Countering Terrorism para. 45, U.N. Doc. A/69/397 (Sept. 23, 2014).

[31] *See, e.g.*, in the United States, the specific protections given to U.S. persons in 50 U.S.C. § 1881(a). In the United Kingdom, see the much broader interception permitted of "external" communications where one or both ends is outside the British Isles, under the Regulation of Investigatory Powers Act 2000, § 8(4).

recognize the right to privacy and security of communications of foreign surveillance targets,[32] but a fierce debate is now underway among international jurists as to the precise nature of those obligations and the best way of demarcating them within the international legal order.[33] Yet, even if some clarity is provided by the United Nations Human Rights Committee through its periodic reviews of State Party compliance with the ICCPR, it will still be left to states parties to the human rights treaties to meet these commitments through domestic law and policy. How can this be achieved and what standards will apply?

In Europe much of the debate about how to protect European citizens from America's foreign intelligence gathering operations has come to rest on E.U. data protection law, which requires foreign companies and third states processing data that originates in the European Union to apply an adequate standard of protection for that data.[34] But that regime has been thrown into disarray by the European Court's ruling that the E.U. Data Retention Directive violated primary European law.[35] The United States is now unusual in explicitly offering (*via* the PPD-28) any kind of guarantee to respect the privacy of foreign persons subject to its foreign intelligence gathering operations, but these protections are still set at a lower standard than those afforded to U.S. persons.

This issue has long hampered E.U.–U.S. cooperation in the area of counter-terrorism, and following the NSA-Affair it has become the greatest impasse between the United States, which has taken only limited steps to amend its privacy framework, and many in the European Union who demand equal treatment and the possibility for European citizens to seek redress for violations of privacy. The U.S. administration has offered to support legislation that would give E.U. citizens the same rights as U.S. citizens under the Privacy Act "to seek judicial redress for intentional or willful disclosures of protected information, and for refusal to grant access or to rectify any errors in that information" where such information was shared for law enforcement purposes.[36] The U.S. Congress is

---

[32] *See* Chapter 5 in this volume.

[33] *See* Marko Milanovic, *Human Rights Treaties and Foreign Surveillance: Privacy in the Digital Age*, 56 HARVARD INT'L L.J. 81 (2015).

[34] *See* European Parliament Report, *supra* note 16, paras. 35–49 & 59–71.

[35] *See* Chapter 21 in this volume. In the meantime, as part of the reform enacted by the US FREEDOM Act, the U.S. has adopted the now-rejected European approach to data retention.

[36] *Attorney General Holder Pledges Support for Legislation to Provide E.U. Citizens with Judicial Redress in Cases of Wrongful Disclosure of Their Personal Data Transferred to the*

considering a Judicial Redress Act that would allow citizens of designated foreign countries to bring civil actions against certain U.S. government agencies for these purposes.[37]

In leveraging data protection in this way, the European Union is essentially advocating for foreign nationals to be able to complain to privacy commissioners or surveillance courts, where these exist, about international data sharing that affects them. Although E.U. data-protection law provides for a reciprocal complaint mechanism, many intelligence agencies in Europe are effectively beyond the scope of national data protection authorities, and it is doubtful that all E.U. Member States provide redress where foreign or military intelligence is concerned (the Investigatory Powers Tribunal in the United Kingdom has considered complaints from nonnationals against GCHQ's bulk collection programs).[38]

An alternative to a top-down standard is for cooperating states to limit SIGINT collection within agreed geographical areas in favor of a commitment to Mutual Legal Assistance Treaties based on due process and a greater degree of protection for one another's citizens. But even in the European Union, where mutual recognition and cooperation between different jurisdictions is most developed, the larger powers clearly retain a strong preference for unilateral intelligence gathering capabilities.[39] This undermines the trust needed for states to commit to greater police and judicial cooperation in sensitive areas such as counter-terrorism. As with the proposed "no-spy" agreements, such cooperation mechanisms raise the prospect of two-tier or even three-tier protection systems. In that regime a state's citizens enjoy the highest level of protection, the citizens of friendly states enjoy reciprocal guarantees, and persons located in the rest of the world remain largely unprotected. In this scenario, the

---

U.S. for Law Enforcement Purposes, DEPARTMENT OF JUSTICE (June 25, 2014), www.justice.gov/opa/pr/attorney-general-holder-pledges-support-legislation-provide-eu-citizens-judicial-redress.

[37] Judicial Redress Act of 2015, H.R. 1428, 114th Cong. (2015–2016).

[38] Complainants include Liberty, Privacy International, Bytes for All (Pakistan), the American Civil Liberties Union, Amnesty International, the Canadian Civil Liberties Association, the Egyptian Initiative for Personal Rights, the Hungarian Civil Liberties Union and the Irish Council for Civil Liberties. *See* Liberty (The Nat'l Council of Civil Liberties) v The Gov't Commc'ns Headquarters & Others, UKIPTrib 13_77-H (2014).

[39] Monica Den Boer, *Counter-Terrorism, Security and Intelligence in the E.U:. Governance Challenges for Collection, Exchange and Analysis,* 30 INTELLI. NAT'L SECUR., 402–19 (2015).

broader goal of a harmonized and universal rights-based international standard for protecting the privacy of foreign nationals goes unrealized.

The third issue is the amount of surveillance that is allowed. SIGINT practice, and the discourse around it, is typically framed in terms of looking for "needles" in data "haystacks"; a narrative that views bulk interception and data-storage as an *a priori* legitimate tool in effective intelligence operations and not an infringement of individuals rights *per se*.[40] Additionally, it is frequently assumed by the Intelligence Community that the infringement of the data subject's rights takes place only at the point at which their data is retrieved from the "haystack" on the basis of a search term, keyword, or another selector. At this point the justification for privacy violations is reduced to a matter of SIGINT operating procedures. But the UN Special Rapporteur on Counter-Terrorism and Human Rights called the bulk collection programs exposed in the NSA-Affair "indiscriminately corrosive of online privacy and imping[ing] on the very essence of the right guaranteed by Article 17. In the absence of a formal derogation from States' obligations under the Covenant, these programs pose a direct and ongoing challenge to an established norm of international law."[41]

If we start from this principle, then the challenge is to think through the contours of legitimate intelligence gathering in today's increasingly data-driven world. Any discussion about the authorization of SIGINT operations and access to communications systems overlaps with debates about private sector mandates for "data retention," that is, the imposition of obligations on service providers to retain metadata for law enforcement and security purposes. The NSA review panel proposed an end to the bulk metadata collection by the NSA, but suggested instead that service providers should keep data for 30 months, with access controlled by the surveillance courts.[42] Carriers offering toll telephone services are

---

[40] E. Nakashima & J. Warrick, *For NSA Chief, Terrorist Threat Drives Passion to "Collect It All*,' WASH. POST (July 14, 2013), www.washingtonpost.com/world/national-security/for-nsa-chief-terrorist-threat-drives-passion-to-collect-it-all/2013/07/14/3d26ef80-ea49-11e2-a301-ea5a8116d211_story.html ("Rather than look for a single needle in the haystack, [NSA Director Gen. Keith B. Alexander's] approach was, 'Let's collect the whole haystack,' said one former senior U.S. intelligence official who tracked the plan's implementation. 'Collect it all, tag it, store it. . . . And whatever it is you want, you go searching for it.'").

[41] Report of the UN Special Rapporteur on the Promotion and Protection of Human Rights and Fundamental Freedoms While Countering Terrorism para. 59, U.N. Doc. A/69/397 (Sept. 23, 2014).

[42] Obama Review Group, *supra* note 15, Recommendation 5.

already required to keep bills containing much of this data for 18 months by FCC regulation.[43]

The substance of this recommendation was implemented by the USA FREEDOM Act of 2015, which requires "specific selection terms" to be used in FBI applications for a Foreign Intelligence Surveillance Act court order requiring the production of call detail records.[44] But the European Union has moved in the other direction. The Court of Justice of the European Union ruled that the EC Data Retention Directive – and the principle that private providers should keep data for 6–24 months – was a violation of European primary law and an intrusion upon a fundamental right, compounded by a lack of safeguards.[45]

The need for some standards in this area is underscored by the tension that arises when one country has retention and access policies that violate the laws of another. The consequences of such a mismatch can be clearly seen in the *Schrems* decision of the Court of Justice of the European Union (CJEU),[46] which invalidated the "Safe Harbor" agreement that previously allowed U.S. companies to transfer personal data from the European Union based on a self-certified commitment to principles providing an "adequate" level of protection under E.U. law, since the European Commission had determined that:

> the United States authorities were able to access the personal data transferred from the Member States to the United States and process it in a way incompatible, in particular, with the purposes for which it was transferred, beyond what was strictly necessary and proportionate to the protection of national security ... data subjects had no administrative or judicial means of redress enabling, in particular, the data relating to them to be accessed and, as the case may be, rectified or erased.[47]

This is a problematic ruling insofar as none of the E.U. Member States give one another this level of protection – despite the fact that they are, in principle, required to do so by the Charter of Fundamental Rights. This misalignment between law and practice could lead to major disruption in commercial data markets, which few believe can be resolved easily – since the U.S. government is unlikely to significantly further change its

---

[43] 47 C.F.R. § 42.6 (1986).   [44] 50 U.S.C. § 1861(b)(2) (2010).

[45] Joined Cases C-293/12 & C-594/12, Digital Rights Ireland Ltd v. Minister for Commc'ns., Marine and Nat. Res. & Others, 2013 EU:C: 845. *See* Chapter 21 in this volume.

[46] Case C-362/14, Maximillian Schrems v. Data Prot. Comm'r., 2015 ECLI:EU:C:627 (hereinafter Schrems).

[47] Schrems, *supra* note 88, § 99.

national security standards of surveillance – and ultimately promises to be a reckoning in the E.U. courts as the Member States' own discriminatory practices toward one another (on national security grounds) are challenged. The "Privacy Shield" to which the United States and the European Union have agreed in response to the CJEU's Schrems Case attempts to resolve the discrepancy but the certainty of renewed challenges before the CJEU leave its long-term value in doubt.[48]

Such standards must therefore address both the powers of national security agencies and the specific role of private sector actors mandated by law to participate in SIGINT operations, including the appropriate legal procedure for responding to intelligence requests.[49]

II   Rules Governing Intelligence Practice

The second key element of privacy-conscious intelligence reform is the need for enforceable standards that restrict authorized surveillance operations to their intended purpose and that guard against abuse. This includes rules on the minimization of data collected during a legitimate operation, limits on the uses for which data can be collected, provisions for the deletion of data not relevant to an investigation, and provisions for retaining data. This set of criteria should also address conduct that should be prohibited or more tightly controlled, such as the undermining of encryption protocols, the use of "zero-day attacks," and the sharing of data internationally where this would have the effect of circumventing domestic privacy safeguards.

With respect to minimization, broadly comparable standards for operational data protection in the police sector exist in many democracies.[50] Part of the challenge is to effectively extend and apply those standards to

---

[48] *See* Mark Scott, *U.S. and Europe in "Safe Harbor" Data Deal, but Legal Fight May Await,* N.Y. Times (Feb. 2, 2016), *available at* www.nytimes.com/2016/02/03/technology/us-europe-safe-harbor-data-deal.html?_r=0; *Swords and Shields: America and the European Union Have Reached a Deal on Data Protection,* The Economist (Feb. 6, 2016), *available at* www.economist.com/news/europe/21690035-america-and-european-union-have-reached-deal-data-protection-swords-and-shields.

[49] *See* Ian Brown & Douwe Korff, *Digital Freedoms in International Law,* Global Network Initiative (June 2012), https://globalnetworkinitiative.org/sites/default/files/Digital%20Freedoms%20in%20International%20Law.pdf.

[50] European states have developed detailed standards in the Council of Europe's *Recommendation No. R(87)15E regulating the use of personal data in the police sector,* September 17, 1987, and the *Data Protection Directive for Police and Criminal Justice Authorities* agreed by the E.U. Council, Parliament and Commission in December 2015. European

the largely unregulated realm of foreign intelligence gathering. The basic provisions in the PPD provide a point of departure.[51]

The "big data" dimension of the SIGINT framework – and the issue of how analytical tools capable of profiling entire personal networks can be regulated or minimized – makes the matter more complex. In this context we should take seriously, as did President Obama's Review Group, the possibility that technology could ultimately minimize infringements of privacy by performing certain techniques in "real time."[52] This could reduce much of the need for bulk interception and storage – although a presidential review committee expressed some skepticism as to the effectiveness of such technology.[53]

With respect to conduct that should be prohibited, the Snowden documents revealed many of the operational practices of U.S. and U.K. intelligence agencies. Comparable information for other countries is not available. Nevertheless, a case-by-case assessment of the legitimacy of the actions that have been revealed can be used to inform standards internationally. More general concerns about the purpose of surveillance – economic espionage and "political policing," for example – can also be addressed. The PPD appears to provide a straightforward prohibition on economic espionage but does so only by ruling out the collection of information for the purpose of gaining a competitive advantage for U.S. business. This has allowed the ongoing surveillance of economic actors for national security purposes.[54]

Commission Press Release IP/15/6321, Agreement on Commission's E.U. data Protection Reform Will Boost Digital Single Market (Dec. 15, 2015).

[51] PPD-28, *supra* note 15, § 4(a)(i) ("The sharing of intelligence that contains personal information is necessary to protect our national security and advance our foreign policy interests, as it enables the United States to coordinate activities across our government. At the same time, however, by setting appropriate limits on such sharing, the United States takes legitimate privacy concerns into account and decreases the risks that personal information will be misused or mishandled. Relatedly, the significance to our national security of intelligence is not always apparent upon an initial review of information: intelligence must be retained for a sufficient period of time for the IC to understand its relevance and use.").

[52] Obama Review Group, *supra* note 15, Recommendation 20.

[53] COMMITTEE ON RESPONDING TO SECTION 5(D) OF PRESIDENTIAL POLICY DIRECTIVE 28: THE FEASIBILITY OF SOFTWARE TO PROVIDE ALTERNATIVES TO BULK SIGNALS INTELLIGENCE COLLECTION, BULK COLLECTION OF SIGNALS INTELLIGENCE: TECHNICAL OPTIONS (2014).

[54] Office of the Director of National Intelligence, *Statement by Director of National Intelligence James R. Clapper on Allegations of Economic Espionage*, IC ON THE RECORD

There is a geopolitical dimension to these issues as well, as evidenced in debates over the existence and extension of "no-spy" agreements, raising the prospect of groups of countries agreeing to limitations with respect to one another's territories and/or citizens.[55] The European Parliament has even suggested that the E.U. principle of "sincere cooperation" requires that Member States refrain from conducting intelligence activities in other Member States' territories.[56] President Obama's Review Group proposed a set of criteria for negotiating special arrangements covering these issues with third states.[57]

III   Methods of Oversight and Accountability

The third element of communications surveillance reform concerns the methods of oversight and accountability that should apply to these laws and practices. Even if detailed new laws restricting the authorization of surveillance operations and strict operational procedures for their conduct were to be put in place, the age old question of "who watches the watchers" requires substantial thought and novel application. Despite comprising the majority of the work undertaken by intelligence agencies, in many countries SIGINT is subject to minimal oversight. This is due to the reasons outlined above, as well as to the outdated notion that SIGINT does not affect citizens or domestic communications. So what role should the executive, judicial, and legislative branches of government play with respect to the operations and activities of SIGINT agencies?

There is growing acknowledgment that existing models of oversight and accountability have failed to ensure that surveillance is both properly authorized and legitimately practiced, but there is no consensus on what constitutes best practices in terms of SIGINT collection and oversight. This is hardly surprising given the difficulty of applying these precepts to organizations that are shrouded in secrecy and fiercely resistant to change.[58]

(Sept. 8, 2013), http://icontherecord.tumblr.com/post/60712026846/statement-by-dir ector-of-national-intelligence.

[55] David E. Sanger, *U.S. and Germany Fail to Reach a Deal on Spying*, N.Y. TIMES (May 1, 2014), www.nytimes.com/2014/05/02/world/europe/us-and-germany-fail-to-reach-a-deal-on-spying.html?_r=0.

[56] European Parliament Report, *supra* note 16, para. 7.

[57] Obama Review Group, *supra* note 15, Recommendation 21.

[58] *But see* GLOBAL INTELLIGENCE OVERSIGHT: GOVERNING SECURITY IN THE TWENTY-FIRST CENTURY (Zachary Goldman ed., *forthcoming* 2016).

Two issues in particular must be addressed. First is the role of the judiciary – both in authorizing intelligence collection and, as noted above, reviewing the legality of specific operations and programs. In the United States the Review Group proposed the introduction of an adversarial counsel at the proceedings of the FISA Court, or some other form of ombudsman to guard the public interest. The USA FREEDOM Act requires the presiding judges of the FISA Court and its Court of Review to appoint at least five individuals to be eligible to act as *amicus curiae* to advise the courts on legal and technological matters.[59] Many European states do not even have clear legal processes in which such individuals could participate.

Second is the capacity for legislative review and democratic oversight within a classified environment. This issue is intimately related to the resources available for oversight, the technical competence of the reviewers, the avoidance of regulatory capture (of the overseer by the overseen), and the intractable difficulty of imposing any mechanism for international oversight of national intelligence agency cooperation.

The Civil Liberties (LIBE) Committee in the European Parliament has called for "minimum European standards or guidelines on the (*ex ante* and *ex post*) oversight of intelligence services ... including the issue of oversight bodies being considered as a third party under the 'third party rule', or the principle of 'originator control', on the oversight and accountability of intelligence from foreign countries."[60] This is the principle that prevents intelligence agencies disclosing the source or content of information received through bilateral cooperation. It undermines in practice the potential for oversight, because it prevents any review of international exchanges of intelligence data.

The LIBE report calls on E.U. Member States to establish the power for oversight bodies to conduct on-site visits of intelligence agencies, interview senior officials, and ensure strict independence of inspectors from their respective governments. For such functions to be credible in the eyes of the public, standards for transparency and reporting requirements – including the methods used to correct instances of noncompliance (whether malicious or otherwise) – must be developed.

The vast majority of data relevant to foreign intelligence collection is gathered, stored, processed, and transmitted by private companies. For this reason, frameworks for oversight and accountability must be

---

[59] 50 U.S.C. § 1803(i) (2010).   [60] European Parliament Report, *supra* note 16, para. 63.

broadened to encompass these entities, who find themselves effectively sandwiched between their legal obligations to provide data to national security agencies, on one side, and their users' reasonable and legitimate expectations with regard to their right to privacy, on the other side. This situation is particularly acute for U.S. companies, whose data represents a highly disproportionate share of the world's Internet traffic.[61] Their role is further compromised because, even when they provide networks and services that are entirely outside the United States, they remain subject to U.S. law.[62]

Transparency is an essential part of any oversight system and provides a good foundation for public accountability more broadly.[63] In the past few years, some Internet service providers have begun publishing comparative international information about government and law enforcement agency demands for their users' data.[64] Since the Snowden revelations, more companies have begun producing transparency reports, and those already doing so have petitioned the U.S. government to let them publish information about their hitherto secret dealings with the NSA.[65] The U.S. government is now cooperating with the private sector to permit some level of transparency with aggregate figures.

The key question is whether the current model of aggregated transparency reporting can provide sufficient detail to allow the public to ascertain the true extent of surveillance practices and the extent to which

---

[61] While difficult to measure conclusively, there are plausible claims that up to 70 percent of global Internet traffic flows through Northern Virginia. *See* Ingrid Burrington, *Why Amazon's Data Centers Are Hidden in Spy Country*, THE ATLANTIC (Jan. 8, 2016), www.theatlantic.com/technology/archive/2016/01/amazon-web-services-data-center/423147/#about-the-authors.

[62] *See, e.g., In the Matter of a Warrant to Search a Certain E-mail Account Controlled and Maintained by Microsoft Corporation*, 15 F.Supp.3d 466 (S.D.N.Y. 2014).

[63] *See* Global Principles on National Security and the Right to Information (June 12, 2013), OPEN SOCIETY FOUNDATIONS, www.opensocietyfoundations.org/publications/global-principles-national-security-and-freedom-information-tshwane-principles (Tshwane Principles); I. Brown, *Transparency to Protect Internet Freedom: A Shared Commitment*, Council of Europe CDMSI (2013) Misc21, (Dec. 2013).

[64] One comprehensive recent example is from Vodafone. *See Law Enforcement Disclosure Report*, VODAFONE, www.vodafone.com/content/index/about/sustainability/law_enforcement.html# (last visited Jan. 24, 2016).

[65] *See, e.g.,* Google Transparency Report, GOOGLE, www.google.com/transparencyreport/userdatarequests/?hl=en; Twitter Transparency Report, TWITTER, https://transparency.twitter.com/information-requests/2015/jan-jun; Yahoo Transparency Report, YAHOO!, https://transparency.yahoo.com; Microsoft Transparency Hub, MICROSOFT, www.microsoft.com/about/business-corporate-responsibility/transparencyhub/.

the private sector is pushing back against undue or overbroad requests. What policy changes would incentivize legal departments to push back on dubious requests for communications data?

A final, related issue involves the steps that data controllers should take to protect data from unauthorized access. A failure on the part of key service providers to fully encrypt communications flowing between their data centers enabled intelligence services to intercept personal information on a grand scale.[66] Some companies have already implemented new encryption standards or announced their intention to do so in future.[67] President Obama's Review Group and the European Parliament are firmly behind mandatory minimum levels of security, including encryption on both commercial services and communications networks.[68] If strong encryption were to become an industry standard, the question would become whether, and under what circumstances, companies could be legally compelled to hand over encryption keys.[69]

D Next Steps

Governments on both sides of the Atlantic have strong political and economic interests in repairing the damage caused by the NSA-Affair. Snowden's revelations have particularly called into question the development of a rights-based Internet that is valued as a trustworthy information system. Yet, despite the severity of the consequences, political

[66] B. Gellman and A. Soltani, *NSA Infiltrates Links to Yahoo, Google Data Centers Worldwide, Snowden Documents Say,* WASH. POST, (Oct. 30, 2013), www.washingtonpost.com/world/ national-security/nsa-infiltrates-links-to-yahoo-google-data-centers-worldwide-snowden-documents-say/2013/10/30/e51d661e-4166-11e3-8b74-d89d714ca4dd_story.html ("According to a top-secret accounting dated Jan. 9, 2013, the NSA's acquisitions directorate sends millions of records every day from internal Yahoo and Google networks to data warehouses at the agency's headquarters at Fort Meade, Md. In the preceding 30 days, the report said, field collectors had processed and sent back 181,280,466 new records – including 'metadata,' which would indicate who sent or received e-mails and when, as well as content such as text, audio and video.").

[67] T. Risen, *NSA Surveillance Spurs Tech Giants to Add Encryption,* U.S. NEWS (Nov. 1, 2013), www.usnews.com/news/articles/2013/11/01/nsa-surveillance-spurs-tech-giants-to-add-encryption.

[68] Obama Review Group, *supra* note 15, Recommendation 29; European Parliament Report, *supra* note 16, para. 82.

[69] *See, e.g.,* Eric Lichtblau & Katie Benner, *Apple Fights Order to Unlock San Bernardino Gunman's iPhone,* N.Y. TIMES (Feb. 17, 2016), *available at* www.nytimes.com/2016/02/18/technology/apple-timothy-cook-fbi-san-bernardino.html?_r=0.

responses have focused either on consolidating power over information networks at the national level (technological sovereignty) or finding a way to manage public alarm without disrupting the practices of the intelligence agencies. Many governments will adopt both of these approaches and, in so doing, they will only deepen the problem. Without better answers we risk diminishing the value of the Internet as a public good, the sanctity of civil and human rights in a digital world, and the commercial imperative of trustworthy online markets.

The European Parliament's report notwithstanding, the loudest response from the European Union has been economic rather than political. Among the most common reactions is a threat to extract penalties from U.S. companies doing business in Europe who do not comply with E.U. data protection rules, a position that will continue to affect negotiations on the Transatlantic Trade and Investment Partnership, the E.U. Data Protection Regulation, the United States's status as a "safe harbor" and the existing E.U.–U.S. agreements on the exchange of Passenger Name Records (of airline travelers), and SWIFT data (on international financial transactions).[70] While these agreements are being leveraged to advocate higher privacy standards, they cannot solve the fundamental problems engendered by a lack of trust in foreign intelligence gathering capabilities and unilateral decisions about what is and is not acceptable.

Even the European governments most critical of the United States have been unwilling to reveal the nature of their own intelligence-gathering practices, or to commit themselves to the specific, rights-based standards that they demand of Washington. None have stepped forward with a clear proposal for bringing communications surveillance under the rule of law, especially to ensure the protection of privacy across borders. At the same time, no national movements have emerged in which political and economic stakeholders are united around a pragmatic call for reform. Silicon Valley has been quick to call for government reform, but it is less sanguine on the digital rights aspect of that agenda. Civil society needs to show how the principles for necessary and proportionate communications surveillance can be applied in practice to legitimate national security operations.

This kind of coalition is most likely to emerge in Germany. It is the most influential country in the European Union, and the public

---

[70] European Parliament Report, *supra* note 16, paras. 28–33, 44–50 & 59.

outrage over the NSA-Affair presents the best opportunity for initiating a reform effort and championing a common standard among European states. The German parliamentary opposition has been among the most outspoken in its demands for restrictions on the NSA, particularly in the wake of revelations that the German Chancellor was a personal target of surveillance, and that the country's foreign intelligence agency (the *Bundesnachrichtendienst*) cooperated with the NSA to monitor the French government, European Commission, and large European businesses such as Airbus.[71] Germany is also a recognized leader in commercial data protection, and German technology companies have been quick to develop "made in Germany" cybersecurity products.

The *Bundestag* has set up a Parliamentary Committee of Inquiry,[72] and the political energy that has animated the public debate over the NSA-Affair continues unabated, refreshed by new revelations published in *The Guardian* or *Der Spiegel*. For many in Germany, the NSA is a serial violator of human and civil rights, and these excesses fit into the narrative of American overreach in the name of counter-terrorism that includes torture, Guantanamo Bay, and unrestricted drone assassinations. If organized around a policy agenda, these politics could fuel a German-led coalition within the European Union that is strong enough to change minds in Washington. Germany has a unique combination of political power in Europe, commercial interest in strengthening its digital economy, and international integrity on issues of data privacy and human rights. The circumstances are ripe for Germany to step forward and link up with parallel movements in Europe and beyond to present a strong and credible alternative to Washington – building on the reforms already introduced by the U.S. Administration and Congress through PPD-28 and the USA FREEDOM Act. If Germany were to show leadership on domestic reform, it could provide a model for the European Union, and in turn become the basis for transatlantic agreement and an international regime.

The European Union and United States already have a particularly close relationship in the areas of economic and security cooperation, and since 9/11 have reached agreements on financial and travel surveillance,

---

[71] Manuel Bewarder & Thomas Sebastian Vitzthum, *Gabriel Zieht Rote Linie für Merkel in BND-Affäre*, DIE WELT (May 4, 2015), www.welt.de/politik/deutschland/art icle140475736/Gabriel-zieht-rote-Linie-fuer-Merkel-in-BND-Affaere.html.

[72] *See* Chapter 12 in this volume.

and mutual legal assistance.[73] Ultimately, the two sides will have to resolve the issues raised in this chapter if existing E.U.–U.S. cooperation is to be maintained or deepened. One potential framework for the approach to the United States is the "New Transatlantic Agenda" (NTA) between the United States and European Union, stemming from the 1990 "Transatlantic Declaration."[74] With sufficient political will this framework could provide a starting point for the adoption of multilateral agreements limiting communications surveillance. Ultimately, it might serve as a model for the rest of the world. In the short term, these issues could be taken up by a core group of E.U. Member States, resulting in some kind of "mini-lateral" agreement that can gradually be extended.

---

[73] Agreement between the European Union and the United States of America on the Processing and Transfer of Financial Messaging Data from the European Union to the United States for the Purposes of the Terrorist Finance Tracking Program 5–14, July 27, 2010, O.J. (L 195); Agreement between the European Union and the United States of America on the Processing and Transfer of Passenger Name Record (PNR) Data by Air Carriers to the United States Department of Homeland Security (DHS) 18–25, Aug. 4, 2007, O.J. (L 204) (2007 PNR Agreement); Agreement on Mutual Legal Assistance between the European Union and the United States of America 34–42, July 19, 2003, O.J. (L 181).

[74] U.S.A., European Community and Its Member States, *Transatlantic Declaration on E.C.-U.S. Relations*, 1990, http://eeas.europa.eu/us/docs/trans_declaration_90_en.pdf (last visited Jan. 24, 2016); U.S.A. and European Union, *New Transatlantic Agenda* (Dec. 5, 1995), http://eeas.europa.eu/us/docs/new_transatlantic_agenda_en.pdf.

18

Espionage, Security Interests, and Human Rights in the Second Machine Age

NSA Mass Surveillance and the Framework of Public International Law

BY SILJA VÖENEKY

"The same tools that make it possible to monitor the world in greater detail also give governments and their adversaries the ability to monitor what people are doing and who they are communicating with. There's a genuine tension between our ability to know more and our ability to prevent others from knowing about us. When information was mostly analog and local, the laws of physics created an automatic zone of privacy. In a digital world, privacy requires explicitly designed institutions, incentives, laws, technologies, or norms about which information flows are permitted or prevented and which are encouraged or discouraged."

– Erik Brynjolfsson/Andrew McAfee, *The Second Machine Age* 253 (2014)

A   Introduction

Many states argue that state security and the safety of their populations depend on the information that they gather without the consent of the subjects of their surveillance operations.[1] For those states, whether to exist or not to exist seems to depend on their decision to spy or not to spy.

The phenomenon of espionage is not a new one, it has been a common practice in international relations in both times of war and times of peace.[2] But, in contrast to the Cold War era when espionage usually meant the

---

[1] *See, e.g.*, Rory Carroll, *NSA Surveillance Needed to Prevent ISIS Attack, Claims Former Intelligence Chair*, THE GUARDIAN (Apr. 22, 2015, 8:52 AM), www.theguardian.com/us-news/2015/apr/22/mass-surveillance-needed-isis-attack-mike-rogers; Angelique Chrisafis, *France Passes New Surveillance Law in Wake of Charlie Hebdo Attack*, THE GUARDIAN (May 5, 2015, 12:11 PM), www.theguardian.com/world/2015/may/05/france-passes-new-surveillance-law-in-wake-of-charlie-hebdo-attack.

[2] Christian Schaller, *Spies, in* MAX PLANCK ENCYCLOPEDIA OF PUBLIC INTERNATIONAL LAW 435 ¶ 2 (Rudiger Wolfrum ed., 2012).

practice of secretly gathering information about a foreign government or state,[3] today we are facing two phenomena that are radically changing the traditional concept of espionage. On the one hand, there has been a revolution in the means of espionage. On the other hand, the twenty-first century has presented a radical change in the focus of security concerns.[4]

The revolution in the means of espionage is caused by the new tools of the digital world, what some have called the "second machine age."[5] Governments' capacity – not to mention companies', non-state actors', and even individuals' – to keep people and foreign governments under surveillance, including the interception and collection of data, has increased to an unprecedented scale.[6] We can now speak of digital mass surveillance and the gathering of bulk information by many different entities.[7] Today, mass surveillance is not only a means for governments to watch people within their own territory but – in the form of cross-border and transnational surveillance collection and analysis of data generated in foreign countries – also a new and additional tool of espionage that is neither difficult nor expensive.[8]

This new tool of espionage intersects with new major security concerns. Most important security concerns today are the unknowns and the so-called "black swans." The two concepts, while separate, are interrelated: "unknowns" are all the facts and people about which nothing is known; "black swans" are understood as very rare cases with the potential for huge consequences but whose probability of occurrence is, if not zero, then very close to it.[9] These are persons and things which we

---

[3] For the historical dimension of espionage, *see* WOLFGANG KRIEGER, GESCHICHTE DER GEHEIMDIENSTE (2009).

[4] For an analysis, *see* BENJAMIN WITTES & GABRIELLA BLUM, THE FUTURE OF VIOLENCE 1 (2015).

[5] ERIK BRYNJOLFSSON & ANDREW MCAFEE, SECOND MACHINE AGE: WORK, PROGRESS, AND PROSPERITY IN A TIME OF BRILLIANT TECHNOLOGIES 7 et seq. (2014).

[6] *See, e.g.*, Human Rights Council, U.N. Doc. A/HRC/27/37, at 3, The Right to Privacy in the Digital Age: Report of the Office of the High Commissioner for Human Rights (June 30, 2014). The report is based on G.A. Res. 69/166, The Right to Privacy in the Digital Age (Dec. 18, 2014). For a comprehensive overview see BRUCE SCHNEIER, DATA AND GOLIATH, 23 et seq., 26 (2015).

[7] UN Doc. A/HRC/27/37, *supra* note 6, at 3.

[8] For the blurring lines between the concepts of espionage and mass surveillance, see B. Schneier, who speaks of government agencies that "could spy on entire populations." *See* SCHNEIER, *supra* note 8, at 24.

[9] *See* NASSIM NICHOLAS TALEB, THE BLACK SWAN: THE IMPACT OF THE HIGHLY IMPROBABLE 44 (2d ed. 2007).

do not yet know about, but which have the potential to kill people, damage our environment and economy, destabilize our governments. In all these ways, "black swans" can endanger the very existence of a state and a society, now or in the near future.

How are these two dynamic phenomena linked? One example comes from a current debate. During the last years there has been an intense discussion about biosecurity issues.[10] The notion of biosecurity describes the problem of dual use in the biological sciences. There nobody knows how to rationalize or quantify the risk of bioterrorism, that is, the misuse of biological agents by terrorists. But if a society and its state organs do not know whether there is a concrete danger of misuse of certain viruses, it is difficult to argue that there is a need for certain tools to prevent these kinds of terrorist attacks, for instance by establishing a new dual-use-research-of-concern commission that evaluates experiments or by setting rules of nonpublication if the results of experiments could be misused by criminals.[11] The tools needed to prevent national and transnational bioterrorism would limit the freedom of research. The freedom of research is protected expressly as a human right by some state constitutions and by the Charter of Fundamental Rights of the European Union.[12] At the international level, scientific research is protected by the freedom of thought and the freedom of expression.[13] The latter freedoms are international human rights protected *inter alia* by Art. 18 and Art. 19 of the International Covenant on Civil and

---

[10] *See, e.g.*, GERMAN ETHICS COUNCIL, BIOSECURITY – FREEDOM AND RESPONSIBILITY OF RESEARCH 9 (2014), www.ethikrat.org/files/opinion-biosecurity.pdf; WITTES & BLUM, *supra* note 4, at 24, 64, 233; Ali Nouri & Christopher F. Chyba, *Biotechnology and biosecurity, in* GLOBAL CATASTROPHIC RISKS 450 (Nick Bostrom & Milan M. Ćirković eds., 2008).

[11] For further details, *see* Silja Voeneky, *Biosecurity – Freedom, Responsibility, and Legitimacy of Research*, ORDNUNG DER WISSENSCHAFT 2/2015, at 117, www.ordnungderwissenschaft.de/2015-2/pdfs/10_2015_voeneky_biosecurity_odw.pdf.

[12] *See, e.g.*, GRUNDGESETZ [GG] [BASIC LAW], art. 5(3), *translation at* www.gesetze-im-internet.de/englisch_gg/ ("Arts and sciences, research and teaching shall be free. The freedom of teaching shall not release any person from allegiance to the constitution.") (Ger.); Charter on the Fundamental Rights of the European Union, Dec. 7, 2000, 2000 O.J. (C 364) 1 art. 13 ("The arts and scientific research shall be free of constraint. Academic freedom shall be respected.") (E.U.).

[13] *See, e.g.*, United Nations Educational, Scientific & Cultural Organization, UNESDOC 29 C/Resolution 16 art. 12, Universal Declaration on the Human Genome and Human Rights, (Nov. 11, 1997) ("Freedom of research, which is necessary for the progress of knowledge, is part of freedom of thought.").

Political Rights (ICCPR)[14] and Art. 9 and Art. 10 of the European Convention for the Protection of Human Rights and Fundamental Freedoms (ECHR).[15] States can limit the freedom of research only if the limits can be justified with a legitimate aim. *Abstract* dangers – by themselves – do not seem to be sufficient to limit this right. Hence, in this conflict, it seems to be a rational response by a government to minimize the unknowns and to substantiate whether it and its citizens face *concrete* dangers.

One can even go a step further. If the unknowns and the so-called "black swans" are the big security concerns of the twenty-first century, then it is not astonishing that information gathering has become one of the main – if not the most important – tools to make a society safe and to secure the existence of a state. Information gathering today, in the second machine age, is a very smooth tool. It is clean and operates beneath the surface of our everyday lives. Usually we do not see or hear it. It is highly questionable whether we "feel" it even if we know that it is taking place: There is no clicking in the telephone line as there once was with wiretapping measures pursued by the East German secret police.[16] Of course, big-data and Internet espionage are not virtual, but they seem to be. Besides, the secretive collection of data in the Internet is something we are used to. Many of us see it as a contribution to personal convenience, and even personal advantage. Digital information gathering is integrated into our daily life in commercial contexts.[17] We have become accustomed to personalized advertisements, which correlate to our desires and wishes, while we are surfing the Internet. Mostly there was no express informed consent given beforehand. This does not mean – and I do not mean to

---

[14] International Covenant on Civil and Political Rights art. 17, Dec. 19. 1966, S. Exec. Doc. No. E, 95-2 (1978), 999 U.N.T.S. 171 [hereinafter ICCPR].

[15] European Convention on Human Rights art. 8, Nov. 4, 1950, E.T.S. 5, 213 U.N.T.S. 221 (as amended by Protocol Nos. 11 & 14) [hereinafter ECHR]. *See* Sorguç v. Turkey, App. No. 17089/03 ¶ 35 f., HUDOC (Jan. 21, 2010), http://hudoc.echr.coe.int/eng?i=001-93161#{"itemid":["001-93161"]}; Vallauri v. Italy, App. No. 39128/05 ¶ 30, HUDOC (Oct. 20, 2009), http://hudoc.echr.coe.int/eng#{"fulltext":["39128/05"],"languageisocode":["FRE"],"documentcollectionid2":["GRANDCHAMBER","CHAMBER"],"itemid": ["001-95150"]} (Fr.); Hans Christian Wilms, Die Unverbindlichkeit der Verantwortung 333 f., 348 f. (2015).

[16] For the comparison of the (expensive) means of the East German government surveilling its population to the modern tools of mass surveillance, see Schneier, *supra* note 8, at 23.

[17] *Id.* at 23 ("Corporate surveillance has grown from collecting as little data as necessary to collecting as much as possible.").

suggest – that the commercial collection of Internet users' data presents the same problems as Internet-based mass surveillance espionage carried out by a state organ, such as the United States' National Security Agency (NSA), but the lines are blurring. In any case, some state-access to communications data may be facilitated by private firms' collection and storage of information, which, in turn, the law requires them to turn-over to the state to aid intelligence gathering operations.

Therefore it is not astonishing that there were massive demonstrations against the plans to base NATO Pershing missiles in Germany during the 1980s. But, despite some anger over the so-called NSA-Affair, there have hardly been any demonstrations against the NSA and other information gathering by foreign States or collaborating companies. The modern tools for fighting today's security dangers are smart, clean, and without an angst-inducing symbolic manifestation.[18]

The situation is made even more complicated by the fact that the persons who endanger a society often lived or live in free and democratic states. It is not the far-off Taliban in Afghanistan that threaten to destabilize France, Germany, the United Kingdom, the United States, or any other western country. The main enemies were or are embedded in our societies: the terrorists of 9/11 studied and lived in Hamburg, Germany; the Boston terrorists studied and lived in the United States.[19] The same is true for the terrorists of the "Charlie Hebdo" attacks that took place in Paris in January of 2015; they were French citizens.[20] Most

---

[18] See, e.g., Meia Chita-Tegmark, Terminator Robots and AI Risk, HUFFPOST TECH (Mar. 2, 2015, 5:59 AM), www.huffingtonpost.com/meia-chitategmark/terminator-robots-and-ai-risk_b_6788918.html.

[19] Mohamed Atta, one of the 9/11 terrorists and the hijacker-pilot of American Airlines Flight 11, studied for many years at the Technische Universität Hamburg-Harburg, Germany; Tamerlan Tsarnaev, one of the terrorists of the Boston Marathon Bombing, studied at the Bunker Hill Community College, Boston, United States; Dzokhar Tsarnaev, the second Boston Marathon Bombing terrorist, studied at the University of Massachusetts Dartmouth in the United States and had been a U.S. citizen since 2012; see Peter Finn et al., Tsarnaev Brothers' Homeland Was War-Torn Chechnya, WASH. POST (Apr. 19, 2013), http://wpo.st/2UP80; Press Release, U.S. Federal Bureau of Investigation, Updates on Investigation Into Multiple Explosions in Boston (Oct. 21, 2013), www.fbi .gov/news/updates-on-investigation-into-multiple-explosions-in-boston/updates-on-investigation-into-multiple-explosions-in-boston; Andreas Ross, Der Körper der Muslime, FRANKFURTER ALLGEMEINE (Mar. 4, 2015), www.faz.net/aktuell/politik/ausland/ amerika/prozess-gegen-boston-bomber-dzokhar-tsarnaev-beginnt-13461975.html.

[20] See Karsten Polke Majewski, et al., Drei Tage Terror in Paris, ZEIT ONLINE (May 11, 2015), www.zeit.de/feature/attentat-charlie-hebdo-rekonstruktion (for the background of the two gunmen, the brothers Kouachi.).

of the terrorists of the latest Paris attacks, in November of 2015, were also citizens of France and Belgium.[21] European newspapers are full of news that terrorist fighters of the so-called Islamic State (IS) or Al Qaida are now streaming back to western countries after having been radicalized by the terror groups and fighting for them in armed conflicts in Syria and Iraq.[22] According to a certain rationale, everyone living in France, Germany, the United Kingdom, the United States, or any other western country could be the next Mohamed Atta, Dzokhar Tsarnaev, "Jihadi John,"[23] or member of an IS militant group. If this is true, everyone seems to be a legitimate aim of secret data collection.

A sometimes very concrete, sometimes very diffuse danger to the public is answered and shadowed by a diffuse and abstract form of observation. Sweeping, comprehensive, and indiscriminate surveillance has a rational aim (i.e., to decrease the unknowns). Often, it is not perceptible and, therefore, it is no burden on our daily lives – at least as long as our assets are not frozen, we are not denied access to another state, we are not detained, and we are not killed by a drone missile strike.[24] But the latter are only rare consequences of mass surveillance that only few of us will hardly ever face.

---

[21] See Andrew Higgins & Milan Schreuer, *Paris Attack Was Work of 3 Teams, an "Act of War" by ISIS, France Asserts*, N.Y. TIMES (Nov. 15, 2015), p. 1, 17; *Was wir über die Attentäter wissen*, FRANKFURTER ALLGEMEINE ZEITUNG (Nov. 15, 2015), www.faz.net/aktuell/politik/terror-in-paris/was-wir-ueber-die-attentaeter-wissen-13913677.html.

[22] Eric Schmitt & David D. Kirkpatrick, *Strategy Shift for ISIS: Inflicting Terror in Distant Lands*, N.Y. TIMES (Nov. 14, 2015), www.nytimes.com/2015/11/15/world/europe/strategy-shift-for-isis-inflicting-terror-in-distant-lands.html; Matthias Gebauer & Raniah Salloum, *German Jihadists: Officials Fear Return of Syrian War Veterans*, SPIEGEL ONLINE (Apr. 26, 2013, 2:22 PM), www.spiegel.de/international/world/german-officials-fear-return-of-islamist-fighters-in-syria-a-896745.html; Thorston Jungholt & Karsten Kammholz, *Deutschland fürchtet die Rückkehr die IS-Kämpfer*, DIE WELT (Dec. 28, 2014), www.welt.de/politik/deutschland/article135787624/Deutschland-fuerchtet-die-Rueckkehr-der-IS-Kaempfer.html; *see also* Jon Henley, *How Do You Deradicalise Returning ISIS Fighters?*, THE GUARDIAN (Nov. 12, 2014, 2:21 PM), www.theguardian.com/world/2014/nov/12/deradicalise-isis-fighters-jihadists-denmark-syria.

[23] The IS militant known as "Jihadi John", who has been pictured in the videos of the beheadings of Western hostages, was a British national from west London who finished his computing degree at the University of Westminster, United Kingdom, in 2009; *see* *'Jihadi John' Named as Mohammed Emwazi from London*, BBC (Feb. 26, 2015), www.bbc.com/news/uk-31637090.

[24] *See* Chapter 8 in this volume.

B   Espionage and General Public International Law

It is not surprising that public international law has an ambivalent approach toward espionage. The very banal reason is that states, the main creators of international law, have an ambivalent approach to espionage. There are several elements to the international law espionage framework.

First, to fight one's enemies and protect one's population from attacks – stemming from terrorists or other states – are legitimate state interests protected by international law. The *right* to self-defense is spelled out by the Charter of the United Nation as an "inherent," that is, natural *right* (Art. 51 U.N. Charter).[25] Some even argue that there is a "responsibility to protect" as an emerging norm of international law[26] and hence sovereignty includes the *duty* of states to protect their populations from mass atrocities and crimes.[27] Even if one does not want to rely on the rather vague concept of "responsibility to protect," then one can deduce such a *duty* from the human right to life that is laid down in human rights treaties: a state has to protect this human right, not only against infringements by state officials, but also against infringements by private actors, and protect its population.[28] The Human Rights Committee expressly stated in its 2015 Draft general comment concerning Art. 6 ICCPR (Right to life) that "state parties must take adequate preventive measures in order to protect individuals against being murdered or killed by criminals and organized crime or militant groups, including armed or terrorist groups."[29]

---

[25] U.N. Charter art. 51 ("Nothing in the present Charter shall impair the inherent right of individual or collective self-defence if an armed attack occurs against a Member of the United Nations, until the Security Council has taken measures necessary to maintain international peace and security.").

[26] *See* Ingo Winkelmann, *Responsibility to Protect, in* MAX PLANCK ENCYCLOPEDIA OF PUBLIC INTERNATIONAL LAW, *supra* note 2, at 965, ¶¶ 1, 22; INTERNATIONAL COMMISSION ON INTERVENTION AND SOVEREIGNTY, THE RESPONSIBILITY TO PROTECT – REPORT OF THE INTERNATIONAL COMMISSION ON INTERVENTION AND STATE SOVEREIGNTY ¶ 2.24 (2001), http://responsibilitytoprotect.org/ICISS%20Report.pdf.

[27] *See* G.A. Res. 60/1, ¶ 138 (Sept. 16, 2005).

[28] *See, e.g.,* ICCPR, *supra* note 14, at art. 6 ("Every human being has the inherent right to life. This right shall be protected by law."); 5 Christian Tomuschat, *International Covenant on Civil and Political Rights (1966), in* MAX PLANCK ENCYCLOPEDIA OF PUBLIC INTERNATIONAL LAW, *supra* note 2, at 639, ¶¶ 18–19; Human Rights Committee, U.N. Doc. CCPR/C/GC/R.36/Rev.2, Draft General Comment No. 36, Article 6 (Right to life), ¶¶ 23 *et seq.* (Sept. 2, 2015).

[29] U.N. Doc. CCPR/C/GC/R.36/Rev.2, *supra* note 28, ¶ 25.

Second, there is neither a general prohibition nor a general justification of espionage in international law.[30] Even according to the laws of war – often referred to as international humanitarian law – a wartime spy does not have the status of a combatant.[31] Hence, once captured he or she is not a prisoner of war and can be prosecuted according to the criminal laws of the capturing state. This has been laid down since 1907 in Art. 29 and 30 of the Annex to the Convention respecting the Laws and Customs of War on Land.[32] In contrast, in an international armed conflict, combatants are allowed to attack and kill enemy combatants as long as there is a military aim and no excessive so-called collateral damage.[33] Spies, however, are not given the same privileges, which means that there is no *per se* justification for espionage according to international law, even in times of war; hence spies can only be subject to prosecution for violating domestic offenses.[34]

Third, espionage for the purpose of preventing terrorism is part of the system of collective security.[35] The U.N. Security Council (UNSC) has repeatedly qualified "any act of terrorism ... as a threat to peace and security"[36] and has strongly urged States to prevent the transit of

---

[30] Richard Baxter, *So-Called "Unprivileged Belligerency": Spies, Guerrillas, and Saboteurs, in* HUMANIZING THE LAWS OF WAR: SELECTED WRITINGS OF RICHARD BAXTER 37, 44 (Detlev F. Vagts *et al.* eds., 2013); Wolfgang Ewer & Tobias Thienel, *Völker-, unions- und verfassungsrechtliche Aspekte des NSA-Datenskandals*, 67 NEUE JURISTISCHE WOCHENSCHRIFT 30, 31 (2014). *But see Ex parte Quirin*, 317 U.S. 1 (1942), at 31: "The spies ... are familiar examples of belligerents who are generally deemed not to be entitled to the status of prisoner of war, but to be offenders against the law of war subject to trial and punishment by military tribunals." *See* Jonathan Hafetz, *Policing the Line: International Law, Article III, and the Constitutional Limits of Military Jurisdiction*, 2014 WIS. L. REV. 681, 729 (2014); Baxter, *supra*, at 52; Jens D. Ohlin, *The Common Law of War*, at 1, 10 (forthcoming article).

[31] *See* Convention (IV) respecting the Laws and Customs of War on Land and its Annex arts. 29–30, Oct. 18, 1907, 205 C.T.S. 277; Protocol I Additional to the Geneva Conventions of August 12, 1949, and Relating to the Protection of Victims of International Armed Conflicts art. 46 ¶ 1, concluded June 8, 1977, 1125 U.N.T.S. 3 [hereinafter Additional Protocol I].

[32] *See* Additional Protocol I, *supra* note 31, at art. 46.

[33] This is part of customary international law; for the laws of targeting in an international armed conflict according to treaty law see Additional Protocol I, *supra* note 31; *see also* Robin Geiß, *Land Warfare, in* MAX PLANCK ENCYCLOPEDIA OF PUBLIC INTERNATIONAL LAW, *supra* note 2, at 678 ¶¶ 22 et seq.

[34] Ohlin, *supra* note 30, at 12.   [35] Schaller, *supra* note 2, at ¶¶ 2, 12.

[36] S.C. Res. 1618, ¶ 1 (Aug. 4, 2005); *see also Resolutions*, SECURITY COUNCIL COUNTER-TERRORISM COMMITTEE, www.un.org/en/sc/ctc/resources/res-sc.html (last visited Dec. 10, 2015).

terrorists to and from countries, the traffic in arms for terrorists, and the financing that supports terrorists.[37] The UNSC has recalled that all States must cooperate fully in the fight against terrorism, in order to find and bring to justice any person who supports, facilitates, participates or attempts to participate in the financing, planning, preparation, or commission of terrorist acts.[38] With these obligations in mind, intelligence cooperation has become an accepted instrument for combating terrorism.[39] Counter-terrorism operations and measures are not only part of the United Nations' system of collective security, but they are also at the center of the new NATO doctrine after 9/11.[40]

Fourth, this does not mean that counter-terrorism trumps everything else and no legal limits exist according to international law. States may adopt counter-terrorism measures only "as may be necessary and appropriate, and in accordance with their obligations under international law."[41] The UNSC has expressly stated that states must ensure that any measures taken "comply with all of their obligations under international law, in particular international human rights law."[42]

C   Espionage, Mass Surveillance, and International Human Rights Law

In the face of general public international law's ambivalence toward espionage, an important question to answer is whether–and if so to what extent–the existing rules of international human rights law limit espionage by means of mass surveillance.

The protection of private life, as enshrined in Art. 8 of the ECHR and Art. 17 of the ICCPR (to which Germany, Russia, and the United States are parties[43]), guarantees information privacy.[44]

---

[37] S.C. Res. 1618, *supra* note 36, ¶ 6.   [38] *Id.* ¶ 7.   [39] Schaller, *supra* note 2, at ¶ 2.

[40] NATO, Active Engagement, Modern Defence: Strategic Concept for the Defence and Security of the Members of the North Atlantic Treaty Organization, ¶ 25, adopted by Heads of State and Government, Nov. 20, 2010, www.nato.int/strategic-concept/pdf/Strat_Concept_web_en.pdf; NATO, Partnership Action Plan against Terrorism, ¶ 16.1.2, Nov. 22, 2002, www.nato.int/cps/en/SID-E86475A7-0E19BA88/natolive/official_texts_19549.htm.

[41] S.C. Res. 1624, ¶ 1 (Sept. 14, 2005).   [42] *Id.* at operative clause 2.

[43] For a list of States Parties, *see 4. International Covenant on Civil and Political Rights*, UNITED NATIONS TREATY COLLECTION, http://treaties.un.org/Pages/ViewDetails.aspx?src=TREATY&mtdsg_no=IV-4&chapter=4&lang=en (last visited Dec. 11, 2015).

[44] ICCPR, *supra* note 14, at art. 17 ("1. No one shall be subjected to arbitrary or unlawful interference with his privacy, family, home or correspondence, nor to unlawful attacks on

But the decisive question is whether states parties to human rights treaties are bound to respect these human rights protections outside their own territory?[45] It is not a convincing argument that human rights protections do not restrict a state's actions with respect to persons acting outside the state's territory and the victims of espionage.[46] In a global order with transnational state activities, it is contrary to the object and purpose of human rights, construed as universal values, to limit their application to the territory of a state party. It is not the territory of a state that is the decisive element. Instead, it is decisive whether a person falls under the *jurisdiction* of a state. Contrary to the view expressed in the *Banković* decision of the European Court of Human Rights,[47] one has to

---

his honour and reputation. 2. Everyone has the right to the protection of the law against such interference or attacks."); ECHR, *supra* note 15, at art. 8 ("1. Everyone has the right to respect for his private and family life, his home and his correspondence. 2. There shall be no interference by a public authority with the exercise of this right except such as is in accordance with the law and is necessary in a democratic society in the interests of national security, public safety or the economic wellbeing of the country, for the prevention of disorder or crime, for the protection of health or morals, or for the protection of the rights and freedoms of others."). See the clear statement of the state community in GA Res. 68/167, *supra* note 6 ("4. *Calls upon* all states: (a) To respect and protect the right to privacy, including in the context of digital communication; (b) To take measures to put an end to violations of those rights and to create the conditions to prevent such violations, including by ensuring that relevant national legislation complies with their obligations under international human rights law; (c) To review their procedures, practices and legislation regarding the surveillance of communications, their interception and the collection of personal data, including mass surveillance, interception and collection, with a view to upholding the right to privacy by ensuring the full and effective implementation of all their obligations under international human rights law".).

[45] For the domestic, constitutional law version of this question, *see* Chapter 15 in this volume; Chapter 10 in this volume. See also Chapter 5 in this volume.

[46] The International Court of Justice (ICJ) and the Human Rights Council clearly supported the extraterritorial application of human right treaties. *See* Legal Consequences of the Construction of a Wall in the Occupied Palestinian Territory, Advisory Opinion, 2004 I.C.J. Rep. 136, ¶ 111 (July 9); Human Rights Committee, U.N. Doc. A/52/50, Report of the Human Rights Committee to the 53rd Session of the United Nations General Assembly (Sept. 15, 1998). *See also* U.N. Doc. A/HRC/27/37, *supra* note 6, at 11. However, the extraterritorial application of human right treaties is still disputed: The U.S. administrations have always contested this view, referring to the history of the ICCPR, see Tomuschat, *supra* note 28, ¶ 24. *See generally* MARKO MILANOVIC, EXTRATERRITORIAL APPLICATION OF HUMAN RIGHTS TREATIES: LAW, POLICY AND PRINCIPLES (2011).

[47] Banković v. Belgium, App. No. 52207/99, HUDOC (Dec. 19, 2001), http://hudoc.echr .coe.int/eng?i=001-22099#{"itemid":["001-22099"]}. *Banković* was subsequently revisited by the European Court of Human Rights; *see* Marko Milanovic, *Human Rights Treaties and Foreign Surveillance: Privacy in the Digital Age*, 56 HARV. INT'L L.J. 81, 115 f; *see also* Loizidou v. Turkey, App. No. 15318/89, HUDOC (Mar. 23, 1995), http://hudoc.echr.coe

conclude that a state's jurisdiction is implicated even if a state merely exercises factual power on the territory of a nonstate or third party.[48] Factual power is exercised in the conduct of espionage on the territory of another state. If the protection of the private sphere is a universal human right – and a global value – then adverse factual effects must be considered to have the same relevance as adverse legal acts. This is at least true if a state has effective control over the adverse factual effects.[49]

If one agrees with this, then the next question concerns the scope of the right to privacy. In the context of espionage and mass surveillance, the scope of this right would have to extend to information privacy to have any protective effect. The object and purpose of the right suggest that it extends to the targeted collection of data as well as the general stockpiling of data.[50] A restriction of this right by one of these forms must have a legitimate aim and must be proportionate.[51] "Proportionate" means that the reasons for the interference have to be sufficient as well as appropriate with respect to the legitimate aim. In this assessment, the disadvantages for the affected individual have to be weighed against the importance of the legitimate aims pursued by the state. Between these poles a fair balance is necessary. On the one hand, one could argue that preventive data collection would always be disproportional – and a violation of the human right of privacy – if no actual terrorist threat exists. On the other hand, Internet-based monitoring and mass surveillance have only minor effects on privacy (as long as we do not see, hear, or feel the observation) and are, therefore, not *per se* disproportionate intrusions on the human right of privacy in the state's pursuit of a terrorist threat, even if the threat is an abstract one.[52]

.int/eng?i=001-57920#{"itemid":["001-57920"]} (as to the extraterritorial application of human rights treaties).

[48] Robert McCorquodale & Penelope Simons, *Responsibility beyond Borders: State Responsibility for Extraterritorial Violations by Corporations of International Human Rights Law*, 70 Mod. L. Rev. 598, 602 (2007).

[49] UN Doc. A/HRC/27/37, *supra* note 6, at 11.

[50] For an even broader view see UN Doc. A/HRC/27/37, *supra* note 6, at 7.   [51] *Id.* at 11.

[52] *See* Klass v. Germany, App. No. 5029/71, HUDOC (Sept. 6, 1978), http://hudoc.echr.coe .int/eng#{"fulltext":["klass v germany"],"documentcollectionid2":["GRANDCHAM-BER","CHAMBER"],"itemid":["001-57510"]} (where the court denied that a German statute, restricting the secrecy of mail and telecommunication would violate the right to privacy of the applicants (ECHR art. 8)); Association for European Integration and Human Rights and Ekimdzhiev v. Bulgaria, App. No. 62540/00, HUDOC (June 28, 2007), http://hudoc.echr.coe.int/eng#{"fulltext":["62540/00"],"documentcollectionid2":

But any infringement of this human right must be based on a legal rule that is clear and precise.[53] Most importantly, the legal rule has to name the type of information, the group of affected people, the circumstances of the surveillance, and the measures to be used.[54] In order to deter abuse, an effective and independent control mechanism is necessary.[55]

In all of these ways, the framework of international human rights law, as applied to espionage by the means of mass surveillance, is clearer and stricter than the framework of general public international law.

D   The Supplementary Agreement to the NATO Status of Forces Agreement[56]

The question remains whether international human rights law trumps other international rules. Apart from the human rights treaties, the 1959/1993 Supplementary Agreement to the NATO Status of Forces Agreement (Supplementary Agreement) could be decisive as far as espionage in and by Belgium, Canada, France, Germany, the Netherlands, the United Kingdom, and the United States is concerned.[57] For these States the treaty governs the exchange of information, even of personal data.

Article 3 of the Supplementary Agreement deals with the cooperation of German authorities with the authorities and forces of the other states parties mentioned above. The provision states:

["GRANDCHAMBER","CHAMBER"],"itemid":["001-81323"]} (upholding the line of argument presented in Klass v. Germany.).

53 UN Doc. A/HRC/27/37, *supra* note 6, at 32.

54 Rotaru v. Romania, App. No. 28341/95, ¶ 57, 2000-V Eur. Ct. H.R. 109, 132.

55 *See id.* ¶ 59. *See also* Human Rights Committee, General Comment No. 16: The right to respect of privacy, family, home and correspondence, and protection of honour and reputation (Art. 17), Apr. 8, 1988, ¶ 1 et seq.; Dumitru Popescu v. Romania (No. 2), App. No. 71525/01, ¶¶ 72 *et seq.*, HUDOC (July 8, 2004), http://hudoc.echr.coe.int/eng# {"itemid":["001-80352"]}.

56 Agreement between the Parties to the North Atlantic Treaty Regarding the Status of their Forces, June 19, 1951, 4 U.S.T. 1792, 199 U.N.T.S. 67, Bundesgesetzblatt [Federal Law Gazette] 1961 II, at 1183.

57 Agreement to Supplement the Agreement between the Parties to the North Atlantic Treaty regarding the Status of their Forces with respect to Foreign Forces stationed in the Federal Republic of Germany, with Protocol of Signature, Aug. 3, 1959, 14 U.S.T. 531, 481 U.N.T.S. 262, Bundesgesetzblatt [Federal Law Gazette] 1961 II, 1218, as amended by the agreement of March 18, 1993, Bundesgesetzblatt [Federal Law Gazette] 1994 II, at 2594 [hereinafter Supplementary Agreement].

1. In accordance with the obligations imposed by the North Atlantic Treaty upon the contracting parties thereto to render mutual assistance, the German authorities and the authorities of the forces shall cooperate closely to ensure the implementation of the NATO Status of Forces Agreement and of the present Agreement.

2. The cooperation provided for in paragraph 1 of this Article shall extend in particular

(a) to the furtherance and safeguarding of the security, as well as to the protection of the property, of the Federal Republic, of the sending States and of the forces, and *especially to the collection, exchange and protection of all information which is of significance for these purposes.*

(b) to the furtherance and safeguarding of the security, as well as to the protection of the property, of Germans, of members of the forces and members of the civilian components and dependents, as well as of nationals of the sending States who do not belong to these categories of persons.

3. (a) German authorities and the authorities of a Force shall, by taking appropriate measures, ensure close and reciprocal liaison within the scope of the cooperation provided for in paragraphs 1 and 2 of this Article. *Personal data shall be passed on solely for the purposes envisaged in the NATO Status of Forces Agreement and in the present Agreement. Restrictions in possible applications based on the legislation of the Contracting Party supplying the information shall be observed.*

(b) This paragraph shall not impose an obligation on a Contracting Party to carry out measures which would contravene its laws or *conflict with its predominant interests with regard to the protection of the security of the State or of public safety.*[58]

The Supplementary Agreement creates the duty to cooperate and exchange all information that is of significance for the security of the states parties and their troops.[59] As can be deduced from the wording of Art. 3 para. 3, states parties are allowed "to pass" even "personal data" for

---

[58] *Id.*

[59] The Supplementary Agreement is currently the only international treaty in force in this area: In June 2013, Germany negotiated with the Governments of France, the United Kingdom, and the United States, and the administrative agreements of 1968 with these States were nullified by mutual agreement in August 2013; *see* Press Release, Federal Foreign Office, Verwaltungsvereinbarungen zum G10-Gesetz mit U.S.A. und Großbritannien außer Kraft (Aug. 2, 2013), www.auswaertiges-amt.de/DE/Infoservice/Presse/Meldungen/2013/130802-G10Gesetz.html; Press Release, Federal Foreign Office, Verwaltungsvereinbarung zum G10-Gesetz mit Frankreich außer Kraft (Aug. 6, 2013), www.auswaertiges-amt.de/DE/Infoservice/Presse/Meldungen/2013/130806_G10_Frankreich.html; *see also* Thomas Gutschker *et al.*, *Amerika darf Deutsche abhören*, FRANKFURTER ALLGEMEINE (July 7, 2013), www.faz.net/-gpg-7b2ag.

the purposes envisaged in the NATO Status of Forces Agreement and in the NATO SOFA Supplementary Agreement. Restrictions on sharing information rooted in domestic law are permitted only if a state party is "supplying" the information.[60] Para. 3 of Art. 3 was included in the treaty in 1993. The object and purpose of the amendment was to determine the limits of the exchange of personal data between the states parties. Nevertheless, the treaty does not seem to impose limits on espionage carried out by mass surveillance. On the contrary, the treaty stresses that security is a legitimate aim and common concern of all states parties and that only the protection of *the security interests of one state party or of the public safety of that party* trumps the common security concern (Art. 3 para. 3 lit. b: *"conflict with its predominant interests with regard to the protection of the security of the State or of public safety"*). This means, as a first result, that espionage is not prohibited by the Supplementary Agreement, and that – if espionage is justified by the security interests of one State Party, which is usually the case – then all the data collected by espionage need not be passed on to another State Party.

E   Espionage by Mass Surveillance: Lost in Fragmentation?

What does this mean for the duties of the state parties stemming from human rights treaties? How can we bring together the different areas and rules of international law, without being lost in fragmentation?[61] According to the *lex posterior* rule, since the ICCPR came into force in 1976, it could have precedence over the Supplementary Agreement that entered into force in 1959.[62] The Supplementary Agreement also does not have precedence over human rights treaties as *lex specialis*, as the Supplementary Agreement regulates different areas than those covered by the human rights treaties. Even para. 3 of Art. 3 of the Supplementary

---

[60] In German, the wording of Supplementary Agreement art. 3 ¶ 3 reads: "Personenbezogene Daten werden ausschließlich zu den im NATO-Truppenstatut und in diesem Abkommen vorgesehenen Zwecken *übermittelt*. Einschränkungen der *Verwendungsmöglichkeiten*, die auf den Rechtsvorschriften der *übermittelnden Vertragspartei* beruhen, werden beachtet." The text of the agreement was authenticated in German, English, and French in the sense of art. 33 Vienna Convention of the Law of Treaties.

[61] As to this phenomenon, *see generally* G.A. Rep. of the Study Group of the International Law Commission, Fragmentation of International Law: Difficulties Arising from the Diversification and Expansion of International Law, U.N. Doc. A/CN.4/L82 (2006).

[62] However, the ECHR entered into force in 1953; therefore one could argue that the NATO Supplementary Agreement has precedence over the ECHR according to the *lex posterior* rule.

Agreement, which was included in the treaty in 1993 and might prevail over the ICCPR norms as *lex posterior*, states that restrictions in applications based on the legislation of the Contracting Party shall be observed. This should be interpreted as including the rules of international human rights treaties, at least as long as they form part of the national law of the respective State.

A different question is whether the Supplementary Agreement might be a justification for the limitation of human rights.[63] Indeed one might argue – as shown above – that the Supplementary Agreement allows espionage by a U.S. organ (including the NSA) or an organ of another State Party in Germany. But Art. 1 of the Agreement must be taken into account. It provides that "the rights and obligations *of the forces* of the Kingdom of Belgium, Canada, the French Republic, the Kingdom of the Netherlands, the United Kingdom of Great Britain and Northern Ireland and the United States of America *in the territory of the Federal Republic of Germany*" form part of the agreement. Therefore (only) espionage by state organs that form part of "the forces" of these states in the territory of the Federal Republic of Germany is allowed as long as the collection of data is relevant for the security or the protection of the population.[64]

F   Conclusion

Public international law leaves us with a very ambiguous picture in regard to espionage carried out by mass surveillance. This is especially true if one looks more closely at the legal situation of espionage by foreign States in Germany.

Fighting transnational terrorism is a legitimate aim of the international order and part of the new NATO doctrine after 9/11. Indeed, fighting transnational terrorism is necessary in a democratic society in the interests of national security.[65] Besides, the Supplementary Agreement, which does not prohibit espionage and even allows the transfer of personal data

---

[63] Some authors, however, argue that the NATO Supplementary Agreement has improved the protection of private data; *see* Frank Burkhardt & Heinrich Granow, *Das Abkommen zur Änderung des Zusatzabkommens zum NATO-Truppenstatut (ZA-NTS)*, 1995 NEUE JURISTISCHE WOCHENSCHRIFT 424, 426 (1995).

[64] *See* Dieter Deiseroth, *Nachrichtendienstliche Überwachung durch U.S.-Stellen in Deutschland – Rechtspolitischer Handlungsbedarf?*, 2013 ZEITSCHRIFT FÜR RECHTSPOLITIK 194, 196 (2013).

[65] Joachim Wolf, *Der verfassungsrechtliche Nebel der deutsch-amerikanischen "NSA-Abhöraffäre,"* 52 JURISTENZEITUNG 1039, 1046 (2013).

by State organs, is part of the legal order of the Federal Republic of Germany as federal law according to Art. 59 para. 2 of the Basic Law.[66]

There are reasons to argue that there is no violation of the right to privacy even if the new tools of the digital age are used for espionage. This might be the case at least if they are used by State organs that form part of the forces of Belgium, Canada, France, the Netherlands, the United Kingdom, or the United States in Germany.

Yet, if one looks at the broader picture of espionage, mass surveillance, and international law, the key question of proportionality emerges: Is secret, preventive mass data collection always disproportional when no actual terrorist threat exists? Or are the minimal negative factual effects of Internet-based observation proportional in the State's struggle against a – mostly – abstract and diffuse terrorist threat.

The global order must be understood as an order with legally-enshrined values. These values are those protected by human rights treaties, as well as the international security and sovereignty of States, whereby the values enshrined in human rights clearly have primacy. In the end, it is up to the states, especially the democratic countries, to emphasize the existence and relevance of human rights. As long as our governments, as long as the citizens of the states, and as long as we are not convinced that large scale secret data collection and large scale espionage is disproportional in regard to the fight against terrorism, then it will be difficult to argue that a human right is violated.

---

[66] GRUNDGESETZ [GG] [BASIC LAW] art. 59(2).

19

The Need for an Institutionalized and Transparent Set of Domestic Legal Rules Governing Transnational Intelligence Sharing in Democratic Societies

BY SUSANA SÁNCHEZ FERRO

A Introduction

In October of 2013, the Spanish newspaper *El Mundo*[1] and the French newspaper *Le Monde*[2] reported that the United States National Security Agency (NSA) had collected millions of phone records of Spanish and French citizens. Gen. Keith Alexander, Director of the NSA, dismissed those reports as "completely false" and told the House Intelligence Committee that the data were collected directly by NATO allies.[3] The French External Intelligence Agency had provided the United States with records of both phone calls and metadata intercepted from Internet traffic flowing via underwater cables that surface in France.[4] Those cables "carry much of the traffic that flows to Africa and Afghanistan."[5] In exchange, the NSA provided the French Intelligence Services information from areas of the world where France had no intelligence presence.[6]

The French and Spaniards are not the only countries closely cooperating with the Americans. The Dutch Ministers of Interior and Defense informed the Dutch Parliament that the NSO (Dutch Signal Intelligence

---

[1] Glenn Greenwald & Germán Aranda, *La NSA espió 60 millones de llamadas en España en sólo un mes*, EL MUNDO (Oct. 28, 2013), www.elmundo.es/espana/2013/10/28/526dcbad61fd3d07678b456b.html.

[2] Jacques Follorou & Glenn Greenwald, *Comment la NSA espionne la France*, LE MONDE.FR (Oct. 21, 2013), www.lemonde.fr/technologies/article/2013/10/21/comment-la-nsa-espionne-la-france_3499758_651865.html.

[3] Ellen Nakashima and Karen DeYoung, *NSA Chief Said NATO Allies Shared Phone Records with U.S. Spy Agency*, WASH. POST (Oct. 30, 2013), www.washingtonpost.com/world/national-security/top-intelligence-officials-called-to-testify-on-nsa-surveillance-programs/2013/10/29/e9e9c250-40b7-11e3-a751-f032898f2dbc_story.html.

[4] *Id.*   [5] *Id.*   [6] *Id.*

Service) had gathered 1.8 million metadata records and had lawfully shared them with the NSA under international cooperation agreements on intelligence issues.[7] The United Kingdom, United States, Australia, New Zealand, and Canada share intelligence as members of the so-called Five-Eyes cooperation group.[8] There are reports of the existence of a broader Nine-Eyes group, which would include France, the Netherlands, Denmark, and Norway. Indeed, there are rumors about a Fourteen-Eyes cooperation group.[9] According to *The Guardian* there is also close technical cooperation and loose alliances between British, German, French, Spanish, and Swedish spy agencies on mass surveillance.[10]

The NSA-Affair shed light on the long-standing practice of international intelligence cooperation. The September 11, 2001 terror attacks merely altered the scope and scale of this well-established practice.[11] Before 9/11, the lack of trust in the ability of others to protect the information shared and the need felt by states to protect their sources

---

[7] COMMISSIE VAN TOEZICHT BETREFFENDE DE INLICHTINGEN – EN VEILIGHEIDSDIENSTEN, REVIEW REPORT ON THE PROCESSING OF TELECOMMUNICATIONS DATA BY GISS AND DISS, CTIVD No. 38, 4 (Feb. 5, 2014), http://english.ctivd.nl/investigations/r/review-report-38/documents/review-reports/2014/03/11/review-report-38-on-the-processing-of-telecommunications-data-by-giss-and-diss [hereinafter REVIEW REPORT ON PROCESSING].

[8] MASS SURVEILLANCE REPORT 9, COMMITTEE ON LEGAL AFFAIRS AND HUMAN RIGHTS, COUNCIL OF EUROPE (2015), http://website-pace.net/documents/19838/1085720/20150126-MassSurveillance-EN.pdf ("The 'Five-Eyes' intelligence sharing alliance is based on the 1946 UKUSA Signals Intelligence Agreement between the United Kingdom and the U.S.A., which was later extended to Australia, New Zealand, and Canada). *See* the UKUSA agreement and related documents at *U.K.U.S.A. Agreement Release 1940–1956*, NAT'L SECURITY AGENCY, www.nsa.gov/public_info/declass/ukusa.shtml (last visited Dec. 5, 2015).

[9] REVIEW REPORT ON PROCESSING, *supra* note 7, at 4. One of Edward Snowden's documents, published by the Spanish newspaper *El Mundo*, outlined four levels of cooperation between U.S. and foreign intelligence agencies. *See* Glenn Greenwald & Germán Aranda, *El CNI facilitó el espionaje masivo de EEUU a España*, EL MUNDO (Oct. 30, 2013, 6:55 AM), www.elmundo.es/espana/2013/10/30/5270985d63fd3d7d778b4576.html.

[10] Julian Borger, *GCHQ and European Spy Agencies Worked Together on Mass Surveillance*, THE GUARDIAN (Nov. 1, 2013, 1:02 PM), www.theguardian.com/uk-news/2013/nov/01/gchq-europe-spy-agencies-mass-surveillance-snowden.

[11] Statement by Professor Ian Leigh & Mr. Aidan Wills, LIBE Committee: Inquiry on Electronic Mass Surveillance of EU Citizens (Nov. 7, 2013); Ian Leigh, *Accountability and Intelligence Cooperation: Framing the Issue*, in INTERNATIONAL INTELLIGENCE COOPERATION AND ACCOUNTABILITY 2, 3 (Hans Born, Ian Leigh & Aidan Wills eds., 2011). *See* Elizabeth Sepper, *Democracy, Human Rights, and Intelligence Sharing*, 46 TEXAS INT'L L.J. 151, 155 (2010) (illustrating that the Canadian Security Intelligence Service (CSIS), for example, has more than 250 information sharing arrangements with foreign security and intelligence organizations, the CIA is connected to more than 400 agencies and the ASIO [Australian Security Intelligence Organization] has 233 liaison partners, distributed across 104 countries.).

and methods hindered cooperation. Today, these concerns continue to be a big obstacle to intelligence sharing,[12] but the tendency has been reversed. 9/11 clearly demonstrated that at least some of the main challenges posed to national security – particularly international terrorism, but also organized crime or the proliferation of weapons of mass destruction – cannot be dealt with only through domestic mechanisms. Given the transnational character of these security threats[13] and the globalization and digitalization of our world, international cooperation has increasingly come to be seen as a necessity in the new security paradigm.[14]

Soon after 9/11, in Resolution 1373, the UN Security Council called on States to work together to prevent and suppress terrorist acts, including through increased cooperation, the exchange of operational information and full implementation of the relevant international conventions relating to terrorism.[15] In this new transnational scenario the help of foreign intelligence services is needed to gain information that no state alone has the capacity to collect.[16] An example of the new transnationalism in the intelligence field is Project A-O Canada.[17] Created by the Royal Canadian Mounted Police (RCMP) after 9/11, Project A-O Canada is meant to facilitate information sharing with the U.S. intelligence agencies. This outside cooperation was important for two reasons. First, members of the Project A-O Canada team lacked in-depth knowledge of, and experience in, counterterrorism investigations. Sharing information with other agencies helped them understand the type of threat they were facing and to develop Canadian capacities.[18] In the same vein, without the cooperation

---

[12] James I. Walsh, *Intelligence Sharing in the European Union: Institutions Are Not Enough*, 44 JCMS 625, 628, 638 (2006).

[13] The 9/11 Commission, The 9/11 Commission Report: Final Report of the National Commission on Terrorist Attacks upon the United States 407 (2004).

[14] Richard Aldrich, *International Intelligence Cooperation in Practice, in* International Intelligence Cooperation and Accountability, *supra* note 11, at 17, 18–19.

[15] S.C. Res. 1373 (Sept. 28, 2001); On the need to strengthen cooperation at the EU level see the *Report by the Secretary General/High Representative to the Council on Intelligence Cooperation*, SN 4546/1/01 REV1 (Nov. 15, 2001), https://s3.eu-central-1.amazonaws.com/euobs-media/1c71c037f423bb9c74e243d62e394196.pdf.

[16] The 9/11 Commission, *supra* note 13, at 361–62. Referring to the myriad of agencies existing in the U.S, the 9/11 Commission stated that "without integrated, all-source analysis it is not possible to 'connect the dots.' No one component [of the intelligence community] holds all the relevant information," in The 9/11 Commission, *supra* note 13, at 408.

[17] Commission of Inquiry into the Actions of Canadian Officials in Relation to Maher Arar, Report of the Events Relating to Maher Arar: Factual Background, Volume I, 47 (2006) [hereinafter Maher Arar Report].

[18] Maher Arar Report, *supra* note 17, at 36.

of other agencies, it would have been difficult to assess whether Canadian intelligence information would be useful to American investigations, or to those being conducted in Europe, Africa, or Asia. Project A-O Canada did not have the resources to gather all of the information it needed on its own, nor did it have direct access to information on the targets' backgrounds, except through other agencies.[19] Second, according to RCMP witnesses, genuine national security concerns – including the potential loss of many lives – provided strong incentives for cooperation. As Inspector Clement explained, law enforcement officers were dealing with "real-time" events occurring against the backdrop of an imminent terrorist attack. "One tidbit of information" could be the missing piece of the puzzle in another agency's database.[20]

The rise of this cooperation in intelligence matters, both in scope and scale, has dramatically increased the possibility of human rights violations due to the lack of regulation, oversight, and accountability. Minimizing that peril is not a minor question.

Transnational cooperation in intelligence matters, with the legitimate aim to further protect the population against global threats, is very important. But it will be necessary to find the right balance between the need to cooperate and the need to protect fundamental rights, particularly the right to privacy.

B   A Legal Framework Regulating Intelligence Cooperation Agreements

There are many well-known formal intelligence cooperation agreements, including the Club of Berne,[21] Europol,[22] IntCen,[23] the European Union Military Staff at E.U. level,[24] and the UKUSA Agreement.[25] Nevertheless,

---

[19] *Id.*   [20] *Id.*

[21] Javier Argomaniz, The EU and Counter-Terrorism: Politics, Polity and Policies After 9/11 50 (2011).

[22] 2009 O.J. (L 121) 37.

[23] IntCen is the EU Intelligence Analysis Center. Over its mandate and structure, *see* Mai'a K. Davis Cross, *A European Transgovernmental Intelligence Network and the Role of IntCen*, 14 Persp. Eur. Pol. & Soc'y 388, at 392–395 (2013). Its existence lacks a legal basis. See *Report on the US NSA Surveillance Programme, Surveillance Bodies in Various Member States and Their Impact on EU Citizens' Fundamental Rights and on Transatlantic Cooperation in Justice and Home Affairs*, ¶ 81, A7-0139/2014, (2014).

[24] As regards the roles and powers of these EU intelligence structures see Aldrich, *supra* note 14, at 27–28.

[25] *See supra*, note 8.

studies indicate that "the great majority of intelligence is shared not through formal or multilateral agreements, but rather through informal, typically bilateral agreements" or even less formal arrangements based on oral agreements or personal friendships.[26] Commonly, "[n]ational intelligence agencies (rather than governments) negotiate memoranda of understanding (MOUs), setting out modalities of intelligence exchange."[27] These memoranda – as opposed to treaties or even executive agreements – "do not require approval by national legislators (or foreign policy ministers) and can be implemented by the agencies themselves."[28] MOUs create a flexible framework for cooperation among intelligence agencies.[29]

Secrecy, flexibility, and informality are common characteristics of these intelligence sharing networks. Intelligence sharing practices are mainly checked by professional peers taking part in the intelligence-sharing, who examine access by third parties to the information given, or the relevance and reliability of the information, applying only professional standards or internal guidelines.[30]

Flexible cooperation may be necessary in emergency situations that require a quick response. But liberal democracies should have a transparent set of legal rules regulating transnational intelligence sharing, even when it is thought that the circumstances necessitate great flexibility. Such a framework would preclude excessively broad agreements that risk a violation of individuals' privacy rights.[31] Only a clear set of legal

---

[26] Sepper, *supra* note 11, at 158. *See* Philippe Hayez, *National Oversight of International Intelligence Cooperation*, in INTERNATIONAL INTELLIGENCE COOPERATION AND ACCOUNTABILITY, *supra* note 11, at 151, 157.

[27] Sepper, *supra* note 11.   [28] *Id.*

[29] *Id.* at 158; Walsh, *supra* note 12, at 638 (pointing to the fact that in relation to the EU there is no obligation of Member States to provide intelligence to fellow members or to deal with such intelligence at the European Level. Member States "have insisted that intelligence sharing remain voluntary.").

[30] Sepper, *supra* note 11, at 160–63.

[31] An example of what is said is the UKUSA agreement, made public recently. The agreement contemplates a broad collaboration between the NSA and the GCHQ but lacks safeguards in order to protect the privacy rights of British and U.S. citizens. It mandates that each party will continue to make available to the other, *continuously, currently*, and without request, all *raw traffic*, COMINT end-product and technical material acquired or produced, and all pertinent information concerning its activities, priorities, and facilities, both present and planned, subject only to the proviso contained in paragraphs 4(b) and 5(b) of the Agreement. There are no rules on acquiring, accessing, using, retaining, or minimizing the information obtained on the other state citizens. U.K.–U.S. Communications Intelligence Agreement, as modified by Amendment No. 4 to the Appendices to the UKUSA Agreement, Appendix C, May 10, 1955, www.nsa.gov/public_info/_files/ukusa/new_ukusa_agree_10may55.pdf.

rules can facilitate oversight and accountability in the shadowy realm of intelligence sharing activities with different partners.

The European Court of Human Rights has sought to shore-up the right to privacy. It has held that the interception of volumes of communications data and the subsequent process of selection to obtain material for further consideration by government agencies amounts to an interference with the rights under Article 8 of the European Convention of Human Rights (ECHR).[32] According to the Courts' jurisprudence, powers like those permitting the examination, use and storage of intercepted communications constitute an interference with the right to privacy under Article 8 of the ECHR.[33] Still, the interference with the right to privacy can be justified if it is in accordance with the law and is necessary in a democratic society in the interests of national security, public safety, or the economic well-being of the country, for the prevention of disorder or crime, for the protection of health or morals, or for the protection of the rights and freedoms of others.[34]

In its jurisprudence, the European Court of Human Rights has demanded that the intrusive measures have some basis in domestic law. The law must be accessible to the person concerned, he or she must be able to foresee the consequences of the law, and it must be compatible with the rule of law (this is known as the quality of the law test).[35]

---

[32] Weber v. Germany, App. No. 54934/00, 2006-XI Eur. Ct. H.R. 309 ¶ 77; Liberty v. U.K., App. No. 58243/00 ¶ 56, HUDOC (July 1, 2008), http://hudoc.echr.coe.int/eng#{"fulltext":["liberty v. uk"], "documentcollectionid2":["GRANDCHAMBER", "CHAMBER"], "itemid":["001-87207"]}.

[33] Weber, supra note 32, at ¶¶ 78–79; Liberty, supra note 32, at ¶ 57.

[34] European Convention on Human Rights, Nov. 4, 1950, E.T.S. 5, art. 8(2).

[35] Liberty, supra note 32, at ¶ 59; Association for European Integration and Human Rights v. Bulgaria, App. No. 62540/00 ¶ 71, HUDOC (June 28, 2007), http://hudoc.echr.coe .int/eng#{"fulltext":["62540/00"], "documentcollectionid2":["GRANDCHAMBER", "CHAMBER"], "itemid":["001-81323"]}; Malone v. The United Kingdom, App. No. 8691/79 ¶ 67, HUDOC (Aug. 2, 1984), http://hudoc.echr.coe.int/eng#{"fulltext": ["malone v. united kingdom"], "documentcollectionid2":["GRANDCHAMBER", "CHAMBER"], "itemid":["001-57533"]}; Kruslin v. France, App. No.11801/85 ¶ 27, HUDOC (Apr. 24, 1990), http://hudoc.echr.coe.int/eng#{"fulltext":["kruslin v. france"], "documentcollectionid2":["GRANDCHAMBER", "CHAMBER"], "itemid":["001-57626"]}; Huvig v. France, App. No. 11105/84 ¶ 26, HUDOC (Apr. 24, 1990), http://hudoc.echr.coe.int/eng# {"fulltext":["huvig v. france"], "documentcollectionid2":["GRANDCHAMBER", "CHAMBER"], "itemid":["001-57627"]}; Kopp v Switzerland, 13/1997/797/1000 ¶ 55, HUDOC (Mar. 25, 1998), http://hudoc.echr.coe.int/eng#{"fulltext":["kopp v. switzerland"], "documentcollectionid2":["GRANDCHAMBER", "CHAMBER"], "itemid":["001-58144"]}; Amann v. Switzerland, App. No. 27798/95, 2002-II Eur. Ct. H.R. 245 ¶ 50.

"Foreseeability in the special context of secret measures of surveillance," the Court explained, "cannot mean that an individual should be able to foresee when the authorities are likely to intercept his communications so that he can adapt his conduct accordingly."[36] But taking into account the risks of arbitrariness intrinsic to the powers of secret surveillance, the law must be sufficiently clear in its terms (particularly precise) so that it gives citizens "an adequate indication as to the circumstances in which and the conditions on which" public authorities are empowered to take such measures.[37] The Court held that "it would be contrary to the rule of law for the legal discretion to be granted to the executive or to a judge to be expressed in terms of an unfettered power"; the law must "indicate the scope of any such discretion conferred on the competent authorities and the manner of its exercise with sufficient clarity to give the individual adequate protection against arbitrary interference."[38] All these requirements seek to account for the risk of abuse that is intrinsic to any system of secret surveillance.[39]

Domestic legal systems should establish minimum conditions as regards the cooperation of their intelligence community with foreign intelligence services in order to try to avoid abuses and violations of human rights and to stop the temptation to use intelligence sharing networks to circumvent statutory and constitutional restraints on domestic activity.[40] It has been said that:

---

[36] Leander v. Sweden, App. No. 9248/81 ¶ 51, HUDOC (Mar. 26, 1987), http://hudoc.echr .coe.int/eng?i=001-57519#{"itemid":["001-57519"]}; Liberty, *supra* note 32, at ¶ 62.

[37] *See* Malone, *supra* note 35, at ¶ 67; Kopp, *supra* note 35, at ¶ 64; Huvig, *supra* note 35, at ¶ 29; Valenzuela Contreras v. Spain, 58/1997/842/1048 ¶ 46(iii), HUDOC (July 30. 1998), http:// hudoc.echr.coe.int/eng#{"fulltext":["Valenzuela Contreras v. Spain"], "documentcollectionid2": ["GRANDCHAMBER", "CHAMBER"], "itemid":["001-58208"]}; Association for European Integration and Human Rights, *supra* note 35, at ¶ 75; Liberty, *supra* note 32, at ¶ 93.

[38] *See, e.g.*, Liberty, *supra* note 32, at ¶ 94.

[39] *See id.*; Rotaru v. Romania, App. No. 28341/95, 2000-V Eur. Ct. H.R. 109 ¶ 55.

[40] Didier Bigo *et al.*, *Mass Surveillance of Personal Data By EU Member States and Its Compatibility with EU Law*, 62 CEPS Pap. Liberty & Secur. 1, 17 (2013) (suggesting that evidence "point to a potential scenario of privacy shopping by services to exploit regimes with the weakest protection/oversight or with the greatest legal loopholes."). Sepper gathers together some examples of cooperation practices impinging on privacy rights. The German BND (Foreign Intelligence Service) "reportedly uses the European Counter-Terrorism Intelligence Center in Paris . . . to read information from German law enforcement agencies it would be barred from obtaining at home as a matter of domestic law." Reports, says the author, "suggest that UKUSA agencies also purposely use ECHELON to exchange surveillance information on each others' citizens in violation of domestic statutes. Sepper, *supra* note 11, at 173.

A country may not be able to tap the lines of its own citizens without legal authorization. But there's nothing to stop it from listening in on some other country's citizen, and then filing very thorough reports to that foreign citizen's government. Just as long as the report does not hand over the specific raw matter – the SIGINT dispatch of nouns and verbs – the letter of various privacy laws would stay intact[41]

This kind of cooperation among intelligence services does not comply with the foreseeability principle. Citizens cannot foresee that they are going to be subjected to unlimited surveillance by a foreign intelligence service only to have that information sent to be used by the *domestic* intelligence services of their country of origin in a cynical maneuver to circumvent domestic limits on intelligence agencies. Such a practice would amount to an infringement of the right to privacy because the action (intelligence sharing or cooperation) lacks a legal basis.[42]

We need a legal framework that tells officials what they can share and with whom, as well as what is prohibited. This would expose transnational information sharing to some limits and controls.

C Assessing the Human Rights Record of the Collaborating Party Before Sharing Intelligence

A preliminary condition for entering into sharing agreements with intelligence or security services of another country should be an evaluation of the compliance of those services with human rights under applicable international conventions. No matter what safeguards we incorporate into our legal systems, when a country does not respect human rights as a matter of fact, intelligence sharing can have negative implications for fundamental rights.

I An Example: The Dutch Intelligence and Security Services Act 2002

Intelligence services, even in the so-called western world, do not have the same mandate and legal powers. Some countries do not even have the same moral standards and responses when they are confronted with

---

[41] Sepper, *supra* note 11, at 174 (citing RON SUSKIND, THE ONE PERCENT DOCTRINE: DEEP INSIDE AMERICA'S PURSUIT OF ITS ENEMIES SINCE 9/11 269 (2006).).

[42] *See* Human Rights Council, U.N. Doc. A/HRC/27/37, ¶ 10, The Right to Privacy in the Digital Age: Report of the Office of the High Commissioner for Human Rights (June 30, 2014).

terrorism and human right issues. With these fundamental differences in mind the Dutch Intelligence and Security Services Act 2002 (ISS Act)[43] requires the Dutch intelligence services to "undertake an assessment of the counterpart's record on human rights" when entering into cooperation agreements with other intelligence services.[44]

The heads of the GISS (Dutch General Intelligence and Security Service) and DISS (the Dutch Defense Intelligence and Security Service) are responsible for maintaining relations with the intelligence and/or security services of other countries, but only with those countries that qualify for such relations.[45] Articles 36 and 59 of the ISS Act govern the cooperation of the DISS and the GISS with other intelligence services. Article 36(1)(d) of the ISS Act applies when the GISS has a direct interest in providing the information to the foreign country, because of the performance of its statutory tasks.[46] Article 59 of the ISS Act applies when the foreign country has made a request for the information. The principle behind this provision is the intelligence service's desire to maintain good cooperative relationships with foreign intelligence services.[47]

According to Article 59(2) of the ISS Act, information may be provided to foreign intelligence services for the purpose of the interests

---

[43] Act of February 7, 2002, Providing for Rules Relating to the Intelligence and Security Services and Amendment of Several Acts (Intelligence and Security Services Act 2002), Bulletin of Acts, Orders and Decrees of the Kingdom of the Netherlands [hereinafter ISS Act].

[44] This is also a practice recommended by Martin Scheinin. U.N. Doc. A/HRC/14/46, ¶¶ 46–47, Report of the Special Rapporteur on the Promotion and Protection of Human Rights and Fundamental Freedoms while Countering Terrorism, Martin Scheinin: Compilation of Good Practices on Legal and Institutional Frameworks and Measures that Ensure Respect for Human Rights by Intelligence Agencies while Countering Terrorism, Including on their Oversight (May 17, 2010) [hereinafter Compilation of Good Practices].

[45] *See* REVIEW REPORT ON PROCESSING, *supra* note 7, at 75.

[46] ISS Act, *supra* note 43, at art. 36.

> 1. Within the context of a proper performance of the duties of the service, the services are authorised to notify the following parties regarding information processed by or on behalf of the service:
>   c. the appropriate intelligence and security services of other countries, and the appropriate international security, signals intelligence and intelligence bodies.

[47] REVIEW COMMITTEE FOR THE INTELLIGENCE AND SECURITY SERVICES, REVIEW REPORT ON THE COOPERATION OF GISS WITH FOREIGN INTELLIGENCE AND/OR SECURITY SERVICES, CTIVD No. 22A, 3 (2009) [hereinafter REVIEW REPORT ON COOPERATION].

served by these services, insofar as: a) these interests are not incompatible with the interests served by the Dutch services and b) a proper performance of the duties by the Dutch services does not dictate otherwise. The legislative history of the ISS Act reveals that the assessment regarding a potential conflict of interest is to be based upon, *inter alia*, Dutch foreign policy, including human rights policy.[48]

It is the responsibility of the head of the GISS to identify the foreign services with which the GISS may cooperate (art. 59 (1)).[49] In order to decide if a country qualifies for cooperation "[t]he services must assess the degree of democratic anchorage of the service and its respect for human rights, its professionalism and reliability, the nature of the service, whether international obligations make cooperation desirable and to what extent cooperation with a service can enhance national security."[50] The enhancement of the performance of statutory tasks by the intelligence services and the degree of reciprocity (*quid pro quo*) are criteria that also may be considered by the services.[51] According to the legislative history, the Minister of Interior and Kingdom Relations must be informed of any cooperation. If the cooperation would involve a relationship with a partner with a dubious human rights record, then the decision to cooperate must be made by the Minister.[52] In this way the legislature made dodgy cooperation an explicit political decision.[53]

It is not easy to assess the degree to which a foreign intelligence service is democratically anchored. In order to make this assessment there are a variety of factors that can be evaluated. Examples include "the general political system of the country in question and the position of the relevant service within the system, the statutory powers of and the (independent) oversight of the service," or whether the country "has ratified international human rights conventions and whether it observes these conventions in actual practice."[54]

---

[48] *Id.* at 2.   [49] *Id.* at 6; ISS Act, *supra* note 43, at art. 59 (1).

[50] REVIEW REPORT ON PROCESSING, *supra* note 7, at 75.

[51] REVIEW REPORT ON COOPERATION, *supra* note 47, at 7. Intelligence services generally cooperate with each other on the basis of this principle of reciprocity. *See* COMMISSION OF INQUIRY INTO THE ACTIONS OF CANADIAN OFFICIALS IN RELATION TO MAHER ARAR, REPORT OF THE EVENTS RELATING TO MAHER ARAR: ANALYSIS AND RECOMMENDATIONS 102 (2006) [hereinafter MAHER ARAR RECOMMENDATIONS]; REVIEW REPORT ON PROCESSING, *supra* note 7, at 29.

[52] Parliamentary Papers II 1999/2000, 25 877, no. 8, p. 102 (Neth.); Appendix to the Proceedings II (Aanhangsel Handelingen II) 2004/05, no. 749 (Neth.).

[53] REVIEW REPORT ON COOPERATION, *supra* note 47 at 7.   [54] *Id.* at 7–8.

II   Analysis of the Implications of the Introduction of a Legal Clause Obliging Intelligence Services to Assess the Human Rights Records of Collaborating Parties

A clause like the one established in the ISS Act is meant to prevent liberal democracies from entering into cooperation with countries that systematically practice torture or do not respect the most fundamental human rights. It also sends a strong signal to the international community that those actions are unacceptable. It aims to preclude cooperation with intelligence services that violate human rights on a structural basis.

The Dutch Minister of Interior stated before the Dutch Parliament that "it is impossible to find out whether information received from a foreign intelligence and security service may perhaps have been obtained by torture. Intelligence and security services keep their sources and their methods secret, also their mutual dealings. Moreover, a service will never say they obtained information by torture."[55] A clause obliging intelligence services to assess a foreign intelligence service's democratic integrity and human rights record before entering into cooperation has a clear objective: to reduce the risk of using information obtained through abominable methods such as torture or the violation of other nonderogable human rights. No information should be solicited or received from a foreign intelligence service where there is a risk that it will cause or contribute to causing torture. On the other hand, data shared with the intelligence services of a regime that supports the use of torture might generate information identifying a possible suspect who might then be arrested and tortured during interrogation.[56]

---

[55] *Id.* at 8.

[56] *See* HANS BORN & IAN LEIGH, MAKING INTELLIGENCE ACCOUNTABLE: LEGAL STANDARDS AND BEST PRACTICE FOR OVERSIGHT OF INTELLIGENCE AGENCIES 66 (2005). Cameron points out, even if there is no case law on this, the convention against torture would seem to run contrary to officials from Convention party N, asking non Convention party P, to interrogate X in Country P in the knowledge that they use torture against "political offenders" but there is no clarity as to how far to stretch the duty not to torture (he asks himself about a situation in which party N just handles information to party P which may or may not result into torture). In any case, the Venice Commission holds that there is a duty of care that can be indirectly derived from the ECHR when entering into intelligence cooperation with states that have a suspect human rights record. Iain Cameron, *Blacklisting and Financial Sanctions against Suspected Terrorists, in* INTERNATIONAL INTELLIGENCE COOPERATION AND ACCOUNTABILITY, *supra* note 11, at 44, 63–64; *see also* Silvia Borelli, *Rendition, Torture and Intelligence Cooperation, in* INTERNATIONAL INTELLIGENCE COOPERATION AND ACCOUNTABILITY, *supra* note 11, at 98, 105–06; *but see* Martin Scheinin & Mathias Vermeulen, *International Law: Human Rights Law and State Responsibility, in* INTERNATIONAL INTELLIGENCE COOPERATION AND ACCOUNTABILITY, *supra* note 11, at 252, 264.

The evaluation of a foreign service's democratic integrity and human rights record is conducted by the intelligence services. The head of the service is responsible for entering into a cooperation relationship. This arrangement is fine as far as there is review of these decisions by an external oversight body. Without this, there is the risk that the Dutch intelligence services will be motivated, by their strong interest in collaborating, to less rigorously apply the controlling standards and establish relationships with services of dubious human rights records in order to accomplish their tasks.

The consequences of introducing this prerequisite into the legal system are not minor. That clause would prevent intelligence services from entering into cooperation with the intelligence services of, for example, Afghanistan or Pakistan, in order to get information about those training in Al-Qaeda training camps. Cooperation with Syrian intelligence services would be also precluded, as it has been proved that torture is practiced in the interrogations by the Syrian intelligence services.[57]

This regime presents some very difficult choices.[58] Well-aware of this, the Minister of Interior and Kingdom Relations, in his statement to the Dutch Parliament, explained that there might not be an absolute preclusion in advance of all forms of cooperation "with certain services."[59] In his assessment, in "a situation in which such a service possesses information concerning an immediate threat of a terrorist attack, such a preclusion could have disastrous consequences."[60] Therefore, communication channels with the appropriate service should always be kept open in the interest of national security.[61]

Noting that the Dutch Intelligence and Security Service (GISS) should exercise the "utmost restraint in cooperating with services of countries that have hardly any tradition of democracy and where human rights are violated (on a structural basis)," the Dutch Review Committee for the

---

[57] See MAHER ARAR RECOMMENDATIONS, *supra* note 51 (discussing interrogatory practices of the Syrian intelligence services relating to Maher Arar, a Canadian citizen.).

[58] Just to give the reader an idea of those hard choices, in the 9/11 Commission Report the Commission recommended the U.S. government to identify actual and potential terrorist sanctuaries. In order to accomplish this goal, the Commission recommended reaching out, listening to, and working with countries that could help. As illustration of those countries, the commission pointed to Pakistan, Afghanistan, and Saudi Arabia. *See* THE 9/11 COMMISSION, *supra* note 13, at 374.

[59] REVIEW REPORT ON COOPERATION, *supra* note 47, at 8.   [60] *Id.*

[61] *Id.* GISS considered it "increasingly advisable to exchange information with foreign counterpart services, in certain situations even with services of which is doubtful whether they satisfy the criteria for cooperation," because of the growing international threat of terrorism.

Intelligence and Security Services determined that, when such services possess information relating to a direct terrorist threat, GISS could ask the services for the information.[62] The Review Committee further conclude that, if GISS "possesses indications of a concrete threat to another country, then, for the purpose of preventing innocent victims, it may be necessary to share information with the service or services concerned."[63]

Intelligence services usually exchange a great variety of information – from raw data, strategic or tactical analysis, and very general information on certain themes, to more "in-depth analysis of phenomena to very concrete information" on particular matters or persons.[64] The GISS should ask itself whether it would be permissible "to provide this specific information to this/these specific service(s) in this particular instance and also whether the GISS itself can afford not to provide certain information to that service."[65] The intensity and frequency of the cooperation within different cooperation relationships does not have to be the same. Cooperation with those foreign services with a dubious human rights record would have to be kept to a minimum.

The RCMP *Operational Manual* goes in a direction similar to the Dutch policy. The *Operational Manual* requires that decisions to share information be made by the RCMP "on a case-by-case basis, and that judgment be applied to determine whether sharing would violate anyone's rights, or otherwise be inappropriate."[66] The policy permits "disclosure of information to a foreign agency that does not share Canada's respect for democratic or human rights, if disclosure is justified because of Canadian security or law enforcement interests, *if it can be controlled by specific terms and conditions and if it will not result in human rights violations.*"[67] Transforming this principle into a legal rule could have the advantage of a stronger commitment to these assessments and the accountability that derives from the need to justify the choices made to the oversight bodies.

---

[62] *Id.* at 8.   [63] *Id.* at ii, 8.

[64] *Id.* at 23. *See also* Loch K. Johnson, *Intelligence, in* INTERNATIONAL ENCYCLOPEDIA OF POLITICAL SCIENCE 1210, 1210 (Bertrand Badie *et al.* eds., 2014) (Strategic intelligence refers to the objective of achieving a global understanding of dangers and opportunities; tactical intelligence is concerned more with threats and opportunities on specific battlefields or theaters of war.").

[65] REVIEW REPORT ON COOPERATION, *supra* note 47, at ii.

[66] MAHER ARAR REPORT, *supra* note 17, at 33 (citing [IC] Cabana testimony (Nov. 1, 2004), p. 3441; [P] Loeppky testimony (June 30, 2004), p. 900.).

[67] MAHER ARAR REPORT, *supra* note 17, at 33 (emphasis added).

Intelligence services do not act in an altruistic manner; they always want something in return.[68] Sepper is right when she explained that "[i]t is one thing for Canadian intelligence to supply 'an assessment on the potential of terrorists to use the avian flu virus as a biological weapon with the Libyan, Saudi Arabian and Egyptian intelligence services.' It is quite another to provide intelligence on individual Chechens to Russian intelligence. Human rights abiding intelligence services have, as a legal imperative, the obligation not to collaborate with torture, so rules the United Nations Convention against Torture."[69] A possible safeguard for those circumstances in which it is necessary to acquire information from someone under the authority of countries with poor human rights records would be to undertake a joint operation with those intelligence services in order to make sure that neither torture nor other violations of human rights occurred in the process of obtaining the desired information.

The political branches have to decide what sort of cooperation can be offered to those intelligence services, in case their cooperation is needed, but must always take into account the protection of human rights recognized in the international conventions.[70] There should be no cooperation that might involve the violation of human rights. Diplomacy should be used to persuade the intelligence services of rights-violating countries that there can be other rewards if they conform their practices with human rights standards as part of their collaboration in the fight against transnational threats. For example, they might be offered aid to support better education in the country, or they might be offered military cooperation to suppress extremists' insurrection.[71] This was precisely the arrangement proposed by the 9/11 Commission with respect to

---

[68] Sepper identifies different demands by illiberal regimes in compensation for their cooperation. *See* Sepper, *supra* note 11, at 175–77.

[69] Sepper, *supra* note 11, at 175 (citing COMMISSION OF INQUIRY INTO THE ACTIONS OF CANADIAN OFFICIALS IN RELATION TO MAHER ARAR, A NEW REVIEW MECHANISM FOR THE RCMP'S NATIONAL SECURITY ACTIVITIES 142 [2006].)

[70] *See* G.A. Res. 217 A(lll), U.N. Doc. A/810, Universal Declaration of Human Rights (Dec. 10, 1948); International Covenant on Civil and Political Rights, Dec. 19, 1966, S. EXEC. DOC. NO. E, 95-2 (1978), 999 U.N.T.S. 171; European Convention on Human Rights, Nov. 4, 1950, E.T.S. 5; Organization of American States, American Convention on Human Rights, Nov. 22, 1969, 1144 U.N.T.S. 123; Organization of African Unity, African Charter on Human and Peoples Rights, June 27, 1981, 1520 U.N.T.S. 217; The Charter of Fundamental Rights of the European Union, 2000 O.J. (C 364) 1.

[71] Although here one must be very careful, as the notion of extremists or terrorists in some countries include domestic dissenters. The EU for example has been able to reach a common definition of terrorism to avoid these difficulties. *See* Council Framework Decision of June 13, 2002 on Combating Terrorism, 2002 O.J. (L 164) 3.

America's collaboration with Pakistan.[72] Alternatively, these collaborations might be confined to the transfer of strategic intelligence, which does not directly implicate personally-identifying data that can be used to violate human rights. It is not easy to resist pressures to collaborate with respect to concrete, personally-identifying data, but it should be done.

Of course, there is an important need for information about threats developing in countries with poor human rights records. If we accept that our collaboration with those countries' intelligence services must be limited, then the question becomes whether we should allow our intelligence services to spy in foreign countries. The answer should be affirmative, but within limits.[73]

The question of respecting human rights arises sometimes in regards to the intelligence or security services of countries with good human rights records and good systems of oversight of those services. In the United States the Central Intelligence Agency (CIA) was accused of practicing torture through its "enhanced interrogation techniques."[74] Would that prevent European Intelligence Services from collaborating with the CIA or with the NSA during the period when that policy or practice was in place, given that the latter is in charge of "providing signals intelligence products, cryptological analysis, and secure communications for the military and civilian members of the Intelligence Community"[75] including the

---

[72] THE 9/11 COMMISSION, *supra* note 13, at 369.

[73] President Obama, for example, has tackled this question in its Presidential Policy Directive/PPD-28 of January 17, 2014. *See* Press Release, The White House Office of the Press Secretary, Presidential Policy Directive – Signals Intelligence Activities Presidential Policy Directive/PPD-28 (Jan. 17, 2014), www.whitehouse.gov/the-press-office/2014/01/17/presidential-policy-directive-signals-intelligence-activities.

[74] The American Civil Liberties Association filed a lawsuit against two of the psychologists who designed and helped oversee the interrogation programs largely based on the findings of the Senate Select Committee on Intelligence Report "Committee Study of the Central Intelligence Agency's Detention and Interrogation Program," whose executive summary was published December 9, 2014. *See Senate Intelligence Committee Study on CIA Detention and Interrogation Program*, DIANNE FEINSTEIN, www.feinstein.senate.gov/public/index.cfm/senate-intelligence-committee-study-on-cia-detention-and-interrogation-program (last visited Dec. 6, 2015) (in the foreword to that study Senator Feinstein regards the enhance interrogation techniques as torture) [hereinafter *CIA Study*]; Press Release, ACLU, ACLU Sues Psychologists who Designed and Ran CIA Torture Program (Oct. 13, 2015), www.aclu.org/news/aclu-sues-psychologists-who-designed-and-ran-cia-torture-program; *A Guide to the Memos on Torture*, N.Y. TIMES, www.nytimes.com/ref/international/24MEMO-GUIDE.html (last visited Dec. 6, 2015) (the memos of the Justice Department that serves as a legal basis for the "enhance interrogation techniques" program.).

[75] *NSA Headquarters*, CENT. INTELLIGENCE AGENCY (Apr. 15, 2007), www.cia.gov/kids-page/k-5th-grade/a-birds-eye-view-of-cia-history-1/nsa-headquarters.html.

CIA? In 2005 the press published the first articles on the use of enhanced interrogation techniques by the CIA.[76] On December 18, 2006 the Consideration of Reports Submitted by States Parties under Article 40 of the Covenant (the ICCP) by the Human Rights Committee was published.[77] The Human Rights Committee expressed its concern because the U.S. authorities did not acknowledge that those practices constituted a violation of Article 7 of the International Covenant on Civil and Political Rights, which forbids torture. It added that, even if the Army Field Manual on Intelligence Interrogation prohibited those techniques, they "may still be authorized or used by other agencies, including intelligence agencies."[78] Given the risks of abuse intrinsic to the secret work of intelligence agencies, once there was some credible evidence that the CIA was using techniques that could amount to torture, other intelligence services should have exercised restraint in sharing information with the CIA or the NSA regarding personal data of individuals if that could lead to their detention and imprisonment in Guantanamo Bay. Alternatively, they should have asked for special assurances from the United States that those individuals detained through the use of shared information would not be imprisoned in Guantanamo and/or subject to such treatment (until the day that policy ceased).[79] Of course, it is one thing when there is a policy behind those violations of human rights, and quite another when there are isolated cases of violations of human rights in countries like the United States with a good system for the oversight of the intelligence services. In this last case, we should be

---

[76] Brian Ross & Richard Esposito, *CIA's Harsh Interrogation Techniques Described*, ABC News (Nov. 18, 2005), http://abcnews.go.com/Blotter/Investigation/story?id=1322866; *History of an Interrogation Technique: Water Boarding*, ABC News, http://abcnews.go .com/WNT/Investigation/story?id=1356870 (last visited Dec. 6, 2015).

[77] Human Rights Committee, Consideration of Reports Submitted by States Parties under Article 40 of the Covenant: Concluding Observations of the Human Rights Committee United States of America, CCPR/C/USA/CO/3/Rev.1 (Dec. 18, 2006), www.state.gov/ documents/organization/133837.pdf.

[78] *Id.* at 3.

[79] Exec. Order No. 13,491, 74 Fed. Reg. 4893 (Jan. 22, 2009). President Obama signed Executive Order 13491 in January 2009, to prohibit the CIA from holding detainees other than on a "short-term, transitory basis" and to limit interrogation techniques to those included in the Army Field Manual. *See CIA Study, supra* note 74, at 4. According to the NGO "human rights first" the last known arrival of detainees in Guantanamo was in 2008.

confident about the mechanisms of oversight in the United States, which have shown themselves to be effective.[80]

D   Additional Proposed Rules That Could Govern Transnational Information Sharing

Cooperation with countries that have a good human rights record also poses important legal problems. Many countries regulate acquisition, access, use, dissemination (to other internal agencies), and retention of personal data. Their aim is to find the right balance between the duty of the state to protect its people and the individual's rights to privacy, free expression, and even free association. According to the same rationale, there should also be a set of legally enforceable rules applicable to personal data disclosed to foreign partners.[81]

When an intelligence service receives a request to provide information to foreign intelligence or law enforcement agencies, it cannot comply without safeguards. National security is not the only interest at stake. The obligation of the state to protect the fundamental rights of the people under its jurisdiction, including the right to privacy enshrined in most constitutions and international conventions – such as the European Convention on Human Rights,[82] the Charter of Fundamental Rights of the European Union,[83] or the International Convention on Civil and Political Rights[84] – obliges national authorities to consider the possible impact of those measures on the rights of their citizens and residents. In

---

[80] In the case of the enhanced interrogation methods, the CIA Inspector General raised the alarm in 2004. *See* Michael Scherer, *Five Important Revelations From The CIA Inspector General Report*, Time (Aug. 24, 2009), http://swampland.time.com/2009/08/24/five-important-revelations-from-the-cia-inspector-general-report/. The Senate Intelligence Committee made a full report on torture after reviewing the program. That report was partially published. *See CIA Study, supra* note 74.

[81] The RCMP for example, has an *Administrative Manual* with a series of requirements that must be abided by when sharing information to other services, but these rules are not enforceable by any external oversight body. Maher Arar Report, *supra* note 17, at 30–34.

[82] European Convention on Human Rights art. 8, Nov. 4, 1950, E.T.S. 5.

[83] The Charter of Fundamental Rights of the European Union arts. 6–7, 2000 O.J. (C 364) 1.

[84] International Covenant on Civil and Political Rights art. 17, Dec. 19, 1966, S. Exec. Doc. No. E, 95-2 (1978), 999 U.N.T.S. 171. In relation to the extraterritorial application of article 17 of the ICCPR, see Chapters 5 and 15 in this volume; *see also*, International Commission of Jurists, Assessing Damage, Urging Action: Report of the Eminent Jurist Panel on Terrorism, Counter Terrorism and Human Rights 55–56 (2009).

United States v. United States Dist. Court, Justice Powell wrote that "Fourth Amendment freedoms cannot properly be guaranteed if domestic security surveillance may be conducted solely within the discretion of the Executive Branch."[85] Today we can say that those freedoms cannot be guaranteed if the relations with foreign intelligence services are left to be conducted "solely within the discretion of the Executive Branch."[86]

In the context of the NSA-Affair, in the *Schrems Case* the Court of Justice of the European Union (CJEU) ruled that the transfer of personal data to third countries constitutes, in itself, the "processing" of personal data as if it had been carried out in a Member State.[87] The Court has also concluded that the protection of personal data resulting from the explicit obligation laid down in Article 8(1) of the Charter is especially important to respect the right to private life enshrined in Article 7 of the Charter.[88] The *Schrems Case* concerned the transfer of personal data from the E.U. to U.S. firms under the Safe harbor Agreement.[89] It did not concern the transfer of personal data by E.U. Member States' intelligence services to the intelligence services of the United States, like the NSA.[90] Yet, by analogy, from a European perspective the transfer of personal data by the European intelligence services to the NSA affects the right to protection of personal data and to private life. As a result, the transfer of personal data (or metadata produced in the context of electronic or network communications) to the NSA must not be done in bulk and without

---

[85] Laura K. Donohue, *Section 702 and the Collection of International Telephone and Internet Content*, 38 HARV. J.L. & PUB. POL'Y 117 (2015) (citing U.S. v. U.S. Dist. Court, 407 U.S. 297, 316–317 (1972)).

[86] *Id.*

[87] Eur. Parl. & Council Directive 95/46/EC ¶ 2(b), O.J. (L 281) (Directive 95/46/EC of the European Parliament and of the Council of October 24, 1995 on the protection of individuals with regard to the processing of personal data and on the free movement of such data.). *See* Case C-362/14, Schrems v. Data Protection Commissioner, INFOCURIA – CASE-LAW CT. JUST. (Oct. 6, 2015), http://curia.europa.eu/juris/document/document.jsf?text=&docid=169195&pageIndex=0&doclang=EN&mode=lst&dir=&occ=first&part=1&cid=391877.

[88] Joined Cases C-293/12 & C-594/12, Digital Rights Ireland & Seitlinger v. Minister for Communications, Marine and Natural Resources, ¶ 53, INFOCURIA – CASE-LAW CT. JUST. (Apr. 8, 2014), http://curia.europa.eu/juris/document/document.jsf?docid=150642&doclang=EN [hereinafter Digital Rights Ireland].

[89] *See* Schrems, *supra* note 87, at ¶¶ 54–58.

[90] The European Union does not have a direct competence to rule on the intelligence services of the Member States. The Charter and the rest of the E.U. legislation are only applicable when the Member States apply EU law. *See* Directive 95/46/EC, pmbl. § 13 (excluding the applicability of this Directive to the activities regarding defense, public safety, or state security.).

safeguards. Indeed, in its Judgment in *Digital Rights Ireland,* the CJEU held that the data retention obligations imposed by Directive 2006/24[91] on providers of publicly available electronic communications services or of public communications networks intrudes on the right to the protection of personal data.[92] This is true, the Court explained, even if there is no retention obligation as regards the contents of the communications.[93] If public authorities want to limit those rights through the transfer of personal data (or metadata generated in the context of everyday electronic communications) to third countries, then they will have to make sure that those limits on the enjoyment of those rights meet several minimum criteria: they must be provided for by law; they must pursue a legitimate aim; they must constitute an adequate measure in pursuit of a legitimate aim; and they must comply with the principle of proportionality.[94]

First of all, when a foreign intelligence service requests some information, it should have to demonstrate its need-to-know.[95] This "need-to-know" principle implies that the requesting agency should only obtain that information necessary for the accomplishment of its tasks.[96] Furthermore, the law should require the foreign intelligence service to give

---

[91] Directive 2006/24/EC of the European Parliament and of the Council of 15 March 2006 on the Retention of Data Generated or Processed in Connection with the Provision of Publicly Available Electronic Communications Services or of Public Communications Networks and Amending Directive 2002/58/EC, 2006 O.J. (L 105) 54.

[92] *See* Digital Rights Ireland, *supra* note 88, at ¶¶ 72–74.

[93] *See* Digital Rights Ireland, *supra* note 88, at ¶¶ 26, 29, 33–34, 42.

[94] See the jurisprudence of the ECtHR in the context of the European Convention of Human Rights and article 52(1) of the Charter of Fundamental Rights of the EU. The CJEU in *Digital Rights Ireland* expressly applied the jurisprudence of the European Court of Human Rights as regards the proportionality principle. *See* Digital Rights Ireland, *supra* note 88, at ¶¶ 54–55. Subject to the principle of proportionality, limitations may be made only if they are necessary and genuinely meet objectives of general interest recognized by the Union or the need to protect the rights and freedoms of others.

[95] In the EU, Member States shall not subject the exchange, by its competent law enforcement authority with a competent law enforcement authority of another Member State, of information or intelligence that in an internal procedure may not be accessed by the requested competent law enforcement authority without a judicial agreement or authorization, to such an agreement or authorization. *See* Council Framework Decision of December 18, 2006 on Simplifying the Exchange of Information and Intelligence Between Law Enforcement Authorities of the Member States of the European Union, art. 3.3, 2006 O.J. (L 386) 89, 91.

[96] Sepper, *supra* note 11, at 160. In the case of the RCMP, for example, the RCMP must be satisfied, before sharing information with a third party, such as the FBI, that there is an operational reason to share the information. *See* MAHER ARAR REPORT, *supra* note 18, at 32. As regards internal sharing of information among U.S. agencies, the 9/11 Commission was critical about the need-to-know principle. The need-to-know principle was criticized because it assumed that "it is possible to know in advance, who will need to use the

proof of a direct link between the data sought and the accomplishment of a legitimate aim. As the Dutch Committee Report on the cooperation of GISS with foreign intelligence and/or security services points out, sometimes it might be convenient to provide information or render technical or other forms of assistance to foreign agencies exclusively for the purposes of the interests to be served by the foreign counterpart.[97] As intelligence services operate on the basis of the principle of *quid pro quo* or reciprocity, "[c]omplying with the request from a foreign service thus serves national security, albeit indirectly," is acceptable, especially insofar as "it is not incompatible with the interests to be served by [the national intelligence service] and the proper performance of its statutory tasks."[98] But there are many forms of cooperation, and when there is not a compelling interest for national security, then the intrusion on privacy rights has to be reduced. For example, if the lives of people are at stake in an allied country, and the information is vital to avoid losing those lives, then this would amount to a compelling interest because the national intelligence service would be interested in receiving the same kind of information when the lives of its citizens are at stake (loyal cooperation between services on the protection of national security). Still, the intrusion on the individuals' privacy rights would be subsequently justified as far as there has been compliance with the principles of necessity and proportionality (the assessment of the proportionality of the measure depends on the seriousness of the interference with those rights).

The German Law regulating the German Intelligence Service (*Bundesnachrichtendienst* or BND) is also interesting in this respect.[99] Article 9 (2) in connection with Article 19 (3) of the *Bundesverfassungsschutzgesetz*[100] (the law regulating the German Domestic Security Service) provides that the

> agency may provide foreign security and other appropriate foreign services, as well as supra and international organizations, with data regarding citizens, provided that the supplying of this data is essential for the pursuit of its duties *or because prevailing security interests of the receiving institution necessitate this*. According to the same provisions, the supplying of

information." The Commission suggested the view that this culture had to be replaced by a "need-to-share" culture. THE 9/11 COMMISSION, *supra* note 13, at 417
[97] REVIEW REPORT ON COOPERATION, *supra* note 47, at 11.   [98] *Id.*
[99] BND-Gesezt [BNDG] [Law on the Federal Intelligence Service], Dec. 20, 1990, BGBl. I at 2954, 2979.
[100] Bundesverfassungsschutzgesetz [BverfSchG] [Federal Act on the Protection of the Constitutiont], Dec. 20, 1990, BGBl. I at 2954, 2970.

information ceases when this would run counter to the predominant foreign concerns of the Federal Republic of Germany or where the pre-eminent interests of the affected private persons deserve to be protected. Furthermore, the law provides that "the supplying of data ought to be recorded in public files. The beneficiary is to be instructed that the infor-mation is transmitted on the understanding that the data may only be used for the specific purpose for which it was sent. The Agency reserves the right to request information on the usage of data by the beneficiary.[101]

Next, it is clear that, in order to effectively protect the right to privacy of their citizens and residents, the provider must establish minimum pro-cedural conditions related to the access of the data by the competent national authorities of the receiver, and to their subsequent use and dissemination.[102] In this regard, the European Union legislature in its Directive 95/46 considers that the receiving country must secure an adequate level of protection similar to that enjoyed by citizens of the European Union.[103] Although this Directive does not apply directly to the transfer of data from the intelligence services of Member States to third countries, the concept can be used here by analogy. But what would qualify as an adequate level of protection? "In view of the important role played by the protection of personal data with regard to the fundamental right to privacy," the CJEU concluded that the third country should offer a high level of protection that is essentially equivalent to that afforded by Directive 95/46.[104] It is accepted that the protection might be imple-mented through means different from those used by the European Union, but "those means must nevertheless prove, in practice, effective in order to ensure protection essentially equivalent to that guaranteed within the European Union."[105]

Taking into account the secret nature of data-transfers to foreign intelligence services, the risks of arbitrariness and serious interferences with privacy increase. Minimum safeguards should be established to ensure effective protection of the data. First, the number of persons authorized to access and subsequently use the data should be limited to that which is strictly necessary in the light of the objective pursued. Second, the retention period should be limited to the length of time that is strictly necessary. Third, requirements for the protection and security

---

[101] BORN & LEIGH, *supra* note 56, at 67 (unofficial translation).
[102] *See, by analogy,* Digital Rights Ireland, *supra* note 88, at ¶¶ 61–62.
[103] *See* Directive 95/46/EC art. 25(1).   [104] Schrems, *supra* note 87, at ¶ 73.
[105] *Id.* at ¶ 74.

of the data should be introduced – along with a rule requiring the destruction of the data once they are no longer useful or upon the expiration of the retention period.[106] According to the third party rule the agency that receives the information will not use this information in any way not envisioned by the collecting agency and will not share it with any other party extraneous to the sharing arrangement without first obtaining the collecting agency's consent.[107] The problem is that "it is not against the law to breach a caveat," though it is true that "there is an implied trust between the lending and receiving agencies" and failure "to respect these caveats can create tension and make agencies reluctant to share information in the future."[108] But, from the point of view of the fundamental rights, it is obvious that the use of caveats does not constitute a sufficient guarantee.[109]

Once the intelligence service receives the request of information from the foreign agency there should be a centralized system to manage the request in order to promote a single policy inside the agency and allow the competent authorities to audit the decision.[110] Martin Scheinin, previous UN Special Rapporteur on the Promotion and Protection of Human Rights and Fundamental Freedoms while Countering Terrorism, recommended that the process for authorizing both the agreements upon which intelligence sharing is based and the *ad hoc* sharing of intelligence should be laid out in the law.[111] This promotes accountability.

---

[106] See Digital Rights Ireland, *supra* note 88, at ¶¶ 62–67.

[107] The collecting agency should seek to avoid the information being used against its interests or being shared with enemy parties or its sources and methods being unveiled. See Craig Forcese, *The Collateral Casualties of Collaboration, in* INTERNATIONAL INTELLIGENCE COOPERATION AND ACCOUNTABILITY, *supra* note 11, at 76–77 (citing several examples).

[108] MAHER ARAR REPORT, *supra* note 17, at 32; Sepper, *supra* note 11, at 187–88; REVIEW REPORT ON PROCESSING, *supra* note 7, at 78–79.

[109] Roach, following the recommendations of the Arar Commission, suggests that caveats must include the contact of a particular official in the sending government that can receive the reports on abuse of the caveats as well as petitions to amend the caveats, and charges the oversight bodies with the task of reviewing the sharing agreements, the information sent by the agency, the caveats, the breaches to the caveats and the sending agency's response. See Kent Roach, *Tool 7: Overseeing Information Sharing, in* OVERSEEING INTELLIGENCE SERVICES: A TOOLKIT 129, 137 (Hans Born & Aidan Wills eds., 2012).

[110] See, e.g., MAHER ARAR REPORT, *supra* note 17, at 33. It is clear that, when there is a concrete significant threat to life from an international terrorist plot, then the intelligence services do not have to wait for a request to share information with another country.

[111] Compilation of Good Practices, *supra* note 44, at practice 32.

Additionally, all the processes leading to a decision to permit surveillance or data collection must be recorded in writing,[112] including: the original request and the justified answer; the name of the authority that decides the dissemination of the information (for traceability purposes); the reasons justifying sharing the information with the foreign intelligence service; and the caveats – with the specific terms and conditions to be followed by the foreign intelligence service – regarding the use, retention, and dissemination of that information.[113]

Intelligence services should assess the reliability and relevance of the information prior to sharing it,[114] and introduce such assessment as part of the limitations on the sharing of the information.[115] Providing inaccurate information to a foreign intelligence service can do much harm to the person involved, as was made painfully clear in the case of the Canadian Maher Arar. Inaccurate information shared by the Canadian Royal Mounted Police with the U.S. Border Agency led to Maher Arar's utterly baseless rendition to Syria, where he was tortured.[116]

What if the requesting country asks for data or information concerning its own citizens, and not data concerning citizens of the third country to which the application is made? In most countries the threshold of suspicion required to justify the use of intrusive intelligence techniques as regards foreigners is not the same as that required for citizens and residents.[117]

---

[112] *See* Roach, *supra* note 109, at 137; Aldrich, *supra* note 14, at 22.

[113] The transmission of data to and their use by others authorities, which enlarges the group of persons with knowledge of the personal data intercepted and can lead to investigations being instituted against the persons concerned, constitutes, according to the European Court of Human Rights a further separate interference with the applicants' privacy rights under Article 8 ECHR. *See* Weber v. Germany, App. No. 54934/00, 2006-XI Eur. Ct. H.R. 309 ¶ 79.

[114] Council of Europe Convention for the Protection of Individuals with regard to Automatic Processing of Personal Data art. 5, Jan. 28, 1981, C.E.T.S. no. 108 (As regards personal data, the principles of fairness, lawfulness, finality, proportionality and accuracy, are supposed to govern all data processing according to article 5 of the Convention.).

[115] The Dutch ISS Act contemplates this duty for example (ISS Act, *supra* note 43.). *See* Articles 12(4) and 15 c) of the ISS Act and REVIEW COMMITTEE FOR THE INTELLIGENCE AND SECURITY SERVICES, REVIEW REPORT ON THE LAWFULNESS OF THE PERFORMANCE BY GISS OF THE FOREIGN INTELLIGENCE TASK 26, CITVD, no. 26 (2011).

[116] *See* MAHER ARAR RECOMMENDATIONS, *supra* note 51, at 119. Sepper proposed creating a position for quality control at the institutional level and converting quality and reliability caveats into a mandatory professional norm. Sepper, *supra* note 11, at 185–87.

[117] *See* 50 U.S.C.A. § 1801 (e) (West 2015); Donohue, *supra* note 85, at 56.

In the United States, in national security cases, the Foreign Intelligence Surveillance Act (FISA)[118] requires the applicant for an order for intelligence surveillance to demonstrate probable cause to the Foreign Intelligence Surveillance Court (FISC).[119] But the probable cause required is unique to the national security context. There must be probable cause that an individual is a foreign power or an agent thereof.[120] For an American, this later status (agent of a foreign power) would involve some criminal activity,[121] including knowingly engaging in clandestine intelligence activities for or on behalf of a foreign power, knowingly engaging in sabotage or international terrorism, or participation in activities that are in preparation for sabotage or international terrorism.[122] In relation to U.S. persons (which include permanent residents), information can only be gathered within the United States when it is necessary to the national defense or the conduct of the foreign affairs of the United States.[123] For non-U.S. persons, however, it suffices if the information relates to the national defense or the conduct of foreign affairs.[124] Moreover, the applicant must submit to the FISC its targeting and minimization procedures and the court must assess whether targeting and minimization procedures are consistent with the Fourth Amendment.[125]

The intelligence agencies could, as has been highlighted, conduct surveillance for each other and then share the information. That would amount to a circumvention of the domestic legal system and should be expressly forbidden as contrary to the rule of law.[126] There could be very exceptional cases where it would be legitimate for an intelligence service to receive personal data about its citizens provided by a foreign intelligence service. In the United Kingdom, the U.K. Investigatory Powers Tribunal had to rule on the validity of the request by British intelligence authorities seeking information from the NSA on individuals located in the United Kingdom[127]

---

[118] 50 U.S.C.A. ch. 36 (West 2015).
[119] 50 U.S.C.A. § 1805(a)(2)(A), § 1805(a)(2)(B), § 1805(b) (West 2015).
[120] 50 U.S.C.A. § 1805(2)(a) (West 2015).
[121] 50 U.S.C.A. § 1801(a), § 1801(b) (West 2015).
[122] 50 U.S.C.A. § 1801 (b)(2) (West 2015).   [123] 50 U.S.C.A. § 1801(e)(2) (West 2015).
[124] Id.
[125] 50 U.S.C.A. § 1805 (c)(2)(A) (West 2015); 50 U.S.C.A. § 1801(h) (West 2015).
[126] Compilation of Good Practices, *supra* note 44, at ¶ 49.
[127] Liberty v. The Secretary of State for the Foreign and Commonwealth Office, [2014] UKIPTrib. 13_77-H, www.ipt-uk.com/docs/IPT_13_168-173_H.pdf

The NSA supplied information to the MI5, MI6, and GCHQ about individuals located in the United Kingdom, information obtained via PRISM and Upstream.[128] The U.K. Investigatory Powers Tribunal was asked to rule on the validity of the U.K. statutory regime, which the claimants found to be contrary to Article 8(2) of the ECHR and not "in accordance with the law" in the sense of the ECHR. The information shared by the NSA was assumed to have been lawfully obtained under section 702 of the FISA and Executive Order 12333.[129] The Tribunal agreed that Article 8 of the ECHR would be affected in such a case and held that the legal regime should comply with the requirements of the ECtHR jurisprudence regarding the storage, sharing, retention, and destruction of the intercepted material once in the hands of the U.K. intelligence agencies.[130]

As to the request of the information by the U.K. intelligence services to the NSA, the Tribunal considered – after the disclosure of some information made by the respondents – that there were adequate arrangements in place for the purpose of ensuring compliance with Article 8 of the ECHR and that those arrangements were subject to oversight.[131] According to the disclosures made by the respondents to the Tribunal, a request

> may only be made by the Intelligence Service to the government of a country or territory outside the United Kingdom for unanalyzed intercepted communications (and associated communications data) otherwise than in accordance with an international mutual assistance agreement if a) either a relevant interception warrant under the Regulation of Investigatory Powers Act 2000 ("RIPA") has already been issued by the Secretary of State, the assistance of the foreign government is necessary to obtain the communications at issue because they cannot be obtained under the relevant RIPA interception warrant and it is necessary and proportionate for the Intelligence Service to obtain those communications; or making the request for the communications at issue in the absence of a relevant RIPA interception warrant does not amount to a deliberate circumvention of RIPA or otherwise contravene the principle established in Padfield v. Minister of Agriculture, Fisheries and Food [1968] AC 997 (e.g., because it is not technically feasible to obtain the communications via RIPA interception), and it is necessary and proportionate for the

---

[128] *Id.* at ¶ 14 ("The U.S. Government's 'Prism' system collects foreign intelligence information from electronic communications service providers under U.S. Court supervision" and "[t]he U.S. Government's 'upstream collection' programme obtains internet communications under U.S. court supervision as they transit the internet.").

[129] *Id.* at ¶ 15.   [130] *Id.* at ¶ 36.   [131] *Id.* at ¶ 55.

Intelligence Services to obtain those communications. In these circumstances, the question whether the request should be made would be considered and decided upon by the Secretary of State personally.[132]

Section a) of the regime does not seem contrary to the right to privacy, as far as the RIPA complies with that right. Section b) poses more problems in practice. If the domestic threshold of suspicion and the principle of proportionality are fulfilled, along with the safeguards of the system (request to an independent authority, who authorizes the request and independent oversight once the information is received), then it may be legitimate to request such information (e.g., because there are no technical means to carry out the interception by the public authorities of the country receiving the information).

E   Oversight of Intelligence Sharing Agreements

Even if the legislature has struck the right balance between liberty and security, a good system of oversight is essential in order to avoid abuses. Nevertheless, domestic oversight bodies face significant barriers to reviewing the intelligence sharing activities carried out between their intelligence services and foreign intelligence agencies.

Independent oversight bodies or parliamentary oversight bodies should be able to review the policy and the individual cases where information is shared, including the caveats attached.[133] These review bodies should have the authority to assess whether the whole process has carefully balanced the needs of national security and foreign relations, on the one hand, with the protection of privacy, on the other hand.

One of the most important rules in these sharing arrangements is the "third party rule." Information coming from a foreign intelligence agency on a sharing agreement cannot be shared with third parties, and that normally includes oversight bodies of the state of the receiving intelligence service, unless the originating body allows it.[134] It seems that some

---

[132] *Id.* at ¶ 47. Where the Intelligence Services receive intercepted communications content or data from the government of a country outside the United Kingdom, they should subject the communications content or data to the same internal rules and safeguards as the same categories of content or data, when they are obtained directly by the Intelligence Services of the United Kingdom as a result of interception under RIPA [*Idem*, §§ 52–54.]. This safeguards should be included in any domestic law dealing with sharing information agreements in order to comply with the international standards regarding the protection of privacy.

[133] *See* Roach, *supra* note 109, at 137.

[134] *Id. See, e.g.,* article 11.2 of the Spanish National Intelligence Centre Act, 2002.

countries understand the third party rule as not excluding oversight activities by their oversight institutions, but this is not yet widespread. Countries want to protect their information from any unwanted disclosure.[135]

Even if the oversight body has access to information coming from a third country, its jurisdiction does not extend to the foreign government authorities. This, undoubtedly, will affect the oversight body's review.[136] Domestic oversight bodies mostly "oversee only one side of the exchange transaction."[137]

Leigh and Wills propose that "a possible workable fall-back arrangement" could be to "establish a system of certification where the oversight institution in the state supplying intelligence at least warrants that it has been collected and handled according to local standards of legality."[138] This could be sufficient when information is provided by liberal democracies and the information concerns its own citizens or residents. But, for example, the NSA can legally gather information on any non-U.S. person living overseas without the protection of the Fourth Amendment. The local standards of legality to obtain that information would not cover a minimum standard of protection for the privacy of those non-U.S. persons concerned.

Sharing information practices that take place through supranational networks (fusion centers) create even more problems as regards accountability.[139] Domestic parliamentary and expert oversight bodies have a limited role and they often lack access to the records of the networks in which intelligence services take part.[140]

There should be mechanisms of redress for those who have suffered a violation of their rights due to information sharing.[141] Probably the only way to ensure this is to negotiate with the other country an agreement by which those citizens affected by an interference with their rights are given standing to sue in the third country. The TFTP agreement[142] between the European Union and the United States, for example, grants any person,

---

[135] Leigh & Wills, *supra* note 11, at ¶ 16.   [136] *Id.* at ¶ 19
[137] Roach, *supra* note 109, at 135.   [138] Leigh & Wills, *supra* note 11, at ¶ §32.
[139] Roach, *supra* note 109, at 132.   [140] *Id.*
[141] *See, e.g.*, Intelligence and Security Services Act, *supra* note 43, at arts. 83–84 (whereby a redress mechanism is established involving the national ombudsman.).
[142] Agreement between the European Union and the United States of America on the processing and transfer of Financial Messaging Data from the European Union to the United States for the purposes of the Terrorist Finance Tracking Program 2010 O.J. (L 195) 5 [hereinafter TFTP Agreement].

regardless of nationality or country of residence, the right to seek effective administrative and judicial redress in accordance with the laws of the European Union, its Member States, and the United States, respectively.[143] Article 12 of the agreement, on the other hand, subjects the enforcement of the agreement (including the terrorism purpose limitation and the provisions on necessity and proportionality) to oversight by independent authorities, including a person appointed by the European Commission, with the agreement of and subject to appropriate security clearances of the United States. This is probably the right path in order to try to assure compliance with the legal regime in such a sensitive field like that of national security. The key issue here is the independence of the oversight authority. In Germany, where the revelations about the close cooperation between the NSA and the BND have outraged the population,[144] in part due to reports that the BND helped the NSA to spy on German and European firms,[145] Chancellor Merkel named a former senior judge as special investigator to inspect a list of targets (search terms) that the BND tracked on behalf of the NSA.[146] She said she did "not expect the U.S. government to formally agree in the immediate future to a public airing of the list. [She] therefore suggested appointing a 'trusted individual' who alone would see its contents"[147] and who would afterwards inform the Bundestag's Committee of Inquiry on the NSA-Affair.[148] The normal oversight systems did not work in a situation like this one because of the particular circumstances of the collaboration with a foreign intelligence service, and Merkel had to look for an imaginative

---

[143] TFTP Agreement art. 18(2).

[144] *Spying Together: Germany's Deep Cooperation with the NSA*, SPIEGEL ONLINE (June 18, 2014, 4:20 PM), www.spiegel.de/international/germany/the-german-bnd-and-american-nsa-cooperate-more-closely-than-thought-a-975445.html; *New NSA Revelations: Inside Snowden's Germany File*, SPIEGEL ONLINE (June 18, 2014, 4:20 PM), www.spiegel.de/international/germany/new-snowden-revelations-on-nsa-spying-in-germany-a-975441.html.

[145] Erik Kirshbaum, *Merkel Defends German Intelligence Cooperation with NSA*, REUTERS (May 4, 2015, 10:19 AM), www.reuters.com/article/2015/05/04/us-germany-spying-merkel-idUSKBN0NP13620150504#ZATsIpcLmideZU9s.97.

[146] Thorsten Severin, *Germany Appoints Senior Judge to Inspect List of NSA Targets*, REUTERS (July 1, 2015, 2:54 PM), www.reuters.com/article/2015/07/01/us-germany-usa-spying-idUSKCN0PB5KO20150701#bvwWOgFiEdbwFhLX.97.

[147] *Id.*

[148] *Neue Turbulenzen um den Bundesnachrichtendienst*, DEUTSCHER BUNDESTAG, www.bundestag.de/dokumente/textarchiv/2015/kw17_pa_1ua/370260 (last visited Dec. 6, 2015) (giving the opinion of the opposition represented in the Budestag Committee of Inquiry.).

solution to ensure that there were no violations of domestic law. The parliamentary opposition was not satisfied with this solution. It had asked to review the list of search terms. But, due to the sensitive nature of the information, foreign intelligence services are not willing to share it with all the members of a committee formed by parliamentarians.

F   Conclusion

If the NSA-Affair has shown us anything, it is that we live in an interconnected world. The need-to-share information to face the threats to our society has grown in scope as our societies have grown more intertwined. Networks in which terrorism-related information is shared must function on a cooperative basis.[149] But intelligence services, even in the so-called western world, do not have exactly the same mandate and legal powers. They may not have the same concept of privacy. And they do not always apply the same guarantees to citizens or residents and foreigners. This poses a real problem when it comes to sharing information. Cooperation is vitally important for the prevention of threats to national security. The only way to surmount this obstacle is to align standards to govern the collection of information among allies. There should be a move to try to reach international agreements between allied partners in order to establish common minimum standards for privacy protection in order to facilitate the legal sharing of information.

On the other hand, domestic legal systems, with all their limitations, have to take into account the transnational perspective if we do not want our liberties to suffer due to the loopholes opened up by these transnational relationships. There is an urgent need to address the problems posed by transnational intelligence cooperation in many domestic legal systems. Obviously, domestic legal systems have a limited role to play. Many solutions to the problems I have outlined cannot be solved through the improvement of national law alone. The international community has to play a role in order to reach a consensus as to privacy protection in democratic states. But improving our domestic legal systems can be a first, although limited, step on the way to improving the protection of our privacy rights as regards transnational intelligence cooperation.

---

[149] MAHER ARAR RECOMMENDATIONS, *supra* note 51, at 102.

II   European Law

20

Developments in European Data Protection Law in the Shadow of the NSA-Affair

BY JENS-PETER SCHNEIDER

A Introduction

Edward Snowden's revelations about the NSA's various large-scale surveillance programs raised major concerns in Europe. Public debate was intense even as the intensity varied among the Member States. This chapter focuses on developments in European data protection law that have been – or might be – influenced by the NSA-Affair. First, I will pay particular attention to judgment of the Court of Justice of the European Union (CJEU) from April 8, 2014.[1] In that decision the Court declared the data retention directive 2006/24/EC invalid due to its unjustified interference with fundamental rights on data protection. In addition, judgments of the CJEU concerning the right to be forgotten (Google Spain)[2] and the Safe Harbor agreement between the United States and

---

[1] Joined Cases C-293/12 & C-594/12, Digital Rights Ireland & Seitlinger v. Minister for Communications, Marine and Natural Resources, INFOCURIA – CASE-LAW CT. JUST. (Apr. 8, 2014), http://curia.europa.eu/juris/document/document.jsf?docid=150642&doc lang=EN [hereinafter Digital Rights Ireland]; see also Joined Cases C-293/12 & C-594/12, Digital Rights Ireland & Seitlinger v. Minister for Communications, Marine and Natural Resources, Opinion of Advocate General Cruz Villalón, INFOCURIA – CASE-LAW CT. JUST. (Dec. 12, 2013), http://curia.europa.eu/juris/document/document.jsf? text=&docid=145562&pageIndex=0&doclang=EN&mode=lst&dir=&occ=first&part= 1&cid=391425.

[2] Case C-131/12, Google Spain SL v. Agencia Española de Protección de Datos (AEPD), INFOCURIA – CASE-LAW CT. JUST. (May 13, 2014), http://curia.europa.eu/juris/document/ document.jsf;jsessionid=9ea7d0f130d58fa348967d244833bad1c86381ec1189.e34KaxiLc3e Qc40LaxqMbN4Oc3aKe0?text=&docid=152065&pageIndex=0&doclang=EN&mode= lst&dir=&occ=first&part=1&cid=385379 [hereinafter Google Spain CJEU]; see also Case C-131/12, Google Spain SL v. Agencia Española de Protección de Datos (AEPD), Opinion of Advocate General Jääskinen, INFOCURIA – CASE-LAW CT. JUS. (June 25, 2013), http:// curia.europa.eu/juris/document/document.jsf?text=&docid=138782&pageIndex=0&doc lang=EN&mode=req&dir=&occ=first&part=1&cid=518199.

the European Union (Facebook/Schrems)[3] will be analyzed as they are part of the whole picture. Second, I will consider the response of the European Parliament, which has been especially active in the European debate on appropriate reactions to the NSA activities. Third, I will survey the European Commission's efforts to foster reform of E.U. data protection law. It is interesting to note, however, that the Commission has seemed to be more reluctant than the Parliament to take-up the issue of E.U.–U.S. data transfers. Fourth, I will remark that the European Council has done the least to react to the NSA-Affair. Despite the seeming outrage across Europe, the modest responses from the European institutions lead me to wonder if the CJEU may again become a driving force for European legal developments.

B   The Judgments of the Court of Justice of the European Union (CJEU)

The most important developments in E.U. data protection to occur since the Snowden revelations have been CJEU judgments. The first, from April 8, 2014, saw the Court strike down EC Directive 2006/24 on data retention for the purpose of combating serious crime.[4] The second, from May 13, 2014, saw the Court articulate the so-called "right to be forgotten" as a privacy limitation on the presentation of information resulting from Internet search engine inquires.[5] The third, from October 6, 2015, saw the Court striking down the so-called "Safe Harbor" decision of the European Commission being the legal basis for many transatlantic data transfers from the European Union to the United States[6]

I   The CJEU's Data Retention Decision

1   Directive 2006/24/EC on the Retention of Data

According to Directive 2006/24/EC communication service providers were obliged to retain traffic and location data of all electronic

---

[3] Case C-362/14, Schrems v. Data Protection Commissioner, INFOCURIA – CASE-LAW CT. JUST. (Oct. 6, 2015), http://curia.europa.eu/juris/document/document.jsf?text=&docid=169195&pageIndex=0&doclang=EN&mode=lst&dir=&occ=first&part=1&cid=391877; Case C-362/14, Schrems v. Data Protection Commissioner, Opinion of Advocate General Bot, INFOCURIA – CASE-LAW CT. JUST. (Sept. 23, 2015), http://curia.europa.eu/juris/document/document.jsf?text=&docid=168421&pageIndex=0&doclang=EN&mode=lst&dir=&occ=first&part=1&cid=391877 [hereinafter Opinion of AG Bot].
[4] Digital Rights Ireland, *supra* note 1.   [5] Google Spain CJEU, *supra* note 2.
[6] Schrems, *supra* note 3; Opinion of AG Bot, *supra* note 3.

communications.[7] For instance, in the case of mobile phone calls, the numbers of communicating phones, the date, time, and duration of communications, the location of the respective phones (cell ID) as well as data of registered users was to be retained by the service providers. Similar obligations applied to fixed network telephony, Internet access, e-mails, and Internet telephony.[8] The Directive did not define an overall retention period or different retention periods for different categories of data or data usages. Instead, the it obliged the Member States to define the retention period in a frame of 6 to 24 months.[9] The last element of the regime established by the Directive was an obligation for the service providers to grant access to retained data to competent security authorities as specified by the Member States.[10]

---

[7] Directive 2006/24/EC of the European Parliament and of the Council of March 15, 2006 on the Retention of Data Generated or Processed in Connection with the Provision of Publicly Available Electronic Communications Services or of Public Communications Networks and Amending Directive 2002/58/EC, 2006 O.J. (L 105) 54 [hereinafter Data Retention Directive]. The most important parts of this directive read as follows:

Article 1 – Subject matter and scope

1. This Directive aims to harmonize Member States' provisions . . . in order to ensure that the data are available for the purpose of the investigation, detection and prosecution of serious crime, as defined by each Member State in its national law.

2. This Directive shall apply to traffic and location data on both legal entities and natural persons and to the related data necessary to identify the subscriber or registered user [of publicly available electronic communications services or of public communications networks]. It shall not apply to the content of electronic communications, including information consulted using an electronic communications network.

Article 3 – Obligation to retain data

1. By way of derogation from Articles 5, 6 and 9 of Directive 2002/58/EC, Member States shall adopt measures to ensure that the data specified in Article 5 of this Directive are retained.

[8] *See* Data Retention Directive art. 5.

[9] *See* Data Retention Directive art. 6 ("Member States shall ensure that the categories of data specified in Article 5 are retained for periods of not less than six months and not more than two years from the date of the communication.").

[10] *See* Data Retention Directive art. 4 ("Member States shall adopt measures to ensure that data retained in accordance with this Directive are provided only to the competent national authorities in specific cases and in accordance with national law. [. . .]").

2   The Judgement of April 8, 2014

The CJEU's judgement was triggered by requests for a preliminary ruling by the Irish High Court and the Austrian *Verfassungsgerichtshof*.[11] Together with other judgments of national constitutional courts striking down national data retention provisions that were meant to implement Directive 2006/24/EC,[12] this indicates the willingness of several E.U. jurisdictions to develop and implement effective data protection safeguards also in the field of national security. Thus, the CJEU's general approach is supported by the courts in a number of E.U. Member States. The basis for such a preliminary ruling is to be found in Article 267 TFEU.[13] The German Federal Constitutional Court (*Bundesverfassungsgericht*), when confronted with a challenge to the German law seeking to implement the Directive, did not refer the case to the CJEU. Instead, on March 2, 2010 the German Federal Constitutional Court issued a decision on the merits in which it found that the German implementing statute was unconstitutional.[14] The German Federal Constitutional Court held that it could refrain from a reference to the CJEU because the EC

---

[11] Joined Cases C-293/12 & C-594/12, Digital Rights Ireland & Seitlinger v. Minister for Communications, Marine and Natural Resources, ¶¶ 17–21, INFOCURIA – CASE-LAW CT. JUST. (Apr. 8, 2014), http://curia.europa.eu/juris/document/document.jsf?docid=150642&doclang=EN [hereinafter Digital Rights Ireland]; *see also* Joined Cases C-293/12 & C-594/12, Digital Rights Ireland & Seitlinger v. Minister for Communications, Marine and Natural Resources, Opinion of Advocate General Cruz Villalón, ¶¶ 10–17, INFOCURIA – CASE-LAW CT. JUST. (Dec. 12, 2013), http://curia.europa.eu/juris/document/document.jsf?text=&docid=145562&pageIndex=0&doclang=EN&mode=lst&dir=&occ=first&part=1&cid=391425.

[12] *See infra* note 46.

[13] Consolidated Version of the Treaty on the Functioning of the European Union art. 267, Dec. 7, 2007, 2012 O.J. (C 326) 1 (entered into force Dec. 1, 2009) [hereinafter TFEU]. Art. 267 TFEU reads as follows:

The Court of Justice of the European Union shall have jurisdiction to give preliminary rulings concerning:

(a) the interpretation of the Treaties;
(b) the validity and interpretation of acts of the institutions, bodies, offices or agencies of the Union.

Where such a question is raised before any court or tribunal of a Member State, that court or tribunal may, if it considers that a decision on the question is necessary to enable it to give judgment, request the Court to give a ruling thereon.

Where any such question is raised in a case pending before a court or tribunal of a Member State against whose decisions there is no judicial remedy under national law, that court or tribunal shall bring the matter before the Court.

[14] Bundesverfassungsgericht [BVerfG] [Federal Constitutional Court] Mar. 2, 2010, 125 BVerfG 260 (2010).

Directive left broad leeway for implementation.[15] As a consequence of this jurisdictional decision, the German Federal Constitutional Court concluded that it could focus its review of the case on the "autonomous" constitutional choices taken by the German Parliament without having to engage with the E.U. law implicated by the case.[16]

a) Interference with the Rights Laid Down in Articles 7 and 8 of the Charter of Fundamental Rights   The CJEU's judgement was straightforward. The first step of its reasoning established the existence of an interference with the fundamental rights to respect for private life, as well as to data protection, which are laid down in Articles 7 and 8 of the Charter of Fundamental Rights.[17] In a comparative perspective, it must be highlighted that the Court sometimes uses the shorter phrase "right to privacy" but

---

[15] *Id.* at ¶ 186.

[16] *Id.* at ¶¶ 185–87; in contrast to this, some commentators observed that the German Court did not only strike down some parts of the implementing statute, but the whole statute. Consequently, Germany did not implement any data retention obligation at all. According to the ECJ judgments concerning Sweden and Austria, this failure to provide for the mandatory data retention constitutes a clear infringement of EU law. *See* Case C-185/09, Commission v. Sweden, INFOCURIA – CASE-LAW CT. JUST. (Feb. 4, 2010), http://curia.europa.eu/juris/document/document.jsf?text=&docid=74925&pageIndex=0&doclang=SV&mode=req&dir=&occ=first&part=1&cid=577032 (Swed.); Case C-189/09, Commission v. Austria, INFOCURIA – CASE-LAW CT. JUST. (July 29, 2010), http://curia.europa.eu/juris/document/document.jsf?text=&docid=84357&pageIndex=0&doclang=DE&mode=lst&dir=&occ=first&part=1&cid=578157. Taking these consequences into account, those commentators question whether the German Constitutional Court was obliged to refer the case to the ECJ. *See* Matthias Bäcker, *Solange IIa oder Basta I? Das Vorratsdaten-Urteil des Bundesverfassungsgerichts aus europarechtlicher Sicht*, 2011 EUROPARECHT 103,114–16 (2011).

[17] Charter on the Fundamental Rights of the European Union, Dec. 7, 2000, 2000 O.J. (C 364) 1 [hereinafter EUCFR]. The relevant provisions in the Charter on the Fundamental Rights of the EU read as follows:

> Article 7 – Respect for private and family life
>
> Everyone has the right to respect for his or her private and family life, home and communications.
>
> Article 8 – Protection of personal data
>
> 1. Everyone has the right to the protection of personal data concerning him or her.
> 2. Such data must be processed fairly for specified purposes and on the basis of the consent of the person concerned or some other legitimate basis laid down by law. Everyone has the right of access to data which has been collected concerning him or her, and the right to have it rectified.
> 3. Compliance with these rules shall be subject to control by an independent authority.

understands this individual liberty interest in a way that is nothing like the U.S. Supreme Court's approach to "privacy." As will become clear form the following, a major difference is that the CJEU does not restrict this right by a very narrow conceptualization of "reasonable expectations" of privacy, which is the approach that dominates American privacy jurisprudence.[18]

With regard to Article 7 the Court held,

> (1) "that it does not matter whether the information on the private lives concerned is sensitive,"
>
> (2) that "the *obligation* [for service providers] imposed by ... Directive 2006/24 ... *to retain* ... *data* relating to a person's private life and to his communications ... *constitutes in itself an interference* with the rights guaranteed by Article 7 [CFR]," and that
>
> (3) "the *access* of the competent national authorities to the data *constitutes a further interference* with that fundamental right."[19]

With regard to Article 8 the Court simply held:

> Likewise, Directive 2006/24 constitutes an interference with the fundamental right to the protection of personal data guaranteed by Article 8 of the Charter because it provides for the processing of personal data.[20]

The Court has derived similar levels of protection from the two Charter provisions. It maintained that practice in this case, concluding that

> [i]t must be stated that the *interference* ... with the fundamental rights laid down in Articles 7 and 8 of the Charter *is* ... *wide-ranging, and it must be considered to be particularly serious.* Furthermore ... is likely to generate in the minds of the persons concerned the *feeling that their private lives are the subject of constant surveillance.*[21]

In an earlier part of the judgement, the Court justified this decisive value judgement in greater detail, explaining that

> [t]hose data, taken as a whole, may allow very precise conclusions to be drawn concerning the private lives of the persons whose data has been retained, such as the habits of everyday life, permanent or temporary

---

[18] For an account of the relevant jurisprudence of the U.S. Supreme Court from a European perspective see PHILIPP WITTMANN, DER SCHUTZ DER PRIVATSPHÄRE VOR STAATLICHEN ÜBERWACHUNGSMASSNAHMEN DURCH DIE US-AMERIKANISCHE BUNDESVERFASSUNG (2014).

[19] Joined Cases C-293/12 & C-594/12, Digital Rights Ireland & Seitlinger v. Minister for Communications, Marine and Natural Resources, ¶¶ 33–35, INFOCURIA – CASE-LAW CT. JUST. (Apr. 8, 2014), http://curia.europa.eu/juris/document/document.jsf?docid=150642&doclang=EN (emphasis added) [hereinafter Digital Rights Ireland].

[20] *Id.* at ¶ 36.   [21] *Id.* at ¶ 37 (emphasis added).

places of residence, daily or other movements, the activities carried out, the social relationships of those persons and the social environments frequented by them.

In such circumstances, even though, as is apparent from Article 1(2) and Article 5(2) of Directive 2006/24, the directive does not permit the retention of the content of the communication or of information consulted using an electronic communications network, it is not inconceivable that the retention of the data in question might have an effect on the use, by subscribers or registered users, of the means of communication covered by that directive and, consequently, on their exercise of the freedom of expression guaranteed by Article 11 of the Charter.[22]

b) Justification of the Interference   The Court then turned its attention to assessing whether there was an adequate justification for the infringement of the rights that would result from the Directive's provisions. The Court was guided in its analysis by Article 52(1) of the Charter of Fundamental Rights.[23] The Court found that the retention of data required by Directive 2006/24 genuinely satisfied an *objective of general interest*. The Court explained that

[i]t is apparent from the case-law of the Court that the fight against international terrorism in order to maintain international peace and security constitutes an objective of general interest ... The same is true of the fight against serious crime in order to ensure public security ... Furthermore, it should be noted, in this respect, that Article 6 of the Charter lays down the right of any person not only to liberty, but also to security.[24]

But, the Court ruled that the *directive did not meet the standard of proportionality*. In this regard, the intensity of control by the Court is decisive. The Court concluded that

[i]n ... view of the *important role* played by the protection of personal data in the light of the fundamental right to respect *for private life* and the extent and *seriousness of the interference* with that right ... the *E.U. legislature's discretion is reduced*, with the result that *review of that discretion should be strict.*[25]

---

[22] *Id.* at ¶¶ 27–28.

[23] EUCFR art. 52 – Scope and interpretation of rights and principles, reads as follows:

1. Any limitation on the exercise of the rights and freedoms recognized by this Charter must be provided for by law and respect the essence of those rights and freedoms. Subject to the principle of proportionality, limitations may be made only if they are necessary and genuinely meet objectives of general interest recognized by the Union or the need to protect the rights and freedoms of others.

[24] Digital Rights Ireland, *supra* note 19, at ¶ 42.   [25] *Id.* at ¶ 48 (emphasis added).

In this respect the Court added that

> the right to respect for private life ... requires, according to the Court's
> settled case-law, in any event, that derogations and limitations in relation
> to the protection of personal data must apply only in so far as is *strictly
> necessary.*[26]

In order to explain the important role for private life, the Court argued
that the directive

> applies to all means of electronic communication, the use of which is very
> widespread and of *growing importance in people's everyday lives.*
> Furthermore ... the directive ... entails an interference with the funda-
> mental rights of *practically the entire European population.* ...

> It therefore applies even to persons for whom there is *no evidence* capable
> of *suggesting that their conduct might have a link,* even an indirect or
> remote one, *with serious crime.*[27]

Under such circumstances, the Court explained,

> the E.U. legislation in question *must lay down clear and precise rules*
> governing the scope and application of the measure in question *and*
> imposing *minimum safeguards ... against* the risk of *abuse* and against
> any unlawful access and use of that data.[28]

According to the Court, Directive 2006/24 failed to satisfy these standards in four ways:

> (1) *Directive 2006/24 covers,* in a generalised manner, all persons and all
> means of electronic communication as well as *all traffic data without any
> differentiation, limitation or exception* being made in the light of the
> objective of fighting against serious crime.[29]

> (2) Directive 2006/24 also *fails to lay down any objective criterion by which
> to determine the limits of the access* of the competent national authorities
> to the data and their subsequent use ... [and ... f]urthermore, Directive
> 2006/24 does not contain *substantive and procedural* conditions relating
> to the access.[30]

> (3) Directive 2006/24 does not provide appropriate determinations con-
> cerning the *data retention period,*[31] and

> (4) Directive 2006/24 does not provide for sufficient *safeguards ... against
> the risk of abuse.*[32] Especially, the directive "does not require the data in

---

[26] *Id.* at ¶ 52 (emphasis added).   [27] *Id.* at ¶¶ 56, 58 (emphasis added).
[28] *Id.* at ¶ 54 (emphasis added).   [29] *Id.* at ¶ 57 (emphasis added).
[30] *Id.* at ¶¶ 60–61 (emphasis added).   [31] *Id.* at ¶¶ 63–64.
[32] *Id.* at ¶¶ 66–67 (emphasis added).

question to be retained within the E.U." with the result that no independent data protection supervision is ensured.[33]

The Court concluded its reasoning with the explanation that

> [h]aving regard to all the foregoing considerations, it must be held that, by adopting Directive 2006/24, the E.U. *legislature has exceeded the limits imposed by compliance with the principle of proportionality* in the light of Articles 7, 8 and 52(1) of the Charter.[34]

It is not clear whether, on their own, each of the four deficiencies identified by the Court would have led to the same result. It is possible that the accumulation of so many deficiencies was decisive for the Court's conclusion. In any event, the final outcome is clear. The Advocate General, who also concluded that the Directive resulted in disproportionate intrusions upon the rights guaranteed in Articles 7 and 8 of the Charter of Fundamental Rights, preferred to temporarily suspend the legal effects of this finding.[35] The Court took the more strict path and declared the Directive to be *invalid*.[36]

3   Analysis of the Judgement

a) The Judgement as a Reaction to the Snowden Revelations?   Some commentators indicated that the judgement's dramatic result, that is, the invalidation of Directive 2006/24, might be attributed to the Snowden revelations.[37]

Indeed, at least on a first glance, the April 2014 judgement contrasts sharply with the CJEU's earlier judgments in which it upheld the Directive. In the case *Ireland v. Parliament and Council* from 2009, for example, the Court dismissed an action seeking to annul the Directive.[38] In that

---

[33] *Id.* at ¶ 68.   [34] *Id.* at ¶ 69 (emphasis added).

[35] Joined Cases C-293/12 & C-594/12, Digital Rights Ireland & Seitlinger v. Minister for Communications, Marine and Natural Resources, Opinion of Advocate General Cruz Villalón, ¶¶ 154–58, InfoCuria – Case-Law Ct. Just. (Dec. 12, 2013), http://curia .europa.eu/juris/document/document.jsf?text=&docid=145562&pageIndex=0&doclang= EN&mode=lst&dir=&occ=first&part=1&cid=391425.

[36] Digital Rights Ireland, *supra* note 19, at ¶ 71.

[37] *See, e.g.*, Wolfgang Durner, *Zum Jagen getragen – der EuGH entdeckt den Datenschutz. Anmerkung zu: EuGH (große Kammer), Urt. v. 8.4.2014, Rs. C-293/12 und C-594/12 –, Digital Rights Ireland, Seitlinger u. a., Nichtigkeit der Richtlinie über die Vorratsdatenspeicherung*, 2014 Deutsches Verwaltungsblatt 712, 713 (2014).

[38] Case C-301/06, Ireland v. Parliament, InfoCuria – Case-Law Ct. Just. (Feb. 10, 2009), http://curia.europa.eu/juris/document/document.jsf?text=&docid=72843&pageIndex= 0&doclang=EN&mode=lst&dir=&occ=first&part=1&cid=585129; *see also* Jörg Gundel,

case Ireland had argued that the Directive was adopted on an incorrect legal basis. In 2010 the Court determined that Sweden and Austria had not fulfilled their duties under E.U. law because they did not enact the necessary national implementing statutes as mandated by Directive 2006/24.[39] Thus, with its 2010 judgment the CJEU demanded that Sweden and Austria establish a data retention scheme that it would find to be an unjustified intrusion upon fundamental rights in its 2014 judgment.

Nonetheless, in all these earlier judgments the Court highlighted that it was not assessing the compliance of the Data Retention Directive with fundamental rights.[40] Although this has been criticized by some commentators,[41] the Court was merely following its longstanding practice of avoiding an annulment decision if judgment in a case can clearly be reached on the basis of other issues.[42] Similar restrain results from the distinction the Court has drawn between infringement procedures and annulment procedures.[43]

Vorratsdatenspeicherung und Binnenmarktkompetenz: Die ungebrochene Anziehungskraft des Art. 95 EGV, 2009 EUROPARECHT 536, 541 (2009); *but see* Durner, *supra* note 37, at 713; Thomas Petri, *EuGH, 10. 2. 2009 – C-301/06: Rechtsgrundlage der EG-Richtlinie zur Vorratsdatenspeicherung – Irland/Parlament*, 2009 EUROPÄISCHE ZEITSCHRIFT FÜR WIRTSCHAFTSRECHT 212, 214–15 (2009); Spiros Simitis, *Der EuGH und die Vorratsdatenspeicherung oder die verfehlte Kehrtwende bei der Kompetenzregelung*, 2009 NEUE JURISTISCHE WOCHENSCHRIFT 1782 (2009); Jörg Philipp Terhechte, *Rechtsangleichung zwischen Gemeinschafts- und Unionsrecht – die Richtlinie über die Vorratsdatenspeicherung vor dem EuGH*, 2009 EUROPÄISCHE ZEITSCHRIFT FÜR WIRTSCHAFTSRECHT 199 (2009).

[39] Case C-185/09, Commission v. Sweden, INFOCURIA – CASE-LAW CT. JUST. (Feb. 4, 2010), http://curia.europa.eu/juris/document/document.jsf?text=&docid=74925&pageIndex=0&doclang=SV&mode=req&dir=&occ=first&part=1&cid=577032 (Swed.); Case C-189/09, Commission v. Austria, INFOCURIA – CASE-LAW CT. JUST. (July 29, 2010), http://curia.europa.eu/juris/document/document.jsf?text=&docid=84357&pageIndex=0&doclang=DE&mode=lst&dir=&occ=first&part=1&cid=578157.

[40] Ireland v. Parliament, *supra* note 38, at ¶ 57; Commission v. Austria, *supra* note 39, at ¶ 15.

[41] *See, e.g.*, Petri, *supra* note 38, at 214–15.

[42] Case C-130/83, Commission v. Italy, ¶¶ 1ff., INFOCURIA – CASE-LAW CT. JUST. (July 11, 1984), http://curia.europa.eu/juris/showPdf.jsf?text=&docid=92555&pageIndex=0&doclang=EN&mode=lst&dir=&occ=first&part=1&cid=593852; Case C-226/87 Commission v Greece. ¶¶ 12ff., INFOCURIA – CASE-LAW CT. JUST. (June 30, 1988), http://curia.europa.eu/juris/showPdf.jsf?text=&docid=95516&pageIndex=0&doclang=EN&mode=lst&dir=&occ=first&part=1&cid=593852; *see also* Claus Dieter Classen, *Datenschutz ja – aber wie? Anmerkung zum Urteil des EuGH vom 8.4.2014, verb. Rs. C-293/12 und C-594/12 (Digital Rights Ireland u.a.)*, 2014 EUROPARECHT 441, 446 (2014). *But see* Nina Wunderlich & Britta Hickl, *Zum Einwand der Grundrechtswidrigkeit von Richtlinien in Vertragsverletzungsverfahren vor dem Europäischen Gerichtshof*, 2013 EUROPARECHT 107 ff. (2013).

[43] *See supra* note 42.

In this respect the judgement does not deviate from the Court's earlier cases concerning the Directive on data retention. Instead, it was the first real opportunity for the Court to review the Directive against the standards of substantive rights. Still, certain parts of the judgement indicate that the Snowden revelations raised the judges' awareness of the possible consequences of such a wide-spread data retention regime. For example, the Court highlighted the potential to use this data to develop extremely probing profiles[44] (based only on statistical assumptions) that may lead to incorrect classification of individuals with potentially serious consequences. It is hard to read the Court's finding that such sensitive data resources must be retained within Europe as anything but a clear indication of the judges' deepening privacy concerns resulting from the NSA-Affair.[45]

Yet, the internal pressures from other important players in the E.U. fundamental rights discourse may have played an even more important role in the judges' deliberations. For the CJEU this judgement was an important chance to establish itself as a fundamental rights court, even in the field of security law. The case presented the Court with a unique opportunity to address public authority in this field. Other data protection cases decided by the CJEU in recent years referred to data protection problems between private actors, such as Internet access providers and their customers.[46]

In any case, Directive 2006/24 was already under attack. As noted earlier, the German Federal Constitutional Court struck down the German implementing statute, as had some other eastern European Constitutional Courts.[47] Several Member States opposed the implementation

---

[44] Joined Cases C-293/12 & C-594/12, Digital Rights Ireland & Seitlinger v. Minister for Communications, Marine and Natural Resources, ¶ 27, INFOCURIA – CASE-LAW CT. JUST. (Apr. 8, 2014), http://curia.europa.eu/juris/document/document.jsf?docid=150642&doc lang=EN (emphasis added) [hereinafter Digital Rights Ireland]; see also Joined Cases C-293/12 & C-594/12, Digital Rights Ireland & Seitlinger v. Minister for Communications, Marine and Natural Resources, Opinion of Advocate General Cruz Villalón, ¶ 74, INFOCURIA – CASE-LAW CT. JUST. (Dec. 12, 2013), http://curia.europa.eu/juris/document/document.jsf?text=&docid=145562&pageIndex=0&doclang=EN&mode=lst&dir=&occ=first&part=1&cid=391425; Chapter 8 in this volume.

[45] Digital Rights Ireland, supra note 43, at ¶ 68.

[46] For an account of the ECJ data protection case law see Jens-Peter Schneider, *Europäische Datenschutzrichtlinie*, ¶¶ 14–34 *in* DATENSCHUTZRECHT IN BUND UND LÄNDERN – KOMMENTAR 12 (Heinrich Amadeus Wolff & Stefan Brink eds., 2013), paras 14–34 (updates available on beck-online).

[47] In addition to the German Constitutional Court, the constitutional courts of the Czech Republic and Romania (decision 1258/2009 and decision 440/2014) have declared

of the Directive due to intense debates in their political institutions and civil society.[48] Even the European Commission was considering a reform of the Directive that would place greater emphasis in civil rights.[49] Against this background it seems likely that the NSA-Affair played a role in the judges' deliberations, but it probably was not a decisive factor.

b) Effects of the Judgement on Third Countries, Such as the United States   The CJEU held that Directive 2006/24 did not provide sufficient safeguards against abuse.[50] In particular, the Court held that the Directive "does not require the data in question to be retained within the E.U." and concluded, as a result, that the Directive did not ensure independent data protection supervision.[51]

As a result, any new attempt to establish an obligation for service providers to retain such traffic data must also oblige them to locate their storage facilities within the European Union and under the supervision of a data protection supervisor of any of the E.U. Member States. This guarantees not only effective supervision, but may also hinder

national data retention statutes unconstitutional. Also, the constitutional courts of Bulgaria, Cyprus, and Hungary undertook partly critical evaluations of national implementing laws. *See* Česká Republika Ústavní Soud [Czech Republic Constitutional Court] Mar. 22, 2011, Pl. ÚS 24/10: Data Retention in Telecommunications Services, *translation at* www.usoud.cz/en/decisions/20110322-pl-us-2410-data-retention-in-telecommunica tions-services/?%3BcHash=bbaa1c5b1a7d6704af6370fdfce5d34c&cHash=a5ac071a9e661 ef4c676332221216657; Curtea Constituțională a României [CCR] [Romanian Constitutional Court] Sept. 18, 2014, Decision 1258/2009, www.ccr.ro/en/comunicate/COMU NICAT-DE-PRES-353; EU Commission, Evaluation Report on the Data Retention Directive (Directive 2006/24/EC), COM (2011) 225 final, 5–6, 20–21 [hereinafter Evaluation Report]. For an evaluation on the significant influences of the judgement of the German Constitutional Court on the reasoning of the ECJ as well as on some interesting differences, see Alexander Roßnagel, *Neue Maßstäbe für den Datenschutz in Europa - Folgerungen aus dem EuGH-Urteil zur Vorratsdatenspeicherung*, 2014 MULTIMEDIA UND RECHT 372, 374–75 (2014).

[48] *See* Case C-185/09, Commission v. Sweden, INFOCURIA – CASE-LAW CT. JUST. (Feb. 4, 2010), http://curia.europa.eu/juris/document/document.jsf?text=&docid=74925&pageIn dex=0&doclang=SV&mode=req&dir=&occ=first&part=1&cid=577032 (Swed.); Case C-189/09, Commission v. Austria, INFOCURIA – CASE-LAW CT. JUST. (July 29, 2010), http:// curia.europa.eu/juris/document/document.jsf?text=&docid=84357&pageIndex=0&doc lang=DE&mode=lst&dir=&occ=first&part=1&cid=578157; *see also* Evaluation Report, *supra* note 46, at 5.

[49] Press Release, European Commission, Commission Evaluates the Directive on Retention of Telecommunications Data (Apr. 18, 2011), http://europa.eu/rapid/press-release_IP-11–484_en.htm?locale=fr.

[50] Digital Rights Ireland, *supra* note 43, at ¶¶ 68–69.   [51] *Id.* at ¶ 68.

third-country security agencies (such as the NSA) from gaining access to those data as easily as was done under the so-called PRISM program. PRISM allowed the NSA to pursue mass surveillance of E.U. citizens through direct access to the central servers of leading United States. Internet, technology, and telecommunications companies.[52] This part of the Court's judgement is all the more noteworthy because it may support an amendment by the European Parliament to the General Data Protection Regulation. I will consider this initiative in a later part of this chapter. In addition, this certainly impacted the negotiations between the European Union and the United States concerning reform of the Safe Harbor agreement,[53] the SWIFT-agreement, and the TTIP-agreement.[54]

c) **The Judgement as a Milestone in the Development of E.U. Data Protection Law**   The judgement has stirred quite different reactions from commentators concerning its strict review of legislative actions that are related to security issues. Some journalists hailed it as a "magna carta of data protection law"[55] comparable with the judgement of the German Federal Constitutional Court's *Census Act Case* from December 1983. In that case the German Court famously derived a right to informational self-determination from Articles 1 and 2 of the Basic Law and applied that right to strike down certain parts of the law authorizing a comprehensive census.[56] In contrast, some politicians criticized the decision as providing a "holiday for organized crime."[57]

---

[52] Policy Department C: Citizens' Rights and Constitutional Affairs, The U.S. Surveillance Programmes and Their Impact on EU Citizens' Fundamental Rights, Directorate-General for Internal Policies of the European Parliament, www.europarl.europa.eu/meetdocs/2009_2014/documents/libe/dv/briefingnote_/ briefingnote_en.pdf; *see also* European Parliament Resolution of March 12, 2014 on the U.S. NSA Surveillance Programme, Surveillance Bodies in Various Member States and their Impact on EU Citizens' Fundamental Rights and on Transatlantic Cooperation in Justice and Home Affairs (2013/2188(INI)), ¶ 2, www.europarl.europa.eu/sides/getDoc .do?pubRef=-//EP//TEXT+TA+P7-TA-2014-0230+0+DOC+XML+V0//EN [hereinafter Resolution].

[53] *See EU Commission and United States agree on new framework for transatlantic data flows: E.U.–U.S. Privacy Shield*, European Commission Press Release (Feb. 2, 2016), *available at* http://europa.eu/rapid/press-release_IP-16-216_en.htm; Schrems v. Data Protection Commissioner (Case C-362/14), Oct. 6, 2015, *availble at* http://curia.europa .eu/juris/liste.jsf?num=C-362/14.

[54] *See also* Roßnagel, *supra* note 46, at 376–77.   [55] *Id.* at 377 n.60.

[56] *Bundesverfassungsgericht* [BVerfG] [Federal Constitutional Court] Dec. 15, 1983, 65 BVerfGE 1, 1 BvR 209/83.

[57] Roßnagel, *supra* note 46, at 377 n.61.

In the scholarly debate the decision was mainly welcomed as a consolidating milestone in the CJEU's fundamental rights and data protection jurisprudence.[58] Nevertheless, Lynskey questioned a "conflating" of Articles 7 and 8 of the Charter of Fundamental Rights, that is, the textually distinct right to respect of one´s private life and the right of data protection.[59] Lynskey argued that the CJEU´s approach would limit the added value of a distinct right to data protection thereby restricting its development into a right to informational self-determination similar to the right the German Constitutional Court derived from the Basic Law. But the German jurisprudence shows that the right to informational self-determination is not an end to itself. It does not, for example, give individuals unlimited power concerning data. Instead, the German constitutional right to informational self-determination serves to enhance a more substantive right such as the right to a personal development, which must and can be balanced against other private, societal, or public interests.[60]

Thus, one might argue that the CJEU's "conflation" of Articles 7 and 8 of the Charter of Fundamental Rights serves exactly such an approach, that is, it links the instrumental right of data protection to a more substantive right, such as the right to respect of private life. Moreover, the right to privacy has proven to be a rather flexible and extensive right in the jurisprudence of the CJEU and the European Court of Human Rights. This has allowed the courts to adjust the right to constitutional challenges in a changing world. With this in mind, the added value of a free-standing right to data protection is questionable.[61]

d) E.U. Competence Creep through Fundamental Rights? One result of the CJEU´s judgement is that any new data retention directive will need to include data protection safeguards. This has been interpreted as a potential expansion of the European Union's competences – at the expense of the Member States – through the articulation of fundamental

---

[58] Durner, *supra* note 37, at 715; Jürgen Kühling, *Der Fall der Vorratsdatenspeicherungsrichtlinie und der Aufstieg des EuGH zum Grundrechtsgericht*, 2014 NEUE ZEITSCHRIFT FÜR VERWALTUNGSRECHT 681, 682, 684–85 (2014); Roßnagel, *supra* note 46, at 377. *But see* Classen, *supra* note 42, at 443–47 (2014).

[59] Orla Lynskey, *Deconstructing Data Protection: The 'Added-Value' of a Right to Data Protection in the EU Legal Order*, 63 INT'L & COMP. L.Q. 569 (2014).

[60] *See* Gabriele Britz, *Informationelle Selbstbestimmung zwischen rechtswissenschaftlicher Grundsatzkritik und Beharren des Bundesverfassungsgerichts*, in OFFENE RECHTSWISSENSCHAFT 561 (Wolfgang Hoffmann-Riem ed., 2010); Schneider, *supra* note 45, at ¶ 20. *See also* Chapter 4 in this volume.

[61] *See* Schneider, *supra* note 45, at ¶¶ 15–16, 18.

rights.[62] This is a complex issue that deserves further analysis. At least with regard to the field of data protection, the consequences might be less dramatic than in other fields of law because the 2009 Treaty of Lisbon included a rather broad legislative competence with regard to data protection for the European Union in Article 16 TFEU.[63]

4   Summary

Five aspects of the CJEU's decision are particularly noteworthy.

First, the Court had no problem at all concluding that the mere storage of electronic traffic data constitutes an interference with the two Charter rights at stake. This is not only true with regard to the innovative and especially broad right of data protection secured by Article 8 of the Charter of Fundamental Rights. It also applies to the rather traditional right to respect for one's private life, which is also enshrined in the 2009 Charter of Fundamental Rights, with more or less the same wording used in the European Convention of Human Rights drafted in 1950.[64]

Second, the Court found that the interference resulting from the data retention was particularly serious. On one hand, the Court reasoned that traffic data allows very precise conclusions about people's behavior. On the other hand, the Court concluded that the data retention in question practically concerns the entire European population in a field of growing importance in everyday life.

---

[62] Classen, *supra* note 42, at 444–46; *see also* Kühling, *supra* note 56 at 684–85 ("ambivalent.").

[63] TFEU art. 16 reads as follows:

> 1. Everyone has the right to the protection of personal data concerning them.
>
> 2. The European Parliament and the Council, acting in accordance with the ordinary legislative procedure, shall lay down the rules relating to the protection of individuals with regard to the processing of personal data by Union institutions, bodies, offices and agencies, and by the Member States when carrying out activities which fall within the scope of Union law, and the rules relating to the free movement of such data. Compliance with these rules shall be subject to the control of independent authorities ...
>
> For a short account of the innovative potential of this provision see Schneider, *supra* note 45, at ¶¶ 35–36.

[64] The European Convention on Human Rights, art. 8, Nov. 4, 1950, E.T.S. 5, www.echr.coe.int/Documents/Convention_ENG.pdf. Article 8(1) of the ECHR reads as follows: "Everyone has the right to respect for his private and family life, his home and his correspondence." For the wording of Article 7 see EUCFR art.7, *supra* note 17.

Third, the Court applied a strict version of the proportionality test. This raises important questions with regard to the interinstitutional balance of powers on the E.U. level, especially the responsibilities of and relationship between the legislative organs and the judiciary.

Fourth, the Court assigned responsibility for developing more detailed data protection safeguards to the E.U.'s legislative organs if they would re-introduce a data retention obligation. This circumvents the Member States on this issue and precludes the emergence of a diverse treatment of this policy question by the Member States.[65] This raises important questions about the federal balance of power between the European Union and its Member States. As a result, data protection rights in the CFR may serve as yet another harmonizing force in the complex multi-level E.U. polity and legal order. This Europeanization of data protection law would be further intensified if the draft General Data Protection Regulation were to be adopted.

Fifth, the Court obliged the E.U.'s legislative organs to require – in any future piece of legislation mandating wide-spread data retention – that the data in question be retained within the European Union in order to guarantee effective, independent data protection supervision as required by Article 8 of the Charter of Fundamental Rights. As U.S. Internet companies are the most important providers of Internet services in Europe, already this judgement raised far-reaching questions about the Court's position toward any transatlantic transfers of data.

II   *The CJEU's* Google Spain Case

Another remarkable recent judgement of the CJEU on data protection is the *Google Spain Case* from May 13, 2014, which involved the European Data Protection Directive 92/46/EC and led to the articulation of a so-called "right to be forgotten."[66] According to the Court

---

[65] Still, in the wake of the CJEU's ruling – and pending action on a new Directive from the Commission and Parliament – the Member States have room for maneuver. *See* Chapter 21 in this volume.

[66] Case C-131/12, Google Spain SL v. Agencia Española de Protección de Datos (AEPD), INFOCURIA – CASE-LAW CT. JUST. (May 13, 2014), http://curia.europa.eu/juris/document/document.jsf;jsessionid=9ea7d0f130d58fa348967d244833bad1c86381ec1189.e34KaxiLc3eQc40LaxqMbN4Oc3aKe0?text=&docid=152065&pageIndex=0&doclang=EN&mode=lst&dir=&occ=first&part=1&cid=385379 [hereinafter Google Spain CJEU]. *See also* Chapter 22 in this volume; Chapter 16 in this volume; Chapter 11 in this volume.

the operator of a search engine is obliged to remove from the list of results displayed following a search made on the basis of a person's name links to web pages, published by third parties and containing information relating to that person, also in a case where that name or information is not erased beforehand or simultaneously from those web pages, and even, as the case may be, when its publication in itself on those pages is lawful.

This ruling did not concern the balance between data protection and security law. Nevertheless, it clearly indicates the Court's willingness to oblige transnational Internet companies to respect the European concepts of data protection law as the Court gave the European Data Protection Directive 95/46/EC a broad interpretation.[67] As a result, U.S. Internet firms such as Google have to comply with E.U. data protection law if data-processing activities of the firm in the United States and those of its establishment situated in an E.U. Member State are inextricably linked.[68]

Unfortunately, the Court did not decide whether a search engine operator is obliged to respect the right to be forgotten only on websites that are the standard access point for searches by European users, for instance in the case of Google sites like Google.de or Google.fr. This option is favored by Google.[69] The company justifies this limited approach because Google actively leads users from Europe to their respective national version of the Google search platform. In contrast, the European (especially the French) data protection authorities prefer a really global approach by ordering that Google is obliged to respect the right to be forgotten with regard to persons from the European Union on all its platforms including the Google.com version or national versions from non-E.U. countries such as Russia.[70] Scholars have been discussing this topic intensively and at the moment it is difficult to identify a leading opinion.[71]

---

[67] Google Spain CJEU at ¶¶ 32–60.   [68] Google Spain CJEU at ¶ 56.

[69] See *Responding to Article 29 Working Party's Questions*, GOOGLE (July 31, 2014), http:// googlepolicyeurope.blogspot.com/2014/07/responding-to-article-29-working-partys.html; *see also* THE ADVISORY COUNCIL TO GOOGLE ON THE RIGHT TO BE FORGOTTEN 18–20 (Feb. 6, 2015), https://drive.google.com/file/d/0B1UgZshetMd4cEI3SjlvV0hNbDA/view.

[70] *See* Article 29 Data Protection Working Party, Guidelines on the Implementation of the Court of Justice of the European Union Judgment on "Google Spain and Inc. v. Agencia Española de Protección de Datos (AEPD) and Mario Costeja González" C-131/12, 14/EN WP 225 (Nov. 26, 2014), http://ec.europa.eu/justice/data-protection/article-29/documen tation/opinion-recommendation/files/2014/wp225_en.pdf [hereinafter Guidelines].

[71] *Compare* Dan Jerker B. Svantesson, *The Google Spain Case: Part of a Harmful Trend of Jurisdictional Overreach* (Eur. U. Inst., Working Paper RSCAS 2015/45, 2015), *and* Brendan van Alsenoy and Marieke. Koekkoek, *The Extra-territorial Reach of the EU's*

III   The CJEU's Schrems/Facebook Decision

The latest landmark decision of the CJEU concerned the Safe Harbor agreement between the United States and the European Union[72] Max-imillian Schrems, an Austrian citizen, has been using Facebook for many years. Schrems lodged a complaint with the Irish supervisory authority, worrying that the data he had provided to Facebook was being trans-ferred from the company's Irish subsidiary to servers located in the United States. Schrems argued that, in the light of the Snowden revela-tions, the law and practice of the United States do not offer sufficient protection of personal data.[73] The Irish data protection authority rejected the complaint, concluding that the European Commission had adopted a decision in 2000 in which it concluded that the United States affords (under the "safe harbor" scheme) an adequate level of data protection.[74]

Schrems appealed to Ireland's High Court, which, in turn, referred the case to the CJEU. The CJEU held that the Commission's adequacy decision does not preclude – or even reduce – the independent review competence granted by the Charter of Fundamental Rights and Directive 95/46/EC to the national data protection authorities.[75] Nevertheless, the Court concluded that it alone has jurisdiction to declare that an E.U. act, such as a Commission decision, is invalid.[76]

The Court had grave misgivings about the Safe Harbor agreement with the United States. First, the Court noted that the limits on access to and use of data established by the agreement applied only to firms who volunteered to abide by them. United States public authorities were not subject to the agreement at all.[77] Second, national security, public interest, and law enforcement requirements were given priority in the agreement. This meant that firms were bound to disregard, without limitation, data protection rules that conflicted with the

---

"*Right to be Forgotten,*" (Interdisc. Ctr. for L. & ICT, Working Paper 20/2015, 2015) (both with further references).

[72] Case C-362/14, Schrems v. Data Protection Commissioner, INFOCURIA – CASE-LAW CT. JUST. (Oct. 6, 2015), http://curia.europa.eu/juris/document/document.jsf?text=&docid=169195&pageIndex=0&doclang=EN&mode=lst&dir=&occ=first&part=1&cid=391877; Case C-362/14, Schrems v. Data Protection Commissioner, Opinion of Advocate General Bot, INFOCURIA – CASE-LAW CT. JUST. (Sept. 23, 2015), http://curia.europa.eu/juris/document/document.jsf?text=&docid=168421&pageIndex=0&doclang=EN&mode=lst&dir=&occ=first&part=1&cid=391877 [hereinafter Opinion of AG Bot].

[73] Schrems, *supra* note 70, at ¶¶ 26–28.   [74] *Id.* at ¶ 29.   [75] *Id.* at ¶¶ 54–60.

[76] *Id.* at ¶¶ 61–62.   [77] *Id.* at ¶ 82.

requirements of U.S. security law.[78] Consequently, U.S. authorities were able to access the personal data transferred into the United States from the Member States in ways that offended European data protection expectations. First, access and use were permitted for purposes that were incompatible with the purposes for which the data had been transferred to the United States. Second, access and use were permitted for purposes beyond those which were strictly necessary and proportionate for the protection of national security.[79] Third, the Europeans affected by the transfer and subsequent access and use were afforded no administrative or judicial means of redress as guaranteed by Article 47 of the Charter of Fundamental Rights.[80] The Court concluded that legislation permitting public authorities to have access – on a generalized basis – to the content of electronic communications must be regarded as compromising the essence of the fundamental right to respect for private life.[81] Having regard to all the foregoing considerations, the CJEU concluded that the Commission's Safe Harbor was invalid.[82]

IV   Reflections on the CJEU's Jurisprudence – In the Shadow of the NSA-Affair

All three judgments indicate clearly that the CJEU will take an active role in developing E.U. data protection law.

C   Initiatives of the European Parliament

When compared with the European Parliament, the CJEU's reaction to the NSA-Affair might seem to have been veiled and coy. The European Parliament became the most active European institution on the issues implicated by the NSA-Affair, also when compared with the Commission and the Council.

I   European Parliament Resolution of March 12, 2014 on the U.S. NSA Surveillance Program

After having commissioned several reports on the topic in 2013, the European Parliament adopted a resolution on the U.S. NSA surveillance

---

[78] *Id.* at ¶¶ 84–86.   [79] *Id.* at ¶¶ 88–93.   [80] *Id.* at ¶ 95.   [81] *Id.* at ¶ 94.
[82] *Id.* at ¶ 106.

programme (2013/2188(INI)) on March 12 2014.[83] In short, the Parliament drafted an action plan called "A European Digital Habeas Corpus – Protecting Fundamental Rights in a Digital Age."[84] The action plan established the following agenda:

- Action 1: Adopt the Data Protection Package in 2014
- Action 2: Conclude the E.U.–U.S. Umbrella Agreement guaranteeing the fundamental right of citizens to privacy and data protection and ensuring proper redress mechanisms for E.U. citizens, including law enforcement purposes in the event of data transfers from the European Union to the United States;
- Action 3: Suspend Safe Harbor agreement for data transfer to the U.S.A. until a full review has been conducted and current loopholes are remedied, [. . .];
- Action 4: Suspend the TFTP agreement until [. . .] all concerns raised by Parliament in its resolution of October 23, 2013 have been properly addressed;
- Action 6: Protect the rule of law and the fundamental rights of E.U. citizens, (including threats to the freedom of the press), [. . .] , as well as ensuring enhanced protection for whistleblowers;
- Action 7: Develop a European strategy for greater IT independence [. . .];
- Action 8: Develop the European Union as a reference player for a democratic and neutral governance of the Internet.

Such action plans tend to be closer to wishful thinking than credible legislative agendas. But it clearly demonstrates the political consequences and the political sensitivity of data protection issues in the E.U. polity.

II European Parliament Legislative Resolution of March 12, 2014 on the Proposal for a General Data Protection Regulation: Amendment 140

A more concrete consequence of the NSA-Affair, especially with regard to the PRISM program,[85] was an amendment adopted by the European Parliament during its first reading of the draft of a General Data-

---

[83] Resolution, *supra* note 51.   [84] *Id.* at ¶¶ 97, 131–33.
[85] *See* WHITMANN, *supra* note 18.

Protection Regulation.[86] This piece of legislation is meant to update the existing data protection framework that was established in 1995 so that it is adapted to the data protection challenges of today.[87] The General Data Protection Regulation has attracted more lobbying than any previous piece of E.U. legislation.[88] It is not clear whether the European institutions can negotiate a compromise concerning this reform package. Nevertheless, the extremely popular parliamentary resolution of March 12, 2014 is a milestone in this discussion.

With respect to the NSA-Affair, amendment 140 is the most interesting.[89] It introduces a complete new Article to the Commission's proposal, which reads as follows:

> Article 43a Transfers or disclosures not authorized by Union law
>
> (1) No judgment of a court or tribunal and *no decision* of an administrative authority *of a third country requiring a controller or processor to disclose personal data shall be recognized or be enforceable* in any manner, without prejudice to a mutual legal assistance treaty or an international agreement in force between the requesting third country and the Union or a Member State.
>
> (2) Where a judgment of a court or tribunal or a decision of an administrative authority of a third country requests a controller or processor to disclose personal data, *the controller* or processor and, if any, the controller's representative, *shall notify the supervisory authority of the request*

---

[86] *See European Parliament Legislative Resolution of 12 March 2014 on the Proposal for a Regulation of the European Parliament and of the Council on the Protection of Individuals with Regard to the Processing of Personal Data and on the Free Movement of Such Data (General Data Protection Regulation),* COM (2012) 0011 – C7-0025/2012 – 2012/0011 (COD) (Ordinary legislative procedure: first reading) www.europarl.europa.eu/sides/getDoc.do?pubRef=-//EP//TEXT+TA+P7-TA-2014-0212+0+DOC+XML+V0//EN [hereinafter *Data Protection Proposal*].

[87] Directive 95/46/EC of the European Parliament and the Council of October 24, 1995 on the Protection of Individuals With Regard to the Processing of Personal Data and the Free Movement of Data, O.J. (L 281) [hereinafter Data Protection Directive]; *see* Case C-131/12, Google Spain SL v. Agencia Española de Protección de Datos (AEPD), INFOCURIA – CASE-LAW CT. JUST. (May 13, 2014), http://curia.europa.eu/juris/document/document.jsf;jsessionid=9ea7d0f130d58fa348967d244833bad1c86381ec1189.e34KaxiLc3eQc40LaxqMbN4Oc3aKe0?text=&docid=152065&pageIndex=0&doclang=EN&mode=lst&dir=&occ=first&part=1&cid=385379 [hereinafter Google Spain CJEU]; *see also* Case C-131/12, Google Spain SL v. Agencia Española de Protección de Datos (AEPD), Opinion of Advocate General Jääskinen, INFOCURIA – CASE-LAW CT. JUS. (June 25, 2013), http://curia.europa.eu/juris/document/document.jsf?text=&docid=138782&pageIndex=0&doclang=EN&mode=req&dir=&occ=first&part=1&cid=518199.

[88] *See Data Protection \ Lobbying,* EUROPEAN DIGITAL RIGHTS, http://edri.org/files/eudatap-03.pdf (last accessed Dec. 4, 2015); *see also* Schneider, *supra* note 45, at ¶ 6.2, 5–7.

[89] *See Data Protection Proposal.*

without undue delay *and must obtain prior authorization* for the transfer or disclosure by the supervisory authority.

(3) The *supervisory authority shall assess the compliance* of the requested disclosure with the Regulation and in particular whether the disclosure is necessary and legally required in accordance with points (d) and (e) of Article 44(1) and Article 44(5). *Where data subjects from other Member States are affected, the supervisory authority shall apply the consistency mechanism* referred to in Article 57.

(4) The supervisory authority shall inform the competent national authority of the request. Without prejudice to Article 21, *the controller or processor shall also inform the data subjects* of the request and of the authorization by the supervisory authority and where applicable inform the data subject whether personal data was provided to public authorities during the last consecutive 12-month period, pursuant to point (ha) of Article 14(1).[90]

This amendment is supported by the Article 29 Data Protection Working Party,[91] which has argued that being transparent about these practices will greatly enhance trust.[92] It is obvious that this amendment would put U.S. Internet technology and service firms in a difficult position by subjecting them to different E.U. and U.S. legal obligations. The probability of an enactment of this or a similar clause causing such a split of regulatory regimes in the market is even greater when one considers paragraph 68 of the CJEU's data retention judgment from 2014. Paragraph 68 can be read as an indication that the Court might contemplate announcing a constitutional obligation to implement this or a similar rule.[93] In addition, the CJEU's *Google Spain* judgement indicates the Court's willingness to oblige transnational Internet companies to respect the European approach to data protection law.[94] Moreover, the CJEU's judgement in *Schrems* obliges the Commission to negotiate

---

[90] *Id.* at amend. 140 (emphasis added).

[91] The Working Party was set up under Article 29 of Directive 95/46/EC and is composed of the national and European Data Protection Supervisors. It is an independent European advisory body on data protection and privacy.

[92] Article 29 Data Protection Working Party, Opinion 04/2014 on Surveillance of Electronic Communications for Intelligence and National Security Purposes 3, 14, 819/14/EN WP 215, (Apr. 10, 2014), www.cnpd.public.lu/fr/publications/groupe-art29/wp215_en.pdf [hereinafter Opinion].

[93] *See also* Roßnagel, *supra* note 46, at 376–77.

[94] Case C-131/12, Google Spain SL v. Agencia Española de Protección de Datos (AEPD), ¶¶ 32–60, INFOCURIA – CASE-LAW CT. JUST. (May 13, 2014), http://curia.europa.eu/juris/ document/document.jsf;jsessionid=9ea7d0f130d58fa348967d244833bad1c86381ec1189 .e34KaxiLc3eQc40LaxqMbN4Oc3aKe0?text=&docid=152065&pageIndex=0&doclang=

an agreement with the United States that contains effective safeguards for E.U. data subjects.[95] Thus, the Court's jurisprudence does not require the E.U.'s legislative organs to enact a provision similar to the one proposed by the European Parliament, but the jurisprudence indirectly supports initiatives of this kind.

D   The Commission and the Council – Reluctant Reaction to the NSA-Affair

During the European Parliament's hearings of newly designated commissioners in 2014, Věra Jourová (the nominated Commissioner for Justice, Consumers and Gender Equality) insisted that she would pursue the swift adoption of a modern data protection reform. Commissioner Jourová shares a mandate over data protection with Andrus Ansip, the Vice-President for the Digital Single Market. Regarding the questions about the "umbrella agreement" (on law enforcement data exchange) and the Safe Harbor agreements with the United States, Jourová stressed that it would be necessary to restore trust between the European Union and the United States and that the Safe Harbor agreement must be made really safe.[96] Also, President Juncker's Mission Letter to Commissioner Jourová highlighted the swift adoption of the data protection reform package as one of the priorities of the new E.U. Commission.[97] Consequently, one might have expected that the new Commission would follow the path of the former 2010–2014 Commission in this regard. The former Commission published a communication in November 2013 expressing deep concerns about the Snowden revelations and the lost trust

---

EN&mode=lst&dir=&occ=first&part=1&cid=385379 [hereinafter Google Spain CJEU].

See Chapter 22 in this volume; Chapter 16 in this volume; Chapter 11 in this volume.

[95] *EU Commission and United States agree on new framework for transatlantic data flows: E.U.–U.S. Privacy Shield*, EUROPEAN COMMISSION PRESS RELEASE (Feb. 2, 2016), *available at* http://europa.eu/rapid/press-release_IP-16-216_en.htm.

[96] *See* Věra Jourová, Commissioner-Designate, Introductory Statement of the Commissioner-Designate to the EWurropean Parliament (Oct. 1, 2014), http://ec.europa.eu/commission/sites/cwt/files/commissioner_ep_hearings/jourova-statement_en.pdf; Věra Jourová, Answers to the European Parliament Questionnaire to the Commissioner-Designate, http://ec.europa.eu/commission/sites/cwt/files/commissioner_ep_hearings/jourova-reply_en.pdf.

[97] *See* Letter from Jean-Claude Juncker, President of the European Commission, to Věra Jourová, Commissioner for Justice, Consumers and Gender Equality (Nov. 1, 2014), http://ec.europa.eu/commission/sites/cwt/files/commissioner_mission_letters/jourova_en.pdf.

concerning E.U.–U.S. data flows. More concretely, the previous Commission recommended renegotiations of important E.U.–U.S. data exchange agreements, including the Safe Harbor agreement.[98] Nevertheless, the previous Commission did not initiate suspensions of the existing agreements as demanded by the European Parliament. Instead, the Commission waited for the CJEU's judgement in the *Schrems Case* before taking action. After the Court delivered its judgement the Commission was forced to renegotiate a data protection agreement for private data transfers to the United States, taking into account the requirements of adequate data protection as developed by the CJEU.[99]

The European Council has been even more cautious. For example, it handled the draft data protection regulation rather reluctantly, although many Member States signaled their desire for a more progressive approach to this dossier in public statements after the Snowden revelations.[100] In October 2014, the Council discussed the regulation at a Council meeting at which it reached a preliminary consensus but did not mention the Parliament's amendment 140. It took several months, interim papers, and meetings before the Council reached an overall consensus as a baseline for the trilogy,[101] which is planned to be finalized at the end of 2015. Still, the positions of the three legislative bodies are quite diverse. This raises concerns about whether the institutions really will be able to find common ground concerning the new regulation.

E   Conclusion

Against the background of the divergent positions in the political and legislative institutions of the European Union, the CJEU again seems to have assumed the role of a driving force of European legal developments.

---

[98] *Communication from the Commission to the European Parliament and the Council, Rebuilding Trust in E.U.–U.S. Data Flows*, at 10, COM (2013) 846 final (Nov. 27, 2013).

[99] *See supra* note 95.

[100] Jens-Peter Schneider, *Europäische Datenschutzrichtlinie* ¶¶ 5.7, 6, *in* BECK OK DATENSCHUTZRECHT IN BUND UND LÄNDERN – KOMMENTAR (Heinrich Amadeus Wolff & Stefan Brink eds., 10th ed. 2014).

[101] *See* Note from the Presidency of the Council of the European Union to the Working Group on Information Exchange and Data Protection (DAPIX), Proposal for a Regulation of the European Parliament and of the Council on the Protection of Individuals with Regard to the Processing of Personal Data and on the Free Movement of such Data (General Data Protection Regulation), Council document 10391/15 (July 8, 2015), www.statewatch.org/news/2015/jul/eu-council-dp-reg-trilogue-10391-15.pdf.

The 2014 *Data Retention Case*, the 2014 *Google Spain Case*, and the 2015 *Schrems Case* demonstrate that the Court increasingly sees itself as a European constitutional court, at least with regard to the protection of fundamental rights enshrined in the Charter for Fundamental Rights. This should be welcomed as a way of developing the European legal community into a more balanced legal system between the poles of a mainly functionalist approach and an excessive protection of individual rights against public powers. Complex legal arrangements are definitely needed with regard to the regulation and supervision of data-processing by security and intelligence services – including those of E.U. Member States or third countries, such as the United States. The Court's case law cannot substitute for detailed legislation. The *Google Spain Case* is a clear example of the limitations of case law in the field of global data-processing. The Court was not able to establish procedures that reflect the multipolar structure of the interests at stake.[102] The 2014 *Data Retention Case* exhibits similar limitations. The Court struck down the existing directive because it did not establish the necessary procedural and material safeguards. The establishment of a legal framework through legislation covering the retention of data from communication traffic remains a task for Europe's legislative organs. Above all, the framework that emerges must be compatible with Europe's high standards for data protection. The CJEU, with its rulings promoting data protection in the shadow of the NSA-Affair, can stimulate the legislative process. Yet, the major forces in this regard must be the E.U.'s political institutions. It remains to be seen whether they will adequately assume their respective responsibilities.

---

[102] Schneider, *supra* note 96, at ¶ 32.

21

Why Blanket Surveillance Is No Security Blanket

Data Retention in the United Kingdom after the European Data Retention Directive

BY LUCIA ZEDNER

A   Introduction: From Targeted to Mass Surveillance

In the wake of 9/11 invasive new security measures were targeted at potential terrorists. Critics were quick to observe that the "security-gains for most people are being balanced against liberty-losses for a few."[1] History suggests, however, that security measures introduced in respect of particular suspect groups spread rapidly to affect the wider population.[2] Perhaps it was unsurprising therefore that the 2004 Madrid and 2005 London bombings prompted a larger shift in Europe from targeted to mass surveillance.[3] A prominent example of this trend was the Data Retention Directive issued by the European Union in 2006, which obliged Member States to require operators to collect and retain all telecommunications traffic data.[4] The Directive constituted a significant move from security measures directed at identified suspects

---

[1] Jeremy Waldron, *Security and Liberty: The Image of Balance*, 11 J. Pol. Phil. 191, 203 (2003); Lucia Zedner, *Securing Liberty in the Face of Terror: Reflections from Criminal Justice*, 32 J.L. & Soc'y 507 (2005).

[2] Paddy Hillyard, *The Normalization of Special Powers from Northern Ireland to Britain*, in A Reader on Criminal Justice 63 (Nicola Lacey ed., 1994).

[3] Marie-Helen Maras, *From Targeted to Mass Surveillance: Is the E.U. Data Retention Directive a Necessary Measure or an Unjustified Threat to Privacy?*, in New Directions in Surveillance and Privacy 74–106 (Benjamin J. Goold & Daniel Neyland eds., 2013).

[4] Directive 2006/24/EC of the European Parliament and of the Council of March 15, 2006, on the Retention of Data Generated or Processed in Connection with the Provision of Publicly Available Electronic Communications Services or of Public Communications Networks and Amending Directive 2002/58/EC, 2006 O.J. (L 105) 54 [hereinafter Data Retention Directive]. In the U.K., the Anti-Terrorism, Crime and Security Act already provided for mass data retention on a voluntary basis. *See* Anti-Terrorism, Crime and Security Act 2001, c. 24, § 102 (Eng.).

to the routine surveillance of *all* E.U. citizens, irrespective of any evidence of their involvement in criminal, let alone terrorist, activity.[5] This trend toward mass surveillance of ordinary citizens was only much later exposed by the Snowden revelations to be vastly greater than suspected.[6]

Well before the NSA-Affair, the shift to universal data retention across Europe was recognized to constitute a serious intrusion on the rights to privacy and protection of personal data. How far privacy should be considered an absolute right, how far it may be qualified or even trumped by countervailing interests, has long been disputed.[7] The European Charter of Fundamental Rights sets out the rights to privacy (Article 7) and protection of personal data (Article 8) in unqualified terms, whereas Article 8 of the European Convention on Human Rights stipulates that privacy may be limited "in the interests of national security, public safety or the economic well-being of the country, for the prevention of disorder or crime, for the protection of health or morals, or for the protection of the rights and freedoms of others." These are potentially significant qualifications since the claims of national and public interest are always liable to weigh heavily against the rights of the lone individual.[8]

This chapter examines the troubled history of data retention in Europe since 2006. It shows that the mass surveillance of communications data was by no means only the child of NSA-led programs and it considers whether the intrusions on civil liberties entailed by such surveillance were

---

[5] Marie-Helen Maras, *The Social Consequences of a Mass Surveillance Measure: What Happens When We Become the "Others"?*, 40 INT'L J.L. CRIME & JUST. 65 (2012a); Elia Zureik, *Theorizing Sureveillance: The Case of the Workplace, in* SURVEILLANCE AS SOCIAL SORTING: PRIVACY, RISK , AND DIGITAL DISCRIMINATION 31 (David Lyon ed., 2002).

[6] *See, e.g.,* Alan Rusbridger, *The Snowden Leaks and the Public*, N.Y. REV. BOOKS (Nov. 21, 2013), http://perma.cc/PEQ7-4GZX. *See also* DAVID ANDERSON Q.C., A QUESTION OF TRUST: REPORT OF THE INVESTIGATORY POWERS REVIEW 18 (2015), https://terrorismlegislationreviewer.independent.gov.uk/wp-content/uploads/2015/06/IPR-Report-Print-Version.pdf.

[7] Judith Jarvis Thomson, *The Right to Privacy*, 4 PHIL. & PUB. AFF. 295 (1975); Ruth E. Gavison, *Privacy and the Limits of Law*, 89 YALE L.J. 421 (1980); AMITAI ETZIONI, THE LIMITS OF PRIVACY (1999).

[8] Lucia Zedner, *Punishment and the Plurality of Privacy Interests, in* PRIVACY AND THE CRIMINAL LAW 163, 165 (Erik Claes, Antony Duff & Serge Gutwirth eds., 2006); David Archard, *The Value of Privacy, in* PRIVACY AND THE CRIMINAL LAW, Id. at 13, 31. On the complex relationship between the European Charter of Fundamental Rights and the European Convention of Human Rights, *see* Sionaidh Douglas-Scott, *The Relationship between the E.U. and the ECHR five years on from the Treaty of Lisbon, in* THE E.U. CHARTER OF FUNDAMENTAL RIGHTS AS A BINDING INSTRUMENT 21 (Sybe de Vries, Ulf Bernitz & Stephen Weatherill eds., 2015).

justified, necessary, and proportionate. It examines the growth of opposition and legal challenges to data retention that led to the landmark European Court of Justice ruling in April 2014, which held that the European Data Retention Directive is – and was from the very outset – invalid for disproportionality. I evaluate this extraordinary judgment and its legal implications before going on to analyze the United Kingdom's desperate bid to restore and maintain data retention powers through emergency legislation and the impassioned debate and legal challenge that followed. My analysis of the twists and turns in the recent history of data retention reflects both upon the enormous pressures imposed by the threat of terrorist attacks in Europe and the exceptional difficulty of ensuring that surveillance powers are consistent with the protection of privacy and individual liberty.

B   A Brief History of the Data Retention Directive

Data retention is a longstanding weapon in the European security arsenal. Limited data retention had been permitted in Europe since 1997, under the E.U. Directive 97/66/EC, which allowed Member States to legislate to retain data "where necessary for the protection of public security, defence or public order, including the economic well-being of the state when the activities related to state security matters and for the enforcement of criminal law."[9] The so-called "ePrivacy Directive" of 2002[10] attempted to protect privacy in Europe by requiring that all electronic communications traffic data be erased or made anonymous when no longer needed for billing purposes, unless the subscriber or user had consented to retention.[11] Yet under this same Directive, E.U. states were permitted to derogate from the principle of confidentiality of communications by retaining data for law enforcement purposes, "when such restriction constitutes a necessary, appropriate and proportionate measure within a democratic society to safeguard national security (i.e., State security), defense, public security, and the prevention, investigation,

---

[9]   Directive 97/66/EC of the European Parliament and of the Council of 15 December 1997 Concerning the Processing of Personal Data and the Protection of Privacy in the Telecommunications Sector art. 14(1), 1997 O.J. (L 24) 1.

[10]   Directive 2002/58/EC of the European Parliament and of the Council of 12 July 2002 Concerning the Processing of Personal Data and the Protection of Privacy in the Electronic Communications Sector (Directive on Privacy and Electronic Communications), 2002 O.J. (L 201) 37 [hereinafter ePrivacy Directive].

[11]   *Id.*

detection and prosecution of criminal offences or of unauthorized use of the electronic communication system."[12] As a consequence data retention was mandated in some jurisdictions but not others, which resulted in widely varied legal regimes and differing obligations imposed upon service providers – notably telecommunications companies – across Europe.[13] This arguably hindered the availability of data for security and law enforcement purposes. The terrorist attacks in Madrid (2004) and London (2005) greatly increased pressure to ensure uniform data retention and harmonization of legal regimes within the European Union.

These factors informed the European Data Retention Directive (2006), which sought to harmonize legal arrangements for retention of data generated or processed by publicly available electronic communications services and public communications networks across Europe.[14] The Directive was intended to ensure that this data was available to help prevent, detect, investigate, and prosecute serious crime, particularly organized crime and terrorism,[15] by obliging E.U. Member States to ensure that providers of publically available electronic communications services and networks retained metadata.[16] This was to include data relating to the originator and recipient of communications (email address or phone number); the type, time, and duration of communication; the equipment used; its location; and details of sites visited on the Internet.[17] In short, the "who, where, when and how" of online communication was to be preserved by the telecommunications operators.

In the interests of privacy, no data about the content of the communication could be retained and Internet searches that might reveal content rather than mere traffic were to be excluded.[18] "Serious crime" was nowhere defined in the Directive, chiefly because the delineation of crime is a matter of national sovereignty. Retained data was to be provided only

---

[12] *Id.* at art. 15(1).

[13] *See* Data Rentention Directive, *supra* note 4, at pmbl. § 5; Federico Fabbrini, *Human Rights in the Digital Age: The European Court of Justice Ruling in the Data Retention Case and Its Lessons for Privacy and Surveillance in the U.S.,* 28 HARV. HUM. RTS. J. 65, 73 (2015).

[14] Data Retention Directive, *supra* note 4.

[15] *Id.* at pmbl. § 9 ("Because retention of data has proved to be such a necessary and effective investigative tool for law enforcement. . . .").

[16] *Id.* at art. 3.

[17] *Id.* at art. 5(1) The Directive applied to fixed network telephones, mobile phones, Internet access, Internet email, and Internet phones.

[18] *Id.* at art. 5(2).

to "competent national authorities," yet states were left to determine which bodies were deemed competent, the procedures to be followed, and the conditions to be fulfilled before data was shared.[19] Despite the avowed aim of harmonization, the Directive left much to the discretion of individual states, whose interpretation and implementation under national law consequently differed widely.[20]

The Directive was passed with unusual speed in just under three months in 2006.[21] This exceptional timetable was said to be justified by the urgency and gravity of the security situation, but it had the effect of limiting opportunity for consultation, debate, and effective opposition. This radical shift to mass surveillance might have been expected to have attracted widespread protest or, at least, the "natural political resistance" ordinarily generated by measures that affect many rather than the few.[22] Yet, despite the fact that the Directive required states to introduce sweeping powers to collect and retain data for up to two years, it prompted relatively little public debate or controversy at the time of its enactment.[23] Small protests were held across Europe but the 15,000 protesters who marched in Berlin – demanding "Liberty instead of Fear – stop the Surveillance Mania!" – were a tiny proportion of the roughly 460 million E.U. citizens affected.[24] Possible explanations for the lack of more generalized public outcry include the speed with which the Directive was passed, the severity of the terrorist threat, and consequent public acceptance of the case made by security agencies.[25] Prior to the shocking disclosures by Snowden and others, it may be that the general public was simply insufficiently alert to the erosion of liberties entailed by data retention and relatively indifferent, therefore, to the attendant loss of privacy. At least as long as data was retained within Europe. Only since

---

[19] *Id.* at art. 4.

[20] Elspeth Guild & Sergio Carrera, *The Political and Judicial Life of Metadata: Digital Rights Ireland and the Trail of the Data Retention Directive*, 65 CEPS PAPERS LIBERTY & SECURITY EUR. 1, 2 (2014), www.ceps.eu/system/files/EG%20and%20SC%20Data%20 retention.pdf.

[21] Instead of the year ordinarily taken to adopt such measures.

[22] CASS SUNSTEIN, LAWS OF FEAR: BEYOND THE PRECAUTIONARY PRINCIPLE 208 (2005).

[23] Marie-Helen Maras, *While the European Union Was Sleeping, the Data Retention Direct-ive Was Passed: The Political Consequences of Mandatory Data Retention*, 6 HAMBURG REV. SOC. SCI. 1 (2011).

[24] Colin J. Bennett, THE PRIVACY ADVOCATES: RESISTING THE SPREAD OF SURVEILLANCE 133 (2008). *See also "Liberty instead of Fear": More Than 15,000 Participants*, www.vorratsdatenspeicherung.de/content/view/142/79/lang,en/ (last visited Dec. 5, 2015)

[25] Maras, *supra* note 23, at 10.

the NSA-Affair has the European public come to appreciate the true scale of the U.S. surveillance program and to contest mass data retention in light of what is now known.[26]

If the genesis of the Directive was unusual, its implementation was no less problematic. Member states were required to transpose the Directive into national law by September 2007, but since the manner in which they did so was left to national determination by the deadline only 25 of 27 had enacted such laws.[27] Significant national differences arose in respect of the purposes for which data was retained; which operators were required to comply; the scope of the data retained; which authorities were granted access; the retention period; the relevant supervisory authorities; the principles by which they exercised their powers; and the restraints upon them.[28] The extent and range of these disparities led the European Data Protection Supervisor to conclude starkly that the Directive "has failed to harmonise national legislation."[29]

Legal challenges soon followed, with the constitutional courts of three Member States (Romania, Germany, and the Czech Republic) annulling their respective data retention legislation. Together with other constitutional courts (Bulgaria and Cyprus) they found the Directive to be unconstitutional, unjustifiably intrusive, or both.[30] A series of cases challenging the Directive, brought by lobby organizations and rights groups, were heard in domestic courts across Europe.[31] They raised issues relating to the legality of its scope, compatibility with fundamental rights, and transposition into national law. Domestic courts questioned whether the provisions were "precise and predictable," "necessary," and

---

[26] Guild & Carrera, *supra* note 20, at 1.

[27] Data Retention Directive, *supra* note 4, at art. 15. Australia and Sweden had implemented no laws on data retention and Belgium had only partially done so.

[28] *Report from the Commission to the Council and the European Parliament: Evaluation report on the Data Retention Directive (Directive 2006/24/EC)*, COM (2011) 225 final (Apr. 18, 2011) [hereinafter *Report*].

[29] *Id.* at 30 n.126 (citing Peter Hustinx, Remarks at the conference "Taking on the Data Retention Directive" (Dec. 3, 2010).).

[30] Curtea Constituţională a României [CCR] [Romanian Constitutional Court] Sept. 18, 2014, Decision 1258/2009, www.ccr.ro/en/comunicate/COMUNICAT-DE-PRES-353; Bundesverfassungsgericht [BVerfG] [Federal Constitutional Court] Mar. 2, 2010, 125 BVerfGE 260; Česká Republika Ústavní Soud [Czech Republic Constitutional Court] Mar. 22, 2011, Pl. US 24/10: Data Retention in Telecommunications Services, *translation at* www.usoud.cz/en/decisions/20110322-pl-us-2410-data-retention-in-tele communications-services/?%3BcHash=bbaa1c5b1a7d6704af6370fdfce5d34c&cHash= a5ac071a9e661ef4c676332221216657.

[31] *See* Fabbrini, *supra* note 13.

"proportionate to the desired aim." Above all, they doubted that the Directive's terms were sufficient to "preserve the essence of the funda- mental rights concerned," including the right to privacy and the protec- tion of personal data.[32] The force of these concerns was partly confirmed when the European Commission later acknowledged that, from its inception to 2014, law enforcement agencies made about 1.5 million requests for retained data under the Directive.[33] The authorities were clearly making extensive use of the retained data despite concern that there was little evidence as to its efficacy as a tool to prevent, combat, or prosecute serious crime or terrorism.[34]

This groundswell of opposition needs to be understood in the context of the Snowden revelations, whose effect was massively to increase public knowledge and alarm about surveillance. In January 2014, the Civil Liberties Committee of the European Parliament summed up the mood of the times when it reported on wide-ranging anxiety about the extent of cooperation and involvement by E.U. Member States with U.S. surveil- lance programs. It deplored the "high risk of violation of E.U. legal standards, fundamental rights and data protection standards,"[35] "the increasingly blurred boundaries between law enforcement and intelli- gence activities, leading to every citizen being treated as a suspect" and the resulting "threats to privacy."[36]

C Digital Rights Ireland (2014) – The Directive Is Dead

It is in light of the intense transatlantic debates about privacy and surveillance prompted by the NSA-Affair that the landmark judgment by the Court of Justice of the European Union (CJEU) in the Digital Rights Ireland case on the legality of the Data Retention Directive needs to be read.[37] The CJEU has a growing reputation for the quality of its

---

[32] *Report* at 8.   [33] Guild and Carrera, *supra* note 20, at 3.

[34] Even the *Report* provides no more than limited, largely anecdotal evidence on the value of retained data in criminal investigations.

[35] *Draft Report on the U.S. NSA Surveillance Programme, Surveillance Bodies in Various Member States and Their Impact on E.U. Citizens' Fundamental Rights and on Transat- lantic Cooperation in Justice and Home Affairs*, at 7, 2013/2188(INI) (Jan. 8, 2014).

[36] *Id.* at 8. All of which it deemed to gravely threaten the mutual trust underpinning ties between Europe and the United States.

[37] Joined Cases C-293/12 & C-594/12, Digital Rights Ireland & Seitlinger v. Minister for Communications, Marine and Natural Resources, INFOCURIA – CASE-LAW CT. JUST. (Apr. 8, 2014), http://curia.europa.eu/juris/document/document.jsf?docid=150642&doc lang=EN [hereinafter Digital Rights Ireland].

jurisprudence on rule of law questions and this was not the first occasion on which the legality of the Directive had been reviewed by the Court.[38] In 2009 the Irish Government had unsuccessfully challenged the legal basis of the Directive but not its compatibility with fundamental rights.[39] A further case was brought in Ireland by the campaign group Digital Rights Ireland, and in Austria by the state government of Carinthia (*Kärntner Landesregierung*) together with by Mr Seitlinger, Mr Tschohl and 11,128 other applicants before the Austrian Constitutional Court (*Verfassungsgerichtshof*). The Austrian Constitutional Court questioned whether the Directive was compatible with the Charter of Fundamental Rights because it allowed so many types of data to be stored concerning such large numbers of people for long periods. The Austrian Constitutional Court took the view that the retention of data almost exclusively affected persons whose conduct in no way justified holding data relating to them: that is to say, the ordinary public.[40]

These cases resulted in preliminary references to the CJEU, which then joined them with the cases *Digital Rights Ireland* and *Kärntner Landesregierung Seitlinger and Others*.[41] The resulting case, heard in April 2014, led to the CJEU's extraordinary judgment that the Data Retention Directive was invalid on the grounds that it entailed a wide-ranging and serious interference with the fundamental rights to respect for private life and the protection of personal data.[42] The Court was particularly troubled by its conclusion that the Directive did not limit this significant interference to circumstances and measures that were strictly necessary.[43] Its conclusion, although based in E.U. law and grounded in very different notions of privacy to those in the United States, had clear resonance for debates on the either side of the Atlantic.

The CJEU found that the Directive significantly interfered in rights of privacy and protection of personal data by requiring universal retention of data and allowing "competent national authorities" access to it. Although the Directive did not require the retention of communications content, the Court found that, taken as a whole, retained data gave very

---

[38] Thomas von Danwitz, *The Rule of Law in the Recent Jurisprudence of the ECJ*, 37 FORDHAM INT'L L.J. 1311 (2014). Prof Dr Dr von Danwitz was a judge at the European Court of Justice since 2006 and President of the fifth chamber of the Court since 2012.

[39] Case C-301/06, Ireland v. Parliament, INFOCURIA – CASE-LAW CT. JUST. (Feb. 10, 2009), http://curia.europa.eu/juris/document/document.jsf?text=&docid=72843&pageIndex=0&doclang=EN&mode=lst&dir=&occ=first&part=1&cid=585129. *See* Guild and Carrera, *supra* note 20, at 3.

[40] Digital Rights Ireland, *supra* note 37, at ¶ 20.   [41] *Id.*   [42] *Id.*   [43] *Id.*

precise information about the private lives of individuals, their habits, residence, movements, activities, social relations, and the social environments they frequented.[44] The fact that data were held for everyone, irrespective of who they were and whether or not they posed a risk to security, was, in the view of the Court, "likely to generate in the minds of the persons concerned the feeling that their private lives are the subject of *constant surveillance.*"[45] The U.K. rights organization Liberty and other campaign groups expressed concern about the sensitivity of such data and its potentially serious political and legal consequences as follows

> just the fact of a single communication and the identity of the parties speaks volumes: the phone call from a senior civil servant to a Times reporter immediately before a major whistle-blower scandal fills the front pages, the email to a civil liberties watchdog from a police officer during the course of an inquest into a death in police custody.[46]

Although the material objective of the Directive was sound – "the fight against international terrorism in order to maintain international peace and security constitutes an objective of general interest"[47] – the Court insisted on the need to verify that measures were proportionate, that is to say appropriate and necessary, to attain this objective. The Court held that the resulting wide-ranging and serious interference in fundamental rights was not sufficiently circumscribed, noting in particular that the Directive covered, "all persons and all means of electronic communication as well as all traffic data without any differentiation, limitation or exception being made in the light of the objective of fighting against serious crime."[48] In short, the CJEU found that the Directive targeted everyone in Europe, even where there was no evidence to suggest that there was any link, even indirectly or remotely, with serious crime. As such it was disproportionate.[49]

In its judgment, the Court's reasoning touched on multiple interrelated grounds. It found that because there was no provision for exceptions, retention applied even to those whose communications are ordinarily protected by law to meet obligations of professional secrecy, including lawyers' privileged professional communication with their

---

[44] Liberty *et al.*, *Briefing on the Fast-Track Data Retention and Investigatory Powers Bill*, at 8, LIBERTY, www.liberty-human-rights.org.uk/sites/default/files/Briefing%20on%20the%20 Data%20Retention%20and%20Investigatory%20Powers%20Bill.pdf (last visited Dec. 5, 2015).

[45] Digital Rights Ireland, *supra* note 37, at ¶ 37 (emphasis added).   [46] *Id.* at ¶ 8.

[47] *Id.* at ¶ 42.   [48] *Id.* at ¶ 57.   [49] *Id.* at ¶ 58.

clients.[50] It noted that the Directive failed to specify criteria to ensure that data would be used only in respect of crimes sufficiently serious to justify the intervention in rights entailed.[51] Instead, the Directive referred simply to "serious crime," leaving the definition of this element to each Member State under national law.[52] Moreover it lacked a requirement that would ensure that access to and use of the data were limited to that which was "strictly necessary" for the purposes of preventing, detecting, or prosecuting serious crimes.[53]

On the question of retention, the Court noted that the Directive required all data be retained for at least six months without distinguishing between different types or categories of data or its possible usefulness.[54] Although the retention period was between six and 24 months, no criteria were stipulated to ensure data were retained for no longer than was strictly necessary.[55] The Court was also troubled by the lack of sufficient safeguards to ensure effective protection of retained data against the risk of abuse and of unlawful access.[56] Given the vast quantity of data held and its sensitive nature, the Court found it particularly significant that there were no rules requiring states to ensure its integrity and confidentiality.[57] The Court found the provisions that allowed service providers (notably telecommunications companies) to have regard for economic considerations especially problematic as they were likely to adversely affect the quality of security maintained.[58] Moreover, it found that the Directive failed to ensure that the data were irreversibly destroyed at the end of the retention period.[59] Finally, the Court noted that the Directive did not require that the collected data be retained within the European Union and, for this reason, could not agree that the collected personal data were ensured adequate protection.[60]

The Court concluded that the Directive entailed a serious interference in fundamental rights; that it did not lay down clear rules governing the

---

[50] *Id.*   [51] *Id.* at ¶ 60.   [52] *Id.* at ¶ 61.   [53] *Id.* at ¶ 62.   [54] *Id.* at ¶ 63.

[55] *Id.* at ¶¶ 64–65.   [56] *Id.* at ¶ 66.   [57] *Id.*

[58] *Id.* at ¶ 67. *See also* Marie-Helen Maras, *The Economic Costs and Consequences of Mass Communications Data Retention: Is the Data Retention Directive a Proportionate Measure?*, 33 EUR. J.L. & ECON. 447 (2012).

[59] Digital Rights Ireland, *supra* note 37, at ¶ 67.

[60] *Id.* at ¶ 68. Charter on the Fundamental Rights of the European Union, Dec. 7, 2000, O.J. (C 364) 1 art. 8 ("Protection of personal data" requires that compliance "shall be subject to control by an independent authority." The fact that transfer of data to non-E.U. countries is lawful may result in data being accessed under national laws that are not necessarily compatible with E.U. rights.).

extent of this interference and could not guarantee it would be limited to that which was strictly necessary. For all these reasons the Court judged the Directive to exceed the limits imposed by the principle of proportionality and held that it was invalid for violation of Charter rights. Although the judgment made no reference to the NSA-Affair, it was significant that just as the United States was contemplating shifting data retention from government to private companies, the Court found that retention of metadata by private companies had violated rights to privacy and data protection. As such, the judgment arguably provided "a clear-cut rebuttal"[61] to the United States hope that such rights might be better secured by shifting data retention to the private sector.

The Court stressed that "the declaration of invalidity takes effect from the date on which the Directive entered into force,"[62] that is, it was void from its inception.[63] In the Member States that had transposed the Directive directly into national law, those laws were automatically invalid, leaving an alarming legal vacuum. Where states gave effect to the Directive by passing laws that varied or deviated from it, their legality depended on whether or not those laws were in accord with the European Charter of Fundamental Rights. In many cases, domestic courts had already found the Directive to be unconstitutional.[64] In others, questions of compatibility with fundamental rights had already been brought before the domestic courts or raised by official bodies (e.g., in Belgium, Bulgaria, France, and Spain).[65] Across Europe, the judgment provoked demands for national debate and review of existing provisions.[66] Significantly, the judgment also raised questions about the soundness of criminal convictions based on evidence taken from data that had been retained under the Directive (or the relevant national laws) and raised the prospect of multiple appeals on the grounds that evidence had been illegally obtained.[67]

---

[61] Fabbrini, *supra* note 13, at 67.

[62] Press Release, Court of Justice of the European Union, The Court of Justice Declares the Data Retention Directive to be Invalid (Apr. 8, 2014), http://curia.europa.eu/jcms/upload/docs/application/pdf/2014-04/cp140054en.pdf.

[63] Judith Rauhofer & Daithí Mac Síthigh, *The Data Retention Directive Never Existed*, 11 SCRIPTED 118, http://script-ed.org/?p=1480.

[64] *See supra* note 30.

[65] *See Report, supra* note 28 at § 4.9 ("Decisions of Constitutional Courts concerning transposing laws").

[66] Guild & Carrera, *supra* note 20, at p.9ff.

[67] Monica Salgado, *Data Retention – What Now?*, PRIVACY & DATA PROTECTION (July–Aug. 2014), at 15.

National governments were left to repeal or revise existing laws or to contrive new legislation compliant with the Charter of Fundamental Rights, the ePrivacy Directive, and the principles set out in the Court's judgment.[68] In light of the tumult created by the judgment, Rauhofer and Mac Sithigh anticipated "a sustained period of legal uncertainty" and they cautioned that "the prudent Member State should hesitate before readopting provisions along the lines of the now invalid Directive."[69] The judgment also constituted a strong caution against the view – widely held in the United States – that transfer of data retention to private companies would better protect against unwarranted government interference and thus limit the reach of the surveillance state.

D   Reactions to *Digital Rights Ireland* – the Directive Is Dead, Long Live the Directive

The April judgment was met by shocked silence by those officials in Europe charged with privacy protection who were arguably its target.[70] Predictably, the ruling was hailed by many observers and lobby organizations as a robust defense of human rights – specifically the Charter rights to privacy (Article 7), data protection (Article 8) and freedom of expression (Article 11).[71] The ruling was widely applauded by privacy organizations and others as "a major victory for civil rights in Europe"[72] and the

---

[68]   ePrivacy Directive, *supra* note 10, at art. 15(1) (permitting "legislative measures providing for the retention of data for a limited period."); ePrivacy Directive, *supra* note 10, at art. 6 (1) (stipulating that retention must be necessary, appropriate, and proportionate to the objectives to be achieved.).

[69]   Rauhofer & Mac Sithigh, *supra* note 63, at 9.

[70]   One of the few E.U. institutions to welcome the judgment was the European Data Protection Supervisor (EDPS) who announced: 'We consider this a *landmark* judgment that limits the blanket government surveillance of communications data' and welcomed the high value it a placed on the protection of fundamental rights. Press Release, European Data Protection Supervisor, The CJEU Rules that the Data Retention Directive is Invalid (Apr. 8, 2014), https://secure.edps.europa.eu/EDPSWEB/webdav/site/mySite/shared/Documents/EDPS/PressNews/Press/2014/14-04-08_Press_statement_DRD_EN.pdf.

[71]   Orla Lynskey, *Deconstructing Data Protection: The "Added-Value" of a Right to Data Protection in the EU Legal Order*, 63 INT'L & COMP. L.Q. 569 (2014).

[72]   Press Release, Privacy International, European Court Invalidates Data Retention Directive, Says Mass Surveillance of Metadata Interferes With Right to Privacy (Apr. 8, 2014), www.privacyinternational.org/node/473; Charles Arthur, *E.U. Court of Justice Overturns Law that Would Enable "Snoopers' Charter"*, THE GUARDIAN (Apr. 8, 2014, 9:43 AM) www.theguardian.com/technology/2014/apr/08/eu-court-overturns-law-snoopers-charter-data-phones-isps.

prevailing sense was that the decision, set against the shocking disclosures made by Snowden, meant that security was "no longer the universal
trump card it once was."[73] Seemingly caught up in this jubilant sentiment
Privacy International went so far as to claim that "this ruling not only
demolishes communications data surveillance laws across Europe, but
sets a precedent for the whole world."[74] Understandable as these
responses were at the time, they overstated the apparent victory of
human rights over the demands of security, their claims proved unduly
optimistic, and their predictions short-lived.

The reaffirmation of the rights to privacy and personal data signaled by
the judgment might have been sustained longer had it not been for the
rapidly growing threat posed to world security by the rise of IS/Daesh. It
proved ephemeral also because in declaring the Directive to be invalid the
CJEU had dug a cavernous hole in the law. Commentators across Europe
expressed concern about the legal uncertainty generated by the judgment,
not least for providers of electronic and telecommunication services.[75]
National security and crime fighting agencies feared that they would
rapidly lose an important intelligence resource if Internet and telecoms
providers were to respond by deleting retained records or ceasing to
collect data.[76] Problems also arose because the Court found that because
the Directive had not required data to be held within the European Union
it was impossible to ensure that retention complied with the requirement
of proportionality. This finding has far-reaching and possibly irresolvable
consequences for data retention for the future. To say that proportionality
can only be assured if data is retained within Europe raises insuperable
difficulties given the global nature of telecoms companies and the growth
of offshore storage.[77] The possible repercussions for the viability of

---

[73] Rauhofer & Mac Sithigh, *supra* note 63, at 5.

[74] Press Release, Privacy International, *supra* note 72.

[75] Salgado, *supra* note 67; Matthias Vierstraete, *ECJ Declares the Data Retention Directive to be Invalid: What's Next?*, Datonomy (Apr. 9, 2014), http://datonomy.eu/2014/04/09/ecj-declares-the-data-retention-directive-to-be-invalid-whats-next/; Carly Nyst, *The Data Retention Directive: Life after Death?*, Privacy Int'l (Apr. 11, 2014), www.privacyinterna tional.org/node/413.

[76] It was claimed that service providers had already begun to delete data. *See, e.g.,* Rob Corbet, Olivia Mullooly & Emma Dunne, *Data Retention Directive Declared Invalid by EU Court of Justice*, Arthur Cox (Apr. 16, 2014), www.arthurcox.com/publications/data-retention-directive-declared-invalid-eu-court-justice/.

[77] In practice, much may depend upon where data is stored and how and by whom it is controlled. See Chapter 19 in this volume. Concern about offshore storage lay at the heart of the subsequent complaint by Mr Schrems to the Irish Data Protection Commissioner

international cooperation among law enforcement agencies are particularly serious given growth of serious crime and terrorism across borders, as both incidents of terrorism in Paris in 2015 made brutally clear.[78]

In sum, the judgment left open difficult questions about the ongoing obligations of service providers and the feasibility of complying with the requirements it laid down. It also led to much speculation about what steps E.U. states should take to give effect to the ruling and what companies retaining metadata should now do.[79]

E   The Data Retention and Investigatory Powers Act 2014 – Emergency, What Emergency?

The *Digital Rights Ireland* judgment undoubtedly created conditions of acute uncertainty for law makers, security officials, and businesses. In the United Kingdom, the situation was exacerbated because the U.K.'s Data Retention (EC Directive) Regulations of 2009 had been introduced specifically to implement the E.U. Directive and were conditional, therefore, on its validity.[80] That the Directive had been found to be invalid from the outset arguably had the effect of retrospectively denying the U.K. Home Secretary the authority to bring in the 2009 Regulations. Again, what this meant for service providers was not immediately clear. On one view, telecommunications companies were no longer obliged to collect and retain data.[81] The U.K. government insisted, however, that the

---

that, in light of the Snowden revelations, the law and practice of the United States did not provide sufficient protection by the public authorities of data transferred to the US. In its judgment, the CJEU declared the Commission's US "Safe Harbour" decision invalid because the level of protection of personal data transferred to US was not "substantially equivalent" to the EU standard, not least because it permitted companies like Facebook, Google, and Microsoft to self-certify the level of protection they provided. Case C-362/14, Schrems v. Data Protection Commissioner, INFOCURIA – CASE-LAW CT. JUST. (Oct. 6, 2015), http://curia.europa.eu/juris/document/document.jsf?text=&docid=169195& pageIndex=0&doclang=EN&mode=lst&dir=&occ=first&part=1&cid=391877.

[78] Ewan MacAskill, *How French Intelligence Agencies Failed before the Paris Attacks*, THE GUARDIAN (Nov. 19, 2015, 1:51 PM) www.theguardian.com/world/2015/nov/19/how-french-intelligence-agencies-failed-before-the-paris-attacks.

[79] Nyst, *supra* note 75.

[80] The U.K. Parliament Constitution Committee noted "We recognise that, given the CJEU's judgment, the 2009 Regulations lack legal authority and that fresh legislation is urgently required to replace them." Constitution Committee, Data Retention and Investigatory Powers Bill §5, www.parlament.uk, www.publications.parliament.uk/pa/ld201415/ldselect/ldconst/31/3103.htm (last visited Dec. 5, 2015).

[81] Liberty *et al.*, *supra* note 44, at 3.

2009 Regulations remained in force[82] and that telecommunication companies were still bound by data retention duties based in other laws.[83] A frantic official search for alternate legal authorities to legitimate continuing data retention raised concerns that the United Kingdom was seeking to circumvent the *Digital Rights Ireland* judgment, even at the risk of subverting the very human rights protections it sought to uphold.

In consequence, the "sustained period of legal uncertainty" predicted by commentators in April 2014, lasted barely three months in the United Kingdom. In the final days of the parliamentary session the government suddenly announced legislation to remedy that uncertainty and to "clarify" the extraterritorial reach of the Regulation of Investigatory Powers Act 2000.[84] Introduced as emergency legislation with cross-party support on July 10, 2014, the Data Retention and Investigatory Powers Act (DRIPA) was enacted just three days later.[85] This exceptionally short timetable did not allow for the public consultation and debate that ordinarily precedes the legislative process. The usual rounds of prelegislative scrutiny[86] were ruled out and the time available for parliamentary debate was so severely curtailed as to make review, amendment, or opposition impossible.[87] The government claimed that resort to emergency powers was necessary to clarify the legislative framework, to replace the 2009 Regulations,[88] and to provide the additional safeguards stipulated in the April judgment.[89] Yet, given that the CJEU's judgment

---

[82] *Id.*

[83] *See* Regulation of Investigatory Powers Act (RIPA) 2000, c. 23, § 12(1) (Eng.) (allowing the Home Secretary to oblige providers to ensure interception capability); Telecommunications Act 1984, c. 12 (Eng.).

[84] Philip Ward, *The Data Retention and Investigatory Powers Bill*, www.parliament.uk (July 16, 2014), http://researchbriefings.parliament.uk/ResearchBriefing/Summary/SN06934.

[85] Data Retention and Investigatory Powers Act 2014, c. 27 (Eng.) [hereinafter DRIPA].

[86] Ordinarily undertaken by the Home Affairs Select Committee, the Constitution Committee, the draft scrutiny Joint Committee, and the parliamentary Joint Committee on Human Rights (JCHR). On this occasion, human rights compatibility was 'satisfied' by a bare assertion by the Minister for Criminal Information, that: 'In my view the provisions of the Data Retention and Investigatory Powers Bill are compatible with the Convention rights.' *See* Data Retention and Investigatory Powers Bill, HL Bill 37, (Eng.), www.publications.parliament.uk/pa/bills/lbill/2014-2015/0037/15037.pdf.

[87] Indeed, the Constitution Committee observed that "It is not clear why these provisions need to be fast-tracked." Constitution Committee, *supra* note 80, at § 11.

[88] Data Retention (EC Directive) Regulations 2009, 2009 S.I. 859 (Eng.), www.legislation.gov.uk/uksi/2009/859/pdfs/uksi_20090859_en.pdf.

[89] EG DRIPA imposed a duty on telecommunications service providers based outside the United Kingdom under Part 1 of the Regulation of Investigatory Powers Act 2000 ("RIPA") to oblige any company providing communication services to customers in the

had been handed down three months earlier, there had been ample time to respond.[90] Certainly no sufficiently grave emergency had arisen in July 2014, to justify overriding the ordinary legislative process. The claim made was that communications companies had declared themselves unwilling to share data for security and investigatory purposes "unless U.K. law is clarified immediately."[91] The threat that companies would otherwise start deleting data, concern about the emergence of the so-called "dark net" (e.g., through use of encryption) and fear of "safe spaces" in which terrorists communicate unmonitored,[92] served to silence opposition and garner unusual all-party support.

Responding to the widespread view that the NSA-Affair had revealed just how far-reaching the surveillance powers of the security services already were, DRIPA was said merely "to strengthen and clarify, rather than extend, the current legislative framework,"[93] by providing for the same types of data to be retained as under the 2009 Regulations.[94] The U.K. government insisted that DRIPA provisions complied with the necessity and proportionality requirements of the April judgment. For example, DRIPA replaced the fixed 12 month data retention period with a retention period *not exceeding* 12 months.[95] It also introduced further safety measures for retained data and a code of practice giving detailed guidelines for service providers.[96] These legislative changes, together with reforms to the working of the independent U.K. Intelligence and Security Committee, suggest a government trying to present a picture of oversight

---

U.K. to comply with requests for communications data and interception warrants issued by the Secretary of State, irrespective of the location of the company providing the service.

[90] *See, e.g.,* Liberty et al., *supra* note 44, at 3.

[91] David Cameron, Prime Minister, & Nick Clegg, Deputy Prime Minister, PM and Deputy PM Speech on Emergency Security Legislation (July 10, 2014), www.gov.uk/government/speeches/pm-and-deputy-pm-speech-on-emergency-security-legislation.

[92] ANDERSON, *supra* note 6, at 18.

[93] *Explanatory Notes: Data Retention and Investigatory Powers Bill* § 3, www.parliament.uk (July 15, 2014), www.publications.parliament.uk/pa/bills/lbill/2014-2015/0037/en/15037en .htm [hereinafter *Explanatory Notes*]. For further reading, see *Bill documents – Data Retention and Investigatory Powers Act 2014,* www.parliament.uk, http://services.parlia ment.uk/bills/2014-15/dataretentionandinvestigatorypowers/documents.html (last visited Dec. 5, 2014).

[94] *Explanatory Notes, supra* note 93, at § 13. *See also* Theresa May, Home Secretary, Home Secretary's Oral Statement About the Use of Communications Data and Interception (July 10, 2014), www.gov.uk/government/speeches/communications-data-and-interception.

[95] *Explanatory Notes, supra* note 93, at § 13.   [96] *Id.*

and restraint of surveillance powers quite at odds with that which had been suggested by the NSA-Affair.[97]

Under pressure from the telecoms companies, British and perhaps also U.S. security services, the DRIPA had been introduced under special provision for "fast-track legislation." In recognition that this tactic precluded proper consultation and debate, ruled out prelegislative scrutiny, and undermined the sovereignty of parliament, the House of Lords Select Committee on the Constitution pressed the government to explain why the legislation should be fast-tracked.[98] The government merely asserted that it was "necessary to urgently make provisions for data retention in United Kingdom law given its importance in protecting the public,"[99] insisting that "retained communications data is of vital importance to law enforcement."[100] Nonetheless, it was obliged to acknowledge that there had been little consultation with the communications industry, law enforcement and intelligence agencies, and limited parliamentary debate.[101] In partial recognition of these concerns, the DRIPA was subject to a "sunset clause," such that the legislation would automatically be repealed on December 31, 2016.[102] Why expedited legislation justified on grounds of a supposed emergency should remain on the statute books for a full two and a half years, rather than a shorter period pegged to the supposed emergency, is unclear. Could it be that the government wanted to postpone robust debate until the furor provoked by the NSA-Affair had died down.[103]

F   Critical Responses to DRIPA – Less a Drip than a Torrent

The speed with which the DRIPA was passed allowed little scope for organized opposition, yet it is curious that there was not more robust,

---

[97]   Answering media questions about the introduction of DRIPA, the U.K. PM asserted, seemingly without irony, 'I looked at this very carefully post-Snowden, and my conclusion is that at the heart of our system is a very sound set of measures.' Cameron & Clegg, *supra* note 91.

[98]   Press Release, Lords Select Committee, Handling of Data Retention and Investigatory Powers Bill "is a matter of concern" says Lords Committee (July 16, 2014), www.parliament.uk/business/committees/committees-a-z/lords-select/constitution-committee/news/data-rentention-report/.

[99]   *Explanatory Notes*, *supra* note 93, at § 29.   [100]   *Id.* at § 33.   [101]   *Id.* at § 38.

[102]   *Id.* at § 41.

[103]   Note the PM's insistence in response to media questions that "The time to debate what more we might need to do, we've agreed, is for the future" and "that debate's for the future. That debate's not for today." Cameron & Clegg, *supra* note 91.

concerted parliamentary resistance to its enactment. Perhaps the heighted threat of serious and organized crime and terrorism[104] rendered the political and reputational risks for opposition parties too great.[105] Although the Act was presented as merely restoring the legal basis for data retention, this claim was swiftly contested by critics who observed that it included new powers that extended the territorial scope of the U.K.'s communications acquisition and intercept capabilities,[106] by enabling interception warrants and orders requiring the maintenance of interception capabilities to be served on bodies overseas. The rights group Liberty argued that, "in extending the territorial reach of the U.K.'s interception regime, the Government seeks to dramatically expand its ability to mandate the interception of communications content across the globe."[107] In short, this was no simple restitution of legal powers but a significant territorial expansion.

Critics from academia, civil liberties organizations, as well as individual Members of Parliament (MPs), pointing to the government's reliance on emergency powers to rush the legislation through, decried the disrespect for the democratic process, sovereignty of parliament, and the rule of law.[108] Members of the upper chamber, the House of Lords, described the hurried timetable variously as "an affront to democracy," "a disgrace," and "a serious abuse of Parliament."[109] In addition to these strong procedural objections, the substance of the Act was widely denounced as treating every member of the public as suspect. Two MPs, Tom Watson and David Davis, subsequently made an application for judicial review

---

[104] Though note that the terror threat level was only later raised from "substantial" to "severe" at the end of August 2014. *UK Terror Threat Level Raised to "Severe,"* BBC (Aug. 29, 2014), www.bbc.co.uk/news/uk-28986271.

[105] It was alleged that U.K. PM David Cameron abandoned his resistance to tightening accountability of the security services as a price for winning Liberal Democrat and Labour support. Patrick Wintour, Rowena Mason & James Ball, *David Cameron Makes Concessions to Rush through Snooping Law,* THE GUARDIAN (July 10, 2014), www.theguardian.com/world/2014/jul/10/david-cameron-concessions-snooping-law-surveillance.

[106] Regulation of Investigatory Powers Act (RIPA) 2000, c. 23 (Eng.).

[107] Liberty *et al., supra* note 44.

[108] Subhajit Basu *et al., Open Letter from U.K. Legal Academic Experts re. DRIP,* PAUL BERNAL'S BLOG (July 15, 2014) http://paulbernal.wordpress.com/2014/07/15/open-letter-from-uk-legal-academic-experts-re-drip/; Shami Chakrabarti, *The DRIP Effect,* LIBERTY (July 14, 2014), www.liberty-human-rights.org.uk/news/latest-news/drip-effect.

[109] Press Release, Privacy International, Passage of DRIP Surveillance Bill Shameful (July 17, 2014), www.privacyinternational.org/press-releases/passage-of-drip-surveillance-bill-shameful.

challenging the legality of the DRIPA on the grounds that "blanket retention of personal data is a breach of fundamental rights to privacy."[110]

In July 2015, just a year after it was hurriedly enacted, the U.K. High Court ruled that s.1 of the DRIPA is "inconsistent with European Union Law" and ordered that it be "disapplied" because "it does not lay down clear and precise rules providing for access to and use of communications data" to ensure that it is "strictly restricted to the purpose of preventing and detecting precisely defined serious offences or of conducting criminal prosecutions relating to such offences."[111] The High Court based its judgment on the additional finding that, under the DRIPA, "access to the data is not made dependent on a prior review by the Court or an independent administrative body whose decision limits access to and use of the data to what is strictly necessary for the purpose of attaining the objective pursued."[112] The Court held that the DRIPA failed to introduce the safeguards necessary to prevent unwarranted interference with the rights to privacy and protection of personal data under the European Charter. Recognising that the DRIPA had been passed in barely 48 hours and observing that "legislation enacted in haste is more prone to error, and it would be highly desirable to allow the opportunity of thorough scrutiny,"[113] the Court suspended the effect of its judgment for seven months to allow the government time to formulate new legislation.[114] Although the decision was widely welcomed, police and security officials again warned that lives would be at risk if data were not retained.[115] Under pressure from the security services, the government appealed to the U.K. Court of Appeal, which immediately referred the case to the CJEU for expedited hearing.[116]

---

[110] Press Release, Liberty, Liberty Represents MPs David Davis and Tom Watson in Legal Challenge to Government's "Emergency" Surveillance Law (July 22, 2014), www.liberty-human-rights.org.uk/news/press-releases/liberty-represents-mps-david-davis-and-tom-watson-legal-challenge-government%E2%80%99s-.

[111] R v. Secretary of State for the Home Department [2015] EWHC (Admin) 2092 at ¶ 114.

[112] Id.   [113] Id. at ¶ 121.

[114] That is 9 months ahead of end date originally set by the sunset clause. DRIPA § 8(3).

[115] Tom Whitehead, *Thousands of Lives at Risk after High Court Rules Snooping Powers Unlawful*, TELEGRAPH (July 17, 2015), www.telegraph.co.uk/news/uknews/terrorism-in-the-uk/11746281/Governments-data-retention-rules-inconsistent-with-EU-law-says-court.html.

[116] Secretary of State for the Home Department v. Davis [2015] EWCA (Civ) 1185.

In times of heightened threat, the security services understandably demand every available means by which to tackle the heightened terrorist threat, and politicians are naturally under enormous pressure to meet this demand. It should surely give pause for thought, however, when the U.K. Prime Minister asserts so readily that "I am confident the powers we need, whether it is on communications data or the content of communications, I am very comfortable they are absolutely right for a modern liberal democracy."[117] Such confidence seems ill-founded given the outraged response across Europe to the NSA-Affair. It fails to reflect and address continuing transatlantic disquiet about how demands for ever-greater surveillance powers are to be squared with the protection of privacy and personal data.[118]

G   Conclusion

In the wake of the NSA-Affair, it is not only America but also Europe that struggles to reconcile the divergent interests of privacy and security. The security mandate rests on the claim that data retention permits law enforcement and security services to identify networks of organized criminals and relations among would-be terrorists. Although data retention permits these services to see which websites suspects have visited, note that it cannot reveal their motivation in so doing or disclose their ulterior intent. As journalist James Ball wryly observed, databases of websites known to be connected with extremists or criminals allow security services to track other users, "If you share such a link, then it is a pretty reliable sign that something is awry. If you do it more than once, even more likely that you are a terrorist. Or a sympathiser. Or a researcher. Or a journalist. Or an employee of a security agency."[119] Or, one might add, an academic writing a chapter such as this.

[117] *David Cameron Says New Online Data Laws Needed*, BBC (Jan. 13, 2015), www.bbc.co.uk/news/uk-politics-30778424.

[118] As evidenced in the U.K. by the introduction of the highly controversial Investigatory Powers Bill in November 2015 – known widely as the "Snoopers' Charter"– that will require Internet companies to retain records of all U.K. citizens' Internet activities for a year. Draft Investigatory Powers Bill, Cm 9152 (presented to parliament Nov. 2015), www.gov.uk/government/uploads/system/uploads/attachment_data/file/473770/Draft_Investigatory_Powers_Bill.pdf. The Investigatory Powers Act was enacted in 2016.

[119] James Ball, *"You're the Bomb!" Are You at Risk from the Anti-Terrorism Algorithms?*, THE GUARDIAN (Dec. 2, 2014), www.theguardian.com/uk-news/2014/dec/02/youre-the-bomb-are-you-at-risk-from-anti-terrorism-algorithms-automated-tracking-innocent-people.

The dismal history of mass surveillance and data retention raises profound concerns about the difficulty of ensuring that data retention regimes are necessary, proportionate, and compliant with human rights.[120] This same history led the Commissioner for Human Rights at the Council of Europe, Nils Muižnieks, to conclude that "[s]uspicionless mass retention of communications data is fundamentally contrary to the rule of law, incompatible with core data protection principles and ineffective."[121] Protection of privacy lies at the heart of a free and democratic society and, as the NSA-Affair made all too clear, mass surveillance has the potential for abuse of the information gathered against political adversaries and damaging effects on press freedom, freedom of speech, and open political debate.[122] Given all that we know now about transatlantic data-sharing and the global interconnectedness of communications technology and of data-storage, it is clear that domestic regulation can, at best, be only part of the solution.[123] A framework agreement between the United States and all E.U. Member States that seeks to protect the privacy rights of citizens on both sides of the Atlantic might be one way to restore transatlantic relations, improve cooperation and, just maybe, to resist overly intrusive surveillance.

This chapter has sought to understand why governments doggedly seek to reassert and reinstate data retention regimes in spite of the intractable difficulties of regulation.[124] In the face of judicial opinion that retention of metadata interferes unwarrantedly with rights to privacy and protection of personal data, the state's determination to ensure the capability to retain and share metadata reflects the gravity of the present security situation. Faced with really serious, even potentially catastrophic, threats to public safety and national security, precaution demands that public officials take all reasonable steps to avert grave risks.[125] The uncertainty that surrounds such serious risks ascribes a special value to

---

[120] Fabbrini, *supra* note 13.

[121] COUNCIL OF EUROPE, THE RULE OF LAW ON THE INTERNET IN THE WIDER DIGITAL WORLD 22 (2014), www.coe.int/t/dghl/standardsetting/media/cdmsi/Rule_of_Law_Inter net_Digital_World.pdf.

[122] *Draft Report, supra* note 35, at 17.

[123] David Cole & Federico Fabbrini, *Bridging the Transatlantic Divide? The United States, the European Union, and the Protection of Privacy across Borders* (iCourts - The Danish Nat'l Res. Found. Ctr. Excellence for Int'l Cts., Working Paper No. 33, 2015).

[124] On the wider issue of meeting the challenges thrown up by preventive measures, *see* ANDREW ASHWORTH & LUCIA ZEDNER, PREVENTIVE JUSTICE (2014).

[125] Claudia Aradau & Rens Van Munster, *Governing Terrorism through Risk: Taking Precautions, (Un)Knowing the Future,* 89 EUR. J. INT'L REL. 89 (2007).

information and perhaps it is the urge to garner every possibly useful scrap of intelligence that motivates mass retention of metadata. Failure by the security services to foresee and forestall terrorist atrocities attracts intense scrutiny and only renews demands for ever greater intelligence capacity.[126]

Technological possibility drives data retention on a hitherto inconceivably grand scale in the hope that "total information awareness" might, one day, contribute to the prevention or prosecution of serious wrongdoing.[127] But mass data retention is a dubious basis upon which to try to find needles in haystacks and might better be characterized as the frantic attempt by states to fashion haystacks in the slim hope of finding needles.[128] The gravity of the threat posed by serious organized crime and international terrorism creates an urgent need to find more powerful means by which to combat it. Whether mass data retention serves as the security blanket it is claimed to be remains open to question. The threat it poses to privacy, however, seems beyond doubt.

---

[126] See, e.g., Jason Burke & Julian Borger, *French Intelligence under Scrutiny in Wake of Paris Attacks*, THE GUARDIAN (Nov. 14, 2015, 9:18 AM), www.theguardian.com/world/2015/nov/14/french-intelligence-under-scrutiny-paris-attacks; Gordon Corera, *Paris Attacks: Security Flaws and Challenges Highlighted*, BBC (Nov. 18, 2015), www.bbc.co.uk/news/world-europe-34853376.

[127] Reg Whitaker, *A Faustian Bargain? America and the Dream of Total Information Awareness*, in NEW POLITICS OF SURVEILLANCE AND VISIBILITY 141 (Kevin D. Haggerty & Richard V. Ericson eds., 2006).

[128] Lucia Zedner, *The Inescapable Insecurity of Security Technologies?*, TECHNOLOGIES OF INSECURITY: THE SURVEILLANCE OF EVERYDAY LIFE 257–70 (Katja Franko Aas, Helene Oppen Gundhus & Heidi Mork Lomell eds., 2009).

22

Do Androids Forget European Sheep?

The CJEU's Concept of a "Right to be Forgotten" and the German perspective

BY BERND HOLZNAGEL AND SARAH HARTMANN

A   Introduction

In 1968 American author Philip K. Dick published the novel *Do Androids Dream of Electric Sheep?*,[1] better known under the title *Blade Runner*, which was a highly regarded film adaptation.[2] The novel's cryptic title alludes to the lack of certain human responses and attributes in the manufactured Android machines featured in the story. Coincidentally "Android" is also the name of the wide-spread operating system for mobile phones developed and distributed by Google. In a certain way, the recent discussion of a so-called "right to be forgotten" seems like an attempt to attribute human qualities to digital technology.

The landmark decision of the Court of Justice of the European Union (CJEU) in the case *Google Spain SL v. González*[3] extended the inherently human concept of forgetting to Internet search engines. The basic message of the decision is simple: Every individual has the right to request that Internet search providers remove content featuring personal data from the results the search engine produces when that applicant's name is queried.[4] The collective knowledge therefore

---

[1] Philip K. Dick, Do Androids Dream of Electric Sheep? (Doubleday 1968).

[2] Blade Runner (Warner Bros. 1982).

[3] Case C-131/12, Google Spain SL & Google, Inc. v. Agencia Española de Protección de Datos (AEPD) & Mario Costeja González, InfoCuria – Case-Law Ct. Just. (May 13, 2014), http://curia.europa.eu/juris/document/document.jsf;jsessionid=9ea7d0f130d58fa348967d244833 bad1c86381ec1189.e34KaxiLc3eQc40LaxqMbN4Oc3aKe0?text=&docid=152065&pageIndex =0&doclang=EN&mode=lst&dir=&occ=first&part=1&cid=385379 [hereinafter Google Spain CJEU].

[4] *Id.* at ¶ 82.

"forgets" about the connection between the data subject and the depicted event or statement.

The *Google Spain* decision generated extensive media coverage.[5] European data protection advocates called the judgment a milestone for digital privacy.[6] European data protection standards had never-before been enforced against global Internet giants. Google is certainly the most iconic giant among these companies and has faced significant public backlash in Europe due to its market dominance.[7] In 2015 the European Commission opened an antitrust investigation into Google's mobile operating system Android and submitted a Statement of Objections on the company's shopping comparison services.[8] Further controversies

---

[5] Matt Warman & David Barret, *Google Must Delete Your Data if You Ask, E.U. Rules*, TELEGRAPH (May 13, 2014, 11:06 AM), www.telegraph.co.uk/technology/google/10827005/Google-must-delete-your-data-if-you-ask-EU-rules.html; David Streitfeld, *European Court Lets Users Erase Records on Web*, N.Y. TIMES (May 13, 2014), www.nytimes.com/2014/05/14/technology/google-should-erase-web-links-to-some-personal-data-europes-highest-court-says.html; Johannes Wendt, *Das Google-Amt*, ZEIT ONLINE (May 19, 2014, 7:45 PM), www.zeit.de/digital/datenschutz/2014-05/google-wird-behoerde-eugh-recht-auf-vergessen; Stefan Schulz, *Google hat ein Problem*, FRANKFURTER ALLGEMEINE ZEITUNG (May 14, 2014), www.faz.net/aktuell/feuilleton/eugh-urteil-google-hat-ein-problem-12939285.html.

[6] Peter Schaar, former Federal Data Protection Commissioner for Germany, called the decision a "victory for data protection." *See* Peter Schaar, *EuGH-Entscheidung zur Google-Suche – Etappensieg für den Datenschutz*, EUROPÄISCHE AKADEMIE FÜR INFORMATIONSFREIHEIT & DATENSCHUTZ (May 13, 2014), www.eaid-berlin.de/?p=375. Jan Philip Albrecht, Member of the European Parliament, assessed the judgment as "the right decision." *See* Press Release, The Greens in the European Parliament, ECJ Ruling: Search Engines Must Respect Data Protection Law (May 13, 2014), www.greens-efa.eu/ecj-ruling-12395.html. The European Commission considered the decision to be in line with their own proposals. *See* Press Release, Europäische Kommission [European Commission], Recht auf Vergessen im Internet: Kommission begrüßt Entscheidung des Europäischen Gerichtshofs (May 13, 2014), http://ec.europa.eu/deutschland/press/pr_releases/12362_de.htm.

[7] *See* Robert M. Maier, *Angst vor Google*, FRANKFURTER ALLGEMEINE ZEITUNG (Apr. 3, 2014), www.faz.net/aktuell/feuilleton/debatten/weltmacht-google-ist-gefahr-fuer die-gesellschaft-12877120.html; *see also* Mathias Döpfner, *Why We Fear Google*, FRANKFURTER ALLGEMEINE ZEITUNG (Apr. 16, 2014), www.faz.net/aktuell/feuilleton/debatten/mathias-doepfner-s-open-letter-to-eric-schmidt-12900860.html (the statement of the CEO of publishing house Axel Springer.); Sigmar Gabriel, *Unsere politische Konsequenzen aus der Google-Debatte*, FRANKFURTER ALLGEMEINE ZEITUNG (May 16, 2014), www.faz.net/aktuell/feuilleton/debatten/die-digital-debatte/sigmar-gabriel-konsequenzen-der-google-debatte-12941865.html (the reaction of the German Minister for Economic Affairs.).

[8] Press Release, European Commission, Antitrust: Commission Sends Statement of Objections to Google on Comparison Shopping Service; Opens Separate Formal Investigation on Android (Apr. 15, 2015), http://europa.eu/rapid/press-release_IP-15-4780_en.htm.

revolved around the privacy impact of specific services, such as Google Street View,[9] and the Autocomplete search predictions.[10] On the other side of the Atlantic, reactions to the judgment showed different tendencies, emphasizing the threat of private censorship.[11] The case once again exposed the culture-clash of privacy regimes.[12]

In this chapter we will consider and critique how this right might be implemented. We think this is far more interesting than the question whether and why a right to removal of personal data from indices exists.[13] Consensus has not yet been reached on whether the delisting decision can and should be left to search engines such as Google. Another critical issue is the notification of publishers affected by the delisting and their possible integration into the delisting evaluation. We believe that the balance between privacy and freedom of expression must be restored through procedural guarantees that frame the final decision to delist Internet content. We propose a two-step approach, including a hearing requirement and an arbitration body. Starting with a summary of the legal proceedings and the subsequent discourse on the "right to be forgotten," we will then consider the differences between the German and the European approach to conflicts between the right to privacy, on one hand, and freedom of expression, on the other hand. Specific attention will also be given to Google's efforts in drafting an evaluation procedure.

B   Background: The *Google Spain* Case

I   Facts of the Case

Mario Costeja González, a Spanish citizen, complained to the Spanish Data Protection Agency (Agencia Española de Protección de Datos [AEPD]) in 2010 about two issues of the *La Vanguardia* newspaper that could be viewed

---

[9] Bernd Holznagel & Pascal Schumacher, *Das Ende der Privatsphäre? – Die verfassungsrechtliche Problematik von Google Street View*, PUBLICUS (Jan. 2010), www.publicusboorberg.de/sixcms/detail.php?template=pub_artikel&id=boorberg01.c.134712.de; Nikol aus Forgó, Tina Krügel & Kathrin Müllenbach, *Zur datenschutz- und persönlichkeitsrechtlichen Zulässigkeit von Google Street View*, CR 2010, 616.

[10] Bundesgerichtshof [BGH] [Federal Court of Justice] May 14, 2013, BGH, VI ZR 269/12, 2013 (the Autocomplete case); Georgios Gournalakis, *Rechtliche Grenzen der Autocomplete-Funktion von Google*, 32 NEUE JURISTISCHE WOCHENSCHRIFT 2321 (2013).

[11] *See* David Streitfeld, *supra* note 5. *See also* Chapter 11 in this volume.

[12] *See* Chapter 2 in this volume.   [13] *See* Chapter 16 in this volume.

at the newspaper's website. The issues in question were originally published in 1998 and included real-estate auction notices of Mr. González's home, which had been repossessed due to social-security debts.

He asked for removal of the announcements or his name, arguing that the information was no longer relevant because the proceedings had been resolved many years ago. His request was denied by the Data Protection Agency, which held that the original publication was legally justified.

Part of the complaint was also directed against Google Inc. and its Spanish subsidiary Google Spain. Mr. González requested that the search engine refrain from displaying his personal data in the search results leading to the announcements at the *La Vanguardia* website. The AEPD upheld this request, which led both Google Inc. and Google Spain to bring actions against this decision before the National High Court. Since the case called for interpretation of the Spanish data protection law enacted in fulfillment of Spain's duties under the European Union's Data Protection Directive, the High Court referred the matter to the CJEU for a preliminary ruling.[14] The High Court posed two questions to the CJEU: (1) whether there were territorial limits on the application of the Data Protection Directive and the related national law and (2) whether the Data Protection Directive applied to search engines and, if so, what the scope of the Directive's right of erasure would be.

II   The Right to Erasure or Objection: Legal Foundation and Prerequisites

The central question referred to the CJEU was whether individuals can request the removal of content with personal information about them from a search engine's index, even if the content itself was lawfully published. The High Court asked whether this right could be derived from either of two provisions, the right to data erasure and blocking established by Article 12(b) of the Directive and the right to object established by Article 14(1)(a) of the Directive.[15]

---

[14] National Courts are obligated to refer to the CJEU for interpretation of European Union law in order to ensure uniform jurisdiction and application throughout the Union.

[15] Case C-131/12, Google Spain SL & Google, Inc. v. Agencia Española de Protección de Datos (AEPD) & Mario Costeja González, ¶ 20, INFOCURIA – CASE-LAW CT. JUST. (May 13, 2014), http://curia.europa.eu/juris/document/document.jsf;jsessionid=9ea7d0f130d58fa348967d 244833bad1c86381ec1189.e34KaxiLc3eQc40LaxqMbN4Oc3aKe0?text=&docid=152065& pageIndex=0&doclang=EN&mode=lst&dir=&occ=first&part=1&cid=385379 [hereinafter Google Spain CJEU].

Erasure or blocking of data can be requested if the processing violates the provision of the Directive.[16] The violation could be constituted in this case by lack of legal legitimation for the processing[17] or by infringement of the criteria for data quality.[18]

For the right to object,[19] on the other hand, data processing is not legitimized by consent but occurs because it is necessary for the controller's legitimate purposes or the purposes of third parties to whom the data are disclosed (Article 7(f)). If this is the case, then the data subject can object "on compelling legitimate grounds relating to his particular situation to the processing of data relating to him."[20]

In order for the data subject to benefit from either of these rights, the Directive must be applicable. The criteria of applicability provided in Article 4(1)(a) call for the processing of personal data by a controller who is established in a Member State, whose activities are carried out in the context of the processing.

Once the Directive's applicability is established it must be kept in mind that the CJEU does not decide upon the details of a specific case. Instead, the Court only resolves questions about the abstract legal framework, leaving the final decision in each case for resolution by the referring national court in conformity with legal standards announced by the CJEU.[21] For this reason the Court did not deliberate at length on the

---

[16] Directive 95/46/EC of the European Parliament and the Council of 24 October 1995 on the Protection of Individuals With Regard to the Processing of Personal Data and the Free Movement of Data, art. 12(b), O.J. (L 281) ("Member States shall guarantee every data subject the right to obtain from the controller: ... as appropriate the rectification, erasure or blocking of data the processing of which does not comply with the provisions of this Directive.") [hereinafter Data Protection Directive].

[17] Id. at art. 7(f) ("Member States shall provide that personal data may be processed only if: [...] processing is necessary for the purposes of the legitimate interests pursued by the controller or by the third party or parties to whom the data are disclosed, except where such interests are overridden by the interests for fundamental rights and freedoms of the data subject which require protection under Article 1 (1).").

[18] Id. at art. 6(1)(c) ("Member States shall provide that personal data must be: [...]adequate, relevant and not excessive in relation to the purposes for which they are collected and/or further processed.").

[19] Id. at art. 14(a) ("Member States shall grant the data subject the right: at least in the cases referred to in Article 7 (e) and (f), to object at any time on compelling legitimate grounds relating to his particular situation to the processing of data relating to him, save where otherwise provided by national legislation. Where there is a justified objection, the processing instigated by the controller may no longer involve those data.").

[20] Id.

[21] Consolidated Version of the Treaty on the Functioning of the European Union, art. 267, OJ 2012/C 326/01.

specific circumstances in González's case. The *Google Spain Case* only established the general criteria for the rights derived from Article 12(b) and 14(1)(a).

III Applicability of the Data Protection Directive

1 Processing Personal Data

The CJEU classified the activity of Google as collecting, retrieving, recording, organizing, and storing of data that is subsequently made available and disclosed to users as search results, which falls under the explicit definition of "data processing" in Article 2(b) of the Directive.[22] This interpretation is not changed by the fact that the data in question had previously been published[23] and remains – as regards its content – unaltered by Google.[24]

It remained uncontested that the processed data included "personal data" as defined by Article 2(a) of the Directive.[25] Having found that the applicability requirements were fulfilled, the Court ruled that Google had "processed personal data."[26]

2 Google as Controller of the Data

Regarding the question of "control" over the data processing, the CJEU distinguished between the processing of data by website providers who publish content and the processing of data by search engines. According to the Court, the search engine plays a pivotal role in the dissemination of the data by making it accessible through search queries without knowledge of the publishing website.[27] Simply entering an individual's name as a search term will result in a structured list of all content containing that name, possibly serving as a profile on the data subject.[28] The Court

---

[22] Case C-131/12, Google Spain SL & Google, Inc. v. Agencia Española de Protección de Datos (AEPD) & Mario Costeja González, ¶ 28, INFOCURIA – CASE-LAW CT. JUST. (May 13, 2014), http://curia.europa.eu/juris/document/document.jsf;jsessionid=9ea7d0f130d58 fa348967d244833bad1c86381ec1189.e34KaxiLc3eQc40LaxqMbN4Oc3aKe0?text=&docid =152065&pageIndex=0&doclang=EN&mode=lst&dir=&occ=first&part=1&cid=385379 [hereinafter Google Spain CJEU].

[23] *Id.* at ¶¶ 29–30; *see also* Case C-73/07, Tietosuojavaltuutettu v. Oy, ¶¶ 48–49, INFOCURIA – CASE-LAW CT. JUST. (Dec. 16, 2008), http://curia.europa.eu/juris/document/document.jsf; jsessionid=9ea7d0f130d57560bbb105d641928d1fa151eebc7c41.e34KaxiLc3eQc40LaxqMb N4Oc3aTe0?text=&docid=76075&pageIndex=0&doclang=EN&mode=lst&dir=&occ=first& part=1&cid=336970.

[24] Google Spain CJEU, *supra* note 22, at ¶ 31. [25] *Id.* at ¶ 27. [26] *Id.* at ¶ 41.
[27] *Id.* at ¶ 36. [28] *Id.* at ¶ 37.

concluded that the heightened visibility and availability of the content resulting from its inclusion in the search engine's index affect the data subject's right to privacy and protection of personal data in addition to the original publication.[29]

The Court considered whether exclusion protocols, such as "robots. txt,"[30] which allow website operators to reject indexing of specified subpages, should preclude the search engine from being considered a controller of data processing.[31] But Article 2(d) of the Data Protection Directive also allows for determining the purposes and means of processing "jointly with others."[32]

Google could not be insulated from the demands of the Directive and, according to the Court, the search engine operator was also a "controller" of the data.[33]

3   In the Context of the Activities of the Establishment

The major challenge with regards to the territorial application of the Directive lay in determining whether, according to Article 4(1)(a) of the Directive, the processing of personal data was "carried out in the context of the activities" of Google Spain.[34]

It was not contested that Google Spain is an establishment of Google Inc. based on and operating in Spanish territory. But the search operation is handled exclusively by the parent company without contribution by Google Spain, which is solely tasked with advertisement sales.[35] The wording of Article 4 does not require the establishment itself to carry out the processing, only that the processing be carried out "in the context of its activities." The Court reasoned that the advertisement sales coordinated by Google's Spanish subsidiary constituted a tangible contribution to the search operation itself, because it is chiefly through this venture that the main service becomes and remains profitable.[36] The

---

[29] *Id.* at ¶ 38.

[30] Robots.txt or the Robots exclusion standard can be used by website operators to instruct web robots, such as search engine crawlers, not to process certain areas or directories of the website. It is often used to avoid indexing of content on websites by search engines. A search for terms appearing on that website will not return any results for that site if the content has not been indexed.

[31] Google Spain CJEU, *supra* note 22, at ¶ 39.

[32] Data Protection Directive, *supra* note 16, at art. 2(d).

[33] Google Spain CJEU, *supra* note 22, at ¶ 41.

[34] Data Protection Directive, *supra* note 16, at art. 4 (1)(a).

[35] Google Spain CJEU, *supra* note 22, at ¶ 51.   [36] *Id.* at ¶ 55.

advertisement sales and the search engine are "inextricably linked," the CJEU explained, because they symbiotically enable each other.[37] This deep co-dependency, the Court noted, can also be graphically demonstrated by the layout of the search result page, which features the result list directly accompanied by advertising.[38]

Google search – constituting a processing of personal data controlled by Google Inc. – was deemed to be carried out in the context of Google Spain's activities as an establishment within a Member State, which rendered the Data Protection Directive applicable.[39]

IV   The Right to Erasure or Objection: Delisting Decisions

1   Balancing Rights and Interests

The rights to erasure or objection provided by Articles 12 and 14 of the Directive essentially involve several balancing mechanisms. First, in order to justify the data processing conducted by search engines under Article 7(f), the interest of the search engine must not be "overridden by the interests for fundamental rights and freedoms of the data subject which require protection under Article 1(1)."[40] The second balancing mechanism is incorporated into the principles for data quality in Article 6(1). According to this provision data must be "kept in a form which permits identification of data subjects for no longer than is necessary for the purposes for which the data were collected or for which they are further processed."[41] The Court held that, in the course of time, processed data may become irrelevant or excessive, even if its original publication was lawful.[42] Finally, the third balancing mechanism is provided by Article 14(1)(a) of the Directive, which allows justified objections on "compelling legitimate grounds." In this respect the CJEU pointed out that this justification does not require the search results to cause prejudice to the data subject.[43] In the specific context of delisting requests addressed to search engines, the balancing mechanism has three steps. In cases where legitimation under Article 7(f) is assumed the processing can still be deemed incompatible with the data quality principles in Article 6 or contested on the basis of Article 14.

The relevant fundamental rights of the data subject include the respect for private and family life and the protection of personal data from

---

[37] *Id.* at ¶ 56.   [38] *Id.* at ¶ 57.   [39] *Id.* at ¶ 60.
[40] Data Protection Directive, *supra* note 16, at art. 7(f).   [41] *Id.* at art. 6(1)(e).
[42] Google Spain CJEU, *supra* note 22, at ¶ 93.   [43] *Id.* at ¶ 96.

Articles 7 and 8 of the Charter of Fundamental Rights of the European Union.[44] The CJEU weighed these rights against the public interest to access information and the search engine operator's economic interests. The Court chose to give a general priority to the right to privacy.[45] In particular, the economic interests of the search engine operator were not deemed significant enough to justify the interference.[46] Other rights, such as freedom of expression, were not seen as an enhancement of the search engine's interests.[47] The Court explained that "the nature of the information in question and its sensitivity for the data subject's private life and [. . .] the interest of the public in having that information" must be considered as factors.[48] Likewise, the identity of the data subject also may be a factor in the balancing in cases where the subject plays an important role in public life.[49]

As to the main proceedings in González's case, the Court held that the auction notices resulting from social-security debts were information of a sensitive nature, with no conceivable public interest 16 years after their first publication.[50] The CJEU assumed that, in a situation like this, the data subject would be entitled to the rights from Articles 12(b) and 14(1) (a) of the Directive. The concrete application of the Court's findings and standards was left to the referring Spanish court.[51]

2 Distinction between Lawful Content and Lawful Reference

The Court approached the publishing of content by website operators and the indexing and processing by search engines as two separate actions with distinguishable impacts on the data subject's rights.[52] The interference caused by the easy availability of content through name-based searches was deemed to be potentially more significant to the fundamental right to privacy than the publication of the content on a single website.[53] The Court also acknowledged the difficulty of approaching the content provider – or multiple content providers – especially in cases where they operate beyond the reach of European Union

---

[44] *Id.* at ¶ 74.   [45] *Id.* at ¶ 81.   [46] *Id.* at ¶ 81.

[47] Search results have been considered by some to benefit from the fundamental right to freedom of speech under German and European law. *See* Alexander Milstein & Matthias Lippold, *Suchmaschinenergebnisse im Lichte der Meinungsfreiheit der nationalen und europäischen Grund- und Menschrechte*, 2013 NEUE ZEITSCHRIFT FÜR VERWALTUNGS-RECHT 182, 186 (2013); *see also* Bernd Holznagel & Pascal Schumacher, *Netzpolitik Reloaded*, 2011 ZEITSCHRIFT FUR RECHTSPOLITIK 74 (2011).

[48] Google Spain CJEU, *supra* note 22, at ¶ 81.   [49] *Id.* at ¶ 97.   [50] *Id.* at ¶ 98.

[51] *Id.* at ¶ 98.   [52] *Id.* at ¶¶ 38, 83.   [53] *Id.* at ¶¶ 80, 87.

legislation.[54] This led the Court to conclude that the data subject might rightfully complain about the search engine operator's processing of data even if the content itself was legally published and remains legitimate.[55] This was precisely the case in the proceedings before the Spanish authorities. The CJEU identified publications "carried out solely for journalistic purposes" (as provided by Article 9 of the Directive) as an example.[56] Journalistic activities benefit from certain privileges that do not extend to search engines.[57] In these situations the data subject can only request removal from search engines, even if the criteria in Articles 12(b) and 14 (1)(a) are not met with regards to the content. This is justified by the search engine's different interests in processing the data.[58] The Court thereby refused to consider any media privileges in favor of the search engine operator, despite admitting its decisive role[59] for the dissemination of information as an intermediary.[60] Reducing the search engine to its economic interests without any further elaboration appears short-sighted considering the First Amendment protection awarded to search engines, in the United States, for example.[61]

3 Procedural Aspects and Judicial Review

The rights provided by Articles 12 and 14 may be exercised by the data subject in addressing requests directly to the search engine operator.[62] In case the request is denied or ignored, the subject can then complain to the national data protection authorities.[63] Member State's data protection or judicial authorities can also directly order search engine operators to delist content.[64] The CJEU did not require any involvement of the affected website publisher. The judgment also contained no tangible clues for the practical implementation of removal evaluation procedures.

V Remarks

The CJEU's judgment is less radical than the reactions of the international press and many scholars suggested. Especially the incendiary

---

[54] *Id.* at ¶ 84.   [55] *Id.* at ¶ 85.   [56] Data Protection Directive, *supra* note 16, at art. 9.
[57] Google Spain CJEU, *supra* note 22, at ¶ 85.   [58] *Id.* at ¶ 86.   [59] *Id.* at ¶ 36.
[60] Kai Lewinski, *Staat als Zensurhelfer – Staatliche Flankierung der Löschpflichten privater nach dem Google-Urteil des EuGH*, 2015 AfP – ZEITSCHRIFT FÜR MEDIEN- UND KOM-MUNIKATIONSRECHT 1, 6 (2015).
[61] Peter Brown, *The Right to be Forgotten: U.S. Rulings on Free Speech Won't Let Google Forget*, 15 COMPUTER L. REV. INT'L 161, 164 (2014). *See* Chapter 11 in this volume.
[62] Google Spain CJEU, *supra* note 22, at ¶ 77.   [63] *Id.* at ¶ 77.   [64] *Id.* at ¶ 82.

concept of a "right to be forgotten" is slightly off target. While the right to object to data processing or to request removal or blocking of data was the central question in the main proceedings in Spain, it was not the most interesting aspect of the CJEU's decision. This "new" right is actually old news and has been part of the Data Protection Directive for a long time.

The judgment was "new" in that it subjects globally operating Internet companies, such as Google, to the present European data protection regime, pursuant to which they can be compelled to assume part of the responsibility for ensuring the privacy of the data they process.[65] Importantly, the pending General Data Protection Regulation, which will replace the Directive, also features an extended scope of application.[66] The strategic orientation and marketing of goods and services to European customers will subject companies to the Regulation, even if they are based outside the European Union.[67]

C Reconciling *Google Spain* with the German Legal Tradition

While some celebrated the judgment as a victory for data protection, the majority of legal scholars reacted with less enthusiasm.[68] German Courts have pursued substantially different approaches to the legal questions raised by the *Google Spain Case*. It is fairly safe to assume that, based on the following presentation of jurisprudence, a German court would have come to a different conclusion when faced with the same facts.

The differences can be highlighted in four aspects. First, by considering the applicability of national data protection law in Internet cases. Second, by considering whether search engines should be the subjects of data protection regulation. Third, by considering the ways in which the right to privacy and freedom of expression are balanced. And fourth, by considering the procedural requirements for delisting requests.

---

[65] For the potential impact on other Internet companies such as Facebook see Eva Beyvers & Tilman Herbrich, *das Niederlassungsprinzip im Datenschutzrecht – am Beispiel von Facebook*, 2014 ZEITSCHRIFT FÜR DATENSCHUTZ 558, 560 (2014).

[66] *See Proposal for a Regulation of the European Parliament and the Council on the Protection of Individuals with Regard to the Processing of Personal Data and on the Free Movement of Such Data (General Data Protection Regulation)*, art. 3 II, COM (2012) 11 final (Jan. 25, 2012).

[67] *Id.*

[68] *See* Marian Arning, Flemming Moos & Jens Schefzig, *Vergiss (,) Europa*, 30 COMPUTER UND RECHT 447 (2014).

I Jurisdiction in Internet Cases

In court proceedings involving Internet companies one of the major legal challenges revolves around the applicability of national law, similar to the constellation in the *Google Spain Case*. In a prominent German example, the *Oberverwaltungsgericht* Schleswig (Higher Administrative Court for the State of Schleswig) presided over a data protection challenge involving the American company Facebook Inc. and its subsidiary Facebook Ireland Ltd.[69] The operator of the globally available social network contested the applicability of the German data protection law. The company argued instead for the application of the Irish regulations. The company also has a German subsidiary, Facebook Germany GmbH, which is tasked with marketing and advertisement sales. The Court considered Facebook Ireland Ltd. to be an establishment of Facebook Inc. and to be the processor of personal data.[70] The classification of Facebook Ireland as controller of the processing was deemed irrelevant, since it is only required that the parent company is the controller of the data processing.[71] This was not contested by Facebook Inc. Concerning Facebook Germany GmbH the Schleswig Court – in accord with the preceding judgment of the lower court[72] – concluded that no processing of personal data was carried out by the German subsidiary itself. The Court saw no relevant connection between the processing carried out by the parent company and the activities of the German subsidiary.[73] For these reasons, German data protection law was ruled to be inapplicable in the case.

The constellation in the *Facebook Case* appears quite similar to the *Google Spain Case*. Still, the CJEU came to a different conclusion regarding the application of the European data protection regime to Google's processing in the United States. In Germany the connection between marketing and advertisement sales by the German subsidiary and the actual processing of personal data by the non-German parent companies, was thought to be too weak to even require further elaboration in the judgment.

---

[69] Oberverwaltungsgericht [OVG] [Higher Administrative Court] Apr. 22, 2013, OVG, 4 MB 11/13, Apr. 22, 2013 (the Schleswig case).
[70] *Id.*, paras 13, 17.   [71] *Id.*, para 15.
[72] Verwaltungsgericht [VG] [Administrative Court] Feb. 12, 2013, VG, 8 B 61/12 (the lower court hearing of the Schleswig case).
[73] 4 MB 11/13, ¶ 16.

II   Search Engines as Subjects of Data and Personality Rights Protection Regulation

While the CJEU ruled that Google processes personal data and is the controller of that data – the *Oberlandesgericht* Hamburg (Higher Regional Court) – came to a different conclusion regarding the responsibility of search engines for the content linked to the results.

In a case from 2009 the plaintiff demanded removal of search results in the defendant's people search engine that linked the plaintiff to content calling him a "murderer." The Court denied the plaintiff's claim, holding that the search engine operator did not store content and had no authority over the data.[74] The mere record of the data's existence exposed through the search results did not constitute storage of their content and did not enable the search engine operator to influence or alter the content.[75] In this regard, the Court ruled, the search engine was not the controller of the plaintiff's personal data and could not be held to the provisions of the German Data Protection Act.

Two similar judgments – from the *Oberlandesgericht* Hamburg (Higher Regional Court) and the *Landgericht* Mönchengladbach (Regional Court) – dealt with the question whether results to name-based searches constituted personality rights infringements. Data-protection law was not at issue in these proceedings, but the courts' considerations regarding responsibility for content on third party websites are relevant to the issues in *Google Spain*.

Both cases involved plaintiffs who sought injunctions against search engine operators who had displayed search results to their name with derogatory content. The courts denied this claim in both cases, concluding that the search results could not be interpreted as a statement by the engine's operator. Search engine operators, the courts reasoned, only reference content from other websites in a neutral way.[76] The courts found that the search engines had not contributed to an infringement of the plaintiffs' personality rights.[77]

---

[74] Oberlandesgericht [OLG] [Higher Regional Court] Nov. 13, 2009, OLG, 7 W 125/09 (the Hamburg case).

[75] *Id.*

[76] *See* Oberlandesgericht [OLG] [Higher Regional Court] May 26, 2011, OLG, 3 U 67/11, ¶¶ 185–86, 210; Landgericht [LG] [Regional Court] Sept. 5, 2013, LG, 10 O 170/12, ¶ 29.

[77] *See* 3 U 67/11, *supra* note 76, at ¶ 182.

III   Right to Privacy and Freedom of Expression in Online Archives

The heart of the CJEU's judgment was the need to balance the data subject's right to privacy and the search engine operator's right to present (as well as the public's interest in accessing) the content in question.[78] The CJEU paid it little attention, but the original publisher's interests in publishing information also should be weighed in the balancing process. This is certainly the most difficult aspect of the *Google Spain Case* to compare with the German jurisprudence. German legal theory does not recognize a general primacy of any of these rights. On one hand, freedom of expression and freedom of the media are recognized as being essential for the functioning of democracy.[79] On the other hand, the right to privacy is derived from the inviolable guarantee and protection of human dignity.[80] Accordingly, the framework applied by German courts to resolve a conflict of rights of this kind has been refined over decades and comprises vast numbers of decisions involving the intricacies of press and media law.[81]

From among that large body of decisions, we will focus on requests from convicted felons to have news coverage of their crimes removed from online archives after having completed their sentences. The *Bundesverfassungsgericht* (Federal Constitutional Court) has treated the general relation between the convict's right to protection of personality and the public interest in receiving information as "reciprocal." With the passage of time (and given that the public has received sufficient information about the crime), the Court has found that a convict's right to a private life without media coverage can come to outweigh the public's and the media's interests in information.[82]

The *Bundesgerichtshof* (Federal Court of Justice) commented on the application of this principle to press publications available in online

---

[78] For a comprehensive summary of the criteria employed by the European Court of Human Rights see Axel Springer AG v. Germany, App. No. 39954/08, ¶ 89–95, HUDOC (Feb. 7, 2012), http://hudoc.echr.coe.int/eng#{"fulltext":["39954/08"],"documentcollectionid2":["GRANDCHAMBER","CHAMBER"],"itemid":["001-109034"]}.

[79] Bundesverfassungsgericht [BVerfG] [Federal Constitutional Court] Jan. 15, 1958, 7 BVerfGE 198 ¶ 33 (Lüth case).

[80] Bundesverfassungsgericht [BVerfG] [Federal Constitutional Court] Apr. 26, 1994, 90 BVerfGE 255, ¶ 20 (Briefüberwachung case); Bundesverfassungsgericht [BVerfG] [Federal Constitutional Court] June 3, 1980, 54 BVerfGE 148 ¶ 13 (Eppler case).

[81] *See* Chapter 16 in this volume.

[82] Bundesverfassungsgericht [BVerfG] [Federal Constitutional Court] June 5, 1973, 35 BVerfGE 202 ¶ 68 (Lebach case).

archives in the *Sedlmayr* cases.[83] Walter Sedlmayr was a German actor who was murdered in 1990. His former protégée and his brother were convicted for the murder in 1993 but never confessed to the crime. After their release in 2007 and 2008 they began fighting online publications for removal of their names from articles and features about the murder.

The first case before the Federal Court of Justice concerned the transcript of an old radio feature that was available in the online archive of a German radio station. The Court emphasized the difference between the archived transcript and a TV broadcast.[84] The presentation of the content in the archive was described as "passive" because users had to actively search for it and it was not accessible through the website's main page.[85] The transcript was clearly marked as old and had no connection to current news coverage.[86] The Court also concluded that the public had a legitimate interest in accessing historic documentation.[87] The freedom of the media and their function in a democratic society, the Court reasoned, justified keeping old publications available online.[88] An obligation to alter or remove these publications after a certain period of time would amount to the deletion of history and an "immunization" of the convicts, a privilege the Court said they had no right to demand.[89] The Court was also concerned that an obligation to manage historical content might create chilling effects for the media, leading to possible self-censorship in an effort to avoid the burden of conducting subsequent reviews of all publications containing references to convicts.[90] The Court ruled that the radio station could continue to make the transcript available to users in its unaltered form.[91] The subsequent decisions followed this reasoning with similar outcomes.[92]

---

[83] Bundesgerichtshof [BGH] [Federal Court of Justice] Dec. 15, 2009, VI ZR 227/08, ¶ 19, http://juris.bundesgerichtshof.de/cgi-bin/rechtsprechung/document.py?Gericht=bgh&Art=en&Datum=Aktuell&Sort=12288&nr=50648&pos=2&anz=599 (Sedlmayr Deutschlandradio); Bundesgerichtshof [BGH] [Federal Court of Justice] Feb. 9, 2010, VI ZR 243/08, http://juris.bundesgerichtshof.de/cgi-bin/rechtsprechung/document.py?Gericht=bgh&Art=en&sid=aa0a227894931853dd0f44a28d9547a7&nr=51316&pos=0&anz=4 (Sedlmayr Spiegel); Bundesgerichtshof [BGH] [Federal Court of Justice] Feb. 22, 2011, VI ZR 346/09, http://juris.bundesgerichtshof.de/cgi-bin/rechtsprechung/document.py?Gericht=bgh&Art=en&Datum=2011-2-22&nr=55559&pos=18&anz=27 (Sedlmayr FAZ); Bundesgerichtshof [BGH] [Federal Court of Justice] May 8, 2012, VI ZR 217/08, http://juris.bundesgericht shof.de/cgi-bin/rechtsprechung/document.py?Gericht=bgh&Art=en&Datum=2012-5-8&nr=60505&pos=18&anz=39 (Sedlmayr rainbow.at).

[84] BGH VI ZR 227/08, *supra* note 83, at ¶ 19.   [85] *Id.* at ¶ 19.   [86] *Id.*

[87] *Id.* at ¶ 20.   [88] *Id.*   [89] *Id.*   [90] *Id.* at ¶ 21.   [91] *Id.* at ¶ 27.

[92] BGH VI ZR 243/08, *supra* note 83; BGH VI ZR 346/09, *supra* note 83; BGH VI ZR 217/08, *supra* note 82.

In its *Apollonia*[93] judgment from 2012, the Federal Court of Justice closely followed its *Sedlmayr* decisions. The public interest in accessing unaltered coverage of historic events,[94] the Court insisted, cannot be limited to print-archives. This would erode the technical efficiency of Internet searches.[95] A complaint against this judgment is currently pending before the Federal Constitutional Court.[96]

The Court accepted the notion that the public's interest in information would diminish over time and give way to the subject's personality interest. But the impact of "passive" archived articles was considered to be less intrusive than an "active" broadcast. The Court also emphasized the public interest in preserving knowledge and preventing the deletion of history.[97] The consideration of online publications as having limited impact and being a less visible form of content compared to TV broadcasts completely contradicts the CJEU's reasoning about the aggravation of personality rights infringements resulting from the interconnected nature of Internet content. The CJEU held in *Google Spain* that personal information was easily accessible and could be gathered to form a partial profile of data subjects by the technical means of the Internet and search engines.[98]

IV   Procedural Aspects

In a case similar to *Google Spain*, the *Landgericht* Mönchengladbach (Regional Court) commented on the ranking order of demands to search engines and host providers. The plaintiff had requested the removal of search results linked to his name, which the search engine had denied. The Court did not validate the plaintiff's claim because he had other, more effective legal remedies available to him. While the removal of the search results would not prevent the further dissemination of the content by other means, the interference by the author and host of the content was more immediate.[99] The Court held that the plaintiff was obliged to demand removal from these parties before contacting the search engine

---

[93] Bundesgerichtshof [BGH] [Federal Court of Justice] Nov. 13, 2012, VI ZR 330/11, http://juris.bundesgerichtshof.de/cgi-bin/rechtsprechung/document.py?Gericht=bgh&Art=en&Datum=2012-11-13&nr=62549&pos=8&anz=17 (Apollonia).

[94] *Id.* at ¶ 18.   [95] *Id.* at ¶ 20.

[96] Bundesverfassungsgericht [BVerfG] [Federal Constitutional Court] BVerfG, 1 BvR 16/13 (not yet delivered).

[97] BGH VI ZR 330/11, *supra* note 83, at ¶ 19.

[98] Google Spain CJEU, *supra* note 22, at ¶ 80.   [99] LG 10 O 170/12, *supra* note 76, at ¶ 32.

operator.[100] The Court referenced the procedural requirements for hosting providers laid down by the Federal Court of Justice as an easy and effective way for the plaintiff to fully resolve the issue.[101]

V   Consequences

Where discord between the German and European jurisprudence can be asserted, the impact for German courts is quite tangible. According to the Federal Constitutional Court's *Solange* doctrine, acts of German authorities based on European Union secondary law are subject exclusively to the European Courts' jurisdiction "so long as" a sufficient level of protection of fundamental rights is guaranteed by the European Union and its institutions.[102] Thus, the Federal Constitutional Court has partially withdrawn its sovereign jurisdiction. European law can no longer be reviewed by the standard of the national constitution (except in specific, extraordinary circumstances). German courts must therefore deviate from past rules that contradict the principles laid down in the CJEU's judgment. We feel this constitutes a setback for the balancing of freedom of expression and the right to privacy. The subtle nuances developed over decades of German legal tradition will partially be replaced by the general primacy of the right to privacy laid down in the *Google Spain Case*.[103]

D   Reaction of Google, European Data Protection Commissioners, and National Data Protection Agencies

I   Delisting Activities

Following the CJEU's judgment Google was faced with the problem of finding a practical process for handling delisting requests. The firm had to define reliable criteria and establish efficient structures in order to manage the high number of requests it would receive.

Immediately after the judgment Google provided an online form for delisting requests.[104] Applicants are asked to provide basic personal

---

[100] *Id.* at ¶ 36.   [101] *Id.* at ¶ 35.

[102] Roughly translated as "so long as." *See* Bundesverfassungsgericht [BVerfG] [Federal Constitutional Court] Oct. 22, 1986, 73 BVerfGE 339 (Solange II).

[103] This has also been pointed out early on by Johannes Masing. *See* Chapter 16 in this volume.

[104] *Search Removal Request under Data Protection Law in Europe*, Google, https://support.google.com/legal/contact/lr_eudpa?product=websearch&hl=en (last accessed Dec. 4, 2015).

information, a copy of a document verifying their identity, and an explanation of how the concerned URL relates to them and why the inclusion of that URL in search results is "irrelevant, outdated, or otherwise objectionable." According to the company's transparency report, after initial publication of the form in May 2014, it received around 330.000 requests as of October 2015), which implicated over 1.1 Mio individual URLs.[105] Google granted 41 percent of these requests, with the respective URLs removed from search results with the applicant's name.[106] More delisting applications were filed against content carried by Facebook.com than by any other website.[107]

Google has disclosed very little information about its evaluation procedure.[108] Webmasters are currently notified of URL removals within their site,[109] as is Google's standard practice for other types of removals (e.g., due to copyright infringement). According to reports by affected webmasters the notification includes a form for reinstatement requests based on public interest or on subsequent alterations of the targeted website that limit access to the challenged content.[110] Users of Google search are informed at the bottom of the search result list that the results may have been modified due to European data protection law.[111] This notice appears as a default for name-based searches and not specifically for search terms that were subject to delisting requests.[112] The delisting affects only European domain extensions of the search engine (e.g., google.de, google.fr.).[113]

---

[105] *European Privacy Requests for Search Removals*, GOOGLE, www.google.com/transparen cyreport/removals/europeprivacy/?hl=en-US (last visited Dec. 4, 2015).

[106] *Id.*

[107] *See id.* (demonstrating that 9,610 Facebook URL's were the subject of delisting applications.).

[108] *Häufig gestellte Fragen*, GOOGLE, www.google.com/transparencyreport/removals/europe privacy/faq/?hl=de (Google Transparency Report – Requests to remove content – European privacy in search, Frequently Asked Questions) (Ger.).

[109] *Id.*

[110] Eli Schwartz, *Google Updates "Right to Be Forgotten" Notification*, SEARCH ENGINE J. (Oct. 18, 2014), www.searchenginejournal.com/google-updates-right-forgotten-notifica tion/117714/.

[111] *Privacy and Terms – FAQ*, GOOGLE, www.google.de/intl/en/policies/faq/ (last visited Dec. 4, 2014).

[112] *Id.*

[113] Peter Fleischer, *Implementing a European, not Global, Right to Be Forgotten*, GOOGLE (July 30, 2015), http://googlepolicyeurope.blogspot.de/2015/07/implementing-european-not-global-right.html.

II *Advisory Council Report*

Shortly after the CJEU issued its judgment, Google established an Advisory Council that held conferences in different European capitals to discuss the implementation procedure with local scholars and experts. Among the members of the council are renowned Internet and media experts such as Jimmy Wales (co-founder of the online encyclopedia Wikipedia), Sylvie Kauffmann (journalist and editor-in-chief of French newspaper *Le Monde*), Frank La Rue (ex-UN Special Rapporteur on the Promotion and Protection of the Right to Freedom of Opinion and Expression), and Sabine Leutheusser-Schnarrenberger (former German Minister for Justice). Eric Schmidt and David Drummond, respectively the Executive Chairman and the Chief Legal Officer/Senior Vice President of Google Inc., co-chaired the council as representatives of the company.[114]

The Council's findings were published in early February 2015. In the introductory remarks the authors emphasize that the CJEU's judgment "should not be interpreted as legitimation for practices of censorship of past information and limiting the right to access information."[115]

Through the consultations the Council identified criteria to evaluate the level of public interest in accessing particular information. One of these criteria is the data subject's role in public life.[116] The source of the information, the Council explained, also should be taken into consideration.[117] If the content was published by journalistic entities, widely known bloggers or established individual authors, or as an official government publication a stronger public interest can be assumed.[118] Another factor in the evaluation is the fluctuating relevance of data at different points in time.[119] If the content deals with past criminal offenses public interest may depend on the subject's current occupation and the nature of the crimes.[120] The most complex criterion with which the Council grappled is the nature of the information in question. The report features a list of types of information that either point toward an overriding privacy interest or a strong public interest.[121] Indicators of the latter include: information relevant to public debates, information

---

[114] *Preface* to THE ADVISORY COUNCIL TO GOOGLE ON THE RIGHT TO BE FORGOTTEN (Feb. 6, 2015), https://drive.google.com/file/d/0B1UgZshetMd4cEI3SjlvV0hNbDA/view (listing the Members of the Council.).

[115] THE ADVISORY COUNCIL TO GOOGLE ON THE RIGHT TO BE FORGOTTEN (Feb. 6, 2015), at 6 [hereinafter ADVISORY COUNCIL].

[116] *Id.* at 7.   [117] *Id.* at 13.   [118] *Id.*   [119] *Id.* at 14.   [120] *Id.*   [121] *Id.* at 9.

concerned with religious and philosophical discourse, or content in connection with public health and consumer protection issues.[122]

The Council's report also suggests a framework for the evaluation of removal requests. Prior notification of publishers was recommended with the option of providing additional information on the publication in "complex cases."[123] Concerning the institution responsible for the evaluation procedure the report clearly favors placing this responsibility in hands of the search engine operators because they possess the necessary competence to handle removal requests in other contexts.[124] The Council strongly advocated for a process before public authorities that would allow for challenges to search engine operators' delisting decisions. The Council suggested that these challenges be open to data subjects and publishers whose rights and interests are affected.[125]

III   Recommendations of the Article 29 Data Protection Working Party

The Artcile 29 Data Protection Working Party (Working Party), an independent advisory body to the European Commission composed of representatives of Member States' Data Protection Authorities (DPAs), also adopted recommendations for the interpretation of the CJEU's judgment.[126] The Working Party's procedural proposals contradict Google's current practice and the Advisory Council's findings. The restriction of URL removal to European versions of search engines is not considered sufficient for guaranteeing the rights of data subjects.[127] Instead, the Working Party urged that delisting should have full effect on all versions and domains, including the ".com" domain.[128]

The Working Party also rejected the idea that third parties should be notified about a delisting procedure. The Working Party also objected to the practice of displaying notifications of delisting decisions – specifically as part of a response to search queries pointing to granted delisting requests.[129] This might allow users to conclude that the data subject, whose name is included in their search term, has made a removal request. This insinuation, the Working Group argued, would subvert the

---

[122] *Id.* at 10–13.   [123] *Id.* at 17.   [124] *Id.* at 18.   [125] *Id.* at 18.

[126] Article 29 Data Protection Working Party, Guidelines on the Implementation of the Court of Justice of the European Union Judgment on "Google Spain and Inc. v. Agencia Española de Protección de Datos (AEPD) and Mario Costeja González" C-131/12, 14/ EN WP 225 (Nov. 26, 2014), http://ec.europa.eu/justice/data-protection/article-29/docu mentation/opinion-recommendation/files/2014/wp225_en.pdf [hereinafter Guidelines].

[127] *Id.* at ¶ 20.   [128] *Id.*   [129] *Id.* at ¶ 22.

intentions of the CJEU's judgment.[130] The Working Party also criticized the practice of notifying webmasters about a delisting decision because the publisher lacks a legitimate interest in receiving notice.[131]

IV   Proceedings in France and the United Kingdom

In the time since the judgment in the *Google Spain Case* was delivered, predictable conflicts over its implementation have arisen between European national data protection agencies and the search engine. These serve to highlight some of the open questions raised up by the Court's decision.

In June 2015, the French national data protection agency, known as the Commission Nationale de l'Informatique et des Libertés (CNIL), ordered Google to extend delisting decisions beyond the European domains of its services.[132] Google refused to comply, stating in a blog post that this would "risk serious chilling effects on the web."[133] The company worried that applying every state's standards for legal content on the Internet worldwide would constitute a "race to the bottom," reducing the Internet to the lowest common denominator of information freedom.[134] In September 2015, the CNIL rejected Google's informal appeal, arguing that original content is not affected by delisting and remains accessible.[135]

Meanwhile, a matter that could be described as an instance of the "Streisand effect" has concerned the Information Commissioner's Office (ICO), the national data protection authority of the United Kingdom. After granting delisting requests Google currently informs the affected webmasters.[136] Several British media outlets have recently published articles about delisting decisions that repeated the data contained in the delisted content, including the data subjects' names.[137] As a consequence,

---

[130] *Id.*   [131] *Id.* at ¶ 23.

[132] Press Release, CNIL, CNIL Orders Google to Apply Delisting on all Domain Names of the Search Engine (June 12, 2015), www.cnil.fr/linstitution/actualite/article/article/cnil-orders-google-to-apply-delisting-on-all-domain-names-of-the-search-engine/.

[133] Fleischer, *supra* note 113.   [134] *Id.*

[135] Press Release, CNIL, Right to Delisting: Google Informal Appeal Rejected (Sept. 21, 2015), www.cnil.fr/english/news-and-events/news/article/right-to-delisting-google-informal-appeal-rejected/.

[136] *See Häufig gestellte Fragen, supra* note 108.

[137] *See, e.g.,* Rhiannon Williams, *Telegraph Stories Affected by E.U. "Right to Be Forgotten,"* TELEGRAPH (Sept. 3, 2015), www.telegraph.co.uk/technology/google/11036257/Telegraph-stories-affected-by-EU-right-to-be-forgotten.html.

the information could once again be found by searching for the data subjects' names, albeit in contemporary news articles focused on the delisting regime and its effects. Following a complaint the ICO ordered the search engine to delist new articles about the delisting of articles that had reported on the complainant's criminal conviction.[138] Google argued, however, that the data contained in the new articles was a matter of current public discussion and no longer irrelevant.[139] It seems likely that Google will appeal the ICO's order.

E Proposal

I Debate over the CJEU's Decision

The debate over the *Google Spain Case* shows pragmatic tendencies. The CJEU's judgment has been widely criticized for distorting the balance between freedom of expression and the right to privacy.[140] The balance can only be restored through the definition of a reliable and proportionate procedure. The evaluation criteria can be derived from the European Court of Human Right's ample case law. Constructive analysis must therefore focus on practical proposals for the judgment's procedural implementation.

It has been suggested that there should be a presumption against delisting lawful content and that data subjects should be required to attempt to resolve matters with the webpage operator prior to contacting the search engine.[141] A closely connected question is the necessity of including publishers in the evaluation process. Some commentators and Google's Advisory Council have argued for the publishers' right to be heard.[142] Others have rejected this proposal.[143]

Given the sensitive nature of the evaluation process for fundamental rights, it is problematic that their fulfillment and application should be

---

[138] ICO, Data Protection Act 1998 Supervisory Powers of the Information Commissioner Enforcement Notice (Aug. 18, 2015), https://ico.org.uk/media/action-weve-taken/enforcement-notices/1432380/google-inc-enforcement-notice-18082015.pdf.

[139] *Id.* at 5.   [140] *See* Arning, Moos & Schefzig, *supra* note 68; Chapter 16 in this volume.

[141] *See* Arning, Moos & Schefzig, *supra* note 68; Chapter 16 in this volume.

[142] ADVISORY COUNCIL, *supra* NOTE 115, at 17; *see also* Jörg Wimmers, *Der Intermediär als Ermittler, Moderator und Entscheider in äußerungsrechtlichen Auseinandersetzungen*, 46 ZEITSCHRIFT FÜR MEDIEN- UND KOMMUNIKATIONSRECHT 202, 209 (2015).

[143] *See* Guidelines, *supra* note 126.

entrusted to a private company.[144] The hazards of this have also been noted by Jimmy Wales and Frank La Rue in their dissenting opinions to the Advisory Council's report. They explained that they "oppose the legal situation in which a private company is forced to become the judge of our most fundamental rights of expression and privacy,"[145] and they insisted that "that the protection of Human Rights is the responsibility of the State."[146]

Further controversy revolves around the geographical scope of delisting actions. The CJEU did not comment on this point. The Working Party proposed global delisting.[147] Google, however, has limited its implementation of the judgment to Europe. After the CNIL's decision in September 2015, this discussion has gained further practical relevance.[148]

II Lawful Content and Lawful Reference

The most radical facet of the CJEU's judgment is the distinction the Court drew between "lawful content," on one hand, and "lawful references to content," on the other hand.[149] It seems counterintuitive to allow the publication of information on the condition that it remains sufficiently obscure. This is, however, in line with the German Federal Court of Justice's *Sedlmayer* decisions in which the Court based the archived articles' continued legitimacy on their low impact compared to a prime-time TV feature.[150] It makes sense that the severity of privacy infringements from the perspective of the affected individual depends on the level of public perception. It is common for people to "google" their acquaintances and potential business partners just to see what comes up in the search. If the search results contain embarrassing or otherwise undesirable information, then this might cause professional or personal repercussions for the data subject. Even if the search result list may be the immediate reminder of past skeletons, these skeletons are still buried on some third party website. In other words, the conflict

---

[144] Jan Freialdenhoven & Philippe Heinzke, *Vergiss mich: das Recht auf Löschung von Suchergebnissen*, GRUR-PRAX 2015, 119, 121; Chapter 16 in this volume; Tabea Rössner, *Grundrechtsabwägung – Das Löschverfahren bei Google sollte reguliert werden*, 6 EPD MEDIEN 5 (2015).

[145] ADVISORY COUNCIL, *supra* note 115, at 27.   [146] *Id.* at 29.

[147] Guidelines, *supra* note 126, at ¶ 20.   [148] *See* Press Release, CNIL, *supra* note 132.

[149] *See* Google Spain CJEU, *supra* note 22, at ¶¶ 38, 80, 83, 84, 87.

[150] BGH VI ZR 227/08, *supra* note 83, at ¶ 19.

should ideally be resolved between the publisher of the content and the individual affected by it.[151] Allowing removal requests for links to lawful content is like giving a store permission to take up a lawful business and then prohibiting every person in town to give directions to customers looking for the store.

III   Geographical Scope of Implementation

The geographical scope of delisting remains a major point of disagreement, made evident by the formal proceedings in France.[152] This question is also discussed in detail in the Advisory Council report.[153] Google currently applies restrictions resulting from delisting decisions exclusively to its European search services. While the Advisory Council concluded that complete protection of data subjects' rights can only be achieved by applying delisting decisions globally, users outside the European Union should not be limited in their access to information and right to free speech by a legal regime operating outside their country of residence.[154] Similarly, European Internet users should not be prevented from accessing international versions of Google's search engine.[155] The Advisory Council expressed concern about setting a precedent for censorship, while the technical measures available to implement such restrictions can be circumvented, making the restriction ineffective.[156]

The Advisory Council report, citing Google's statistics, found that 95 percent of users located within the European Union access the local versions of Google search in any case.[157] With this in mind, the Advisory Council concluded that the practice of limiting link removals to European versions of the search engine affords the affected data subject sufficient protection while adhering to the principle of proportionally.[158] In her dissenting opinion attached to the Advisory Council report, Sabine Leutheusser-Schnarrenberger expressed the opposite view, which was also advanced by the Working Party.[159] Leutheusser-Schnarrenberger explained that "the Internet is global, the protection of user's rights must also be global."[160]

Given the profound differences between privacy regimes around the world it would be presumptuous for one regime to assume sovereignty of

---

[151] *See* Wimmers, *supra* note 142.   [152] *See* Press Release, CNIL, *supra* note 132.
[153] ADVISORY COUNCIL, *supra* note 115, at 19.   [154] *Id.*   [155] *Id.* at 20.   [156] *Id.*
[157] *Id.* at 19.   [158] *Id.* at 20.   [159] Guidelines, *supra* note 125, at ¶ 20.
[160] ADVISORY COUNCIL, *supra* note 115, at 27.

interpretation over the content accessible to users through search engines worldwide. For example, data protection has historically been valued differently in the European Union than in the United States.[161] On one hand, the data protection concept in the European Union employs a preemptive approach by prohibiting all processing of personal data in the private and public sector by default unless it can be legitimized under one of the enumerated provisions. On the other hand, U.S. data protection law does not provide a catch-all clause and is comprised of fragmented, sector-specific regulations.[162] Dissemination of information contained in official releases of government entities, including personal data, is not subject to restrictions.[163] The validity of other sovereign state's approaches to data protection should not be subject to European evaluation.[164] It is our opinion that delisting decisions resulting from the procedure implemented in response to the CJEU's decision should be limited to European Internet search engine domains.

VI   Procedural Implementation

As a compromise between the sole responsibility of private companies, on one hand, and strict state organization of delisting evaluations, on the other hand, we suggest a two-step procedure. The first level comprises a notice and counter-notice approach under the supervision of an independent arbitration entity at the second level.

1   Notice and Counter-Notice

In the first step, there should be an effort to resolve conflicts between the content provider/author and the data subject directly. If search engine operators receive removal requests from data subjects, then they should forward these requests to the webmaster of the website hosting the content. Depending on the situation, the webmaster should then contact the content's author, if possible, and present him with the options to remove the content, remove the subject's personal data, or object to the removal request. In the event that the author cannot be contacted, or

---

[161] Brown, *supra* note 61, at 162; Chapter 2 in this volume.

[162] Paul Schwartz, *The E.U.–U.S. Privacy Collision*, 126 Harv. L. Rev. 1966, 1975 (2013).

[163] John Kropf, *Google Spain SL v. Agencia Española de Protección de Datos (AEPD)*. Case C-131/12, 108 Am. J. Int'l L. 502, 506 (2014).

[164] *See* Brown, *supra* note 61; *Europe's Expanding "Right to Be Forgotten*," N.Y. Times (Feb. 4, 2015), www.nytimes.com/2015/02/04/opinion/europes-expanding-right-to-be-forgotten.html.

when the webmaster is the author, then the decision should revert back to the content provider. If, after a set period of time, the webmaster has not received a response from the author (or the webmaster does not respond to the inquiry by the search engine operator), then the link in question may be removed from the search engine's index. Afterwards, the search engine should notify the webmaster of the removal and inform him or her of the option to challenge the decision. If the content is removed or altered to exclude the subject's personal data, then the request has been resolved and data subjects should be notified. The case should be forwarded to the arbitration entity, our proposed second step, only if the author or the webmaster objects to the delisting decision.

The concept of systematically including both parties in the decision is comparable to the notice and counter-notice mechanism in Section 512 of Title 17 of the U.S. Code, which was introduced by the Digital Millennium Copyright Act.[165] The Federal Court of Justice insisted on similar requirements for Internet service providers who receive complaints about third party content.[166]

Search engines would only act as intermediaries between data subjects and content providers, and their evaluation capacities would be limited to the formal requirements of a data subject's request. The publishers, however, would have an active role in this process and they would have the option to object to delisting requests. This is the approach that was suggested by the Advisory Council's report.[167] The entities originally responsible for the challenged content should be approached before resorting to the removal of a search engine's links. A similar "sequential approach" has been suggested in the Advisory Council's consultations.[168] This opinion is not shared by the Working Party, which rejects the notion of a data subject's obligation to contact the publisher.[169] We recognize that it might be difficult for the data subject to identify and contact the responsible publisher, but this difficulty can be circumvented by positioning the search engine operator as an intermediary who is obliged to provide easily accessible mechanisms to submit delisting requests and then to forward them to the involved parties on the data

---

[165] 17 U.S.C. § 512 (c)(3), (g)(3).

[166] Bundesgerichtshof [BGH] [Federal Court of Justice] Oct. 25, 2011, VI ZR 93/10, ¶ 27, 2011, http://juris.bundesgerichtshof.de/cgi-bin/rechtsprechung/document.py?Gericht= bgh&Art=pm&Datum=2011&Sort=3&anz=169&pos=0&nr=58574&linked=urt&Blank =1&file=dokument.pdf.

[167] ADVISORY COUNCIL, *supra* note 115, at 18.   [168] *Id.* at 35.

[169] Guidelines, *supra* note 126, at ¶ 11.

subject's behalf. Another advantage of this approach is that delisting will be the default result if the original publisher of the content fails to react. In our proposal, a single delisting request can be submitted for multiple URLs with the same content and the delisting will either be granted or it will be forwarded to the arbitration entity for evaluation.

2 Arbitration

An independent arbitration body should be established to review delisting requests that were contested by authors or webmasters and to consider later objections by webmasters upon receiving notification of delisting decisions.[170] The search engine operator would submit the cases and all documentation received from either party to this body, which will determine whether the data subject's rights override the public interest in accessing the content. The arbitration body should be able to prompt both the data subject and the publisher to submit further evidence or explanations for their respective positions. It would then notify both parties of its decision and its reasoning and submit the decision to the search engine operator in case the data subject's request is deemed to be legitimate.

In our opinion it makes sense to establish this arbitration body at a European level to ensure uniform application of evaluation criteria. A similar suggestion of a voluntary European arbitration body has been brought forward by Leutheusser-Schnarrenberger in the appendix to the Advisory Council's report.[171]

The arbitration body should be independent from state authorities. Its membership should be drawn from representatives of Member States' data protection and media regulation authorities, press and media associations, and search engine operators. The most important facet of this part of our resort to arbitration is our conviction that the public interest – and all parties involved – would be best served by not imposing the responsibility of balancing fundamental rights on private companies.

The legal basis for the procedure could be introduced in the upcoming General Data Protection Regulation.[172] The German Government has

---

[170] This has also been suggested by Tabea Rössner, *supra* note 144, at 6.

[171] ADVISORY COUNCIL, *supra* note 115, at 25.

[172] *See Proposal for a Regulation of the European Parliament and the Council on the Protection of Individuals with Regard to the Processing of Personal Data and on the Free Movement of Such Data (General Data Protection Regulation)*, COM (2012)11 final, http://eur-lex.europa.eu/legal-content/EN/TXT/HTML/?uri=CELEX:52012PC0011& from=EN.

already submitted an amendment note to the draft Regulation.[173] It proposes a similar dispute settlement process in §17c of the Regulation, which provides the affected third party (publisher) the opportunity to submit an opinion on the data subject's request and obligates the search engine to inform both the data subject and the publisher about the decision. The German proposal would establish independent dispute settlement units within the Member States.

F Closing Remarks

It is inaccurate to refer to the CJEU's delisting procedure as the "right to be forgotten." Still, there is no doubt about the immense relevance of the decision for Internet service operators. Indeed, the right itself will not soon be forgotten. It will influence future interpretation of the fundamental rights in Articles 7 and 8 of the Charter of Fundamental Rights and might be incorporated into the forthcoming General Data Protection Regulation. Its implementation offers ample opportunity to improve the balancing of rights while compensating for some of the judgment's weaknesses.

Concerning the transatlantic relationship, the judgment might prove problematic in negotiations of free trade agreements, such as the proposed Transatlantic Trade and Investment Partnership (TTIP) that has already sparked conflicts over data protection standards.[174] This is aggravated by the CJEU's *Schrems Case*,[175] which declared the Commission's "Safe Harbor" decision void. "Safe Harbor" had previously facilitated data transfers between the European Union and the United States. But the idea of a "right to be Forgotten" in the digital era is not entirely foreign to the United States either.[176] The Californian Online Privacy Protection Act, for example, provides minors with the right to request

---

[173] German Delegation to the Council of the European Union, Note on the Regulation of the European Parliament and of the Council on the Protection of Individuals With Regard to the Processing of Personal Data and on the Free Movement of Such Data (General Data Protection Regulation) – Right to be Forgotten: Dispute Settlement (Feb. 9, 2015), http://lobbyplag.eu/governments/assets/pdf/CD-6032_15.pdf.

[174] Sam Schechner, *Online Privacy Could Spark U.S.–E.U. Trade Rift*, WALL ST. J. (Jan. 8, 2014), www.wsj.com/articles/SB10001424052702304361604579291041878017398.

[175] Case C-362/14, Schrems v. Data Protection Commissioner, INFOCURIA – CASE-LAW CT. JUST. (Oct. 6, 2015), http://curia.europa.eu/juris/document/document.jsf?text=&docid=169195&pageIndex=0&doclang=EN&mode=lst&dir=&occ=first&part=1&cid=421175.

[176] *See* Chapter 11 in this volume.

removal of content that they published themselves under section 22581 (a). Website operators whose services are directed to minors also must inform their users of this right and provide instructions for removal or removal requests. Still, a full-blown "right to be forgotten" would be contrary to the U.S. Constitution.[177]

It remains to be seen how the Member States' courts, DPAs, and possibly legislators will substantiate the right to be forgotten. In the absence of a clear and unified European approach, such as the dispute settlement proposed here, national DPAs must fend for themselves at this point. As discussed above, France and the United Kingdom have already contested Google's current implementation of the judgment. Other States may choose to use their margin of appreciation to emphasize freedom of expression and the media.

---

[177] Brown, *supra* note 61.

23

Adequate Transatlantic Data Exchange in the Shadow of the NSA-Affair

BY ELS DE BUSSER

A Introduction

No interstate cooperation can function without an exchange of information. In most cases information will include personal data, including highly sensitive personal data for use in law enforcement activities. From an E.U. perspective, every outgoing transfer of personal data should be preceded by an assessment of the level of data protection in the receiving state.[1] This should be "adequate," or the transfers is prohibited. It is not hard to rubberstamp a third state's data protection system as adequate when it has ratified the same data protection provisions as the other E.U. Member States. But when the United States is concerned this becomes a more complicated analysis. In commercial matters, the Safe Harbor scheme was thought to ensure the required "adequate" level of data protection.[2] For criminal matters, fair trial rights are at stake and the consent requirement does not work. Additionally, in the European Union, investigations undertaken in support of law enforcement are strictly separated from intelligence gathering. That is not the case in the United States. Academic research published in 2009 showed that for data transferred for law enforcement purposes (preventing, investigating and prosecuting criminal offenses) the U.S. data protection system could not be labeled as "adequate."[3] Much has taken place since 2009. In

---

[1] Directive 95/46/EC, arts. 25–26, 1995 O.J. (L281) 23, 11.

[2] Commission Decision of July 26, 2000, pursuant to Directive 95/46/EC of the European Parliament and of the Council on the adequacy of the protection provided by the Safe Harbor privacy principles and related frequently asked questions issued by the US Department of Commerce, 2000 O.J. (L215) 25, 08 [hereinafter Commission Decision of July 26, 2000]. *But see* Case C-362/14, Maximillian Schrems v. Data Prot. Comm'r., 2015 ECLI:EU:C:627.

[3] ELS DE BUSSER, DATA PROTECTION IN E.U. AND U.S. CRIMINAL COOPERATION 293–302 (2009).

2012 the European Commission presented its legislative proposals to reform the data protection legal framework in commercial matters and in criminal matters. At the time this chapter was written the proposals had not yet been adopted.[4] Still, in the context of both the draft regulation on data protection in commercial matters and the draft directive on data protection in criminal matters a general approach had been agreed upon.[5] This means that both files were set to be considered by the European Parliament. The reform proposals also include new rules governing the adequacy assessment. In 2013 the former NSA contractor Edward Snowden leaked a large number of documents revealing the NSA's extensive data-collection and retention programs.[6] The revelations led to policy changes announced in 2014.[7] Finally, in 2015 several sunset clauses in the USA PATRIOT Act expired, leading to a significant reform in the United States.[8]

In this chapter I will examine developments since 2009 to draw conclusions on the adequacy of the level of data protection in the United States – with a special focus on the "purpose limitation" principle. It is important to note that this is done from an E.U. perspective, a point of viewed justified by the fact that the adequacy requirement is an E.U. requirement. This research is limited to publicly accessible legislation, policy documents, and the applicable court decisions. For the European Union the relevant sources consist of the applicable European Union and Council of Europe (CoE) legal

---

[4] Proposal for a Regulation of the European Parliment and of the Council on the Protection of Individualswith Regard to the Processing of Personal Data and on the Free Movement of Such Data, COM (2012) 11 final; *Commission Proposal for a Regular of the European Parliament and of the Council on the Protection of Individuals with Regard to the Processing of Personal Data and on the Free Movement of Such Data*, art. 3(1), COM (2012) 10 final.

[5] Proposal for a Regulation of the European Parliament and of the Council on the Protection of Individuals with Regard to the Processing of Personal Data and on the Free Movement of such Data (General Data Protection Regulation) Preparation of a General Approach, Council Doc., 9565/15, (June 11, 2015) and Proposal for a Directive of the European Parliament and of the Council on the Protection of Individuals with Regard to the Processing of Personal Data by Competent Authorities for the Purposes of Prevention, Investigation, Detection or Prosecution of Criminal Offences or the Execution of Criminal Penalties and the Free Movement of such Data – General approach, Council Doc. 12555/15, (Oct. 2, 2015).

[6] GLENN GREENWALD, NO PLACE TO HIDE (2014).

[7] Directive on Signals Intelligence Activity (PPD-28), 2014 DAILY COMP. PRES. DOC. (Jan. 17, 2014), www.fbi.gov/about-us/nsb/fbis-policies-and-procedures-presidential-policy-directive-28-1 (last visited, Nov. 18, 2015).

[8] USA FREEDOM Act, H.R. 2048, 114th Cong. (2015).

instruments, excluding national laws. In view of the ongoing reform of the E.U.'s data protection legal framework, differences between the currently applicable legal instruments and the proposals are emphasized where relevant. For the United States the research focused on federal legislation. In a first step, I present the basic concepts and their meaning on both sides of the Atlantic, with due consideration for the distinction between law enforcement and intelligence activities. In a second step, the concept of adequacy will be scrutinized, especially in view of the mentioned reform of the E.U.'s data protection framework. In a third step, from the point of view of the E.U. data protection standards, recent relevant developments in the United States are assessed. In a final step, I deal with the question of E.U. citizens' rights in the United States.

B   Concepts

To examine the adequacy of data protection in the United States, the first part of this chapter is dedicated to the relevant concepts in both the European Union and the United States, including: personal data; privacy; law enforcement; and intelligence gathering. Due to the ongoing reform of the E.U.'s data protection framework, the pending proposals were included in this research together with the currently applicable legal instruments (and the interpretation of the latter by the European courts and the Article 29 Data Protection Working Party [29 WP]).

I   Personal Data and Data Protection

In the European convention that is widely seen as the starting point for data protection, "personal data" is defined as "any information relating to an identified or identifiable individual."[9] The 1980 OECD Guidelines governing the protection of privacy and transborder flows of personal data were drafted at the same time.[10] This explains why the definition is identical in both texts. Even after the 2013 revision of the

---

[9] Convention for the Protection of Individuals with regard to Automatic Processing of Personal Data, Jan. 28, 1981, ETS No. 108.

[10] *OECD Guidelines on the Protection of Privacy and Transborder Flows of Personal Data*, OECD (2013), www.oecd.org/sti/ieconomy/privacy.htm (last visited, Nov. 18, 2015).

OECD Guidelines and in the currently ongoing modernization of the Convention, the definition remains unchanged.[11] The same definition for personal data was copied into Directive 95/46/EC.[12] Still, it was not until 2007 that the 29 WP explained how to define personal data. In accordance with the jurisprudence of the European Court of Human Rights (ECtHR), which cited the Convention, the 29 WP endorsed a broad interpretation and illustrated this with examples drawn from the field of European Community activity.[13]

It is not necessary to know a person's name or address in order to identify or single out an individual from a group of individuals.[14] Even an IP address can constitute personal data,[15] as could a string of search terms or surfing behavior.[16] The preamble to Directive 95/46/ EC includes a reasonable-means test.[17] This could change because the Commission has reformulated the concept "personal data" in its data protection reform based on the identification question. Personal data, in the new formulation, is defined as any information relating to a "data subject." A data subject is defined as "an identified natural person, or a natural person who can be identified, directly or indirectly, by means reasonably likely to be used by the controller or by any other natural or legal person, in particular by reference to an identification number, location data, online identifiers, or to one or more factors specific to the physical, physiological, genetic, mental, economic, cultural or social identity of that person."[18] The proposed definition integrates the reasonable-means test into the description

---

[11] *Information Document – Text of the Modernised Convention 108 with Reservations*, (June 17, 2015), www.coe.int/t/dghl/standardsetting/dataprotection/TPD_documents/Informa tion%20doc%20Modernised%20Convention%20108%20with%20reservations.pdf   (last visited, Nov. 18, 2015).

[12] Directive 95/46/EC, *supra* note 1.

[13] *Opinion 4/2007 on the Concept of Personal Data*, art. 29, (June 20, 2007), ec.europa.eu/ justice/data-protection/article-29/documentation/opinion-recommendation/files/2007/ wp136_en.pdf (last visited Nov. 18, 2015).

[14] LEE A. BYGRAVE, DATA PROTECTION LAW 43 (2002).

[15] *Opinion 4/2007 on the Concept of Personal Data, supra* note 13.

[16] *Opinion 2/2010 on Online Behavioural Advertising*, art. 29 (June 22, 2010), ec.europa.eu/ justice/data-protection/article-29/documentation/opinion-recommendation/files/2010/w p171_en.pdf (last visited Nov. 18, 2015).

[17] Recital 26, Directive 95/46/EC and Committee of Ministers, Recommendation No. R(89) 2, Jan. 18, 1989.

[18] *Commission Proposal for a Regular of the European Parliament and of the Council on the Protection of Individuals with Regard to the Processing of Personal Data and on the Free Movement of Such Data*, art. 3(1), COM (2012) 10 final.

of what constitutes a data subject and, thus, personal data. The definition does not, however, refer to information that would allow authorities to single out an individual.[19]

The U.S. data protection framework consists of specific laws, sectoral legislation, and self-regulation.[20] This fragmented approach differs from the umbrella Convention applicable in Europe. The 1974 Privacy Act is the law that protects citizens' information stored in systems of records held by the government.[21] Despite its discrete purpose and coverage, the Privacy Act comes closest in the United States to the European omnibus approach. Drafted in the context of the Watergate-scandal, one of the policy objectives of the Privacy Act is to restrict disclosure of personally identifiable records maintained by federal agencies.[22] As used in the Privacy Act the term "record" refers to any item, collection, or grouping of information about an individual that is maintained by an agency – including but not limited to, education, financial transactions, medical history, and criminal or employment history. The record must contain a name, identifying number, symbol, or other identifying particular assigned to the individual, such as a fingerprint, voiceprint, or a photograph.[23] The term record refers to any item of information that includes an individual identifier and can include as little as one descriptive item about an individual.[24] Explicitly mentioning identifying factors corresponds to the proposed definition in the E.U. data protection reform package, which is expected to bring clarity to those situations in which data concerning online behavior or geolocation data are collected.[25] Nevertheless, substantial differences on other points remain between the E.U. and the U.S. systems.

---

[19] Opinion 01/2012 on the Data Protection Reform Proposals, art. 29, (Mar. 23, 2012), ec.europa.eu/justice/data-protection/article-29/documentation/opinion-recommenda tion/files/2012/wp191_en.pdf (last visited Nov. 18, 2015).

[20] David Banisar and Simon Davies, *Global Trends in Privacy Protection: An International Survey of Privacy, Data Protection and Surveillance Laws and Developments*, 18 J. Marshall J. Comput. & Info. L. 1, 13–14 (1999).

[21] 5 U.S.C. § 552(a) (2012).

[22] U.S. Dep't of Justice's Office of Privacy and Civil Liberties, Overview of the Privacy Act of 1974, www.justice.gov/opcl/file/639731/download (last visited Nov. 18, 2015).

[23] 5 U.S.C. § 552a(a)(4) (2012).

[24] OMB Guidelines, 40 Fed. Reg. 28,948, 28,951 (July 09, 1975).

[25] *Commission Proposal, supra* note 18.

In spite of their involvement in drafting the text as an observer, the United States never signed or ratified the Convention.[26] Even if the Commission seemed to think differently when outlining negotiation directives for a possible E.U.–U.S. general data exchange agreement, it is not expected that such ratification would ever occur.[27]

II Privacy

The right to a private life is strongly embedded in the European Convention on Human Rights (ECHR)[28] and the E.U. Charter of Fundamental Rights and Freedoms.[29] The latter also introduced an explicit right to data protection.[30] The ECtHR has linked data protection and privacy, stressing that storing data related to an individual's private life falls within the application of Article 8 of the ECHR.[31] Later, the ECtHR even referred to the American concept of a "reasonable expectation of privacy" but concluded that it should not to be a conclusive factor when defining the right to a private life.[32] The Court preferred not to define privacy in a restrictive way. But analyzing the Court's rulings over several decades shows a distinction between two overlapping categories. On the one hand, the Court has considered the public or nonpublic nature of the situation in which an individual exercises his or her right to privacy. On the other hand, the Court has considered the moral or material characteristic of the right to privacy. Public or relational privacy refers to an individual's professional or personal relationships, including the privacy of telephone conversations or e-mail.[33] Nonpublic privacy represents those aspects of a person's life that do not involve relationships with

---

[26] Convention for the protection of individuals with regard to automatic processing of personal data, Jan. 28, 1981, ETS No. 108, § 15.

[27] COM (2010) 252/2, Annex, Negotiating Directives, § 17, May 12, 2010. *See* Els De Busser, *The Adequacy of an E.U.–U.S. Partnership*, in European Data Protection: In Good Health? 185, 198–99 (Serge Gutwirth *et al.* eds., 2011).

[28] Convention for the Protection of Human Rights and Fundamental Freedoms, Mar. 9, 1953, C.E.T.S. No. 005.

[29] Charter of Fundamental Rights of the European Union, 2000 O.J. (C364) 1.

[30] Charter of Fundamental Rights of the European Union, art. 8, 2000 O.J. (C364) 1. *See* Herke Kranenborg, *Protection of Personal Data*, in The E.U. Charter of Fundamental Rights 223–66 (Steve Peers *et al.* eds., 2014).

[31] Amman v. Switzerland, App. No. 27798/95, Eur. Ct. H.R. ¶¶ 65–67 (2000).

[32] P.G. and J.H. v. the UK, App. No. 44787/98, Eur. Ct. H.R., ¶57 (2001).

[33] Paul De Hert, *Artikel 8 - Recht Op Privacy*, in Handboek EVRM, Artikelsgewijze Commentaar 701, 723 (Johan Vande Lanotte & Yves Haeck eds., 2004).

others.[34] Moral privacy focuses on the human personality itself, such as making decisions regarding health and sexual life.[35] Exercising moral privacy can result in material elements – the category known as material privacy – that includes information in any format, whether containing personal data or not.

It is essential to stress that "personal data protection" and "privacy" are not the same.[36] Personal data refers to data that identify or enable the identification of an individual. They can overlap with the right to privacy but they are not co-extensive with privacy because an individual can exercise his or her right to privacy without identifying data being involved.

An explicit right to a private life, as secured by the ECHR, does not exist in the U.S. legal framework. Still, aspects of the right are protected by the Bill of Rights. The protection most relevant for this chapter is the Fourth Amendment, which is concerned with searches and seizures.[37] In 1886 the U.S. Supreme Court linked the Fourth Amendment to privacy.[38] It was further interpreted as "the right to be let alone," reaching further than material objects and encompassing a person's beliefs, thoughts, emotions, and sensations.[39] Justice Brandeis saw the right to privacy as the most comprehensive and the most valued right enjoyed by civilized societies and described it – in a landmark essay co-written with Samuel Warren – as "the right to be let alone."[40] With respect to the Fourth Amendment, the Supreme Court developed a subjective test based on a reasonable expectation of privacy.[41] After establishing that the right protects people and not places,[42] the right to privacy extends to those activities and areas of life in which an individual has a subjective expectation of privacy. The limits of privacy are determined by what society is prepared to recognize as reasonable from among those subjective expectations.[43] These limits were recently tested with regard to smart

---

[34] Els De Busser, Data Protection in E.U. and U.S. Criminal Cooperation 51–52 (2009).

[35] Z v. Finland, App. No. 22009/93, § 95, Eur. Ct. H.R. (1997); Dudgeon v. the United Kingdom, App. No. 7525/76, § 60, Eur. Ct. H.R. (1981).

[36] Opinion 4/2007, supra note 13.   [37] U.S. Const. amend. IV.

[38] Fred Cate, Privacy in the Information Age 57 (1997); Boyd v. United States, 116 U.S. 616 (1886).

[39] Olmstead v. U.S., 277 U.S. 438 (1928) (Brandeis, J., dissenting).

[40] Samuel D. Warren and Louis D. Brandeis, The Right to Privacy, 4 Harv. L. Rev. 193, 193–220 (1890).

[41] Katz v. United States, 389 U.S. 347 (1967).   [42] Id.

[43] Smith v. Maryland, 442 U.S. 735 (1979).

phones when the U.S. Supreme Court held that a warrantless search and seizure of the digital contents of a smart phone during an arrest is unconstitutional.[44] In 1973 the connection between privacy and the right to data protection was made in the Fair Information Practice Principles, which stated that an individual's personal privacy is directly affected by the disclosure and use made of identifiable information in a record.[45] Drafted in the context of the nascent but increasing use of automated data systems, the Principles were later integrated as general standards for the protection of records containing identifiable information in the Privacy Act.

III   Law Enforcement and Intelligence

In the European Union, collecting data for law enforcement purposes should be clearly distinguished from collecting data for intelligence and security purposes. Criminal investigations conducted by law enforcement authorities are based on the suspicion of a criminal offense and have the goal of using the data as evidence in criminal proceedings. Intelligence activities are carried out without such suspicion and aim to protect national security. In the case of intelligence activities, the data usually is collected in secret.[46] In spite of this, legal limits and safeguards for collecting and processing personal data for the detection, investigation, and prosecution of criminal offenses are stronger than those applied to the activities of intelligence agencies. Control on the gathering of information to be used as evidence in criminal proceedings requires transparency; an aspect inherently at odds with the function and purpose of secret intelligence activities.[47] This becomes problematic when the results of intelligence activities come to be used as evidence in criminal proceedings and, thus, lead to severe consequences for the individual involved who has not benefited from the safeguards that apply to information-gathering in a criminal investigation. Besides the difference in purpose, national security remains an exclusive

---

[44] Riley v. California, 134 S. Ct. 2473 (2014).

[45] U.S. DEP'T OF HEALTH, EDUC. AND WELFARE, REPORT OF THE SECRETARY'S ADVISORY COMMITTEE ON AUTOMATED PERSONAL DATA SYSTEMS, 40–41 (1973), www.justice.gov/opcl/docs/rec-com-rights.pdf (last visited Nov. 18, 2015).

[46] John A.E. Vervaele, Gegevensuitwisseling en Terrorismebestrijding in de VS en Nederland: Emergency Criminal Law?, PANOPTICON 27, 27–52 (2005).

[47] MARIANNE F.A. HIRSCH BALLIN, ANTICIPATIVE CRIMINAL INVESTIGATION 127–29 (2012).

national competence and the E.U. law-makers do not have the authority to draft any provisions in this area. The area of judicial and police cooperation in criminal matters, however, can be regulated to a certain extent by E.U. legal instruments.[48]

The European tradition of separating law enforcement from intelligence does not, as such, have an equivalent in the U.S. system. In principle the divide was present in laws such as the National Security Act of 1947.[49] Even with agencies that have double competences, such as the FBI, a legislative wall was firmly in place to prevent the use of data gathered for intelligence purposes in criminal investigations.[50] This wall has gradually been dismantled,[51] with the most significant steps taken in the 2001 PATRIOT Act.[52] Transatlantic discussions revealed how difficult it is to agree on a definition of "law enforcement purposes," with the United States having a much wider understanding of the term that includes national security.[53]

C   Adequate Transatlantic Data Transfers

I   The Adequacy Requirement: Inconsistencies and Assumptions

Transfers of personal data from the European Union to third states should only be carried out after an assessment has found that the third state's data protection framework is adequate, or that adequate safeguards have been agreed upon. First included in Directive 95/46/EC,[54] the adequacy requirement was also included in the 2008 Framework Decision[55] and in the 2001 Additional Protocol of the Convention.[56] The latter made the requirement applicable to several – but not

---

[48] Consolidated Version of the Treaty on European Union, art. 4, §2, 2010 O.J. C 83/01 [hereinafter TEU]; Consolidated Version of the Treaty on the Functioning of the European Union art. 82–89, 2008 O.J C115/47 [hereinafter TFEU].

[49] Fred F. Manget, *Intelligence and the Criminal Law System*, 17 STAN. L. & POL'Y REV. 415, 416–17 (2006).

[50] Description of "Intelligence Community" by Executive Order 12333 including only the "intelligence elements of the Federal Bureau of Investigation." Executive Order 12333, 3. C.F.R. 1981, § 2, § 1(7)(g) (1981).

[51] *See* Manget, *supra* note 49, at 417; Cyrille Fijnaut, *Inlichtingendiensten in Europa en Amerika*, 3 JUSTITIËLE VERKENNINGEN 10, 16–18 (2004).

[52] 50 U.S.C. §§ 1804(a)(7)(B), 1823(a)(7)(B) (2012).

[53] Council, 9831/08, 28.05.2008 and Council, 13696/1/02, 28.11.2002.

[54] *See* Directive 95/46/EC, *supra* note 1.

[55] Art.13 Framework Decision 2008/977/JHA, O.J. L350, 30.12.2008.

[56] Art. 2 Additional Protocol, ETS No. 181.

all – Member States.[57] The 2008 Framework Decision is only applicable to data that the providing Member State receives from another Member State and not to domestically collected data.[58] Domestically collected data can still be sent to a third state without having to check the third state's level of data protection (unless the providing Member State has incorporated the adequacy procedure in its national law on its own initiative).[59] The only type of data transfer for which an adequacy assessment should always be made is the transfer for commercial purposes.[60]

Besides the requirement's lack of general application, the meaning of "adequacy" has posed problems for policymakers, academics, and practitioners. Even if it was clear that an "adequate level of data protection" did not mean that the receiving state's system should be identical, the precise content of what should be assessed remained uncertain.[61] Adequacy decisions reached by the Commission offered guidance,[62] but the reform started in 2012 was an opportunity to improve the existing provisions. The adequacy requirement creates unacceptable confusion with respect to cooperation in criminal matters. This is particularly unfortunate because the sensitive nature of the data used in criminal matters counsels for the strong privacy protection provided by E.U. standards with respect to transfers to a third state.

Other inconsistencies raise questions, especially when studying how adequacy has been assessed by Europol and Eurojust. The two agencies have their own provisions. Since both are E.U. agencies dealing with personal data for the purpose of investigations and prosecutions involving the same range of cross-border criminal offenses, one should expect their methods of adequacy assessment to be similar. Europol has introduced a four-step filtering system for reaching a decision on a third state's level of data protection, except for urgent circumstances.[63] For

---

[57] Belgium, Greece, Italy, Malta, Slovenia, and the United Kingdom have not yet ratified.

[58] Art. 1 (2) Framework Decision 2008/977/JHA.

[59] Nonetheless, a 2010 study ordered by the Commission concluded that Member States' national laws do not fully comply with the adequacy rules of Directive 95/46/EC. Douwe Korff, *Comparative Study on Different Approaches to New Privacy Challenges, in Particular in the Light of Technological Developments*, EUROPEAN COMMISSION DG JUSTICE, 92–94 (2010), ec.europa.eu/justice/policies/privacy/docs/studies/new_privacy_challenges/final_report_working_paper_2_en.pdf (last visited Nov. 20, 2015).

[60] *See* Directive 95/46/EC, *supra* note 1.

[61] C-362/14, Schrems v. Data Protection Commissioner, § 73, 2015.

[62] *See e.g.*, Commission Decision 2002/2/EC, 2002 O.J. L2.

[63] Council Decision 2000/C, 2000 O.J. (C 106) (EC).

Eurojust the assessment of its data protection officer is sufficient.[64] Transatlantic cooperation involving Europol and Eurojust also resulted in different approaches. Exchange of personal data in accordance with the 2002 Europol-U.S. Agreement was initiated without a full adequacy assessment but based on the urgency exception.[65] Eurojust concluded a cooperation agreement with the United States in 2006 and used the same formulation that was included in the 2003 E.U.–U.S. Mutual Legal Assistance Agreement,[66] namely no "generic" restrictions for processing of data with respect to the legal standards of the receiving party may be imposed as a condition for delivering information.[67] This is a rejection of the adequacy procedure, since the assessment that is part of the procedure amounts to a condition without which information should not be transmitted.

The 2010 Agreement between the European Union and the United States on the processing and transfer of financial messaging data from the European Union to the United States for the purposes of the Terrorist Finance Tracking Program (TFTP Agreement)[68] made history even before it was adopted due to the European Parliament's decision to reject the first version based on, *inter alia*, data protection concerns.[69] The TFTP Agreement also introduced the concept of "assumed adequacy," by stating that "subject to ongoing compliance with the commitments on privacy and protection of personal data set out in this Agreement, the U.S. Treasury Department is deemed to ensure an adequate level of data protection for the processing of financial payment messaging and related data transferred from the European Union to the United States for the purposes of this Agreement."[70] This provision was identical to the text

---

[64] Rules of Procedure on the Processing and Protection of Personal Data at Eurojust, 2005/ C, 2005 O.J. (C 68) (EC).

[65] Els De Busser, *Transatlantic Adequacy and a Certain Degree of Perplexity*, 1 EU CRIM. 31, 31–34 (2010).

[66] Commission Regulation 606/2013, 2003 O.J. (L 181).

[67] Agreement between Eurojust and the U.S., art. 10, Nov. 6, 2006, *available at* www.eurojust.europa.eu/doclibrary/Eurojust-framework/agreements/Agreement%20Euro just-USA%20%282006%29/Eurojust-USA-11-06-EN.pdf (last visited Dec. 16, 2015).

[68] Council Decision 2000/412, 2010 O.J. (L 195) (EC).

[69] EP Recommendation, A7-0013/2010, Feb. 5, 2010; European Parliament Press Release, SWIFT: European Parliament votes down agreement with the U.S. (Feb. 11, 2010).

[70] Agreement between the United States of America and the European Union on the Processing and Transfer of Financial Messaging Data from the European Union to the United States for the Purposes of the Terrorist Finance Tracking Program, E.U.–U.S., art. 6, Nov. 27, 2013. [hereinafter TFTP Agreement].

that was initially rejected and to the text that was ultimately adopted. Joint reviews of the TFTP Agreement were not always positive.[71] The same goes for the inspection reports of Europol's Joint Supervisory Body.[72] The report mentioning the U.S. Treasury's oral instructions to Europol regarding Europol's verification of the requests under the TFTP Agreement makes the assumption of adequacy sound rather cynical.[73] Recently the U.S. Treasury refused to release documents on the TFTP's operational functions to the European Ombudsman.[74] This demonstrated again the difficulty of transparency and oversight in this context. Nevertheless, after the European Parliament asked for proof that the data gathered under the TFTP was "necessary," the U.S. Treasury published a report giving concrete examples of the ways in which these data were used in counter-terrorism efforts in the United States, Europe, and elsewhere.[75]

It should be pointed out that a general E.U.–U.S. agreement for the protection of personal data exchanged for the purpose of criminal investigations was negotiated and awaits approval by the European Parliament. When preparing this chapter, a draft text had not yet been made

---

[71] *Report from the Commission to the European Parliment and the Council on the Joint Review of the Implementation of the Agreement between the European Union and the United States of America on the Processing and Transfer of Financial Messaging Data from the European Union to the United States for the Purposes of the Terrorist Finance Tracking Program*, COM (2014) 513 final (Aug. 11, 2014).

[72] Joint Supervisory Body of Europol, Implementation of the TFTP Agreement: assessment of the follow-up of the JSB recommendations, Ref. 13-01 (Mar. 38, 2013), www.europarl.europa.eu/meetdocs/2009_2014/documents/libe/dv/jsb_inspection_rep2013 /JSB_inspection_rep2013EN.pdf (last visited Nov. 21, 2015); Joint Supervisory Body of Europol, Data Protection Inspection Report (Dec. 9, 2014), europoljsb.consilium.europa .eu/media/267640/14-41%20final%20data%20inspection%20report%20september% 202014-%20v07.pdf (last visited Nov. 21, 2015).

[73] Joint Supervisory Body of Europol, Public Statement on the second inspection of the implementation of the TFTP Agreement, (Mar. 14, 2012), europoljsb.consilium.europa.eu/ media/205081/tftp%20public%20statement%20-%20final%20-%20march%202012.pdf (last visited Nov. 21, 2015).

[74] Decision of the European Ombudsman closing the inquiry into complaint 1148/2013/TN against the European Police Office (Europol), EUROPEAN OMBUDSMAN (Aug. 22, 2013), www.ombudsman.europa.eu/en/cases/decision.faces/en/54678/html.bookmark (last visited Nov. 21, 2015).

[75] *Communication from the Commission to the European Parliament and the Council on the Joint Report from the Commission and the U.S. Treasury Department Regarding the Value of TFTP Provided Data Pursuant to Article 6 (6) of the Agreement between the European Union and the United States of America on the Processing and Transfer of Financial Messaging Data from the European Union to the United States for the purposes of the Terrorist Finance Tracking Program*, COM (2013) 843 final (Nov. 27, 2013).

public. But the Commission released a statement accompanied by a list of questions and answers on the agreement.[76] These confirm that final conclusion of the agreement is dependent on the adoption of a bill by the U.S. Congress extending the core of the judicial redress provisions of the Privacy Act to E.U. citizens. This Judicial Redress Bill was approved by both houses of Congress but at the time of this writing the President had not yet signed the act into law.[77]

II   Reforming the Adequacy Requirement in the European Union

The nature of the data transfer determines the content of the adequacy assessment.[78] The 2008 Framework Decision provided a general list of aspects to consider when making such an assessment.[79] More precise, and therefore more useful, are the Europol Decision[80] and a document by the 29 WP[81] in the context of Directive 95/46/EC. These efforts hone in on the aspects to be considered for adequacy checks that could, *mutatis mutandis*, be used for criminal matters. Both documents especially rely on limiting transfers according to the purpose for which data were collected. When criminal investigations are the purpose of the data transfer, for example, it is of principal concern that these may include data about suspects to whom the presumption of innocence must apply. Also, improper application of the proportionality principle can have crucial consequences for individuals involved in a criminal investigation – either as suspect, witness, or victim.

The revision of the E.U.'s data protection rules is an excellent opportunity to correct the lack of clear guidance in what to assess and the inconsistencies surrounding adequacy assessments. The Commission's proposal for a directive on data protection in criminal matters introduced a more precise list of elements to be given

---

[76] European Commission Press Release, The Commission, Statement by E.U. Commissioner Věra Jourová on the Finalization of the E.U.–U.S. Negotiations on the Data Protection "Umbrella Agreement," http://europa.eu/rapid/press-release_STATEMENT-15-5610_en.htm (last visited Nov. 21, 2015) [hereinafter Umbrella Agreement].

[77] *See* Judicial Redress Act of 2015, H.R.1428, 114th Cong. (2015).

[78] Explanatory Report to the Additional Protocol to the Convention for the Protection of Individuals with Regard to Automatic of Personal Data, Regarding Supervisory Authorities and Transborder Data Flows, Nov. 8, 2001, E.T.S. 181.

[79] Framework Decision 2008/977/JHA, art. 13(4), 2008 O.J. (L 350) 60 (EC).

[80] 2009 O.J. (L 121) 52.

[81] First Orientations on Transfers of Personal Data to Third Countries – Possible Ways Forward in Assessing Adequacy, 29 WP, June 26, 1997.

consideration.[82] These elements included, first and foremost, the rule of law and relevant legislation, jurisprudential precedents as well as redress for E.U. residents whose data are transferred. Second, it was proposed that the assessment should consider the existence and effective functioning of independent supervisory authorities in the third state. This draws on the 29 WP, which stressed that it is more efficient to define the objectives to be achieved by certain mechanisms and their ability to achieve them rather than requiring their mere presence.[83] Third, it was proposed that the third state's international commitments be treated as a factor in the adequacy assessment. Derogations from the adequacy requirement were already based on necessity. But the European Parliament reinforced this by adding that transfers based on derogations "shall be duly justified and limited to what is strictly necessary and frequent massive transfers of data shall not be allowed."[84] The proposed directive still lacks a mandatory reassessment of adequacy when legislation or practice in the third state undergoes significant changes. It requires continuous monitoring of developments that could affect the fulfillment of the adequacy assessment only when the Commission takes an adequacy decision by means of a delegated act.[85] Continuous monitoring should be included for all adequacy decisions because new developments in the third state could change the level of data protection considerably, as was shown by the NSA-Affair in the United States.

[82] *Proposal for a Directive of the European Parliament and of the Council on the Protection of Individuals with Regard to the Processing of Personal Data by Competent Authorities for the Purposes of Prevention, Investigation, Detection or Prosecution of Criminal Offences or the Execution of Criminal Penalties, and the Free Movement of such Data*, art. 34(2), COM (2012) 10 final (Jan. 25, 2012).

[83] Assessing Adequacy, *supra* note 81,

[84] Resolution of March 12, 2014, on the Proposal for a Directive of the European Parliament and of the Council on the Protection of Individuals with Regard to the Processing of Personal Data by Competent Authorities for the Purposes of Prevention, Investigation, Detection or Prosecution of Criminal Offences or the Execution of Criminal Penalties, and the Free Movement of such Data, amendment 99, Eur. Parl. Doc, TA/2014/219/ P7 (2014).

[85] Resolution of March 12, 2014, on the Proposal for a Directive of the European Parliament and of the Council on the Protection of Individuals with Regard to the Processing of Personal Data by Competent Authorities for the Purposes of Prevention, Investigation, Detection or Prosecution of Criminal Offences or the Execution of Criminal Penalties, and the Free Movement of such Data, amendment 97, Eur. Parl. Doc, TA/2014/219/ P7 (2014).

III Safe Harbor and Adequacy

Having established a common policy on data protection for commercial matters in the Member States, the purpose of Directive 95/46/EC was to apply the adequacy requirement to transfers to third states. As partners in trade, this new condition meant that the United States had to comply with an adequate level of data protection to maintain its commercial relations with the European Union. A compromise was found with the Safe Harbor Framework consisting of seven principles to which U.S. companies could commit when processing personal data while doing business with an E.U.-based partner. The Commission confirmed the adequacy of these Safe Harbor principles in 2000.[86] The European Parliament, joined by the 29 WP,[87] immediately voiced concerns about the level of data protection offered by the United States and called on the Commission and the Member States to review the decision in the light of experience and legislative developments.[88] This did not happen.

Thirteen years later, Edward Snowden leaked documents revealing the NSA's interception and surveillance programs involving Internet and telecommunications systems. Max Schrems, an Austrian law student, seized on these revelations as evidence that no effective data protection system exists in the United States and that the NSA could access personal data on Facebook users sent from its E.U. office in Ireland to its U.S. head office. He pressed his concerns in a plea to the Irish data protection commissioner to stop personal data transfers from Facebook to the United States. The Irish data protection commissioner, relying on the Commission decision that created the Safe Harbor Framework,[89] did not investigate further. Therefore, one of the questions raised by Schrems in his appeal to the Irish High Court involved the validity of an adequacy decision taken in 2000 on a data protection system that is operational today.[90] The Irish High Court referred the matter to the CJEU for a preliminary ruling. The CJEU was asked to determine whether, as a matter of E.U. law, the data protection commissioner was bound by a

---

[86] Commission Decision of July 26, 2000, *supra* note 2.

[87] Opinion 4/2000 on the Level of Protection Provided by the "Safe Harbor Principles," 29 WP, May 16, 2000.

[88] Report on the Draft Commission Decision on the Adequacy of the Protection Provided by the Safe Harbor Privacy Principles (C5-0280/2000 – 2000/2144(COS)), (June 22, 2000), http://ec.europa.eu/justice/policies/privacy/docs/adequacy/0117-02_en.pdf (last visited, Nov. 21, 2015).

[89] Commission Decision of July 26, 2000, *supra* note 2.

[90] Schrems v. Data Protection Comm'r [2014] 2013 No. 765JR (H. Ct.) (Ir.).

finding of the Commission from an adequacy decision from 2000 (regarding data protection in the law and practice of the United States) when there had been considerable developments in the years since, especially including the entry into force of the Charter of Fundamental Rights in the E.U. legal system.[91] This was relevant because Article 8 of the Charter provides a right to data protection besides the right to a private life in Article 7.

On October 6, 2015, the CJEU declared the adequacy decision from 2000 invalid, concluding that E.U. legislation involving interference with fundamental rights guaranteed by Articles 7 and 8 of the Charter must lay down clear and precise rules governing the scope and application of a measure and imposing minimum safeguards. According to the CJEU, the American legislation does not limit the government's access to the transferred data to cases of strict necessity. Instead, the relevant American law authorized the storage of all the personal data of all the persons whose data has been transferred from the European Union to the United States. The law recognizes no differentiation, limitation, or exception relative to the objective pursued. The law does not provide objective criteria by which to determine the limits of access to the data and its subsequent use. Finally, the law does not identify specific, strictly restricted purposes that can justify the access to and use of the data.[92] The CJEU also suggested that the Commission should, after deciding on a third state's adequacy, conduct periodic checks to determine whether a finding of adequacy is still factually and legally justified.[93] In my view, the CJEU here has recognized that adequacy assessments are a snap-shot of a system at a certain moment in time and require reassessment when the data protection system in question changes considerably.

D Data Protection Standards

I Accuracy and Reliability

The 2008 Framework Decision obliges authorities to take all reasonable steps to prevent the transmission of personal data that are inaccurate, incomplete, or no longer up-to-date.[94] As far as practicable, data should

---

[91] Charter of Fundamental Rights of the European Union, 2000 O.J. (C 364).
[92] Case C-362/14, Schrems v. Data Protection Comm'r, §§ 91–92, 2015 E.C.R.
[93] *Id.* § 76.   [94] Art. 8 Framework Decision 2008/977/JHA.

be verified before transmission. Since criminal investigations often contain information from different sources, it is essential that information is added that enables the receiving Member State to assess the degree of accuracy, completeness, and reliability. The proposed directive has made this provision more precise by adding that personal data based on facts should be distinguished from personal data based on personal assessments, in accordance with their degree of accuracy and reliability.[95] Intelligence data should, thus, be separated from information that can be used as evidence in a criminal proceeding. This provision appeared in the first proposal of the Framework Decision in 2005 but not in the adopted text.[96]

Accuracy, completeness, timeliness, and pertinence are also requirements in the American Privacy Act;[97] but when an interagency transfer of data takes place, law enforcement and intelligence agencies are exempted from the accuracy standard. The exemption does not apply to requests under the Freedom of Information Act and to transfers to persons other than an agency.[98] Furthermore, in the Privacy Act there is a general exemption from the accuracy standard for data maintained by the CIA and agencies that have criminal law enforcement as their principal function. This general exemption applies when these agencies process data for the purpose of identifying an offender, aiding a criminal investigation, or for use at any stage in the criminal justice process (from arrest to release from supervision).[99] It is important to note here that the Privacy Act is only applicable to U.S. citizens and residents.[100] It extends no rights to E.U. citizens whose data are processed. The lack of rights for E.U. data subjects was made painfully clear in the aftermath of the Snowden revelations.[101] The Judicial Redress Act aims to resolve this

---

[95] *Communication from the Commission to the European Parliment and the Council Assessment of the Action Taken by Latvia and Hungary in Response to the Council Recommendations of 7 July 2009 with a View to Bringing an End to the Situation of Excessive Government Deficit,* art. 6(2) COM (2010) 10 final (Jan. 27, 2010) [hereinafter Assessment of the Action Taken by Latvia and Hungary].

[96] *Proposal for a Council Framework Decision on the Protection of Personal Data Processed in the Framework of Police and Judicial Co-Operation in Criminal Matters,* COM (2005) 475 final (Oct. 4, 2005).

[97] 5 U.S.C. § 552a(e)(5) (2012).   [98] 5 U.S..C § 552a(e)(6) (2012).

[99] 5 U.S.C. § 552a(j)(1)–(2) (2012).   [100] 5 U.S.C. § 552a(a)(2) (2012).

[101] Report on the U.S. NSA Surveillance Program, Surveillance Bodies in Various Member States and Their Impact on E.U. Citizens' Fundamental Rights and on Transatlantic Cooperation in Justice and Home Affairs, 2013/2188(INI), Feb. 21, 2014.

by allowing citizens of designated foreign countries to bring civil actions under the Privacy Act.[102]

II   Purpose Limitation and Necessity

One of the most eye-catching differences between the E.U. and the American data protection systems is the fact that the "purpose limitation" is a general standard in the European Union but not in the United States. This does not mean that purpose plays no role in the American data-transfer regime. It can be found in specific laws such as the Children's Online Privacy Protection Act.[103] Remarkably, the risk for "mission creep" and use of data for unlawful purposes was also explicitly recognized in the Privacy and Civil Liberties Oversight Board (PCLOB) report on bulk collection of telephone data.[104]

The European Union's reliance on purpose as a limitation for data transfers generally prohibits processing of personal data for a purpose that is incompatible with the purpose for which the data were gathered. In accordance with the 2008 Framework Decision, derogations from this principle are allowed if the law permits it and if the derogation is necessary in the interests of, *inter alia*, criminal investigations and the prevention of an immediate and serious threat to public security.[105] The 29 WP clarified the purpose limitation, in particular by defining the term "compatible," which previously had not been defined outside the academic literature.[106]

The purpose limitation will remain a basic principle even as the European Union's data protection regime is reformed. Nevertheless, the requirements for derogating from this principle have been restructured and spread over several articles.[107] This development has been criticized

---

[102] Judicial Redress Act of 2015, H.R. 1428, 114th Cong. (2015).

[103] Also, the exemption of routine use in the Privacy Act strongly resembles purpose limitation except that its ratio is not data protection but efficiency in avoiding a request for consent to disclose personal data. *See* 5 U.S.C. § 552a(a)(7) (2012).

[104] Privacy and Civil Liberty Oversight Bd., Report on the Telephone Records Program Conducted under Section 215 of the USA PATRIOT Act and on the Operations of the Foreign Intelligence Surveillance Court, 160, Jan. 23, 2014, www.pclob.gov/library/215-Report_on_the_Telephone_Records_Program.pdf (last visited Nov. 23, 2015) [hereinafter PCLOB Report on the Telephone Records Program].

[105] Arts. 3, 11 Framework Decision 2008/977/JHA.

[106] Opinion 03/2013 on Purpose Limitation, 29 WP, Apr. 2, 2013. *See also* LEE A. BYGRAVE, DATA PROTECTION LAW 340 (2002).

[107] Assessment of the Action Taken by Latvia and Hungary, *supra* note 95, arts 4, 7.

by the EDPS.[108] In any case, the revised provisions must conform to the Convention and that means that any change of purpose should fulfill the requirements of proportionality and necessity.

III Necessity, Proportionality, and the NSA-Affair

In the context of U.S. authorities' uses of European data for criminal or national security purposes, the Foreign Intelligence Surveillance Act (FISA) and the Foreign Intelligence Surveillance Court (FISC) are the most important parts of the framework.[109] This is especially true in light of the NSA programs that involved cooperation with private companies as well as upstream interception of communication.[110] Two sections inserted in the FISA by the PATRIOT Act are crucial. Section 215 provides access to certain business records for foreign intelligence and international terrorism investigations.[111] Section 702 provides procedures for targeting "persons outside the U.S. other than U.S. persons."[112] The key issue with Section 215 lies in the massive amount of data that can be collected because it allows the government to request orders for documents or other tangible items when they are relevant to an authorized national security investigation. These are orders for telephone providers to cooperate and deliver metadata, such as numbers dialed and the length of calls. Even when no content of communication, financial information, or location data were obtained, the data collected under rolling or renewing court orders is staggering. It is just one glimpse into this massive haystack, but the 2015 ODNI report confirmed that call records were collected based on individual target identifiers.[113] In 2014, for

---

[108] *EDPS Opinion on the Data Protection Reform Package*, §§ 33–34, EUROPEAN DATA PROTECTION SUPERVISOR (Mar. 7, 2012), https://secure.edps.europa.eu/EDPSWEB/ webdav/site/mySite/shared/Documents/Consultation/Opinions/2012/12-03-07_EDPS_ Reform_package_EN.pdf (last visited Nov. 23, 2015).

[109] Foreign Intelligence Surveillance Act, Pub. L. No. 95–511, 95 Stat. 1783 (1978), amended by Pub. L. 110–261 (2008).

[110] Barton Gellman, Julie Tate & Ashkan Soltani, *In NSA-Intercepted Data, Those not Targeted Far Outnumber the Foreigners Who Are*, WASH. POST (July 5, 2014), www.washingtonpost.com/world/national-security/in-nsa-intercepted-data-those-not-targeted-far-outnumber-the-foreigners-who-are/2014/07/05/8139adf8-045a-11e4-8572-4b1b969b6322_story.html (last visited Nov. 23, 2015).

[111] 50 U.S.C. § 1861 (2012).   [112] 50 U.S.C. § 1881a (2012).

[113] Office of the Direction of National Intelligence, Signals Intelligence Reform, 2015 Anniversary Report, icontherecord.tumblr.com/ppd-28/2015/privacy-civil-liberties#section-215 (last visited Nov. 23, 2015).

example, the FISC approved 161 target identifiers,[114] but the calls made
by those targets led to a second range of identifiers and, in a "second
hop," added all identifiers who communicated with the second range of
identifiers.[115] If, over a one year period, the average person communicates 100 times by phone, then that would mean that in 2014 hypothet-
ically 16,100 numbers would have been checked and a second hop
would mean that over 1.6 million numbers would have been collected.[116] Adding a third hop to the data collection would implicate
more than twice the population of Germany. Enhancing the minimization procedures, as announced by the Presidential Policy Directive 28
(PPD-28), would reduce the number of hops in this practice from three
to two.[117] This will reduce the number of data subjects involved, but it
will still amount to a large number of persons whose data are collected
on nothing more than an incidental call with no relation to a crime or
security threat whatsoever. It will be extremely difficult to maintain a
link between the data that are sought and the crime or threat that is
investigated – in other words – to ensure compliance with the necessity
requirement.

The traditional standard for issuing a warrant in American criminal
law – probable cause to believe that a crime has been or is about to be
committed – was not required for the FISC to authorize Section 215
orders.[118] Instead, a warrant can issue if there are reasonable grounds to
believe that the tangible items are relevant to an authorized investigation.[119] In a decision reached in October 2013, the FISC concluded that
this lower threshold was not a violation of the Fourth Amendment.[120]
Still, the ODNI report concluded that, in accordance with PPD-28,

---

[114] *Id.*, at Chapter "Strengthening Privacy & Civil Liberties Protections – New Privacy
Protections for Bulk Telephony Metadata Collected under Section 215."

[115] *Id.*

[116] The White House, Report and Recommendations of The President's Review Group on
Intelligence and Communications Technologies (2013), www.whitehouse.gov/sites/
default/files/docs/2013-12-12_rg_final_report.pdf (last visited Nov. 23, 2015) [herein-
after Report and Recommendations on Intelligence].

[117] Directive on Signals Intelligence Activity (PPD-28), 2014 DAILY COMP. PRES. DOC.
(Jan. 17, 2014), www.fbi.gov/about-us/nsb/fbis-policies-and-procedures-presidential-
policy-directive-28-1 (last visited, Nov. 18, 2015).

[118] U.S. CONST. amend. IV. *See* Illinois v. Gates, 462 U.S. 213, 232 (1983).

[119] 50 U.S.C. § 1861(b)(2)(A) (2012).

[120] FISC Amended Memorandum Opinion, BR-13-109, fas.org/irp/agency/doj/fisa/fisc-
082913.pdf (last visited Nov. 23, 2015).

reasonable, articulable suspicion findings should be approved by the FISC in advance.[121]

As one of the sunset clauses, Section 215 expired on June 1, 2015. In spite of intense efforts on Capitol Hill in the last days of May a compromise was not reached. One day later, on June 2, 2015, the USA FREEDOM Act was enacted, stirring mixed reactions.[122] On the one hand, this Act imposes new restrictions on the bulk collection of telecommunication data on U.S. citizens by U.S. intelligence agencies, such as the aforementioned standard of reasonable, articulable suspicion findings and a stronger purpose limitation rule.[123] On the other hand, it allows the NSA to restart bulk collection of data for a six months transition period and it does not touch upon data collected under Section 702 of the PATRIOT Act.[124] This is far from a thorough reform of America's data collection programs.

Section 702 of the PATRIOT Act permits the collection of information on non-U.S. persons who are reasonably believed to be located outside the United States.[125] This means that if the target of foreign intelligence surveillance is an E.U. citizen reasonably believed to be located outside the United States, then his or her communication can be intercepted and the U.S. government neither has to have probable cause to believe that he or she is an agent of a foreign power nor obtain an individual warrant from the FISC. This is the case even if the interception takes place in the United States.[126] On the contrary, the FISC approves categories of targets subject to minimization procedures.[127] The disclosed NSA minimization procedures regarding Section 702 reveal a set of provisions aimed at filtering out the relevant data,[128] but the procedures aim more at removing incidentally obtained data on U.S. persons rather

---

[121] Office of the Direction of National Intelligence, Signals Intelligence Reform, 2015 Anniversary Report, icontherecord.tumblr.com/ppd-28/2015/privacy-civil-liberties#section-215 (last visited Nov. 23, 2015).

[122] USA FREEDOM Act of 2015, H.R. 2048, 114th Cong. (2015).

[123] USA FREEDOM Act of 2015, § 103, H.R. 2048, 114th Cong. (2015).

[124] Harley Geiger, Q & A on the USA FREEDOM Act of 2015, CENTER FOR DEMOCRACY AND TECHNOLOGY (Apr. 28, 2015), https://cdt.org/blog/q-a-on-the-usa-freedom-act-of-2015/ (last visited Nov. 23, 2015).

[125] 50 U.S.C. § 1881a(a) (2012).

[126] See Report and Recommendations on Intelligence, supra note 116, at 135.   [127] Id.

[128] Minimization Procedures used by the NSA in Connection with Acquisitions of Foreign Intelligence Information Pursuant to Section 702 of the FISA of 1978, as amended, http://www.dni.gov/files/documents/ppd-28/2014%20NSA%20702%20Minimization%20Procedures.pdf (last visited Nov. 23, 2015).

than at minimizing data obtained on non-U.S. persons. In view of the lack of privacy and data protection rights of E.U. citizens in the United States, this is a crucial point for future discussion that reaches further than just Section 702.

The President's Review Group concluded that Section 702 has served an important function in helping the United States to uncover and prevent terrorist attacks in and outside the United States, but acknowledged that Section 702 may achieve this goal in a way that unnecessarily sacrifices individual privacy and damages foreign relations.[129] Despite these concerns, Section 702 was reauthorized until 2017.[130]

E   Adequate Rights

Missing from the analysis of Section 215 by the PCLOB and the ODNI is the impact on non-U.S. persons, even though the program's objective is "to obtain foreign intelligence information not concerning a U.S. person or to protect against international terrorism or clandestine intelligence activities."[131] In its report on Section 702 the PCLOB acknowledged that, compared with the traditional FISA process, it imposes significantly fewer limits on the government when it targets foreigners located abroad.[132] The report of the President's Review Group goes so far as to conclude that, if Section 702 was drafted to intercept communications of U.S. persons, then it would violate the Fourth Amendment.[133] Section 702 is directed at non-U.S. persons located outside the United States and, therefore, it does not breach the Fourth Amendment.[134] Besides the aforementioned "reasonable belief" standard, which replaces the traditional "probable cause" standard, the President's Review Group recognized that non-U.S. persons can be targeted by Section 702 without a warrant – but with *post factum* review – and confirmed that the minimization requirements do not fully apply to them.[135] Interestingly, the Review Group's

---

[129] *See* Report and Recommendations on Intelligence, *supra* note 116, at 144–45.   [130] *Id.*
[131] 50 U.S.C. § 1861(a)(1) (2012). *See also* Casper Bowden, The U.S. Surveillance Programmesand their Impact on E.U. Citizen's Fundamental Rights, Report for the EP Committee on Civil Liberties, Justice and Home Affairs 20 (2013).
[132] *See* PCLOB Report on the Telephone Records Program, *supra* note 104, at 106.
[133] *See* Report and Recommendations on Intelligence, *supra* note 116, at 153.
[134] United States v. Verdugo-Urquidez, 494 U.S. 259, 265–66 (1990).
[135] *See* Report and Recommendations on Intelligence, *supra* note 116, at 156–57.

recommendation was to extend the Privacy Act to non-U.S. persons rather than to amend Section 702.[136]

The Judicial Redress Act extends the Privacy Act to citizens of designated foreign countries. In any case, the wording is narrower than that used by the PPD-28, which stated that "all persons should be treated with dignity and respect, regardless of their nationality or wherever they might reside, and that all persons have legitimate privacy interests in the handling of their personal information."[137] It is unclear what is meant by designated foreign countries and whether or not this includes the European Union but the European Commission stressed that the conclusion of the E.U.–U.S. umbrella agreement on data transfers for law enforcement purposes is frozen until the Judicial Redress Act is adopted at last adopted as law.[138]

The fact that the Fourth Amendment and other U.S. legislation do not provide rights for E.U. citizens to claim data protection is not only an issue with regard to the NSA programs exposed by Edward Snowden. It is equally significant in the context of cloud computing.[139]

F   Adequate Transatlantic Data Exchange: A Work in Progress

From the overview provided by this chapter, it can be concluded that the question of the transatlantic data exchange for the purpose of criminal investigations and national security is a "work in progress." The basic concepts of information exchange in criminal matters are relatively similar in the European Union and the United States, with an important exception for the term "law enforcement" that should be handled with care in transatlantic relations. The similarity of terms, however, does not translate to similarities in legislation and policy. On the contrary, from an E.U. perspective, some provisions of U.S. law are unacceptable. Most prominently, this includes the lack of rights for E.U. citizens and the bulk collection of data without necessity. These practices have now been acknowledged on the U.S. side as impermissible departures from privacy

---

[136] *Id.* at 157.
[137] Directive on Signals Intelligence Activity (PPD-28), 2014 DAILY COMP. PRES. DOC. (Jan. 17, 2014), www.fbi.gov/about-us/nsb/fbis-policies-and-procedures-presidential-policy-directive-28-1 (last visited, Nov. 18, 2015).
[138] *See* Umbrella Agreement, *supra* note 76.
[139] Casper Bowden, *The U.S. Surveillance Programmesand Their Impact on E.U. Citizen's Fundamental Rights*, REPORT FOR THE EP COMMITTEE ON CIVIL LIBERTIES, JUSTICE AND HOME AFFAIRS 21–24 (2013).

rights. The momentum should be used for legislative improvements beyond the USA FREEDOM Act, especially in view of the *Schrems Case* and the defunct Safe Harbor Framework. Nonetheless, there is room for improvement with respect to E.U. legislation as well.

The issue clearly is a "work in progress" on the U.S. side of the relationship because legislative amendments have been recommended and announced in several reports. Most likely it is exactly the publication of the reports cited in this paper that embody the most significant change since the revelations by Edward Snowden.[140] They identify what the precise issues are and they also promote transparency and inspire debate. In some circumstances they inspire legal action such as the case initiated by Max Schrems. All of this has led to legislative reforms on the U.S. side. For the purpose of the transatlantic relations it is most significant whether and how the U.S. government will create a solution for the rights of E.U. citizens. An extension of the Privacy Act to non-U.S. persons will not suffice if data collection continues under the existing programs. In the words of the 29 WP when explaining adequacy: it is more efficient to define the objectives to be achieved by (supervisory and oversight) mechanisms and their ability to achieve these objectives rather than requiring their mere presence.[141]

The European Union's framework is equally a "work in progress" in this area. Negotiations on the data protection reform continue. E.U. lawmakers would be missing a perfect opportunity if they fail to insert a continuous monitoring requirement for adequacy in the proposed Directive inspired by the *Schrems Case*. Already introduced by the European Parliament as an amendment but limited to delegated acts, this should be mandatory for all adequacy decisions.

Finally, transatlantic negotiations on a future general agreement on exchanging personal data for law enforcement purposes also must be characterized as a "work in progress." An understanding of the terms "law enforcement" by both parties should be reached without reservations. The adequacy requirement should be taken seriously by both parties without relying on hollow assumptions or rejecting generic restrictions.

---

[140] *See also* Sarah Childress, *How the NSA Spying Programs Have Changed since Snowden*, FRONTLINE (Feb. 9, 2015), http://www.pbs.org/wgbh/pages/frontline/government-elec tions-politics/united-states-of-secrets/how-the-nsa-spying-programs-have-changed-since-snowden/ (last visited Nov. 21, 2015).

[141] Assessing Adequacy, *supra* note 81.

This chapter only touched upon a fraction of the issues regarding transatlantic data exchange and it is without a doubt one of the most complicated matters to solve in interstate cooperation in criminal matters. With many human, political, and economic interests involved – not to mention the continuous development of technology – the making of new law and international agreements often seems to move too slowly to answer questions that must be resolved if we are to create mechanisms that safeguard citizens' personal data. Still, it is a process by which patience and deliberation should produce high-quality provisions that have the objective, on one hand, of effective data transfers, and on the other hand, that guarantee data protection. Again the words of the 29 WP are fitting: it is more efficient to define the objectives to be achieved by mechanisms and their ability to achieve these objectives rather than requiring their mere presence.[142]

---

[142] *Id.*

PART FIVE

Transatlantic Reflections on the Cultural Meaning
of Privacy and Intelligence Gathering

24

The Intimacy of Stasi Surveillance, the NSA-Affair, and Contemporary German Cinema

BY LAURA HEINS

A Introduction

Recent objections to surveillance and demands for intensified data-protection laws in the wake of revelations about NSA spying in Germany have often drawn comparisons between the NSA and totalitarian state apparatuses, while employing surprisingly retrograde conceptual frameworks. One of the most widespread images used by anti-surveillance protesters during demonstrations held in Berlin and Frankfurt in July 2013 compared the American security agency to the East German Ministry for State Security (Stasi) via an illustration of Obama wearing headphones along with the subscript "Stasi 2.0."[1] The style of the headphones in this image alludes to those worn by the central character of *The Lives of Others* (*Das Leben der Anderen*), Florian Henckel von Donnersmarck's Oscar-winning film from 2004. Consequently, this image codes Obama as another incarnation of the sympathetic Stasi officer in the film. The use of the image of Obama blended with the fictional Stasi officer Gerd Wiesler not only testifies to the deep impact that *The Lives of Others* has had on public memory, but it also indicates that the East German state security service has become a dominant model for the public's thinking about the nature of surveillance, despite this model's anachronicity.

Such references to *The Lives of Others* add no small degree of ambiguity to the German response to the NSA-Affair, since they highlight a conflict in the popular imagination between twenty-first century surveillance methods that are conceived of as oppressive by way of their anonymity and twentieth century surveillance imagined in ambivalent terms as intimate. I would like to propose that an examination of *The Lives of Others* along with two other

---

[1] For examples of the "Stasi 2.0" icon, *see* Anti-Prism Demo, ANTI PRISM, www.antiprism.de/ (last visited Nov. 28, 2015).

recent German films about Stasi surveillance, *Barbara* (Christian Petzold, 2012) and *Two Lives* (*Zwei Leben*, Georg Maas, 2012), might serve to illuminate such contradictory tendencies in German ways of envisioning surveillance, tendencies that can resurface in political protests and in discussions regarding privacy and data protection regulations. As in *The Lives of Others*, both *Barbara* and *Two Lives* feature central protagonists who work for the Stasi, but who elicit strong audience identification. In all three films, Stasi agents or collaborators are represented as taking a personal and empathetic interest in the victims of the GDR's paranoid authoritarianism. The representation of Stasi surveillance in these films follows earlier and similarly ambivalent depictions of surveillance in German literature, most notably in the work of Christa Wolf, where Stasi agents are described in surprisingly familiar terms.

The use of Stasi imagery in anti-NSA demonstrations proposes negative historical continuities at the same time that it hints at problematic undercurrents of nostalgia that give preference to surveillance as conducted by human agents over that of automated mass data collection. Along with their invocation of *The Lives of Others*, German protesters' signs have sometimes referred to other Cold War-era visions of totalitarianism such as the Orwellian "Big Brother" or classic James Bond films with Russian villains.[2] Yet such imagery hardly seems appropriate to our contemporary era of dataveillance and "liquid surveillance," the term Zygmunt Bauman and David Lyon use to describe the mobile, unstable, and fragmentary nature of contemporary surveillance and the ungraspable supra-state powers that lie behind it.[3] On the one hand, the use of anachronistic totalitarian imagery serves to code the contemporary U.S. and German governments as dystopian continuations of the state security agencies of the past, as they implicitly critique the legacy of Cold War politics as unresolved. Paradoxically, however, and particularly in the case of Obama-as-Wiesler, the Cold War imagery can also evoke positive connotations. Given that sympathy for Obama remains significantly higher in Germany than in the United States, the blending of his image with that of Stasi officer Wiesler in the German context also may take on the character of a wish.[4]

---

[2] For images from the August 2014 protest in Berlin, *see* Images, SPIEGEL ONLINE (Aug. 30, 2014), www.spiegel.de/fotostrecke/freiheit-statt-angst-anti-ueberwachungs-demo-in-berlin-fotostrecke-118484-4.html. *See* Chapter 27 in this volume.

[3] ZYGMUNT BAUMAN & DAVID LYON, LIQUID SURVEILLANCE (2013).

[4] According to a 2013 poll by the Allensbacher Institute, Obama had a 78 percent approval rate among Germans. This contrasts with an American rate of less than 50 percent. Thomas Petersen, *Schleichende Zunahme des Antiamerikanismus*, FAZ (Jan. 23, 2013),

The double character of this fantasy is extended by Petzold's film *Barbara*, which depicts the East German state's violence against its citizens while also offering seductive images of the intimacy of in-person surveillance, and Maas's *Two Lives*, which takes close relations between the Stasi and its victims even further. Considering these partially alluring cinematic depictions of Stasi surveillance, the Stasi's secret policing might actually be imagined positively when compared to the NSA's impersonal data collection and analysis, even as the Stasi serves as the central example of surveillance's potential excesses. It must be stressed that none of these films endorses Stasi violence or engages in simplistic *Ostalgie*, the whitewashing of the history of oppression in East Germany and the commodification of memories of life in the GDR. Instead, *The Lives of Others* and *Barbara* reflect a widespread mourning for what many Germans still see as the lost opportunities to build an alternative form of socialism in East Germany, while *Two Lives* explains affective connections to the Stasi as a desire for harmonious international qua familial relations. The ambivalence of the depiction of Stasi surveillance in all three of these films, I would like to suggest further, also reflects undercurrents of nostalgia for the solidity of past power relations in contradistinction to today's "liquid" institutions. The Stasi thus functions as the central figure of a solid power politics that no longer exists, a corporeal solidity that is imagined as supporting intimacy, which likewise no longer seems attainable in our now more radically postprivate and instable world.[5]

B   The Stasi's Embodied Surveillance

The representation of Stasi surveillance in *The Lives of Others*, *Barbara*, and *Two Lives* does have some basis in historical facts, and it also has literary precedent. One of the most salient characteristics of surveillance in the GDR was its bizarre quality of intimacy between the victims and the perpetrators of the surveillance, a phenomenon that now inspires a curious mixture of horror and fascination. One example of the ways in which the Ministry for State Security intruded into the private sphere of

www.faz.net/aktuell/politik/deutsche-fragen-deutsche-antworten-schleichende-zunahme-des-antiamerikanismus-12034804.html; Presidential Approval Ratings – Barack Obama, GALLUP, www.gallup.com/poll/116479/barack-obama-presidential-job-approval.aspx (last visited Nov. 28, 2015).

[5] I am leaning here on Todd Herzog's notion of the "post-private world." Todd Herzog, *The Banality of Surveillance: Michael Haneke's Caché and Life after the End of Privacy*, 43:2 MOD. AUSTRIAN LIT. 26–40 (2012).

East German citizens has become an almost archetypal image of the perversions of Stasi surveillance: the notorious smell samples that were collected from detainees under interrogation and used to train dogs to detect whether a suspected dissident had attended illicit meetings. In Henckel von Donnersmarck's account, rather than having those under interrogation sit on pieces of fabric in order to document the suspects' personal scent – as depicted in *The Lives of Others* – detainees were more often directed to simply rub the fabric between their legs, and these intimate scents were then stored in glass jars in Stasi archives.[6] This can be seen as emblematic of the intensely physical, sensory, and personal nature of Stasi "data collection," along with the invasive corporeal presence of the Stasi agent.

Despite their intrusions into the privacy of GDR citizens, the agents of the Ministry for State Security were not universally despised and even encountered some level of tacit approval among a portion of the population. As historian Jens Gieseke has asserted, the Stasi functioned as an "*ersatz* public sphere," because in addition to intimidating dissidents, they also had the task of writing up public opinion or "mood" reports to be submitted to the SED (Socialist Unity Party) leadership.[7] The Stasi collected complaints and conveyed them to the Politbüro, and so surveillance, according to Gieseke, also functioned as a sort of suggestion box for the regime, a substitute for democratic processes. The German columnist and cultural critic Henryk Broder has even gone so far as to suggest that the fall of the Wall in 1989 was actually the result of Stasi surveillance and the work of its agents, who supposedly recognized as they were collecting intelligence for their mood reports that public opinion had turned irrevocably against the SED. Broder argued in 1994 that "the Stasi perfected its work with the so-called *Wende*. The 'peaceful revolution' was its magnum opus."[8]

Many members of the East German intelligentsia had, of course, accommodated themselves to Stasi surveillance. Probably the most well known example is the writer Christa Wolf, who was likely an inspiration for the character of the playwright Georg Dreyman in *The Lives of*

---

[6] Alan Riding, *Behind the Berlin Wall, Listening to Life*, N.Y. TIMES (Jan. 7, 2007), www.nytimes.com/2007/01/07/movies/awardsseason/07ridi.html?pagewanted=all&_r=0.

[7] JENS GIESEKE, THE HISTORY OF THE STASI: EAST GERMANY'S SECRET POLICE, 1945–1990 109 (2014).

[8] Henryk Broder, *A Beautiful Revolution, in* A JEW IN THE NEW GERMANY 77 (Sander L. Gilman & Lilian M. Friedberg eds., 2004).

Others.[9] Like the fictional Dreyman, Wolf was one of the few GDR authors who was widely read and appreciated in the West. As a result, she was a privileged member of the GDR's cultural scene, one of the select group of East Germans who was allowed to travel abroad and even hold multiple guest professorships in Western countries, including the United States.[10] She was also under surveillance for much of this time, a fact of which she was fully aware, as her novella *What Remains* evidences.[11] Even though it might have been possible for her to defect during one of her many extended stays abroad, she made a conscious decision to continue living in East Germany because of her continued attachment to the project of socialism.[12]

What Remains, written in 1979 but not published until 1990, is an autobiographical account of the effects of surveillance on her own subjectivity. Wolf relates in this book how she had begun to internalize the surveillance and function as her own self-censor in classic panoptic fashion.[13] She also wrote of conversations with a less privileged writer who had been brutally persecuted by the regime, a young woman who was imprisoned and forced to undergo sterilization as a punishment for her oppositional viewpoints.[14] Yet Wolf's text also is full of ambiguity, in a similar manner to the films that will be examined in more detail later. The following passages from *What Remains* particularly resonate with the depiction of the Stasi in contemporary German cinema:

> They had been there for three minutes, I noticed them right away ... The young gentleman or comrade had had dark hair, which was beginning to thin along the part, this I could see from upstairs. For a brief moment I reveled in the notion of being the first one to notice this young gentleman's encroaching baldness, even before his own wife, who presumably never studied him so attentively from above ... Our feelings in situations such as these are complicated ... one could not ask the men in cars whether they were equipped with listening devices and, if so, what their range was. Other intimacies, however, were not out of the question ... For example, I still regretted the fact that I hadn't followed my first impulse right away, back then when it started, on those cold November nights, and

---

[9] Mary Beth Stein, *Stasi with a Human Face? Ambiguity in* Das Leben der Anderen, 31 GERMAN STUD. REV. 572 (2008).
[10] SONJA HILZINGER, CHRISTA WOLF 137–39 (2007).   [11] *Id.* at 42.
[12] Eve Pormeister, *"Aber die Frage begleitete mich: Wie lebt man in einer Diktatur?" Christa Wolf – Hoffnungen und Enttäuschungen einer DDR-Autorin,* 18 INTERLITTERARIA 450–1 (2013).
[13] *See* Chapter 1 in this volume.
[14] CHRISTA WOLF, WHAT REMAINS AND OTHER STORIES 273–76 (1993).

brought them down some hot tea. That could have developed into a habit; we had nothing against each other personally, after all, we were all doing what we had to, we could have struck up a conversation – not about business, God forbid! – but about the weather, about illnesses or family matters.[15]

What is notable about Wolf's account of Stasi surveillance here is her striking use of the term "intimacies" and her autobiographical narrator's desire to enter into familial relations with the agents of surveillance. The corporeality of the Stasi agents in Wolf's account – and the pleasure the narrator takes in feeling a physical closeness with them – are remarkable; as she observes the Stasi agents eating sausages in their cars and she ruminates on the fabric of their coats, the narrator speaks of seeking a "loving" and "protective" language to describe her experiences.[16] She concludes that she is simply not capable of employing a bestializing, alienating language of hatred in regard to the "young gentlemen" out on the street watching her.[17] Notable, furthermore, is the reciprocity of the surveillance here, which transcends the purely panoptic: while the Stasi agents spy on her, the narrator places herself in an inverted version of Bentham's tower, looking down at the thinning hair of the man she calls a "comrade." This literary account of intimacy, corporeality, and the reciprocity of the observing gaze in the experience of Stasi surveillance is mirrored in the depiction of the Stasi in *The Lives of Others*, *Barbara*, and *Two Lives*.

C   A Man Who Really Listens and Narrates: Surveillance in *The Lives of Others*

Many reviewers of *The Lives of Others* have remarked on the "scandal" of a positively portrayed Stasi officer, and much of the initial reception of the film circled around the question of historical authenticity and the plausibility of such a character.[18] Others have noted that *The Lives of Others* relies on a conventional redemption plot in its tale of an initially "bad" Stasi agent who becomes converted to humanistic compassion and resistance against state violence. The medium for this conversion is the aesthetic education the agent receives from the

---

[15] *Id.* at 236–39.   [16] *Id.*   [17] *Id.* at 237–38.

[18] Paul Cooke, *Introduction: The Lives of Others and Contemporary German Film*, in THE LIVES OF OTHERS AND CONTEMPORARY GERMAN FILM: A COMPANION 6–11 (Paul Cooke ed., 2013).

artists who are the targets of his surveillance. This plot allows the film to address the mass fantasy of individual heroism in the face of a corrupt system and the hope for reconciliation between the perpetrators and the victims of Stasi surveillance.[19] Yet, as I would like to suggest, the reasons for the film's prize-winning success with audiences also have to do with the way in which it engages with the fantasy of intimacy with a benevolent authority figure and the desire for a directly sensory and meaningful access to the lives of other people. This is an access that is not provided by the forms of surveillance characteristic of our contemporary "liquid" age, by the remote and amateur mutual surveillance of one citizen by another via Facebook and Google, the invisible and impersonal surveillance of the entire world by the NSA, or the fluid and uncontained surrender of consumer data to corporate entities. *The Lives of Others* presents images of surveillance with a solid human face, which are connected to the utopian fantasy of socialism with a human face, a particularly potent fantasy in the age of faceless dataveillance.

The psychological ambiguity of *The Lives of Others* has to do with an almost perverse undercurrent of nostalgia for an era when surveillance was conducted by actual, visible human beings. Wiesler is repeatedly shown observing intimate relations between the main objects of his surveillance, the dramatist Georg Dreyman and the actress Christa-Maria Sieland. But rather than taking sexual pleasure in his observations, Wiesler's intrusions into their privacy allow him greater insight into the emotional intricacies of the couple's relationship, which in turn allows him to develop empathy with them and to ultimately use his powers to act on their behalf. Correspondingly, in the sequence in which the dissident writer Paul Hauser has a conspiratorial meeting with fellow writers in Treptower Park, he remarks on the Stasi agent who trails him wherever he goes, "My own bodyguard. I call him 'Rolf,'" as the agent awkwardly and somewhat endearingly tries to hide behind a tree. The ever-presence of this visibly embodied Stasi "bodyguard" then appears almost reassuring rather than threatening, as it suggests a familiarity akin to that expressed by Christa Wolf's autobiographical narrator in regard to the men who were watching her apartment. The mise-en-scène of surveillance here is a far cry from the sinister,

---

[19] Daniela Berghahn, *Remembering the Stasi in a Fairy Tale of Redemption: Florian Henckel von Donnersmarck's* Das Leben der Anderen, 38 OXFORD GERMAN STUD. 324–30 (2009).

disembodied omnipotence of remote-controlled cameras and darkly lit command centers with massive banks of screens and the video game aesthetics that typify depictions of espionage in contemporary Hollywood cinema.[20]

The scene toward the end of *The Lives of Others* in which the main protagonist, Dreyman, reads his Stasi files after the fall of the Wall also suggests another side of surveillance besides that of persecution. As the archivist wheels out a cart full of files and says "My respects!," the film suggests that to have been under surveillance in the GDR was to have accomplished something, to have been important and recognized, not simply a suspect. This recognition may have been part of Christa Wolf's motivation for tolerating the "young gentlemen" who spied on her from 1969 onward, or like her narrator, for even having the impulse to share tea with them. Stasi surveillance ensured artists an audience, *The Lives of Others* suggests, and it also allowed citizens to be heard in some fashion. In the key scene in which Wiesler approaches Christa-Maria in a bar, Wiesler displays his talent for understanding other people's psychology and his benevolent capacity to empathize with others: he professes to know Christa-Maria's true self behind her actress's mask, and he also expresses love for her and admiration for her art. Wiesler, as the man who listens to those under surveillance carefully and writes reports on them as would a psychoanalyst listening to his patients, comes to know them better than they know themselves. This scene suggests that artists in the GDR had an attentive following. It also suggests that the GDR's citizens were personally known to the state, and that this state had the potential to also be benevolent. A loving form of socialism seems to be possible here, whether this is an impossible fantasy or not. The rogue Stasi agent Wiesler is of course depicted as anomalous among his cynical and self-interested colleagues, yet his character functions as the figure of the state's potential, one that might have been realized if the state had listened *more* attentively to its citizens.

The primary reason that Christa Wolf gave for refusing to emigrate was her sincere hope that the socialist experiment could in fact work, that the GDR could become the better, the antifascist Germany.[21] Similarly,

---

[20] The *Bourne* franchise is paradigmatic for the Hollywood mise-en-scène of disembodied and omniscient surveillance. On Paul Greengrass's 2007 installment, *see* Pat Brereton & Eileen Culloty, *Post-9/11 Counterterrorism in Popular Culture: The Spectacle and Reception of* The Bourne Ultimatum *and* 24, 5 CRIT. STUD. TERROR. 483–97 (2012).

[21] Pormeister, *supra* note 12, at 449.

the film *The Lives of Others* also reflects a wish for a more humane version of socialism. The undercurrent of nostalgia in *The Lives of Others* is not a longing for the actually existing, utterly dystopian, and repressive East German regime, but rather for the lost opportunity to find a "third way" between the seemingly unchecked neoliberal capitalism of the West and the exploitative socialism that was the Soviet/Stalinist system. This sense of longing is reinforced by the fact that the two main figures of identification in the film, Wiesler and Dreyman, maintain their faith in socialism even while rejecting the abuses of the SED leadership. Wolf may have believed to some degree that surveillance was necessary to maintain the state that would eventually make true socialism possible. In any case, this sentiment is expressed by Dreyman, who shows understanding for the fact that the oppositional writer Hauser is being monitored by the Stasi and is not allowed to travel abroad.

At times, Wiesler, the representative of the GDR's unrealized potential, seems to develop an almost telepathic intimacy with the targets of surveillance. After Christa-Maria has been raped by the villainous culture minister Hempf, Wiesler intuits her pain and mirrors her contorted body position while she showers, thus seeming to see through the walls into the apartment below.[22] As Daniela Berghahn has observed, the film's editing and mise-en-scène create an equivalence between the Stasi man and the playwright, especially in the scenes in which the two characters are placed in the same position in the doorway of Dreyman's apartment building.[23] As other scholars have noted, *The Lives of Others* turns the Stasi officer himself into a writer as he takes on aspects of the identity of his would-be victim.[24]

The film's attention to the process of writing surveillance reports is also highly ambivalent. Wiesler and his assistant Udo record the minutiae of everyday life and produce from it a narrative, an interpretation. Their form of espionage is almost a literary act. Indeed, *The Lives of Others* implicitly draws comparisons between the writing of surveillance reports and literature: Wiesler's reports create a narrative out of real lives, and sometimes he adds his own fictional elements. In such scenes and in

---

[22] Andrea Rinke, *Fear and (Self-) Loathing in East Berlin: Gender and Melodrama in the Lives of Others, in* THE LIVES OF OTHERS *and* CONTEMPORARY GERMAN FILM 114 (Paul Cooke, ed., 2013).

[23] Berghahn, *supra* note 19, at 328.

[24] Martina Kolb, *"Immerhin Brecht": Literacy and Theatricality in* Das Leben der Anderen, 43 OXFORD GERMAN STUD. 332 (2014).

the scenes of Dreyman at the archive, the film presents the Stasi agent almost as a personal narrator who writes a (semi-fictionalized) journal for the man under surveillance and provides him with an interpretation of events and circumstances to which he himself did not have access. (By contrast, Udo is shown to be a lesser writer than Wiesler, an inadequate interpreter of character motivation, as when he surmises in his report that the tensions between the couple are a result of Christa-Maria's inadequate devotion to housekeeping.) The film clearly engages with the fantasy of recognition by an embodied yet powerful other – another potent fantasy in our contemporary digital age, when everyone generates a lot of data but not a lot of personal attention. *The Lives of Others* is less a film about *Ostalgie* than a film about nostalgia for a time when a human agent processed and interpreted the data of surveillance, formed it into a narrative, and could potentially care about the people under his watch, even if there is little evidence that such a thing ever actually occurred in the GDR.[25]

Furthermore, *The Lives of Others* is a film about a no longer existing "solid" form of surveillance. As Bauman and Lyon have commented, surveillance today is marked by the dissolution of previously fixed institutions such as state security apparatuses, and thus the agents of surveillance are now impossible to grasp, both physically and intellectually: "Today's world ... is post-panoptical. The inspectors can slip away, escaping to unreachable realms. Mutual engagement is over."[26] A further element of contemporary "liquid" surveillance is the splitting of power from politics: "Power now exists in global and extraterritorial space, but politics, which once linked individual and public interests, remain local, unable to act at the planetary level."[27] The semi-panoptic state depicted by *The Lives of Others* and its literary precursor *What Remains* (which are marked by a greater physical presence and visibility of the "inspectors" than in the classic Foucauldian model[28]) is one in which power and party politics were still identical and highly visible, in which mutual engagement seemed possible, even in the limited and highly inadequate form of Stasi public opinion reports.

---

[25] On the historical authenticity of the film, *see* Jens Gieseke, *Stasi Goes to Hollywood: Donnersmarcks The Lives of Others und die Grenzen der Authentizität*, 31 GERMAN STUD. REV. 580–88 (2008).

[26] BAUMAN & LYON, *supra* note 3, at 4.   [27] *Id.* at 5.

[28] MICHEL FOUCAULT, DISCIPLINE AND PUNISH 202 (1995).

Surveillance in *The Lives of Others* is likewise solid in its medial form. The recurrent stress in the film on the physical process of writing surveillance reports – the close-ups of Wiesler typing and correcting his observations – seems almost fetishistic, as if holding in abeyance the threat of nonphysical data collection. This is another reason why the scene in which Dreyman visits the Stasi archives to read his files contains an element of fascination, despite the horror the files hold in their revelation of Christa-Maria's betrayal. The close-up of the red indexical mark of Wiesler's finger that Dreyman finds on one of the files once again insists on the corporeality of Stasi surveillance. This stands in contrast to Bauman and Lyon's account, in which "liquidity" also describes the unstoppable flow of twenty-first century surveillance data from one database to another: "Old moorings are loosened as bits of personal data extracted for one purpose are more easily deployed in another ... Without a fixed container, but jolted by 'security' demands and tipped by technology companies' insistent marketing, surveillance spills out all over."[29] The glass jars and paper files locked away in the massive Stasi archives provide a solid counter-image to this liquidity. The archivists in the film, as physically present gatekeepers of data who hold paper files within the semi-private and solid walls of the archive and only wheel out carts of data to those who have demonstrated a legal right to it, are the very opposite of Google's uncontrollable spillage.

D   The Seduction of Sensory Intimacy: Surveillance in *Barbara*

The agents of surveillance in Christian Petzold's *Barbara* are likewise solid in their physical presence and lack of anonymity, which in this film proves both threatening and attractive. The main protagonist and title character of the film, a doctor who is under constant observation by the Stasi because she has applied to emigrate from the GDR, is in this case the victim rather than the perpetrator of surveillance. Petzold has described his choice to film from the viewpoint of the character who is under observation as an effort to avoid the "moral problem" of asking spectators to identify with the surveilling gaze, as most espionage dramas do.[30] Yet *Barbara*, set around the same time as *The Lives of Others* (the

---

[29] BAUMAN & LYON, *supra* note 3, at 3.
[30] Megan Ratner, *Building on the Ruins: Interview with Christian Petzold*, 66 FILM Q. 17 (2012).

early 1980s) and explicitly intended by Petzold as a response to Henckel von Donnersmarck's film,[31] also develops into a love story between a man working for the Stasi and the object of his surveillance.[32] Here, the representative of the Stasi, the IM (*Inoffizieller Mitarbeiter* or unofficial collaborator) and head doctor in Barbara's new workplace, André, is even more corporeally present than Wiesler in *The Lives of Others*. His sensual and empathetic presence is so alluring that it induces Barbara to abandon her plans to escape to the West and instead to make a renewed commitment to working in the socialist East. Petzold does not neglect to depict and denounce East Germany's repressive state violence in this film, but he invests surveillance with an ambivalent duality by making one Stasi agent the embodiment of its repressive aspects and the other, André, into a positive figure of solidity and intimacy.

Petzold has commented in interviews that his concept for *Barbara* was to provide a warmer, more lifelike, and sensual image of the GDR than created by the dark, forbidding mise-en-scène of *The Lives of Others*.[33] On Henckel von Donnersmarck's film, Petzold commented: "The GDR is only a studio here. A studio for a story that does not arise out of the GDR itself . . . [It is a] Western nightmare."[34] Even the choice to shoot *Barbara* on 35mm Kodak film stock was made to humanize the GDR, Petzold said, because this technique brings the film's images closer to his own memories of vacationing in the country with his parents, former refugees from the East: "I wanted to give the GDR colors. I was in the GDR every year, and I remember a colorful country.[35] The warm color palette of *Barbara* opposes the cool, muted greens and blues of *The Lives of Others*, and the many outdoor scenes in *Barbara* with a natural soundtrack of wind and birdsong contrasts with the studio interiors and melodramatic music of *The Lives of Others*. The sensory appeal of *Barbara*'s vivid colors

---

[31] Jaimey Fisher, Christian Petzold 140 (2013).

[32] As Slavoj Žižek has insisted, the principal romance in *The Lives of Others* is between the two central male protagonists. Slavoj Žižek, *The Dreams of Others*, These Times (May 18, 2007), http://inthesetimes.com/article/print/3183/the_dreams_of_others (last visited Nov. 28, 2015).

[33] Fisher, *supra* note 31, at 140.

[34] Stefan Schirmer & Martin Machowecz, *Regisseur Christian Petzold: "Was es da an Irren gab!,"* Zeit Online (Jan. 31, 2013, 7:00 AM), www.zeit.de/2013/06/Christian-Petzold-Filme-DDR-Osten.

[35] Cristina Nord, *Regisseur Christian Petzold über 'Barbara': 'Ich wollte, dass die DDR Farben hat,'* Taz.de, www.taz.de/!87469/ (last visited Nov. 28, 2015); Petzold stated that Kodak stock has "the most human colors." Ratner, *supra* note 30, at 18.

was intended to give the audience an understanding of the allure of the utopian project of socialism, as Petzold has commented:

> Here the country shows what might be possible in it, and thereby makes it difficult for the woman who is fleeing. There is sensuality ... The GDR was of course also a utopia. A dream of a place where all needs were provided for, a place of anti-fascism, equality between the sexes, life far away from the greed for profits. That the film seems so colorful now has no doubt to do with the fact that capitalism is [now] in the middle of a deep crisis.[36]

For Petzold the socialist dream continues to be alluring, particularly from the vantage point of the present condition of gaping inequalities under neoliberalist austerity. In the sunny yellow hospital clinic of *Barbara*, the East German doctors have the time to read to patients and to intuit the causes of their maladies, rather than hustling through the factory-like, profit-oriented health facilities more common in the West. The inhumanely accelerated pace of life characteristic of contemporary Western society can make the sensory experience of the GDR depicted in *Barbara* attractive by comparison.

Even the treatment of Stasi surveillance in *Barbara* is more sensual than the depiction of postunification surveillance in Petzold's other films. Surveillance is a running theme throughout his work, but before *Barbara*, it always appeared in its "liquid" state, in films set after the dissolution of Cold War power blocs and the global surge of neoliberal capitalism. Petzold's *Pilots* (*Pilotinnen*, 1995), *The Sex Thief* (*Die Beischlafdiebin*, 1998), *The State I Am In* (*Die innere Sicherheit*, 2001), and *Wolfsburg* (2003) depict surveillance in commercial environments in the form of closed-circuit television monitors or camera-monitored job interviews, while *Dreileben* (2011) depicts the use of cell phone cameras as privacy-invasive surveillance devices.[37] *Wolfsburg* introduces one of the main protagonists, Laura, with a high angle shot from above, as she appears in the security cameras of the discount supermarket where she works. The cold, black-and-white, low resolution, high angle image of the CCTV surveillance camera is not shown in *Wolfsburg* to have a human agent; no return shot anchors the free-floating gaze of commercial surveillance here, though the protagonist is subsequently subjected to demeaning harassment by the supermarket's security guards as she undergoes a

---

[36] Schirmer & Machowecz, *supra* note 34.
[37] On the issue of surveillance in all of these films, *see* Fisher, *supra* note 32.

search meant to protect the merchandise against theft by the underpaid, mostly female workforce.

Barbara's opening sequence likewise offers a high angle shot of the main protagonist, but this time the image is warmly colored and the gaze of surveillance does have a human agent. Right after Barbara is shown from above as she exits a bus and sits on a bench to smoke, a counter shot shows André at the window, observing her with a sympathetic and curious expression. "Is that her?," André asks the man in the room with him, a Stasi agent who is holding a file folder, thus indicating that André has read about Barbara before meeting her and that he is collaborating with the Stasi as an IM. André's collaboration is further confirmed in later sequences when he shows that he is privy to extensive information about Barbara. He not only knows where she lives before she tells him, but he also makes allusions to information that could only be known through auditory surveillance. When Barbara asks for a night off from work, for example, André asks if she plans to use the time to go to a parade in Berlin, which was exactly the (weak and implausible) alibi suggested by Barbara's West German boyfriend for the night of her planned escape. Yet André's gaze remains sympathetic throughout the film. The introductory sequence of *Barbara* codes Stasi surveillance as marked by intimate knowledge of the individuals under observation, unlike the remote or exploitative depiction of surveillance in Petzold's other films. The Stasi officer, Klaus Schütz, remarks, "She won't come a second too early. She's like that ... If she were six years old, you would call it being sulky." Schütz here shows knowledge of Barbara's character that appears almost familial (though patronizingly so) in comparison to the anomie that typifies Petzold's films set in the post-Wall period.

Indeed, part of the conception of the film was to explore the intimate nature of social relations that can develop precisely because of the ever-presence of watchers. As one reviewer of the film noted, Petzold staged the conversations between Barbara and André so that the border between interrogation and a lover's attentiveness is blurred beyond distinction.[38] André, the character in the film who most represents the unrealized potential of the GDR, has a strongly sensual presence that is heightened by the way he is often framed in close physical proximity to Barbara, watching her intently but tenderly. In comparison to most of Petzold's other films, there are a greater number of shot/counter-shot structures in

---

[38] Elisabeth von Thadden, *Film Barbara: Wer bleibt*, ZEIT ONLINE (Mar. 8, 2012, 07:00 AM), www.zeit.de/2012/11/Film-Barbara.

Barbara, which allows a greater sense of intimacy between Barbara and André than most of the characters in Petzold's films set in the neoliberal era. According to the actor who played André, Ronald Zehrfeld, the conditions of life under surveillance in the GDR produced a greater awareness of others, a phenomenon that he experienced first-hand as he was growing up in East Germany: "[There was] a more social way of being together, which people miss more and more today, which used to exist back then ... The fascinating thing is that people looked at each other more closely in the GDR. It is precisely this distrust that people had that also produced a particular attentiveness to my counterpart, because people looked at each other in the eyes in a completely different way." Nina Hoss, the actress who played Barbara, added in the same interview: "In this atmosphere, there always lies a subliminal distrust. And yet it has a great warmth. This country [the GDR] also makes love possible."[39] Even the warmth of the would-be villain in this film, the Stasi officer Schütz, is portrayed in the scenes in which he cries over his wife as she lies dying from cancer and, significantly, he calls André to come treat her in her own bedroom rather than in an impersonal hospital room.

In contrast to the staging of scenes between Barbara and André, the scenes in which Barbara meets up with her West German boyfriend Jörg and temporarily evades the gaze of the Stasi are staged to give a sense of distance and lack of intimacy. In the first scene, she meets Jörg in the forest, while holding a basket that makes her appear like Little Red Riding Hood awaiting the wolf (though, ironically, Barbara's own last name is Wolff).[40] When the two lovers first catch sight of each other, Petzold gives a somewhat ominous shot from behind Jörg's head, with Barbara in the distance, the Western man looming in the foreground like a predator.[41] This shot is a reversal of the scene between André and Barbara in the sequence just preceding the meeting of Barbara and Jörg. The previous scene had André placed in the background, looking at Barbara

---

[39] *Liebe und Lügen: Christian Petzold, Nina Hoss und Ronald Zehrfeld über die Arbeit an* Barbara, BARBARA 10, http://susanne-bormann.info/Barbara/Barbara_Presseheft.pdf (last visited Nov. 28, 2015).

[40] Nick Hodgin makes a similar observation. Nick Hodgin, *East Germany Revisited, Reimagined, Repositioned: Representing the GDR in Dominik Graf's Der rote Kakadu (2005) and Christian Petzold's Barbara (2012)*, in EAST, WEST, AND CENTRE: REFRAMING POST-1989 EUROPEAN CINEMA 246 (Michael Gott & Todd Herzog eds., 2014).

[41] In an interview, Petzold extended the sense of predation here to a colonial allusion, by comparing Jörg to John Smith and Barbara to Pocahontas, and thus the Western man exploits the Eastern/"native" woman. Ratner, *supra* note 30, at 19.

in the closer foreground with attentive and admiring eyes as she peered into a microscope. In the encounter between Barbara and Jörg, however, there is a disorientingly rapid series of cuts that change screen direction and that add to the impression of awkwardness in their rushed and businesslike sex on the forest ground, an act that culminates in the exchange of consumer goods.

The second time that Barbara meets Jörg, in the Interhotel, the cool, neon lighting of the sparsely decorated room underlines the relative lack of warmth in the couple's interactions, contrasting Jörg with the warm presence of André, and thus by extension the culture of the West with that of the East. As Petzold commented, Barbara and Jörg "make an effort at sensuality, but they cannot manufacture it," while André is "sensually present, and that confuses her."[42] Instead of the intimacy-producing shot/counter-shot structures and close-ups in bright light typical of the sequences with André, Petzold stages the cross-border couple in a manner that suggests a power imbalance, by showing Jörg lying on top of Barbara in murky dim light or Barbara sitting on his lap in a childlike position. Unlike André, the socialist believer in the equality of the sexes, Jörg fails to appreciate Barbara's medical expertise when he states that she will no longer have to work once she moves to the West. It is at this moment that Barbara realizes that the West, the land she thought she had longed for, might actually prove to be – in Petzold's words – a "cold chamber" for her, a place where she might be stripped of her profession.[43] An abrupt cut from the Interhotel to a shot of Barbara sitting stone-faced in the train on the way home is followed by a shot out the window of two young couples on motorcycles near the tracks, cheerfully waving at her as the train whistles past. This image of joyful, summery East German youth seems to disprove Barbara's earlier assertion to Jörg that "you can't become happy in this country," and indicates the beginnings of a shift in conviction.

Despite the portrayal of the warmth and attractive sensory experiences of the East, Petzold is careful to not endorse the violence of East German state surveillance. The two scenes in which Barbara is subjected to strip searches are akin to Christa-Maria's rape in *The Lives of Others*, as the shot of Barbara painfully curled up on her couch in her bathrobe after the first search corresponds to the shots of Christa-Maria

---

[42] *Liebe und Lügen: Christian Petzold, Nina Hoss und Ronald Zehrfeld über die Arbeit an Barbara*, Barbara 9, http://susanne-bormann.info/Barbara/Barbara_Presseheft.pdf (last visited Nov. 28, 2015).

[43] *Id.*

in a fetal position in her bed after her own violation by a representative of the regime. The intimacy of Stasi surveillance is clearly shown to have a perverse side when Barbara is commanded by the female Stasi agent in the familiar form of address ("*du*") to bend over and spread her legs. In another example of the critique of Stasi oppression in *Barbara*, the dialogue implicitly compares Barbara's young patient Stella's forced labor in a GDR juvenile reformatory to the crimes of Nazi Germany: Barbara refers to the *Jugendwerkhof Torgau*, the reformatory where Stella is imprisoned, as a "*Vernichtungsanstalt*" (extermination institute), which resonates with the term "*Vernichtungslager*" (extermination camp) as a synonym for Auschwitz.[44]

Yet the rejection of Stasi oppression does not equate here with a complete rejection of the GDR, and Petzold opens the possibility of resisting oppression from within the system. As Petzold has commented, he intended the figure of André as one who struggles subtly against the violence of the East German state, even while endorsing its utopian ideal of socialism, including that of gender equality. In reference to the opening sequence of the film, Petzold stated: "A man looking at a woman from above without her knowledge is like state surveillance. The entire film is the story of a man trying to get out of this position. He's attempting to be at eye level."[45] The story that André tells Barbara about why he ended up working in a provincial hospital suggests that he too is a victim of the regime, having been forced into becoming an IM in exchange for immunity in a malpractice case. André is repeatedly shown struggling to prove to Barbara that he does not intend to subject her to a violating gaze and instead has great respect for her work. As in *The Lives of Others*, his empathetic observation of her functions as a counter-model of surveillance under socialism – his empathy is also a product of the surveillance apparatus, not just in spite of it. *Barbara* does not argue that the abuses endemic to surveillance are a necessary precondition of intimacy, however. Instead, the film suggests that the experience of living under surveillance produces an intensified attentiveness to others while also nurturing the search for free spaces within the system that can take on a more passionate character due to pressure from the outside.[46]

---

[44] Petzold has explicitly called the GDR system of reformatories "a fascist legacy." Ratner, *supra* note 30, at 19.

[45] Ratner, *supra* note 30, at 18.

[46] This insight might be derived from the films of Rainer Werner Fassbinder, whom Petzold cites as an influence on *Barbara*. Christian Petzold, *Director's Note*, BARBARA 3, http://susanne-bormann.info/Barbara/Barbara_Presseheft.pdf (last visited Nov. 28, 2015).

In Petzold's account, it is not only the nascent Eastern couple, but the whole of the GDR that is under pressure in *Barbara*. As Petzold commented in an interview: "Before I started *Barbara*, I thought about the GDR as an island, surrounded by bodies of water. I tried to do as much with water as possible: Barbara [repairing] the bike inner tube underwater, her wet hair, Stella's work in the canal ... There's always a water motif."[47] Although Petzold alluded in the same interview to the GDR as being like the prison island Alcatraz, he insisted once again that this island state had once possessed a utopian foundation: "The GDR was actually built on yearnings: no fascism, no anti-Semitism, no more war."[48] Petzold decided to set *Barbara* in 1980 because this was the year when the external pressure on the GDR began crumbling away, since the end of the Brezhnev Doctrine in the early 1980s meant that the island GDR would soon no longer be propped up by Soviet power. The GDR was then like the punctured inner tube that Petzold shows in close-up, a system with holes, one that would be entirely liquidated only nine years later.

These last years of dissolution, before Eastern Germany finally transitioned to the entirely "liquid" condition of post-Wall neoliberalism, were a time of unrealized potential, *Barbara* suggests. For Petzold, genuine intimacy is no longer possible in our contemporary society, because capitalism's demand for mobility and flexibility has irrevocably dissolved the private sphere: "We can't really say that the world is a neoliberal place, but at least our love is pure. People try to return to proper families with piano lessons for their children, for example, but the middle class they pretend exists is kaput."[49] In contrast, the bourgeois class seems, oddly enough, to have been preserved in the GDR of *Barbara*, where Barbara's state-allotted apartment comes with a piano, and André's highly inviting apartment is decorated with objects that signify a socialist *Bildungsbürgertum* (similar to Dreyman's painting- and piano-filled apartment in *The Lives of Others*).[50] It is in these spaces that the potential for a more humane form of socialism seems to reside. About the clinic in the film and the "communal life" that it promoted, Petzold said: "I miss that alternative to capitalist property."[51] Accordingly, the final sequences

---

[47] Ratner, *supra* note 30, at 20.   [48] *Id.*   [49] *Id.*
[50] On the covert language of the many cultural objects surrounding the characters in *Barbara*, see Debbie Pinfold, *The End of the Fairy Tale? Christian Petzold's Barbara and the Difficulties of Interpretation*, 67 GERMAN LIFE & LETT. 290–300 (2014).
[51] Ratner, *supra* note 30, at 23.

of the film suggest that Barbara has developed an awareness that an alternative version of life under socialism might still be possible. Barbara makes the decision to return to the island GDR, to her work in the clinic, and to the solidity of André, giving up her opportunity to escape to the "liquid" West via the cold Baltic Sea.

When Barbara comes back to face André's attentive eyes at the end of the film, she returns to a form of surveillance that holds out a promise of reciprocity. She turns her back on the uncertainties of emigration and submits to a surveillance state that not only seeks to discipline its subjects, but also desires to retain its citizens as a unified community. This stands in contrast to our contemporary situation of liquidity, in which digital techniques of tracking are employed not to prevent escape, but rather to exclude. As Bauman and Lyon have emphasized, surveillance is now most often used to prevent undesired migrants from slipping through the porous borders of chaotic failed states and into the heavily policed territories of Western capitalism.[52] From the vantage point of these neoliberal territories of today, where intimate bonds have been significantly weakened by the economic insecurity of the majority, older institutions of surveillance and state power may appear almost reassuring in their constancy.

E   The Familiar Agent: Surveillance in *Two Lives*

Two Lives, which premiered seven months after *Barbara*, is about a woman who claims to have taken exactly the escape route from the GDR that Barbara decides to abandon. The protagonist of *Two Lives* allegedly survived a perilous escape across the Baltic Sea. As eventually becomes clear during the unfolding of the complicated thriller plot that brings Stasi spying to an international level, the heroine who calls herself Katrine and is supposedly a victim and escapee of the GDR is actually an undercover Stasi agent named Vera who was sent to Norway to report on the activities of the Norwegian navy. Despite the film's complex narrative with scenes from multiple time frames arranged next to each other like a puzzle, director Georg Maas in many ways employs more conventional representations of the Stasi in this film, by showing the GDR in unsensuous, grainy, and indistinct images and by narrating the film from the position of the observer rather than those under observation. Like both

---

[52] BAUMAN & LYON, *supra* note 3, at 63-4.

The Lives of Others in 2007 and *Barbara* in 2013, *Two Lives* was Germany's official submission for the Oscar for Best Foreign Language Film in 2014, though critics have been fairly unanimous in proclaiming *Two Lives* as artistically weaker.[53] Nevertheless, the level of identification with the main Stasi agent that *Two Lives* demands of the spectator is remarkable, as is the depiction of intensified intimacy between the observer and the observed, extending the affective relations between agent and victim depicted in *The Lives of Others* and *Barbara* much further. In *Two Lives* the Stasi agent marries and has a child with a submarine captain (who is the object of the Stasi's interest) after insinuating herself into a Norwegian family via a fabricated biography. Yet it is the Stasi agent's emotional pain that is at the center of the narrative, and as the film intermingles the codes of the espionage thriller with those of the television family drama, the spectator is asked to identify strongly with the spy's love for the man she spies on, as well as for the Stasi officer who commands her.[54]

Two Lives touches on issues of memory and the documentation of life histories under both of Germany's tyrannical pasts, the Nazi and the Stasi. As in *The Lives of Others*, there is a prominent scene in *Two Lives* set in an archive which suggests the ease of containing and even erasing data contained in paper files, though the documents here date back to the Third Reich. The heroine of the film is shown cutting out and destroying names in the paper files that ostensibly deal with her childhood, files that the archivist indicates are originals with no copies, and thus the archive of *Two Lives* again stands in contrast to our present digital era, in which personal records migrate uncontrollably – an era without forgetting.[55] Although most of the film is set in 1990, right after the end of the GDR, flashbacks and dialogue elaborate the prehistory of Vera's espionage activities, including her early childhood in the Nazi era, her youth in the GDR, her recruitment for the Stasi, and the beginnings of her marriage with the submarine captain Bjarte. Claiming to have been the product of a romance between a Norwegian woman and a member of the

---

[53] *See, e.g.,* Elmar Krekeler, *Im Irrgarten der guten Absicht,* DIE WELT (Sept. 9, 2013), www.welt.de/120167267; Birgit Roschy, *Deutsche Vergangenheitsbewältigung am Fjord,* ZEIT ONLINE (Sept. 17, 2013), www.zeit.de/kultur/film/2013-09/film-zwei-leben-norwegen-lebensborn.

[54] The television drama *12 Means: I Love You* (*12 heißt: Ich liebe dich,* Connie Walther, 2008) might be considered another precedent for *Two Lives,* since it depicts a love affair between a Stasi agent and a woman under interrogation that is even more developed than in *Barbara.*

[55] *See* Chapter 22 in this volume; Chapter 11 in this volume.

occupying Nazi forces during the World War II – the false biography that allowed her to pass herself off as the long-lost daughter of a Norwegian mother and thus to infiltrate Norwegian society – Vera, as the spectator later learns, was actually a German-born child orphaned by Allied bombs. Or at least this is what she asserts once her cover has finally been blown and she must explain her true past to her Norwegian family. Memories of both the Nazi and the Stasi pasts are never narrated in this film with absolute certainty, and this is perhaps *Two Lives*'s most intriguing stylistic attribute. The grainy flashbacks interspersed throughout the plot that indicate the workings of memory are sometimes contradictory and undermine the plot set in the present. To cite one example, the flashbacks that seem to be originating from Vera's memories in the court sequence could not possibly be her own memories, since they are the recollections of the genuine refugee Katrine, whose identity Vera has assumed, falsely, as her own.

Two Lives intentionally leaves the question of Vera's motivation for working for the Stasi somewhat murky. In the confrontation scene with her daughter Anne, who asks to know who she really is and why she joined the Stasi, Vera explains that she was recruited to work for the Ministry of State Security while still a youth in a GDR orphanage, where, as she says, "Nice men came to visit us. They gave us presents and took us on outings. And they gave us what we were longing for. You can easily mistake it for love." Her decision to join the Stasi is thus at first explained in nonideological terms as the search for an ersatz family rather than as an attachment to the GDR's utopian ideals. Yet this explanation is somewhat undermined by the fact that Vera begins telling this story as she has her back turned to Anne and while she smokes a cigarette, since smoking often serves as a sign of Vera's strategic cunning, such as when she lights a cigarette and then burns part of the archival file with the same match. Vera's explanation is further undermined by a grainy memory sequence inserted earlier in the film that shows her performing an aptitude test in the Stasi headquarters while she was in her 20s, and then her surprised delight when the Stasi officer Hugo tells her that she has passed the exam. In this sequence, her face is framed next to a portrait of Karl Marx, indicating some influence of Marxist ideology over Vera's actions. Vera professes her deep gratitude to Hugo, who then calls her a "scout for peace," suggesting that these Stasi agents might have genuinely believed that they were promoting harmonious international relations while spying on the Norwegian navy. (Curiously, the Stasi officer Schütz from *Barbara* seems to make a reappearance in this scene, since Hugo is played by the same actor, Rainer Bock.) Vera is primarily depicted as a victim of history who becomes a perpetrator due to her need for affection, yet it is suggested that she might have also once held an attachment to the GDR's utopian ideals, just like the Stasi collaborators in *The Lives of Others* and *Barbara*.

Nonetheless, most of the scenes set in East Germany are conventional depictions of a gray and dreary country, while the scenes set in Norway are coded as the utopian spaces. The shots of decrepit buildings lining the East German streets in *Two Lives* have none of the summery warmth of the provincial town in Petzold's *Barbara*. In contrast, Vera's home in Bergen, Norway, is shown as embedded in nature, located right next to a picturesque fjord, and her family's wooly sweaters and the wood-paneled interiors of her cozy house are designed to give a sense of the warmth of this environment. Interestingly, though, in regard to the notion of the West as "liquid," the very first shot of the Norwegian location is a close-up of the waves of the sea through which Vera is subsequently shown paddling her kayak under a cold rainy sky. But she then gets out of the boat and enters the house to find her husband and her law student daughter awaiting her, the former of whom proceeds to serve her break-fast in his navy uniform, indicating that Norway is to be seen in this film as the idealized space of gender equality. Yet the attractive mise-en-scène of Vera's house primarily serves to suggest how much she has to lose through the revelation of her past if her efforts to expunge the archival data are not entirely successful. As a result, the spectator becomes invested in hoping that Vera's Stasi activities will not be revealed, so that her familial idyll may stay intact. The defense of privacy that this film mounts is above all a defense of the former Stasi agent's right to be forgotten, rather than the right to not be spied upon by state agencies.

The depiction of East Germany and Western Europe in *Two Lives* is therefore not intended as a binary opposition, and neither is Stasi surveillance coded as unequivocally oppressive here. It is significant that Vera's family does not begin to break apart until after the fall of the Wall; the end of the GDR leads to the end of love for the heroine of *Two Lives*. The introductory title sequence of the film, with its voice-overs of media speakers announcing the dissolution of the GDR along with slow piano chords full of pathos, paints the reunification in melancholy tones. In the post-1989 scene in which Vera is told by the former Stasi agent Kahl-mann that she will have to come to terms with her problems on her own because the Ministry for State Security no longer exists, Vera appears to have lost a cherished support system. It is also significant that Vera's marital relationship begins in the same (and only) scene that depicts her in the midst of spying on the Norwegian navy; just after she succeeds in secretly photographing military plans with a hidden camera, Captain Bjarte approaches her, introduces himself, and then exchanges flirtatious glances with her. This effectively ties romantic intimacy to the act of surveillance, since the ensuing happy marriage would not have come about in the absence of Vera's espionage activities. The "solid," physically present surveillance of the Stasi seems to carry benefits in *Two Lives*, just as it does in *The Lives of Others* and *Barbara*.

Evidently, the depiction of the Stasi in *Two Lives* is not intended to be entirely condemnatory. This ambivalence is produced in part by the film's mixture of generic codes, by Maas's blending of the conventional elements of the espionage thriller, such as the scenes in the airport where Vera changes into her disguise, with elements of the family drama during the scenes of confrontation between Vera and her family members inside her house in Bergen. Unlike the sparse soundtrack and startling cuts of Petzold's *Barbara*, this film makes use of extensive musical guidance of the spectator's emotions and expectations, as the music often swells before the end of a scene and the beginning of the next. The result is that *Two Lives* appears less cinematic and more like a television drama, an effect to which the limited number of exterior location shots and high number of close-ups contributes. The GDR is almost exclusively depicted within the tight confines of Hugo's office. But this only intensifies the effect of intimacy in the film's treatment of the topic of surveillance. Multiple scenes underline Vera's emotional attachment to Hugo, including the flashback scene in which he offers her an empathetic embrace, and the one in which he tells her while bidding her farewell at the airport that he was always fond of her.

Vera's attachment to her superiors is revealed to be tragically misplaced when the genuine Katrine is killed and her corpse burned by Vera's Stasi colleagues in horror film-like hand-held camera sequences that show Katrine's attempted escape from arrest for the "crime" of leaving the GDR without authorization. Yet even Katrine's killing is rendered somewhat ambiguous because she is shot just as she is attacking Vera, after having knifed Hugo in the stomach. As Maas commented in an interview, he expected spectators to identify with the Stasi agents rather than viewing them unequivocally as villains: "While writing the script, I noticed at some point that there was the possibility of representing the main protagonist in an ambivalent manner. The violence of both dictatorships is based on black-and-white [representations]. The dramaturgy of the film attempts to dissolve this kind of thinking . . . I did not want the spectators to condemn the characters."[56] Maas' equivocal treatment of the Stasi and its surveillance methods was no doubt reinforced by the fact that there was a representative of the Ministry for State Security on set observing the production of the film: Thomas Lawincky, who played the agent Kahlmann, is himself a former Stasi agent.[57] Maas added in regard to his refusal to entirely condemn the agents of Stasi surveillance: "This is a film about forgiving."[58]

F Conclusion: Stasi Surveillance and the NSA

The German cinematic and literary imagination of Stasi surveillance has coalesced around contradictory figures of a repressive state apparatus that simultaneously supports emotional intimacy; intimacy and privacy are thus conceived of as partially separate phenomena. Instead of being unambiguous defenses of the right to privacy against an oppressive and largely invisible state panopticon, these recent German films imagine the watchers to be highly embodied and capable of entering into interpersonal relations with those under surveillance. This suggests that the German reaction to NSA spying might not be exclusively characterized as a hypersensitive public response to all instances of surveillance or state intrusions into the private realm. What is at play in the cinematic and literary expressions of mass cultural tendencies examined in this chapter, as well as their echoes in anti-surveillance protests, is instead a more complex dialectic between fears of tyranny, on the one hand, and utopian fantasies, on the other hand: between the concrete historical experience of state terror and the widespread and as-yet-unrealized hopes for social progress and communal harmony that once resided in socialism. These hopes now seem fully unrealizable in the wake of the detachment of power from (democratic) politics. The solidity of older, even Cold War, forms of state power are imagined to have had the potential to promote more intimate bonds than the unstable social relations of the post-Wall, digital era.

---

[56] Violetta Rjabko, *Regisseur Georg Maas und sein Film "Zwei Leben,"* DEUTSCHE WELLE (Jan. 16, 2014), http://dw.de/p/1AmLb.

[57] Marieke Reimann, *Die Art, wie Liv Ullmann guckt' – Georg Maas über seinen Film "Zwei Leben,"* GOETHE INSTITUTE, www.goethe.de/ins/fr/lp/kul/mag/flm/ksf/de12564285.htm (last visited Nov. 28, 2015).

[58] Rjabko, *supra* note 56.

The contemporary iconography of Stasi surveillance also responds to an undercurrent of anxiety surrounding the "liquid" nature of surveillance in the twenty-first century, the agents of which continually evade our grasp. Although comparisons to the Stasi are meant to denounce the NSA as totalitarian on the first level, ambivalent depictions of the Stasi itself must necessarily inflect the popular image of the NSA. The fact that the twenty-first century surveillance apparatus is often imagined through the lens of the twentieth century in anti-NSA protests and in contemporary cinema might be explained in part as a covert desire, while also indicating the conceptual difficulties in visualizing and comprehending security systems that are remote and impersonal. When Obama is depicted in the guise of the main protagonist of *The Lives of Others*, this expresses not only the fear of the repressive potential of American spying, but also a wish that the president might empathetically listen to his European counterparts, and that effective power could continue, anachronistically, to reside in the solid figure of the democratically elected leader, rather than in fluid power networks that cannot be easily visualized or contained.

25

Hans Fallada, the Nazis, and the Defense of Privacy

BY ROGER CROCKETT

A Introduction

The Nuremberg Trials had recently ended. On October 16, 1946, ten war criminals were hanged in a gymnasium next to the Hall of Justice. Among the executed was Ernst Kaltenbrunner, head of the RSHA (*Reichssicherheitshauptamt*, or Reich Main Security Office) from 1943–1945, the umbrella organization created by Heinrich Himmler that controlled the SS intelligence agency, formally called the *Sicherheitsdienst* but better-known (and feared) as the Gestapo.[1] Two prisoners died by their own hand before the Allies could execute them: Robert Ley, head of the German Workers' Front, who hanged himself in his cell before the trial;[2] and Hermann Goering, who swallowed poison the night before the executions.[3] Ley's suicide had the effect of tightening security on the remaining prisoners, throughout their trials and up to the time of their executions. Guards posted in front of every cell were required to observe each prisoner once a minute, around the clock.[4] Thus, ironically, the chief perpetrators of a system that denied millions of Germans any vestige of privacy for twelve years, lived their last months under constant surveillance.

Ten days after the executions – to the east in the Soviet Occupation Zone – Hans Fallada completed the first postwar novel to chronicle the horror the Nazis' institutions of surveillance and control had inflicted on the home front.[5] Unlike several of his postwar literary compatriots – Böll,

---

[1] RICHARD OVERY, INTERROGATIONS: THE NAZI ELITE IN ALLIED HANDS, 1945 164–65 (2001).

[2] Ronald Smelser, *Robert Ley: The Brown Collectivist, in* THE NAZI ELITE 153 (Ronald Smelser & Rainer Zitelmann eds., 1993); OVERY, *supra* note 1, at 168.

[3] Alfred Kube, *Hermann Goering: Second Man in the Third Reich, in* THE NAZI ELITE, *supra* note 2, at 68.

[4] OVERY, *supra* note 1, at 168–69.

[5] HANS FALLADA, EVERY MAN DIES ALONE (Michael Hofmann trans., 2009).

Borchert, Andersch – Fallada had done no military service. Still, he had barely survived the regime and its war. Now, in his new novel, he would describe the terror the Nazis perpetrated on the civilian population, including the persecution and murder of its best and brightest. Their aim was to silence all progressive elements; their tools included intense surveillance and, in many ways worse, the chilling threat of surveillance.[6] In this chapter, as part of this book's broader contribution to a transatlantic dialogue on the issues of privacy and surveillance in the shadow of the NSA-Affair, I will consider the insights Fallada and his work can give us into Germans' anxious and alarmed response to Edward Snowden's revelations.

B   Fallada and the Fragility of Privacy

Hans Fallada's given name was Rudolf Ditzen. When he began his literary career he took his *nom de plume* from two Grimm Brothers' tales. He chose Hans from *Hans im Glück* (Lucky Hans), the story of a man who receives a lump of gold for seven years work, then, through a combination of treachery and his own stupidity progressively loses it all while remaining optimistic – because he is relieved to be freed from the burden of wealth.[7] Falada (Ditzen added the extra "l") is the talking horse in *Die Gänsemagd* (The Goose Girl), which, even after being decapitated, continues to talk, and eventually helps reveal the truth to the prince about how an imposter took the place of his intended bride.[8] There is an unintended irony in this pen name, which he took in 1919, long before the Nazis assumed power. In keeping with the talking horse, Ditzen might have been the courageous mouthpiece of truth that even death could not silence. In fact, the Nazis effectively silenced him – not the least because decapitation or some other cruel death remained an intermittent

---

[6] Robert Gellately, *Surveillance and Disobedience: Aspects of the Political Policing of Nazi Germany, in* THE THIRD REICH: THE ESSENTIAL READINGS 191(Christian Leitz ed., 1999) (Gellately surmises that a few spectacular "successes" led to the Gestapo's overall strength being over-estimated.)" *See also* RICHARD J. EVANS, THE THIRD REICH IN POWER 1933–1939 115–16 (2005).

[7] DIE BRÜDER GRIMM, KINDER UND HAUSMÄRCHEN: AUSGABE LETZTER HAND 407-13 (Heinz Rölleke ed., 1997).

[8] *Id.* at 436–42. *See* GUNNAR MÜLLER-WALDECK & ROLAND ULRICH, NEUES VON DAHEIM UND ZU HAUS: ERINNERUNGEN AND HANS FALLADA 13–23 (1993); JENNY WILLIAMS, MORE LIVES THAN ONE: A BIOGRAPHY OF HANS FALLADA 48 (1998).

threat. Fairytale endings for undesirable writers in the Third Reich were too rare, unless they managed to emigrate before it was too late.[9]

Germany in the Wilhelminian era, which paralleled the Victorian era in England, was a difficult place in which to grow to maturity. Frank Wedekind described in his 1891 drama *Spring Awakening* a society that was long on rules for moral conduct and short on counsel for the youth experiencing the hormonal turbulence that is puberty.[10] Youth existed in an information vacuum about sex, imposed by parents who considered it a violation of the ethical code even to discuss such things with their inquiring offspring.[11] Children were told what to do, without being told why or, more importantly, how. Left to their own devices, they learned what they needed to know on the street, often with disastrous results. Pubescent suicide was not uncommon in this environment.[12] Ditzen's upbringing was in this same mold. Biographer Jürgen Manthey explained that "[Ditzen's] parents still lived totally in the hermetic world of ideas for which the following generation coined the term prudishness . . . For example, Fallada's mother didn't send her children to the toilet, but only ever 'there'. Even more so, the sexual realm was not only beyond all mention, it remained for one's own sensibilities in darkness and was repressed into semi-consciousness."[13]

Ditzen's childhood, lived in this psycho-sexual vacuum, was predictably troubled. Already as an eight year old he was compelled to attend a strict, authoritarian school – the *Prinz Heinrich Gymnasium* – in Berlin's Schöneberg District. It was a school for the sons of the nobility and military officers that could have stood model for the one in *Spring*

---

[9] To cite but a few examples: Ödön von Horváth left Germany under threat in 1934 and moved to Salzburg. He left Austria two days after the Annexation and fled through six countries before reaching Paris, where, in relative political safety, he died in a freak accident. Walter Benjamin took his own life in a village in the Pyrenees, feeling that his flight from the Nazis was hopeless. Walter Hasenclever poisoned himself in the French detainment camp Les Milles. Historian and Journalist Egon Friedell committed suicide as the Nazis were trying to arrest him. Erich Maria Remarque succeeded in escaping to America, but the Nazis took their revenge on his sister, whom they tried on a bogus charge and beheaded.

[10] FRANK WEDEKIND, SPRING AWAKENING (Tom Osborn trans., 1969).

[11] WILLIAMS, *supra* note 8, at 16.   [12] WILLIAMS, *supra* note 8, at 14.

[13] JÜRGEN MANTHEY, HANS FALLADA IN SELBSTZEUGNISSEN UND BILDDOKUMENTEN 24 (1963) ("[Seine] Eltern leben noch ganz in der geschlossenen Welt von Vorstellungen, für die erst die folgende Generation das Wort Prüderie fand. . . . So schickte Falladas Eltern ihre Kinder zum Beispiel nicht etwa auf die Toilette, sondern immer nur, dahin'. Erst recht war der sexuelle Bereich nicht nur jenseits aller Erörterung, er blieb auch für das eigene Empfinden im Dunkeln und war ins Halbbewusste verdrängt.").

Awakening. On the first day the school's director is said to have hissed at the terrified Rudolf: "We'll soon straighten you out."[14] Ditzen had the wrong temperament for the *Prinz Heinrich Gymnasium*, where he was brought to tears daily by his teachers and exposed to the constant ridicule of his classmates.[15] Particularly cruel and arbitrary was Ditzen's Latin teacher, Herr Olearius, who delighted in humiliating him before he could even answer a question: "Now, let's call on our dimwit. He doesn't know anything, and won't know anything this time either, but he may serve us all as a warning example."[16] Ditzen's German teacher, Herr Gräber, was less hostile, but perhaps as damaging to the pupil's psyche. He would spend most of the class period standing before Ditzen's desk and playing with the youngster's hair, thereby calling attention to his abnormally long front locks and bringing derisive laughter from the other pupils.[17] On the playground Ditzen fared even worse. His patched trousers caused unabated teasing from his "finer" classmates.[18] It is difficult to claim that Ditzen's experience was paradigmatic for a generation. Yet it is a reasonable assumption that schools like *Prinz Heinrich* were partly responsible for creating the lick-up, kick-down ethic of the Third Reich. The strong emerge as leaders with authoritarian tendencies and little regard for the rights of the weak, while the weak learn the survival strategy of making themselves very inconspicuous and doing what they are told without questioning authority.

At age twelve, Ditzen attempted to run away. Finally realizing the *Prinz Heinrich Gymnasium* was to blame, his parents transferred him to another school where he began to flourish.[19] But, when Ditzen was fifteen, his father took a position in Leipzig. Uprooting was traumatic enough for Ditzen, but after only a few weeks in Leipzig he nearly died in an accident. While riding his bicycle he ran into a butcher's cart, was kicked in the head by the horse, and run over by the wagon.[20] In addition to long-term stomach problems, the experience stirred in the

---

[14] MANTHEY, *supra* note 13, at 14 ("Dich werden wir schon zurechtkriegen."). WERNER LIERSCH, HANS FALLADA: SEIN GROSSES KLEINES LEBEN 26 (1981).

[15] MANTHEY, *supra* note 13, at 14; HANS FALLADA, DAMALS BEI UNS DAHEIM 46 (1955).

[16] LIERSCH, *supra* note 14, at 26; FALLADA, *supra* note 15, at 46 ("Jetzt wollen wir einmal unser Schwachköpfchen anrufen. Zwar weiß er nichts und wird auch diesmal nichts wissen, aber er diene uns allen zum abschreckenden Beispiel.").

[17] FALLADA, *supra* note 15, at 45–46.   [18] *Id.* at 44; MANTHEY, *supra* note 13, at 15.

[19] FALLADA, *supra* note 15, at 52; MANTHEY, *supra* note 13, at 18; WILLIAMS, *supra* note 8, at 9.

[20] MANTHEY, *supra* note 13, at 20–21; LIERSCH, *supra* note 14, at 34.

boy grave religious doubts.[21] By age 17 he had renounced Christianity, replacing it with a vague love of beauty, which, in turn, inspired him to write poetry.[22] His fascination with Oscar Wilde's *The Picture of Dorian Gray* induced him to begin calling himself "Harry" after the evil Lord Harry Wotton.[23] At age 17 he spent the summer in Holland with the *Wandervogel* youth group, where he contracted typhus. As punishment for his tipping over the kettle and spilling their supper, the other boys had held Ditzen under the water so long that he passed out. The infection likely entered his lungs though the water.[24] His personality changed after that illness. He rejected his parents and also the school system, declaring in a speech before a local literary society: "Modern schools can only produce criminals or madmen."[25] Ditzen's views of the educational establishment were in part affected by the suicides of three of his classmates that year.[26] He, in turn, became suicidal. A likely cause can be found in his sexual frustration as he struggled with his awaking urges, in particular for one girl in his circle named Käthe Matzdorf. He wrote her suggestive letters, and his exposure as the writer prompted his first suicide attempt.[27] At age eighteen, in the autumn of 1911, Ditzen became romantically involved with a fifteen year old girl and, at the same time, was tormented by an irrational desire to kill her.[28] He decided instead to kill himself. He and an equally suicidal friend, Hanns-Dietrich von Necker, devised a plan to kill each other in a duel, ostensibly over the honor of the girl.[29] Things did not go as planned. Necker fired twice and missed. Ditzen wounded Necker, who then begged him to finish the job. Ditzen fired again into Neckar's heart and then fired two shots into his own chest.[30] He survived and escaped prosecution for murder only because he was deemed mentally unfit to stand trial.[31] Still, he spent the next two years in psychiatric care,

---

[21] LIERSCH, *supra* note 14, at 33; WILLIAMS, *supra* note 8, at 11.

[22] Williams, *supra* note 8, at 13.   [23] *Id.* at 12; LIERSCH, *supra* note 14, at 36.

[24] FALLADA, *supra* note 15, at 193–94; MANTHEY, *supra* note 13, at 24. *But see* LIERSCH, *supra* note 14, at 40 (Werner Liersch disputes that Ditzen could have contracted the typhus in Holland considering the incubation period.).

[25] WILLIAMS, *supra* note 8, at 13.   [26] *Id.* at 14–15; LIERSCH, *supra* note 14, at 39.

[27] WILLIAMS, *supra* note 8, at 16.

[28] Williams cites this motivation for the duel. Werner Liersch collaborates it with a report of a brief conversation between Rudolf and his father in the former's hospital room after the duel. LIERSCH, *supra* note 14, at 66.

[29] WILLIAMS, *supra* note 8, at 22.

[30] *Id.* at 24; MANTHEY, *supra* note 13, at 37–38; LIERSCH, *supra* note 14, at 62.

[31] WILLIAMS, *supra* note 8, at 26.

primarily in the sanatorium at Tannenfeld.[32] Among comparable institutions, this sanatorium was a relatively humane place. Ditzen was not content with the restrictions imposed, but during his stay, shielded from the outside world and aided by private tutoring from his aunt, Ditzen began to develop his talent as a writer and a translator.[33]

These were the significant events that shaped Ditzen's adult life. On the one hand, he was able to develop the nonconformity and creative talent that led to a literary career. On the other hand, depression and illness led to alcohol and drug dependency. Declared physically unfit for military service in 1914,[34] Ditzen earned his living working on agricultural estates.[35] But as early as 1917 he came under the influence of the morphine given to him for the pain of stomach ulcers, and had to undergo an addiction cure.[36] Ditzen's father was never enthusiastic about his son's literary aspirations. Still he grudgingly provided financial support to the budding writer for a trial year, during which Ditzen was sick much of the time.[37] When he began to write novels, he took the pseudonym Hans Fallada at his father's suggestion. The public's memory of the duel with Necker was still too fresh.[38] In 1923, drug and alcohol dependent again and in need of money, Fallada traded a large amount of grain from the estate where he was working on the black market. He was caught and sentenced to six months in prison, a sentence he finally served in 1924, after his writing career was well-underway.[39] Two years later he was back in prison, this time serving a two-year sentence for embezzlement.[40] Of his Weimar Republic novels, the one that gained Ditzen (now Fallada) international recognition was *Kleiner Mann, was nun?* (Little Man, what now?), a tale of the victory of morality over materialism amid the economic hardships of 1931–32.[41] As 1932 drew to a close, Fallada had

---

[32] *Id.* at 26–32; MANTHEY, *supra* note 13, at 38; LIERSCH, *supra* note 14, at 79.

[33] MANTHEY, *supra* note 13, at 41.

[34] LIERSCH, *supra* note 14, at 106; WILLIAMS, *supra* note 8, at 34.

[35] WILLIAMS, *supra*, 35–38; LIERSCH, *supra* note 34, at 100–02, 108–10; MANTHEY, *supra* note 13, at 43–47.

[36] MANTHEY, *supra* note 13, at 47.   [37] WILLIAMS, *supra* note 8, at 45–47.

[38] LIERSCH, *supra* note 14, at 130.

[39] The biographers here are not in agreement. Williams dates the embezzlement to October 1922 and lists the prison term as 6 months, WILLIAMS, *supra* note 8, at 60–62; Liersch confirms the six-month prison term, but dates the offense to summer of 1923, LIERSCH, *supra* note 14, at 134. Manthey dates the offense to summer of 1923, but reports a three-month sentence, MANTHEY, *supra* note 13, at 55.

[40] WILLIAMS, *supra* note 8, at 76–77; LIERSCH, *supra* note 14, at 146–148.

[41] HANS FALLADA, KLEINER MANN – WAS NUN? (1932).

emerged as a widely-popular author in Germany. His friendship with publisher Ernst Rowohlt, with whose publishing house he had contracts for future projects, insured him a steady income. Fallada was debt-free, married, with a son, and looking optimistically to the future.

This all changed dramatically in January 1933. The National Socialists – a despised and ridiculed splinter party – came to power with modest plurality of votes, an aggressive and revolutionary agenda, a well-developed persecution complex, a panoply of "martyrs," and an impressive list of enemies. Indeed, for the Nazis, enemies were everywhere. Each had committed particular heresies or exhibited particular "weaknesses" that qualified them, by definition, as *Staatsfeinde*: Communists, Jews, certain Christian sects, homosexuals, Gypsies, and eventually all those who were not convinced enough of the Führer's mission to join the Party. It is common knowledge today how quickly the rule of terror replaced the rule of law and how quickly the expectation of privacy disappeared from German society. By means of *Gleichschaltung* (forced assimilation) the National Socialists quickly brought all the significant organs of social interaction – churches, labor unions, youth organizations, press, universities, courts – under control of the Party. The *Volksgerichtshof* (Peoples' Court), whose judges Hitler appointed personally, supplanted the Imperial Court's jurisdiction over "political crimes." And through the Enabling Laws, Hitler kept the Weimar Constitution ostensibly in place while according himself the ability to change it at will without consulting the legislature.[42] The changes happened quickly, even if it was not so obvious at the time. Those who misread the signals, who believed that Germany was still a nation of laws and that German humanistic traditions would hold sway under the new regime, misapprehended the Nazis. If they opposed the regime, then they risked imprisonment – or worse.

Hans Fallada was one of the naïve Germans who took too long to understand the severity of the situation. He clearly did not comprehend the speed with which the Nazis dismantled the Weimar Constitution and replaced it with the dictatorship of Hitler and the Party's elite. As a patriotic German who knew, or thought he knew, what it meant to be German, Fallada lacked the cynicism he would have needed to adapt

---

[42] For a discussion of Hitler's measures to secure power immediately after taking power, *see* Albrecht Tyrell, *Towards Dictatorship: Germany 1930 to 1934, in* THE THIRD REICH, *supra* note 6, at 27–48. *See also* JACQUES DELARUE, THE GESTAPO: A HISTORY OF HORROR 3–13 (Mervyn Savill trans., 1987).

more quickly. He also was possessed of a stubbornness that delayed his acquiescence to Nazi authority until it became a matter of survival for himself and his family. Ultimately he would make certain concessions, but there were many more Fallada refused to make. Every act of contrition or submission left him feeling embittered, eroded his self-respect, and drained him of any optimism he held for the future of Germany. "What will Germany be like after the war?" he wrote in 1944 in his *Prison Diary*.[43] "What kind of Germans will one have to live with? A terrible thought! How few of them will have retained vestiges of their true selves! And they won't even feel the change that has happened to them! They'll just say: 'We were always like this.'"[44]

Fallada was incarcerated in the fall of 1944, but not for political reasons. He had escaped the consequences of denunciation by nosy and vindictive neighbors on several occasions, as his diary entries attest. Instead, he was imprisoned because of an emotional outburst in his farmhouse in Carwitz. His marriage to his wife Anna, nicknamed Suse, had just ended in divorce. But due to the shortage of living space, he and Suse had to continue to live together. The situation was stressful for both of them and, on one occasion during an argument, Fallada discharged a gun in the house. He had not aimed at Suse, but he was extremely drunk at the time and, after she disarmed him and called a doctor to help Fallada, the doctor sent for the police who arrested the writer.[45] The incident eventually led to the most dangerous of all his incarcerations, which he suffered in a hospital for the criminally insane. Fallada was fortunate to survive the experience, confined as he was alongside "murderers, thieves and sex offenders,"[46] and with the omnipresent threat of the Nazis' purifying euthanasia agenda. Ironically, the incarceration may have saved his life because it spared him from Josef Goebbels' end-of-days call for total mobilization, which not even the sickly Fallada would have escaped.[47] Fallada kept the *Prison Diary* at great personal peril and despite constant observation by guards. The Neustrelitz State Psychiatric Hospital was indeed a microcosm of what Robert Gellately calls (with reference to Michel Foucault[48]) the "'surveillance' or 'panoptic' society"

---

[43] Hans Fallada, A Stranger in my Own Country: The 1944 Prison Diary 186–87 (Jenny Williams & Sabine Lange eds., Allen Blunden trans., 2015).

[44] *Id.* at 186–87.   [45] Williams, *supra* note 8, at 236.

[46] Fallada, *supra* note 43, at viii.   [47] Williams, *supra* note 8, at 237.

[48] Michel Foucault, Discipline and Punish: the Birth of the Prison (Alan Sheridan trans., 2d ed. 1995).

created by the Gestapo in Nazi era Germany.[49] Werner Liersch describes
the conditions Fallada faced daily: "Everywhere eyes and ears are directed
toward him. The State's Attorney reads his letters. The institution's
doctors control his reactions. The uniformed guards pay attention to
the following of the rules. The trusties keep the strange man under
observation as he sits on a stool and writes, sits and writes . . . ."[50] The
diary Fallada produced under these conditions is especially revealing
about the climate of surveillance in the 1930s before the war. It is mere
good fortune that Fallada was permitted a brief visit home in October
1944, that allowed him to smuggle the diary to safety in Carwitz. Unfortunately, he dared not risk a resumption of his diary writing when he
returned to the institution. His perceptive and passionate personal narrative does not include the war years. It may be technically inaccurate to
label this desultory autobiographical narrative a "diary." In essence,
Fallada was writing an exposé of a corrupt, inhumane regime right under
the noses of his captors, with the hope that he would survive the war with
a text to publish. Using very fine print and writing upside down between
lines he had already written, Fallada fooled the wardens into believing
that he was writing children's stories.[51] The narrative juxtaposes his own
experiences under constant surveillance in the countryside with the fates
of friends and acquaintances who fell victim to monitoring and control in
Berlin.

The Gestapo played a larger role in the city, but the common denominator in both contexts was the informant. This might have been a true
believer doing his or her duty for the fatherland by reporting on seditious
speech. Very often it was simply an opportunist who hoped for material
gain or some other advantage by denouncing neighbors to the Gestapo or
the SS.[52] "The Nazi Party and the government that emerged from it made

---

[49] Gellately, "Surveillance and Disobedience," 183.

[50] LIERSCH, *supra* note 14, at 350 ("Überall sind Augen und Ohren auf ihn gerichtet. Der
Staatsanwalt liest seine Briefe. Die Anstaltsärzte kontrollieren seine Reaktionen. Die
uniformierten Wärter achten auf die Einhaltung der Vorschriften. Die Kalfaktoren
belauern den merkwürdigen Mann, der auf einem Schemel sitzt und schreibt, sitzt und
schreibt . . .").

[51] Jenny Williams & Sabine Lange, *afterword* to FALLADA, *supra* note 43, at 233–34.

[52] Walter Otto Weyrauch conducted a study of the nature and types of confidential informants and their motivations using the Gestapo card files. He determined that the most
valuable informants were neither the true believers nor the members of fringe groups, but
rather the inconspicuous, apolitical community members who had the trust of their
neighbors and simply blended in. *See* W. O. Weyrauch, *Gestapo Informants: Facts and
Theory of Undercover Operations*, 24 COLUM. J. TRANSNAT'L L. 553 (1986).

a point of investigating every report from an informer," Fallada wrote, "even the ones that were obviously motivated by spite or greed."[53] Such was the motivation of an elderly couple named Sponar, from whom the Falladas rented an apartment in a country villa at Berkenbrück on the Spree in 1932. The Sponars had come on hard times when their lamp-shade business failed, and the couple was facing foreclosure. Fallada, who liked the couple and felt sorry for them, proposed buying the mortgage to the villa at auction, and guaranteeing the couple a rent-free apartment in it for the rest of their lives, plus a generous monthly annuity.[54] In repayment for Fallada's strategic kindness on their behalf, the Sponars waited until the mortgage was safely out of the bank and in Fallada's hands. They then denounced him on a trumped-up charge of "conspiracy against the person of the Führer."[55] The occasion for the charge was a visit Fallada had received from a man who told a political joke too loudly within earshot of the Sponars. Using their Party connections, the Sponars tried to arrange to have him "shot while trying to escape," and when that failed, they conspired to keep Fallada in prison indefinitely without a trial.[56] In this way the Sponars could continue to live in the whole house without having to worry about the mortgage payments (assumed by Fallada) or the rent payments Fallada had expected from them.[57] Fallada should have been wizened by this experience, but denial and stubborn-ness continued to render him incautious. In his diary he wondered, "which of us can keep in mind that someone downstairs only needs to leave a door ajar in order to hear every word that's spoken upstairs?"[58] The *Sturmabteilung* (Storm Detachment or SA), the paramilitary prede-cessor to the SS, tore up Fallada's apartment without finding a shred of evidence against him. Yet, despite his confinement in "protective cus-tody" for over a week, the true extent of the abrogation of civil liberties did not fully sink in. "Child that I was," Fallada would lament, "I still didn't get it: since January 1933 Germany had ceased to be a country under the rule of law, and now was a police state pure and simple, where those in charge decided what was lawful and what was not."[59]

After an interlude in Berlin, where the Falladas took up residence in a Jewish guest house, "which couldn't be kept secret, given the growing number of spies and informers – another fruit of the Nazi regime,"[60] they returned to Carwitz in the Mecklenburg countryside in autumn of 1933. When they arrived there were not many party members in Carwitz, a

---

[53] FALLADA, *supra* note 43, at 178.   [54] *Id.* at 16.   [55] *Id.* at 33.   [56] *Id.* at 41–42.
[57] *Id.* at 48.   [58] *Id.* at 19.   [59] *Id.* at 33.   [60] *Id.* at 57.

dynamic that gave Fallada a false sense of security. He spoke his mind freely. The mayor, named Stork, was a power-hungry, weak, and cowardly caricature of the ambitious class in this area. Their means for advancement was to hide behind their Party affiliation, but their "sole concern was how to get on in the world and ingratiate [themselves with their] superiors."[61] To this end "Mr. Stork made a habit of initiating compromising conversations . . ., subsequently reporting what was said, either to the Party or to the district council leader, as appropriate. He was constantly gathering material – to incriminate others, and to assist his own advancement."[62] Stork and his "mercurial wife" tormented the village, including the Falladas, by turning those who were willing to be informers against everyone else. A drunken farmer got a long prison term after joking at the local pub that "he had a cow in his shed that looked just like Adolf Hitler."[63] Fallada, by now painfully conscious of being constantly observed, noted, "I had long known that [Stork] had his eye on me, too, and his confidantes, old women for the most part, had been leaking information for a long time."[64] When Fallada fired an old housekeeper who had a son in the SS, she denounced Fallada, but on charges so ridiculous that not even the Gestapo took an interest in them.[65] When Fallada fired his gardener, his former employee did the same thing. Fallada again avoided the worst because it could be proven that the gardener had denounced his previous two employers on equally trumped-up charges after both had fired him.[66] Stork even had a poor chemist jailed for telling a joke about Winter Aid, the Nazi "charity" program.[67] But Stork's most odious offense, according to Fallada, was spying on a lonely local woman who, while her husband was off fighting the war, entertained a male visitor in her home. Stork wrote a letter to the soldier detailing the liaison.[68]

Such was the blatant invasion of privacy prevalent in the small farming community of Carwitz in the 1930s. Fallada's experience with this pervasive state of observation, control, and distrust equipped him to give voice to the victims in the city as well, in particular, two well-known publishers. One was Peter Suhrkamp, who had been Fallada's friend before they had a falling out. Suhrkamp secretly hated the Nazis, but knew how to disguise it and to cooperate in order to survive.[69] Nevertheless he was arrested on a charge of treason. Fallada knew few details, but logically assumed an informer was involved, writing:

---

[61] *Id.* at 171.   [62] *Id.* at 172.   [63] *Id.* at, 174.   [64] *Id.* at 174.   [65] *Id.* at 175.
[66] *Id.* at 195   [67] *Id.* at 177.   [68] *Id.* at 192–93.   [69] *Id.* at 84.

"Perhaps [Suhrkamp] was drunk, or perhaps even he needed a confidant eventually, someone to whom he could unburden his heart of the hatred he felt inside. And this confidant then reported him to the authorities. I don't know. I just heard that he said too much, and that he was arrested for treason, and for all I know he is already dead as I write."[70] Fallada did not know at the time that Suhrkamp was in Sachsenhausen Concentration Camp and would improbably survive the experience to resume his publishing career.[71]

A man Fallada knew much more intimately was his longtime friend and publisher Ernst Rowohlt. Rowohlt, in the same way as Fallada, had trouble holding his tongue in moments when he should have been cautious. Rowohlt was particularly lax, Fallada reports, about the government order that required Germans to present to the Gestapo immediately any seditious letter they received without showing it to anyone else.[72] One Gestapo agent warned him: "We send these things out ourselves from time to time, just as a test, to separate the sheep from the goats."[73] Unless they were committed Nazis, it was especially difficult for publishers to survive economically in those years. This was particularly the case for a publishing house such as Rowohlt, which had a large number of successful Jewish authors whose works were suddenly banned. Ernst Rowohlt tried to defend both his Jewish authors and the Jewish workers in his business, which kept him at odds with the authorities.[74] One such attempt – to keep a Jewish woman from losing her livelihood – ultimately cost Rowohlt his. Forced to fire her formally, Rowohlt was secretly dictating letters to the woman in the evenings and on Sundays and paying her under the table. "But no matter how secretively they went about their business, the Nazi spy had been even more secretive," Fallada reported.[75] Rowohlt was arrested and expelled from the German publishing profession.[76] This, however, was not the reason he had to flee Germany to save his life. That was the result of his wife's horrified public outburst at the atrocities committed against Jews during the *Kristallnacht* (Night of Broken Glass).[77] "Back then in Germany," Fallada explained,

---

[70] *Id.* at 84.

[71] Siegfried Unseld, Peter Suhrkamp: Zur Biographie eines Verlegers in Daten, Dokumenten und Bildern 106-07 (2004).

[72] Fallada, *supra* note 43, at 93.   [73] *Id.* at 94–95.

[74] *Id.* at 92–93 (An example of Rowohlt's beneficent attitude toward Jews was his refusal to fire translator Franz Fein after being ordered to do so by the Reich Chamber of Literature.).

[75] *Id.* at 97.   [76] *Id.* at 97.   [77] *Id.* at 100.

"whenever three people were gathered together, one of them was bound to be an informer. That same night they began to pack. It was high time: the concentration camp beckoned."[78]

A most poignant example of the fragility of privacy in which Fallada lived was the fate of Fallada's admired acquaintance, the cartoonist E.O. Plauen. After Plauen's Berlin office was destroyed in an air raid, he took new quarters in Fürstenwalde with a friend. Fallada continued the story: ". . . and when the two of them were talking and laughing together in the evening, their landlord was sitting next door and taking down every word in shorthand! Plauen's deafness meant that every word could be clearly heard. This vile creature kept it up for six months, then went and handed all the material over to the Gestapo."[79] Plauen committed suicide in prison before his trial, with a revolver the authorities placed in his cell for that purpose.[80] Another of Fallada's acquaintances, Alfred Schmidt-Sas, had once been a Communist but had long since given up any Communist activity. An old party comrade gave him a suitcase and asked him to hold it a few days until he returned. The request had seemed innocent enough. When it became clear the old friend was not going to return, Schmidt-Sas put it in the attic and forgot about it. Eventually caught by the Gestapo, the old party comrade claimed Schmidt-Sas was an accomplice and revealed the suitcase. It contained a printing press, once used to print Communist leaflets.[81] Fallada concluded that this was "revenge on the former party comrade who had abandoned the fight."[82] An innocent favor for an old friend, turned traitor, cost Alfred Schmidt-Sas his life.

In an excursus about his present situation in the asylum, Fallada describes receiving a letter from a soldier at the front, an admirer of his literature. Fallada, of course, never received the letter himself, as all his mail was being read in advance. But he was given to understand that there was some seditious content that rendered the letter dangerous to both the soldier and to himself, for the Nazis considered the recipient of a letter equally as culpable as the sender. Reflecting on this episode, Fallada summed up the experience he had made in this perverted world of observation and control:

> But will I not find myself lying in the same bed? Won't the recipient of such remarks come under the same suspicion as the writer? Won't they go through all my post at home? Won't they haul me off somewhere else to

---

[78] *Id.* at 100.   [79] *Id.* at 117.   [80] *Id.* at 118.   [81] *Id.* at 107–08.   [82] *Id.* at 108.

be cross-examined about defeatism, before I've had a chance to destroy this MS? Won't they pounce upon these pages, and will not even the tiniest handwriting fail to save me, once they have deciphered a single sentence?[83]

These agonizing questions haunted Fallada and contributed to his decision to stop writing his diary as soon as he got an opportunity to smuggle the text out of the asylum. It would be two more years before this life-long experience with brutally (and sometimes fatally) diminished privacy – his own experiences and those of his friends and acquaintances – would find expression in Fallada's fiction. These would be the themes of his final and most significant novel.

C   Nazi Surveillance, Control, and Terror – Fallada's Literary Portrayal

As he was about to smuggle his diary to safety, Fallada wrote: "I regret that I was not able to complete it. Another ten days or maybe just a week, and I would have finished the chapter about the war, and the one about my trip to France."[84] The trip to France notwithstanding, we can assume that Fallada's experiences in the war years found an accurate rendering in his novel, *Every Man Dies Alone*. Characters and episodes depicted in the prison diary reappear in altered form in the novel. The fictional former Communist Karl Hergesell, for example, makes the same mistake and suffers the same fate as Alfred Schmidt-Sas, that is, he takes a suitcase containing a printing press from an old associate, and ultimately dies for this innocent act of friendship.[85] The petulant schoolmaster and Mayor Stork of Carwitz and his "mercurial wife" reappear as the Schwochs in Eva Kluge's otherwise idyllic farm village. Schoolmaster Schwoch, "a rampant Nazi, a cowardly little yapper and denouncer," loudly proclaims his desire to fight for the fatherland, but uses every party protection to avoid service at the front.[86] Jenny Williams points out a number of other characters in the novel that seem to be drawn from real life: Dr. Stark, the lawyer who intentionally denies Otto Quangel a defense at his trial, is based upon the lawyer with the same name who advised Fallada against taking the Sponars to court. The courageous and principled Justice Fromm who lives in the Quangel's apartment block and keeps a

---

[83] *Id.* at 119–20.   [84] *Id.* at 215.   [85] FALLADA, *supra* note 5, at 286, 401.
[86] *Id.* at 335.

benevolent eye on the residents may likely reflect Fallada's father, and the courageous prison chaplain Pastor Lorenz represents Fallada's maternal grandfather, a prison chaplain of the same name.[87]

The impetus for the novel was delivered by Fallada's friend Johannes R. Becher, a Communist author who had spent the Nazi years in exile in the Soviet Union. Becher suggested Fallada fictionalize the story of Otto and Elise Hampel, who had been executed for writing anti-Hitler propaganda on postcards and leaving them in public places. Fallada obtained the Gestapo file through Becher, who was a high ranking official in the Soviet-controlled provisional government of East Germany after the war.[88] The history behind the fiction began in 1940, when Elise Hampel's brother died fighting in France. The loss turned her and her husband – who until that event had been supporters of the regime – into opponents. Otto Hampel began writing the cards because Elise could not print well. Otto dropped hundreds of cards calling for civil disobedience in public places for two years without being caught. Ultimately, Otto was betrayed by a supervisor at his factory, who was a Gestapo informer. The couple signed confessions after Gestapo interrogation and they were tried in January 1943, before the infamous hanging judge Roland Freisler of the People's Court in Berlin. Two months later they were executed at Plötzensee Prison.[89] Fallada changed the names to Otto and Anna Quangel and motivated their rebellion more strongly by changing the person killed in action from her brother to their only son.[90] Other small cosmetic differences are not important, but Fallada spares Anna the guillotine, allowing her to die as a bomb falls on the prison where she is being held.[91]

A major false lead in the real criminal case against the Hampels was the arrest in January 1942, of a gambling addict named Heinz Klaus, who acted strangely in a dentist's office where one of the cards was found.

---

[87] WILLIAMS, *supra* note 8, at 261–62.

[88] *The True Story behind Every Man Dies Alone*, afterword to FALLADA, *supra* note 5, at 529 [hereinafter *The True Story*].

[89] *Id.* (This appendix from the publisher without attribution contains documents from the Gestapo file against the Hampels including their confessions and copies of four of the cards.).

[90] WILLIAMS, *supra* note 8, at 263.

[91] FALLADA, *supra* note 5, at 505. For a detailed study of the similarities and differences between the historical figures in the Hampel case and Fallada's fictional characters, *see* MANFRED KUHNKE, DIE HAMPELS UND DIE QUANGELS: AUTHENTISCHES UND ERFUNDENES IN HANS FALLADAS LETZTEM ROMAN (2001).

In the novel Fallada casts this character as Enno Kluge. The historical Klaus was eventually released.[92] The fictional Kluge dies at the hands of Commissar Escherich, who does not want his sloppy police work to come to light.[93] Fallada introduces the fictional characters Karl and Trude Hergesell. Their struggle to rationalize their submission to the Nazis and their disavowal of the resistance cell to which they once belonged have their roots in the guilt Fallada felt about his compromises with the regime and the self-loathing he experienced as a result of his realization that he lacked the courage and character to resist actively. "I do not like grand gestures," Fallada had lamented in the prison diary, "being slaughtered before the tyrant's throne, senselessly and to the benefit of no one and to the detriment of my children. That is not my way"[94]

Fallada sets the tone of paranoia in the novel at the outset and maintains it throughout. In the forward to the first edition, he wrote:

> Many readers will find that in this book a large amount of torturing and dying is going on. The author allows himself to draw the reader's attention to the fact that the book deals almost exclusively with people who fought the Hitler regime, and with their persecutors. In these circles between 1940 and 1942, and before and afterward, there was rather much death. A good third of this book is set in prisons and insane asylums, and there, too, death was quite common. The author was often appalled at having to paint such a gloomy picture, but more brightness would have been a lie.[95]

Omnipresent surveillance and observation is as prevalent as death. Barely seven pages into the novel, at the beginning of chapter 2, we are reminded by the author, that

> "Doing things" meant reporting on others, for instance: So-and-so was listening to a foreign radio station. Ideally, Quangel would have packed up all the radios in Otto's room and stashed them in the basement. You couldn't be careful enough in times like these, when everyone was spying

---

[92] *The True Story, supra* note 88, at 538.   [93] FALLADA, *supra* note 5, at 263–73.
[94] FALLADA, *supra* note 43, at 136.
[95] "Mancher Leser wird finden, daß in diesem Buch reichlich viel gequält und gestorben wird. Der Verfasser gestattet sich, darauf aufmerksam zu machen, daß in diesem Buch fast ausschließlich von Menschen die Rede ist, die gegen das Hitlerregime ankämpften, von ihnen und ihren Verfolgern. In diesen Kreisen wurde in den Jahren 1940 bis 1942 und vorher und nachher ziemlich viel gestorben. Etwa ein Drittel dieses Buches spielt in Gefängnissen und Irrenhäusern, und auch in ihnen war das Sterben sehr im Schwange. Es hat dem Verfasser oft nicht gefallen, so ein düsteres Gemälde zu entwerfen, aber mehr Helligkeit hätte Lüge bedeutet."

on everybody else, the Gestapo had their eyes on all of them, and the concentration camp in Sachsenhausen was expanding all the time.[96]

Even the worst of the Nazi snitches in the novel, the Persickes, are constantly afraid that they are also being watched. They express the oppressive mood with the reflection: "Take someone like the man in the flat above us, old Quangel. You never hear a squeak out of him, and I'm quite sure he sees and hears everything, and probably has someone he reports to. And if he reports that you can't trust the Persickes, they're unreliable, they don't know how to keep their mouths shut, then we've had it."[97]

Vertrauensleute (informants) were spies for the Gestapo, recruited from the ranks of those lower and middle classes willing to report on their fellow citizens. They were either paid for their service, or forced to inform in return for the remission of a minor offense they had committed with potentially serious consequences. One such example in the novel is Frau Gesch, a neighbor of Eva Kluge. Eva is the estranged wife of the deadbeat Enno Kluge, previously mentioned as the man the inspector suspects of writing the cards, then murders when his suspicions prove false. Inspector Escherich demands that Frau Gesch reveal everything she knows about Eva, who has quit her job with the post office, resigned her party membership, slipped out of town, and is hiding out in a farm village. Though initially defiant, Frau Gesch eventually succumbs to the inspector's threats of an interrogation at Gestapo headquarters. She gives him vital information about her former neighbor, but that is only the beginning of a long-term relationship. "When Inspector Escherich said good-bye to Frau Gesch, he left behind not only a couple cigars for her husband, but also an eager, unpaid, and invaluable spy for the Gestapo. She would keep a vigilant eye on the Kluges' apartment, but more than that, she would listen to everything that went on in the house and in the shops, and she would call the kindly inspector the moment she heard anything she felt would be useful to him."[98]

Another eager but less reliable informant in the novel is Emil Borkhausen, a petty criminal who reports Enno Kluge to the Gestapo for the reward money, but not before blackmailing him with the threat of denunciation. This game does not work and Borkhausen gets neither the blackmail money nor the reward. But he does get Enno arrested. The factory where Otto Quangel works as a foreman is full of spies. Workers

[96] FALLADA, *supra* note 5, at 15.   [97] *Id.* at 17.   [98] *Id.* at 200.

who let a misguided word fall in an innocent conversation disappear with regularity. A brownshirt Nazi, at a meeting of the factory foremen, thunders "[A]nyone who helps get a defeatist man or woman put away will have done something for the German nation, and will be a man after the Führer's heart ... Anyone who is weak-willed and mealy-mouthed and doesn't immediately denounce anything and everything wrong will wind up in a concentration camp himself."[99]

In the fictional world of the novel, Trude and Karl Hergesell make the same discovery that Fallada had made in real life. Weary of the atmosphere of denunciation in the city, they seek the rural idyll. The book's narrator explains

> Like many city dwellers, they'd had the mistaken belief that spying was really bad only in Berlin and that decency still prevailed in small towns. And like many city dwellers, they had made the painful discovery that recrimination, eavesdropping and informing were ten times worse in the small towns than in the big city. In a small town everyone was fully exposed; you couldn't ever disappear in the crowd.[100]

Karl and Trude do not belong to the Party. They do not contribute much to the Nazis' Winter Aid chairty. Worse, Trude lets slip that she feels sorry for the Jews. Then, too, there are some old Gestapo files from the days when they were suspected of Communist activity. All this gives them the reputation of being politically unreliable. As a result, they remained under tighter surveillance than they could have imagined. A bartender in Berlin suffered the same fate when he failed to report Enno Kluge's presence in his bar to the Gestapo. Fallada remarks that Escherich would not forget the bartender's lack of communication. "He would inform a certain department about it, whereupon a file would be opened on the bartender, in which the word 'unreliable' would appear prominently. One day, perhaps sooner rather than later, the bartender would get to know what it meant to be thought of as unreliable by the Gestapo."[101] Nearly every character in the novel, insofar as he is not a ranking Gestapo agent, is either an informant or the victim of one.

Where there is no immediate spy, the chilling effect that results from the well-justified fear that there could be one works its own damage on the characters' lives. It is the actor Harteisen, a man alternately adored and persecuted by Dr. Goebbels, who finds Otto Quangel's first treasonous card. He has just been visiting his friend, Toll, who is also his lawyer.

---

[99] *Id.* at 51.   [100] *Id.* at 277.   [101] *Id.* at 228.

Terrified, Harteisen's first instinct is to run back into Toll's office with the card. Prompted by nothing more than the prevailing fear and certainty of surveillance, the friends suspect each other immediately. Toll refuses to take the card, intimating that Harteisen could be trying to entrap him. They could burn the card and no one would know, Harteisen protests. "You would know," says Toll, suggesting that a witness to a political crime, even a close friend, was potentially dangerous. "He's an actor, thought the attorney. Maybe he's putting on a show for me, to draw me into something. Comes here with instructions to test my reliability."[102] And Harteisen cannot help but doubt his friend in turn: "He's acting against me. Who knows whether this postcard – you hear so much about traps being set for people."[103] Eventually the friends agree to trust each other: "What were we thinking? The son betrays his mother, the sister her brother, the boyfriend his girlfriend . . . ." "But not you and me!"[104] Life had not always been so suffocatingly insecure, as an innocuous anecdote only a few pages later reveals. In a time before the start of the Thousand-Year Reich, when Anna Quangel was just a schoolgirl, "[S]he was well-liked in the village, because, stubborn and brave as she was, she had rebelled against all forms of injustice. Once, she had even hit a tyrannical schoolteacher three times in a row with a snowball – and had never been betrayed. Only Ulrich had known it was she, and Ulrich never tattled."[105] While it has no bearing on the plot, this harmless reflection stands in subtle but intentional contrast to the stifling atmosphere of the novel, a time when "[t]he son betrays his mother, the sister her brother, the boyfriend his girlfriend." Perversely, the success of the Nazis' surveillance state capitalized on the residual socialization of those more trusting times, which too-often led people to let down their guard.

While the Gestapo's methods of breaking down a prisoner's will to resist were state of the art, they did not always get at the truth. Rather they could easily elicit merely what the interrogator wanted to hear, as in the case of Enno Kluge, who is bullied into a confession that both the interrogator and the confessor know is false.[106] Escherich simply needs someone to take the fall. Under a similar interrogation Ulrich Heffke, Otto Quangel's brother-in-law, confesses not only to distributing the cards, but also to industrial espionage at his factory. Both charges are false and later disproven, but as a result, Heffke turns into a pitiful wreck who suffers a nervous breakdown at Otto's trial.[107]

---

[102] *Id.* at 150.   [103] *Id.* at 150   [104] *Id.* at 151.   [105] *Id.* at 159.   [106] *Id.* at 186–89.
[107] *Id.* at 459–60.

Anna Seghers, in her novel of individual heroisms in the face of Nazi terror, puts the following words into the mouth of a man who has just survived a night of Gestapo interrogation and has been released: "They threatened me with every imaginable thing. Hell-fire was the only thing they left out. But in every other respect they apparently wanted me to think they were the Day of Judgment ... but they are a long way from knowing everything. They only know what they are told."[108] Yet, as later revelations made clear, Seghers' assessment, which matches Fallada's in *Every Man Dies Alone*, was not entirely accurate.

The Gestapo was not exclusively reliant on information from willing and unwilling informants. It also was not exclusively dependent on confessions and denunciations exacted from prisoners. The Gestapo also made use of electronic surveillance – what we might today call "signals intelligence." While the Germans did not invent wiretapping, they put it to use beginning in 1933. Fallada was not privy to this top-secret information at the time he wrote the novel. Certainly wiretapping gets no mention in the book. Despite the fact that it employed three thousand German citizens at the height of its operation,[109] Hermann Goering's "*Forschungsamt*" (Office of Research) – a crude euphemism for Nazi Germany's surveillance agency for telephone, telegraph and radio transmissions – was successfully kept secret from the German population until the end of the war. Beginning in 1933 the *Forschungsamt* was the personal domain of Goering, who controlled the flow of information to other agencies, such as the RSHA, and even the Gestapo.[110] Goering used some of the information gathered for his own purposes, to neutralize personal enemies (such as Ernst Roehm), to increase his own power at the expense of those enemies, and to secure his own business interests.[111] He monitored the secret conversations of industrialists who opposed the growing nationalization of industry under Goring's "Four Year Plan."[112] But the bulk of information obtained dealt with "national security." Unlike the information gathered daily by the Gestapo, however, the *Forschungsamt* data focused mainly on big fish and not the general public. The primary targets of wiretaps were journalists, foreign leaders, ambassadors and embassies, German military officers and cabinet

[108] ANNA SEGHERS, THE SEVENTH CROSS 377 (James A. Galston trans., 2004).

[109] LEONARD MOSLEY, THE REICH MARSHAL: A BIOGRAPHY OF HERMANN GOERING 187 (1974).

[110] DELARUE, *supra* note 42, at 86.   [111] *Id.* at 86; MOSELY, *supra* note 109, at 187–90.

[112] EVANS, *supra* note 6, at 373.

ministers, and ranking party functionaries.[113] It is not surprising that, even had Fallada known about these intelligence practices, he and his family in rural Carwitz would have been completely unaffected by this form of surveillance. They had their hands full with the day to day harassment of informers and denunciation. Although denied unrestricted access to Goering's wiretaps, the Gestapo was not without technology of its own to spy on the populace. Jacques Delarue reports that "the Gestapo acted on its own by secretly installing microphones and tape recorders in the homes of suspects. In the absence of the victim, or on the pretext of making repairs or of checking the telephone lines or the electric installations, a few microphones were discretely installed, allowing the individual to be spied upon even in the bosom of his family."[114] Whether its information was gathered from crude denunciations or sophisticated technology, the Nazi state was built around the premise of pervasive and total observation and control. This distinctly corrupt and corrupting climate, experienced first-hand by Fallada, is profoundly and artistically depicted in his marvelous and heartbreaking novel.

D   Conclusion

The extent of the *Forschungsamt's* invasions of privacy only became clear at the Nürnberg Trial. These methods were then improved upon and widely employed in East Germany in the next four decades by the Stasi. In the lifetimes of the majority of East Germans before 1990, there was no time when their phone conversations could not be secretly bugged and transcribed for political reasons. The experiences of these practices – from the Nazi era and in East Germany – shed light on Germany's angry reaction to the NSA's programs for mass surveillance and data collection. For Germans living in the American, British and French occupation zones that ultimately formed the Federal Republic in 1949, the first decade since the "zero hour," or the moment of capitulation, brought not only economic recovery, not only reconstruction of the infrastructure, but also the restored right of privacy. And just as the citizens voraciously devoured the spoils of the economic miracle, they equally reveled in the freedom from

---

[113] MOSELY, *supra* note 109, at 187.   [114] DELARUE, *supra* note 42, at 86.

surveillance and denunciation. For East Germans the release from the terror of surveillance is more recent but no less welcome.

Hans Fallada dreamed of this release, even as he was languishing in the mental hospital under constant guard. He fantasized about constructing a tunnel under his farmhouse in Carwitz, where his family would inhabit a space far underground, unknown to the world outside. There they would remain, with food for years and a constant fresh air supply, until the war was over and the Nazis were gone. The dream has several variants and runs on for pages in his diary, but Fallada summed it up this way: "My dream of a refuge deep in the bowels of the earth takes me away from my enemies each day, and strengthens me for the day to come. I was alone, and down here, twenty meters below ground, I'm out of reach. Here the banned books line the shelves, the walls are hung with degenerate art, and traitorous thoughts run through my brain – free from interference! Here is the source of my strength, which no Nazi can violate!"[115] Fallada outlived the Thousand-Year Reich, but by less than two years. He wrote his final novel, *Every Man Dies Alone*, with the blessing and support of the occupying Soviet authorities, who appointed him Mayor of Feldberg and the outside villages, which included Carwitz, in the months immediately after the war.[116] Ironically, had he lived, he likely would have become an author in the German Democratic Republic, where, to his certain bitter disappointment, he would have experienced a new generation of equally oppressive surveillance techniques similar to those under which he had suffered and against which he had achieved a degree of literary revenge.

The *Prison Diary* and the novel *Every Man Dies Alone* are documents drawing on a twelve-year span when all vestiges of privacy disappeared from everyday life, when the son betrayed the mother, the sister her brother, the boyfriend his girlfriend, and when dissidents like Hans Fallada, who chose to remain in Germany rather than emigrate, could only find solace in dreams. For an understanding of the Germans' principled defense of their privacy rights today, one Fallada's texts provide a compelling argument.

---

[115] FALLADA, *supra* note 43, at 214.
[116] LIERSCH, *supra* note 14, at 366; MANTHEY, *supra* note 13, at 150; WILLIAMS, *supra* note 8, at 247.

26

"It Runs Its Secret Course in Public"

Watching the Mass Ornament with Dr. Mabuse

BY SUMMER RENAULT-STEELE

A Introduction

In the wake of what has come to be called the NSA-Affair, whistleblower Edward Snowden has become a popular icon in Germany.[1] At the same time, his image has been quickly embraced by a culture of mass production and consumption. Snowden's face has appeared on merchandise from shoulder bags to skateboards, and his story has been integrated into advertisements for lingerie and a travel agency.[2] In a particularly iconic portrait, generated by the German advertising firm Zitrusblau, Snowden's visage was printed on one million stickers and plastered across walls and lampposts.[3] The same portrait also graced T-shirts sold by the German lobbying organization Compact, for the equivalent of $28.00 per shirt.[4] Snowden's idolization rose to crescendo with an award winning documentary in 2014, co-produced between Germany and the United States,[5] and may return soon enough with the Hollywood thriller *Snowden*, set to be released in 2016.[6] Curiously, the figure of Edward Snowden is thus both antisurveillance hero and ubiquitous, best-selling symbol.

---

[1] Jonathan Jones, *Edward Snowden: 21st Century Revolutionary Icon?*, THE GUARDIAN (Aug. 20, 2013, 12:10 PM) www.theguardian.com/world/shortcuts/2013/aug/20/edward-snowden-21st-century-revolutionary-icon.

[2] Joanna Slater, *Adoring Germans Embrace Edward Snowden as Pop Culture Icon*, THE GLOBE AND MAIL (Nov. 2, 2014, 11:02 AM). www.theglobeandmail.com/news/world/adoring-germans-embrace-edward-snowden-as-a-pop-cultureicon/article21422337/.

[3] *Id.*   [4] *Id.*

[5] Amy Davidson, *Why "Citizenfour" Deserved Its Oscar*, THE NEW YORKER (Feb. 22, 2015), www.newyorker.com/news/amy-davidson/is-citizenfour-worth-celebrating. *But see* Chapter 28 in this volume.

[6] *Snowden: First Trailer for Oliver Stone's Movie Hits the Web*, THE GUARDIAN (June 30, 2015, 01:07 PM), www.theguardian.com/film/2015/jun/30/snowden-first-trailer-for-oliver-stone-movie-joseph-gordon-levitt.

On one hand, his image serves as a grave reminder of the dangers of contemporary mass culture: That cellular and digital technologies can be monitored by corporate and state power on a global scale. On the other hand, that very reminder is forged and propagated with the tools of contemporary mass culture.

Significantly, the paradox of Snowden's iconicity is not new. There is a legacy of cultural production in twentieth-century Germany that performs the same reflexive twist: Using tools of mass culture and modern technology to meditate upon the dangers of mass culture and modern technology. This chapter opens a small window onto that legacy by tracing unexpected lines of convergence between two storied antagonists: Cultural critic Siegfried Kracauer, and filmmaker Fritz Lang. Key articles by Kracauer from the Weimar period, paired with an analysis of Lang's film series on the master criminal Dr. Mabuse, reveal a number of shared concerns: Both Kracauer and Lang were apprehensive about the malignant growth of unseen power in modern German life, and both were concerned about how technologies of mass culture could be used to facilitate that surreptitious growth. Retracing this relationship between critic and filmmaker can disclose an unexplored facet of the cultural imagination that today embraces Snowden as popular icon.

B   Reconsidering A Storied Antipathy: Kracauer and Lang

In *Weimar Cinema and After: Germany's Historical Imaginary* Thomas Elsaesser outlines the antipathy that developed between Siegfried Kracauer and Fritz Lang, after critic and filmmaker had managed to escape the National Socialist reign.[7] Nowhere was this antipathy more apparent, Elsaesser writes, than in Kracauer's 1947 study, entitled *From Caligari to Hitler: A Psychological History of the German Film*, which explored the relationship between cinema and psychosocial development in the Weimar Republic.[8] Building on E. Ann Kaplan's authoritative claim that Kracauer "effectively damaged Lang's critical reputation for at least a decade,"[9] Elsaesser suggests Lang's cinema was considered

---

[7] Thomas Elsaesser, Weimar Cinema and After: Germany's Historical Imaginary (2000).

[8] Siegfried Kracauer, From Caligari to Hitler: A Psychological History of the German Film (2004).

[9] E. Ann Kaplan, Fritz Lang: A Guide to References and Resources 2 (1981).

replete with authoritarian figures projecting conservative-nationalist values, its mystic-mythical iconography of … Weimar Germany was underpinned by fables that offered protofascist solutions to economic and social ills. The name "Fritz Lang" stood for films where human relations revolved around power, control and domination, and the individual was a mere puppet of hostile forces, malevolent tyrants or superspies.[10]

On Elsaesser's account, *From Caligari to Hitler* ties Germany's descent into totalitarianism directly to Lang's depictions of Dr. Mabuse, consequently painting Lang as "very nearly the evil genius of the faltering Republic's film culture."[11] According to Elsaesser, Lang's *Dr. Mabuse, Der Spieler* (*Dr. Mabuse, the Gambler*) (1922) and *Das Testament Des Dr. Mabuse* (*The Testament of Dr. Mabuse*) (1933) in particular fell prey to Kracauer's indictment. Lang apparently objected to Kracauer's criticism, noting in an interview as late as 1975 that if he had predicted the rise of Hitler with his films, "then Kracauer was pinning the blame for the bad news on the messenger."[12]

Despite the dramatic legacy of this feud between critic and filmmaker, when we return to Kracauer's text itself and place it in the context of his larger critical oeuvre, it is not clear that Lang is "blamed" for paving the path to fascism by authoring prophetic parables. Indeed, it is curious to suggest Kracauer would center his analysis around the "evil genius" of one filmmaker at all. In the introduction to *From Caligari to Hitler* he explains "films are never the product of an individual."[13] Rather, he argues that cinema is a collective enterprise because the medium demands collaborative production efforts. Kracauer quotes Russian director Vsevolod Pudovkin, who describes the collective nature of work on the film set:

> The technical manager can achieve nothing without the foremen and workmen and their collective effort will lead to no good result if every collaborator limits himself only to a mechanical performance of his narrow function. Teamwork is that which makes every, even the most insignificant, task a part of the living work and organically connects it to the general task.[14]

Because film production is necessarily collaborative, Kracauer continues, any particular film will always "embody a mixture of heterogeneous interests and inclinations," thereby "suppressing individual peculiarities

---

[10] ELSAESSER, *supra* note 7, at 145.   [11] *Id.* at 157.   [12] *Id.* at 157.
[13] KRACAUER, *supra* note 8, at 5.   [14] *Id.* (quoting Vsevolod Pudovkin, 136)

in favor of traits common to many people."[15] Thus, no film can be the work of a solitary filmmaker. Moreover, Kracauer continues, cinema is not only a medium of mass production; it is also a medium of mass consumption. Films "address themselves, and appeal, to the anonymous multitude."[16] According to this line of reasoning, from genesis to screened completion, cinema transcends the individual. And for Kracauer, as well as other first generation Critical Theorists, it is precisely this aggregate existence that makes cinema worth attending to in the first place. Given this inconsistency, it seems important to question the prevailing reception of Kracauer's analysis when it comes to the Mabuse series and to reevaluate it in the light of Kracauer's larger scholarly frame of reference. Indeed, to do so points to unexpected lines of convergence between Kracauer and Lang.

In what follows I revisit key portions of Kracauer's cultural criticism, published in a daily newspaper during *Dr. Mabuse*'s initial rise to prominence. The focus is on Kracauer's understanding of mass culture under modern capitalism as "the mass ornament," a "monstrous figure" that "runs its secret course in public."[17] This "monstrous figure" penetrates both entertainment and work, and because it is ubiquitous – with no discernable end – it works away unnoticed, growing and consolidating through self-propelled animation. Next, I suggest Lang's Dr. Mabuse functions in much the same way as Kracauer's mass ornament. Mabuse is the author of an empire that erases his own presence, the head of a headless machine that drives forward indiscriminately. Through the figures of the mass ornament and Mabuse respectively, I contend both critic and filmmaker warn about the danger posed by unmonitored power that draws upon the tools of mass culture and modern technology to operate on a grand scale. Both, of course, are also drawing on tools of mass culture and modern technology to issue this warning. This point of connection, in turn, is what can help illuminate the creation of Snowden as popular antisurveillance icon in the wake of the NSA Scandal.

C The Mass Ornament

Before his forced exile from Germany in 1923, Kracauer wrote cultural criticism for the *Frankfurter Zeitung*, a liberal daily of which he became

---

[15] KRACAUER, *supra* note 8, at 5. [16] *Id.* at 78.
[17] Siegfried Kracauer, *The Mass Ornament*, *in* THE MASS ORNAMENT: WEIMAR ESSAYS 75, 78 (Thomas Y. Levin ed., Thomas Y. Levin trans., 1995).

feuilleton editor in 1924. The *feuilleton* section was traditionally reserved for literary and artistic criticism, but began to play an important political role in German culture in the wake of World War I.[18] According to Thomas Y. Levin, this was a moment when "the inherited cultural vocabulary" of German academic institutions was proving less and less adequate for left leaning intellectuals seeking to explain their new climate.[19] In this sense, Levin suggests, the *feuilleton* in the Weimar era took on "an avant-garde function," serving as the locus of a concerted effort "to articulate the crisis of modernity."[20] Significantly, the genesis of Kracauer's work on film took place within this larger project. He published two thousand articles in the *feuilleton* before his exile, close to seven hundred of which were dedicated to an analysis of the cinema.[21]

Like Walter Benjamin, Theodor W. Adorno, Max Horkheimer, and other first generation Critical Theorists, Kracauer approached cultural phenomena in general – and cinema in particular – as a symptomatic element within a larger philosophy of history aimed at grasping the nature of modernity.[22] For Kracauer, cinema functioned as a sign of its time, pointing to the larger social, political, and economic conjuncture from which it arose. In a piece for the *feuilleton* entitled "Der heutige Film und sein Publikum" ("Contemporary Film and its Audience") Kracauer declared: "The critique of current film production is . . . by no means directed exclusively against the industry, but forces just as much on the public sphere which allows this industry to flourish."[23] Kracauer's criticism at the *feuilleton* – and his mediations on cinema generally – stemmed from a broader and more complex diagnostic aim than simple castigation of "the industry" itself.

Specifically, Kracauer theorized that Weimar cinema (and other attendant cultural products) functioned as catalysts for a new kind of urban public defined by a culture of leisure and consumption, and

---

[18] THOMAS Y LEVIN, THE MASS ORNAMENT: WEIMAR ESSAYS 5 (Thomas Y. Levin ed., Thomas Y. Levin trans., 1995).

[19] *Id.*   [20] *Id.*

[21] MIRIAM BRATU HANSEN, CINEMA AND EXPERIENCE: SIEGFRIED KRACAUER, WALTER BENJAMIN, AND THEODOR W. ADORNO 3–4 (2012).

[22] *Id.* Prominent examples include Walter Benjamin's 1936 piece, "The Work of Art in the Age of its Technological Reproducibility," and his fragments on film, including "Chaplin," (1928)"Chaplin in Retrospect," (1929) and "The Formula in Which the Dialectical Structure of Film Finds Its Expression," (1935) as well as Theodor W. Adorno and Max Horkheimer's 1947 book *Dialectic of Enlightenment.*

[23] Siegfried Kracauer, *Film 1928, in* THE MASS ORNAMENT: WEIMAR ESSAYS 307, 307–08 (Thomas Y. Levin ed., Thomas Y. Levin trans., 1995).

dominated by principles of mass production.[24] As Inka Mülder-Bach puts it, "Kracauer is the first to describe the functional connection between work and leisure, between economic rationalization and the distraction provided by the culture industry."[25] A particularly illustrative example of how Kracauer pursued these connections can be found in his piece for the *feuilleton* entitled "Kult der Zerstreuung: Über die Berliner Lichtspielhäuser" ("Cult of Distraction: On Berlin's Picture Palaces"). Here Kracauer meditates on the refrain that, with the proliferation of movie theaters, the residents of Berlin have become addicted to the distractions of popular culture. He concedes that the consumption of films and other diversions is greater in Berlin than in the provinces. But, Kracauer ascribes this to more than the triumph of "poor taste" among the masses. Rather, he puts his finger upon a "formal tension" that binds white collar and industrial work with popular film:

> [T]he tension to which the working masses are subjected is also greater and more tangible: it is essentially a formal tension, which fills the day without making it fulfilling. Such a lack demands to be compensated, but this need can be articulated only in terms of the same surface sphere that imposed the lack in the first place. The form of free-time busy-ness necessarily corresponds to the form of business.[26]

Kracauer argues that the "tension" endured at the office or the factory is somehow mirrored – formally, and at the level of the "surface" – by films watched in leisure. This formal, surface-level mirroring also provides a kind of counterbalance to, or "compensation" for, the working day. "Surface" here can be taken both figuratively and literally. Kracauer is concerned with the "surface" of culture (the popular and putatively superficial) as well the literal "surface" of the screen at the movie theater. These surfaces display an aesthetic punctuation that, Kracauer suggests, link up with the rhythm of the workplace. We can more readily discern the form these shared surface-level tensions assume by turning to one of

---

[24] HANSEN, *supra* note 21, at 6.

[25] INKA MÜLDER-BACH, THE SALARIED MASSES: DUTY AND DISTRACTION IN WEIMAR GERMANY 5 (Quintin Hoare Trans., 1998). Mülder-Bach is no doubt implicitly referring to the patent similarities between Theodor W. Adorno and Max Horkheimer's claims in *Dialectic of Enlightenment* (1947) with Kracauer's earlier Weimar era writings. Incidentally, Kracauer served as Adorno's philosophy teacher and colleague. For more on their relationship, see Martin Jay, *Adorno and Kracauer: Notes on a Troubled Friendship*, 40 SALMAGUNDI 42–66 (1978).

[26] Siegfried Kracauer, *Cult of Distraction: On Berlin's Picture Palaces*, in THE MASS ORNAMENT: WEIMAR ESSAYS 323, 325 (Thomas Y. Levin ed., Thomas Y. Levin trans., 1995).

Kracauer's more prominent pieces for the *feuilleton*, "Das Ornament der Masse" ("The Mass Ornament").

"The Mass Ornament" begins with Kracauer's viewing experience of the celebrated dance troupe the Tiller Girls, whose performance can be seen in the film *Half Shot at Sunrise* (1930) and whose aesthetic was later adopted and hyperbolized by famed Hollywood choreographer Busby Berkeley. The Tiller Girls' choreography elaborated upon the basic form of the kick-line. They were known for producing large-scale, abstract patterns through the tight coordination of kicking legs, waving arms, and nodding heads. Upon viewing the Tiller Girls' performance Kracauer describes the dancers as "no longer individual," but instead, "indissoluble girl clusters."[27] As the dancers condense into massive geometric figures, he writes, their movements become nothing more than perfect "demonstrations of mathematics," leaving the audience with only "the plastic expression of erotic life."[28] Unlike the regularity of, for example, military exercises, the Tiller Girls' choreography serves no purpose beyond the production of a dazzling, human kaleidoscope. "No matter how regular [military exercises] turn out to be," Kracauer explains, "that regularity was considered a means to an end; the parade march arose out of patriotic feelings."[29] Thus, even if the Tiller Girls' dance resembles the rhythmic uniformity of a military drill, unlike soldiers, Kracauer argues that the Tiller Girls are not a "moral unit."[30] Instead, their movements have no end beyond the movements themselves: "the girl-units drill in order to produce an immense number of parallel lines ... The end result is the ornament ... [as] an *end in itself*."[31]

In the pages that follow, Kracauer blends his vision of The Tiller Girls with a description of modern industrial labor processes: "The hands in the factory correspond to the legs of the Tiller Girls."[32] Labor ruled by Taylorist principles,[33] Kracauer suggests, has a striking formal

---

[27] Siegfried Kracauer, *The Mass Ornament, in* THE MASS ORNAMENT: WEIMAR ESSAYS 75, 76 (Thomas Y. Levin ed., Thomas Y. Levin trans., 1995).

[28] *Id.* at 76.   [29] *Id.* at 77.   [30] *Id.*   [31] *Id.* at 76–77 (emphasis in the original).

[32] *Id.* at 79.

[33] Taylorism, sometimes called Fordism but referred to in Kracauer's work as capitalist "rationalization" or "Ratio," is an early twentieth-century formula for the production process intended to increase efficiency and maximize profit. It is characterized by fracturing the work process into numerous, simple tasks to be completed in rapid, serial succession. Taylorism was implemented heavily in Germany in conjunction with the Dawes Plan after the Treaty of Versailles. For more on Taylorism, see DANIEL NELSON, FREDERICK W. TAYLOR AND THE RISE OF SCIENTIFIC MANAGEMENT (1980). For more on the Dawes Plan, *see* LISA JAYE YOUNG, ALL-CONSUMING: THE TILLER-EFFECT AND THE AESTHETICS OF AMERICANIZATION IN WEIMAR PHOTOGRAPHY, 1923–1933 (2008).

resemblance to the choreography of the Tiller Girls. "Everyone does his or her task on the conveyor belt" and, like the Tiller Girls, these workers "perform a partial function without grasping the totality."[34] Dancers and workers closely mirror and reinforce one another. Thus, despite the purported opposition between leisure and work, there is a larger, pervasive form that organizes them both. Kracauer calls our attention to this shared "tension," this shared "form." It is conceived, he explains, "according to rational principles which the Taylor system merely pushes to their ultimate conclusion" and is merely "the aesthetic reflex of the rationality to which the prevailing economic system aspires."[35] Just as the Tiller Girls' choreography was an end in itself, so is the Taylorist production process:

> The commodities that it [modern industrial production] spews forth are not actually produced to be possessed; rather, they are made for the sake of a profit that knows no limit ... The producer does not labor for private gains whose benefits he can enjoy only to a limited extent ... No. The producer labors to expand the business. Value is not produced for the sake of value. Though labor may well have once served to produce and consume values up to a certain point, these have now become side effects in the service of the production process. The activities subsumed by that process have divested themselves of their substantial contents.[36]

Similar to the aesthetic of the Tiller Girls' dance, modern industrial production enacts an indiscriminate, self-propelled animation. It is fueled by production for production's sake, growth for growth's sake. On Kracauer's account this dynamic deserves urgent attention because limitless growth has an inverse relationship to the integrity of the individual dancers – or individual workers – involved in the performance. "Community and personality perish," Kracauer laments, "when what is demanded is calculability."[37] People become interchangeable within the vast machinery of production, and their solidarity loses its footing. Indeed, one is hard-pressed to find a deviant dancer among the tightly coordinated Tiller Girls, just as any disorderly worker at the conveyor belt can be promptly replaced.

Even more worrisome, Kracauer continues, is that so few notice this exploitative link between popular culture and labor. It is allowed to run "its secret course in public."[38] Protected precisely because it is on display, the mass ornament is everywhere, and yet goes almost entirely unnoticed.

---

[34] KRACAUER, *supra* note 17, at 78.   [35] *Id.* at 79.   [36] *Id.* at 78.   [37] *Id.*   [38] *Id.*

It "stands above the masses, a monstrous figure whose creator withdraws it from the eyes of its bearers, and barely even observes it himself."[39] This is Kracauer's warning about the power of the unseen: Germans are "bearing" the logic of the mass ornament, it saturates their movie screens and it disciplines their work life, and yet, still it "withdraws" from their vision. For Kracauer, that is the most insidious form of power, a power that propels and organizes with massive force, and yet hides in the everyday.

In this sense, Kracauer's concern in "The Mass Ornament" parallels the antisurveillance sentiment fueling Snowden's idolization. Namely, there is a shared concern about the danger posed by unseen power drawing upon the tools of mass culture and modern technology to operate on a grand scale and infiltrate everyday operations. Granted, Kracauer was primarily concerned with the unmitigated dominance of Taylorist capitalism, as opposed to the NSA. Furthermore, he necessarily critiqued the technology of his own historical moment – film and the infrastructure of the factory – as opposed to the cellular and digital technology at the center of the NSA Scandal. Nonetheless, there appears to be a similar preoccupation at work in both moments.

More compelling still, both the mass ornament and the NSA Scandal are understood to present specifically American incursions on German life. On the very first page of "The Mass Ornament," Kracauer refers to the Tiller Girls as "products of American distraction factories."[40] This is despite the fact the Tiller Girls were British,[41] but factual error here is beside the point. What is significant is that Kracauer denounced the Tiller Girls – and the phenomenon of the mass ornament at large – as part of a creeping American influence on German life. Kracauer's misgivings in this regard were not idiosyncratic. Indeed, the term *Amerikanismus* was coined in the late Weimar period to express a broad concern with the so-called Americanization of cultural and economic life in Germany, (associated in large part with the transformative effects of the Dawes Plan).[42] Part of the expository function of Kracauer's article was thus, to locate the mass ornament as part of the cultural and

---

[39] *Id.*   [40] *Id.* at 75.   [41] YOUNG, *supra* note 33, at 3.

[42] *Id.* at 1–2. Young notes "The debate around Americanization [was] a European-wide phenomenon in the 1920s [and was] debated more widely in Germany than in any other country at the time due to its close economic ties with the United States after WWI." For more on the reception of Americanization and specifically, the reception of Taylorism or Fordism in Germany, *see* MARY NOLAN, VISIONS OF MODERNITY: AMERICAN BUSINESS AND THE MODERNIZATION OF GERMANY (1994).

economic imperialism of the United States. A likeness of this narrative is replaying in the wake of the NSA Scandal and in particular, in the idolization of Snowden. For clearly, there is a natural alliance between the antipathies directed at the American state and the NSA, and the elevation of Snowden as antisurveillance icon. In this way, both Kracauer's mass ornament and the present-day idolization of Snowden betray a similar critique: Both are directed at a specifically American power perceived to pull the levers of mass culture and modern technology in order to surreptitiously infiltrate German life.

D   Dr. Mabuse

A similar concern about the danger posed by unseen power drawing upon mass culture and modern technology resonates throughout Lang's *Dr. Mabuse* film series. As Elsaesser notes, many of Lang's films are hyperconscious of how modern culture and technology affects the way power can operate.[43] The following analysis of Lang's *Dr. Mabuse* films illustrates the similarity between Kracauer's theorization of the mass ornament, Lang's vision of the master criminal, and the attendant worries expressed by critic and director alike about modern, urban German life.

In 1921 Norbert Jacques hatched the master criminal Dr. Mabuse in his novel *Dr. Mabuse, der Spieler*. Directly after the book's publication Lang transformed the novel into a film with the same title.[44] Both incarnations enjoyed wild commercial success in Germany and abroad, propelling a succession of tales about Mabuse including three more pieces authored by Jacques,[45] and two more films by Lang.[46] As Erik Butler explains, Mabuse "quickly became a German and even an international *Kulturgut*," earning a place in the pop culture pantheon of the early twentieth century.[47]

Throughout Lang's series, Mabuse successfully "traffics in images," and this constant dissimulation functions to inject his environment with uncertainty.[48] This capacity to foment doubt becomes the quintessence of Mabuse's particular breed of power, which Lang escalates from film to

---

[43] Elsaesser, *supra* note 7, at 150.   [44] Dr. Mabuse, der Spieler (Fritz Lang, 1922).

[45] Norbert Jacques, Ingenieur Mars (1923); Norbert Jacques, Mabuses Kolonie (1930); Norbert Jacques, Chemiker Null (1934).

[46] Das Testament des Dr. Mabuse (Fritz Lang, 1933); Die 1000 Augen des Dr. Mabuse (Fritz Lang, 1960). *See* Eric Butler, *Dr. Mabuse: Terror and Deception of the Image*, 78 German Q. 481 (2005).

[47] Butler, *supra* note 46, at 481.   [48] *Id.* at 484.

film. In *Mabuse, the Gambler,* for example, we are introduced to the villain who "traffics in images" as the head of a counterfeiting operation that is staffed with blind employees. The operation performs a double-deceit: Employees generate the means to deceive others, while they are deceived about the identity of their boss. Already, we learn one imitation alone is too simple a ruse for Mabuse. Throughout the course of the film artifice is layered upon artifice in this way. Mabuse uses real bank notes for writing paper and counterfeit notes for transactions; he distributes misleading signs throughout his city, contributing to the confusion of those who would track him.[49] And, as the title of the film suggests, *Dr. Mabuse, der Spieler* is not just a gambler, but also an actor who disguises himself in turn as a stockbroker, a drunken sailor, a scientist, and a political radical.[50] As the film catalogues this subterfuge it fuels the eerie sense that Mabuse and his activities have an indefinite reach. At any given moment he could be doing anything, anywhere, as anyone.[51] This is Mabuse's infamous magic: He affects ubiquitous influence while remaining, paradoxically, untraceable.

Crucially, it is the cultural and technological infrastructure of modern urban existence in *Gambler* that allows Mabuse to exercise the power he does. Here his crimes take place in an unnamed city, generally thought to be Berlin but which Butler claims is more like "the 20th century in microcosm."[52] To be sure, Mabuse relies upon major signifiers of the early twentieth century in order to carry out his operation. He relies upon the impersonal, crowded spaces of the city to pass unnoticed in which-ever disguise he chooses. He harnesses the labor practices and technology of mass reproduction to generate artificial bank notes. He relies upon rapid communication and coordination by way of telephones, trains, and cars in order to pull off heists. In this way, as Tom Gunning notes, "Mabuse appears as the evil genius of modernity, able to extend his power ... like a spider sitting in the center of a technological web."[53] In other words, the possibility of Mabuse's power – ironically – relies upon the very character of the society he abuses. Without his "web" of modern urban alienation and instruments, this "spider" would be at a loss.

Beyond Mabuse's exploitation of early twentieth century urban ano-nymity and technology, Gunning suggests the figure of the master

---

[49] *Id.* at 484–85.   [50] *Id.* at 484.   [51] *Id.*   [52] *Id.*
[53] Tom Gunning, The Films of Fritz Lang: Allegories of Vision and Modernity 97 (2000).

criminal himself is also unique product of the modern Western imagination.[54] This is because the master criminal is "not simply a clever or prodigious criminal with a long array of crimes to his credit, but the ... organizer, head of a vast conspiracy."[55] Only the modern author could conceive of a criminal network that paralleled the sweeping organization of modern industry. Gunning traces the figure of the master criminal back to the literary character Vautrin, from Honoré de Balzac's early nineteenth century, multivolume work *La Comédie Humaine*.[56] Gunning finds two aspects of Vautrin define the master criminal. The first is that he orchestrates, "a vast system of underlings whose intricately organized interactions mirror those of a vast industry."[57] The same characteristics are apparent in the character of Professor Moriarty, from Arthur Conan Doyle's late nineteenth and early twentieth century detective fiction.[58] Doyle described Moriarty as "the organizer of half that is evil and nearly all that is undetected" and, yet, "[Moriarty] does little himself. He only plans ... his agents are numerous and splendidly organized."[59] On Gunning's account, both Vautrin and Moriarty function like captains of industry, directing immense, intricate operations. Furthermore, their administration must occur in secret. According to Gunning, it is this concealed – yet ubiquitous influence – that confers upon Vautrin, Moriarty, and Mabuse their virtuoso status. The second aspect of Vautrin that defines the master criminal, Gunning suggests, is "a desire for power itself, rather than a simple personal gain or revenge, as the motivating force behind the criminal's activity."[60] And indeed, Mabuse's motives are never quite made clear; it appears as if the empire he constructs exists for its own sake. He certainly accrues power and influence, but to what end? To the end of accruing more power and influence, it seems.

---

[54] The figure of the master criminal in modern literature was generally male. For more on the question of why or how this particular kind of criminality is tied to conceptions of modern European masculinity, particularly in the works of Arthur Conan Doyle, see EMELYNE GODFREY, MASCULINITY, CRIME AND SELF-DEFENCE IN VICTORIAN LITERATURE (2011).

[55] GUNNING, *supra* note 53, at 94.

[56] HONORÉ DE BALZAC, LA COMÉDIE HUMAINE (1799–1850).

[57] GUNNING, *supra* note 53, at 95.

[58] This includes four novels, *A Study in Scarlet* (1887), *The Sign of the Four* (1890), *The Hound of the Baskervilles* (serialized 1901-1902), *The Valley of Fear* (serialized 1914-1915), in addition to 56 short stories.

[59] GUNNING, *supra* note 53, at 95 (quoting Sir Arthur Conan Doyle, *The Final Problem*, in THE COMPLETE SHERLOCK HOLMES 471 (1930)).

[60] *Id.*

Vautrin, Moriarty, and Mabuse are also all described as difficult to capture. Indeed, simply proving their existence becomes problematic for the various authorities on their trail.[61] Lang's second Mabuse film amplifies the problem of getting hold of the elusive Mabuse. In *Testament* the very nature of Mabuse's existence is thrown into question and it becomes unclear whether he is threatening because he is a person, an idea, or a spirit. The corporeal Mabuse has a minimal presence in the second film. He is trapped in an insane asylum cell for half of the story, before purportedly suffering a quiet "death." And yet, as Butler observes, death seems to make Mabuse "more powerful than ever. Instead of changing disguises, he changes bodies."[62] He leaves behind a last will and testament that enchants Professor Baum, the head of the asylum. As if studying the document could release Mabuse's contagious essence, Baum comes to embody the late criminal, carrying out the conspiracies outlined in the will. In this sense Mabuse's veiled ubiquity is not simply a question of manipulation through disguise or proxy, as it was in the first film. Here, his criminal activities touch upon the metaphysical: Mabuse is able to influence reality because he transcends it. In this sense, what Butler aptly refers to as Mabuse's "diffuse wickedness" spills over from its urban, material birthplace in the first film, to psychological, supranatural channels in the second.[63]

The percolation of Mabuse's identity, from corporeal subject – to testament – to Baum, presents an even "more perfect system of terror" than the first film dared imagine "because its operation does not necessarily require anyone to oversee it."[64] In *Gambler*, even though Mabuse presides over pervasive manipulations, the film's narrative still depends on the fact that he could be caught and the manipulations would cease. *Gambler's* Mabuse still relies on the simple cause-and-effect logic of locating a perpetrator in order to neutralize his machinations. This Mabuse – although a master criminal – has not escaped the laws of nature, or at least causality. But, in the second film, Mabuse's activities are no longer contingent upon the existence of Mabuse. Or, Mabuse's activities are no longer contingent upon the kind of agent touched by the laws of nature or man. Lang has upset our hypothetical recourse to law enforcement, doubling down on the insecurity fomented by Mabuse. This, in essence, presents us with a most extreme extension of the deceit Mabuse initially establishes in *Gambler*. In the first film Mabuse hid his

---

[61] *Id.*   [62] Butler, *supra* note 46, at 486.   [63] *Id.* at 487.   [64] *Id.* at 485.

identity from his employees and moved about incognito. In *Testament* Mabuse fades from mortal existence and, at the same time, recreates himself in the text of the will and in the person of Baum. Mabuse no longer has an identity that must be hidden behind multifarious masks; he has instead multiplied and *become* multifarious masks.

In Lang's final contribution to the series, the specter of Mabuse returns to the urban center decades later to harness new technologies of dissimulation. Although *Thousand Eyes* was created a full 39 years after Lang's original Mabuse film, the filmmaker aims to maintain a sense of continuity with this third installment. "The first moments of *The Thousand Eyes of Dr. Mabuse* unwind as if Lang had never left Germany," Gunning observes, "so smoothly does [he] resume the style of editing and sound links that characterized his last German films, *The Testament of Dr. Mabuse* in particular."[65] But Gunning also notes an important difference. In the opening to *Gambler*, Lang makes ample use of cross cutting to pull together a rapidly synchronized murder and heist.[66] This sequence finds its center in the subject of Mabuse, sitting at his desk, timing every maneuver and ready at the telephone. But, in *Thousand Eyes*, the engineer of the initial murder and heist remains hidden. The first minutes of *Thousand Eyes* are peppered with approximately a dozen short scenes. We slice back and forth between a traffic filled road, and Police Commissioner Kras in his office receiving a call from the blind psychic Cornelius. "Someone's life has been threatened by a deadly foe" Cornelius warns, "There's danger!" Kras rolls his eyes at the blind psychic, but the frame shifts back to the stalled traffic and confirms Cornelius' prophecy only moments later: A man is shot from behind and slumps over his steering wheel. "I'm afraid I see far better than most," laments the blind psychic.

While these first minutes convey a tightly coordinated murder, it is not clear who coordinates the crime. This, Gunning observes, further develops the techniques of dispersion that Lang deployed in *Testament*. Since the opening crime in *Thousand Eyes* cannot be attributed to an identifiable agent, it seems to "wander astray in a flurry of associations, cued by Lang's free-roaming, associative editing."[67] Nonetheless, Lang continues to toy with the audience's latent desire to find a perpetrator at the center of the discord. In the next shot Mabuse's name is invoked at a smoky meeting in police headquarters. "I feel a sense of discomposure

---

[65] GUNNING, *supra* note 53, at 461.   [66] *Id.*   [67] *Id.* at 462.

about this case," chimes in one of the inspectors. "I mean ... it's like I've already gone through it. It's hard to explain ... What does the name, Dr. Mabuse convey?" The other officers murmur: "Nothing." But the inspector interjects: "A genius! He wanted to terrorize and provoke all kinds of strange fears. He was finally caught and very soon afterwards committed to an asylum ... he died in 1932 completely mad." The camera pans over Dr. Mabuse's gravestone as the inspector's monologue continues. "However, if you speak to the old hardened criminals who knew him, they all say the same thing 'Dr. Mabuse isn't dead, he can never die!'" "Old wives tales!" exclaim the other officers. This vague speculation about Mabuse hangs uncomfortably in the air, like the smoke from the officer's cigarettes. Mabuse is gone and yet he is present, as tangibly as in *Gambler* and *Testament*, commanding unease because of his ambiguous existence.

Most of *Thousand Eyes* takes place in the Luxor Hotel, a location designed to stoke the unease Mabuse's name stirred at police headquarters. The hotel was built to allow its owners to spy on guests; it features hidden cameras and one-way mirrors throughout. This is the main site of intrigue where four main characters try to get behind each other's acts.[68] The two characters who appear to be heroes throughout the better part of the film are eventually revealed as imposters, and what's more, we learn they are in fact only pawns in a game played by other characters, who are relatively marginal until the last minute.[69] Gunning explains that

> [t]hroughout *The Thousand Eyes of Dr. Mabuse* characters are framed within plots devised by others without the characters being aware of their own manipulation by these unseen forces. But Lang parallels the fates of these blindly manipulated characters with his own manipulation of the film viewer, blindly following misleading clues, unaware of the total design until the end of the film.[70]

In other words, just as the characters are deceived time and again, so is the audience. The ultimate betrayal occurs when a fight scene in the hotel is suddenly reframed within a television monitor. The point of view that belonged to the audience actually belongs to another; someone else, whom we cannot see, has also been watching. This is Lang's most penetrating disruption, for the audience is suddenly made aware that their purportedly objective frame of vision is itself subject to the technologies of manipulation at Luxor Hotel.

---

[68] Butler, *supra* note 46, at 491.   [69] *Id.* at 491–92.
[70] GUNNING, *supra* note 53, at 461.

If finally locating Mabuse is the relief the audience needs to feel that all is right with the world, Lang never gives it to them. To watch the *Dr. Mabuse* series is to learn the power to see is the power to control; and to be denied that power, all at once. The films, in other words, show just enough to make the audience aware they can never see it all, and therefore, they can never be in complete control. They must remain vigilant; the hunt for Mabuse is never ending. Lang hyperbolizes this lesson through his varying representations of Mabuse manipulating mass culture and modern technology – and yet ironically, the lesson is itself is delivered through film – a medium of mass culture and modern technology. In this respect, the nature of the *Mabuse* series and the nature of Snowden as antisurveillance icon are remarkably similar. Both cultural products aim to insinuate a nagging suspicion in their audience, and at the same time, offer a reflexive critique upon the very medium of their distribution.

E   Conclusion

Reexamining Lang's Mabuse series in the light of Kracauer's work on the mass ornament has not only illuminated key points of convergence between two purported antagonists, it also suggests a cultural inheritance from which to begin making sense of contemporary antisurveillance iconography. Kracauer's mass ornament is ubiquitous, penetrating both leisure and work, and yet, it is also virtually untraceable, completely normalized and unseen. Like Kracauer's mass ornament, Lang's Mabuse is the author of an empire who erases his own presence, the head of a headless machine. Indeed, Kracauer himself describes Mabuse as "an omnipresent threat that cannot be localized," a figure who succeeded in communicating the essential nature of life under tyranny.[71] On Kracauer's account, the Mabuse films rendered a society "in which one fears everybody because anybody may be the tyrant's ear or arm."[72] Further, he suggests this was part of Lang's conscious effort to render "the whole society" by way of a single tale.[73] That is also the aim of "The Mass Ornament": To theorize the formal unity of "the whole society" at that particular moment and place in history. Kracauer articulates what binds entertainment and production in the Weimar Republic, seeing an omnipresent totality that resists "localization" or, resists being seen. In this sense, Kracauer cannot have "blamed" Lang for predicting fascism, anymore than he ought to have "blamed" himself for it.

---

[71] KRACAUER, *supra* note 8, at 83.   [72] *Id.*   [73] *Id.*

And this is the point of connection between the works of both Kracauer and Lang: Through the figures of the mass ornament and Mabuse respectively, both critic and filmmaker warn about the danger posed by unmonitored power, and in particular, unmonitored power that draws upon the tools of mass culture and modern technology to operate on a grand scale. Moreover, both critic and filmmaker render this warning through newspaper and film respectively, paradigmatic technologies of mass culture and modernity in the early twentieth century. Recognizing this correspondence suggests the paradox of Snowden's iconicity is not a completely new phenomenon. That is to say, Snowden as antisurveillance hero *and* Snowden as ubiquitous best-selling symbol, are part of a critical inheritance in modern German culture: Using tools of mass culture and technology to reflect upon the dangers of mass culture and technology.

27

Secrecy, Surveillance, Spy Fiction

Myth-Making and the Misunderstanding of Trust in the Transatlantic Intelligence Relationship

BY EVA JOBS

"In civilizations without ships, dreams dry up, espionage takes the place of adventure, and the police that of the corsairs."[1]

A Introduction

Edward Snowden's revelations about the NSA's global surveillance operations have enlivened and helped to focus an old discussion about intelligence activities. They also disclosed a chasm in transatlantic relations over the different weight the United States and Germany give to privacy and security. Snowden's disclosures cast a bright light on an otherwise shadowy realm that is usually distinguished by the lack of trustworthy information – even in democracies. With respect to intelligence and privacy, an unholy mix of rumors, stereotypes, and fiction creates a breeding ground for speculation and conspiracy theories. Depictions of intelligence and espionage in the news media, political debates, and popular culture have shaped citizens' perception. These varied representations have also had an impact on officers and agents themselves. Importantly, these cultural manifestations, which also deviate substantially between Germany and the United States, contribute to the tensions in transatlantic affairs that have been stirred by the NSA-Affair.

It is often claimed that in Germany intelligence agencies enjoy a less romantic reputation.[2] This has two main sources. First, intelligence institutions and operations make many Germans think about troubling

---

[1] MICHEL FOUCAULT, AESTHETICS, METHOD, AND EPISTEMOLOGY 185 (James D. Faubion ed., 1998).

[2] *See, e.g.*, Eva Horn, *Zeig' mir dein Staatsgeheimnis* 1, GKND (July 2006), www.gknd.de/SB-2006-07-31.pdf.

institutions from the past – namely the Nazi Gestapo (*Geheime Staatspolizei*) and East Germany's infamous Stasi – which developed and deployed brutally effective systems of surveillance and oppression. It is important to remember that, aside from *"Hauptverwaltung Aufklärung,"* the Stasi was first and foremost a domestic secret police rather than a foreign intelligence service.[3] Nevertheless, the Stasi is now best known for the army of spies and informants it maintained.[4] Second, historically Germans have held disdain for spies and spying, which was (and continues to be) widely considered a dishonorable craft. This view is expressed in the old Prussian motto: "A German officer does not spy."[5] Yet, despite the fact that espionage was publicly disparaged, it was an integral part of military reconnaissance in the Prussian (and later in the German) military – just like everywhere else.[6] Nevertheless, one looks in vain for positive cultural (literary or cinematic) representations of spies, secret services, or spycraft in Germany.[7] This is accompanied by a lack of public knowledge: little or no attention has been paid to the relevant legal framework, mandate, or personnel matters relating to Germany's Intelligence Community. Few Germans, for example, can name the president of the *Bundesnachrichtendienst* (Foreign Intelligence Services or BND).[8] With the recent events, slowly more people have begun to take an interest in these topics.[9] But there is nothing like the exposure and awareness of the Intelligence Community in the United States where the current

---

[3] Jens Gieseke, *Deutsche Demokratische Republik, in* HANDBUCH DER KOMMUNISTISCHEN GEHEIMDIENSTE IN OSTEUROPA 1944–1991, 199 (Lukasz Kaminski, Krzystof Persak & Jens Gieseke eds., 2009) ('Die DDR Sataatssicherheit war zuallererst Geheimpolizei.").

[4] The number of "unofficial informants"(IM) was at times as high as 200,000. *See* Helmut Müller-Enbergs, *Die inoffiziellen Mitarbeiter, in* MFS-HANDBUCH 35–38 (2008), *available at* www.nbn-resolving.org/urn:nbn:de:0292-97839421302647.

[5] *See e.g.,* the Prussian criminal code of 1851, § 69, ¶¶ 4, 5. Espionage is listed as an offense that carries death penalty. http://koeblergerhard.de/Fontes/StrafgesetzbuchPreussen1851 .pdf

[6] JOHANNES EHRENGRUBER, GEHEIM-UND NACHRICHTENDIENSTE DES DEUTSCHEN KAISERREICHS VOR AUSBRUCH DES ERSTEN WELTKRIEGS (2014).

[7] *But see* Chapter 24 in this volume. In fact, Heins' claim is that Germany's popular culture celebrates spies whose humanity outshines their sinister function or activities. In this sense spies and informants are portrayed positively for *not* doing their jobs, rather than for being good at their work as spies.

[8] Bruno Kahl took office as BND President in 2016.

[9] In March 2014 the German Parliamentary Committee investigating the spying scandal started its work, a media research network between Süddeutsche Zeitung, NDR and WDR (radio and TV stations) has formed to cover intelligence activities investigatively, and the Bundestag reformed the BND Act in October 2016.

Director of National Intelligence (DNI) regularly appears on the news. Usually, the knowledge in Germany about the CIA, whether accurate or not, greatly exceeds that about the BND.

Instead of looking into the underlying causes for German suspicions toward intelligence gathering, or offering a comparative perspective, I want to consider why it looks so different on the other side of the Atlantic, paying particular attention to the role popular culture plays. The Intelligence Community has a much more favorable image in English speaking countries (and Russia, as well) than in Germany.[10] One explanation for this is the generally positive, romantic depiction British or American agencies are given in popular culture. In this chapter I will examine this phenomenon in the United States with a study of some of prominent cultural portrayals of the Intelligence Community. I will proceed in three steps.

First, I will elaborate the historical backgrounds that inform modern myths about secret intelligence institutions that traditionally and frequently merge fact and fiction. Up until the middle of the Cold War period, the American experience yielded a favorable Western image of intelligence with heroes and often unchallenged narratives. Myth-making appeared rather ambivalent, but yet included an "end justifies the means" kind of thinking. The two significant turning points have shifted that traditional, romantic narrative in the United States. The first was the revelations of the Congressional Church and Pike Committees, which conducted searing investigations of American intelligence activities in the shadow of the Watergate scandal and exposés published by the press. The second was the 9/11 attacks, which raised painful questions about the shortcomings and effectiveness of intelligence work. Therefore, I will explore how the discourse in popular culture about intelligence reflected shifting social and political attitudes as well as expectations toward the "business." Despite these traumas, the genre still resorts to romantic, heroic narratives, possibly to capitalize on nostalgia for a lost sense of certainty that seemed to shape the Cold War. But the genre has increasingly produced critical undertones. The film *Three Days of the Condor* (1975) is a leading example of this development. This critical turn may have reached its peak with the genre's embrace of the digital age and the

---

[10] The reasons for a greater appreciation of intelligence in Russia are manifold, and I cannot go into the details here. A main difference lies in the political system, and the unique opportunity of intelligence jobs within that.

unique threats it implicates. This is exemplified by the film *Enemy of the State* (1998).

Second, I will propose that the basic trust that the public grants intelligence services in the United States derives from a strong belief in purifying self-regulation. While the above-mentioned films fathom worst-case scenarios of political abuse and misappropriation of intelligence methods, they also offer a way out and the possibility of deliverance. What is particularly and exaggeratedly reflected in such cultural works are cathartic moments and turns offering a remedy for rotten systems.

Third, I will consider how cultural representations vary and are able to shape people's opinion, how they create an artificial, but nevertheless powerful space that is exploited to openly discuss otherwise clandestine practices. Governments and politicians as well as the media and the public have been equally susceptible to this mythology. It is futile to argue about causality here, but it is important to critically assess the impact of ideas, fiction, and sensationalism on the Intelligence Community – and the impact the Intelligence Community has had on culture.

B   The Intelligence Evolution

Intelligence activities are by no means a modern phenomenon.[11] After all, they are often characterized as the second oldest profession.[12] Still, the public's perception of and broad interest in espionage has increased considerably since the end of the nineteenth century. This interest reached a climax during the Cold War. The reasons for that development are complex and multilayered. First, the process of democratization affected the arcane sphere of politics.[13] Secret diplomacy based on individual and personal trust had to be translated into increasingly professionalized institutions. Confidential correspondence, information-gathering, and propaganda activities were increasingly carried out by special bureaus or departments within governments. For example, since the eighteenth century, Austria and France have had institutions such as

---

[11] *See* WOLFGANG KRIEGER, GESCHICHTE DER GEHEIMDIENSTE, VON DEN PHARAONEN BIS ZUR CIA 20–66 (2009).

[12] Support for this claim is often drawn from the Bible. *See* Joshua, Ch. 2, vs. 1. *See also* Paul Reynolds, *The world's Second Oldest Profession*, BBC (Feb. 26, 2004, 05:01 PM), http://news.bbc.co.uk/2/hi/americas/3490120.stm.

[13] *See* EVA HORN, DER GEHEIME KRIEG: VERRAT, SPIONAGE UND MODERNE FIKTION 112 (2007) ("Die Verdrängung der Arkana in der Moderne").

the *Geheime Ziffernkanzlei* or the *Cabinet Noir*, both of which were engaged in elaborate postal espionage.[14] At the same time, the media landscape changed dramatically. News could easily spread via newspapers, and politics became an increasingly public and popular phenomenon. These same processes opened up new channels of information for the intelligence services to exploit. The notorious Dreyfus affair, which started in 1894, is the classic example of public interest in nepotism and secrecy.[15] Furthermore, the strategic value of information became more and more obvious, at least since the Napoleonic Wars. Bonaparte supposedly said: "One spy in the right place is worth 20,000 men in the field."[16] The so-called "Great Game,"[17] the conflict between Great Britain and Russia for dominance in Central Asia (Hindukush), is commonly regarded as the first major use of institutionalized espionage activities.[18] In keeping with my thesis, this conflict came to be represented through a literary work and, therefore, it became a public preoccupation. Rudyard Kipling's novel *Kim* tells the story of a road trip during which the protagonists collect information for the British intelligence services.[19]

With World War I the professionalization of intelligence gathering continued. The German *Kaiserreich* upgraded the section IIIb in the General Staff and enhanced its competences, both financially and concerning personnel.[20] At the same time, Great Britain, Russia, and others

---

[14] *See* KLAUS BEYRER, DIE SCHWARZEN KABINETTE DER POST (2007). *See, e.g.,* ZENSUR IM JAHRHUNDERT DER AUFKLÄRUNG: GESCHICHTE, THEORIE, PRAXIS 45–59 (Wilhelm Haefs, York-Gothard Mix eds., 2007).

[15] *See, e.g.,* John Ehrman, *The Dreyfus Affair: Enduring CI Lessons,* 55 STUD. IN INTELLIGENCE no. 1, 21–30 (2011).

[16] This quote has only been attributed to Napoleon. *See, e.g.,* THE LITERARY SPY: THE ULTIMATE SOURCE FOR QUOTATIONS ON ESPIONAGE & INTELLIGENCE 135 (Charles E. Lathrop ed., 2004).

[17] FREDERICK P. HITZ, THE GREAT GAME: THE MYTH AND REALITY OF ESPIONAGE 6 (2004).

[18] JOHNSON, ROBERT, SPYING FOR EMPIRE: THE GREAT GAME IN CENTRAL AND SOUTH ASIA, 1757–1947 (2006). Hayden Peake stated in 51 STUD. INTELL., no. 2 (2007), that the author demonstrates that "by the end of the 19th century, British military intelligence in India had become a professional service that did more than monitor the northern frontier. It also maintained India's domestic security through collaboration with the local Indian police."

[19] RUDYARD KIPLING, KIM (1901).

[20] For further information on German military intelligence, *see* Stefan Weiß, Wilhelm Stieber, August Schluga von Rastenfeld & Otto von Bismarck, *Zu den Anfängen des deutschen Geheimdienstes, in* 31 FORSCHUNGEN ZUR WESTEUROPÄISCHEN GESCHICHTE DHI PARIS 87–112 (Francia ed., 2004); JÜRGEN W. SCHMIDT, GEGEN RUSSLAND & FRANKREICH, DER DEUTSCHE MILITÄRISCHE GEHEIMDIENST 1890–1914 (2006). However, this armament was enforced despite the poor reputation of espionage.

intensified their intelligence activities.[21] This reflected Europe's newly emerging security architecture, which no longer was based on the agreements of the Congress of Vienna but on competing and often unstable alliances.[22] Those alliances posed threats to nonallied states and states sought to meet this menace with a massive intelligence build-up.[23] It was not long until spectacular cases of double agents, such as the one involving Austrian Colonel Alfred Redl (who sold military secrets to the Russians on the eve of World War I) triggered a new kind of espionage hysteria and sensationalism.[24]

From the beginning, the intelligence build-up of the early twentieth century provided compelling material for popular culture, sometimes following extensive media coverage of actual events or based on investigations. Robert Erskine Childers' bestseller *The Riddle of the Sands* (1903) is widely accepted as the novel that founded the genre, which is seen as distinct from detective fiction.[25] Remarkably, the first edition in German was only released in 1975.[26] Other works from that period include John Buchan's *The Thirty-Nine Steps* (1915),[27] and stories by Somerset Maugham.[28] British authors dominated the genre in the Western hemisphere[29] and common topics included the threat of a Russian invasion and the conflict between an allegedly civilized Western world and the barbaric East.[30] The literature of the time overtly advanced

---

[21] Michael Warner, *Building a Theory of Intelligence Systems, in* NATIONAL INTELLIGENCE SYSTEMS: CURRENT RESEARCH AND FUTURE PROJECTS 11–38 (Gregory F. Treverton & Wilhelm Agrell eds., 2009).

[22] BRETT F. WOODS, NEUTRAL GROUND: A POLITICAL HISTORY OF SPY FICTION 27 (2008).

[23] For examples of the intelligence built up around 1914, *see* WOLFGANG KRIEGER, GESCHICHTE DER GEHEIMDIENSTE. VON DEN PHARAONEN BIS ZUR CIA 156-169.

[24] By way of example, reference is made to the infamous case of Austrian colonel Alfred Redl: Albert Pethö, *Der Fall Redl, in* GEHEIMDIENSTE IN DER WELTGESCHICHTE: SPIONAGE UND VERDECKTE AKTIONEN VON DER ANTIKE BIS ZUR GEGENWART (Wolfgang Krieger ed., 2003).

[25] WOODS, *supra* note 22, at 28 (2008); ROBERT ERSKINE CHILDERS, THE RIDDLE OF THE SANDS (1903).

[26] ERSKINE CHILDERS, THE RIDDLE OF THE SANDS (Diogenes Verlag 1975) (1903).

[27] JOHN BUCHAN, THE THIRTY-NINE STEPS (1915).

[28] W. SOMERSET MAUGHAM, ASHENDEN: OR THE BRITISH AGENT (1928).

[29] Regarding the distinction from detective fiction and the British dominance, *see* LUC BOLTANSKI, MYSTERIES AND CONSPIRACIES 121–28 (2014).

[30] John Buchan, author of The Thirty-Nine Steps and other novels also worked extensively for British propaganda (Wellington House). For further reading see Rebecca Bordon, *John Buchan and the Emerging Post-Modern Fact: Information Culture and the First World War, in* JOHN BUCHAN AND THE IDEA OF MODERNITY 97–110 (Kate Macdonald & Nathan Waddell eds., 2013). The Western enemy image during the Cold War also

political propaganda; popular fiction was an easy way to disseminate ideologies, images of the enemies, and agendas.[31] In Germany spy fiction was met with less enthusiasm. Translations of the British stories were published and sold, but the lack of German protagonists with a positive connotation might have been one reason for the lukewarm interest.[32] During the World War II, when intelligence agencies were established globally and enjoyed celebrated successes (such as the Allies' success in breaking Germany's ENIGMA code), the literary field also expanded to the United States and France.[33] Nonetheless, British writer Eric Ambler remained the bestselling spy-fiction author of the period.[34]

Two phenomena interacted after WWII to initiate a cultural era – at least for Germans, the British, and Americans – that has now come to almost definitively shape the image of the Intelligence Community: the start of the Cold War and the emergence of television as a major force in entertainment. The imminent threat coming from the Soviet Union, scarce knowledge of the actual situation, and the feeling of being jostled about by developments in world politics nurtured both anxiety and curiosity.[35] The assessment of intelligence work shifted from prosaic analysis to speculation, rumor, or conspiracy theories. In the United States, the CIA was founded as the first permanent service to act in peacetime.[36] A growing fear of a third – possibly nuclear – world war fueled political action that sought to gain an information-advantage no

referred toward the East, it had only expanded to Communism and Soviet citizens. Beginning in the 1980s and definitely since the 9/11 attacks Islamist terror replaced Communism as the greatest threat factor. This is also reflected in pop culture (*Syriana* 2005, *Homeland* 2011, *Zero Dark Thirty* 2012, *A Most Wanted Man* 2014).

[31] On literature's deployment for the purpose of propaganda, *see, e.g.*, A. P. FOULKES, LITERATURE AND PROPAGANDA 71–82 (1983).

[32] For the first comprehensive approach to research "cultures of intelligence," *see Kulturen der Intelligence: Ein Forschungsprojekt zur Geschichte der militärischen Nachrichtendienste in Deutschland, Großbritannien und den U.S.A., 1900-1947*, GERDA HENKEL STIFTUNG, www.gerda-henkel-stiftung.de/?page_id=80594 This project includes a study on German intelligence literature (last visited Dec. 4, 2015).

[33] WOODS, *supra* note 22, at 9–10 (2008).

[34] ERIC AMBLER, EPITAPH FOR A SPY (1938); ERIC AMBLER, EPITAPH FOR A SPY (1991); ERIC AMBLER, THE MASK OF DIMITRIOS (1939). *See also* IAN FLEMING, CASINO ROYALE (1953).

[35] *See, e.g.*, JOHN LEWIS GADDIS, DER KALTE KRIEG. EINE NEUE GESCHICHTE 63–64 (2008).

[36] The CIA stands here as the most prominent example; almost ever since its foundation in 1947 it has been a synonym for a huge, modern foreign intelligence service. *See* Phyllis Provost McNeil & Aspin-Brown Commission, *The Evolution of the U.S. Intelligence Community - An Historical Overview, in* STRATEGIC INTELLIGENCE: WINDOWS INTO A SECRET WORLD: AN ANTHOLOGY 9–12 (Loch K. Johnson & James J. Wirtz eds., 2004).

matter what that required.[37] This was true on both sides of the Iron
Curtain. And citizens' fantasies thrived accordingly. The ultimate and
universal imminence of mutually assured destruction served as justification for military armament and intelligence expansion alike. Only the
former was openly debated.[38] Because of the arcane process of intelligence evolution, public opinion seemed sometimes unsympathetic and
included suspicions of total control, on one hand, and intelligence
incompetence, on the other hand.[39]

C Merging Fact and Fiction

The debate right after the World War II was particularly fueled by
fictional treatments of intelligence abuses – such as George Orwell's
dystopian novel *Nineteen Eighty-Four* (1949).[40] Ever since, the cultural
portrayal of intelligence services has been contradictory, all the more so
after several "real" intelligence failures.[41] Many people on both sides of
the Atlantic tend to perceive them as omnipotent surveillance institutions with legally and morally questionable methods.[42] Others deem their
work to be irrelevant and overestimated.[43] Still others prefer an image of
excitement, patriotism, and masculinity.[44] The contradictory clichés are
blended with fragments stemming from several cultural sources, including ambiguous fictional heroes such as James Bond, Carrie Mathison, or
George Smiley. These characters offer a treatment of the eternal antagon-
ism between good and evil. "Real" persons – such as the convicted spies

---

[37] *See, e.g.,* ROBERT HIGGS, DEPRESSION, WAR, AND COLD WAR: STUDIES IN POLITICAL
ECONOMY (2006). In connection to nuclear threats he cites Senator Patrick Moynihan
"knowledge is power, and the ability to define what others take to be knowledge is the
greatest power." *Id.* at 140.

[38] GADDIS, *supra* note 35, at 56.

[39] On the notion of control and accountability, *see* Hans Born & Thorsten Wetzling,
Intelligence Accountability: Challenges for Parliaments and Intelligence Services, in HAND-
BOOK OF INTELLIGENCE STUDIES 315–28 (Loch Johnson ed., 2009).

[40] GEORGE ORWELL, NINETEEN EIGHTY-FOUR (1949). The novel that condemns surveillance and totalitarian regimes was influenced by Orwell's rejection of Stalinism had a
cultural impact on various fields, including language ("Big Brother"). Sales figures
increased heavily after the Snowden affair, highlighting the topicality. Dominique
Mosbergen, *George Orwell's "1984" Book Sales Skyrocket In Wake Of NSA Surveillance
Scandal,* HUFFINGTON POST (June 11, 2013, 05:25 PM), www.huffingtonpost.com/2013/
06/11/orwell-1984-sales_n_3423185.html.

[41] Recognized failures include the Iranian coup d'état in 1953, the Guatemalan coup d'état
in 1954, and the Bay of Pigs invasion in 1961.

[42] Horn, *supra* note 2, at 2.   [43] *Id.*   [44] WOODS, *supra* note 22, at 11.

Kim Philby and Jonathan Pollard – seem to play only a minor role in our broader perception, unless they confirm preexisting prejudices. Apart from that, stereotypes about the spy's outward appearance – fedoras, trench coats, or extreme inconspicuousness – are invoked with both pleasure and popular success. The hybrid nature of intelligence services, the fact that they provide a projection screen for deep-rooted fears as well as for hope for security and heroism, predestines them for myth-making. Precisely because knowledge about governments' clandestine activities is necessarily scarce, the public has embraced a classic modern myth about these services that very neatly fits Roland Barthes' definition of a "myth" as a firmly established belief that it is "a system of communication, that it is a message. This allows one to perceive that a myth cannot possibly be an object, a concept, or an idea; it is a mode of signification, a form."[45] In this way, verifiability of events – be it a scandal or an intelligence success – becomes less important. People's attitude and expectation to some extent develop independently from official (political, rational) portrayals.

Beginning in the 1970s the activities of America's secret services, mostly the CIA, came under increasing scrutiny for torture, *coups d'états*, and assassinations, in the United States and elsewhere.[46] Until then, agents were generally held in high esteem as smart, brave, and patriotic.[47] The work they were doing was assumed to be serving the common good. The world of intelligence was associated with excitement, danger, and the struggle for freedom. Here, the thin line between fact and fiction becomes remarkably blurry. Particularly when former intelligence professionals became writers – John le Carré and Graham Greene are just two prominent examples – and cast light on the obscure sphere of the Intelligence Community.[48] These writers' success, and the sometimes unflattering picture they painted of the Intelligence Community, benefited immensely from their status as insiders. This is true even if their work admittedly

---

[45] ROLAND BARTHES, MYTHOLOGIES 109 (Annette Lavers trans., 1973).

[46] *See, e.g.*, RHODRI JEFFREYS-JONES, THE CIA AND AMERICAN DEMOCRACY (1989); JOHN PRADOS, SAFE FOR DEMOCRACY: THE SECRET WARS OF THE CIA (2009).

[47] Gaddis, Krieg, *supra* note 35, at 220; Gaddis states that the CIA "survived" the many crises (U-2, Bay of Pigs, beginning of the Vietnam War) up until the Watergate affair. The German posture mentioned above contrasts with that in Great Britain and the United States where there was a greater appreciation for spycraft, at least until the Vietnam War.

[48] JOHN LE CARRÉ, THE SPY WHO CAME IN FROM THE COLD (1963); JOHN LE CARRÉ, A PERFECT SPY (1986); JOHN LE CARRÉ, A MOST WANTED MAN (2008); GRAHAM GREENE, OUR MAN IN HAVANNA (1958).

had little or nothing to do with reality. John le Carré, for example, clarified that his novel *The Spy Who Came in from the Cold* was nothing but fiction. He explained:

> As it was, they [the agency for whom he had worked][49] seem to have concluded, rightly if reluctantly, that the book was sheer fiction from start to finish, uninformed by personal experience, and that accordingly it constituted no breach of security. This was not, however, the view taken by the world's press, which with one voice decided that the book was not merely authentic but some kind of revelatory Message From The Other Side, leaving me with nothing to do but sit tight and watch, in a kind of frozen awe, as it climbed the bestseller list and stuck there, while pundit after pundit heralded it as the real thing. [...] I was the British spy who had come out of the woodwork and told it how it really was, and anything I said to the contrary only enforced the myth.[50]

Scholars of conspiracy theories, such as the American sociologist Shibutani, have pointed out that a knowledge vacuum generated by unavailable information and intransparency often is offset with imagined action and possibilities – with rumors, speculation, and plausibility.[51] The flimsy base of information concerning states' intelligence activities, which is most thoroughly covered when it has failed,[52] is an instance of this. The Bay of Pigs invasion in Cuba is an example. So is the East German government's surprising erection of the Berlin Wall. The Iran-Contra affair fits this model. More recently – and tragically – so do the September 11 attacks. Events that involve (or seem to involve) questionable intelligence participation lead to a vague alertness to the possible power and omniscience of the intelligence services.

The only upside of this pessimistic *Weltanschauung* are apparently the juicy, lurid tales, and factoidal buzz that keep people entertained. As the quest for sufficient answers to endless questions is often quixotic in the face of national security considerations, this discussion becomes self-perpetuating. As a result, intelligence agencies in general are widely seen as mysterious and potentially evil institutions, possessing seemingly

---

[49] Here, he refers to MI6, the foreign intelligence branch of the British service, though he had also been working for MI5, the domestic intelligence bureau.

[50] John le Carré, *John le Carré: "I Was a Secret Even to Myself,"* THE GUARDIAN (Apr. 12, 2013), www.theguardian.com/books/2013/apr/12/john-le-carre-spy-anniversary.

[51] *See* TAMOTSU SHIBUTANI, IMPROVISED NEWS: A SOCIOLOGICAL STUDY OF RUMOR (1966).

[52] One detailed evaluation on intelligence failure is the 9/11 commission report, see THE 9/11 COMMISSION REPORT 399, www.9-11commission.gov/report/911Report.pdf (last visited Dec. 26, 2015).

infinite financial, political, and moral leverage. Questions pointing to the moral high-ground or judging the legitimacy of intelligence practices become a matter of political conviction, personal concern, and interest. And at this point fiction and creativity meet a need. As John le Carré puts it: "We are living in a world of virtual news. This being considered, it falls within the responsibility of authors and film-makers to fill this gap of information."[53] As a matter of fact, novels and movies (often film adaptations), TV series, comics, video and computer games dealing with spies, intelligence agencies, and espionage are "as marketable as ever."[54] Popular examples include the omnipresent James Bond movies or the contemporary series *Homeland*. Their plots and protagonists are in many cases based on "true" stories or real persons (e.g., supporting the Taliban in the film *Charlie Wilson's War*, or CIA officer Tony Mendez in the Academy Award winning film *Argo*), they reflect contemporary debates and *Zeitgeist* via technological innovations, fashion, or political circumstances. But fiction, spy fiction in particular, might serve another need – at least in the United States, where Americans seem to treat scandals and disclosures with pragmatic equanimity rather than only seeing their worst misgivings affirmed. By fictionalizing intelligence nightmares, dystopias, or potential misuse of power, a critical debate can actually take place.[55] Fears and perceived threats can be expressed, pros and cons can be negotiated as if it was just a game or a part of our entrainment culture.

D   *Three Days of the Condor* and *Enemy of the State*: Waking Up from a Nightmare?

Pop-cultural references illustrating a skeptical or even hostile perception of real-life surveillance by intelligence services are manifold. In the film *Good Will Hunting* (1997) a protagonist goes on a rant on the role of the Intelligence Community in failed U.S. foreign policy during a job interview with the NSA. The scene has become part of collective cultural memory.[56] Even *The Simpsons* almost clairvoyantly referred to the NSA's

---

[53] John le Carré: *"Ich bin zorniger geworden,"* DIE WELT, (Jan. 3, 2003), www.welt.de/print-welt/article188220/Ich-bin-zorniger-geworden.html.

[54] Sam Goodman, *James Bond, Spy Fiction and the Decline of Empire*, THE GUARDIAN (SEPT. 5, 2015, 06:00 AM), www.theguardian.com/books/2015/sep/05/spy-fiction-james-bond-why-spy-fiction-sells.

[55] *See* Chapter 28 in this volume.

[56] This is difficult to confirm, I refer to numerous youtube clips, blog posts, and mentions in online quotation lists.

eavesdropping practices against U.S. citizens in a 2007 cinematic release, years before Edward Snowden's revelations.[57]

Here, I would like to introduce two Hollywood movies that present a peculiar American tension. They both identify and point out the dangers the Intelligence Community poses while also presenting a solution to the problem. Sidney Pollack's film *Three days of the Condor* (1975) and Tony Scott's *Enemy of the State* (1998) very critically depict systematic abuse of power by the CIA and the NSA. In this way they support the "catharsis through fiction" thesis I proposed earlier by showing the Intelligence Community's dark side. But they also illustrate how control and account-ability can be reestablished – often initiated by a single hero who is an outsider or an unlikely agent of change. Viewed through this lens, Snowden is playing a well-established part in an old American narrative.

Joe Turner, a rather harmless CIA analyst (played by Robert Redford), is the protagonist in the film *Three Days of the Condor*. Turner discovers that seven of his co-workers were murdered in their safeguarded NYC office while he was out for lunch. After an attempt to "finish" the job by killing Turner fails (he manages to escape the assassination attempt), he finds out that the agency (or "the company" as they call it here) is behind the murders and that he can no longer trust anyone anymore. With the help of a young woman Turner abducts Higgins, a CIA division chief, and even holds the director of operations at gunpoint to learn about the background of the events and how to save his life. A group within the CIA has hired contract killers to eliminate Turner because one of his reports accidently unveiled a secret plan to take over Middle Eastern oil fields. In the film's climactic show-down a highly-skilled Alsatian con-tract killer surprisingly spares Turner and instead shoots the director of operations because he has been ordered to do so by an even higher level within the CIA. His advice for Turner is to leave the country for he will never be safe in the United States again.

A similarly grim sentiment infuses *Enemy of the State* (1998), which also deploys dystopian images of intelligence agencies that misuse their capabilities to go after their own citizens. This time, however, technology plays a much more important role – represented by a mixture of real and possible means of surveillance and eavesdropping – and a flattering accumulation of powers and competences carried out by the NSA. It is

---

[57] This video clip taken from the movie *The Simpsons* illustrates an Orwellian scenario: bin proker, *the simpsons are the real nsa whisleblowers 360*, YouTube (June 16, 2013), www.youtube.com/watch?v=gtBpmljNaZE.

the story of a manhunt for lawyer Robert Dean who is accidently handed video footage with extremely explosive content: It shows the murder of a congressman. Dean's former college friend, who put the disc in Dean's shopping bag, dies in a car accident as he is chased by NSA agents. For a long time the audience is ahead of Dean's understanding of the matter and drawn into the hectic hunt emphasized by rapid cuts and zooms. The perspective changes frequently, depicting the NSA's effort of running the surveillance machinery (by accessing cameras and satellite images in high resolution) to capture Dean. This is contrasted with Dean's desperate confusion. He soon finds himself in the middle of a smear campaign; he loses his job and reputation, his wife, and eventually his life as he knew it. Via his ex-girlfriend, Dean comes into contact with a secretive lone-wolf named Brill, a former NSA communications expert who left the agency under mysterious circumstances and has remained in the shadows ever since. Brill identifies the murderer as well as the bigger picture behind the murder and the raid: The murdered politician was blocking a bill in Congress that would have severely eroded Americans' privacy rights. Together, Dean and Brill begin to fight back by bugging a promiscuous congressman who was supporting the bill. Their aim is to have the congressman believe that the NSA was behind the surveillance. Brill also manipulates the bank account of a high ranking NSA officer, suggesting he was taking bribes. The two outlaws essentially defeat their overpowering opponent with its own weapons.

Both movies – separated by a generation – present the potential threats posed by America's Intelligence Community. But they also depict ways out of the looming crises. Interestingly, in the case of these two movies, the solution for the problem comes from the margins of society. Joe Turner is a book-loving intellectual whose unconventional style drives his employers crazy. Robert Dean is a black lawyer who gets help from a former NSA operative (portrayed by Gene Hackman) whose behavior is on the border of the socially acceptable. These protagonists are cultural representations of a very basic American model: salvation comes from the lone-wolf outsider who is capable of thinking outside the box.[58] Their

---

[58] The myth of outsiders as an innovative driving force in American history started with the pilgrims who left Britain as religious outcasts to establish a new political community and is has been a part of the American Dream narrative ever since. *See* R. Laurence Moore, *Insiders and Outsiders in American Historical Narrative and American History*, 87 AM. HIST. REV. 390–412 (1982); Sebastian Jobs, *American Dream*, *in* Metzler Lexikon Moderne Mythen 18–21 (Juliane Ebert & Stephanie Wodianka eds., 2014).

vantage point from the margins defies cold-blooded realpolitik and the logic of political inevitability based on security considerations. In these stories morality gets re-infused through the fresh look of outsiders. Other "unlikely" fictional heroes that are able to change a system of structural power abuse in intelligence agencies from within include Carrie Mathison (Claire Danes) from the TV show *Homeland*. Mathison is a bipolar woman working most effectively when off her medication. Another example is Jason Bourne, an amnesic CIA assassin who finds himself at the top of a hit list. Both of these characters struggle with opaque bureaucratic structures within their services that hide the institutions' true motives and safeguard powerful yet inhuman masterminds.

A second remedial source for the abuses of America's Intelligence Community has been the mass media. Investigative journalism has revealed disturbing facts about the Intelligence Community, which often generates more fictionalization and conspiracy theories. The media coverage might reveal actual crimes, illegal covert operations, and political schemes, such as those the CIA conducted during the 1960s and 1970s. One prominent example of this is the work of Seymour Hersh, a journalist for the *New York Times*, who reported the story of the My Lai massacre in 1969 and covered the Watergate scandal (together with Carl Bernstein and Bob Woodward of the Washington Post). Hersh also uncovered the CIA's illegal operation against America's antiwar movement and civil rights activists.[59] This story, among others, led to the U.S. Senate's Church Committee investigation in the mid-1970s.[60] The media, especially newspapers, again played an important role in the more recent NSA-Affair. Glenn Greenwald, writing for *The Guardian*, was among the few journalists responsible for unveiling the Snowden documents in June 2013.[61] These stories set off enormous public outrage and a new debate about the duties and limits of the Intelligence

---

[59] Seymour Hersh, *Huge CIA Operation Reported in U.S. against Antiwar Forces, Other Dissidents During Nixon Years*, N.Y. TIMES (Dec. 22, 1974), http://s3.documentcloud.org/documents/238963/huge-c-i-a-operation-reported-in-u-s-against.pdf.

[60] *See, e.g.*, HARRY ROSITZKE, THE CIA'S SECRET OPERATIONS. ESPIONAGE, COUNTERESPIONAGE, AND COVERT ACTION (1988); JOHN M. DIAMOND, THE CIA AND THE CULTURE OF FAILURE: U.S. INTELLIGENCE FROM THE END OF THE COLD WAR TO THE INVASION OF IRAQ (2008).

[61] Glenn Greenwald published his first article about the Snowden documents. *See* Glenn Greenwald, *NSA Collecting Phone Records of Millions of Verizon Customers Daily*, THE GUARDIAN (June 6, 2013), www.theguardian.com/world/2013/jun/06/nsa-phone-records-verizon-court-order.

Community in the digital age.[62] In Germany, the weekly *Der Spiegel* and the daily newspaper *Süddeutsche Zeitung* are among the most outspoken outlets of critical investigative journalism that are particularly interested in the BND or other intelligence issues.[63] The fact that the BND had spied on inconvenient German journalists during the 1990s added fuel to the fire and sometimes gave the impression of a personal vendetta.[64] The more difficult the process of unraveling and publishing classified stories and documents, the greater the concern is for even more secret scandals and conspirators in politics, the military, and business. This is a fruitful breeding ground for disillusion, conspiracy, and also opposition. And yet, with obedient resignation, many people seem to accept the Intelligence Community's great power and the necessity – or at least inevitability – of surveillance. Some citizens even defiantly declare they have nothing to hide and that they consensually let democratic governments and their agencies collect data. Few seem willing to sing the song of the outraged.

The mass media link also is an element of the film *Three Days of the Condor*. In the last scene Turner again meets up with Higgins, the CIA operative, to tell him he had leaked the whole story to the *New York Times*, in order to protect himself and to bring justice to the conspirators. Higgins, however, doubts that the newspaper will publish stories about the disclosures, suggesting that Turner's efforts have been in vain. Here, the worst dystopian idea of the abuse of power through an intelligence agency that has taken on a life of its own emerges. Neither the rule of law nor rationality can intervene and produce consequences. In the end there is no relief for the virtuous and upright hero; the power of intimidation even silences the press and the public. This is as depressing a treatment of the subject as one can imagine. But the silver lining consists of the mere existence of people like Joe Turner within the corrupted system, "inside the CIA." People who will not fall but bring the evil elements to justice

---

[62] GLENN GREENWALD, NO PLACE TO HIDE (2014).

[63] Matthias Gebauer & Hubert Gude, *Neuer Geheimdienstskandal: Die willigen Helfer vom BND*, SPIEGEL ONLINE (Apr. 23, 2015, 07:32 PM), www.spiegel.de/politik/deutschland/bundesnachrichtendienst-schindler-in-nsa-affaere-a-1030290.html; BND, SPIEGEL ONLINE www.sueddeutsche.de/thema/BND.

[64] Annette Ramelsberger, *BND bespitzelte Journalisten in großem Stil*, SUEDDEUTSCHE.DE (May 11, 2006, 10:40 PM), https://web.archive.org/web/20080428020629/http://www.sueddeutsche.de/deutschland/artikel/694/75619/; Von Hans-Jürgen Jakobs, Intrigen, Gerüchte, Verräter, SZ.DE (May 19, 2010 07:40 PM), www.sueddeutsche.de/politik/bnd-intrigen-geruechte-verraeter-1.884968.

with the help of an incorruptible media and the public. It trades on justice Louis Brandeis' famous quote: "sunlight is said to be the best disinfectant."[65]

A striking punch-line from the film *Three Days of the Condor* lies in Turner's remit: He is mining information about national security from fiction. Therefore, he reads all sorts of print media in order to find hidden messages, ideas, or conspiracy plots. Within a fictitious CIA a plausible intelligence method is introduced that symbiotically interweaves fact and fiction.

E   The Power of Secrecy and Vagueness

There is a kind of interaction between popular culture and the Intelligence Community's reality. We can presume that intelligence professionals know about their industry's public image. It is rare for anyone from the "inside" to comment on this, and when they do, they merely sweep it away or seem to be somewhat allergic to it.[66] Occasionally, however, fiction can have an impact on intelligence reality, even though it is usually the other way round. The CIA's own journal, *Studies in Intelligence*, frequently features a section "Intelligence in Public Literature/ Recent Public Media" where CIA officers review movies, spy fiction, but also historical or other scholarship concerned with intelligence.[67] Michael Hayden took office as the Director of the NSA in 2001, shortly after the release of *Enemy of the State*. During a CNN program recorded at that time and entitled "Inside the NSA: The Secret World of Electronic Spying," Hayden explains: "I made the judgment that we couldn't survive with the popular impression of this agency being formed by the last Will Smith movie." David Ensor, the CNN National Security

---

[65] Louis D. Brandeis, Other People's Money and How the Bankers Use It 92 (1914).

[66] Reinhard Gehlen, Der Dienst 247 (1971).

[67] For A very critical review/roundtable on "The Good Shepard," *see* David Robarge, Gary McCollim, Nicholas Dujmovic & Thomas G. Coffey, *The Good Shepherd: Intelligence in Recent Public Media*, CIA, www.cia.gov/library/center-for-the-study-of-intelligence/csi-publications/csi-studies/studies/vol51no1/the-good-shepherd.html (last visited Dec. 8, 2015); Michael Bradford & James Burridge, *Intelligence in Public Literature: Tinker, Tailor, Soldier, Spy: the movie*, CIA, www.cia.gov/library/center-for-the-study-of-intelli gence/csi-publications/csi-studies/studies/vol.-56-no.-3/tinker-tailor-soldier-spy-the-movie.html (last visited Dec. 8, 2015); Hayden B. Peake, Section *Intelligence in Recent Public Literature: The Intelligence Officer's Bookshelf*, CIA, www.cia.gov/library/center-for-the-study-of-intelligence/csi-publications/csi-studies/studies/vol52no2/intelligence-in-recent-public-literature.html (last visited Dec. 8, 2015).

Correspondent replied, "When General Michael Hayden saw the movie, he saw a problem – an image problem. That is in part why the NSA decided to let CNN inside the NSA to see where code breakers gather, and code makers protect the nation's secrets. Above all, Hayden knows the NSA cannot afford to be seen as trampling on the privacy rights of U.S. citizens."[68] But others have argued that popular depictions of intelligence activities could achieve quite the opposite. John Patterson, a journalist with *The Guardian*, suggests in his article "How Hollywood Softened Us up for NSA Surveillance"[69] that intelligence operatives could exploit the cultural input. Through frequent exposure to espionage in fictional scenarios spectators might become accustomed to the normality of surveillance. Yet, these two lines of argument invite intelligence services to reflect on their own reputation – both good and bad. Sometimes, a shady image can be liberating.

Building and establishing this aura of secrecy can be an instrument to deceive, to create room to maneuver. If the assumed adversary – and that can also be the general public or the government – believes that a secret intelligence service is capable of doing almost anything, even wiping out their own loyal employees, then the "bad guys" but also a critical public or media are obliged to overestimate the Intelligence Community's actual abilities. This will require them to act with awestruck respect and, perhaps, to engage in self-restraint. Thus, the mixture of fact and fiction, of uncertainty, rumors and imminent threat lead to a dubious perception that is not necessarily unfavorable to agents and officers or their employers and clients. It can also be seized upon by intelligence personnel and their political subordinates. There is the clear message that an intelligence agency is capable of solving serious security problems, for example fighting international terrorism, in ways that no other existing institution – including the military – can. Furthermore, it is designed to fulfill this task by means about which many people would prefer to remain ignorant.[70] Taking the burden of knowing – and not bedeviling citizens – is often regarded as a noble and necessary aspect of day-to-day

---

[68] For the transcript of the show, *see Inside the NSA: The Secret World of Electronic Spying*, CNN (Mar. 25, 2001), http://edition.cnn.com/TRANSCRIPTS/0103/25/sm.16.html.

[69] John Patterson, *How Hollywood Softened Us up for NSA Surveillance*, THE GUARDIAN (June 16, 2013, 02:00 PM), www.theguardian.com/film/shortcuts/2013/jun/16/hollywood-softened-us-up-nsa-surveillance.

[70] *See* Chapter 6 in this volume.

intelligence work. In this way, intelligence agencies are able to create their own arcane sphere of action.

This is a Faustian bargain because the arrangement moves the Intelligence Community ever-farther from lawful oversight and public control. Even the best informed oversight committee members can only ask for aspects and components about which they have been made aware, usually as a result of leaks by intelligence personnel. Listening to official NSA statements in the wake of the Snowden revelations it seems that many employees almost expect more gratefulness and respect, not dismay; they cannot understand the harsh critique coming from Germany in particular, but also from various groups within the United States.[71] One of the greatest talents of the intelligence services seems to lie in building a mysterious Arcanum; a vacuum that is easily and voluntarily filled with plausible answers, explanatory efforts, and positive and negative wishful thinking. It functions like a *perpetuum mobile*: The less responsive and transparent the agencies are, the more curiosity they stir, as well as fear and attributions of power. This can be and is reflected in the way popular culture depicts intelligence services.

In other words, real-life intelligence spills into fiction through insider knowledge, imagination, speculation, and open source information. At the same time, some invented or artistic discourses and images do not exclusively remain within their fictional framework, where they deal with authentic fears and problems. Fiction also influences real-life intelligence behavior, encourages a certain self-fashioning of intelligence personnel and creates a productive co-dependency between fact and fiction.

When we look back on the state of affairs, at the factors that got the ball rolling and that fortunately increased public interest in intelligence matters, it is clear that the NSA-Affair has an historical genealogy. But that is not the whole story.[72] Underlying our different interpretations of the past there is a fundamental rift that divides the German and the American publics on the issues of privacy and intelligence gathering. Great parts of the U.S. population seem to have accepted the need for intelligence

---

[71] *See* Chapter 6 in this volume.

[72] Here, the popular proverb is valid: "there are friendly nations but no friendly intelligence services." James M. Olson, *The Ten Commandments of Counterintelligence*, 45 Stud. Intell. 5, 11 (2001), www.cia.gov/library/center-for-the-study-of-intelligence/kent-csi/vol45no5/html/v45i5a08p.htm (last visited Dec. 8, 2015). For the history of the West-German postwar intelligence built up, that was substantially supported by U.S. authorities, *see* Forging and Intelligence Partnership: CIA and the Origins of the BND, 1945–49 (Kevin C. Ruffner ed., 1999).

services as part of their political and private sphere. The majority of Americans seems to take a critical, yet constructive, approach to the Intelligence Community. This pragmatic – perhaps even balanced approach – is fostered by fiction and popular culture. On the one hand, abuses and Orwellian scenarios are "exposed" and "debated." On the other hand, the rule of law and democratic integrity can be seen to prevail. As long as this approach neither becomes uncritical nor becomes entangled in the twilight zone between fact and fiction, it should be taken seriously as in any effort to understand Americans' response to the NSA-Affair.

28

CITIZENME

What Laura Poitras Got Wrong About the NSA-Affair

BY RUSSELL A. MILLER AND STEPHEN CHOVANEC

A   Introduction

Throughout her award-winning documentary film *CITIZENFOUR* Laura Poitras resorts to the image of a car traveling through a darkened tunnel toward the light.[1] The tunnel is clearly meant to represent the world's trajectory over the last several years: first groping in unknowing and unseeing darkness and then bursting into the light shed on the NSA's activities by Edward Snowden.[2] The image also suggests a reasonable standard by which documentary films might be judged: does the movie cast useful light on its subject, leaving us better informed about (if not also inspired to respond to) the issues it addresses.[3]

Despite its success, Poitras' film does not live up to this standard. The film released to critical and popular acclaim,[4] winning many awards,

---

[1] *CITIZENFOUR*, RADiUS-TWC, 2014.

[2] *See* Spencer Ackerman, *CITIZENFOUR Review – Poitras' Victorious Film Shows Snowden Vindicated*, THE GUARDIAN (Oct. 11, 2014), *available at* www.theguardian.com/film/2014/ oct/11/citizenfour-review-snowden-vindicated-poitras-nsa-journalism. For the meaning of this image we are also indebted to our insightful conversations with Dr. Martin Holtz at the Institut für Anglistik/Amerikanistik at the University of Greifswald.

[3] The genre-defining film *Nanook of the North* (1922) is praised for exactly this achievement: it provided a great deal of valuable insight into the traditional modes of living of Nanook and his people." *See* ERIK BARNOUW, DOCUMENTARY 33–45 (2d. Revised ed., 1993).

[4] *See* Godfrey Cheshire, *CITIZENFOUR*, RogerEbert.com (Oct. 24, 2014), www.rogerebert.com/reviews/citizenfour-2014 (scoring the film four out of four stars and calling it "the movie of the century (to date)."); Peter Bradshaw, *CITIZENFOUR Review – Gripping Snowden Documentary Offers Portrait of Power, Paranoia and One Remarkable Man*, THE GUARDIAN (Oct. 16, 2014, 10:00 AM), www.theguardian.com/film/ 2014/oct/16/citizen-four-review-edward-snowden-documentary (a five star review calling the movie "a gripping record of how our rulers are addicted to gaining more and more

including the Emmy for "Exceptional Merit in Documentary Filmmaking," the BAFTA Award for "Best Documentary," the American Cinema Editors' Eddie-Award for "Best Edited Documentary – Feature," and the Academy Award for "Best Documentary – Feature."[5] Spencer Ackerman's gushing review for *The Guardian* credited the film for "accessibly explaining how surveillance works, and why it matters," a task he said "only gets more challenging the deeper you dig into the NSA trove."[6] Whatever the film's merits may be, this is not its great achievement. Watching the documentary gives the viewer a front-row seat to the week's events surrounding Snowden's initial leaks, his emergence from the shadows to take responsibility for and explain his actions, and his flight to asylum in Russia. This is gripping and dramatic stuff (even if not at all new to most viewers who, by the time of the film's release, could have followed the same events in the mainstream media). Poitras captures it all with her open and uncritical lens. But the film does not do the hard work of explaining what the NSA is, how its intelligence gathering and data collection systems work, what framework exists to ensure accountability for and the legality of its operations, why the NSA's operations are viewed by Poitras (as well as Snowden and the film's other protagonists) as such a grave threat to freedom, and how each of us is complicit in the technological-telecommunications complex that makes the entire surveillance regime possible. No expert on these issues appears in an independent capacity in the film to address these central concerns. Instead, film of their testimony, interviews, and speeches on these subjects in other venues is chopped down to just the most conspiratorial chunks. Americans know very little about the NSA and the context and contours of its

---

power and control over us."); Peter Travers, *CITIZENFOUR*, RollingStone (Oct. 24, 2014), www.rollingstone.com/movies/reviews/citizenfour-20141024 (a 3 1/2 out of 4 star review); Ann Hornaday, *"CITIZENFOUR" Movie Review: Laura Poitras Reintroduces Edward Snowden*, Wash. Post (Oct. 23, 2014), www.washingtonpost.com/goingout guide/movies/citizenfour-movie-review-laura-poitras-reintroduces-edward-snowden/2014/ 10/23/e6915dc8-59ea-11e4-8264-deed989ae9a2_story.html?tid=kp_google (3 1/2 out of 4 stars). See also *See CITIZENFOUR*, metacritic, www.metacritic.com/movie/citizenfour (last visited Dec. xx, 2015) (giving the film a critical aggregated approval score of 88 percent and a user-voted score of 7.7); *CITIZENFOUR*, Rotten Tomatoes, www .rottentomatoes.com/m/citizenfour/ (last visited Dec. xx, 2015) (giving an aggregate score of "98 percent fresh" from critics and an audience approval score of 87 percent).

[5] *CITIZENFOUR: Awards*, IMDb, www.imdb.com/title/tt4044364/awards?ref_=tt_awd (last visited Dec. xx, 2015).

[6] Ackerman, *supra* note 2.

operations.[7] Poitras' film leaves viewers stalled in her dark tunnel on the complex issues of technology and law that are implicated by the NSA-Affair.

If it does not set out to grapple with the issues, then what are the film's aims? At its best, it very effectively stokes the emotions and conveys the anxieties that are part of a distinct (but not necessarily widespread) view of privacy and intelligence gathering.[8]

In this effort, however, the film makes two profound mistakes. First, *CITIZENFOUR* is so preoccupied with the members of the coterie assembled by Snowden – including the journalist Glenn Greenwald and the film's director Poitras – that it largely ends up serving as a platform for their aggrandizement. This is true for Snowden, even as he insists that he wants his actions (and media coverage about them) to draw attention to the issues and not to him as a personality. But why, then, invite a documentary filmmaker to record your apotheosis? This is true for Greenwald, who is (and clearly wants to be) portrayed as part of the story and not just as a journalist reporting and commenting on the issues of privacy and intelligence gathering. And it is true for Poitras, who makes herself (and her career) a part of the narrative despite her seeming absence from the film. It is no longer a surprise that a documentary filmmaker would place himself or herself at the center of the film. We have a few documentarians, perhaps most notably Michael Moore, to thank for this sad trend in the genre.[9] But it is troublingly ironic that Snowden, Greenwald, and Poitras would submit themselves to such personally revealing documentary "surveillance" as the means for criticizing the NSA's personally revealing surveillance. Second, it is hard to understand why a film that expresses such deep unease about the NSA's opacity would itself resort to opaque, unarticulated threats to justify its agenda. But this is exactly what the film does. Instead of hard proof of the

---

[7] *See, e.g.*, Patrick Toomey & Brett Max Kaufman, *How did we let the NSA spying get this bad?*, THE GUARDIAN (Nov. 20, 2013, 1:31 PM), www.theguardian.com/commentisfree/2013/nov/20/how-nsa-spying-got-this-bad-fisa-secret-court.

[8] *See* Kenneth Turan, *Message from Documentary "CITIZENFOUR": Be Afraid (Of Surveillance)*, NPR (Oct. 24, 2014, 4:43 AM), www.npr.org/2014/10/24/358471536/message-from-documentary-citizenfour-be-afraid-of-surveillance.

[9] JEFFREY GEIGER, AMERICAN DOCUMENTARY FILM: PROJECTING THE NATION 195 (2011) ("McElwee, Moore, Nick Broomfield and others were stressing the 'I' of the presenter/director: the 'filmmaker-as-star syndrome.'). *See also* Cowie, *infra* note 62, at 584 (commenting on the "personal direct-filming approach of Michael Moore and Nick Broomfield ... becoming the subject of, as well as investigator in the film.").

NSA's invidiousness, Poitras gives us only innuendo and suggestions: phones ring ominously; unrevealed notes are scribbled and raise eyebrows. Naturally, government surveillance and intelligence gathering is an elusive target. Still, the problem with Poitras' conspiratorial approach is that opacity and vague threats are precisely the tactics the Intelligence Community uses to justify its agenda. "Trust us," the sentiments runs. "If only you knew what we knew, then you wouldn't object to surveillance."[10] It is fair to expect Poitras to do better than this. While holding transparency out as the standard against which the NSA should be judged, she nevertheless adopts the government's scaremongering approach. Trust her, she seems to be saying. If only we knew what she knows. Perhaps this approach is necessary because, as a matter of the facts, the film simply cannot show that the Intelligence Community is wreaking irrevocable harm on our freedoms. To the contrary, the film demonstrates – and is itself significant evidence of – the absence of the ominous chilling effect about which Snowden, Greenwald, and Poitras are so concerned.[11] Rather than documenting the ways in which government surveillance has eroded our democratic culture, the film contains scenes of quite a lot of civil society engagement, including citizens, citizen groups, and political institutions advocating against government surveillance. Of course, the film's success is the most damning evidence of the very rich possibilities for democratic discourse and civic action that exist, even in the shadow of the NSA-Affair.

We develop these critiques of the film *CITIZENFOUR* in this chapter.

B Synopsis of *CITIZENFOUR*

The film opens with a simple card stating that in 2006 Poitras "was placed on a secret watch list after making a film about the Iraq War. In

---

[10] *See* Kevin Johnson, *NSA Director Defends Surveillance Programs as Necessary*, USA Today (Dec. 11, 2013, 5:17 PM), www.usatoday.com/story/news/nation/2013/12/11/alexander-nsa-surveillance-snowden/3989233/; Rory Carroll, *NSA Surveillance Needed to Prevent ISIS Attack, Claims Former Intelligence Chair*, The Guardian (Apr. 22, 2015, 8:52 AM), www.theguardian.com/us-news/2015/apr/22/mass-surveillance-needed-isis-attack-mike-rogers; Charlie Savage, *N.S.A. Chief Says Surveillance Has Stopped Dozens of Plots*, N.Y. Times (June 18, 2013), www.nytimes.com/2013/06/19/us/politics/nsa-chief-says-surveillance-has-stopped-dozens-of-plots.html?_r=0. *See also* Sandy Fitzgerald, John McCain: NSA Phone Surveillance Program Is Necessary, Newsmax (May 7, 2015, 12:35 PM), www.newsmax.com/Newsfront/John-McCain-NSA-surveillance-ISIS/2015/05/07/id/643210/.

[11] *See, e.g.* Glenn Greenwald, No Place to Hide (2014).

the following years [she] was detained and interrogated at the U.S. border dozens of times."[12] Poitras then sets the stage for the film by reading (off-screen) the email correspondence between her and a mysterious source calling himself or herself *CITIZENFOUR*.[13] The source is Snowden and he tells Poitras that she "chose herself" to tell his story, presumably because of her previous documentary films, which were critical of the U.S. occupation of Iraq.[14]

The film documents Snowden's early, aborted attempts to communicate with journalist Glenn Greenwald, a reporter at that time for *The Guardian*. Greenwald is the other person Snowden chose to disseminate the stolen NSA materials and to tell his story.[15] Greenwald himself recounts this in more detail in *No Place to Hide*, the book he wrote detailing these events from his perspective.[16] According to Greenwald, Snowden first contacted him via email in an effort to establish a secure form of communication.[17] Snowden, calling himself "Cincinnatus," urged Greenwald to secure his email via encryption to enable secure communication.[18] Greenwald ignored him and after a couple of follow-up efforts Snowden turned his attention to Poitras.[19] Poitras convinced Greenwald of the magnitude of the information Snowden was offering them and she brought Greenwald back into story.[20]

Poitras then introduces William Binney in a vignette. Binney is a former NSA cryptologist and mass-data analyst.[21] Brief commentary

---

[12] *CITIZENFOUR, supra* note 1. Poitras made two films prior to *CITIZENFOUR*, both dealing critically with the post-9/11 "war on terror." *See* My Country, My Country (Zeitgeist Films 2006); and The Oath (Zeitgeist Films 2010). *See also* Glenn Greenwald, *U.S. Filmmaker Repeatedly Detained at Border*, SALON (Apr. 8, 2012, 6:37 AM), www.salon.com/2012/04/08/u_s_filmmaker_repeatedly_detained_at_border/ ("But Poitras' work has been hampered, and continues to be hampered, by the constant harassment, invasive searches, and intimidation tactics to which she is routinely subjected whenever she reenters her own country. Since the 2006 release of "*My Country, My Country*," Poitras has left and reentered the United States roughly forty times. Virtually every time during that six-year period that she has returned to the United States, her plane has been met by DHS agents who stand at the airplane door or tarmac and inspect the passports of every de-planing passenger until they find her (on the handful of occasions where they did not meet her at the plane, agents were called when she arrived at immigration). Each time, they detain her, and then interrogate her at length about where she went and with whom she met or spoke.").

[13] *CITIZENFOUR, supra* note 1.   [14] *Id.*   [15] *Id.*   [16] Greenwald, *supra* note 11.

[17] *Id.*, at 7–10.   [18] *Id.*, at 7–8.   [19] *CITIZENFOUR, supra* note 1.

[20] Greenwald, *supra* note 11, at 12–14.

[21] *CITIZENFOUR, supra* note 1. *See also* Interview by Jim Gilmore with William Binney, 36 year NSA Veteran (Dec. 13, 2013), www.pbs.org/wgbh/pages/frontline/government-elections-politics/united-states-of-secrets/the-frontline-interview-william-binney/.

from Binney appears throughout the film, with him decrying his former employer. In the initial episode, Binney travels to the HOPE (Hackers On Planet Earth) Conference, where he cursorily recounts the initial development of the metadata analysis program.[22] He then mournfully informs the audience that "9/11 happened, and it must have been right after, a few days, no more than a week after 9/11 that they decided to begin actively spying on everyone in this country."[23] During his presentation at the conference Binney reports that he protested the existence of the mass-data collection programs to an aide with the House Intelligence Committee, who took his complaint "up the chain."[24] Binney claims that the government's response was an armed raid on him and three other NSA officers in an effort to "keep us quiet."[25]

The stage is set with a few more vignettes aimed at developing the narrative of an overwhelming police state with eyes everywhere. Poitras presents archival footage of congressional hearings (in which Generals Keith Alexander, then-Director of the National Security Agency, and James Clapper, the Director of National Intelligence, both swear that the NSA is in no way gathering data on or from U.S. citizens).[26] She provides several minutes of footage from legal proceedings (oral arguments in the case *Jewel v. National Security Agency* before the U.S. Court of Appeals for the Ninth Circuit, a case brought about by a technician revealing the NSA wiretaps on AT&T's network).[27] And there is video from a presentation made by Jacob Appelbaum, a notorious hacker, to members of Occupy Wall

---

[22] *CITIZENFOUR, supra* note 1. *See also* HOPE NUMBER 9, www.hopenumbernine.net/ (last visited Feb. 4, 2016) (the official website for the ninth Hackers On Planet Earth conference).

[23] *CITIZENFOUR, supra* note 1.

[24] *See* Jane Mayer, *The Secret Sharer*, NEW YORKER (May 23, 2011), www.newyorker.com/ magazine/2011/05/23/the-secret-sharer (providing detail of Binney's interactions with "Diane Roark, a staff member on the House Permanent Select Committee on Intelligence," which oversaw the NSA. The article also claims that Binney filed a complaint with the Pentagon's Inspector General.).

[25] *CITIZENFOUR, supra* note 1. *See also* David Welna, *Before Snowden: The Whistleblowers Who Tried to Lift the Veil*, NPR (July 22, 2014, 4:44 AM), www.npr.org/2014/07/22/ 333741495/before-snowden-the-whistleblowers-who-tried-to-lift-the-veil.

[26] *Id. See, generally* Savage, *supra* note 10; Kim Zetter, *The NSA Hearing, by the Numbers*, WIRED (June 18, 2013, 3:00 PM), www.wired.com/2013/06/nsa-hearing-by-the-numbers/.

[27] *CITIZENFOUR, supra* note 1. *See also* Jewel v. Nat'l Security Agency, 673 F.3d 902 (9th Cir., 2011).

Street. Applebaum's talk is supposed to inform the audience on methods for beating modern surveillance.[28]

CITIZENFOUR then turns to its central narrative arc. It documents Poitras' and Greenwald's travel to Hong Kong to meet the still anonymous source in a claustrophobic hotel room. The film covers the events of the next several days, providing a small slice of each day's meeting in Snowden's room.[29] Snowden explains who he is and he contemplates his motivations. It is an impressive performance, made more convincing by the fact that it is clearly unscripted and unrehearsed, qualities that are lacking in his subsequent interviews.[30] Snowden is depicted as a man of many qualities. At times he exudes a confidence that is just short of arrogance,[31] while at other times he appears vulnerable, especially in the quiet shots Poitras makes of Snowden staring pensively into the Hong Kong skyline as he seems to contemplate the personal and public turmoil his actions have caused. Snowden shows brief flashes of humor, too, such as when he gives the reporters a "pro-tip" encouraging them to "not leave the same SD cards in our laptops forever in the future."[32]

Snowden is initially adamant that the stolen materials, and the surveillance operations they document, should be the focus of Greenwald's reporting. He claims that he does not want personal exposure because "the more we focus on [me], the more the media is going to use that as a distraction."[33] Despite Snowden's protests, Greenwald (and, implicitly,

---

[28] *CITIZENFOUR, supra* note 1. *See, generally* Nathaniel Rich, Jacob Appelbaum: The American Wikileaks Hacker, ROLLING STONE (Dec. 1, 2010), www.rollingstone.com/culture/news/meet-the-american-hacker-behind-wikileaks-20101201.

[29] *CITIZENFOUR, supra* note 1.

[30] *See* Mark Kermode, *CITIZENFOUR Review – Edward Snowden Documentary Is Utterly Engrossing*, THE GUARDIAN (Oct. 19, 2014, 4:00 AM), www.theguardian.com/film/2014/oct/19/citizen-four-review-edward-snowden-nsa-engrossing (calling Snowden "positively camera-shy."). For an example of the scripted nature of media interviews, *see* Matt Agorist, *MSM Scripting Exposed On Live TV by Olympic-Level Troll Replacing Edward Snowden with Scissorhands*, FREE THOUGHT PROJECT (Oct. 1, 2015), http://the freethoughtproject.com/man-exposes-msm-scripted-live-tv-referencing-edward-scissor hands-snowden/.

[31] *CITIZENFOUR, supra* note 1 (e.g., while discussing the ability to protect the stolen documents from acquisition by others, Snowden boldly proclaims that he was "comfortable in [his] technical ability to protect them … [He has] the sophistication to do that." At another point, Snowden is being interviewed by Ewen MacAskell about going public, and part of the reason Snowden gives is to show the government that he is "not afraid of you [the government]. You're not going to bully me into silence like you've done to everybody else.").

[32] *Id.*   [33] *Id.*

Poitras' documentary eye) can hardly think of anything but the story's personal dimension. Greenwald turns the conversation back to Snowden as a personality in the unfolding drama, explaining that he wanted to "dichotomize" his reporting, with one prong being the content of the leaked documents and the second prong being the "you [Snowden] story."[34] Greenwald insists that Snowden's story be explored first because Snowden "is the only one" who can guide him to the details that are essential to the overall narrative he is constructing.[35]

Having acquiesced to Greenwald's instinct to personalize the story the film then captures Snowden's answers to questions about his motivation for stealing an unprecedented trove of top-secret materials and leaking them to the press.[36] Snowden explains that he was alarmed by the technical capabilities of the U.S. government. He also says that he was driven to act by the disappointment he felt over his dashed hopes for the Obama administration. Obama the candidate had promised to curtail the so-called "war on terror," Snowden explains. Instead, Obama, the president, had enhanced the Intelligence Community's powers and expanded surveillance programs. These events, Snowden explains, "hardened me to action."[37] Snowden also says that he has grown increasingly troubled by the chilling effect that surveillance has had on the great promise of freedom in the Internet. His actions, he says, are an attempt to fight back against the "curtailment" of his "intellectual freedom."[38]

The film's next scene takes place the next day, again in the nondescript hotel room. Greenwald (and ever-present Poitras) are joined by Ewen MacAskill, another journalist from *The Guardian*. MacAskill starts the questioning anew and, just as Greenwald had done, he immediately steers the conversation to Snowden, asking where he was from and how his actions might affect his family in the United States. "I don't know who you are," MacAskill implores. When Snowden points out that his family would be pressured by the government if they were portrayed as being closely associated with him, Greenwald and MacAskill have a brief aside during which they contemplate not reporting on Snowden's family. Greenwald suggests that they "move on to the documents and come back to" the

---

[34] *Id.*   [35] *Id.*
[36] *See* Luke Harding, *How Edward Snowden Went from Loyal NSA Contractor to Whistle-blower*, THE GUARDIAN (Feb. 1, 2014, 6:00 AM), www.theguardian.com/world/2014/feb/01/edward-snowden-intelligence-leak-nsa-contractor-extract (calling Snowden's leak "the biggest intelligence leak in history.").
[37] *CITIZENFOUR, supra* note 1.   [38] *Id.*

story's personal prong.[39] Snowden is shown giving MacAskill a primer on the programs the documents reveal. He even tries to tailor the information to what he presumes to be MacAskill's greater interest in the staggering scope of the United Kingdom's surveillance and intelligence gathering operations. But MacAskill – just as much as Greenwald – seems to struggle to understand the technical complexities involved. He, too, is more interested in the personal, human elements of the story.

Greenwald publishes the first article based on the Snowden documents and the film shifts to excerpts from Greenwald's television interviews. Snowden is shown sitting on his bed engaged in an electronic messaging conversation with his girlfriend of ten years, Lindsay Mills. He is contemplating never seeing her again, and Poitras (in a rare audible appearance) asks him to describe to her what "they" (meaning government investigators) asked Mills.[40] Snowden then describes to Greenwald how the government had sent an agent to his house to "break in," but that his girlfriend was home.[41] This establishes a troubling trend in the film. Poitras does not distinguish between the strategic intelligence gathering activities to which she objects and the criminal investigation that Snowden's theft and flight trigger. By conflating the two, she is able to depict the Intelligence Community as intrusive and ominous, even if the government's pursuit of Snowden is an altogether different undertaking, motivated by a criminal prosecution.

Once the story breaks, the film confirms its – and Greenwald's – central interest in Snowden. In the hotel room Greenwald reassures Snowden that public exposure will help keep him safe.[42] Greenwald expresses to Snowden that he wants to begin putting forward the idea that there is a single person that leaked the documents, but that he does not want to introduce Snowden as a character in the ongoing drama because he did not want to "do [the government's] work for them."[43] Greenwald quickly reverses himself, saying that perhaps Snowden might want to go ahead and announce his presence to the world not "because you think inevitably they're going to catch you and you want to do it first, you're coming out because you want to fucking come out."[44] Snowden agrees that it would be "powerful" to "come out and be like 'look, I'm not afraid.'"[45] Together, Snowden and Greenwald agree that the world

---

[39] *Id.*   [40] *Id.*   [41] *Id.*
[42] *Id* ("I think the more public we are out there, you know, as journalists, the more protection that's going to give as well.").
[43] *Id.*   [44] *Id.*   [45] *Id.*

deserves to feel the power of Snowden's choice, and they decide that Snowden should be revealed. Greenwald conducts a video interview of Snowden that is circulated to the news media. The film documents the resulting media frenzy, showing what appears to be Hong Kong residents gathered beneath a giant television monitor displaying the Snowden interview. The same interview footage is seen on video screens in what appear to be crowded Hong Kong trams.

The film also documents the personal fallout (for Snowden, but also for Poitras and Greenwald) from the release of the stolen materials. An increasingly exhausted Snowden consults with hurriedly arranged legal counsel. The film, probably unintentionally, depicts the contribution from the Hong Kong lawyers as nothing short of slapstick. In the moment that Snowden is prepared to at last flee the Mira Hotel (under cover of sun glasses and an umbrella), the lawyer explains that he has no car to help spirit Snowden to the local United Nations representation. "We could take a taxi," the lawyer offers.[46] It is a bumbling start to Snowden's flight from the law. Snowden initially disappears in Hong Kong and at the same time he is charged with three felonies, two of which arise under the Espionage Act.[47] Armed with an indictment, U.S. authorities request that Hong Kong extradite Snowden.[48] In response, Snowden flees Hong Kong on a jet to Russia (funded by WikiLeaks and Julian Assange). Once in Russia, Snowden's passport is revoked, which leads eventually to him taking asylum there.

The film tells us that Snowden is not the only member of the circle affected by the story. Greenwald returns to Brazil where he meets with reporters at *O Globo* to describe the breadth of data being "stolen" from Brazil by the NSA.[49] Greenwald is also called upon by the Brazilian government to testify in senate hearings regarding the capture of data. The film, with much drama and very little explanation, shows Greenwald's partner arriving at the Rio de Janeiro airport at the end of an international flight during which he was detained at Heathrow International Airport in the United Kingdom for nine hours under schedule 7 of the Terrorism Act 2000.[50] People normally detained under this Act are held for less than an hour.[51]

---

[46] *Id.* [47] *Id.* [48] *Id.* [49] *Id.*

[50] *Id. See also Glenn Greenwald's partner detained at Heathrow airport for nine hours*, THE GUARDIAN (Aug. 18, 2013, 7:33 PM), www.theguardian.com/world/2013/aug/18/glenn-greenwald-guardian-partner-detained-heathrow.

[51] *Glenn Greenwald's partner detained at Heathrow airport for nine hours*, THE GUARDIAN (Aug. 18, 2013, 7:33 PM), www.theguardian.com/world/2013/aug/18/glenn-greenwald-guardian-partner-detained-heathrow.

And Poitras lets the viewer know from the start that she has already been pressed into exile, choosing to live in Germany in order to avoid government interference with her work. Once Snowden goes underground in Hong Kong, Poitras attempts to stay and shoot more film, but she notices that she is being followed. She returns to Germany and the film's following scenes capture some of the media and legal activity undertaken on Snowden's behalf in Berlin. This includes the reappearance of Binney, whose arrival for testimony at the German *Bundestag* is documented. In a text conversation with Greenwald (who is living in Brazil), neither Poitras nor Greenwald seem confident about ever returning to the United States.[52]

The film concludes in Russia, showing Snowden and his girlfriend cooking together in the kitchen of a house. Especially these images suggest the film's assumption of the surveillance posture. Shot from outside in the darkness, Snowden and Mills are seen through a window in an obviously intimate moment, much as a nosy neighbor (or an intelligence agent) would observe. It also shows a last meeting between the principals. Greenwald arranged the meeting to discuss with Snowden a new "source" that had approached him.[53] We are not told who it is, but Snowden seems suitably impressed by the identity of Greenwald's new source, calling the source "bold." But Snowden expresses concern about the source's ability to remain undetected.[54] Throughout this scene Snowden and Greenwald communicate largely via notes scribbled on paper, some of which Poitras quickly zooms in to capture on film. One of the notes indicates that the drone strikes being carried out in the Middle East "are done through Ramstein Air Base in Germany," with the other proclaiming that "there are 1.2 m (sic) people on various stages of their watch list."[55] Snowden finds this last bit of information "fucking ridiculous," noting that the number of people is the equivalent of the population of a small country.[56] The only other note to which the viewer is partially privy features a sketch of the chain of command associated, presumably, with America's secret drone campaign. At the apex of the chart is the acronym "POTUS" for "President of the United States."[57] This conversation's unremarked shift to the American drone campaign, despite the film's

---

[52] *CITIZENFOUR, supra* note 1.   [53] *Id.*   [54] *Id.*   [55] *Id.*   [56] *Id.*

[57] *Id.* This is hardly a revelation for anyone with a basic understanding of the constitution, which makes the president both Commander in Chief of the armed forces and the head of the federal government's executive branch.

earlier focus on data collection through telecommunications surveillance, is a crude last stroke meant to both expand and deepen the nature of the threat animating *CITIZENFOUR*. It does not seem to matter to Poitras – or Snowden and Greenwald – that the drone campaign involves a different range of issues altogether.[58] Greenwald tears the handwritten notes to smallish pieces. This is a laughable security measure, as suggested by the film's closing scene, which features an anonymous hand gathering up the scraps.[59] Surely they will be scrutinized and reassembled by unseen, intrusive forces.

C CITIZENME

CITIZENFOUR largely serves as a vehicle for the aggrandizement of Snowden and the members of the coterie he assembled, including the film's director Laura Poitras and *The Guardian* reporter Glenn Greenwald. Considering the film's sharp critique of government surveillance, it is troubling that Snowden, Greenwald, and Poitras would submit themselves to such personally revealing documentary "surveillance" as the means for criticizing the NSA's personally revealing intelligence gathering.

Documentarians, by the nature of the artistic component of their work, have individual styles. Poitras claims that her "films have always kind of been about protagonists – *they* are the lens through which the film happens."[60] This focus on the "protagonists" means that *CITIZENFOUR* is as much a personality study as it is an examination of the issues of privacy and intelligence gathering. Poitras exhaustively studies her subjects, tracking their movements and knowing their thoughts.[61] This is just one example of how the modern documentary has "potentially taken on more sinister, totalizing, and authoritarian tones."[62]

---

[58] *But see* Chapter 8 in this volume.   [59] *Id.*

[60] Andrea Peterson, *Snowden Filmmaker Laura Poitras: 'Facebook Is a Gift to Intelligence Agencies,'* WASH. POST (Oct. 23, 2014), www.washingtonpost.com/news/the-switch/wp/2014/10/23/snowden-filmmaker-laura-poitras-facebook-is-a-gift-to-intelligence-agencies/. (emphasis added).

[61] This can go so far as to involve interfering with the subjects themselves. Such interference can be seen as early as *Nanook*, where Flaherty insisted that his subjects go on hunts using only traditional methods, rather than using guns. *See* BARNOUW, *supra* note 3.

[62] Alexandra Juhasz & Alisa Lebow, *Introduction: A World Encountered, in* A COMPANION TO CONTEMPORARY DOCUMENTARY FILMS 8 *(Alexandra Juhasz & Alisa Lebow eds.,* 2015).

Furthermore, the entire process of editing together the hours and hours of documentary footage into an accessible, digestible form requires the documentarian to provide only pieces of the events being recorded – in effect, they are no less involved in constructing an imaginary world for the viewer to explore than any of the great masters of fiction.[63] Except that the documentarian's raw material is the stuff of real life, observed and recorded. The use of such "an observing camera" can generate "a sadistic, surveilling gaze that exposes its subjects as objects for our view."[64] The pursuit of this kind of deep documentary "surveillance" is an almost inexcusable mechanism for a film that wants to be a critique of surveillance.

Poitras does not see the irony in this. Instead, her chief aesthetic choice for the film is to make long, lingering, vulnerable takes of Snowden, but also the journalists Greenwald and MacAskill. Especially Snowden is laid bare for us in his cramped Hong Kong hotel room across several days of filming in various states of casual or intimate dress. He discusses the nature of the materials he has stolen from the NSA; he talks about his ideas of privacy, democracy, and freedom. He and the reporters debate how best to go about disclosing the documents. But Poitras does not limit her gaze to these moments of exposition on the issues that might have been the heart of the film. Instead, she provides us with several shots of Snowden staring out the window, arranging his hair in the bathroom mirror, emailing and telephoning with his girlfriend, and watching television news coverage of the leaks.

She seems to revel in these intimate, deeply revelatory personal moments, even if the aesthetic choice constitutes a kind of surveillance more intrusive than the intelligence gathering to which she objects.[65]

---

[63] Elizabeth Cowie, *The World Viewed: Documentary Observing and the Culture of Surveillance,* in A COMPANION TO CONTEMPORARY DOCUMENTARY FILMS, *supra* note 61, at 580.

[64] *Id.* at 589. *See also* Brian Winston, *Surveillance in the Service of Narrative,* in A COMPANION TO CONTEMPORARY DOCUMENTARY FILMS, *supra* note 61, at 611, 620–24 (this discusses the documentary *The Bridge,* a film about suicides committed by jumping off the Golden Gate Bridge. The centerpiece of the film is surveillance footage taken of the bridge depicting actual people jumping to their deaths. For example, one of the jumpers surveilled was Gene Sprague. He was watched by the film crew for 90 minutes before jumping off of the bridge and ending his life – the final scene of the film.).

[65] *See, e.g.,* Sonia Saraiya, *HBO's Political Call to Arms: "CITIZENFOUR" Has More in Common with "Girls" Than You'd Think,* SALON (Feb. 24, 2015), www.salon.com/2015/02/24/hbos_political_call_to_arms_citizenfour_has_more_in_common_with_girls_than_youd_think/. For the meaning of intimacy in surveillance, *see* Chapter 24 in this volume.

Poitras wants to evoke in the audience the emotional context of Snowden's courage and isolation. But she does not hesitate to instrumentalize Snowden – and sacrifice his privacy – for the purposes of her critique. We are left with the eerie juxtaposition of using documentary "surveillance" to contest surveillance.

Poitras is not the only participant in the drama who is determined to make exposing Snowden a part of the critique of government surveillance. Snowden says he wants the stolen documents to be the focus of the story and that he does not want the media's interest in him to overshadow the revelations contained in the documents themselves. He claims that he wants to share the documents only because of his concerns about privacy and intelligence gathering.[66] But why, then, does he invite a documentary filmmaker to chronicle the affair? Snowden might have been satisfied to work with a print journalist, such as Greenwald, who had already shown himself to be a vociferous opponent of "the radical and extremist theories of power the U.S. government had adopted in the wake of 9/11."[67] Greenwald had crossed swords with the NSA over the warrantless wiretapping scandal, which was the subject of his bestselling 2006 book.[68] That man, and the print journalist's medium, would have been adequate and far less personally revealing vehicles for his agenda. But agreeing to have himself documented by Poitras exhibits a comfort with public exposure that contradicts his exaggerated concern for privacy.

Poitras is undoubtedly aware of this contradiction and she builds an awkward explanation into the start of the film. She establishes that Snowden originally reached out to Greenwald. But after the two failed to establish secure communications and Greenwald seemed to lose interest, Snowden reached out to Poitras. "You asked why I picked you." Snowden is quoted as saying. "I didn't. You did."[69] Poitras wants us to know that this is because of the respect Snowden has for her earlier work challenging the American government's post-9/11 policies. But it should have been adequate to rely on Poitras' help in gaining secure access to Greenwald. What motivated him to agree to be the subject of her documentary film, including the personally revealing documentary surveillance this would involve? Did he desire fame? Did he need it?[70] By

---

[66] *CITIZENFOUR, supra* note 1. [67] GREENWALD, *supra* note 11, at 1. [68] *Id.*, at 2.

[69] *CITIZENFOUR, supra* note 1.

[70] Snowden has detractors. *See, e.g.,* Jeffery Toobin, *Edward Snowden is No Hero,* NEW YORKER (June 10, 2013), www.newyorker.com/news/daily-comment/edward-snowden-is-no-hero; Michael B. Kelley, *We Now Know A Lot More About Edward Snowden's Epic Heist – And*

announcing himself and his deeds to the world (especially through the medium of a bio-doc) Snowden was ensuring that he would be under one form of surveillance or another for the rest of his life. If the government was not watching him, the media would be. He has traded his resentment for a lack of privacy for a life spent in the public eye.

At least as portrayed in the film, Greenwald and *The Guardian* are also determined to expose Snowden despite the intrusive consequences this will have for his privacy. Waving off Snowden's objections that the story has to be about the issues (perhaps because it is so hard to take that claim seriously with a documentary filmmaker in the room), a significant portion of the interviews presented in the film involve Greenwald and MacAskill redundantly probing Snowden's personal background and talking with Snowden about when it will be best to finally expose him to the public. Greenwald, in the initial meeting, suggested that Snowden might want to "do that early, because it might be necessary, or you might choose to have that done early."[71] There is a journalistic justification for the evident pleasure Greenwald takes in exposing Snowden. This gave the issues a human face and helped bolster the drama by making him a martyr. But it is also a deeply ironic strategy if one's agenda is the affirmation of privacy.

More than just compromising Snowden's privacy, Poitras and Greenwald also want to be seen in the film. Through the medium of film, and through his book about the Snowden revelations, Greenwald has become more than a conduit for information about intelligence gathering practices – he has become an active participant in the narrative. A number of scenes in the film show Greenwald giving interviews and being congratulated by other journalists for breaking the story and testifying before government bodies. Although she makes only a fleeting, ghost-like appearance in the film (when her image behind the camera is briefly visible in a mirror in the hotel room), Poitras very effectively turns the

---

It's Troubling, Bus. Insider (Aug. 17, 2014, 9:32 AM), www.businessinsider.com/snow den-took-level-1-and-level-3-documents-2014–8; Michael B. Kelley, *Snowden Won't Talk About His Time In Hong Kong – And Now We Know Why*, Bus. Insider (June 30, 2014, 3:21 PM), www.businessinsider.com/snowden-in-hong-kong-2014–6#ixzz381uUaUZU; Michael B. Kelley, *There's An 11-Day Hole In Snowden's Story About Hong Kong*, Bus. Insider (July 20, 2014, 2:00 PM), www.businessinsider.com/snowden-says-he-didnt-cover-his-tracks-in-hong-kong-2014–7#ixzz3ALSZpsWo; Bryan Burrough *et al.*, *The Snowden Saga: A Shadowland of Secrets and Light*, Vanity Fair (Apr. 30, 2014, 8:00 PM), www.vanityfair.com/news/politics/2014/05/edward-snowden-politics-interview.
[71] *CITIZENFOUR, supra* note 1.

film's spotlight on herself. The documentary opens with a list of her films. Poitras' voice is the first we hear in the film and she speaks her name as the film's first words: "Laura."

CITIZENFOUR's critique of state surveillance through documentary, voluntary exposure raises another irony: the interplay between the millennial obsession with attention via social media and constant linkages with the network have been a data windfall for the Intelligence Community. But Poitras also does not grapple with our contributions to the intrusive state of affairs she detests.[72]

D   Opacity and Loathing

It is hard to understand why a film that expresses such deep unease about the NSA's opacity would itself resort to opaque, unarticulated threats to justify its agenda. But this is exactly what *CITZENFOUR* does. Instead of hard proof of the NSA's invidiousness, Poitras gives us only innuendo and suggestions: phones ring ominously; unrevealed notes are scribbled and raise eyebrows. Naturally, government surveillance and intelligence gathering are elusive targets. Still, the problem with this choice is that this is precisely the tactic the Intelligence Community uses to justify its agenda. "Trust us," the sentiments runs. "If only you knew what we knew, then you wouldn't object to surveillance."[73] It is fair to expect Poitras to do better. While holding transparency out as the standard

---

[72] Zygmunt Bauman *et al.*, *After Snowden: Rethinking the Impact of Surveillance*, 8 Int'l Pol. Soc. 121, 143 ("One suspects that a significant role in this reaction (or rather absence of reaction) was played by the conscious or subconscious satisfaction felt by billions of Internet users engaged, with abandon, in 24/7 self-spying. After all, one of the main attractions of the Internet is the freedom of constant, on-demand access to the (online version of) the "public sphere," previously open solely to the chosen few, with big radio, TV, or press companies sternly guarding the entry. For uncountable millions, scared by the specter of loneliness and abandonment, the Internet offers an unprecedented chance of exit/salvation from anonymity, neglect, and oblivion. A collateral effect of Snowden's revelations was making Internet users aware just how big, and stuffed with important people, "people who truly matter," that public sphere is. It rendered their half-conscious hope look suddenly much more realistic, and supplied the resounding proof, if proof they needed, of just how sound is their investment of time and energy into virtual friends and the virtual public arena. If anything, the most profound and lasting effects of the whole affair will be another leap upwards in the dedication and enthusiasm of Do It Yourself (DIY) – voluntary and unpaid – spying, to the gleeful joy and comfort of consumer and security markets.")

[73] *See supra*, note 10.

against which the NSA should be judged, she nevertheless adopts the government's opaque, scaremongering approach. It is as if she is saying: Trust her. If only you knew what she knows. Perhaps this approach is necessary because the films shows – and is itself – profound evidence of the absence of the ominous chilling effect about which Snowden, Green-wald, and Poitras are so concerned. Rather than documenting the ways in which government surveillance has eroded our democratic culture, the film shows quite a lot of civil society engagement, including citizens, citizen groups, and political institutions advocating against government surveillance. Of course, the film's success is the most damning evidence of the still-present, very rich possibilities for democratic discourse and civic action.

Poitras – and especially Greenwald – are most concerned about the potential for government abuse of the vast trove of data it is collecting. Snowden himself says that his chief concern was a potential change in administration or government policy that could lead to intelligence abuses. "I'm sitting there every day," Snowden claims, "getting paid to design methods to amplify [the] state power [of surveillance]. And I'm realizing that if the policy switches – that are the only thing that restrain these states – were changed, then you couldn't meaningfully oppose these [surveillance programs]. I mean, you would have to be the most incredibly sophisticated technical actor in existence."[74] Snowden's fear about the illicit and troubling uses to which the NSA's data *might* be put is enough to motivate Snowden's dramatic, illegal actions. But the film – just as it neglects a deeper treatment of many other related issues – does not offer much evidence of abuse. The most harrowing event presented by the film involves the detention and questioning of Greenwald's partner David Miranda at London's Heathrow airport. But Poitras manipulates the episode, giving it no context and thereby imbuing it with the most arbitrary and sinister possible tones. She does not, for example, explain that Miranda was detained and questioned shortly after Poitras and Greenwald began reporting from the Snowden mater-ials. And she does not reveal that Miranda was "stopped in transit between Berlin and Rio de Janeiro after meeting the filmmaker Laura Poitras" and that "he had been carrying encrypted files, including an external hard drive containing 58,000 highly classified U.K. intelli-gence documents, 'in order to assist the journalistic activity of

---

[74] *CITIZENFOUR, supra* note 1.

Greenwald.'"[75] The episode involved a concrete suspicion that Miranda was in possession of stolen classified information and was nothing like the suspicionless and random intrusions on privacy that Poitras and the rest of the film's protagonists want us to fear. In fact, Miranda's detention was conducted in strict observation with English law, as confirmed by a three judge court panel, which found that the detention "was legal, proportionate and did not breach European human rights protections of freedom of expression."[76]

The film also shows the burden borne by Snowden as the government's net begins to close around him. After an online conversation with his girlfriend Snowden reports that there are "construction trucks all over the street at [his] house," with the obvious implication that the NSA is watching his place of residence. Snowden's suffocating retreat to the Hong Kong hotel room where most of the film takes place contributes to the atmospherics of government oppression. But none of this is fair evidence of the generalized privacy concerns that the film is meant to raise. After all, Snowden had just perpetrated one of America's largest and most revealing security breaches, in knowing violation of the law. Snowden is not the victim of unconstrained intelligence surveillance in the film. Instead, he is a fugitive from the law who is enduring a robust and legitimate criminal investigation.

Surely it is hard to capture evidence of "chilling" on film because, by its nature, it involves *not doing*. How, then, can Poitras depict the very phenomenon that is meant to animate the film? She allows her protagonists to set the ominous tone. Trust them. If only you knew what they know. So, we learn of the dreadful consequences of intrusive government surveillance from Snowden's insistence on draping himself in a shroud when he types passwords and encryption codes into his laptop. But Poitras does not try to discover whether that was actually necessary in that hotel room. And Poitras allows Snowden's suspicions to characterize the meaning of a fire alarm that rings repeatedly and disturbingly through one scene in the film. It does not matter that Snowden's call to the hotel lobby confirms that it was merely a routine test. Obviously,

---

[75] Owen Bowcott, David Miranda allowed to appeal against ruling on Heathrow detention, THE GUARDIAN (May 15, 2014, 9:24 AM), www.theguardian.com/world/2014/may/15/david-miranda-appeal-high-court-ruling-detention-heathrow.

[76] Alan Travis *et al.*, David Miranda detention at Heathrow airport was lawful, high court rules, THE GUARDIAN (Feb. 19, 2014, 2:38 PM), www.theguardian.com/world/2014/feb/19/david-miranda-detention-lawful-court-glenn-greenwald. *See also id.*

Poitras wants us to understand, the Intelligence Community is behind unexpected phone calls, our lost car keys, and weather forecasters' persistent inaccuracies. Or, at least we should fear that it is so.

The worst of these banal, conspiracy-tinged moments, which are meant to convey the threat posed by government intelligence gathering, occurs in the film's ridiculous final scene. Snowden, having successfully fled to Russia, meets again with Greenwald in what looks like another (but much classier) hotel room. Greenwald wants to give Snowden an update on the impact of the leaks. But unlike the film's earlier, Hong Kong hotel room scenes, in this episode Greenwald can only communicate with Snowden by way of half-uttered thoughts that are completed as frantically scribbled notes. Poitras does not bother to distinguish the potential Russian surveillance of that room from the American Intelligence Community's surveillance and intelligence gathering activities, despite the fact that there are significant and material differences between the two contexts. Worse, except for a few fleeting hints, Poitras does not allow us to see the content of those notes. Instead, we have to accept on faith the gravity of their content as it is expressed by Greenwald's smug gestures and by Snowden's increasingly alarmed grimace. What assurances do we have that their alarm is justified? We have to trust them. The most profound bit of information conveyed by the notes, only teasingly observed by Poitras (who keeps moving the camera into and out of focus in this scene in order to enhance the moment's tension and mystery), shows written on one of the shredded scraps the acronym POTUS – although it is obviously not from the sketch Greenwald drew to lay out the decision making process. Does the mysterious new source have a role that places them near the President? Poitras does not deign to provide any hints. We just have to trust them.

The fear evoked in *CITIZENFOUR* is, in many ways, less well articulated than the fearmongering done by those that claim mass surveillance is necessary. The threat of terrorism may be exaggerated by the government – and the intelligence–industrial complex. But we are reminded all too frequently that it is real.

The vocal protest of surveillance goes beyond *CITIZENFOUR* in many other ways. As is established elsewhere in this volume, there were many civilian protest groups planned and organized via the Internet.[77] Websites

---

[77] *See* Chapter 12 in this volume (citing *February 11TH, 2014 was the Day We Fought Back Against Mass Surveillance*, https://thedaywefightback.org/the-results/; *STOP WATCHING US*, https://rally.stopwatching.us/; *Congress: This Is a Blackout*, www.blackoutcon

and social media pages raged with debate. Petitions were signed by U.S. citizens demanding that Congress act to repeal the laws that granted the NSA such sweeping surveillance powers. Congress, in a rare moment of cooperation and productivity, responded by enacting the USA FREEDOM Act. These actions seem to demonstrate the opposite of a chilling effect.

Apart from CITIZENFOUR, both Poitras and Greenwald (along with scores of other journalists and pundits) have spoken out against the surveillance programs. There have been debates and conferences scheduled across the globe whose sole purpose is to dispute the legitimacy and legality of government surveillance programs. Citizens across the globe have also taken their problems with corporate involvement with the NSA data-collection programs directly to the companies they do business with.[78] This protest, which occurred largely via social media, caused "several media giants such as Google and Apple to introduce encryption into consumer communication."[79] These actions stand as a testament to the fact that political and social discourse has not been stunted by the revelation of the NSA's mass surveillance. Instead, it has been reinvigorated.

The success of CITIZENFOUR may be the most damning evidence that the chilling effect about which Poitras is so concerned has not emerged. It is evidence that discourse about Snowden's revelations has been given broad acceptance, at least by the panels that issue film awards.

E   Conclusion

CITIZENFOUR is the very thing it sets out to criticize. It is an act of surveillance justified by innuendo and unarticulated fear. The film's true genius is in evading criticism on this basis. Viewers are instead invited to focus on the gripping, real-life spy drama of a small group of rebels taking on the monolithic United States government. And if they do not triumph in the film, at least they survive. What goes unrecognized, however, are the layers of troubling irony in the film's choices, proving that it is not only the Intelligence Community that can make productive use of a darkened tunnel.

gress.org/; Adam Gabbat, *Protesters Rally for 'The Day We Fight Back' Against Mass Surveillance*, THE GUARDIAN (Feb. 11, 2014, 1:12 PM), www.theguardian.com/world/ 2014/feb/11/day-fight-back-protest-nsa-mass-surveillance.).

[78] W. Lance Bennett, *Forward*, in CIVIC ENGAGEMENT AND SOCIAL MEDIA: POLITICAL PARTICIPATION BEYOND PROTEST 1 (Julie Uldam & Anne Vestergaard eds., 2015).

[79] *Id.*, at 2.

INDEX